THE PRINTING PRESS AS AN AGENT OF CHANGE

*Communications and cultural
transformations in early-modern Europe*

THE PRINTING PRESS AS AN AGENT OF CHANGE

Communications and cultural transformations in early-modern Europe

Volumes I and II

ELIZABETH L. EISENSTEIN
PROFESSOR OF HISTORY, UNIVERSITY OF MICHIGAN

CAMBRIDGE UNIVERSITY PRESS

CAMBRIDGE

LONDON NEW YORK NEW ROCHELLE

MELBOURNE SYDNEY

Published by the Press Syndicate of the University of Cambridge
The Pitt Building, Trumpington Street, Cambridge CB2 1RP
32 East 57th Street, New York, NY 10022, USA
296 Beaconsfield Parade, Middle Park, Melbourne 3206, Australia

First published in two volumes 1979
First paperback edition 1980

Printed in the United States of America
Typeset by Cambridge University Press
Printed and bound by Halliday Lithograph Company
West Hanover, Massachusetts

Library of Congress Cataloguing in Publication Data

Eisenstein, Elizabeth L.

The printing press as an agent of change.

Bibliography
Includes index.
1. Printing-Influence. 2. Reformation.
3. Renaissance. 4. Technology and civilization.
I. Title.
Z124.E37 686.2 77–91083

ISBN 0 521 21967 1 volume I
ISBN 0 521 21969 8 volume II
ISBN 0 521 22044 0 set of two volumes
ISBN 0 521 29955 1 combined paperback edition

TO THE MEMORY OF
JOHN EISENSTEIN 1953-1974

CONTENTS

CONTENTS

PREFACE

I do ingenuously confess that in attempting this history of Printing I have undertaken a task much too great for my abilities the extent of which I did not so well perceive at first...

Joseph Ames, June 7, 1749[1]

This book has been composed over the course of some fifteen years. Its inception goes back to 1963 when I read Carl Bridenbaugh's presidential address to the American Historical Association. This address which was entitled 'The Great Mutation' belonged to an apocalyptic genre much in vogue at that time (and unfortunately still ubiquitous).[2] It raised alarms about the extent to which a 'run-away technology' was severing all bonds with the past and portrayed contemporary scholars as victims of a kind of collective amnesia. Bridenbaugh's description of the plight confronting historians; his lament over 'the loss of mankind's memory' in general and over the disappearance of the 'common culture of Bible reading' in particular seemed to be symptomatic rather than diagnostic. It lacked the capacity to place present alarms in some kind of perspective – a capacity which the study of history, above all other disciplines, ought to be able to supply. It seemed unhistorical to equate the fate of the 'common culture of Bible reading' with that of all of Western civilization when the former was so much more recent – being the by-product of an invention which was only five hundred years old. Even after Gutenberg, moreover, Bible reading had remained *un*common among many

---

[1] Dibdin, ed. *Typographical Antiquities*, preface of 1749 by Joseph Ames, I, 12.
[2] Bridenbaugh, 'The Great Mutation.' Other essays on the same theme appearing at the same time are noted in Eisenstein 'Clio and Chronos.'

highly cultivated Western Europeans and Latin Americans who adhered to the Catholic faith.

In the tradition of distinguished predecessors, such as Henry Adams and Samuel Eliot Morison, the president of the American Historical Association appeared to be projecting his own sense of a growing distance from a provincial American boyhood upon the entire course of Western civilization.[3] As individuals grow older they *do* become worried about an unreliable memory. Collective amnesia, however, did not strike me as a proper diagnosis of the predicament which the historical profession confronted. Judging by my own experience and that of my colleagues, it was recall rather more than oblivion which presented the unprecedented threat. So much data was impinging on us from so many directions and with such speed that our capacity to provide order and coherence was being strained to the breaking point (or had it, perhaps, already snapped?). If there was a 'run-away' technology which was leading to a sense of cultural crisis among historians, perhaps it had more to do with an increased rate of publication than with new audio-visual media or even with the atom bomb?

While mulling over this question and wondering whether it was wise to turn out more monographs or instruct graduate students to do the same – given the indigestible abundance now confronting us and the difficulty of assimilating what we have – I ran across a copy of Marshall McLuhan's *The Gutenberg Galaxy*.[4] In sharp contrast to the American historian's lament, the Canadian professor of English seemed to take mischievous pleasure in the loss of familiar historical perspectives. He pronounced historical modes of inquiry to be obsolete and the age of Gutenberg at an end. Here again, I felt symptoms of cultural crisis were being offered in the guise of diagnosis. McLuhan's book itself seemed to testify to the special problems posed by print culture rather than those produced by newer media. It provided additional evidence of how overload could lead to incoherence. At the same time it also stimulated my curiosity (already aroused by considering Bible-printing) about the specific historical consequences of the fifteenth-century communications shift. While studying and teaching aspects of

---

[3] Henry Adams, *The Education*, p. 5, felt cut off from the eighteenth century by the opening of the Boston and Albany Railroad, the first Cunard steamer and the advent of the telegraph. Samuel Eliot Morison *Vistas in History*, p.24, saw *his* generation being cut off from preceding ones 'by the internal combustion engine, nuclear fission and Dr Freud.'

[4] McLuhan's book was brought to my attention by Frank Kermode's 1963 *Encounter* review: 'Between two Galaxies.'

the history of Western Europe over the course of several decades, I had long been dissatisfied with prevailing explanations for the political and intellectual revolutions of early-modern times. Some of the changes to which McLuhan alluded might well be helpful for providing more satisfactory solutions to long-standing problems and at least seemed to offer a possible way out of some circular arguments and inconclusive debates. But McLuhan's oracular pronouncements did not provide an adequate starting point. A large number of questions about the actual effects of the advent of printing would have to be answered before other matters could be explored. What were some of the most important consequences of the shift from script to print? Anticipating a strenuous effort to master a large and mushrooming literature, I began to investigate what had been written on this obviously important subject. As I say in my first chapter, there was not even a small literature available for consultation. Indeed I could not find a single book, or even a sizeable article which attempted to survey the consequences of the fifteenth-century communications shift.

While recognizing that it would take more than one book to remedy this situation, I also felt that a preliminary effort, however inadequate, was better than none, and embarked on a decade of study – devoted primarily to becoming acquainted with the special literature (alas, all too large and rapidly growing) on early printing and the history of the book. Between 1968 and 1971 some preliminary articles were published to elicit reactions from scholars and take advantage of informed criticism before issuing a full-scale work. The reader who has seen these articles will be familiar with some portions of the first three chapters, although each has been extensively revised. Fresh content increases as the chapters progress; most of chapter 4 and all of the rest appear in this book for the first time.[5]

My treatment falls into two main parts. Part 1 focuses on the shift from script to print in Western Europe and tries to block out the main features of the communications revolution. Parts 2 and 3 deal with the relationship between the communications shift and other developments conventionally associated with the transition from medieval to early

---

[5] Preliminary articles for chaps. 1, 2, and 3 respectively are Eisenstein, 'The Position of the Printing Press in Current Historical Literature'; 'Some Conjectures about the Impact of Printing on Western Society and Thought'; and 'The Advent of Printing and the Problem of the Renaissance.' A thirty-page abridgement of parts of chap. 4 appeared as 'L'Avènement de l'Imprimerie et la Réforme.'

modern times. (I have concentrated on cultural and intellectual movements, postponing for another book problems pertaining to political
ones.) The last two parts thus take up familiar developments and
attempt to view them from a new angle of vision. The first part, however, covers unfamiliar territory – unfamiliar to most historians, at
least (albeit not to specialists in the history of the book) and especially
exotic to this historian (who had previously specialized in the study
of the French Revolution and early nineteenth-century French
history).

While trying to cover this unfamiliar ground I discovered (as all
neophytes do) that what seemed relatively simple on first glance
became increasingly complex on examination and that new areas of
ignorance opened up much faster than old ones could be closed. As
one might expect from a work long-in-progress, first thoughts had
to be replaced by second ones, even third thoughts have had to be
revised. Especially when I was writing about the preservative powers
of print (a theme assigned special importance and hence repeatedly
sounded in the book), I could not help wondering about the wisdom
of presenting views that were still in flux in so fixed and permanent
a form. I am still uncertain about this and hope that my decision to
publish at this point will not be misinterpreted. I have not reached any
final formulation but have merely become convinced that beyond this
provisional resting point, diminishing returns will set in.

It also should be noted at the outset that my treatment is primarily
(though not exclusively) concerned with the effects of printing on
written records and on the views of already literate élites. It is the shift
from one kind of literate culture to another (rather than from an oral
to a literate culture) that I have in mind when referring to an 'un-
acknowledged revolution.' This point needs special emphasis because
it runs counter to present trends. When they do touch on the topic of
communications, historians have been generally content to note that
their field of study, unlike archeology or anthropology, is limited to
societies which have left written records. The special form taken by
these written records is considered of less consequence in defining
fields than the overriding issue of whether any have been left. Concern
with this overriding issue has been intensified recently by a double-
pronged attack on older definitions of the field, emanating from African
historians on the one hand and social historians dealing with Western

civilization on the other. The former have had perforce to challenge the requirement that written records be supplied. The latter object to the way this requirement has focused attention on the behavior of a small literate élite while encouraging neglect of the vast majority of the people of Western Europe. New approaches are being developed – often in collaboration with Africanists and anthropologists – to handle problems posed by the history of the 'inarticulate' (as presumably talkative albeit unlettered people are sometimes oddly called). These new approaches are useful not only for redressing an old élitist imbalance but also for adding many new dimensions to the study of Western history. Work in progress on demographic and climatic change, on family structure, child rearing, crime and punishment, festivals, funerals and food riots, to mention but a few of the new fields that are now under cultivation, will surely enrich and deepen historical understanding.

But although the current vogue for 'history from below' is helpful for many purposes, it is not well suited for understanding the purposes of this book. When Jan Vansina, who is both an anthropologist and an historian of pre-colonial Africa, explores 'the relationship of oral tradition to written history' he naturally skips over the difference between written history produced by scribes and written history after print.[6] When Western European historians explore the effect of printing on popular culture they naturally focus attention on the shift from an oral folk culture to a print-made one.[7] In both cases, attention is deflected away from the issues that the following chapters will explore. These issues are so unfamiliar that some readers of my preliminary sketches jumped to the mistaken conclusion that my concerns were the same as Vansina's.

This misunderstanding, alas, is more easily explained than forestalled. For one thing, the advent of printing did encourage the spread of literacy even while changing the way written texts were handled by already literate élites. For another thing, even literate groups had to rely much more upon oral transmission in the age of scribes than they did later on. Many features which are characteristic of oral culture, such as the cultivation of memory arts and the role of a hearing public, were also of great significance among scribal scholars. Problems associated

[6] Vansina, *Oral Tradition*, part I, section 2, pp. 2 ff.
[7] See e.g. Natalie Z. Davis' essay on 'Printing and the People.'

with oral transmission thus cannot be avoided even when dealing with literate groups. Nevertheless the experience of the scribal scholar was different from that of his preliterate contemporaries and the advent of printing had a different effect on Latin-reading professors than on unlettered artisans. To leave out the former and consider only the latter is to lose a chance of helping to explain major intellectual transformations of early-modern times.

In dealing with these transformations one cannot ignore how printing spurred the spread of literacy. New issues posed by vernacular translation and popularization had significant repercussions within the Commonwealth of Learning as well as outside it. Nevertheless it is not the spread of literacy but how printing altered *written communications within the Commonwealth of Learning* which provides the main focus of this book. It is primarily concerned with the fate of the *un*popular (and currently unfashionable) 'high' culture of Latin-reading professional élites. I have also found it necessary to be unfashionably parochial and stay within a few regions located in Western Europe.[8] Thus the term 'print culture' is used throughout this book in a special parochial Western sense: to refer to post-Gutenberg developments in the West while setting aside its possible relevance to pre-Gutenberg developments in Asia. Not only earlier developments in Asia, but later ones in Eastern Europe, the Near East and the New World have also been excluded. Occasional glimpses of possible comparative perspectives are offered, but only to bring out the significance of certain features which seem to be peculiar to Western Christendom. Because very old messages affected the uses to which the new medium was put and because the difference between transmission by hand-copying and by means of print cannot be seen without mentally traversing many centuries, I have had to be much more elastic with chronological limits than with geographical ones: reaching back occasionally to the Alexandrian Museum and early Christian practices; pausing more than once over medieval bookhands and stationers' shops; looking ahead to observe the effects of accumulation and incremental change.

The developments covered in Parts 2 and 3, however, do not go

---

[8] My earlier training and special interests have led to a preference for selecting French and English examples. I realize that there are rich yields to be found elsewhere in Western Europe (that German literature is especially large on the subject of a German invention, that Venetian pride has led to a scholarly industry focused on Venetian printers, etc.) but I have not managed to do more than scratch the surface of a few regions as it is.

beyond the first two centuries of printing, with the story carried beyond Galileo's Trial only in order to see the Copernican Revolution completed and periodical publication embarked on, and to provide an appropriate prelude to Enlightenment thought. The age of Newton and Locke coincides with the interval when the leadership of the Republic of Letters is taken over from the great merchant publishers and scholar–printers by the editors of literary reviews such as Pierre Bayle and Jean LeClerc. The point at which the print shop gives way to the editorial office represents the passing of the heroic age of the master-printer and forms an especially appropriate stopping-point for my book.

I am fond of Marc Bloch's dictum: 'The good historian is like the giant of the fairy tale...wherever he catches the scent of human flesh, there his quarry lies,'[9] and I would have liked to underline the human element in my title by taking the early printer as my 'agent of change.' But although I do think of certain master printers as being the unsung heroes of the early-modern era and although they are the true protagonists of this book, impersonal processes involving transmission and communication must also be given due attention. In the end, practical considerations became paramount. I decided that cataloguing would be simplified if I referred to the tool rather than its user. Of course not one tool but many were involved in the new duplicating process. As I try to make clear in the first chapters, the term printing press in the context of this book serves simply as a convenient labelling device; as a shorthand way of referring to a larger cluster of specific changes – entailing the use of movable metal type, oil-based ink, etc. My point of departure, in any case, is not one device invented in one Mainz shop but the establishment of print shops in many urban centers throughout Europe over the course of two decades or so.

One final comment on the title is in order: it refers to *an* agent not to *the* agent, let alone to *the only* agent of change in Western Europe. Reactions to some of my preliminary articles make it seem necessary to draw attention to these distinctions. The very idea of exploring the effects produced by any particular innovation arouses suspicion that one favors a monocausal interpretation or that one is prone to reductionism and technological determinism.

Of course disclaimers offered in a preface should not be assigned too much weight and will carry conviction only if substantiated by the

[9] Bloch, *The Historian's Craft*, p. 26.

bulk of a book. Still it seems advisable to make clear from the outset that my aim is to enrich, not impoverish historical understanding, and that I regard monovariable interpretations as antipathetic to that aim. It is perfectly true that historical perspectives are difficult to preserve when claims made for a particular technological innovation are pressed too far. But this means that one must exercise discrimination and weigh the relative importance of diverse claims. To leave significant innovations out of account may also skew perspectives. I am convinced that prolonged neglect of a shift in communications has led to setting perspectives ever more askew as time goes on.

As *an* agent of change, printing altered methods of data collection, storage and retrieval systems and communications networks used by learned communities throughout Europe. It warrants special attention because it had special effects. In this book I am trying to describe these effects and to suggest how they may be related to other concurrent developments. The notion that these other developments could ever be *reduced* to *nothing but* a communications shift strikes me as absurd. The way they were reoriented by such a shift, however, seems worth bringing out. Insofar as I side with revisionists and express dissatisfaction with prevailing schemes, it is to make more room for a hitherto neglected dimension of historical change. When I take issue with conventional multivariable explanations (as I do on several occasions) it is not to substitute a single variable for many but to explain why many variables, long present, began to interact in new ways.

Interactions of many kinds – between old messages and new medium, cultural context and technological innovation, handwork and brain work, craftsmen and scholars, preachers and press agents – crop up repeatedly in the chapters which follow. One friendly scholar suggested that I should take as my epigraph E. M. Forster's celebrated plea: 'Only connect!' It does seem suitable – to genre as well as content. For despite some analytical and critical portions, this is primarily a work of synthesis. It brings together special studies in scattered fields and uses monographs on limited subjects to deal with problems of more general concern.

Needless to say it has the defects as well as the virtues of any large-scale synthetic work. It is based on monographic literature not archival research, and reflects very uneven acquaintance with relevant data. I have consulted specialists, sat in on seminars and colloquia and taken advantage of informed criticism wherever possible. Yet I cannot rule out the likelihood that I will blunder – either by relying on some authorities who are outdated or unsound, or by drawing incorrect inferences on my own. Nevertheless I am convinced that the dangers of neglecting this large and important topic far outweigh the disadvantages of my inevitably inadequate, necessarily tentative treatment. As I note in the following chapter, neglect by conscientious scholars has allowed the topic to go by default into incautious hands. Although Marshall McLuhan's work stimulated my historical curiosity, among many of my colleagues it has been counter-productive, discouraging further investigation of print culture or its effects. Concern with the topic at present is likely to be regarded with suspicion, to be labelled 'McLuhanite' and dismissed out of hand. I hope my book will help to overcome this prejudice and show that the topic is not incompatible with respect for the historian's craft.

During the long interval this work has been in progress, I have incurred more than the usual number of scholarly debts. Where my memory has not failed, contributors of special pieces of information have been thanked in footnote references. The following acknowledgements are limited to those who have furnished general guidance and instruction and support.

   Among the small group of senior scholars who provided sustained encouragement, I owe a special debt to the late Crane Brinton. From the 1940s, when he supervised my dissertation, until shortly before his death he urged me to persist with research and writing despite other demands on my time. That this book was finally written is due, in no small measure, to the strong backing he provided when it was in an unpromising early phase. At a somewhat later stage, I was heartened by unexpected encouragement from Robert K. Merton, thanks in part to the good offices provided by Elinor Barber, who has taken an informed interest in my work throughout. I have also profited from many hours of conversation with J. B. Ross. The names of Natalie Z. Davis and Robert M. Kingdon appear in my annotations with sufficient frequency to indicate my heavy reliance on their special studies of sixteenth-century print culture. Both deserve additional thanks for the many other services they have performed. Margaret Aston helped me over the course of many years, by reading and commenting on the drafts that I sent her after our weekly meetings in the Folger Library ended and we had to resort to correspondence overseas.

For introducing me to some of the 'mysteries' of early printing and the history of the book I am grateful to Frederick Goff, who let me attend his informative seminar on incunabula at the Folger Library and to Rudolf Hirsch, who guided me around the rare book collection at the University of Pennsylvania, sent me articles and books and discussed controversial issues with remarkable amiability. John Tedeschi of the Newberry Library and Francis J. Witty of the Library Science department of The Catholic University of America provided me with many offprints, references and helpful advice.

For more than a decade I took full advantage of the opportunities extended to its readers by the Folger Shakespeare Library and feel especially indebted to its hard-working staff. At the Folger I sat in on a seminar given by A. G. Dickens, received helpful counsel from Paul O. Kristeller and had useful conversations with Jan van Dorsten. I am grateful to R. J. Schoeck who supervised research activities when I was there; to the Library's Directors: Louis B. Wright and O. B. Hardison; to Nati Krivatsky, Reference Librarian; to Letitia Yeandle, Curator of Manuscripts; and, above all, to the three staff members: Elizabeth Niemyer, Rachel Doggett and Sandra Powers, who cheerfully participated in my first seminar on early printers while teaching me more than I taught them.

For clarification of problems associated with the manuscript booktrade in Renaissance Italy I have turned repeatedly to Albinia de la Mare of the Department of Western Manuscripts at the Bodleian Library. She has generously shared with me her unparalleled knowledge of the world of Vespasiano da Bisticci and of the notaries who served him as scribes. Some of the 'secrets' of medieval codicology have been unlocked for me by Richard Rouse of the University of California, Los Angeles. He corrected several misconceptions and supplied me with useful studies I would not otherwise have seen. That I could take advantage of this expertise before completing the first part of my book was due to Elizabeth Kennan, who – as a friend and as a medievalist – has helped in many ways. My acquaintance with medieval studies has been further enriched by Mary M. McLaughlin.

For an opportunity to meet various luminaries of the Warburg Institute and for sharing with me his special knowledge of Renaissance

Aristotelianism I owe much to Charles Schmitt. I am indebted to Paul Lawrence Rose for imparting to me the results of his research on the librarians and mathematicians of Renaissance Italy. Martin Lowry shared with me his work in progress on Aldus Manutius; Paul Grendler has kept me informed about his work on Venetian bookmen. Miriam Chrisman, John Elliott, Edmund Fryde, Donald Kelley, Benjamin Kohl, Nancy Roelker, Charles Nauert, Orest Ranum, Thomas Tentler, Charles Trinkaus are among the many historians of early-modern Europe who have helped me in diverse ways. Myron Gilmore, who guided the studies of several of those named above, has also helped me directly by supplying offprints and reacting promptly and positively to my requests for aid.

When working on the last part of the book, I received help from a different group of specialists, associated with the history of science and technology. I am particularly grateful to Robert Palter and Robert Westman for being faithful correspondents; checking early drafts, sending me relevant data and keeping me informed about current work. Owen Gingerich also deserves special thanks for enabling me to participate in a Copernican conference at the Smithsonian Institution and for supplying me thereafter with his own pertinent studies. Additional services were provided by William Wallace of The Catholic University who read and commented on a draft; by Uta Merzbach and D. J. Warner at the Smithsonian who helped me with mathematical and astronomical data; and by Francis Maddison of the Museum of the History of Science at Oxford. A chance to give a paper to Oxford scholars at a Linacre College seminar sponsored by Margaret Gowing was made possible through the kind offices of Christopher Hill, who has during the last decade provided heartening encouragement.

Although I was greatly assisted by the advice and support of those named above, I must naturally assume full responsibility for the contents of this book. I must also extend apologies to those contributors who have gone unmentioned because inadequate records were kept. I may be forgetful, but I am, nonetheless, truly grateful to every one who helped me.

In addition to aid from individuals, I owe much to institutional support, which came just when it was most needed, and enabled me to complete a final draft. By granting me a Fellowship for Independent Study and Research, the National Endowment for the Humanities provided the necessary incentive for spending six months of hard labor at a desk. The Rockefeller Foundation made it possible for me to spend a month as a scholar-in-residence at the Villa Serbelloni Conference and Study Center in Bellagio, Italy, where the concluding chapter was written. I am grateful to Joel Colton, director of the Humanities Division of the Foundation who alerted me to this opportunity and to Dr and Mrs William Olson, the resident Director of the Center and his wife, who did everything possible to make my stay enjoyable.

Several editors helped with the publication of both my preliminary articles and of this full-length book. For their acceptance of my early essays together with their tactful suggestions for revision, I am grateful to Trevor Aston, Hanna H. Gray, Richard Vann and Robert Webb. Responsibility for handling the book-length typescript from beginning to end was assumed by a single editor, whose present post is that of Publisher at the Cambridge University Press. Michael Black, who first came to my attention as an authority on early printed bibles, has exhibited remarkable patience and unflagging good humor over the course of many years of negotiations with a procrastinating author. He also obtained the services of N. Carol Evans to help with indexing. In completing both indexes, Clarissa Campbell Orr proved invaluable. The assistance of Andrew Brown and Maureen Leach was provided at the stage of copy-editing; Jane Majeski of the Cambridge University Press New York office cheerfully performed the thankless task of relaying messages overseas. For unexpected assistance with plans for a French edition I am much obliged to Philippe Ariès – who has been a remarkably sympathetic listener, stimulating conversationalist and helpful correspondent.

I am also indebted to those who typed and retyped several versions of a long manuscript. Over the course of some fifteen years I have relied on services cheerfully supplied by Phyllis Levine. She made herself available on short notice, and proved skillful in unravelling snarled footnotes and deciphering illegible scrawls. For help with the exacting work of retyping, proof reading, correcting, and checking for consistency, I have turned to Flora Symons, who has put in long hours of painstaking work on my typescript and relinquished more than one holiday trip to help me out.

In concluding with a note of thanks to members of my immediate family I regret that this procedure has become so conventional; that readers are likely to dismiss as superficial the very statements which are most deeply felt. In this instance, my feelings are stronger than my powers of expression. My husband and all three of my children contributed in different ways to shaping my thoughts and strengthening my determination to finish the book. My daughter, Margaret, who is pursuing graduate study in history and my son, Ted, who has cast type and operated hand presses, repeatedly refreshed my interest in work that was often on the verge of seeming stale. My husband's support of all my professional activities has been manifested for more than thirty years. It was never more helpful than after our oldest son's fatal stroke. Along with his sister and brother, John had taken a lively interest in my work-in-progress. Engaged in graduate study of neuro-biology, he was interested in the humanities as well as the sciences and valued clarity and precision in assessing writing styles. When he looked over an early version of one of my chapters, he expressed concern about excess verbiage and urged me to reduce what he described (by means of an equation) as the 'fog-count.' Had John lived, the 'fog-count' of this book would have been lower. His father's editorial help prevented it from becoming higher, and thus placed the reader as well as this author in Julian Eisenstein's debt.

PART ONE

INTRODUCTION TO AN
ELUSIVE TRANSFORMATION

I

THE UNACKNOWLEDGED
REVOLUTION

In the late fifteenth century, the reproduction of written materials began to move from the copyist's desk to the printer's workshop. This shift, which revolutionized all forms of learning, was particularly important for historical scholarship. Ever since then, historians have been indebted to Gutenberg's invention; print enters their work from start to finish, from consulting card-files to reading page-proofs. Because historians are usually eager to investigate major changes and this change transformed the conditions of their own craft, one would expect the shift to attract some attention from the profession as a whole. Yet any historiographical survey will show the contrary to be true. It is symbolic that Clio has retained her handwritten scroll. So little has been made of the move into new workshops, that after five hundred years, the muse of history still remains outside. 'History bears witness to the cataclysmic effect on society of inventions of new media for the transmission of information among persons. The development of writing and later the development of printing are examples...'[1] Insofar as flesh-and-blood historians who turn out articles and books actually bear witness to what happened in the past, the effect on society of the development of printing, far from appearing cataclysmic, is remarkably inconspicuous. Many studies of developments during the last five centuries say nothing about it at all.

Those who do touch on the topic usually agree that the use of the invention had far-reaching effects. Francis Bacon's aphorism suggesting that it changed 'the appearance and state of the whole world' is cited

---

[1] St John, book review, *The American Journal of Sociology*, p. 255. (For full citation of all footnote references, consult Bibliographical index at end of volume II.)

repeatedly and with approbation. But although many scholars concur with Bacon's opinion, very few have tried to follow his advice and 'take note of the force, effect, and consequences' of Gutenberg's invention. Much attention is paid to developments that paved the way for this invention. Many efforts have been made to define just what Gutenberg did 'invent,' to describe how movable type was first utilized and how the use of the new presses spread. But almost no studies are devoted to the consequences that ensued once printers had begun to ply their new trades throughout Europe. Explicit theories as to what these consequences were have not yet been proposed, let alone tested or contested.

There is, to be sure, a large and ever growing literature devoted to the history of printing and related topics.[2] Although much of it seems to be written by and for specialists – custodians of rare books and other librarians; experts on typography or bibliography, literary scholars concerned with press-variants, and the like – this literature does contain material of more wide-ranging interest. Historians working in neighboring fields – such as economic history, comparative literature, or Renaissance studies – have also contributed useful treatments of special aspects. The field of social history has probably yielded the richest harvest. There one finds a bewildering abundance of studies on topics such as investment in early presses and the book trade in various regions; labor conditions and social agitation among journeymen typographers; scholar–printer dynasties and publication policies; censorship, privileges, and regulation of the trade; special aspects of pamphleteering, propaganda and journalism; professional authors,

---

[2] According to 'Nouvelles du Livre Ancien' (Fall, 1974) no. 1 (a tri-annual newsletter issued by the 'Institut de Recherche et d'Histoire des Textes'), almost a thousand periodicals are covered by the new *Annual Bibliography of the History of the Printed Book and Libraries* issued from the Hague since 1970. In the 1972 volume (which excludes all U.S. publications as well as those of several European countries) there are some 2,800 entries. *The Selective Check Lists of Bibliographical Scholarship* issued at five-year intervals by the Bibliographical Society of the University of Virginia are especially helpful for keeping up with recent output. The *Archiv für Geschichte des Buchwesens* which first appeared in 1956 under West German auspices covers a wider, geographic and topical, area than the old *Archiv für Geschichte des Deutschen Buchhandels* and, along with two new journals launched since 1970 from Holland and France, enables one to sample the dazzling variety of research activities undertaken in the second half of this century. Like the *Archiv*, *Quaerendo: A Quarterly Journal from the Low Countries Devoted to Manuscripts and Printed Books* (Amsterdam) (a successor to *Het Boek*) and *Revue Française d'Histoire du Livre* (Bordeaux) (sponsored by the *Société Française d'Histoire du Livre*) stress the broader cultural implications of the history of the book. A useful selective bibliography is in Berry and Poole, *Annals of Printing*, pp. 287–94, but note the caution given by Gaskell, *A New Introduction to Bibliography*, p. 392. For a basic introduction to topic, Gaskell should be consulted in any case.

patrons and publics; the sociology of reading and the sociology of literature. The list could be extended indefinitely.[3]

Furthermore, several works that synthesize and summarize parts of this large literature have recently appeared. Thus Rudolf Hirsch surveys problems associated with 'printing, selling, reading,' during the first century after Gutenberg, for the benefit of 'the general reader of social and intellectual history' as well as for the specialist.[4] A more extensive, well-organized volume by Febvre and Martin, which skillfully covers the first three centuries of printing, has appeared in the *Evolution de L'Humanité* series. An even broader coverage, embracing 'five hundred years,' is provided by Steinberg's remarkably succinct semi-popular English survey.[5] All three of these books summarize data drawn from many scattered studies. But although the broader historical implications of these data are occasionally hinted at, they are never really spelled out. Like the section on printing in the *New Cambridge Modern History*[6] the contents of these surveys rarely enter into treatments of other aspects of the evolution of humanity.

According to Steinberg: 'The history of printing is an integral part of the general history of civilization.'[7] Unfortunately the statement is not applicable to written history as it stands although it is probably true enough of the actual course of human affairs. Far from being integrated

---

[3] The wide range of periodicals containing relevant material is suggestive. Apart from numerous journals specifically devoted to special aspects (such as *The Library* or the *Gutenberg Jahrbuch*), I have also found useful data in the *Journal des Savants*, the *UCLA Law Review*, *Bibliothèque d'Humanisme et Renaissance*, *Archiv für Reformationsgeschichte*, *Isis*, *Shakespeare Studies*, and other seemingly unrelated specialized journals.

[4] Hirsch, *Printing, Selling*. In my view the specialist will profit more than the general reader from sampling the richly detailed findings contained in this work. For a second printing in 1974, the author has added a bibliographical introduction but has left intact the text. The latter provoked perhaps an unduly harsh critical review in the *Times Literary Supplement* (Sept. 21, 1967), p. 848.

[5] Febvre and Martin, *L'Apparition*. (Febvre died before the book was completed and credit for most of it should go to Martin.) Martin's later master work: *Livre, pouvoirs et société à Paris au XVIIe siècle* has been described as a 'splendid sequel.' (See 'Books in France,' *Times Literary Supplement* (Nov. 20, 1969), p. 1344.) It is indeed a splendid work encompassing more than its title suggests. But two volumes on conditions in seventeenth-century France do not really serve as a 'sequel' to one volume covering all of Europe during three centuries. As a synthesis, the one volume is, as yet, unsurpassed and, unlike the other surveys, contains a large classified bibliography. An English translation which has just been issued: *The Coming of the Book*, tr. David Gerard (London, 1976) unfortunately omits the bibliography, which is by now in need of updating. Steinberg, *Five Hundred Years*, covers a wider interval in fewer pages but lacks the richness and depth of the French volume. In dealing with the most recent centuries, Steinberg's work is especially thin. But in covering the first century after Gutenberg, he offers some data that is not duplicated in the other surveys despite their traversal of the same ground.

[6] Hay, 'Literature: The printed book,' pp. 359–86. See n. 64 below.

[7] Steinberg, *Five Hundred Years*, p. 11.

into other works, studies dealing with the history of printing are isolated and artificially sealed off from the rest of historical literature. In theory, these studies center on a topic that impinges on many other fields. In fact, they are seldom consulted by scholars who work in any other field, perhaps because their relevance to other fields is still not clear. 'The exact nature of the impact which the invention and spread of printing had on Western civilization remains subject to interpretation even today.'[8] This seems to understate the case. There are few interpretations even of an inexact or approximate nature upon which scholars may draw when pursuing other inquiries.[9] The effects produced by printing have aroused little controversy, not because views on the topic coincide, but because almost none have been set forth in an explicit and systematic form. Indeed those who seem to agree that momentous changes were entailed always seem to stop short of telling us just what they were.

The following two citations may suffice to illustrate the range of evasive tactics that are employed. The first comes from a justly celebrated study of comparative literature by an eminent literary historian: 'The immense and revolutionary change which it [the invention of printing] brought about can be summarized in one sentence: Until that time every book was a manuscript.'[10] The author goes on to discuss scribal book production, in a somewhat fanciful and romantic vein.[11] Nothing more is said about what happened *after* books ceased being manuscripts and perhaps this explains how Curtius can assert: 'we have modernized our railroads but not our system of transmitting tradition.'[12] In my view, the transmission of literary traditions was 'modernized' several centuries before the steam engine appeared; but this cannot be seen unless one takes a longer look at the 'immense and revolutionary change,' than Curtius does. That an otherwise careful scholar entertains

---

[8] Hirsch, *Printing, Selling*, p. 2.

[9] The casual treatment given to the topic by most historians has often been underlined by students of library science, without much effect. See e.g. remarks by Uhlendorf, 'The Invention and Spread of Printing,' p. 179.

[10] Curtius, *European Literature*, p. 238.

[11] Compare Curtius' remarks about the diligent, loving, sedulous scribe (p. 328) with Ivins' 'sloppy, clumsy, inelegant, hastily and carelessly written manuscript' as reported by Bühler, *The Fifteenth Century Book*, p. 87. Curtius says that 'every book produced by copying' was 'a personal achievement,' overlooking all the evidence that shows piecemeal copying was common – at least as far back as the ninth century. See Destrez, *La Pecia*, pp. 21; 44. The misleading impression of manuscript books conveyed by the beautiful specimens preserved in library treasure rooms is underlined by Butler, *Origin of Printing*, p. 11.

[12] Curtius, *European Literature*, p. 16.

the notion of summarizing such a change in a single sentence is surely remarkable. A less exceptional approach is provided by the author of the second citation, who has contributed much to the special literature on printing and whose competence in this field gives his views added weight. 'It would require an extensive volume to set forth even in outline the far-reaching effects of this invention in every field of human enterprise.'[13] This is probably so. Yet no volume, whether slim or extensive, can set forth or present in outline form, effects that have not yet been described or explicitly defined. Douglas McMurtrie's reference to an immense unwritten volume turns out to be scarcely more satisfying than Ernst Curtius' summary sentence. In both instances we learn nothing more about seemingly momentous consequences save that they occurred. Nor is the curious reader offered any guidance as to where one might go to learn more.

Since we are concerned with 'far-reaching effects' that, by common consent, left no field of human enterprise untouched, one might well wonder why such effects still remain undetermined. 'Neither political, constitutional, ecclesiastical, and economic events, nor sociological, philosophical, and literary movements can be fully understood without taking into account the influence the printing press has exerted upon them.'[14] All these events and movements have been subjected to close scrutiny by generations of scholars with the aim of understanding them more fully. If the printing press exerted some influence upon them, why is this influence so often unnoted, so rarely even hinted at, let alone discussed? The question is worth posing if only to suggest that the effects produced by printing are by no means self-evident. Insofar as they may be encountered by scholars exploring different fields, they are apt to pass unrecognized at present. To track them down and set them forth – in an outline or some other form – is much easier said than done.

When McMurtrie or Steinberg refer to the impact of printing on every field of human enterprise – political, economic, philosophical and so forth – it is by no means clear just what they have in mind. In part at least they seem to be pointing to indirect consequences which have to be inferred and which are associated with the consumption of printed products or with changed mental habits. Such consequences are, of course, of major historical significance and impinge on most forms of human enterprise. Nevertheless it is difficult to describe them

[13] McMurtrie, *The Book*, p. 136.   [14] Steinberg, *Five Hundred Years*, p. 11.

precisely or even to determine exactly what they are. It is one thing to describe how methods of book production changed after the mid-fifteenth century or to estimate rates of increased output. It is another thing to decide how access to a greater abundance or variety of written records affected ways of learning, thinking, and perceiving among literate élites. Similarly, it is one thing to show that standardization was a consequence of printing. It is another to decide how laws, languages, or mental constructs were affected by more uniform texts. Even at present, despite all the data being obtained from living responsive subjects; despite all the efforts being made by public opinion analysts, pollsters or behavioral scientists; we still know very little about how access to printed materials affects human behavior.[15] (A glance at recent controversies on the desirability of censoring pornography shows how ignorant we are.) Historians who have to reach out beyond the grave to reconstruct past forms of consciousness are especially disadvantaged in dealing with such issues. Theories about unevenly phased changes affecting literacy rates, learning processes, attitudes and expectations, do not lend themselves, at all events, to simple, clear-cut formulations that can be easily tested or integrated into conventional historical narratives.

Problems posed by some of the more important effects produced by the shift from script to print, by indirect consequences that have to be inferred and by imponderables that defy accurate measurement, probably can never be overcome entirely. But such problems could be confronted more squarely if other impediments did not lie in the way. Among the far-reaching effects that need to be noted are many that still affect present observations and that operate with particularly great force upon every professional scholar. Thus constant access to printed materials is a prerequisite for the practice of the historian's own craft. It is difficult to observe processes that enter so intimately into our own observations. In order to assess changes ushered in by printing, for example, we need to survey the conditions that prevailed before its advent. Yet the conditions of scribal culture can only be observed through a veil of print.

Even a cursory acquaintance with the findings of anthropologists or casual observations of pre-school age children may help to remind us of the gulf that exists between oral and literate cultures. Several studies,

15 Berelson and Janowitz, *Reader in Public Opinion* contains several relevant articles.

accordingly, have illuminated the difference between mentalities shaped by reliance on the spoken as opposed to the written word.[16] The gulf that separates our experience from that of literate élites who relied exclusively on hand-copied texts is much more difficult to fathom. There is nothing analogous in our experience or in that of any living creature within the Western world at present. The conditions of scribal culture thus have to be artificially reconstructed by recourse to history books and reference guides. Yet for the most part, these works are more likely to conceal than to reveal the object of such a search. Scribal themes are carried forward, post-print trends are traced backward in a manner that makes it difficult to envisage the existence of a distinctive literary culture based on hand-copying.[17] There is not even an agreed-upon term in common use which designates the system of written communications that prevailed before print.[18]

Schoolchildren who are asked to trace early overseas voyages on identical outline maps are likely to become absent-minded about the fact that there were no uniform world maps in the era when the voyages were made. A similar absent-mindedness on a more sophisticated level is encouraged by increasingly refined techniques for collating manuscripts and producing authoritative editions of them. Each successive edition tells us more than was previously known about how a given manuscript was composed and copied. By the same token, each makes it more difficult to envisage how a given manuscript appeared to a scribal scholar who had only one hand-copied version to consult and no certain guidance as to its place or date of composition, its title or

[16] For suggestive imaginative use of the distinction between oral and literate cultures to illuminate diverse phases of Greek thought, see Havelock, *Preface to Plato*. The same distinction is discussed from the viewpoint of anthropologists by Goody and Watt, 'The Consequences of Literacy,' 304–45. See also collection of essays, edited by Goody, *Literacy in Traditional Societies* for pertinent discussion and references. Despite passing reference to the work of McLuhan and Ong in Goody's introduction, the difference between scribal culture and print culture tends to be blurred by arguments which contrast alphabetic with ideographic writing and oral with written transmission but not script with print. For an earlier, somewhat neglected essay comparing oral with written transmission, see Gandz, 'The Dawn of Literature.' As noted in my preface, recent interest in African studies has stimulated a new, large and mushrooming literature on this question. See bibliography given by Vansina.

[17] For elaboration on this point, see my essay, 'Clio and Chronos.'

[18] I have found the term 'scribal culture' useful as a shorthand way of referring to such activities as producing and duplicating books, transmitting messages, reporting news and storing data after the invention of writing and before that of movable type. 'Chirographic' is more correctly opposed to 'Typographic' by Father Ong but seems somewhat too recondite for my purposes. As noted in my preface, the term 'print culture' is used to refer only to post-Gutenberg developments in the West. How printing affected pre-Gutenberg Asia must be left to others to investigate.

9

author. Historians are trained to discriminate between manuscript sources and printed texts; but they are not trained to think with equal care about how manuscripts appeared when this sort of discrimination was inconceivable[19] – when everything was off the record, so to speak, save that which was read to those who were within earshot. Similarly, the more thoroughly we are trained to master the events and dates contained in modern history books, the less likely we are to appreciate the difficulties confronting scribal scholars who had access to assorted written records, but lacked uniform chronologies, maps and all the other reference guides which are now in common use.

Efforts to reconstruct the circumstances that preceded printing thus lead to a scholarly predicament. Reconstruction requires recourse to printed materials, thereby blurring clear perception of the conditions that prevailed before these materials were available. Even when the predicament is partly resolved by sensitive scholars who manage to develop a genuine 'feel' for the times after handling countless documents,[20] efforts at reconstruction are still bound to be frustratingly incomplete.

For the very texture of scribal culture was so fluctuating, uneven and multiform that few long-range trends can be traced. Conditions that prevailed near the bookshops of ancient Rome, in the Alexandrian library, or in certain medieval monasteries and university towns, made it possible for literate élites to develop a relatively sophisticated 'bookish' culture.[21] Yet all library collections were subject to contraction, and all texts in manuscript were liable to get corrupted after being copied over the course of time. Outside certain transitory special centers, moreover, the texture of scribal culture was so thin that heavy

19 The need to distinguish between the pre-Gutenberg manuscript and the post-print one has been recognized by specialists in the history of the book. For general discussion of the 'archeology' of the manuscript book, see Josserand, 'Les Bibliothèques.' One scholar has suggested reserving the term 'codicology' for the study of the pre-print manuscript book and using the term 'manuscriptology' for the study of mss. after Gutenberg. See important article by Gruijs, 'Codicology or Archeology of the Book?' where pertinent remarks of W. Hellinga at a Dutch Philological Congress in 1952 are cited (p. 107, n. 4). The absent-mindedness of most modern book users about the nature of manuscript books handled by scholars before print is brought out by Goldschmidt, *Medieval Texts*, p. 9.

20 A remarkable imaginative reconstruction of the European mentality before print is offered by Febvre, *Le problème*. See especially the sections devoted to the printing press and hearsay, pp. 418–87. For another example of sensitivity to the conditions of scribal culture, see Smalley, *English Friars*, pp. 9–10. A pioneering effort to describe how medieval literature was shaped by scribal procedures is Chaytor's *From Script to Print*.

21 I have not mentioned Moslem or Byzantine centers simply because they are off limits for this book. It is a truism that scribal culture flourished more vigorously in certain centers outside Latin Christendom than within it during much of the medieval millennium.

reliance was placed on oral transmission even by literate élites. Insofar as dictation governed copying in scriptoria and literary compositions were 'published' by being read aloud, even 'book' learning was governed by reliance on the spoken word – producing a hybrid half-oral, half-literate culture that has no precise counterpart today. Just what publication meant before printing or just how messages got transmitted in the age of scribes are questions that cannot be answered in general.[22] Findings are bound to vary enormously depending on date and place. Contradictory verdicts are especially likely to proliferate with regard to the last century before printing – an interval when paper had become available and the literate man was more likely to become his own scribe.

Specialists in the field of incunabula, who are confronted by ragged evidence, are likely to insist that a similar lack of uniformity characterizes procedures used by early printers. To generalize about early printing is undoubtedly hazardous and one should be on guard against projecting the output of modern standard editions too far back into the past.[23] Yet one must also be on guard against blurring a major difference between the last century of scribal culture and the first century after Gutenberg. Early print culture is sufficiently uniform to permit us to measure its diversity. We can estimate output, arrive at averages, trace trends. For example, we have rough estimates of the total output of all printed materials during the age of incunabula. Similarly, we can say that the 'average' early edition ranged between two hundred and one thousand copies. There are no comparable figures for the last fifty years of scribal culture. Indeed we have no figures at all. What is the 'average edition' turned out between 1400 and 1450? The question verges on nonsense. The term 'edition' comes close to being an anachronism when applied to copies of a manuscript book.[24]

Some of the difficulties of trying to estimate scribal output are

[22] Although very old, the article by Root, 'Publication before Printing,' still provides the best introduction to this topic. See also Bennett, 'The Production and Dissemination of Vernacular Manuscripts.'

[23] How operations performed by actual early printers differed from those imagined by bibliographers is vividly described by McKenzie, 'Printers of the Mind.' A warning against attributing modern standardization to early editions is offered by Black, 'The Printed Bible.' See also discussion in chap. 2, section 2 below.

[24] Here, as elsewhere, opinions vary. For references to an 'edition' of a thirteenth-century Paris Bible, see Branner: 'Manuscript Makers' and 'The Soissons Bible Paintshop.'

illustrated in the following chapter. As examples given there will show, quantification is not suited to the conditions of scribal culture. The production figures which are most often cited, on the basis of the memoirs of a Florentine manuscript bookdealer, turn out to be entirely untrustworthy.[25] Quattrocento Florence, in any case, is scarcely typical of other Italian centers (such as Bologna), let alone of regions beyond the Alps. But then *no* region is typical. There is no 'typical' bookdealer, scribe or even manuscript.[26] Even if we set aside problems presented by secular book producers and markets as hopelessly complex and consider only the needs of churchmen on the eve of printing, we are still faced by a remarkable diversity of procedures. Book provisions for diverse monastic orders varied; mendicant friars had different arrangements from monks. Popes and cardinals often turned to the 'multifarious activities' of the Italian *cartolai*; preachers made their own anthologies of sermons; semi-lay orders attempted to provide primers and catechisms for everyman.

The absence of an average output or a typical procedure poses a stumbling-block when we try to set the stage for the advent of print. An earlier version of this chapter, for example, asserted that book production moved from scriptoria to printers' workshops in the late fifteenth century. The assertion was criticized by a medievalist scholar on the grounds that book production had already left the monasteries in the course of the twelfth century, when lay stationers began to handle book provisions for university faculties and the mendicant orders. With the so-called 'book revolution' of the twelfth century and university supervision of copying, there came a 'putting-out' system. Copyists were no longer assembled in a single room, but worked on different portions of a given text, receiving payment from the stationer for each piece (the so-called 'pecia' system). Book production, according to my critic, had thus moved out of scriptoria three centuries *before* the advent of print.

The objection seems worth further thought. Certainly one ought to pay attention to the rise of the lay stationer in university towns and other urban centers during the twelfth and thirteenth centuries.[27] The

---

25 See reference to Albinia de la Mare's research on Vespasiano da Bisticci in n. 28 below.
26 For useful warning against the notion of a 'typical' manuscript book, see Delaissé, *Le Manuscrit Autographe*, I, 50.
27 For terse description of twelfth-century 'book revolution' see Humphreys, *The Book Provisions*, p. 13. The system of the 'pecia' handled by university stationers in Oxford, Paris,

contrast between the free labor of monks working for remission of sins and the wage labor of lay copyists is an important one. Recent research has stressed the use of a putting-out system and has also called into question long-lived assumptions about the existence of lay scriptoria attached to stationers' shops.[28] Thus one must be especially cautious about using the term scriptoria to apply to conditions in the later middle ages – more cautious than I was in my preliminary version.

Yet on the other hand one must also be wary about placing too much emphasis on trends launched in twelfth-century Paris, Oxford, Bologna and other university towns where copies were multiplied rapidly to serve special institutional needs. Caution is needed when extending university regulations on the system of the 'pecia' to the actual practices of university stationers – let alone to bookdealers serving non-university clientèle.[29] That relatively clear thirteenth-century patterns

Bologna who farmed out pieces of a given ms. for copying and were meant to have their mss. periodically checked against an exemplar by university officials is described in exhaustive detail by Destrez.

[28] Compare categorical statement in Febvre and Martin, *L'Apparition*, pp. 18–19, concerning 'véritables ateliers de copistes' with penetrating critique by Delaissé questioning the existence of any such 'workshops' in his *Art Bulletin* review of Millard Meiss' work. The dispersal of the diverse individuals responsible for turning out manuscript Bibles in thirteenth-century France is also described by Branner: 'Manuscript Makers;' 'The Soissons Bible Paintshop.' The long lived notion that Vespasiano da Bisticci (the most celebrated Florentine bookdealer of the quattrocento) had an actual scriptorium attached to his shop is not sustained by the intensive research of de la Mare, 'Vespasiano' and 'Messer Piero Strozzi, A Florentine Scribe.' She says that Vespasiano farmed out manuscripts for copying to notaries like Strozzi who did the work in their spare time. There are no records showing that he ever kept any group of copyists regularly employed on any task. For further comment on Vespasiano and de la Mare's findings see chap. 2, notes 6, 13, 14 below. On the other hand, I have not seen anyone challenge the 'secular scriptorium' in early fourteenth-century London which was uncovered by Loomis, 'The Auchinleck Manuscript,' or John Shirley's 'publishing firm,' as noted by Raymond Irwin, introduction, *The English Library Before 1700*, p. 5. The oft-cited 'book factory' run by Diebold Lauber in Hagenau (Alsace), and other similar lay scriptoria in Strassburg and Stuttgart are noted by Lehmann-Haupt, 'The Heritage of the Manuscript,' and *Peter Schoeffer*, pp. 64–5. For discussion and references offering a conventional (now outmoded? view) see Harrington, 'The Production and Distribution of Books.' Chapter 5 is devoted to 'public commercial scriptoria' from the twelfth to the fifteenth centuries. Evidence that Paris college chambers were used as scriptoria even in the late middle ages is given by Willard, 'The Manuscripts of Jean Petit's justification.' For the purpose of rapid simultaneous copying, the advantages of gathering many copyists to receive dictation in one room seem so obvious, it is difficult to envisage a complete abandonment of the scriptorium at any point during the centuries of hand-produced books.

[29] Although authorities often assume that the 'pecia' actually performed as university statutes intended it to – that it arrested corruption and encouraged the production of uniform texts (see e.g. Febvre and Martin, *L'Apparition*, pp. 10–11; Hirsch, *Printing, Selling*, p. xi) – a careful reading of Destrez, *La Pecia* shows the contrary was often the case (see discussion of *pecia corrupta* or *falsa*, pp. 70–1; also passages on pp. 35; 40–1). The numerous categories of manuscript books that were not subject to this system although carefully noted by Destrez (pp. 20, 43) are also often overlooked in more general accounts.

get smudged by the late fourteenth century must also be kept in mind. It is a mistake to imply that the 'pecia' once introduced, continued down to the advent of printing. Available evidence suggests that it declined a full century before the first presses appeared.[30] During the interval between 1350 and 1450 – the crucial century when setting our stage – conditions were unusually anarchic and some presumably obsolete habits were revived. Monastic scriptoria, for example, were beginning to experience their 'last golden age'.[31]

The so-called 'book revolution' of the twelfth century had not entirely extinguished the tradition of copying as part of the *opus dei*. It was energetically revived in the Netherlands by the orders founded by Gerhard Groote. 'No religious community had ever concentrated its energies on book production as Groote's brethren did.'[32] This revival was not confined to regions where the *devotio moderna* flourished. Elsewhere the tradition of Cassiodorus was also given a new lease on life. The early fifteenth-century treatise by Jean Gerson *In Praise of Scribes* was written in reply to queries from Carthusians and Celestines about permission to copy books on feast days.[33]

The existence of monastic scriptoria right down to and even beyond the days of early printing is most intriguingly demonstrated by that anomalous treatise which owed much to Gerson and is often cited as a curiosity in books on early printing: Johannes Trithemius' *De Laude Scriptorum*. This is the treatise where the Abbot of Sponheim not only exhorted his monks to copy books but enriched an ancient topos by explaining why 'monks should not stop copying because of the invention of printing.'[34] Among other arguments (the usefulness of keeping idle hands busy, encouraging diligence, devotion, knowledge of scripture, etc.) Trithemius somewhat illogically compared the written word on parchment which would last one thousand years with the printed word on paper which would have a shorter life-span. The possible use of paper (and scraped parchment) by copyists, or of skin for

---

[30] Destrez, p. 25, notes that the system of the 'pecia' declined by the time paper came into common use, for reasons that are unclear. Its relatively short-lived existence is underlined by Hajnal, *L'Enseignement*, p. 238. In Oxford it existed from the 1230s until the mid-fourteenth century according to Pollard, 'The University and the Book Trade.'

[31] Klaus Arnold, introduction to Johannes Trithemius' *In Praise of Scribes – De Laude Scriptorum*, p. 14.   [32] Southern, *Western Society*, p. 350.   [33] Gerson, 'De Laude.'

[34] Trithemius *Praise of Scribes* (ed. Arnold), chap. 7, p. 63. Versions of this advice are cited by several authorities: Clapp, 'The Story of Permanent Durable Book Paper,' ii, 108; Bühler, *Fifteenth Century Book*, p. 35; Fussner, *The Historical Revolution*, p. 8 (who cites a relevant passage from Ivy, 'Bibliography of the Manuscript Book.')

a special printed version went unmentioned. As a hebraist, a Christian scholar and a reader of Gerson, the Abbot was clearly familiar with the topos which had first set durable parchment against perishable papyrus.[35] His arguments show his concern about preserving a form of manual labor which seemed especially suitable for monks. Whether he was genuinely worried about an increased use of paper – as an ardent bibliophile and in the light of ancient warnings – is an open question. But his activities show clearly that as an author he did not favor handwork over presswork. He had his *Praise of Scribes* promptly printed, as he did his weightier works.[36] Indeed he used one Mainz print shop so frequently that 'it could almost be called the Sponheim Abbey Press.'[37]

Even before the Abbot of Sponheim made his trip from scriptorium to print shop, the Carthusian monks of Saint Barbara's Charterhouse in Cologne were turning to local printers to extend their efforts, as a cloistered order bound by vows of silence, to preach 'with their hands.'[38] As many accounts note, the same thing happened outside Cologne and not just among the Carthusians.[39] A variety of reformed

---

35 Trithemius' dependence on Gerson for other sections is noted by Arnold, introduction, p. 20. Febvre and Martin, *L'Apparition*, p. 31, note how Gerson advised durable parchment rather than perishable paper (given the date, nothing is said about presswork as against handwork, of course). One of Saint Jerome's fourth-century epistles describes the damage done to papyrus (paper) volumes in the great library of Pamphilus at Caesarea and how they were replaced by more durable vellum ones. There are also injunctions in the *Talmud* about writing on skin rather than paper. (See Kenyon, *Books and Readers*, pp. 44–5; 115.)

36 On Trithemius' contacts with Basel printers, German humanist circles and his significant roles as bibliographer, chronicler, cryptographer and necromancer, see pp. 94–7 below.

37 Arnold, introduction, p. 15, notes that Trithemius closely supervised the presswork of Peter von Friedberg at Mainz and that thirteen of the twenty-five editions this printer produced during the decade 1490–1500 were works by Trithemius (1494–8); another six were by the Abbot's friends.

38 Collaboration between the Carthusian monk, Werner Rolevinck and the Cologne printer, Arnold Therhoernen in the 1470s is discussed by the former in his preface to his *Sermo de Presentacione Beate Virginis Marie* (Cologne, 1470) and is now being investigated by Richard B. Marks. Marks is following up his recent monograph: *The Medieval Manuscript Library* with a series of articles on the late mss. and early printed versions produced by the Cologne Carthusians and has kindly supplied me with advance copies of his papers – upon which I have drawn. For further references to the theme of 'preaching with one's hands' (which goes back at least to Cassiodorus), see pp. 316–17, 373–4 below.

39 According to Hirsch, *Printing, Selling*, p. 54, at least seven monastic presses were established in German areas by the 1470s. Kristeller, 'The Contribution of Religious Orders to Thought and Learning,' p. 99, n. 13 offers references to early monastic presses in Italy and England (p. 99 discusses the Convent of San Jacopo of Ripoli as one of the chief early presses in Florence). Febvre, *Au Cœur Religieux*, p. 33n notes the setting up of presses by French monks in Chartres. Febvre and Martin, *L'Apparition*, p. 264, mention several French abbeys in Burgundy. The adoption of printing by the Brethren of the Common Life in the Netherlands and the large output of the Deventer press, which had an uncertain affiliation with Groote's

Benedictine orders also kept local printers busy and, in some cases, monks and nuns ran monastic presses themselves. The possible significance of this intrusion of a capitalist enterprise into consecrated space belongs to other sections of this book.[40] Monastic copying and presswork have been mentioned here merely to suggest what might be missed if the rise of the lay stationer in the twelfth century is overplayed. To rule out the formula 'scriptorium to printshop' completely seems almost as unwise as to attempt to apply it in a blanket form.

As these comments may suggest, it is easier to generalize about the new system of book production than about the old, especially when considering the interval 1350–1450. Uniformity and synchronization have become so common since the advent of printing, that we have to remind ourselves repeatedly that they were usually absent in the age of scribes. When one has been trained to view phenomena at a distance, however, one is prone to myopia about those that occur, so to speak, directly under one's eyes. The apparent blindness of most scholars to effects exerted by the medium they look at every day has been most emphatically stressed and elaborately treated by Marshall McLuhan.[41] According to his thesis, subliminal effects are engendered by repeatedly scanning lines of print presented in a standardized format. Habitual book readers are so subjectively conditioned by these effects that they are incapable of recognizing them. The bizarre typographical format of *The Gutenberg Galaxy* is presumably designed to counteract this conditioning and to jolt the reader out of accustomed mental ruts. McLuhan attributes his own awareness of and ability to withstand the quasi-hypnotic power of print to the advent of new audio-visual and electronic media. By affecting our senses and conditioning our perception differently, he holds, the new media have begun to break the bookish spell that held literate members of Western society in thrall during the past five centuries.

It is noteworthy that the author, while presenting his thesis in an

order is covered by Sheppard, 'Printing at Deventer.' The intellectual influence of the Brethren in general and their involvement in Deventer in particular has been overstated, according to Post, *The Modern Devotion*, pp. 8–10; 551–3. The transition from scriptorium to press in Zwolle is well documented in the *Narratio de Inchoatione Domus Clericorum in Zwollis*, ed. M. Schoengen (1908), cited by Southern, *Western Society and the Church*, p. 349.

40 See reference to Hellinga article, chap. 2, n. 55, and discussion of Luther's attitudes and the Weber thesis, chap. 4, sect. 5 below.

41 McLuhan, *The Gutenberg Galaxy*. The same theme is elaborated in *Understanding Media: The Extensions of Man*. For further comment on McLuhan, see below pp. 40–1.

unconventional format, tends to undermine it at the same time by drawing heavily for substantiation on conventional scholarly literature even while reiterating conventional nineteenth-century literary themes. The chaotic format of *The Gutenberg Galaxy* probably owes less to the impact of new media than to the old-fashioned difficulty of trying to organize material gleaned from wide-ranging reading – evaded in this instance by an old-fashioned tactic, by resorting to scissors and paste. When its author argues that typography has become obsolescent and that an 'electric age' has outmoded the 'technology of literacy' he is himself (in my view, at least) failing to take full note of what is under his own eyes and that of the reader he addresses.

Elaborate media-analysis does not seem to be required to explain current myopia about the impact of print. Since Gutenberg's day printed materials have become exceedingly common. They ceased to be newsworthy more than a century ago and have attracted ever less attention the more ubiquitous they have become. But although calendars, maps, time-tables, dictionaries, catalogues, textbooks and newspapers are taken for granted at present (or even dismissed as old-fashioned by purveyors of novelties) they continue to exert as great an influence on daily life as ever they did before.[42] Indeed the more abundant they have become, the more frequently they are used, the more profound and widespread their impact. Typography is thus still indispensable to the transmission of the most sophisticated technological skills. It underlies the present knowledge explosion and much of modern art. In my view, at least, it accounts for much that is singled out as peculiarly characteristic of mid-twentieth century culture.[43] But, I repeat, the more printed materials accumulate, the more we are inclined to overlook them in favor of more recent, less familiar media. Articles speculating about the effects of television will thus find a larger market than conjectures about the impact of print. Because the latter has become increasingly less visible, repercussions that are actually being augmented and amplified at present are paradoxically believed to be diminishing instead.

---

[42] The extent to which 'ours is a typographical culture' and the accompanying tendency to take the functions wrought by printing too much for granted is brought out clearly by Butler, *Origin of Printing*, pp. 2–4.

[43] As noted in Eisenstein, 'Clio and Chronos,' p. 63, present nihilistic and chaotic aesthetic trends owe more to the preservative powers of print than is often realized. See also the concluding chapter of volume II of this book.

The prolonged ubiquity of printed materials, however, does not completely explain current myopia. The era of incunabula had ended well before Bacon, Campanella, Galileo or Kepler were born. But none of them was inclined to take typography for granted; on the contrary, each commented on its great significance. To be sure, by present standards, printed materials were relatively scarce in the early seventeenth century. Nevertheless, by contemporary standards they were remarkably abundant and were already being described as a glut on the market; 'begotten only to distract and abuse the weaker judgements of scholars and to maintain the Trade and Mystery of Typographers' according to Sir Thomas Browne.[44] Since the scanning of printed pages had become a familiar daily routine in seventeenth-century scholarly circles and yet letterpress was still being discussed as a conspicuous innovation, our present tendency to overlook it needs further explanation.

Some additional points are worth considering. In the seventeenth century, many scholars and intellectuals were on much closer terms with print shops and typographers than they have been since the industrialization of printing led to new divisions of labor. Down through the Age of Enlightenment, genteel publishers and mechanic printers had not yet come to a parting of the ways. An early seventeenth-century virtuoso, such as Kepler, who spent hours in print shops himself, closely supervising scientific presswork, was likely to be more alert to print technology than are contemporary astronomers, who send off their findings to the editors of journals and assume publication will be forthcoming, after receiving a favorable verdict from referees. How this growing distance from printing plants has affected the attitudes of men of knowledge remains to be assessed.[45] Has it helped, perhaps, to reinforce a disdain for technology and applied science on the part of those who are engaged in 'pure' research?

In addition to the industrialization of printing trades and new divisions of intellectual labor, problems of censorship and ideology also

---

[44] *Religio Medici* (1643), sect. 24 in *The Prose of Sir Thomas Browne*, p. 32. See also citation from Lope de Vega in Preserved Smith, *A History of Modern Culture* II, 276. Although Smith implies that it was only in the seventeenth century that the multiplication of books began to be felt as an oppression, Erasmus had already complained about the swarms of new books. See 'Festina Lente,' *The 'Adages' of Erasmus*, pp. 182–3. This complaint probably owed something to ancient scribal literary conventions. Both Petrarch and Juvenal had, after all, complained about the number of scribblers at work in their day.

[45] See discussion of Mannheim's views p. 154, below.

need to be brought into the picture. In the early-modern era, gaining access to publication outlets often entailed circumventing censors and engaging in illicit activities. A man of letters who had to smuggle out a manuscript for publication by a foreign press or locate a clandestine press in his native land was less likely to take the services of printers for granted than are most men of letters (in Western Europe, at least) today. This was especially true of Campanella, Galileo and Kepler, as it was of the later *philosophes* who lived under Catholic rule. Tributes to the power of the press were more compatible with patriotic themes in Protestant realms; emphasis on the epoch-making functions performed by printing had anti-papist and anti-Roman overtones. The theme was thus developed by anti-Italian German humanists, amplified by Lutherans and other Protestants, carried on by Huguenots, Puritans, freethinkers and Enlightenment *philosophes*, reaching a final climax in the writings of Whig historians, such as Macaulay, and anti-clerical ones, such as Michelet.[46] Thereafter, however, the apostles of progress were diverted from gunpowder and printing, first to the steam engine and then to the dynamo. By the late nineteenth century, the hand press itself was becoming something of a museum piece – a point that also helps to explain why it seems less conspicuous to us than to Francis Bacon or Condorcet.

The cumulative impact of recent technological advance thus has also helped to relegate the fifteenth-century invention to the position of an antique; of more interest to rare book dealers than to observers of the modern scene. It is symptomatic that incunabula have joined hand-produced books as highly valued scarce objects to be placed in glass cases and cherished as vestiges of a distant, lost past.[47] Given the

[46] On Condorcet's influential scheme and its use by Michelet, see chap. 3, n. 420 below; Protestant historiography is discussed on pp. 304–5 below. The recently published *Mémoires de Louis Philippe* I, 4 start with describing the invention of printing as perhaps 'the most decisive event in the history of man' and assign it a prime role in destroying feudalism.

[47] The present 'museum-culture' veneration of manuscripts and incunabula is in marked contrast to the careless approach of earlier eras. The fact that sixteenth-century men often discarded manuscripts 'like old newspapers' once a printed edition had been made (see Destrez, *La Pecia*, p. 18) or that seventeenth-century Oxford librarians sold off Shakespeare's first folio as superfluous after the third had appeared (Bühler, *Fifteenth Century Book*, p. 101, n. 44) is sometimes taken to indicate a benighted contempt for manuscripts that came with printing. See e.g. Allen, *The Age of Erasmus*, pp. 159–60. But even before Gutenberg, some humanist book-hunters showed singularly little interest in preserving the manuscript from which they copied a given text. See Reynolds and Wilson, *Scribes and Scholars*, p. 116. On the other hand, as an editor working for Sweynheim and Pannartz, de Bussi complained of niggardly collectors withholding their loan of manuscripts to the firm he served because 'they esteemed the

recent rapid pace of innovation, moreover, the Renaissance convention of coupling printing with other post-classical inventions has also helped to diminish the attention focused upon it. The more rapidly new inventions proliferate, the less conspicuous earlier ones tend to become. The expansion of the so-called modern knowledge industry has produced similar results, with modern scholars uncovering old inventions almost as rapidly as modern technology has brought forth new ones.[48] As just one more item in an increasingly cluttered inventory, the printing press has also become less distinctive.

In this respect we have come around almost a full circle since the press was first tacked on to a long list of post-classical novelties. This list had been drawn up before Gutenberg, by a Papal librarian who mentioned some twenty-two items (including the stirrup, the mechanical clock, the compass, and gunpowder) to illustrate a possible reason for using non-Latin words.[49] In the course of the sixteenth century this concern over a philological departure from pure Latinity was transmuted into a celebration of technological advance. The written word was powerfully reinforced by graphic presentation. 'Nova Reperta,' an often reproduced series of copper-plate engravings celebrating 'modern' inventions and discoveries, designed by Vasari's pupil 'Stradanus' (Jan van der Straet) in the 1580s (engraved and published repeatedly by the Antwerp firm of Galleus) probably did as much as any written treatise to fix the theme in its present familiar form.[50] After interest had shifted from the study of words to the invention of things, items were reordered and assigned varying degrees of importance.[51]

art of printing to be a depreciation of their property.' Botfield, *Praefationes*, pp. vi–vii. Franklin, 'Conjectures on Rarity,' suggests that the ethos of the 'rare book room' first appears in the seventeenth century.

[48] Publications by the Society of the History of Technology during the past decade suggest the problem of squeezing Gutenberg's invention onto crowded inventories. References to printing are infrequent in the articles, reviews, and cumulative bibliographies published in *Technology and Culture*.

[49] On Giovanni Tortelli's list, see Keller, 'A Renaissance Humanist.' Composed in 1449, 'De Orthographia' was first printed in 1471 in both Rome (by Gallus and Nicholaus) and in Venice. It ran through thirteen incunable editions.

[50] Keller, 'Mathematical Technologies,' pp. 22–3. An interesting view of the Antwerp firm of engravers who produced 'Nova Reperta' is offered by Bataillon, 'Philippe Galle et Arias Montano.' The role of engraver–publisher *and* of the caption writer (Cornilis Kiliaan or A. C. Kilianus Dufflaeus) – both of whom were affiliated with Plantin's circle in Antwerp – points to a collaborative effort. The series is too often credited to Stradanus alone.

[51] Both Sarton, *Six Wings*, pp. 248–9, n. 35, and White, *Medieval Technology*, p. 135, n. 1, note how the title page of *Nova Reperta* series places printing, compass, and gunpowder in the company of the stirrup, the mechanical clock, the discovery of America, silk, distilling and a purported cure for syphilis. This seems fairly cluttered, yet it reduces the number of items

Printing, gunpowder and the compass were singled out for special prominence on many different lists.[52] By the time Francis Bacon wrote about the need to take note of 'the force, effect and consequences' of human inventions or discoveries, he could assume that the 'most conspicuous' numbered only three.[53] No such assumption can be made at present. Although headline writers manage to discriminate among unprecedented events, by varying the scale of their captions, twentieth-century historians seem to have lost the knack.[54] Once again, our lists of innovations have become cluttered and confused. In view of the oddly assorted company Gutenberg's invention keeps at present (I have found it placed between the insurance contract and advances in metallurgy in one account; between the mechanical clock and the university in another; between double-entry bookkeeping and spectacles in a third)[55] one wonders, indeed, where to look for it.

Does it belong where we are most accustomed to finding it, in the context of late medieval technology? In many ways it does seem appropriate to couple letterpress printing with other instruments of power and precision, and to place it in a sequence which includes developments in metallurgy and textiles and experiments in oil-based pigments and ink.[56] But if one is in the company of librarians and bibliophiles it will seem equally appropriate to place it in quite a different sequence associated with the history of the book. There it will be

inherited from Tortelli, whose list had been augmented earlier, not only by printing but also by other lesser items, such as the long hose and berets in Polydore Vergil's *De Inventoribus Rerum* (Venice, 1499). The title page of 'Nova Reperta' also discriminates by means of scale and position between the press and the cannon (which are large and central), the discovery of America and the magnetic compass (large and flanking the centerpieces) and other lesser objects which are smaller and scattered somewhat randomly on the ground. (I am grateful to Alice McGinty, whose dissertation on Stradanus was recently completed at Boston University, for providing me with a look at the full series and guiding me to literature on this subject.)

[52] In addition to Keller's articles, cited above, useful background on the coupling of gunpowder and compass with printing is offered by Wolper, 'The Rhetoric of Gunpowder'; and Kinser, 'Ideas of Temporal Change.'

[53] See Aphorism 129, *Novum Organum* – an excerpt is cited as an epigraph for chap. 2. Among other sixteenth-century comments, those of Budé and Rabelais (1532), Jean Fernel (1542), du Bellay (1549), Cardano (1551), Jean Bodin (1556), Frobisher (1578), Louis Le Roy (1557), Guillaume Postel (1560) contributed to making printing conspicuous by Bacon's time. For an Englishman like Bacon, Protestant propagandists, such as John Bale and John Foxe ought to be added to any such list.

[54] How perspectives are skewed by a recent proliferation of epoch-making events, strategic inventions, ages of crisis and decisive breaks with the past is discussed in my essay, 'Clio and Chronos,' pp. 38–9.

[55] Lopez, 'Hard Times and Investment in Culture,' p. 33; Mumford, *Technics and Civilization*, pp. 134–7; Durand, *The Vienna-Klosterneuberg Map Corpus*, p. 282.

[56] See Clapham, 'Printing.'

viewed as just one more stage of a long process which goes back at least to the slave labor of antiquity and to the shift from roll to codex.[57] Not late medieval metallurgy but the twelfth-century book revolution will be taken as the most significant point of departure. As we have seen, this context favors a gradual, evolutionary view. Once manuscript book-publishing has been organized on a new basis and paper production developed to handle an expanding trade, little room is left for innovation by the printer and his new machines.

Yet another different context is supplied by the economic historian. The latter is much more likely than the librarian to place the stationer's successor in an innovative role. Accordingly, the early printer is viewed as an urban entrepreneur who substituted machine-made products for hand-produced ones, who had to recoup large investments and secure financial aid; who pioneered in early mass production and extended trade networks beyond the limits of late medieval guilds and towns; who experienced labor problems, including early strikes, and who confronted constant competition from profit-driving rival firms. For the economic historian, then, the first printers belong in the company of other early capitalists rather than with the manuscript bookdealers of an earlier age.[58]

To portray early printers as early capitalists enables one to regard them as innovators. But it also places them uncomfortably close to the company of philistines and invites other misleading inferences associated with the behavior of economic man. It means losing sight of many other roles that were performed – in connection with the arts

[57] For English language studies of classical book production, libraries and book-trade, see Kenyon, *Books and Readers*; Reichmann, 'The Book Trade at the Time of the Roman Empire'; Pfeiffer, *History of Classical Scholarship*. By comparison, Putnam's *Authors and Their Public* is not worth consulting. Putnam's survey of medieval *Books and Their Makers*, is old-fashioned anecdotal and rambling but contains some useful data (albeit in a disorganized state). Reynolds and Wilson, *Scribes and Scholars* is intended to explain problems of transmission to 'beginners in the field of classical studies' but also serves as a most useful succinct introduction to medieval scribal culture. In addition to McMurtrie, two books by Diringer: *The Hand Produced Book* and *The Illuminated Book* also offer a useful general introduction. Book provisions in medieval English monasteries are covered by Knowles, *The Religious Orders in England* II, 331–51. For examples of the smooth transition from the late medieval manuscript book-trade to the early printed book-trade, see Lehmann-Haupt, 'Heritage of the Manuscript' and Harrington's dissertation.

[58] For discussion of far-flung markets and pioneering publicity developed by expanding firms during the first half century of printing, see Ehrman, 'The Fifteenth Century.' The use of printers' account books to illustrate facets of early capitalism is exemplified by Edler de Roover's articles, 'Cost Accounting in the Sixteenth Century;' 'New Facets on the Financing and Marketing of Early Printed Books,' and by F. Geldner, 'Das Rechnungsbuch des Speyrer ...Grossbuchhändlers Peter Drach.'

and sciences or with the learning and letters of the day. 'Printing was a mechanical art' writes Edgar Zilsel, 'and the publishers, though themselves classical scholars, were not literary dispensers of glory but business men.'[59] It seems more accurate to describe many publishers as being *both* businessmen *and* literary dispensers of glory. They served men of letters not only by providing traditional forms of patronage but also by acting as press agents and as cultural impresarios of a new kind. 'To make illustrious this author's name and to benefit the world' – Tartaglia's Venetian publisher thus described his motives in printing a posthumous translation of Euclid by the self-made artisan-engineer. Doubtless, he hoped to make money as well as win for Tartaglia a measure of fame. The point is that the profit motive was combined with other motives that were self-serving *and* altruistic, and even evangelistic, at times. The printer could take satisfaction in serving humanity at large even while enhancing the reputation of authors and making money for himself. This distinctive mixture of motives entered into the rapid expansion of early printing industries. A variety of interests were served and not merely those represented by economic man.

As pioneers in new manufacturing and marketing techniques, early printers shared something in common with other urban entrepreneurs; but as pioneers in advertising and publicity, in agitation and propaganda, in lexicography and bibliography they must be placed in a class by themselves. Their shops were different from those run by earlier manuscript bookdealers and lay stationers, because they contained new machines and mechanics trained to operate them. At the same time, the new workshops also differed from those run by other contemporary manufacturers because they served as gathering places for scholars, artists, and literati; as sanctuaries for foreign translators, emigrés and refugees; as institutions of advanced learning, and as focal points for every kind of cultural and intellectual interchange.

As these remarks may suggest, the establishment of print shops in urban centers throughout Europe rather resembles another topic described by Frances Yates as being everybody's business and thus nobody's business.[60] Diverse aspects of the multi-faceted topic are handled by diverse specialists engaged in tracing different sequences and sharing few common concerns. Although problems relating to

---

[59] Zilsel, 'The Origins of Gilbert's Scientific Method,' p. 24.
[60] Yates, *The Art of Memory*, p. 374.

book production and distribution come under the aegis of economic and social historians; those relating to consumption are more likely to be handled by literary scholars or media analysts. Although the history of the book is normally allocated to courses in library studies; the topic of printing itself is assigned to historians of technology while type design, layout and lettering are treated as part of a subspecialty taught in schools of design. Given a topic that is segmented, subdivided and parcelled out in this fashion, it is little wonder that one rarely gets a sense of its significance as a whole. Even the wide-ranging studies produced by social historians have failed to provide a full-length, well-rounded study of the new occupational culture represented by the early printer or a full assessment of his many roles.[61]

Thus a steady division of intellectual labor (perhaps an inevitable concomitant of the expanding knowledge industry) has also diminished the number of those who might be interested in following Bacon's advice. If printing often receives a somewhat cursory treatment in large volumes devoted to the history of the book, of Western technology or of early capitalism, it gets even shorter shrift elsewhere. Countless standard histories of Western philosophy, religion, and science, of political and economic theory, of historiography, literature or the fine arts pass over the topic entirely. Not only modern specialization, but also the persistence of a venerable philosophical tradition of proud ignorance concerning material and mechanical phenomena, may help to account for neglect by intellectual and cultural historians. Because of this neglect the history of ideas is weakened as a discipline. When ideas are detached from the media used to transmit them, they are also cut off from the historical circumstances that shape them, and it becomes difficult to perceive the changing context within which they must be viewed. This point is not only pertinent to most histories of Western philosophy or literature; it also applies to most treatments of the history of science and of historiography.[62]

The shift from script to print affected methods of record-keeping and the flow of information. We cannot, each of us, study all aspects

---

[61] Of his *or her* many roles. That daughters and widows of printers often took over the family enterprise is noted by Lenkey and others. See references in chap. 2, n. 136 below.

[62] See part 3, volume II below for attempts to suggest how the so-called 'external' advent of printing may be related to the so-called 'internal' history of science. Issues pertaining to historiography are touched on at various points in chap. 3 and in my essay, 'Clio and Chronos,' but full coverage would require another book.

of the past, and intellectual historians may be well advised to leave many inventions, such as stirrup or grist mill, to other specialists. To treat Gutenberg's invention in this way, however, is to miss the chance of understanding the main forces that have shaped the modern mind. The problem of relating intellectual history to the rest of history could also be handled more effectively if greater attention were paid to the impact of print. Attempts to relate ideas to social action, to link the Marxist 'superstructure' to actual modes of production, or to develop a 'sociology of knowledge' are likely to produce strained and awkward solutions when the communications revolution is not taken into account. Most speculation about mind and society or mentalities and material conditions seems premature and excessively abstract. Before theorizing in general about these issues, should we not consider more concretely how specific forms of book learning may be related to specific techniques for producing and distributing books?

The printing press, of course, is not merely classified topically as a special kind of innovation and assigned to bibliographers, historians of technology, and other specialists in neighboring fields. It is also classified chronologically and thus falls within the general area cultivated by historians who specialize in fifteenth-century studies. As a period-piece, it usually appears on time-charts coupled with the Fall of Constantinople and gets mentioned under the appropriate chapter-heading in general surveys and textbooks. Placed somewhere between the Black Death and the Discovery of America in the minds of attentive students, it occupies a relatively inconspicuous position among all the events that are passed in review when thousands of years are surveyed. Most professional historians, specializing in various periods, are even less apt to pause over the advent of printing than those who read introductory surveys. It is likely to escape the attention of most ancient historians and of many medievalists. Nor does it attract much more notice from scholars who specialize in the periods that post-date its advent. Discussion of the historical significance and broader social consequences of the shift from script to print is generally left to those who specialize in the problematic era (or is it a cultural movement?) known as the 'Renaissance.'[63]

---

[63] The usefulness of restricting the term to a cultural movement and distinguishing 'movements' from 'periods' is brought out by Gombrich, *In Search of Cultural History*. But textbook writers are impervious to such advice. For discussion of the problem, see chap. 3, below.

The field of Renaissance studies is not well designed to accommodate the consequences of printing, however. Its chronological limits are too narrow, and its usual concentration on Italy too intense to do justice to the topic. In the early sixteenth century, praise of Gutenberg's inventive genius came from Germans trying to counter prior claims to cultural supremacy made by Italian literati. Insofar as these prior claims have been reasserted by Renaissance scholars, they are more likely to stress the advent of early humanism than the later establishment of the new press. Furthermore the output of early presses drew on a backlog of scribal work; the first century of printing produced a bookish culture that was not very different from that produced by scribes. The more closely one observes the age of incunabula the less likely one is to be impressed by changes wrought by print. To see how a process of cultural transmission was transformed by the shift, one must take a more wide-angled, long-range view than is common among specialists in the Renaissance. Scholars engaged in tracing a sequence which unfolds in a single region from the trecento to the cinquecento have no good reason to make much of the difference between printer and scribe. On the contrary, they are likely to be impressed by the unity and continuity of the cultural movement Petrarch launched. In their scheme of things, Gutenberg's invention may have helped to propel existing trends (by popularizing humanist bookhands, for example) but its advent should not be taken as a cultural demarcation point. It appeared too late for that – well after the first-born sons of modern Europe had already started to ring down the curtain on the medieval scene.

Ever since Burckhardt, this view has become conventional in a way that dissident scholars have been powerless to change. New course-catalogues and textbook chapters reinforce it every year. Although some early philosophers of history, such as Condorcet, regarded printing as an epoch-making event and arranged epochal divisions accordingly, most periodization schemes at present place printing in a kind of limbo – so that it comes somewhere in the middle of an ill-defined age of transition. Its consequences receive less attention than the characteristics of the hypothetical era in which it is placed. In more general works, earlier chapters frequently postpone discussion of Gutenberg's invention until the Renaissance has ended. The shift from script to print is never discussed; the age of incunabula is permitted to close as inconspicuously as it opened and the subject is relegated to miscellaneous aspects of the Reformation.[64]

When the innovation is placed, more accurately, in the fifteenth century, it is usually mentioned in an off-hand and casual manner and treated as an incidental example of some other concurrent development – if not as an instance of early capitalist enterprise, then to illustrate the expansion of a literate laity or to demonstrate late medieval technological advances or to discuss diffusionist theories and Western importation of Far Eastern techniques.[65] It is indicative that Fernand Braudel, one of the most distinguished living historians of early-modern Europe, has relegated printing to a subordinate position between artillery and ocean navigation. No longer does it lead the trio that Bacon singled out for having changed the state of the world. Instead it 'shared equally between the retrograde and progressive thought of Europe,' 'accelerated currents the hand written book created' and bore 're-sponsibility for the slow development of mathematics...' In Braudel's view, 'only ocean navigation ended by creating any upheaval or asymmetry in the world';[66] a fundamental misapprehension – as I hope readers of this book will see.

Nevertheless, George Sarton has described movable type as 'the greatest invention of the Renaissance' and, in a symposium devoted to the era, tried, however briefly, to spell out some of its consequences.[67] So, too, has Myron Gilmore, who devotes several paragraphs to the topic in his volume in 'the rise of modern Europe' series. When we consider the treatments of specialists in the periods that postdate the

---

[64] Thus Denys Hay's chapter on printing in *The New Cambridge Modern History* appears in vol. II: *The Reformation 1520-59* although the end of the age of incunabula belongs within the interval covered by vol. I: *The Renaissance 1493-1520*. Instead of being associated with 'intellectual tendencies' during the Reformation, I think Hay's chapter should precede and set the stage for R. Weiss, 'Learning and Education in Western Europe, 1490-1520.'

[65] The theme of Chinese priority in the inventions of 'gunpowder' and printing was developed from sixteenth-century missionary reports and popularized by Renaissance men of letters, such as Montaigne. See 'On Coaches,' (1588), (tr. John Florio, 1600) as cited in *The Portable Renaissance Reader*, ed. Ross and McLaughlin, p. 157. Early seventeenth-century works comparing block-printing in China unfavorably with Gutenberg's movable type are described by Keller, 'Mathematical Technologies,' p. 24. For standard treatments of this topic see Carter and Goodrich, *The Invention of Printing in China* and Fuhrman, 'The Invention of Printing.' That movable metal type was developed in pre-Gutenberg times in Asia (by the Koreans) has been uncovered since the seventeenth century. Discussion now centers on the advantages of an alphabetic as against an ideographic written language for full use of letterpress printing.

[66] Braudel, *Capitalism*, chap. 6, pp. 285; 300.

[67] Sarton, 'The Quest for Truth,' p. 67. For discussion of Sarton's changed opinion of the impact of print, which is muffled in his early work, see pp. 507 ff, volume II below.

age of incunabula, a Renaissance scholar such as Gilmore will appear to be farsighted indeed.

The invention and development of printing with movable type brought about the most radical transformation in the conditions of intellectual life in the history of western civilization. It opened new horizons in education and in the communication of ideas. Its effects were sooner or later felt in every department of human activity.[68]

Although he thus points toward later repercussions, the chronological limits of Gilmore's volume prevent his describing them in any detail. Subsequent volumes in the series that might be expected to describe somewhat more fully effects that were eventually 'felt in every department of human activity' contain no explicit reference to these effects at all. This tendency to curtail discussion of a continuing transformation at the very point, in the early sixteenth century, when it was just beginning to gather momentum is unfortunately typical. Studies devoted to the centuries that followed the era of incunabula relegate consideration of printing to a variety of fringe areas and minor subspecialties.

Separate marginal plots within the large, somewhat amorphous, field of social history are cultivated by authors of monographs devoted to the book-trade, to patronage and censorship, to belles lettres, journalism, and education, to public opinion and propaganda analysis or to the internal organization of printing industries in diverse regions. Save for occasional references to the 'rise' of the 'reading public' and the emergence of 'professional' authors in the eighteenth century, to the role of the 'press' and of 'public opinion' in the nineteenth century, one might conclude from the vast bulk of current history books, that the social and intellectual transformations introduced by printing had petered out with the last Reformation broadside. That the new presses disseminated Protestant views is, probably, the only aspect of the impact of printing which is familiar to most historians of modern Europe. In accounts of the Reformation as in accounts of other movements, the effects produced by printing tend to be drastically curtailed and restricted to the single function of 'spreading' ideas. That new issues were posed for churchmen when the scriptural tradition 'went to

[68] Gilmore, *The World of Humanism*, p. 186. See also informative discussion at the very outset of survey by Rice, *The Foundations of Early Modern Europe*, pp. 1–10. An unusually perceptive passage on the new presses is contained in Hale, *Renaissance Europe*, pp. 188–90.

press', and that print contributed to dividing Christendom before spreading Protestantism are possibilities that have gone unexplored.[69] At all events, once chapters devoted to the Reformation are closed and the spread of Protestantism has been achieved, the activities of printers and publishers seem to become less newsworthy. The spotlight of history is focused on later, seemingly more significant developments.

Among historians dealing with the post-Reformation era, the invisibility of the cumulative impact exerted by the new communications system is particularly marked. The intellectual and political revolutions of the seventeenth and eighteenth centuries are placed in the context not of a post-print but of a pre-industrialized society. In setting the stage for the rise of modern science, for example, the state of communications in seventeenth-century Europe is often discussed. One is told about the rise of postal systems, the building of canals and other improvements in transport. But the previous replacement of hand-copied tables, charts and maps by printed ones, is likely to be left out of account. The significance of a growing handwritten correspondence among virtuosi is frequently underlined; the more novel appearance of 'open letters' addressed to scattered observers tends to be ignored. The distribution of scientific talent is often examined; the distribution of scientific publication outlets is seldom explored.[70]

The same point may be made about efforts to set the stage for Enlightenment thought or for the political revolutions of early-modern times.[71] In attempting to explain these revolutions, shifts associated with trade routes and prices, land use and crops, status groups and classes, are discussed at length. Changes which affected duplication

[69] For further discussion, see chap. 4 below.

[70] See sections on 'improvements in communication' in G. N. Clark, *The Seventeenth Century*, pp. 47–60; 330–333. See also treatment of slide rules and logarithms (p. 235); education (chap. 18) and literature (chap. 20) in same work. Clark's approach has been carried over into the influential work of Robert K. Merton on the sociology of science and hence is still noteworthy despite its age. For further discussion see pp. 460ff., volume II below.

[71] Since this was written there have appeared many volumes sponsored by two sections of the École Pratique des Hautes Études (the IVe Section publications by H.-J. Martin and his colleagues and those of the VIe Section by Robert Mandrou, François Furet and their colleagues), which suggest that the history of the book is being broadened to encompass cultural and political trends. See essays in *Livre et Société au XVIIIe Siècle* and review articles by Dupront, 'Livre et Culture;' Trénard, 'L'Histoire des Mentalités Collectives;' Mandrou, 'Le Livre: Ce Ferment.' But in my view even these new studies muffle the impact of print in a manner suggested by Dupront's comment: 'Le Livre retarde,' p. 895. More explosive implications emerge from Robert Darnton's many pioneering articles (cited in the bibliographical index). For updated review of literature to 1976 see Birn, '*Livre et Société* after ten years.'

of maps, charts and tables, of law books and reference works, calendars and treaties, bills and petitions are noted infrequently, if at all. The rise of the middle class and the role of the bourgeoisie is always related to the growth of a money economy; yet the rise of men of letters and the role of the intelligentsia is rarely related to the expanding powers of the press. We hear much about the effects of the commercial revolution but nothing about those of the communications revolution.[72]

Like the fast growing bibliography on the history of technology, a long-lived, ever thickening literature on the 'industrial revolution' has also helped to distract attention from the invention Bacon once regarded as conspicuous. In general works, for example, more emphasis will be placed on shifts affecting textile production and the cloth trade than on those affecting book production and the book-trade. The two areas are related, to be sure. Not only did textile printing precede book-printing but textiles also entered into rag paper production and thus helped to pave the way for the use of the press. Nevertheless letterpress printing had a more direct effect on the flow of information than did either textile mills or paper mills.

The flow of information, a review article tells us, is an important and neglected area of institutional innovation which economic historians ignore at their peril, especially if they are concerned with commercial expansion and theories of economic growth.[73] The article stops short of suggesting any possible effects produced by printing on the interchange of economic information. The relationship, if any, between expanding printing industries and the growth of capitalist enterprise during the early-modern era still remains to be explored. Most surveys of economic history move from the later middle ages to early-modern times without giving any indication of how the advent of printing might have affected commerce and industry in general or methods of advertising, insurance schemes, stock market reports and systems of currency in particular. In any attempt to cover the last two centuries, there are too many changes affecting agriculture, industry, and transportation to be noted for later phases of the continuing revo-

---

72 This statement, made in 1970, now must make room for a welcome exception. Klaits' *Printed Propaganda under Louis XIV* contains a section on 'The Sun King and the Communications Revolution.' This entire monograph is devoted to the implications of new developments which came after print. In applying the term 'communications revolution' to specifically seventeenth-century phenomena, such as the new periodical press, however, Klaits still uses the term more narrowly than I do in this book.

73 North and Paul, 'An Economic Theory of the Growth of the Western World.'

lution – the advent of new paper mills and the use of iron and steam for presswork – to receive more than cursory notice. Even the earliest phases are now overshadowed by the cluster of changes that came three centuries later; so that the advent of printing instead of being treated as an event that is *sui generis* and that should be examined on its own terms is made to serve merely as another precursor of later mass-production techniques. Coupled with sixteenth-century mining and shipbuilding, instead of the compass and gunpowder, it is relegated to the position of forerunner and made to anticipate later large-scale industrial enterprises.

As one among numerous inventions, the 'divine art' has become less illustrious. As a revolutionary process that helped to usher in early-modern times, the shift from script to print is overshadowed by later transformations and placed by periodization schemes into a closed chapter. Still, historians are presumably well equipped to open closed chapters. It is, after all, their main stock in trade. The contents of this particular chapter are, however, curiously difficult to decipher. For when we stay in the brief interval allotted to typography in most texts and surveys and try to focus the spotlight more narrowly on its advent, we find that the more closely we look, the less certain we become about what it is that we are to examine. The enigmatic phrase 'movable metal type' appears, like the grin of the vanished Cheshire cat, to be all that is left of the first of Bacon's most conspicuous inventions.

Not only have lists grown longer and boundaries between specialties more formidable; our analyses of 'inventions and discoveries' have also become increasingly sophisticated in a way that tends to muffle our sense of their force and effectiveness. We are more aware than were Bacon and his contemporaries that major innovations do not spring to life abruptly and full blown, like Minerva from Jove's brow. They are now regarded less as single events than as complex social processes, representing in turn the end-products of other vaster social changes.[74]

To account for the utilization of movable type, it is no longer sufficient merely to go to Gutenberg's workshop in Mainz – or even to argue that one should first go to Coster's in Haarlem, or possibly also to examine the business operations of Johannes Fust and Peter Schoeffer.

[74] See Clapham, 'Printing,' p. 377 for comment on naiveté of sixteenth-century views. That inventions and discoveries have now come to be treated as highly problematic events is noted, with pertinent references, in my essay, 'Clio and Chronos,' p. 39, n. 9.

Instead one must investigate the prior expansion of a literate laity and a manuscript book-trade, account for the accumulation of capital required for investment in early plants, or try to explain why printing industries expanded so rapidly in Western Europe during the late fifteenth century and why the invention of movable type did not have similar consequences in the Far East. Furthermore, the first presses now appear merely as the end-products of many other innovations drawn from home and abroad. Changes affecting all manner of industries, arts, and crafts – ranging from wine-making, cheese-making, seal-cutting, oil-painting and card-playing, to metallurgy and textile production have to be taken into account. Together with the prior establishment of paper mills and the production of block-printed books, such innovations have been examined in sufficient detail to fragment our concept of 'printing' as an invention. 'It requires a long treatise to say what actually constituted Gutenberg's "invention." '[75] Insofar as we are nonetheless apt to locate the 'printing press' on our time charts in the 1450s, it rests there as a convenient abstraction – as a summary statement of concrete particulars that must, for the most part, be located elsewhere.

To describe the 'force and effect' of such an abstraction leads to difficulties. On the one hand, it seems to have changed nothing; on the other, it appears to have transformed everything. Almost all historians agree that no sharp line should be drawn dividing the first half of the fifteenth century from the second. All of them concur with the following judgment. 'It was not the production of books that was revolutionized by the use of moveable type or its application to the machine-made edition. In fact printed books were at first hardly distinguishable from manuscripts...'[76] Yet they are also apt to note how Gutenberg 'introduced into Europe, more than three centuries ahead of its general adoption by industry, the "theory of interchangeable parts" which is the basis of all modern mass-manufacturing technique.'[77] Possibly a sharp line *should* be drawn severing the last part of the fifteenth century from preceding eras. By 1480, 'the basic difference between the effects created by the metal worker and those produced by the quill driver...brought about the victory of the punch cutter over the scribe and with it the supersession of the imitation manuscript by the authen-

---

[75] Steinberg, *Five Hundred Years*, p. 23.
[76] *Ibid.* p. 22.   [77] *Ibid.* p. 25.

tic book.'[78] In the end, even sophisticated moderns fall back on ancient mythology: 'Again and again the historian is struck by the fact that... various offshoots of Gutenberg's art sprang into existence full-grown and armed like Athena from Zeus' forehead.'[79]

As these passages suggest, it is difficult to deal with the advent of typography without skewing perspectives by resorting simultaneously to two incompatible models of change: one gradual and evolutionary; the other, abrupt and revolutionary. There are cogent arguments for regarding Gutenberg's invention as part of a continuously unfolding process; for presenting it (as Febvre and Martin do) as one element in a larger 'ensemble' of transformations. Thus, the invention and utilization of movable type may be viewed as one by-product of previous developments, such as the spread of lay literacy, and as a factor, which, in turn, helped to pave the way for later developments, such as modern mass literacy. Printers and scribes copied each other's products for several decades and duplicated the same texts for the same markets during the age of incunabula. In the mind of the Italian humanists 'there was no distinct line of demarcation between the manuscript book and that printed by movable type.'[80] For at least fifty years after the shift there is no striking evidence of cultural change; one must wait until a full century after Gutenberg before the outlines of new world pictures begin to emerge into view.

It seems plausible, in the light of such considerations, to favor a gradualist, evolutionary approach. But there are also compelling reasons for regarding the shift from script to print as a large 'ensemble' of changes in itself and for contrasting the talents that were mobilized and the functions that were performed by copyists and *cartolai* on the one hand and by early printers on the other. As various studies show, historical imagination is required to bridge the gap between the age of scribes and that of the printer.[81] But before it can be bridged, the gap must be acknowledged, and this acknowledgement, in turn, implies acceptance of discontinuity. A persuasive case, then, can also be made out for regarding the age of incunabula as a major historical great divide and for viewing the advent of printing as inaugurating a new cultural era in the history of Western man.

[78] *Ibid.* p. 29.   [79] *Ibid.* p. 133.
[80] Hugh H. Davis, book review, *Renaissance Quarterly* (1973), p. 353. The Italian book under review shows that the same word 'codex' was used for both.
[81] See e.g. works by H. J. Chaytor, E. P. Goldschmidt, and Lucien Febvre cited above.

In current literature, there is much more reluctance to adopt the second line of approach than the first one.[82] Whenever possible, discontinuities are glossed over; significant distinctions between the two modes of production are not fully spelled out and various implications of the shift from one to the other are overlooked. At the same time, however, the thesis of evolutionary gradualism is employed intermittently and inconsistently. Indeed, one must read between the lines to determine which model, if any, is being used. Interpretations are conveyed indirectly and obliquely. On those rare occasions when a relevant question is posed, an uncertain answer is obtained.

The road from manuscript to print was continuous *and* broken and I venture to say that all great discoveries, all so-called new movements, harbor the same contrasting elements, continuity and radical change. This dichotomy accompanies Humanism, Renaissance, nationalism, capitalism, the Reformation and...the splitting of atoms...Jacob rightly called the xvth century a 'remarkable admixture of the old and the new...'
His characterization fits the xvth-century book as well. Old elements remained unchanged, others were transformed, new techniques were developed and the uses of books changed.[83]

In many ways, the paradoxical model of a line which is both continuous and broken does seem to suit the odd nature of effects produced by a new process designed to duplicate old products. The difficulty of handling changes initially wrought by printing without shattering conventional 'linear' sequential patterns is certainly worth further thought. On the other hand, special problems presented by the shift are likely to be obscured by considering other assorted developments such as humanism, capitalism or atom-splitting. It is also disappointing to be told that all movements contain elements of continuity and radical change and that a given century is an admixture of old and of new. To be reminded of eternal verities is rarely helpful in dealing with specific historical problems. In the end, the passage simply deflects attention away from the wider implications of the problem and towards a more limited range of issues. The general reader recedes and the bibliophile

---

[82] This reluctance seems more common among professional historians and college professors than among secondary school history teachers. The latter are likely to assign more significance to Gutenberg's invention than the former regard as justified. For a recent work by a former secondary school teacher which starts out by stressing 'the impact of printing' see McLean, *Humanism and the Rise of Science in Tudor England*, chap. 1. Later sections of this work, however, seem to follow more conventional guidelines. See n. 85 below.
[83] Hirsch, *Printing, Selling*, p. 2.

comes to the fore; the impact of print on the fifteenth-century book rather than on European society is discussed in the paragraphs that follow the citation. Even when dealing with this narrower topic and bringing his special competence to bear on it, the author's approach is sufficiently ambiguous to leave open the question of how abrupt or gradual, major or minor, were the changes typography entailed.

A similar ambiguity and uncertainty marks the more ambitious broad-gauged historical synthesis composed by Febvre and Martin. The very title of their volume: *L'Apparition du Livre* underlines a failure to come to grips with basic issues. Although the work is really devoted to 'l'apparition du livre imprimé' (as Marcel Thomas tells us on the first page) the reference to print is omitted from the title. The uninformed reader is left in the dark as to when the advent of the book really occurred. The more knowledgeable scholar cannot help wondering why the advent of printing, rather than of the book, was not clearly presented as the subject under review. As it is, the theme of a major cultural metamorphosis is muffled by the authors' oblique approach. Lucien Febvre's preface stresses the larger ensemble of transformations within which Gutenberg's invention should be viewed and also presents the shift to print as a mere prologue to later and greater transformations. The first chapter is devoted to the prior advent of paper and to tracing an evolutionary pattern. It describes the gradual expansion of both manuscript book production and of a cosmopolitan lay reading public. Thereafter, the same pattern recurs, divisions between manuscripts and incunabula are blurred and the lack of important changes in book-production techniques during the next three centuries is stressed.[84] We are also told that the new presses, by duplicating outmoded scribal works more efficiently, did 'nothing to speed up the adoption of new theories or knowledge' and, on the contrary, contributed to cultural inertia.[85] In certain scattered passages, however, the typographical industry is 'very rapidly modernized'; 'medieval' workshops are transformed into 'modern plants' as early as the 1480s; a 'bouleversement' of literate Europe is produced by the immensely

---

[84] See preface (by Lucien Febvre) xxiii–xxix, introduction (by Marcel Thomas), pp. 1–24 and chap. 1 in Febvre and Martin, *L'Apparition*. In contrast to Steinberg's treatment, evolutionary as opposed to revolutionary changes in book format are stressed by Martin, p. 108.

[85] Febvre and Martin, *L'Apparition*, pp. 420–1. This passage is cited by many authorities (see e.g. McLuhan, *Gutenberg Galaxy*, p. 142; McLean, *Humanism*, p. 22) all of whom tend to overlook the possibility that an increased output of old texts may have contributed to the shaping of new ideas. Further discussion of this crucial point is offered in later chapters of this book.

increased output of books during the age of incunabula; the concern of sixteenth-century printers to attract the greatest number of buyers to their wares is described as a step toward 'mass culture'; in mid-sixteenth-century Lutheran regions a 'mass literature' 'directed at everyone and accessible to everyone' had already been achieved.[86]

It is noteworthy that the scattered passages which hint at remarkably rapid modernization and 'bouleversement' are at odds with the general tenor of the work. Insofar as they tend to play down discontinuous and revolutionary implications and stress the themes of gradualism and continuity, Febvre and Martin appear to be conforming to deep-rooted historical conventions. 'Here as always,' wrote Carl Stephenson in a passage devoted to the printing press, 'the historian finds that his epoch-making event was not a sudden innovation, but a gradual transition.'[87] Denys Hay seems to speak for the entire historical profession when – even while noting the exceptional character of the event – he warns against overdramatizing consequences.

Some inventions...have taken centuries to be widely adopted and even more have taken generations. Printing was an exception. It spread at a phenomenal speed from Mainz and by the 1490s each of the major states had one important publishing centre and some had several...
It is impossible to exaggerate the rapidity of the transformation. It is all too easy to exaggerate the consequences...[88]

Given the tendency of uninformed laymen to overlook the development of manuscript book production; to underrate the extent of lay literacy before printing and overrate the rapidity of its spread thereafter, it is probably necessary to issue some kind of warning. But although some of Hay's readers may need to be cautioned in this way, most of his scholarly colleagues do not. They are, if anything, more likely to underestimate changes wrought by printing than to overestimate them.

The dangers of exaggerating the significance of the initial shift have in any case already been sufficiently emphasized in current scholarly literature. It is the opposite danger – that of forcing an evolutionary

---

[86] Febvre and Martin, *L'Apparition*, pp. 193; 377; 394; 443.
[87] Stephenson, *A Brief Survey of Medieval Europe*, p. 369.
[88] Hay, introduction, *Printing and the Mind of Man*, p. xxii. (The sub-title of this work, which refers to 'the impact of print on the evolution of Western civilization,' is misleading. It is an enlarged descriptive catalogue containing over 400 entries on early editions of great books displayed at a London exhibition of 1963.) In his introduction to the *New Cambridge Modern History* I, 4, Hay similarly warns against overestimating the impact of print.

model on a revolutionary situation – which now ought to arouse more concern. For specific illustration of this point, let me turn to a 1975 article in a library journal.[89] The author sets out to reaffirm an evolutionary thesis and to refute some of the views I presented in preliminary sketches for this book. He begins by warning against the temptation of projecting 'upon the fifteenth century and the Renaissance the influence which printing clearly had at the time of the Reformation.' He goes on to discuss the activities of a Bruges scribe-turned-printer, who seems to have used his press much as he did his pen in order to turn out the books which were desired by his noble Burgundian patrons.

In no instance did Mansion's production of printed editions outnumber manuscript copies of the same work...As it existed in Bruges, printing offered no guarantee of a larger audience. The largest editions of Mansion and his successors barely equaled the normal distribution of contemporary manuscript books. The usual Mansion printed edition was four or five copies, a modest figure in comparison to manuscript editions which numbered twenty or more.[90]

Having demonstrated to his own satisfaction that the output of Colard Mansion, printer, was not significantly different in terms of quantity or quality from that of Colard Mansion, scribe, the author seems to feel that an evolutionary thesis has been proved. Yet merely because a given printer, who served noble patrons in Bruges, failed to exploit the duplicative powers of the new press is no reason to assume these powers went unused elsewhere in Europe. Let me set aside doubts about the validity of comparing manuscript 'editions' with printed ones or of designating an edition as 'usual'; a distribution as 'normal'; and take the estimates we are given at their face value. Four or five copies is indeed a 'modest' figure, not merely in comparison with multiple copies made of manuscripts but, much more strikingly, in comparison with estimates of the number of copies issued from pre-Reformation presses.[91] 'As it existed at Bruges,' printing may have 'offered no

[89] Saenger, 'Colard Mansion.'
[90] Saenger, 'Colard Mansion,' p. 414. The reference to Mansion's 'successors' is somewhat puzzling. According to Erich von Rath, 'Printing in the Fifteenth Century,' p. 79, nothing more is heard of Mansion after his flight from Bruges in 1484. Other authorities concur. What editions 'his successors' turned out or who they were is unclear.
[91] See estimates given both by Hirsch, *Printing, Selling*, pp. 66–7, and Febvre and Martin, *L'Apparition*, pp. 327–8, both of whom start by citing the findings of K. Haebler, *The Study of Incunabula* and thus note that Sweynheim and Pannartz, the first printers in Italy, listed 275 as their usual press output between 1465 and 1471. In the 1480s, between 400 and 500 copies became usual. This was also the decade when printed book prices dropped. (Saenger's com-

guarantee of a large audience' but Bruges was not as important a printing center as were other towns at the same time. Like Colard Mansion himself, indeed, Bruges crops up in printing history chiefly because of associations with William Caxton.[92] Bruges *had* been a center of deluxe manuscript book production. Its relative insignificance as a continental book-production center after the advent of printing is worth noting. The establishment of presses in diverse regions did not leave book-trade patterns unaltered. Before 1500 new centers of production and exchange had appeared.

In view of such considerations it seems incautious to conclude that pre-Reformation printing left European book production virtually unchanged.

By the early part of the sixteenth century, the number of large printed editions reproduced and distributed by the printing press clearly exceeded the capabilities of the scriptorium. By radically increasing the number of books and reducing their cost, printing had great social, economic and intellectual impact on European civilization at the time of the Reformation. However none of the factors which made printing important in the 1500s existed at the time of Colard Mansion when printing was an adjunct to the scriptorium and not its rival...[93]

According to a recent authority Mansion was ruined by the outlay required for his lavishly illustrated printed edition of Ovid so that he had to flee Bruges and his creditors in 1484 and 'is heard of no more.'[94] This suggests that Mansion failed to adapt his business to new require-

ment: 'In general the first printed books were no cheaper than manuscripts' (p. 411, n. 14) is not helpful on this point.) In the 1490s, the number of copies became still larger. Up to 900 copies of a Latin Bible, 1,000 of a commentary on canon law, 1,025 of an edition of Plato, 1,500 copies of Aristotle's *Politics* are some of the figures cited by Lenhart, *Pre-Reformation Printed Books: A Study in Statistical and Applied Bibliography*, p. 9. Lenhart's study which is devoted solely to pre-Reformation output contains just the sort of data Saenger would have us place in the post-Reformation epoch. For detailed evidence of rapid multiplication by Venetian presses of three manuscripts in vernacular translation provided by the Florentine merchant: Gerolamo Strozzi, see Edler de Roover, 'Per la Storia dell'arte della Stampa in Italia: come furono stampati a Venezia tre dei primi libri in volgare.' Over 1,500 volumes were produced between 1475 and 1476 to be distributed by Strozzi's Italian agents in Rome, Siena, Pisa and Naples or transported to Bruges and London on galleys. Venetian presses were thus serving Bruges markets even while Colard Mansion was at work.

92 On Mansion's association with Caxton the most useful recent account is Painter, *William Caxton*, chap. 9. The most richly documented study is still Blades' *Life of William Caxton*, I, 39 ff. See also Bühler, review article *The Library* (1953); Blake, *Caxton and His World*, p. 62.

93 Saenger, 'Colard Mansion,' p. 416. Whether the use of the term scriptorium is justified in this case is a question for Delaissé's students to decide. See n. 28 above.

94 Painter, *William Caxton*, p. 102.

ments posed by printing and that his preference for deluxe small editions was not easily reconciled with operating a successful early press. The view that printing was an adjunct and not a rival to the hand-copying of books thus is not substantiated even by the one atypical case we are offered. Mansion's career, however atypical, may still serve as a reminder that Gutenberg's invention by itself is insufficient to account for the fifteenth-century communications revolution. His unusually small output points up the need to consider the myriad diverse factors which encouraged or discouraged the spread and full use of the new presses. But to say that 'none of the factors' which made printing important 'existed at the time of Colard Mansion' is to make a sweeping judgment which seems to fly in the face of available evidence. To blow up the obscure case of Mansion while ignoring the celebrated one of his one-time colleague, William Caxton, also seems perversely calculated to set historical perspectives askew.

As this example may suggest, it is not necessarily prudent and may even be rash to insist on gradual and evolutionary change when dealing with the shift from script to print. Few authorities are as explicit about rejecting the revolutionary model as is the article discussed above. But all seem reluctant to employ it. When dealing with our topic scholars are more likely to err in the direction of understating the change than of overstating it. More often than not, as previous remarks suggest, they fall back on evasive tactics and play safe by not dealing with the topic at all.

But here again, playing safe is not really a safe solution, for it invites unqualified judgments to preempt the field. Where historians are prone to be over-cautious, others are encouraged to be over-bold. Evasion on the part of careful scholars allows the topic to go by default into more careless hands. The fifteenth-century 'media revolution' is also of interest to those who cultivate various avant-garde fields (communications theory, media analysis and the like) and who scrutinize the current scene without paying much heed to the past.[95] Non-historians of this sort, however, are almost certain to go astray if they try to thread their way unaided through five centuries of

---

[95] The absence of historical perspectives in such fields is underlined by Jowett, 'Toward a History of Communication.' See also Katzman, 'The Impact of Communication Technology.' Some of the propositions set forth by Katzman might be worth examining with regard to the shift from script to print.

unevenly phased change. It is not surprising that they may become impatient with the absence of clear guidelines and decide to try short-cuts on their own.

In *The Gutenberg Galaxy*, Marshall McLuhan provides a good case in point. The author has solved his difficulties by the simple (albeit inelegant) device of dispensing with chronological sequence and historical context altogether. Far from appearing to be concerned about preserving proportion and perspective, he impatiently brushes aside all such concerns as obsolete. Developments that have been unfolding over the course of five hundred years, affecting different regions and penetrating to different social strata at different intervals, are randomly intermingled and treated as a single event – most appropriately described, perhaps, as a 'happening.'

According to some critics and the author himself, the jumbling of data and disregard for sequence are deliberate. *The Gutenberg Galaxy*, we are told in the *Times Literary Supplement*, is an 'anti-book.' The author has set out to subvert 'traditional modes of philosophic-historical argument' and to persuade his readers 'that books – a linear progression of phonetic units reproduced by movable type – are no longer to be trusted.'[96] It seems unlikely that readers of the *Times Literary Supplement* (or of *The Gutenberg Galaxy* for that matter) are in much need of persuasion on this point. Few of them have ever put much trust in books *per se*; most of them are trained to approach all publications with caution and are inclined toward disbelief when presented with arguments (whatever the format) that are not solidly substantiated.

McLuhan's 'non-linear' presentation at all events has not inspired confidence in his arguments. The way he justifies his handling of the topic only increases the reader's sense of distrust. In addition to old mosaics and new media, he invokes the 'field theories' of modern physics. His special training, not in electromagnetic theory but in literature and philosophy, his close study not of Einstein but of James Joyce, seems to me to be more to the point. To be well versed in modern literary criticism is to be predisposed against chronological narrative regardless of other avant-garde trends. Indifference to mundane temporal sequence also has venerable religious antecedents. Catholic theology may well be more of an influence than twentieth-

96 'Battle of the Senses.'

century physics on recent efforts at understanding media.[97] Paradoxically enough, *The Gutenberg Galaxy* also owes something to the work of the most influential school of historians in our time. Not only the general critique of conventional narrative history by the *Annales* school, but also Lucien Febvre's special thesis concerning the shift from 'the age of the ear' to 'the age of the eye' enters into McLuhan's interpretation.[98] When the *Annalistes* reject a conventional narrative form or Febvre seeks to reconstitute the psychological experience of earlier generations, however, it is in order to enrich and deepen historical understanding. Whatever his purpose may be, this, clearly, is not McLuhan's aim.

If indeed he did set out to subvert traditional modes of historical argument, he selected an unsuitable topic. Almost any other subject would provide a better target than the shift from script to print. Historical guidelines still fall short of encompassing this shift. They need to be extended rather than undermined. It is not really accurate to say that McLuhan has taken data out of context, for an adequate context has not yet been supplied. As noted earlier, I think the author has shirked the difficult task of organizing his material coherently. His insistence that coherence is itself outdated strikes me as unconvincing. *The Gutenberg Galaxy* performs a useful function, nevertheless, by pointing to a large number of significant issues that cry out for historical investigation and have, as yet, received almost none.

Perhaps historians are too often discouraged in advance by being reminded repeatedly of the magnitude of the task:

The cumulative effect of the continuing revolution wrought in every aspect of human thought and activity by the invention associated with the city of Mainz is too immense ever to be fully describable. Its consequences to religion, politics and industry are far too vast for assessment by available historians and bibliographers or by any assemblage of scholars to be foreseen at present.[99]

[97] This is suggested by one of many recent publications by Ong, *The Presence of the Word.* Father Ong, who mastered intellectual history under the guidance of the late Perry Miller and produced a solid scholarly study of Ramus, seems to be more favorably inclined toward historical modes of argument than McLuhan. His speculations about the effects of media shifts on language, consciousness and rhetoric may be sampled in his collection of essays: Ong, *Rhetoric, Romance and Technology* which provides a list of his other works.

[98] According to Burke, introduction, *A New Kind of History*, p. x, 'Marshall McLuhan has built his career on the reiteration of Febvre's thesis.' In view of the many other authorities McLuhan acknowledges in his work, the statement seems too strong. On Harold Innis, Lewis Mumford and several others who preceded Febvre as influences on McLuhan, see Kuhns, *The Post-Industrial Prophets*, part 2.   [99] Morison, 'The Learned Press as an Institution,' p. 153.

The prospect of tackling a subject that is 'far too vast' to be assessed by any present or future assemblage is apt to daunt even the most audacious individual. If it is too vast to be handled by any single scholar, however, it is, by the same token, also too vast to be avoided by any single scholar. Given its almost limitless dimensions, the cumulative effect of the 'continuing revolution' is bound to impinge, one way or another, on all fields of inquiry, even highly specialized ones. Hence individual specialists, who are careful and cautious about their work, must, sooner or later, come to terms with it. Consequences entailed by a major transformation have to be reckoned with, whether we acknowledge them or not. In one guise or another, they will enter into our accounts and can best be dealt with when they do not slip in un-observed. Enough warnings have already been issued. Historians scarcely need to be alerted again to the difficulties of following Bacon's advice. But the importance of trying to surmount these difficulties does need to be stressed. Although the task may never be completed, it should, at least, be begun.

2

DEFINING THE INITIAL SHIFT; SOME FEATURES OF PRINT CULTURE

We should note the force, effect, and consequences of inventions which are nowhere more conspicuous than in those three which were unknown to the ancients, namely, printing, gunpowder, and the compass. For these three have changed the appearance and state of the whole world...

Francis Bacon, *Novum Organum*, Aphorism 129

To dwell on the reasons why Bacon's advice ought to be followed by others is probably less helpful than trying to follow it oneself. This task clearly outstrips the competence of any single individual. It calls for the pooling of many talents and the writing of many books. Collaboration is difficult to obtain as long as the relevance of the topic to different fields of study remains obscure. Before aid can be enlisted, it seems necessary to develop some tentative hypotheses relating the shift from script to print to significant historical developments.

This task, in turn, seems to call for a somewhat unconventional point of departure and for a reformulation of Bacon's advice Instead of trying to deal with 'the force, effect, and consequences' of a single post-classical invention that is coupled with others, I will be concerned with a major transformation that constituted a large cluster of changes in itself. Indecision about what is meant by the advent of printing has, I think, helped to muffle concern about its possible consequences and made them more difficult to track down. It is difficult to find out what happened in a particular Mainz workshop in the 1450s. When pursuing other inquiries, it seems almost prudent to by-pass so problematic an event. This does not apply to the appearance of new occupational groups who employed new techniques and installed new equipment in new kinds of workshops while extending trade networks and seeking new markets to increase profits made from sales. Unknown anywhere in Europe before the mid-fifteenth century, printers' workshops would be found in every important municipal center by 1500. They added a new element to urban culture in hundreds of towns.[1] To pass by all that, when dealing with other problems, would seem to be incautious. For this reason, among others, I am skipping over the perfection of a new process for printing with movable types and will not pause over the massive literature devoted to explanations of Gutenberg's invention.[2] Instead, I will begin where many studies end, after the first dated printed products had been issued and the inventor's immediate successors had set to work.

By the advent of printing then, I mean the establishment of presses in urban centers beyond the Rhineland during an interval that begins in the 1460s and coincides, very roughly, with the era of incunabula.[3] So few studies have been devoted to this point of departure that no conventional label has yet been attached to it. One might talk about a basic change in a mode of production, about a book revolution, or a media revolution, or perhaps, most simply and explicitly, about a shift from script to print. Will Durant refers to a 'typographical revolution.' Partly because it can be neatly coupled with the already well entrenched commercial revolution and also because it points to a major dimension of history which needs more attention, I believe 'communications revolution' best suits my purposes in this book. Whatever label is used, it should be understood to cover a large cluster of relatively simultaneous, closely interrelated changes, each of which needs closer study and more explicit treatment – as the following quick sketch may suggest.

First of all, the marked increase in the output of books and the drastic

---

[1] For estimate of numbers of printing offices and places of printing, see Lenhart, *Pre-Reformation Printed Books*, p. 7. For graphic presentation, see maps in Febvre and Martin, *L'Apparition*, p. 273, covering the two intervals: 1471 to 1480 and 1481 to 1500, and discussion in Hirsch's 1974 edition of *Printing, Selling*, p. x, concerning the updating of R. Teichl's more detailed rendering, 'Der Wiegendruck im Kartenbild.' Uhlendorf's 1932 article, 'The invention and spread of printing,' has not been superseded as a brief suggestive treatment of possible socioeconomic factors contributing to the rapid spread of printing, and the clustering of early presses in certain centers. When one considers the massive literature devoted to shifts in trade routes during the early-modern era, it is remarkable how little work has been done on shifts in communications centers.

[2] Stillwell, *The Beginning of the World of Books* offers useful guidance. See especially appendix A, pp. 75–87. Stillwell selects 1470 as a take-off point for the rapid spread of the new art (p. x).

[3] That the age of incunabula should be extended to encompass the life-spans of the founders of early firms and hence to embrace the first few decades of the sixteenth century is persuasively argued by Steinberg, *Five Hundred Years*, pp. 15–17.

reduction in the number of man-hours required to turn them out deserve stronger emphasis. At present there is a tendency to think of a steady increase in book production during the first century of printing. An evolutionary model of change is applied to a situation that seems to call for a revolutionary one.

A man born in 1453, the year of the fall of Constantinople, could look back from his fiftieth year on a lifetime in which about eight million books had been printed, more perhaps than all the scribes of Europe had produced since Constantine founded his city in A.D. 330.[4]

The actual production of 'all the scribes of Europe' is inevitably open to dispute. Even apart from the problem of trying to estimate numbers of books that went uncatalogued and then were destroyed, contemporary evidence must be handled with caution, for it often yields false clues to the numbers of books involved. Since it was customary to register many texts bound within one set of covers as but one book, the actual number of texts in a given manuscript collection is not easily ascertained.[5] That objects counted as one book often contained a varying combination of many provides yet another example of the difficulty of quantifying data provided in the age of scribes. The situation is similar when we turn to the problem of counting the man-hours required to copy manuscript books. Old estimates based on the number of months it took forty-five scribes working for Vespasiano da Bisticci to produce 200 books for Cosimo de Medici's Badia library have been rendered virtually worthless by recent intensive research.[6]

Thus the total number of books produced by 'all the scribes of Europe' since 330 or even since 1400, is likely to remain elusive. Nevertheless, some comparisons are possible and they place the output

[4] Clapham, 'Printing,' p. 37. It is not clear whether Clapham takes 'all the scribes of Europe' to include those of Byzantium or not. If not, the statement becomes much more plausible.

[5] The problematic and often composite nature of the medieval 'book' and the absence of any uniform conventions among medieval cataloguers who recorded them is discussed with many pertinent examples by E. P. Goldschmidt, *Medieval Texts*, pp. 95–101.

[6] On the classic version derived from Vespasiano's *Lives*, see Burckhardt, *The Civilization of the Renaissance* I, part 3, chap. 3, p. 201. Doubts expressed by Ullman, *The Origin*, p. 132, have been thoroughly documented from surviving Fiesole accounts and mss. by de la Mare, 'Vespasiano,' pp. 74–76 and appendix. (Her forthcoming study on 'Vespasiano and the Library of the Badia at Fiesole' to be published by the Warburg Institute will supply additional data.) She shows that Vespasiano obtained the books that filled the library by diverse methods, including the purchase of second-hand copies and reliance on other *cartolai*, and that the work took more than two years, encompassing an interval from 1461 until at least 1466-7. For recent use of the now discredited figures to estimate 'average' scribal output, see Burke, *Culture and Society*, p. 59.

of printers in sharp contrast to preceding trends. 'In 1483, the Ripoli Press charged three florins per quinterno for setting up and printing Ficino's translation of Plato's *Dialogues*. A scribe might have charged one florin per quinterno for duplicating the same work. The Ripoli Press produced 1,025 copies; the scribe would have turned out one.'[7] Given this kind of comparison, it seems misguided to suggest that 'the multiplication of identical copies' was merely 'intensified' by the press.[8] Doubtless, hand-copying could be quite efficient for the purpose of duplicating a royal edict or papal bull.[9] Sufficient numbers of copies of a newly edited Bible were produced in the thirteenth century for some scholars to feel justified in referring to a Paris 'edition' of a manuscript Bible. To turn out one single whole 'edition' of any text was no mean feat in the thirteenth century, however. The one thirteenth-century scribal 'edition' might be compared with the large number of Bible editions turned out in the half century between Gutenberg and Luther.[10] When scribal labor was employed for multiplying edicts or producing a whole 'edition' of scripture, moreover, it was diverted from other tasks.

Many valued texts were barely preserved from extinction; untold numbers failed to survive. Survival often hinged on the occasional copy being made by an interested scholar who acted as his own scribe. In view of the proliferation of 'unique' texts and of the accumulation of variants, it is doubtful whether one should refer to 'identical copies' being 'multiplied' before print. This point is especially important when considering technical literature. The difficulty of making even one

---

[7] De la Mare, 'Vespasiano,' p. 207. The remarkable success of this 'uncommonly large edition' which was 'sold out in six years' when another printing took place is noted by Reynolds and Wilson, *Scribes and Scholars*, p. 130. According to Kristeller, 'Contribution of Religious Orders,' p. 99, the Ripoli Press was 'one of the chief early presses in Florence.' In addition to the first edition of Ficino's Plato, which appeared in 1484, a 'Donatus' of 1476 and a *Book of Revelations* of 1478 are also noteworthy. The nuns of the Convent of San Jacopo di Ripoli, who ran the press, were 'the first women actually to print,' according to Gies, 'Some Early Ladies,' p. 1421. For basic work, see Nesi, *Il Diario della Stamperia di Ripoli*.

[8] Harrington, 'The Production and Distribution,' p. 3. This seems especially true when considering the fifty years before Gutenberg, when the system of the 'pecia' which had helped to speed duplication of large academic texts was no longer employed.

[9] From conversation with Joseph Strayer, I learned that fourteenth-century French royal edicts were rapidly multiplied and distributed by a kind of 'chain letter' technique. At court, ten scribes were put to work producing ten copies each, some of which were carried by couriers to numerous provincial centers where the same procedure was repeated so that thousands of copies were quickly produced. See also evidence on Burgundian propaganda offered by Willard, 'The Manuscripts of Jean Petit.'

[10] On the thirteenth century Paris Bible, see two articles by Branner cited above, chap. 1, n. 28. On output of printed editions before Luther, see chap. 4, n. 148, below.

'identical' copy of a significant technical work was such that the task could not be trusted to any hired hands. Men of learning had to engage in 'slavish copying' of tables, diagrams and unfamiliar terms. The output of whole editions of sets of astronomical tables did not 'intensify' previous trends. It reversed them, producing a new situation which released time for observation and research.[11]

The previous introduction of paper, it should be noted, did not have anything like a 'similar' effect, any more than did 'the organization of a regular trade in manuscript books.'[12] Paper production served the needs of merchants, bureaucrats, preachers and literati; it quickened the pace of correspondence and enabled more men of letters to act as their own scribes. But since the same number of man-hours was still required to turn out a given text, the increase in book production was sluggish and copies continued to be made at an irregular rate. Shops run by stationers or *cartolai* multiplied in response to an increasing demand for tablets, notebooks, prepared sheets and other supplies.[13] In addition to selling writing materials and school books as well as book-binding materials and services, some merchants also helped book-hunting patrons by locating valued works. They had copies made on commission and kept some for sale in their shops. But their involvement in the book-trade was more casual than one might think.

The activities of the *cartolai* were multifarious, although they usually specialized in one or another branch of their trade. The preparation and selling of book materials and binding were probably their commonest occupations. Some *cartolai* were also illuminators or employed illuminators in their shops...Scribes who mostly had other occupations (they were often notaries or priests) seem usually to have worked at home or in their shops, on commission...Many of the *cartolai* especially those who specialized in the sale and preparation of book materials or in bindings were probably

11 See discussion in part 3, volume II, below.
12 The 'enormous number' of manuscript copies of the Latin classics produced after the advent of paper is stressed by Kristeller, *Renaissance Thought*, pp. 14–15, who writes as a scholar concerned about the neglect of later Latin works and as an assiduous energetic investigator of Renaissance manuscript book lists. The compiler of *Iter Italicum* and *Latin Manuscript Books before 1600* is bound to be impressed by the remarkable output of copyists before print. Nevertheless, one must also make allowance for the fact that handmade copies, however 'enormous' their number may seem, were still in very short supply compared to the number issued after printing. Paper was incapable of reducing the man-hours required for copying and hence could not achieve effects 'similar' to those produced by the press.
13 For a close-up view of the shop of an ordinary Florentine *cartolaio* who was engaged in binding books and selling writing materials rather than in procuring or producing books (although he kept some texts on hand for sale), see de la Mare, 'The Shop of a Florentine "cartolaio" in 1426.'

concerned little if at all, with the production or sale of manuscripts and (later) printed books, either new or secondhand...[14]

Even the retail book-trade that was conducted by Vespasiano da Bisticci, the most celebrated Florentine book merchant, who served prelates and princes and 'did everything possible' to attract patrons and make sales, never verged on becoming a wholesale business. Despite Vespasiano's unusually aggressive tactics in promoting sales and matching books with clients, he showed no signs of ever 'having made much money' from all his transactions.[15] He did win notable patrons, however, and achieved considerable celebrity as 'prince of publishers'. His shop was praised by humanist poets along lines which were similar to those used in later tributes to Gutenberg and Aldus Manutius.[16] His posthumous fame – achieved only in the nineteenth century after the publication of his memoirs and their use by Jacob Burckhardt – is perhaps even more noteworthy. Vespasiano's *Lives of Illustrious Men* contains a reference to the beautifully bound manuscript books in the Duke of Urbino's library and snobbishly implies that a printed book would have been 'ashamed' in such elegant company. This one reference by an atypical and obviously prejudiced bookdealer has ballooned into many misleading comments about the disdain of Renaissance humanists for vulgar machine-made objects. Thus the catalogue to the beautiful Morgan Library 1973 Exhibition on 'The Art of the Printed Book' asserts that the Medici [sic] 'considered newly printed books a degradation and would not allow them in their libraries.'[17] The same error was amplified by an article in *The New York Times*: 'The Medici and other Florentine Princes [sic] considered printing a degradation and barred it from their sacred manuscript libraries.'[18] Similar distortions, all emanating from Burckhardt's use of Vespasiano's *Lives*, have been multiplied and amplified in so many varying contexts that scholarly disclaimers cannot catch up with them.[19]

---

[14] De la Mare, 'Bartolomeo Scala's Dealings,' 240.   [15] De la Mare, 'Vespasiano,' pp. 95–7; 226.

[16] See de la Mare, 'Vespasiano,' pp. 108–9 for laudatory verses.

[17] *Art of the Printed Book 1455–1955*, introduction by Joseph Blumenthal, p. 9. The same assertion was made on the label attached to entry no. 55 in this exhibition.

[18] Shenker, 'Books as an Art Form Through Five Centuries,' *The New York Times* (10 Sept., 1973), 2nd sect., p. 1.

[19] See Burckhardt, *The Civilization of the Renaissance in Italy* 1, p. 204 where Duke Federigo's shame is attributed to the idea of owning a printed book and Cardinal Bessarion's envoys when seeing a printed book in the house of Constantine Lascaris 'laughed at the discovery made among the barbarians in some German city.' Burckhardt's use of Vespasiano is discussed by Wieruszowski, 'Burckhardt and Vespasiano.' See also chap. 3, n. 420, below.

The need to make Renaissance bibliophiles and patrons into snobbish enemies of machine-made objects seems oddly compelling. Why else is the story so often told with no real hard evidence to support it and expanded to Florence with no supporting evidence at all? Actually, Florentine bibliophiles were sending to Rome for printed books as early as 1470. Under Guidobaldo da Montefeltro, the ducal library at Urbino acquired printed editions and (shamelessly or not) had them bound with the same magnificent covers as manuscripts. The same court also sponsored the establishment of an early press in 1482.[20] That Vespasiano was indulging in wishful and nostalgic thinking is suggested by his own inability to find sufficient support from princely patrons to persist in his exclusive trade. His chief rival in Florence, Zanobi di Mariano, managed to stay in business right down to his death in 1495. 'Zanobi's readiness to sell printed books – a trade which Vespasiano spurned – explains his survival as a bookseller in the tricky years of the late fifteenth century. Vespasiano dealing exclusively in manuscripts was forced out of business in 1478.'[21]

One must wait for Vespasiano to close shop before one can say that a genuine wholesale book trade was launched.

As soon as Gutenberg and Schoeffer had finished the last sheet of their monumental Bible, the financier of the firm, John Fust, set out with a dozen copies or so to see for himself how he could best reap the harvest of his patient investments. And where did he turn first of all to convert his Bibles into money? He went to the biggest university town in Europe, to Paris, where ten thousand or more students were filling the Sorbonne and the colleges. And what did he, to his bitter discomfiture find there? A well organized and powerful guild of the book-trade, the Confrérie des Libraires, Relieurs, Enlumineurs, Ecrivains et Parcheminiers...founded in 1401... Alarmed at the appearance of an outsider with such an unheard of treasure of books; when he was found to be selling one Bible after another, they soon shouted for the police, giving their expert opinion that such a store of valuable books could be in one man's possession through the help of the devil himself and Fust had to run for his life or his first business trip would have ended in a nasty bonfire.[22]

The story may be just as unfounded as the legend that linked the

[20] Bühler, *Fifteenth Century Book*, p. 62; de la Mare, 'Vespasiano,' p. 112; Moranti, *L'Arte Tipografia in Urbino*, p. 9.
[21] De la Mare, 'Bartolomeo Scala's Dealings,' p. 241.
[22] Goldschmidt, *Gothic and Renaissance Bookbindings* I, 43–4.

figure of Johann Fust with that of Dr Faustus.[23] The adverse reaction it depicts should not be taken as typical; many early references were at worst ambivalent.[24] The ones that are most frequently cited associate printing with divine rather than diabolic powers. But then the most familiar references come either from the blurbs and prefaces composed by early printers themselves or from editors and authors who found employment in print shops.[25] Such men were likely to take a more favorable view than were the guildsmen who had made a livelihood from manuscript books. The Parisian *libraires* may have had good reason to be alarmed, although they were somewhat ahead of the game; the market value of hand-copied books did not drop until after Fust was dead.[26] Other members of the *confrérie* could not foresee that most book-binders, rubricators, illuminators, and calligraphers would be kept busier than ever after early printers set up shop.[27] Whether the new art was considered a blessing or a curse; whether it was consigned to the Devil or attributed to God; the fact remains, that the initial increase in output did strike contemporary observers as sufficiently remarkable to suggest supernatural intervention. Even incredulous

---

[23] By 1910, when the article for the eleventh edition of the Britannica was written, Phillips, 'Faust,' *Encyclopedia Britannica* x, 210, n. 1, could assert that 'the opinion, long maintained' of Faust and Fust being identical was 'now universally rejected.' Evidence showing that Fust was in Paris selling books in 1466 when he was killed by the plague suggests that the outcome of his first business trip did not discourage him from making a later one.

[24] The ambivalence of scholars who cursed the errors made by careless printers much as earlier authors had cursed careless scribes is brought out by Bühler, *Fifteenth Century Book*, pp. 50–1, and by Hirsch, *Printing, Selling*, p. 48, n. 20. Early tributes to the 'divine' art are conveniently collected by Stillwell, *The Beginning of the World of Books*, appendix A: 2, pp. 88 ff. They often echo tributes to the labors of scribes – a topos that goes back at least to Cassiodorus and which was publicized by early printings of both Gerson's and Trithemius' *De Laude Scriptorum*. See discussion in chap. 1 above.

[25] Gianandrea de' Bussi, a minor cleric, one-time private secretary to Nicholas of Cues and later Bishop of Aleria, helped to edit texts for Sweynheim and Pannartz (after they established the first press in Rome). In his dedicatory letter to Pope Paul II which appeared in the 1469 Roman edition of Saint Jerome's *Epistles* de' Bussi attributes the phrase 'divine art' ('Haec sancta ars') to Cusanus. Needless to say, early printers saw to it that the phrase received maximum exposure. A thoughtful essay on less well-publicized reactions – particularly some unpublished diatribes against early printing by a Dominican friar who had served as a copyist and reacted unfavorably to the Venetian press in the late fifteenth century – is contained in an article by Martin Lowry, 'Intellectuals and the Press in fifteenth century Venice' to appear in a forthcoming issue of the *Bulletin of the John Rylands University Library*.

[26] De la Mare, 'Vespasiano,' p. 113. On prices, see also Hirsch, *Printing, Selling*, pp. 68–73; Febvre and Martin, *L'Apparition*, chap. 4; Pettas, 'The Cost of Printing a Florentine Incunable.'

[27] Of course, hindsight is required to show that technological unemployment was not severe, and fears, whether ultimately justified or not, may well have been aroused. On the new jobs created by printing, see Bühler, *Fifteenth Century Book*, pp. 25–7; Hirsch, *Printing, Selling*, pp. 48–9. In Florence the number of stationers' shops rose from twelve to thirty during the first half-century after the advent of the press. De la Mare, 'Vespasiano,' p. 44.

modern scholars may be troubled by trying to calculate the number of calves required to supply enough skins for Gutenberg's Bible.[28] It should not be too difficult to obtain agreement that an abrupt rather than a gradual increase did occur in the second half of the fifteenth century.

Scepticism is much more difficult to overcome when we turn from consideration of quantity to that of quality. If one holds a late manuscript copy of a given text next to an early printed one, one is likely to doubt that any change at all has taken place, let alone an abrupt or revolutionary one.

Behind every book which Peter Schoeffer printed stands a published manuscript...The decision on the kind of letter to use, the selection of initials and decoration of rubrications, the determination of the length and width of the column, planning for margins...all were prescribed by the manuscript copy before him.[29]

Not only did early printers such as Schoeffer try to copy a given manuscript as faithfully as possible, but fifteenth-century scribes returned the compliment. As Curt Bühler has shown, a large number of the manuscripts made during the late fifteenth century were copied from early printed books.[30] Thus handwork and presswork continued to appear almost indistinguishable, even after the printer had begun to depart from scribal conventions and to exploit some of the new features inherent in his art.

That there were new features and they were exploited needs to be given due weight. Despite his efforts to duplicate manuscripts as faithfully as possible, the fact remains that Peter Schoeffer, printer, was following different procedures than had Peter Schoeffer, scribe. The absence of any apparent change in product was combined with a complete change in methods of production, giving rise to the paradoxical combination, noted above, of seeming continuity with radical change. Thus the temporary resemblance between handwork and presswork seems to support the thesis of a very gradual evolutionary change; yet the opposite thesis may also be supported by underlining the marked difference between the two different modes of production and noting

[28] See amusing speculations on sales of veal by Bühler, *Fifteenth Century Book*, p. 41.
[29] Lehmann-Haupt, *Peter Schoeffer*, pp. 37–8.
[30] Bühler, *Fifteenth Century Book*, p. 16. A detailed description of particular cases found in the Beinecke Library at Yale is offered by Lutz, 'Manuscripts Copied from Printed Books.'

the new features that began to appear before the fifteenth century had come to an end.

Concern with surface appearance necessarily governed the handwork of the scribe. He was fully preoccupied trying to shape evenly spaced uniform letters in a pleasing symmetrical design. An altogether different procedure was required to give directions to compositors. To do this, one had to mark up a manuscript while scrutinizing its contents.[31] Every manuscript that came into the printer's hands, thus, had to be reviewed in a new way – one which encouraged more editing, correcting and collating than had the hand-copied text.[32] Within a generation the results of this review were being aimed in a new direction – away from fidelity to scribal conventions and toward serving the convenience of the reader. The highly competitive commercial character of the new mode of book production encouraged the relatively rapid adoption of any innovation that commended a given edition to purchasers.[33] Well before 1500, printers had begun to experiment with the use 'of graduated types, running heads... footnotes...tables of contents...superior figures, cross references... and other devices available to the compositor' – all registering 'the victory of the punch cutter over the scribe.'[34] Title pages became increasingly common, facilitating the production of book lists and catalogues, while acting as advertisements in themselves.[35] Hand-drawn illustrations were replaced by more easily duplicated woodcuts and engravings – an innovation which eventually helped to revolutionize

[31] Some Yale mss. marked up by early printers to be used as copy are noted by Lutz, 'Manuscripts Copied,' p. 262, who also offers evidence of the irritation of a thirteenth-century scribe at a correction made by a bookdealer which destroyed the surface symmetry of two pages of a copy of a commentary by Thomas Aquinas.

[32] For a pertinent example, see the account of the procedure used by Aldus Manutius' chief editor, Marcus Musurus, when preparing the printer's copy for the 1498 edition of Aristophanes' works. Reynolds and Wilson, *Scribes and Scholars*, pp. 132–3.

[33] Lehmann-Haupt, *Peter Schoeffer*, pp. 53–4 contains relevant data.

[34] Steinberg, *Five Hundred Years*, p. 28.

[35] Steinberg, *Five Hundred Years*, p. 145. Along with many other authorities, both Steinberg (pp. 145 ff.) and Hirsch, *Printing, Selling*, p. 25 overstate the novelty of the title page when describing it as a purely post-print phenomenon. The Folger Library has a copy of Lorenzo Valla's *De Elegantiis Linguae Latinae* – Phillipps Ms 2966 (Folger 'v.a. 102') which is identified by A. M. de la Mare as being by the hand of a Veronese scribe: Cristoforo Schioppo. The name of the book's author, 'Lauretii Vallae,' and part of the title are clearly placed on a single page as if engraved on a stone tablet. That this is by no means the only ms. 'title page' of its kind is attested to by Dr de la Mare. But the basic points made by Steinberg in his section on the title page are not really invalidated by his overlooking quattrocento humanist manuscripts and taking Northern ms. styles for his norm. Title pages did not become common and information contained in colophons did not get shifted until after print.

technical literature by introducing 'exactly repeatable pictorial statements' into all kinds of reference works.

The fact that identical images, maps and diagrams could be viewed
simultaneously by scattered readers constituted a kind of communications revolution in itself. This point has been made most forcefully by
William Ivins, a former curator of prints at the Metropolitan Museum.[36]
Although Ivins' special emphasis on 'the exactly repeatable pictorial
statement' has found favor among historians of cartography,[37] his
propensity for overstatement has provoked objections from other
specialists. Repeatable images, they argue, go back to ancient seals and
coins; while *exact* replication was scarcely fostered by woodblocks
which got worn and broken after repeated use. Here as elsewhere one
must be wary of underrating as well as of overestimating the advantages
of the new technology. Even while noting that woodcuts did get
corrupted when copied for insertion in diverse kinds of texts, one
should also consider the corruption that occurred when hand-drawn
images had to be copied into hundreds of books. Although pattern
books and 'pouncing' techniques were available to some medieval
illuminators,[38] the precise reproduction of fine detail remained elusive
until the advent of woodcarving and engraving. Blocks and plates did
make repeatable visual aids feasible for the first time. In the hands of
expert craftsmen using good materials and working under supervision,
even problems of wear and tear could be circumvented; worn places
could be sharpened; blurred details refined and a truly remarkable
durability achieved.[39]

It is not so much in his special emphasis on the printed image but
rather in his underrating the significance of the printed text that Ivins
seems to go astray. In his work the use of movable type is oddly described as 'little more than a way to do with a smaller number of proof
readings.' A reference by Pliny the Younger to one thousand copies of

---

[36] Ivins, *Prints and Visual Communication*. Some specific examples discussed by Ivins are treated
in later discussion of scientific data collection and early field trips. See pp. 262 ff below.

[37] See e.g., Bagrow, *History of Cartography*, p. 89; Skelton, *Maps*, p. 12; Robinson, 'Map making,'
Five Centuries of Map Printing, p. 1. The illustrations (in this last mentioned work) of
relevant tools and techniques are unusually clear and helpful.

[38] On medieval pattern books, see n. 123 below.

[39] Thus the second edition of Vesalius' *De Fabrica* profited from the sharpening of indistinct
letters and lines by a Basel woodcarver using a fine knife. Woodblocks impressed only on
moist paper and made of birchwood treated with hot linseed oil can remain unspoiled even
after running off 3,000 to 4,000 copies, according to Willy Wiegand (who printed an edition
of Vesalius' *Icones anatomicae* from old woodblocks in 1935). See Herrlinger, *History of Medical
Illustration*, p. 113.

a book being made in the second century A.D. is cited repeatedly as evidence that the duplicative powers of print were relatively feeble.[40] The incapacity of any two scribes (let alone one thousand) to produce identical copies while taking dictation is overlooked. Although he mentions in passing that 'the history of prints as an integrated series' begins with their use 'as illustrations in books printed from movable types'[41] Ivins' analysis elsewhere tends to detach the fate of printed pictures from that of printed books. His treatment implies that the novel effects of repeatability were confined to pictorial statements. Yet these effects were by no means confined to pictures or, for that matter, to pictures and words. Mathematical tables, for example, were also transformed. For scholars concerned with scientific change, what happened to numbers and equations is surely just as significant as what happened to either images or words. Furthermore, many of the most important pictorial statements produced during the first century of printing employed various devices – banderoles, letter-number keys, indication lines – to relate images to texts.[42] To treat the visual aid as a discrete unit is to lose sight of the connecting links which were especially important for technical literature because they expressed the relationship between words and things.

Even though block-print and letterpress may have originated as separate innovations and were initially used for diverse purposes (so that playing cards and saints' images, for example, were being stamped from blocks at the same time that hand illumination continued to decorate many early printed books), the two techniques soon became intertwined. The use of typography for texts led to that of xylography for illustration, sealing the fate of illuminator along with that of the scribe.[43] When considering how technical literature was affected by the shift from script to print, it seems reasonable to adopt George

[40] Ivins, *Prints and Visual Communication*, pp. 2, 11, 163.

[41] Ivins, *Prints and Visual Communication*, p. 27.

[42] See fascinating section on 'indication lines' in Herrlinger, *History of Medical Illustration*, pp. 54–60. I owe thanks to Karen Reeds for bringing this to my attention.

[43] Questions pertaining to the relationship between block-printing and book-printing and to whether the block book preceded the invention and use of movable type have given rise to a massive controversial literature that cannot be examined here. To sample recent arguments see Musper, 'Xylographic Books,' pp. 341–7 (esp. bibliography p. 347) and Lehmann-Haupt, *Gutenberg and the Master of the Playing Cards*. A close-up view of the overlap between hand illumination and early Mainz printing is offered by Vaassen, *Die Werkstatt der Mainzer Riesenbibel in Würzburg und Ihr Umkreis*. See review article by Labarre, 'Un Atelier Mayençais d'Enluminure vers 1450–1500.' For stimulating speculation relating changes in shop structure to new handbooks for illuminators, see Bober's review of *The Göttingen Model Book*.

Sarton's strategy of envisaging a 'double invention; typography for the text, engraving for the images.'[44] The fact that letters, numbers and pictures were *all* alike subject to repeatability by the end of the fifteenth century, needs more emphasis. That the printed book made possible new forms of interplay between these diverse elements is perhaps even more significant than the change undergone by picture, number or letter alone.

Intellectual historians may find the new interplay between 'literate, figurative and numerate' forms of expression of particular interest.[45] Social historians also need to be alerted to the new interplay between diverse occupational groups which occurred within the new workshops that were set up by early printers. The preparation of copy and illustrative material for printed editions led to a rearrangement of all book-making arts and routines. Not only did new skills, such as typefounding and presswork, involve veritable occupational mutations;[46] but the production of printed books also gathered together in one place more traditional variegated skills. In the age of scribes, book-making had occurred under the diverse auspices represented by stationers and lay copyists in university towns; illuminators and miniaturists trained in special ateliers; goldsmiths and leather workers belonging to special guilds; monks and lay brothers gathered in scriptoria; royal clerks and papal secretaries working in chanceries and courts; preachers compiling books of sermons on their own; humanist poets serving as their own scribes. The advent of printing led to the creation of a new kind of shop structure; to a regrouping which entailed closer contacts among diversely skilled workers and encouraged new forms of cross-cultural interchange.

Thus it is not uncommon to find former priests among early printers or former abbots serving as editors and correctors.[47] University pro-

---

[44] Sarton, *The Appreciation of Ancient and Medieval Science During the Renaissance 1450–1600*, p. xi.

[45] I borrow these terms from Derek da Solla Price's article, 'Geometrical and Scientific Talismans.'

[46] How the diverse skills of the punchcutter, matrix-maker and mold-maker got lumped under the heading of 'typefounder' is discussed by Harry Carter, *A View of Early Typography*, p. 92.

[47] The widely varying social and occupational origins of early printers, extracted from biographical dictionaries such as those compiled by E. Voullième and Joseph Benzing for German-speaking regions, are indicated by Hirsch, *Printing, Selling*, pp. 18–23. A 'flocking of priests into printing' is noted on p. 22 and the numbers of priests and bishops involved in proof-reading, on p. 4). How a former monk and abbot abandoned his monastery to work full-time as an editor for Peter Schoeffer's early firm is noted by Lehmann-Haupt, *Peter Schoeffer*, p. 83, n. 6. A recent finely detailed study of the Paris book-trade in the mid-sixteenth century confirms the impression of diverse backgrounds among those entering the trade: Parent, *Les*

fessors also often served in similar capacities and thus came into closer contact with metal workers and mechanics. Other fruitful forms of collaboration brought astronomers and engravers, physicians and painters together, dissolving older divisions of intellectual labor and encouraging new ways of coordinating the work of brains, eyes and hands. Problems of financing the publication of the large Latin volumes that were used by late medieval faculties of theology, law, and medicine also led to the formation of partnerships that brought rich merchants and local scholars into closer contact. The new financial syndicates that were formed to provide master printers with needed labor and supplies brought together representatives of town and gown.[48] As the key figure around whom all arrangements revolved, the master printer himself bridged many worlds.[49] He was responsible for obtaining money, supplies and labor, while developing complex production schedules, coping with strikes, trying to estimate book markets and lining up learned assistants.[50] He had to keep on good terms with officials who provided protection and lucrative jobs, while cultivating and promoting talented authors and artists who might bring his firm profits or prestige. In those places where his enterprise prospered and he achieved a position of influence with fellow townsmen, his workshop became a veritable cultural center attracting local literati and celebrated foreigners; providing both a meeting place and message center for an expanding cosmopolitan Commonwealth of Learning.

Métiers du Livre, pp. 175 ff. Parent also notes that publication of devotional literature was often supervised by a priest who was sent by a bishop to receive room and board from the printer (p. 122).

[48] References to pertinent studies are given by Hirsch, *Printing, Selling*, p. 51. Bühler, *The University and the Press in 15th Century Bologna*, pp. 15–16 gives an example of a contract drawn up in 1470 to build and run a press for academic purposes. The complex arrangements that went into the printing for academic purposes of a massive commentary on Avicenna's *Canon* (comprising over a thousand double column large folio-sized pages of text) are described by Mardersteig, *Remarkable Story*.

[49] He was such a protean figure that no one label such as 'printer' adequately designates his many-faceted role. On my unorthodox use of this label, see n. 136 below.

[50] Mardersteig's *Remarkable Story* shows the printer, Petrus Maufer, coping with strikes and many other complications before triumphantly concluding the actual printing which began in May 1477 when the first reams of paper were delivered. From then until December 1, 1477 when the last sheet came off the press, 'not a working day was wasted.' Four hand presses had been in operation from daybreak to nighttime without interruption, and 6,800,000 separate pieces of type had been procured and used. For general description of the complex working routines observed in most print shops during the first centuries after Gutenberg, McKenzie's article, 'Printers of the Mind,' is unexcelled. A useful glimpse of Plantin's operational plan is given by Lotte and Wytze Hellinga, 'Regulations.' That routines were somewhat more orderly than either McKenzie or the Hellingas imply is suggested by K. I. D. Maslen and John Gerritsen, correspondence in *The Library* (June, 1975).

Some manuscript bookdealers, to be sure, had served rather similar functions before the advent of printing. That Italian humanists were grateful to Vespasiano da Bisticci for many of the same services that were later rendered by Aldus Manutius has already been noted. Nevertheless, the shop structure over which Aldus presided differed markedly from that known to Vespasiano. As the prototype of the early capitalist as well as the heir to Atticus and his successors, the printer embraced an even wider repertoire of roles. Aldus' household in Venice, which contained some thirty members, has recently been described as an 'almost incredible mixture of the sweat shop, the boarding house and the research institute.'[51] A most interesting study might be devoted to a comparison of the talents mobilized by early printers with those previously employed by stationers or manuscript bookdealers. Of equal interest would be a comparison of the occupational culture of Peter Schoeffer, printer, with that of Peter Schoeffer, scribe. The two seem to work in contrasting milieux, subject to different pressures and aiming at different goals. Unlike the shift from stationer to publisher, the shift from scribe to printer represented a genuine occupational mutation. Although Schoeffer was the first to make the leap, many others took the same route before the century's end.[52]

Judging by Lehmann-Haupt's fine monograph, many of Schoeffer's pioneering activities were associated with the shift from a retail trade to a wholesale industry which led the printer to turn peddler and to launch what soon became an annual book fair at Frankfurt. 'For a while the trade in printed books flowed within the narrow channels of the manuscript book market. But soon the stream could no longer be contained.' New distribution outlets were located; handbills, circulars and sales catalogues were printed and the books themselves were carried down the Rhine, across the Elbe, west to Paris, south to Switzerland. The drive to tap markets went together with efforts to hold competitors at bay by offering better products or, at least, by printing a prospectus advertising the firm's 'more readable' texts, 'more complete and better arranged' indexes, 'more careful proof

---

[51] Martin Lowry's forthcoming biography of Aldus Manutius contains this description.

[52] In sustaining a gradual evolutionary approach to the impact of printing, authorities on the history of the book naturally emphasize the stationer as the true precursor of the printer. Yet the use of the term *scriptor* for *impressor* by printers showed that they considered themselves the successors not of stationers but of copyists. (See Hirsch, *Printing, Selling*, p. 19, n. 21.) It seems fair to say that early printers took over functions performed *both* by copyists *and* by stationers (or 'publishers') while diverging from both in significant ways.

reading' and editing. Officials serving archbishops and emperors were cultivated, not so much as potential bibliophiles, nor even as potential censors, but rather as potential customers, who issued a steady flow of orders for the printing of ordinances, edicts, bulls, indulgences, broadsides and tracts. By the end of the century, Schoeffer had risen to a position of eminence in the city of Mainz. He commanded a 'far-flung sales organization,' had become a partner in a joint mining enterprise, and had founded a printing dynasty. His supply of types went to his sons upon his death and the Schoeffer firm continued in operation, expanding to encompass music printing, through the next generation.[53]

As the foregoing may suggest, there are many points of possible contrast between the activities of the Mainz printer and those of the Paris scribe. All need to be brought out more clearly when considering fifteenth-century trends. The movement of centers of book production from university towns, princely courts, patrician villas and monasteries to commercial centers; the organization of new trade networks and fairs; the new competition over lucrative privileges and monopolies; the new restraints imposed by official censors have been covered in special accounts.[54] But the implications of such changes need to be underlined so that they may be related to other concurrent developments. Competitive and commercial drives were not entirely absent among the stationers who served university faculties, the lay scribes who were hired by mendicant orders, or the semi-lay copyists who belonged to communities founded by the Brethren of the Common Life. But they were muted in comparison with the later efforts of Schoeffer and his competitors to recoup initial investments, pay off creditors, use up reams of paper, and keep pressmen employed. The manuscript bookdealer did not have to worry about idle machines or striking workmen as did the printer. It has been suggested indeed that the mere act of setting up a press in a monastery or in affiliation with a religious order was a source of disturbance, bringing 'a multitude of worries about money and property' into space previously reserved for meditation and good works. When one considers that such an event

---

[53] See Lehmann-Haupt, *Peter Schoeffer, passim.*
[54] Much of this is covered in detail by Febvre and Martin, *L'Apparition*, chap. 6, and is also well documented by Pollard and Ehrman, *The Distribution of Books.* Hirsch, *Printing, Selling,* pp. 63–4 points out how Schirokauer's (1951) study drastically underestimates the size of markets tapped by early printers.

occurred in several places in the late fifteenth century, it seems to warrant more attention in studies of changes affecting late medieval religious life.[55]

We also need to hear more about the job-printing that accompanied book-printing. It lent itself to commercial advertising, official propaganda, seditious agitation, and bureaucratic red tape as no scribal procedure ever had.[56] The very term 'avertissement' underwent an intriguing change. In the Low Countries, books copied during holy days in medieval scriptoria were regarded as specially consecrated. A note placed in the colophon designating holy-day work served as a warning (or 'avertissement') against sale.[57] Of course such a warning can be interpreted as indicating the commercialization of the manuscript book-trade. Books were being copied not just for the love of God but for sale, on all save holy days. But a different, more muted commercial theme was sounded by this kind of 'avertissement' than would be the case after presses were established.

As self-serving publicists, early printers issued book lists, circulars and broadsides. They put their firm's name, emblem and shop address on the front page of their books. Indeed, their use of title pages entailed a significant reversal of scribal procedures; they put themselves first. Scribal colophons had come last. They also extended their new promotional techniques to the authors and artists whose work they published, thus contributing to the celebration of lay culture-heroes and to their achievement of personal celebrity and eponymous fame. Reckon masters and instrument makers along with professors and preachers also profited from book advertisements that spread their fame beyond shops

[55] Wytze Hellinga, 'Thomas A Kempis', 4–5. For references to monastic presses in diverse regions, see chap. 1, n. 39 above.

[56] Although Steinberg, *Five Hundred Years* (p. 22) stresses this aspect of Gutenberg's invention as the most far-reaching, it receives little attention from Febvre and Martin, *L'Apparition* because of their focus on 'the book.' 'Jobbing printing' was also, with one exception, omitted from the exhibition on 'Printing and the Mind of Man' assembled at the British Museum and at Earl's Court, July 16–27, 1963. See British Museum Catalogue (London, 1963) p. 8. Official printing for ecclesiastical and secular governments is discussed by Hirsch, *Printing, Selling*, pp. 52–3. It furnished an important part of Peter Schoeffer's output, according to Lehmann-Haupt, *Peter Schoeffer*, pp. 78–9.

[57] See item 7, Catalogue of Exhibition held in the Royal Library of Brussels (Sept.–Oct. 1973): *Le Cinquième Centenaire de L'Imprimerie dans les Anciens Pays-Bas* (Brussels, 1973), pp. 11–12 and footnote reference to B. Kruitwagen, 'Het Schrijven op Feestdagen in de Middeleuwen.' One might compare this medieval approach to holy-day book making with the indignation of a member of the Royal Society at printing delays caused by 'the holy days sticking in the workman's hands,' cited by Hill, book review, *English Historical Review* (1973).

and lecture halls.[58] Studies concerned with the rise of a lay intelligentsia, with the new dignity assigned to artisan crafts or with the heightened visibility achieved by the 'capitalist spirit' might well devote more attention to these early practitioners of the advertising arts.

Their control of a new publicity apparatus, moreover, placed early printers in an exceptional position with regard to other enterprises. They not only sought ever larger markets for their own products; but they also contributed to, and profited from, the expansion of other commercial enterprises. What effects did the appearance of new advertising techniques have on sixteenth-century commerce and industry? Possibly some answers to this question are known. Probably others can still be found. Many other aspects of job printing and the changes it entailed clearly need further study. The printed calendars and indulgences that were first issued from the Mainz workshops of Gutenberg and Fust, for example, warrant at least as much attention as the more celebrated Bibles. Indeed the mass production of indulgences[59] illustrates rather neatly the sort of change that often goes overlooked, so that its consequences are more difficult to reckon with than perhaps they need be.

In contrast to the changes sketched above, those that were associated with the consumption of new printed products are more intangible, indirect, and difficult to handle. A large margin for uncertainty must be left when dealing with such changes. Many of them also have to be left for later discussion because they involved prolonged, unevenly phased transformations which occurred over the course of several centuries. This seems especially true of those changes which are most commonly associated with the impact of printing: changes, that is, which hinge on the spread of literacy and which entail a variety of popularizing trends.

On the difficult problem of estimating literacy rates before and after printing, the comments of Carlo Cipolla seem cogent:

It is not easy to draw a general conclusion from the scattered evidence that I have quoted and from the similarly scattered evidence that I have not quoted...I could go on to conclude that at the end of the sixteenth century 'there were more literate people than we generally believe'...I could

---

[58] Printed announcements of university lectures containing blurbs for pertinent books on sale are described by Hirsch, *Printing, Selling*, p. 51 and Parent, *Les Métiers*, p. 142. For further discussion of changed status of artists, authors, instrument-makers, etc. see pp. 232 ff and chap. 6, vol. II, below.   [59] On indulgence-printing, see pp. 375 ff, below.

equally conclude that 'there were less literate people than we generally believe' for in all truth one never knows what is it that 'we generally believe'...one could venture to say that at the end of the sixteenth century the rate of illiteracy for the adult population in Western Europe was below 50 percent in the towns of the relatively more advanced areas and above 50 percent in all rural areas as well as in the towns of the backward areas. This is a frightfully vague statement...but the available evidence does not permit more precision.[60]

Statements about literacy rates during the fourteenth and early fifteenth centuries are likely to be just as vague – perhaps even more so. In the absence of hard data, plausible arguments may be developed to support sharply divergent opinions and there is no way of settling the inevitable conflict between revolutionary and evolutionary models of change. Thus one may envisage a relatively swift 'educational revolution' in the sixteenth century, in which case, the effects produced by printing will loom large; or, one may instead describe a 'long revolution' which unfolds so slowly that these effects are completely flattened out.[61]

In view of the fragmentary evidence that is available and the prolonged fluctuations that were entailed, it would seem prudent to bypass vexed problems associated with the spread of literacy until other issues have been explored with more care. That there are other issues worth exploring – apart from the expansion of the reading public or the 'spread' of new ideas – is in itself a point that needs underlining (and that will be repeatedly underscored in this book). When considering the *initial* transformations wrought by print, at all events, changes undergone by groups who were already literate ought to receive priority over the undeniably fascinating problem of how rapidly such groups were enlarged.

Once attention has been focused on already literate sectors, it be-

---

60 Cipolla, *Literacy*, p. 60.
61 See Cipolla, *Literacy*, p. 52 where he discusses whether Lawrence Stone's concept of an 'educational revolution' in England is relevant to continental trends. In his article on 'Literacy and Education,' p. 78, Stone underlines the importance of cheap paper and movable type whereas Williams, *The Long Revolution*, pp. 132–3 discusses the interval encompassed by Stone's 'educational revolution' without mentioning printing at all. On pp. 156–7, Williams mentions printing but traces the growth of the reading public back to the eighth century and beyond to Rome. When this approach is coupled with emphasis on the advent of a mass reading public after the steam press, the fifteenth-century typographical revolution is bound to recede. Williams does bring out the importance of printing as against writing in his brief study of *Communications*, p. 22. The topic is especially likely to be underplayed in connection with the history of education. See e.g. Talbott, 'The History of Education,' where a survey of the literature shows printing to be omitted from among factors which 'triggered educational expansion' in early-modern England (p. 136).

comes clear that their social composition calls for further thought. Did printing at first serve prelates and patricians as a 'divine art' or should one think of it rather as the 'poor man's friend'? It was described in both ways by contemporaries, and probably served in both ways as well. When one recalls scribal functions performed by Roman slaves or later by monks, lay brothers, clerks and notaries, one may conclude that literacy had never been congruent with élite social status.[62] One may also guess that it was more compatible with sedentary occupations than with the riding and hunting favored by many squires and lords.[63] In this light, it may be misguided to envisage the new presses as making available to low born men, products previously used only by the high born. That many rural areas remained untouched until after the coming of the railway age seems likely. Given the large peasant population in early-modern Europe and the persistence of local dialects which imposed an additional language barrier between spoken and written words, it is probable that only a very small portion of the entire population was affected by the initial shift. Nevertheless within this relatively small and largely urban population, a fairly wide social spectrum may have been involved. In fifteenth-century England, for example, mercers and scriveners engaged in a manuscript book-trade were already catering to the needs of lowly bakers and merchants as well as to those of lawyers, aldermen, or knights.[64] The proliferation of literate merchants in fourteenth-century Italian cities is no less notable than the presence of an illiterate army commander in late sixteenth-century France.[65]

It would be a mistake, however, to assume that a distaste for reading was especially characteristic of the nobility, although it seems plausible that a distaste for Latin pedantry was shared by lay aristocrat and com-

---

[62] The very term 'poor man's book' ('Liber Pauperum') goes back at least as far as the twelfth century in England where a Lombard master arranged a compilation of the Code and Digest for poor law clerks. Cf. Haskins, *The Renaissance of the Twelfth Century*, p. 211.

[63] Thus in Richard Pace's celebrated anecdote about the early Tudor squire, who questioned the need to teach his sons how to read, hunting and hawking are opposed to armchair study. See chap. 4, n. 315, below.

[64] Jacob, *The Fifteenth Century*, pp. 663–667. See also Adamson, 'The Extent of Literacy in England,' 163–93; Bennett, *English Books and Readers 1475-1557*, p. 20; Parkes, 'The Literacy of the Laity'. Thrupp, *The Merchant Class*, p. 157 provides a useful table as well as relevant data.

[65] See Renouard, *Etudes d'Histoire Médiévale*, I, pp. 419–26; Jeannin, *Merchants of the Sixteenth Century*, pp. 80–6; Sapori, *The Italian Merchant*, passim; Bec, *Les Marchands Ecrivains*, passim, has data on the numerous merchants who kept diaries as well as accounts. On the reputed illiteracy of a famous Marshal of France (Montmorency) see anecdote cited below, p. 395.

moner alike. It also remains uncertain whether one ought to describe the early reading public as being 'middle class.' Certainly extreme caution is needed when matching genres of books with groups of readers. All too often it is taken for granted that 'low-brow' or 'vulgar' works reflect 'lower class' tastes, despite contrary evidence offered by authorship and library catalogues.[66] Before the advent of mass literacy the most 'popular' works were those which appealed to diverse groups of readers and not just to the plebes.

Divisions between Latin and vernacular reading publics are also much more difficult to correlate with social status than many accounts suggest. It is true that the sixteenth-century physician who used Latin was regarded as superior to the surgeon who did not, but also true that neither man was likely to belong to the highest estates of the realm. Insofar as the vernacular translation movement was aimed at readers who were unlearned in Latin, it was often designed to appeal to pages as well as apprentices; to landed gentry, cavaliers and courtiers as well as to shopkeepers and clerks. In the Netherlands, a translation from Latin into French often pointed away from the urban laity who knew only Lower Rhenish dialects and toward relatively exclusive courtly circles. At the same time, a translation into 'Dutch' might be aimed at preachers who needed to cite scriptural passages in sermons rather than at the laity (which is too often assumed to be the only target for 'vernacular' devotional works). Tutors trying to educate young princes; instructors in court or church schools; and chaplains translating from Latin in response to royal requests had pioneered in 'popularizing' techniques even before the printer set to work.

But the most vigorous impetus given to popularization before printing came from the felt need of preachers to keep their congregations awake and also to hold the attention of diverse outdoor crowds.[67] Unlike the preacher, the printer could only guess at the nature of the audience to which his work appealed. Accordingly, one must be especially careful when taking the titles of early printed books as trustworthy guides to readership. A case in point is the frequent description of the fifteenth-century picture Bible, which was issued in

[66] Useful warnings on this point are offered by Natalie Z. Davis, 'Printing and the People.'
[67] A thirteenth-century Dominican manual: *De Arte Predicandi* issued on 'how to sew a sermon together quickly' and how to appeal to special interest groups such as 'rich women in towns' or 'crowds at fairs' or 'young girls' is described by Murray, 'Religion among the Poor.'

both manuscript and then blockbook form, as the 'poor man's' Bible. The description may well be anachronistic, based on abbreviating the full Latin title given to such books. The *Biblia Pauperum Praedicatorum* was not aimed at poor men but at poor preachers who had a mere smattering of Latin and found scriptural exposition easier when given picture books as guides.[68] Sophisticated analysts have suggested the need to discriminate between 'audiences' – that is, actual readership as determined by library catalogues, subscription lists and other objective data – and 'publics,' the more hypothetical targets envisaged by authors and publishers, those to whom they address their works.[69] Given the tendency to cite titles or prefaces as evidence of actual readership, this distinction is worth keeping in mind.

> To arrive at valid conclusions...we must proceed with care and caution. Information on the spread of reading and writing...is limited and must be supplemented by analysis of the subject contents of the total production (in itself not an easy task); this in turn provides circumstantial evidence on the composition of the reading public: a cookbook...reprinted eight or more times in the xvth century was obviously read by people concerned with the preparation of food, the *Doctrinal des Filles*...a booklet on the behavior of young women, primarily by 'filles' and 'mesdames.'[70]

Such 'circumstantial evidence,' however, is highly suspect. Without passing judgment on the audience for early cookbooks (its character seems far from obvious to me), booklets pertaining to the behavior of young ladies did not necessarily attract feminine readers and were probably also of interest to male tutors, or confessors, or guardians. As a later chapter suggests, the circulation of printed etiquette books had wide-ranging psychological ramifications; their capacity to heighten the anxiety of parents should not go ignored. Furthermore such works were probably also read by authors, translators and publishers of other etiquette books. That authors and publishers were wide-ranging readers needs to be perpetually kept in mind. Even those sixteenth-century court poets who shunned printers and circulated

---

68 James Strachan, *Early Bible Illustrations*, p. 7 raises the question of whether the abbreviated title *Biblia Pauperum* is appropriate or not.

69 This distinction, suggested by T. J. Clark in his study of Courbet is discussed in connection with problems posed by sixteenth-century 'popular' culture by Natalie Davis, 'Printing and the People.' It seems futile to try to restrict usage of terms already employed interchangeably in a large literature. I prefer the phrase: 'assumed public' (which is used by Davis elsewhere in the same article) since it is less likely to be misinterpreted.

70 Hirsch, *Printing, Selling*, p. 7.

their verse in manuscript form[71] took advantage of their own access to printed materials. It has been suggested that books describing double entry bookkeeping were read less by merchants than by the writers of accountancy books and teachers of accountancy. One wonders whether there were not more playwrights and poets than shepherds who studied so-called *Shepherd's Almanacks*. Given the corruption of data transmitted over the centuries, given the false remedies and impossible recipes contained in medical treatises, one hopes that they were studied more by poets than by physicians. Given the exotic ingredients described, one may assume that few apothecaries actually tried to concoct all the recipes contained in early printed pharmacopeia, although they may have felt impelled to stock their shelves with bizarre items just in case the new publicity might bring such items into demand.[72] The purposes, whether intended or actual, served by some early printed handbooks offer puzzles that permit no easy solution. What was the point of publishing vernacular manuals outlining procedures that were already familiar to all skilled practitioners of certain crafts?[73] It is worth remembering, at all events, that the gap between shoproom practice and classroom theory was just becoming visible during the first century of printing and that many so-called 'practical' handbooks and manuals contained impractical, even injurious, advice.

While postponing conjectures about social and psychological transformations, certain points should be noted here. One must distinguish, as Altick suggests, between literacy and habitual book reading. By no means all who mastered the written word have, down to the present, become members of a book-reading public.[74] Learning *to read* is different, moreover, from learning *by reading*. Reliance on apprentice-

---

[71] Saunders, 'From Manuscript to Print,' pp. 507–28.

[72] On accountancy books, almanacs, pharmacopeia and other 'practical' guide-books see Natalie Davis, 'Printing and the People' and discussion on pp. 243ff. and 554ff. below.

[73] In his *Speculum* review of *The Göttingen Model Book*, Harry Bober suggests that the detailed instructions for illumination contained therein (which included sixteen separate steps for painting one acanthus leaf) must have been aimed at a new group of untrained craftsmen mobilized by printers since scribal illuminators had no need of such a manual – any more than 'an experienced chef needs the numbered instructions on soup cans.' Even if this argument holds good for book-making, it still leaves open questions raised by other craft manuals in trades where there was no dramatic change in shop structure nor influx of neophytes. The purposes served by the early publication of vernacular booklets by the two German master masons: Matthias Roriczer and Hans Schmuttermayer, for example, remain somewhat baffling, as I have learned from two articles by Shelby, 'The Education of Medieval English Master Masons,' 1–26; 'The Geometrical Knowledge,' 395–421, and correspondence with their author.

[74] Altick, *The English Common Reader*, p. 31.

ship training, oral communication and special mnemonic devices had gone together with mastering letters in the age of scribes. After the advent of printing however, the transmission of written information became much more efficient. It was not only the craftsman outside universities who profited from the new opportunities to teach himself. Of equal importance was the chance extended to bright undergraduates to reach beyond their teachers' grasp. Gifted students no longer needed to sit at the feet of a given master in order to learn a language or academic skill. Instead they could swiftly achieve mastery on their own, even by sneaking books past their tutors – as did the young would-be astronomer, Tycho Brahe. 'Why should old men be preferred to their juniors now that it is possible for the young by diligent study to acquire the same knowledge?' asked the author of a fifteenth-century outline of history.[75]

As learning by reading took on new importance, the role played by mnemonic aids was diminished. Rhyme and cadence were no longer required to preserve certain formulas and recipes. The nature of the collective memory was transformed.

In Victor Hugo's *Notre Dame de Paris* a scholar, deep in meditation in his study...gazes at the first printed book which has come to disturb his collection of manuscripts. Then...he gazes at the vast cathedral, silhouetted against the starry sky...'Ceci tuera cela,' he says. The printed book will destroy the building. The parable which Hugo develops out of the comparison of the building, crowded with images, with the arrival in his library of a printed book might be applied to the effect on the invisible cathedrals of memory of the past of the spread of printing. The printed book will make such huge built-up memories, crowded with images, unnecessary. It will do away with habits of immemorial antiquity whereby a 'thing' is immediately invested with an image and stored in the places of memory.[76]

To the familiar romantic theme of the Gothic cathedral as an 'encyclopedia in stone,' Frances Yates has added a fascinating sequel. Not only did printing eliminate many functions previously performed by stone figures over portals and stained glass in windows but it also affected less tangible images by eliminating the need for placing figures and objects in imaginary niches located in memory theatres. The way was paved for a more thorough-going iconoclasm than any Christian

---

75 Jacobo Filippo Foresti, *Supplementum Chronicarum* (Venice, 1483) cited by Martin Lowry in his forthcoming biography of Aldus.   76 Yates, *Art of Memory*, p. 131.

church had ever known. 'The "Ramist man" must smash the images both within and without, must substitute for the old idolatrous art, the new image-less way of remembering through abstract dialectical order.'[77]

This line of argument dovetails neatly with Walter Ong's earlier studies of Ramism and print culture – perhaps too neatly in the judgment of some medieval scholars who see evidence in medieval manuscripts of those diagrammatic features which Ong reserves for the printed page.[78] But even if all parts of the argument are not deemed equally acceptable, the basic point still seems valid. Printing made it possible to dispense with the use of images for mnemonic purposes and thus reinforced iconoclastic tendencies already present among many Christians. Successive editions of Calvin's *Institutes* elaborated on the need to observe the Second Commandment. The favorite text of the defenders of images was the dictum of Gregory the Great that statues served as 'the books of the illiterate.'[79] Although Calvin's scornful dismissal of this dictum made no mention of printing, the new medium did underlie the Calvinist assumption that the illiterate should not be given graven images but should be taught to read. In this light it may seem plausible to suggest that printing fostered a movement 'from image culture to word culture,' a movement which was more compatible with Protestant bibliolatry and pamphleteering than with the Baroque statues and paintings sponsored by the post-Tridentine Catholic Church.

Yet the cultural metamorphosis produced by printing was really much more complicated than any single formula can possibly express.[80] For one thing, the graven image became more, rather than less, ubiquitous after the establishment of print shops throughout Western

[77] Yates, *Art of Memory*, p. 271.
[78] See n. 154 below, for references. In slide lectures given at Catholic University during the 1974 Medieval Academy Summer Institute program on 'The Archeology of the Book,' Professor Richard H. Rouse of U.C.L.A. demonstrated graphically the frequent use of diagrams, brackets, cross-references, marginal guides and other devices in scribal compilations (especially in concordances and guides to patristic works) produced by medieval teachers and preachers.
[79] Myron Gilmore, 'Italian Reactions to Erasmian Humanism,' pp. 87–8.
[80] Although Stone, 'Literacy and Education,' p. 76 cites my preliminary 'Conjectures' as suggesting that the printed book caused Europe to move 'decisively from image culture to word culture' I am not convinced that this formulation is valid and regret any inadvertent implication that such a movement occurred. That Protestant bibliolatry and iconoclasm were more compatible with early print culture than Tridentine Catholicism was suggested in my article (and is now spelled out more fully in chapter 4) but that is a different matter than suggesting that European culture moved from image to word. For objections to the latter formulation, see paragraphs following this note in text above.

Europe. For another thing, Protestant propaganda exploited printed image no less than printed word – as numerous caricatures and cartoons may suggest. Even religious imagery was defended by some Protestants, and on the very grounds of its compatibility with print culture. 'If graving were taken away we could have not printing,' wrote Stephen Gardiner, putting the case for images against Nicholas Ridley in 1547. 'And therefore they that press so much the words of *Non facies tibi sculptile*...they condemn printed books, the original whereof is graving to make *matrices literarum*.'[81] A close study of two versions of sixteenth-century Dutch Bibles, one Protestant, the other Catholic, suggests that there was indeed a tendency for Protestants to deemphasize pictures and stress words; yet at the same time, they did engage in illustrating Bibles – a movement which Lutherans, at least, encouraged.[82] Luther himself commented on the inconsistency of iconoclasts who tore pictures off walls while handling the illustrations in Bibles reverently. Pictures 'do no more harm on walls than in books,' he commented and then, somewhat sarcastically, stopped short of pursuing this line of thought: 'I must cease lest I give occasion to the image breakers never to read the Bible or to burn it.'[83]

If we accept the idea of a movement from image to word, furthermore, we will be somewhat at loss to account for the work of Northern artists, such as Dürer or Cranach or Holbein, who were affiliated with Protestantism and yet owed much to print. As Dürer's career may suggest, the new arts of printing and engraving, far from reducing the importance of images, increased opportunities for image makers and helped to launch art history down its present path. Even the imaginary figures and memory theatres described by Frances Yates did not vanish when their mnemonic functions were outmoded, but received a 'strange new lease on life.' They provided the content for magnificent emblem books and for elaborate Baroque illustrations to Rosicrucian and occult works in the seventeenth century. They also helped to inspire an entirely new genre of printed literature – the didactic picture book for children. Leipzig boys in Leibniz' day 'were brought up on Comenius'

[81] *The Letters of Stephen Gardiner*, pp. 258–9. I owe this reference and the one from Luther below (n. 83) to Margaret Aston, who is completing a major study of iconoclasm in Tudor England.
[82] Hindman, 'The Transition from Manuscripts.' See esp. p. 205.
[83] 'Against the Heavenly Prophets in the Matter of Images and Sacraments,' (1525), *Luther's Works*, XL 99–100. On Lutheran Bible illustration, see Ph. Schmidt, *Die Illustration der Lutherbibel 1522–1700*.

picture book and Luther's Catechism.'[84] In this form, the ancient memory images re-entered the imagination of Protestant children, ultimately supplying Jung and his followers with evidence that suggested the hypothesis of a collective Unconscious. Surely the new vogue for image-packed emblem books was no less a product of sixteenth-century print culture than was the imageless 'Ramist' textbook.

Furthermore, in certain fields of learning such as architecture, geometry or geography and many of the life sciences as well, print culture was not merely incompatible with the formula offered above; it actually increased the functions performed by images while reducing those performed by words. Many fundamental texts of Ptolemy, Vitruvius, Galen and other ancients had lost their illustrations in the course of being copied for centuries and regained them only after script was replaced by print.[85] To think in terms of a movement going from image to word points technical literature in the wrong direction. It was not the 'printed word' but the 'printed image' which acted as a 'savior for Western science' in George Sarton's view. Within the Commonwealth of Learning it became increasingly fashionable to adopt the ancient Chinese maxim that a single picture was more valuable than many words.[86] In early Tudor England, Thomas Elyot expressed a preference for 'figures and charts' over 'hearing the rules of a science'[87] which seems worth further thought. Although images were indispensable for prodding memory, a heavy reliance on verbal instruction had also been characteristic of communications in the age of scribes. To be sure, academic lectures were sometimes supplemented by drawing pictures on walls; verbal instructions to apprentices were accompanied by demonstrations; the use of blocks and boards, fingers and knuckles were common in teaching reckoning and gestures usually went with the recitation of key mnemonics. Nevertheless, when seek-

---

[84] Yates, *Art of Memory*, pp. 134; 377. The magnificent Baroque engravings that made visible the elaborate memory systems developed in the sixteenth and seventeenth centuries may be sampled by examining almost any work by Robert Fludd. How much Comenius' *Orbis Pictus* (1658) owed to Campanella's *City of the Sun* and Rosicrucian manifestoes is noted by Yates, p. 377.

[85] For references to loss of maps, architectural and anatomical illustrations, see chap. 5, volume II below.

[86] Sarton, *Appreciation*, pp. 91; 95. As is noted in chap. 3, the notion that the ancient Egyptians had compressed valuable data in each hieroglyph was believed by would-be decipherers of hieroglyphs until the nineteenth-century discovery of the Rosetta Stone.

[87] See citation from the *Boke Called the Gouvernour* (1531) in Watson, *The Beginning of the Teaching of Modern Subjects in England*, p. 136. It is given in my conclusion, p. 698, volume II below.

ing rapid duplication of a given set of instructions, words simply had to take precedence over other forms of communication. How else save by using words could one dictate a text to assembled scribes? After the advent of printing, visual aids multiplied, signs and symbols were codified; different kinds of iconographic and non-phonetic communication were rapidly developed. The fact that printed picture books were newly designed by educational reformers for the purpose of instructing children and that drawing was considered an increasingly useful accomplishment by pedagogues also points to the need to think beyond the simple formula: image to word.

As these comments may suggest, efforts to summarize changes wrought by printing in any one statement or neat formula are likely to lead us astray. Even while acknowledging that there was an increased reliance on rule books and less on rules of thumb, or that learning by reading gained at the expense of hearing or doing; one must also consider how printing encouraged new objections to bookish knowledge based on 'slavish' copying and how it enabled many observers to check freshly recorded data against received rules. Similarly, one must be cautious about assuming that the spoken word was gradually silenced as printed words multiplied or that the faculty of hearing was increasingly neglected in favor of that of sight. Surely the history of Western music after Gutenberg argues against the latter suggestion. As for the many questions raised by the assertion that print silenced the spoken word; a few are noted elsewhere in this chapter; all must be passed over here.

The purpose of this preliminary section has been simply to demonstrate that the shift from script to print entailed a large ensemble of changes, each of which needs more investigation and all of which are too complicated to be encapsulated in any single formula. But to say that there is no simple way of summarizing the complex ensemble is not the same thing as saying that nothing had changed. To the contrary!

Granted that some sort of communications revolution did occur during the late fifteenth century, how did this affect other historical developments? Since the consequences of printing have not been thoroughly explored, guidance is hard to come by. Most conventional surveys stop short after a few remarks about the wider dissemination of humanist tomes or Protestant tracts. Several helpful suggestions – about the effects of standardization on scholarship and science, for example – are offered in works devoted to the era of the Renaissance or the history of science. By and large, the effects of the new process are vaguely implied rather than explicitly defined and are also drastically minimized. One example may illustrate this point. During the first centuries of printing, old texts were duplicated more rapidly than new ones. On this basis we are told that 'printing did not speed up the adoption of new theories.'[88] But where did these new theories come from? Must we invoke some spirit of the times, or is it possible that an increase in the output of old texts contributed to the formulation of new theories? Maybe other features that distinguished the new mode of book production from the old one also contributed to such theories. We need to take stock of these features before we can relate the advent of printing to other historical developments.

I have found it useful, in any case, to make a start at taking stock by following up clues contained in special studies on printing. After singling out certain features that seemed to be distinctive, I held them in mind while passing in review various historical developments. Relationships emerged that had not occurred to me before and some possible solutions to old puzzles were suggested. Conjectures based on this approach may be sampled below under headings that indicate my main lines of inquiry.

I. A CLOSER LOOK AT WIDE DISSEMINATION: INCREASED OUTPUT AND ALTERED INTAKE

Most references to wide dissemination are too fleeting to make clear the specific effects of an increased supply of texts directed at different markets. In particular they fail to make clear how patterns of consumption were affected by increased production. Just as the 'spread' of literacy tends to take priority over changes experienced by already literate sectors, so too the 'spread' of Lutheran views or the failure of Copernican theories to 'spread' as rapidly as Ptolemaic ones seems to outweigh all other issues. Too often the printer is assigned the sole function of serving as a press agent. His effectiveness is judged by circulation figures alone. Perhaps the term 'dissemination' is distracting

---

[88] Febvre and Martin, *L'Apparition*, pp. 420–1.

and more emphasis on cross-fertilization or cross-cultural interchange might be helpful. For even while more copies of one given text were being 'spread, dispersed, or scattered' by the issue of a printed edition,[89] different texts, which had been previously dispersed and scattered were also being brought closer together for individual readers. In some regions, printers produced more scholarly texts than they could sell, and flooded local markets.[90] In all regions, a given purchaser could buy more books at lower cost and bring them into his study or library. In this way, the printer, who duplicated a seemingly antiquated backlist, was still providing the clerk with a richer, more varied literary diet than had been provided by the scribe. 'A serious student could now endeavor to cover a larger body of material by private reading than a student or even a mature scholar needed to master or could hope to master before printing made books cheap and plentiful.'[91] To consult different books it was no longer so essential to be a wandering scholar. Successive generations of sedentary scholars were less apt to be engrossed by a single text and expend their energies in elaborating on it. The era of the glossator and commentator came to an end, and a new 'era of intense cross referencing between one book and another'[92] began.

That something rather like a knowledge explosion was experienced in the sixteenth century has often been suggested, in connection with the Northern Renaissance if not with the advent of printing. Few studies of the literature of the era fail to cite relevant passages from Marlowe or Rabelais indicating how it felt to become intoxicated by reading and how bookish knowledge was regarded as if it were a magic elixir conferring new powers with every draught. 'All the world is full of learned men, of most skilled preceptors, of vast libraries...neither in Plato's time nor in Cicero's was there ever such opportunity for

---

89 Insofar as this enabled scattered readers to consult the same book, I agree with Sarton that the appearance of the edition has to be considered in connection with standardization. See comment on p. 81 below.

90 Early crises of overproduction of humanist works are noted by Hay, 'Literature, the Printed Book,' p. 365. The failure of printers to assess their markets shrewdly, accounting for some of these crises, is noted by Bühler, *Fifteenth Century Book*, pp. 59–61. Inadequate distribution networks at first were largely responsible. Zainer's firm, for example, turned out 36,000 books when the population of Augsburg was half that number (p. 56).

91 Craig Thompson, *The Colloquies of Erasmus*, tr. and ed. p. 458 (note to 'The Art of Learning,' 1529).

92 Hay, 'Literature, the Printed Book,' p. 366. By the mid-sixteenth century, 'even obscure scholars could possess a relatively large collection of books on a single topic' according to A. R. Hall, 'Science,' p. 389.

studying. . .'[93] In commenting on the comprehensive program of study which accompanied this passage from Rabelais, H. O. Taylor notes that a very similar program had been set forth by Roger Bacon three centuries earlier. Renaissance humanism had intervened between the two eras, Taylor says, so that Bacon did not have the 'literary feeling for the classics' that the sixteenth-century humanist had. Otherwise, his program reflected the same goals. But because theology was still enthroned in the thirteenth century, the friar's program, unlike Rabelais', went unfulfilled.

This line of argument which implies a rise in 'secularism' and decline of religiosity, although often employed, seems to raise more questions than it answers. Just how had theology lost ground in the age of Luther and polyglot Bibles? Could anything be more 'Rabelaisian' than the vernacular sermons of medieval friars? Instead of spinning out debate over 'the religion of Rabelais' perhaps more attention should be devoted to 'the vast libraries' and new opportunities for study that marked his age. The desire to master original tongues and an encyclopedic urge to comprehend every part of creation were manifested in the middle ages. Both played significant roles in the sixteenth-century knowledge explosion. Special research programs developed by scribal scholars and book-hunting humanists in quattrocento Italy also helped to fill library shelves. But when searching for the strategic element which had been lacking in the thirteenth century and was available in Rabelais' time it is worth pausing longer over the invention that Rabelais and other Christian humanists described as 'divine.'

The same point applies to the remarkable erudition displayed by the most celebrated polymaths of the sixteenth century – by scholars such as Conrad Gesner, who pioneered in both bibliography and zoology[94] or by J. J. Scaliger who seemed to fulfill Gargantua's grotesque ambition for Pantagruel by becoming a 'bottomless pit of erudition.'[95] 'The most richly stocked mind that ever spent itself on knowledge' – Mark Pattison's description of Scaliger – seems fair enough. But in all fairness

---

[93] Cited from Urquhart's (1653) translation of Gargantua's letter in *Pantagruel* (chapter 8) by Henry Osborn Taylor, *Thought and Expression* I, part 3: 'The French Mind,' chapter 4.

[94] On Gesner, see pp. 97–9, below.

[95] For vivid account of erudite circles frequented by Scaliger, see Pattison, *Isaac Casaubon*. Although Casaubon took as his second wife the daughter of Henri Estienne II, he failed to get the scholar–printer's library he hoped to inherit. For contemporary epithets applied to Joseph Justus Scaliger as 'the light of the world,' 'the sea of sciences' etc., see Preserved Smith, *Origins of Modern Culture 1543–1687*, p. 268.

to earlier scholars one ought to take into consideration the fact that Scaliger was better served by printers than his predecessors had been by scribes.

This point is especially worth keeping in mind when considering developments associated with classical scholarship or scientific advances. As later chapters may suggest, when dealing with any major intellectual change in the sixteenth century, the ferment engendered by access to more books is likely to receive much less attention than the effect of the voyages of discovery or of the Lutheran revolt, or of humanist attacks on Aristotle and scholasticism. In a recent perceptive account of the sense of intellectual crisis reflected in Montaigne's writing, for example, we are told about the shattering impact of the Reformation and wars of religion and 'the extension of mental horizons' produced by geographical discoveries and humanist recoveries.[96] It would be foolish to assert that the most newsworthy events of the age made no impression on so sensitive an observer as Montaigne. But it also seems misguided to overlook the event that impinged most directly on his favorite observation post. That he could see more books by spending a few months in his Bordeaux tower-study than earlier scholars had seen after a lifetime of travel also needs to be taken into account. In explaining why Montaigne perceived greater 'conflict and diversity' in the works he consulted than had medieval commentators in an earlier age, something should be said about the increased number of texts he had at hand.

More abundantly stocked bookshelves obviously increased opportunities to consult and compare different texts. Merely by making more scrambled data available, by increasing the output of Aristotelian, Alexandrian and Arabic texts, printers encouraged efforts to unscramble these data. Some medieval coastal maps had long been more accurate than many ancient ones, but few eyes had seen either.[97] Much as maps from different regions and epochs were brought into contact in the course of preparing editions of atlases, so too were technical texts brought together in certain physicians' and astronomers' libraries. Contradictions became more visible; divergent traditions more difficult to reconcile. The transmission of received opinion could not proceed

96 Rattansi, 'The Social Interpretation of Science,' p. 7.
97 The superiority of manuscript charts to early printed maps is noted by Penrose, *Travel and Discovery*, chap. 16. The logical conclusion – that intelligent, literate sixteenth-century printers did not know what cartographers and mariners in coastal regions did – is, however, not drawn.

smoothly once Arabists were set against Galenists or Aristotelians against Ptolemaists. Even while confidence in old theories was weakened, an enriched reading matter also encouraged the development of new intellectual combinations and permutations.

Viewed in this light, cross-cultural interchanges fostered by printing help to explain Sarton's observations: 'The Renaissance was a transmutation of values, a "new deal," a reshuffling of cards, but most of the cards were old; the scientific Renaissance was a "new deal," but many of the cards were new.'[98] Combinatory intellectual activity, as Arthur Koestler has suggested, inspires many creative acts.[99] Once old texts came together within the same study, diverse systems of ideas and special disciplines could be combined. Increased output directed at relatively stable markets, in short, created conditions that favored new combinations of old ideas at first and then, later on, the creation of entirely new systems of thought.

It should be noted that cross-cultural interchange was experienced first of all by the new occupational groups responsible for the output of printed editions. Even before a given reference work had come off the press fruitful encounters between typefounders, correctors, translators, copy editors, illustrators or print dealers, indexers and others engaged in editorial work had already occurred. Early printers themselves were the very first to read the products that came off their own presses. They also kept an anxious eye on their competitors' output. The effects of access to more books (and indeed of all the varied features associated with typography) were thus first and most forcefully experienced, within printers' workshops, by the new book producers themselves. Whereas other libraries were nourished by the output of scholar–printers such as the Estiennes or Christopher Plantin, the valuable collections they themselves built up contained many by-products of their own daily shopwork.[100]

---

[98] Sarton, 'Quest for Truth,' p. 57.
[99] Koestler, *Act of Creation.* For a close-up view of a fruitful interaction produced by reading two books on separate topics and combining their themes in one mind, see Vorzimmer, 'Darwin, Malthus.' The veritable explosion of 'creative acts' during the seventeenth century – the so-called 'century of genius' – can be explained partly by the great increase in possible permutations and combinations of ideas.
[100] Plantin's library, which began as a collection of books needed by correctors and included the lexicons, thesauruses, and other major reference works produced by the Estiennes, is described by Voët, *The Golden Compasses* I, 339. On the Estiennes and the valuable collection of books amassed by the dynasty (partly through marriage and litigation) see Elizabeth Armstrong, *Robert Estienne*, and Robert Kingdon, 'The Business Activities of Printers Henri and François Estienne.'

That a remarkable amount of innovative work in both scholarly and scientific fields was done outside academic centers in the early-modern era is often noted. The new attraction exerted by printers' workshops upon men of learning and letters who had previously frequented college lecture halls helps to explain this noteworthy development.[101] The same point holds good for discussion of the new interchanges between artists and scholars or practitioners and theorists which proved so fruitful in early-modern science. As we shall see in a later chapter, the printer's workshop attracted diverse talents in a way that was conducive to cross-fertilization of all kinds.[102] Printing encouraged forms of combinatory activity which were social as well as intellectual. It changed relationships between men of learning as well as between systems of ideas.

Cross-cultural interchange stimulated mental activities in contra-dictory ways. The first century of printing was marked above all by intellectual ferment, and by a 'somewhat wide-angled, unfocused, scholarship.'[103] Certain confusing cross-currents may be explained by noting that new links between disciplines were being forged before old ones had been severed. In the age of scribes, for instance, magical arts were closely associated with mechanical crafts and mathematical wizardry. As later discussion suggests, when 'technology went to press' so too did a vast backlog of occult lore, and few readers could discriminate between the two. Historians who are still puzzled by the high prestige enjoyed by alchemy, astrology, 'magia and cabala' and other occult arts within the Commonwealth of Learning during early modern times might find it helpful to consider how records derived from ancient Near-Eastern cultures had been transmitted in the age of scribes. Some of these records had dwindled into tantalizing frag-ments, pertaining to systems of reckoning, medicine, agriculture, mythic cults, and so forth. Others had evaporated into unfathomable glyphs. Certain cosmic cycles and life cycles are experienced by all men, and so common elements could be detected in the fragments and glyphs. It seemed plausible to assume that all came from one source and

---

101 During his stay in Basel, Ramus was drawn toward the presses rather than toward the academic centers. In his 'Panegyrique de Bâle' (1571), he eulogized the university and local academy but reserved his highest praise for the firms of Amerbach, Froben, Bischoff, Petri, Isingrin, Oporinus *et al.* Fleckenstein, 'Petrus Ramus,' pp. 119-33. That town and gown were not necessarily opposed but were often drawn into fruitful collaboration by early printers should also be kept in mind. See critique of Stillman Drake's thesis pp. 524ff., volume II below.
102 See discussion, pp. 251ff., below.   103 Harbison, *The Christian Scholar*, p. 54.

to take seriously hints in some patristic works about an Ur-text set down by the inventor of writing, which contained all the secrets of Creation as told to Adam before the Fall. The teachings contained in this corpus, it was believed, had been carefully preserved by ancient sages and seers, before becoming corrupted and confused in the course of the dark ages and barbarian invasions. A large collection of writings containing ancient lore was received from Macedonia by Cosimo de Medici, translated from Greek by Ficino in 1463, and printed in fifteen editions before 1500. It took the form of dialogues with the Egyptian god Thoth, and seemed to come from the same corpus of texts as other fragmentary dialogues long known to medieval scholars. It was, accordingly, also attributed to 'Hermes Trismegistus.' The hermetic corpus ran through many editions until 1614 when a treatise by Isaac Casaubon showed it had been compiled in the post-Christian era. On this basis we are told that Renaissance scholars made a 'radical error in dating.' No doubt they had. A neo-Platonic, post-Christian compilation had been mistaken for a work which preceded and influenced Plato. Yet to assign definite dates to scribal compilations, which were probably derived from earlier sources, may be an error as well.[104]

The transformation of occult and esoteric scribal lore after the advent of printing also needs more study. Some arcane writings in Greek, Hebrew or Syriac, for example, became less mysterious. Others became more so. Thus hieroglyphs were set in type more than three centuries before their decipherment. These sacred carved letters were loaded with significant meaning by readers who could not read them. They were also used simply as ornamental motifs by architects and engravers. Given Baroque decoration on one hand, and complicated interpretations by scholars, Rosicrucians, or Free Masons on the other, the duplication of Egyptian picture writing throughout the Age of Reason presents modern scholars with puzzles that can never be solved. In the next chapter the fate of hieroglyphs will be discussed in more detail. Here I just wanted to suggest that one should not think only about new

104 Yates, *Giordano Bruno, passim.* That some ancient Egyptian ingredients were present in the post-Christian compilation is noted on pp. 2–3, n. 4; 431. Yates implies that Baroque argument about 'hermetica' ended with Isaac Casaubon's early seventeenth-century proof that Ficino had translated works dating from the third century A.D. But Greek scholarship alone could not unlock the secrets of the pyramids. Interest in arcana associated with Thoth and 'Horapollo' continued until Champollion. By then the cluster of mysteries that had thickened with each successive 'unveiling of Isis' was so opaque, that even the decipherment of the Rosetta Stone could not dispel them. See discussion below, pp. 279–84.

forms of enlightenment when considering the effects of printing on scholarship. New forms of mystification were encouraged as well.

In this light it seems necessary to qualify the assertion that the first half-century of printing gave 'a great impetus to wide dissemination of accurate knowledge of the sources of Western thought, both classical and Christian.'[105] The duplication of the Hermetic writings, the Sybilline prophecies, the hieroglyphics of 'Horapollo' and many other seemingly authoritative, actually fraudulent esoteric writings worked in the opposite direction, spreading inaccurate knowledge even while paving the way for a purification of Christian sources later on. Here as elsewhere there is need to distinguish between initial and delayed effects. An enrichment of scholarly libraries came rapidly; the sorting out of their contents took more time. Compared to the large output of unscholarly vernacular materials, the number of trilingual dictionaries and Greek or even Latin editions seems so small, one wonders whether the term: 'wide dissemination' ought to be applied to the latter case at all.

Dissemination, as defined in the dictionary, seems especially appropriate to the duplication of primers, ABC books, catechisms, calendars and devotional literature. Increased output of such materials, however, was not necessarily conducive either to the advancement of scholarship or to cross-cultural exchange. Catechisms, religious tracts, and Bibles would fill some bookshelves to the exclusion of all other reading matter. The new wide-angled, unfocused scholarship went together with a new single-minded, narrowly focused piety. At the same time, practical guidebooks and manuals also became more abundant, making it easier to lay plans for getting ahead in this world – possibly diverting attention from uncertain futures in the next one. Sixteenth-century map-publishers thus began to exclude 'Paradise' from this world as being of too uncertain a location.[106] Eventually Cardinal Baronius would be cited by Galileo as distinguishing between 'how to go to heaven' – a problem for the Holy Spirit – and 'how the heavens go' – a matter of practical demonstration and mathematical reasoning.[107] It would be a mistake to press this last point too far, however. As noted above, many so-called 'practical guides' were impractical. Moreover, until Newton's *Principia*, the output of conflicting theories and astro-

---

[105] Gilmore, *World of Humanism*, p. 190.
[106] See comment by Ortelius cited, p. 227 below.
[107] Galileo, 'Letter to the Grand Duchess Christina,' p. 186.

nomical tables also offered very uncertain guidance on 'how the heavens go.' Manuals on devotional exercises and guidebooks on spiritual questions provided clear-cut advice. Readers who were helped by access to road maps, phrase books, conversion tables and other aids were also likely to place confidence in guides to the soul's journey after death. Tracts expounding the Book of Revelation entailed a heavy reliance on mathematical reasoning. The fixing of precise dates for the Creation or for the Second Coming occupied the very same talents that developed new astronomical tables and map projection techniques.[108]

It is doubtful, at all events, whether 'the effect of the new invention on scholarship' was more significant than its effect on vernacular Bible reading at the beginning of the sixteenth century.[109] What does need emphasis is that many dissimilar effects, all of great consequence, came relatively simultaneously. If this could be spelled out more clearly, seemingly contradictory developments might be confronted with more equanimity. The intensification of both religiosity and secularism could be better understood. Some debates about periodization also could be by-passed. Printing made more visible long-lived and much used texts which are usually passed over and sometimes (mistakenly) deemed obsolete when new trends are being traced. Many medieval world-pictures were duplicated more rapidly during the first century of printing than they had been during the so-called middle ages. They did not merely survive among conservative Elizabethans 'who were loth to upset the old order.'[110] They became more available to poets and playwrights of the sixteenth century than they had been to minstrels and mummers of the thirteenth century.

In view of such considerations, I cannot agree with Sarton's comment: 'It is hardly necessary to indicate what the art of printing meant for the diffusion of culture but one should not lay too much stress on diffusion and should speak more of standardization.'[111] How printing changed patterns of cultural diffusion deserves much more study than

---

108 The efforts of such distinguished virtuosi as Napier and Newton to determine the number of the Beast are well known. An excellent example of how rational theory and mathematical techniques were applied to the calculation of the year of the Second Coming is offered by John Craig's *Mathematical Principles of Christian Theology* (London, 1699), tr. from Latin in *History and Theory, Beiheft 4* (1963). The date, calculated by Craig, hinges on the growth of disbelief in the gospels which is described as the 'velocity of suspicion' and is held to increase in an arithmetic progression until it becomes sufficiently probable to make the Second Coming inevitable.

109 Gilmore, *World of Humanism*, p. 189 suggests that its effect on scholarship was most important.

110 Tillyard, *The Elizabethan World Picture*, p. 8.   111 Sarton, 'Quest for Truth,' p. 66.

it has yet received. Moreover, individual access to diverse texts is a different matter than bringing many minds to bear on a single text. The former issue is apt to be neglected by too exclusive an emphasis on 'standardization.'

2. CONSIDERING SOME EFFECTS PRODUCED BY STANDARDIZATION

Although it has to be considered in conjunction with many other issues, standardization certainly does deserve closer study. One specialist has argued that it is currently overplayed.[112] Yet it may well be still under-stressed. One must be careful not to skew historical perspectives by ignoring the difference between early printing methods and those of more recent times. But it is equally important not to go too far in the other direction and overestimate the capacity of scribal procedures to achieve the same results as did the early presses. Doubtless medieval university faculties 'attempted to achieve what the presses succeeded later in doing';[113] but the production of identical copies remained an unobtainable goal even when academic regulations pertaining to the 'pecia' were actually enforced. Indeed the division of exemplars into separate segments probably hastened corruption while speeding up the multiplication of copies of much desired academic texts. Moreover not one master copy but many exemplars (no two of which were quite the same) were distributed to the many stationers who served a given university.[114]

Although early printing methods made it impossible to issue the kind of 'standard' editions with which modern scholars are familiar, they represented a great leap forward nevertheless. Certainly press variants did multiply and countless errata were issued. The fact remains that Erasmus or Bellarmine could issue errata; Jerome or Alcuin could not. The very act of publishing errata demonstrated a new capacity to locate textual errors with precision and to transmit this information simultaneously to scattered readers. It thus illustrates, rather neatly,

---

112 On what follows, see remarks by Black, 'The Printed Bible,' pp. 408–14 and same author's review of Steinberg's *Five Hundred Years*.

113 Hirsch, *Printing, Selling* (1974 edition), pp. xl; 13.

114 See chap. 1, n. 29 above for pertinent references to misinterpretations of Destrez' thesis. Saenger, 'Colard Mansion,' p. 413 writes of manuscripts being 'highly standardized' in a fifteenth-century Burgundian court where only a single master copy, the *minute*, was used. How mss. could be copied *accurately*, in *quantity* and *with speed* by using only one exemplar is puzzling to me.

some of the effects of standardization. However late medieval copyists were supervised – and controls were much more lax than many accounts suggest – scribes were incapable of committing the sort of 'standardized' error that led printers to be fined for the 'wicked Bible' of 1631.[115] If a single compositor's error could be circulated in a great many copies, so too could a single scholar's emendation.

The mere fact that a single emendation by a great scholar could now be circulated in thousands of copies without the danger of a copyist's error signified a complete revolution in the conditions of activity of the learned world.[116]

Those who may overstate the case by overlooking compositors' errors in early editions still seem to me to be less wide of the mark than those who understate it and who underestimate the diversity that made every manuscript error unique. The need to qualify the thesis of standardization is less urgent than the need to pursue its ramifications. Sarton's remark: 'Printing made it possible for the first time to publish hundreds of copies that were alike and yet might be scattered everywhere'[117] is too important to get lost in quibbling over the fact that early printed copies were not all precisely alike. They were sufficiently uniform for scholars in different regions to correspond with each other about the same citation and for the same emendations and errors to be spotted by many eyes.[118]

In suggesting that the implications of standardization may be underestimated, however, I am not thinking only about textual emendations and errors, but also about calendars, dictionaries, ephemerides and other reference guides; about maps, charts, diagrams and other visual aids. The capacity to produce uniform spatio-temporal images is often assigned to the invention of writing without adequate allowance being made for the difficulty of multiplying identical images by hand.[119] The

---

[115] On the 'wicked' Bible of 1631 which omitted 'not' from the seventh commandment, see Black, 'The Printed Bible,' p. 412. Other editions of English Bibles celebrated for containing standardized errors, such as the 'Judas Bible' of 1611; the 'Printers' Bible' of 1702 and the 'Vinegar Bible' of 1717 are noted by Steinberg, *Five Hundred Years*, p. 204.

[116] Gilmore, *World of Humanism*, p. 189. The significance of standardization for erudition was brought out clearly by Allen, *Erasmus: Lectures and Wayfaring Sketches*, pp. 4–5.

[117] Sarton, 'Quest for Truth,' p. 66.

[118] This point is especially pertinent to classical scholarship. According to Kenney, *The Classical Text*, p. 19, n. 1, classical texts were relatively unaffected by the unfortunate practice of mixing sheets from different states. 'The multiplication of textually uniform copies became the norm.'

[119] See discussion of the 'disassociated transcript' by Boulding, *The Image*, pp. 64–8, and my criticism of Boulding's treatment pp. 478ff, volume II, below.

same point applies to systems of notation whether musical or mathematical. How different fields of study and aesthetic styles were affected by exact repeatability remains to be explored. It does seem worth suggesting that both our so-called two cultures were affected. This feature of print technology impinged on the disciplines of the *quadrivium* as well as on those of the *trivium*, on poetry and painting along with mathematics and medicine.

Too many important variations were, indeed, played on the theme of standardization for all of them to be listed here. This theme entered into every operation associated with typography, from the replica casting of precisely measured pieces of type to the making of woodcuts that were exactly the right dimension for meeting the surface of the types.[120] It also involved the 'subliminal' impact upon scattered readers of repeated encounters with identical type-styles, printers' devices, and title page ornamentation.[121] Calligraphy itself was affected. Sixteenth-century specimen books stripped diverse scribal 'hands' of personal idiosyncrasies.[122] They did for hand-writing what style books did for typography itself; what pattern books did for dressmaking, furniture, architectural motifs or ground plans. Writing manuals, like pattern sheets and model books, were not unknown in the age of scribes.[123] But like the manuscript grammar books and primers used by different

---

[120] Steinberg, *Five Hundred Years*, p. 25; Goldschmidt, *The Printed Book of the Renaissance*, p. 38.

[121] The probable effect of title page ornamentation on sixteenth-century fine arts and the necessity of taking printing into account when dealing with new aesthetic styles is noted by Chastel, 'What is Mannerism?' p. 53. See also Adhémar, 'L'Estampe.'

[122] An illustration of a fifteenth-century type specimen sheet, issued from Augsburg by Erhard Ratdolt dated April 1, 1486, is given by Steinberg, *Five Hundred Years* (facing p. 54). The same author discusses Ludovico degli Arrighi's pioneering writing manual of 1522 (pp. 57 ff). See also Hofer, 'Variant Issues,' p. 95. According to Hofer, Sigismondo Fanti's *Theoria et Practica* (Venice, 1514) was the first printed treatise on writing for professional scribes. An earlier printed treatise on letter forms by Damianus Moyllus printed in Parma between 1477 and 1483 is noted by Goudy, *The Capitals from the Trajan Column at Rome*, pp. 11–12. Arrighi's *Operina*, at all events, is a good example of how an early printed edition although not free of variants still contributed to a new kind of standardization.

[123] On a medieval writing master's specimen sheet, see von Dijk, 'An Advertisement Sheet.' The 'everpresent need of the medieval craftsman for patterns,' the methods employed to transfer patterned outlines by first pricking a piece of parchment and then 'pouncing' with charcoal dust, and some albums of useful sketches and models compiled by diverse masters are well described by Dorothy Miner's Library of Congress pamphlet on *The Giant Bible of Mainz*. The use of a 'pattern book' by a thirteenth-century painter is shown and described by Egbert, *The Medieval Artist at Work*, pp. 38–9, plate IX. For a close-up study of a unique sketch book by an early 15th century Lombard master see Pächt, 'Early Italian Nature Studies,' 13–47. The problem of distinguishing between the so-called medieval 'sketch book' and 'pattern book' is noted by D. J. A. Ross 'A Late Twelfth Century Artist's Pattern Sheet.' For conjectures about the remarkable *Göttingen Model Book*, see n. 73, above on Harry Bober's review.

teachers in different regions in fifteenth-century England, they were variegated rather than uniform.[124]

It seems likely that the very concept of a 'style' underwent transformation when the work of hand and 'stylus' was replaced by more standardized impressions made by pieces of type. Distinctions between bookhand and typeface are such that by placing a given manuscript against a printed text one may see much more clearly the idiosyncratic features of the individual hand of the scribe.[125] When set against a printed replica, a given sketch or drawing offers an even more dramatic contrast. It appears much fresher and more 'original' than when it is set against a hand-drawn copy. Thus distinctions between the fresh and original as against the repeatable and copied were likely to have become sharper after the advent of printing. The process of standardization also brought out more clearly all deviations from classical canons reflected in diverse buildings, statues, paintings and *objets d'art*. 'Gothic' initially meant not yet classic; 'barocco,' deviation from the classic norm. Ultimately the entire course of Western art history would be traced in terms of fixed classical canons and various deviations therefrom: 'That procession of styles and periods known to every beginner – Classic, Romanesque, Gothic, Renaissance, Mannerist, Baroque, Rococo, Neo-Classical, Romantic – represent only a series of masks for two categories, the classical and the non-classical.'[126]

With the disappearance of variegated bookhands, styles of lettering became more sharply polarized into two distinct groups of typefonts: 'Gothic' and 'Roman.'[127] A similar polarization affected architectural designs. A heightened consciousness of the three orders set down by Vitruvius accompanied the output of architectural prints and engravings along with new treatises and old texts.[128] Heightened awareness of distant regional boundaries was also encouraged by the output of more uniform maps containing more uniform boundaries and place names.[129] Similar developments affected local customs, laws, languages,

[124] On the standardization of English primers and grammars, see p. 350 below.
[125] Bühler, *Fifteenth Century Book*, p. 37.
[126] Gombrich, *Norm and Form: Studies in the Art of the Renaissance*, pp. 83; 84.
[127] See below, pp. 201ff.
[128] Burns, 'Quattrocento Architecture,' chap. 27, pp. 285–7 describes how preoccupation with the ancient orders became dominant after the printing of the first edition of Alberti's *De Re Aedificatoria* in 1485.
[129] Hay, 'Geographical Abstractions' contains useful speculation about the influence of cartography on regional consciousness.

and costumes. A given book of dress patterns published in Seville in the 1520s made 'Spanish' fashions visible throughout the far-flung Habsburg Empire. New guidance was provided to tailors and dressmakers and, at the same time, the diversity of local attire became all the more striking to the inhabitants of Brussels or of Lima.

A fuller recognition of diversity was indeed a concomitant of standardization. Sixteenth-century publications not only spread identical fashions but also encouraged the collection of diverse ones. Books illustrating diverse costumes, worn throughout the world, were studied by artists and engravers and duplicated in so many contexts that stereotypes of regional dress styles were developed. They acquired a paper life for all eternity and may be recognized even now on dolls, in operas, or at costume balls.

Concepts pertaining to uniformity and to diversity – to the typical and to the unique – are interdependent, they represent two sides of the same coin. In this regard one might consider the emergence of a new sense of individualism as a by-product of the new forms of standardization. The more standardized the type, indeed, the more compelling the sense of an idiosyncratic personal self. No period was without some sense of the typical and of the individual but concepts pertaining to both were, nevertheless, transformed by the output of standard editions. Even while an author such as Montaigne was developing a new informal and idiosyncratic genre of literature and laying bare all the quirks and peculiarities that define the individual 'me, myself' as against the type, other genres of literature were defining ideal types – setting forth the requirements of service to king or country and delineating the role played by priest, merchant, and peasant; by nobleman and lady, husbandman and wife, well-bred boy and girl.[130]

Here again the 'exactly repeatable pictorial statement' helped to reinforce the effects of issuing standard editions. Repeated encounters with identical images of couples, representing three social groups: noble, burgher, peasant, wearing distinctive costumes and set against distinctive regional landscapes probably encouraged a sharpened sense of class-divisions and regional groupings.[131] At the same time the cir-

---

[130] For further discussion of this point, see pp. 230–1 below.
[131] Sixteenth-century costume manuals and engravings displaying diverse groups of citizens against views and plans of different towns are described and illustrated by Yates, *The Valois Tapestries*, pp. 12–15.

culation of royal portraits and engravings of royal entries made it possible for a reigning dynast to impress a personal presence in a new way upon the consciousness of all subjects. The difference between the older repeatable image which was stamped on coins and the newer by-product of print is suggested by one of the more celebrated episodes of the French Revolution. The individual features of emperors and kings were not sufficiently detailed when stamped on coins for their faces to be recognized when they travelled incognito. But a portrait engraved on paper money enabled an alert Frenchman to recognize and halt Louis XVI at Varennes.

It should be noted that a new alertness to both the individual and the typical was likely to come first to circles frequented by those printers and engravers who were responsible for turning out the new costume manuals, style books, commemorations of royal entries, and regional guides. Just as the act of publishing errata sharpened alertness to error within the printer's workshop, so too did the preparation of copy pertaining to architectural motifs, regional boundaries, place names, details of dress and local customs. It seems likely that a new alertness to place and period and more concern about assigning the proper trappings to each was fostered by the very act of putting together illustrated guidebooks and costume manuals. To be sure, the use – in *The Nuremberg Chronicle*, for example – of the same engraving of silhouetted buildings to designate many different cities, or of the same portrait head to designate many different historic personages, may seem to argue against such a thesis. There are many examples of early printers frugally using a few prints to do service for many diverse purposes.[132] An Ulm edition of 1483 'has one cut which is used thirty-seven times and altogether nineteen blocks do duty for one hundred and thirty-four illustrations.'[133] Nevertheless during the same decade of the 1480s, two Mainz publications contained illustrations made by a travelling artist-engraver sent out to the Holy Land with the specific purpose of producing fresh renderings of cities and plants encountered on the pilgrimage. Erhard Reuwich's illustrations of cities for Breydenbach's *Peregrinatio in Terram Sanctam* (1486) and of plants for Schoeffer's

---

[132] See amusing discussion by Ivins, *Prints and Visual Communication*, p. 38. The re-use of the same blocks for various scenes in the same book and by diverse printers for diverse books is discussed by Hirsch, *Printing, Selling*, p. 49. Specific examples affecting Bible illustration are given by Hindman, 'Transition from Manuscripts,' p. 199.

[133] Bland, *A History of Book Illustration*, p. 106.

vernacular herbal *Gart der Gesundheit* (1485) did point the way to an increasingly precise and detailed recording of observations in visual form.[134] The careless re-use of a few blocks for many purposes also needs to be distinguished from the deliberate re-use of a 'typical' town or portrait head, to serve as pointers or guide marks helping readers find their way about a text.[135] Whatever the purpose served by the cuts of towns and heads in a work such as *The Nuremberg Chronicle*, previous remarks about individuation and standardization also seem cogent. The more standardized the image of typical town, head or plant, the more clearly the idiosyncratic features of separate towns, heads, or plants could be perceived by observant draughtsmen. Painters and carvers had been rendering natural forms on manuscript margins, church vestments or stone fonts during previous centuries. But their talents were used for new ends by technical publication programs initiated by master printers and learned editors from the days of Peter Schoeffer on.

Here as elsewhere, we need to recall that early printers were responsible not only for publishing innovative reference guides but also for

[134] On Breydenbach volume and the vernacular versions that appeared soon after the first Latin edition of 1486, see H. W. Davies, *Bernhard von Breydenbach*. The likelihood that Erhard Rewich (or Reuwich) of Utrecht was not only responsible for the illustrations to Breydenbach's *Peregrinatio* but was also the 'wise and skillful painter' who accompanied the chief author of the *Gart der Gesundheit* (a Frankfurt physician named von Cube) and receives thanks in the preface to this Peter Schoeffer publication of 1485 is noted by Hind, *An Introduction to a History of Woodcut*, 1, 350; 354. In *Prints and Visual Communication*, p. 36, Ivins oddly regrets not knowing the names of any one who contributed to *Gart der Gesundheit* while referring two paragraphs later to Reuwich accompanying Breydenbach and producing the celebrated fold-out views of towns such as Venice, Rhodes, and Jerusalem. An earlier collection of Ivins' essays: *Prints and Books: Informal Papers* contains a paper on 'Breydenbach's Itinerary,' pp. 10–21 which describes Reuwich's role not only as illustrator but also as 'printer' of both the Latin and German versions of the Breydenbach volume. There Ivins notes Reuwich's own reference in the German edition (Mainz, 1486) to his carrying out 'the printing in his own house' and that the type used came from Peter Schoeffer's firm. On the significance of the illustrations in *Gart der Gesundheit* (Peter Schoeffer's Mainz publication of 1485) see below, pp. 262ff. The fact that the plants were drawn on a trip to the Holy Land made at the same time that Breydenbach's pilgrimage occurred, as well as stylistic similarities, leads Hind to concur with L. Baer's 1925 opinion that Reuwich illustrated both books. His closeness to Peter Schoeffer also makes it a reasonable assumption that he had a hand in the vernacular herbal. This assumption is taken for granted by Herrlinger, *History of Medical Illustration*, p. 47 who suggests that the illustrator of *Gart der Gesundheit* may also be the 'master of the Housebook' – a celebrated early copper-plate engraver.

[135] Bland, *History of Book Illustration*, p. 107 credits Paul Kristeller (the author of *Early Florentine Woodcuts*) with the suggestion that the *Nuremberg Chronicle* cuts were intended to act as signposts for the benefit of readers rather than as detailed visual aids. An interesting case where successive editions of a sixteenth-century encyclopedia show stereotyped cuts being replaced by actual town profiles and genuine likenesses is described by Gerald Strauss, 'A Sixteenth-Century Encyclopedia,' pp. 154–5.

compiling some of them.[136] To those of us who think in terms of later divisions of labor, the repertoire of roles undertaken by early printers seems so large as to be almost inconceivable. A scholar–printer himself might serve not only as publisher and bookseller but also as indexer-abridger-lexicographer-chronicler. Whatever roles he performed, decisions about standards to be adopted when processing texts for publication could not be avoided. Suitable type styles had to be selected or designed and house conventions – relating to orthography, punctuation, abbreviation and the like – had to be determined.[137] Textual variants and the desirability of illustration or translations also had to be confronted. Insofar as such decisions entailed consultation with the professors and physicians, print dealers, painters, translators, librarians and other learned men, it is not surprising that printers' workshops served as cultural centers in several towns or that the most advanced work in scholarship and science during the sixteenth century seemed to gravitate away from older lecture halls and academic precincts. Moreover, printers were in the unusual position of being able to profit from passing on to others systems they devised for themselves. They not only practiced self-help but preached it as well. In the later middle ages, practical manuals had been written to guide inquisitors, confessors, priests and pilgrims – and lay merchants as well. Although large *summae* now attract scholarly attention, medieval scribes also turned out compact *summulae*, comprehensive guidebooks designed to offer practical advice on diverse matters – ranging from composing a sermon to dying in one's bed.[138] Here, as in many other ways, the printer seems

---

[136] This applies particularly to the publisher-printer (or printer-bookseller) as described e.g. by Armstrong, *Robert Estienne*, pp. 18, 68. It is also applicable to many independent master-printers, to some merchant-publishers (who, literally defined, were not printers at all and yet closely supervised the processing of texts – even editing and compiling some themselves), and finally to some skilled journeymen (who served as correctors or were charged with throwing together from antiquated stock, cheap reprints for mass markets). The divergent social and economic positions occupied by these groups are discussed by Natalie Z. Davis, 'Strikes and Salvation in Lyons,' p. 48: and 'Publisher Guillaume Rouillé,' pp. 73–6. Within workshops down through the eighteenth century, divisions of labor varied so widely and were blurred so frequently, they must be left out of account for the purpose of developing my conjectures. Accordingly, I use the term 'printer' very loosely to cover all these groups I have also blurred gender when describing 'his' print shop and never mentioning 'hers.' As noted by Lenkey, 'Printers' wives,' p. 331, although widows and daughters of printers did take over the family enterprise, it was more common for male relatives to do so. On a noteworthy sixteenth-century woman printer, see references to Charlotte Guillard's Paris firm in Parent, *Les Métiers*, p. 138

[137] On English compositors' sense of obligation to amend orthography and grammar, see Hereward T. Price, 'Grammar and the Compositor,' 540–8.

[138] Peters, 'Editing Inquisitors' Manuals,' 95–107.

to have taken over where the clerical scribe left off. But in so doing, he greatly amplified and augmented older themes. There is simply no equivalent in scribal culture for the 'avalanche' of 'how-to' books which poured off the new presses, explaining by 'easy steps' just how to master diverse skills, ranging from playing a musical instrument to keeping accounts.

Many early capitalist industries required efficient planning, methodical attention to detail, and rational calculation. The decisions made by early printers, however, directly affected both tool-making and symbol-making. Their products reshaped powers to manipulate objects, to perceive and think about varied phenomena. Scholars concerned with 'modernization' or 'rationalization' might profitably think more about the new kind of brainwork fostered by the silent scanning of maps, tables, charts, diagrams, dictionaries, and grammars. They also need to look more closely at the routines pursued by those who compiled and produced such reference guides. These routines were conducive to a new *esprit de système*. In his preface to his pioneering atlas which contained supplementary texts and indexes, Abraham Ortelius likened his *Theatrum* to a 'well furnished shoppe' which was so arranged that readers could easily find whatever instruments they might want to obtain.[139] 'It's much easier to find things when they are each disposed in place and not scattered haphazardly' remarked another sixteenth-century publisher.[140] He was justifying the way he had reorganized a text he had edited. He might equally well have been complaining to a clerk who had mislaid some account papers pertaining to the large commercial enterprise he ran.

3. SOME EFFECTS PRODUCED BY REORGANIZING TEXTS AND REFERENCE GUIDES: RATIONALIZING, CODIFYING, AND CATALOGUING DATA

Editorial decisions made by early printers with regard to layout and presentation probably helped to reorganize the thinking of readers. McLuhan's suggestion that scanning lines of print affected thought-processes is at first glance somewhat mystifying. But further reflection suggests that the thoughts of readers are guided by the way the contents

---

[139] Ortelius, 'Message to the Reader,' *Theater of the Whole World.*
[140] Cited by Natalie Z. Davis, 'Guillaume Rouillé,' p. 100.

of books are arranged and presented. Basic changes in book format might well lead to changes in thought-patterns. To handle printed reference works, for example, readers had to master certain skills that are now considered rudimentary but were previously esoteric, even among learned men. A 1604 edition of an English dictionary notes at the outset that 'the reader must learne the alphabet, to wit: the order of the letters as they stand.'[141] One wonders why defining the meaning of the term alphabet was thought to be needed in England at so late a date. Numerous editions of ABC books, which had made profits for privileged printers such as John Day, might be expected to have made the definition unnecessary. At all events, printed reference works did encourage a repeated recourse to alphabetical order. Ever since the sixteenth century, memorizing a fixed sequence of discrete letters represented by meaningless symbols and sounds has been the gateway to book learning for all children in the West. This was so little the case before printing, that a Genoese compiler of a thirteenth-century encyclopedia could write that

'Amo' comes before 'bibo' because 'a' is the first letter of the former and 'b' is the first letter of the latter and 'a' comes before 'b'...by the grace of God working in me, I have devised this order.[142]

This is not to say that systems based on full use of alphabetical order were unknown before the thirteenth century, but only that they were sufficiently esoteric to be unfamiliar to the compiler of the *Catholicon*.[143] Other ways of ordering data were no less likely to be used in reference works. As for library catalogues, the full use of alphabet systems by the fabled custodians of the Alexandrian Library had vanished with the

---

[141] Cited (from Robert Cowdrey's 'table alphabetical') by Daly, *Contributions to a History of Alphabetization*, p. 91.

[142] Cited in Daly, *Contributions*, p. 73 from remarks by 'Giovanni di Genoa' (or Friar Johannes Balbus of Genoa) in his *Catholicon* of 1286. This popular thirteenth-century encyclopedia is celebrated for being printed by Gutenberg in Mainz, 1460, with a colophon describing how the 'noble book' was printed 'without help of reed, stylus, or pen but by the wondrous agreement, proportion and harmony of punches and types...in the noble city of Mainz of the renowned German nation' which 'by God's grace' has been endowed 'above all other nations of the earth with so lofty a genius.' Steinberg, *Five Hundred Years*, p. 19. Should this claim for Gutenberg's invention be taken in the same spirit as the friar's claim to have 'devised' alphabetic order? See Butler's perceptive comments on how claims set forth concerning 'invention' of typography entail a different concept of 'invention' than ours. *Origin of Printing*, p. 97. For further discussion of problematic nature of 'invention,' see n. 251 and n. 252 below.

[143] For data on medieval alphabets, see Wolpe, 'Florilegium Alphabeticum.'

institution itself.[144] 'When it comes to cataloguing, a poem is a far cry from a card index,' note Reynolds and Wilson, in connection with some verses attributed to Alcuin describing the eighth-century library at York.[145] The rhymed book list was incomplete because metrical exigencies required the exclusion of various works. Medieval library catalogues, to be sure, were not usually in verse but they were, nevertheless, far from being ordered along the lines of modern card indexes – or, for that matter, along any kind of uniform lines. They reflected the multiform character of scribal culture and were, for the most part, idiosyncratically arranged, designed to help a given custodian find his way to the books which reposed in cupboards or chests or were chained on desks in a special chamber.[146]

The increasing use of full alphabetical order, both for book catalogues and also for indexes, has been attributed to the introduction of paper, which made it less costly to prepare the necessary card-files.[147] Doubtless cheaper writing-materials made indexing and cataloguing less costly, but they did little to overcome a natural resistance to repeatedly copying out long lists by hand. Occasional efforts were made to make one index valid for several copies but they were invariably thwarted by scribal errors of diverse kinds. For the most part the owner of a medieval compendium, preparing an index for his own use, felt no obligation to employ anybody else's system but rather followed whatever method he chose.[148] Similarly a custodian keeping track of a library collection had no incentive to arrange his records in accordance with those of other librarians – and no incentive, either, to make the arrangement of volumes follow any clear order at all. (On the basis of encounters with some living guardians of rare books, one suspects

---

[144] In addition to Daly *Contributions*, see also Francis Witty, 'Early Indexing Techniques,' 141–8. A review of Daly's book by Sherman Kuhn discusses the repeated loss and recovery of partial alphabetization. Kuhn's article 'The Preface to a Fifteenth Century Concordance,' also has useful data on arrangements of glossaries and vocabularies going back to the eighth century.

[145] Reynolds and Wilson, *Scribes and Scholars*, p. 76.

[146] Even the catalogues of libraries maintained in university towns by members of the mendicant orders retained the character of inventories or shelf lists. Humphreys, *The Book Provisions*, p. 83.

[147] This seems to be Daly's conclusion in *Contributions* and that of Sherman Kuhn's *Speculum* book review. Although Kuhn notes that full alphabetization is established only after printing, this review suggests 'that it came not so much as a direct result' of printing as of the 'greater availability and cheapness of paper.'

[148] On the frustration of efforts to make the index of one manuscript valid for other copies see Smalley, *English Friars*, pp. 33–5. The idiosyncratic and highly particularized character of indexing by owners of compendia is noted by Hay, introduction, *Printing and Mind of Man*, pp. xviii–xix.

that the more unfathomable the arrangement of a given inventory the better some medieval custodians were pleased.) After the advent of printing, however, shelf lists were supplemented by sales catalogues aimed at readers outside library walls, while any index compiled for one text could be duplicated hundreds of times. Thus the competitive commercial character of the printed book-trade when coupled with typographical standardization made more systematic cataloguing and indexing seem not only feasible but highly desirable as well. To tap markets and attract potential purchasers while keeping competitors at bay called for booksellers' lists that presented titles in a clear and coherent arrangement, and for editions that could be described as well indexed, as well as 'new and improved.'

Peter Schoeffer's prospectus which claimed that his firm offered 'more complete and better arranged' indexes as well as 'more readable' texts than those of his competitors[149] should not be taken at face value. The early printer, like the modern press agent, often promised more than he could deliver. Nevertheless the pressure of competition did spur efforts to look for ways of improving familiar products and worked against the inherent resistance to change which had hitherto characterized the copying of valued texts. A rationalization of format helped to systematize scholarship in diverse fields. Robert Estienne's five Paris book catalogues issued between 1542 and 1547 reflect a rapid advance along many fronts. Divided along trilingual lines, with each section arranged in a uniform progression, beginning with alphabets in Hebrew, Greek and Latin, going on to grammars, dictionaries and texts; these catalogues have justly been described as 'a miracle of lucid arrangement.'[150] The same skills were used by Estienne for his pioneering work in lexicography[151] and his succession of biblical editions. Much as Estienne's successive improved editions of the Bible produced in sixteenth-century Paris might be compared to the one so-called 'edition' turned out by scribes in thirteenth-century Paris; so, too, his many contributions to lexicography might be compared with that single unique bilingual lexicon produced

149 See citation above, p. 57.
150 Pollard and Ehrman, *Distribution of Books*, p. 53.
151 DeWitt T. Starnes, *Robert Estienne's Influence on Lexicography*, pp. 86–7. Starnes also notes how Estienne expanded on earlier thesauruses dealing with Greco-Roman literature by including the vast array of biblical references he had compiled in the course of producing his Bible editions and how his reference works furnished English poets (down to Milton and beyond) with classical and biblical allusions.

by thirteenth-century schoolmen under the direction of Robert Grosseteste.[152]

Such comparisons are useful, not only because they show what the new power of the press could achieve, but also because they suggest that attempts at lexicography had been made before print. Efforts at codifying and systematizing which pre-dated the new presses had long been made by preachers and teachers who had compiled concordances for the use of other churchmen or arranged scriptural passages, sermon topics, and commentaries for themselves. A poem is not only 'a far cry from a card index'; it is also fairly distant from many scholastic treatises on medical and legal as well as theological subjects. Such treatises were surrounded by glosses, and bristled with abbreviations and marginal notations. Some contained diagrams which showed the branches of learning, schematized abstract concepts or connected human organs with heavenly bodies.[153] Others were furnished with small tabs made of parchment or paper to permit easy reference. One must be wary, in other words, of overstating the novelties introduced by printing or of overlooking how previous developments helped to channel the uses to which the new tool was put.[154] Such devices as diagrams and brackets, along with the habit of cross-referencing be-

---

[152] Daly, *Contributions*, p. 70 notes that this Greek–Latin lexicon – a rare example of such a bilingual reference work – was also unusual because it came close to achieving a complete alphabetical order. Grosseteste's own considerable skills as an indexer are indicated by Hunt, 'The Library of Robert Grosseteste.' On Estienne's Bible printing, see p. 328 below.

[153] Medical and astrological diagrams are abundantly illustrated in Herrlinger, *History of Medical Illustration, passim.* Saxl, 'A Spiritual Encyclopedia,' pp. 82–136 presents a number of diagrams showing relationships between abstract concepts. The large number in this fifteenth-century manuscript strikes Saxl as unusual and possibly due to contemporary agitation over theological issues during the Hussite Wars (p. 83). See also Yates' *Art of Memory* (plate 11), where a fourteenth-century miniature depicting the art of Ramon Lull suggests the kind of diagramming that was associated with memory arts and may be found in many manuscripts. Other illustrations in Yates' book, which come from early printed versions, are also of interest. See e.g. visual alphabet given in figure 7c.

[154] In several suggestive studies, Walter Ong has brought out the 'diagrammatic tidiness' imparted by print to the world of ideas in a way that might lead hasty readers to discount the extent to which diagramming and graphing preceded print. See e.g. *Ramus*; 'System Space and Intellect'; 'From Allegory to Diagram in the Renaissance Mind.' Actually Ong does credit medieval scholasticism with many of the habits of mind that became more pronounced after printing and in one article: 'Tudor Writings on Rhetoric, Poetic and Literary Theory' (1968) *Rhetoric, Romance*, p. 85 notes that the 'resort to diagrams and other visual models' was a 'procedure encouraged *both by scholastic logic and by typography.*' [Italics mine.] Nevertheless, the actual use of such devices as brackets, diagrams and cross-references in medieval compendia and concordances does not receive much notice in Ong's studies. For a fully documented account of medieval anticipations of modern scholarly apparatus see Parkes, 'The Influence of the Concepts of Ordinatio and Compilatio on the Development of the Book.'

tween one passage and another, were not uncommon among medieval compilers and commentators, even though such practices took idiosyncratic and variegated forms. Just as the uniform use of alphabetic order for all reference words did not result from the invention of printing alone but required an alphabetic written language as a base, so too much of the cataloguing, cross-referencing and indexing that marked sixteenth-century scholarship should not be regarded only as by-products of typographic culture but also as reflecting new opportunities among clergymen and clerks to realize old goals.

At his most characteristic, medieval man...was an organizer, a codifier, a builder of systems. He wanted a place for everything and everything in the right place. Distinction, definition, tabulation were his delight...There was nothing medieval people did better or liked better than sorting out and tidying up. Of all our modern inventions, I suspect that they would most have admired the card index.[155]

As this citation suggests, one need not think only of 'well furnished shops' when considering the urge to rationalize Western institutions. A desire to have 'everything in its right place' was shared by the medieval schoolman and the early capitalist alike. The print shop performed a significant, albeit neglected function – by bringing together intellectual and commercial activities which reinforced each other and thus created an especially powerful – almost 'overdetermined' – drive.

On the other hand, one must be on guard against the temptation to make too much of occasional medieval anticipations of trends that could not be really launched until after printing. The schoolmen might have admired our card index but their sense of order was not based upon its use. A unique bilingual lexicon cannot do the same work as hundreds of thousands of trilingual reference guides. There is simply no counterpart in medieval houses of studies or monastic libraries for the printed polyglot Bibles of the sixteenth and seventeenth centuries or for the reference apparatus which accompanied them. The same point applies to the clarity of organization and readers' aids contained in the Geneva Bible. As for attempts at cross-referencing and indexing, one may marvel at the 'vast amount of labor and ingenuity' that scribal compilers expended on such thankless tasks; even while recognizing that the results were bound to appear inadequate by later

---

[155] C. S. Lewis, *The Discarded Image*, p. 10.

standards, given the inevitable errors made by copyists and foliation sequences which were 'usually incomplete' and 'nearly always wrong.'[156]

In describing the scholarly abbot he has singled out as the true 'father of bibliography,' Theodore Besterman comments on Johannes Trithemius' 'inexplicable ardor for system.'[157] As the abbot of Sponheim who compiled the *Liber de Scriptoribus Ecclesiasticis* – a three-thousand-page list of titles and authors, first printed by Johann Amerbach in Basel, 1494 – Johannes Trithemius probably deserves the title Besterman assigns him.[158] His path-breaking printed bio-bibliography contained an innovative alphabetical index and went well beyond medieval catalogues of Christian authors. 'Almost one thousand authors are listed, with information on their life and work, from the Church Fathers to living writers, including Trithemius himself.' An excerpt from the main work, the *Catalogus illustrium virorum Germaniae* (Mainz, 1495), introduced the concept of a 'Carolingian Renaissance' to European history, and also enabled literati such as Johann Reuchlin and Sebastian Brant to pay tribute to each other's work. In the guise of a bibliographer ostensibly devoted to sacred studies, the abbot thus served as a kind of press agent for a German humanist coterie.[159] His publications reflect the ambiance of print shops in Mainz and in Basel – at least as much as they do that of the Sponheim monastery.

Sponheim was situated in a remote corner of Germany away from all political, economic and cultural centers, yet it was the focus of a lively intellectual exchange. A never-ending stream of visitors kept open the lines

---

156 In addition to comments on indexing by Smalley noted above, see also remarks on foliation by Ivy, 'The Bibliography of the Manuscript-Book,' p. 57.

157 Besterman, *The Beginnings of Systematic Bibliography*, pp. 7–10.

158 The most recent monograph is Arnold's *Johannes Trithemius (1462–1516)*. Arnold has summarized this biography in his introduction to the English-Latin edition of Trithemius' *In Praise of Scribes* (see pp. 14–15 above). A very useful selective bibliography of studies of Trithemius is given by Kristeller, 'Contribution of Religious Orders,' appendix B, p. 156.

159 *De Scriptoribus Ecclesiasticis* contained an eulogistic article on Reuchlin written by Sebastian Brant (who was an editor for Amerbach at the time). The same eulogy appeared also in the excerpt from *de Scriptoribus* which was printed (at Wimpfeling's request) by Amerbach in 1495: the *Catalogus illustrium virorum Germaniae* (Mainz, 1495). Brant's tribute to Reuchlin, Reuchlin's tribute to Agrippa and Trithemius' praise of Brant are noted by Zeydel, 'Johann Reuchlin and Sebastian Brant,' 117–39. On the German circle around Trithemius and Amerbach see Arnold, introd. pp. 6–7; also Febvre, *Au Coeur Religieux*, p. 140. A glimpse of efforts made by a German Benedictine monk in the summer of 1514 to get fresh materials for a new edition of a work that had come to serve as a kind of literary *Who's Who*, the *Schriftstellerlexikon* also points to the new kind of literary celebrity achieved by ecclesiastical careerists who took advantage of print. See Schweibert, 'New Groups and Ideas,' 69.

of communication between the remote monastery and the world. They came for many reasons: to inspect the library, to use it for research, to study under the abbot. The flow of . . . visitors increased in the 1490s after his first major works had appeared in print and contributed to his growing reputation as a writer. Those who could not come – and they were the majority – kept in touch by letters. . . [160]

Trithemius' policies in Sponheim aroused the enmity of other Benedictines and he was forced out of the abbey in 1505. In his new post as abbot of a monastery outside Würzburg, he won the patronage of Emperor Maximilian I, wrote several chronicles, using his own fabricated genealogies and concocted Carolingian documents to enlarge upon the glories of the Benedictine order and of the Frankish–German Empire.[161] In this later period, he resorted less frequently to the presses and left many annals, chronicles and treatises for posthumous publication. Did the patronage of the Emperor seem to render resort to printers less necessary? Or did the unexpected opposition to his magical writings, expressed by the French scholar Bovillus (Charles Bouelles) make him more wary of publicity in general? His decision to 'condemn to perpetual silence all my marvelous discoveries' rather than 'incur' suspicion of 'pernicious magical or necromantic' activities is set forth in his own posthumously published *Polygraphia* (1518) and his advice to the young Agrippa to avoid the profanation by vulgar minds of sacred mysteries is contained in the letters Agrippa cites in his preface to his own *De Occulta Philosophia*.[162]

Nevertheless, in his later writings, the abbot did, repeatedly, pay tribute to the wonderful art of printing devised 'in the city of Mainz in Germany near the Rhine and not as certain men say falsely in Italy . . .' citing his own conversations with Peter Schoeffer concerning the role of Gutenberg as inventor and of Fust as financial backer.[163] One

160 Arnold, introd. p. 5.
161 Arnold, introd. p. 10. Arnold seems to be disconcerted by the falsification of historical documents and invention of fictitious chroniclers although the practice was in no way exceptional for a fifteenth-century monastic chronicle. In his acceptance of Trithemius' story about Dr Faust fearing to meet the abbot and his contrast of Trithemius 'the scholar' with Dr Faust 'the charlatan' (p. 11) Arnold also seems to adopt a somewhat simplistic view.
162 Brann, 'The Shift from Mystical to Magical Theology,' presented a detailed account of Trithemius' encounter with Bovillus and its consequences. I owe the citations given above to this paper. Brann also notes how a pun on Bovillus' name is included in the letter from Trithemius presented in Agrippa's preface to *De Occulta Philosophia*; the latter work, dedicated to Trithemius, was published in Cologne, 1520.
163 See citations in Butler, *Origin of Printing*, pp. 106, 107. (Is it possible that Trithemius' references to Gutenberg's financial backer combined with his anecdote about Dr Faustus, the necromancer, contributed to confusing the two figures?)

of his last contributions as a chronicler also served as a vehicle for Peter Schoeffer's son to pay a filial tribute to his father and grandfather (Johann Fust) as the first authors of the art of printing, and to render homage once again to the city of Mainz as the birthplace of the press.[164] His posthumous fame owed much to the way he carried his 'ardor for system' beyond cataloguing and chronicling – into such fields as cryptography and numerology and necromancy, as shown in his two treatises: the *Steganographia* and *Polygraphia*.[165] It was not only his mastery of library sciences, it was also his command of 'magia and cabala' which excited his later disciples and admirers, such as Agrippa and Dr John Dee.[166] 'Allready I have purchased one boke for wch a Thousand Crownes have ben by others offered and yet could not be obteyned,' wrote Dee, from the Antwerp house of his Dutch printer, Willem Sylvius, to Cecil on February 16, 1563. 'The Steganographia Joannis Tritemij mentioned in his Polygraphia & in his epistles & in sundry other mens bokes' was 'so meet, so hedefull and commodious' that 'with continuall Labor the most part of ten days' Dee had copied at least half of it.[167] The fame of the unpublished treatise, it seems, owed something to other books already in print and to Dee's contacts with knowledgeable Antwerp printers. At all events, it contained such 'fantastically complex calculations'[168] that authorities are likely to

---

164 John Schoeffer's tribute to his grandfather, Johann Fust and father, Peter Schoeffer in the colophon of Trithemius' *Compendium...de origine regum et gentis francorum* (Mainz: J. Schoeffer, 1515) is cited in Butler, *Origin of Printing*, p. 93. The interweaving of filial and patriotic civic themes in this colophon is typical. How civic pride found a new outlet in the colophons of early printers, and was in turn reinforced thereby, is worth more study – especially in connection with the German imperial cities where the Reformation took root.

165 These two works were posthumously printed. The first edition of the *Polygraphia* appeared in 1518; that of the *Steganographia* only in 1606. How the former work helped to publicize the latter is shown by John Dee's comments, as noted in my text, below.

166 D. P. Walker, *Spiritual and Demonic Magic*, pp. 85–8. Agrippa's inclusion of Trithemius' approving letter to him in *De Occulta Philosophia* (1533) is noted on p. 85.

167 Bailey, 'Dee and Trithemius' Steganography,' pp. 401–2. This transcription by Bailey is accompanied by further notes on pp. 422–3.

168 Peter French, *John Dee*, pp. 36–7. This helpful biography guided me to the indispensable letter transcribed by Bailey as noted above. Dee's explicit reference there to meeting with 'sundry Dutch printers' and requests to extend his trip to 'deale with Printers of high Germany' point to an aspect of his activities that has been somewhat neglected. It is clear that the publication of *Monas Hieroglyphica* by Sylvius in 1564 and its arrival in England before Dee's return helped him with his patrons. His visit to Commandino in Urbino on this same continental journey was also aimed at a publication. Sylvius' own skills as a calligrapher and fascination with lettering must have made him an especially valuable collaborator in preparing a work such as the *Monas Hieroglyphica* for publication. He may have met Dee while acting as a writing master and tutor to the sons of William of Orange at the University of Louvain, 1548–50. See Clair, 'Willem Silvius,' pp. 192–205 (esp. 195–6). Dee's other encounters during his 1564 stay on the continent which included a visit with Conrad Gesner in Zurich are noted by

remain at odds over whether the invocation of angels and demons was concealed beneath an apparent discourse on cryptography or whether there was more method than madness in a presentation of ciphers which commended itself to spy masters and secret couriers of all kinds.[169]

However obsessive or even irrational Trithemius' propensity for every kind of system-making may appear to disenchanted modern scholars, it can scarcely be described as 'inexplicable.' To the contrary, many forces combined to produce it. Numerous concordances – not to mention calendrical computations and astrological and alchemical treatises – show that a similar 'ardor for system' had long been present in medieval monasteries, colleges and houses of studies.[170] But there it was perpetually held in check by the conditions of scribal culture. In the workshops of the printers, who were visited by Trithemius, passions for systematizing could be given freer rein.

The abbot's successor as 'father of bibliography' – the remarkably energetic young Swiss scholar, Conrad Gesner – took full advantage of his predecessor's work and went well beyond it. In his effort to produce the first (it would also be the last) truly comprehensive 'universal' bibliography listing all Latin, Greek and Hebrew works published during the first century of printing, Gesner made full use of the publishers' catalogues and booksellers' lists which were being issued in his day. His first edition of the *Bibliotheca Universalis* (1545) listed some ten thousand titles and some three thousand authors (the number would triple by the time of his posthumous third edition three decades later). As a companion piece to this colossal work, in 1548, he issued another vast folio: the 'all-embracing' *Pandectae* which contained some thirty thousand topical entries, each cross-referenced to the appropriate author and book, arranged under headings and sub-headings which

Josten, 'A Translation of John Dee's "Monas Hieroglyphica,"' pp. 84ff. The *Monas Hieroglyphica* is coupled with Trithemius' *Steganographia* in a list of Rosicrucian works compiled by Gabriel Naudé in 1623. See Yates, *The Rosicrucian Enlightenment*, p. 107.

[169] At present the former theory commands the support of such formidable authorities as D. P. Walker and Yates. Nevertheless it seems possible that part of the excitement generated by the *Steganographia* may be attributed to the hope of learning more about number-letter codes. Although admittedly in the case of Dee the summoning of spirits was entailed, it does not follow that everyone in search of the *Steganographia* had magic-making aims in mind.

[170] It is intriguing to find two posthumously published medieval 'calculatores' of the Merton school coupled with Dee and Trithemius in Naudé's list of Rosicrucian authors. Yates, *Rosicrucian Enlightenment*, p. 108. Trithemius' efforts to synchronize chronologies and coordinate astrological with historical events is noted by Arnold, introd. p. 10.

were associated with diverse branches of learning.[171] The nineteen separate sections of the Pandects, each devoted to a separate scholarly discipline, contained dedications to the outstanding scholar–printers of Gesner's day listing their publications and their accomplishments.[172] Gesner thus acted as a press agent for some of the better known master printers of his generation, much as Trithemius had done for his German humanist friends. As was the case with Trithemius also, Gesner's passion for cataloguing and systematizing went well beyond the library sciences. But, unlike the abbot, his remarkable flair for classification (his 'compulsive quest for orientation' as Fischer puts it) was applied to beasts rather than spirits. Working for more than twenty years, beginning with his early botanical studies, he continued to collect an immense mass of information relating to the animal kingdom. Making excerpts from books consulted for his universal bibliography, enlisting the help of some fifty correspondents in different regions, soliciting drawings, copying woodcuts and always acknowledging his sources with care,[173] he finally produced the first edition of his celebrated four-volume text supplemented by three volumes of illustrations which won him posthumous fame as the 'father of zoology.' Fischer comments that Gesner's enormous labors were all the more remarkable because they were undertaken without being commissioned and represented the voluntary work of a lay scholar who had no special patron or institution to spur him on. It is true that, compared to Abbot Trithemius, or even to a lay humanist, such as Marsilio Ficino, who could count on Medici backing, Gesner lacked princely patrons or church-governed institutional support. Yet it is also significant that he did receive unflagging encouragement and help from flourishing printing firms.[174] He obtained a post as Greek pro-

---

171 Besterman, *Beginnings*, p. 21 suggests that Gesner's attempt to deal with the vast increase in knowledge and to reorganize learning anticipated Bacon and later encyclopedists.

172 Hans Fischer, 'Conrad Gesner (1516–1565),' pp. 269–81 shows the use Gesner made of printed indexes supplied by the firms of Manutius and Estienne as well as of booksellers' catalogues in compiling his massive bibliography. Gesner's achievements and his acknowledgements to the master printers of his day are also noted by Sarton, *Appreciation*, pp. 108–13; see esp. pp. 109–10.

173 Gesner's acknowledgements of those whose specimens, illustrations, descriptions, etc. he used include a reference to Dürer for supplying the celebrated rhinocerus woodcut. *Historia Animalium* (Zürich: Froschauer, 1551), p. 952.

174 Gesner's scrupulosity is indicated by his services to the posthumous reputation of Valerius Cordus whose botanical writings Gesner edited for publication in Strasbourg in 1561. See Dannenfeldt, 'Wittenberg Botanists,' pp. 230, 233. This essay seems to underrate the role of publication programs undertaken outside Wittenberg in bringing Lutheran scholars' research

fessor at the Academy of Lausanne when barely twenty-one partly because he had already won support from the Basel firm of Heinrich Petri (Henricpetreius) for publication of his Graeco-Latin Lexicon.[175] His mature work owed much not only to the lists and catalogues issued by diverse printers but also to the active encouragement provided by Christopher Froschauer's Zürich firm. Froschauer may have had a hand in Gesner's dedicating two of his volumes to imperial councilors and may have suggested the tributes Gesner paid to the nineteen master printers.[176] As a lay Protestant scholar then, Gesner did not exist in an institutional vacuum. He was closely affiliated with early printers, and indeed the completion of his major publication programs was inconceivable without their aid.

Under the aegis of Trithemius' publishers, both in Mainz and in Basel, or that of Gesner's publisher Christopher Froschauer in Zürich or that of John Dee's friend Willem Silvius, in Antwerp, a long-lived desire to comprehend the divine scheme for creation and to classify and order all of God's creatures was given a new impetus. The older religious and intellectual 'ardor for system' was combined with the stringent disciplines required for editing copy and with the rationality of profit-seeking merchants who had to be skillful at keeping accounts, operating machines and marketing products. The output of catalogues, dictionaries, atlases and other reference works satisfied both practical and religious impulses. Christopher Froschauer served the founding father of Swiss Protestantism, Ulrich Zwingli, as well as the father of bibliography and zoology. Much of Robert Estienne's work on lexicography came as a 'fall-out' from his biblical editions. On the other hand, one of Christopher Plantin's lexicographic contributions came simply from his position as an immigrant business man. After settling in Antwerp and establishing ties with Leiden, Plantin decided to learn Dutch. Never one for wasted effort, he 'placed in piles and in alphabetical order' each word that he learned. Thus was launched a collaborative venture which resulted in the *Thesaurus*

to fruition. The importance of the Strasbourg printing industry in determining the shape of scientific work there is brought out by Thibodeau, 'Science and the Reformation,' p. 49.

[175] This is the same Basel firm that published the second edition of Copernicus' *De Revolutionibus* in 1566. As the son of Adam Petri who married the widow of Jerome Froben (son of Johann) and worked with Michael Isingrin on a Greek lexicon, Heinrich Petri (1508–79) was well entrenched in Basel printing circles. See entry no. 16 in Benzing, *Buchdrucker-lexicon*, p. 24.

[176] Sarton, *Appreciation*, p. 110. On Froschauer, see also Potter, 'Zwingli and His Publisher.'

Theutonicae Linguae of 1573 – the 'first Dutch dictionary worth its name.'[177]

Placing words (and letters) in piles according to alphabetical order was indeed a ubiquitous routine in the printer's workshop. The preparation of each index was in itself an exercise in textual analysis – one which was applied to many works which had never been indexed before. Here again one could develop an interesting contrast between the Florentine manuscript bookdealer Vespasiano, who persuaded notaries with fine bookhands to copy manuscripts for him in their spare time and the Florentine printer N. Laurentii, who persuaded Bernardo Machiavelli (father of Niccolò) to index Livy's *Decades* as a spare-time job. Nine months were spent by Bernardo in 1475 listing the cities, provinces, islands, mountains, and rivers mentioned in the text.[178] While engaged in this exercise, the elder Machiavelli was approaching Livy's text in a somewhat different way than had been employed by earlier generations of copyists and commentators. Petrarch, for example, was fond of citing St Augustine against the medical faculties of Padua, Bologna, and Paris. He upheld 'the investigation of the nature of man' while condemning 'the vain search for knowledge about mere things.'[179] But an indexer of Livy's works could not afford to keep these two forms of knowledge quite so separate. Investigation of references to natural phenomena and other 'mere things' was built into the act of indexing all the major classical texts that were most admired by the early humanists.

Not only was the difference between the activity of copying and that of indexing in itself likely to produce diverse attitudes toward given texts; but the difference between collecting moral examples (as medieval preachers were wont to do when engaged in indexing compendia) and simply collecting neutral data pertaining to place names, flora or fauna, is also worth underlining. The act of indexing and cross-referencing which had been animated by the religious purposes of the teaching and preaching orders became more neutral and even amoral

---

[177] Vöet, *Golden Compasses* I, 132. Whereas Plantin is made solely responsible for this work in Vöet's version, the more detailed account, by Clair, *Christopher Plantin*, pp. 118–24 points to contributions made by Cornelius Kiel ('Kilianus') (b. Cornelius Duffel, 1528), an expert lexicographer and caption writer for the series: *Nova Reperta* noted in chap. 1, n. 50 above.

[178] Relevant references in Bernardo Machiavelli's *Libro di Ricordi*, ed. C. Olschki (Florence 1954), pp. 14; 35; 222–3 are noted by Clough in *Machiavelli Researches*, p. 87 and introd. to *The Discourses of Niccolò Machiavelli* I, xliv.

[179] Garin, *Italian Humanism*, p. 23. See also citation on pp. 251–2 below, denigrating the 'mechanical' arts of the anatomist.

when applied to all manner of texts by printers who thought in terms of sales appeal.

This new, more business-like approach to copy-editing may be related to the more neutral, amoral treatment of politics and history which is often associated with the writings of Bernardo's son, Niccolò Machiavelli. The latter made several trips to printers on his father's behalf; he would have seen his father working over Livy and might have recalled Bernardo's marked-up copy when he wrote his 'Discourses' on Livy later on. The fact that his most 'notorious treatise' did not get printed until well after its author's death has been cited to demonstrate that printing was less consequential than I seem to assume. If printing 'was so crucial,' the argument goes, then why did the *Prince* exercise its 'notorious influence' while still in manuscript form?[180] Here again it seems worth stressing that the consequences of printing were not limited to spreading ideas. Just how Niccolò's views might have been affected by watching his father index a classical text for a publisher or simply by using indexes and printed reference guides on his own, are questions that must be left to specialists and cannot be handled here. But even a non-specialist may be allowed to suggest that Machiavelli's views should not be detached from the context of print culture simply because he had not seen the *Prince* through the press before he died.

The same point applies to many other writers and scholars who were contemporaries of Machiavelli – who belonged, that is, to the same generation as the earliest scholar–printers. The preparation of indexes and other procedures entailed in copy-editing pointed scholarly activities in a somewhat different direction than had the preparation of orations, dialogues, and other occasional commemorative pieces which had preoccupied earlier humanists. Objections posed by the latter to the barbarous language and bookhands used by the schoolmen were supplemented by new objections to the barbarous arrangement of medieval compendia with their great mass of elaborate digressions and seemingly unrelated details. The earliest printed editions were faithful replicas of these 'barbarous' scribal compendia, to be sure; but the very act of duplication was a necessary preliminary to later rearrangement. A disorder previously concealed by oral presentation and piecemeal copying became more visible to copy-editors and

---

[180] Rabb, 'Debate,' *Past and Present*, p. 138.

indexers and more offensive to publishers who valued systematic routines. Classical criteria of unity, internal consistency and harmony were extended beyond orations, poems, and paintings to encompass the rearrangement of large compilations and of entire fields of study which were not within the early humanist domain.

Clarity and logic of organization, the disposition of matter on the printed page became...a preoccupation of editors, almost an end in itself. It is a phenomenon familiar to a student of encyclopedic books of the late sixteenth century, relating to the increased fascination with the technical possibilities of typesetting and the great influence exerted by the methodology of Peter Ramus...The Ramist doctrine that every subject could be treated topically, that the best kind of exposition was that which proceeded by analysis was enthusiastically adopted by publishers and editors...[181]

As Neal Gilbert suggests, the term 'methodus' which had been banned as barbarous by early humanists came into its own a full century before Descartes – appearing 'with almost unbelievable frequency in the titles of sixteenth-century treatises.'[182] The Ramist movement, as discussed by Father Ong, may be regarded as the most striking and widely diffused manifestation of this new vogue.[183] But it probably owed less to any one proselytist than to the fact that printing made of textbook-writing a new and profitable genre. The mere preparation of differently graded textbooks for teaching varied disciplines encouraged a reassessment of inherited procedures and a rearrangement of approaches to diverse fields.[184] An example is offered by Vives' *On The Teaching of Disciplines* (1531), which contained, in a section on the proper method for reading history, a list of relevant narratives arranged in chronological order. The list was later picked up by Jean Bodin, who used it in his 'Method for the easy comprehension of Histories.' Bodin delineated, not a succession of book titles, but a sequence of peoples whose rise and fall formed part of an ordered

---

[181] Gerald Strauss, 'Sixteenth Century Encyclopedia,' p. 152.

[182] Gilbert, *Renaissance Concepts of Method*, p. 66.

[183] Ong's seminal study, *Ramus*, focuses on the *trivium*. Ramus' energetic insistence on pedagogical reform was directed at the *quadrivium* disciplines as well. Ramism entered into the teaching of mathematics and astronomy in particular. See discussion below p. 542, volume II.

[184] This point is well demonstrated in a recent monograph on the emergence of chemistry as a distinctive discipline with the publication of Andreas Libavius' textbook in 1597. See Owen Hannaway, *The Chemists and the Word* (pp. 110–14 esp.). Hannaway's approach owes much to Ong's Ramus studies, as he acknowledges repeatedly. On textbook writing, see also discussion below, volume II, chap. 6, section 2.

world-historical scheme.[185] As may be seen from Bodin's own work, the new emphasis placed on system and method was not exclusively pedagogical or confined to textbook-writing. It was also related, as Gilbert suggests, to 'the severe discipline of editing *editiones principes* of classical authors.'[186] An even greater challenge was presented by editing non-classical texts used for graduate studies by the faculties of theology, law and medicine.

The medieval teacher of the *Corpus Juris*, for example, was 'not concerned to show how each component was related to the logic of the whole,'[187] partly because very few teachers on law faculties had a chance to see the *Corpus Juris* as a whole. The accidental separation of portions of the manuscript of the *Digest* had given rise to two separate 'ordinary' and 'extraordinary' lecture series even before successive layers of commentary were deposited by the glossators and post-glossators.[188] The subdivision of portions into 'puncta' to be read aloud within time-limits set by academic calendars also led to frag-mentation and to throwing sequences into further disarray.[189] To gain access to the most important manuscript source for the *Digest* required a pilgrimage to Pisa, where the Florentine Codex was closely guarded and could be examined, if at all, only for a short time.[190] For a full century after the advent of printing, this problem of access continued to plague those who tried to clean 'the Augean stables of law' by cutting through the thicket of commentaries and reconstructing the corpus in its ancient form. The legal scholars were barred (quite literally in the case of Budé, who saw the manuscript only through a grate) by the guardians of the precious Codex who allowed visitors only fleeting glimpses of the relic.[191] Its publication in 1553 was thus an event of some significance – one which enabled a new generation, led by Jacques Cujas, to complete what earlier scholars, such as Budé,

---

[185] Julian Franklin, *Jean Bodin*, pp. 14–15; 137–8. Along parallel lines is Jacopo Aconcio's pre-Cartesian *De Methodo* (Basel, 1558) and his treatise on how to read history which entered into the first English treatise on the subject: Thomas Blundeville's *The True Order and Methode of Wryting and Reading Hystories* (London, 1574).

[186] N. Gilbert, *Renaissance Concepts*, pp. 71–5.

[187] J. Franklin, *Jean Bodin*, pp. 27–8.

[188] Rashdall, *The Universities of Europe in the Middle Ages*, I, 205.

[189] Destrez, *La Pecia*, p. 14 discusses how these 'puncta', which were designed to begin and end on fixed days, were noted on manuscripts used for teaching civil and canon law. Haskins, *Renaissance of the Twelfth Century*, pp. 202–3 gives the order and division of the course of study of the *Corpus Juris* pursued at Bologna.

[190] Rashdall *Universities of Europe*, I, 255 describes pilgrimages made by the glossators at Bologna.

[191] Kelley, *Foundations of Modern Historical Scholarship*, pp. 67; 113.

Alciato and Amerbach, had begun.[192] Cujas's corrections ranged from 'the simplest textual errors' to 'anachronistic substitutions.' He also undertook 'the job of indexing the citations.' By the end of the century the whole compilation had been made available in an emended and indexed form.[193] Stripped of the encrustation of glosses, the ancient compilation was rendered ever more stylistically coherent and internally consistent. By the same token, it came to seem less and less relevant to contemporary jurisprudence. Very much as was the case with Ciceronian Latin, when complete restoration had been successfully applied to the letter of the ancient code, its living spirit vanished for good.[194]

On the other hand, a body of living law was also affected by copy-editing, indexing and emendation. Even while ancient compilations such as the *Corpus Juris* seemed less relevant to current practice, a sharper cutting edge was given to some statutes and *ordonnances* which were in effect. In Valois France, distinctions between royal *ordonnances* (which were already being printed in the reign of François I) and private contracts, which continued to be notarized in manuscript form, may have been sharpened – so that the difference between 'public' and 'private' law became more marked.[195] In Tudor England, royal proclamations, once printed, were no longer merely fixed to walls and doors and other public places but were collected into a convenient octavo volume and furnished with a table of contents for easy reference.[196] Beginning with Caxton's little-known contemporary, W. de Machlinia, in the 1480s, English law-printing attracted an increasing number of enterprising Londoners such as Pynson, Redman,

192 The contributions of Budé and Alciato are discussed by Kelley, *Foundations*, chaps. 3 and 4. On those of Boniface Amerbach, son of the founder of the Amerbach-Froben firm, Erasmus' closest friend, literary executor and heir, see Gilmore, *Humanists and Jurists*, chap. 6, pp. 146–77. That Erasmus, the Amerbachs and Beatus Rhenanus, all of whom belonged to the same Basel printers' circle, provided the main inspiration for Alciato is noted by Kelley, p. 93, but Budé's relationship to Badius is not explored and a misprint on pp. 56–7, n. 5 makes Robert Estienne (who married Perrette Badius) the son-in-law of Budé rather than of Budé's chief printer. Badius' career, as sketched by Febvre and Martin, *L'Apparition*, pp. 183; 224, over-lapped with the Amerbach circle. In general, I think that the scholar–printers' workshops played a more significant role in sixteenth-century legal studies than most accounts suggest.
193 Kelley, *Foundations*, p. 114.
194 Gilmore, 'The Renaissance Conception of the Lessons of History,' p. 85 cites a pertinent comment by Jacques Cujas. See below, p. 194.
195 See relevant discussion between Francois Masai and John Gilissen in *Individu et Société à la Renaissance: Colloque International* (April, 1965), pp. 86–7, following Gilissen's paper on 'Individualisme et Sécurité Juridique,' (pp. 35–58).
196 Bennett, *Books and Readers 1475–1557*, pp. 135–6, offers a pertinent excerpt from Grafton's note to the reader.

Berthelet and Thomas More's versatile brother-in-law, John Rastell.[197]

Keenly aware of one another's output, each made efforts to keep their own wares up to date and attractive to the legal public. It was probably to counter the complete abridgement of the Statutes...published by Redman in 1528, that Pynson reissued his 1521 edition...with a new title page and four folios of 'newe addicions'...Rastell could not let these actions go un-challenged and replied with his *Magnum Abbreviamentum* listing the statutes down to 1523 abridged in...Latin, Anglo-French and English.[198]

Publications of abridgements and lists of statutes issued by John Rastell and his son offer a good illustration of how a rationalized book-format might affect vital organs of the body politic. The systematic arrangement of titles; the tables which followed strict alphabetical order; the indexes and cross-references to accurately numbered para-graphs all show how new tools available to printers helped to bring more order and method into a significant body of public law.[199] Until the end of the fifteenth century, it was not always easy to decide just 'what a statute really was' and confusion had long been compounded concerning diverse 'great' charters.[200] In 'Englishing and printing' the 'Great Boke of Statutes 1530-1533' John Rastell took care to provide an introductory 'Tabula': a forty-six page 'chronological register by chapters of the statutes 1327 to 1523.' He was not merely providing a table of contents; he was also offering a systematic review of parlia-mentary history – the first many readers had ever seen.[201]

This sort of spectacular innovation, while deserving close study, should not divert attention from much less conspicuous, more ubiqui-tous changes. Increasing familiarity with regularly numbered pages, punctuation marks, section breaks, running heads, indices, and so forth, helped to reorder the thought of *all* readers, whatever their profession

[197] As a pioneering law printer, playwright, theater builder, lexicographer, music printer and promoter of overseas colonization, John Rastell (whose wife was Elizabeth More, Thomas' sister) seems to exemplify the versatility of the early sixteenth-century printer. Aspects of his career may be glimpsed in A. W. Reed, *Early Tudor Drama*, pp. 11-12; 187-201; Quinn, *England and the Discovery of America 1481-1620*, pp. 166-9; H. J. Graham, 'The Rastells and the Printed English Law Book of the Renaissance.' On Pynson and others, see section on law printers in Bennett, *Books and Readers 1475-1557*, pp. 76-85.

[198] Bennett, *Books and Readers 1475-1557*, p. 77.

[199] Cowley, 'The Abridgement of Statutes,' See esp. p. 128.

[200] See below, p. 119.

[201] H. J. Graham, 'Our Tong Maternall Marvellously Amendyd and Augmentyd.' This article also brings out Rastell's patriotic (and profiteering) crusade to 'English' all law, which was at that time still largely in Latin or 'law-French.'

or craft. Hence countless activities were subjected to a new 'esprit de système.' The use of arabic numbers for pagination suggests how the most inconspicuous innovation could have weighty consequences – in this case, more accurate indexing, annotation, and cross-referencing resulted.[202] Most studies of printing have, quite rightly, singled out the regular provision of title pages as the most significant new feature associated with the printed book format.[203] How the title page contributed to the cataloguing of books and the bibliographer's craft scarcely needs to be spelled out. How it contributed to new habits of placing and dating, in general, does, I think, call for further thought.[204]

On the whole, as I have tried to suggest throughout this discussion, topics now allocated to bibliophiles and specialists on printing are of general concern to historians at large – or, at least, to specialists in many different fields. The way these very fields are laid out could be better understood if we opened up the one assigned to printing. A case in point is offered by a 'Catalogue of English Printed Bookes' printed in 1595 for Andrew Maunsell, a London bookseller. Over 6,000 titles were presented in a well-organized three-part sequence each 'gathered into alphabet' – devoted first to 'Divinitie,' second to 'The Sciences' and third to the 'Humanities.' In his introduction to each part, Maunsell provides three separate dedications beginning with Queen Elizabeth and the Earl of Essex, going on to interested professionals (such as 'Reverend Divines' for part one and 'Professors of the Sciences Mathematical and of Physicke and Surgery' for part two) and ending with 'the Worshipfull, the Masters, Wardens and Assistants to the Companie of Stationers and all other Printers and Booksellers in general.' In his initial remarks addressed to the latter he notes that his

---

202 Sarton, 'Incunabula Wrongly Dated,' pp. 322–3. Arabic numerals (already used in the thirteenth century by Robert Grosseteste for cross-referencing) appear for the first time on each page of a printed Bible with Froben's first edition of Erasmus' New Testament of 1516 which also 'set the style' for the well-differentiated 'modern' book-and-chapter headings employed by other Bible-printers. Black, 'Printed Bible,' p. 419. See also Witty, 'Early Indexing Techniques.'

203 As already noted, n. 35 above, occasional anticipations in quattrocento humanist mss. do not diminish the significance of title pages becoming a regular phenomenon after print.

204 The specific contributions made by early publishers to this habit are also worth further attention. Erhard Ratdolt's Venetian edition of Eusebius' *Chronicle* (1483), for example, listed events that were important in the publisher's own life. Under 1476, he listed the death of Regiomontanus and the publication of his own 'Kalendar.' Whereas monastic necrologies tend to dominate chronology in the age of scribes, the march of time would be associated with events considered significant by urban entrepreneurs after printing.

system includes mention of 'the Author, the Matter, the Translator, the Printer' and boasts that he has improved on the systems employed by earlier compilers of 'Latine Catalogues' such as Gesner, Simler, or John Bale. 'They make their Catalogue by the Christen name, I by the Sir name. They mingle Diuinitie Law, Phisicke etc together. I set Diuinitie by itself.'[205] Maunsell's system not only set Divinity by itself; it also gathered all the disciplines we now describe as scientific, both mathematical and medical, under one heading labelled 'Science'; while placing all the disciplines we now describe as humanistic: 'Gramer, Logicke, Rethoricke, Lawe, Historie, Poetrie, Policie, &c which for the most part Concerne matters of Delight and Pleasure,' under the heading of the 'Humanities.'[206] In addressing doctors of divinity in Part One and professors of the Sciences mathematical, together with physicians and surgeons, in Part Two he was also defining the profession of the scientist in a manner that is often attributed to a much later era.[207]

4. THE NEW PROCESS OF DATA COLLECTION: FROM THE CORRUPTED COPY TO THE IMPROVED EDITION

In developing separate categories and opposing them to the indiscriminate 'mingling' of previous cataloguers, Maunsell was reacting to the same competitive pressures that led each law printer to try to issue a more complete index or a more systematic compilation. He was also taking advantage of a new opportunity to improve on the work of predecessors such as Gesner, much as Gesner had improved on Trithe-

205 The Folger copy of this 'Three Part Catalogue' (listed under Maunsell, Andrew in the STC no. 17669) was obtained from the Harmsworth collection and was Item no. 318 in the Pembroke sale of March, 1920. The 'First Part, printed by John Windbet for A. Maunsell, 1595,' is bound separately; the second part, printed by James Roberts for A. M., 1595, is bound with the third. (I am indebted to Kate Frost for this material.)
206 'The seconde parte of the Catalogue...concerneth the Sciences Mathematicall, as Arithmetick, Geometrie, Astronomie, Astrologie, Musik, the Arte of Warre and Navigation and also ...Physicke and Surgerie...' The fact that 'Musicke' includes titles relating to easy lessons in lute playing and collections of psalms and that books on 'Architechture, Bathes, Cookerie, Dreames and Prognostications' are also listed suggests that the division between fields was still not quite like our own. Nevertheless, the grouping of main topics seems remarkably similar to later procedures and quite unlike earlier ones.
207 See discussion of use of term 'scientific' in Middleton, The Experimenters, p. 81 which notes how the O.E.D. attributes the first use of the term, as contradistinguished from art, to Moxon in his Mechanick Exercises of 1678. See also 'Science' in the O.E.D. (1961 ed.), p. 221. In 1421 the three fields of graduate study: 'Divinity, Fisyk, and Lawe' are described as the 'three sciences' in the Rolls of Parliament – an interesting contrast with Maunsell's tripartite scheme which places law under the humanities and medicine under science.

mius. Whereas large compilations or catalogues tended to become progressively more systematic and orderly in the hands of printers, increasing confusion and disorganization had been more characteristic of a compendium that was handled by scribes. When dealing with the output of successive editions of a given reference-work or set of maps, printers not only competed with rivals and improved on their predecessors. They were also able to improve on themselves. The succession of Latin Bibles turned out by Robert Estienne, or the succession of atlases turned out by Ortelius suggest how the immemorial drift of scribal culture had been not merely arrested but actually reversed.

In making this point, one is likely to run up against objections posed by scholars who have good reason to be sceptical about all claims made on behalf of early printers. Prefaces and blurbs which repeatedly boast of improvement are belied by actual evidence of uncritical copying and – even worse – of ignorant emendation.[208] After comparing copies of a given reference work with early printed versions it is often found that an age-old process of corruption was aggravated and accelerated after print. In the field of Bible illustration, for example, inferior quality blocks used repeatedly led to unintelligible lettering; misinterpretations of blurred captions by ignorant craftsmen produced mystifying juxtapositions; while all errors were compounded by pirated editions issued over the course of decades.[209]

Early printed botany books underwent much the same kind of degradations as did early printed Bibles. A sequence of printed herbals beginning in the 1480s and going down to 1526 reveals a 'steady increase in the amount of distortion,' with the final product – an English herbal of 1526 – providing a 'remarkably sad example of what happens to visual information as it passed from copyist to copyist.'[210] But in the very course of accelerating a process of corruption, which had gone on in a much slower and more irregular fashion under the aegis of scribes, the new medium made this process more visible to learned men and offered a way of overcoming it for the first time. As noted above, cuts for Vesalius' second edition were not blurred and degraded, but were sharpened and refined.[211] In the hands of ignorant printers driving to make quick profits, data tended to get garbled at an ever more rapid

[208] Kenney, *The Classical Text* stresses the advantages of 'slavish copying' over the emendations made by ostensibly learned editors in preserving the authenticity of ancient texts.
[209] Strachan, *Early Bible Illustrations, passim.*
[210] Ivins, *Prints and Visual Communication*, p. 40.   [211] See above, n. 39.

pace. But under the guidance of technically proficient masters, the new technology also provided a way of transcending the limits which scribal procedures had imposed upon technically proficient masters in the past.

How the sequence of corrupted copies was replaced by a sequence of improved editions may be demonstrated by drawing on a recent close-up study of successive editions of a sixteenth-century encyclopedia. Sebastian Munster's *Cosmography*, which was first published in 1544, went through eight editions in its author's lifetime and thirty-five more down to 1628. As each edition became bigger, more crammed with data, and more profusely illustrated, each was also provided with more tables, charts, indexes which made it possible for readers to retrieve the growing body of information that was being stored in the work. Editors worked conscientiously to keep each edition updated and to provide more thorough coverage for regions that had received short shrift in earlier versions. Like Gesner's 'universal' bibliography, Munster's *Cosmography* was fated to be supplanted by less comprehensive reference guides; for a rapid accumulation of data made it impossible 'to contain between covers of a single narrative volume all that was useful and interesting to know.'[212]

This rapid accumulation of data, it should be noted, was itself spurred from the workshops of master printers who issued reference works of various kinds. Sixteenth-century editors and publishers, who served the Commonwealth of Learning, did not merely store data passively in compendia. They created vast networks of correspondents, solicited criticism of each edition, sometimes publicly promising to mention the names of readers who sent in new information or who spotted the errors which would be weeded out.

By the simple expedient of being honest with his readers and inviting criticism and suggestions, Ortelius made his *Theatrum* a sort of cooperative enterprise on an international basis. He received helpful suggestions from far and wide and cartographers stumbled over themselves to send him their latest maps of regions not covered in the *Theatrum*.

The *Theatrum* was...speedily reprinted several times...Suggestions for corrections and revisions kept Ortelius and his engravers busy altering plates for new editions...Within three years he had acquired so many new maps that he issued a supplement of 17 maps which were afterwards incorporated

---

[212] Gerald Strauss, 'Sixteenth Century Encyclopedia,' p. 158. According to Strauss, thirty-one of the editions were issued from Heinrich Petri's Basel press (p. 145). This is the same firm which gave Gesner his early start. See n. 175 above.

in the *Theatrum*. When Ortelius died in 1598 at least 28 editions of the atlas had been published in Latin, Dutch, German, French and Spanish...The last edition was published by the House of Plantin in 1612...[213]

Not every edition, to be sure, eliminated all the errors that were spotted; good intentions stated in prefaces failed to be honored in actual manufacture. Even so, the requests of publishers often encouraged readers to launch their own research projects and field trips which resulted in additional publication programs. Thus a knowledge explosion was set off. The 'fall-out' from Ortelius' editions, for example, encompassed treatises on topography and local history ranging from Muscovy to Wales.[214]

The solicitor or recipient of new data was not always a printer or publisher. Often it was the author or editor of a given series of editions who heard from readers about errors or additions to be incorporated in a later edition. As Mattioli's commentaries on Dioscorides, first published in 1554, ran through one edition after another, they were periodically revised and corrected on the bases of specimens and information received from correspondents. Exotic plants were thus introduced to Europeans (so that the horse chestnut, lilac and tulip came from Turkey into botanical gardens in Europe via Mattioli's edition of 1581). The proliferation of foreign reports pertaining to fruits and seeds also led to more complete and precise descriptions of domestic plants.

By the middle of the sixteenth century, botanists were vying with each other to obtain novelties from India, from the New World, from frozen countries, marshes, and deserts – from anywhere and everywhere. The plants and animals of distant exotic countries were either radically new or sufficiently different from those already known to cause perplexities and to

---

213 Lloyd A. Brown, *The Story of Maps*, pp. 163–4. Ortelius' plea for new information and assurance of 'honorable mention' for any correspondent providing it is in his 'Message to the Reader,' pp. 31–2. Preliminary research in the Clements Library by a University of Michigan graduate student, Gail Bossenga, shows that Ortelius incorporated the corrections his correspondents spotted on an irregular and occasional basis, but did take advantage of addenda more frequently. Ortelius' correspondence which was collected in J. H. Hessels' multi-volume *Epistulae Ortelianae* of 1887 has been issued in a single-volume edition of 965 pp. by Otto Zeller. Mercator's correspondence has also been collected by van Durme (ed.), *Correspondance Mercatorienne*. Ancient as well as modern geography was subject to the same process. Stevens, *Ptolemy's Geography*, p. 9 notes that almost every succeeding edition was re-edited and expanded with new maps being added and old ones redrawn. For further discussion of geography and cartography, see pp. 479–83, 512–18, volume II below.

214 For some by-products of Ortelius' venture, see F. J. Levy, 'The Making of Camden's Britannia,' pp. 70–97, also E. G. R. Taylor, *The Mathematical Practitioners*, p. 32.

invite further investigation...There emerged a new kind of scientist, the traveling naturalist...The greedy adventurers of early days were now replaced by men in search of knowledge...

The discoveries made in foreign lands excited the naturalists who were obliged to stay at home, such as physicians, professors and keepers of botanical gardens and greenhouses, and forced them to describe more accurately and completely the faunas and floras of their own countries...So much new knowledge was amassed that it tended to create confusion and there was an increasing need for new surveys...[215]

The new surveys led, in turn, to further interchanges which set off new investigations; the accumulation of more data making necessary more refined classification, and so on – *ad infinitum*. The sequence of improved editions and ever-expanding reference-works was a sequence without limits – unlike the great library collections amassed by Alexandrian rulers and Renaissance princes. The destruction of the Alexandrian Library in the distant past and the destruction of the great collection amassed by Matthias Corvinus in the recent past were noted by Conrad Gesner in the dedication of the first edition of his own more open-ended universal 'bibliotheca.'[216] The natural sciences and the library sciences which Gesner helped to found were capable of unlimited expansion. They entailed an open-ended indefinitely continuous process. The term 'feed-back' is ugly and much over-used, yet it does help to define the difference between data-collection before and after the communications shift. After printing, large-scale data-collection did become subject to new forms of feed-back which had not been possible in the age of scribes.

Here as elsewhere, there are advantages to spelling out the consequences of the new communications system, instead of merely noting in passing that, of course, printing was a prerequisite for early modern scholarship and science, before going on to cover other things. If the new system received more attention one might be less inclined to attribute unusual moral virtues to sixteenth-century scholars or to set 'greedy adventurers' against disinterested naturalists. If authors, editors and publishers adopted 'the simple expedient of being honest' by citing contributors it was not because they were unusually noble but because this simple expedient had become more satisfying to mixed motives after printing than had been the case before. When Ortelius

[215] Sarton, *Six Wings*, p. 137.
[216] Fischer, 'Conrad Gesner,' p. 271.

listed contributors to his atlas, he was manifesting the 'modern idea of scientific cooperation,' just as Edgar Zilsel suggests. But that is no reason to draw invidious comparisons between 'honest' and cooperative craftsmen who sought to benefit others and vain, devious, self-serving schoolmen or literati who worked only for themselves.[217] No occupational group had a monopoly on a given virtue or vice. A collaborative approach to data-collection and the acknowledgement of sources and contributions were by no means confined to scientific disciplines, classical scholarship, art history and literary studies were also affected.[218] As we have seen, bibliography as well as zoology became collaborative and subject to incremental change. Indeed the father of these two disciplines was the same man.

Insofar as the change from a sequence of corrupted copies to a sequence of improved editions encompassed all scholarly fields, it might be expected to have a fairly widespread effect upon the entire Commonwealth of Learning. It needs to be taken into consideration, I think, when dealing with massive intellectual movements such as the growing orchestration of themes associated with limitless progress and the muting of the older 'decay of nature' themes. In later chapters this point will receive more attention. Here let me just note that the transmission of written records no longer reinforced the sense that corruption was an inevitable consequence of any sequence over time. 'The Power which Printing gives us of continually improving and correcting our Works in successive Editions,' wrote David Hume to his publisher, 'appears to me the chief Advantage of that art.'[219] What was true of a single author's work applied with even greater force to large collaborative reference works. A series of new and augmented editions made the future seem to hold more promise of enlightenment than the past.

[217] Zilsel, 'The Genesis of the Concept of Scientific Progress,' pp. 344–5. See also discussion on pp. 241 ff and 558 ff (volume II) below.

[218] On Vasari's expanded (1568) edition of his *Lives of the Artists* and the correspondence and field trips this edition entailed, see chap. 3, n. 198, below. John Bale's offer to include mention of any authors who sent him biographical data is noted by Leslie Fairfield, *John Bale*. Moran, 'William Caxton,' 63, points to the interchange between Caxton and a reader of his first edition of the *Canterbury Tales* (1478) which is noted in Caxton's preface to the 1484 version. The reader sent Caxton a 'better' text to be used as a basis for the second edition. Although Blake, *Caxton: England's First Publisher*, p. 99 denigrates the haphazard and irregular emendations Caxton made after receiving the Chaucer ms., the fact remains that the printer did take the time and trouble to change his first edition on the basis of a complaint and new data from an unknown correspondent.

[219] Cited by J. A. Cochrane, *Dr. Johnson's Printer*, p. 19, n. 2.

'Until half a century after Copernicus' death, no potentially revolutionary changes occurred in the data available to astronomers.'[220] But Copernicus' life (1473-1543) spanned the very decades when a great many changes, now barely visible to modern eyes, were transforming 'the data available' to all book-readers. A closer study of these changes could help to explain why systems of charting the planets, mapping the earth, synchronizing chronologies, codifying laws and compiling bibliographies were all revolutionized before the end of the sixteenth century. In each instance, one notes, Hellenistic achievements were first reduplicated and then, in a remarkably short time, surpassed. In each instance, the new schemes once published remained available for correction, development, and refinement. Successive generations could build on the work left by sixteenth-century polymaths instead of trying to retrieve scattered fragments of it. The varied intellectual 'revolutions' of early-modern times owed much to the features that have already been outlined.[221] But the great tomes, charts, and maps that are now seen as 'milestones' might have proved insubstantial had not the preservative powers of print also been called into play. Typographical fixity is a basic prerequisite for the rapid advancement of learning. It helps to explain much else that seems to distinguish the history of the past five centuries from that of all prior eras – as I hope the following remarks will suggest.

5. CONSIDERING THE PRESERVATIVE POWERS OF PRINT: FIXITY AND CUMULATIVE CHANGE

Of all the new features introduced by the duplicative powers of print, preservation is possibly the most important.[222] To appreciate its importance, we need to recall the conditions that prevailed before texts could be set in type. No manuscript, however useful as a reference

---

[220] Thomas Kuhn, *The Copernican Revolution* p. 131. For further discussion of printing and developments in astronomy, see chap. 7, volume II, below.

[221] The issues dealt with by studies such as Fussner, *The Historical Revolution* and Sypher, 'Similarities between the Scientific and Historical Revolutions,' 353-68, need particularly to be reviewed in the light of the above discussion.

[222] Butler, *Origin of Printing*, p. 23; Sarton, 'Quest for Truth,' p. 67 and Steinberg, *Five Hundred Years*, flyleaf, all underline the preservative powers of print. How printing arrested and froze the classical text (after corruption by copyists had been followed by ill-advised editorial emendation) is noted by Kenney, *Classical Text*, pp. 2-3. See also pp. 18-19, 69, where Kenney discusses the 'uniquely stable point of reference' provided by the so-called 'textus receptus.'

guide, could be preserved for long without undergoing corruption by copyists, and even this sort of 'preservation' rested precariously on the shifting demands of local élites and a fluctuating incidence of trained scribal labor. Insofar as records were seen and used, they were vulnerable to wear and tear. Stored documents were vulnerable to moisture and vermin, theft and fire. However they might be collected or guarded within some great message center, their ultimate dispersal and loss was inevitable. To be transmitted by writing from one generation to the next, information had to be conveyed by drifting texts and vanishing manuscripts.

This aspect of scribal culture is not often appreciated by modern scholars. It is completely concealed by recent anthropological studies which focus on the contrasts between oral and written records exhibited during the last few hundred years. Thus anthropologists are likely to assign to handwriting the capacity to produce 'permanently recorded versions of the past.'[223] A single manuscript record, even on parchment, was fairly impermanent, however, unless it was stored away and not used. More than one record required copying, which led to textual drift. Durable records called for durable materials. Stone inscriptions endured; papyrus records crumbled. These tangible differences gave rise to the rule: 'Much is preserved when little is written; little is preserved when much is written.'[224] After the advent of printing, however, the durability of writing material became less significant; preservation could be achieved by using abundant supplies of paper rather than scarce and costly skin. Quantity counted for more than quality. Even while time-tested rules were being duplicated, they were being made obsolete. One is reminded of the way modern scholars smile at the notion of an abbot instructing his monks to copy printed books so that texts would not perish.[225] Yet modern scholars are just as prone as fifteenth-century monks to be deceived by appearances, and appearances have become increasingly deceptive.

By and large, printing required the use of paper – a less durable material than parchment or vellum to begin with, and one that became ever more perishable as the centuries have passed and rag content has diminished. Whereas the scraping and reuse of skin does not obliterate letters completely, the scrapping or reconversion of discarded printed

[223] Goody and Watt, 'Consequences of Literacy,' p. 345. See also chap. 1, n. 16 above.
[224] Innis, *Empire and Communication*, p. 10 cites passage from Pirenne in this connection.
[225] On Trithemius' instructions, see p. 14 above.

matter leaves no palimpsests behind. When written messages are duplicated in such great abundance that they can be consigned to trash bins or converted into pulp, they are not apt to prompt thoughts about prolonged preservation. Manuscripts guarded in treasure rooms, wills locked in vaults, diplomas framed behind glass do appear to be more indestructible than road maps, kitchen calendars, or daily newspapers.[226] Moreover we are repeatedly reminded of the remarkable survival-value of ancient documents which have been buried under lava or stored in jars for thousands of years. A process of retrieval that was launched after printing has led to the uncovering of so many long-lost records that we are likely to underestimate the perishability of manuscripts which were not buried but were used. The development of new techniques for restoration and duplication, which bring lost writings to light, also encourage absent-mindedness about losses which were incurred before the new techniques were employed.

Earlier scholars were less absent-minded. Thomas Jefferson, for one, was keenly aware of the preservative powers of print.

Very early in the course of my researches into the laws of Virginia [he wrote to George Wythe], I observed that many of them were already lost, and many more on the point of being lost, as existing only in single copies in the hands of careful or curious individuals, on whose deaths they would probably be used for waste paper. I set myself therefore to work to collect all which were then existing....In searching after these remains, I spared neither time, trouble, nor expence....But...the question is What means will be the most effectual for preserving these remains from future loss? All the care I can take of them, will not preserve them from the worm, from the natural decay of the paper, from the accident of fire, or those of removal when it is necessary for any public purpose....Our experience has proved to us that a single copy, or a few, deposited in MS in the public offices cannot be relied on for any great length of time. The ravages of fire and of ferocious enemies have had but too much part in producing the very loss we now deplore. How many of the precious works of antiquity were lost while they existed only in manuscript? Has there ever been one lost since the art of printing has rendered it practicable to multiply and disperse copies? This leads us then to

---

226 Clapp, 'Story of Durable Book Paper,' makes this point. Some early medieval mss. also appear to be more indestructible than many eighteenth-century novels. According to Chambers, 'The Lost Literature of Medieval England,' p. 297, it is likely that a larger percentage of eighteenth-century novels are already lost than of the works of the Venerable Bede. There were many distinguished medieval scholars, however, who were less fortunate than Bede. On the random survival of medieval mss. see Goldschmidt, *Medieval Texts*, p. 12; J. W. Thompson, 'The Wanderings of Manuscripts,' p. 659.

the only means of preserving those remains of our laws now under consideration, that is, a multiplication of printed copies.[227]

This revealing letter is described by Julian Boyd as leading directly to the publication of Hening's *Statutes of Virginia*. According to Boyd, it reflects the same views Jefferson expressed much earlier 'to the author of Hazard's *Historical Collections*: "the lost cannot be recovered; but let us save what remains: not by vaults and locks which fence them from the public eye and use, in consigning them to the waste of time, but by such a multiplication of copies, as shall place them beyond the reach of accident." '[228]

It seems in character for Jefferson to stress the democratizing aspect of the preservative powers of print which secured precious documents not by putting them under lock and key but by removing them from chests and vaults and duplicating them for all to see. The notion that valuable data could be preserved best by being made public, rather than by being kept secret, ran counter to tradition, led to clashes with new censors, and was central both to early–modern science and to Enlightenment thought. In deploring the loss of the 'precious works of antiquity' while 'they existed only in manuscript' Jefferson also sounded an older humanist theme which linked the rebirth of ancient learning to the new art of printing. Problems associated with this linkage will be discussed in the next chapter. Here let me merely note that a classical revival, which was already underway when the first printers moved into Italy, persisted despite Ottoman advances in eastern Europe, the French invasions of Italy, the despoiling of English monasteries and all the horrors of the religious wars. Once Greek type fonts had been cut, neither the disruption of civil order in Italy, the conquest of Greek lands by Islam, nor even the translation into Latin of all major Greek texts saw knowledge of Greek wither again in the West. But the implications of typographical fixity are scarcely exhausted by thinking about the permanent retrieval of Greek letters. Nor are they exhausted by reckoning the number of other ancient languages that have been retrieved and secured after being lost – not just to Western Europe but to the entire world – for thousands of years. They involve the whole modern 'knowledge industry' itself, with its

227 Boyd, 'These Precious Monuments of. . . Our History,' pp. 175–6. (I am indebted to Mr Reid Beddow for bringing this citation to my attention.)
228 Boyd, 'These Precious Monuments,' pp. 175–6.

ever expanding bibliographies; its relentless pressure on book shelf space and library facilities.

They also involve issues that are less academic and more geopolitical. The linguistic map of Europe was 'fixed' by the same process and at the same time as Greek letters were. The importance of the fixing of literary vernaculars is often stressed. The strategic role played by printing is, however, often overlooked.[229] How strategic it was is suggested by the following paraphrased summary of Steinberg's account:

Printing 'preserved and codified, sometimes even created' certain vernaculars. Its absence during the sixteenth century among small linguistic groups 'demonstrably led' to the disappearance or exclusion of their vernaculars from the realm of literature. Its presence among similar groups in the same century ensured the possibility of intermittent revivals or continued expansion. Having fortified language walls between one group and another, printers homogenized what was within them, breaking down minor differences, standardizing idioms for millions of writers and readers, assigning a new peripheral role to provincial dialects. The preservation of a given literary language often depended on whether or not a few vernacular primers, catechisms or Bibles happened to get printed (under foreign as well as domestic auspices) in the sixteenth century. When this was the case, the subsequent expansion of a separate 'national' literary culture ensued. When this did not happen, a prerequisite for budding 'national' consciousness disappeared; a spoken provincial dialect was left instead.[230]

Studies of dynastic consolidation and/or of nationalism might well devote more space to the advent of printing. Typography arrested linguistic drift, enriched as well as standardized vernaculars, and paved the way for the more deliberate purification and codification of all major European languages. Randomly patterned sixteenth-century

---

[229] Compare the abundance of relevant data in Febvre and Martin, L'Apparition, chap. 8, with what is missing in Hughes, History as Art and as Science, pp. 38–40, where the relation between linguistic fixity and nationalism, individualism, capitalism, the nation-state is discussed. Hughes urges historians to make use of linguistic studies, but linguists, like anthropologists, while careful to discriminate between 'spoken' and 'written' languages, say little about scribal as opposed to printed ones. Judging by my own experience, books on linguistics are difficult to master and seem to lead far afield. I found the reverse to be true when consulting literature on printing.

[230] Steinberg, Five Hundred Years, pp. 120–6. Cases pertaining to Cornish, Cymric, Gaelic, Latvian, Estonian, Lithuanian, Finnish, Pomeranian, Courlander, Czech, Basque, etc. are cited. Of course, other factors may have been at work in other instances than those cited, but the number of instances where sixteenth-century type-casting seems to have been critical is noteworthy. One detailed case study which suggests some of the complications Steinberg's survey does not cover is offered by Huffines, 'Sixteenth Century Printers and Standardization of New High German,' pp. 60–72. Unfortunately, Huffines deals mainly with a dispute two German authorities which seems somewhat peripheral to the questions with which I am concerned.

type-casting largely determined the subsequent elaboration of national mythologies on the part of certain separate groups within multi-lingual dynastic states. The duplication of vernacular primers and translations contributed in other ways to nationalism. A 'mother's tongue' learned 'naturally' at home would be reinforced by inculcation of a homogenized print-made language mastered while still young, when learning to read. During the most impressionable years of childhood, the eye would first see a more standardized version of what the ear had first heard. Particularly after grammar schools gave primary instruction in reading by using vernacular instead of Latin readers, linguistic 'roots' and rootedness in one's homeland would be entangled.

Printing contributed in other ways to the permanent fragmentation of Latin Christendom. Erastian policies long pursued by diverse rulers could, for example, be more fully implemented. The duplication of documents pertaining to ritual, liturgy, or canon law, handled under clerical auspices in the age of the scribe, was undertaken by enterprising laymen, subject to dynastic authority, in the age of the printer. Local firms, lying outside the control of the papal curia, were granted lucrative privileges by Habsburg, Valois, or Tudor kings to service the needs of national clergies. An Antwerp printer joined forces with a King of Spain to supply all Spanish priests with some 15,000 copies of a sixteenth-century breviary – its text having been slightly altered from the version authorized by post-Tridentine Rome. Philip II thus demonstrated royal control over the clergy of his realm, and Christopher Plantin thus evaded payments to the privileged Roman printer (none other than Paul Manutius) who had won a lucrative monopoly on the newly authorized Roman version.[231] The other varied ways in which printers by pursuing their own interests contributed to loosening or severing links with Rome, to nationalist sentiment, and to dynastic consolidation cannot be explored here. But they surely do call for further study.[232]

Many other consequences of typographical fixity also need to be explored. As a later chapter suggests, sixteenth-century religious divisions within Latin Christendom proved to be peculiarly permanent.

---

[231] Kingdon, 'Patronage, Piety, and Printing,' *A Festschrift for Frederick B. Artz*, pp. 32–3. See also Kingdon's article: 'The Plantin Breviaries.'

[232] By pursuing this line of inquiry, one could usefully supplement the theoretical views developed by Deutsch, *Nationalism and Social Communication* with a more empirical, historically grounded approach. For further discussion, see pp. 356–7, 363–4 below.

When a heresy was condemned or a schismatic king excommunicated, such actions left a more indelible imprint than had been the case in earlier centuries. Similarly, as edicts became more visible, they also became more irrevocable. Magna Carta, for example, was ostensibly 'published' (i.e. proclaimed) twice a year in every shire. By 1237 there was already confusion as to which 'charter' was involved.[233] In 1533, however, Englishmen glancing over the 'Tabula' of the 'Great Boke' could see how often it had been repeatedly confirmed in successive royal statutes.[234] In France also the 'mechanism by which the will of the sovereign' was incorporated into the 'published' body of law by 'registration' was probably altered by typographical fixity.[235] It was no longer possible to take for granted that one was following 'immemorial custom' when granting an immunity or signing a decree. Much as M. Jourdain learned that he was speaking prose, monarchs learned from political theorists that they were 'making' laws. But members of parliaments and assemblies also learned from jurists and printers about ancient rights wrongfully usurped. Struggles over the right to establish precedents became more intense, as each precedent became more permanent and hence more difficult to break.

On the other hand, in many fields of activity, fixity led to new departures from precedent, marked by more explicit recognition of individual innovation and by the staking of claims to inventions, discoveries, and creations. It is no accident, I think, that printing is the first 'invention' which became entangled in a priority struggle and rival national claims. Arguments over Gutenberg versus Coster or Jenson set the pattern for all other 'Columbus Day' type disputes.[236] One might compare the anonymity of the inventor of spectacles with later disputes over Galileo's right to claim priority in the case of the telescope.[237] How much credit should be assigned to map-publishers

[233] Holt, *Magna Carta*, pp. 288–90. [234] Graham, 'Our Tong Maternall,' p. 93.
[235] Ford, *Robe and Sword*, p. 80, describes this mechanism – not, however, how it was altered. See also his remarks about 'great advance in publicity techniques' and how the major remonstrances of the French parlements were being 'published' by 1732 in printed form (p. 101).
[236] See Butler, *Origin of Printing*, pp. 88–110, for discussion of various claims, relevant citations from early printed literature and comments on ambiguity of terms such as 'inventor' during the sixteenth century. On Gutenberg's claims, see also n. 142 above.
[237] See two studies by Rosen, 'The Invention of Eyeglasses,' and *The Naming of the Telescope* and n. 251, n. 252 below for pertinent data. The fact that a sermon is our chief source for dating the invention of eye-glasses suggests the difference between publicity sources before and after print. See discussion of technical literature on p. 553, volume II below. On the list of post-classical 'inventions' compiled before printing by a papal librarian who was concerned with philology, see above, chap. I, n. 49.

and printers for the naming of the New World itself?[238] The way names were fixed to human organs and to the craters of the moon also seems to be indicative of the new kind of eponymous 'discovery' that came only after print.

By 1500, legal fictions were already being devised to accommodate the patenting of inventions and the assignment of literary properties.[239] Upon these foundations, a burgeoning bureaucracy would build a vast and complex legal structure. Laws pertaining to licensing and privileges have been extensively studied. But they have yet to be examined as by-products of typographical fixity. Both the dissolution of guild controls and conflicts over mercantilist policies might be clarified if this was done. Once the rights of an inventor could be legally fixed and the problem of preserving unwritten recipes intact was no longer posed, profits could be achieved by open publicity provided new restraints were not imposed. Individual initiative was released from reliance on guild protection, but at the same time new powers were lodged in the hands of a bureaucratic officialdom.[240] Competition over the right to publish a given text also introduced controversy over new issues involving monopoly and piracy. Printing forced legal definition of what belonged in the public domain.[241] A literary 'Common' became subject

---

[238] Conventional references to Martin Waldseemüller's *Cosmographiae Introductio* (St Dié, 1507) need to be supplemented by considering that Vespucci was not only a 'much more effective publicist than Columbus' but also the first to spell out the implications of voyaging to a new continent in his *New World* (*Mundus Novus*) which he got published by presses in nine different European centers between 1503 and 1508. Vespucci's role in advertising himself is described by Quinn, 'The New Horizons of Geographical Literature.' Many aspects of the significance of printing for the age of discovery are brought out by Richard B. Reed, 'The Expansion of Europe.'

[239] A landmark in the history of literary property rights which came in 1469 when a Venetian printer obtained a privilege to print and sell a given book for a given interval of time is noted in many accounts. See e.g. Blagden, *The Stationers Company*, p. 32. According to Forbes and Dijksterhuis, *History of Science* I, 147, the state of Venice was also the first to provide legal protection for inventors in 1474. See chap. 3, n. 218 below, for further references.

[240] Elizabethan privileges which allocated to different firms exclusive rights over Bibles, law books, almanachs, school books, ABC books and catechisms, music and paper ruled for music, etc. are conveniently outlined by McKerrow, 'Booksellers, Printers and the Stationers Trade' II, 222. Problems created by patent monopolies which blocked innovation are discussed, in connection with Francis Bacon's activities, by Webster, *The Great Instauration*, pp. 343–55.

[241] Birn, 'Journal des Sçavans sous L'Ancien Régime,' pp. 29; 33, shows how diverse fields of learning (and a division between 'serious' and 'frivolous' literature) were clearly defined by the terms of the official privilege granted this journal to cover a wide variety of different topics of serious concern. Both this article and Siebert, *Freedom of the Press in England 1476–1776*, *passim* suggest how laws regulating printing raised new issues pertaining to privilege and monopoly which became an acute source of conflict down through the eighteenth century.

to 'enclosure movements' and possessive individualism began to characterize the attitude of writers to their work. The 'terms plagiarism and copyright did not exist for the minstrel. It was only after printing that they began to hold significance for the author.'[242]

Personal celebrity is related to printed publicity at present. As later discussion will suggest, the same point may be applied to the past – in a manner that is especially relevant to debates over the difference between medieval and Renaissance individualism. When dealing with these debates, it is useful to recall that both the eponymous inventor and personal authorship appeared at the same time and as a consequence of the same process. Cheaper writing materials encouraged the separate recording of private lives and correspondence. Not paper mills but printing presses, however, made it possible to preserve personal ephemera intact. The 'drive for fame' itself may have been affected by print-made immortality. The urge to scribble was manifested in Juvenal's day as it was in Petrarch's. But the 'insanabile scribendi cacoethes' may have been re-oriented once it became an 'itch to publish.'[243] The wish to see one's work in print (fixed forever with one's name in card files and anthologies) is different from the desire to pen lines that could never get fixed in a permanent form, might be lost forever, altered by copying, or – if truly memorable – be carried by oral transmission and assigned ultimately to 'anon.' Until it became possible to distinguish between composing a poem and reciting one, or writing a book and copying one; until books could be classified by something other than incipits; how could modern games of books and authors be played?

The thirteenth-century Franciscan, St. Bonaventura, said that there were four ways of making books:

A man might write the works of others, adding and changing nothing, in which case he is simply called a 'scribe' (*scriptor*). Another writes the work of others with additions which are not his own; and he is called a 'compiler' (*compilator*). Another writes both others' work and his own, but with others' work in principal place, adding his own for purposes of

---

[242] Kline, 'Rabelais and Printing,' p. 54. See also Delaissé's pertinent comment, *Le Manuscrit Autographe* I, 149 and Chaytor, *From Script to Print*, p. 193. Just as lists of post-classical 'inventions' had been compiled before printing in conjunction with philological concerns so too notions of plagiarism existed in a different context among medieval friars. Concern about having a good anecdote stolen before it got used in a sermon, is described by Smalley, *English Friars*, pp. 37–8.

[243] See witty discussion of these terms by Merton, *On the Shoulders of Giants*, pp. 83–5.

explanation; and he is called a 'commentator' (*commentator*)...Another writes both his own work and others' but with his own work in principal place adding others' for purposes of confirmation; and such a man should be called an 'author' (*auctor*).

This passage is remarkable, not only for its omission of completely original composition from the otherwise symmetrical scheme, but also for the unitary conception of writing which it implies. A writer is a man who 'makes books' with a pen just as a cobbler is a man who makes shoes on a last.[244]

Many problems about assigning proper credit to scribal 'authors' may result from misguided efforts to apply print-made concepts where they do not pertain. The so-called 'forged book of Hermes' is only one of many illustrations of this point. Who *wrote* Socrates' lines, Aristotle's works, Sappho's poems, any portion of the scriptures? 'God was not the author' of the written text of Scripture, writes a reviewer of a recent book on *Biblical Inspiration*;

but who was? That is the new and radical question which has since been raised by scholarship, disclosing to us centuries of development and complex multiplicity of authorship in the biblical documents as we now read them. Isaiah did not 'write' *Isaiah*.[245]

The new forms of authorship and literary property-rights undermined older concepts of collective authority in a manner that encompassed not only biblical composition but also texts relating to philosophy, science, and law. Veneration for the wisdom of the ages was probably modified as ancient sages were retrospectively cast in the role of individual authors-prone to human error and possibly plagiarists as well.[246] Treatment of battles of books between 'ancients and moderns' might profit from more discussion of such issues. Since early printers were primarily responsible for forcing definition of literary property rights, for shaping new concepts of authorship, for exploiting best sellers and trying to tap new markets, their role in this celebrated quarrel should not be overlooked. By the early sixteenth century, for example, staffs of translators were employed to turn out vernacular versions of the more popular works by ancient Romans and con-

---

[244] Burrow, 'The Medieval Compendium,' p. 615.
[245] 'The Author and his Ghosts,' p. 1121. See also discussion by McLuhan, *Gutenberg Galaxy*, pp. 130–7 of issues pertaining to authorship and authority.
[246] See citation from Glanvill's *Essays* of 1676 cited by Merton, *Shoulders of Giants*, p. 68, and discussion concerning authorship of scripture, pp. 320–3, below.

temporary Latin-writing humanists.[247] The tremendous impetus given by printers to the vernacular translation movement in diverse countries needs to be taken into account when discussing debates between Latinists and the advocates of new vulgar tongues.[248]

It is also worth considering that different meanings may have been assigned terms such as ancient and modern, discovery and recovery, invention and imitation before important departures from precedent could be permanently recorded.[249] 'Throughout the patristic and medieval periods, the quest for truth is thought of as the *recovery* of what is embedded in tradition...rather than the *dis*covery of what is new.'[250] Most scholars concur with this view. It must have been difficult to distinguish discovering something new from recovering it in the age of scribes. To 'find a new art' was easily confused with retrieving a lost one, for superior techniques and systems of knowledge *were* frequently discovered by being recovered.[251] Probably Moses, Zoroaster, or Thoth had not 'invented' all the arts that were to be found.[252] But many were retrieved from ancient giants whose works re-entered the West by circuitous routes bearing few traces of their origins, even while testifying to remarkable technical expertise. Some

[247] On vernacular translation movements, see discussion and references pp. 360 ff, below, also Febvre and Martin, *L'Apparition*, p. 410.

[248] See Baron, 'The *Querelle* of the Ancients and Moderns,' 3–22, and also chap. 3, n. 51 below.

[249] Curtius, *European Literature*, pp. 251–6, covers the scribal use of terms such as 'ancients' and 'moderns' but fails to note how they were altered after printing. All of Merton's (tongue-in-cheek) treatment of the giant and dwarf aphorism is also relevant, and points to vast literature on topic.

[250] Harbison, *Christian Scholar*, p. 5.

[251] Rosen, 'Invention of Eyeglasses,' p. 34, n. 99 regards an early fourteenth-century preacher as inconsistent when he is recorded as saying in one sermon, 'Nothing remains to be said... today a new book could not be made nor a new art' and in a preceding one as referring to 'all the arts that have been found by man and new ones yet to be found.' *Finding* a new art was not, however, necessarily equivalent to *making* one. This point and the number of authors who are cited as responsible for the same arts by Hugh of St Victor in the twelfth century are discussed by Rose, *The Italian Renaissance of Mathematics*, pp. 255–6.

[252] A search made by Rosen turned up only one reference to the Italian word for invention in fourteenth-century literature. He found Petrarch described Zoroaster as the 'inventore' of the magic arts, Rosen, 'Invention of Eyeglasses,' p. 192. Thoth (or 'Hermes Trismegistus') was responsible for inventing writing and numbering or measurement. Adam had, of course, named all things and (in a pre-lapsarian state) may have also known all things as well. A full inventory would include countless other overlapping ancient claimants to the role of originators. Although the 7th Book of Pliny's *Natural History* is often held to be the oldest surviving catalogue of 'inventors'; Yates, *Art of Memory*, p. 43, notes that the so-called 'Parian Chronicle' a marble tablet of about 264 B.C. records legendary dates for the invention of the flute, the introduction of corn and even the 'publication of Orpheus' poetry.' But this tablet was not discovered until the seventeenth century. It still can be said that Pliny was the chief source for all the Renaissance inventories.

pagan seers were believed to have been granted foreknowledge of the Incarnation. Possibly they had also been granted a special secret key to all knowledge by the same divine dispensation. Veneration for the wisdom of the ancients was not incompatible with the advancement of learning, nor was imitation incompatible with inspiration. Efforts to think and do as the ancients did might well reflect the hope of experiencing a sudden illumination or of coming closer to the original source of a pure, clear, and certain knowledge that a long Gothic night had obscured.

When unprecedented innovations did occur, moreover, there was no sure way of recognizing them before the advent of printing. Who could ascertain precisely what was known – either to prior generations within a given region or to contemporary inhabitants of far-off lands? 'Steady advance,' as Sarton says, 'implies exact determination of every previous step.' In his view, printing made this determination 'incomparably easier.'[253] He may have understated the case. *Exact* determination must have been impossible before printing. Given drifting texts, migrating manuscripts, localized chronologies, multiform maps, there could be no systematic forward movement, no accumulation of stepping-stones enabling a new generation to begin where the prior one had left off. Progressive refinement of certain arts and skills could and did occur. But no sophisticated technique could be securely established, permanently recorded, and stored for subsequent retrieval. Before trying to account for an 'idea' of progress we might look more closely at the duplicating process that made possible not only a sequence of improved editions but also a continuous accumulation of fixed records. For it seems to have been permanence that introduced progressive change. The preservation of the old, in brief, launched a tradition of the new.

The advancement of learning had taken the form of a search for lost wisdom in the age of scribes. This search was rapidly propelled after printing. Ancient maps, charts, and texts once arranged and dated, however, turned out to be dated in more ways than one. Map-publishers turned out genuinely new and improved editions of atlases and star maps which showed that modern navigators and star gazers knew more things about the heavens and earth than did ancient sages. 'The simple sailors of today,' wrote Jacques Cartier in his *Brief Narration* of

[253] Sarton, 'The Quest for Truth,' p. 66.

1545, 'have learned the opposite of the philosophers by true experience.'[254] New improved editions of ancient texts also began to accumulate, uncovering more schools of ancient philosophy than had been dreamed of before. Scattered attacks on one authority by those who favored another provided ammunition for a wholesale assault on all received opinion.

Incompatible portions of inherited traditions could be sloughed off, partly because the task of preservation had become less urgent. Copying, memorizing, and transmitting absorbed fewer energies. Useful reference books were no longer blotted out or blurred with the passage of time. Cadence and rhyme, images and symbols ceased to fulfill their traditional function of preserving the collective memory. Technical information could be conveyed directly by plain words, unambiguous numbers, diagrams and maps. The aesthetic experience became increasingly autonomous and the function of works of art had to be redefined. Although books on the memory arts multiplied after printing, the need to rely on these arts decreased. Scribal systems, elaborated in print, ultimately petrified and are only now being reassembled, like fossil remains, by modern research. The special formulas that had preserved recipes and techniques among closed circles of initiates also disappeared. Residues of mnemonic devices were transmuted into mysterious images, rites, and incantations.[255]

Nevertheless, scribal veneration for ancient learning lingered on, long after the conditions that had fostered it had gone. Among Rosicrucians and Freemasons, for example, the belief persisted that the 'new philosophy' was in fact very old.[256] Descartes and Newton had merely retrieved the same magical key to nature's secrets that had once been known to ancient pyramid builders but was later withheld from the laity or deliberately obscured by a deceitful priesthood. In fact, the Index came only after printing, and the preservation of pagan learning owed much to monks and friars. Some enlightened freethinkers, however, assigned counter-Reformation institutions to the Gothic Dark

254 Cited by Haydn, *The Counter Renaissance*, p. 208.
255 According to Finegan, *Handbook of Biblical Chronology*, p. 57, the term 'Amen' encapsulated in the three Hebrew letters: Aleph, Mem, Nun (to which different numbers were assigned) a scheme for remembering four 91-day seasons of the solar year. When consulting works on this topic I find it difficult to decide whether the ingenuity of modern scholars or that of ancient ones is being displayed. This seems especially true of studies of how the pyramids or Stonehenge may have served astronomical purposes, but the perplexity extends to almost all modern theories pertaining to ancient schemes for preserving data.
256 Walker's *The Ancient Theology* contains several relevant essays on this phenomenon.

Ages and turned Zoroaster into a Copernican.[257] Similarly, once imitation was detached from inspiration, copying from composing, the classical revival became increasingly arid and academic. The search for primary sources which had once meant drinking from pure wellsprings came to be associated with dry-as-dust pedantry. But the reputation of ancient seers, bards, and prophets was not, by the same token, diminished. Claims to have inherited their magic mantle were put forth by new romanticists who re-oriented the meaning of the term 'original,' sought inspiration by dabbling in the occult, and tried to resurrect scribal arts in the age of print. Even the 'decay of nature' theme, once intimately associated with the erosion and corruption of scribal writings, would be reworked and re-oriented by gloomy modern prophets who envisaged a 'run-away technology' and felt regress, not progress, characterized their age.

6. AMPLIFICATION AND REINFORCEMENT: THE PERSISTENCE OF STEREOTYPES AND OF SOCIO-LINGUISTIC DIVISIONS

Many other themes embedded in scribal writings, detached from the living cultures that had shaped them, were propelled as 'typologies' on printed pages. Over the course of time, archetypes were converted into stereotypes, the language of giants, as Merton puts it, into the clichés of dwarfs. Both 'stereotype' and 'cliché' are terms deriving from typographical processes developed three-and-a-half centuries after Gutenberg. They point, however, to certain other features of typographical culture in general that deserve closer consideration. During the past five centuries, broadcasting new messages has also entailed amplifying and reinforcing old ones. I hope my use of these terms (amplify and reinforce) will not distract attention from the effects they are meant to designate. I am using them simply because I have found no others that serve as well. Some such terms are needed to cover the effects produced by an ever more frequent repetition of identical chapters and verses, anecdotes and aphorisms, drawn from very limited scribal sources. This repetition is not produced by the constant republication of classical, biblical, or early vernacular works, although it undoubtedly sustains markets for such works. It is produced by an

---

[257] See discussion below, pp. 283–4.

unwitting collaboration between countless authors of new books or articles. For five hundred years, authors have jointly transmitted certain old messages with augmented frequency even while separately reporting on new events or spinning out new ideas. Thus if they happen to contain only one passing reference to the heroic stand at Thermopylae, a hundred reports on different military campaigns will impress Herodotus' description on the mind of the reader who scans such reports with a hundredfold impact. Every dissimilar report of other campaigns will be received only once. As printed materials proliferate, this effect becomes more pronounced. (I have encountered several references to Thermopylae in the daily newspaper during the past year.) The same is true of numerous other messages previously inscribed on scarce and scattered manuscripts. The more wide-ranging the reader at present, the more frequent will be the encounter with the identical version and the deeper the impression it will leave. Since writers are particularly prone to wide-ranging reading, a multiplying 'feed-back' effect results. When it comes to coining familiar quotations, describing familiar episodes, originating symbols or stereotypes, the ancients (that is, those who went to press first) will generally outstrip the moderns. How many times has Tacitus' description of freedom-loving Teutons been repeated since a single manuscript of *Germania* was discovered in a fifteenth-century monastery? And in how many varying contexts – Anglo-Saxon, Frankish, as well as German – has this particular description appeared?

The frequency with which all messages were transmitted was primarily channeled by the fixing of literary linguistic frontiers. A particular kind of reinforcement was involved in relearning mother-tongues when learning to read. It went together with the progressive amplification of diversely oriented national 'memories.' Not all the same portions of an inherited Latin culture were translated into different vernaculars at the same time.[258] More important, entirely dissimilar dynastic, municipal, and ecclesiastical chronicles along with other local lore, both oral and scribal, were also set in type and more permanently fixed. The meshing of provincial medieval *res gestae* with diverse classical and scriptural sources had, by the early seventeenth century, embedded distinctively different stereotypes within each

---

[258] Bennett, *English Books and Readers 1475–1557*, p. 158, notes a 'striking difference' between the large number of 'pagan' classics translated into French in the sixteenth-century and the greater number of 'edifying' devotional works translated into English.

separate vernacular literature.[259] At the same time, to be sure, a more cosmopolitan *Respublica Litterarum* was also expanding, and messages were broadcast across linguistic frontiers, first via Latin, then also in French, to an international audience. An even more effective means of transcending language barriers was being developed by contributors to technical literature. Mathematical and pictorial statements conveyed identical messages to virtuosi and scientific correspondents in all lands without need for translation. Although Latin learned journals, a lively French-language press and scientific transactions did reach a sizable portion of the reading public by the eighteenth century, the diverse cosmopolitan literary cultures did not have the powers of amplification that the separate vernaculars had. Messages received in foreign languages from abroad only intermittently and occasionally reinforced the shared references that were learned in familiar tongues at home.[260]

On the other hand, the fixing of religious frontiers that cut across linguistic ones in the sixteenth century had a powerful effect on the frequency with which certain messages were transmitted. Passages drawn from vernacular translations of the Bible, for example, would be much more thinly and weakly distributed throughout the literary cultures of Catholic regions than of Protestant ones.[261] The abandonment of Church Latin in Protestant regions made it possible to mesh ecclesiastical and dynastic traditions more closely within Protestant realms than in Catholic ones – a point worth noting when considering how Church–State conflicts were resolved in different lands. Finally, the unevenly phased social penetration of literacy, the somewhat more random patterning of book-reading habits, the uneven distribution of

---

259 How this was done in sixteenth-century England is traced with remarkable clarity by Haller, *The Elect Nation, passim* – an exceptional work that integrates printing with other historical developments. Children's books about Elizabeth I are still being written from bits and pieces drawn from Foxe's massive apologia.

260 The most important exceptions are France and Geneva, where by the mid-seventeenth century two differently-oriented native literary cultures coincided with a single cosmopolitan one. A sounding board was thus provided for Rousseau, Mme de Staël, Sismondi and other Genevans who might otherwise have been as obscure as their German, Swiss or Dutch counterparts. The reasons for the conquest of the Gallic tongue (which paradoxically linked the most populous and powerful consolidated dynastic Catholic state with the tiny canton that had served as the Protestant Rome and with the cosmopolitan culture of civilized Europe) deserve further study. Réau, *L'Europe Française au Siècle des Lumières*, although devoted to this important topic, slides over issues that need more rigorous analysis. Pottinger, *The French Book Trade*, offers some useful statistics, pp. 19–23. See also Steinberg, *Five Hundred Years*, p. 118. Some further consequences of the spread of French are touched on below. See p. 145.

261 The contrast between the deep penetration of vernacular scriptural versions into the literary culture of Scandinavian, Dutch, German, and English-speaking peoples and the shallow effect of Spanish, Italian and French Bible translations is discussed below, pp. 351–2.

costly new books and cheap reprints of old ones among different social sectors also affected the frequency with which diverse messages were received within each linguistic group.

From a hearing public to a reading public: some unevenly phased social and psychological changes

These last remarks are relevant to most of the issues that have been raised by Marshall McLuhan in connection with the 'making of typographical man.' By making us more aware that both mind and society were affected by printing, McLuhan has performed, in my view at least, a most valuable service. But he has also glossed over multiple interactions that occurred under widely varying circumstances in a way that may discourage rather than encourage further study. 'The print-made split between heart and head is the trauma that affects Europe from Machiavelli to the present.'[262] Since this sort of statement cannot be tested, it provides little incentive for further research. Granted that the replacement of discourse by silent scanning, of face-to-face contacts by more impersonal interactions probably did have important consequences: it follows that we need to think, less metaphorically and abstractly, more historically and concretely about the sort of effects that were entailed and how different groups were affected. Even at first glance, both issues appear to be very complex.

In many cases, for example, spoken words would be conveyed by printed messages without being replaced by them. While often transposed into print, sermons and public orations thus continued to be delivered orally. These traditional forms of discourse were nonetheless altered by the new possibility of silent publication. The printing of parliamentary debates probably affected exchanges between members of parliament. The printing of poems, plays, and songs altered the way 'lines' were recited, sung, and composed. Academic dialogues were conducted along different lines after the advent of the 'closet philosopher.' On the one hand, some 'dying speeches' were fabricated for printing and never did get delivered; on the other, printed publicity enabled evangelists and demagogues to practice traditional arts outdoors before large hearing publics. A literary culture created by typography was conveyed to the ear not the eye by classroom lectures,

---

[262] McLuhan, *Gutenberg Galaxy*, p. 170.

repertory companies, and poetry readings. Beyond the age of Dickens and even that of Dylan Thomas, print continues to propel authors away from their desks and onto the podium. No simple formula will cover the changes these new activities reflect.

The same is true of how different groups were affected. Most rural villagers, for example, probably belonged to an exclusively hearing public down to the nineteenth century. Yet what they heard had, in many instances, been transformed by printing two centuries earlier. For the storyteller was replaced by the exceptional literate villager who read out loud from a stack of cheap books and ballad sheets turned out anonymously for distribution by peddlers.[263] A fairly sleazy 'popular' culture, based on the mass production of antiquated vernacular medieval romances, was thus produced well before the steam press and mass literacy movements of the nineteenth century. Yet the bulk of this output was consumed by a medieval hearing public, separated by a vast psychological gulf from their contemporaries who belonged to an early-modern reading one.[264]

The disjunction between the new mode of production and older modes of consumption is only one of many complications that need further study. Members of the same reading public, who confronted the same innovation in the same region at the same time, were nonetheless affected by it in markedly different ways. Trends pointing to modernism and to fundamentalism, for example, were both launched by Bible-printing – as later discussion suggests. Pornography as well as piety assumed new forms. Book reading did not stop short with guides to godly living or practical manuals and texts, any more than printers stopped short at producing them. The same silence, solitude, and contemplative attitudes associated formerly with pure spiritual devotion also accompanied the perusal of scandal sheets, 'lewd Ballads', 'merry bookes of Italie', and other 'corrupted tales in Inke and Paper'.[265] Not a desire to withdraw from a worldly society or the city

---

263 Robert Mandrou, *De la Culture Populaire aux 17e et 18e Siècles: La Bibliothèque Bleue de Troyes*, *passim* and Natalie Z. Davis, 'Printing and the People,' illustrate this topic in detail for early modern France. Bennett's three volumes and Altick's first chapter touch on it, in scattered passages, for England. There is a much larger literature on developments in all regions from the eighteenth century on.

264 This gulf may be found even within some printers' workshops during the sixteenth century, separating some journeymen typographers from master printers. See Natalie Z. Davis, 'The Protestant Printing Workers of Lyons in 1551,' pp. 252–3, 256–7. The illiterate journeymen, however, sang psalms composed by Marot and Beza which were written for the press and circulated in printed form.   265 Cited by Wright, *Middle Class Culture*, pp. 232–3.

of man but a gregarious curiosity about them could be satisfied by silent perusal of eighteenth-century journals, gazettes, or newsletters. Increasingly the well-informed man of affairs had to spend part of each day in temporary isolation from his fellow men.

As communion with the Sunday paper has replaced church-going, there is a tendency to forget that sermons had at one time been coupled with news about local and foreign affairs, real estate transactions, and other mundane matters. After printing, however, news gathering and circulation were handled more efficiently under lay auspices. Such considerations might be noted when thinking about the 'secularization' or 'desacralization' of Western Christendom. For in all regions (to go beyond the eighteenth century for a moment) the pulpit was ultimately displaced by the periodical press and the dictum 'nothing sacred' came to characterize the journalist's career. Pitted against 'the furious itch of novelty' and the 'general thirst after news,'[266] efforts by Catholic moralists and Protestant evangelicals, even Sunday Schools and other Sabbatarian measures[267] proved of little avail. The monthly gazette was succeeded by the weekly and finally by the daily paper. More and more provincial newspapers were founded.[268] By the last century, gossiping churchgoers could often learn about local affairs by scanning columns of newsprint in silence at home.

The displacement of pulpit by press is significant not only in connection with secularization but also because it points to an explanation for the weakening of local community ties.

The actual reality, the tangible quality of community life in earlier towns or villages...is puzzling...and only too susceptible to sentimentalisation. People seem to want to believe that there was a time when every one belonged to an active, supportive local society, providing a palpable framework for everyday life. But we find that the phenomenon itself and its passing – if that is what, in fact happened – perpetually elude our grasp.[269]

Perhaps this phenomenon might become somewhat less elusive if the relationship between communications systems and community struc-

---

[266] Citations from the British *Mercury* of 1712 and Addison in Preserved Smith, *The Enlightenment 1687-1776*, p. 284.

[267] See Altick, *English Common Reader*, p. 128.

[268] The thirty-odd provincial newspapers established by 1760 in England are discussed by Wiles, *Freshest Advices, passim*. See also references and discussion by Plumb, 'The Public, Literature and the Arts in the 18th Century,' pp. 22–4. The French provincial press, which developed somewhat later is covered by Trénard, 'La Presse Française,' pp. 323–402.

[269] Laslett, 'Philippe Ariès and "La Famille,"' p. 83.

tures was more carefully explored. To hear an address delivered, people have to come together; to read a printed report encourages individuals to draw apart. 'What the orators of Rome and Athens were in the midst of a people *assembled*,' said Malesherbes in an address of 1775, 'men of letters are in the midst of a *dispersed* people.'[270] His observation suggests how the shift in communications may have changed the sense of what it meant to participate in public affairs. The wide distribution of identical bits of information provided an impersonal link between people who were unknown to each other.

By its very nature, a reading public was not only more dispersed; it was also more atomistic and individualistic than a hearing one. Insofar as a traditional sense of community entailed frequent gathering together to receive a given message, this sense was probably weakened by the duplication of identical messages which brought the solitary reader to the fore. To be sure, bookshops, coffee houses, reading rooms provided new kinds of communal gathering places. Yet subscription lists and corresponding societies represented relatively impersonal group-formations while the reception of printed messages in any place still required temporary isolation – just as it does in a library reading room even now. The notion that society may be regarded as a bundle of discrete units or that the individual is prior to the social group seems to be more compatible with a reading public than with a hearing one. The nature of man as a political animal was less likely to conform to classical models after tribunes of the people were transmuted from orators in public squares to editors of news-sheets and gazettes.

But even while communal solidarity was diminished, vicarious participation in more distant events was also enhanced; and even while local ties were loosened, links to larger collective units were being forged. Printed materials encouraged silent adherence to causes whose advocates could not be found in any one parish and who addressed an invisible public from afar. New forms of group identity began to compete with an older, more localized nexus of loyalties.

Propaganda wars developed, exacerbating traditional friction between crown and estates, court and country, church and state, laying the basis for the formation of political parties as distinct from the mere 'factions' of an earlier age. During the first two centuries after Gutenberg, beginning with the crusade against the Turks, religious warfare

[270] Cited by Arthur Wilson, *Diderot: the Testing Years*, p. 162. [Italics mine.]

took top billing. But 'martyrs' and 'massacres' were eventually secularized, along with the word 'propaganda' itself.[271] Riots, rebellions and seditions acquired more threatening dimensions when boosted by partisan presses.[272] (By the nineteenth century, when Paris sneezed, all Europe would be said to catch cold.) But urban populations were not only pulled apart, they were also linked in new ways by the more impersonal channels of communication. Personal attendance was increasingly supplemented by vicarious participation in civic functions and municipal affairs. Beginning perhaps with the early broadsides and cheap versions of the magnificent prints which commemorated civic ceremonies, such as royal entries, even public festivals could be experienced by some stay-at-homes. The elaborate symbols and visual effects employed at these civic ceremonies reveal the exposure of their designers to printed literature and book illustration.[273] Peaceful forms of urban social action, such as the exchange of goods and services, real estate transactions, the provision of charity, also were increasingly to be affected by the advent of a silent, impersonal medium of interchange.[274]

Private life as well as public affairs underwent transformation; indeed the new medium encouraged a sharper division between these two zones. An unending stream of moralizing literature penetrated the privacy of the home and helped to precipitate a variety of domestic dramas. The 'family' was not only endowed with new educational and religious functions, especially in regions where the laity was trusted with printed Bibles and catechisms; but the family circle also became the target of a complicated literary cross-fire. As book markets ex-

[271] See Kelley, 'Martyrs, Myth and the Massacre.' The four-hundredth anniversary of Saint Bartholomew's Eve has precipitated a large output of relevant studies. See e.g. essays in Soman, ed. *The Massacre*.

[272] How chronic problems presented by riots and seditions were affected by printing – well before the age of John Wilkes – needs to be investigated. A vast literature on subversive pamphlet warfare – such as that entailed in the 'Mazarinades' – generally stops short of relating press output to either the uprisings or government handling of them.

[273] Peter Burke's review, 'Fanfare for Princes,' of the magnificent 4 vol. facsimile series: *Renaissance Triumphs*, ed. Margaret McGowan, devoted to festivals celebrating the entry of princes into sixteenth-century cities, raises intriguing questions about the purpose of the ceremonies and the limited circulation of official accounts. The duplication of costly woodcuts in cheaper versions and the importance of prints in structuring these ceremonies also merits further consideration.

[274] The beginning of this process in seventeenth-century Paris is described in a recent study of projects launched by Théophraste Renaudot: the so-called 'father of French journalism' working under Richelieu's patronage: Solomon, *Public Welfare*. How print helped to standardize poor-law reforms in sixteenth-century German cities is suggested by Cole, 'The Dynamics of Printing,' pp. 101–3.

panded and divisions of labor increased, feminine readers were increasingly differentiated from masculine ones, and children were supplied with reading matter different from their parents'. Previous overlapping amorphous categories assigned to different 'ages of man' were replaced by chronologically numbered age-grades.[275] Newly segregated at schools, receiving special printed materials geared to distinct stages of learning, separate 'peer groups' ultimately emerged. A distinctive 'youth culture' that was somewhat incongruous with the 'family' came into being. So, too, did a distinctive feminist movement. The rise of a specifically feminine reading public represents an aspect of the age-old battle between the sexes that has yet to be fully explored. Such developments, however, did not really crystallize until the last century, after both typography and schooling underwent new transformations.

Public life was nonetheless profoundly transformed from the sixteenth to the eighteenth centuries, as many historical studies suggest. With a few notable exceptions, these studies make little room for the advent of printing. It must have affected traditional governing groups in many ways. The printing of emblems of heraldry and orders of chivalry, for example, probably encouraged class consciousness among hereditary nobles and helped to codify notions about rank, priority, and degree.[276] One may learn from Mark Curtis how 'drastic changes introduced by printing' affected undergraduate studies at Oxford and Cambridge and how 'well born successors to medieval clerks' profited thereby.[277] Unfortunately this approach seems to be exceptional. The effect produced by printing on medieval curricula and academic institutions usually has to be inferred by reading between lines. The same thing is true of works devoted to other pertinent topics such as the

---

[275] On the question of domestic guides, the 'family' and the 'child,' see discussion in chap. 4, below, pp. 427ff. There is a large and growing literature on learned ladies and women authors, but somewhat less attention is given to the formation of a special feminine reading public. P. J. Miller, 'Eighteenth Century Periodicals for Women,' pp. 279 ff points to a relatively early proliferation of printed materials aimed specifically at this special market. For eighteenth-century France, the 'débuts de la presse féminine' are discussed by Trénard, 'La Presse Française,' pp. 315–19.

[276] See reference to Caxton's Ordeyne de Chevalrie and other early books on heraldry in Jacob, Fifteenth Century, p. 665. On the very different form taken by the art of heraldry before printing, see Denholm-Young, History and Heraldry 1254–1310. The hardening of the concept of 'degree' is treated by Altick, English Common Reader p. 31. The printing of the Almanach de Gotha down to the present has helped to perpetuate hereditary aristocracies in Europe despite their legal non-existence.

[277] Curtis, Oxford and Cambridge, pp. 89–111.

appearance of the 'articulate citizen in Elizabethan England,'[278] the greater impersonality of political discourse in seventeenth-century France,[279] or the growth of 'Leviathan States,' swarming with officials and bureaucrats, everywhere in *ancien régime* Europe.

Even while taking note of the extended powers conferred on an impersonal officialdom, one should also make room for the heightened visibility assigned to the features and activities of individual rulers, with the circulation of broadsides and engravings.[280] Both of the 'king's two bodies' – the royal office and the royal person – were more sharply defined for subjects by the output of printed materials. The effect of duplicating images and portraits of rulers – which were eventually framed and hung in peasant hovels throughout Catholic Europe along with saints and icons – has yet to be assessed by political scientists. The *mass* following of a single leader and the nation-wide extension of his charismatic appeal, at all events, are possible by-products of the new communications system which ought to be further explored. How early-modern rulers deliberately set out to exploit the new presses has, at long last, begun to attract attention. As a recent monograph on the age of Louis XIV suggests:

Princes who had employed the cumbersome methods of manuscript to communicate with their subjects switched quickly to print to announce declarations of war, publish battle accounts, promulgate treaties or argue disputed points in pamphlet form. Theirs was an effort...'to win the psychological war which prepared and accompanied the military operations' of rulers...The root idea was to evoke the notion of the *patrie* as the realm of France and to represent the king as the personification of this *patrie*. In similar fashion the English crown under Henry VIII and Thomas Cromwell made systematic use of both Parliament and press to win public support for the Reformation...

In France the regency of Louis XIII saw the last meeting of the Estates General before 1789; it also saw the founding of the first royally sponsored newspaper in Europe. The replacement of the volatile assembly by the controlled weekly *Gazette* is a concurrence symptomatic of the importance Cardinal Richelieu attached to print in his state-building objectives.[281]

---

[278] Arthur B. Ferguson, *The Articulate Citizen*, passim.
[279] Rothkrug, *Opposition to Louis XIV*, pp. 458–9.
[280] Heightened visibility is indicated in the recognition of Louis XVI from an assignat, noted above, p. 85.
[281] Klaits, *Printed Propaganda*, pp. 6–7. The citation in this passage comes from the useful study by Seguin, *L'Information en France de Louis XII à Henri II* and the reference to Thomas Cromwell's propaganda machine is drawn from Elton, *Policy and Police*, chap. 4. Some effects of the new publicity on royal activities in France are also noted by Martin, *Livre à Paris*, I, 258 ff.

On the related and equally significant problem of the conduct of early-modern warfare, recent studies by John Hale point to some of the effects of printing both on military strategy and on the training of an officer class.[282] But, of course, much remains to be done on both military and political fronts.

How access to printed materials affected attitudes towards estates of the realm, the cultivation of landed estates, the collection of seigneurial dues, the conduct of courtiers, the strategies of councillors, diplomatic and fiscal policies, even the aspirations of would-be gentlemen – also could be usefully explored. Recently some historians have begun to abandon, as fruitless, older debates about the 'rise' of a new class to political power in early-modern times. They seek to focus attention instead on the re-education and re-groupment of older governing élites – and have, thereby, precipitated new debates.[283] Both lines of inquiry might be reconciled and fruitfully pursued if the consequences of printing received more attention.

The republic of letters and the printed book-trade

In addition to the re-groupment of old élites and enhanced political consciousness among literate commoners, social historians might also take into consideration the formation of new groups engaged in the production and distribution of printed materials. For all the attention devoted to 'alienated intellectuals' in Tudor and Stuart England or to the 'desertion of intellectuals' in Bourbon France, very little has been written about the rise of intellectuals as a distinctive social class.[284] The distance which separated the most eminent culture-heroes, such as Erasmus and Voltaire, from the unknown grub-street hack remains to be assessed. The early-modern Grub Street itself awaits its historian. A series of fascinating studies by Robert Darnton has illuminated the 'low-life of literature' in eighteenth-century France and the strategic role played by frustrated literary careerists in translating Enlightenment doctrines into radical political action. Glimpses of a distinctive sub-

---

282 See e.g. John Hale, 'War and Public Opinion,' 18-36. Hale notes the increasing importance of mastering a 'copious flow of books on weaponry and strategy' (pp. 20-2) among military leaders.

283 See e.g. Hexter, *Reappraisals in History*, chap. 4; Stone, *The Crisis of the Aristocracy 1558-1641*, p. 673; Ford, *Robe and Sword*, and further discussion, pp. 395 ff, below.

284 Curtis, 'The Alienated Intellectuals of Early Stuart England,' 25-41. Brinton, *The Anatomy of Revolution*.

culture associated with literary hackwork are offered in scattered studies devoted to early sixteenth-century Venice and Elizabethan London;[285] but the full picture, which would provide a needed perspective on French eighteenth-century developments, has not yet been sketched. The same point applies to the development of a profitable clandestine book-trade and black markets for forbidden books. Again glimpses of this phenomenon can be obtained from studies of assorted topics – ranging from the smuggling of vernacular Bibles in the early sixteenth century to Galileo's evasion of the officials who placed him under house arrest. But the full dimensions of the topic remain, like those of a gigantic iceberg, submerged.[286] Only the tip is visible – largely defined by debates on the significance of inflammatory literature in pre-revolutionary France. Beginning with the remarkably versatile occupational groups associated with the early printed book trade and ending, perhaps, with the staffs of the journals who took over the government of France in 1848, the story of the rise of a 'fourth estate' also remains to be told.

Largely because the growing power of the press as an independent force in early-modern Europe is concealed, men of letters tend to be regarded as spokesmen for the interests of all classes save their own. The values which were common to members of the Commonwealth of Learning and the institutions which were peculiar to the Republic of Letters still remain undefined.[287] It is clear enough that 'News from

[285] On Darnton's studies, see above n. 71. Paul Grendler's *Critics of the Italian World*, chap. 1 describes the emergence of a Venetian Grub Street in the wake of Aretino's success. Edwin H. Miller, *The Professional Writer in Elizabethan England*, is one of many studies on the Elizabethan phenomenon.

[286] On the complex problem of defining the literary 'underground' for the early modern era, see chap. 3, n. 333 below.

[287] The very concept of a 'Republic of Letters' has received inadequate attention. As a late seventeenth-century institution it has been well described by Barnes, *Jean Le Clerc et la République des Lettres*, pp. 14–15. A somewhat earlier seventeenth-century phase associated with Grotius' *Respublica Literaria Christiana* has been discerned by Dibon, "L'Université de Leyde et la République des Lettres au 17e Siècle,' pp. 25–32. On the origin of the term Dibon says only that 'it is in dispute'. The earliest reference I have tracked down is associated with the idea of a 'rinascita' and the recovery of ancient texts. It comes from a letter of July 6, 1417 written by the Venetian humanist, Francesco Barbaro (1398–1454) to Poggio extravagantly congratulating the latter for restoring the lost literature of antiquity. Phyllis W. G. Gordan (ed.), *Two Renaissance Book Hunters*, appendix: letter IV, p. 199. From there it can be traced through Valla's much published *Elegantiae* to Erasmus, Lefèvre d'Etaples, Vadianus, Beatus Rhenanus, et al. A reference to the 'Republic' crops up in John Dee's letter to Cecil about Trithemius' secret ciphers and in the dedication of Dee's *Monas Hieroglyphica* (Antwerp, 1564) (see references to Bailey and Josten above, n. 167 and n. 168). Dee was writing from the Antwerp shop of his printer, Sylvius, who had ties with Plantin and other Netherlands printers. His reference thus links up with the early seventeenth-century Leiden phase described by Dibon.

the Republic of Letters' as edited by Pierre Bayle came from Rotterdam. Rotterdam also provided 'the only patron Bayle needed,' namely Reiner Leers, his publisher. Leers 'in turn relied on the relative freedom enjoyed by Dutch printers and on the existence of a sufficiently large international reading public' for support.[288] It is also clear that the language of the inhabitants of the literary Republic had shifted in the course of the seventeenth century from Latin to French.[289] Its central city in the eighteenth century was neither Paris nor Rotterdam, however. According to most authorities, it was Amsterdam[290] – which had earlier provided Europeans with their first newspapers, and which continued until the eve of the French Revolution to service newspaper readers in France.[291]

But a margin for uncertainty has to be left when one pinpoints the headquarters or designates the frontiers of this 'Republic' on real maps. It remained, from the beginning, a somewhat elusive, often deliberately mysterious, domain. Its inhabitants rarely used their proper names – preferring more elegant Latinate or Greek versions, when not deliberately concealing their identity behind vernacular pseudonyms or complete anonymity.[292] Even the colophons of the printers they relied on often reflected a desire not to attract potential customers to bookshops (as was the usual purpose of early colophons), but to distract officials and avoid fines or arrest. Products issued from 'Utopia' and 'Cosmopolis' helped to publicize these novel terms,[293] but also

288 Haley, *The Dutch in the Seventeenth Century*, p. 173. See also references in chap. 4, n. 394 below.

289 Since this is not true of the audience addressed by Leibniz's *Acta Eruditorum* or Newton's Latin versions of the *Principia*, it may be desirable to distinguish between a learned cosmopolitan Latin-reading 'Commonwealth of Learning' and the more 'worldly' cosmopolitan French-reading 'Republic of Letters.' The persistence of Latin as a means of transmitting significant scholarly and scientific findings is too often forgotten. The difference between the French review (perhaps by John Locke) of Newton's *Principia* in Jean Le Clerc's *Bibliographie Universelle* and the Latin one (by Leibniz) in the *Acta Eruditorum* (chap. 8, n. 6, volume II below) shows that Latin was by no means a vehicle only for Catholic churchmen and old-fashioned pedants – as is sometimes suggested – but that it was still used for communication among innovative mathematical scientists in Newton's day.

290 Febvre and Martin, *L'Apparition*, p. 298.

291 Dahl, *Dutch Corantos 1618–1658 A Bibliography*, p. 23; Trénard, "La Presse Française,' p. 295; Yardeni, 'Journalisme et Histoire Contemporaine à l'Epoque de Bayle.'

292 An early defense of using a Latinized name is offered by the Swiss humanist, 'Vadianus' (Joachim von Watt). The custom goes back at least to the literary coterie formed by Lorenzo Valla's successor as professor of literature in Rome namely 'Laetus' (Giulio Pomponio Leto). Archer Taylor and Frederick Mosher, *The Bibliographical History*, pp. 18–19. The diverse strategies used in seventeenth-century France to deceive censors are succinctly described by Delof, 'Comment déjouait-on la Censure en France au XVIIe Siècle?'.

293 See invented accommodation addresses mentioned by Steinberg, *Five Hundred Years*, pp. 264–5, and by Kronenberg, 'Forged Addresses.' As early as 1516, Kronenberg notes (p. 82) 'Utopia' was used as an accommodation address by a Leiden printer to mask an Erasmian satire.

added to the sense of unreality and impracticality associated with the circulation of ideas. Yet those who took advantage of the new careers opened to the talents of skillful writers were not disembodied spirits who must be materialized to be believed. They were, rather, complex flesh-and-blood human beings. (Some forty-odd volumes were required to cover the lives of the more celebrated inhabitants of the 'Republic of Letters' by the mid-eighteenth century.)[294] Moreover, real foundries, workshops and offices were built to serve the needs of this presumably fictitious realm; real profits were made by tapping the talents which gravitated to it.[295]

A mixture of shrewd practicality with a seemingly idealistic preference for places such as 'Cosmopolis' and 'Utopia' (not to mention Eleuthera and Philadelphia) was exhibited by many early leaders of the expanding printing industries. Paradoxically enough, the same presses which fanned the flames of religious controversy also created a new vested interest in ecumenical concord and toleration; the same wholesale industry which fixed religious, dynastic, and linguistic frontiers more permanently also operated most profitably by tapping cosmopolitan markets. Paradoxically also, the same firms made significant contributions to Christian learning by receiving infidel Jews and Arabs, schismatic Greeks and a vast variety of dissident foreigners into their shops and homes. Circles associated with the firms of Daniel Bomberg or Aldus Manutius in Venice; with the Amerbachs or Oporinus in Basel; with Plantin in Antwerp or the Wechels in Frankfurt point to formation of 'polyglot' households in scattered urban centers throughout the continent. In the age of the religious wars, such print shops represented miniature 'international houses'. They provided wandering scholars with a meeting place, message center, sanctuary and cul-

'Juan Philadelpho of Venice' was a favorite pseudonym of Jean Crespin of Geneva as noted in The Cambridge History of the Bible III, 126. Grendler, Critics of the Italian World, p. 33 describes Ortensio Lando's use of 'Utopia' for diverse pseudonyms. Bennett, Books and Readers 1475–1557, p. 210, provides an amusing early English example: 'Printed in Jerico in the land of Promes by Thome Truth' (London, 1542). During the first centuries after Gutenberg, a considerable amount of illicit literature (both pornographic and political) was circulated in manuscript form. See Bühler, Fifteenth Century Book, pp. 30–1. This tradition persisted in eighteenth-century France as shown by Wade, The Clandestine Organization. It persists (with the typewriter and mimeographing machine often replacing the scribe) even now. Fascinating though it is, the circulation of hand-copied political lampoons or scatological verse should not distract attention from the more massive effect of an organized underground trade in printed books.   [294] Niceron, Mémoires.

[295] The large profits made from printing and reprinting the Grande Encyclopédie alone are described in Darnton's article, 'The Encyclopédie Wars.'

tural center all in one. The new industry encouraged not only the formation of syndicates and far-flung trade networks, similar to those extended by merchants engaged in the cloth trade or in other large-scale enterprises during early-modern times. It also encouraged the formation of an ethos which was specifically associated with the Commonwealth of Learning – ecumenical and tolerant without being secular, genuinely pious yet opposed to fanaticism, often combining outward conformity to diverse established churches with inner fidelity to heterodox creeds.

A later chapter will offer a closer look at this development, and at some varied factors which contributed to the formation of the new ethos.[296] Here let me just underline the need to distinguish between the ecumenical ideology associated with the printed book-trade in general and the more sectarian secret societies and heterodox sects to which certain master printers belonged. By now it is well documented that there were a few influential publishers and booksellers who used their shops as headquarters for undercover activities while carrying on normal business operations at the same time.[297] As a result of this kind of double dealing, one can never be sure whether one is extending the influence of a given secret society unwisely by confusing it with the normal operations of a large international book firm or, conversely, whether one is drastically underestimating the powerful levers of influence exerted by a seemingly small and obscure secret group.

Printers and publishers were frequently centres for obscure religious movements in those days. We know that the great Antwerp printer Christopher Plantin was secretly a member of the Family of Love...The printer Wechel at Frankfurt had been resorted to by Philip Sidney and his friends after the Massacre of St. Bartholomew in 1572. Another Frankfurt printer, also called Wechel, had harbored Giordano Bruno[298]...Through his long family

---

[296] See pp. 443 ff below. Notes 463-73 point to relevant studies, bearing on discussion in text.

[297] There are some intriguing points of overlap between different firms and printing centers which point to a certain continuity over the course of centuries. To take but two examples: the Bomberg firm links an early sixteenth-century Venetian press with Plantin in Antwerp later on, See chap. 4, n. 468 below. The Basson firm in Leiden served both Familists and Rosicrucians, as shown by Jan van Dorsten, 'Garter Knights.' See also van Dorsten's *Thomas Basson*. Govert Basson also printed for Louis Elsevier (according to Dibon, 'L'Université,' p. 19).

[298] Sidney's host was Johann Wechel; Bruno's was Andreas Wechel, a Huguenot who had continued his father Chrétien's work as a learned Parisian printer until the Massacre led to his emigration to Frankfurt. He thus escaped the fate of his friend, Peter Ramus, whose memory he perpetuated by printing some 180 editions of Ramus' separate works. The relation of Johann to Andreas is uncertain. Possibly they were uncle and nephew. In 1591 Johann issued

association with printing in Frankfurt it is likely that Johann Theodore De Bry would have had knowledge of deep European currents of thought moving and mingling in that great international centre of the book trade....

All the secret movements of the late sixteenth century might have had a secret sympathy with the movements around the Elector Palatine. We know that the Family of Love was a secret society...which allowed its members to belong ostensibly to any religious denomination whilst secretly maintaining their affiliation with the Family. These attitudes of the Family... have something in common with Freemasonry. We know that secret membership of the Family was widespread among printers...the De Bry family of printers, who had connections with the Plantin firm might have been Familists...the movement of this firm into Palatine territory where it published...works...in the 'Rosicrucian' interest might have been because of secret sympathy with movements in the Palatinate.[299]

In these passages from an otherwise most illuminating study, dissimulation and secrecy have been exploited, incautiously, as the common denominator of diverse groups and activities. Events in the Palatinate are linked up with the operations of large printing centers on the one hand and to all clandestine activities on the other. Insofar as the Familists observed officially sanctioned religious practices while secretly remaining faithful to their own brethren, they were practicing a form of dissimulation which was common, not only among many other sixteenth-century 'Nicodemite' sects[300] but also among many 'crypto-Christians' or 'conversos' of Spanish–Jewish origin as well as many later Huguenots who chose to remain in Bourbon France. To note that all these groups had 'something in common with Freemasonry' does not take us very far – or, rather, carries us much too far by extending masonry in an awesome and indefinite manner. To speculate that 'all the secret movements of the late sixteenth century might have had a secret sympathy with the movements around the Elector Palatine' seems equally unwise. 'All the secret movements' takes us even beyond religious dissimulation to encompass any number of undercover agents and spies, and to embrace also all the varied

reprints of Dee's *Monas Hieroglyphica* and of the last published writings of Giordano Bruno; the previous year, he printed the first volumes of the de Bry narrative accounts of the American continent. See authoritative monograph by Evans, 'The Wechel Presses: Humanism and Calvinism in Central Europe 1572–1627,' pp. 3–4, 12, 17.

299 Yates, *The Rosicrucian Enlightenment*, pp. 73; 216. See also p. 219 for explicit use of 'theme of secrecy' to link Renaissance occult currents with early modern science.

300 A recent study of Nicodemite movement traces it back to the ex-Carthusian and celebrated Strasbourg herbalist of the early sixteenth century: Otto Brunfels. Ginzburg, *Il Nicodemismo: Simulazione e Dissimulazione religiosa nell' Europa del '500.*

subterranean activities which are labelled by the ambiguous term 'underground.' In particular, given the involvement of major printing centers in Antwerp and Frankfurt, this speculation extends the repercussions of one short-lived and localized political episode to encompass the vast territory covered by a far-flung clandestine book-trade.

The need to evade censors and to engage in clandestine activities was so common that it characterized many 'normal' large-scale book-trade ventures in early-modern Europe. As a result, definite lines between overt and covert operations are peculiarly difficult to draw. Much activity occurs in that twilight zone described by such ambiguous terms as 'semi-legal,' 'semi-secret' or *permission tacite*.' Even in England after the Glorious Revolution, freethinkers with republican leanings could not rely on a completely 'free' press:

> The charge that freethinkers formed a cabal or a party occurs consistently in their opponents' literature. The historian is tempted to dismiss it entirely as ...official paranoia but that would be unwise. Sufficient evidence exists, most of it unpublished, that many of the freethinkers knew one another, socialized together, engineered literary projects...John Toland belonged to a secret society...as early as the 1690s which can best be described, for lack of a better term as an early Masonic lodge. Freethinkers...did on many occasions resort to secrecy. In a society where prosecution for disagreeable publications was still very possible we should hardly be surprised that they preferred a private and even secret life-style.[301]

Fear of prosecution for disagreeable publications, however, did not deter Toland and his circle from resort to printed publicity. Toland himself is probably best described as a 'publicist'. Whether editing (and altering) the works of English commonwealthmen, seeking patronage from Whig aristocrats, consorting with grub-street hacks, or working for the continental Dutch-centered French-language press, he was never far from one print shop or another.[302] Only recently has it become clear that his 'secret life-style' included significant surrepti-

---

[301] Margaret C. Jacob, *The Newtonians*, chap. 6, esp. pp. 206–7; 217–31. Jacob notes that discussion of Giordano Bruno's work was featured in Toland's secret group. In view of Bruno's views and Toland's *Pantheisticon*, she believes Toland is better described as a 'pantheistic materialist' than (as is common) as a deist (p. 227). The strong influence of Bruno and the Hermetic Tradition on Toland's *Letters to Serena* is also stressed (p. 234) in a manner which supports Frances Yates' earlier speculations about Bruno as a precursor of later Freemasonry.

[302] In addition to references cited by Jacob, p. 210, n. 29, see also Venturi, *Utopia and Reform*, pp. 48–68. Toland's skill as a committed republican in doctoring the writings of Sidney, Ludlow, Milton, Nevile, Harrington and thus contributing to the tradition of the Commonwealthman is brought out by Worden, 'Edmund Ludlow,' pp. 15–16.

tious ties with the cosmopolitan book-trade network via a group called the 'Knights of the Jubilation' who met at the Hague in 1710 and whose members were prominent in that part of the Dutch publishing trade which was run by French Huguenots.[303] The secretary of this group, Prosper Marchand, was a publisher–bookseller who wrote an early history of printing and helped to edit and issue the 1720 edition of Bayle's *Dictionnaire*.[304] Another noteworthy member was the celebrated engraver, Bernard Picart, whose frontispiece for Marchand's edition of Bayle's *Dictionnaire* has given rise to speculation concerning a special 'Minerval' branch of masonry. The figure of Minerva, often in conjunction with Mercury and other special symbols, occurs repeatedly in frontispieces of works favored by freethinkers of a certain kind.[305] Minerva, we recall, was also singled out for special honor as patron of the printing trades. Picart was such a fine engraver that his services were much in demand and his prints were widely copied.[306] Here is another instance of a phenomenon one encounters over and over again. The involvement of an engraver, like that of a printer, in a given secret society leads to an indefinite extension of the influence of that society; for engravings, like printed books, travelled far and wide.

[303] In addition to chap. 6 in her book on *The Newtonians*, Jacob's forthcoming article, 'Clandestine Culture in the Early Enlightenment,' soon to appear in a Festschrift to Henry Guerlac, contains new data on the 'Knights' which she found in unpublished papers in London and Leiden, while tracking down Toland's movements.

[304] Berkvens-Stevelinck, 'Prosper Marchand, Auteur et Editeur,' gives relevant data, mentioning Marchand's *L'Histoire de L'Origine et du Premier Progrès de L'Imprimerie* (The Hague, 1740).

[305] Schlegel, 'Freemasonry and the Encyclopédie Reconsidered.' The frontispiece of the *Encyclopédie* was designed by Charles-Nicolas Cochin, who was probably a mason. The printing trade also crops up in other connections in the debate over masonic influence on *L'Encyclopédie*. One of its four bookseller–publishers: Laurent Durand designed emblems for its title page which Schlegel deems masonic. Another André François Le Breton (who was chiefly responsible for financing and supervising the work), is the subject of a prolonged argument over whether he was or was not the same Le Breton who appears on a list of members of a French lodge. For a sceptical review of the literature, see Shackleton, 'The Encyclopédie and Freemasonry.' For recent review article on Le Breton, see Frank Kafker, 'The Fortunes and Misfortunes of a leading French Bookseller–Printer: André François Le Breton, Chief Publisher of the Encyclopédie.'

[306] How Picart's 1707 engraving displaying Minerva expelling ignorance on the theme, 'Veritas Filia Temporis,' was reworked to allude to Newton's natural philosophy instead of Descartes is described by Saxl, 'Veritas Filia Temporis,' pp. 220–3. This reworking fits in well with John Locke's review of the *Principia* and Voltaire's later espousal of Newton vs Descartes. A tract on the same theme, 'Temporis Filia Veritas' had been issued in 1589 by the Familist publisher–bookseller, Thomas Basson in Leiden, according to van Dorsten, 'Garter Knights,' p. 187. But again, like Minerva and Mercury, the Latin tag does not necessarily have a special sectarian significance since it was widely distributed and reduplicated in pottery, medals as well as in books. See Saxl, 'Veritas Filia Temporis,' p. 199, n. 2.

The problem of disentangling the normal operations of a wholesale business with far-flung (and occasionally clandestine) distribution networks from the abnormal special covert operations of a given secret order may well be incapable of a complete solution. But any effort in this direction seems better than none. Every name that crops up on the list of Plantin's vast correspondence, or even on the list of those who stayed in his house for some time, should not be assigned to the 'Domus Charitatis,' the 'House' or 'Family of Love.' Every eighteenth-century book containing an engraving by Bernard Picart should not be taken to be a product of early eighteenth-century masonry. Every reference to Minerva even when coupled with Mercury does not have an alchemical, hermetic or masonic significance. Every printer, bookseller or bookshop visited by John Dee when he travelled on the continent should not be characterized as part of the 'Dee connection' nor should Dee be presumed to have roots in the 'Familist world' because he visited and corresponded with the most notable map-publishers, cosmographers, and booksellers of his day. On such matters, useful guidance is provided by the late Rosalie Colie (who did much to illuminate Anglo-Dutch intellectual interchange).

To postulate the Family of Love as a universal solvent to the problems raised in trying to consolidate any loose group of men with common interests seems to outrun what is known – or perhaps knowable – of that group...it seems risky to make [this] central to a group of intellectuals...who can be demonstrated to have ordinary connections with one another.[307]

The risk is even higher when 'ordinary connections' among publishers, printers and booksellers are brought into the picture. For then one must cope with 'ordinary connections' which were, almost routinely, supplemented by some kind of complicity in clandestine activities.

In 1517 when Erasmus first wrote about a 'conspiracy' of men of letters, it was in a relatively light-hearted vein:

All over the world, as if on a given signal, splendid talents are stirring and conspiring together to revive the best learning. For what else is this but a conspiracy when all these great scholars from different lands share out the work among themselves?[308]

Soon after these hopeful words were issued, the Lutheran revolt broke out, precipitating civil war in Christendom. Thereafter a different kind

---

[307] Colie, book review, *Renaissance Quarterly* (1973)   [308] Harbison, *Christian Scholar*, p. 87.

of 'conspiracy' was required to get Erasmus' works into bookshops and private libraries in Catholic lands.[309] After the Council of Trent, almost the entire Republic of Letters had to go 'underground' in Catholic Europe. Black-market prices brought profits not to local printers and publishers but to rival firms in foreign Protestant lands. As a later discussion of the Reformation book-trade makes clear, an intriguing asymmetry was introduced by the workings of the Index. It provided Protestant firms with a list of profit-making titles and free advertising while alerting potential Catholic purchasers to the existence of forbidden fruit.

From the sixteenth century on, the Republic of Letters expanded in Catholic Europe despite official disapproval, not only because lay rulers were often at odds with churchmen or because censors were over-burdened, inefficient or easily bribed. Expansion occurred also because hard-driving Protestant publishers extended alternative opportunities to writers who found Catholic publication outlets blocked. This particular asymmetry tilted early-modern science toward the Protestant cause, as is later discussed. It also has a significant bearing on the question of the 'desertion of intellectuals' in *ancien régime* France. For the conquests of the French language had created special opportunities for literati of French descent. Their command of their native tongue made them useful when translation was required and still sought after when it could be by-passed. The cosmopolitan French-language press, however, flourished better in Holland than in France. Numerous other small states fringing the great Bourbon realm also set up presses to take advantage of the lucrative clandestine trade and to tap populous French markets for censored works. 'For a century, from 1690 to 1790, the works of the most famous French writers were read throughout all Europe in editions published outside France.'[310]

---

[309] A succinct account of the Catholic censorship of Erasmus' works, beginning with condemnations by the Sorbonne in 1526 and climaxed by the banning of the *opera omnia* in the Pauline Index of 1559, is given by Paul and Marcella Grendler, 'The Survival of Erasmus in Italy.' When the *opera omnia* was issued in a new edition it would be from Protestant Holland by one of the Huguenot leaders of the 'Republic of Letters': Jean LeClerc. On the movement of colophons of separate works of Erasmus from Catholic to Protestant printing centers, see Trevor-Roper, 'Desiderius Erasmus,' p. 51. For further discussion and references, see chap. 4, below.

[310] Febvre and Martin, *L'Apparition*, p. 278. Pottinger, *French Book Trade*, p. 76 notes the large proportion of French works that came from Protestant regions. The role of the small buffer states and principalities is illuminated by Birn, *Pierre Rousseau*, a finely detailed case study of a French playwright turned foreign publisher and propagandist for the Encyclopedists. Bachman, *Censorship in France from 1715 to 1750*, *passim*, is one of several studies which

Ambitious and talented subjects of the French Catholic king, who had previously served as writing masters, tutors, secretaries and clerks in law courts or in noble households, thus found new employment serving foreign Protestant firms. To understand why they 'deserted' the Bourbon régime, the opening of new career opportunities is worth keeping in mind. The lure of international celebrity channeled aspirations toward achievement away from local élites. Would-be writers from varied backgrounds who set out on a 'perilous voyage to prosperous distinction'[311] in the seventeenth century found their way to acceptance at Parisian salons and foreign courts (as well as to prison and penury) in the next century by wielding their pens for printers everywhere. Some were treated as lackeys by unenlightened aristocrats; some served other nobles as hired hands; while a number of the most celebrated Enlightenment authors: Condorcet, Condillac, Mably, Helvetius, *et al.* were of noble birth themselves. In no other eighteenth-century region would the hope of obtaining an independent eminence and international prestige be similarly encouraged by aid forthcoming from foreign workshops.

Drawn from diverse strata, and detached from local loyalties, the new careerists appear to posterity either as ghost writers for others or as free-floating intellectuals. Most often they appear as ideologists of a rising 'bourgeoisie' or, in less explicitly Marxist terms, as representatives of the growing middle class. Yet their position was different from that of French merchants, manufacturers, doctors and lawyers. It must also be distinguished from the specific interests of the businessmen who ran privileged firms within France.

The philosophes were men of letters. This is more than a phrase. It defines their vantage point and eliminates the stale debate over their status as philosophers...devotion to the art of writing gave the philosophes the strength that comes from membership in a respectable guild...No matter how varied their concerns they were men with a single career...[312]

The 'art of writing' is too segregated from the business of printing for this comment to cover the case it describes. Even in the eighteenth

describes difficulties with parlements, bureaucrats, and censors experienced by French publishers. As in all Catholic regions, the local bookmen were hit harder than authors, who could and did turn to foreign printers in neighboring regions. The eighteenth-century French book-trade and censorship is the subject of a huge and rapidly growing literature. For review of recent works, see Birn, 'Livre et Société,' after ten years.'

[311] Pottinger, *French Book Trade*, p. 11.   [312] Gay, *The Party of Humanity*, p. 117.

century, some poets and literati were still devoted to the 'art of writing' in the old scribal sense, but this was certainly not true of the *philosophes*. Since their 'single career' entailed the harnessing of pens to the new powers of the press, their 'vantage point' is not adequately defined by referring to the pen alone.[313] Still the comment has the merit of relating the Enlightenment *philosophes* to a distinctive occupational culture.

As a new class of men of letters and not as spokesmen for the robe nobility, the *Tiers Etat*, or the royal power, the *philosophes* urged men to trust their own understanding, assailed the Church, fought for a free trade in ideas, and hoped to wean enlightened monarchs away from collaboration with the Index and the presses of the Catholic Propaganda. Their political attitudes and the pressures they exerted were distinctive and need to be considered as such. They should not be classed among traditional parvenus seeking offices closed by the so-called 'feudal reaction.'

In 1789, did not the fall of the Bastille signify something of particular importance to men of letters in comparison with all other social groups? Over eight hundred authors, printers, booksellers, and print dealers had been incarcerated there between 1600 and 1756.[314] Its image as a dreadful symbol of royal tyranny had been built up by publicists who had been 'embastillé.' 'The métier of Aretino has always been risky' commented Grimm when Simon Nicholas Henri Linguet was thrown into the Bastille in 1780.[315] Even now, guides at the Place de la Bastille, like many historians, dwell on the irony of expending so much effort to storm a fortress which contained only seven residents: four men accused of forgery, two 'mental cases' and the Marquis de Sade. But to those who followed the 'métier of Aretino' – and they were the same men who harangued the crowds assembled at the Palais Royal on the afternoon of July 12 – the aim of completely destroying the Bastille was not anomalous at all. The crowds who stormed the fortress seeking gunpowder may have seen cannon trained on crowded quarters and thought about toll-barriers and bread prices. To the pamphleteers

---

313 The 'stale debate over their status as philosophers' also could be viewed in a fresh light if the effect of printing on the traditional vocation of philosophers received more attention. The shift from an esoteric to an exoteric approach noted by Leo Strauss in *Persecution and the Art of Writing*, p. 33, and the reorientation of Horace's 'Sapere Aude!' noted by Venturi, *Utopia and Reform*, pp. 5–9, seem to me to be related to the new publicity system. The same is true of issues raised in article by Ginzburg, 'High and Low.'

314 Pottinger, *French Book Trade*, p. 79. Symbolically enough, thousands of copies of the *Encyclo-pédie* were also locked up in the Bastille between 1770 and 1776. Lough, *Essays on the Encyclopédie of Diderot and d'Alembert*, p. 62.   315 Cited by Trénard, 'La Presse Française,' p. 280.

who hailed its fall, it appeared as a symbol of a different sort of tyranny. The meaning of its capture would be continuously amplified by the publicists who kept the republican tradition alive under a succession of kings and emperors, until ultimately July 14 would become an official holiday, annually celebrated on a national scale.

The sort of influence that was exerted by this new class of men of letters has been the topic of a prolonged argument without end.[316] General theories about the relationship between ideas and social action are frequently invoked. Seldom, if ever, do the specific effects of the advent of printing enter into the discussion. Yet both the thrust of Enlightenment propaganda and the invisible meeting of minds that came with its diffusion can scarcely be understood without taking these effects into account. It was after all printing that made possible vicarious encounters with famous philosophers who turned out to be kindred spirits. They boldly spelled out the repressed content of interior dialogues. They argued at length with persuasive power about matters one could not discuss in front of one's servants, parents, or neighbors. Few visible traces, save thumbprints on well-worn volumes or a chance remark about a youthful enthusiasm for a favorite author, would be left by such encounters. Yet fear of disapproval, a sense of isolation, the force of local community sanctions, the habit of respectful submission to traditional authority – all might be weakened among many obscure provincial book readers by recognition that their innermost convictions were shared by fashionable and famous men of letters. Moreover, print is a singularly impersonal medium. Lay preachers and teachers who addressed congregations from afar often seemed to speak with a more authoritative voice than those who could be heard and seen within a given community.

The publication in numerous editions of thoughts hitherto unthinkable involved a new form of social action that was indirect and at a distance.

The revolutionary spirit was surely not formed in silence and solitude. One might write revolutionary works but they would remain pure and inoffensive speculations if their ideas had not fermented in the heat of conversation, discussion and battles of words. In order for such ideas to become *idées forces* they required a public...[317]

316 For brief review, see Peyre, 'The Influence of Eighteenth Century Ideas.'
317 Mornet, *Les Origines Intellectuelles de la Révolution Française (1715–1787)*, p. 281.

A most important consequence of the printing press, however, was that it did create a new kind of public for *idées forces*.[318] The reading public was not necessarily vocal, nor did its members necessarily frequent cafés, clubs, or salons of known political complexion. It was instead composed of silent and solitary individuals who were often unknown to each other and who were linked only by access to bookshops, lending libraries, or *chambres de lecture* and, here and there, also by membership in 'corresponding societies'.[319]

There is no way of knowing, with certainty, what really went on in the minds of silent, solitary readers who have long since gone to their graves. Authors are often surprised by what gets read into their works. A wide margin for uncertainty must be left whenever one tries to read the minds of other readers. It is precisely because it shows where this margin lies and why it cannot be eliminated that speculation on this matter may be useful. Interactions that cannot be determined with certainty in retrospect could not be foreseen or controlled in prospect. Failure to speculate about the indirect effects exerted by the *philosophes* on their public prolongs the search for some alien invisible hand that set Frenchmen in motion by 1789. The law-abiding subjects of Bourbon France did behave in a manner that astounded contemporaries. If we side-step the problem in social psychology that their unexpected behavior poses, the myth-makers are apt to step in, and debates will center on thickly-documented solutions that leave no margin for uncertainty at all.

The conspiratorial myths that have been woven around masonic lodges, reading societies and the French Revolution could themselves be better understood if various effects produced by printing were taken into account.[320] New forms of secrecy, publicity, duplicity and

---

[318] This view conflicts not only with Mornet's work but also with more recent French studies of the eighteenth-century bookish world – currently the topic of intensive investigation. Much as Febvre and Martin hold that printing retarded the adoption of new ideas by duplicating old ones in the sixteenth century, so Dupront argues that far from contributing to revolutionary dynamics, eighteenth-century book production reinforced tradition and acted as a brake. See n. 71, chap. 1, above.

[319] On *chambres de lecture* see Cochin, *Les Sociétés de Pensée* I, 20. On the corresponding societies that circulated hundreds of thousands of copies of Paine's *Age of Reason* between 1791 and 1793 in the British Isles, see Altick, *English Common Reader*, p. 70; E. P. Thompson, *Making of English Working Class*, chap. 5. The large number of editions of Paine's writings that circulated in France after 1776 is described by Echeverria, *Mirage in the West*, p. 44.

[320] Roberts, *The Mythology of the Secret Societies* provides a survey of the literature from a sceptical, liberal viewpoint. Some of the limitations of this approach are noted in my review of Roberts' book, *The American Historical Review* (1973).

censorship underlie all modern myths of this genre. Examination of these issues cannot be undertaken here. Let me just note in passing that conspiratorial hypotheses in general are more often propelled than dispelled by efforts that stop short with disproving them. Bibliographies grow thicker, the atmosphere more charged, as sceptics and true believers fail alike to convince each other.[321] The possibility that multiple invisible interactions *were* introduced by a silent communications system is a point that both parties tend to ignore, and that the sceptical liberals, at least, should be persuaded to explore. Most of them agree that pens can poison the atmosphere when they are used to accuse Protestants or Papists, Masons or Jacobins, Jesuits, Jews or Bolsheviks of sinister plots. If this is true, then it would seem that climates of opinion can be affected by pens, at least when they are harnessed to the power of the press. A closer look at the nature of 'media events' in early-modern Europe and more alertness to the possibility of social 'action at a distance' is needed if we want to understand how earlier views of conspiracy – pertaining to assassination plots or rabble-rousers hired by seditious factions – gave way to the more awesome image of a vast network, controlled from secret headquarters, that set men to do its bidding from afar.[322]

Many other developments could be clarified by exploring the new complex interplay between different groups of writers and readers. Vicarious experiences with newly created fictional worlds, for example, affected human hearts as well as heads.[323] Empathy induced by novel-reading probably helped to sustain humanitarian movements of various kinds. Powers of calculation and abstraction were sharpened by access to printed materials. But new imaginative and sympathetic faculties were also brought into play. That poets, artists, social reformers and visionaries ought to be numbered among users of printed materials is often overlooked. 'Through the habit of using print and paper,

---

[321] A cogent example is Cohn's *Warrant for Genocide* which deals with the concocted 'Protocols of the Elders of Zion.' The work ends with useful insights but it also unwisely duplicates lurid tales and vicious cartoons which keep the old virus in circulation and may even revive some dormant strains. It was, incidentally, a satire on Napoleon III's regime as 'journalism incarnate' which provided a model for the Protocols. Kulstein, 'Government Propaganda and the Press during the Second Empire.'

[322] For discussion of Rosicrucian 'media events' see chap. 3, pp. 275–6 below. The effect of printing on collective psychopathology urgently needs further study. Richard Hofstadter's suggestive work on the 'paranoid style in politics' as well as a spate of recent studies on the witch craze and the differences between medieval and modern anti-semitism ought to be reappraised from this angle.   [323] Q. D. Leavis, *Fiction and the Reading Public, passim.*

thought lost something of its flowing...organic character and became abstract, categorical, stereotyped, content with purely verbal formulations and verbal solutions....'[324] Although 'typographic man' as defined by Mumford and McLuhan is a post-romantic construct and thus different from the more 'classical' figures of 'economic man' and 'political man', the creature is no less abstract and stereotyped than its forebears. Indeed McLuhan's eighteenth-century man who is 'locked into a closed visual system' seems to be symptomatic of the very ailment he purports to diagnose: a print-and-paper creation, a fit companion only for McLuhan's other ingenious creation: the 'mechanical bride.'

Such constructs may well be plausibly related to the habit of using print and paper. Certainly, unfortunate consequences have ensued when flesh-and-blood human beings are viewed as statistical averages or become stereotyped role-players. But many readers were also made more conscious of the limitations of book learning after the fifteenth century. Readers in the sixteenth century learned from Paracelsus and his followers, for example, that 'the sick should be the doctor's books.'[325] As a later section of this book will try to demonstrate, a closer observation of human bodies, not verbal formulations about them, was fostered by typography. The discrepancy between bookish theories about the behavior of all bodies – political, human, heavenly, or terrestrial – and how things *do* behave in this world was sharply perceived and forcefully articulated by so many early-modern authors that denunciation of book learning became itself a bookish cliché. By the eighteenth century, long hours of schooling were already beginning to replace apprenticeship training. However, readers did not have to wait for John Dewey or Marconi and electronic media[326] to appreciate the value of 'learning by doing.' The precepts set forth in *Emile* were closely heeded by many eighteenth-century parents and tutors. Self-consciousness or a somewhat artificial effort at naturalness was one by-product of 'learning by reading.' An alertness to the fallacies of print-made abstractions was another.

Variety, moreover, did not cease to be the spice of life for human book-readers. Tactile, auditory, and sensory experiences were, possibly,

---

[324] Mumford, *Technics and Civilization*, pp. 136–7.
[325] Cited by Haydn, *Counter-Renaissance*, p. 198. For discussion of Haydn's thesis and other relevant questions, see below, pp. 475ff., volume II.
[326] McLuhan, *Gutenberg Galaxy*, p. 144.

more sharply and keenly experienced by being alternated with reading, as country air is enjoyed by city folk; or the outdoors after intervals spent indoors. Insofar as such experiences were more deliberately courted as aesthetic, autonomous areas of activity, they were also more consciously enjoyed. Concert-going, gardening, bird-watching, or gourmandizing, are entirely compatible with 'typographic man'. The remarkable virtuosity displayed by new literary artists who managed to counterfeit taste, touch, smell, or sound in mere words required a heightened awareness and closer observation of sensory experience that was passed on in turn to the reader.

All the creative arts were, indeed, transformed by typography in ways that need to be taken into account by those who suggest that human experience was impoverished once the age of scribes had come to an end and the great age of Western music, art, and literature began. Ears attuned to Bach's fugues or Beethoven's symphonies had surely not grown more insensitive. Nor was human vision atrophied by painterly renditions of landscapes or figures on canvas. Visual perception was altered, as Gombrich has suggested, by 'seeing' a Corot when walking through the woods in early spring; or a 'Cezanne' when glancing at a bowl of fruit. The capacity of artists to alter perception of sounds or sights extended to the realm of literature in a manner that enriched rather than stunted sensuous response to external stimuli, expanded rather than contracted sympathetic response to the varieties of human experience. Successive generations of skillful narrators learned to simulate the colorful, odorous, noisy, thick-textured stuff of life; to imitate the voices of different generations and convey the passage of time as old bards never had. Many diverse milieux would be vicariously inhabited, many different lifetimes vicariously lived by generations of novel-readers – with somewhat paradoxical consequences.

It is frequently suggested that reading 'light fiction' provided an 'escape' for many who lived dull, monotonous, or humdrum lives. Less often is it noted that the one real life of the novel-reader invariably appears more drab and monotonous after vicarious participation in so many vividly realized fictional worlds. The most frequent complaints about ennui, boredom, or the grinding monotony of daily routines come, indeed, in the nineteenth century not from toiling workers, hard pressed businessmen, or shopkeepers but from the literati themselves. It was Lamartine who proclaimed that 'France was bored' and de Musset who spoke of a 'mal de siècle'. The conviction that the past is more colorful than the present, exotic locales more attractive than home, and drabness the hallmark of modern social life would be altogether characteristic of 'typographic man', especially after bestselling novels had appeared.

Here again, one might note that novelists are also apt to be novel-readers. The literary artist, whether poet, fiction-writer or historical romancer, not only exploited the new media most fully and deliberately. Like the early printer, he also registered most forcefully the consequences of access to proliferating printed materials. His vision of the society he inhabited was no less affected by a swelling flow of books and journals than that of his expanding audience. It was largely as a reader that he mirrored the Zeitgeist and transposed into a new key the grey abstractions of bookish philosophers by embodying them in vivid concrete immediate images.[327] Even while power to alter perception was conferred on image makers, intellectual responsibility was placed in the hands of dry-as-dust pedants and scientists – a division of labor which remains characteristic of print culture even now.

The many tensions created by the expansion of literary markets after printing have been illuminated by several recent studies.[328] Despite these studies, however, there is a tendency when discussing the commercialization of belles lettres or the disappearance of patronage to take too much at face-value the images purveyed by literary artists. The advent of an 'industrial' society is too often made responsible for conditions that were shaped by the momentum of an on-going revolution in communications. From the first, authorship was closely linked to the new technology. As Febvre and Martin suggest, it is a 'neologism' to use the term 'man of letters' before the advent of printing.[329] The romantic figure of the aristocratic or patrician patron has tended to obscure the more plebeian and prosaic early capitalist entrepreneur who hired scholars, translators, editors and compilers when not serving in these capacities himself. Partly because copyists had, after all, never

---

[327] How Walter Scott 'transposed into the key of fiction' the doctrines of Edmund Burke is noted by Somervell, *English Thought*, pp. 8–9.

[328] Apart from Altick, *English Common Reader*, see Dudek, *Literature and the Press*; Escarpit, *Sociologie de la Littérature*; Grana, *Bohemian versus Bourgeois*; Raymond Williams, *Culture and Society 1780–1950*; Coser, *Men of Ideas*; Molnar, *The Decline of the Intellectuals*.

[329] Febvre and Martin, *L'Apparition*, p. 18.

paid those whose works they copied, partly because new books were a small portion of the early book-trade, and partly because divisions of literary labor remained blurred, the author retained a quasi-amateur status until the eighteenth century. During this interval, printers served as patrons for authors, acted as their own authors, and sought patronage, privileges and favors from official quarters as well. This was the era when men of letters and learning were likely to be familiar with print technology and commercial trade routes in a manner that later observers overlook.

The intelligentsia are thus singled out by Karl Mannheim as peculiarly lacking 'direct access to any vital and functioning segment of society.'

The secluded study and dependence on printed matter afford only a derivative view of the social process. No wonder this stratum remained long unaware of the social character of change...The proletariat had already perfected its own world view when these latecomers appeared on the scene.[330]

For Mannheim, 'the rise of the intelligentsia marks the last phase of the growth of social consciousness'. In my view, however, he has put first things last. Most inhabitants of the sixteenth-century Republic of Letters spent more time in printers' workshops than in 'secluded studies'. They were thus in direct contact with a 'vital and functioning segment of society.' Authors who 'composed' their work with a composing stick in hand were not uncommon in the age of Erasmus – nor in that of Benjamin Franklin. Indeed, the simplicity of the early press made it possible for American men of letters to act as their own printers – much as Italian humanists had acted as their own scribes.

A literate person – man or woman by the way – with a copy of Moxon's *Mechanick Exercises* (1683) in hand could teach himself or herself the trade, from beginning to end. Simplicity of operation was not a factor of prime importance in London...But it was crucially important in the provinces and colonies, where printing-houses were small and pressmen few. There, if necessary, one man who knew his business could mix his own ink, compose his folio halfsheet page at the type cases, operate the press himself, dry the pages and even take the papers in his own hands to the neighboring taverns and coffee houses for sale and distribution if he did not have a printer's devil and could not find a boy who would do it for him for a penny. The process was a natural school for the autodidact and the way was open for the de-

---

[330] Mannheim, *Essays on the Sociology of Culture*, part 2, section 2, p. 101.

velopment of authors who could complete the process by actually composing their work, in both senses of the word, with the composing stick. Two who did so were those autodidact printers Mark Twain and Benjamin Franklin.[331]

Benjamin Franklin's involvement in the print shop might be expected to intrigue a sociologist of knowledge such as Mannheim who is concerned with the way social activities enter into world views. But, as later discussion of Max Weber's thesis will suggest, sociologists are strangely oblivious of Benjamin Franklin's particular occupation. In Mannheim's coverage of intellectual associations during the early-modern era, we are told about universities, chancelleries, courts, salons and academies; but of the print shop, which provided jobs, food, lodging and all manner of interchanges nothing is said. Because of its presence in numerous urban centers the 'historical and social consciousness' of men of letters in early modern Europe was well in advance of that of other groups. Even in the early nineteenth century, a professional man of letters such as Sir Walter Scott could write, 'I love to have the press thumping, clattering and banging in my ear. It creates the necessity which always makes me work best'.[332] The 'secluded study' which now provides a setting for many sociologists of knowledge, should not be projected too far back into the past. Between the sixteenth and eighteenth centuries, at all events, intellectuals, mechanics and capitalists were not out of touch.

But even during this interval, a somewhat more indirect and more ambivalent relationship to the new technology was experienced by poets, playwrights, fabulists, satirists, and romancers who were linked both to 'la cour et la ville' and poised somewhat uncertainly between royal patronage and publishers' stipends. Ambivalence over whether they were serving the muses or mechanic printers, engaged in a 'divine art' or a 'mercenary métier', was already manifested in French literary circles during the seventeenth century.[333] Often treated with contempt by aristocrats, these 'scribblers' belonged to a highly volatile, unstable status group. No traditional institutions or systems pertaining to rank, priority, and degree took their existence into account. They wavered between the lofty position of arbiters of taste and inspired 'immortals' and the lowly role of supplying, for favor or payment, commodities

---

[331] Winton, 'Richard Steele,' pp. 22–3.   [332] Cited by Coser, *Men of Ideas*, p. 55.
[333] See citation from Boileau and discussion by Lough, *An Introduction to Seventeenth Century France*, p. 177.

sold for profit on the open market. Tension between these two extreme and entirely contradictory roles thus existed before the advent of new paper mills, steam presses and a mass fiction-reading public. It simply became more acute as the literary marketplace expanded and new groups of readers were tapped.

The competent business or professional man, who had been the natural ally of the early printer, was the natural enemy of the professional fiction writer or lionized poet. A hard-working man who relied on facts and figures, any man who worked hard for a living, could not afford to spend much time reading novels or poetry. Adolescent bookworms, young apprentices and clerks and a wide spectrum of feminine readers were more apt to have hearts that could be touched and imaginations that could be held in thrall. A vested interest in idleness, in promoting the value of pleasure-seeking and leisure, in cultivating consumption of the 'finer' things of life, was built into the trade of all novelists and poets (and of other artists as well). The romantic creed of the nineteenth-century aesthete is little more than an inversion of the values of censorious moralists and practical utilitarians. The aesthetic vision, so the rationale went, was *more* moral and *more* useful than any other. Claims to superior historical dignity and spiritual value were uneasily reconciled with turning out bestselling works that sold like drugs on the market – and were similarly advertised in the daily press. The complaint of being misunderstood by heartless, unimaginative philistines had, as Grana notes, a paradoxical aspect,[334] for it implied merely that a work was not selling well.

Anxiety about getting attention and holding it was also built into the trade of the new professional author. Not only did his work have to hold its own against energetic competition from rivals. Once space had been secured for serial publication or favorable notice from literary journalists had been won, the distracting effect of headline-grabbing politicians, advertising space-buyers, and news-making reporters had to be countered. His pecuniary rewards and prestige depended on printed publicity – like those of any business firm. But an inversion of values here again occurred. A reputation was gained not by respectability but by a *succès de scandale*; *épater le bourgeois* was also a profitable venture. Business or professional men might be offended, but few of them would be attracted to fiction in any case. A feminine and youthful

---

[334] Grana, *Bohemian*, p. 56.

audience was more likely to be captivated than deterred by vicarious participation in this particular sport.[335] The courting of scandal was by no means confined to the assault on ostensibly respectable family men. 'The reader refused to be caught save by a book baited with a small corpse in the first stage of putrefaction...Men are not as unlike fishes as most people seem to think.'[336] May not this search for ever more thrilling or shocking effects account for the syndrome described by Mario Praz as the 'romantic agony'?

Although many authors expressed disgust at the vulgar sensationalism of others, none could afford to abandon the hope of creating a sensation himself. Alone with his quill pen, altogether remote from workshops and foundries, equally remote from the fickle readers upon whom his fame and fortune hinged, the professional author did not simply mirror the alienation of others from an industrial or urbanized society. He was himself an alienated man who worked hard to promote leisure, fought for a commercial success that he despised, set wives against husbands, fathers against sons, and celebrated youth even in his old age. Even if new factories, mines, and slag heaps had never appeared, given the momentum of the on-going communications revolution, he would probably still have felt nostalgia for scribal culture, worried about cultural anarchy and the vulgarization of taste, seen the public in the guise of a many-headed beast, and assailed the 'cash nexus' as well as the heartless businessman.[337]

During the nineteenth century, among many of the most sensitive artists and most gifted image makers, the effort to reconcile a commercial métier with the role of immortal was abandoned altogether. Earning daily bread was divorced from turning out a *succès d'estime*. Increasingly, the most strikingly 'original' and arresting images were shaped within secluded ivory towers for small groups of connoisseurs. Keeping faith with the muses was rewarded, often posthumously, by a place in the last chapter of a literary anthology. But the preservative powers of print also made this loftier ambition ever more difficult for

[335] That the novel-reading public in nineteenth-century England was largely feminine and that women increasingly took over supplying the fiction market there is noted in a pertinent review article by Collins, 'The Fiction Market.'

[336] Gautier, Preface to *Mademoiselle de Maupin* (1835), p. 82. All of this celebrated preface illuminates the diverse pressures, censors, and competitors confronting the professional fiction-writer in early nineteenth-century France.

[337] On earlier political use of this 'many-headed beast' theme, see Hill, 'The Many-Headed Monster.' Carlyle's tirade against the garbage being fed millions of readers and the 'cash nexus' which governed literature is noted by Dudek, *Literature and the Press*, p. 207.

each new generation to achieve. The more strident the voice of one generation, the more deafening the static interference became for the next. Among the variety of reactions that ensued two might be singled out: on the one hand, a museum culture, preserved in anthologies and taught in the schoolroom, was savagely assaulted; on the other, modern cultural 'anarchy' and the society that sustained it were nostalgically repudiated. Nihilistic images pertaining to a 'dustbin of the past' and a 'wasteland of the present' were, in turn, dutifully recorded and expounded. Several last chapters of current anthologies now contain such images. (They serve, one might note, to introduce the present generation of students to the society in which they are coming of age.) Thus the same process that had, earlier, introduced eponymous authorship and harnessed the drive for fame to print-made immortality, led to an overpopulation of Parnassus. An ever more strenuous effort was required to handle an increasing 'burden of the past.' How the later phases of the on-going revolution contributed to cultural pessimism and the multiple variations played upon this theme cannot, however, be explored here.

This brief excursion beyond the early-modern era has been offered merely to suggest that particular perturbations, emanating from a permanent, cumulative, print-made culture, need to be taken into account when trying to reconstruct the experience of literate élites during the last few centuries. They also need to be taken into consideration when attempting to understand the sense of cultural crisis which has become ever more acute in recent years. This last point needs special emphasis in view of the possible distracting effect of new electronic media. Whatever damage has been done to youthful reading habits, old literary themes continue to be amplified by script writers and song writers over air waves even now. Moreover, there is no sign that our libraries and museums without walls have begun to contract, or that the burden of the past is diminishing for the literati of today. Thus, although I believe that scribal culture did come to end, I am not persuaded that one can say the same about print culture. The effects of printing seem to have been exerted always unevenly, yet always continuously and cumulatively from the late fifteenth century on. I can find no point at which they ceased to be exerted or even began to diminish. I find much to suggest that they have persisted, with ever-augmented force, right down to the present. Recent obituaries on the

Age of Gutenberg show that others disagree.[338] As yet, however, so few historians have been heard from that final verdicts seem unacceptable and, in more ways than one, premature.

It would also be premature at this point to make any final remarks. This introductory section was intended to open up a field for future study and not to provide a basis upon which conclusions may be drawn. Let me simply recapitulate: A new method for duplicating handwriting – an *ars artificialiter scribendi* – was developed and first utilized five centuries ago. 'It brought about the most radical transformation in the conditions of intellectual life in the history of western civilization... its effects were sooner or later felt in every department of human life.' At present we must reckon with effects 'felt in every department of human life' without knowing which came sooner, which later, and, indeed, without any clear notions as to what these effects were. Explicit theories, in short, are now overdue. To make a start at providing them, a preliminary sketch has been offered. It was designed to block out the topic as a whole, to indicate some of its neglected ramifications and to suggest its possible bearing on many different forms of historical change.

In the following sections, selected developments receive closer attention. Possible relationships and connections are explored with the aim of providing a basis for some tentative conclusions concerning the effect of the communications shift upon three movements which seem strategic in the shaping of the modern mind.

[338] The obsolescence of print technology and its supersession by electronic media has been repeatedly asserted by McLuhan, not only in *The Gutenberg Galaxy* but also in *Understanding Media*. See also Steiner, 'The Retreat from the Word'; and Winetrout, 'The New Age of the Visible.'

CLASSICAL AND CHRISTIAN TRADITIONS REORIENTED; RENAISSANCE AND REFORMATION REAPPRAISED

3

A CLASSICAL REVIVAL
REORIENTED: THE TWO PHASES
OF THE RENAISSANCE

I. INTRODUCTION

We all know...that down to the fifteenth century all European books were pen written and that ever since that time most of them have been printed. We know likewise that in that same fifteenth century Western culture laid off its medieval characteristics and became distinctively modern. But we are quite unable to conceive realistically any connection between these technological and cultural changes except that they happened in the same period.[1]

This statement, which was made in 1940 by a professor of library science, describes a situation which seems current even now. Although the relationship between technology and culture in general has been the subject of a growing literature, the more specific relationship between the advent of printing and fifteenth-century cultural change has not yet been explored. This is partly because the very act of drawing connections is not as easy a task as one might think. Butler goes on to refer to an 'intimate connection' which becomes apparent 'the moment our thought penetrates through bare facts,' but I must confess I cannot imagine just what connection he had in mind. Although the shift from pen-written book to printed one may be taken as a known fact, it is not the kind of fact that can be said to 'speak for itself.' As the previous chapter suggests, a complex ensemble of many interrelated changes was involved.

When one turns to the other side of the equation, matters are no less complicated and even more obscure. Do we really 'all know' in which century Western culture became 'distinctively modern'? Historians are more likely to claim knowledge of the large literature of contro-

[1] Butler, *Origin of Printing*, p. 9.

versy which has grown around this very point. In the absence of any consensus, and given prolonged inconclusive debate, one may be tempted simply to dismiss the question as a semantic booby trap. There is a difference, however, between historical theory and practice. In theory, periodization problems may never get solved, but in practice, definite lines have to be drawn. In most course-catalogues and scholarly journals, the lines which are drawn seem to support Butler's view. Judging by academic divisions of labor, reflected in courses and articles, the fifteenth century does seem to be taken as an interval where the expertise of medievalists ends and that of specialists in early-modern Europe begins.

But here again, matters are not as simple as an outsider might think. The same division which seems only natural when one considers the policies of journals such as *Speculum* or the *Journal of Modern History* will seem arbitrary and even misguided when one considers *Studies in the Renaissance*. From the viewpoint of most Renaissance scholars, the advent of printing comes too late to be taken as a point of departure for the transition to modern times. From their viewpoint this transition begins with the generations of Giotto and Petrarch and with a classical revival that was already under way by the early quattrocento – well before Gutenberg had set to work. Before making much headway in drawing the connections to which Butler alludes, one must first deal with the argument that his technological and cultural changes do not really coincide and that the major cultural metamorphosis had occurred under the auspices of scribes.

That the 'rinascita' came to Italy before printing was developed in Mainz may be taken as firmly established. But although the question of chronology is easily settled, the problem of periodization remains. It is one thing to show that the Petrarchan revival was flourishing in Italy in the age of hand-copied books. It is another to show why Petrarch and his successors should be taken as agents of epochal change. This latter point is far from being firmly established. Ever since Jacob Burckhardt suggested that we ought to take the Italians of Petrarch's day as the 'first born sons of modern Europe,' his thesis has given rise to an argument without end. In the absence of any consensus concerning the specific agents of epochal change, many historians have tended to fall back on the notion of a transitional age – an elastic period encompassing some three hundred years during which Western Europe is seen to have experienced the cultural equivalent of a chemical change of phase.[2] Unlike the chemical change of a liquid into a solid or into a gas, however, the precise nature of the cultural transition is never defined. We are told that 'something rather decisive' or 'of crucial importance' or 'immeasureably different' happened.[3] 'Something important and revolutionary occurred...and we might as well go on calling that something the Renaissance'[4] – a review thus sums up a recent book on the familiar theme. The nature of the 'something' is elusive, however; uncertainty persists as to how to track it down. To the question posed by Huizinga in 1920: 'What actually was the cultural transformation we call the Renaissance? What did it consist of, what was its effect?'[5] no clear answer has been found.

Accordingly, other scholars object that the question is based on a false premise. They see certain decisive changes occurring in the twelfth century or before; others, in the seventeenth century or after; but none of major consequence in the interval in between. By prolonging the middle ages for some purposes, by advancing the advent of modern times for others, they close the conjectured gap and eliminate the need for a transitional era to bridge it. These conflicting views are swathed in semantic confusion since the term 'Renaissance' is used by both schools to designate a specific classical revival and aesthetic style. Confusion arising over the extension of the label to encompass a transitional epoch provokes additional dispute. The basic issue is whether the period, however labelled, contains a major historical transformation and hence should be set apart; or whether it is a spurious construct and should be discarded. One objectionable feature of this debate is the way it encourages both sides alike to pass over in silence an actual transformation in order to argue about a hypothetical one that cannot be clearly defined.

To solve the problem of the Renaissance, Huizinga suggests, we should begin by contrasting the middle ages with the Renaissance and the Renaissance with modern culture.[6] Similarly, Ferguson calls for

[2] Ferguson, 'The Interpretation of the Renaissance,' offers an explicit justification for creating this transitional epoch. The Dannenfeldt anthology of excerpts is a useful guide to chief works dealing with the problem.
[3] Panofsky, *Renaissance and Renascences*, p. 40; Ferguson, *The Renaissance in Historical Thought*, p. 393; Santillana, *The Age of Adventure*, p. 12.
[4] Warnke, 'Mazzco on the Renaissance,' p. 288.
[5] Huizinga, 'The Problem of the Renaissance,' p. 278.
[6] Huizinga, 'The Problem,' p. 278.

a 'systematic analysis both of the essential differences between medieval and modern civilization and of what was peculiar to the transitional age itself.'[7] It would be more sparing of scholarly energies, I think, to begin by answering the question: 'what was peculiar to the transitional age itself?' directly and tersely. Among new things reserved to this age, we might say, echoing a sixteenth-century chronicler, 'printing deserves to be put first.'[8] By adopting this tactic we can by-pass debates about equivocal labels and constructs. We can direct attention to something that really did happen, that was obviously of crucial importance, that occurred in the second half of the fifteenth century and at no other time in the history of the West.

Verbal labels such as 'medieval' and 'modern' cannot be operationally defined. The specific phenomena they are meant to designate can be shuffled around so easily that systematic analysis or useful comparisons are almost impossible to achieve. But to analyse the differences between hand-copied texts and printed ones requires examining tangible objects and the activities of definite groups. Varying interpretations must, perforce, be grounded on examining the same empirical data. Not only did it entail a specific cluster of changes (unlike the notion of a 'transitional age') but the shift from script to print also involved a European-wide transformation which occurred in a relatively short span of time. In a few decades, printers' workshops were established in urban centers throughout Europe. By 1500, various effects produced by the output of printed materials were already being registered. Compared with the three centuries that stretch from 1250 to 1550 or 1300 to 1600, the age of incunabula is short indeed. Nor is it necessary to move from one region to another in order to locate a major shift. One must leave Paris and its environs with its Gothic cathedrals and faculties of theology, cross over the Alps and journey into Italy to find an early Renaissance. When one considers what was happening elsewhere on the continent between 1350 and 1450, one may wonder if an encounter with peculiar local conditions has not been mistaken for the advent of a new age. But one may move freely across all sorts of European frontiers – from Mount Etna to regions north of Stockholm, from Atlantic coasts to the mountains of Eastern Montenegro – during the last half of the fifteenth century and one will find that the same sort of new

[7] Ferguson, *Renaissance in Historical Thought*, p. 391.
[8] Louis Le Roy, excerpt from *De la Vicissitude ou Variété des Choses en l'Univers* (1575), tr. J. B. Ross in *The Portable Renaissance Reader*, p. 98.

workshops in major urban centers are producing books in almost all the languages of Western Europe.[9] New trades such as that of compositor or typefounder are being created; traditional skills developed by metal workers, merchants and scholars are being directed toward new ends. New occupational groups are, in all regions, being mobilized by lay entrepreneurs driving to tap new markets, extend new trade networks, and get their products on display at annual book fairs. By 1500, one may say with some assurance that the age of scribes had ended and the age of printers had begun.

Why then is there so much controversy about where to end one era and begin another; so much debate about a hypothetical transition instead of an actual occurrence; and, above all, such an abundance of false starts? To put the question less rhetorically, why has it become common practice to lump together developments that occurred during the last century or so of scribal culture with those that occurred during the first century or so of typographical culture, thereby creating a troublesome transitional era even while concealing a genuine revolutionary transformation? One might argue that the impact of the new mode of book production was bound to be muffled or delayed since it could have no effect on unlettered folk and hence initially affected only a very small literate élite. Fortunately we can dismiss this sort of argument without having to worry about inadequate data on fifteenth-century literacy rates. For scholars who deal with the problem of the Renaissance – who point to the survival of a 'medieval world picture' beyond the sixteenth century or who take Petrarch's inversion of pagan darkness and Christian light as their point of departure for a new cultural epoch – are looking only at literate élites.

To bring the problem in a sharper focus: the advent of printing, we are told, was the most important event 'in the *cultural* history of mankind'; it 'brought about the most radical transformation in the conditions of *intellectual* life in the history of Western civilization.'[10] Yet intellectual and cultural historians, in particular, have been unable to find room for it in their periodization schemes. To account for this paradox it seems necessary to look more closely at the peculiar, almost paradoxical, nature of the radical transformation itself. Instead of coupling the advent of printing with other innovations or regarding it

9 Bühler, *Fifteenth Century Books: An Address*, pp. 21–2.
10 McMurtrie, *The Book*, p. 136; Gilmore, *World of Humanism*, p. 186. [Italics mine.]

as an example of some other development, it has to be singled out as an event which was *sui generis* and to which conventional models of historical change cannot be applied.

The advent of printing transformed the conditions under which texts were produced, distributed and consumed. But this was accomplished in a most deceptive way – not by discarding the products of scribal culture but by reproducing them in greater quantities than ever before. The *ars artificialiter scribendi*[11] was first and foremost a duplicating process. Even while the conditions of scribal culture were being outmoded, texts reflecting these conditions were becoming more abundant, and different spirits from different times were being simultaneously released.

Later scholars, looking back on the first century of printing, will necessarily see few signs of the advent of a new culture, unless they know in advance what to look for. The most significant changes ushered in by typography cannot be detected by scanning booksellers' catalogues in search of new titles. This very activity inhibits recognition that a frequent use of title pages was new (and booksellers' catalogues were too) during the first century of printing. To be sure, living authors were better served by printers than they had been by scribes. But so too were dead authors better served in the same way. The most revolutionary impact of the new technology was initially exerted simply by increasing the output of extant texts – whatever their original provenance.

This point is worth stressing because it is often overlooked. Attention is usually centered on trying to determine whether early printers drew on scribal backlists or contemporary authors to furnish their main stock-in-trade. The somewhat naive assumption is made that such evidence will show whether printers encouraged the circulation of new ideas or not. Upon this basis, judgments are formed concerning the contribution made by printing to cognitive advance. Since the evidence is itself ambiguous;[12] since most 'new' works in the fifteenth century

---

[11] This very term which is translated by Bühler, *Fifteenth Century Books: An Address*, p. 96 as the 'art of writing by mechanical means' may have been used *before* printing to refer to skills taught by certain writing masters or 'artificers', according to Alfred Swierk in 'Was bedeutet "ars artificialiter scribendi"?' *Der Gegenwaertige Stand der Gutenberg-Forschung*, pp. 243–51.

[12] The thorny problems involved are noted by Hirsch, *Printing, Selling*, pp. 30–1, and well covered by Goldschmidt, *Medieval Texts, passim*, see esp. pp. 14–15; 41–2. Goldschmidt says that the preponderance of books published for academic markets during the first century of printing 'originated' (an ambiguous term) in the thirteenth and fourteenth centuries. With regard to the whole field, however, Bühler, *Fifteenth Century Books: An Address*, p. 15, con-

consisted of epitomes of old works while many old texts yielded much that seemed new in this era, conflicting interpretations are bound to result. Far from sweeping away the old, writes one authority, 'printers contributed to the artificial prolongation of the dying medieval culture.' Another regards early printers as so anxious to market new works that they cut off contemporary readers from the 'immediate' past.[13] The conviction that printing made a definite impact on Western culture is weakened by this kind of contradiction. It conveys an impression of cultural change that is too blurred and confused to leave much of a mark upon historical accounts.

As previous discussion of dissemination may suggest, printers initially contributed to 'the advancement of disciplines' less by marketing so-called 'new' works than by providing individual readers with access to *more* works. The sheer increase in the quantity of copies in circulation was actually of immense significance. Augmented book production altered patterns of consumption; increased output changed the nature of individual intake. The literary diet of a given sixteenth-century reader was qualitatively different from that of his fourteenth-century counterpart. His staple diet had been enriched, and intellectual ferment had been encouraged, whether he consulted living authors or dead ones, 'new' books or 'old' ones. But a twentieth-century observer, intent on tracing trends or shifts in styles of thought and expression, is poorly situated to see this.

Whether he counts titles relating to law, theology, science, and belles lettres or actually peruses relevant texts, he will find that the bookish culture of Europe between 1450 and 1550 was not markedly different from that which prevailed between 1350 and 1450.[14] At the same time he is aware of a continuously unfolding cultural movement sustained by successive generations of Italian artists and literati from the trecento through the cinquecento and beyond. Accordingly he will be inclined to group together the last century of scribal culture and the first century of printing. Renaissance scholarship has prepared him to find classical and humanist texts multiplying as he moves toward the end of the

cludes that over seventy per cent of all incunabula were 'composed' (also ambiguous) by contemporaries of Gutenberg. On the other hand, Hay states in his introduction to *Printing and the Mind of Man*, p. xxiii, that 'old' texts constituted the 'bulk' of works printed during the first century of printing.

[13] Compare Verwey, 'The Netherlands Book,' p. 9, with Clark, *Early Modern Europe*, p. 35.

[14] See e.g. Steele, 'What Fifteenth Century Books are About.' Also Lenhart, *Pre-Reformation Printed Books*; Haebler, *The Study of Incunabula*.

fifteenth century. He is less well prepared to find that time-tested epitomes, scholastic compendia, commentaries on Aristotle, and chivalric romances are also proliferating well after Gothic styles had been stigmatized and the 'new learning' launched. If he detects any shifts as he moves on into the early sixteenth century they will probably entail some sort of subtle retrogression. But newly composed Latin and vernacular works also become more abundant, so allowances must be made for certain confusing cross-currents. He will, in any case, have seen nothing in his mental voyage from the mid-fourteenth to the mid-sixteenth century to indicate that a cultural and intellectual revolution had occurred. With regard to the social history of art, we are informed by one authority: 'In the fifteenth century...it is true, a number of things come to fruition but as good as nothing absolutely new begins.'[15] Another account dealing with developments in astronomy finds that 'no mutational elements of significance appear to have been introduced in the fifteenth century.'[16]

In a later chapter I hope to suggest that a mutational element of significance was introduced into the study of astronomy during the fifteenth century when Regiomontanus set up his Nuremberg press. In this chapter, I want to suggest that printing produced a mutation of the classical revival itself. This entails adopting a somewhat different strategy from that employed in the citation at the head of this chapter. The relationship between a given technological and a given cultural change will be approached, not by taking them to coincide, as Butler does; but, rather, by acknowledging that they came at different times and by investigating how they affected each other. Let us then set aside for the moment, the problem of locating a transition from medieval to modern times and take as a starting point the Italian cultural revival which antedated printing. Given a cultural revival already under way, we may then ask: how was it affected by the shift from script to print?

The question seems so unexceptional that one is surprised to find it has seldom if ever been posed. The debate over periodization has probably blocked it from view. On the one hand, those who launch a new era with the trecento revival endow it from the beginning with

---

15 Arnold Hauser, *The Social History of Art*, II, 3.
16 Durand, 'Tradition and Innovation,' p. 35. The statement is based on evidence similar to that used by Sarton in his early work. Durand holds that early printed editions of Ptolemy's *Almagest* and of Archimedes' and Euclid's works simply duplicated 'crabbed medieval' Latin translations made by twelfth and thirteenth-century scribal scholars. See discussion pp. 508–17; 588 volume II below.

all its modernizing attributes and leave little or nothing for the new technology to do. On the other hand, those who question the Burckhardt thesis regard the Petrarchan revival as a limited and local episode and are rarely curious about how it might have been transformed. At all events the approach tried out here seems sufficiently unfamiliar for readers to have misinterpreted earlier versions of this chapter. To forestall further misunderstanding, some preliminary comments are in order. Before taking up specific issues, let me clarify some general points concerning the relationship between printing and the Renaissance.

In suggesting that something happened of great significance in the second half of the fifteenth century, I am not trying to depreciate the importance of what happened earlier, in the days of Petrarch and his immediate successors, nor am I denying that the Petrarchan revival introduced certain new elements into European culture. In suggesting that the Italian Renaissance underwent a mutation or a metamorphosis after the advent of printing, I am not arguing that there was nothing one may describe as a Renaissance before this event.

These disclaimers have to be made, not only to forestall misunderstanding but also to make clear that my approach is somewhat different from that of others who have also taken the advent of printing as a cultural demarcation point. I am referring not only to the sweeping and sensational claims made by Innis and McLuhan[17] but also to the more limited and cautious verdicts rendered by respected specialists. H. J. Chaytor, for example, asserts that 'the middle ages ended so far as literary style is concerned with the invention of printing' and George Sarton, in his later works defines the scientific Renaissance as beginning with printing and engraving.[18] I believe it would be a mistake to extend this line of analysis, which seems to obliterate the early phases of the Italian Renaissance. To investigate the effect of printing on the Petrarchan revival requires acknowledging the prior existence of the revival first of all. Moreover there is a difference between observing a mutation and performing an amputation. The movement which runs from the trecento to the cinquecento exhibits too much continuity to be completely split apart. Later generations of Italian artists and literati were

---

[17] See chap. 1, above. A single cogent sample is offered in Innis, *Empire and Communications*, pp. 7–8.

[18] Chaytor, *From Script to Print*, p. 82; Sarton, *Appreciation*, p. xi. Sarton's verdict provoked an interesting riposte from Kristeller in his preface to *Iter Italicum* I, XXII. On Sarton's 'ambivalent' views see pp. 507–8, volume II below.

not cut off from their predecessors merely because they could take advantage of printing and engraving for the first time. They carried on where their predecessors left off, working under different circumstances to be sure, but still toward the same goals. Many elements in the movement remained the same even while undergoing a change of phase. As previous discussion of amplification and reinforcement may suggest, when making more room for the advent of a new medium, the persistence of old messages should not be ignored. Even while trying to distinguish more clearly between the two different phases associated with script and with print, I have no intention of denying that a unified movement did unfold.

Furthermore, I can see few advantages in trying to describe the movement by some other term than that used by the early humanists when they wrote of a 'rinascita' and celebrated the rebirth of letters and learning in their own day. Far from holding that the term 'Renaissance' should be discarded, I would oppose this suggestion as both futile and undesirable.[19] For one thing, there is no way of eradicating a label that has been used for so many book titles, chapter-headings, course outlines, college catalogues, bibliographies, card-files, museum labels, art books, record albums and the like. This list has been extended deliberately to suggest how the duplicative powers of print act as a fixative. Given print culture, one may *add* to the contents of card catalogues; but there is no way of subtracting from them. To write an article questioning the use of the term 'Renaissance' only swells the bibliography that is filed under the questionable term. Not only does it seem futile to try to discard a label that is firmly fixed, but there are also some compelling reasons for continuing its use. My sympathies are with those who dislike the term because it perpetuates a self-congratulatory propaganda movement. One need not be a medievalist to find it dismaying that students still take the humanist version of history at face-value and think of the entire medieval millennium as a 'dark' interval which lasted down to Petrarch's cultural rebirth. Yet the very existence of so much promotional literature celebrating the end of the dark ages points to a movement which seems sufficiently distinctive to require using a distinctive label.

Moreover, the subjective appraisal of Renaissance literati is coupled

---

[19] In a paper given at an American Historical Association Meeting, Dec. 28, 1971, Walter J. Ong welcomed the suggestion and attributed it to me.

with objective indications of a distinctive cultural movement. Evidence supplied by equestrian statues and free standing nudes, commemorative bronze medals, classical motifs combined with classical subjects, circular churches, the use of focused perspective, the new styles of lettering and of manuscript illumination, all seems to justify the opening of a new chapter in art history with the early Renaissance in Italy. Given texts attacking scholasticism and celebrating civic humanism, intellectual historians have good reason for doing the same thing. It is not possible, in this account, to do justice to all the reasons why new chapters are opened, by various specialists, when they come to the Petrarchan revival. Yet the issue is too pivotal to be passed over entirely.

Let me list in quick succession some of the elements that were present in the quattrocento movement even before printers set to work. There is the new cycle of studies, connected with the new occupational groups who were engaged in speech-writing and undergraduate teaching and who developed a unique blend of moral philosophy and literary concerns. There is the pursuit of eloquence and repudiation of 'Gothic' styles; the increasing concern with language arts, especially with rhetoric and philology; the new spirit of civic humanism and celebration of the city of man.[20] In conjunction with all these developments there is also the persistent search for specific ancient texts neglected by medieval graduate faculties, the support of city state rulers, prelates and popes, and of a thriving literate merchant community. One should also note the demand for cheaper writing materials and the development of paper as a by-product of textile production, leading to a quickening pace of literary interchange in Italy well before printing. Given the concatenation of all these developments in an urban Mediterranean setting, it is not surprising that there is, finally, a special sense of kinship and closeness to the literati and civic spirit of ancient Rome.

The urban Mediterranean setting, the sense of kinship with certain ancient poets and artists, the sense of distaste for Gothic styles of thought and expression must be numbered among the special features that made the quattrocento revival different from the ninth-century Carolingian revival or the so-called twelfth-century Renaissance. Nevertheless, all three revivals also shared in common their reliance on the limited resources of scribal culture. Each depended on libraries that

[20] For pertinent references, see studies by P. O. Kristeller, Hanna Gray, Hans Baron mentioned elsewhere in this chapter.

were walled, on books that were chained or locked in chests, on manuscript collections that expanded only within certain limits and then
contracted – destroyed by fire, or war or looting. All three revivals
were marked also by a heavy reliance on oral transmission, the cultivation of speech arts and memory arts, and on the use of mnemonic aids.
All show the same tendency toward keeping sketchbooks closed and
toward handing down new techniques and craft skills within closed
circles of apprentices.

In the case of the quattrocento revival, these limits were transcended
in a manner that reoriented the Italian movement and, in my view,
reflected the impact of print. The new learning and the new art were
thus detached from a Mediterranean setting, and from the special civic
loyalties engendered by the city states of Italy. Humanism not only
crossed the Alps but it also expanded to encompass the very occupational groups who had been the special enemies of early humanists.
The Petrarchan revival had reflected departmental rivalries within the
groves of academe, with arts faculties promoting a humanistic cycle of
studies and the creation of new lectureships and chairs; while attacking
the graduate faculties of medicine, theology and law.[21] The later phases
of Renaissance humanism saw many physicians, theologians and jurists,
who collaborated with scholar printers, becoming advocates of the
humanistic disciplines themselves.[22] New divisions appeared within
every graduate faculty giving rise to lively pamphlet wars. Like
theology, medicine and jurisprudence, pulpit oratory was also caught
up in the conflict. Advocacy of the 'new learning' and the pursuit of
eloquence was taken up by preachers and teachers seeking to implement
traditional evangelical goals.[23] At the same time, Italian civic consciousness was transmuted and transplanted. Self-congratulatory themes and

---

[21] This issue is exemplified by Petrarch's polemic against the medical faculties, which is cited
below, pp. 251–2.

[22] In 'Erasmus and the Visual Arts,' pp. 200–27, Panofsky regards Erasmus as taking a 'restrictive
concept' of the Renaissance when he heralds the revival of 'good letters' in such fields as
medicine, philosophy and jurisprudence. But it can be argued that an 'expanded' concept is
being expressed. Even though Erasmus fails to mention the visual arts and refers only to Latin
learning, he is still extending the concept to fields excluded by earlier scribal scholars who
celebrated the *rinascita* and developed the cycle of studies associated with the 'studia humanita-
tus.' See Kristeller, *Renaissance Thought*, p. 10.

[23] Chester, 'The New Learning,' notes that the phrase 'new learning' was first used by English
theologians who were objecting to Lutheran teachings and was employed ironically thereafter
by defenders of the Reformation who held that they were merely reviving the teachings of
Augustine and Jerome. (I use it more loosely throughout this chapter in its more recent conventional sense which includes the pre-Reformation cycle of humanist studies described by
P. O. Kristeller.)

laudatory orations were extended beyond Italian city-state boundaries and used to glorify German imperial courts as well as Spanish, French and English dynasties. Even the concept of a barbaric 'Dark Age', which had earlier been elaborated by librarians and scholars at the papal court, was reoriented and turned against the papacy in the end.[24]

The distinction between an early and a later phase of the Renaissance: one limited to specific disciplines; the other expansive and intellectually comprehensive; one confined to Italy; the other encompassing the North, is implicit in many studies. The two phases have even received occasional explicit treatment – notably by P. S. Allen who anticipated my position by connecting the later phase with changes wrought by print.[25] In the decades that followed the appearance of Allen's studies on Erasmus, however, other interpretations prevailed. The two phases, which were 'easily distinguished' around the turn of the century when Allen was studying history, have become much less distinct in recent years. They have been blurred by the practice of bisecting the Renaissance in other ways by dividing a 'classical' from a 'Christian' Renaissance for example, or an Italian from a Northern one, and by other dichotomized schemes.[26] Recent debates over the difference between the 'Renaissance of the Twelfth Century' and that of the quattrocento also leave less room for contrasting two different phases of the latter movement itself. That Allen's phases are no longer 'easily distinguished' is shown by the inclusion, in a volume of papers presumably devoted to the 'Early' Renaissance, of an essay on Michelangelo's poetry.[27] However much he was indebted to the poets and artists of the early quattrocento, all of Michelangelo's oeuvre, along with that of Raphael, Titian and others, surely belongs to a later, post-

---

[24] How anti-papist propagandists manipulated the theme of the 'dark ages' is brought out by W. K. Ferguson, *Renaissance in Historical Thought*. See also citations on pp. 304–5, below.

[25] Allen, *The Age of Erasmus*, pp. 260–3. Woodward's 1897 study of *Vittorino da Feltre and Other Humanist Educators*, pp. 182; 206; also points to differences between an early period, running from the death of Petrarch to the 1470s, and the later 'age of Erasmus' and Vives in a manner that brings out the impact of print.

[26] The concept of a Christian Renaissance has itself become complicated by the proliferation of diverse and contradictory schemes. Hyma's *Christian Renaissance* concerns the *Devotio Moderna* movement which goes back to the fourteenth century; Lewis Spitz's *Religious Renaissance* (of the German Humanists) commences after the mid-fifteenth century. Despite its title, Enno van Gelder's *Two Reformations of the Sixteenth Century* is mainly concerned with the 'Religious Aspects of the Renaissance' during the sixteenth century – an interval also covered by Hiram Haydn's 'Counter-Renaissance' movement.

[27] *Developments in the Early Renaissance* (ed. Bernard S Levy), Another paper in the same collection, by Rudolph Wittkower on Renaissance hieroglyphics, also seems to fall outside the 'early' phase, given its concern with the Aldine edition of 'Horapollo' and Alciati's *Emblemata*.

print phase of the Renaissance. But the principles of art history have never left much room for the impact of printing upon the work of the greatest Renaissance masters.

It is noteworthy that the two phases which are conspicuous in the studies of Erasmus by Allen are inconspicuous in the studies of Dürer by Panofsky, although the German artist no less than the Dutch humanist was profoundly indebted to print.[28] In his many erudite and fascinating studies the art historian seems to be so intent on distinguishing between earlier renascences and the Italian Renaissance and between Northern and Italian trends, that he leaves little room for distinguishing between diverse phases of the Italian movement itself. When he does bring up the topic of 'multiplying media' in one article, it is to contrast a so-called 'Northern' propensity for popularization and egalitarianism with a so-called 'Italian' élitism and secrecy.[29] Yet surely Italian printers and engravers showed themselves just as ready to exploit new publicity techniques as did the Flemings, the Germans or the Dutch. Did not the Venetians pioneer as publicists and provide the first example of Grub Street that Europe knew?[30] The contrast between keeping things secret and publicizing them seems to be more closely related to conditions before and after printing than to differences between Italian and Northern Europe.[31] Raphael and Michelangelo profited from printed publicity just as Dürer did. Indeed Vasari tells us that Dürer's engravings prompted Raphael to have his own works engraved by Marcantonio Raimondi of Bologna.[32] The number of presses that dotted the peninsula soon after the new art was born and the number of print shops clustered in Venice by 1500, also suggest that 'multiplying media' were no less welcome in Italy than elsewhere in the North.

As these remarks may suggest, current interpretations of the Re-

---

[28] In *Albrecht Dürer* I, 33–4ff, Panofsky does underline how much Dürer owed to engravings for his view of antiquity and discusses the artist's use of varied media, but still places him in the context of a Northern rather than a post-print Renaissance. That the latter concept is foreign to his general historical scheme is also clear from his other work. See second section of this chapter below.

[29] In 'Erasmus and Visual Arts,' pp. 218–20, Panofsky develops this contrast with reference to the Italian habit of putting portraits under lock and key as against the multiplication of Holbein's portraits of Erasmus in copies of *Praise of Folly*. The first author portrait to be multiplied in a printed book appeared under Italian, not Northern, auspices (in Milan, 1479). See Hirsch, *Printing, Selling*, p. 60.

[30] See discussion of Aretino's métier and references in n. 181, below.

[31] For further discussion of secrecy–publicity issues see section 4 of this chapter and pp. 562ff., volume II below.   [32] Vasari's *Lives of the Artists*, p. 228.

naissance often fail to distinguish between what was peculiar to Italy and what was peculiar to print. This is especially apparent in studies devoted to the later phases of the Italian movement. The spread of humanism to Northern Europe is discussed without considering how traditional forms of cultural diffusion, both within and without Italy, may have been changed. This point may be illustrated by drawing on studies dealing with the 'mechanics of diffusion' to use Peter Burke's phrase. In surveying this problem, Burke passes in review what various authorities have written and poses questions concerning the agents of diffusion himself. 'Who were the middlemen?' he asks and replies 'The translators, the printers, the travellers; foreigners who visited Italy...Italians who came to live abroad and in a sense Italy as a whole ...'[33] The roles of translators, travellers and of 'Italy as a whole' were not merely supplemented by the addition of printers but were changed by their arrival. Staffs of vernacular translators were mobilized; fewer trips over the Alps had to be made; dictionaries and thesauruses lessened reliance on personal encounters and the service of emigrés. In this light it seems desirable to distinguish between the old agents of cultural diffusion and those who were newcomers to the scene. The same point is cogent in Roberto Weiss' discussion of the 'spread of Italian humanism.' Weiss singles out the papacy as 'a powerful propagating factor'[34] without making clear whether he is referring to the period before or after printing. It seems likely that the very power of the papacy as a 'propagating factor' was affected by the shift from script to print. The reliance of Northern scholars on the uncertain sporadic interchanges entailed in church council conclaves and visits to papal courts was lessened as the output of scholar printers increased.

Not only do changes introduced by the Petrarchan revival need to be more clearly distinguished from those introduced by printing, but the relationship between the two developments also needs much more careful thought. A recent large volume on the history of the book put out by UNESCO contains a chapter by its editor, H. D. L. Vervliet, who says, 'It is not so much that printing made the Renaissance possible as

---

[33] Burke, *The Renaissance*, section VII, pp. 119ff.

[34] Weiss, *The Spread of Italian Humanism*, pp. 86–7. There is mention of the 'timely' invention of printing on p. 46, but less attention is devoted to this propagating factor than to the papacy. It also seems an understatement to say that the role of printed books in the spread of Italian humanism was 'no less impressive' than that of ms books before, Kristeller, 'The European Diffusion,' p. 82.

that the Renaissance contributed to the successful spread of printing.'[35] Both clauses seem to me to need revising. If the movement launched by Petrarch is considered, the first part seems much too weak. Not at all did printing make the Petrarchan revival 'possible,' Gutenberg came too late for that. The second part of the statement: that the Renaissance contributed to the spread of print, requires substantiation which the author fails to give and which seems elusive to me. How was the *spread* of printing propelled by the new cycle of studies, or by the classical revival? Did not early editions of Cicero which flooded markets contribute less to the spread of printing than to the bankruptcy of early printers? No doubt there is a relation between increased literacy rates and paper production in Italy. Paper in turn was indispensable for the development of and spread of printing. But so too were Northern workshops which spread the new art in regions that were remote from Renaissance Italy and in order to serve the needs of preachers and teachers pursuing traditional Christian ends. A manuscript bookdealer such as Vespasiano may well be taken both as a precursor of the humanist printer Aldus Manutius and as an embodiment of the quattrocento Renaissance; yet, clearly he did nothing to encourage the spread of the new art. If anything, the shoe was on the other foot; Gutenberg may have forced Vespasiano to close shop. Early Rhenish workshops did not flourish in response to demands coming from Italy, except for demands coming from ecclesiastical Rome. The crusade against the Turks brought envoys to Gutenberg's workshop requesting printed indulgences. Bibles, sermons, breviaries, indulgences, calendars and almanacks were among the main staples of early Rhineland trade. The first attempt to use the new medium to arouse widespread mass support was not in connection with Florentine humanism but with a late medieval crusade, that is with the war against the Turks.

In this regard it is difficult to understand the persistence of the notion that printing came as a 'by-product of the Renaissance spirit.'[36] However that elusive 'spirit' may be defined, it was not strongly manifested in the regions where the first printers set shop. The new technology

---

[35] Vervliet, 'Printing,' p. 356. Almost the same point was made in a bibliophile's lecture in 1921: 'Printing did not make the Renaissance; the Renaissance made printing.' Slater, *Printing and the Renaissance*, p. 1. I remain mystified by the second clause.

[36] DeMolen, 'The Age of the Renaissance and Reformation,' p. 16. See also Randall's much used text: *The Making of the Modern Mind*, p. 119. 'The demand for learning seemed insatiable. The answer was the production of books printed on paper.'

and occupational culture, it should be recalled, spread beyond Mainz to German and Swiss–German towns during the 1460s even while the first German printers were crossing the Alps. The spread of printing to towns such as Strasbourg, Cologne, Augsburg, Nuremberg and Basel accompanied its spread into Italy. The route followed by Caxton: Cologne–Bruges–London also points to currents that were remote from the 'Renaissance spirit' of mid-quattrocento Italy. Recent studies of how printing came to Lyons similarly show that a negligible role was played by Italian humanism there.[37] One may even suggest that Venice like Lyons became a main center of the new form of book production more because of late medieval trade-patterns than because it participated in the new art and letters cultivated in Renaissance Italy.

When considering elements which contributed to the success of Gutenberg's invention, 'by-products of the Renaissance spirit' ought to be coupled with by-products of medieval Christian concerns. The first business trip that was made by one of Gutenberg's associates, Johann Fust, was to carry Bibles to the University of Paris. Fust was thus hoping to tap markets for the Old Learning rather than the New. A mental voyage from Mainz and the Gutenberg Bible to Strasbourg and the Mentelin Bible, to Wittenberg and the Lutheran Bible suggests how forces propelling the new industry were rooted more in the Christian than in the classical tradition, even while also stemming from early capitalist, profit-seeking drives.[38] For the initial impetus given to the expansion of early printing, one should look first to the book which Westerners regard as the perennial 'bestseller'. The evangelical urge to spread glad tidings ultimately resulted in establishing presses in Africa and Asia. It probably did more to propel printing in the West than did the effort to bring back the muses to quattrocento Florence.

It would be a mistake to separate classical and Christian traditions too sharply, however. Just as Italian paper-making and Northern metallurgy were brought together by the new technology, so too were diverse textual traditions, long separated in lecture halls, newly intertwined in the workshops of scholar–printers. Work on Greek texts, for example, as pursued in Venice or Basel or Lyons, brought the old and new learning closer together. So too did the editing of polyglot Bibles and the output of new vernacular translations. Once they could

---

[37] Fedou, 'Imprimerie et Culture,' pp. 1–27.
[38] This point is neatly illustrated by Robert Kingdon, 'Patronage, Piety and Printing.'

be duplicated in quantity Greek grammars and dictionaries proved useful for many diverse purposes – they served not only poets, mythographers and astronomers but anatomists and theologians as well. Divisions maintained in old lecture halls were not sustained in the new workshops. Humanists and Bible printers became close allies even while humanists and schoolmen often remained at odds.

Thus the second part of Vervliet's formula might hold up better if the terms were reversed. The Renaissance probably did less to spread printing than printing did to spread the Renaissance. To say this is to repeat what others have also said[39] rather than to offer a new insight on how the classical revival may have been changed. Yet old truths often need to be repeated. Given numerous studies which pass over printing when discussing the 'spread of Italian humanism,' this particular point seems worth underlining once again. Let me recall the warning given to the Venetian printer, Aldus Manutius, as reported by Erasmus' biographer and friend. According to Beatus Rhenanus, the printer was told that if he published his Greek commentaries on Euripides and Sophocles he would encourage the 'barbarians' to remain at home and thus cut down on tourist traffic into Italy.[40] As it turned out, the Aldine editions did have the predicted effect, enabling Northern scholars to learn Greek and to teach it to successive generations without leaving their homes. In this regard, dissemination may be linked to a significant reorientation which diminished the cultural influence exerted over the Alps by 'eternal' Rome.

Nevertheless it would be a mistake to confine discussion to the 'spread' of Italian humanism and thus focus attention on dissemination – the one function performed by printing which is invariably singled out. As the preceding chapter suggests, several other functions ought to be assigned equal prominence. In particular, the preservative powers of printing ought to be given higher priority, especially when considering a revival which has been singled out for being more permanent than previous movements of a similar kind.

[39] E.g. Hirsch, 'Printing and the Spread of Humanism,' pp. 24–37.
[40] 'The Life of Erasmus by Beatus Rhenanus' (1540), *Christian Humanism and The Reformation: Selected Writings of Erasmus*, ed. and tr. by J. C. Olin, p. 48.

2. DISTINGUISHING BETWEEN TRANSITORY REVIVALS AND A PERMANENT RENAISSANCE

Let me turn then to the question of how the advent of printing may be related to the emergence of a so-called permanent Renaissance. Given a classical revival that was still under way when new preservative powers were brought into play, one might expect that this revival would acquire peculiar characteristics. Since it was initiated under one set of circumstances and perpetuated under different ones, it would probably begin by resembling previous revivals and yet take an increasingly divergent course. Among other differences that would become apparent with the passage of time, one would expect this revival to be more permanent than previous ones.

'To put it briefly, the two medieval renascences were limited and transitory; the Renaissance was total and permanent.'[41] As Panofsky's now celebrated formulation suggests, the issue of permanence does figure prominently in current debates. However, typographical fixity does not. To be sure, one scholar has suggested that 'humanism may have owed the ultimate survival of its ideas to Gutenberg's invention.'[42] But this comes as a casual aside, qualifying the author's main argument that the distinctive features of the 'Italian Renaissance, as such' owed nothing to the 'novelties of the printing press.' 'The pattern of the movement had been clearly established' he contends before printing began to exert an impact. Since he does not deal with the question of how printing affected the patterning of cultural movements, I find Bolgar's argument ambiguous and incomplete, but that is somewhat beside the point. My basic concern is that his casual remark about 'ultimate survival' has not been followed up. The implications of typographical fixity do not often get brushed aside in Renaissance studies, but only because they are usually left out of account altogether.

This unfortunate omission may be attributed in part to the somewhat subtle, intangible nature of the preservative powers of print – a feature already discussed in the preceding chapter. Previous discussion may suffice to suggest that there are good reasons for believing that preservation was an important feature introduced by typography. There seems

41 Panofsky, *Renaissance and Renascences*, p. 106.
42 Bolgar, *The Classical Heritage*, p. 280.

to be no reason at all for believing that this feature was introduced by artists or literati associated with the humanist movement in quattrocento Italy. If the muses returned to stay, this was because of something that happened after they were recalled that had not happened before. Moreover, the preservative powers of print changed the character of *all* forms of survival and revival; their impact was by no means confined to the return of the muses in quattrocento Italy. Medieval survivals and early Christian revivals were also affected by typographical fixity in ways that need to be investigated.

The immense consequences of the preservative powers of print are at present, however, concealed by the problem of the Renaissance. Instead of being attributed to the new technology, or even recognized as a new cultural trait that needs to be accounted for, permanence currently serves as a debating point. As an inherent virtue, somehow exuded by Renaissance culture, it is invoked to save the appearances of a century-old theory that has been under attack. No explanation is offered as to why medieval classical revivals were more transitory than that which occurred in quattrocento Italy.[43] The fact that the latter did prove more permanent and hence lent itself to continuous systematic development is taken to justify setting it apart from prior revivals and inaugurating a new epoch with its advent. In this way objections posed to Burckhardt's thesis can be countered and a seemingly interminable debate prolonged.

By now it is evident that most of the criteria employed to distinguish the Italian Renaissance from prior revivals may, with equal validity, also be employed to distinguish these prior revivals from each other. Each of the revivals in question, from the days of Charlemagne to those of the Medici, was sponsored by different élites, served the needs of different professional groups, and occurred within the context of dissimilar regional cultures. That the Italian Renaissance had certain peculiar features which deserve to be singled out as novel and significant has been noted already.[44] But so too did the Carolingian revival and

---

[43] Unless one accepts as an explanation the passage that precedes Panofsky's remark, 'this is why the medieval renascences were transitory; whereas the Renaissance was permanent,' *Renaissance and Renascences*, p. 113. To say that the Renaissance 'stood weeping' at the grave of antiquity and succeeded in resurrecting 'its soul' represents a poetic rephrasing of the problem but does not, in my opinion, constitute a genuine explanation.

[44] See above, p. 173. Insofar as Bolgar is suggesting that these features had emerged before printing began to exert an impact, I would agree with him. But I also think they might have been smudged or erased during Italy's 'time of troubles' in the early sixteenth century had not typographical fixity intervened.

that of the twelfth century have significant new features. Why, then, attribute a special epoch-making role to the quattrocento revival? It seems to be difficult to justify this attribution without straining the evidence, by reading back into quattrocento cultural products anticipations of later developments. In the nineteenth century, early humanist texts were made to point to the secular and modernist heresies that were being listed in the Syllabus of Errors. At present, Renaissance humanists look less like nineteenth-century freethinkers than they once did. But they look more like twentieth-century historians instead. As 'the ancestors of modern philologists and historians'[45] they resemble contemporary professional scholars too closely, in my view, for their true likeness to be caught.

In the Middle Ages there was in relation to the Antique a cyclical succession of assimilative and non-assimilative stages. Since the Renaissance the Antique has been constantly with us, whether we like it or not. It lives in our mathematics and natural sciences. . .it is firmly entrenched behind the thin but thus far unbroken walls of history, philology and archeology.

The formation and, ultimately, formalization of these three disciplines – foreign to the Middle Ages in spite of all the Carolingian and twelfth century 'humanists' – evince a fundamental difference between the medieval and modern attitude toward. . .antiquity. . . .In the Italian Renaissance the classical past began to be looked at from a fixed distance, quite comparable to the 'distance between the eye and the object' in that most characteristic invention of this very Renaissance, focused perspective. . .this distance prohibited direct contact. . .but permitted a total and rationalized view.[46]

It is undeniable that there is a fundamental difference between medieval and modern views of antiquity. Medieval scholars did not see the classical past from a fixed distance as we do now. They did not regard it as a container of objects to be placed in glass cases and investigated by specialists in diverse scholarly fields. Nor were they familiar with the historical disciplines as they are practiced today. Agreement on these points, however, still leaves open to dispute the views of Renaissance humanists and the correct interpretation of their attitude toward the past. Given their celebration of a revival based on classical models and their passion for recovering, collecting and examining antique

---

[45] Kristeller, *Renaissance Thought*, p. 98.
[46] Panofsky, *Renaissance and Renascences*, p. 108. The passage is frequently cited or paraphrased with approval by others. See e.g. Gilmore, *World of Humanism*, p. 236.

works, given also their more novel belief that a dark interval of barbarism separated them from antiquity, were they the harbingers of a new and distinctively modern historical consciousness? Did their sense of temporal distance come close to resembling our own? Panofsky, of course, answers affirmatively, and many other distinguished authorities agree with him. Passages drawn from a variety of Renaissance texts – ranging from Petrarch to Erasmus – are cited to support him.[47] It is almost taken for granted at present that a capacity to view the past from a fixed distance may be singled out as a distinguishing feature of Renaissance thought – one that links the Italian revival with later developments and separates it from prior ones.

Despite the formidable support it commands, I think this interpretation is open to dispute. It has to be sustained by straining a good deal of evidence on the one hand and ignoring a good deal of counter-evidence on the other hand. For example, when Renaissance expressions of nostalgic longing for a past that has gone forever are taken as equivalent to our modern sense of 'fixed' distance, the evidence *is* being strained, in my view. Similar expressions of regret for a vanished past also crop up in medieval texts. That 'every age has found its own modernity displeasing and has preferred a past age to itself'[48] was already expressed in the twelfth century.

Although Panofsky argues that Carolingian and twelfth-century revivals were 'free' from 'nostalgia,' his opinion is not sustained by evidence supplied by other authorities. For example, Federico Chabod cites an early twelfth-century elegy on ancient Rome by Hildebert of Le Mans, in order to contrast the medieval poet's sense of finality with Renaissance beliefs that antique culture could be revitalized. According to Chabod, the most distinctive characteristic of the Petrarchan movement lay in its optimism about the possibility of reviving antiquity instead of forever mourning its loss.

Imitatio: here we find uttered the all-important word that divides the world of Cola from the world of Hildebert of Le Mans. In place of admiration mingled with regret, for what can never return, we find a determination to act in scrupulous conformity with the teachings of the Ancients. *Legere*

---

47 Gilmore, *World of Humanism*, p. 236 and Harbison, *The Christian Scholar*, p. 93, provide relevant citations accompanied by apposite interpretations.

48 Cited by Chenu, *Nature, Man and Society*, p. 320. Many other twelfth-century passages are cited by Chenu which contain sentiments conventionally attributed to the new historical consciousness of the quattrocento Renaissance.

becomes *exercere*. And instead of an elegy we have an exhortation to revive the ancient splendors, the glories of Rome.[49]

Hans Baron, similarly, argues that Renaissance humanism was distinctive because it viewed antiquity 'not melancholically as a golden age never again to be realized but as an exemplary parallel to the present, encouraging the moderns to seek to rival antiquity in their vernacular languages and literatures.'[50] Whereas Chabod emphasizes the Petrarchan theme of cultivating true Latinity and praising Rome, Baron suggests that early quattrocento Florence was peculiarly innovative in adapting antique themes to non-Roman institutions and in placing the Tuscan *volgare* on an equal footing with ancient Latin.[51]

Whether one stresses *imitatio* as does Chabod or *emulatio* as does Baron, the fact remains that for both it was not a sense of distance but of closeness to antiquity which animated the Italian revival. The distinctive feature was a determination to rekindle the ancient spirit rather than a nostalgic elegiac mood. If one accepts this analysis, it seems that the sense of distance described by Panofsky – a 'distance which prohibited direct contact...but permitted a total and rational-

---

[49] Chabod, *Machiavelli*, pp. 168–9. Like Chabod, Theodore Mommsen contrasts the humanist 'hope of resurrection' with the sense of final loss inspired by the sight of Roman ruins. But he cites Gibbon's late eighteenth-century nostalgia as a foil for Petrarch's views rather than medieval poetry. Mommsen, 'Petrarch's Conception,' p. 233. Roberto Weiss *does* cite Hildebert's elegy and yet insists that medieval man 'failed to notice a fracture between the classical age and their own.' *The Renaissance Discovery of Classical Antiquity*, p. 3.

[50] Baron, *The Crisis of the Early Italian Renaissance*, pp. 460–1. Baron's emphasis on the modernity inherent in the Florentine break with the notion of 'perennial Rome' needs to be balanced against Chenu's discussion of the medieval political 'translatio' theme (developed by Otto of Freising) of the movement of empire from Rome to Byzantium to the Franks, Lombards and then to the Germans. Chenu, *Nature, Man*, pp. 1–2, 186–7, 200–1. The theme of cultural 'translatio studii' which led from Greece to Rome to Paris (in the opinion of University of Paris scholars before the Italian Renaissance) is also discussed by Weisinger, 'Who Began the Revival of learning?' and by Kinser, 'Ideas of Temporal Change,' pp. 720–1. To be sure, a transplanted empire may be more compatible with themes of continuity than the idea of linking the fall of Rome with the birth of new nation states. Nevertheless, the medieval idea that 'Westward runs the course of Empire' was just as significant for later historiography as any of the quattrocento Florentine concepts underlined by Baron. The 'translatio' theme also belies the idea that there was an inherently static quality to belief in a perennial Rome. For a well-rounded sympathetic account of medieval historiography see Southern, 'Aspects of the European Tradition.'

[51] In both *Crisis*, chap. 15 and his article on the '*Querelle* of the Ancients and the Moderns' Baron treats the defense of vernaculars against the claims of Latin as a particularly 'humanist' development without noting the powerful boost given by printers to the promotion of translation movements in every realm and for all kinds of texts. Even without scattered early quattrocento arguments in favor of the *volgare* (and they were counterbalanced by arguments in favor of Latin) the vernaculars would probably have been defended and become triumphant after printing.

ized view' – was foreign not only to the middle ages but also to the interval he allots to the Italian Renaissance.

In this regard, the art historian's suggestion that the capacity to see the past from a fixed distance is 'quite comparable' to the 'distance between the eye and the object' in central perspective renderings[52] needs to be taken with caution. In the present century, images of the past which appear in one's mind's eye (and on the covers of books dealing with historical subjects) do seem to entail a resort to Renaissance perspective devices; but this tells us nothing about the historical circumstances governing both developments. An especially incautious use of the suggestion is evident in McLuhan's work where much is made of the fact that historians use terms such as 'perspective' and 'point of view.'[53] As medieval etymologies suggest, almost anything can be proved by playing with words. In my view, the difference between a treatise on optics and one on chronology needs to be more carefully assessed.

That a 'total rationalized' view of any past civilization could be developed before the output of uniform reference guides and gazetteers seems implausible to me. How could the entire classical past be viewed 'from a fixed distance' until a permanent temporal location had been found for antique objects, place names, personages, and events? The capacity to see the past in this way could not be obtained by new optical effects devised by Renaissance artists. It required a rearrangement of documents and artifacts rather than a rearrangement of pictorial space.

The Middle Ages did not lose the classical interest in inscriptions and archeological remains. Inscriptions were occasionally collected. Monuments were noticed. What was lost was...the idea of a civilization recovered by systematic collection of all the relics of the past....The great antiquarians of the sixteenth century...combined literary, archeological and epigraphical texts. They slowly pieced together Roman chronology, topography, law and religion....[54]

No doubt quattrocento humanists, eager to imitate and emulate, had begun to copy inscriptions and images and to collect ancient objects,

---

[52] Panofsky's suggestion first appeared in *Studies in Iconology*, p. 28 and is reiterated in his *Renaissance and Renascences*.
[53] See McLuhan, *Gutenberg Galaxy*, pp. 56, 111–12. Here as elsewhere McLuhan's interpretation owes much to Giedion's *Space Time and Architecture*. Giedion follows Panofsky in assigning a pivotal cultural role to the invention of focused perspective.
[54] Momigliano, 'Ancient History,' pp. 5–6.

before printing. It required at least a century of printing however before a 'systematic collection' of relics, a 'slow piecing together' of records and a mastery of ancient chronologies could occur.[55] It was not only the loss of the *idea* of systematically reconstructing a past civilization, it was also the absence of adequate equipment for such an undertaking which made earlier views of antiquity so fundamentally different from our own.

It took at least a century of printing before the multiform maps and tangled chronologies inherited from scribal records were sorted out, data reworked, and more uniform systems for arranging materials were developed. Before then, there was no fixed spatial-temporal reference frame which men of learning shared. This is not to deny that a growing sensitivity to anachronism was manifested by quattrocento scholars. There was discrimination between Gothic and antique styles, medieval and Ciceronian Latin, republican and imperial institutions, the Rome of ancient Caesars and of medieval popes. But it occurred within an amorphous spatio-temporal context that was still fundamentally different from the modern one.[56] Within this context some portions of the past might appear to be very close at hand, even while others might be placed at a great distance. Since we are told that an Attic stele from the fifth century B.C. could not be distinguished by sixteenth-century connoisseurs from a piece of sculpture by Michelangelo,[57] it would appear that some portions of the Greco-Roman past must have seemed very close at hand even after the quattrocento had ended.

Panofsky regards it as characteristic of the medieval mind that it viewed classical antiquity as 'too strongly present' and at the same time as 'too far removed' to be 'conceived as an historical phenomenon... Linguists looked upon Cicero and Donatus as their forefathers... mathematicians traced their ancestry back to Euclid' even while there was awareness of 'an unsurmountable gap' between pagan and Christian eras. 'These two tendencies were as yet not balanced so as to

---

[55] For interesting data on role of Basel printers in promoting the output of guides to ancient coins, costumes, and other artifacts see Bietenholz, *Basle and France*, chap. 4.

[56] For a sensitive description of this spatio-temporal context which persisted down through the sixteenth century see Lucien Febvre's *Le Problème*, pp. 418–37.

[57] Panofsky, *Renaissance and Renascences*, p. 41. Other examples of an inability to distinguish Renaissance products from ancient ones are given by Gilmore, *World of Humanism*, p. 237. The extent to which classical form and non-classical subject matter were still joined by sculptors of the early quattrocento is brought out by Janson, 'The Revival of Antiquity.'

permit a feeling of historical distance.' 'No medieval man could see the civilization of antiquity as a phenomenon complete in itself... belonging to the past...detached from the contemporary world.'[58] His discussion seems equally pertinent to the mind of the quattrocento humanists and indeed to that of many cinquecento scholars.

In this regard, the mentality of those artists and literati who collected ancient art works and copied ancient inscriptions during the quattrocento needs to be distinguished from that of modern curators and scholars who are still engaged in similar activities. The latter are alert to the difference between ancient Roman styles of lettering and those of Carolingian scribes. They are unlikely to confuse the work of an ancient artist with that of a cinquecento one. The contrary was true of Renaissance scholars and connoisseurs. Even Dürer's work, which was modelled on copies and engravings, was mistaken for the art of classical antiquity – as Panofsky himself demonstrates.[59] Moreover the successors of Dürer and Michelangelo continued to embody Christian subject matter in classical forms just as medieval artists had. In the late sixteenth century a student of Vasari presented an Apollonian sun god which

was patterned after Michelangelo's 'Risen Christ'...At a time when artists, as Dürer expressed it, had learned to fashion the image of Christ...in the likeness of Apollo, the image of Apollo could be fashioned in the likeness of Christ; in the judgement of his contemporaries and followers, Michelangelo and the Antique had become equivalent.[60]

Not only were the works of contemporary artists confused with ancient ones and pagan forms still employed for Christian subjects, but some medieval bookhands (notably Carolingian minuscule) were also mistakenly attributed to antiquity.[61] When they handled manuscript books copied by eleventh and twelfth-century scribes, quattrocento literati thought they were looking at texts that came right out of the bookshops of ancient Rome. When they sat down and wrote out their own books in a similar bookhand, they must have also experienced a sense of closeness to ancient authors that is quite unlike our own. We might compare the experience of a humanist who was engaged in copying one of Livy's books, and thus, in a sense, was engaged in

58 Panofsky, *Studies in Iconology*, p. 27.
59 Panofsky, *Meaning in the Visual Arts*, p. 294.
60 Panofsky, *Meaning in the Visual Arts*, p. 158. This student of Vasari was Giovanni Stradano (or Stradanus) (or Jan van der Straet) whose *Nova Reperta* is discussed above, p. 20.
61 Kristeller, *Renaissance Thought*, p. 21.

'writing' one of Livy's books,[62] with our experience in taking down a bound volume in the Loeb series from some library shelf.

Doubtless the very activity of copying and commenting on books by ancient authors such as Livy did help to sharpen awareness of the difference between ancient and contemporary Latin grammar as well as between ancient styles of thought and expression and those reflected in the medieval Latin texts which were used in the schools. A sophisticated approach to philology as a key to dating documents was manifested by some Renaissance scribal scholars, most notably by Lorenzo Valla.[63] But the heavy reliance on memory training and speech arts, combined with the absence of uniform conventions for dating and placing, worked against any reinforcement of this embryonic consciousness. Given ubiquitous training in the *ars memorandi*, classical images were more likely to be placed in niches in 'memory theatres' than to be assigned a permanent location in a fixed past.[64]

Given the absence of fixed guidelines, moreover, the copying of ancient artifacts and of ancient texts often contributed less to setting antiquity at a distance than to making it appear closer at hand.

Petrarch learned direct from Livy and wrote direct to him; Salutati's and Bruni's Florence learned direct from republican Rome and envisaged itself as Rome's revival. Later...Machiavelli's famous letter...describes how he ...puts on formal clothing and enters into the presence and conversation of the ancients by reading their books. The conversation is meant to restore Machiavelli not only to the understanding of politics but indirectly to actual civic participation. The idea of direct conversation with antiquity is a key concept in all forms of humanism...[65]

[62] See definition of authors given by Bonaventura, cited above, pp. 121–2. Poggio is told by Bruni that he will be honored as the 'second author' of all the texts he has recovered and restored. Letter of September 15, 1416 in Gordan (ed.), *Two Renaissance book hunters*, p. 191. Variations on this scribal theme are elaborated in later celebrations of Copernicus as a 'second Ptolemy' or Vesalius as a 'second Galen.'

[63] A full appreciation of Valla's many contributions to the development of historical scholarship is given by Kelley, *Foundations*, chap. 2. In applying the scheme developed by Thomas Kuhn's *Structure of Scientific Revolutions* to Renaissance historiography and in suggesting Valla could be cast as a 'Copernicus of the Historical Revolution,' Kelley seems to overlook the difficulty of applying Kuhn's analysis to circumstances before printing, that is, before anything equivalent to 'normal science' or 'normal research' existed. (See critique of Kuhn offered on pp. 605ff., volume II below.) Valla's position as a precursor seems to be related to the new continuous and systematic character of research activities launched after printing. His posthumous reputation also owed much to the numerous printed editions of his own works that were issued. See n. 114 below.

[64] The use of vividly presented classical images, personages, myths, etc. to help memorize abstract Christian teachings is brought out by Yates, *Art of Memory* and helps to explain the disjunctions assigned to the 'Gothic mind' by Panofsky.

[65] Pocock, *The Machiavellian Moment*, p. 62.

The idea of a 'direct conversation' with ancient Romans seems to point to an intimacy that is incompatible with our 'total rationalized' view of antiquity. Even when due allowance is made for the conventional character of rhetorical exercises, the writing of letters to long dead authors still seems to work at cross-purposes with holding the ancients at a fixed distance.[66] When Petrarch dated his letters to Livy as being in such and such a year 'of the Incarnation of Him of whom you would have heard had you lived a little longer' he was conveying a sense of distance which seems somewhat similar to Dante's addressing Virgil as 'poet, by the God you did not know.'[67] In both cases we are offered evidence of a mentality which lacked modern perspective – which simultaneously could envisage ancient poets as being kindred spirits and also as belonging in a remote pre-Christian context.

How the early humanists were inhibited from developing a sense of fixed distance is also suggested by their ignorance concerning events that occurred in the more recent past. The hundreds of years that had elapsed after the barbarians first sacked Rome could be counted and were known – as Petrarch's dating of his letters to the ancients shows. But the events that took place during those hundreds of years were more obscure than the events that had occurred earlier. Ancient historians were closely studied, but medieval chronicles were not.[68] Insofar as dark, dimly lit figures are likely to seem more distant than bright, clearly lighted ones, the lives of the Caesars must have seemed closer to quattrocento scholars than did the Holy Roman Emperors of more recent times. In contrast to 'the canonical history of Greece and Rome'[69] the medieval past presented a confusing tangle of incongruous local chronicles coupled with conflicting papal and imperial grand designs. The political history of the most recent millennium was merely confused and tangled; its cultural history was even darker than

---

[66] The composition of fictitious letters, which goes back to ancient rhetorical exercises, and Petrarchan and Erasmian variations on this genre, are discussed by Gerlo, 'The *Opus de Conscribendis Epistolis*,' pp. 103–15. Gerlo notes the proliferation of manuals and anthologies on epistolography after the second half of the fifteenth century without commenting on the role played by printers in catering to this vogue.

[67] Pocock, *The Machiavellian Moment*, p. 61. It is only fair to note that Pocock cites Dante in order to contrast rather than to liken his view with that of Petrarch and to bring out the difference between the extra-historical realm inhabited by the poet and the 'social and secular' context of Petrarch's prose.

[68] According to Aeneas Sylvius Piccolomini, there was no point in studying local chronicles, which he characterized as a 'farrago' of 'nonsense.' Woodward, *Vittorino da Feltre*, p. 152 (see also pp. 216–18).

[69] Momigliano, 'Ancient History,' p. 7.

that.[70] 'Beginning with Boethius and Isidore of Seville, Valla's sense of discrimination diminished as his disgust grew.'[71] Cramped unreadable letters, ungrammatical Latin, twisted and distorted images seemed to leave little room for the exercise of discrimination. By piercing through the black interval one might perceive the radiance of an earlier golden age. But the activity of pulling aside a curtain or removing dirt from a painting, is not at all the same as looking across a fixed distance. Time intervals were still contracted, and distances were still shortened by the very blankness and blackness of the dark age.[72]

The contraction of time intervals, the sense of closeness to the book-shops of ancient Rome, the celebration of the return of the muses and of the reappearance of a golden age lasted through the first century of print and beyond. During the first century of printing, the spirit which had animated the Italian revival was quickened, even as the texture of book culture was enriched and the skills of artists and craftsmen were perfected. Divinely inspired artists and artificers seemed ever more successful in mastering the secrets of the ancients and in emulating their finest feats. Erasmus was celebrated for redoing St Jerome, Copernicus and Vesalius for 'restoring' astronomy and anatomy, Luther for return-ing the church to the age of the fathers and pure Christianity.[73] The more Greek texts were unearthed, the more corrupt Latin translations were purified, the more there was a sense of getting closer to the pure well-springs of inspiration, to the pristine origins of all the wisdom that God had initially imparted to man. As one scholar has observed with a certain air of puzzlement, 'reliability' was 'connected with temporal priority' in a way quite uncharacteristic of post-Renaissance thought.[74]

[70] The incongruity of the periodization schemes adopted by Renaissance political chroniclers with those developed by literati tracing cultural change is underlined by Rubinstein, 'Il Medioevo nella Storiagraphia Italiana della Rinascimento,' pp. 429–48. Rubinstein also notes the disparities between Florentine, Milanese and Venetian chronicles.

[71] Kelley, *Foundations*, p. 37.

[72] The sense of blankness which led Renaissance writers to 'feel themselves the contemporaries of the ancients' is underlined in Weisinger's 1945 essay, 'Ideas of History during the Renais-sance.' See esp. p. 76.

[73] That Luther's affection for Saint Paul had the same directness and personal quality as Petrarch's attachment to Cicero and Erasmus' to Saint Jerome is noted by Harbison, *Christian Scholar*, p. 134.

[74] Shumaker, *The Occult Sciences in the Renaissance*, p. 256. See also question posed by Shumaker on p. 255 concerning the high value placed on the wisdom of the earliest authors. Von Leyden, 'Antiquity and Authority,' simply asserts that Renaissance authors assigned a 'privileged' position to the most ancient and earliest utterances without explaining why. In my view, the conditions of scribal culture are primarily responsible for this phenomenon.

We might note in this connection the changed meaning of the term original. Its old meaning was 'closest to divine inspiration; closest to the fount, to the well-spring, to the original, or to the source.' This inspired the slogan, 'To the sources,' *Ad Fontes!* The modern meaning is quite different. As every art-critic knows, to be original is to break with precedent, to depart from tradition. A given artist, scholar or scientist is being original when he does *not* go back to an earlier work but strikes out in some new direction on his own.

This change provides a clue to the reorientation of the classical revival and to the new sense that a fixed distance separated the living present from the antique past. It reflects the difference, noted earlier, between the two modes of transmission sustained on the one hand by scribal culture and on the other by print; with the former entailing a sequence of corrupted copies and the latter a series of improved augmented editions. In the former instance, the advancement of disciplines was geared to retrieving old texts; the activities of ancients and moderns seemed aimed at the same goals; it was possible to envisage moving toward a golden past and brighter future at the same time. In the latter case, the first edition or 'original' manuscript gets consigned to the treasure room, innovators must avoid repeating acts previously performed. Although the new cult of literary originality did not really crystallize until the mid-eighteenth century and the 'burden of the past' was not experienced as oppressive until the age of Dryden,[75] the sixteenth century had already witnessed a marked shift in spatial and temporal orientation which placed antiquity at a greater distance from the present world.

This shift may be illustrated by discussing developments in diverse disciplines. For my purposes the most cogent example is offered by the replacement of Ptolemy's *Geography* as an authoritative guide for constructing a true model of the globe. In its initial phases the Ptolemaic revival of the fifteenth century helped to spur new developments in both science and art. It inspired new techniques for surveying, for mapping, for developing coordinate systems and for rendering three-dimensional forms.[76] As a sophisticated treatise on large-scale cartography it was welcomed by contemporaries of Henry the Navigator

[75] See Mann, 'The Problem of Originality.' Also Bate, *The Burden of the Past.*
[76] Fruitful innovations associated with the 'Ptolemaic Renaissance' are explored by Gadol, *Leon Battista Alberti*, pp. 157–95. See also Edgerton, *The Renaissance rediscovery.*

and seemed to point to the future no less than to the past. By the early seventeenth century, however, this was no longer true. Under the spur of competition between map-publishers, new atlases were being turned out in an unprecedented sequence of ever-expanding and up-dated editions. Alexandrian world pictures were less and less likely to be consulted by armchair travellers who were curious about the fron-tiers of the known world. Here as elsewhere the *Theatrum* of Abraham Ortelius (issued in successive editions from 1570 on) represents a land-mark. Before Ortelius, contemporary maps had been presented as supplements to Ptolemaic ones. In the *Theatrum* the ancient maps were set off in a separate section which followed the representation of the contemporary known world. The limits of ancient knowledge were graphically and textually underlined so that the reader could see 'how maimed and imperfect' were ancient world views which comprised 'scarce one quarter of the whole globe now discovered to us.'[77] Classical scholars went on digging, as they continue to do even now, but navigators and explorers could be seen to be moving in a different direction. The recovery of old maps had been clearly detached from the discovery of new lands. Ptolemy's *Geography*, which had spurred innovation for a century and a half, was drained of its vitality and in-creasingly became of antiquarian concern.

This example not only suggests how notions of recovery and dis-covery were themselves reoriented after print. It also shows why the invention of focused perspective needs to be distinguished from the development of a sense of fixed distance through time. Whereas the former innovation was spurred by the recovery of Ptolemy's *Geo-graphy*, the latter was associated with setting aside the very same treatise and replacing it by successive new editions of a recent atlas. In this respect it seems necessary to qualify Panofsky's assertion that 'antiquity still lives in modern mathematics and science.'[78] Some of antiquity still lives in that way, but much of it was set aside, like Ptolemy's treatises. When considering views of antiquity, the discarding of Roman numerals or of Galen's anatomy or of Aristotle's physics deserves at least as much emphasis as does the survival of theorems established by Pythagoras, Euclid or Archimedes. This discarding had not occurred until after a century of printing. No less than 660 editions of Galen

---

[77] Ortelius, 'Message to the Reader,' p. vj. (Thanks are due to Gail Bossenga for bringing this reference to my attention.) [78] Panofsky, *Renaissance and Renascences*, p. 108.

were issued between 1490 and 1598. They were issued for use by physicians who had no better medical textbooks on hand. Forty-six editions of the elder Pliny's vast encyclopedia were turned out before 1550. They were valued for content, not style.[79] As long as scientific and technical advance was geared to recovering lost texts of the ancients, classical culture could not be set apart or placed at a distance. It still had too many vital messages to convey. As George Sarton notes

Renaissance editions of ancient scientific treatises were never produced for the sake of curiosity or disinterested scholarship (as happens today) but for practical use...The discovery of the new text was not simply of archeological importance; it was (or might be, at least) a positive addition to the workable knowledge of contemporary men of science or physicians...hunting for medical manuscripts was a form of medical research.[80]

The loss of vitality which affected certain ancient sources after they ceased to add to the workable knowledge of contemporaries was especially dramatic in scientific fields. But it was by no means confined to such fields. How it affected the study of jurisprudence is well described by Myron Gilmore's memorable passage concerning Jacques Cujas, a sixteenth-century professor of law at the University of Paris.

Cujas...dedicated all his life to the restoration of the juridical texts of the pre-Justinian period and to the preparation of critical editions and learned commentaries...When his pupils came to him to ask what course they should follow in the terrible crisis of the wars of religion, he replied 'Nihil hoc ad edictum praetoris.' This has nothing to do with the edict of the praetor... It was his task to teach history and not draw from it lessons for the present. The image of antiquity had been recovered but at the same time it ceased to speak directly to the modern world.[81]

Cujas' response to the students seems to epitomize the new outlook which Panofsky attributes to the Renaissance. 'The classical past was looked upon for the first time as a totality cut off from the present.'[82] That this outlook was actually quite foreign to the spirit of the Petrarchan revival is suggested by Gilmore's observation that

History was becoming academic. The opposition between Bodin and Cujas would have seemed incomprehensible to a Petrarch or to a Valla. For these humanists the truths of history, discovered by means of philological analysis,

---

[79] Oestreich, 'Die Antike Literatur als Vorbild der Praktischen Wissenschaften im 16. und 17. Jahrhundert,' pp. 315–25.   [80] Sarton, *Appreciation*, p. 4.
[81] Gilmore, 'The Renaissance Conception of the Lessons of History,' p. 85.
[82] Panofsky, *Renaissance and Renascences*, p. 108.

were always truths which could be applied to the present. But by the time Cujas gave his reply to his students, the Renaissance was already over.[83]

From the mid-sixteenth century on, philology, archeology and classical scholarship brought more and more of antiquity into view, but the past could come no closer although a permanent process of recovery went on. This permanent process is going on right now. It extends indefinitely into the future, beyond the deciphering of a new Linear B, or the uncovering of more Dead Sea Scrolls. But although more and more of the ruins of antiquity continue to come into view we are never brought closer to the bookshops of Rome or to the libraries of Alexandria. They remain fixed forever at a distance, a part of a world that is forever gone. This sense of a past that can never be recaptured, however many artifacts are dug up, is the hallmark of our modern consciousness. It presents a striking contrast to the sense of a past on the verge of being reborn. Insofar as the latter, not the former, view characterized the Petrarchan *rinascita*, the outlook of the quattrocento humanists is being distorted when treated as anticipating our own.

It requires an effort of the historical imagination for us to recapture the sense of closeness to antiquity which was experienced in the quattrocento. When the outlook of Renaissance scholars is prematurely modernized, the effort is less likely to be made. Moreover, sixteenth-century scholarship will appear to be strangely retarded when earlier scholarship is prematurely advanced. This point may be demonstrated by drawing on Jean Seznec's otherwise splendid monograph: *The Survival of the Pagan Gods*. In Seznec's view, the chief guidebooks to mythology that were compiled in the sixteenth century represent 'a striking regression, a return to the Middle Ages.' The pagan gods who had just been restored to their rightful position were 'forced back into the matrix of allegory' by mythographers such as Giraldi, Conti, and Cartari who proved to be not only too 'barbaric' but also too 'bookish' at the same time.[84]

---

[83] Gilmore, 'Renaissance Conception,' p. 85. Gilmore seems to see more of a difference between the position of Valla and that of Cujas than does Kelley who links Valla's views to that of later historical relativists. *Foundations*, pp. 36–46. In passing over Valla's 'particular brand of classicism' and in holding that he called for a return to the original sources simply in order to allow antiquity to 'speak in its own ultimately inimitable accents' (p. 46) Kelley seems to modernize Valla's outlook in a manner that conflicts with other interpretations. See e.g. Hanna Gray, 'Valla's Encomium...and the Humanist Conception of Christian Antiquity,' pp. 37–51.

[84] Seznec, *The Survival of the Pagan Gods*, p. 256.

They are even more lacking in historical sense than in critical faculty. They pay no attention to place or time. They mix together all the gods...Giraldi does not even distinguish between Greek and Roman deities.[85]

Ideas of milieu and evolution are, admittedly, recent achievements and it would be a manifest injustice to reproach scholars of the sixteenth century for not having possessed them. Furthermore, classical antiquity itself had... encouraged mingling and disorder....

Even with this reservation however we are forced to pass rather severe judgement...they offer us a confused mass of erudition, a jumble....[86]

If it is a manifest injustice to reproach sixteenth-century scholars for not possessing later ideas, then so severe a judgment may not be required. Seznec's unfavorable verdict is largely due to his belief that the 'notion of antiquity as a distinct historical milieu, as a period that had run its course' had already crystallized before the mid-sixteenth century. Unlike the middle ages he suggests in his conclusion 'the Renaissance...perceived...historical distance.'[87] Sixteenth-century scholars who failed to perceive this distance and paid 'no attention to place or time' are accordingly judged to be regressive. But it seems just as plausible, perhaps even more so, that modern expectations rather than sixteenth-century performers are at fault. Before sixteenth-century mythographers are condemned for being backward, some evidence is needed to show that some earlier mythographers were more advanced. There is no such evidence. There is only the 'curious fact that the Renaissance in its most brilliant phase produced no work in this field...perhaps...the very contact with and immediate intuition of antiquity rendered such scholarly aids unnecessary.'[88]

Lacking the requisite Renaissance scholarly aids, the author substantiates his thesis by describing the representation of pagan gods in contemporary works of art. A continuous allegorical textual tradition is artificially interrupted and a flood of early printed works is temporarily dammed up.[89] Armed with well-illustrated modern reference

[85] The absence of any agreed-upon methods for estimating the competence of Renaissance scholars is shown by contrasting Seznec's severe judgment with Panofsky's glowing tribute to Giraldi's 'truly scholarly' treatise which brought to fruition the 'critical and scientific' approach initiated by Boccaccio. Panofsky, *Studies in Iconology*, p. 23 (same essay republished in *Meaning in the Visual Arts*, p. 47). There is no consensus about Boccaccio, either, for Seznec does not regard the *Genealogy* as 'critical and scientific.' He sees it as a continuation of medieval mythography (p. 224). Insofar as Giraldi *et al.* merely carry on where Boccaccio left off, I find it hard to understand why Seznec describes sixteenth-century mythography as 'regressive.'
[86] Seznec, *Survival*, pp. 241–2.   [87] Seznec, *Survival*, p. 322.   [88] Seznec, *Survival*, p. 224.
[89] Although Seznec stresses as significant the fact that 'no Italian history of the gods appeared between Boccaccio and Giraldi' (p. 320), he shows elsewhere how Europe was inundated by

guides and studies of iconography, Seznec turns to frescoes, medallions, drawings and engravings and demonstrates just how Renaissance artists stripped visual images of the gods of their bizarre medieval disguises and returned them to Mount Olympus.[90] Unfortunately, early sixteenth-century scholars, trying to unravel a great tangle of old tales, were much less well-equipped. Armed with recently printed scribal compendia, they necessarily lacked a uniform sense of time and place. They could not readily identify Hercules' scimitar with Arabic sources or his club with classical ones. Nor could they easily examine the transposition into Latin of Greek myths centered on Herakles. Given multiform maps and conflicting chronologies, lacking a standardized orthography and nomenclature they were almost bound to produce what modern eyes see as a 'confused mass of erudition, a jumble.'

Scribal texts had woven an allegorical web around pagan myths that was eventually unravelled by later scholars. Artifacts excavated by Renaissance collectors and images turned out from Renaissance workshops certainly contributed to this unravelling. But old words and new engravings were only beginning to be juxtaposed in the mid-sixteenth century. Some Renaissance bookworms were also collectors of antiquities,[91] but there were many hard-working pedants in the sixteenth century for whom contact with classical art – far from being interrupted – had yet to be made.

relevant works (including new editions of Boccaccio and other scribal works) during this interval (pp. 20–1, 103, 226–8). His exclusion of new texts (such as Textor's *Officina*, Basel, 1503, or Pictor's *Treatise*, Freiburg and Antwerp, 1532) like his characterization of Giraldi's Latin manual published in Basel as 'Italian' also seems unjustified to me.

90 Although the importance of engraving is noted: Seznec, *Survival* (pp. 203, 209, n. 75), the extent to which *indirect* contact with classical models (via woodcuts and engravings as against actual coins and artifacts) accounted for restoring authentic images is not spelled out. Dürer's *oeuvre*, assigned a key role by Seznec (pp. 185–7, 209–11), was based entirely on indirect contacts, as noted above, n. 28. A good example of reintegration occurring in a post-print context is Stradano's 'Sol-Apollo' (also mentioned above, p. 188) as being patterned after Michelangelo's 'Risen Christ.' Thus Seznec's conclusion should be modified: 'Iconographical types that had been "handed down" and therefore altered were almost everywhere abandoned in favor of types "rediscovered" in their primal purity' (p. 320) partly because new duplicating techniques had been developed and printed replicas were placed in circulation. A work in printed replica is surely different from one of 'primal purity.' 'To look at the surrounding world and listen to the voice of instinct' (p. 320) did not suffice during the quattrocento any more than it had in earlier eras.

91 Thus the editor of the late fifteenth-century *Nuremberg Chronicle*, Hartmann Schedel, collected and copied antique objects and images as assiduously as he collected old texts. Panofsky, *Dürer* I, p. 31. The same passage, however, has a revealing note about Pirckheimer's collection of Greek and Roman coins which he exploited for a treatise on economics while ignoring its archeological and cultural significance. The medieval flavor of the *Nuremberg Chronicle*, moreover, suggests how little its editor was affected by the spirit of the classical artifacts he collected.

The authors of the 'regressive' manuals are chided for failing to make use of 'coins, reliefs, and statues being excavated by the thousands, collections...overflowing with marbles and bronzes.' Unlike fourteenth-century scholars, it is argued, the sixteenth century 'mythographers did have at their disposal a documentation of infinite value.' Quattrocento artists had already made use of excavated artifacts and one would 'naturally expect' to see Giraldi and his colleagues follow suit. The treasures of antiquity were within their reach, 'being listed, reproduced and made available. At the same moment as our manuals, in the very year of the first publication of Cartari (1556) the catalogue of Aldrovandi appeared as an appendix to the *Antichità* of Lucio Mauro.'[92]

Much is concealed by the phrase, 'at the same moment.' On the date of publication a book has not left the printer's workshop. Unless one is dealing with a scholarly coterie gathered in the same workshop, time is required for the distribution, purchase, and perusal of a relevant work. In the sixteenth century, allowance for this time must be generous indeed. Furthermore, even at present, one may not assume that two works published in the same year will be studied by the same reader when the topics with which they deal have not been correlated before. To expect instantaneous assimilation of the contents of the catalogues is to indulge in the fallacy of being wise after the event. Seznec knows that the appendix he cites was followed by more extensive publication on classical archeology – a field which developed 'above all in the second half of the sixteenth century.'[93] The mythographers did not know this, however. For their first editions, they did not, in fact, have 'at their disposal' even the appendix that is mentioned above. It was published *after* two of the manuals in question had first appeared and while the third was going to press.[94]

One cannot naturally expect scholars to consult works that are only beginning to appear after their own studies have already been completed. Unjustified expectations of this kind are sufficiently ubiquitous in historical literature to call for some sort of explanation. Failure to allow for the advantages conferred by hindsight is probably accountable. Scholars who consult a sixteenth-century first edition that appears to have launched some new trend are apt to forget that contemporaries

[92] Seznec, *Survival*, p. 243.   [93] Seznec, *Survival*, n. 89.
[94] Giraldi's *De Deis Gentium* was published (by Oporinus in Basel) in 1548. Conti's *Mythologiae* by the Manutius firm in Venice, 1551 according to Seznec, *Survival*, p. 229.

were necessarily blind to its future significance and – since a single edition often consisted only of a few hundred copies – were sometimes unaware of its very existence. The historian who can now take down from library shelves and place on his desk many books published in 1556 is, similarly, apt to forget that scholars who were at work in that year could not even begin to do what comes so easily to him now.

Even with regard to hindsight, sixteenth-century scholars were disadvantaged. They did not have access to well-ordered collections of printed books that had accumulated over the course of centuries. Most of the texts that they handled were of uncertain origin, and labelled with titles only recently assigned them. There were no agreed conventions pertaining to chronology, geography, nomenclature, orthography. When Seznec comments on the failure of sixteenth-century scholars to 'organize their material along geographical or historical lines' he seems to forget that geography and history were, themselves, still in a disordered state. Early printed compendia did not provide the sort of guidelines that are now supplied by modern reference works. Lacking uniform procedures for filing data, material was bound to be disorganized.

Eventually, of course, new procedures were devised and new guidelines supplied. Texts could be allocated to the intervals in which they were composed and arrayed in a uniform sequence. Various traditions would be traced and developments seen to unfold in terms of a fixed sequential array. When Seznec describes the allegorical tradition by beginning with ancient works and taking up medieval texts in the order in which they were composed, he follows a procedure that is now taken for granted by intellectual historians – taken too much for granted, perhaps. The automatic adoption of modern conventions often masks earlier conditions, and this seems to be particularly true when we try to trace textual traditions that were shaped in the age of scribes. Before the advent of printing, for example, the order in which texts were composed was by no means the same as that in which they became available to Latin-reading scholars within Western Christendom. Any history of Western philosophy must make some allowance for the migration of manuscripts (must place the works of Aristotle after those of Augustine, and certain dialogues of Plato after both, for instance) when accounting for the views of medieval schoolmen. By lining up texts in the order in which they re-entered the West we may come closer to understanding certain medieval developments. But this approach still leaves us far from grasping the chaotic conditions with which sixteenth-century scholars had to reckon. One way or another, we are encouraged to order in sequence texts that they found in a state of almost complete disarray.

At all events, the mythological manuals however bookish or barbaric do seem to reflect the state of scholarship in the early sixteenth century. The disciplines of 'history, philology, and archeology' which Panofsky describes as foreign to the middle ages, were still foreign to Seznec's mythographers, and when they were writing the three centuries Panofsky allots to the Renaissance had almost elapsed.[95] Many inscriptions and images had been copied, classical forms in lettering and architecture had been revived. The system of focused perspective had been fully developed and the art of the high Renaissance fully achieved. Nevertheless the revision of chronology undertaken by Scaliger, and the great age of map-publishing, launched by Mercator and Ortelius, had not yet begun.

I would argue then that 'a total rationalized view' of antiquity began to appear only after the first century of printing rather than in Petrarch's lifetime and that the preservative powers of print were a prerequisite for this new view. It is not 'since the Renaissance' but since the advent of printing and engraving, that 'the antique has been continuously with us.' Furthermore it seems likely that the same changes which affected the classical revival in Italy also affected medieval survivals on both sides of the Alps. The so-called 'historical revolution' of the sixteenth century owed perhaps as much to the 'systematization and codification of existing customary law' as it did to the systematic investigation of the legal heritage from Rome.[96] Views of the medieval past were altered in much the same manner as the classical past, so that it, too, came to be observed from 'a fixed distance.'[97] Even Gothic art was eventually entrenched behind the same museum walls as classical art. Are there not many medieval institutions and styles of thought and expression – like the English Inns of Court, the Sorbonne, Thomist philosophy, romantic love and the Arthurian legend – that may also be

95 1250 to 1550. Panofsky, *Renaissance and Renascences*, p. 40.
96 Julian Franklin, *Jean Bodin*, pp. 36–8 discusses this development in sixteenth-century France.
97 Trithemius' *Catalogus Illustrium Virorum Germaniae* (1495) represents a landmark as one of the first cultural chronicles to make room for a 'Carolingian' revival. Arnold, introduction to *De Laude*, p. 7.

described as having been 'continuously with us'? To be sure, the term 'Gothic' was used pejoratively by Renaissance humanists, by Enlightenment *philosophes* and by most arbiters of taste for three centuries or more. But the neo-classic vogue did not deter jurists, antiquarians, philologists, and other early-modern scholars, both clerical and lay, from developing an idealized image of the golden age of chivalry and the ancient constitution. Even during the interval when Gothic was synonymous with 'barbaric', there were some barbarian folkways that evoked admiration (as numerous citations from Tacitus' *Germania* suggest). From the fifteenth century on, praise for feudal institutions and pride in vernacular literatures was scarcely less common in learned circles than the cult of antiquity. 'We were having a little Renaissance of our own; or a Gothic revival if you please.'[98] Maitland's comment seems to apply, beyond developments in Tudor and Stuart England, to the contemporaneous continental scene as well.[99] It was, finally, in opposition to a full blown Gothic revival that the nineteenth-century concept of a 'Renaissance' was shaped.

Such considerations are worth keeping in mind when we look at the way Panofsky tries to illustrate his thesis:

Our own script and letter press derive from the Italian Renaissance types patterned in deliberate opposition to the Gothic upon Carolingian and twelfth century models which in turn had been evolved on a classical basis. Gothic script one might say symbolizes the transitoriness of the medieval renascences; our modern letter press, whether Roman or Italic, testifies to the enduring quality of the Italian Renaissance. Thereafter the classical element in our civilization could be opposed (though it should not be forgotten that opposition is only another form of dependence) but it could not entirely disappear again.[100]

The end of this passage seems to apply with equal force to the 'Gothic' element in our civilization.[101] That so-called 'Gothic' type-forms

---

98 Cited by Pocock, *The Ancient Constitution*, p. 15, n. 4. Much of Pocock's study is relevant to above discussion. See also Gossman, *Medievalism*; Kelley, *Foundations*, chap. 10; Franklin, *Jean Bodin, passim.*

99 'The French humanists stood humanism on its head' and 'began to celebrate the Middle Ages...' In so doing they fashioned 'the model of modern historiography' according to George Huppert, 'The Renaissance Background of Historicism,' p. 54.

100 Panofsky, *Renaissance and Renascences*, p. 108.

101 Beginning with quattrocento humanists, going on through Gibbon to Burckhardt, opposition to (hence dependence on?) the Gothic has been a persistent theme. Like the concept of revival or 'rebirth' of classical culture, the idea of a 'Gothic' style was of scribal origin having been applied to architecture by Alberti, to scribal hands by Valla before being propelled as a typology in print. On origin of term, see Frankl, *The Gothic*, p. 260.

competed on equal terms with 'antiqua' in most regions during the first century of printing;[102] that they outlasted the Renaissance in Dutch, Scandinavian, and German regions; that they continued to impress their mark on German texts through the nineteenth century and beyond – all this also seems to have been left out of account. As is suggested below, modern letter-forms testify to a complicated cluster of changes which came in the wake of printing. These changes cannot be understood by thinking about the 'enduring quality of the Italian Renaissance' or the 'transitoriness' of medieval revivals but only by examining the effects of typography on fifteenth-century bookhands. By the seventeenth century, the patterning of type-styles reflected the fixing of new religious frontiers and markedly departed from Renaissance conventions. 'The twentieth century reader,' writes Panofsky, 'finds Carolingian script easier to decipher than Gothic and this ironic fact tells the whole story.'[103] What is ironic is that this is by no means the whole story, and that it comes from a twentieth-century reader who probably learned to read his native language as a schoolboy from texts which were set in a 'Gothic' type.

The contrast of 'Gothic script,' taken as a symbol of transience, with 'our modern letter press,' taken to signify the enduring Renaissance, suggests how confusion is compounded when Renaissance humanism is credited with functions performed by the new technology. To understand stylistic developments, it makes sense to contrast different bookhands with each other or different type-forms with each other. But to contrast one sort of bookhand with another sort of type-form is to muddle things from the start. When the author refers to 'Renaissance types patterned in deliberate opposition to the Gothic,' it is not clear whether he means that 'Roman' and 'Italic' types were designed with the aim of deliberately opposing 'Gothic' ones or, instead, that these early types reproduced earlier manuscript bookhands which had been designed previously in a spirit of 'deliberate opposition.' The latter interpretation is likely to be the correct one. Nevertheless, it is

[102] Labels assigned various fonts such as 'Antiqua,' 'roman,' 'italic,' 'Gothic,' 'Fraktur,' 'Schwabacher' were the 'fanciful inventions of later writers' according to Steinberg, *Five Hundred Years*, p. 30. The etymology of the terms 'type' and 'style' and the new meanings assigned to both after Gutenberg would make an interesting essay. How choice of type-styles related to new ideas about national 'caractères,' defense of vernaculars, and early Gothic revivals is suggested by patriotic propaganda associated with introduction of Granjon's 'civilité' type designs in sixteenth-century France. Carter and Vervliet, *Civilité Types*, p. 15.

[103] Panofsky, *Renaissance and Renascences*, p. 107.

not supported by all specialized studies. Insofar as deliberation entered into the adoption for copying classical texts of one bookhand that resembled Carolingian minuscule, we are told on good authority that presbyopia may have played a role but 'aesthetic revulsion did not' and further, it is a mistake to view 'humanist scribal reform as a battle waged by Roman against Goth.'[104]

Given the complicated evolution of late medieval bookhands from earlier ones, given distinctions between bookhands used for different texts in different regions and all the subtle differences now used to trace the provenance of manuscripts to separate abbeys, universities, and courts; it would seem that no one dichotomy is adequate to describe the situation.[105] Panofsky makes the point that Carolingian bookhands 'evolved on a classical basis' while overlooking the way 'Gothic' bookhands evolved from Carolingian ones.[106] Carolingian minuscule, moreover, rested on a shaky 'classical basis.' The only genuine classical prototypes for humanist bookhands were supplied by the inscriptions on ancient Roman monuments which were copied and reproduced as the Alphabetum Romanum.[107] These capital letters were believed to be based on principles of geometry and associated with Pythagorean harmonies, golden sections, perfect ratios and the like. Efforts to reconstruct them in accordance with given formulas preoccupied the talents of artists, scribes and type designers for a century or more.[108] Insofar

---

[104] Wardrop, *The Script of Humanism*, pp. 4–5. For fascinating speculation on the possible presbyopia of Carolingian scribal reformers (such as Boniface) and of later humanists (such as Petrarch and Salutati), see B. L. Ullman, *The Origin and Development*, pp. 13–14. According to Updike, *Printing Types* I, 83, presbyopia also contributed to equipping the first press established in France with 'antiqua' fonts; the rector of the Sorbonne had poor eyesight and wished to facilitate proof-reading.

[105] Distinctions between bookhands used in abbeys as against universities, at different universities, and for different faculties are illuminated by Destrez, *La Pecia*, pp. 44–8. (An Arezzo bookhand designated as 'de bona littera antiqua' in a 1227 catalogue is noted on p. 48.) Other distinctions (involving categories of texts, such as missals not turned out by university scribes) are noted by Febvre and Martin, *L'Apparition*, pp. 109–11.

[106] On the stages by which Carolingian bookhands evolved into those which formed a basis for 'Gothic' type-styles, see Updike, *Printing Types* I, 50–3, esp. p. 53, n. 1.

[107] This is brought out especially clearly by Harry Carter, *A View of Early Typography*, pp. 46–7.

[108] Carter, *A View of Early Typography*, p. 71 points to the influence exerted by Felice Feliciano's neo-platonic approach to the ideal forms of letters. On Feliciano (1433–79), a writing master and bookbinder of Verona who was a friend of Mantegna's and dedicated a book of inscriptions to him, see Giovanni Mardersteig's edition of Feliciano's *Alphabetum Romanum*. Feliciano turned to printing toward the end of his life, establishing a press in Verona before dying in Rome. On 'geometrical' alphabets sponsored by Luca Pacioli, Dürer and Geoffroy Tory, see below, volume II, chap. 6, n. 82. The effort to inscribe ideally proportioned human bodies on ideally constructed letters takes an amusing non-classical form in Book 2 of Tory's *Champ Fleury* (1529) where we are instructed to place the cross bar of the A unusually low

CLASSICAL AND CHRISTIAN TRADITIONS REORIENTED

as lower case letters were designed by typefounders to combine with antique capital letters, a 'classical basis' for the Renaissance letter-forms was eventually supplied. Even here however some non-classical, barbaric or medieval elements often intruded, in the form of ornamental interlacing and lattice work designs. There was no classical ancestry for the decorated initial letters and ornamental borders which were favored by the Italian humanists.[109] The Renaissance book, whether written or printed, was a culturally hybrid product from first to last. Neither the variety of bookhands and decorative motifs employed by fifteenth-century scribes nor the profusion of early types designed to imitate extant manuscripts[110] lend themselves to being classified in terms of any simple bi-polar scheme.

What happens when attempts are made to dichotomize the spotted actuality of the age of incunabula is suggested by the celebrated case of the Subiaco 'Cicero.' Often heralded as one of the first books to come off the first press established in Italy, this 1465 edition of *De Oratore* is sometimes described as being set in 'Roman' type.[111] According to humanist conventions, as portrayed by later scholars, it would have been unthinkable to set Cicero in anything else.[112] In fact, authorities cannot agree about how to classify the hybrid type-styles actually used by Sweynheim and Pannartz for this edition: 'Semi-Gothic or *fere humanista*, take your choice!'[113] Bühler's summation of the vexing problem suggests how little 'deliberate opposition to Gothic' there was in the early design of Renaissance types.

To question the statement that Renaissance bookhands and/or type-fonts were 'patterned in deliberate opposition to the Gothic' is not to deny that large clear rounded letters *were* set against crabbed pointed ones with deliberate polemical intent by certain Renaissance humanists. That cramped letters, ligatures, and abbreviations should be associated with the

in order to conceal the genitals of the male body signifying that 'Modesty and Chastity are required before all else.' Tory, *Champ Fleury*, p. 48.

[109] Pächt, 'Notes and Observations,' p. 189.

[110] How this initial profusion conferred on a vast variety of bookhands and less formal cursive scripts 'the permanence and ubiquity of print' is noted by Wardrop, *Script of Humanism*, p. 42. He also describes (pp. 39–42) how displaced scribes became writing masters and outmoded bookhands were preserved in calligraphic manuals or specimen books. The preservation of styles abandoned by book-printers also occurred via display fonts and other forms of job-printing, as noted by Steinberg, *Five Hundred Years*, p. 40.

[111] It is described as the 'earliest humanist fount' by Scholderer, *Fifty Essays*, p. 151.

[112] See Steinberg, *Five Hundred Years*, p. 31 and Goldschmidt, *Printed Book of the Renaissance*, p. 2.

[113] Bühler, 'Roman Type and Roman Printing in the Fifteenth Century,' p. 101. This whole essay (pp. 101–10) is relevant to the above discussion.

204

corruption of texts and the loss of ancient learning was only natural. Copyists' errors were encouraged by writing that was hard to read. The shape of the letter, the nature of the texts and the quality of learning were, in any case, linked by scholars such as Lorenzo Valla in a way that encouraged polarization and set the terms for a prolonged battle of books.

But although modern historians find texts such as Valla's scribal treatise highly significant,[114] there were many early type-designers, printers, and patrons who did not. Some flouted humanist conventions unwittingly or followed them with other aims in mind.[115] Others, while espousing the new learning, far from rejecting Gothic styles, contributed to their survival. Type designs modelled on Gothic bookhands and on more informal Gothic cursive script were sponsored in Northern humanist circles and associated with the flowering of vernacular literatures.[116] During the first century of printing, decisions relating to the equipment of presses with different types and the employment of type-styles for different texts hinged on so many rapidly shifting local circumstances and individual choices, that it is almost impossible to perceive any all-over design.[117] Efforts to simplify the intricate pattern

[114] Although Harbison, *The Christian Scholar*, p. 43, describes Valla's *De Elegantiis Linguae Latinae* as 'published' in 1444 and Valla himself boasted: 'I have published many books in almost every branch of learning' I think the assignment of a publication date probably should be reserved for printed editions. Valla's treatise ran through sixty editions between 1471 and 1536. Similarly, his *Notes on the New Testament*, which were composed and revised between 1444 and 1452, became a 'landmark,' in the history of biblical scholarship only after Erasmus got a manuscript copy found in a monastery to the printer in 1505. What publication meant before printing is by no means clear and could entail reading out loud as well as making several copies. See chap. 1, n. 22 above.

[115] That Italians did not feel strongly about the merits of Gothic as against Roman styles is asserted by Harry Carter, *A View of Early Typography*, p. 89. Bühler, 'Roman Type,' pp. 102–3, lists incunabula in the British Museum that ran counter to convention by presenting classical texts in 'Gothic' and medieval law-books in 'Roman' styles. Salutati's request for a copy of Abelard's (medieval theological) work in 'antiqua littera' shows how unconventional a humanist scribal reformer could be. B. L. Ullman, *Origin and Development*, p. 14.

[116] The design of an influential Gothic or 'black-letter' type-style originated in Nuremberg humanist circles which may have included Dürer himself, according to Degering, *Lettering*, xvi–xvii. Dürer's attempt to apply classical canons and geometrical construction devices to 'Gothic' as well as 'Roman' letters is illustrated by Panofsky himself in his biography of *Dürer*, pp. 258–9, fig. 7a and b). Granjon's 'civilité' types based on a semi-Gothic cursive hand used for French vernacular texts, were sponsored by the great scholar-printer Robert Estienne and by circles associated with the Pléaide. Carter and Vervliet, *Civilité Types*, pp. 15 ff. These types were conceived as a French *riposte* to the Aldine italic.

[117] In Spain, e.g. Salamanca sponsored 'Roman'; Alcala 'Gothic' styles. The French typographer Nicholas Jenson, who pioneered 'Roman' type design, re-equipped his Venetian presses with 'Gothic' types. The first press established in France was equipped with 'Roman' types; but until the mid-sixteenth century, French book-printing reflected no clear preference. The decision also hung in the balance in the Lowlands and England. See Harry Carter, *A View of Early Typography*, pp. 28, 88–9.

or to correlate the distribution of type-styles with one particular trend or development during this interval are almost certain to lead us astray.

Thus, it seems unwarranted to explain the establishment of 'a four hundred year tradition of black letter Gothic in Germany' by a 're-sistance to the spirit of humanism' or by the fact that theological works predominated in Cologne and Wittenberg.[118] Theological works pre-dominated almost everywhere in the era of Reformation and Counter-Reformation. In view of Spanish and Italian Counter-Reformation tracts it also seems unwise to take the adoption of 'humanistic letters' as indicating a 'repudiation of medieval dogmatism.'[119] Actually a particular theological work, the Bible, probably played a crucial role in fixing later typographical frontiers. The shift from Antwerp to Geneva as a principal center of Bible printing seems to have been strategic in the spread of Roman type, outside regions where Luther's translation had set the mode.[120] Far from 'symbolizing the enduring quality of the Italian Renaissance,' the adoption of Roman type for the Vulgate and for certain vernacular Bibles marked a decisive break with humanist conventions. Ironically, the use of Gothic type for Luther's German translation of the Bible, which *conformed with Italian humanist practices* (by using non-classical lettering for a vernacular theological work) did much to fix what later appeared to be an eccentric tradition.[121] In view of such considerations, Denys Hay's statement: 'Noth-ing illustrates better the diffusion of...certain elements in Italian

118 Steinberg, *Five Hundred Years*, p. 126. Actually the demand for classical texts favored by the humanists was fairly strong in Cologne despite its being stigmatized as the home town of 'obscure men.' Bühler, *Fifteenth Century Book*, p. 182. Among other printing firms, the one founded by Heinrich Quentell in 1479 helped to counter academic orthodoxy and to en-courage humanist activity in this city before the Reformation. See Bissels, *Humanismus und Buchdruck: Vorreden Humanistischer Drucke in Köln*; Benzing, *Die Buckdrucker des 16. und 17. Jahrhunderts*, pp. 220; 223. (I owe these references to James V. Mehl's unpublished dissertation: 'Ortwin Gratius: Cologne Humanist' which contains a relevant chapter on the Quentell Press.) That English importers got their Roman and Italic types from Cologne is noted by Hirsch, *Printing, Selling*, p. 118. In Wittenberg, as elsewhere, the decision hung in the balance. The first edition of Luther's theses was set in Roman type but was followed by a flood of pamphlets in Gothic styles. Goldschmidt, *Printed Book*, pp. 14–16.
119 Lehmann-Haupt, *Peter Schoeffer*, p. 23. See also p. 368, n. 8 where a reference to Goebbels and Nazi propaganda is introduced into a discussion of German preference for Gothic type-styles. Was not this preference more pronounced in nineteenth-century Germany than after Hitler's rise?
120 This point is persuasively argued by Black, 'Printed Bible,' pp. 436–54; also Black, book re-view, *The Library*, p. 302. According to Carter and Vervliet, *Civilité Types*, p. 18, the use of 'Roman' for the 1541 French edition of Calvin's *Institutes* also helped to set a permanent vogue. See also Harry Carter, *A View of Early Typography*, p. 88.
121 Black, 'The Typography of Luther's Bible,' pp. 110–13.

humanism than the spread in Northern Europe of the civilized typography of Italy'[122] seems to be wide of the mark. Thus a work expounding Vitruvian architectural principles was set in Gothic type by a Netherlands' publisher 'so ordinary people can read it more easily.'[123] Bringing Vitruvius to lay architects was in keeping with the spirit of Italian humanism even though the 'wrong' type was employed for this purpose. Typographical frontiers that divided Geneva from Amsterdam and Madrid from Vienna while linking Sorbonnistes with Florentines[124] appear to be entirely unrelated to disputes between schoolmen and humanists, theologians and advocates of the new learning. By the seventeenth century, these frontiers cut across intellectual, cultural, and religious divisions, completely obliterating distinctions once reflected by scribal hands. That the spread of 'Roman' type should not be taken as a token of the diffusion of humanism is suggested by a glance at the sort of texts that were printed in 'Gothic' Sweden or Holland and banned in 'Roman' Spain or Italy or by reflecting on the fate of Erasmian humanism in diverse regions where 'Roman' type-styles prevailed.

It seems to be equally misleading to take Gothic script as a symbol of the transitoriness of medieval renascences. Insofar as bookhands are involved, Gothic is a singularly inappropriate symbol for the sort of revival that sponsored Carolingian minuscule; while the type-form that was popularized by Lutheran Bible printers never was medieval and has not proved to be transitory. A twentieth-century American singling out today's copy of *The New York Times* or *The Washington Post* from newsstand piles has no trouble deciphering Gothic letters.[125] The Renaissance type-form left a permanent imprint not because it drew on one style of lettering rather than another but because it was impressed by type and not by a human hand.

[122] Hay, 'Literature: The Printed Book,' p. 366. See also same author's introduction to *Printing and the Mind of Man*, xxvi, where the victory of Italian typestyles is similarly characterized. The use of the adjective 'civilized' suggests how humanist propaganda continues to be amplified today. [123] Verwey, 'Pieter Coecke van Aelst,' p. 192.

[124] See summary in Febvre and Martin, *L'Apparition*, p. 118, and Harry Carter, *A View of Early Typography*, pp. 89ff. The Netherlands vogue for 'civilité' type (used by Plantin's Leiden presses) down through the eighteenth century, is discussed by Verwey, 'Les Caractères de Civilité et la Propagande Réligieuse,' p. 27.

[125] That the use of Gothic for the titles of English language newspapers is a late eighteenth-century English 'Gothic revival' development (to be classed with 'Ye Olde Tea Shoppe' spelling) is amusingly discussed by Hutt, 'The Gothic Title-piece and the English Newspaper.' The repudiation of this style by 'working class' republican and radical journals is also noted with approval by Hutt. His article suggests how anti-Gothic polemics acquired anti-aristo-cratic overtones in a manner that would have surprised Renaissance cardinals and princely patrons.

This brings me to some other variations played on the theme of permanence, centering on the rise of classical scholarship and the recovery of classical texts. In his seminal studies on Renaissance thought, Kristeller applies Panofsky's thesis to intellectual history and points to the unprecedented range and scope of classical studies in the Renaissance.[126] Instead of being subordinated to theology, he notes, these studies became more autonomous. At the same time, the selection of texts known to medieval scholars was greatly enlarged, almost reaching present limits. The novelty of these Renaissance developments is emphasized without reference to the novel elements introduced by printing. The humanist movement in general is thus credited with presenting the Western world with all those ancient texts that are, even now, still regarded as standard classics.

It would be wrong to maintain that classical Latin literature...was neglected during the Middle Ages...It would be equally wrong to deny that as a result of humanist discoveries the available patrimony of Latin literature was extended almost to its present limits...

Almost the entire body of extant Greek literature was deposited in Western libraries and diffused through handwritten copies and printed editions.

Thus...both in the Latin and Greek fields, the Middle Ages possessed a significant selection of classical sources but...Renaissance humanism extended its knowledge almost to the entire range of its extant remains, that is to the point where modern scholarship has made its further discoveries from palimpsests and papyri.[127]

It is difficult to ascertain just how far short of 'present limits,' humanist discoveries extended and just at what point modern scholarship took over, to make possible the 'further discoveries' mentioned in the final sentence. From the advent of printing on, one must deal with a continuous process of recovery and with a continuous development of techniques for investigating the past. Further discoveries have never ceased to be made (e.g., certain plays of Menander were only retrieved in this century) and in this sense the Renaissance has never come to an end. But more recent discoveries did come too late to be inserted into an undergraduate curriculum that was fixed, in a more or less permanent form, in the course of the sixteenth century. Hence they are regarded as being somewhat peripheral to the central corpus of Greek and Latin texts. The fixing of this corpus in a permanent mold *was* unprecedented, but Renaissance copyists were no more capable of

126 Kristeller, *Renaissance Thought*, p. 104.   127 Kristeller, *Renaissance Thought*, pp. 14–17.

208

accomplishing this than medieval copyists had been.[128] If 'Renaissance humanism extended its knowledge' almost to present limits, this is surely because ancient texts recovered by the humanists were not again 'lost' i.e., actually destroyed, progressively corrupted, transplanted or mislaid.

In fact, many of the manuscripts that Petrarch and his successors managed to track down and get copied *have* since been lost. Some of the libraries in which the 'recovered' texts were found have also disappeared.[129] The same fate awaited quattrocento transcriptions and the new collections that were made of them. One example may suffice to illustrate this point. '*De Rerum Natura* had been practically unknown for centuries and for a time its survival seems to have depended on a single manuscript. Then Poggio found it late in 1414.'[130] This familiar version breaks off the story before the crucial event occurred. The manuscript of Lucretius' poem that Poggio found also got lost. Fortunately he had had one more copy made. How many scribes would, thereafter, be set to work to preserve Lucretius' poem; how many friars might ferret out and destroy all extant copies; whether a few might be 'discovered' again by later book-hunters – these are questions that cannot be certainly answered. But surely the future of the text was still uncertain until 1473 when it reached a printer's workshop in Brescia. Possibly it still remained uncertain thereafter – but not for long. By the end of the sixteenth century, thirty whole editions had been issued. A school of pagan philosophy, long frowned upon by many churchmen, intermittently revived and repeatedly extirpated, had secured a permanent position within Western culture for the first time.[131] Was it Poggio or was it a Brescian printer who transformed the ancient Epicurean into the author of a standard classic?

[128] The way printing made it possible to 'fix' a given text (albeit in a regrettably corrupted form) and thus provided a common basis for scholarly discussion concerning variant readings and versions is described by Kenney, *The Classical Text*, p. 69.

[129] The dispersal of several famous Renaissance collections is noted by Gilmore, *World of Humanism*, p. 185. The not atypical fate of the Verona library which disappeared so completely that even its site was unknown to Mabillon is described by Deuel, *Testaments of Time*, pp. 45–6. The disappearance of such collections during the fourteenth and fifteenth centuries is not taken into account by Kenney, *The Classical Text*, p. 78, when he refers to mss. being placed 'in cold storage' by monks and describes the interval before printing as one of 'relative stability.'

[130] Gay, *The Enlightenment*, I, 262.

[131] Sailor, 'Moses and Atomism,' p. 4. On the cult of Lucretius during the Enlightenment, see Gay, *The Enlightenment*, I, who notes (p. 99) that Voltaire alone owned six editions of *De Rerum Natura* and that other *philosophes* collected the work just as assiduously.

As this question suggests, the book-hunting of quattrocento humanists was of immense significance for the future development of Western culture because – unlike texts which had been retrieved previously only to be lost again – the texts which the humanists rescued were duplicated in print and permanently secured.

The great age of discovery of manuscripts in the West had preceded the fall of Constantinople. The generation of Poggio, Niccoli and Nicholas of Cusa had brought to light the most important works of Latin antiquity and nothing quite like the experience of the age was to be seen again.[132]

The statement is accurate as far as it goes, but I believe it does not go far enough. To stop short of the 1450s is to exclude the event that made the age especially remarkable. The experience of the age was not seen again because the works that were 'brought to light' shortly before 1453 remained in the public domain forever after. The experience itself was not entirely unprecedented. Viking landfalls may or may not have preceded the great age of maritime discoveries; there can be no doubt that Western scholars who were contemporaries of Gerard of Cremona or Adelard of Bath witnessed a previous great age of manuscript discoveries. It was not the experience but what became of it that was completely unprecedented.

The distinction between making discoveries and securing them may seem somewhat subtle. Nevertheless, troublesome questions can be handled more easily if it is drawn. Why, for example, should humanists be credited with 'discovering' ancient works that were obviously known already to some medieval scholars since they were found in the form of medieval copies? It is conventional to sidestep the question and suggest that the 'merit' of humanist discoveries is 'unduly disparaged' by posing it.[133] Yet unless it is posed, medieval contributions to the survival of ancient classics are apt to be concealed from view.

If an ancient Latin text survived only in one or two Carolingian copies and if there are but scanty traces of its having been read during the subsequent centuries the fact that such a text was found by a humanist and made generally available through numerous copies does constitute a discovery...the fact that some classical Latin authors such as Virgil or Ovid or Seneca or Boethius were widely known throughout the Middle Ages does not refute the equally obvious fact that some other authors such as Lucretius or Tacitus or Manilius were discovered by the humanists.[134]

The more closely one looks at the 'obvious fact' the less obvious it

---

[132] Gilmore, *World of Humanism*, p. 182. [133] Kristeller, *Renaissance Thought*, pp. 13–14.
[134] Kristeller, *Renaissance Thought*, p. 14.

becomes. Recent research has refuted (what was once regarded as) the 'obvious fact' that Vitruvius was 'unknown' until 'discovered' by Poggio in 1416. The same point applies to Archimedes, since Marshall Clagett's research. Further findings will probably refute other claims of discovery made by the humanists.[135] 'Finding' a text and making it 'generally available', moreover, are two different activities. If they are lumped together under the ambiguous term 'discovery,' confusion is likely to ensue. It is a fact that numerous medieval copies of certain works by Virgil or Ovid can be found, and very few of certain works by Lucretius or Tacitus. But it is also true that evidence pertaining to the circulation of ancient works after the break-up of Charlemagne's empire is too shaky to make firm conclusions possible.[136] Even apart from uneven documentation, there are no standard citations of authors or titles to go by.[137] Medieval readers were not unfamiliar, for example, with the 'lost apology of Aristides.' Although it was not formally 'discovered' until the nineteenth century, it had long been present in the popular romance of 'Barlaam and Josaphat.'[138]

The question remains: if Poggio is credited with 'discovering' Lucretius on the basis of a single copy, should not the eleventh-century scribe who provided quattrocento book-hunters with the valuable Tacitus–Apuleius codex also be credited with 'discovering' Tacitus? When three manuscript copies of a humanist work can be cited to show that it 'attained a certain diffusion'[139] should not the 'one or two Carolingian copies' that survived centuries of disorder show the same thing? As these questions suggest, claims made for Renaissance humanism often seem to be based on a kind of double standard. Successive generations who actually collaborated to salvage the same fragments of antiquity are made to compete in an unequal contest. The eponymous humanist who got the text to the printer – whether by stealing it from a monastery, importing it by routine purchase, or making several copies – goes down in the history books as a culture hero. The anony-

---

[135] See Krinsky, 'Seventy-eight Vitruvius Manuscripts,' pp. 36–40; and on Clagett, see pp. 496–7. volume II below.

[136] R. M. Wilson, 'The Contents of the Medieval Library,' p. 85, notes some of the difficulties entailed.

[137] On 'the extraordinary uncertainty and elusive fluidity' of scribal authors' names, see Goldschmidt, Medieval Texts, p. 86. An instructive example of different possible meanings one might read into a given label, such as Sermones Bonaventurae is offered on p. 98.

[138] Deuel, Testaments of Time, pp. 329–32.

[139] Kristeller, Renaissance Thought, p. 152, n. 20, cites three mss. of Manetti's version of the Psalms to show 'that it attained a certain diffusion.'

mous medieval scholar, scribe or copyist who got the text to the human-ist recedes into the mist of the dark ages.

It ought to be possible to give both groups their just due without 'unduly disparaging' either. This might be done by discarding the term 'discovery' (which is troublesome at best and particularly so when applied in the context of scribal culture) and by stressing pre-carious recovery instead. Several important works which were re-trieved by quattrocento humanists seem to have been on the verge of being totally lost. But these precious texts could be retrieved only because they had been repeatedly rescued by copyists from the same plight before. As Bolgar puts it, in a passage which provides welcome support for my views: 'The work of Petrarch and his circle was in this tradition which had been the glory of Tours and Monte Cassino. If the invention of printing had not supervened, their labors would have had to be re-peated again and again as had been the case after similar efforts in the past.'[140]

By prolonging a precarious lifeline that carried fragments of antiquity down to the age of print, Petrarch and his successors performed much the same function that had been performed long before by Carolingian scribes and court scholars. By importing Greek texts from Byzantium and working with Greek scholars to translate them, Renaissance humanists functioned in much the same way as had the twelfth-century schoolmen who reintroduced the works of Aristotle, Galen, Euclid *et al.* into the West. Different cross-cultural routes were involved in the twelfth-century revival and the early Italian Renaissance. But both shared common limitations imposed by the conditions of scribal culture. They were thus confined to restricted regions and to the transmission of a limited portion of the classical heritage. They were also primarily aimed at regaining ground that had been lost in preceding eras. The ground that humanist book-hunters sought to regain and the manner in which it had been lost is worth special consideration. Not only are the limitations inherent in scribal book production revealed but at the same time a possible connection between the twelfth century and quattrocento revivals is suggested. Does it not seem likely that the particular classical texts which were sought by Italian humanists were in short supply, partly because other classical texts, recently retrieved via Arabic routes, had been made more available?

[140] Bolgar, *The Classical Heritage*, p. 263.

Before pursuing the implications of this suggestion, it is worth noting that it runs counter to the line of analysis developed by art historians, such as Panofsky. In this respect, there is need for caution about accepting advice to extend Panofsky's thesis to 'other fields of intellectual history.'[141] Panofsky's interpretation stresses an extreme estrangement from classical tendencies during the thirteenth century. He holds that a 'radical alienation from the antique' was represented by 'high Gothic' styles in art and letters. Earlier medieval revivals had entailed a partial assimilation of the classical heritage but full assimilation was perpetually blocked. Classical form remained separate from classical content. A Greek god such as Mercury might be portrayed as a bishop; Jupiter and the eagle were transmogrified into Pope Gregory and the Holy Dove. Such disjunctions, in the eyes of the art historian, expressed a characteristic ambivalence toward classical antiquity which was ultimately resolved by complete repudiation. In the high Gothic period, classical ornaments were stripped from the capitals of columns, classical influences were banned and purged, reaching a 'zero point' or a 'nadir' 'in all genres in all countries.' The 'total resurrection' of the antique spirit which is attributed to the great Renaissance is predicated on a previous 'total' extinction, under the aegis of scholasticism. 'It is only by beginning as it were from zero that the real Renaissance could come into being.'[142]

I think this description of a 'total' Gothic extinction of classical elements goes too far and endows medieval Gothic culture with a kind of consistency and stylistic unity that could come only after print. It is as if one incorrectly imagined scribes deliberately removing all traces of round Carolingian letters and designing 'Gothic' script, much as nineteenth-century Gothic revivalists actually did. Many of the disjunctions singled out by Panofsky seem to have been inadvertent rather than deliberate; less a product of ambivalence than of accidents of transmission.[143] Conditions which led to the mislabeling of inherited materials and to lifting classical images and motifs out of context for mnemonic purposes need to be considered before invoking the idio-

---

[141] See Kristeller, *Renaissance Thought*, p. 93. Panofsky's thesis has been applied very widely by many authorities.

[142] Panofsky, *Renaissance and Renascences*, p. 162. See also pp. 42, 101–3.

[143] Although Panofsky, *Renaissance and Renascences*, specifically rejects 'accidents of transmission' as sufficient to explain the disjunctions he describes (p. 106), his account of the dissolution of classical representational traditions does seem to illustrate just how these very 'accidents' repeatedly occurred.

syncrasies of the 'high medieval mind.' One source of disjunction has been well described by Jean Seznec.

Either the artist has a visual model but...lacking an explanatory text is unable to render it correctly or he has nothing but the text and there is no model to check against his version.

Even where the model is handed down, it engendered more and more debased replicas so that understanding was obscured and lost.[144]

Not only was this true for the pagan gods whose metamorphosis Seznec has traced. It also occurred with classical descriptions of plants and animals and with accounts of architectural orders, coast-lines, constellations and the like. Separation of textual passages from images reflected a necessary division of labor between artisans copying models in materials like wood, stone, ivory, or metal and illuminators copying images traced in ink on parchment. (It is worth noting that recent reproductive techniques make the distinction between the diverse media ever more difficult for us to perceive. Images which were originally rendered in a variety of different materials are now reproduced side by side in a single book. We are so accustomed to their being juxtaposed in this manner, we are likely to forget how rarely this could occur in the past.)

Scribal culture did not merely encourage disjunctions between images and texts. It entailed repeated losses as well as occasional gains. When one portion of antiquity was retrieved, another was likely to slip away. Where classical *belles lettres* were revived, classical law and science were likely to languish. Insofar as the schoolmen were concerned with law and science, they were trying to preserve and transmit, not destroy or repudiate portions of inherited classical culture. In urging more study of Greek during the 'high Gothic' era, Roger Bacon was seeking to come closer to the texts of antiquity, and not reflecting 'scholastic' alienation. But the effort to recover all of Aristotle, as well as Euclid, Galen, Ptolemy and Roman law was at the expense of other parts of antiquity. The Grecian heavens were reconstructed in the high Gothic period under the aegis of the schoolmen. But even while Hellenistic astronomy was being recovered, the names and attributes of the Greek gods were being lost. The two phenomena were not unrelated.

---

[144] Seznec, *Survival*, pp. 180, 213. See also discussion of separation between scribe and painter by Kurt Weitzmann, *Illustration in Roll and Codex (Studies in Medieval Illumination)*, pp. 144, 151, 160–1. How illustrations were transferred from ancient rolls to bowls, friezes and sarcophagi is discussed on pp. 5–7.

The so-called 'high medieval' or Gothic extinction of classical elements was so far from being total that it stopped short of the cosmos. In the very era when Gothic spires were being built, a spherical earth and domed heavens were being recovered. As Lovejoy pointed out 'the most classical thing in the Middle Ages may be said to have been the universe...The architecture of the heavens was not a piece of Gothic design...it was a Grecian edifice.'[145] In this sense, thirteenth-century rejection of the classical heritage was, to put it mildly, incomplete. One also should be on guard against taking the appearance of seemingly bizarre non-classical elements to indicate a deliberate rejection of the antique. The metamorphoses undergone by certain pagan heroes offer a case in point. Perseus and Hercules, for example, underwent exotic transformations during the later middle ages and became 'thoroughly Orientalized in physiognomical appearance, costume and equipment.' For Panofsky, this suggests that the Gothic mind was so alienated from classical culture that it destroyed even those representational traditions that the Carolingian revival had managed to transmit.[146] His readers might infer that the Greek gods were being stigmatized as Saracens and infidels, much as 'Sir Pilate, the Saracen Knight' was cast as a villain in medieval mystery plays. The inference would be wrong. The pagan figures acquired their oriental accessories inadvertently, as part of an Arabic astronomical textual tradition which offered a more precise indication of the location of stars than did corrupted copies of Carolingian texts. Rather than representing alienation from (or even ambivalence about) classical culture, the orientalized images reflected an effort by learned men to retrieve portions of a technically sophisticated Hellenistic astronomy which had survived in Arab hands.

The use of mythical figures to pinpoint configurations of stars brings to mind another aspect of scribal transmission that also helps to explain medieval disjunctions. In addition to the tendency of pictures to drift away from texts and other accidents of transmission, one must take into account the deliberate exploitation of vivid images and motifs as memory aids. As already noted, classical images were necessarily

---

[145] Lovejoy, *The Great Chain of Being*, p. 101. That the later 'architecture of humanism' harmonized better with Aquinas' heavens than did the pointed arches and groin vaults of the thirteenth century suggests that the dichotomy Gothic–Classical may be pressed too far even in the realm of art history. See e.g. Geoffrey Scott, *The Architecture of Humanism*, *passim*.

[146] Panofsky, *Renaissance and Renascences*, p. 104; see also Seznec, *Survival*, pp. 185–7.

detached from their historical contexts when placed in imaginary 'memory theatres.' Reliance on the *ars memorandi* contributed to anachronistic juxtapositions. Insofar as men of learning mastered memory arts, their efforts to reconstruct the totality of a past civilization were weakened rather than reinforced. The orientalizing of Hercules and Perseus could thus be interpreted as indicating the incapacity of scribal culture to transmit the entire classical heritage at once. The recovery of classical astronomy entailed a loss of classical mythology. Different portions of the heritage could be recovered for different groups in diverse regions. But all of Greco-Roman civilization could not be restored as a complete and coherent cultural system as long as learned men had to depend on the limited means of transmission supplied by scribes.

The effort to recover and transmit the architecture of Grecian heavens along with other portions of antique wisdom; the effort to assimilate Aristotelian and Alexandrian learning (not to mention Roman law and Arabic science) must have taxed the resources of scribal culture to the utmost. Even as some Gothic abbreviations and bookhands suggest the problem of cramming a lot of data, recently retrieved, onto scarce supplies of skin;[147] so too does the relative dearth of texts relating to classical belles lettres suggest the problem of recruiting scribes to keep older works in circulation even while copying out newly retrieved ones. Large numbers of professional copyists had to be recruited to preserve the bulky technical works that had been recovered during the eleventh and twelfth centuries, to make them more available, to copy the recensions and syntheses, glosses and commentaries that were based upon them. A diversion of scribal labor at the main center of academic book production (in regions between Paris and Orleans) probably underlies the dwindling supply of texts relating to ancient belles lettres, previously used at the cathedral schools and later sought by quattrocento book-hunters.

To be sure, few developments were coordinated and synchronized during the middle ages. As noted in a preceding chapter, not all monastic scriptoria declined when new book-production centers were

---

[147] According to Destrez, *La Pecia*, p. 44, the abbreviations which made late medieval bookhands hard to read reflected the shift of book production from monastery to university, where clerks and lay copyists, working for money, looked for shortcuts in order to speed up their output. Bookhands derived from the slave labor of antiquity and the free labor of monks working for remission of sins might be contrasted with those developed by wage labor in the thirteenth century.

organized by the teaching and preaching orders. It seems unlikely that all fourteenth-century monasteries resembled Monte Cassino as Boccaccio purportedly found it, or that the earlier 'craze for the new dialectic' had diverted all groups of scribes simultaneously. But it does seem plausible that the particular works sought by Petrarch and his successors (which were usually 'recovered' in the form of copies made before the thirteenth century) had dwindled in supply because of new efforts to assimilate other portions of the classical heritage. These efforts were spurred by newly created graduate faculties who enthroned theology as queen of the sciences and supervised the book-trade conducted by lay stationers. Theology did not reign at Italian universities, but law and medicine flourished there. Significantly the Florentines could import and export texts relating to literature and the arts more freely than works in fields such as law and medicine which were subject to customs regulations and stringent academic controls.[148] Given access to the supplies of writing materials and clerical labor commanded by the papal court and city state despots, it was probably easier for quattrocento bookdealers to supply the growing demand for 'the periods of Cicero and the rules of Quintilian' in Northern Italy than elsewhere on the continent. But the copying of texts cherished by the humanists could scarcely have been sustained for very long on the peninsula let alone diffused beyond the Alps, without exacting some sort of toll – had not the 'divine art' been discovered, 'miraculously discovered' (as Louis Le Roy put it) 'in order to bring back to life more easily literature which seemed dead.'[149]

Until the advent of printing, classical revivals were necessarily limited in scope and transitory in effect; a sustained and permanent recovery of all portions of the antique heritage remained out of reach. This was true even after the introduction of paper. Cheaper writing material encouraged the recording of more sermons, orations, adages, and poems. It contributed greatly to more voluminous correspondence and to the keeping of more diaries, memoirs, copybooks and notebooks. The shift from parchment to paper thus had a significant impact upon the activities of merchants and literati.[150] Nevertheless, as noted

[148] De la Mare, 'Vespasiano,' pp. 64–5.
[149] Le Roy, excerpt from De la Vicissitude, tr. J. B. Ross, Portable Renaissance Reader, p. 98.
[150] The importance of keeping copybooks and notebooks, their use as memory aids, and the approach to the classics the practice entailed, is illuminated by Bolgar, The Classical Heritage, pp. 272–5.

above, paper could do nothing to lighten the labors or increase the output of the professional copyist.[151] As long as texts could be duplicated only by hand, perpetuation of the classical heritage rested precariously on the shifting requirements of local élites. Texts imported into one region depleted supplies in others; the enrichment of certain fields of study by an infusion of ancient learning impoverished other fields of study by diverting scribal labor. For a full century after the coronation of Petrarch, the revival of learning in Italy was subject to the same limitations as had been previous revivals. If we accept the distinction between several limited and transient renascences on the one hand and a permanent Renaissance of unprecedented range and scope on the other; then we must wait for a century-and-a-half after Petrarch before we can say that a genuinely new pattern was established.

This point seems especially pertinent to interpretations which center on the 'historical revolution' of early-modern times.[152] It ought to be considered before assigning responsibility to any one group of scholars for launching new disciplines such as philology, classical archeology, and other varieties of historical research. In one sense, it seems valid to single out the Italian humanists as the founders of these modern disciplines. Insofar as they influenced the publication programs pursued by master printers such as Aldus Manutius, they did initiate trends that became subject to continuous development after print. Nevertheless, the humanists were no more capable than any other group of scribal scholars of ensuring continuity for any branch of learning or of bringing about a permanent revolution in the handling of texts. Classical scholarship and historical research along with a variety of auxiliary disciplines became subject to a new form of continuous development only after, and not until, the establishment of printing plants in the second half of the fifteenth century.

Here a comparison with scribal precedents presumably established at Alexandria may prove instructive. For five centuries or more, successive generations of scholars worked over records deposited in a

[151] Chap. 2, n. 12.

[152] I have in mind the studies already cited above in this chapter, such as: Weiss, *Renaissance Discovery*; Kelley, *Foundations*; Kristeller, *Renaissance Thought*; Panofsky, *Renaissance and Renascences*; Gilmore, 'Renaissance Conception.' For further references see review article by Kelley, 'Faces in Clio's Mirror.' According to Momigliano, 'Ancient History and the Antiquarian,' p. 2, 'the whole modern method of historical research is founded on the distinction between original and derivative authorities.' Although this distinction became common 'only at the end of the seventeenth century,' it was, perhaps, more likely to be drawn after hand-written records could be set against printed secondary accounts.

great library. The catalogues and bibliographies they produced did not disappear entirely. But the remnants that remained, when contrasted with what passed for book learning thereafter, offer striking evidence of discontinuity. Neither the skills that were developed to classify rolls and codices, nor knowledge of the languages in which they were written could be preserved in the West after the contents of the Museum had been dispersed. Four or five centuries after the advent of printing, scholarly collaboration had produced entirely dissimilar results in the form of 'bibliographies of bibliographies of bibliographies.' A rapidly expanding bookish universe was being charted and catalogued by scholars all over the world using ever more refined systems and techniques. In an adage where he paid tribute to the Venetian printer, Aldus Manutius, Erasmus aptly described the difference. Aldus, he wrote, had taken up the task which had in other ages been undertaken by great rulers, such as the legendary founder of the Alexandrian library. But whereas the library of Ptolemy 'was contained between the narrow walls of its own house' the printer was 'building up a library which has no other limits than the world itself.'[153]

The implications of the difference to which this adage alludes, are too far-reaching for all of them to have been envisaged by Erasmus. They are also too far-reaching to be contained within the confines of this chapter. The new flow of information led far beyond the classical Christian horizons which bounded the world of humanism. The seemingly endless expansion of the library without walls helps to account for the sense of limitless vistas forever unfolding which characterized arts and letters in the age of the Baroque. The difference between the circumscribed contents of the walled libraries of antiquity and the open-ended data banks which were developed after printing ought to be considered in conjunction with developments such as the 'denial of limit,' the 'breaking of the circle,' and other similar conceptual shifts which were not yet dominant themes in Erasmus' day. In a later section of this book I hope to suggest how the shift from a 'closed world' to the 'infinite universe of the new cosmology' may be related to the advent of a 'library without walls.'[154] Here I will

---

[153] 'Festina Lente,' tr. from the 1508 edition of the *Adages* by Margaret Mann Phillips (ed.), *The 'Adages' of Erasmus*, pp. 180–1.

[154] On the cosmological shift see Koyré, *From the Closed World*. Haydn, *The Counter Renaissance* and Marjorie Nicolson, *The Breaking of the Circle* describe related developments and cite relevant texts. For further discussion, see pp. 517ff., volume II below.

merely note that an astronomer such as Copernicus was just as indebted as was Erasmus to the new kind of library that was created by Aldus and other early printers. The classical editions, dictionaries, grammars and reference guides issued from print shops made it possible to achieve an unprecedented mastery of Alexandrian learning even while laying the basis for a new kind of permanent Greek revival in the West.

The fate of Greek studies after the fall of Constantinople offers a dramatic example of how printing transformed traditional patterns of cultural change.

One of the strangely persistent myths of history is that the humanist study of Greek works began with the arrival in Italy in 1453 of learned refugees from Constantinople who are supposed to have fled the city in all haste, laden with rare manuscripts. Aside from the essential improbability of their doing any such thing, and the well-established fact that the opening years of the fifteenth century had seen intense activity,...there is the testimony of the humanists themselves that the fall of Constantinople represented a tragedy to them. Characteristic is the cry of the humanist Cardinal, Aeneas Sylvius Piccolomini...who wrote despairingly to Pope Nicholas in July, 1453: 'How many names of mighty men will perish ! It is a second death to Homer and to Plato. The fount of the Muses is dried up forever more.'[155]

The 'strangely persistent' myth points to a remarkable reversal of previous trends. To the best of my knowledge, it represents the very first time that the dispersal of major manuscript centers ever got associated with a revival of learning rather than with the onset of a dark age. The humanist cardinal was expressing expectations that were based on all the lessons of history which were available in his day and which showed how learning was eclipsed when great cities fell. We now tend to take for granted that the study of Greek would continue to flourish after the main Greek manuscript centers had fallen into alien hands and hence fail to appreciate how remarkable it was to find that Homer and Plato had not been buried anew but had, on the contrary, been disinterred forever more.

Surely Ottoman advances would have been catastrophic before the advent of printing. Texts and scholars scattered in nearby regions might have prolonged the study of Greek but only in a temporary way. By 1520, according to Burckhardt, the study of Greek literature was dying out 'with the last of the colony of learned Greek exiles.' He

[155] Marie Boas, *The Scientific Renaissance*, p. 24.

notes as 'a singular piece of good fortune that Northerners, like Agricola, Reuchlin, Erasmus, the Stephani and Budæus had meanwhile made themselves masters of the language.'[156] It was this 'singular piece of good fortune' which led later generations to elaborate the myth that Erasmus and Reuchlin, rather than Petrarch and Boccaccio had initiated a revival of letters and had 'rescued' learning from ignorant monks.[157]

As Northern scholars, Erasmus and Reuchlin were actually 'rescued' themselves by an Italian printer and his Greek editions. According to Reuchlin's own testimony he could not have taught Greek in Germany without the aid of the Aldine editions.[158] Aldus Manutius also helped to fill the shelves of the Wittenberg University Library where Reuchlin's nephew, Philip Melanchthon, was appointed as a professor of Greek and later won renown as the 'preceptor of Germany.' As a Northern astronomer on a visit to Italy, Copernicus found a Greek teacher. The Greek teacher died. Copernicus went on with the help of new dictionaries and editions.[159] Although he elsewhere pays tribute to the Aldine press, Burckhardt does not help his readers to connect the 'singular piece of good fortune' with the new enterprise in which 'Northerners like the Stephani' were engaged.[160] The same point applies to many other treatments of the Greek revival, which simply trace continuous trends from the early fifteenth century on, without pausing over the remarkable way the revival withstood Constantinople's fall.

---

156 Burckhardt, *Civilization of the Renaissance* I, 205.

157 Weisinger, 'Who Began the Revival,' p. 629 cites relevant passages from Thomas Campion which praises Northern humanists while belittling illiterate 'Monks and Friers [sic].' The tendency to launch the revival with Gutenberg was boosted by patriotic, anti-Italian German and French literati, thus paving the way for the misappropriation of the term 'Renaissance' by later French scholars such as Naudé and Michelet, as is noted below, n. 420. Use of the theme of disinterring buried authors and restoring mangled ones by the early humanists, who preceded both printing and the capture of Constantinople, is vividly demonstrated in the correspondence of Poggio, Gordan (ed.), *Two Renaissance book hunters*. See e.g. Bruni to Poggius, letter of Sept. 15, 1416, pp. 191ff.

158 Reuchlin's comment that he could not have taught Greek in Germany without the aid of Aldine editions is cited by Geanokoplos, *Greek Scholars in Venice*, pp. 297–8. How Aldus was warned his editions would cut down on tourist traffic into Italy is noted above, p. 180. The difficulty of persuading Greek emigrés to go to cold Northern regions ought to be included in any discussion of Greek studies before printing.

159 On Aldus and Wittenberg library, see Grossman, *Humanism*, chap. 7 and Schweibert, *Luther and his Times*, pp. 249–53. On Copernicus, see pp. 578ff., volume II below.

160 'Hellenistic studies owed a priceless debt to the press of Aldo Manucci at Venice,' Burckhardt, *Civilization of the Renaissance* I, 206. It seems inconsistent that 'Aldo's' name is given in its Italian guise whereas the Estiennes are presented as the 'Stephani.'

By the early sixteenth century, contacts with Byzantium had been severed, Ottoman advances were being consolidated, refugee enclaves were dying out, and Italy itself was the scene of invasions from the North. Given this constellation of events, and keeping in mind that all major Greek texts had been translated into Latin by 1520,[161] one might expect that the impulse given by the humanists to the study of Greek would have died out 'nstead it was the scribal phrase 'Graeca sunt ergo non legenda' that gradually disappeared from Western texts – never to appear again.[162] The study of Greek was permanently inserted into the curriculum of academic institutions throughout Europe and the reach of classical scholars was gradually extended to encompass earlier phases of Hellenic civilization.[163] If old forms of collaboration had produced entirely novel results, this was probably because Greek typefonts had been cut, dictionaries and grammars had been compiled and printed and original texts had been made available in the form of whole editions.

In this regard some caution is needed about blurring the difference between earlier groups of scribal scholars, book collectors and copyists and later groups who gathered in printers' workshops, when we discuss the contribution made by Greek expatriates to Western scholarship during the Renaissance.[164] It is useful to learn how much the remarkable output of the Aldine press between 1494 and 1515 owed to aid furnished by Cretans and other Greek exiles who became members of the printer's household, formed the nucleus of his academy, and served him in innumerable ways. It is worth noting that these scholars accomplished more during a quarter century in Venice than had their predecessors in Florence during an interval four times that

---

[161] On printing and translation of Greek classics see Bolgar, *The Classical Heritage*, p. 375; Kristeller, *Renaissance Thought*, pp. 16, 96.

[162] In early printed editions of patristic or classical works that were published outside Italy, blanks *were* often left for Greek passages. See Proctor, *The Printing of Greek*, p. 48. The Oxford University Press did not acquire Greek types until 1586, according to Pattison, *Isaac Casaubon*, p. 111.

[163] The recent steady accumulation of documents (largely papyrus) covering the span of a millennium which enables scholars to note changes affecting the Greek language and script is summarized by Deuel, *Testaments of Time*, p. 157.

[164] Welcome support for my views on this question is offered by M. J. C. Lowry, 'Two Great Venetian Libraries.' Lowry shows how difficult it was to gain access to any of Bessarion's collection (which the Cardinal had started to amass after the fall of Constantinople and had bequeathed to Venice in 1468) and why Aldus should not be viewed simply as the beneficiary of the Marciana (or of the Grimaldi collection either). Lowry's more recent article, 'The "New Academy" of Aldus Manutius,' points to his forthcoming full-scale study of Aldus and suggests that the Aldine 'academy' was less substantial than others indicate.

long.[165] But the Greeks who aided Aldus in Venice did not merely perform more efficiently the same functions that similar enclaves had previously performed. Since they were employed by a printer and engaged in processing copy for the new presses, they were bound to perform entirely new functions as well. When presenting their activities as a 'chapter in the transmission of Greco-Byzantine learning to the West'[166] it is essential to underline the unusual nature of this particular chapter. It covers an interval that saw major changes in the way all forms of learning were transmitted. Intellectual trade routes were drastically reoriented in a manner that revolutionized traditional contacts between East and West – to the extent of outmoding previous reliance on personal intercourse and diminishing the impact of emigré movements. The Aldine editions drew on Greek aid. But they also emancipated Western scholars from their traditional reliance upon this kind of aid. Not only Germans beyond the Alps but also Englishmen across the Channel – and, ultimately, Western colonists in the new world – could pursue Hellenic studies regardless of what happened to Greeks in Constantinople or Athens, in Crete, Venice, Florence, or Rome.

The flourishing of Hellenic studies in the West, despite the disruption of peaceful contacts with the Greek learned world, provides only one of many indications that typography endowed scholarship with new powers. Hebrew and Arabic studies also gained a new lease on life.[167] Medieval Bible studies had depended on Christian contacts with Jews as well as Greeks. Until after the fifteenth century, Western Christendom had been unable to sustain 'an unbroken tradition of skill in

---

[165] Geanakoplos, *Greek Scholars in Venice*, p. 293. It is disappointing that the central figure of this useful study never emerges from a marginal position. The author notes that almost every scholar discussed is associated with Aldus Manutius and promises that 'a later chapter' will discuss 'the printer's work and significance' (p. 60). But although each associate has a separate chapter assigned to him, Aldus does not. Even his biography is interwoven with other data in a chapter presumably devoted to Marcus Musurus. See pp. 116–22, 128–32, 156–7.

[166] Geanakoplos, 'Erasmus and the Aldine Academy.' This 'chapter' is incorporated into the book-length study cited above. It contains fascinating data on Erasmus' stay in Aldus' household during 1508, but presents the episode as 'only a single example, albeit a climactic one, of the traditional medieval function of Venice as an intermediary between Byzantium and the Latin West' (p. 134). In my view, it reveals much about the early phases of a major cultural revolution and also should be examined in this light.

[167] It is indicative of how advanced erudition shifted away from university to printer's workshop that Erasmus perfected his Greek during his sojourn with Aldus and then turned to the son of a Basel printer, Bruno Amerbach, for help with Hebrew. See his description of his work on Saint Jerome's letters, 'Hercules' Labors,' *The Adages*, pp. 208–9. Johann Amerbach's circle is outlined by Febvre and Martin, *L'Apparition*, pp. 218–19.

semitic languages.'[168] A Venetian printing firm run by Daniel Bomberg, an emigré from Antwerp, laid new foundations for Western semitic scholarship, spurring studies in Hebrew and Arabic much as Aldus Manutius had spurred the study of Greek.[169] Other languages, hitherto completely foreign among Europeans, became available to Western scholars for the first time. Polyglot Bibles were turned out by presses located in Alcalà, Antwerp, Paris, and London between 1517 and 1657. Each of the four editions surpassed its predecessors in the number of languages used; no less than nine (including Persian and Ethiopic) had to be mastered by the compositors and correctors of the London edition of 1657.[170] Once fonts had been cut and multilingual dictionaries and grammars had been issued, durable foundations for the development of new erudite disciplines had been laid.[171]

The recovery of ancient languages followed the same pattern as the recovery of ancient texts. A process which had hitherto been intermittent became subject to continuous, incremental change. Once a finding could be permanently secured by being registered in print, the way was paved for an unending series of discoveries and for the systematic development of investigatory techniques. Probes into the past were steadily extended; texts and languages lost, not merely to the West, but to all men everywhere for thousands of years, were retrieved from the dead, reconstructed and deciphered. Compared to the refined techniques employed at present, sixteenth-century methods appear crude and clumsy. Yet however sophisticated present findings have become, we still have to call upon a fifteenth-century invention to secure them. Even at present, a given scholarly discovery, whatever

[168] Beryl Smalley, *The Study of the Bible in the Middle Ages*, p. 44. See also two essays: Singer, 'Hebrew Scholarship in the Middle Ages,' and Box, 'Hebrew Studies in the Reformation.' For a more recent account, suggesting the ambivalent and complex nature of medieval Christian contacts with Jewish teachers and Hebrew scholarship, see Grabois, 'The *Hebraica Veritas*.'

[169] According to Box, p. 333, Elias Levita the 'real founder of modern Hebrew grammar' emigrated to Venice after the sack of Rome and worked for Daniel Bomberg from 1527 to 1549. Dannenfeldt, 'The Renaissance Humanists' notes how Daniel Bomberg helped to finance Guillaume Postel's trip to the Orient and also aided a Louvain scholar who was trying to master Arabic. On Bomberg's Antwerp connections (which overlapped with Plantin's circle) see chap. 4, n. 468 below. On Levita, see also Weil, *Elie Lévita: Humaniste et Massorète (1469–1549)*.

[170] Updike, *Printing Types* II, 98. The types, all made in England, used for this Bible provided models for eighteenth-century Oriental fonts.

[171] The importance of printing in laying these foundations is acknowledged by Bolgar, *The Classical Heritage*, pp. 374–5, but in such an understated way that other scholars who cite Bolgar's opinion are apt to pass over typography altogether. See e.g. Pocock, *Ancient Constitution*, pp. 4–5.

its nature (whether it entails using a shovel or crane, a code book, a tweezer or carbon 14), has to be registered in print – announced in a learned journal and eventually spelled out in full – before it can be acknowledged as a contribution or put to further use.

Archeology, writes Roberto Weiss, 'was a creation of the Renaissance. Reverence for the antique has...nearly always existed. But one would search the classical world or the Middle Ages in vain for a systematic study of antiquity.'[172] Systematic study, however, was still in the future during the century which followed Petrarch. As Weiss himself points out, during the first half of the quattrocento, classical studies were still in an unsystematic state. Systematization came only after the humanist impulse could be combined with new features supplied by print culture. Furthermore, the systematic development of the investigation of antiquity had medieval as well as Renaissance antecedents. Curiosity about ancient artifacts and languages was perpetually stimulated by the need to copy and emend both the writings of Church fathers and the sacred scriptures themselves.

In this light, it seems misleading to stop short with the humanist movement in Italy when trying to account for the so-called rise of classical scholarship and the development of auxiliary disciplines. Humanism may have encouraged the pursuit of classical studies for their own sake, sharpened sensitivity to anachronism, and quickened curiosity about all aspects of antiquity; but it could not supply the new element of continuity that is implied by the use of the term 'rise.' Findings relating to lost texts and dead languages began to accumulate in an unprecedented fashion not because of some distinctive ethos shaped in quattrocento Italy but because a new technology had been placed at the disposal of a far-flung community of scholars.

3. THE SHIFT TOWARD MODERN FORMS OF CONSCIOUSNESS

A wide variety of other developments that are usually associated with the culture of the Italian Renaissance and that seem to point toward modern times lend themselves to a similar interpretation. We might look, for example, at the developments covered by Burckhardt's most celebrated passage:

In the Middle Ages both sides of human consciousness...lay dreaming or

---

172 Weiss, *The Renaissance Discovery of Antiquity*, p. 203.

half awake beneath a common veil. The veil was woven of faith, illusion, and childish prepossession, through which the world and history were seen clad in strange hues. Man was conscious of himself only as a member of a race, people, party, family, or corporation – only through some general category. In Italy this veil first melted into air; an objective treatment of the state and of all the things of this world became possible...at the same time... man became a spiritual individual and recognized himself as such...It will not be difficult to show that this result was owing above all to the political circumstances of Italy.[173]

Certain portions of this passage seem to me to be invalid – especially the assertion about medieval man lacking consciousness of self. It is probably misguided to assign group-consciousness to one era and individual consciousness to another. The sense of belonging to a 'general category' *and* of being a 'spiritual individual' seems to have coexisted in Western Christendom in the days of Saint Augustine and in those of Saint Bernard. If, indeed, there was a change in human consciousness during the early-modern era, it probably entailed *both* the sense of a group identity and of an individual one.[174] Other portions of the passage also need to be reformulated. As they stand, they are so ambiguous that one cannot be certain just what Burckhardt means by 'this result.'

Nevertheless, I would not join those who argue that the passage contains no substantive issues or that there was no real shift in human consciousness that needs to be explained. Unlike certain critics, moreover, I do not doubt that political circumstances in Italy helped to shape a distinctive ethos which contained much that was new and proved historically significant. At the same time, I think much more is owed to the advent of printing and much less to local circumstances in Italy than is suggested by the passage or by later interpretations of it. Given a shift in human consciousness and a concurrent revolution in communications, it seems far-fetched to attribute the shift to political conditions in Italy.

Of the two sides of human consciousness discussed by Burckhardt, the so-called 'objective' aspect need not detain us for long, since changing views of 'the world and history' have entered into previous

[173] Burckhardt, *Civilization of the Renaissance* I, 143. That this passage which opens Part II ('The Development of the Individual') contains Burckhardt's 'basic theme' or 'the heart' of his work is noted by Nelson and Trinkaus (p. 8), and by Huizinga, 'Problem of the Renaissance,' p. 257. The same point is also underlined in a pertinent essay by Gombrich, *In Search of Cultural History*, pp. 19–20.   [174] See above, chap. 2, n. 130.

discussion. Let me note in passing, however, that the problem might be handled more satisfactorily if it were posed somewhat differently. Whether or not the medieval mentality was peculiarly childlike or credulous is in my view an unedifying question. I would prefer instead to stress the common acceptance on the part of otherwise hard-headed, intelligent and literate adults (belonging to ancient, medieval, and/or Renaissance élite groups) of what has been described elsewhere as 'fantastic history and imaginary geography.'[175] An inability to discriminate between Paradise and Atlantis on the one hand, Cathay and Jerusalem on the other, between unicorns and rhinoceroses, the fabulous and the factual, does seem to separate earlier mentalities from our own in a way that arouses curiosity and requires explanation. How may we account for this strangely colored vision? In my view, it is not adequately explained by Burckhardt's vague poetic allusions to medieval dreams and veils which melted into air under the impact of political circumstances in Italy. As previous comments suggest, I think more adequate explanations can be found by considering the conditions of scribal culture and how they changed after print. After reviewing the controversy over the location of Paradise which contemporaries were placing in such dissimilar places as Syria and the Arctic Pole, Ortelius decided to exclude it as a problem for geographers: 'By Paradise I do think the blessed life be understood.'[176] When considering how veils were lifted, the publication programs of map makers should not be ignored. The absence of uniform maps delineating political boundaries seems to me to be more relevant to blurred political consciousness during prior eras than has been yet noted in most historical studies.[177] For Ortelius, as for Herodotus, geography was the 'eye of history.' The media shift altered what could be seen by this metaphorical eye. An atlas such as the *Theatrum* did enable men to envisage past worlds and the present one more clearly. This was because methods of data collection rather than political circumstances in Italy had been changed.

Without dwelling longer on this point, let me turn now to Burckhardt's treatment of the 'subjective' side of human consciousness and

[175] Chaytor, *From Script to Print*, p. 26.
[176] Ortelius, preface, *Message to the Reader*, facsimile of 1606 English ed. p. ij.
[177] As noted above (chap. 2, n. 129) there is a suggestive paper by Denys Hay on the influence of cartography on awareness of regional groupings, 'Geographical Abstractions,' p. 11. But how the difference between scribal and printed cartography may have affected political consciousness remains to be discussed.

consider some of the issues that he covers in his most celebrated section on 'The Development of the Individual.' Even at first glance it is evident that the theme of growing self-awareness is handled unevenly. The author begins on shaky grounds and ends on firmer ones, when he moves from the age of scribes to that of printers. His opening passages, describing how 'at the close of the thirteenth century, Italy began to swarm with individuality,' seem vulnerable to criticism from many quarters.[178] The section closes, however, with a much more straightforward account of a new career, one which pointed the way to the future and was based on exploiting the new power of the press.

Aretino affords the first great instance of the abuse of publicity...The polemical writings which a hundred years earlier Poggio and his opponents interchanged are just as infamous in their tone and purpose but they were not composed for the press...Aretino made all his profit out of a complete publicity and in a certain sense may be considered the father of modern journalism. His letters and miscellaneous articles were printed periodically after they had already been circulated among a tolerably extensive public.[179]

The title of 'father of modern journalism' may be somewhat too dignified for one of the founders of the gutter press. Although Aretino was not the first blackguard to pursue a literary career,[180] he was the first to take advantage of the new publicity system. His activities, like those pursued by his Grub Street successors, do at least suggest that new powers were placed at the disposal of men of letters after the advent of printing.[181]

That these powers could be used by literati on their own behalf needs to be kept in mind when considering Renaissance individualism. As Pierre Mesnard has noted, the Republic of Letters, during the sixteenth century resembled a newly liberated state where every citizen felt he

---

178 Burckhardt, *Civilization of the Renaissance* I, 143. As one might expect, Morris, *The Discovery of the Individual* makes out a plausible case for finding in twelfth-century France what Burckhardt found peculiar to trecento Italy. An historian who is skilled in exploiting selected sources and painting vivid word pictures with his pen can make almost any region at any time seem to 'swarm with individuals.'

179 Burckhardt, *Civilization of the Renaissance* I, 170–1.

180 An intriguing account of how bards tried to frighten patrons into filling their pot with silver by threatening to blight crops and sicken people with curses is given by Holznecht, *Literary Patronage*, p. 4. Holznecht notes that printed blackmail à la Aretino represented a significant innovation.

181 How Aretino used the epistolary genre for promotional purposes is brought out by Mesnard, 'Le Commerce Epistolaire,' pp. 17–18. The rapid emergence of 'Grub Street' in the wake of Aretino's success and the irreverent vernacular literature turned out by the so-called 'poligrafi, low-born adventurers of the pen' are illuminated by Paul Grendler, 'The Rejection of Learning.' See also Grendler's book, *Critics of the Italian World*, chap. 1.

had an irresistible vocation for serving as prime minister.[182] Many of the devices which are still being used by press agents, were first tried out during the age of Erasmus. In the course of exploiting new publicity techniques, few authors failed to give high priority to publicizing themselves. The art of puffery, the writing of blurbs and other familiar promotional devices were also exploited by early printers who worked aggressively to obtain public recognition for the authors and artists whose products they hoped to sell.[183]

In general, the new powers of the press seem to be so pertinent to the heightened recognition accorded to individual achievement that it is disconcerting to find them unmentioned in most treatments of the latter topic.[184] The testimony of prophets and preachers may be cited to suggest that public curiosity about private lives, like the desire for worldly fame and glory – like avarice, lechery, or vanity, for that matter – had venerable antecedents. The process which made it possible to supplement tales of great men teaching by example and the lives of saints and saintly kings, by biographies and autobiographies of more ordinary people pursuing more variegated careers;[185] the industry which encouraged publishers to advertise authors and authors to advertise themselves – such phenomena are less ancient and more in need of historical examination. Scribal culture could not sustain the patenting of inventions or the copyrighting of literary compositions. It worked against the concept of intellectual property rights.[186] It did not lend itself to preserving traces of personal idiosyncrasies, to the public

---

[182] Mesnard, 'Le Commerce Epistolaire,' p. 26. See also p. 17 for suggestive comments about the Republic of Letters as a new 'third force' in European affairs. On the need to explore this concept further, see above, chap. 2, n. 287.

[183] On the efforts at self-promotion made by Erasmus when he was an obscure young man 'on the make,' see below, pp. 400 ff, where other literary careerists such as Rabelais and the young Calvin are also mentioned.

[184] For examples see Walter Ullmann, *The Individual and Society in the Middle Ages*; Cassirer, 'On the Originality of the Renaissance'; and Arnold Hauser's effort to deal with the issue of intellectual property, *Social History of Art* II, 70. No mention of the advent of printing entered the otherwise wide ranging session on 'Society and the Individual: Medieval and Renaissance.' Meeting of the *American Historical Association* at Toronto, December 29, 1967. The topic comes up, only incidentally, in the Brussels colloquium of 1965 on *Individu et Société*.

[185] On the emergence of new genres of biography and autobiography, see Zimmerman, 'Confession and Autobiography'; Delany, *British Autobiography*, chap. 2; Fairfield, 'The Vocacyon of Johan Bale and Early English Autobiography,' pp. 327 ff.

[186] That the concept of 'the artist as a genius' is related to the new notion of 'intellectual property rights' is underlined by Arnold Hauser, *Social History of Art* II, 70. Hauser seems at a loss to explain the latter notion, however, and merely notes that it followed 'from the disintegration of Christian culture': a dubious proposition in my view.

airing of private thoughts, or to any of the forms of silent publicity that have shaped consciousness of self during the past five centuries.

Despite precedents established by scribal works, such as Augustine's 'Confessions,' Abelard's 'Calamities' or Petrarch's 'Secret'; the paradoxical implications of making private thoughts public were not fully realized until authors began to address an audience composed of silent and solitary readers.[187] Classical rhetorical conventions had allowed for the difference in tone between addressing a large assemblage in a public arena, where strong lungs and broad strokes were required, and pleading a case in a courtroom, which called for careful attention to detail and a more soft-spoken, closely argued, intimate approach.[188] But no precedent existed for addressing a large crowd of people who were not gathered together in one place but were scattered in separate dwellings and who, as solitary individuals with divergent interests, were more receptive to intimate interchanges than to broad-gauged rhetorical effects. Perhaps the most ingenious solution devised to meet the new situation was the informal essay which was first successfully used by Montaigne.

Montaigne's special gift for achieving an intimate relationship with his many unknown readers has often been noted; so too, has his peculiar cult of the self.[189] The two phenomena, however, are more likely to be discussed in connection with the problem of Renaissance individualism than in relation to changes wrought by print.[190] More attention to the latter might diminish puzzlement about the former. As noted in the previous chapter, a sharper sense of individual difference was fostered by repeated encounters with identical types.[191] It was just this sense that Montaigne exploited to the hilt. The state of being he portrayed – idiosyncratic, volatile, involved with trivial concerns – contrasted in every way with the fixed norms and forms conveyed by other books. The latter dealt with the behavior of ideal typical figures who were defined by their membership in a given group. Princes, courtiers, councillors, merchants, schoolmasters, husbandmen

---

187 For illuminating treatment of the paradoxical implications of a public display of intimate thoughts, see Colie, *Paradoxia Epidemica*, chap. 12.

188 Trimpi, 'The Meaning of Horace's "Ut Pictura Poesis,"' pp. 4–7.

189 See references given by Winter, 'Mon Livre et Moi.'

190 Cassirer, 'On the Originality of the Renaissance' singles out the case of Montaigne without reference to printing. The new division between the role-playing personage and the 'authentic' inner self is described by Delany, *British Autobiography*, p. 11 as a novel development whose origins remain obscure.   191 See above, p. 84.

and the like were presented in terms which made readers ever more aware, not merely of their shortcomings in their assigned roles, but also of the existence of a solitary singular self – characterized by all the peculiar traits that were unshared by others – traits which had no redeeming social or exemplary functions and hence were deemed to be of no literary worth. By presenting himself, in all modesty, as a unique individual and by portraying with loving care every one of his peculiarities, Montaigne brought this private self out of hiding, so to speak. He displayed it for public inspection in a deliberate way for the first time. By drawing on a recently recovered sceptical tradition,[192] he gave his idiosyncrasies a respectable classical ancestry; as a consummate literary artist, he endowed them with the lustre of lasting fame. He also established a new basis for achieving intimate contact with unknown readers who might admire portraits of worthy men from a distance but felt more at home when presented with an admittedly unworthy self. Above all he provided a welcome assurance that the isolating sense of singularity which was felt by the solitary reader had been experienced by another human being and was, indeed, capable of being widely shared. The 'universal' appeal of Montaigne's claim to be different may become more understandable when it is related to the new silent means of communication, and not simply kept as a familiar bone of contention in debates about the Renaissance.

The enhanced awareness of singularity which resulted from standardization probably affected the visual arts no less than the literary ones. When a given painting by an artist, such as Raphael, was duplicated in quantity by printmakers, such as Marcantonio, it seems likely that a new value would be assigned to the 'original' painting or drawing which came directly from the artist's own hand.[193] One wonders if the personal hand and signature of the artist did not also become

---

[192] On the recovery of the work of Sextus Empiricus, the revival of the classical sceptical tradition and contributions made by Henri II Estienne (member of the printing dynasty) and Montaigne, see Popkin, *The History of Scepticism*, pp. 34–5, and Haydn, *Counter-Renaissance*, chap. 2. As noted below, volume II, chap. 5, many of the currents of thought Haydn describes as part of his 'Counter-Renaissance' seem to me to be related to changes wrought by print. His discussion of Montaigne and the 'Vanity of Learning' tradition provides a case in point.

[193] How prints helped to 'broadcast' the 'inventions' of artists such as Raphael is noted by Shearman, *Mannerism*, pp. 46–7. Vasari's account of Raphael's collaboration with Marcantonio is mentioned above, n. 32. A relevant exhibition: 'Titian and the Venetian Woodcut' held at the National Gallery of Art, Washington D.C., December, 1976, included a supplement on 'Titian and Engraving' which showed how the artist received a publication copyright from the Venetian government in 1567 to cover prints issued from his house (executed by Dutch engraver, Cornelius Cort, who took up residence there).

more highly prized after hand-copied books became less common.[194] It can scarcely be doubted, at all events, that the relationship between artists, patrons and publics was changed by the power of the press in ways that still need to be explored.

In accounting for the emergence of uniquely distinguished, personally celebrated artists out of the ranks of more anonymous artisans, the preservative powers of print deserve more attention. This is not to deny that individual artists were already being singled out for praise as eminent citizens (especially in Florence) well before the advent of printing.[195] Nor is it to overlook the evidence of heightened self-esteem and self-consciousness which was provided by several scribal treatises written by Florentine artists about themselves and their craft.[196] It is merely to say that the cult of personality was repeatedly undermined by the conditions of scribal culture and was powerfully reinforced after the advent of printing. The personal histories of even the most celebrated masters could not be recorded until writing materials became relatively abundant. And until such records could be duplicated they were not likely to be preserved intact for very long. When fifteenth-century manuscripts found their way into print, ephemeral materials were secured along with formal work. Treatises, orations, intimate correspondence, anecdotes and drawings all were collected by Vasari for his celebrated *Lives*.

Vasari's work is often heralded as the first book devoted specifically to art history. The novelty of his theory of cultural cycles also is often stressed.[197] But there are other less familiar aspects of his enterprise

---

194 The increasingly high value assigned to drawings, sketches, and other evidence of work in progress by artists is noted by Arnold Hauser, *Social History of Art* II, 71. Hauser makes no mention of possible changes wrought by printing, but does, however, refer to a relevant passage from Filarete's treatise where the forms of a work of art are compared to the pen-strokes of a manuscript revealing the hand of the writer.

195 Baxandall, *Giotto*; Larner, *Culture and Society*, chap. 11 are among many studies which cover relevant scribal works including the tributes paid to Giotto by Dante and his successors, Filippo Villani's inclusion of painters in his tribute to Florentine citizens, Alberti's treatise on painting, Filarete's on architecture and the section on painters (which included Flemish masters) in *De Viris Illustribus* by Bartolomeo Facio.

196 A key work here is Lorenzo Ghiberti's three-part *Commentaries* (written over the course of decades and left unfinished at the author's death in 1455) especially the artist's autobiography provided at the end of Book 2. See Richard Krautheimer and T. Krautheimer-Hess, *Lorenzo Ghiberti* and R. Krautheimer, 'The Beginnings.' Ghiberti's work is also cited as evidence of a new kind of self-consciousness by Wittkower, 'Individualism in Art and Artists: A Renaissance Perspective.' See also the Wittkowers' *Born Under Saturn*, chap. 3 and Gombrich, 'The Renaissance Conception.'

197 See R. Krautheimer, 'The Beginnings,' p. 268; Gombrich, 'Art and Scholarship'; Blunt, *Artistic Theory*, chap. VII, p. 98.

which deserve more attention because they show how the art of biography profited from changes wrought by print. The sheer number of separate individuals, all engaged in a similar endeavor, covered by the second edition of his multi-volumed work is, in itself, noteworthy. To match art-works with biographical records for 250 separate cases represented an unprecedented feat. In addition to the expansion in scale, there was a new effort at research in depth. Vasari's was the first systematic investigation based on interviews, correspondence, field trips, of the procedures used and the objects produced by generations of European artists.[198] The *Lives* also reflect the new opportunity offered by print to extend the scope of a given work from one edition to another. The second edition of 1568 was a vastly expanded version of the first one of 1550. It broke out of the limits imposed by Florentine civic loyalties and introduced no less than seventy-five new biographical sketches. Among other notable innovations, woodcut portraits were designed to go with each biographical sketch. Significantly enough, despite the special effort made to match faces with names, purely conjectural portraits had to be supplied for artists who lived before the fifteenth century.[199]

Before the fifteenth century, even artists' self-portraits were deprived of individuality. The conditions of scribal culture thus held narcissism in check. A given master might decide to place his own features on a figure in a fresco or on a carving over a door; but, in the absence of written records, he would still lose his identity in the eyes of posterity and become another faceless artisan who performed some collective task. The same point also applies to those occasional author portraits which survived from antiquity. In the course of continuous copying, the face of one author got transferred to another's text and distinctive features were blurred or erased.[200] After the passage of centuries, the

[198] Petrucelli, 'Giorgio Vasari's Attribution of the Vesalian Illustrations to Jan Stephan of Calcar.' The Mellon lectures, given at the National Gallery, Washington, D.C., on the theme of 'Vasari: The Man and the Book' by T. R. Boase also contain much relevant data. One might compare the scale and scope of Vasari's investigation with that undertaken by Bartolomeo Facio for the section on artists in the latter's *De Viris Illustribus*. (Evidence that Facio did request information from Poggio about his own writings and those of Bruni, Manetti and Traversari is offered by Kristeller, 'Bartolomeo Facio and his Unknown Correspondence.') A similar expansion in scope and scale and a similar development from edition to edition may be demonstrated by looking at Polydore Vergil's *De Inventoribus* which was issued in some thirty editions during the second half of the sixteenth century and which contains abundant references to 'an amazingly rich array of literature.' Hay, *Polydore Vergil*, pp. 56–8.   [199] Rud, *Vasari's Life and Lives*, provides this information.

[200] Pächt, 'Early Italian Nature Studies,' p. 26, n. 3, describes how authors' portraits in herbals of the sixth century got interchanged.

figure at the desk or the robed scholar holding a book simply became an impersonal symbol of the author at large. As a previous chapter suggests, these impersonal images did not disappear when print replaced script. On the contrary, they were subject to a greater degree of standardization and multiplied by woodcuts and engravings.[201] Just as the same city profile might be labelled with different place names in an early printed chronicle, so too, an identical human profile served to illustrate diverse individuals performing the same occupational role. Careless handling of corrupted woodcuts also led to further comedies of errors and mistaken identities. At the same time, however, the drive for fame moved into high gear; the self-portrait acquired a new permanence, a heightened appreciation of individuality accompanied increased standardization, and there was a new deliberate promotion by publishers and print dealers of those authors and artists whose works they hoped to sell. Along with title pages and booksellers' catalogues, came portrait heads of authors and artists.[202] More and more, distinct physiognomies became permanently attached to distinct names. Sixteenth-century portraits of Erasmus, Luther, Loyola *et al.* were multiplied with sufficient frequency to be duplicated in innumerable history books and to remain recognizable even now.

When historical figures can be given distinct faces, they also acquire a more distinctive personality. The characteristic individuality of Renaissance masterpieces in comparison with earlier ones is probably related to the new possibility of preserving by duplication the faces, names, birth-places, and personal histories of the makers of objects of art. The hands of medieval illuminators or stone carvers were in fact no less distinctive – as investigations by art historians show. But the personalities of the masters (who are usually known only by their initials or by the books, altarpieces, and tympana they produced) are as unfamiliar to us as those of cabinet makers or glaziers. Even those masters whose names are known because they lacked the modesty

[201] See above, pp. 85–6.

[202] The replacement of 'stereotyped' profiles and portrait heads by more authentic ones in a sixteenth-century encyclopedia is noted above, chap. 2, n. 135. 'Medallions of portraits' which were issued by an early sixteenth century Lyonnais publisher are described by Natalie Z. Davis, 'Publisher Guillaume Rouillé,' p. 89. See also N. Z. Davis, 'Printing and the People,' p. 215. Sarton's *Six Wings* contains thirty portraits based on contemporary renderings. Their 'authenticity' is noted in the preface (p. IX) and their provenance is described beside the space where they appear. The three figures on p. 134 representing the two artists and the engraver who drew the plants for Fuchs' herbal of 1542 are good examples of the kind of self-advertisement which could flourish in early printers' workshops.

often attributed to 'humble' medieval craftsmen and took pains to carve their names on permanent materials – even such men seem to lack individuality because there are no other written records to accompany the proud inscriptions they left behind.

At the turn of the eleventh and twelfth centuries...the sculptor Wiligelmo placed a tablet in the façade of Modena cathedral bearing the words:

> Among sculptors how greatly are you worthy in honor
> Now, oh Wiligelmo, your sculpture shines forth.

On the portals of Ferrara and...of Verona cathedral, a pupil of Wiligelmo working in the 1130s announced his own fame in a similar way:

> Coming together men will praise for generations
> That Niccolò the skilled *artifex* who carved these things.

...From this period, inscriptions of this type appeared quite frequently in other centres in northern Italy, as they did at the same time in France.[203]

Sculptors such as Wiligelmo and Niccolò were, clearly, conscious of themselves as individuals, but they were also powerless to transmit the sense of their individuality beyond their graves.

Every hand-copied book, it is sometimes said, 'was a personal achievement.' Actually a great many hand-produced books were farmed out piecemeal to be copied and worked over by several hands.[204] But even where a single hand runs from incipit to colophon and a full signature is given at the end, there is almost no trace of personality left by the presumably 'personal achievement.'[205] Paradoxically we must wait for impersonal type to replace handwriting and a standardized colophon to replace the individual signature, before singular experiences can be preserved for posterity and distinctive personalities can be permanently separated from the group or collective type.

Thus we know that architects and musicians were ranked fairly high in the hierarchy of medieval arts. Certain master builders and master singers must have achieved considerable local celebrity, but few traces of it remain. They must now be portrayed, just as Burckhardt envisaged them, according to the garb they wore or the life-style

---

[203] Larner, *Culture and Society*, p. 266.

[204] See reference to Curtius' comment, chap. 1, n. 11 above.

[205] The contrast felt by paleographers, who move from the anonymous bookhand of the medieval scribe to the more 'human documents' provided by eponymous humanists, is vividly conveyed by Wardrop, *Script of Humanism*, p. 3. Walter Ullmann, *Individual and Society*, pp. 32–4, with a certain insensitivity to historical circumstances, is 'annoyed' by the anonymity of medieval 'writers, scholars, pamphleteers, chancery personnel, architects, scribes.'

they shared with other members of their occupational group. There is ample evidence – at least enough to arouse the indignation of medievalists – to suggest that a sense of spiritual individuality was not lacking in the middle ages. But there is also a dearth of the homely details needed by historians who want to flesh out portraits of those individuals whose spiritual life they can trace.[206] For centuries the pulpit served as the chief public address system of Christendom. Yet we know very little about the personal style of medieval preachers. The very language in which they delivered their sermons is veiled by the conventional Latin outline form used by auditors who recorded what was said.[207] How different is our sense of the style of a Savonarola or a Geiler von Keysersberg, whose sermons were swiftly transmuted into print.

If we turn to a different occupational group, an even more striking comparison may be drawn. Think of the two celebrated Italian mathematicians: Leonardo of Pisa (also called Fibonacci) and Girolamo Cardano (Jerome Cardan). A biographer of the thirteenth-century man can tell us nothing about his personal appearance or private life. Cardano's biographer has an embarrassment of riches: location of warts, style of beard, foot-size, sex-life, etc., etc., placed at his disposal.[208] To be sure, the number of details provided by Cardano, in his posthumously published *De Vita Propria*,[209] is sufficiently unusual to raise doubts about exceptions and rules. As controversies over Shakespeare and some later authors suggest, not all lives during the past five centuries are as fully documented as his. But there can be little doubt about the case of Fibonacci. The lives of most medieval masters of the abacus were even less well documented than his. Whether or not medieval men were conscious of themselves 'only through some general

---

[206] The troublesome absence of basic details concerning year, place of birth, and family background is noted by Benton, ed. and introd., *Self and Society*, appendix 1, pp. 229-33. An amusing account of the shock experienced by an historian accustomed to handling the modern abundance of biographical data when confronting fourteenth-century scarcity is given by Tuchman, 'Hazards on the Way to the Middle Ages.'

[207] Gallick, 'A Look at Chaucer and His Preachers.' See esp. p. 458.

[208] Vogel, 'Fibonacci, Leonardo,' notes the few details supplied by the preface to the *Liber Abaci*. See also J. and F. Gies, *Leonardo of Pisa*; Ore, *Cardano*.

[209] Cardano's *De Vita Propria* did not get into print until 1643, sixty-seven years after his death. Similarly, Cellini's autobiography had to wait for publication until 1728. These delays lead Delany, *British Autobiography*, p. 7, to discount the significance of printing for the new genre of autobiography. As I see it, however, works such as Cardano's and Cellini's reflected new features introduced by print culture even though their writings remained for a long time in manuscript form.

category,' as Burckhardt would have us believe, it is very difficult for historians to portray them in any other way, without trespassing into the domain of fiction or deserting Clio for some other muse.

The same point applies to the celebrated mathematicians, philosophers or artists of antiquity. Classical ideals pertaining to 'mens sanus in corpore sano' have to be somewhat abstractly embodied by idealized figures. Images of discus throwers and scribes, young men and old, maidens and matrons are collected; shards registering how daily life was lived are assembled; lyric poems, satiric gossip, orations, and apocrypha are sorted out. But despite the work of generations of classical archeologists and social historians, we still have to envisage Sophocles the playwright, Aristotle the philosopher, Hippocrates the physician, or Euclid the geometer as marble statues, as fanciful engravings contained in the Bettmann Archives, or merely as names listed on incompleted employment forms. The occasional glimpses of personal lives which we do get at second hand – when we learn about Socrates' shrewish wife or about Archimedes taking a bath – tend also to be transmuted and frozen into archetypical symbols. As architect, physician, astronomer, and court councillor, Imhotep would be worshipped as a deity. Hadrian was perhaps as versatile as Jefferson, but he does not come alive for us in the same way. It seems doubtful that Alberti was the first architect to embody Vitruvius' ideal of the versatile man and display so many talents as athlete, orator, scholar, and artist. He was, however, probably the first whose after-dinner speeches and boasts about boyhood feats were preserved for posterity along with treatises on aesthetic theory and descriptions of the buildings he designed.

Thus Burckhardt's often cited tribute: 'In all by which praise is won, Leon Battista was from his childhood the first...his serious and witty sayings were thought worth collecting...'[210] needs to be supplemented by an additional consideration. The 'serious and witty sayings' of this architect could be not only collected but also preserved and transmitted to posterity. It was in part because he could be displayed in a variety of moods and activities, as an athletic youth and as a scholarly sage – moving through all the 'ages of man' – personifying as a single individual multiple archetypes and collective social roles that he appears to Burckhardt in the guise of 'l'uomo universale.' 'An acute and practised eye might be able to trace, step by step, the increase in the number

---

[210] Burckhardt, *Civilization of the Renaissance* I, 149–150.

of complete men during the fifteenth century.'[211] This apparent increase may in part be explained by the fact that it becomes easier to see men 'in the round,' so to speak, as we move from the age of copyists and illuminators to that of printers and engravers. The preservation of records by duplication does not, however, completely explain the apparent increase. For although documentation proliferates as we continue moving toward the present, the number of 'complete men' does not. Instead, versatility appears to diminish. Collective biographies begin to be written which trace distinctive genealogies for separate arts and sciences.[212] New divisions of labor and increasing specialization of function become increasingly apparent as the centuries wear on.

'The age which we commonly think of as characterized by versatility and the universal man was in fact the period when the walls between art and science, between politics and ethics, began to be built.'[213] Because the walls were still low during the first century of printing, they could be straddled with relative ease; while the higher they grew, the more remarkable an earlier versatility would seem. Living in an age when 'the barriers which kept things in order – but also apart – during the Middle Ages'[214] were dissolving and the foundations for new walls were only beginning to be laid, Renaissance man would appear to have the best of both worlds.

New opportunities to master technical literature while profiting from the expertise of generations of unlettered men in arts, crafts, and sports also contributed to his protean appearance. He was among the last who could handle a lute or a sword with ease; among the first to read musical scores or chart the path of a cannon's projectile. The 'well-rounded man' described in courtier literature 'can fight, dance, swim, hunt, woo, and warble. His mind introduces system into every field. War becomes strategy, business is bookkeeping, statecraft is diplomacy, art is perspective.'[215] On the one hand, the old arts are perfected; on the other, new professions are initiated.

Leonardo da Vinci, notes Burckhardt, 'was to Alberti as the finisher to the beginner, the master to the dilettante.' Along with Raphael and Michelangelo, Leonardo brought to a point of perfection an artistic tradition that had flourished in Italy at least since Giotto's day. Cele-

---

[211] Burckhardt, *Civilization of the Renaissance* I, 147.
[212] See Rose, *The Italian Renaissance of Mathematics*, pp. 256–7 for discussion of this new development during the sixteenth century. [213] Gilmore, *World of Humanism*, p. 265.
[214] Panofsky, 'Artist, Scientist, Genius,' p. 128. [215] Bainton, 'Man, God and Church,' p. 80.

brated among contemporaries for having perfected an old art, he was credited by posterity with having originated the new sciences. The painter of the 'Last Supper' is acknowledged as old master; the designer of flying machines is heralded as a kind of infant prodigy. In point of fact, most of Leonardo's ingenious designs and precisely rendered pictorial observations went unpublished. As is noted in later discussion, although he absorbed many useful lessons from the technical literature of his day he made no direct contribution to technical literature himself.[216] Centuries later, after the celebrated notebooks had finally appeared in print and the cult of genius had been thoroughly romanticized and modernized, he would be credited, nevertheless, with anticipating twentieth-century developments in sophisticated specialized fields, such as aeronautics or embryology.

Although romantic biographers tend to overplay the theme (by failing to allow for later professionalization and specialization), there are good reasons for associating a new versatility with the Renaissance man. Polymaths who took advantage of opportunities extended by printing did contribute to a dazzling variety of disciplines. Artisans who learned to master letters became more well-rounded as well as more upwardly mobile and more conscious of their own worth. Professions which required a coordination of brain work with handwork were given a new impetus, as the hybrid terms: scholar-printer, anatomist-printer, astronomer-printer may suggest. Where I disagree with Burckhardt is not in his suggesting that 'many-sided men' appeared during the Renaissance, but rather in his insistence that they 'belonged to Italy alone' and in his failure to account for their emergence save by referring to an 'impulse.' The group of changes he describes in conjunction with the 'perfecting of the individual' can best be accounted for, I think, not by resorting to theories about willpower or volition but by considering new circumstances which enhanced opportunities to combine learning by doing with learning by reading.

Similarly, I agree with Panofsky on the need to account for 'the

---

[216] For further discussion, see pp. 564–6, volume II below. (The technical literature consulted by Leonardo is described by many authorities. See references given in chap. 6, volume II, n. 135 for relevant titles.) Panofsky's speculation that Vesalius *may* have had a look at Leonardo's anatomical drawings *if* he paid a visit to Melzi's house seems to be the only way Leonardo could have posthumously contributed to the *De Fabrica* and the only basis for describing him as 'founding anatomical science.' Since Vesalius collaborated with a living artist from Titian's workshop, whatever he saw had a remote bearing on the actual drawings for his plates and Leonardo's contribution, if any, was very indirect. See Panofsky, 'Artist, Scientist, Genius,' pp. 142, 147–51, n. 31, and discussion on p. 269, below.

new prestige of the inventor, the military and civilian engineer and quite particularly the artist,'[217] but feel that his discussion leads us unnecessarily far afield, toward metaphysical speculation about the relationship between 'ideas' and social 'reality.' By examining specific changes introduced by the printing press, it might be possible to by-pass such issues in favor of others that are more down-to-earth. The growing prestige of the inventor, for example, was probably connected with new forms of intellectual property rights that printing introduced. It is noteworthy that 'authors' are coupled with 'inventors' by article 1 of the United States Constitution, which guarantees to both an exclusive right, for a limited time, to their 'respective writings and discoveries,' in order to promote 'the progress of science and useful arts.' The first privilege granted to a printer and the first law pertaining to patenting both appeared in the same place in the same decade: in Venice between 1469 and 1474.[218] Such laws transformed the anonymous artisan into the eponymous inventor, released individual initiative from the secretive cocoon of the guild, and rewarded ingenuity with the luster of fame as well as the chance to make a fortune.

The mathematical practitioners...had no guild to protect them. Literate without being scholars, they had to make their own way, and, often moving from place to place in search of pupils, they felt a need to advertise their presence. And what better way than by inventing a *new* mathematical instrument? So the book fairs were flooded, from the 1530's on with holometres, mecometres, pantometres, and even Henry-metres (not, however, to measure Henrys), all–purpose instruments of calculation in rich variety. Jacques Besson had led a career of this type, as a wandering teacher of mathematics, and one of his earlier books is devoted to the 'cosmolabe', a mathematical instrument to end all mathematical instruments and of incredible complexity...It may be that the success of these books of instruments gave Besson the idea of publishing his machines, too.[219]

Before book fairs could be flooded or advertisements pay off, fairs for books had to be established and printed handbills produced. The emergence of mathematical practitioners and instrument-makers as a distinctive occupational group is often associated with new demands

---

[217] Panofsky, 'Artist, Scientist, Genius,' p. 166.

[218] Frumkin, 'Early History of Patents' contains much relevant data but no explicit discussion of effects of printing on issues discussed. Other useful references are offered by Lynn White, 'Jacopo Aconcio.' Problems associated with scribal inventions are illuminated (again without explicit reference to communications techniques) in the late medieval case study offered by Rosen, 'The Invention of Eyeglasses,' and in the survey of ancient developments by Finley, 'Technical Innovation.' [219] Keller, *A Theatre of Machines*, p. 3.

for greater precision made by monarchs, bureaucrats and merchants during early-modern times. The output of mathematical instruments, atlases, globes and theatres of machines also hinged on the advent of a new publicity apparatus which made it possible to profit from disclosing, instead of withholding, the tricks of varied trades.

The new prestige of the inventor was thus related to his new role as eponymous author – a role that was assumed, in part, because of the practical need to advertise products and bring trade to shops. Many of the technical manuals which were issued during the first century of printing may be regarded as promotional literature. They assigned new dignity and worth to the mechanical arts, and at the same time called the attention of readers to special services and products which were for sale in local shops. Not all of the new breed of technicians were as peripatetic as the mathematical practitioners described above. Specific locations were sometimes given for the benefit of readers who were close at hand. An example is provided by the English translator of Simon Stevin's treatise on decimals. Henry Lyte's booklet 'The Art of Tens or Decimall Arithmeticke' (London, 1619) invites the reader to 'repaire' to Mr Griffin (his publisher) to learn the author's address and, it is hoped, hire him as a private tutor. Those who want to have a ruler 'made very well according to the Arte of Tens' as set down in the booklet are also advised to go to 'Mr Tomson dwelling in Hosier Lane, who makes Geometricall Instruments.'[220] Three birds: the interests of publisher, author, and instrument-maker are thus neatly killed with one stone. Another, more celebrated, example is the treatise by the instrument-maker Robert Norman on the lodestone: 'The Newe Attractive...concerning the declyning of the Needle' (London, 1581). The preface makes much of Norman's fear of publicity and reluctance to reveal his secret. In order to 'glorify God' and help his country, however, he manages to overcome his hesitation, to the point of including a notice that he resides in Ratcliffe.[221]

In view of these examples, and others given later on, the strong contrast drawn by some authorities between the self-serving élitist

[220] Cited by Sarton, 'The First Explanation of Decimal Fractions and Measures,' pp. 189–90.
[221] See the long citation from Norman's work given by Zilsel, 'The Origins of William Gilbert's Scientific Method.' Several authorities note that the Parisian potter, Bernard Palissy, suggests that readers can get his address from his publisher and come for a free demonstration to his shop. See Rossi, *Philosophy, Technology and the Arts*, pp. 70–1; N. Z. Davis, 'Printing and the People,' p. 216. That Palissy may have hoped to attract potential purchasers by this offer is worth more consideration than is given in diverse accounts.

Latin-reading literati and a cooperative public-spirited artisanate does not seem to be sustained. The evidence suggests that both groups – like most human beings – were spurred by a mixture of selfish and altruistic motives. Moreover, the output of technical literature tapped the talents of both groups. As a later discussion of Agricola's *De Re Metallica* suggests, technology went to press with the aid of scholars and school-masters. Vernacular editions of Euclid, Archimedes or Vitruvius also required collaboration with Latin-reading literati.[222] Numerous trans-lations of classical technical texts in turn raised the status of builders, surveyors, draughtsmen, and engineers, by providing them with a lustrous classical lineage. To have some share in the fabled wisdom of the ancients helped to elevate the practitioners of diverse arts and crafts.

Once profits could be achieved by publicity and inventions spelled out in print, ambitious or ingenious artisans had new incentives both to master letters and to contribute to a growing literature themselves. As readers and authors, artisans and mechanics were viewed more favorably by élites. The muses themselves were eventually affected by the simple vernacular style which artisan–authors used. It was primarily as authors – as early beneficiaries of the title page and the printed edition – that Palissy the potter, Paré the barber-surgeon, and many other sixteenth-century guildsmen emerged from obscurity to achieve eponymous fame.

Like the learned writer they present themselves to the unknown buyers of their books in proud author portraits quite different from the humble donor picture characteristic of medieval manuscripts. Thus Miles de Norry, previously a modest reckon master in Lyon, gazes from his 1574 commercial arithmetic fitted out with a ruff and a Greek device...practicing apothecaries get into print...surgeons write on their art...Sailors publish accounts of their travels to the new world.

Female writers also appeared...in noticeable numbers...Louise Labé, the rope-maker's daughter,...Nicole Estienne, printer's daughter and physi-cian's wife...and the Midwife, Louise Bourgeois....Bourgeois wrote on her art, believing herself the first woman to do so. Her wide practice, she claimed would show up the mistakes of Physicians and Surgeons, even of Master Galen himself...[223]

Such authors were often less inclined than were university professors

---

[222] See critique of Zilsel's approach (pp. 558 ff.) and discussion of Agricola (p. 545), volume II below.

[223] N. Z. Davis, 'Printing and the People,' pp. 215–17. That a midwife was sufficiently familiar with Galen to criticize him (whether rightly or wrongly) indicates the services rendered by vernacular translations of ancient technical literature.

to treat masters such as Galen with reverence. For the most part, they had not gone through the schools and had not mastered Latin or the rules of rhetoric; nor had they learned to see the world in terms of schemes inherited from ancient philosophers. They set down plainly and directly what they had seen and done in the course of long experience practicing their craft. In this way urban craftsmen gained an entry into the Commonwealth of Learning and won a hearing from royal ministers and Latin-reading philosophers in foreign lands. Francis Bacon knew of Bernard Palissy, the French potter;[224] Sir William Cecil placed Albrecht Dürer in the company of Vitruvius and Alberti as an authority on military fortifications.[225]

Burckhardt connects the 'awakening of personality' with a new spirit of independence and a new claim to shape one's own life – apart from one's 'parents and ancestors.'[226] He seems to ascribe this phenomenon also to 'Italy alone.' The careers of Palissy or Paré were not shaped by Italian developments, however. Nor was it on Italian soil that Ulrich von Hutten revealed a concern with the problem of self-education, a novel concern for a Teutonic knight.[227] New forms of self-help and self-awareness owe more to the mid-century German invention than one is likely to realize if too much attention is concentrated on quattrocento Italy. As numerous studies have documented, the sixteenth century saw a flood of treatises come off the new presses which were aimed at encouraging diverse forms of self-help and self-improvement – ranging from holding family prayers to singing madrigals and keeping accounts.[228] Even a superficial observer of sixteenth-century literature cannot fail to be impressed by the 'avalanche' of treatises which were issued to explain, by a variety of 'easy steps,' (often supplemented by sharp-edged diagrams) just 'how to' draw a picture, compose a madrigal, mix paints, bake clay, keep accounts, survey a field, handle all manner of tools and instruments, work mines, assay metals, move armies or obelisks, design buildings, bridges and machines.[229] How actual practices may have been affected by all these

---

[224] Rossi, *Philosophy, Technology*, pp. 8–9.
[225] See letter of 1559, cited by Lynn White, 'Jacopo Aconcio,' p. 430.
[226] Burckhardt, *Civilization of the Renaissance* I, 147, n. 1.
[227] Hajo Holborn, *Ulrich von Hutten and the German Reformation*, p. 2.
[228] Many examples are offered by Wright, *Middle Class Culture, passim.*
[229] This 'avalanche' is documented in many studies. In addition to Wright, see e.g. Gille, *Renaissance Engineers*; Charlton, *Education in Renaissance England*, p. 298; Curtis, 'Education and Apprenticeship.'

'teach-yourself' manuals is a complex question, as later discussion suggests.[230] But it can scarcely be doubted that the new genre extended new opportunities for would-be authors and would-be autodidacts alike.

It was accompanied by promotional literature which probably stimulated aspirations toward self-improvement even while being aimed simply at spurring sales. If only they purchased works such as Thomas Morley's *Plain and Easy Introduction to Practical Music*, Elizabethan readers were assured, they could overcome their shameful ignorance and ineptitude when music books were brought out by their host.[231] It is, of course, possible that a natural ineptitude on the part of many readers became more apparent, and that self-confidence was undermined the more such claims were put to the test. (The manipulation of shame by commercial advertisers needs to be set beside the manipulation of guilt by indulgence sellers and confessors during the sixteenth century.) On the other hand, the chance to master new skills without undergoing a formal apprenticeship or schooling also encouraged a new sense of independence on the part of many who became self-taught. Even though the new so-called 'silent instructors'[232] did no more than duplicate lessons already being taught in classrooms and shops, they did cut the bonds of subordination which kept pupils and apprentices under the tutelage of a given master.

The opportunity to teach oneself affected learned élites as well as artisanal groups – a point that warrants further emphasis when considering intellectual innovation in diverse fields. Guillaume Budé 'was one of those rare beings,' writes Bolgar, 'who can instruct themselves primarily from books with a minimum of outside help. With writings of Italian and German humanists at his elbow he could mount to the level they had attained and move beyond.'[233] Much the same kind of activity may be observed, later on, in the young Isaac Newton, who

---

[230] The inefficacy of books and engravings compared to human operators for transmitting technical skills is brought out by Cipolla, *Before the Industrial Revolution*, chap. 6. (See esp. relevant citation from Oakeshott, p. 176.) For further discussion of this issue, see pp. 554 ff., volume II below.

[231] Morley, *A Plain and Easy Introduction*, pp. 9–10.

[232] The term was used by Isaac Joubert, a professor of medicine at Montpellier, in his preface to his reissue of his father's edition of *La Grande Chirurgie de M. Gui de Chauliac restituée par M. Laurent Joubert* (1578) (Tournon, 1598), cited by Charles Sherrington, *The Endeavour of Jean Fernel*, p. 111. Both Jouberts were ardent proponents of increasing the literacy of surgeons and making more technical literature available to them in vernacular form. See pp. 538–9, volume II below.

[233] Bolgar, *Classical Heritage*, p. 309.

took full advantage of local book fairs and libraries. With editions of ancient and modern mathematicians at his elbow, he mounted to the level attained by Descartes and then moved beyond during his 'miraculous' year.

Newton was self-taught in mathematics, deriving his factual knowledge from the books he bought or borrowed with little or no outside help...The transformation of a youth who knew no more mathematics than simple arithmetic and who could not read a treatise on astrology for want of trigonometry into the profound creator of higher mathematics is marvelous to follow...a small notebook in which Newton had begun to make a Hebrew-English dictionary lists the...Pythagorean theorem...Before long he is deep in the geometry combinations...This is 1664 but before long he has gone deeply into number theory and algebra and...mastered 'the arithmetical symbols of Oughtred' and the 'algebraical from Descartes.'[234]

Acceptance of diverse traditions, which had hitherto been transmitted by personal interchange between masters and disciples, was probably modified when one no longer needed to sit at a master's feet before standing on one's own. The fact that young men could master an inherited body of knowledge more efficiently by reading for themselves than by listening to their elders was a significant, albeit neglected, stimulus to the quarrel between ancients and moderns. Similarly (as is later suggested) the transmission of sacred traditions was also affected and the authority of the priesthood weakened, once the laity had an opportunity to read God's words for themselves.[235]

'The ultimate origins of faith in unaided human capacity remain mysterious,' writes Keith Thomas, in a passage which attributes to the Lollards a new 'spirit of sturdy self help.'[236] Thomas goes on to note that although the urban occupations of 'the carpenters, blacksmiths, cobblers and above all textile workers' who espoused the Lollard cause are often cited as an explanation; urban trades are not really any more compatible with the new spirit than rural ones. Granted that all 'ultimate origins' tend to be shrouded in mystery, and that many puzzles about Lollardy are still unsolved, the increased visibility of a 'spirit of self-help' – during the sixteenth and seventeenth centuries,

---

[234] I. B. Cohen, review of Whiteside ed. *The Mathematical Papers of Isaac Newton*. On Leibniz as an autodidact, see Meyer, *Leibniz and the Seventeenth Century Revolution*, pp. 85–6. See also discussion of Tycho Brahe's self-instruction pp. 596–7, 623–4, volume II below.

[235] See pp. 387ff., below.

[236] Thomas, *Religion and the Decline of Magic*, pp. 663–4.

at any rate, – may become less mysterious when new occupations associated with the printed book-trade are taken into account.

Indeed some of the central problems posed in Thomas's seminal study would become easier to handle if the effects of printing received more attention. There is, for example, his puzzlement over the fact that the Reformation did not 'coincide with any technological revolution: the men of the sixteenth century were as vulnerable in the face of environmental hazards as their medieval predecessors. Yet many were able to discard the apparatus of the Church without devising a new magic in its place.'[237] But the Reformation did coincide with the early phases of a communications revolution – which provided new incentives to publicize trade secrets and which changed the character of magic and the quality of religious experience as well.[238] The 'breathtaking faith in the potentialities of human ingenuity' that Thomas sees being reflected in early patent application[239] also becomes less puzzling when one considers the new incentives and opportunities extended to inventors and instrument-makers by print. That a 'spirit of practical self-help' was manifested in the field of medicine well before any real progress had been made in prevention or cure,[240] once again, seems less anomalous when the output of 'silent instructors' is given due weight.[241]

An excellent example of how printing might encourage new kinds of medical self-help, even while physicians were killing more patients than they cured, is offered by a study of a seventeenth-century medical reformer who is also described as the 'father of French journalism':

In 1642, he published 'a formulary for the use of *malades absens*, so simple that not only the country apothecary or surgeon or those who might have the least knowledge of illnesses and their forms but also simple peasant women and their children, provided that they can read will be able to indicate the condition of the sick person, of his malady and of all the symptoms and circumstances so that we may treat him as methodically and as well as if he were present.' The blue covered 60-page pamphlet sold for 5 sous and had a very complete index, its format and price indicating it was intended for

237 Thomas, *Religion and the Decline of Magic*, p. 657.
238 See next section of this chapter: 'Arcana Disclosed.'
239 Thomas, *Religion and the Decline of Magic*, p. 662.
240 Thomas, *Religion and the Decline of Magic*, p. 659.
241 This anomaly is by no means self-evident. The very failure of early-modern medicine to cope with disease might be expected to engender distrust of traditional authority, and a recourse to some form of self-help – whether 'magical' or 'practical' or both.

a wide audience. It consisted of diagrams of the human body upon which the absent could mark the location of the malady and extended lists of possible symptoms from which he could select those that applied. He then sent the filled out formulary to Renaudot's staff for evaluation. Such long distance diagnosis would force everyone to be more exact in the recognition and discernment of their maladies...With his enthusiasm for chemical medicine Renaudot's clinic attracted a large number of syphilitics...those with 'shameful' maladies [could]...use the Bureau's services without appearing in person.[242]

To be sure, Théophraste Renaudot was an exceptional figure among his compatriots, and his diverse pioneering experiments occurred almost two hundred years after Gutenberg. But even if attention is confined to an earlier period and focused on a more 'common, ordinary, garden-variety' of printed products, one can scarcely avoid noting that self-reliance was being encouraged in new ways. Sixteenth-century Europe 'was deluged with small convenient school manuals' where traditional subjects were 'reduced to rules so simple that any child, literally, could learn them[243] – any child, that is, who could read. But book markets were also deluged with ABC books and primers which made it feasible to teach oneself reading and writing, so that a new element of self-selection entered even into acquisition of literacy. The autodidact like the printer himself was a new kind of self-made man – one who was necessarily set apart from his parents and ancestors.

As a Northern painter and draughtsman, Albrecht Dürer was pursuing the sort of career one might expect a Nuremberg goldsmith's son to pursue. As the author of widely circulated treatises on human proportions, geometry and fortifications, however, he broke the conventional mold. In this latter guise he came to the attention of foreign noblemen. He was also placed by his fellow citizens in a select circle of Nuremberg savants – a circle which included the most distinguished mathematicians and astronomers of the day.[244] The prefaces he wrote

[242] Solomon, *Public Welfare*, pp. 175–6.   [243] Gilbert, *Renaissance Concepts of Method*, p. 73.
[244] Dürer's reputation as a Nuremberg savant, associated with Regiomontanus' successors such as Schöner and Werner, is brought out in a pertinent essay by Margolin, 'La Réalité Sociale.' (See esp. 215–18.) The actual relationship between Dürer and Regiomontanus' successors is documented by Rose, *The Italian Renaissance of Mathematics*, pp. 108; 116 n.; 135. Rose refers to a pertinent monograph by de Haas, *Albrecht Dürer's Engraving*, suggesting a possible link between Dürer's engraving of 'Melancholia I' and the first astronomer–printer. For further discussion of Regiomontanus and later contributions to the Copernican revolution made by Nuremberg printers, see pp. 586–8, volume II below.

to his much translated treatises are now singled out as anticipating a later 'Baconian' vision of scientific enterprise as an organized cooperative and cumulative disclosure of nature's secrets for the benefit of mankind.[245] As artisan–author, as autodidact and as print-maker, the Nuremberg master with the initials 'A.D.' departed from the late medieval guildsman's accustomed role.

That Dürer's 'Weltanschauung' was different from that of earlier Nuremberg guildsmen is recognized by many authorities, who often attribute the difference to Italianate influences or more vaguely to the 'spirit of the Renaissance.' A recent essay has attempted to be more specific in assessing the varying factors which shaped this particular 'new man.' Civic loyalties, class structure, military technology, the peasant rebellion, Erasmian humanism, Lutheran Protestantism and other contemporary developments are discussed in an effort to portray the social forces which shaped Dürer's life and work.[246] Nothing is said of the occupational culture of early printers which was, in my view, a most significant new element both in late fifteenth-century Nuremberg and in the life and work of Albrecht Dürer, where it played an absolutely fundamental role.[247] After all, Dürer was not merely a goldsmith's son who became a great print-maker. He was also the godson of Anton Koberger, the greatest entrepreneur of the printed book-trade in the fifteenth century. Dürer's wife was uneasy about the company her husband kept and objected to his spending time away from his studio with patrician humanists like Willibald Pirckheimer. She took the traditional view. A man who earned an honest living working with his hands should not waste time discussing books and antiquities and did not belong with gentlemen and scholars.[248] Dürer, however, had frequented printers' workshops since his early boyhood and if for no other reason, held different views than his wife. In these workshops, scholars *did* mingle with artisans. Often the versatile master printer combined both roles.

---

245 Zilsel, 'The Genesis,' pp. 334–5.
246 See Margolin, 'La Realité Sociale,' *passim*. For further discussion of other works which overlook the novelty of print shops when considering the social ambiance of fifteenth-century Nuremberg, see below, pp. 403–5.
247 For interesting contrast drawn by George Sarton between Dürer's affinity for print and Leonardo's antipathy to it, see pp. 564–6, volume II, below. How much Dürer's 'singular fame' owed to the power of the press is noted by Goldschmidt, *The Printed Book*, pp. 55–6. The extent to which his 'earliest prints' exercised an 'overwhelming influence' upon Italian engravers, opening a new chapter in Italian print-making shortly before 1500 is brought out by Oberhuber, introduction to *Early Italian Engravings*, p. xx.   248 Panofsky, *Dürer* I, 7–8.

'The Renaissance bridged the gap which had separated the scholar and thinker from the practitioner.'[249] Of course, the 'Renaissance' is too much of an abstraction to have done this. Like others who discuss the issue, Panofsky really means that the gap was bridged *during* the Renaissance and, like others also, he has certain specific factors in mind. Whereas others focus on certain socio-economic factors, he stresses the versatility displayed by quattrocento artists: The 'demolition of barriers between manual and intellectual labor was first achieved by the artists (who tend to be neglected by Zilsel and Strong).'[250] Actually, many diverse groups – medical and musical as well as architectural – sought to combine handwork with brainwork at different times. In my view, the permanent achievement of this combination, however, could not come until after printing. When it did come, it resulted in occupational mutations which affected anatomy no less than art.[251]

In seeking to explain new interactions between theory and practice, schoolman and artisan, few authorities even mention the advent of printing. Yet here was an invention which made books more accessible to artisans and practical manuals more accessible to scholars; which encouraged artists and engineers to publish theoretical treatises and rewarded schoolmasters for translating technical texts. Before the Renaissance, says Panofsky,

the absence of interaction between manual and intellectual methods...had prevented the admirable inventions of medieval engineers and craftsmen from being noted by what were then called the natural philosophers and... conversely had prevented the equally admirable deductions of logicians and mathematicians from being tested by experiment.[252]

The printing press was one invention that did not escape the attention of natural philosophers. Although it came from Vulcan's workshop and was capable of provoking snobbish disdain it served grammarians

---

[249] Panofsky, 'Artist, Scientist, Genius,' pp. 135–6.
[250] Panofsky, 'Artist, Scientist, Genius,' p. 136, n. 13.
[251] The demolition of barriers which divided choirmasters and instrumentalists from scholarly musicologists is discussed by Lowinsky, 'Music of the Renaissance as Viewed by Renaissance Musicians'; 'Music in the Culture of the Renaissance.' By considering the effects of printing – not only of scores but also of books about music – I think many of the issues Lowinsky discusses could be illuminated. Santillana, 'The Role of Art,' p. 48 suggests that architecture played a key role in the integration of brainwork with handwork. The claims of Vesalius and Fernel show that medical faculties were equally insistent on the Vitruvian theme. For Jean Fernel medicine was an art which encompassed all others: 'from the bared bowels of the earth to the wheeling of heavens,' See Sherrington, *The Endeavour of Jean Fernel*, pp. 3–22.
[252] Panofsky, 'Artist, Scientist, Genius,' p. 137.

and philosophers no less than artisans and engineers. It was also associated with Minerva, goddess of wisdom and was esteemed by literati and churchmen as a 'divine art.'[253]

Bacchus and Ceres were made divinities for having taught humanity the use of wine and bread but Gutenberg's invention is of a higher and diviner order, for it furnishes characters by the aid of which all that is said or thought can be written, translated and preserved to the memory of posterity.[254]

The new mode of book production not only brought the work of philosophers to the attention of craftsmen and vice versa. It also brought bookworms and mechanics together in person as collaborators within the same workshops. In the figure of the scholar–printer, it produced a 'new man' who was adept in handling machines and marketing products even while editing texts, founding learned societies, promoting artists and authors, advancing new forms of data collection and diverse branches of erudite disciplines. The sheer variety of activities, both intellectual and practical, sponsored by the more celebrated firms of the sixteenth century is breathtaking. Greek and Latin classics, law books, herbals, Bible translations, anatomy texts, arithmetic books, beautifully illustrated volumes of verse – all these, issued from one print shop, pointed to fertile encounters of diverse kinds. Contemporary tributes to master printers and their products must be taken in a sceptical spirit – just as one takes the overblown claims made by blurb writers and publicists today. But hyperbole does not seem misplaced when applied to the number and variety of interchanges fostered by the master printers of Venice, Lyon, Basel, Paris, Frankfurt, Antwerp and other major centers of the sixteenth–century trade.[255]

[253] As is noted above p. 48 the repetition in many secondary works of remarks made by one manuscript book dealer who had a clear vested interest in denigrating printed books has led to the false impression that printed books were disdained as inferior mass-produced objects by Renaissance patricians. 'Aristocrats opposed printing as a mechanical vulgarization and feared it would lower the value of their mss. libraries' says Durant in *The Reformation*, p. 159. Actually, most aristocratic book collectors sought printed books as eagerly as they did mss. and often valued them *more* highly than mss. Bühler, *Fifteenth Century Book*, p. 62. On Minerva as 'the Mother of Printing and Goddess of Knowledge' see discussion of journeymen's festival in sixteenth–century Lyon and plate no. 1 in N. Z. Davis, 'Strikes and Salvation in Lyon,' p. 5. On the later use of Minerva both as patron of printing and guardian of a secret wisdom see p. 143, above.

[254] Letter from Guillaume Fichet to Robert Gaguin attached to gift copy of the second book to be printed on the first Paris press, which was set up in the Sorbonne 1470–2: *Gasparini Orthographia* (a treatise on orthography by Gasparini Barzizi of Bergamo) cited in Updike, *Printing Types* I, 84.

[255] For pertinent data, see Febvre and Martin, *L'Apparition*, chap. 5, section III.

It is, indeed, surprising that the figure of the scholar–printer does not loom larger in discussion of the 'formation of groups and friendships conducive to cross-fertilization between all kinds of people...'[256] In his hands the work of editing, translating and textual analysis was removed from cloistered precincts, such as monastic scriptoria, houses of study, college chambers and walled patrician villas. Instead texts were handled in a bustling commercial establishment where robed scholars and merchants worked alongside craftsmen and mechanics. The master-printer's activities combined forms of labor, which had been divided before and would be divided again, on a different basis, later on. His products introduced new interactions between theory and practice, abstract brainwork and sensory experience, systematic logic and careful observation.

Recognition of the need to combine empirical and theoretical knowledge went back to the medical literature as well as the architectural literature of antiquity.[257] In the middle ages, there were enlightened surgeons such as Gui de Chauliac who insisted that book learning was needed for practitioners of his demanding craft. But the conditions of scribal culture worked against such reformers.[258] They supported a continuation of ancient quarrels between 'head and hand.'[259] The celebrated invective of Petrarch and of his successors, such as Salutati, perpetuated this state of affairs:

Carry out your trade, mechanic, if you can. Heal bodies, if you can. If you can't, murder; and take the salary for your crimes...But how can you dare...relegate rhetoric to a place inferior to medicine? How can you make the mistress inferior to the servant, a liberal art to a mechanical one?

256 Panofsky, 'Artist, Scientist, Genius,' p. 138. See also very similar discussion of the appearance of new 'lay circles,' by Baron, 'Toward a More Positive Evaluation,' p. 42.

257 That a combination of theoretical with empirical knowledge was urged in ancient Roman treatises, notably by Cornelius Celsus (whose De Medicina was published in Milan in 1481) is brought out by Kemp, 'Il Concetto dell'Anima,' see esp. pp. 116; 130.

258 See references given in chap. 6, n. 46 and 47, volume II below.

259 Practical inventions were derogated as 'vile, low, mercenary' and deemed unworthy of being recorded in antiquity, according to Frumkin, 'Early History of Patents,' p. 47. According to Finley, 'Technical Innovation in the Ancient World,' pp. 33–4: 'Only the tongue was inspired by the Gods, never the hand.' The use of slave labor for manual work (including that of scribe and copyist) may have contributed to this ancient contempt, while the medieval church by encouraging monks to engage in manual labor (including scribal work) may have reduced it. On the twelfth-century scheme of seven 'mechanical arts' which Hugh of Saint Victor devised as a counterpart to the seven liberal arts and other pertinent references, see Kristeller, 'The Modern System of the Arts,' p. 175; Chenu, Nature Man and Society, p. 43. The affirmative view of Western Christendom toward the mechanical arts is brought out by Lynn White, 'The Iconology.'

It is your business to look after bodies. Leave the care and education of the mind to genuine philosophers and orators.[260]

The long-lived division between the 'liberal' arts practiced by freemen and the 'mechanical' by slaves was thus carried over into early humanist attacks on the practitioners of the medical arts.

The situation confronting artists during the quattrocento was, of course, quite different from that of the medical faculties who provoked Petrarchan wrath. There were, to be sure, guilds which linked painters with apothecaries; both, after all, used mortar and pestle as tools. Similarly stone carvers and surgeons shared in common certain technical concerns. Nevertheless, in their quarrels with graduate faculties of law and medicine, the humanists regarded artists not as foes but as natural allies. Thanks to unusual municipal schools moreover, the young apprentice in architecture, painting or sculpture was also well ahead of his Northern counterparts in his mastery of the written word.[261] Some quattrocento Tuscan artists were familiar with pertinent technical literature – not only on how to mix paints but also on geometry and optics. A few masters, such as Piero della Francesca, Lorenzo Ghiberti and Leon Battista Alberti, authored significant treatises themselves. But these treatises were designed for the edification of a given prince or patron,[262] and not for would-be artists or readers-at-large. Indeed, vernacular treatises on perspective and proportion were unavailable in artists' ateliers, even in quattrocento Florence – just as most technical texts lacked useful visual aids until after the advent of printing. Only after then would the gap between manual and mental labor be permanently closed and new institutions be created to implement professional training of new kinds.

Here, as elsewhere, early printers, who had to be proficient in mechanics and in book learning, did much to point the way. In the printing trades particularly, literacy was required for journeymen who hoped to become their own masters. As the pace of publication

---

[260] Petrarch's *Invectiva in Medicum Quendam* is cited and discussed by Eugenio Garin, *Italian Humanism*, p. 24. See also pp. 35 ff. for references to other aspects of 'La disputá delle arti' and to Garin's own monograph on this topic. Of course there is also counter-evidence showing that several humanists were less biased against manual labor and mechanical arts than this passage suggests. See Keller, 'A Renaissance Humanist,' esp. p. 345.

[261] For pertinent data (in addition to Baxandall, cited above) see Zervas, 'The *Trattato dell'Abbaco.*' Zervas notes the difference between the Italian situation she describes and Shelby's articles on medieval master masons in Northern Europe.

[262] See chap. 6, n. 81 and n. 88, volume II below for comment on treatises by Piero and Alberti.

quickened, the same requirement pressed harder on certain other trades and crafts as well. In some instances an entire craft was transformed; in others, a split occurred. Wherever it took hold, the new combination of book learning with manual labor resulted in some sort of occupational mutation. Academies were founded, learned journals published, professional standards fixed and practitioners, who still worked with their hands, began to mingle with other literate élites. The changed status of artists in sixteenth-century Italy provides a celebrated case:

> The three visual arts, painting, sculpture and architecture were...clearly separated from the crafts with which they had been associated...The term *Arti del disegno* upon which 'Beaux Arts' was probably based, was coined by Vasari who used it as a guiding concept for his famous collection of biographies...in 1563, in Florence, again under the personal influence of Vasari, painters, sculptors and architects cut their previous connections with craftsmen's guilds and formed an Academy of Art (Accademia del Disegno) ...that served as a model for later, similar institutions...The Art Academies followed the same pattern of the literary Academies that had been in existence for some time and they replaced the old workshop tradition with a regular kind of instruction that included such scientific subjects as geometry and anatomy.[263]

Insofar as a new combination of manual and mental labor resulted, the shift from artisan to artist thus appears to be similar to other occupational mutations.[264] Of course, each case requires separate analysis. The impact of print affected musicians in one way, medical practitioners in another. Even with regard to medicine, the fate of apothecaries differed from that of surgeons while within the latter group military surgeons formed a special category of their own. Furthermore different regions had diverse professional and academic traditions. No two university faculties responded to the challenge presented by new claims in the same way. The reactions of rulers and of patrons also were far from uniform. To explain how craftsmen who wielded chisel or paint brush were transformed into practitioners of the 'fine arts,' we must deal with a set of special problems which are exceedingly complex. In discussing all such cases, however, it is helpful to keep the

---

[263] Kristeller, 'Modern System of the Arts,' p. 182. See also Jack, 'The *Accademia del Disegno*,' which is based on author's unpublished doctoral dissertation on same topic. (Chicago 1972.)

[264] On the shift from the medieval master mason to the Renaissance architect, see Shelby, 'The Geometrical Knowledge'; 'The Education of Medieval English Master Masons.' How musicians were affected by the bridging of the gap between instrumentalists and teachers of the quadrivium is discussed by Lowinsky in the articles noted above, n. 251.

advent of printing in mind. When attempting to account for the changed role of artists during the Renaissance, it is not enough to point to humanist antagonism to graduate faculties or to the recovery of texts showing that artists were esteemed in antiquity or to parvenu patrons who invested in beautiful objects to satisfy various needs. The position of the artist and the nature of his products were fundamentally changed by the shift from script to print.

Printing diminished reliance on memory aids and hence altered significant social functions performed by image-makers in the past. At the same time it enabled artists 'to publish their own designs for profit and in the way they wished their inventions to be seen.'[265] The artist thus acquired a share in the new prestige assigned to eponymous artisan–engineers, authors, and inventors.[266] He

was no longer a purveyor of goods which every one needed and which could be ordered like any other material goods, but an individual facing a public...by the beginning of the sixteenth century, it became an accepted idea that the educated layman could give a useful opinion on the arts and there was even a small outcrop of treatises on the arts written by laymen...

The artist was now faced with a wide public...and in this spirit of competition he began to carry out works other than those directly commissioned...[267]

At the same time, new links between *beaux arts* and *belles lettres* were forged. A continuous interchange between book-reading painters and image-viewing literati was initiated – one that is still going on to this day.[268] Printed publicity, skillfully exploited by new academies, expanded markets – not only for art works, but also for books about artists and their works.[269] Critics and dealers, collectors and connoisseurs, aesthetes and middlemen of all kinds found immortality of sorts by praising, 'discovering' or patronizing new 'immortals.' An ever more elaborate literature of explication helped to transform products turned out in workshops into cult objects guarded in museums. Beginning with quattrocento eulogies of Giotto, precedents were noted

---

[265] Oberhuber, introduction, *Early Italian Engravings*, p. xv.
[266] For use of term 'inventio' in classical rhetoric and how it was transposed to the craft of the painter by Renaissance theorists even before the advent of printing, see Rensselaer W. Lee, *Ut Pictura Poesis*, p. 17 and appendix 2, p. 70.   [267] Blunt, *Artistic Theory in Italy*, p. 56.
[268] How cinquecento artists were already reacting to the 'gadfly of criticism' is described by Gombrich, 'The Leaven of Criticism.' See also pertinent data in Blunt, *Artistic Theory in Italy*, chap. VI.
[269] Academic publicity is well demonstrated by *The Divine Michelangelo, The Florentine Academy's Homage on his death in 1564.*

and landmarks recorded, so that imitation and innovation became more deliberate.

Typographical fixity affected the way images were shaped, partly by changing the way they could be collected, catalogued and reproduced. By encouraging a recurrent recycling of identical motifs, the duplicative powers of print also placed an increasingly high premium on the development of new visual vocabularies. Images initially designed to be placed on walls or on parchment were duplicated in woodblocks and engravings, purveyed by print dealers, reworked by cabinet-makers, glaziers, potters and tapestry weavers, taken up by a new generation of artists as elements in large-scale compositions, only to be copied again by print-makers and redistributed for the benefit of craftsmen all over again.[270] In this way visual clichés were created which later generations had to manipulate self-consciously or attempt, with increasing desperation, to evade. 'An immense new variety of types and themes' was stimulated,[271] but the creativity of one generation proved all the more burdensome to the next. Thus the move from craftsman to creative artist was not as liberating in the long run as it seemed to be at first. Along with other culture-heroes such as composers, playwrights or poets, artists were raised to the rank of 'immortals' by the preservative powers of print; as aspirants to this elevated position, they were caught up in an ever more frantic pursuit of novelty and threatened by an ever more oppressive 'burden of the past.'

To be sure, several centuries had to elapse before such cumulative effects became apparent and a 'tradition of the new' was fully launched. Other changes, however, came more immediately. After Alberti had counselled painters to read the *rhetorici*, there came printers who made it easier to implement this advice, followed by critics who would not let it be ignored. The canons governing literary composition and the time-honored rules of rhetoric anchored pictorial design to poetic

---

[270] For a striking example of sixteenth-century transfers of printed book illustrations to enamels, ceramics, windows, dressers, cabinets, and 'objets d'art' see illustrated article by Thirion, 'Bernard Salomon.' Note how one of Salomon's designs was, in turn, drawn from one of Marcantonio Raimondi's engravings of Raphael's composition (p. 65, n. 22).

[271] A shift from the output of a few master themes and archetypical visual forms to a torrential outpouring of myriad diverse themes and forms is noted by Kubler, *The Shape of Time*, p. 29. Kubler locates this shift roughly around A.D. 1400 but also notes that 'the torrent of new forms has been rising ever since the fifteenth century' a development I would attribute to typographical fixity. Kubler's stimulating study makes no mention of the shift from script to print, but does contain relevant speculations about such issues as 'prime objects and replications,' 'invention and variation,' and 'aesthetic fatigue.'

construction. Parallels between painting and poetry, drawn from the ancient sayings of Horace and Simonides, began to appear with increasing frequency in treatises on painting from the sixteenth century on.[272] To produce a major 'history painting' became the equivalent of composing an epic poem. The 'learned painter' was coupled with the 'learned poet' and assigned an ever more ambitious program of research. It demanded no less of the painter than is furnished today by the staff of experts who are hired to check out authentic costumes and furnishings, buildings and grounds, flora and fauna, for films dealing with historical themes. Alberti thought the painter should glean enough from his reading to talk intelligently with the learned men of his day and select subjects of universal interest. Later critics required that he 'be learned not only in sacred and profane literature, but also in geography, climatology, geology, theology, and the manners and customs of various countries...'[273] As Lee points out, the learned painter represented an almost unattainable ideal – so much time spent in the library would leave little for the workshop. Still the theory does suggest how increased book production extended the mission assigned the artist, even while enhancing his powers to reach toward new goals.

Much as the collaboration of artist with anatomist contributed to the so-called 'scientific revolution,' so too did the coupling of artist with antiquarian contribute to the so-called 'historical revolution.' Detection of anachronism and of stylistic change expanded beyond the philological concerns of Latinists such as Lorenzo Valla to encompass all the objects that were entailed in precise visual reconstruction of past events.

The prudent painter should know how to paint what is appropriate to the individual, the time and the place...so that he does not represent Aeneas as coming to Italy in the time of the Emperor Justinian, or the battles of the Carthaginians in the presence of Pontius Pilate...

Is it not an error to paint Saint Jerome with a red hat like the one cardinals wear today? He was indeed a cardinal but...it was Pope Innocent IV, more than seven hundred years later, who gave cardinals their red hats and red

272 Confusion between the precepts drawn from Simonides ('painting is speechless poetry and poetry is speaking painting') and from Horace ('a poem is like a picture') is discussed and skillfully analyzed by Trimpi, 'The Meaning of...Ut Pictura Poesis,' pp. 31–4. Kristeller, *Renaissance Thought* II, 182, notes that the parallel 'appeared prominently for the first time' in sixteenth-century treatises and retained 'its appeal down to the eighteenth.'
273 R. W. Lee, *Ut Pictura Poesis*, pp. 40–1.

gowns...All this proceeds from the ignorance of painters. If they were educated they would not make such elementary and obvious mistakes.[274]

Failure to portray a given historical event in accurate detail was thus scored as an error unworthy of the 'learned painter.' The effort to spot errors helped to propel antiquarian research and contributed to the unscrambling of historical data.

The new pedantic insistence on 'correct' presentation of costumes and setting entailed a more literal, timebound interpretation of episodes which hitherto had been presented in more timeless context. The demand for fuller visual information thus encompassed mythical figures such as Aeneas as well as Church fathers such as Saint Jerome. Not all episodes lent themselves easily to this new demand. To envisage in convincing graphic detail the building and provisioning of Noah's ark, for example, posed special problems. Diagrams of the ark had been drawn by medieval scholars; Hugh of Saint Victor and Nicholas of Lyra had suggested possible plans and elevations;[275] the possible size of a Hebrew cubit had been learnedly discussed.[276] But the visual imagination of medieval schoolmen was more flexible than that of sixteenth-century pedants who were accustomed to envisaging creatures rendered in proper scale according to central perspective devices. When attempting to cope with the logistics involved in Noah's ark, the new insistence on 'correct presentation' was unhelpful, and may have encouraged speculation whether scripture should be taken literally after all.[277]

[274] Excerpt from G. A. Gilio da Fabriano, *The Errors of Painting* (1564) cited by Burke, *Sense of the Past*, p. 28. The extent to which Poussin in the following century took pains to avoid such errors is underlined by Burke in his comment on this excerpt.

[275] Strachan, *Early Bible Illustration*, p. 23, notes how sectional drawings of Noah's ark done by Paul of Burgos, commenting on Nicholas of Lyra's work, appeared in early printed editions of Lyra's *Postillae* turned out by Koberger and others beginning in 1481. Victorine manuscript diagrams are discussed on p. 17. Fig. 50 offers a small woodcut produced in Venice for a Czech Bible of 1506 where the absence of natural proportions is striking – Noah and his family standing with their heads level with the ark.

[276] Medieval glosses on the cubit and its allegorical religious significance are discussed by Milburn, 'The "People's" Bible,' pp. 294–6.

[277] Problems posed by these logistics crop up in Sebastian Castellio's mid-sixteenth century biblical annotations (Basil Hall, 'Biblical Scholarship', p. 83) and serve as ammunition against scholasticism and literalism in the hands of later freethinkers and *philosophes*. The diverse problems (Would extra sheep be needed to nourish carnivores? How much space was needed for food supplies and equipment for cleaning out stables?) and the ingenious solutions proposed are summarized in Abbé Mallet's article on Noah's Ark in the *Grande Encyclopédie*. The straight-faced presentation has a comical effect on modern readers and doubtless was intended to arouse scepticism among readers by the editors. The author, however, seems to have been a conservative theologian and oblivious to the effect his summary produced. See

It is also worth noting that heightened critical insistence on 'learned' painters went hand in hand with the careless output of ignorant print-makers. A pedantic concern with appropriate context on the part of sixteenth-century literati may be partly explained by the numerous blunders committed by early printers and by the notoriously inappropriate uses to which many early woodcuts and engravings were put. As we have already seen, errors in captioning, reversed images, repeated use of identical blocks, made many early printed illustrations seem more like visual hindrances than like visual aids.[278] Crude woodcuts, contained in texts which ranged from Bibles to botany books, often fell short of faithfully duplicating the handwork of medieval scribes. Ironically, the contempt of sixteenth-century cognoscenti for the barbarous ignorance of early times may have owed something to the clumsy handling of the new medium; a garbled and inferior woodcut could be, all too easily, mistaken for a true artifact of the benighted 'dark age.'[279] Whether they served as visual hindrances or furnished visual aids it does seem clear, at all events, that the new forms of book illustration did not simply perpetuate earlier scribal conventions or leave them unperturbed.

In this regard there is need to qualify the view, expressed by several authorities, that a reunion of pictorial and textual traditions characterized high Renaissance culture.[280] In the field of book illustration, at least, what happened in the late fifteenth century resembled a divorce rather more than a reunion. When the graceful lines that linked text to marginal decoration were severed, pictures and words were disconnected. The former even while being reproduced were removed from their initial context and became more liable to being used indiscriminately. Relationships between text and illustration, verbal description and image were subject to complex transpositions and disruptions.

Calligraphy had been intertwined with manuscript illustrations. Even where many hands were at work, rubricators and illuminators

Rex, 'Arche de Noé and Other Religious Articles by Abbé Mallet.' Fig. 1 facing p. 340 in this article shows a plate from a 1777 Supplement to the Encyclopédie illustrating the ark – a testament to l'esprit géométrique, it depicts a vast structure which appears quite incapable of floating.
278 See discussion p. 108, above.

279 McLuhan's comment in Gutenberg Galaxy, that Renaissance men saw 'more of the Middle Ages' than medieval men ever did, needs to be qualified by this consideration. Even though medieval texts 'became more portable and easier to read' after printing, the woodcut also conveyed a somewhat different, often distorted view, of what the illuminator had drawn.

280 Both Seznec, Survival, p. 213 and Panofsky, Renaissance and Renascences, p. 100, stress the theme.

usually worked over the same texts as did copyists and scribes.[281] But printed illustrations drew on the talents of goldsmiths, woodcarvers and armorers.[282] Such workers did not necessarily have their hands on the pages of texts at all; nor were they always informed about the destination of their products. A middleman – the print publisher – frequently intervened. The frugal custom, already discussed, of reusing a small assortment of blocks and plates to illustrate a wide variety of textual passages[283] also helped to set picture and words at odds with each other. Sacred images borrowed from manuscript books of hours were oddly juxtaposed with news of battles and royal entries in sixteenth-century broadsides and gazettes. At least it seems unlikely that God the Father supporting Christ on the Cross was deliberately chosen to illustrate the Entry of Margaret of Flanders in Cambrai, 1528.[284] Other even more 'ludicrous' effects resulted when literal-minded craftsmen who were unfamiliar with scribal convention tried to render the visual equivalents of certain poetical phrases or cut the wrong inscription under the image on the block. Certain encounters between prosaic print and poetical text had special comical implications – much as if Sancho Panza had been called on to illustrate Don Quixote's favorite tales of chivalry. There is one engraving, which may have inspired Sir Philip Sidney, where the juxtaposition of Breughel's peasant girl with Virgil's pastoral verse reminds one of Bottom blundering into Oberon's realm.[285] The servant with the pig's snout and padlocked mouth who was used to point up a moral, and the use of Leda and the swan to decorate the Epistle to the Hebrews, are other examples of incongruous imagery which arrests the attention of modern scholars.[286]

[281] Usually but not always. In fifteenth-century Utrecht, divisions of labor were carried so far that texts and miniatures were separately produced and copies of miniatures were often subject to being sold for export separately. Delaissé, *A Century of Dutch Manuscript Illumination*, pp. 70–1. As Delaissé notes, however, the *modus operandi* of these Dutch miniaturists bears less resemblance to the usual procedures of ms. illustrators than to those of painters. Guidance concerning the appropriate images to be placed in medieval academic texts was supplied by a master who indicated what should be shown by a marginal comment and sometimes even sketched a preliminary draft, according to Destrez, *La 'Pecia'*, pp. 58–9.

[282] Ivins, *Prints and Visual Communication*, p. 24.   [283] See chap. 2, n. 132 above.

[284] Trénard, 'La Presse Française,' pp. 32–3.

[285] A 'glaringly inappropriate' quotation from Virgil's Eighth Eclogue, appended by either publisher, engraver, or artist himself, to an engraved reproduction of Breughel's picture of 'The Ugly Bride' (a Flemish folk motif) furnished Sir Philip Sidney with the inspiration for a comical character in his *Arcadia*, according to McPherson, 'A Possible Origin.'

[286] The literalism of woodcuts and the case of the servant is discussed by Saxl, 'A Spiritual Encyclopedia,' pp. 100–1, n. 3. The so-called 'notorious Leda Bible' of 1572 is mentioned by Steinberg, *Five Hundred Years*, p. 158 to show the careless use of the wrong woodcut.

All such evidence of incongruity, however, should be approached with caution. Traps lie in wait for the unwary; modern scholars may on occasion be cast as comical blunderers themselves. Ovid's tale of Leda, for example, had long been imbued with Christian significance by medieval allegory. As we have learned from scholars at the Warburg Institute, pagan tales were scarcely stripped of religious associations during the Renaissance: 'Renaissance humanists contemplated Ammannati's "Leda and the Swan" (based on a Michelangelo design) not as the portrayal of an event but as a symbol of the power of love to free the soul and to unite it with Deity.' [287] The 'Leda Bible' thus may provide evidence of refined discrimination rather than carelessness. (One wonders when and how it became 'notorious'?) Similarly the juxtaposition of Virgilian Eclogue with Flemish genre scene, which possibly inspired Sir Philip Sidney, may well have been an intentional sophisticated witticism[288] rather than an accidental blunder.

Such problems make sixteenth-century iconography peculiarly baffling. One can rarely be certain whether a subtle allusion was intended or a simple mistake was made. For any given image, there is no sure way of allocating responsibility; too many possible agents – artists, engravers, caption writers, editors, print dealers, publishers – were at work. Even the ingenuity of modern scholars may lead to obfuscation; in seeking recondite allusions, connections may be drawn which were not apparent to sixteenth-century eyes. The vision of the modern observer is liable to distortion not only by being myopic; but also by being *too* keen. Apart from vexed questions of intentionality, moreover, one must also consider that the categories of literal and allegorical scarcely exhaust the diverse uses to which images were put. Other purposes – ranging from mnemonic and didactic to purely decorative – need consideration as well.

While making due allowance for wide margins of uncertainty, one may at least suggest that the imagination of sixteenth-century poets and playwrights was stimulated by the new interplay between pictures and words. A variety of Mannerist and Baroque inventions – conceits, puns and paradoxes – might be traced to the altered forms assumed by early printed images and their diverse encounters with printed texts. May not the same thing be said of other kinds of inventions – of those

[287] Rosenthal, 'The Renaissance,' pp. 61–2.
[288] McPherson 'A possible Origin,' argues that it was intentional.

which had scientific implications or technical applications? Certainly the stimulating effect of the new forms of book illustration was by no means confined to imaginative literature. New combinations and permutations were probably suggested by the provision of illustrations for diverse genres of technical literature – genres which proliferated rapidly after printers set to work.[289] Gutenberg's invention 'released a stream of mining and metallurgy handbooks'; while 'the chemical industry went to print even earlier than metallurgy.'[290] As the tools of all trades and professions, the contents of workshops, and the routines of working men came to be rendered in specific graphic detail, a vast backlog of unpatented innovations and of naturalistic observation was brought into view.

Much as the new medium was used to publicize the names and faces of authors and artists so too it was exploited by the designers of siege engines, canal locks and other large-scale public works. The new woodblocks, engravings, broadsheets and medallions made more visible and also glamorized a variety of 'ingenious' devices. Major 'public works,' once published, became tourist attractions which vied with old pilgrimage sites and Roman ruins.[291] In the hands of skillful artists, the somewhat prosaic functions of levers, pulleys, gears and screws were dramatized; engineering feats were illustrated in the same heroic vein as epic poems. At least some of these sixteenth-century engineering epics may be described as promotional ventures undertaken by ambitious technicians in search of patrons and commissions. As the winner of a competition to move an obelisk for Sixtus V, Fontana was not crowned with laurel wreaths but he did manage to publicize his successful achievement with a lavishly illustrated vast folio, which was followed by a flurry of pamphlets.[292] Other elaborate picture books, devoted to presenting 'theatres of machines,' not only served as advertising for instrument makers but also pointed the way to the plates of the eighteenth-century *Encyclopédie* and even to the real displays

[289] A Gilbert and Sullivan patter song might be composed about sixteenth-century Italian illustrated treatises on matters 'architectural, mathematical and medical, anatomical, physiognomical...' etc. noted in a recent review by Trapp, 'The High Renaissance at Harvard,' p. 41 (of part 2 of Ruth Mortimer's magnificent descriptive catalogue of illustrated printed books at the Houghton Library). According to Trapp, 'it is the new genre of scientific-practical rather than fabulous-moral instruction that steals the show.'

[290] Forbes and Dijksterhuis, *A History of Science and Technology* II, 313, 316. Chapter 16 is aptly titled, 'Technology goes to Press.'

[291] Keller, 'Mathematical Technologies,' p. 22, cites Montaigne's report of 1580-1 as well as other relevant contemporary journals. [292] Keller, 'Mathematical Technologies,' p. 22.

mounted in nineteenth-century industrial exhibition halls.[293] Presented by artful engravers as three-dimensional objects on two-dimensional planes, even the grimiest mining machinery acquired a certain dignity and aesthetic appeal. Similarly, corpses raised from demonic depths seemed to lose their odor of decay and fearful appearance when displayed (as in *De Fabrica*) performing stately pavanes against idyllic Italian landscapes.

The use of the same visual devices to delineate machine parts and human organs – both hidden from readers before – may have encouraged new analogies between pump and heart or between mechanical piping and plumbing and human venous or arterial systems. This particular suggestion (which I borrow from A. R. Hall)[294] is difficult to substantiate.[295] So too is the possibility (suggested in a later chapter) that repeated encounters with the new sharp-edged visual aids, which illustrated printed treatises on proportion, perspective, optics and geometry, may help to account for the special concern with 'fixed symmetry' exhibited by Copernicus and Kepler.[296] Although I find such speculation illuminating, others may regard it as too far-fetched. There can be no doubt, however, that the character of scientific data collection was changed by the output of printed visual aids.

This point is probably best demonstrated by looking at developments in fields such as botany and anatomy where visual information plays an especially crucial role. A pertinent example is offered by Ivins' discussion of two early printed herbals.[297] One, printed in Rome in 1480, contained replicas of corrupted scribal images which had long since drifted away from the much-copied Latin text. Crudely rendered by draughtsmen who had their eyes trained on books, these woodcuts raise a problem that crops up repeatedly in this book.[298] They show

[293] See introduction by Keller to Jacques Besson's 1579 work: *A Theatre of Machines*. Some forty plates from Agostino Ramelli's *Le Diverse ed Artificiose Macchine Composte in Lingua Italiana ed Francese* (Paris, 1588) which contained 195 full-page illustrations, were copied, clarified and used by a German instrument-maker, Leupold, for his multi-volumed *Theatrum Machinarum* (Leipzig, 1724–39) which was in turn consulted by James Watt (who studied German for this purpose). See Eugene Ferguson, 'Leupold's *Theatrum Machinarum*,' pp. 64–6. How Diderot borrowed from Ramelli for his *Encyclopédie* plates is noted by Proust, *Diderot et l'Encyclopédie*, pp. 177–8.   [294] A. R. Hall, 'Science,' p. 391.

[295] A passage from Fabricius noting that nature's device of valves placed in veins is 'strangely like that which artificial means have produced in the machinery of mills,' cited by Whitteridge, *William Harvey*, p. 21, suggests that analogies between machinery and anatomy were at least being drawn.   [296] See p. 588, volume II below.

[297] Ivins, *Prints and Visual Communication*, pp. 33–6.

[298] See above p. 108, and chap. 5, section 3, volume II below.

how indiscriminate use of the new medium perpetuated and indeed multiplied the defects inherent in the old. Furthermore they appeared at the very time when master drawings based on real plants were being rendered by skilled pens. If advances in visual aids are sought in the fifteenth century, should we not examine the work of artists who drew from nature rather than inferior printed images copied from old books? That the new medium simply prolonged the half life of archaic conventions has indeed been argued in several works.[299] But further reflection suggests that this argument fails to allow for the limitations imposed, before printing, by scribal procedures. It assumes that fresh drawings based on direct observation would somehow remain intact so that corruption could be recognized and inferior copies discarded. Until printing intervened, however, conventions now labelled as 'archaic' had an indefinitely long lease on life. Fresh observations could be preserved, only precariously and temporarily, in special chart-houses, workrooms or houses of studies. They could not be used for long, or circulate outside closed circles without undergoing corruption.

As a medium for *repeated* copying, drawing compares most un-favorably with woodcut or engraving but this is a difference that can-not be seen at first glance. (As noted below, modern reproductive techniques have made it hard to see this difference at all.) Insofar as 'seeing is believing' indeed the woodcut will appear inferior even on second glance. Pen-and-ink drawing is a better medium than is the woodcut for the accurate rendering of a given observation. A drawing is not only fresher and more spontaneous but is also better suited to the precise handling of fine detail. In addition to these intrinsic differences between the two media, the late quattrocento also saw a marked con-trast in the state of the two arts which placed the new forms of book illustration at a further disadvantage. Draughtsmen and illuminators had developed a high degree of sophistication in wielding their pens and brushes. In contrast to the refinement and elegance of manuscript illustration early printed visual aids seem especially clumsy and crude.[300] Most important of all any visual comparison will convey no informa-

[299] See *appendix A:* 'Botanical Illustration' in A. R. Hall, *The Scientific Revolution*, p. 396. References given there and others offered on same topic by Hirsch, *Printing, Selling*, p. 147, n. 50 omit Ivins' seemingly relevant treatment.

[300] For vivid contrast between delicate, lively spontaneous pen and ink designs and drawings as against clumsy, crude and rough woodcuts see Lehmann-Haupt, 'The Heritage,' pp. 18–19.

tion about the relative merits of the two media for transmitting exact images over space and over time.

Thus we are not accustomed to distinguishing between the much-copied hand-drawn image in the much-used reference work and the freshly drawn image in the unique sketchbook or manuscript. The visual contrast between 'fine' pen drawing and 'crude' woodcut is so powerful, the difference between fresh and copied handwork is especially likely to be overlooked. This is unfortunate. The difference between the hand-copied image that decays over the course of time and the repeatable engraving that can be corrected and improved is essential for understanding how visual aids were affected by print. The fate of the much-copied image was so decisively reversed, however, that its very existence has almost faded from view. In this respect modern reproductive techniques have been unhelpful and block our vision of an earlier process of change. The simultaneous duplication of old master drawings in hundreds of copies of books is achieved so effortlessly now that it is difficult to remember this feat was utterly impossible when the old masters were at work.

Before printing, indeed, the detailed rendering of natural phenomena for readers was a 'marginal activity' in the most literal sense of the word. Given our present capacity to spot some 'real' birds or plants on the margins of certain manuscripts or within the landscapes of certain paintings, we are prone to forget that earlier readers lacked plant guides and bird watchers' manuals, and could not discriminate between a fanciful or factual rendering.[301] This is not to deprecate the ability to render lifelike insects, plants or birds which was highly developed by certain masters in certain ateliers. It is merely to note that this ability was just as likely to be employed decorating the borders of psalters or embroidered church vestments[302] as to appear in books. It was rarely, if ever, used to demonstrate visually points made in technical texts.

[301] See e.g., discussion of so-called 'Cocharelli Ms.,' produced near Genoa in the fourteenth century, by Hutchinson, 'Aposematic Insects' (especially p. 161), where Crombie is cited on how such marginalia contributed to the 'rise of modern biology' and Hutchinson himself describes a movement that continued 'producing the formal natural history treatises...in the sixteenth century and...has never stopped.'

[302] Pächt, 'Early Italian Nature Studies,' p. 19 describes the 'astonishingly life-like creatures' interspersed on the borders of early fourteenth-century East Anglian psalters and embroidered church vestments. The absence of any relation between the fine figures drawn by a certain artist (Cybo of Hyères) and the text they adorn is noted by A. R. Hall, *Scientific Revolution* in appendix A.

In the age of scribes one might hire a particular illuminator to decorate a unique manuscript for a particular patron, but there would be little to gain by hiring illustrators, as Agricola did, to make detailed drawings of 'veins, tools, vessels, sluices, machines and furnaces' for embellishing a technical text.[303] Agricola provided illustrations 'lest descriptions which are conveyed by words should either not be understood by the men of our times or should cause difficulty to posterity.' In this approach he seems to prefigure the spirit of Diderot and the encyclopedists. He was also departing from scribal precedents by taking for granted that words and images would not be corrupted or drift apart over time.[304]

Historians have often been puzzled to account for the shocking difference between the crude and conventional woodcuts illustrating fifteenth-century herbals and the accuracy and artistic merit of the work of painters and miniaturists of the same period. It is reasonable to suppose that the fifteenth century saw no conflict; the woodcuts were copied from the illustrations of the manuscript whose text was also faithfully copied; the illustrations illustrated the text, not nature, a peculiar view, no doubt, but there was as yet no really independent botanical (or zoological) study.
    That was to be the contribution of the sixteenth century...in herbals... a revolution took place as authors, in despair at the inadequacies of purely verbal description, sought the aid of skilled draughtsmen and artists, trained to observe carefully and well.[305]

In duplicating crude woodcuts, the publishers of early printed herbals were simply carrying on where fifteenth-century copyists left off. Reversals, misplacements, the use of worn or broken blocks may have served to compound confusion, but the basic gap between master-drawing and misshapen image was an inheritance from the age of scribes. It was not so much a new awareness of the 'inadequacies of purely verbal description' as it was the new means of implementing this awareness that explains the 'sixteenth-century revolution.' For the first time the work of skilled draughtsmen could be preserved intact in hundreds of copies of a given book.
    In short, Ivins seems justified in taking the inferior printed herbal of 1480 to represent an end-product of scribal transmission. For compari-

---

[303] On Agricola's new approach see pp. 469–70, 545, volume II below.
[304] The separation of textual and illustrative materials associated with the medieval Dioscoridean herbal is discussed by Stannard, 'The Herbal,' p. 217. For other references see p. 485, volume II below.   [305] Marie Boas, *Scientific Renaissance*, p. 52.

son, he points to another book, a vernacular herbal entitled the *Gart der Gesundheit*, which was printed by Peter Schoeffer in Mainz in 1485. This pioneering book contains a preface describing how some new drawings were commissioned for the purpose of publication. A master learned in medicine (that is, one who had edited the works of Galen, Avicenna and others) was first consulted and asked to go over the text that was to be freshly illustrated. It turned out that many of the plants mentioned were not indigenous and could not get drawn 'in their true colors and forms save by hearsay.' Accordingly, a new kind of secular pilgrimage was organized (aptly described by Ivins as the first scientific expedition to be recorded in print and illustrated) – and a painter 'with a subtle and practised hand' was hired to accompany it.[306] His drawings were copied on blocks and put in the work, along with other woodcuts of indifferent quality. The edited text was translated into the vernacular for the benefit of a German-reading lay public. This herbal was a forerunner. Although it contained much-copied as well as freshly drawn images and was atypical in its day, it pointed the way to future developments.

By the mid-sixteenth century, botanical illustration was not being based simply on direct observation. It was departing from scribal and painterly precedents with schematic presentations that facilitated classification of a rapidly expanding data pool.[307] By this time multilingual 'pocket' editions of freshly illustrated herbals, expressly designed to be carried on field trips, were being prepared[308] and new large-scale botanical publication programs were being orchestrated in diverse European print shops. Distant correspondents began to supply actual seeds and specimens along with reports and drawings to cele-

---

306 As noted above, Ivins oddly regrets that we know none of the names of those responsible for this collaboration (*Prints and Visual Communication*, p. 36) although the names of publisher Peter Schoeffer, of the town physician Johann von Cube of Frankfurt and of the probable painter Erhard Reuwich are noted in many secondary accounts. Reuwich's name is actually cited by Ivins as the illustrator of von Breydenbach's *Peregrinations* on the very same page where he regrets the anonymity of the artist who contributed to *Gart der Gesundheit*. See discussion above, chap. 2, n. 134 for further information.

307 Technical advances made by new illustrations placed in printed herbals are well documented and graphically demonstrated by Arber, 'From Medieval Herbalism,' pp. 317–36. Note plates showing three successive illustrations of henbane.

308 A gift of Ruth G. Bush to the Vassar College Library provides a fine example of a pocket edition of Leonhart Fuchs' *De Stirpium*...(Basel: Isengrin, 1549) which contains 516 full page woodcuts, the illustrations from the great folio edition of 1542 having been executed under Fuchs' supervision, in reduced form. In addition to Latin and German letterpress titles, the sixteenth-century owner has added French titles in a contemporary hand, showing how this pocket guide was used for the field trips for which it was intended.

brated editors such as Mattioli and Clusius.[309] Once records based on direct observations and actual specimens drawn from distant regions began to be sent to editors of technical publications, one may say that modern scientific data collection was launched on its present path.

The 'subtle and practised' hands of Renaissance draughtsmen also began to contribute to the study of anatomy after print-makers replaced illuminators.[310] Only specialists are competent to enter into the dispute over whether Joannes Stephanus of Calcar *did* have a hand in illustrating Vesalius' *De Fabrica*, how large were the contributions made by other draughtsmen from Titian's studio and the extent to which Vesalius himself guided the hands of the artists and artisans he employed.[311] The non-specialist can only note that the evidence is incomplete on these points and verdicts appear to be inconclusive. Whatever the verdict in this case, it is clear that new kinds of collaboration between the learned anatomist–author, who had studied in the schools, and the artisan–draughtsman, who acquired his skills through apprenticeship, were encouraged by the new anatomical publication programs.

The significant role played by printed illustration in anatomy texts and the 'elaborate system of cross-reference between image and word' developed in works such as *De Fabrica* have been brought out so well by various authorities, few additional remarks are needed.[312] Rupert Hall's account seems to be especially well balanced. Hall not only indicates how illustrating textbooks helped to guide scientific observation, he also makes due allowance for the prior development of new pictorial conventions by quattrocento artists even before the advent of print.[313] In view of the tendency of some media analysts to overlook the way image making was transformed by draughtsmen before printed book illustration had begun, this point seems worth restating here.

[309] Sarton, *Six Wings*, pp. 137, 144 gives relevant references. For further discussion, see pp. 484 ff., volume II below.

[310] For vivid graphic contrast of scribal with printed visual aids in this field, see pictures of 'wound-men' used by barber-surgeons in Kurz, 'The Medical Illustrations.'

[311] Ivins' views (echoed by Panofsky, 'Artist, Scientist, Genius,' pp. 163–4, n. 36) which assign a predominant role to Calcar are challenged by O'Malley, *Andreas Vesalius*, pp. 124 ff. He argues that Vesalius (himself an accomplished draughtsman) closely supervised work done by others in his employ and that Vasari's assignment of credit to Calcar is untrustworthy. The debate has been reviewed and evidence reassessed by Kemp, 'A Drawing for the *De Fabrica*.' Kemp holds that Vasari's account is more reliable than O'Malley's.

[312] See description of *De Fabrica* as a 'servo-mechanism' in O'Malley and Saunders, *Leonardo da Vinci*, pp. 20–1.   [313] A. R. Hall, *Scientific Revolution*, pp. 41–50.

A glance at ambiguous medieval medical drawings may be sufficient to call in question the dictum (which tends to be taken for granted in an age of photography) that one picture is always worth more than many words. A picture may be unclear or misleading and no easier to decipher than a foreign phrase. As Gombrich's brilliant studies suggest, all pictures require some measure of decoding, and all 'fool the eye' one way or another.[314] But Gombrich also indicates that pictures can clarify as well as obfuscate our perception of natural phenomena. Images conveying correct information may be distinguished from those providing false reports. Artists may come closer to achieving verisimilitude by means of correction and feedback – provided of course that correct information is their chosen goal.[315] Quattrocento artists were working toward this goal even before printed book illustrations had become common. By developing new aesthetic conventions which stressed unified composition and focused perspective and by striving for clarity as well as verisimilitude, they provided sixteenth-century anatomists with a new and useful vocabulary of forms.[316]

But although the development of a new visual vocabulary needs to be acknowledged as an important ingredient, it did not in itself suffice to launch anatomy as a science. To overlook the sketch pads of Renaissance masters is misguided, but it is also misguided to ignore how new pictorial statements were transferred onto editions of technical books.

Anatomy as a science (and this applies to all other observational and descriptive sciences) was simply not possible without a method of preserving observations in graphic records, complete and accurate in three dimensions. In the absence of such records even the best observation was lost because it was not possible to check it against others and thus to test its general validity. It is no exaggeration to say that in the history of modern science the advent of perspective marked the beginning of a first period, the invention of the

---

314 Gombrich, *Art and Illusion*. The output of drawing books which helped to disseminate Renaissance pictorial conventions after printing is discussed on pp. 157–67.

315 See Gombrich, *Art and Illusion*, pp. xi; 276, 299 and Robert Palter's review (of *Hypothesis and Perception* by E. E. Harris). Palter notes (pp. 208–9) the tendency for Gombrich's discussion of Dürer's stylized rhinoceros (which was borrowed by Conrad Gesner for his zoological works) to become over-stylized itself.

316 The importance of retrieving Alexandrian technical literature, particularly Ptolemy's geography, in the development of new perspective renderings by quattrocento artists is shown by both Edgerton, *The Renaissance Rediscovery* and Gadol, *L. B. Alberti*. Although I think she underestimates the importance of printing in the development of geodetic surveying and mapping, by limiting its function to making 'manuals more numerous' (p. 171); Gadol brings out clearly how much Alberti's early work in Rome in the 1430s on cartography, surveying and mapping contributed to the shaping of these new conventions.

telescope and the microscope that of a second; and the discovery of photo-graphy that of a third: in the observational or descriptive sciences illustration is not so much the elucidation of a statement as a statement in itself.[317]

In my view, it is an exaggeration to launch modern science with the advent of perspective renderings and to regard pictorial statements as sufficient in themselves. 'A method of preserving observations in graphic records' and a chance to check them against others should not be presumed to lie in an artist's sketchpad. An exaggerated empha-sis on pictorial statements alone leads Panofsky to describe Leonardo as 'founding anatomical science.' But the case of Leonardo (as is later discussed) actually seems to show that eagle-eyed observation (even when combined with masterful drawing and dissection) was not in itself sufficient to set the study of anatomy on a new course. Familiarity with books as well as bodies was required. Knowledge of medieval and ancient nomenclature, command of Greek and Arabic as well as Latin terms and other skills gained from editing ancient works, also entered into the anatomist's art. To say that Vesalius' work 'does not essentially differ' from Leonardo's 'in purpose and method' is to overlook all the differences which distinguish a collaborative publica-tion program from the keeping of a single sketchbook.

In this regard one must be wary of placing too much emphasis upon the new visual aids and upon the special skills of artists when considering developments in such fields as anatomy or botany. A fuller discussion of other changes which affected these fields must be postponed for a later chapter. Let me merely note here that questions relating to collaboration and coordination deserve more consideration when 'dealing with observational or descriptive sciences. Doubtless certain ateliers, academies, courts and colleges have to be singled out for special attention. Contributions made by particular masters do loom large. But it is also a mistake to linger too long in any one region or focus too much attention on any one activity. For the chief new feature that needs to be considered is the simultaneous tapping of many varied talents at the same time. Publication programs launched from urban workshops in many regions made it possible to combine and coordinate scattered investigations on a truly unprecedented scale.

The new interactions which were encouraged, both within the printer's workshop and by the circulation of his products, would

[317] Panofsky, 'Artist, Scientist, Genius,' p. 146.

probably not have proved so fruitful had it not been for typographical fixity. The preservative powers of print made it possible to dispense with the 'barriers' of which Panofsky speaks. 'The Renaissance was a period of decompartmentalization: a period which broke down the barriers that had kept things in order – but also apart – during the Middle Ages.'[318] As he notes, these barriers had previously divided different forms of knowledge into separate compartments and had conveyed them by separate 'transmission belts.' Whereas he regards the 'irresistible urge to compartmentalize' as an 'idiosyncrasy of the high medieval mind,'[319] I am inclined to think, instead, of discontinuities which were inherent in the conditions of scribal culture. Keeping channels of transmission apart probably helped to prevent the dilution or corruption of information as it was passed from one generation to another.

Many forms of knowledge had to be esoteric during the age of scribes if they were to survive at all. Quite apart from issues associated with religious orthodoxy and heterodoxy; closed systems, secretive attitudes and even mental barriers served important social functions. Despite drifting texts, migrating manuscripts and the dispersal or destruction of record collections, much could be learned by trial and error over the course of centuries. But advanced techniques could not be passed on without being guarded against contamination and hedged in by secrecy. To be preserved intact, techniques had to be entrusted to a select group of initiates who were instructed not only in special skills but also in the 'mysteries' associated with them. Special symbols, rituals, and incantations performed the necessary function of organizing data, laying out schedules, and preserving techniques in easily memorized forms.

In these circumstances, opportunities for cross-cultural interchange were necessarily restricted and limited. An apprentice learning to wield the tools of the surgeon–barber, and a university student transcribing passages from Latin translations of Greek and Arabic medical texts were acquiring skills that were conveyed by entirely separate 'transmission belts.' Even within the university itself, the conditions of scribal culture prevented an interchange between disciplines that now seem to be closely related: astronomy and physics, for example. To be sure,

318 Panofsky, 'Artist, Scientist, Genius', p. 128.
319 Panofsky, *Renaissance and Renascences*, p. 106.

the very migration of manuscripts occasionally resulted in a fruitful encounter between two previously separate textual traditions. A new fusion of theology with natural philosophy was worked out by the fortunate schoolmen who received the newly recovered Aristotelian corpus. Although the synthesis was at first resisted by conservatives, it did ultimately win acceptance. Hellenic and patristic cosmologies were dovetailed sufficiently well that the orders of angels and orbits of planets could be simultaneously memorized and held in mind. It is noteworthy, however, that the more complicated calculations which traced every planet's apparent path by means of deferents and equants were omitted from Aquinas' grand design. Wobbling and retrograde motions did not interfere with Dante's stately ascension toward the empyrean heavens. The charts and tables of the *Almagest* were preserved, outside circles frequented by philosophers and poets, by a select group of professional astronomers, from which Copernicus ultimately emerged.[320] Records containing precise computations required special training for copyists, close supervision of scriptoria, careful custody of relevant texts and detailed instruction in how to use them. Mastery of planetary astronomy under such conditions was almost bound to isolate this discipline from other branches of learning.

Curiously enough, doctrines cultivated by cloistered monks and veiled nuns were less hedged in by secrecy than trades and mysteries known to lay clerks and craftsmen. The Church with its armies of apostles and missionaries, its oral and visual propaganda, its pervasive exoteric symbols and rituals, seems to have represented a remarkable exception to prevailing rules. Despite reliance on scribes, it succeeded in transmitting Christian doctrine even while proclaiming it openly and eschewing the sort of secrecy that had characterized pagan priesthoods and mystery cults. But the Church, which controlled most centers of book production and the recruitment and training of copyists, was probably the only institution that was capable of instructing its priests while openly proclaiming the Truth to the laity. Heroic efforts were required to ensure that the special meaning associated with Christian symbols, ritual and liturgy would not be lost or diluted over the course of centuries but would become increasingly available

[320] The limited audience that was equipped to handle the *Almagest* and the special position occupied by astronomy in medieval universities are discussed in pp. 536-7, p. 604 n., volume II below.

to a partly Latinized, largely barbarian population. Energies mobilized for this evangelical task tended to exhaust the capacities of scribal culture to transmit other messages without restricting access to select minorities who perpetuated divergent closed systems of knowledge by using separate channels of transmission.

4. ARCANA DISCLOSED: THE CULT OF ANTIQUITY AND THE IDEA OF A 'RINASCITA' TRANSFORMED

The process of cross-fertilization that occurred when these compartmentalized systems entered the public domain was by no means a neat or elegant one. Retrospective studies of the interlocking of the relatively rigorous trades and disciplines practiced by artists, anatomists, mechanics, astronomers, and the like are misleading in this regard. According to Frances Yates, mechanics and machines were 'regarded in the Hermetic tradition as a branch of magic.'[321] During the age of scribes, the tendency to associate magical arts with mechanical crafts was not, however, confined to those who followed the doctrines of Hermes Trismegistus. As long as trade skills had been passed down by closed circles of initiates, unwritten recipes of all sorts seemed equally mysterious to the uninitiated. Even when instructions were written down and preserved in lodgebooks, they might still appear as 'mysteries' to people on the outside. The mason's apron might serve just as well as the eye of Horus to indicate secrets veiled from the public at large.[322] Secret formulas used by the alchemist could not be distinguished from those used by apothecaries, goldsmiths, glaziers or luthiers.[323] All had belonged to the same 'underworld of learning,'[324] and emerged into view at more or less the same time.

Thus when 'technology went to press' so too did a vast backlog of occult practices and formulas and few readers were able to discriminate between the two. For at least a century and a half confusion persisted. Publications dealing with unseen natural forces wandered all over the map and into the spirit world as well. What later came to be described

---

[321] Yates, *Art of Memory*, p. 340; see also her intriguing account of belief in ancient Egyptian proficiency in mathematics and mechanics, 'The Hermetic Tradition,' pp. 259–60.

[322] On problems associated with defining the so-called 'secret' of the master masons, see Shelby, 'The "Secret." '

[323] That Paracelsus considered the weaver, the baker, the cultivator to be 'alchemists' is noted by Rossi, *Francis Bacon*, p. 20.

[324] Bolgar, *The Classical Heritage*, p. 180.

as a 'natural history of nonsense' was greatly enriched.[325] The same publicity system that enabled instrument-makers to advertise their wares and contribute to public knowledge also encouraged an output of more sensational claims. Discoveries of philosophers' stones, the keys to all knowledge, the cures to all ills were proclaimed by self-taught and self-professed miracle workers who often proved to be more adept at press agentry than at any of the older arts. At the same time medieval secretive attitudes persisted among many artisans, even after the decline of craft guilds. More than two centuries after Gutenberg, Joseph Moxon was still complaining, 'Letter cutting is a handy-work hitherto so conceal'd among artificers of it that I cannot learn anyone hath taught it any other.'[326]

Fear of new censors as well as ambivalence about new publicity also provoked widely varying reactions among professional and academic élites. Deliberate resort to 'Aesopian language,' the use of veiled allusions and cryptic comment were, if anything, more common after printing than had been the case before. Ancient esoteric injunctions to withhold the highest truths from the public were amplified and reinforced, at first.[327] As a later discussion suggests, whereas some natural philosophers followed Francis Bacon in urging the opening of closed shops and a freer trade in ideas, others, like Sir Walter Raleigh, reacted against new publicity by praising ancient sages for withholding or disguising certain truths.[328] Copernicus and Newton were as reluctant as Vesalius or Galileo were eager to break into print. 'The conception of scientific collaboration as a meeting of illuminati jealously guarding their precious and mysterious discoveries'[329] was by no means decisively defeated in Francis Bacon's day. Nevertheless, the basis for this

---

[325] This is richly documented by Thorndike's two volumes on the sixteenth century: *A History of Magic*. Thorndike's view that printing had a largely pernicious effect – by flooding book markets with pseudo-scientific stuff – is discussed on p. 529, volume II below.

[326] Cited by Clapham, 'Printing,' p. 385. Moxon's 'Mechanick Excercises,' published serially from 1667 on (a one-volume edition appearing in 1683) represents a landmark in publicizing technology. His account of printing is especially notable and was later incorporated in the celebrated article in *L'Encyclopédie*. How he visited Amsterdam (and made contact with Blaeu's firm) in 1652 to study printing before setting up shop as a globe and instrument maker in Cornhill is noted by E. G. R. Taylor, *Mathematical Practitioners*, pp. 231–3.

[327] For detailed account of a German humanist who adhered to a cautious, prudential position and avoided publishing anything in his lifetime, see Baumann, 'Mutianus Rufus,' 567–98. Baumann refers to a key work by Leo Strauss, *Persecution*. The shift, noted by Strauss (p. 33), from esoteric to exoteric philosophical approaches seems to me to be predicated on printing and has many implications for early-modern science which remain to be explored.

[328] See p. 563, volume II below.

[329] Rossi, *Francis Bacon*, p. 27.

conception had been drastically transformed almost as soon as the first booksellers' catalogues appeared.

Views which were shaped by the need to preserve data from corruption were incongruous with mass-produced objects sold on the open market. Insistence on concealment, as Bishop Sprat later noted, came oddly from authors who were turning out bestsellers and 'ever printing their greatest mysteries.'[330] 'We ask you,' writes Paracelsus, 'to handle and preserve this divine mystery with the utmost secrecy.'[331] The request, which seems appropriate when addressed to a select group of initiates, becomes absurd when disseminated, via commercial promotion, to the public at large. Similarly, to hear someone talk of protecting pearls from swine when he is trying to sell gems to all comers is to provoke scepticism both about his intentions and about the real worth of the products he purveys. The sorcerer who exploited fear of the unknown eventually became the charlatan who exploited mere ignorance – at least in the eyes of 'enlightened' professional and academic élites. Having emerged from an old 'underworld of learning' in the company of artisans and craftsmen, the master of occult arts would end by being submerged once again – but into different subterranean regions and with a different motley assortment of companions: ranging from Rosicrucians and Freemasons and Mesmerists to faith healers, spiritualists, and pseudo-scientists of all kinds. 'The Rosicrucians represent the tendency of Renaissance Hermeticism and other occultisms to go underground in the seventeenth century, transforming what was once an outlook associated with dominant philosophies into a preoccupation of secret societies and minority groups.'[332]

There are many significant differences between the old 'underworld' which contained unlettered artisans and unwritten recipes and the new 'underground' which was inhabited by men of letters – too many to be analyzed here.[333] Let me merely note that the new 'secret' societies

---

330 For fuller citation and discussion, see p. 562, volume II below.

331 Cited by Rossi, *Francis Bacon*, p. 29. Other relevant references (including warnings about pearls of wisdom) are given in this passage. John Dee ended his *Monas Hieroglyphica* with a published request to his printer to limit the edition since it contained 'mysteries' not intended for the 'vulgar.' Trattner, 'God and Expansion,' p. 23.

332 Yates, *Giordano Bruno*, p. 407. According to Yates, Isaac Casaubon's redating of the Hermetic corpus in 1614 and his proof that the assemblage was compiled in the post-Christian era was *the* event which 'shattered the position of the Renaissance magus' and forced Hermeticism underground.

333 Among other complications, the one term 'underground' is used – with reference to early modern European intellectual history – to designate quite different phenomena by different

presented an especially dramatic contrast with the older guilds and lodges in their paradoxical exploitation of publicity. Far from being restricted to small closed circles of adherents, they extended invitations to unknown readers and by hinting at mysteries revealed only to the initiated, appeared to use secrecy as a recruiting device. The Rosicrucian manifestoes 'were highly publicized statements thrown provocatively out into the world. Since the prime aim of a secret society must ever be to keep itself secret, it would seem an odd thing for a real...secret society to do, to publicize itself so dramatically.'[334]

The normal way of trying to get into touch with the R.C. Brothers, after reading the manifestoes was to publish something addressed to them or expressing admiration for them. These replies were not answered; the R.C. Brothers did not reply either to their admirers or to their critics...

The Rosicrucian furore which arose in response to the stirring...manifestoes soon became inextricably confused through the large numbers who tried to join without inside knowledge of what it was about being merely attracted by the exciting possibility of getting in touch with mysterious personages... or angered and alarmed by the imagined spread of dangerous magicians or agitators.[335]

authorities. Yates, *Giordano Bruno*, is referring to a region created by new boundaries set by the Commonwealth of Learning in accordance with newly developed rules of evidence and consensual validation. More often, the term designates a more clearly subversive region created – not by learned élites – but by official censors, who determined the contents of a clandestine book-trade. In this latter sense, much of the Commonwealth of Learning itself was forced 'underground,' and in Catholic regions, a Protestant scholar, such as Isaac Casaubon, would be an 'underground' author. [334] Yates, *Rosicrucian Enlightenment*, p. 207.

[335] Yates, *Rosicrucian Enlightenment*, pp. 74, 91. The 'amazing response' elicited by the first manifesto: the 'Fama Fraternitas,' which was published in four languages and issued in nine editions between 1614 and 1617 is also noted by Debus, *Science and Education*, pp. 21–4. See also Debus' article, 'The Chemical Debates of the Seventeenth Century.' Both Debus and Yates note that Robert Fludd made his first appearance in print (under the aegis of the Basson firm in Leiden which was allied to the Familists, see above, chap. 2, n. 297) in reply to the appeal of the 'invisible' brethren and in an effort to defend them from the attacks of Libavius, the Lutheran schoolmaster who fought the Paracelsians and wrote textbooks on chemistry. How print entered into the quarrels between Libavius and the Paracelsians is discussed by Hannaway, *The Chemist and the Word*. Libavius' insistence on public disclosure as against Paracelsian secretiveness is noted on p. 84; how much his didactic approach owed to the printed book is handled along lines that follow Father Ong's work on Ramus (pp. 112–13). But the paradoxical exploitation of the printed word by Paracelsians – who often denounced book learning even while making good use of both printing and engraving – is not brought out. Plates from the magnificently illustrated volumes turned out by the de Bry firm in Oppenheim for both Fludd and Michael Maier appear in Yates, *Rosicrucian Enlightenment*, chap. 6. One of Johann Theodore de Bry's sons-in-law was William Fitzer, the publisher of Harvey's *De Motu*. Another was the Swiss engraver, Matthieu Merian, the celebrated illustrator of Maier's *Atlanta Fugiens* (Oppenheim: de Bry, 1618). On connections between the de Bry firm and that of the Wechels when both were in Frankfurt, see Evans, 'The Wechel Presses,' pp. 12, 28. The Wechel firm published the works of Libavius' opponent, the Paracelsian, Oswald Croll. See discussion on p. 474, volume II below.

Just 'what it was about' remains baffling to this day. The sequel proved equally strange. Soon after the initial furore, a new commotion was produced. As reported by Gabriel Naudé in 1623, placards appeared throughout Paris proclaiming that 'the deputies of the principle [sic] college of the Brothers of the Rosy Cross are making a visible and invisible stay in this city.'[336] Perhaps no placards were actually printed and posted, and it was merely the publication of Naudé's report that caused rumors to fly. At all events there was another outpouring of pamphlets defending and attacking the Rosicrucians. However invisible or incredible, the Brethren thus provoked sufficient controversy to make an indelible historical mark. Modern scholars seem to be no more in agreement than were seventeenth-century observers as to whether the matter warrants a serious investigation or whether it should be dismissed as a hoax. The brothers of the Rosy Cross took their secrets to their graves. Whatever their intentions we may at least agree that they succeeded in producing a long-lasting 'media event.'

The old 'underworld of learning' was signally devoid of events of this kind. A significant difference between the medieval alchemist and the later Paracelsian was that the latter found the role of publicist congenial. Early printers and engravers indeed were among his closest friends.[337] The same point could be made of other claimants to the role of 'Renaissance magus,' a peculiarly protean figure who seems to be half revealing and half concealing the diverse tricks of his long-lived trade. The shift from sorcerer to sage and the re-evaluation of magic which occurred in the age of Trithemius, Agrippa and John Dee have been noted in several recent accounts.[338] This transformation recalls several other occupational mutations which we have already discussed. Indeed Frances Yates compares the elevation of the magician to that of the artist in a manner that suggests how the acquisition of letters and learning affected both.[339] The position of conjurers was

---

[336] Yates, *Rosicrucian Enlightenment*, p. 103.

[337] Paracelsus received his position as physician in Basel through Froben's good offices and had employed Oporinus as an assistant. Croll's relationship to the Wechel firm and Fludd's to the Basson firm in Leiden and the de Brys in Oppenheim is noted above n. 335. On John Dee's important stay with his Antwerp printer, Sylvius, and Trithemius' use of Mainz printers, see chap. 1, n. 37; chap. 2, n. 158 and n. 167 above. In her *Rosicrucian Enlightenment* Yates traces to John Dee many strands which seem to me to have indigenous continental roots. Trithemius' work on magic and ciphers preceded Dee's after all. (See also discussion of Pacioli, pp. 547 ff., volume II below.)

[338] Rossi, *Francis Bacon*, pp. 17-19; Yates, *Giordano Bruno*, pp. 107-11; Nauert, *Agrippa, passim*.

[339] Yates, *Giordano Bruno*, p. 107.

probably enhanced when sorcerers' apprentices learned to handle books as well as brooms and their masters could acquire a reputation for erudition. To be adept at sleight-of-hand was merely to be allied with shady tricksters and pickpockets. To publish books on hidden powers was to join the company of learned men and often to achieve eponymous fame as a scholarly author oneself.[340]

Moreover, efforts to translate ancient texts or to decipher inscriptions and glyphs were naturally linked with the study of magic squares and cabalistic signs. Works used in all manner of advanced studies were liable to the suspicion of being 'conjuring books' in an age when geometry was considered a 'black art,' and Arabic numerals, like Greek letters, were still arcane.[341] The Hebrew alphabet not only entered into efforts to emend scriptural passages but also figured prominently in necromancy. Since many medieval scholars developed their own idiosyncratic methods for cross-referencing and indexing large compilations, it was (and still is) unclear whether the presence of ciphers, acrostics and letter-number codes should be taken to indicate study of the Cabala or not.[342] In addition to all the special trade secrets associated with scribal arts, there were numerous key mnemonics associated with the memory arts which helped to compound confusion. Given centuries of reliance on mnemotechnics, moreover, it was a reasonable hypothesis that clues to the properties of things were contained in the names used to designate them.[343] Belief that divine secrets had been entrusted by God to Adam and that these secrets entered into the names Adam gave all things is often associated with the influence exerted by the so-called Hermetic tradition. The textual assemblage attributed to the Egyptian scribal god (whom the Greeks called Hermes Thrice-Blessed) was only one among several textual compilations which pointed in the same direction.[344] The Hermetic corpus would

---

[340] Or even, perhaps, as a scholar–printer. The now discredited, long-lived legend linking Gutenberg's partner Johann Fust with the historical prototype for Dr Faustus (see chap. 2, n. 161, n. 163 above) suggests the new status-role achieved by the Renaissance magus. Printing itself was originally regarded as a 'magical' invention.

[341] See references cited by Thomas, *Religion and the Decline of Magic*, p. 362.

[342] This is brought out in a discussion of the key mnemonics, acrostics and ciphers used in Roger Bacon's work by Derek de Solla Price, introduction to Chaucer's *The Equatorie of the Planetis*, ed. Price, pp. 182–3.

[343] Mystico-magical properties associated with names and etymology are discussed by Borchardt, 'Etymology,' p. 417.

[344] Others such as the *Orphica*, the Sybylline Prophecies, the Pythagorean *Carmina Aurea*, the *Oracula Chaldaica* are noted by D. P. Walker in his introduction to his collected studies on 'Christian Platonism': *The Ancient Theology*, p. 27. The names of the gods sung in Orphic

scarcely have exerted such great authority had it not expressed views which conformed to the experience of learned men who relied on forms of transmission which have now dissappeared. The same point applies to the enthusiasm for study of Cabala shown by Christian scholars such as Pico, Reuchlin and Lefèvre d'Etaples.[345]

The hidden meaning of hieroglyphs was concealed until the nineteenth century; that of Hebrew vowel points remained mysterious for a shorter time.[346] Yet for Renaissance Hebraists such as Pico or Reuchlin, the same mystical magical properties were locked up in both Egyptian and Hebrew letters; the mystery of the Trinity as well as the secrets of Creation having been engraved on the tablets handed to Moses and entrusted first to Adam when he was told the names of all things. Now it was common for the most ignorant wizards, a Tudor bishop complained, to boast that their cunning was derived from Adam, Moses or the Archangel Raphael.[347] As ignorant possessors of corrupted lore, such wizards were regarded with contempt, not only by orthodox bishops, but also by heterodox scholars. The grounds for rejection were quite different, however. When Pico della Mirandola contemptuously dismissed the medieval wizard – who invoked the names of Adam and Moses and used Hebrew letters – as 'ignorant and barbarous,'[348] he did so in much the same spirit as the critic who objected to ignorant history-painting. The practitioner and not the art was called into question. The practice of 'magia and cabala' in other words was probably viewed by Pico in the same way as all other arts and letters were. Cabala had been subjected to 'Gothic' barbarism much

hymns concealed the names of natural and divine powers distributed in the world by the Creator according to a citation from Pico.

345 Blau, *The Christian Interpretation, passim.* Yates, *Giordano Bruno,* chap. 5; Spitz, 'Reuchlin's Philosophy.' How his study of cabala entered into Reuchlin's theories about scriptural composition is discussed by Schwarz, *Principles and Problems of Biblical Translation,* pp. 64–82.

346 The key work was the anonymously published *Arcanum Punctationum Revelatum* (Leiden, 1624) by Louis Cappel (Capellus), a Huguenot professor at the college of Saumur. Controversial publication about the vowel points goes back at least to the editing and publication of Plantin's Antwerp polyglot Bible of 1560, but reached a climax in the early seventeenth century as is noted on p. 332 below. The fact that Cappel's 'mystery of the vowel points revealed' appeared ten years after Isaac Casaubon's publication, placing the Hermetic corpus in post-Christian times, suggests that cabala as well as Hermeticism lost intellectual prestige during roughly the same interval. That 'old magical systems were robbed of their capacity to satisfy the educated élite' during the seventeenth century is noted casually and only in passing by Thomas, *Religion and the Decline of Magic,* p. 645, despite its seeming relevance to the central theme of his book.

347 Thomas, *Religion and the Decline of Magic,* p. 271.

348 Yates, *Giordano Bruno,* p. 107 refers to Pico's rejection of 'wicked magics going under the name of Solomon, Moses, Enoch or Adam.'

as Ciceronian Latin had been. What had been garbled and corrupted needed to be purified and restored.

As a recipient of ancient secrets passed down through the centuries, the magician seemed to hold a key to the fabled body of knowledge that had been guarded by scribal priesthoods before old temples had been destroyed and a confusion of tongues let loose on the world. His fortunes were linked to a cult of antiquity which had been shaped by the conditions of scribal culture – a cult which was rapidly propelled before being dispelled by the output of scholar–printers.

In his review of Yates' work on Giordano Bruno, Giorgio de Santillana points to certain problems presented by the 'churning turbid flood of Hermetic, cabalistic, Gnostic, theurgic, Sabean, Pythagorean and generally mystic notions that broke over Europe with the Renaissance carrying everything before it.'[349] Here again, I would argue that the flood was released not 'with the Renaissance' but by means of printer's ink. It came, I think, with the casting of typefonts, the duplication of old inscriptions, and with the piecemeal publication of what at first appeared to be fragments drawn from some vast Ur-book of Knowledge. As is suggested by the dating of diverse post-Christian compilations and the prosaic explanation of Hebrew vowel points, some of these writings gradually became less mysterious after typefonts were cut; grammars and lexicons were issued; and scholarly findings accumulated. Printed side by side in polyglot reference books, Greek and Hebrew letters could be seen as equivalent to the familiar Latin alphabet.

But not all arcane letters lent themselves to this treatment. The Aldine press contributed to enlightenment by publishing Greek texts and lexicons; it also contributed to mystification with its editions of the 'Hieroglyphics of Horapollo.'[350] For the next three hundred years, Egyptian picture-writing was loaded with significant meaning by readers who could not read it. Most of them could and did read Erasmus' bestselling *Adages*, however; and many agreed that these 'sacred carved letters' had been devised by ancient priests to conceal

---

[349] de Santillana, book review, *American Historical Review*. This review contains hints of de Santillana's later collaborative book with Hertha von Dechend: *Hamlet's Mill*. The authors argue that a variety of ancient myths were designed to transmit information concerning the long-term slow-motion precession of the equinoxes.

[350] Early publications by Aldus and previous history of ms. versions are given by George Doas (ed. and tr.), *The Hieroglyphics of Horapollo*, pp. 22 ff. See also Iversen, *The Myth of Egypt*, pp. 48–9, 151, n. 34. David, *Le Débat*.

secret wisdom from the vulgar, even while preserving it for well-trained minds to decode.[351] Described by Alberti as 'ageless symbols of universal knowledge which had lasted when ordinary letters perished and their meanings had disappeared,'[352] the sacred glyphs became ever more fascinatingly mysterious as other mysteries were unveiled.

A printer's device had provided the occasion for Erasmus' comments, and these much publicized trademarks often conveyed special occult meanings to those who moved in the circles to which printers and engravers belonged.[353] Printers thus led the way in emulating the wise Egyptians; but other well-read laymen soon followed, until entire books were filled with veiled messages conveyed by means of picture-writing. Learned artists produced engravings which covered Roman arches with replicas of picture-writing drawn from recent books. With new printers' devices and emblem-books added to ancient hieroglyphics, there came a profusion of symbols that engendered further confusion.[354] Successive attempts to unveil the secrets of the pyramids not merely failed to clarify issues but actually seemed to obscure them more completely. Even after the riddle of the sphinx could be deciphered, other unfathomable glyphs and engravings remained – like John Dee's *Monas Hieroglyphica*, emblems containing a rose and a cross, or the libretto of *The Magic Flute* – to tantalize later scholars.

The fact that new meanings continued to be read into hieroglyphics over the course of three centuries of printing helps to account for some of the more puzzling aspects of the later phases of the Hermetic tradi-

---

351 The occasion for this discussion is Erasmus' description of how Aldus showed him a Roman silver coin given by Cardinal Bembo, stamped with an effigy of Titus Vespasianus and an anchor-and-dolphin. The meaning of the latter, 'Festina Lente,' had been Augustus' motto, according to the 'books on hieroglyphics,' writes Erasmus and he goes on to discuss these enigmatic carvings (from the 1508 edition of the *Adages*, tr. M. M. Phillips, pp. 174–6). He thus stimulated curiosity about his publisher's books on hieroglyphics as well as publicized the firm's trademark in this adage.

352 Iversen, *Myth of Egypt*, pp. 65ff. See also intriguing discussion of Ficino's view of hieroglyphs, Gombrich, 'Icones Symbolicae,' pp. 171–2.

353 Some of the alchemical symbols (such as the griffon, the pelican, etc.) used in printers' devices are described by Rosarivo, 'Simbolos Alquimicos.' Since these symbols were also imbued with Christian significance by medieval allegorists, and were also used for mnemonic purposes, a wide margin for uncertainty needs to be left when labelling them as 'alchemical.' See discussion of 'Leda Bible' above, p. 260.

354 On tremendous vogue initiated by Alciati's *Emblemata*, its links with the Aldine edition of 'Horapollo's' *Hieroglyphics* and suggestive treatment of printers' devices, see Goldschmidt, *Printed Book of the Renaissance*, pp. 85–6; also Praz, *Studies in Seventeenth Century Imagery*, pp. 23ff. On Dürer's use of hieroglyphics for his engraving of the Triumphal Arch for Emperor Maximilian, see Panofsky, *Dürer* I, 177.

tion. For the reputation of the Egyptian scribal God was not really dealt a fatal blow in 1614 when Isaac Casaubon demonstrated that the assemblage translated by Ficino was written in the early Christian era.[355] The Hermetic corpus may have been post-Christian, but Thoth-Hermes obviously was not. His venerable antiquity (attested to by Saint Augustine) and his role as an inventor of arithmetic, geometry, astronomy and writing (recalled by Plato in the *Phaedrus*) were, if anything, confirmed. That such a figure had existed long before Jesus and also before Plato was in no way disproved by the imputation of 'forgery.'[356] Dating the 'forged' Donation of Constantine showed that the Emperor had not made it. Dating the Hermetic assemblage showed that the Egyptian scribal God was not responsible for it. Just what he *was* responsible for, however, still remained unclear. Did the inscriptions found on obelisks provide clues to the secrets of Creation or show foreknowledge of Christian truths? As long as they remained undeciphered, how could anyone be sure?

Moreover the *Hermetica* presented all the familiar problems associated with an ancient assemblage of diverse writings drawn from different places and times. It did not really lend itself to being handled as a printed treatise, assigned a single publication date or attributed to an individual author. This point, to be sure, was not likely to be perceived by most seventeenth-century scholars. In an era when imputations of forgery and imposture were being directed at Aristotle and Homer, it was natural that they be used to deflate the reputation of 'that supposititious semi-Platonic also semi-Christian, but however erudite writer who is commonly called Hermes Trismegistus.'[357] Nevertheless the point is worth keeping in mind. Even now there is no agreement about how much or how little genuine ancient Egyptian material entered into the post-Christian assemblage.[358] Those Cambridge Platonists

355 Walker, *Ancient Theology*, p. 192 warns against exaggerating the destructive effects of Casaubon's dating.

356 Trevor-Roper, review essay, *History and Theory* (1966), p. 80, n. 32 notes that Walter Raleigh inconsistently praised the 'excellent work of Master Casaubon' who showed 'the books of Hermes were no better than counterfeited pieces' and then later calmly referred to the prophecies of 'Hermes who lived at once with or soon after Moses, Zoroaster...' In thus dismissing the 'counterfeited pieces' while upholding the antiquity of the real sage, perhaps Raleigh was not really being so inconsistent after all.

357 Walker, *Ancient Theology*, p. 193, cites this description of Hermes from Gerard Vossius' *De Idolatria* (1642).

358 Yates, *Giordano Bruno*, p. 431. Shumaker, *The Occult Sciences*, p. 210 says we may be confident that Egyptian religious doctrines were not 'preserved accurately and in detail' in the corpus, but this leaves open a wide margin for uncertainty.

who were not entirely persuaded by Casaubon's arguments, and who believed some ancient Egyptian teachings to be contained in the corpus, may have been less wide of the mark in certain respects than their more sceptical contemporaries.[359] The 'forged books of Hermes which contain a philosophy not Egyptian' were being used, Bishop Warburton complained, 'to explain and illustrate old monuments not philosophical.'[360] But how could the Bishop be certain that a given philosophy was not that of ancient Egyptians when writings which *were* ancient Egyptian could not be read?

Warburton's complaint was aimed at a celebrated Baroque monument to Jesuit erudition, Athanasius Kircher's *Oedipus Aegyptiacus* (1652–4), described by Frank Manuel as an 'elephantine set of four Latin folio volumes' and 'one of the most learned monstrosities of all times.'

Hieroglyphs were there demonstrated to be the secret repositories of a great fund of ancient Egyptian wisdom. Using analogies and indulging freely in flights of scholarly fancy... – his text was bedecked with quotations from twenty different tongues – Kircher showed that every branch of knowledge ...had already been fully developed among the Egyptian priests. He knew the classical corpus, rabbinic literature, the cabala, Hebrew and Arabic philosophy and through his devious interpretations, every Egyptian pictorial image on a mummy, an obelisk, on the wall of a tomb, on papyrus, assumed concrete scientific or theological significance.[361]

In thus amassing all the drawings of genuine Egyptian hieroglyphs that he could obtain from correspondents, Kircher actually performed a scholarly service which later Egyptologists acknowledged.[362] But his work provoked considerable ridicule from the Jesuit-baiters of the day. Not that the futility of reading meaning into undeciphered picture-writing was acknowledged. On the contrary, the volume of controversial publication simply thickened; new layers of interpretation were deposited over the old.

---

[359] See discussion of Cudworth's argument in Yates, *Giordano Bruno*, pp. 427–31. Walker shows how this argument was used by the eighteenth-century French freemason, André Michel Ramsay, author of *The Travels of Cyrus* (who made the celebrated announcement that a *Universal Dictionary* was to be undertaken as a masonic project in 1737). *The Ancient Theology*, pp. 231, 241.

[360] Cited by Manuel, *The Eighteenth Century*, p. 191.

[361] Manuel, *The Eighteenth Century*, p. 190. See also Yates' discussion of Kircher, *Giordano Bruno*, pp. 416–23.

[362] Iversen, *The Myth of Egypt*, pp. 86–97 calls Kircher the 'true founder of Egyptology' and regards his work more respectfully than does Manuel.

By the eighteenth century some 'enlightened' scholars were prepared to dismiss the sphinxes as mere fetishes and the Egyptians as 'primitive' brute worshippers.[363] But others were persuaded that the pyramid builders had mastered sophisticated techniques for measuring the earth and charting the heavens. Alberti's 'ageless symbols of universal knowledge' were assigned new astronomical and geodetic significance – much as the pillars of Stonehenge have been in our age.[364] The sacred carved letters, while retaining their significance, at least among some Jesuits, as arcane symbols of a special revelation, lost much of their mystical–magical significance for adherents of the 'new philosophy.' At the same time they gained new attributes in accordance with the shift from occult and revealed to demonstrable and observed.[365] In some interpretations, notions of concealment were retained although occult content was denied. The glyphs stood for a pure, clear and certain knowledge which had been withheld from the populace by ancient priests, much as Latin treatises seemed to withhold religious and scientific truths according to vernacular translators in the seventeenth century. How 'ancient wise men concealed mysteries from the vulgar in Hieroglyphics' thereby enhancing 'reverence' but not advancing the 'philosophy of nature' was noted by, among others, the propagandist for the Royal Society, Bishop Sprat.[366] The secrecy imposed by priests who prevented lay Bible-reading was coupled with that imposed by censors who required circumvention. In his *Tachygraphy* of 1641, Thomas Shelton pushed his scheme for shorthand as a way of using Bibles and other books without danger of 'bloudy Inquisitours.'[367] That hieroglyphs might be a kind of shorthand designed not so much by priests to fool the populace but by initiates to deceive censors was a possibility that fitted the purposes of the literati, printers and engravers who contributed to a clandestine book-trade. If they did represent a kind of shorthand, then the ancient glyphs were esoteric

[363] Manuel, *The Eighteenth Century*, pp. 189–90.

[364] Tompkins, *Secrets of the Great Pyramids* cites the measurements of the pyramids made in 1638 by John Greaves (later Savilian Professor of Astronomy at Oxford) and by Tito Livia Burattini, a Venetian sent to Egypt by Father Kircher. This book contains an appendix by L. C. Stecchini which shows how the art of reading hidden meanings into hieroglyphs is continued in our day. Stecchini's first insight into 'the Egyptian geodetic system' came from reading 'Italian Renaissance Scientists, influenced by Cabalists' (p. 301).

[365] The relevance of this distinction to Hermeticism is spelled out by Nock, introduction, *Corpus Hermeticum* I, i–ii.

[366] Sprat, *History of the Royal Society*, p. 5. The attack on Latin and the defense of vernaculars by translators is discussed in chap. 4, below. (See pp. 360ff.)

[367] Cited by Manuel, *A Portrait of Isaac Newton*, p. 409, n. 17.

only in the sense that Latin or Greek or mathematical symbols were esoteric to the uninstructed. Perhaps the wise Egyptians had possessed a truly universal language, as Alberti held, one which transcended linguistic boundaries much as Comenius' picture books and Leibniz's mathematical symbols managed to do.[368] By the end of the Enlightenment, all these possibilities had been explored. The still undeciphered images had come to stand for everything that was secret and everything that was known.

In this regard the contrast which is often drawn between Renaissance syncretism and seventeenth-century criticism needs to be modified. Renaissance neoplatonists, it has been said, tried

> to abolish the borderline not only between philosophy, religion and magic, but between all kinds of philosophies, all kinds of religions and all kinds of magic, including Hermeticism, Orphism, Pythagoreanism, Cabala, and the ancient mysteries of Egypt and India. This wild mixture could not resist the criticism, both scientific and philological, that was to set in during the seventeenth century.[369]

Seventeenth-century scholars did solve certain puzzles and separated out some of the disparate ingredients which had earlier been combined. But, as we have just seen, they also contributed to puzzlement on their own by venturing somewhat further than their philology could take them – much as the earlier 'neoplatonists' had done. In both cases, I think, the scholars involved were not mixing things up deliberately but rather perpetuating a deep-rooted monotheistic tradition while being flooded with an unprecedented output of data drawn from disparate cultures and presented in scrambled form.

'The Renaissance thirst for synthesis, for syncretism, was unquenchable.'[370] This point has become a scholarly commonplace. But, as in many other cases, what is commonly attributed to the Renaissance seems no less characteristic of medieval movements. To produce a synthesis from apparent antitheses was part of the schoolman's training – at least since the era of Abelard's *Sic et Non* and Gratian's *Concordance of Discordant Canons*. Certainly the great *summas* of the thirteenth century contained a smoother blend of ingredients than did the 'wild

---

368 David, *Le Débat*, pp. 31–7, discusses the confusion between ancient writing systems and modern attempts to invent a universal language.
369 Panofsky, 'Artist, Scientist, Genius,' pp. 129–30. Much of the 'wild mixture' is, incidentally, still fermenting – as a glance at brochures sent out by occult book clubs and the output of the Bollingen Press suggests.   370 Shumaker, *The Occult Sciences*, p. 205.

mixture' of the fifteenth and sixteenth centuries. This may have been partly because lay humanists, despite the disapproval they often provoked, were less restrained by church authorities than were the medieval friars.[371] But it was also because fewer ingredients were available to the latter.[372] In my view, at least, the mixture resulted less from a deliberate effort to abolish boundaries or to concoct a new syncretist faith than from making available to a Latin-reading public, inspired by medieval traditions, an unprecedented profusion of old texts which had never been published before.

In this light, one wonders whether the term 'syncretist' is really suited to the endeavors of Renaissance neoplatonists. Syncretism implies an effort to combine conflicting schools of thought or variegated materials which have previously been placed apart. The texts, attributed to Zoroaster, Orpheus, Hermes, Plato and Plotinus, which were translated into Latin and made available in the late fifteenth century, had not yet been sorted out. They arrived in the wake of rumors which credited them to a single source. Later feats of scholarship were required to date and place them. The neoplatonists were indeed in much the same position as the sixteenth-century mythographers mentioned earlier in this chapter who found 'history and geography' in a disordered state.[373]

Much as the mythographers were described as 'bookish and barbaric' by Jean Seznec; so too the neoplatonists provoke criticism from Wayne Shumaker – not for regressing to the middle ages but for never leaving there: 'The Renaissance mind was medieval or pre-medieval in many of its assumptions.'[374] Although he thus departs from Burckhardt's schema, Shumaker uses the term 'medieval' in the same pejorative sense that Burckhardt did – to mean childlike, credulous, incapable

---

[371] Condemnations, such as that delivered by the Archbishop of Paris in 1277, against the acceptance of certain Aristotelian doctrines, may be cited as examples of restraint. Savonarola's inconclusive debates with Pico della Mirandola over the value of the *Hermetica* are discussed by Walker, *The Ancient Theology*, chap. 2.

[372] Roger Bacon's belief in the revelations which passed from Adam through Zoroaster, Hermes, and others to Solomon, Plato, Aristotle and finally to Avicenna is noted by Rossi, *Francis Bacon*, pp. 69–70. But Roger Bacon did not have on hand as did Pico the full corpus of texts attributed to Hermes, Zoroaster, Plato *et al.* See Walker, *The Ancient Theology*, pp. 12–13. For run-down of mss. and of early printed editions of Ficino's Latin translation of the Hermetic corpus, see Festugière, *La Révélation* II, 1–28. On the numerous French editions that were printed after Lefèvre D'Etaples's 1494 edition of Ficino's translation of the *Pimander*, see Walker, *Ancient Theology*, pp. 67–9.

[373] See above, pp. 196–9, for reference to Seznec's interpretation.

[374] Shumaker, *The Occult Sciences*, p. 204.

of facing reality or of separating fact from fantasy. A common effort to defend Western science and rationality links the nineteenth-century Swiss professor combatting romantic medievalism and the twentieth-century American professor objecting to the content of occult bookstores proliferating on campuses today. One wonders how much their vision of an easily deluded 'medieval' mind owes to encounters with the youth culture of their own age. The question seems worth posing if only because it helps to draw attention to the difference between the modern retreat from reason and attitudes expressed in a pre-scientific age. However much one is opposed (as I am) to the anti-scientific posture of many literati today, one is also obliged (if only in one's interest) to grant respectful consideration to the work of mature scholars who lacked the advantages hindsight confers. Concern with the occult was far from being anti-scientific in the late quattrocento and cinquecento. Indeed a fairly plausible case has been made that it contributed much to later Cartesian and Newtonian conceptual schemes.[375] Without passing judgment on the merits of this case, the fact that it can be made does at least point to significant differences between the occult sciences of the Renaissance and those of today. Not even the handsomely illustrated expensive volumes of the Bollingen Press can be said to contribute in any way to modern astronomy, physics or chemistry.

One of the many merits of Frances Yates' work is that such significant differences are made clear. The alert scientific curiosity, philological grounding and intellectual discipline of the Renaissance magus that she depicts contrasts sharply with later science-baiting dabblers in the occult. But even Yates expresses occasional mild surprise at the failure (f Renaissance scholars to discriminate between disparate textual traditions – at the way Marsiglio Ficino, for example, 'happily combined the *Summa* of Thomas Aquinas with his own brand of Platonic theology.' 'The Renaissance occult philosopher,' she observes, 'had a great gift for ignoring differences and seeing only resemblances.'[376] It is precisely this 'great gift' which leads Shumaker to write somewhat condescendingly of a culture still given to 'syncretism and superstition' and to invoke 'the desire of the human mind to reduce psychic conflict

---

375 Apart from Yates' *Bruno,* and *Rosicrucian Enlightenment,* see esp. McGuire and Rattansi, 'Newton,' and Pagel, *Paracelsus.* For critique, see Hesse, 'Hermeticism and Historiography,' and Westman, 'Magical Reform.' Further discussion and references are given in chap. 8, n. 15 and n. 16, volume II below.   376 Yates, *Art of Memory,* p. 168.

by modifying discrete bits of information so that they no longer exist in tension.'[377]

Before concluding that Renaissance syncretism served as a kind of mental balm 'designed to reduce psychic conflict' it seems worth giving more thought to different procedures for transmitting 'discrete bits of information.' For objective as well as for subjective reasons, they appeared in a different guise to earlier scholars from the way they look to us now.

By the fifteenth century many ancient records had evaporated into tantalizing fragments and glyphs. They hinted at resemblances which were only later shown to be false. At the same time, many differences now familiar to us had been obscured. Lines between pagan error and Christian truth, drawn sharply by Augustine, had been erased and retraced so frequently that they had become increasingly blurred. The distance between Athens and Jerusalem was often discussed but never clearly fixed; texts from Alexandria could be located almost anywhere in between. The reconstruction of diverse ancient civilizations had not yet arrived at a point where Egyptian, Persian, Hellenic and Hellenistic could be clearly distinguished one from another. Whereas we instinctively place ancient records and unfamiliar scripts in the separate contexts of diverse ancient cultures, Renaissance scholars, who were more familiar with memory theatres than with maps and textbooks, instinctively sought a single context.

They were accustomed to think of monotheism as the oldest religion and of one Ur-language as preceding a later confusion of tongues.[378] Whereas we see them handling materials drawn from disparate schools and cultures, they saw themselves as trying to reassemble portions of a single corpus which had been broken up. Nor was this belief unreasonable, requiring a leap of faith. Behind the vestiges of ancient records which remained, certain uniformities could be glimpsed. After all, letter-number codes, incantations, pictograms and lines of verse had been used to record and transmit useful data.[379] That they might provide a clue to uniform movement in the heavens

---

[377] Shumaker, The Occult Sciences, pp. 208; 235.

[378] A useful general discussion of belief in an Ur-sprache is given by Steiner, After Babel. See esp. chap. 2.

[379] See e.g., above account (chap. 2, n. 255) of contraction 'Amen' in Finegan, Handbook of Biblical Chronology, p. 57. When Shumaker, The Occult Sciences, p 254 comments on a 'remarkable failure' to recognize that poetry is metaphorical rather than factual he overlooks the many fact-bearing functions performed by rhyme and verse before printing.

or the mastery of natural forces on earth was not an unreasonable hypothesis.

Long before Ficino's day, ancient glyphs were seen to emanate from the same 'Logos' which had presided over creation and had taught Adam the names and properties of all things.[380] This belief was enriched with new content when whole systems of knowledge, detached from their actual historical context, began to re-enter the West after the eleventh century. Imported from Islam and Byzantium, texts by Euclid, Archimedes, Galen, Aristotle, and the like confronted the separate groups who tried to master them with staggering testimony of immense technical sophistication.[381] Even now, the degree to which the *Almagest* or the *Digest* depended upon unusual facilities for prolonged cooperative ventures in record-keeping and research goes overlooked. That ancient giants could take advantage of certain exceptional libraries and abundant scribal labor was even less obvious to earlier scholars. By the seventeenth century when Francis Bacon sought to dispel the awe still engendered by the ancients, he suggested (ironically overlooking the changes in communications) that they had simply 'thought it superfluous and troublesome to publish their notes, minutes and commonplaces, and therefore followed the example of builders who removed the scaffolding and ladders when the building is finished.'[382] In prior centuries, such structures seemed to have sprung abruptly into existence, like the fabled codes of Lycurgus or the goddess of wisdom herself. They had been contrived by ancient seers who seemed to require neither scaffolding nor ladders and who must have had special access to supernatural aid.

Thus it seemed plausible that the same God who had handed the Tablets to Moses and the same grace which had granted some pagan poets prophetic powers to anticipate the Incarnation, had also endowed ancient philosophers with uncanny insights into the secrets of nature. Ancient texts were greeted with excitement and scanned for possible hidden meanings. The Bible itself was probed with cabalistic code-

---

[380] George Boas, *Hieroglyphics of Horapollo*, p. 22. Hieroglyphics were still being regarded as emanating from the Logos by clergymen in the seventeenth century, according to Gombrich, 'Icones Symbolicae,' p. 183. They were thought to have been invented by Hermes and to conceal theological truths by some sixteenth-century Frenchmen. Walker, 'The Prisca Theologica in France,' p. 232.

[381] When Shumaker, *The Occult Sciences*, p. 205, suggests that the intellectual superiority which was attributed to the ancient giants came as an afterthought – tacked on to legends of their unusual longevity and size – he seems to me to stress the least important features most of all.

[382] Francis Bacon, Aphorism no. 125, *Novum Organum*.

books on hand. Orthodox limits had been strained by the reception of Aristotle surrounded by Arabic and Hebrew commentaries. These limits snapped when the new presses released the turbulent 'turgid flood.' Eventually Christian doctrine was purified; and after the Church split apart more sharply defined limits were set by Catholic and Protestant alike. The study of 'magia and cabala' was gradually detached from scholarly research. By now, the detachment is so complete that it is difficult for us to imagine how the study of dusty records and dead languages could have ever caused such a stir.

Modern historians who work in the field of Renaissance studies find it necessary to remind their readers that a 'sense of revivification... accompanied the effort to interpret the original sources.'[383] It is difficult for us to recapture this sense because the meaning of the term 'original source' (or, for that matter, 'primary source') has long since been emptied of its inspirational associations. When deciphering an ancient inscription, a modern philologist or archeologist is more apt to anticipate finding a merchant's bill of lading or even a grocery list than a clue to the secrets God entrusted to Adam. Awesome powers *are* still associated with decoding the Book of Nature, to be sure, but the key is not sought by studying Linear B or the Dead Sea Scrolls.

'How...could a critical theory like that of close imitation secure a strong hold on intelligent people or how could there have been such extravagant and servile worship of men who had lived many ages before?'[384] asks a scholar who is trying to explain the defense of the 'Ancients' after the battle of books had commenced. His inadequate answer is that the classical 'decay of nature' theme simply lingered on. I think it more likely that this theme was transformed after it had been detached from the conditions of scribal culture. Although it was propelled by print, it lost its relevance to the living experience of literate élites and became ever more artificial and conventional.[385] Before printing, however, no artifice was required to sustain the belief that loss and corruption came with the passage of time. As long as ancient learning had to be transmitted by hand-copied texts, it was more likely

[383] Gilmore, *World of Humanism*, p. 199.
[384] Richard Foster Jones, *Ancients and Moderns*, p. 49.
[385] At least it became more artificial down to the mid-nineteenth century. Thereafter the old decay-of-nature theme was filled with new content by philosophers of history who invoked the second law of thermodynamics while experiencing new pressures produced by an unprecedented and continuing communications overload. For further speculation on this matter, see my essay, 'Clio and Chronos,' pp. 36–65 (esp. p. 57).

to be blurred or blotted out than to be augmented and improved over the course of centuries. 'The ascription of "exact and absolute knowledge of all naturall things" to the earliest writers' is especially puzzling, in Shumaker's view, 'because the sources of the prestige are never dilated upon sufficiently to satisfy my curiosity...'[386] The assumption that 'the ancientest must needs be the right, as nearer the Fountain the purer the streams and the errors sprang up as the ages succeeded'[387] conformed so completely with the experience of learned men throughout the age of scribes that it was simply taken for granted. Only after that age came to an end would the superior position of the ancients require a defense.

Whereas a succession of scribal copies of an Alexandrian text led to an ever more diffuse and corrupted textual tradition, successive printed editions of sixteenth-century reference works became easier to use and more useful. As previous comments suggest, the data contained in early editions were supplemented, clarified, codified, and surpassed by later ones. A first edition, to be sure, became increasingly valuable to the antiquarian or bibliophile. But it was discarded in favor of the latest edition or most up-to-date work by professional groups, who relied on such works in the practice of their craft.[388] An updated technical literature, moreover, enabled young men, in certain fields of study, to circumvent master–disciple relationships and to surpass their elders at the same time. Isaac Newton was still in his twenties when he mastered available mathematical treatises, beginning with Euclid and ending with an updated edition of Descartes. In thus climbing 'on the shoulders of giants' he was *not* re-enacting the experience of twelfth-century scholars for whom the retrieval of Euclid's theorems (and of Aristotle's natural philosophy) had been a major feat.

We are like dwarfs standing on the shoulders of giants. Thanks to them, we see farther than they, busying ourselves with the treatises of ancients we take their choice thoughts, buried by age and the neglect of men and raise them ...from death to renewed life.[389]

Peter of Blois is thus cited by M. D. Chenu to demonstrate medieval awareness of the 'progress of civilization.' The passage does suggest why medievalists question the distinctiveness of those themes of secular

---

386 Shumaker, *The Occult Sciences*, p. 255.
387 Cited by R. E. Burns, book review, *American Historical Review* (1968), p. 181.
388 See chap. 2, section 4, above.
389 Citation from Peter of Blois by Chenu, *Nature, Man and Society*, p. 290.

rebirth which are attributed to the early Italian Renaissance. But it also points to a way of thinking about the advancement of learning which had ceased to be taken for granted by Newton's day. When seventeenth-century virtuosi 'busied themselves with the treatises of the ancients,' it was not to preserve them by slavish copying, to transmit them by delivering lectures, to emend them by judicious editing, or to gather choice passages for new compendia. It was rather to find out what had been done in order to surpass it – to go beyond the limits prior generations had set. With fixity came cumulative cognitive advance which called into question traditional concepts pertaining to growth and decay. In a celebrated passage Francis Bacon played with the paradox: *Antiquitas saeculi juventus mundi*:

Just as we look for greater knowledge of human things and riper judgement in the old man than in the young...so in like manner from our own age... much more might be fairly expected than from ancient times inasmuch as it is a more advanced age of the world and stored and stocked with infinite experiments and observations...[390]

For scribal scholars the longer-lived age was more likely to suffer from loss of memory and senility than to be endowed with an increased stock of knowledge. Not only could more be learned from retrieving an early manuscript than from procuring a recent copy but the finding of lost texts was the chief means of achieving a breakthrough in almost any field. In this regard it is misleading to invoke an 'eager desire to increase knowledge' and 'an active impatience with all its hindrances' as 'causes' of the 'revolt from the ancients.'[391] A similar desire to increase knowledge had been manifested for centuries before Francis Bacon's day but methods of obtaining the desired goal were necessarily quite different before printing. Neither an 'irrational hatred of novelty' nor 'an equally irrational love for the old and the tried' had entered into the reverence for antiquity manifested during the age of scribes. On the contrary, energies were expended on the retrieval of ancient texts because they held the promise of finding so much that still seemed new and untried.

there had been a great deal of technological progress throughout the Middle Ages...it is puzzling that its psychological effects seem to have been very

---

[390] Citation from Francis Bacon in R. F. Jones, *Ancients and Moderns*, p. 40 For similar views expressed earlier by Bruno, see citation in Butterfield, *The Statecraft of Machiavelli*, pp. 37-46.
[391] R. F. Jones, *Ancients and Moderns*, p. 145.

slight before the fifteenth or sixteenth centuries. It certainly generated no diffused concept of technical progress...an inventor was...a person who found something which had been lost, not one who devised a new solution unknown to previous generations.[392]

What had been 'unknown to previous generations' was so obscured before printing that finding 'something which had been lost' was often equivalent to devising 'a new solution.' If early modern scientists 'represented their contributions as the mere restoration of ancient wisdom, lost since the Fall and surviving only in coterie circles' it was not necessarily because 'they wanted to conceal the fact of innovation.' Rather they were living in an era when the process of innovation was just beginning to be detached from renovation and just beginning to assume the meaning assigned to it today.

Because the 'mere restoration of ancient wisdom' has by now been completely drained of its inspirational content, we are likely to overlook its many contributions to cognitive advance in an early age. We are also likely to misinterpret the effect of attributing superior feats in all fields to the ancients. Far from hindering innovation, belief in prior superlative performance encouraged emulators to reach beyond their normal grasp. The notion that supreme mastery of a given art had been obtained under divine dispensation in an earlier golden age linked imitation to inspiration. Much as a new form of music-drama, the opera, was created as a way of resurrecting Greek drama, so too new ocean routes were developed while searching for fountains of youth and cities of gold. Even the 'invention' of central perspective may have been sparked by efforts to reconstruct lost illustrations to an ancient Alexandrian text. Only after ancient texts had been more permanently fixed to printed pages would the study of 'dead' letters or the search for primary sources seem incompatible with the release of creative energies or the claim to be specially inspired.

'Back to the classics' and 'back to nature' are now seen as two separate themes which the humanists managed to intertwine; when Giotto won praise from Boccaccio and the painter's capacity to render lifelike forms was celebrated as part of the revival. 'The inclusion of painting in the theory of revival...resulted...in a kind of bifurcation...To Petrarch's principal theme, "back to the classics," Boccaccio... opposed as a counterpoint, the theme, "back to nature"; and the

---

[392] Thomas, *Religion and the Decline of Magic*, p. 430.

interweaving of these two themes was to play a decisive role in human-ist thought...'[393] I think these slogans have been coined too recently, however, to convey scribal themes accurately. 'Back to the classics' evokes games of books and authors which scribal scholars could not play, and bound volumes arrayed on bookshelves in a format they never saw. 'Back to nature' also has anachronistic, post-romantic over-tones and points to later divisions between academician and artist, pedant and poet.

In Boccaccio's words as cited by Panofsky: 'Giotto brought the art of painting' not back to nature but 'back from the grave.' This theme was scarcely 'opposed as a counterpoint' to that favored by Petrarch. Arts and letters (as quattrocento literati never seemed to tire of saying) had been reborn together and had begun to flourish together just as they had in the days of Pliny and Cicero.[394] Insofar as praise was given to the Florentine painter for simulating nature, it was because Pliny had thus described the praise given to painters in antiquity[395] rather than because some new naturalistic theme was being introduced. In other words, the two slogans were still fused. No bifurcation took place. The recovery of lost arts was firmly linked to the retrieval of old books. Thus when Ghiberti deplored the destruction of antiquities by zealots he had in mind book-burnings as well as iconoclasm: '...thus were destroyed not only statues and paintings, but the books and commentaries and handbooks and rules on which men relied for their training in this great and excellent and gentle art...'[396] From the viewpoint of quattrocento artists and writers, removing distortion from images was naturally related to removing corruption from texts. Retrieving the writings of the ancients went together with the idea of restoring forms to their natural state.

By recognizing that veneration for the ancients took a different form in the age of scribes from the one it took later on, we may be in a better position to understand changing views of the Renaissance itself.

[393] Panofsky, Renaissance and Renascences, p. 19. That Boccaccio was actually reweaving a theme he derived from Dante, when he praised Giotto, is noted on p. 13.

[394] A discussion of how art history was patterned by Renaissance humanists on models furnished by Aristotle, Cicero and Pliny is in Gombrich, Norm and Form, pp. 100–1. Also pp. 1–10. For the most illuminating recent full-length treatment see two books by Baxandall, Giotto and Painting and Experience in 15th Century Italy.

[395] Petrarch's copy of Pliny's Natural History was heavily annotated especially at passages concerning Apelles, according to Baxandall, Giotto, pp. 62–3.

[396] Cited in Chabod, Machiavelli, p. 153.

With this change of emphasis from things religious to things secular, the significance of the old metaphor became reversed: Antiquity, so long considered as a 'Dark Age' now became a time of 'light' which had to be restored: the era following Antiquity, on the other hand was submerged in obscurity.[397]

Those who first celebrated a rebirth of ancient arts and letters, however, were not necessarily registering a shift of emphasis from religious to secular concerns. The 'metaphor of light and darkness' did not necessarily 'lose its original religious value as it came to have a literary connotation.'[398] In early fourteenth-century Avignon the application of luminary metaphors to recent recovery of ancient texts was not peculiar to the Florentine poet. Clerical compilers of preachers' manuals – of the very compendia Petrarch disliked – used the same metaphor, and with a 'literary' connotation.[399] As for the special interest of the early humanists in the restoration of the classical canons – in achieving eloquence in speech or symmetry and natural proportions in art; it may be misconstrued if taken as pointing away from 'things religious to things secular.' Even the rejection of Gothic styles as barbaric and corrupt might well indicate spiritual aspirations in an age when the very heavens – the abode of God and His angels – were believed to be fashioned along classical lines. Here it is useful to recall a point made earlier – one that believers in a unified *Zeitgeist* neglect: Grecian heavens had been recovered in the age of the Gothic cathedral and scholastic philosophy.[400] The domes and the circular floor plans of Renaissance churches echoed a divine order envisioned in Aquinas' age.

Post-romantic generations find it natural to relate the summas of schoolmen, medieval Latin and Gothic cathedrals with Christian faith; but early humanists were unaware that stained glass, pointed arches, or Church Latin reflected the 'Génie du Christianisme'. They saw nothing edifying in scholastic glosses or stone gargoyles. Artifacts produced between the fall of Rome and the Black Death had not been

---

[397] Mommsen, 'Petrarch's Conception,' p. 228. This influential article is acknowledged by Panofsky, *Renaissance and Renascences*, p. 10, n. 1 as the basis for his own similar interpretation.

[398] Franco Simone is thus cited by Mommsen, 'Petrarch's Conception,' p. 227.

[399] See discussion by Richard H. and Mary A. Rouse, 'The Texts Called Lumen Anime,' esp. pp. 12, 22. One of these compilations was sponsored by an Avignon Pope during the period of Petrarch's residence there. On the role of Avignon in the Petrarchan revival and Petrarch's distate for florilegia and compendia, see Simone, *The French Renaissance*, chap. 1, esp. p. 47.

[400] See reference to Lovejoy's interpretation, above, p. 215.

classified – let alone viewed as tokens of a distinctive Christian culture. Garbled syntax and grotesque imagery simply testified to the havoc wrought by heathen hordes. Panofsky refers to Petrarch's 'almost heretical notion of the Christian Middle Ages as a period of darkness.'[401] Whereas Gibbon *did* link the triumph of Christianity to that of barbarism, it seems likely that Petrarch did not and that the notion of a 'Christian Middle Ages' was foreign to his thought. That Christian truths had been obscured by barbarism was not an 'almost heretical notion' and was more compatible with Petrarch's outlook.[402] Vandalism, like plague and war, still signified God's wrath for the early humanists. The tower of Babel, the confusion of tongues, the loss and corruption of texts went together with other catastrophes.[403] All pointed to a withdrawal of divine guidance.

What did Petrarch mean to say by using this word 'tenebrae?' asks Mommsen. He is referring to Petrarch's letter to Agapito Colonna where the poet excuses himself for failing to mention the Colonna family. After citing Petrarch's comment: 'I did not wish for the sake of so few famous names to guide my pen so far and through such darkness. Therefore...I have determined to fix a limit to my history long before this century,' Mommsen poses the question:

What did Petrarch mean to say by using this word 'tenebrae'? In his opinion was this period dark simply because the lack of sources prevented the historian shedding light on it? Or was it dark because the 'lamps had gone out all over Europe' for a time of more than a thousand years? With this alternative we come to the crucial point in the interpretation of Petrarch's conception of history. For the acceptance of the second assumption would mean that Petrarch passed a very definite judgement of value upon the long era in question.[404]

Before accepting the second assumption (and marvelling at the way Petrarch anticipated Sir Edward Grey) one might pause longer over the first alternative – if only to wonder why it is so casually dismissed.

---

[401] Panofsky, 'Erasmus and the Visual Arts,' p. 201. On Panofsky's neo-Hegelian desire to demonstrate the organic unity of the Christian, Gothic and scholastic middle ages, see perceptive comment by Gombrich, *In Search of Cultural History*, p. 28.

[402] That Petrarch sought to corroborate Christian truths in returning to pure classical sources and never imagined that classical and Christian truths might diverge is stressed by Simone, *French Renaissance*, p. 47.

[403] Did the Black Death, which was associated with a decline of learning in prefaces to the charters of Perugia, Siena, Pavia and other city states, contribute to the sense of a recent dark age among the early humanists? See Campbell, *The Black Death*, pp. 149, 161.

[404] Mommsen, 'Petrarch's Conception,' p. 395.

A 'lack of sources,' which is treated by Mommsen as a trivial excuse, was probably of crucial concern to a scribal scholar. It also appears to be less an alternative than a complement to the second assumption. Would not regret over barbarian invasions be complementary to regret over a dearth of usable records? As an earlier discussion has suggested, the sheer difficulty of unravelling the tangled chronicles of barbarian kingdoms should not be underestimated.[405] Petrarch's dark age, Hanna Gray has suggested, was not completely devoid of talented or noble men but did lack the eloquence needed to preserve the memory of such men.[406] A loss of eloquence meant an impairment of the collective memory. It led to a prolonged 'slumber of forgetfulness,' as Petrarch put it. Of course, a negative value-judgment was entailed in assigning darkness to the age. But this negative judgment was passed on a millennium that was relatively blank as well as black – not filled with the specific Christian significance assigned to it later on.

'This slumber of forgetfulness will not last forever. After the darkness has been dispelled, our grandsons will be able to walk back into the pure radiance of the past.'[407] When Petrarch wrote this celebrated passage, he was probably not attributing a 'gloomy ignorance' to Christian culture after the conversion of Constantine, but rather evoking a loss of memory which scribal scholars attributed to a fall from grace.[408] When he expressed hope that darkness would be dispelled and former radiance restored, was he 'transferring to the state of intellectual culture' a metaphor previously applied to 'the state of the soul?'[409] It seems more likely that he coupled soul with intellect, thought of knowledge as a form of recalling what was imprinted on the soul, regarded divine wisdom as the source of all radiance and attributed what he admired about antiquity to inspiration from this source. That he was preoccupied, as a poet and scholar, with the loss of classical texts – particularly those relating to the *ars memorandi* and rules of rhetoric – seems very probable. That he objected to florilegia and glosses and sought a return to 'pure' sources is evident. That he

---

405 See reference to Aeneas Sylvius Piccolomini above, n. 68.
406 Gray, 'Renaissance Humanism,' p. 503.
407 Citation from Petrarch in Panofsky, *Renaissance and Renascences*, p. 10.
408 On Petrarch's concern with the *ars memorandi*, and how this concern linked him with Aquinas see Yates, *Art of Memory*, pp. 109–13. How preoccupation with loss of memory (which loomed large in all scribal endeavors) may have entered into early humanist ideas about a revival and also into their 'pursuit of eloquence,' as described by Hanna Gray is worth further thought. Eloquence was regarded as a 'fixative' by the Christian humanists according to Rice, 'The Humanist Idea,' p. 130.   409 Panofsky, *Renaissance and Renascences*, pp. 10–11.

hoped true eloquence and Roman glory could be revived is also quite clear. But I cannot see why it is necessary to assume that he was effecting a 'complete reversal of accepted values' or revolutionizing the interpretation of history when he contrasted recent darkness with past radiance.

In medieval monasteries, where the love of learning went together with the desire for God, distinctions between sacred and profane had long been blurred by a complex system of correspondences between earthly and heavenly kingdoms and by the use of historic personages as mnemonic devices to reinforce Christian truths.[410] Even in the most orthodox religious circles, the concept of antiquity contained too many Christian ancestors and prophets – was too well illuminated by 'the light from the East' and too richly embroidered by allegory – to be simply described as a 'dark age.' At the time Petrarch was writing, it was difficult to distinguish between pagan poets in the guise of Christian prophets and church fathers in the guise of men of letters. Both demonstrated mastery of Latin prose-styles; both seemed by their eloquence to have been specially inspired.[411] It is not entirely clear just where Petrarch placed the onset of darkness (with the conversion of Constantine or the accession of barbarian emperors) but wherever he placed it, pagan prophecy had already been fulfilled and the Incarnation had occurred. Petrarch's golden age included witnesses, apostles and martyrs to the true faith. It encompassed the crucifixion and resurrection. Surely no traditional values had to be reversed in order to describe this interval as bright; only impious men could describe it as dark. Similarly, Petrarch's program of purifying Latin and reviving Greek went together with reverence for Gospel truths and patristic teachings – as later Christian humanists would spell out.

To be sure, Jerome had worried about being a better Ciceronian than he was a Christian and this same concern seems to have troubled Petrarch and Boccaccio – as it did Erasmus later on.[412] If they were

---

[410] That antiquity was *not* viewed as a dark age by monastic scholars is documented by Leclercq, *The Love of Learning, passim.* How the memory arts were used for didactic Christian purposes (including memorizing sermons) is shown by Yates, *Art of Memory,* pp. 55–7, 85. The use of figures such as Plato and Aristotle to stand for groups of things to be memorized is discussed on p. 250.

[411] That the Church fathers were considered as classical men of letters is spelled out by Rice, 'The Humanist Idea,' p. 130. An example of the way lines drawn by Augustine between pagan and Christian were blurred by a fourteenth-century Dominican commenting on the *City of God* is noted by Smalley, *English Friars,* pp. 61–3.

[412] See description of Boccaccio's crisis of conscience in Meiss, *Painting in Florence,* chap. 7.

troubled, however, this was not because values had been reversed but because a traditional ambivalence, which had always marked the vocation of Christian scholars, was still being manifested.[413] The point is that the 'dark ages' as perceived by the humanists had obscured the wisdom of Ciceronian and Christian alike. The words of apostles and disciples had been garbled along with those of senators and sages; patristic texts disfigured along with pagan ones. Even the human form, molded by the Creator, had been twisted out of shape by graceless clumsy hands – so that the miracle of Incarnation itself was obscured.[414] The urge to penetrate Gothic darkness was, in short, still not detached from the hope of coming closer to Christian truth.

the whole idea of the Italian 'rinascita' is inseparably connected with the notion of the preceding era as an age of obscurity. The people living in that 'renascence' thought of it as a time of revolution. They wanted to break away from the medieval past and all its traditions and they were convinced that they had effected such a break...[415]

Significantly enough, most of the terms used in this citation, insofar as they *were* current during the quattrocento[416] have shifted their meaning since then. The wish 'to break away from the medieval past and all its traditions' no longer conveys a desire to master Latin grammar, read the Church fathers, or restore texts and images to their original state. Revolution (as many studies note) also means something quite different to us than it did to Machiavelli and Copernicus. The idea of a 'rinascita' was similarly affected. 'While the humanists' antiquity and the philosophes' antiquity were not the same, they were kin' writes Peter Gay; 'the first was to the second as an illuminated manu-

---

[413] It seems likely that some of the concern expressed by quattrocento humanists about the wrecking of ancient Roman culture reflected dismay about the 'burning of vanities' by zealots in Florence. An illuminated manuscript of Petrarch's own works went up in flames on one such occasion in the 1490s. Wardrop, *Script of Humanism*, p. 9, n. 1.

[414] That a shift from a 'spiritual and abstract' concern with the Logos or Godhead to a more 'naturalistic' concern with the Incarnation can be detected in medieval art is discussed by Kitzinger's review of Ladner's *Ad Imaginem Dei: The Image of Man in Medieval Art*. See also Trinkaus' *In Our Image and Likeness*, for evidence concerning the way Italian humanists tended to humanize God while deifying man. This movement which occurred within the context of scribal culture was amplified, reinforced and turned in new directions in the context of print culture.

[415] Mommsen, 'Petrarch's Conception,' p. 241.

[416] The phrase 'medieval past' seems somewhat anachronistic, implying as it does a safely distant closed chapter rather than the disorder of recent times. Insofar as the early humanists wrote about a *medium aevum* it was to characterize the *saecula recentiora* and the culture of the *moderni*. See perceptive comment by Trinkaus, 'Humanism, Religion, Society...Recent Studies,' p. 684.

script is to a printed book – an ancestor, a little archaic perhaps but manifestly within the same family.'[417] That a process of transmission had been transformed when the bookhand was replaced by the very similar looking typeface is concealed by this kind of simile. When Petrarch hoped that his descendants might walk back into the 'pure radiance' of the past, his outlook was oriented in an opposite direction from that of Condorcet. Insofar as the Enlightenment may be regarded as an heir of the Renaissance, the notion of a movement away from darkness toward radiance has been preserved. But when the direction of the movement was reversed (so that it pointed toward a clear light of reason that grew ever brighter and away from the pristine sources of ancient wisdom), its implications were transformed as well. The advancement of disciplines was detached from the recovery of ancient learning. Inspiration was set against imitation, moderns against ancients; and the early humanists, themselves, increasingly appeared in a Janus-like guise, looking hopefully in two opposite directions at once.

This is not to deny that the early Italian humanists made much of the 'notion of belonging to a new time.' My point is, rather, that this notion was fundamentally reoriented after it had been introduced, so that an imaginative leap is required for modern scholars to get at its original context. Although intuition or a 'feel for the times' is helpful in making such a leap, it is even more useful to be able to gauge the objective dimensions of the gap that must be bridged. Indiscriminate use of the term 'Renaissance' – which was employed by scribal scholars to describe their cultural revival and later extended to cover changes associated with printing, Protestantism and the Copernican Revolution – seems to be singularly unhelpful for this purpose. 'The breadth of the gulf which separates the age of manuscripts from the age of print is not always nor fully realized by those who read and criticize medieval literature,'[418] notes Chaytor. The remark can be applied much more widely outside Chaytor's own field, but it does seem particularly cogent to Renaissance studies. For in this field, where the gulf must be constantly traversed, its dimensions are still unfathomed and its very existence almost completely concealed.

To return to a remark cited at the beginning of this chapter: I agree that 'something important and revolutionary occurred' between the fourteenth and sixteenth centuries; but disagree with the suggestion

---

[417] Gay, *Enlightenment*, I, 259.   [418] Chaytor, *From Script to Print*, p. 1.

that 'we might as well go on calling that something the Renaissance.'[419] Instead I propose that we break with precedents set by Michelet and Burckhardt and distinguish between the disparate developments now covered by the same label.[420] It makes sense to employ the term Renaissance when referring to a two-phased cultural movement which was initiated by Italian literati and artists in the age of scribes and expanded to encompass many regions and fields of study in the age of print. But needless confusion is engendered when the same term is also used to cover the ensemble of changes which were ushered in by print. Not only is a major communications revolution obscured by this practice; but so, too, is the reorientation of the cultural movement. It becomes difficult to guard against prematurely endowing the Petrarchan revival with the attributes of print culture. A later sense of antiquity 'as a totality cut off from the present' is thus confusingly coupled with an early sense of antiquity on the verge of being reborn.

In an interesting comment which prepares the way for my next chapter, Peter Burke points out that the demand of early sixteenth-century reformers to return to early Christian practices had both an historical and an 'unhistorical' aspect. The demand illustrates a 'new sense of history' Burke asserts, 'for it implies an awareness that the Church had changed over time. Of course the reformers also thought that it would be possible to go back to the primitive Church, a view we might find "unhistorical" – but that is a separate point.'[421] When these two separate points are not kept separate, paradoxical hybrid

[419] See citation from Warnke's review, above, p. 165.
[420] In using the term 'Renaissance' to cover an epoch which featured 'the discovery of the world and of man,' Michelet did not merely precede Burckhardt (as is noted by Simone, *The French Renaissance*, pp. 33–4; 112–13 and W. K. Ferguson, *Renaissance in Historical Thought*, pp. 177–8). He also combined the practices of Gabriel Naudé, who applied the term to a phase of French culture, with those of Condorcet, who dropped the term from his scheme of world history. Michelet thus renamed Condorcet's 8th period – which ran from the invention of printing to the age of Bacon, Galileo, Descartes. See Michelet, *Histoire de France* VII, introduction, chaps. 7 and 17. (Michelet's profession of faith as the son of a printer, pp. 294–5, links him to Condorcet whose 'hymn to print' is in the opening sections of the 'Huitième Période' of the *Esquisse*, pp. 177–83.) While repeating Michelet's phrases, and continuing to point to the same era (of Galileo *et al.*) Burckhardt, *Civilization of the Renaissance*, took an opposite tack, completely by-passing printing while remaining in Italy. He started with the Petrarchan *rinascita*, drew heavily on the memoirs of the ms. bookdealer, Vespasiano da Bisticci (who scorned the new presses) and credited to Italian native genius all the discoveries encompassed by Michelet's 'Renaissance.' (The distracting effect of this 'primacy of Italy' thesis upon the history of science is noted in chap. 5, volume II below.) Thus Burckhardt did not merely restore to the Italian movement a label which French historians had, in a sense, misappropriated. He also fused the scribal *rinascita* in Italy with all the developments in world history that Condorcet had launched with printing.
[421] Burke, *Renaissance Sense of the Past*, p. 40.

constructs are created – such as the notion of a 'permanent Renais-sance.' A rebirth which is permanent is a contradiction in terms. Living things are perishable; only dead ones can be embalmed and indefinitely preserved. The idea of permanent post-mortem, which (alas) may be compatible with modern academic history, is at odds with the sense of quickening manifested in the cultural movement called the Renaissance.

Please note that this point is intended to apply to both phases of the cultural movement – to the age of Erasmus as well as that of Petrarch. In terms of the scheme tried out in this chapter, the communications shift does *not* coincide with the beginning of a modern historical con-sciousness but rather precedes it by a century or more. The past could not be set at a fixed distance until a uniform spatial and temporal framework had been constructed. This did not occur until the age of Mercator, Ortelius, Scaliger and Gesner – that is until after the first century of printing. By then, as an earlier citation from Myron Gil-more suggests, the Renaissance was over. As with most vital move-ments, it proved to be impermanent after all.

By prolonging a process of retrieval while draining it of its inspira-tional significance, the preservative powers of print seem to have had a negative and largely deadening effect. From the viewpoint of roman-tic critics of modern culture at all events, the academic historian appears to be a bloodless desiccated creature in comparison with the Renais-sance Man. Yet it must be remembered that early humanists, from Petrarch to Valla, owe their still vital reputation as culture-heroes to the prosaic print-made knowledge industry. They would not now be heralded as founding fathers of historical scholarship if it were not for the new forms of continuity and incremental change which came after their work was done. Earlier scholars had been less fortunate.

Perhaps a counterfactual proposition should be entertained to bring out the significance of the accident of timing which produced the two-phased cultural movement now called the Renaissance. In view of the thriving manuscript book trade in thirteenth-century university towns, it is at least conceivable that movable type (had it been developed by a goldsmith at the time) might have been welcomed by the teaching and preaching orders and by medieval merchants in the age of Inno-cent III. It is also possible that the invention might have been delayed until the early sixteenth century and thus come after the French invasions of Italy, the sack of Rome and the dispersal of Greek refugee colonies. In either case it seems likely that a different kind of cultural movement – one which owed less to the native genius, civic loyalties, mercantile activities and Mediterranean traditions of quattrocento Italians – would now be heralded as supplying the 'first-born sons of modern Europe.' Had printing not come until the sixteenth century the Italian revival might well have resembled the so-called 'proto-humanist' movement of the twelfth century. Instead of a gradual loss of vitality, there would have been swift death – even before a full flowering could occur.

It also should be noted (no longer in a counter-factual vein) that the full flowering of high Renaissance culture in cinquecento Italy owed much to early printers – especially to those in Venice where not only Greek and Hebrew publishing but vernacular translations, new compositions in the 'lingua volgare,' the arts of woodcut and engraving, and the first Grub Street sub-culture, also thrived. In this light, emphasis on the devitalizing and negative effects of the new medium needs to be balanced by considering its stimulating effect on inventive and imaginative faculties and its contributions to a heightened sense of individuality and personality – a sense which continues to distinguish Western civilization from other civilizations even now.

One more observation is in order before moving on to the next chapter. It would be a mistake to assume (as media analysts sometimes do) that the advent of printing affected all vital movements in the same way. As our brief indulgence in counter-factual speculation suggests, the regional location of the movement, the specific content of the textual tradition, and above all the 'accident' of timing have to be taken into account. Under the aegis of the early presses, a classical revival in Italy was reoriented. Under the same auspices, German Protestantism was born.

4

THE SCRIPTURAL TRADITION
RECAST: RESETTING THE STAGE
FOR THE REFORMATION

I. INTRODUCTION

Between 1517 and 1520, Luther's thirty publications probably sold well over 300,000 copies... Altogether in relation to the spread of religious ideas it seems difficult to exaggerate the significance of the Press, without which a revolution of this magnitude could scarcely have been consummated. Unlike the Wycliffite and Waldensian heresies, Lutheranism was from the first the child of the printed book, and through this vehicle Luther was able to make exact, standardized and ineradicable impressions on the mind of Europe. For the first time in human history a great reading public judged the validity of revolutionary ideas through a mass-medium which used the vernacular languages together with the arts of the journalist and the cartoonist...[1]

As this citation suggests, the impact of print, which is often overlooked in discussions of the Renaissance, is less likely to go unnoted in Reformation studies. In this latter field, historians confront a movement that was shaped at the very outset (and in large part ushered in) by the new powers of the press. 'The Reformation was the first religious movement,' it has been said, 'which had the aid of the printing press.'[2] Even before Luther however, Western Christendom had already called on printers to help with the crusade against the Turks. Church officials had already hailed the new technology as a gift from God – as a providential invention which proved Western superiority over ignorant infidel forces.[3]

Although the anti-Turkish crusade was thus the 'first religious movement' to make use of print, Protestantism surely was the first fully to

---

[1] Dickens, *Reformation and society*, p. 51.   [2] Louise Holborn, 'Printing,' p. 1.
[3] Geoffroy Atkinson, *Les Nouveaux Horizons*, p. 57. See also Bohnstedt, *The Infidel Scourge of God*.

exploit its potential as a mass medium. It was also the first movement of any kind, religious or secular, to use the new presses for overt propaganda and agitation against an established institution. By pamphleteering directed at arousing popular support and aimed at readers who were unversed in Latin, the reformers unwittingly pioneered as revolutionaries and rabble rousers. They also left 'ineradicable impressions' in the form of broadsides and caricatures. Designed to catch the attention and arouse the passions of sixteenth-century readers, their antipapist cartoons still have a strong impact when encountered in history books today. By its very nature then, the exploitation of the new medium by Protestants is highly visible to modern scholars.

Moreover the reformers were aware that the printing press was useful to their cause and they acknowledged its importance in their writings. The theme of printing as proof of spiritual and cultural superiority, first sounded by Rome in its crusade against 'illiterate' Turks, was taken over by German humanists trying to counter Italian claims. Gutenberg had already joined Arminius as a native culture-hero before he gained added stature for providing Lutheran preachers and princes and knights with their most effective weapon in their gallant struggle against popes.[4] Luther, himself, described printing as 'God's highest and extremest act of grace, whereby the business of the Gospel is driven forward.' It was typical of the Protestant outlook that he also regarded it as 'the last flame before the extinction of the world.'[5] Others who did not share his religious outlook might regard man's future on earth as being indefinitely extended and could thus associate printing with progressive enlightenment. Luther believed, on the contrary, that the forward movement of history was soon to be terminated by the day of judgment. Many later Protestants, like early humanists, still looked back and not ahead when seeking to overcome Gothic darkness and move toward an age of light. When John Foxe heralded 'the excellent arte of printing most happily of late found out...to the singular benefite of Christe's Church' he was thinking about the restoration of 'the lost light of knowledge to these blynde times' and 'the reneuing of holsome and auncient writers whose doinges and teachinges otherwise had lyen in oblivion.'[6]

---

[4] Spitz, *The Religious Renaissance*, pp. 84–5. See also Hajo Holborn, *Ulrich von Hutten*, p. 42.
[5] Luther's remarks cited by Black, 'The Printed Bible,' p. 432.
[6] John Foxe, preface to a collection of Protestant texts (1572) cited by Aston, 'Lollardy,' p. 169. See also Aston, 'John Wycliffe's Reformation Reputation,' pp. 23–52, for account of how Foxe

Nevertheless the epoch-making role assigned printing in Protestant schemes marked a departure from previous historiography. From Luther on, the sense of a special blessing conferred on the German nation was associated with Gutenberg's invention, which emancipated the Germans from bondage to Rome and brought the light of true religion to a God-fearing people. The mid-century German historian, Johann Sleidan developed this theme in an *Address to the Estates of the Empire* of 1542, a polemic which was republished more than once.

As if to offer proof that God has chosen us to accomplish a special mission, there was invented in our land a marvelous new and subtle art, the art of printing. This opened German eyes even as it is now bringing enlightenment to other countries. Each man became eager for knowledge, not without feeling a sense of amazement at his former blindness.[7]

The same theme was taken over by the Marian exiles and exploited in a manner that suited Elizabethan statecraft. By associating printing with the providential mission of a prospering expansive realm, the English Protestants pointed the way to later trends – to revolutionary messianism in the Old World and Manifest Destiny in the New. '...the art of Printing will so spread knowledge, that the common people, knowing their own rights and liberties will not be governed by way of oppression and so, little by little, all kingdoms will be like to Macaria...'[8] Protestant divines diverged from Enlightened *philosophes* on many issues. But both viewed printing as a providential device which ended forever a priestly monopoly of learning, overcame ignorance and superstition, pushed back the evil forces commanded by Italian popes, and, in general, brought Western Europe out of the dark ages.[9]

followed 'where John Bale had led' and of early use of 'luminary metaphors' by eulogists of Wycliffe. A reference to the 'cleare light which God hath now reveiled' accompanies the translators' preface to the Geneva Bible and represents their recognition of the work of the first generation of scholar–printers on biblical texts. Lloyd Berry, introduction, *The Geneva Bible*, pp. 10–11.

[7] Cited by Gerald Strauss, 'The Course of German History,' p. 684. The theme of Germany opening her eyes after the scholastics had wrapped religion in darkness was already sounded by Ulrich von Hutten during the pre-Lutheran controversy over Reuchlin and the 'obscure men.' See passage cited by Overfield, 'A New Look at the Reuchlin Affair,' p. 205.

[8] Gabriel Plattes, 'A Description of the Famous Kingdome of Macaria' (1641) in Webster, *Samuel Hartlib*, p. 89. Compared with Luther's 'last flame' before the end of the world, this interpretation provides a fine example of the movement from millennium to utopia, described by Ernest Tuveson, and recently documented by Webster, *The Great Instauration*, chap. 1. (That Gabriel Plattes rather than Samuel Hartlib was the author of 'Macaria' is noted by Webster on p. 47.)

[9] Foxe's world-historical scheme which stresses printing is discussed by W. Ferguson, *The Renaissance in Historical Thought*, pp. 54; 97. References linking papal control of the 'kingdom

The Lord began to work for His Church not with sword and target to sub-
due His exalted adversary, but with printing, writing and reading...How
many presses there be in the world, so many block-houses there be against
the high castle of St. Angelo, so that either the pope must abolish knowledge
and printing or printing must at length root him out.[10]

Printing and Protestantism seem to go together naturally as printing
and the Renaissance do not, partly because vestiges of early historical
schemes are carried over into present accounts. The new presses were
not developed until after Petrarch's death and had no bearing on early
concepts of a 'rináscita'; whereas they were in full operation before
Luther was born and did enter into his views of a religious reformation.
In the latter case, moreover, they affected events as well as ideas and
actually presided over the initial act of revolt.

When Luther proposed debate over his Ninety-Five Theses his
action was not in and of itself revolutionary. It was entirely conventional for professors of theology to hold disputations over an issue such
as indulgences and 'church doors were the customary place for medieval publicity.'[11] But these particular theses did not stay tacked to the
church door (if indeed they were ever really placed there).[12] To a
sixteenth-century Lutheran chronicler, 'it almost appeared as if the
angels themselves had been their messengers and brought them before
the eyes of all the people.'[13] Luther himself expressed puzzlement, when addressing Pope Leo X six months after the initial
event:

It is a mystery to me how my theses, more so than my other writings, indeed,
those of other professors were spread to so many places. They were meant
exclusively for our academic circle here...They were written in such a

of darkness' with unenlightened superstitions about 'fairies, ghosts, and spirits' may be found
in Hobbes' *Leviathan*, as noted by Willey, *The Seventeenth Century Background*, p. 96.

[10] Cited from Foxe's *Book of Martyrs* by Haller, *The Elect Nation*, p. 110. See also pertinent
citation and discussion in Heath, *The English Parish Clergy*, p. 193.

[11] G. R. Elton, *Reformation Europe*, p. 15.

[12] Iserloh, *The Theses Were Not Posted* does not prove the event did not occur but shows there is
no reliable contemporary evidence that it did occur. Heinrich Grimm, 'Luther's "Ablassthesen,"' pp. 139–50, believes a hand-copied text was nailed on the church door but in mid-Nov-
ember rather than October 31. Harold J. Grimm, 'Introduction to Ninety-Five Theses', *Career
of the Reformer* I, 22–3 states that the text was printed before being nailed. That the last word
on whether the Theses were nailed or mailed has not been spoken is noted by McNally, 'The
Ninety-Five Theses of Martin Luther,' p. 461n. I imagine the same point applies to whether
they were first duplicated by hand or in print. The literature cited in Heinrich Grimm's
article should be consulted in any case.

[13] Myconius, selection from *Historia Reformationis*, *The Reformation*, ed. and tr. Hans Hillerbrand, p. 47.

language that the common people could hardly understand them. They...
use academic categories...[14]

According to a modern scholar, it is still 'one of the mysteries of Reformation history how this proposal for academic disputation, written in Latin, could have kindled such enthusiastic support and thereby have such far-reaching impact.'[15]

Precisely when were Luther's theses first printed outside Wittenberg? Just who was responsible for their being translated into German at first and then into other vernaculars? How did it happen that, soon after being printed in a handful of towns, such as Nuremberg, Leipzig and Basel, copies were multiplied in such quantities and distributed so widely that the Theses won top billing throughout central Europe – competing for space with news of the Turkish threat in print shop, book stall and country fair?[16] These questions cannot be answered in detail here.[17] I have posed them simply to direct attention to the important intermediate stages between the academic proposal and the popular acclaim. The mystery, in other words, is primarily the result of skipping over the process whereby a message ostensibly directed at a few could be made accessible to the many. If we want to dispel it, instead of jumping directly from church door to public clamor, we should move more cautiously, a step at a time, looking at the activities of the printers, translators, and distributors, who acted as agents of the change. Probably we ought to pause with particular care over the interval in December 1517 when three separate editions were printed almost simultaneously by printers located in three separate towns.[18]

[14] Luther, letter May 30, 1518 in Hillerbrand, ed. *The Reformation*, p. 54. That 'Luther took no steps to spread his theses among the people...' and 'General dissemination was not in Luther's mind when he posted the theses,' is asserted by Bainton, *Here I Stand*, pp. 63 4.

[15] Hillerbrand, ed. *The Reformation*, p. 32.

[16] The rapid distribution of news about Luther's protest is brought out by Hillerbrand, 'Spread of the Protestant Reformation,' and Kortepeter, 'German Zeitung Literature,' p. 115.

[17] According to Harold J. Grimm, 'Introduction to Ninety-Five Theses,' pp. 22–3, and Schweibert, *Luther and His Times*, p. 315, the first printing was done by Johann Grünenberg of Wittenberg. Heinrich Grimm, 'Luther's "Ablassthesen,"' p. 142 disagrees, stating that there was no suitable Wittenberg printer so that Luther had to turn to the Leipzig shop of Jacob Thanner. His low opinion of Grünenberg's presswork and suitability runs counter to that offered by Grossman, 'Wittenberg Printing.' For data on the printer: Johannes Rhau-Grünenberg, active in Wittenberg 1508–25, see Benzing, *Buchdrucker-lexicon des 16 Jahrhunderts* (*Deutsches Sprachgebiet*), p. 181. There is agreement, at all events that three separate printers: Hölzel of Nuremberg, Thanner (or Herbipolensis) of Leipzig and Petri of Basel had issued editions by December, 1517.

[18] The likelihood that a 'single directing hand' guided this triple publication is noted by Heinrich Grimm, 'Luther's "Ablassthesen,"' p. 145. The important role played by the 'Sodalitas

It is possible that Luther helped his friends on this occasion. His surprise at the interest he aroused may have entailed self-deception. One of his letters, written in March 1518, reveals his anxious ambivalence over the question of publicity. Although he 'had no wish nor plan to publicize these Theses,' he wrote, he was willing to have his friends do the job for him and left it to them to decide whether the Theses were to be 'suppressed or spread outside.'[19] Given this choice, did he doubt how his friends would choose? 'It is out of the question,' writes Heinrich Grimm, 'for Luther not to have known of the publication of his theses or for them to have been published against his will.'[20] Although Wittenberg was not yet a major printing center, Brother Martin was well acquainted with the new powers of the press. He had already acquired experience editing texts in Latin and German for printers. He had already demonstrated sensitivity to diverse German book markets and discovered that vernacular works appealed to a diversified clientèle.[21]

In addition to investigating just how the message was spread, we also need to look more carefully at the so-called 'academic circle' to which it was first addressed. In this regard, the conventional medieval format of the invitation to debate the Theses was somewhat deceptive. By 1517, the audience for learned disputation had been extended – far beyond earshot of pulpit or lectern. Pre-Reformation controversies had already seen scholars, such as Peter of Ravenna, 'consciously appealing over the heads of...university authorities to general educated opinion through published tracts.'[22] The educated élite who could understand Latin and theological debate was no longer composed only of church-

Staupitziana' in Nuremberg – especially by Christoph Scheurl and Kaspar Nutzel – in getting the Theses printed, in German as well as Latin, is noted by several authorities. See Bebb, 'The Lawyers,' p. 59; also, Gerald Strauss, *Nuremberg*, pp. 160 ff.

[19] Letter to Scheurl, March 5, 1518, cited by Schweibert, 'The Theses and Wittenberg,' p. 142, n. 55.

[20] Heinrich Grimm, 'Luther's "Ablassthesen,"' p. 144. Luther's expressions of disapproval and surprise excluded the printing of the Leipzig version, according to Grimm and were directed only at the Basel and Nuremberg editions. Since Petri in Basel received his copy from Wittenberg friends of Luther and the Staupitz circle sponsored the Nuremberg version Luther's reaction still strikes me as disingenuous. (It is hard to reconcile Grimm's argument here with his reference to a 'single directing hand' noted above, n. 18.)

[21] In a letter of May 6, 1517, Luther wrote to Scheurl saying that he was aiming his German translation of the penitential psalms at 'rude Saxons' not at cultivated Nurembergers and was dismayed that *Die Sieben Busspsalmen* was being read by the latter. Grossman, 'Wittenberg Printing,' p. 73. For other data, see rest of Grossman's article.

[22] Nauert, 'The Clash of Humanists,' p. 7. See also same author's 'Peter of Ravenna.' (The transformation of intra-university disputes into more public forms of controversy is well described on p. 639.)

men and professors. The scholar–printer who presided over the new centers of erudition was usually a layman and rarely had a university degree. Although it was closer to commercial crossroads than to cloistered precincts, the printer's workshop attracted the most learned and disputatious scholars of the day. His products made it possible for academic disputation to be followed from afar. Whether or not the Theses were actually tacked on the door of the castle church in Wittenberg on All Hallows Eve, they were initially read by a small group of learned laymen who were less likely to gather on the church steps than in urban workshops where town and gown met to exchange gossip and news, peer over editors' shoulders, check copy and read proof.[23] There, also, new schemes for promoting bestsellers were being tried out. Given access to presses and booksellers' routes in the early sixteenth century, it required only a small following in a handful of towns to create an unprecedented stir.

A letter from Beatus Rhenanus to Zwingli in 1519 suggests how the tactics employed by the small Latin-reading audience, whom Luther addressed, might produce distant repercussions in a short time. 'He will sell more of Luther's tracts if he has no other to offer,' Zwingli was told by Beatus in a letter recommending a book peddler. The peddler should go from town to town, village to village, house to house, offering nothing but Luther's writings for sale. 'This will virtually force the people to buy them, which would not be the case if there were a wide selection.'[24] The linking of concern about salvation with shrewd business tactics and a so-called 'hard-sell' seems to have been no less pronounced in the early sixteenth century than among Bible salesmen today. Deliberate exploitation of the new medium helps to explain the paradox, which is noted in many Reformation studies, that a return to early Christian Church traditions somehow served to usher in modern times.

'Rarely has one invention had more decisive influence than that of printing on the Reformation.' Luther 'had invited a public disputation and nobody had come to dispute.' Then 'by a stroke of magic he found

[23] A good view of Erasmus at work in Froben's press room in Basel surrounded by a boisterous group who read what he set down and responded to it on the spot is offered by Tracy, 'Erasmus,' p. 288.

[24] Letter of June 2, 1519 from Beatus to Zwingli in Hillerbrand, ed. *The Reformation*, p. 125. (See also pp. 123ff. for correspondence pertaining to distribution of Ninety-Five Theses.) On Zwingli's organizing colportage of Luther's books and for other relevant data, see Hillerbrand, 'Spread of the Protestant Reformation,' p. 274.

himself addressing the whole world.'[25] Here is an example of revolutionary causation where normally useful distinctions between precondition and precipitant are difficult to maintain.[26] For there seems to be general agreement that Luther's act in 1517 *did* precipitate the Protestant Revolt. October 31 'continues to be celebrated in Lutheran countries as the anniversary of the Reformation and justly so. The controversy over indulgences brought together the man and the occasion: it signalled the end of the medieval Church.'[27] To understand how Luther's Theses served as such a signal, we cannot afford to stand at the door of the Castle Church in Wittenberg looking for something tacked there. If we stay at the Wittenberg church with Luther we will miss seeing the historical significance of the event. As Maurice Gravier pointed out, it was largely because traditional forms of theological disputation had been transformed by entirely new publicity techniques that the act of the German monk had such a far-reaching effect.[28]

The theses...were said to be known throughout Germany in a fortnight and throughout Europe in a month...Printing was recognized as a new power and publicity came into its own. In doing for Luther what the copyists had done for Wycliffe, the printing presses transformed the field of communications and fathered an international revolt. It was a revolution.[29]

The advent of printing was an important precondition for the Protestant Reformation taken as a whole; for without it one could not implement a 'priesthood of all believers.' At the same time, however, the new medium also acted as a precipitant. It provided 'the stroke of magic' by which an obscure theologian in Wittenberg managed to shake Saint Peter's throne.

In this respect, the contrast drawn by several authorities between the fate of Luther who had the new vehicle at his disposal and that of earlier heretics who did not is worth more extended discussion.[30] According to Dickens, Lollardy 'could become no more than an abortive Reformation' partly because 'it lacked access to the printing press until after 1530.'[31] One wonders whether the same thing could be said about

[25] Rupp, *Luther's Progress*, p. 54.   [26] Stone, *Social Change*, p. xxii discusses this distinction.
[27] G. R. Elton, *Reformation Europe*, p. 15.   [28] Gravier, *Luther et L'Opinion Publique*, p. 19.
[29] Aston, *The Fifteenth Century*, p. 76.
[30] That Hus and Wycliffe were separated from Luther by a technical discovery as well as by time, circumstances and conviction is noted by Aston, *The Fifteenth Century*, p. 50. Apart from citations given above, see also more extended treatment in Dickens, *The English Reformation*, chap. 2 and pertinent discussion by Henri Hauser, *La Naissance du Protestantisme*, pp. 51ff.
[31] Dickens, *English Reformation*, p. 37.

Waldensians or Hussites. John Foxe had no doubts that it could: 'although through might be stopped the mouth of John Huss,' he wrote, 'God hath opened the press to preach, whose voice the Pope is never able to stop with all the puissance of his triple crown.'[32] Protestant polemics however are far from offering adequate guidance. Just how did the advent of printing actually affect the heresies that were current during the later middle ages? The problem calls for much more thought and study than can be given here.[33] Previous discussion of the problem of the Renaissance, however, points to a line of analysis that might be worth pursuing further. It may be helpful, in other words, to keep typographical fixity in mind when comparing the sixteenth-century upheaval with previous religious developments. Thus medieval heresies can be distinguished from the Protestant Revolt in much the same manner as medieval revivals from the Italian Renaissance. In both instances, localized transitory effects were superseded by widespread permanent ones. In both, lines were traced back as well as forward, so that culture heroes and heresiarchs gained increased stature as founding fathers of movements that expanded continuously over the course of time. Partly because religious dissent was implemented by print, it could leave a much more indelible and far-reaching impression than dissent had ever left before.[34]

For example, there had been many schisms within the Western Church. Popes had often been at odds with emperors and kings; with

[32] Cited from a nineteenth-century edition of the *Book of Martyrs* by D. M. Loades, in 'The Theory and Practice of Censorship,' p. 146.

[33] According to Leff, *Heresy* I, 47, the heresies were defined within the context of a Catholic Church that was co-extensive with Western Christendom and could only exist within that context. After the Protestant revolt, they came to an end, almost by definition, along with the medieval church. Just how they 'passed into the Reformation,' however, is left open by Leff. The Lollard revival, undertaken by Foxe and others who fully exploited print, retrieved texts and wrote eulogies has been examined by Dickens, Aston and others. How the Waldensians (by contributing to the printing of Olivetan's French translation of the Bible, for example) entered into Calvinist developments might be worth more study. That early waves of Protestantism in southern France came to regions already penetrated by Waldensian propaganda and vernacular Bibles and psalters is noted by LeRoy Ladurie, *Les Paysans* I, 334. (The section of this work entitled 'Les Chemins de L'Ecriture,' pp. 333–56 is full of relevant data.) A program for studying the effect of print on Italian heresies is outlined by de Frede, 'Per la Storia.' See Gravier, *Luther et L'Opinion Publique*, p. 22 and p. 220, n. 16 for comments on Hussite survival and revival in central Europe.

[34] This line of analysis was already set forth at the 1962 Colloque de Royaumont by Mandrou, 'La Transmission de l'Hérésie.' Mandrou's discussion of the role played by printing in transmitting heresies across space and over time and his analysis of the genres of printed matter: learned tomes, pamphlets, placards used by sixteenth-century heresiarchs deserves to be better known. I owe thanks to J. B. Ross for bringing this highly relevant contribution to my attention and regret that I was unaware of it until after this chapter was written.

church councils, and with rival claimants to the throne. But no episode that occurred from Canossa to Constance – not even a contest between three rival popes – shattered the unity of the Church as decisively or permanently as did the contested divorce case of a sixteenth-century English king. 'The first... campaign ever mounted by any government in any state in Europe' to exploit fully the propaganda potential of the press was that conducted by Thomas Cromwell to back up the actions of Henry VIII.[35] The English minister proved to be as skillful as Luther's German friends in mobilizing propagandists and attracting a large public by vernacular translations. The output of polemical tracts to sway opinion in favor of an anti-papist royal action had occurred before printing, as the campaigns mounted by the councillors of Philip the Fair may suggest. But scribal campaigns had had a shorter wave-resonance and produced more transitory effects.[36] When implemented by print, divisions once traced were etched ever more deeply and could not be easily erased.

Sixteenth-century heresy and schism shattered Christendom so completely that even after religious warfare had ended, ecumenical movements led by men of good will could not put all the pieces together again. Not only were there too many splinter groups, separatists, and independent sects who regarded a central Church government as incompatible with true faith; but the main lines of cleavage had been extended across continents and carried overseas along with Bibles and breviaries. Colonists who crossed a great ocean to arrive safely in the new world offered prayers to the same God, much as had medieval pilgrims or crusaders. But the sign of the cross had become divisive. There was no longer any one language to serve for common prayer. The forms of worship shared by congregations in New England markedly diverged from those of fellow Christians who attended mass in the Baroque churches of New Spain. Within a few generations, the gap between Protestant and Catholic had widened sufficiently to give rise to contrasting literary cultures and life-styles.[37] Long after theology

---

35 Geoffrey Elton, Policy and Police, p. 206. (See also pp. 171ff. for extended discussion and relevant references.) Many other studies note the exploitation of print by Cromwell and his coterie and describe how they promoted vernacular Bibles as well as various tracts.
36 For useful data on just how a given political argument was propagated by being dictated to a group of copyists, see Willard, 'The Manuscripts,' pp. 274–7.
37 For further discussion of Protestant–Catholic cultural divergence centered on disparate reactions to printing, see pp. 409ff., and discussion of scientific publication in chap. 8, volume II below.

had ceased to provoke wars, Christians on both continents were separated from each other by invisible barriers that are still with us today.

2. THE END OF THE MEDIEVAL CHURCH:
ORTHODOX CHRISTIANITY TRANSFORMED

The lasting establishment of anti-papist churches, and the continuous propagation of heterodox faiths was of enormous consequence to Western civilization. But the impact of print on Western Christendom was by no means confined to the implementation of protest or the perpetuation of heterodoxy. Orthodox beliefs and institutions were also affected in ways that should be taken into account.

The invention of the printing press made it possible, for the first time in Christian history, to insist upon uniformity in worship. Hitherto the liturgical texts could be produced only in manuscript, and local variations were inevitably admitted and indeed tolerated. But now printed editions were produced with uniform texts and rubrics. Since the Latin language was retained as the medium of worship in all western countries of the Roman obedience, the same texts could be recited and the same ceremonies performed, in the same way, throughout the Catholic world. At the same time all spontaneous growth and change and adaptation of the liturgy was prevented, and the worship of the Roman Catholic Church fossilized.[38]

This picture of complete uniformity, needless to say, oversimplifies the 'spotted actuality.' As noted above, kings were just as eager as popes to take advantage of printing. Erastian as well as ultramontane tendencies were reinforced. Not precisely the same texts but slightly different ones were recited in churches located within the dominions of the Spanish monarch Philip II.[39] Nevertheless, in comparison with earlier times, one may say that Catholic liturgy *was* standardized and fixed for the first time in a more or less permanent mold – at least one that held good for roughly four hundred years.

Nor was liturgy the only field in which printing enabled orthodox churchmen to implement long existing goals. Repeated efforts to ensure that priests mastered the rudiments of Latin, that parish registers were kept in order, that various instructions of popes and councils were carried out in scattered dioceses had met with uneven success during the medieval millennium. Printing made it possible to move ahead

---

[38] Daniélou, A. H. Conratin and John Kent, *Historical Theology*, p. 233.
[39] See reference to actions of Philip II and Plantin as described by Kingdon, on p. 118 above.

and consolidate gains on all these fronts.⁴⁰ In this sense the Catholic reformation – as distinct from the Counter-Reformation – owed much to the powers of the press. Not only was the Roman Church able to implement long delayed internal reforms and institute more rigorous training of the clergy, it was also able to fulfil its apostolic functions more successfully. The thesis recently propounded by Jean Delumeau: that missionary movements within sixteenth-century Europe were required by the survival of paganism – even at that late date – and that a Christianization of Europeans accompanied efforts to convert heathen overseas; this thesis also may be usefully related to the communications shift. That the barbarian peoples of Europe were still not fully Christianized, despite all the efforts made by the medieval Church, becomes more plausible when the limits of scribal culture have been taken into account.⁴¹ In this respect, Reformation studies, while they do make room for printing, almost always say too little and bring the topic in too late. It is with regard to the spread of Luther's ideas that the author of the citation at the head of this chapter finds it 'difficult to exaggerate the significance of the Press.' It is almost always when discussing the dissemination of Protestant tracts that historians pause over printing at all.

Actually, church traditions were already being affected by the advent of printing, well before Martin Luther had come of age. When fixed in a new format and presented in a new way, orthodox views were inevitably transformed. The doctrines of Thomas Aquinas, for example, acquired a new lease on life after appearing in print and becoming the subject of a deliberate revival – even before winning official approval at the Council of Trent.⁴² Acceptance of Aristotle's cosmology had

⁴⁰ Binz, *Vie Religieuse* I, 338–56, offers a close-up view of the problems of implementing reforms in one diocese and points to the specific advantages which came after printing – especially after 'Guy de Montrocher's' (or Guido de Monte Rocherii) *Manipulus Curatorum* could be purchased instead of having to be copied out by parish priests.

⁴¹ See e.g., Delumeau, *Le Catholicisme*, pp. 227–92. Delumeau's thesis is sharply contrasted with that of O'Connell, *The Counter Reformation* by Eric Cochrane, book review, *American Historical Review* (1977), 7, p. 88. The views of both authors seem to me to become compatible when the effects of printing are taken into account.

⁴² The Thomist *Summa* failed to supplant Peter Lombard's *Sentences* for three hundred years after its composition and became the textbook *par excellence* only in the sixteenth century according to Knowles, *The Evolution of Medieval Thought*, p. 182. Kristeller, *Le Thomisme*, pp. 36–9 sees a 'second period in the history of Thomism opening in the late fifteenth century when the *Summa* begins to replace the *Sentences* among German Dominicans.' This period culminates in the adoption of the *Summa* by the Jesuits and by the fathers at Trent. Is it possible that the *Sentences* came under attack from all sides partly because they were better suited to the needs of scribal culture than of print?

caused some difficulty among faculties of theology in the thirteenth century. Rejection of the same cosmology would cause even more trouble after the scholastic synthesis had been fixed in a more permanent mold. Mysticism, like scholasticism, was also transformed when spiritual exercises moved out of the cloisters. 'Meditative forms of mental prayer' became subject to rulebooks issued in uniform editions.[43] Attempts to inspire lay devotion, previously characteristic of a localized movement, such as the Northern 'devotio moderna', became much more widespread. In Southern Europe, friars began to address the lay public through printing as well as preaching, and devotional works were turned out in large editions aimed less at monks than at worldly men:

Alongside the immense output of hagiographical and other books catering for the more popular cults, there grew throughout the early and middle decades of the sixteenth century an extensive literature dealing with the interior life and intended for the use of people in the world as distinct from the cloister. These range from simple primers to sophisticated guides, mostly by members of religious orders.[44]

That this movement preceded attempts to counteract Protestant heresy is suggested by the dramatic 'sudden flaring' in Spain around 1500. Even before the Ninety-Five Theses had provoked a reaction, a 'literary mass-movement' was already under way which would result in the output of some three thousand Spanish works before the vogue declined in the late seventeenth century.[45] The 'spiritual energy' associated with the Spanish revival was carried over into Italy and France by publishers who found it profitable to cater to the new vogue.[46]

Sermon literature also underwent significant changes as pulpit oratory became increasingly affected by the new powers of the press. The living word was threatened by some of these changes. Pedantic handbooks for preachers set forth rigid rules governing pulpit oratory. A revival of classical rhetoric, initially sparked by an ardent pursuit of eloquence and later animated by geniune Christian zeal was drained

---

[43] Evennett, *The Spirit*, pp. 32–4.

[44] Dickens, *The Counter-Reformation*, p. 28. See also p. 19 for reference to the Thomist Revival which began in the 1490s.

[45] Dickens, *Counter-Reformation*, pp. 25–6. The stream of Spanish mystical publication was temporarily blocked in the 1550s by the Erastian policy of Philip II. See Martin, *Livre à Paris* I, 17–20.

[46] Evennett, *The Spirit*, pp. 17–19. A similar phenomenon is evident in the printing of Lullist texts which started in the 1480s in Spain and moved by 1510 to France. Victor, 'The Revival of Lullism,' pp. 530–1.

of vitality when transmuted into printed regulations. The new rule books, it has been suggested, ultimately killed off flexible medieval Latin speech.[47] On the other hand, lively sermons designed to keep congregations awake proved especially well suited to the new mass medium. When the Carthusian prior, Werner Rolevinck, wrote that he was having a sermon printed to 'communicate' with more people, he was simply providing a model for many priests, not comparing a hearing to a reading public.[48] As a Carthusian, Rolevinck belonged to an order which had to 'preach with its hands.' But there were many others whose actual performances were transmuted into print. The most gifted preachers, such as Savonarola or Geiler von Keysersberg, were able to send their messages from beyond the grave, as editions of their collected sermons continued to be published long after their deaths.

Ultimately, gifted boys who might have become preachers simply became publicists instead. 'The preaching of sermons is speaking to a few of mankind,' remarked Daniel Defoe, 'printing books is talking to the whole world.'[49] As an English journalist, a dissenter and a pioneering novelist, Defoe presents many contrasts with the Christian humanists of the early sixteenth century. Yet Erasmus sounded a similar theme. When he was attempting to win the favor of a lay patron, he compared those who preached obscure sermons and were heard in one or two churches with his own books which were 'read in every country in the world.'[50]

In thus celebrating the carrying power of their publications, both Defoe and Erasmus were actually ringing variations on an old scribal theme.

Praise for the apostolate of the pen...is met with at every period and...had been developed perhaps for the first time by Cassiodorus. Alcuin took it up in a poem which was inscribed over the entrance to the scriptorium at Fulda. Peter the Venerable was thinking of it when he spoke of the solitary... cloistered life: 'He cannot take up the plow? Then let him take up the pen ...He will preach without opening his mouth; without breaking silence he

---

47 See e.g. discussion by Rickard, *La Langue Française*, p. 2 of *De Corrupti Sermonis Emendatione* (1530) by Mathurin Cordier.
48 This is not clear from the citation and comment offered by Hirsch, *Printing, Selling*, p. 8. On Rolevinck's collaboration with a Cologne printer, see Marks 'The Significance of Fifteenth-Century Hand Corrections,' and chap. 1, n. 38 above.
49 Cited from *The Storm* (1704) by Watt, *The Rise of the Novel*, p. 103.
50 Cited by Harbison, *Christian Scholar*, p. 80.

will make the Lord's teaching resound in the ears of the nations; and without leaving his cloister he will journey far over land and sea.'[51]

Thus monastic scriptoria supplied the topos which lay publicists adapted to new ends. Once harnessed to the press the 'apostolate of the pen' – like Erasmus himself – left the monastery for the world. By the nineteenth century, 'glad tidings' would be almost drowned out by the flood of news from other quarters. Yet even then Christian missionaries continued to set up print shops in remote parts of the world to turn out gospels and psalters as had been done in Mainz four hundred years earlier.[52]

The notion of an 'apostolate of the pen' points to the high value assigned to the written word as a means of accomplishing the Church's mission on earth. As later discussion suggests, this made Christianity peculiarly vulnerable to the shift from pen to press. It also helps to account for the rapid expansion of the infant industry. The enthusiastic welcome given to the press by the fifteenth-century Roman Church, not only for its help in the anti-Turkish crusade but also for domestic purposes ought to be noted in connection with the prelude to Protestantism. In hailing printing as God's highest act of grace, Luther was elaborating on a theme which found favor not only among other monks but also among prelates and popes. The very phrase 'divine art' was attributed to a cardinal (Nicholas of Cusa) by a churchman who was later made bishop (Gianandrea de' Bussi, Bishop of Aleria). Even the censorship edicts issued by archbishops and popes from the 1480s down through 1515 hail the invention as divinely inspired and elaborate on its advantages before going on to note the need to curtail its abuses.[53] Not only did the Church legitimate the art of printing, it provided a large and lucrative market for the infant industry. The poor priest needed books even more urgently than did the prosperous layman. For fifty years before the Protestant Revolt, churchmen in most regions welcomed an invention which served both.

Although the Holy Ghost through printing had opened up hidden treasures of wisdom, wrote a Nuremberg priest in 1510, yet learned

[51] Leclercq, *The Love of Learning*, p. 128. On Luther's use of this theme and the question of preaching versus printing, see below, pp. 373–4.
[52] See e.g. accounts offered by Khan, 'The Early Bengali Printed Books'; Barnett, 'Silent Evangelism'; McDonald, 'The Modernizing of Communication.' See also Boxer *et al.* *Exotic Printing*, 1972 for useful survey of relevant presses.
[53] See e.g. texts and references cited by Hirsch, 'Bulla Super Impressione Librorum, 1515.'

confessors had not yet produced vernacular guides for lay sinners. Instead lay readers were being offered silly rhymes and secular guide-books as if law-suits were more important than sacred things. To counter this trend, the priest wrote, he was offering his manual of instruction: *Peycht Spigel der Sunder*.[54] He thus unwittingly offered a preview of behavior which was soon to be described as Protestant. A conservative religious impulse to counterbalance secular distractions and guide sinners toward salvation resulted in action which was not conservative at all – that is, in the output of materials which were aimed at religious self-help.[55] The role of the confessor and the sacrament of confession became more problematic than had been the case when there were no books to intervene between sinner and priest. At the same time, the role of the confessor was also becoming subject to more rigorous impersonal standards while the output of manuals directed at priests classifying categories of sins and listing penalties and pardons made visible the complexities and contradictions in orthodox doctrines, posing problems that seemed insoluble without advanced training in casuistry. The contrast between the simplicity of Christ's own teachings and the complex rigmarole of officially approved doctrines became sharper and more dismaying to those who felt a genuine religious vocation. For even while ecclesiastical rules and regulations were being more rigorously enforced and more rigidly fixed, the *Imitation of Christ* was being printed in all tongues, and the Bible was being promoted as a bestseller for the first time.

Thus although the new presses did much to invigorate religious piety and zeal, they also had the unfortunate consequence of setting churchmen at odds with each other. The same winds of change which favored lay evangelism and vernacular sermons also threatened prerogatives long held and cherished by conservative prelates. The question of whether one should encourage or block the new forces which were unleashed became a bone of contention within every church. Conflict was further aggravated by problems of exegesis which were

---

54 Cited by Tentler, *Sin and Confession*, p. 21.
55 As a 200-page manual the *Peycht Spigel* was not well designed for easy reading. A shorter printed guide – written in simple Latin rather than in the vernacular – the *Manual for Parish Priests* is also discussed by Tentler, *Sin and Confession* who suggests that it actually touched the lives of more laymen than the *Peycht Spigel*. Since the latter was aimed at by-passing priests, its implications were more revolutionary nevertheless. Other aspects of printed confessional literature are discussed by Ozment, *The Reformation in the Cities*, pp. 22–8. He emphasizes the use of picture books to dramatize penalties for sinning in a manner that offended the Reformers.

posed by copy-editing and which set off furious and interminable disputes between biblical scholars and theologians. In view of the carnage which ensued, it is difficult to imagine how anyone could regard the more efficient duplication of religious texts as an unmixed blessing. Heralded on all sides as a 'peaceful art,' Gutenberg's invention probably contributed more to destroying Christian concord and inflaming religious warfare than any of the so-called arts of war ever did. Much of the religious turbulence of the early modern era, I think, may be traced to the fact that the writings of church fathers and the scriptures themselves could not continue to be transmitted in traditional ways. As a sacred heritage, Christianity could be protected against most forms of change. As a heritage that was transmitted by texts and that involved the 'spreading of glad tidings,' Christianity was peculiarly vulnerable to the revolutionary effects of typography.

Processing texts in new workshops was, to be sure, a peaceful activity undertaken by pacific urban craftsmen and merchants. Nevertheless, it brought into focus many troublesome issues which had always been blurred, or glossed over, before. Oral testimony, for example, could be distinguished much more clearly from written testimony when poets no longer composed their works in the course of chanting or reciting them and when giving dictation or reading out loud became detached from the publication of a given work.[56] Accordingly, questions were more likely to arise about the transmission of the teaching that came from the lips of Christ or from the dictation of the Holy Spirit to the Apostles. Was the Gospel meant to be 'passed on by telling others of the presence'?[57] Was the Word affected by being silently transmitted and the presence experienced by the solitary Bible-reader?[58] Was all of the Christian heritage set down in written form

[56] Apart from standard references, such as Crosby, 'Oral Delivery'; Root, 'Publication before Printing,' and Chaytor, *From Script to Print, passim*, see also interesting account of Boccaccio being paid by Florentines to read Dante's *Commedia* out loud every day (save for holidays) during the year 1373, 'Boccaccio's Dante,' p. 969. Diverse rules governing oral and written discourse had, of course, been debated by classical philosophers (see e.g. citations in Trimpi, 'The Meaning of Ut Pictura Poesis'). But the distinction surely became sharper when publication no longer required giving dictation or reading out loud.

[57] Preus, *The Inspiration of Scripture*, pp. 5 ff. and Tavard, *Holy Writ*, p. 3 offer pertinent data. Teeple, 'The Oral Tradition' shows the issue is still controversial.

[58] It is intriguing to note that the Lutherans held the 'essence' of scripture to be unaffected by the means used to transmit it (see Preus, *Inspiration of Scripture*, pp. 17–18). McLuhan's insistence that the medium is as significant as the message seems more compatible with Catholic than Protestant doctrines. The providential nature of scribal culture – which was perfectly designed to ensure the 'maximum presence through history' of the divine Word – is underlined by Ong, *The Presence of the Word*, pp. 190–1.

and contained solely in scripture? Was not some of it also preserved 'in the unwritten traditions which the Apostles received from Christ's lips or which, under the inspiration of the Holy Spirit, were by them, as it were, passed down to us from hand to hand'?[59] Was it meant to be made directly available to all men in accordance with the mission to spread glad tidings? Or was it rather to be expounded to the laity only after passing through the hands of priests, as had become customary over the course of centuries? But how could the traditional mediating role of the priesthood be maintained without a struggle when lay grammarians and philologists had been summoned by scholar–printers to help with the task of editing old texts? The priest might claim the sacred office of mediating between God and man, but when it came to scriptural exegesis many editors and publishers were in agreement with Roger Bacon and Lorenzo Valla. They felt that Greek and Hebrew scholars were better equipped for the task.[60]

The scholar–printer, who was often more erudite than the university theologian of his day, was much less likely to defer to clerical judgment than the scribe or copyist had been. As a layman he owed loyalty to princes and magistrates. The ruling of churchmen, unless backed by lay officials, seemed less compelling to him than the rules of evidence, and he reserved his most scornful epithets for the grammar of school-men and the learning of monks. His viewpoint was shared, moreover, by most of the editors, translators and authors whom he gathered in his workshop.

'I show how in some places Hilary has been mistaken. So of Augustine and Thomas Aquinas,' wrote Erasmus concerning his edition of the New Testament in a letter of 1516. 'They were men of the highest worth, but they were men.'[61] Along with the new learning and erudition came new forms of intellectual property rights and eponymous authorship. The reputation of church fathers or angelic doctors was diminished not merely because they were found to have made grammatical errors but also because they were, in retrospect, cast in the role of

59 Draft of Decree on the Acceptance of the Holy Scriptures and the Apostolic Traditions, March 22, 1545, in Jedin, *A History of the Council of Trent* II, 74.
60 An early example is offered by John of Piacenza, editor of a *Psalterium Graecum cum Versione Latinâ*, printed in Sept. 1481, whose preface consisted of a letter to the Bishop of Bergamo defending a critical approach to the biblical text against the views of 'ignorant' men who believed scripture should not be subject to the grammatical rules. Botfield, ed. *Praefationes*, pp. 13–14.
61 Erasmus' letter to Henry Bullock, in *The Portable Renaissance Reader*, p. 405.

men of letters. Defoe envisaged Homer not only as a plagiarist but also as an entrepreneur who hired hacks to turn out ballads in his name.[62] When the collective authority associated with the 'auctores' of medieval clerks was replaced by more individualized concepts of authorship, ancient prophets and sages dwindled in stature. As fallible individuals, prone to human error, apparently guilty of plagiarism on many counts, old giants began to look more like modern dwarfs. The ancients were men like ourselves, said Budé, and often wrote about things they little understood.[63] According to Ramus, all that Aristotle said was forged.[64] The anti-Aristotelian movement formed part of a more general repudiation of the ancients which had Christian as well as classical implications.

By the seventeenth century an inexorable advance in trilingual studies made it difficult to ignore discrepancies in scriptural texts. Scriptural authorship itself became problematic. The same techniques that were used by a Greek scholar like Casaubon to show that the 'forged book of Hermes' actually dated from the post-Christian era were used by Hebrew scholars to show that the Pentateuch could not have been written by Moses. Moses might have founded the archives from which the first books of the Old Testament were based, according to Richard Simon, but later groups of annalists and archivists were responsible for the actual composition of the Pentateuch.[65] The very idea of casting in the role of an archivist the prophet who was once believed to have received the Ten Commandments from God on Sinai suggests how the mythopoeic scribal vision of the past was deflated by the habits of mind which were engendered by reading proof and checking copy.

Richard Simon...first clearly recognized the complicated process of revision and change to which the sacred text had been exposed from the time of its composition until recently. The canonical books of the Old Testament, he said, had been handed on from generation to generation by a guild of scribes who had constantly...altered them. He thought that in the course of time, the loose sheets on which the text was written became mixed...such a process would destroy the theory of the verbal inspiration of the text...[66]

[62] Watt, *The Rise of the Novel*, pp. 240–1.   [63] Kinser, 'Ideas of Temporal Change,' p. 738.
[64] Cited by Baker, *The Wars of Truth*, p. 93.
[65] Barnes, *Jean Le Clerc*, p. 111. For evidence that U.S. Baptists still insist that the Pentateuch was composed by a single hand, identified with Moses, see *The New York Times* (Thurs., June 4, 1970), pp. 1, 9.
[66] Preserved Smith, *Origins of Modern Culture 1543–1637*, p. 255.

But it was not only an enhanced awareness of the process of scribal transmission which helped to undermine confidence in a direct revelation from on high. It was also the increasing difficulty of reconciling older ideas of divine inspiration with new methods of literary composition. Compositions by singers of songs or tellers of tales thus had a natural affinity with belief in revelation and inspiration. 'Golden-voiced' orators and bards striking their lyres were in some ways akin to actors or instrumentalists today. They relied on well trained memories and on skills developed through exercise and drill. But they also achieved some of their most memorable effects, much like modern preachers, trial lawyers, or jazz trumpeters, by leaving room for spontaneous improvisation. They allowed 'the spirit to move them' and let themselves be 'carried away' – sometimes to the point of 'divine madness' or 'frenzy.'[67] Of course not all authors were bards in the age of scribes and there were scribal poets who did not compose before an audience. Moreover the hand press lent itself to more flexible uses than is often recognized. One gains the impression that Erasmus managed to compose certain satires fairly spontaneously and directly, surrounded by friends who peered over his shoulder as he corrected copy and actually handled pieces of type. Nevertheless, it seems fair to say that opportunities for spontaneous improvisation were curtailed once authors began to compose with the new presses in mind. Not only was the act of writing more likely to be detached from performing before a live audience, but all works, however composed, had to go through additional stages of copy-editing after the printer replaced the scribe. A last minute change-of-phrase or spur-of-the-moment addition, which seemed to come as an act of grace to the hard-pressed bard, was likely to be viewed as a troublesome extravagance by the hard-pressed editor or printer. As creative activities in general and literary compositions in particular became less impulsive and more responsive to the demands of the new medium, standards of excellence shifted accordingly. Among editors, translators and critics, true eloquence became less and less associated with 'inspired' improvisation, more and more with obedience to the rules of rhetoric reflected in carefully polished, flawless prose. But the more men of letters came to take such standards for granted, the more early scriptural texts, which presumably reflected

---

67 On the effect of the disappearance of a live audience, see Bronson, 'The Writer.' On problems associated with the Platonic doctrine of inspiration, see Trimpi, 'The Meaning of Ut Pictura Poesis'; Tigerstadt, 'Furor Poeticus.'

the pristine perfection of a divine order,[68] appeared to be strangely flawed. 'To find solecisms, barbarisms and poor Greek in the speeches and writings of the holy apostles, is to reflect on the Holy Ghost who spoke through them...' noted a reproof issued against an audacious German scholar by the theological faculty of Wittenberg.[69] Given the belief that true eloquence was a token of divine inspiration, Biblical scholars faced a painful predicament: either they had to conceal all the discrepancies and lapses they uncovered, or else they cast doubt on the divine authorship of the scriptures.[70] However individual scholars resolved the conflict, polemicists made sure that the reading public was kept informed. The failure of prophets and apostles to live up to the standards followed by even mediocre scholars and authors was broadcast in all regions where the Inquisition was not feared.

He finds so many mistakes and so many errours at the beginning of *Genesis*, that he gives you to guess his meaning, though he will not speak it, to be that the Jewish religion is little else than a forgery and that it has but small evidence of a Revelation from God Almighty.[71]

This accusation was directed at an English apostate by a pious Protestant in an era when 'the road to preferment lay as much through polemics as through political subservience. The cleric who did not publish was likely to perish in some remote village and he had every reason to be grateful' to writings which gave him a chance to display 'pious indignation.'[72]

Indignation of a different kind was soon displayed by anti-clerical French *philosophes* who were no less persuaded that they had to publish or perish. As expert polemicists they effectively countered pious pro-

[68] His belief in the true eloquence of Gospel writers was important in Lorenzo Valla's effort to reclaim the New Testament from corruption and also animated Erasmus' attempt to continue Valla's work. Gray, 'Valla's Encomium,' pp. 49–50.

[69] Reproof issued to Joachim Jungius (1587–1657) cited by Preserved Smith, *Origins of Modern Culture*, p. 263. That seventeenth-century Lutheran dogmatists viewed it as blasphemy to suggest that solecisms or barbarisms marred scriptural versions is noted by Preus, *Inspiration of Scripture*, pp. 64–6.

[70] An amusing example of present-day irreverence, based on applying modern concepts of authorship to the scriptures, is offered by a graffito (reported in *Time*, April 13, 1970, p. 61): 'GOD IS NOT DEAD! HE IS ALIVE AND AUTOGRAPHING BIBLES TODAY AT BRENTANO's (110 St. subway station, New York City).' The same issue (p. 58) reports that a computer study of the Book of Isaiah gives odds of 1 to 100,000 against one prophet having authored the entire text.

[71] Citation from Thomas Bambridge, *An Answer to a Book Entituled Reason and Authority* (1687), in L. I. Bredvold, *The Intellectual Milieu of John Dryden*, p. 96.

[72] Gay, introduction to *Deism*, p. 9.

CLASSICAL AND CHRISTIAN TRADITIONS REORIENTED

testations by adapting theological disputes to their own ends. Whenever attribution seemed doubtful and documentary evidence confused, they did not hesitate to believe the worst and to assume that forgers and counterfeiters had been at work. As authors in an age of print, they did not make allowance for the conditions of scribal culture. Forced themselves to obey rules pertaining to intellectual property, they were naturally irritated at the negligence of earlier writers. Engaged in a life-and-death struggle with living priests and monks, they were in no frame of mind to be generous about dead ones. The somewhat hesitant tone of biblical scholars and English deists was abandoned by eighteenth-century freethinkers. They took the offensive, went straight to the jugular, and attacked the central miracle of Christianity at its source:

The evangelists contradict each other about the length of Jesus's life, about the miracles, about the day of the last supper, about that of his death...in a word about almost all the facts. The Christians of the early centuries made forty-nine Gospels which all contradict one another...in the end, they picked the four...which remain to us...They imagine the Trinity, and to make it credible they falsify the earliest Gospel.

They add a passage about this Trinity; just as they falsify the historian Josephus to have him say a word about Jesus...They...make up Sybilline verses...Apostolic canons, Apostles' Creeds...there is not a trick, a fraud, an imposture that the Nazarenes do not bring into play...

O miserable deceivers...what proof do you have that these apostles wrote what has been put over their names? If it was possible to make up canons, could one not make up gospels? Do you not yourselves recognize forgeries?...There is not a single contemporary historian who even mentions Jesus and his apostles. Admit that you support lies by lies...[73]

With this explicit statement that the central miracle of the Christian faith was nothing more than deliberate trickery, practiced by forgers and impostors – a pack of tricks played on the dead to enslave men's minds – we reach a critical point in the history of Western Christendom, where men cease to attribute evil to witches and demons and start blaming wicked priests instead.[74]

[73] Excerpts from Voltaire's 'Sermon of the Fifty,' in Gay, *Deism*, pp. 154–6.
[74] Of course Protestants had also attacked priests as confidence men (see discussion of Tyndale by Dickens, *English Reformation*, p. 73), but in order to uphold scriptural faith against ecclesiastical hierarchies. Voltaire's cynical view of sacred history gives a new twist to the pyrrhonist arguments of Catholic apologists who tried to bolster faith by attacking reason and who opposed Protestant reliance on the scriptures. A paranoid Jesuit priest, Jean Hardouin, may have helped pave the way for Voltaire (who was educated at a Jesuit college) by questioning

Many troublesome questions concerning scriptural composition and authorship were new and came after print. There were also several long-standing chronic problems that printing rendered more acute. The question of lay Bible-reading, for example, had provoked occasional disturbances throughout the middle ages. But these episodes had been sporadic and localized, capable of being handled on a haphazard piecemeal basis and attributed to a minority of trouble-makers. Not only had the issue been handled differently during the early Christian era than later on; but different approaches were used in different regions during the later middle ages. Thus the Brethren of the Common Life seem to have encouraged lay evangelism without encountering much opposition in the Netherlands during the late fourteenth century, even while rebellion and repression, over much the same issue, was occurring across the channel where Lollard martyrs were being made. After it became possible (and, indeed, profitable) to boost Bible sales, the issue forced itself upon all churchmen and statesmen in a much more urgent and acute form. Policy decisions had to be made on an either-or basis; there was no way of avoiding taking a stand; pressures on both sides became more intense and compromise almost impossible.

In this regard, Bible printing helps to cast light on the phenomenon which has been well described by Eugene Rice:

The medieval Church was more ecumenical, more genially encompassing, more permissive doctrinally than the...sixteenth century...churches... There was more room in it for doctrinal maneuver...for disagreement and debate among the orthodox...All the bits and pieces that were to make up the sixteenth-century theologies of Protestantism and Catholicism were in solution in medieval thought. What so dramatically happened during the age of Reformation is that they crystallized into two distinct and opposed systems, each more exclusive, more consistent, and more rigid than the medieval tradition from which they both derived...[75]

Although the shift from script to print is not mentioned in the passage, I think it helps to account for the developments that are therein described. Given the possibility of fully implementing old evangelical

the validity of all scriptural texts dating before the fourteenth century. He claimed they were all forged by 'atheistical monks.' See Palmer, *Catholics and Unbelievers*, p. 66. Hardouin's 'pathological' suspicions did not stop short with sacred texts. His study of 'hard' evidence supplied by coins led him to conclude that almost *all* ancient texts had been forged by a gang of fourteenth-century Italians. See Momigliano, 'Ancient History,' p. 16.

[75] Rice, *The Foundations*, p. 143. See also remarks of Blunt, *Artistic Theory*, pp. 108-9 on the 'surprisingly broad-minded' attitude toward heretical paintings taken by the Church before the Counter-Reformation.

goals, given the pressure to expand markets for books, new policy decisions had to be made, and made on an either-or basis. One could defend priestly prerogatives or encourage lay Bible-reading; one might even, like Henry VIII, first do one and then the other; but one could not, for very long, countenance both policies at once. Doctrines that could co-exist more or less peacefully because full implementation was lacking, thus came into sharp conflict after printers had set to work.

With typographical fixity, moreover, positions once taken were more difficult to reverse. Battles of books prolonged polarization, and pamphlet wars quickened the process. Where Lutherans and Anglicans pioneered, Catholic authorities soon followed. It was from a new Catholic congregation, which was established at Rome in 1622, and provided with its own printing office, that the term 'propaganda' emerged.[76] Polemical disputes developed a momentum of their own; passions were enflamed as Protestant and Papist saw the devil at work in the enemy camp. It soon became impossible to play down provocative issues; too many pens were being employed in playing them up.

Moderates trapped in the withering crossfire were rapidly deprived of any middle ground on which to stand. Those who relied solely on scripture did not stop short of casting doubt on the legitimacy of priestly authority and church *traditio*. Embattled Papists did not hesitate to attack bibliolatry. Skillful Jesuits questioned grounds for authenticating scriptural texts. They exploited sceptical arguments in order to undermine confidence in the Book and strengthen faith in the Church.[77] According to one angry Huguenot, they went so far in their desperate defense of 'the authoritie of unwritten traditions' as to defame the sacred scriptures 'by calling it the booke of heretikes, the blacke Gospell, Inke-Divinitie...the apple of Discord...'[78] In fact, the printed Bible did prove to be 'an apple of discord,' even within the Protestant camp. For Gospel writers had failed to anticipate doctrines

---

[76] Activities of the 'Tipografia della Congregazione de Propaganda Fide' (established in 1626) are outlined by Steinberg, *Five Hundred Years*, p. 234, who notes how the French revolutionaries destroyed the Roman office and transferred its impressive equipment to the Imprimerie Nationale. On the secularization of the term 'propaganda,' during the same interval, see Leith, *Media and Revolution*, pp. 11–21.

[77] The arguments of the early seventeenth-century French Jesuit, François Véron (1575–1625) were particularly persuasive on this point. See Popkin, *The History of Skepticism*. Also Preus, *Inspiration of Scripture*, pp. 137ff.; Bredvold, *Intellectual Milieu*, pp. 78ff.

[78] Cited by Bredvold, *Intellectual Milieu*, p. 77 from a refutation by Tillenus (published in 1606) of a French bishop's arguments upholding unwritten tradition and questioning scripture.

formulated at the Council of Nicea. Trinitarians who pitted the Bible against Church tradition were forced onto shaky grounds.

sola scriptura was...the harbinger not of peace but of a sword; and a sword of such sharpness as to pierce...the joints and marrow of Protestantism. Welcomed first as a...defense against...Rome...and Trent...it was now suffering an assault from the rear at the hands of Socinius and his followers ...Socinian views...offered an obvious and tempting target for Roman Catholic polemic against Protestantism in general...It became evident that 'The Bible Only' was an insecure basis even for so fundamental a tenet of orthodoxy as the doctrine of the Trinity.[79]

Between Protestant attacks on church authority and unwritten tradition, and Catholic efforts to undermine sole reliance on scripture, little was left. Efforts to restore or to preserve the traditional faith thus only sharpened tools of analysis that helped, in the end, to subvert it.

That a clash of warring faiths eventually dethroned theology and undermined confidence in Christianity itself has often been noted. My point is not that disputes between rival churches paved the way for later views but rather that printing (by revolutionizing all processes of transmission) made it necessary for churchmen to depart from earlier views and set them at odds with each other. Given the shift from script to print, it was quite impossible to preserve the status quo, and hence some kind of disruption was inevitable.

A specific illustration of this point is provided by the status of Holy Writ itself. To preserve the Vulgate in the age of scribes meant securing the text against corruption by copyists. To this end, churchmen enlisted aid from the most learned men of the day, encouraged study of Greek and Hebrew and sponsored frequent review and emendation. To preserve the Vulgate in the age of printers, however, meant to defend Jerome's translation against new revised versions; hence to side with obscurantists against biblical scholars, to discourage emendation based on new findings and to insist on the authenticity of an obviously corrupted text. This last position became official Catholic policy after the Council of Trent. But it had already become a bone of contention between theologians in the early sixteenth century. Thus Caspar Schatzgeyer directed a pamphleteering campaign against his former friend, Osiander, in 1525 over the issue, holding that the Vulgate had

<hr />

[79] Sykes, 'The Religion of the Protestants,' pp. 178–9.

been perfected and not polluted over the course of the centuries it had served the Church.[80]

In the thirteenth century, theologians at the University of Paris had sponsored correction of the Vulgate and given their assent to the issue of an emended exemplar.[81] In the sixteenth century, the same faculty at the same institution censured a scholar–printer who was engaged in just the same sort of work. Robert Estienne's apparatus of notes, indices, and comments grew larger with each of his successive editions of the Vulgate and the alarm of Sorbonnistes increased accordingly.

he was a layman working without their control, and yet he was correcting the received contemporary version of the Vulgate by pointing to...variants from earlier sources and adding...interpretative notes...One example of the censures to which his Bible was exposed...may suffice:....*Annotation*: 'L'Eglise c'est à dire a l'assemblée publique.' Censure: 'Ceste proposition... favorise à l'erreur des Vauldois et Vicléfistes: et aussi elle derogue à la puissance des prélats de l'Eglise'[82]

In the end, Estienne left France for Geneva in time to escape the Edict of Châteaubriant which expressly forbade 'the printing or selling of books, commentaries, scholia, annotations, tables, indexes, or summaries of Holy Scripture and the Christian religion written during the past forty years.'[83] Clerical controls imposed from any one center were incapable of containing the sixteenth-century book-trade and forty years of biblical scholarship could not be effectively blotted out. The attempt was made, nevertheless. The Edict of Châteaubriant was only one of a series of similar measures taken by Catholic officials in Europe to protect the Vulgate against the new biblical scholarship. These defensive measures culminated in the edict of 1592 in which the post-Tridentine papacy turned to the version revised under Pope Clement VIII and proclaimed it 'authentic.' Unlike Estienne's version, the Clementine Vulgate contained no variant readings and was pro-

---

[80] Nyhus, 'Caspar Schatzgeyer.' The polemic against Osiander is discussed on p. 201.

[81] Smalley, *The Study of the Bible*, p. 366; Samuel Berger, *Histoire de la Vulgate*, p. 329; and Branner, 'The Soissons Bible Paintshop,' all convey an impression of the 'emended' Paris version that is more favorable than that given by Loewe, 'The Medieval History of the Latin Vulgate,' pp. 134ff. Loewe holds that this 'heavily interpolated and corrupt version' was 'in one sense specially edited or officially sponsored' but was simply the result of enterprising Paris stationers who went in for irresponsible copying on a large scale (p. 147). According to Sutcliffe, 'Jerome,' pp. 99ff. the term *textus vulgatus* was often applied to the thirteenth-century Paris recension but the term Vulgate does not become a standard term for Jerome's translation until the sixteenth century. During the middle ages it might refer to the earlier version in Old Latin as well as to Jerome's.   [82] Basil Hall, 'Biblical Scholarship,' p. 67.

[83] Black, 'The Printed Bible,' p. 438.

tected by a series of bulls from further revision making 'new critical work…difficult for Catholics' until the nineteenth century.[84]

The policy of sixteenth-century Catholics with regard to biblical scholarship was thus markedly different from that which had been pursued in the thirteenth century. A patristic tradition of scholarship inherited from Jerome was not merely abandoned or allowed to lapse. It was taken up by lay scholars and blocked by Catholic clergymen who were driven to this action less by Protestants than by print. Moreover, Jerome had deployed his learning in order to convert the scriptures of his day into a language better understood by his contemporaries. To authorize only the Vulgate after new vernaculars had superseded Latin also went against precedents set by Church fathers and against an apostolic mission derived from Christ himself. Indeed the chief spokesman for the anti-vernacular position at Trent questioned the value of following ancient customs and argued that changing times called for changing policies.[85]

Even when assuming a conservative posture, then, sixteenth-century churchmen could not avoid being innovators – as the Index, the Imprimatur and many Jesuit policies suggest. Nor should one exclude Lutheran policies when making this point. Actually one might argue that the position of most churchmen was basically conservative during the first century after printing. They might press for reform or for preserving the status quo; they might seek to restore early Christian customs or be eager to prolong late medieval ones. Whatever they advocated, a basic change had occurred in the circumstances they faced. Any position a given churchman might take on questions pertaining to the Gospel was bound to mark a departure from precedent because the terms of all such questions had changed along with the format of the Gospel itself.

3. GOSPEL TRUTHS RECAST: THE VULGATE IN PRINT

'It is not sufficiently emphasized that the printing of vernacular bibles …long preceded the Reformation in several countries.'[86] Partly

[84] Basil Hall, 'Biblical Scholarship,' p. 69. Loewe, 'The Medieval History of the Latin Vulgate,' p. 152 describes the Clementine version as being based on the corrupt Paris version of the thirteenth century (see n. 81 above).

[85] See citation from Alphonse de Castro, *De Justa Haeriticorum Punitione* (Salamanca, 1547) in Cavallera, 'La Bible en Langue Vulgaire,' p. 55.   [86] Black, 'The Printed Bible,' p. 423.

because it is conventional to begin with Luther rather than Gutenberg, most studies of the Reformation rarely pause to note that a new
·means of editing and spreading the Gospel was an important antecedent
of the division of Christendom. We are told much about the role of
print in the spread of Protestantism, little about its prior role in the
spread of Bibles. There are some Catholic scholars, to be sure, who
take note of pre-Lutheran Bible-printing when defending the Church
against Protestant attacks. Daniel-Rops, for example, somewhat
sarcastically, repudiates the notion that the Bible 'which ought to have
been found in the hands of all pious men day and night was lying
hidden under the benches between the seats and the dust, fallen into
universal oblivion.' Between the invention of the printing press and
1520, he says, 'one hundred and fifty-six Latin editions of the Bible
had been published, together with seventeen German translations, not
to mention the manuscript copies which have been estimated at more
than a hundred.'[87] But the significance of duplicating Bibles at this
new rapid rate remains to be explored.

There are remarkably few discussions, if any, of how the new mode
of book production affected a biblical faith. The issue has cropped up
in one instance, but in an inverted form: the effect of a scriptural faith
on printing industries, rather than the effect of print on a scriptural
faith, has provoked some disagreement. Thus Robert Kingdon suggests
(correctly, I think) that reliance on sacred scripture as an ultimate
source of truth was an important factor in the development and expansion of printing industries in the West.[88] This thesis is questioned by
Lawrence Stone who argues that the Koran has served Islam much as
the Bible served medieval Christianity without generating comparable
pressures. The 'critical element,' Stone thinks, was

not so much Christianity as Protestantism. In the early sixteenth century the
Catholics were fearful of heresy because of Bible study whereas the Reformers were fearful of superstition because of lack of Bible study. But this
new Protestant demand for familiarity with a book was made upon a society
where there was no popular tradition of oral memorizing and recitation of
the sacred text, since it was in a dead language.[89]

[87] Daniel-Rops, *The Protestant Reformation*, p. 47.
[88] Kingdon, 'Patronage, Piety, and Printing,' p. 26.
[89] Stone, 'Literacy and Education,' p. 77. The importance of the premium Protestants placed on
literacy is also noted by George Foster, *Traditional Cultures*, p. 146. For discussion of the
Protestant emphasis on literacy as an important variable in the early-modern era, see
pp. 414–15, 421–6 below.

In my view, the 'new Protestant demand' was a by-product of older evangelical drives that could be fully implemented for the first time. The same point applies to biblical humanism, which received a new impetus after typefonts could be cast. Dissension generated by biblical scholars who feared 'superstition' more than 'heresy' not only predated the Lutheran revolt but was never precisely congruent with Catholic–Protestant polarities. Beginning with the outbreak of several pre-Reformation controversies, a continuous battle of books was fought over the extent to which trilingual studies should be encouraged and scholarly disciplines be brought to bear on the received text of the day. This struggle, which was spearheaded by editions issued by scholar-printers, cut across confessional lines. It divided Catholic scholars from Catholic theologians and forced divisions among Protestants as well.

Thus disputes over the Hebrew studies of Pellican and Reuchlin in Germany; over Lefèvre d'Etaples' analysis of the 'three Marys' in France; or over the introduction of Greek studies into English universities found Catholics quarreling among themselves.[90] Scholars who joined forces over the issue of Bible studes, moreover, were divided by the Lutheran revolt. More died as a Catholic martyr; Melanchthon, as a Protestant Church father. Erasmus ran into opposition from Lutherans and Catholics alike. The same point applies to debates provoked in Spain by work on the Complutensian Polyglot.[91] Robert Estienne was forced to leave Paris for Geneva, but Cardinal Ximenes completed his scholarly biblical editions while remaining at the Spanish university of Alcalà. Although decisions taken at Trent wounded Catholic biblical scholarship severely, later scholars continued to face dogmatic opposition from both camps.

The question of which was the true text of the Bible was central to sixteenth-century theological disputes. Both Catholics and Protestants believed in its infallibility. The crucial question was which was the correct text of Revelation. In the opinion of reactionary scholastics, the Hebrew text of the Old Testament had been falsified by rabbis. They based their opinion on the fact that the masoretic points, indicating vowel sounds, were added to the original text by Jewish scholars...Moreover they believed in a special grace granted to Saint Jerome for his translation...In addition there was an

---

90 Richard Cameron, 'The Attack on the Biblical Work of Lefèvre d'Etaples'; Harbison, *Christian Scholar*, pp. 88–9; Hufstader, 'Lefèvre d'Etaples'; McConica, *English Humanists*, p. 217; Nauert, 'Peter of Ravenna,' and 'Clash of Humanists and Scholastics'; Nyhus, 'Caspar Schatzgeyer.'   91 Basil Hall, 'The Trilingual College.'

emotional protest based on the anti-Semitism rife in Spain which opposed the use of Jewish sources.[92]

The 'reactionary scholastics' referred to in this passage were Spanish Catholics who condemned a supplementary treatise added to Plantin's Antwerp Polyglot. This treatise explained problems associated with translating from the Hebrew and had already alarmed friendly censors in Louvain who advised its author to cut it out.

If the faithful were to learn that a 'literal' translation from Hebrew could be one of several possibilities because this language lacks vowels and several literal meanings could be taken from a single word, the authority of the Vulgate would be entirely undermined. In fact, the censors' fears were justified, for this very treatise was to be censured severely in Rome.[93]

In the end the alarming treatise was issued from the Leiden press of Plantin's Protestant son-in-law, Raphelengius. It appeared as a separate work under the title of *Antiquitates Judaicae* in 1593.[94]

Given this particular example, one might be tempted to contrast the benighted censors of Catholic Spain, Rome and Louvain with the enlightened Protestants of Leiden who allowed the scholarly supplement to appear. Yet the supplementary treatise had been written by an eminent Spanish Catholic churchman, and when a later Protestant scholar pursued the same line of research, Protestant reaction was strongly hostile from the first. Theories about the transcription of Hebrew scriptures, proposed by the French Protestant scholar Louis Cappel, were not only refuted by English Puritans but more solemnly repudiated by an official Protestant assemblage: the *Consensus Helveticus* of 1674.[95] In view of Protestant leanings toward literalism, the refutation of Cappel is not surprising. But it suggests how easily the usual formula could be reversed, making the Reformers appear more fearful than the Catholics of too much Bible study. The French Catholic priest, Richard Simon, did indeed try to exploit this reverse formula;

---

[92] Rekers, *Benito Arias Montano*, p. 25.   [93] Rekers, *Benito Arias Montano*, p. 52.

[94] Rekers, *Benito Arias Montano*, p. 63, n. 1. For further data on Raphelengius' relations to both Plantin and Montano see pp. 95–6; 121. Rekers' monograph supplies evidence that Montano, the Spanish Catholic churchman sent by Philip II to supervise Plantin's work, got caught up in a heterodox network in the course of working in Antwerp with Plantin and ended by creating a subversive 'cell' in the Escorial itself. See below, pp. 443–4.

[95] Louis Cappel's *The Mystery of the Vowel Points Revealed (Arcanum Punctationum Revelatum)* was, like Montano's earlier treatise, published at Leiden (in 1624). See Preserved Smith, *Origins of Modern Culture*, pp. 250–1; Barnes, *Jean Le Clerc*, p. 26. Controversy over vowel points during the seventeenth century is discussed by Preus, *Inspiration of Scripture*, pp. 141ff.

coupling an attack on Protestants and Socinians with an analysis of all the 'caprices of copyists' which made reliance on scripture less dependable than reliance on the Church. But French Catholics under Bossuet were no more tolerant of the Oratorian priest Simon than the Swiss Reformers had been of the Protestant scholar Cappel.[96]

In addition to the opposition various projects aroused, the patronage given to biblical scholars also suggests that divisions over Bible study cut across confessional lines. Polyglot publication programs were sponsored by Catholic authorities in Spain and in France.[97] On the other hand, the pursuit of Oriental studies and trilingual scholarship was propelled more vigorously by Protestant presses in Holland than by any Catholic firms, as the Dutch editions of Montano's, Cappel's and Simon's treatises may suggest. Here, as with pro-Copernican treatises, the existence of a relatively free press rather than of a particular confession may have been strategic.[98]

At all events, it does seem necessary to distinguish between Bible study in the sense of scholarly exegesis and Bible study in the sense of lay Bible reading. In this latter field, Protestant–Catholic contrasts did become extremely important. It was printing, to be sure, that made it possible fully to implement long-lived evangelical aims. Nevertheless, Protestant doctrines which stressed Bible-reading as necessary for salvation did generate unusual pressures toward literacy; while the Catholic refusal after Trent to authorize alternatives to the Latin Vulgate worked in the opposite direction. Indeed a modern English Jesuit seems to approve of the conventional formula when discussing the eighteenth-century condemnation of Jansenism. The Church, he

---

96 Whereas Sykes, 'Religion of Protestants,' notes Simon's expulsion from his Order; F. J. Crehan, 'The Bible in the Roman Catholic Church,' pp. 218–20, has Simon merely leaving the Oratory in 1678. On implications of Simon's work, see also Preserved Smith, *Origins of Modern Culture*, pp. 254–6. Hazard, *La Crise* I, 243–64. The publication of Simon's later critical edition of the New Testament (1702) precipitated a fateful struggle between the Gallican Church led by Bossuet and royal officials headed by Pontchartrain over the right to censor religious works which resulted in a stunning defeat for the Archbishop. See recent account by Woodbridge, 'Censure Royale et Censure Episcopale.'

97 Hendricks, 'Profitless Printing.' See also Martin, *Livre à Paris* I, 9; Kingdon, 'Christopher Plantin and His Backers,' pp. 311, 314–15; B. Hall, 'Biblical Scholarship,' p. 54.

98 See Martin, *Livre à Paris* II, 894. For discussion of scientific publication programs, see chap. 8, below. A vigorous polemic against oriental studies pursued by Dutch biblical scholars was conducted by the French Catholic virtuoso, Friar Mersenne, as is noted by Bréhier, 'The Formation of our History,' p. 161. One gains the impression that biblical research entailing Hebrew and Oriental languages was propelled more rapidly by Protestant than by Catholic scholars during the seventeenth and eighteenth centuries despite Catholic polyglots of the earlier epoch and the remarkable erudition displayed by the Bollandists and Jesuits such as Athanasius Kirchner, later on.

says, 'held it was safer to have less Scripture-reading than more heresy.' He hastens to add, 'There was no desire to hold back the spread of education.'[99] Of course not. In the opinion of Protestants, however, the unwanted result was nonetheless obtained: 'The struggle against analphabetism was almost invariably...the struggle against the papist church where the priest reads for all.'[100]

The rest of Stone's argument: that unusual pressure toward literacy was also generated by a sacred book which did not lend itself to oral transmission, as did the Koran, points to a problem in comparative religions that is worth further exploration. One may want to question parts of the argument by doubting whether Latin was really dead in the late middle ages, by objecting that vernacular versions of scripture circulated in manuscript form, or by noting that Christians had occasionally resorted to oral transmission.[101] But one must still agree that the basic contrast with the Koran holds good. The written text of their sacred book was of strategic significance even for early Christians. Christian insistence on circulating *written* versions of the Bible had indeed helped to reshape the very format of the ancient book by encouraging the shift from roll to codex.[102]

This unusual prolonged reliance on written rather than oral transmission meant that the Christian religion was especially vulnerable to changes ushered by print. 'With us the natural seat of the book is something material such as paper which may or may not be committed to memory. With the Arab, it is memory which may or may not be committed to writing.'[103] Manuscripts were much more likely than were memories to be affected by a new mode of book production.

99 Crehan, 'The Bible in the Catholic Church,' p. 223.
100 Henri Hauser, *Naissance du Protestantisme*, p. 58. See also Droz, 'Bibles Françaises,' pp. 210–15.
101 That Latin was not a 'dead language' during the middle ages is stressed by Auerbach, *Literary Language*, p. 269. It was still a 'living tongue,' used for ordinary conversation in some sixteenth-century households, such as that of the Estiennes. See p. 447 below. The so-called 'Gothic' vernacular owed its alphabet to a scriptural translation by Ulfilas and there were many medieval versions made in more modern vernacular tongues for early printers to duplicate. See n. 148 below. The 'oral memorizing' tradition was strong enough to preserve memory of Old Latin passages among the copyists of early mss. of Jerome's version. See Loewe, 'The Medieval History of the Latin Vulgate,' p. 104. It was also used by the Waldensians to teach scriptures to unlettered followers.
102 According to Kenyon, *Books and Readers in Ancient Greece and Rome*, p. 120, the dominance of the vellum book over the papyrus roll corresponds almost exactly with the Christian millennium: 400–1400. He also assigns importance to Constantine's conversion and the great demand for Bibles created throughout the Empire (pp. 113–15). Reichman, 'The Book Trade of the Roman Empire,' p. 55, asserts that the parchment codex was developed by the Roman book industry but did not become ubiquitous until used for the Christian Bible.
103 Gandz, 'The Dawn of Literature,' p. 495.

On the other hand, while oral recitation remained important for transmission, the Koran had been committed to writing and Islam was served by scribes. A further consideration is worth pondering: Christendom was not only more committed to an 'apostolate of the pen'; it was also much less reluctant to accept the substitution of press for pen. The same thing, curiously enough, can be said of Judaism. By 1494, the Jews had already set up a press in Istanbul for Hebrew printing. Among Ottomans, it was regarded as a sin to print religious books.[104]

The hybrid, Judeo–Christian character of Biblical texts points to yet another issue that needs exploring. Compared with the more homogeneous Koran, the diversity of ingredients contained in the Bible, the sheer number of dissimilar materials drawn from different places, eras, and linguistic groups, is particularly striking. Apart from all the centuries and cultures spanned by both testaments taken together, portions of each, taken separately, still show a remarkably variegated texture.

Is there anything in the Koran to equal the cultural complexity of the Septuagint, a Greek version of the Hebrew Old Testament made in Egypt? Is there any equivalent of the mixture in the New Testament of Aramaic sermons with Greek epistles? The Koran comes closer to resembling a single prophetic book of the Old Testament, but even then it seems more homogeneous. The Book of Isaiah, for example, was composed over several centuries whereas the compilation of Mohammed's sayings occurred over the course of a few decades. Of course, the Prophet drew heavily on the Jewish scriptures himself. But all of the Koran's varied ingredients were filtered through one mind, articulated in one tongue, and shaped in terms of a single lifespan. However controversial the Arabic textual tradition, it can be traced back to a few manuscripts made in one language in one region a few decades after Mohammed's death. What a contrast is offered by the numerous prophets, annalists, and Gospel writers, languages and folkways, centuries and regions encompassed by the Bible! How much more intricate the puzzles offered by its texts, how much more difficult it is to determine their provenance, how much farther back in time and further afield must one go to retrieve and decipher them!

Reverence for a sacred book inspired the search, and a new

---

[104] Inalcik, *The Ottoman Empire*, p. 174.

technology made it possible. The richly variegated contents of the Bible were strategic, nevertheless, in determining the course taken by Western scholars. As soon as they were equipped, they embarked on a never-ending, seemingly impossible, quest which might be described as 'quixotic,' or perhaps as 'Faustian.' Whatever their goal – whether they sought the date of Creation, the name of the fruit which led to Adam's fall, the location of Ararat or the actual year of the birth of the Savior himself – Western scholars were fated always to fall short of obtaining it.[105] Nevertheless, a remarkable impetus was given to erudite studies of all kinds as exotic territory was explored, strange languages mastered and archeological data stored.

Research inspired by the scriptures, indeed, set the pattern followed by Western scholarship in general. A comparison of how the Bible was handled before and after print helps to illuminate the basic shift which affected all forms of knowledge. The sacred book had been laboriously transmitted (much as had Roman law, the Aristotelian corpus or Ptolemy's *Almagest*) by dint of 'slavish' copying and with the aid of diverse memory arts, from generation to generation, throughout the age of scribes. In the hands of scholar–printers, however, it became the focus of an open-ended process of investigation, with researchers pressing against continuously receding frontiers. The transmission of a single closed system – a body of inherited lore – gave way to the steady accumulation of data which enabled each generation to probe deeper into the past and advance beyond the position of its predecessor – in knowledge of *this* world, albeit not of the next.

How attempts to edit the Bible in the scholar–printer's workshop led to a rapid accumulation of findings is suggested by the output of Robert Estienne, who began by compiling an index to the Vulgate and ended with pioneering work in lexicography.[106] Between 1500 and 1800 more than seventy lexicons devoted solely to Hebrew would be issued.[107] In the second half of the sixteenth century, Plantin set out to produce a slightly revised edition of the Complutensian Polyglot of 1517–22. He ended by publishing a monumental new work containing five volumes of text and three of reference materials, which included

---

[105] The Faustian metaphor seems particularly apt in view of Sir Thomas Browne's attribution to Satan of all the troublesome factual questions pertaining to the Ark, the Golden Calf, manna, etc. which tantalized him and his contemporaries. See Willey, *The Seventeenth Century Background*, pp. 57–8. [106] Starnes, *Robert Estienne's Influence*, pp. 13, 17, 33.
[107] D. R. Jones, 'Aids to the Study of the Bible,' appendix I, 524.

grammars and dictionaries for the Greek, Hebrew, Aramaic and Syriac languages.[108] Further expansion came with the Paris polyglot edition of 1645 and the climax came in mid-seventeenth-century England. The London 'Polyglotte' of 1657 was announced by a prospectus which boasted of its superiority to all prior editions (in terms which were later echoed by Bishop Sprat in his praise of the Royal Society).[109] Its contents suggest how much territory had been conquered after two centuries of printing. It presented texts in 'Hebrew, Samaritan, Septuagint Greek, Chaldee, Syriac, Arabic, Ethiopian, Persian and Vulgate Latin' thus adding to the stock of typefonts used by Western scholars for oriental studies. Its elaborate appendices showed how Bible-printing spurred the modern knowledge industry. They comprised

a vast apparatus including a table of ancient chronology prepared by Louis Cappel, descriptions and maps of the Holy Land and of Jerusalem; plans of the temple; treatises on Hebrew coins, on weights and measures, on the origin of language and of the alphabet, on the Hebrew idiom; an historical account of the chief editions and principal versions of the Scriptures; a table of variant readings, with an essay on the integrity and authority of the original texts and other matter.[110]

This 'vast apparatus' demonstrates how texts attributed to Moses forced scholars to reach further back and wander farther afield than texts attributed to Mohammed. Obviously scriptural texts were more vulnerable than the Koran to questions provoked by new forms of authorship and intellectual property rights.[111] Problems arising from words and phrases which shifted their meanings in the course of translation were also much more troublesome for Western scholars than for those of Islam – as one can see from the number of languages and tables of variants in polyglot Bibles. Increasingly the words of God seemed subject to perplexing flux. No sooner had one generation of scholar–printers become confident that they had produced 'reasonably authenticated' and 'reasonably authoritative versions of the Hebrew and Greek texts of the Old and New Testaments' than another polyglot

---

[108] Vöet, The Golden Compasses I, 60.

[109] Hendricks, pp. 110–13 describes this prospectus. On its resemblance to Bishop Sprat's apologia, see p. 695, volume II below. For data on Paris polyglot of 1645 see Martin, Livre à Paris I, 100. On all editions see also Darlowe and Moule, Historical Catalogue.

[110] Preserved Smith, Origins of Modern Culture, p. 251.

[111] After studying distinctions between 'Q' and 'M' utilized for the Gospel of Matthew, it even becomes difficult to assign the Sermon on the Mount to any one author. See 'The Man Behind the Sermon,' Times Literary Supplement (Feb. 27, 1964), p. 175.

publication project was launched and confidence again slipped away. Protestants might scoff at the obstinate obscurantists who proclaimed the Clementine Vulgate authentic. But sooner or later they themselves deemed it necessary to agree upon one 'textus receptus' – a term first employed not by a church synod, but by the Leiden branch of the Dutch publishing firm of Elsevier, as a blurb.[112]

It may be partly because the words of their God gave rise to so many variants and translation problems after the advent of printing, that learned men in Western Christendom became increasingly attracted by His works.[113] By tracing the scriptures to their true Hebrew and Greek sources, argued the young Philip Melanchthon (in his inaugural lecture as Professor of Greek at Wittenberg) their 'true meaning will light up for us as the midday sun.'[114] The more Greek and Hebrew studies progressed, however, the more wrangling there was over the meaning of words and phrases. The quibbles of schoolmen about the nature of angels were no more destructive of piety than learned disputes between biblical scholars. It was all very well for Richard Bentley to argue that

far from leading to uncertainty and justifying Pyrrhonism, a large number of manuscripts containing a large number of variant readings provided a surer means of reconstructing an original text than a single manuscript. 'If there had been but one manuscript of the Greek Testament at the restoration of learning about two centuries ago,' he asked '...would the text be in a better condition then, than now we have 30,000 (variant readings)?'[115]

Thousands of variant readings, however enlightening, could not make things as clear as Melanchthon's midday sun. The ceaseless accumulation of scriptural commentaries resulted in

---

112 See B. Hall, 'Biblical Scholarship,' p. 63; Bouyer, 'Erasmus in Relation to the Medieval Biblical Tradition,' p. 499; and Metzger, *The Text of the New Testament*, pp. 102–3 for relevant data. It is not entirely clear which Greek text of the New Testament, one of Erasmus' editions or the emended version of Beza and Estienne, was accepted in the late sixteenth century as the 'textus receptus.' The term was first used in a blurb put out by the Elsevier press in Leiden to advertise the merits (of the Beza-Estienne version according to Hall) of Erasmus' version according to Metzger. See Jarrott, 'Erasmus's Biblical Humanism,' p. 121, n. 14. According to Kenney, *The Classical Text*, pp. 59–69, Daniel Heinsius was the scholarly editor, serving the Elseviers, who applied the term to the 1633 edition of Erasmus' version. Kenney underlines the need for a base text from which departures can be noted.

113 The juxtaposition of 'the book of God's word' and the 'book of God's works' occurs in many texts – and goes back to medieval sermon literature. Francis Bacon's *The Advancement of Learning* (1605), Book I: 'To the Kings,' offers one of many examples. For further discussion of this topos see first section of the next chapter, volume II below.

114 Cited in Hillerbrand, ed. *The Reformation*, pp. 59–60.

115 In his riposte to Anthony Collins, *Remarks upon a...Discourse of Free Thinking* (1713) cited by Gossman, *Medievalism*, pp. 227–8.

the gradual decay of the ordinary Christian's sense that he can read the Bible for himself without an interpreter and discover its unambiguous meaning... The Bible came to be regarded as a book for experts requiring an elaborate training in linguistic and historic disciplines before it could be properly understood...[116]

As long as book production depended on scribal labor, no permanent remedy could be found for the corruption that provoked the young Melanchthon's scorn. It was not uncommon for the Old Testament to be preceded by a life of Alexander the Great in manuscript Bibles.[117] Extracts from the New Testament were often mixed with other matter, especially in handbooks for teachers and preachers. The tendency for a compendium such as the *Sentences* to replace the actual scriptures themselves had aroused objections from at least one thirteenth-century schoolman, namely Roger Bacon.[118] But here as elsewhere, the Franciscan scholar was well 'ahead of his times.' Much as was the case with the glosses that veiled the *Corpus Juris*, the text of Jerome's translation was buried 'fathoms deep' under layers of comment.[119]

Scribal transmission not only threatened to bury the Vulgate but it also concealed the full complexity of the textual tradition that lay beneath Jerome's version. In this regard the pollution of pure streams went together with a kind of ignorance that engendered bliss. The very idea of going back to Greek and Hebrew texts was 'revolutionary' in the sixteenth century,[120] even though it had been advocated inter-mittently by biblical scholars ever since Jerome. To preserve the Vulgate from the persistent threat of corruption and to locate the texts that were needed for emending portions of the corrupted versions usually ex-hausted the resources of those exceptional centers where scribal scholars engaged in research. The thousands of variants available to Bentley might be compared with the complete absence of any manuscript at all which confronted John the Scot – as he searched in vain for a copy of the Septuagint to help him with his labors.[121] Alcuin's slender know-ledge of Greek and complete ignorance of Hebrew did not equip him very well for the emendations he undertook.[122] Moreover, when the

---

[116] Alan Richardson, 'The Rise of Modern Biblical Scholarship,' p. 301.
[117] Delaissé, *A Century of Dutch Manuscript Illumination*, p. 16.
[118] Aidan (Cardinal Gasquet), 'Roger Bacon and the Latin Vulgate.'
[119] Harbison, *Christian Scholar*, p. 59.
[120] Schwarz, *Principles and Problems*, pp. ix–x.
[121] Smalley, *Study of the Bible*, p. 44. See also Smalley, *English Friars*, p. 56.
[122] Loewe, 'The Medieval History of the Latin Vulgate,' p. 134.

dearth of linguistic aids and texts was partly overcome and schools of exegesis formed around manuscript collections, their labors were fated to resemble those of Sisyphus. Scribal Bible study, as pursued in Antioch and later by the Victorines, was undertaken without knowledge of previous accomplishments; whatever was found by one school could not be passed on to the next.[123]

Thus, although Greek and Hebrew studies were supported in theory during the middle ages they could not be pursued very far in fact. The idea of a trilingual Bible was 'as old as Origen' and some fragments of late medieval efforts have been found.[124] Yet when Aldus Manutius set about procuring types for producing such a Bible in 1498, the project still could be described as a 'complete novelty.'[125] Similarly, the idea of providing multilingual studies at universities had been approved and new chairs decreed by a Church Council at Vienne in 1311. The permanent establishment of chairs in Greek and Hebrew at colleges throughout Europe, however, had to wait for the permanent recovery of ancient languages by the West.[126] After the new lectureships had been founded and the collaboration of heterodox Greeks and Jews had been enlisted, trilingual studies came under a new vigorous attack. Theologians at the older universities soon began to defend the Vulgate and forget the Council of Vienne. The Sorbonne tried to suppress lectureships as well as scholarly editions; despite the protection of Cardinal Ximenes, scholars who contributed to the Complutensian Polyglot were persecuted by the Inquisition.[127] Everywhere the very same scholarly programs, which had been supported by earlier church authorities, were attacked as subversive by later authorities. For the most part, the obscurantists were fearful that contact with infidel scholars and texts would prove subversive, and lead to apostasy and heresy. The contaminating effect of studying Talmudic materials was

---

123 Smalley, *Study of the Bible*, p. 357.
124 Part of a Greek column survives from a trilingual Bible proposed by the Latin Archbishop of Thebes in Boetia (1336–85) but the project was 'without perceptible influence' according to Singer, 'Hebrew Scholarship,' p. 301.
125 Morison, 'The Learned Press as an Institution,' p. 154.
126 See preceding chapter for discussion of contribution of typography to this permanent recovery. Bouwsma, *Concordia Mundi*, pp. 88–9, discusses the multilingual decree passed by the Council of Vienne in 1311 and reasserted at Basel as evidence of influence exerted by Raymond Lull. Although he attributes later implementation to other factors than print he notes that the Vienne decrees themselves became more available, because the *Constitutiones Clementinae* were frequently reprinted from 1460 on.
127 B. Hall, 'Trilingual College,' pp. 115–16.

particularly feared.[128] In the long run, subversion came from other quarters. Even when Christian scholars remained unshaken in their true faith, their search for pure sources led to complications that were unforeseen. The pursuit increased rather than diminished perplexity about the Divine Word. It could be argued, indeed, that the peace-loving Christian humanist who abhorred theological disputes disturbed the old order by his quiet Bible study just as effectively as did the noisiest most militant Protestant or Papist pamphleteer

Early in 1517, when Erasmus was envisaging the dawn of a new golden age, and writing about a conspiracy to revive the best learning, he was confident that he and his friends were merely doing for their age 'what Jerome had done for him: restoring and purifying the Christian tradition.'[129] It was not merely his failure to anticipate the outbreak of a 'monkish quarrel' set off by a stubborn Wittenberg theologian that makes Erasmus' optimism seem ironic in retrospect. It was also his blindness about his own historical role. Despite his close collaboration with printers (or, perhaps, just because he was so close that perspective was lacking) he did not take full stock of the new powers he commanded; powers that had not been envisaged by Church fathers and that he wielded most skillfully before Luther turned them to other ends. In this regard it may be a mistake to take Erasmus' self-estimate at face value, to follow his lead too faithfully and make too much of his sense of affinity with Saint Jerome. 'Spiritual affinities' between the scholarly humanist and early Christian saint should not be ignored; but the material distance between Jerome's study and Froben's workshop must be brought into the picture as well. This distance has to be correctly assessed if we want to place the Reformation in its appropriate historical setting.[130] Humanists and Reformers looked back to Church fathers for guidance. They were faithful to earlier Christian traditions and consciously engaged in tasks of restoration.

[128] See problems posed for Pellican when trying to obtain a copy of the Talmud and a Talmudic lexicon at a Dominican chapterhouse in Ratisbon. Copying the text was forbidden on the grounds that the copyist might be injured by exposure to the infidel work. Nyhus, 'Caspar Schatzgeyer,' pp. 188–9. Grendler, 'The Roman Inquisition,' pp. 52–3 describes the order to burn all Talmuds in Italy in 1553 and how compliance by the Venetians led to a ten year hiatus in Jewish publishing in Venice.

[129] Harbison, *Christian Scholar*, p. 95. See p. 144 above for citation concerning Erasmus' 'conspiracy.'

[130] The popular engraving by Wolfgang Stuber portraying Luther in the position assigned by Dürer to 'Saint Jerome in his Study' (see frontispiece to Bluhm, *Martin Luther, Creative Translator*) is also full of historic irony. Like Erasmus, Stuber, Dürer and Luther, all owed their historical stature to a medium which was never envisaged by the early Christian saint.

They were unwitting innovators nevertheless. The means they employed to achieve their goal of 'reformatio' were radically new, and this made all the difference in the end.

The disruptive effect of pressures generated in new workshops becomes even more apparent when we turn from the question of how the Gospel should be studied to the equally controversial issue of how it should be spread. Here again, the golden age of Christian humanism was necessarily short-lived, and sharp division among churchmen impossible to prevent. Erasmus had expressed a sense of evangelical mission forcefully in his famous 'paraclesis' or introduction to the New Testament:

> I wish that every woman would read the Gospel and the Epistles of Paul...
> I wish these were translated into each and every language...read and understood not only by Scots and Irishmen, but also by Turks and Saracens...
> I hope the farmer may sing snatches of Scripture at his plough, that the weaver may hum bits...to the tune of his shuttle, that the traveller may lighten...his journey with stories from Scripture...[131]

By producing his French translation of the New Testament, Lefèvre d'Etaples acted in accordance with Erasmus' words. Lefèvre himself remained within the Catholic fold; but his French Bible did not. It went on the Index and circulated widely only after passing through Calvinist hands.[132] Those who tried only to follow the Church fathers by making vernacular scriptures available were fated to outdistance them in an age of print. Bible translators in the post-Gutenberg era found themselves breaking new paths for Erastian princes and Protestant rebels – even while claiming, with justice it seems, that precedents set by the Church fathers were on their side.

When Erasmus talked hopefully of versions in Celtic or Turkish, he could claim that he was merely following earlier leads. The very term, Vulgate, reminds us that Jerome had converted the scriptures of his day into a vulgar tongue. Similarly, the numerous ancient languages that had to be mastered to edit later polyglots – Syriac, Ethiopian, Persian and the like – show that vernacular translations had been encouraged by the early Church. Even before the new art of printing had become known, argued a Huguenot pamphleteer of 1554, the Apostles had

---

[131] Harbison, *Christian Scholar*, p. 101.
[132] Droz, 'Bibles Françaises,' p. 211 discusses editions of Lefèvre's version from the first printing in 1523 (by Robert Estienne's stepfather, Simon de Colines) to its appearance on the Index of 1569.

'imprinted' the Gospels on the hearts and souls of their audience aided by the Grace of the Holy Spirit and using a language the people could understand. Errors came not from reading the Bible in French but from learned theologians who read Latin – like the Pope![133] Whereas the anti-vernacular party at Trent had difficulty finding historical arguments to support their cause and had to stretch the evidence at every point, evangelical reformers could turn to the past with confidence. Saint Paul was on their side and could be cited against the actions of Pope Paul II.[134] Even today, Protestant historians who deal with the question approach early Church practices confidently and find clear and certain precedents at hand. Ever since the Council of Trent, however, Catholics tend to be much more equivocal.[135]

Place every book of Scripture in the hands of children is an instruction of the fourth-century Apostolic Constitution...Besides being read in church, the Bible is distributed by sales says Augustine...The principle is plain: in the formative years of the Christian Church, the Bible was available in the vernacular...the laity: men, women, and children were expected to hear it read in church and to read it for themselves at home.[136]

'The principle is plain' to the Regius Professor at Oxford. It was plain to the Erasmians who upheld it at Trent. But post-Tridentine Catholic scholars are likely to argue that early Church policy was, in fact, quite obscure.[137] This division of opinion, interestingly enough, follows the same lines as debates held at Trent. The vernacular translation movement went together with a belief that Gospel truths were so simple that they could be understood by ordinary men. The only role

---

[133] Droz, 'Bibles Françaises,' pp. 214–15. This pamphlet, first published in 1554 went through many editions according to Droz.

[134] See remark: 'Popes err; St. Paul does not,' made by the Cardinal of Trent at the Session of March 17, 1546, Cavallera, 'La Bible en Langue Vulgaire,' p. 41. On divisions at Trent over vernacular translation see also Herman A. P. Schmidt, *Liturgie et Langue Vulgaire*, pp. 85ff.; Droz, 'Bibles Françaises,' p. 209; Jedin, *History of the Council of Trent* II, 67ff. The latter repeatedly describes this issue as 'burning.' It did, indeed, lead to the burning of men as well as of books.

[135] Equivocation is particularly marked in discussion by Crehan, 'The Bible in the Catholic Church,' pp. 199ff.

[136] Greenslade, 'Epilogue,' pp. 490–1.

[137] Thus Schmidt, *Liturgie et Langue Vulgaire* argues that Protestants are indulging in anachronisms when pointing to patristic acceptance of vernaculars because antiquity had no sense of 'linguistic principles,' pp. 179 ff. Bouwsma, *Concordia Mundi*, pp. 241–2 notes that Postel's eagerness to spread the work in all possible tongues moved him away from a Catholic stress on the 'sacerdotal custody of sacred truth' and toward a Protestant position. (It also brought him into the orbit of Plantin's heterodox circle.) Postel thus applauded St Jerome, was fond of citing early Christian translations into Armenian, Coptic and other tongues and got into trouble for saying mass in French.

ɔf the pastor was to convey God's word as clearly as possible. Bibles should be stripped of extravagant glosses, laid bare in unadorned guise, and presented in everyday language. Once plain texts, plain speaking and open books were associated with Protestant doctrine, Catholic reaction took the contrary path justifying mystification, élitism and censorship. The use of Latin was defended not only because it was a time honored ecclesiastical practice, but also because it was esoteric and kept mysteries veiled from the profane.[138] The power of the press could be used to improve clerical education but had to be controlled by clerical censors to foster lay obedience.[139]

A deliberate cultivation of mystery, an insistence on withholding pearls of wisdom from the swinish multitude and more emphatic distinctions between educated clergy and uninformed laity characterized the anti-vernacular arguments made at Trent. 'After reading the decrees of April 8, 1546, one may understand how and why innumerable Catholics are, even today, almost totally ignorant about the Bible.'[140] Even where vernacular translation was allowed, in lands held by Protestant rulers, Catholic Bibles were marked by Latinate expressions and elaborate glosses. 'It was only the plain text that was thought harmful,' notes a Catholic scholar about his church's policy in England.[141] To regard the plain text as harmful in lay hands, however, meant to encourage obfuscation and to deny to laymen the most direct access to the divine Word. This fearful approach to spreading the Gospel led, in turn, to much hedging about patristic precedents.

It is often noted that Protestant policies followed patterns set by early church assemblies more closely than did those of Catholic reformers. It cannot be too often stressed, however, that Catholic post-Tridentine policies were different from those pursued by the medieval

---

138 Schmidt, *Liturgie et Langue Vulgaire*, pp. 130–4, gives an account of debates at Trent which shows how the élitist and authoritarian position of the anti-vernacular party extended to a defense of Latin literature as elevated and noble as against low, base vulgar tongues. R. F. Jones, *The Triumph*, pp. 63ff. describes English Catholic disdain for 'Unlearned... rifferaffe' and their use of the 'pearls before swine' argument. How this same argument was used by the chief spokesman for the anti-vernacular cause at Trent is described by Cavallera, 'La Bible en Langue Vulgaire,' p. 46.

139 Schmidt, *Liturgie et Langue Vulgaire*, p. 177, reveals stress on lay obligations of obedience, respect and devotion which contrasts with the Protestant goal of educated laymen.

140 Droz, 'Bibles Françaises,' p. 210.

141 Crehan, 'The Bible in the Catholic Church,' p. 223. Craig Thompson, *The Bible in English*, pp. 12–13, comments on the difficult Latinate English and the preface warning against indiscriminate Bible-reading which made the Catholic (Rheims-Douai) version different from Protestant ones. For complaints by English Protestants about Papist obfuscation, even in vernacular translations, see R. F. Jones, *Triumph*, pp. 113–14.

church. The clergy appeared somewhat more élitist and their doctrines somewhat more esoteric in the middle ages than during the later Roman empire, to be sure. But such changes may be attributed to the same kind of factors which led to linguistic drift, the emergence of new vernaculars, and the development of canon law. A quasi-monopoly of learning by the Church and a sharp separation between clergy and laity as belonging to different orders resulted, that is, more from historical circumstances than from a deliberate policy. It was a formidable task to preserve the Christian faith by scribal transmission for more than a millennium, even while coping with successive waves of barbarian invasions. It was difficult enough to provide every region with a steady supply of priests who could read some Latin and who were adequately trained to handle routine tasks. Additional demands for lay education had to be met on an irregular, haphazard basis. The cause of lay evangelism, in other words, was pursued intermittently after the collapse of imperial Rome, largely because there was no other way of pursuing this cause until after the advent of printing.

Nevertheless, those who pressed the cause of lay evangelism in the sixteenth century did not always have to reach back to the early Church for precedents. Protestant scholars, who stress persecution of Lollards and Hussites, often leave the mistaken impression that Counter-Reformation policies were typical of the medieval Church and that the latter consistently deprived the laity of access to 'Christian records.'[142] As noted above, however, the position of the Church on vernacular Bibles was more flexible and less consistent before the sixteenth century than afterwards. When one remembers, for example, that a French translation of the Bible had appeared under the sponsorship of the University of Paris in 1235, Lefèvre d'Etaples' work appears somewhat more traditional and less pioneering.[143] Even closer to the lives of many reformers were the Brethren of the Common Life, whose efforts at lay evangelism had not been proscribed.

Gerhard Groote, the founder of the order, had been an ardent biblio-

[142] See e.g. Deanesly, The Lollard Bible, p. 2. The tendency to overstress religious monopoly and persecution of dissidents by the medieval church goes back to early eulogists of Wycliffe who was portrayed as a martyr although he died a natural death. See Aston, 'Wycliffe's Reformation Reputation,' p. 38.

[143] Robson, 'Vernacular Scriptures in France,' p. 451, notes that French vernacular Bibles were neither prohibited nor licenced in fourteenth-century northern France in contrast with England. He also suggests that the chief original contribution made by Lefèvre's translation was the elimination of glosses (p. 437).

phile. He 'had pressed the book' into the service of his movement from its start,[144] and his movement combined a somewhat unconventional drive for lay literacy with more customary monastic devotions. Book provisions and schooling sponsored by the Brethren were thus not exclusively designed for the benefit of the clergy. Even the more learned branch of the order, the scholarly houses of the Windesheim congregation, contributed to the output of vernacular sermons and tracts.[145] Like the *Imitation of Christ*, composed by one or more of their copyists, the Brethren's primers and prayer books flowed with unusual continuity from old scriptoria and new presses alike.[146] The young Erasmus himself had profited thereby.

The *devotio moderna*, as promulgated by Groote's order in the Netherlands, was only one indication of the way lay evangelism flourished in the later middle ages. Perhaps ecclesiastical Rome provides the most striking example of late medieval permissiveness in contrast with post-medieval restrictions. The church in Italy 'showed no hostility to the translation of the Bible and placed no serious obstacle in the way of rendering it to the people in their own language.'[147] Here, as elsewhere, it is useful to place the issue in a wider comparative perspective than that familiar to Anglo-Americans who take the persecution of Lollards to be the rule. By the fifteenth century, there were numerous versions of vernacular Bibles, especially in German and Italian, but also in many other tongues, to suggest the wide latitude allowed to local initiative by church policy during the later middle ages.[148]

Efforts to control or curtail the output of vernacular Bibles and prayer books continued to vary in accord with local decisions after the advent of printing. The output of printed Bibles and prayer books,

[144] Post, *The Modern Devotion*, pp. 98ff.
[145] Verwey, 'The Netherlands Book,' p. 7. The Gothic script used by one of the Brethren's copyists left a lasting mark on Dutch Bible-printing (p. 15). That Groote's order influenced many scriptural translations into southern Dutch and low German is noted by Lockwood, 'Vernacular Scriptures,' pp. 431ff.
[146] Sheppard, 'Printing at Deventer' points out that the first printer at Deventer lived with the rector of the school there (pp. 116–17). The installation of new presses by the orders founded by Groote is discussed in many studies. See Verwey, 'Netherlands Book,' and chap. 1, n. 39, above, for references.
[147] Kenelm Foster, 'Vernacular Scriptures in Italy,' p. 465.
[148] A number of editions in German, Saxon, French, Italian, Spanish, Bohemian, Dutch are mentioned by Steele, 'What 15th Century Books Are About,' p. 340. A chronology of editions of vernacular Bibles printed in Europe between 1466 and 1552 is offered by Hirsch, *Printing, Selling*, pp. 92–3. The absence of any clear, uniform Church policy on vernacular translation before Trent is also noted by Jedin, *History of the Council of Trent* II, 67. On mss. versions, see K. Foster 'Vernacular Scriptures in Italy,' pp. 338–491.

however, posed new problems, and new forms of censorship were devised to cope with them. The first landmark came in 1485 from the same region as the Gutenberg Bible. With a statement which specifically mentioned the 'divine art,' complained about its misuse and noted the need to protect the purity of divine books from being converted into 'incorrect and vulgar German,' the archbishop of Mainz issued an edict requiring the licensing of all German vernacular translations.[149] There followed a series of papal bulls and edicts which indicated a growing concern about the dangers posed by print, particularly within the Empire. These measures culminated in the sweeping censorship decree issued by Leo X following the May 4 session of the Lateran Council of 1515:

> It may have been under the influence of the Reuchlin controversy (and now not directed against any particular territory or town) that Leo X ordered censorship to be applied to all translations from Hebrew, Greek, Arabic, and Chaldaic into Latin and from Latin into the vernacular. The regulations were to be enforced by bishops, their delegates or the *inquisitores haereticae pravitatis*. The decree bemoaned the fact that readers were supplied by printers with books...which promote errors in faith as well as in daily life...The Pope saw acute danger that the evil 'may grow from day to day' (as indeed it did)...[150]

The Roman Church had thus moved against Bible-printing and developed new forms of censorship backed by the Inquisition even before Luther's revolt. The imperial and papal edicts of 1520, which were aimed at arresting the spread of Protestant heresy, singled out Lutheran tracts rather than scriptural translations for prohibition. But of course the Lutheran heresy also entailed the output of unauthorized biblical editions and vernacular translations. Earlier local measures were soon polarized along Protestant–Catholic lines. Separate edicts, directed against new editions and translations of the Bible, had been issued in the Empire, in France and in Spain by the mid-sixteenth

---

[149] An English translation of parts of this edict is given by Hirsch, 'Pre-Reformation Censorship,' p. 102. It is the first landmark only with regard to censoring vernacular Bibles. An earlier censorship trial centering on a different 'misuse' of the 'new art' comes in Cologne in 1478 (where precursors of the 'nihil obstat' and 'imprimatur' also first appear). The Mainz edict is often misdated 1486 and 1487; it was reissued in both years. In addition to 'Pre-Reformation censorship,' and summary offered in *Printing, Selling*, pp. 87–91, Hirsch gives guidance to literature and early church edicts in 'Bulla Super Impressione Librorum.' The need for a solid, impartial study of Church censorship policies noted in 1906 by G. H. Putnam, *Censorship* I, vii, is still clear. Of the two standard works on the Index, Reusch's *Der Index der Verbotenen Bücher* is essentially a catalogue and Hilgers' *Der Index der Verbotenen Bücher* is an apologia. [150] Hirsch, *Printing, Selling*, p. 90.

century; they were followed by a series of far-reaching, long-lasting measures taken by the Counter-Reformation Papacy.[151] Thus the first Papal Index of 1559 under Paul IV repeated earlier prohibitions, and Bible-reading as well as Bible-printing was singled out for censorship in the list of ten general rules, first promulgated in the 1564 Index of Pius IV and reiterated in all later lists.[152]

By implementing these measures, the post-Tridentine Church put an end to serious Bible translations by Catholics in Italy for the next two hundred years.[153] Significant repercussions resulted from this reversal of previous trends. Venetian printers were especially hard hit by the new prohibition imposed on some of their bestselling wares.[154] The cause of lay evangelism in Italy was thereafter linked to a clandestine book-trade.[155] Beyond the Alps, the situation was more confused. Erastian rulers in Catholic lands saw to it that Tridentine decrees were not enacted everywhere. The Catholic clergy in Protestant regions wanted to counter heretical translations with versions of their own. Catholic Bible translation, while never officially sponsored and often regarded with suspicion, did not entirely cease in every region. Division of opinion had been so troublesome at Trent, moreover, that equivocation was required, some room for local option was left, and it is still difficult to find out precisely what the Council meant by 'declaring the Vulgate authentic.'[156]

Nevertheless, guidelines set by Rome, upholding the Vulgate and Church Latin, generally prevailed throughout Catholic territories. Thus during the second century of printing, vernacular Bibles were rarely sponsored by Catholic rulers. 'The Roman Church did not publish vernacular versions save in countries where she was threatened

---

151 Imperial and national edicts aimed against printing vernacular Bibles are noted in various articles in *The Cambridge History of the Bible* vol. 3. See pp. 113, 125, 430–1. The persistent opposition of the Sorbonne, beginning in 1487, to French vernacular versions is noted by Rickard, *La Langue Française*, pp. 9–10.

152 Putnam, *Censorship* I, 176–7; 182–9. See also discussion of ten rules by Jackson, 'Printed Books,' pp. 45–6.

153 Kenelm Foster, 'Italian Versions,' p. 112. The lasting effect of this prohibition is conveyed by an interview with the Italian director of a film on the Bible: 'Five years ago, I had never read the Bible, because in Italy we learn everything about religion from the priests,' said Dino de Laurentiis as cited by Lillian Ross, 'Our Far-Flung Correspondents,' p. 197.

154 See de Frede, 'Per la Storia...,' pp. 175–7; Grendler, *The Roman Inquisition, passim*.

155 McNair, *Peter Martyr in Italy, passim*, supplies much relevant data, as does Grendler.

156 See e.g. F. J. Crehan, 'The Bible in the Catholic Church,' p. 204. On the 'supple formula' devised by clever councillors, who were inspired by the 'Holy Ghost,' according to a modern Jesuit, see Schmidt, *Liturgie et Langue Vulgaire*, pp. 82; 95. Varying interpretations of the formula given by earlier Catholic scholars are noted by Palmer, *Catholics and Unbelievers*, p. 64.

by Protestant translations and with the sole aim of replacing these translations with a text adapted to Catholic dogmas.'[157] Publication of vernacular Bibles in Catholic regions moreover often led to persecution and imprisonment. Vernacular versions were generally handled under foreign or heterodox auspices. Spanish translations were thus printed in London, Geneva, Basel, Amsterdam and on a Jewish press in Ferrara; the Protestant Giovanni Diodati had his celebrated Italian translation printed in Geneva; French translations of scripture were 'almost always produced abroad' or else produced clandestinely by Lyons publishers who resorted to false addresses.[158] Even the Anglo-Catholic (Rheims-Douai) version was produced outside England. It seems characteristic that one project for a vernacular French version (which was temporarily authorized under Louis XIII) resulted only in arousing a successful opposition movement which was climaxed by a book entitled: 'The Sanctuary Closed to the Profane or the Bible Prohibited to the Vulgar.'[159]

In marked contrast to Catholic policy, vernacular Bibles, prayer books and catechisms were adopted by all reforming churches. Sooner or later, scriptural translations were officially authorized by all rulers who broke with Rome, and thus entered into the mainstream of national literary cultures in Protestant lands. Late medieval currents in England and in France were significantly reversed by these developments.[160] At the same time that French Bibles and Psalters were being banned by the edicts of Valois courts, English translations, which had been proscribed since the Lollards, were gaining official approval under Cromwell and Cranmer. The timing of the reversal was crucial. For after printing, primers, catechisms, and school books of all kinds could be made more uniform, and national characters began to be cast into more permanent molds.

In England, the crown put its stamp of approval, not only

---

[157] Victor Baroni, *La Contre Réforme devant la Bible*, introduction, article IX.

[158] See Droz, 'Bibles Françaises,' p. 211. (The intriguing case of René Benoist's French version, which was condemned after getting permission to be printed in Paris in 1566 and was reissued by Plantin with the approval of Philip II is described on p. 222. See also Black, 'The Printed Bible,' pp. 447–8; Martin, *Livre à Paris* I, 102.)

[159] *Le Sanctuaire Fermé au Prophane ou la Bible défendue au Vulgaire* by the royal confessor, Le Maire, is discussed by Martin, *Livre à Paris* II, 610–11.

[160] That the 'machinery for persecution was rusty in France' compared to England at the time of the Lutheran revolt is noted by Knecht, 'The Early Reformation,' pp. 6 ff. That the French had been ahead of the English in medieval and Renaissance Bible translation is noted by Sidney Lee, *The French Renaissance*, pp. 139–45.

on a vernacular Bible and Book of Common Prayer but also on the grammars and primers that paved the way for lay reading. Education and religion were cast in the same uniform vernacular mold.

> And as his maiesty purposeth to establyshe his people in one consent and harmony of pure & tru religion: so his tender goodnes toward the youth & chyldhode of his realme, entedeth to have it brought up under one absolute and uniforme sorte of lernynge...consideryng the great encombrance and confusion of the young and tender wittes...by reason of the diversity of grammar rules and teachinges.[161]

Thus ran the introduction to the 1542 edition of William Lily's celebrated grammar: 'An Introduction of the Eyght Partes of Speche.' Three years later in 1545 came the authorized Primer, published by Grafton 'for avoyding of the dyversitie of primer bookes that are now abroade...and to have one uniform ordre of al suche bokes through out all our dominions.'[162] This small and cheap authorized Primer placed in the hands of English readers a guidebook that served the cause of uniformity, the Anglican religion and popular education all at once.[163] Nothing of the sort occurred under Valois or Bourbon kings. The *ratio studiorum* of the Jesuits shared much in common with that of Lutheran educators in Strasbourg and of the Calvinists who ran Huguenot academies. But there was a sharp contrast between Catholic and Protestant practices when it came to Bible study; this was integrated into all stages of learning by the latter but left in Jesuit schools for priests and theologians to expound.[164] The revised Catholic catechisms, which were issued in response to Tridentine decrees, calling for improving elementary religious instruction were also directed at priests and curés. Learning the catechism remained an oral exercise for French children long after English children had become accustomed to the printed word. Indeed, no full French version of the Roman catechism authorized at Trent was printed in Paris before 1670.[165] Only after the dissolution of the Jesuit order in France in the 1760s was a concerted effort made to devise a new, more uniform lay vernacular educational system. It was under anti-clerical auspices that French

---

[161] Cited by Baldwin, *William Shakespere's Small Latine* I, 179–80.
[162] Cited from royal injunction, May 6, 1545, by Butterworth, *The English Primers*, p. 257.
[163] Wood, *The Reformation and English Education*, p. 261.
[164] R. Chartier, M. M. Compère, D. Julia, *L'Education en France*, p. 162.
[165] Martin, *Livre à Paris* I, 104, 127.

triumphed over regional tongues and the basis for a truly national system of lay education was laid.[166]

Despite its patriotic orientation and hostility towards ultramontanism, the Gallican Church was never as completely integrated as the Anglican Church was into a national culture. Bossuet preached in French but his sermons, however well publicized, could not enter the minds and hearts of his countrymen as deeply as did scriptures read during prayer meetings and alone. After the Huguenots were expelled, Bourbon rhetoric centered on the theme of unity: 'One King, One Faith, One Law.' Although French religious uniformity appeared to contrast with English toleration of dissent, the English Church was cemented to the state in a way that the French Church was not.[167] In France, unlike England, a permanent language barrier separated a liturgy which remained Latin from the law of the land which was converted into the vernacular. Greco-Roman authors were successfully converted into French classics, so that Amyot's Plutarch entered the mainstream of French letters along with Montaigne. But the Bible remained outside. The fine translation by Sacy was known by Racine, but it was published outside France, and failed to achieve anything like the depth of penetration of the version sponsored by King James. Like French lay Bible-reading in general, Sacy's version hinged largely on the fate of French Jansenism.[168] Its popularity waned when Jansenism was condemned.

One result of the absence of a standard version has been that biblical ways of expression have penetrated much less deeply into French than English. Quotation comes less easily when the form of the text is not fixed. For most educated Frenchmen...the authoritative text is the Vulgate and readers of

---

[166] The principal pre-revolutionary French program for educational reform was set forth in conjunction with the dissolution of the Jesuit order in 1762–3 by La Chalotais, the attorney-general of the Parlement of Brittany. His *Essay on National Education* which later influenced revolutionary legislation, upheld the cause of lay as opposed to clerical teaching and urged that more use be made of printed catechisms among other things. La Chalotais, *Essay on National Education, or Plan of Studies for The Young, passim.*

[167] The separatist tendencies of the Gallican as against the Anglican episcopacy have been analyzed by Ravitch, *Sword and Mitre.* Ravitch stresses fiscal and political policies rather than literary and cultural issues.

[168] Isaac Le Maistre de Sacy, a member of the Jansenist group at Port-Royal, began work on the Old Testament in the Bastille, was refused a privilege for his New Testament which was printed by the Elsevier Press in Amsterdam, although credited to Gaspard Migeot at Mons and known as the 'Mons Testament' (1667). Sayce, 'French Versions,' pp. 348–9. The Jansenist preference for instruction in French as opposed to the Jesuit preference for Latin is noted by Artz, *The Development of Technical Education,* p. 14.

Pascal, or for that matter of Gide, will know how often the Latin quotation is preferred to the French.[169]

When the bonds of dynastic loyalty snapped under the Stuart kings, and civil war broke out, Englishmen – however else they were divided – continued to draw on the same store of scriptural reference and to speak the same language. Even where the Bible itself was a bone of contention, conflicting groups cited chapter and verse in the same tongue. At the solemn ceremony of beheading a king, English regicides were inspired by the sonorous cadences of their Authorized Version. In addition to law books and chronicles, Old Testament precedents came readily to mind. Among French regicides in the eighteenth century, a markedly different situation prevailed. Biblical precedents were rarely invoked, the crowd who gathered round the guillotine carried no prayer books along. For the presence of psalm-singing sans-culottes in the streets of French cities one must return for a fleeting glimpse to the sixteenth century (when an interlude of toleration permitted the circulation of the famous Marot-Beza Huguenot psalter).[170] 'If only Robespierre had appeared,' wrote Sebastian Mercier 'with an old Bible under his arm and told his countrymen to become Protestant he might have succeeded.'[171] But for such an event to have occurred, several centuries of French history would have had to be repealed. By the late eighteenth century furthermore, few Parisian artisans were likely to connect an old Bible with any of the causes they held dear. French working class agitation was not leavened by religious nonconformity.[172] Insofar as an element of mimesis entered into the revolutionary drama, classical authors such as Plutarch furnished the necessary materials. Republican Rome was remote to those who lacked a secondary education, however, and for most of the populace who observed the event, the beheading of Louis XVI occurred in a kind of void; religious sanction was significantly lacking; a new patriotic mystique, centered on 'the nation in arms,' had to do service instead.

[169] Sayce, 'French Versions,' p. 114.
[170] On mass distribution of psalters in France during 1561–2, see Kingdon, 'Patronage, Piety and Printing,' pp. 28–30. For a glimpse of militant psalm-singing journeymen in the streets of Lyons, see Natalie Z. Davis, 'The Protestant Printing Workers,' pp. 252–7.
[171] Cited by McManners, The French Revolution, p. 105.
[172] On the dissenting tradition that entered into English Jacobinism and the competing sects and chapels to which English nonconformist artisans belonged, see E. P. Thompson, The Making of the English Working Class, p. 51. See also discussion of reading public of Bunyan, Defoe and Milton by Q. D. Leavis, Fiction and the Reading Public, pp. 97–118.

This brief look at later developments is offered merely to suggest that sixteenth-century division over the question of Bible translation had long-range implications, and the relationship between Protestantism and nationalism might be clarified if they were explored. In view of their far-reaching consequences, one may agree with Dickens that the decisions made at Trent 'have attracted too little attention':

the divided Fathers failed...to establish any priority for Biblical studies or ...to encourage the laity to read the Scriptures, or to prepare the Scripturally-oriented catechism for laymen which the humanist group had... planned. This great refusal of 1546 had permanent effects...At no stage did the spirit of Erasmus and Lefebvre suffer a more catastrophic defeat and in no field did the fear of Protestantism leave deeper marks upon the development of Catholic religion.[173]

Something that ran even deeper than fear of Protestantism was also at stake in the 'great refusal of 1546.' The decision to stand by the Vulgate, to veil Gospel texts, and stress lay obedience over lay education was certainly framed as a reaction to the Protestant threat. Fear of the spread of Lutheran heresy undoubtedly loomed large in the debates. Actions taken by Catholic churchmen, however, were also designed to counteract forces which had begun to subvert the medieval church before Luther was born and which continued to menace Roman Catholicism long after Protestant zeal had ebbed.[174]

It was printing, not Protestantism, which outmoded the medieval Vulgate and introduced a new drive to tap mass markets. Regardless of what happened in Wittenberg or Zürich, regardless of other issues taken up at Trent; sooner or later the Church would have had to come to terms with the effect on the Bible of copy-editing and trilingual scholarship on the one hand and expanding book-markets on the other. Whether or not the Lutheran heresy spread, whether or not clerical abuses were reformed, the forces released by print, which pointed to

---

[173] Dickens, *The Counter Reformation*, p. 115. This (Protestant) interpretation is quite different from the (Catholic) one given by F. J. Crehan, 'The Bible in the Catholic Church,' p. 203. The latter asserts that 'the Christian humanists at the Council' 'swept aside' conservative arguments in arranging for lectureships in Scripture and says nothing about other issues.

[174] That the suppression of Protestantism by the Roman Curia was incidental to the containment of other more basic and more long-range forces is also argued by Bouwsma, *Venice and the Defense*, pp. 293–5. Whereas he associates the threat with 'Renaissance values' and sees Rome's 'primary adversaries...symbolized by Florence and Venice rather than by Wittenberg and Geneva,' (p. 294) I think the threat was posed by forces unleashed by print. In my view, both Venice and Geneva, as important printing centers, represented 'primary adversaries' of sixteenth-century Rome. The role of Genevan presses in stirring French opinion against Rome is well documented by Kingdon, *Geneva and the Coming of the Wars*, pp. 93–129.

more democratic and national forms of worship, would have had to be contained or permitted to run their course.

The argument that Catholic policies no less than Protestant ones reflected adaptation to 'modernizing' forces in the sixteenth century, needs to be qualified by considering the divergence over lay Bible-reading. According to Evennett, for example, Gutenberg's invention 'cut both ways' by helping Loyola as well as Luther and by spurring a Catholic revival even while spreading Lutheran tracts.[175] Of course it is true that many Catholic teachers and preachers were well served by early printers; although, even here, Protestants seemed to have an early edge.[176] During the decade after 1517, one finds a chorus of complaints suggesting that the new medium did not 'cut both ways' but was, on the contrary, biased against the traditional faith.

Scholars complained that the whole book market was devoted to books by Luther and his followers and that nobody wished to print anything for the pope or any material which would offend Luther...Catholic polemsts and authors had a difficult time finding printers and publishers for their manuscripts...Georg Witzel from Mainz, a Catholic convert from Lutheranism, complained that the printer had kept his manuscript for a whole year with promises. 'If I were a Lutheran,' he said, 'there would be no difficulty, but as a Catholic I am writing in vain.'[177]

By the second half of the sixteenth century, however, the post-Tridentine Church had successfully mobilized printers for its counter-offensive. The Catholic Reformation of the sixteenth century, as Evennett suggests, used printing for proselytizing just as the Protestant churches did. Catholic firms made profits by serving the Roman church. They produced breviaries and devotional works for priests on far flung missions; school books for seminaries run by new orders; devotional literature for pious laymen, and tracts which could later be used by the seventeenth-century office of the Propaganda. Furthermore, in England, after the Anglicans gained the upper hand, Catholic printers proved as skillful as their Puritan counterparts in handling problems posed by the surreptitious printing and the clandestine marketing of books.[178]

[175] Evennett, The Spirit, p. 25.
[176] For data on the pro-Lutheran, anti-Catholic bias of German printers, see Gravier, Luther et L'Opinion Publique, pp. 20, 72-4, 251.
[177] Louise Holborn, 'Printing and the Growth,' p. 11.
[178] See e.g., Allison and Rogers, A Catalogue of Catholic Books.

If one confines the scope of inquiry to the mere spreading of books and tracts, then, one may be inclined to argue that the new medium was exploited in much the same way by Catholics and Protestants alike. But, as I have argued throughout this book, new functions performed by printing went beyond spreading tracts. Catholic policies framed at Trent were aimed at holding these new functions in check. By rejecting vernacular versions of the Bible, by stressing lay obedience and imposing restrictions on lay reading, by developing new machinery such as the Index and Imprimatur to channel the flow of literature along narrowly prescribed lines, the post-Tridentine papacy proved to be anything but accommodating. It assumed an unyielding posture that grew ever more rigid over the course of time. Decisions made at Trent were merely the first in a series of rear-guard actions designed to contain the new forces Gutenberg's invention had released. The long war between the Roman Church and the printing press continued for the next four centuries and has not completely ended yet. The *Syllabus of Errors* in the mid-nineteenth century showed how little room was left for maneuver after four hundred years.[179] Even after Vatican II, a complete cessation of hostilities between popes and printers' devils is still not clearly in sight.[180]

As these remarks suggest, the fate of the medieval Vulgate was closely intertwined with that of the medieval church. By examining the effects of print on Jerome's version one might also illuminate the forces that disrupted Latin Christendom.[181] Once again I must offer a sketchy summary of a topic that deserves more extended treatment by suggesting that printing subjected the Vulgate to a two-pronged attack. It was threatened by Greek and Hebrew studies on the one hand, and by vernacular translation on the other. Accordingly, the authority of the medieval clergy was undercut on two levels: by lay erudition on the part of a scholarly élite and by lay Bible-reading among the public at large. On the élite level, laymen became more erudite than church-

---

[179] It seems altogether fitting that the chief objection posed by the papacy to the French *Declaration of the Rights of Man* of 1789 was to the clause proclaiming freedom of the press.

[180] See e.g. 'Pontiff says Media Lead Youth Astray,' *The Washington Post* (Tuesday, May 5, 1970), p. A14. The headline sums up Pope Paul VI's message for 'World Social Communications Day.'

[181] The fate of the medieval *Corpus Juris* (also described as the 'legal *Vulgate*') seems to me to be similar to that of Jerome's version of the Scriptures. (See remarks, pp. 103–4, above.) That the twelfth-century 'glossa ordinaria' on Scripture is akin to the Bolognese glosses on the *Corpus Juris*, is evident in Milburn, 'The People's Bible,' p. 294. It would be useful to study the impact of print on the medieval legal textual tradition as well as on the medieval scriptural one.

men; grammar and philology challenged the reign of theology; Greek and Hebrew studies forced their way into the schools. On the popular level, ordinary men and women began to know their scripture as well as most parish priests; markets for vernacular catechisms and prayer books expanded; Church Latin no longer served as a sacred language which unified all of Western Christendom. Distrusted as an inferior translation by humanist scholars, Jerome's version was also discarded as too esoteric by evangelical reformers.

These two levels were not entirely discrete, of course, and were actually linked in many different ways. For one thing, Erasmian scholarship and Lutheran heresy were coupled by the opposition they provoked. Biblical scholarship and vernacular translation thus came under a common prohibition when the Vulgate was proclaimed authentic. For another thing, they were coupled by all who tried to re-do the work of Saint Jerome. A conscientious translator required access to scholarly editions and some command of trilingual skills. A Tyndale or a Luther necessarily took advantage of the output of a scholar–printer such as Robert Estienne; while scholar and translator could easily be combined in one person – as was the case with Lefèvre d'Etaples.[182] Finally the two-pronged attack was mounted from one and the same location – that is, from the newly established printer's workshop. The new impetus given scholarship by compilers of lexicons and reference guides went together with a new interest in tapping mass markets and promoting bestsellers. Robert Estienne working on his successive editions to the distress of Sorbonnistes provides one illustration of the disruptive effects of sixteenth-century Bible printing. Richard Grafton, pestering Thomas Cromwell to order the placing of the Matthew Bible in every parish church and abbey, provides another.[183]

Although they were coupled in various ways, there are good reasons nonetheless for considering the two prongs of the attack separately. There is no need to dwell on the distinctions that are inherent in my reference to two *levels* – that is, distinctions based on social stratification and market definition. The fact that scholarly editions circulated among a select readership and vernacular translation was aimed at a mass

---

[182] For data on uses made of printed reference guides and typographical resources by biblical translators such as Luther and Lefèvre, see Bluhm, 'The Sources of Luther's September Testament.'

[183] On persistent pressure to obtain government sponsorship of English Bibles, see Dickens, *Thomas Cromwell*, p. 115.

audience, in other words, seems too obvious to call for extended discussion. There are other distinctions, however, which seem less obvious and need more attention. For example, the approaches of scholars and evangelists to the sacred Word did not always converge and were sometimes at odds. Jerome and Augustine had themselves disagreed over Bible translation and in the sixteenth century, old arguments flared anew. At first, Luther felt indebted to Erasmus and his Greek edition, but later he

came to believe that a mere grammarian and historian concerned to get at the literal meaning and historical context of a sacred writing could do positive harm...Luther thought of himself as a theologian rather than as a grammarian. If he were asked to define the function and scope of Christian scholarship, it was clear where he would look for guidance...'Jerome is a babbler like Erasmus. Augustine...is the best theologian since the apostles...'[184]

Luther attacked Erasmus for being more of a grammarian than a theologian. From a different standpoint, Thomas More attacked Lutheran translators such as Tyndale, and objected to placing vernacular scriptures instead of Latin grammars in schoolboy hands. More stood with Erasmus and against obscurantists in working to introduce Greek studies into English universities. But he parted company with the author of the 'paraclesis' over the question of lay evangelism.[185]

Moreover, Renaissance princes tended to share More's position. As patrons of learning they sponsored scholarly editions but exhibited more caution about vernacular translation. The latter issue was much more politically explosive and complicated delicate negotiations over church affairs. Catholic kings might act as did Philip II by sponsoring polyglot Bibles and by providing local clergy with special breviaries and missals. But they stopped short of substituting vernaculars for Church Latin or of displacing the Vulgate. The tortuous policy of Henry VIII illustrates rather well the half-Catholic, half-Protestant position of the schismatic Tudor king. He began by persecuting Tyndale and other Lutheran translators; then encouraged Cromwell to turn loose his coterie of publicists and printers against the Pope; then accused his minister of

---

[184] Harbison, *Christian Scholar*, p. 110. See also discussion of different 'philological' and 'inspirational' approaches to scriptural translation problems, represented by Jerome and Augustine in Schwarz, *Principles and Problems*, pp. 16, 27–9, 37, 40.

[185] Deanesly, *The Lollard Bible*, p. 12, and Wood, *The Reformation and English Education*, pp. 229–30, both discuss differences between Erasmus and More. Devereux, 'English Translators,' pp. 47 ff. also mentions Tyndale's sly dig at More for failing to follow Erasmus' 'paraclesis.'

having false books translated into the mother tongue.[186] In 1543 the government seemed to grant with one hand what it withdrew with the other:

an Act of 1543 prohibited the use of Tyndale or any other annotated Bible in English and forbade unlicensed persons to read or expound the Bible to others in any church or open assembly...Yet in 1543 Convocation ordered that the Bible should be read through in English, chapter by chapter every Sunday and Holy Day after *Te Deum* and *Magnificat*.[187]

There was no logical contradiction; but the two acts worked at cross-purposes, nevertheless. Prohibiting the use of annotated English Bibles, forbidding unlicensed persons to read or expound scripture and placing Bible-reading out of bounds for 'women, artificers, apprentices, journeymen, yeomen, husbandmen and laborers'[188] were not logically incompatible with ordering the clergy to read from an English Bible in church. But if one wanted to keep English Bibles from lay readers it was probably unwise to tantalize congregations by letting them hear a chapter per week. Appetites are usually whetted by being told about forbidden fruit. The actions of 1543 probably worked together to increase the market for English Bibles. After Henry's death, of course, the prohibitions were abandoned and a less ambivalent royal policy was pursued. Despite a sharp setback under Mary Tudor[189] and intermittent reactions against Puritan zealots, the Englishing of the Bible moved ahead under royal auspices, reaching a triumphant conclusion under James I. With the Authorized Version, the English joined other Protestant nations to become a 'people of the Book.'

Once a vernacular version was officially authorized, the Bible was 'nationalized,' so to speak, in a way that divided Protestant churches and reinforced extant linguistic frontiers.

Translation of the Bible into the vernacular languages lent them a new dignity and frequently became the starting point for the development of national languages and literatures. The literature was made accessible to the

---

[186] Henry's abruptly changing policy is well described by Devereux, 'English Translators,' pp. 50–3.
[187] Greenslade, 'English Versions,' p. 153, n. 1.
[188] Categories of those forbidden to read by the act of 1543 are taken from Bennett, *Books and Readers 1475–1557*, p. 27.
[189] How the pace of Bible-printing accelerated under Edward VI and came 'almost to a standstill' under Mary Tudor is described by Bennett, *Books and Readers 1558–1603*, p. 141. The English experience during this brief interval offers a miniature model of what happened elsewhere when Protestant and Catholic rulers were enthroned.

people at the very time that the invention of printing made the production of books easier and cheaper.[190]

As this chapter indicates, I think it more than a mere coincidence that these developments occurred 'at the very time' book-production costs were lowered by printing. Nevertheless, Kohn's suggestion that the vernaculars were dignified by their association with the sacred book contains a valuable insight. And so does his observation that 'Latin was dethroned at the very moment when...it had started to become the universal language for a growing class of educated men...'[191] Thus Kohn shows why it is necessary to keep the two prongs of the attack on the Vulgate separate; for vernacular translations, by reinforcing linguistic barriers, ran counter to the cosmopolitan fellowship encouraged by biblical scholarship.

Although the authority of Jerome's version was undermined by Greek and Hebrew studies, the sense of belonging to the same Commonwealth of Learning remained strong among Christian scholars in all lands. A network of correspondence and the actual wanderings of scholars thus helped to preserve ties between Catholic Louvain and Protestant Leiden during the religious wars. Collaboration on Plantin's polyglot Bible pulled together scholars of diverse faiths from different realms.[192] Even after Christianity was regarded as divisive and French had displaced Latin as the international language, a common grounding in the same classical education and a shared interest in trilingual studies helped to unify the Republic of Letters. This cosmopolitan Republic, moreover, seemed to grow more expansive in its sympathies as the centuries wore on. Even in the sixteenth century, collaboration with heterodox enclaves of Jews and Greeks had encouraged an ecumenical and tolerant spirit, particularly among scholar–printers who often provided room and board in exchange for foreign aid and were, thus, quite literally 'at home' with travellers from strange lands.[193] Work on polyglot Bible editions encouraged scholars to look beyond

---

[190] Kohn, *Nationalism*, p. 14.

[191] Kohn, *The Idea of Nationalism*, p. 143; also pp. 618–20 where data are given on formation of literary languages such as Polish, Lithuanian, Latvian, Slovenian, etc. The importance of Bible translation in the development of Scandinavian literary languages, including Finnish, is noted by Dickens, *Reformation and Society*, pp. 90–1. See also Steinberg, *Five Hundred Years*, pp. 120–6.

[192] See discussion of travels and conversions of Justus Lipsius, who spent twelve years in Leiden before moving to Louvain, in Martin, *Livre à Paris* I, 23–4.

[193] The polyglot households of scholar–printers are discussed below, pp. 446–8.

the horizons of Western Christendom toward exotic cultures and distant realms. Vernacular Bible translation, while it owed much to trilingual studies, had precisely the opposite effect. It led to the typical Protestant amalgam of biblical fundamentalism and insular patriotism.

Sixteenth-century vernacular translation movements also had anti-intellectual implications which worked at cross-purposes with the aims of classical scholars. Of course, this was not true of the group which produced the Geneva Bible in the 1550s or of the committee which labored over the King James translation. Authoritative translations could not be produced save by erudite scholars, who were indebted to polyglot Bibles and trilingual studies.[194] There were many publicists, however, who championed the cause of Englishing the Bible by roundly condemning erudition and pedantry.[195] Several special studies have revealed the complex interplay of diverse elements (ranging from court councillors, Puritan pressure groups, and the Inns of Court to London theatres and the Elizabethan Grub Street) which resulted in the Englishing of law and letters during the sixteenth century.[196] Under the aegis of patrons like the Earl of Leicester, corps of translators labored to convert useful and edifying works of every kind into the mother tongue. The missionary zeal of lay evangelists, who objected to withholding Gospel truths from any man, was completely compatible with the new movement.[197] 'Loth he and other printers be to printe any Lattin booke bicause they will not heare be uttered and for that Bookes printed in Englande be in suspition abroad.'[198] Thus Archbishop Parker wrote in 1572 about John Day's reluctance to carry

---

194 Berry, *The Geneva Bible*, pp. 10–11 discusses the Hebrew and Greek studies of the Marian exiles who were in close contact with scholar–printers in Geneva, Strasbourg, etc. On the King James committee, see facsimiles of the notes of John Bois, tr. and ed. by Ward Allen, *Translating for King James, passim.*

195 See e.g. Thomas Becon's defense of the English Bible and his native tongue as conveyed by R. F. Jones, *Triumph*, p. 61.

196 In addition to R. F. Jones' *Triumph* on the English movement, see Ebel, 'Translation and Cultural Nationalism'; Graham, '"Our Tongue Maternall,"' pp. 58–98; Rosenberg, *Leicester.* A comparative study of sixteenth-century translation movements (perhaps based on translators' prefaces to diverse works) would be useful, judging by data sampled in scattered articles: e.g. Grendler, 'Francesco Sansovino,' p. 141; Beardsley, 'The Classics and Their Spanish Translators,' pp. 3ff.; Rickard, *La Langue Française, passim*; Gerald Strauss, 'The Course of German History.'

197 The first printed book on the art of translation was by the French Huguenot printer and martyr, Etienne Dolet, *La Manière de bien Traduire d'une Langue à L'Autre* (1540). See Hirsch, *Printing, Selling*, p. 133.

198 Letter of Archbishop Parker to Cecil, 1572, cited by Oastler, *John Day*, p. 19.

out a commission for him – a commission that Day did undertake, after compensation had been arranged. Day was not at all reluctant, needless to say, to undertake printing the 'A B C with the Little Catechism' and the 'Psalms in Metre' – the two most lucrative privileges available to printers in Elizabethan England. But he reserved his wholehearted enthusiasm for the promotion of the Protestant cause. Profits made from his monopoly of the two elementary texts were ploughed back into his major publication program which entailed issuing the tracts and sermons of Marian martyrs and returned exiles and which culminated in the successive editions of the ever expanding *Book of Martyrs*, whose author he kept in his employ.[199] That Day was also the printer for the first English translation of Euclid, the celebrated version by Henry Billingsley which contained an equally famous preface by John Dee, and that he also printed Dee's *Perfecte Arte of Navigation*, was probably not due to the printer's initiative.[200] Vernacular technical literature and translations of Euclid were however quite in keeping with the publication programs of other early printers who hired translators in order to supply the growing demand.

Protestant objections to veiling Gospel truths were adopted by the translators and used for more secular ends. For example, they argued that the liberal arts and sciences should not be 'hidden in Greke or Latin tongue' but made familiar to the 'vulgare people.' In 'blunt and rude English,' they set out 'to please ten thousand laymen' instead of 'ten able clerkes.'[201] They sought to close the gap not so much between priest and laity as between academic or professional élites and 'common' readers who were variously described as 'unskilfull,' 'unlettered' and 'unacquainted with the latine tounge.'[202] In this way, they linked the lay evangelism of Protestants with the cause of so-called popularizers who campaigned against academic monopolies and professional

[199] Oastler, *John Day*, p. 15; Haller, *The Elect Nation*, pp. 114–17. Oastler corrects Haller's view that Parker was a special patron of Day.
[200] Oastler, *John Day*, p. 16. (Dee's preface to Billingsley is assigned great significance by Frances Yates in her theory about the Globe theatre.)
[201] Thomas Norton, *The Ordinall of Alchemy* (1477) cited by R. F. Jones, *Triumph*, p. 5, n. 8.
[202] Altick, *The English Common Reader*, p. 18. See also Caxton's reference to 'rude and unconnynge men' cited by Bennett, *Books and Readers, 1475-1557*, pp. 16–17. By defining markets, such prefaces also articulated class distinctions in a new way. A Bible Concordance of 1631 has a preface noting that it is not 'for the most learned or for the most unlearned but for the middle sort.' Cited by Wright, *Middle Class Culture*, p. 235. This very special use of the term 'middle' to cover an 'assumed public' is probably the only justification for linking Tudor court culture with that of an English middle class. See objections posed by Hexter, *Reappraisals*, p. 75.

élites.[203] Scholastic theologians, Aristotelian professors and Galenic physicians were attacked in much the same way by diverse opponents of Latin learning. Nicholas Culpeper, an aggressive and prolific medical editor and translator during the Commonwealth, made his debut with an unauthorized translation of the official guide to London apothecaries: the *Pharmacopeia Londinensus* and accused the College of Physicians of being Papists because they resisted using vernaculars in medicine.[204]

The assault on old professional élites did not always stop short of political élites. Indeed the two motifs were combined during both the English and French revolutions. The Englishing of lawbooks had been defended on patriotic grounds under the early Tudors by the versatile law printer and publicist, John Rastell.[205] The same theme was turned against both the legal profession and the Stuart monarchy by rebellious subjects such as John Lilburne. The latter held that the law of the land should not be hidden in Latin and old French but should be in English so that 'every Free-man may reade it as well as the lawyers.'[206] In their insistence on converting knowledge which had been esoteric, 'rare, and difficult,' into a form where it was 'relevant and useful for all,' and in their confidence in the intelligence of the reading public at large, the prefaces of the translators seem to have anticipated much of the propaganda of the Enlightenment. In their expressed desire to bring learning within reach of artisans they reflected a drive toward new markets that was powered by the new presses. 'Learning cannot be too common and the commoner the better...Why but the vulgar should not know all,' said Florio, whose translations and dictionaries put the dictum into practice.[207] The common reader could only be reached by using a mother tongue, however. Unlike many disciples of Comenius and Hartlib and unlike the French *philosophes* as well, the translators played insistently on chauvinistic themes – reworking and democratizing the defense of the 'volgare' which had been sponsored by princes and despots during the Renaissance.

The same combination of democratic and patriotic themes accom-

203 In sixteenth-century France, arguments defending vernacular medical treatises (issued for the benefit of surgeons, midwives, apothecaries *et al.*) 'resembled those used in defense of vernacular Bibles' according to Natalie Z. Davis, 'Printing and the People,' p. 223.
204 Webster, *The Great Instauration*, p. 268. Further discussion of vernacular versus Latin scientific literature is offered below. See pp. 531, 545-7, 657-8, volume II.
205 A. W. Reed, *Early Tudor Dramas*, p. 204.
206 'England's Birth-Right Justified' (1645) cited by Gregg, *Free-born John*, p. 128.
207 For citations, see Ebel, 'Translation and Cultural Nationalism,' pp. 595-8.

panied Protestant Bible translation. Indeed the drive to bring the Bible within reach of everyman had paradoxical aspects which help to illustrate the contradictory effects of the communications revolution as a whole. Everyman spoke in many tongues, and the Christian scriptures had to be nationalized to be placed within his reach. 'What is the precise meaning of the word universal in the assertion that *Pilgrim's Progress* is "universally known and loved?"' asks a reviewer.[208] The question is worth posing, for it draws attention to an important process which is often overlooked. The desire to spread glad tidings, when implemented by print, contributed to the fragmentation of Christendom. In the form of the Lutheran Bible or the King James version, the sacred book of Western civilization became more insular as it grew more popular. It is no accident that nationalism and mass literacy have developed together. The two processes have been linked ever since Europeans ceased to speak the same language when citing their scriptures or saying their prayers.

In questioning the familiar equation of Protestantism with nationalism, J. H. Hexter points out that the claims of the Calvinists 'were *not* national...they were quite as universal, quite as catholic and in that dubious sense quite as medieval as the claims of the Papacy.'[209] The case of Calvinism, to be sure, is somewhat exceptional because the language spoken by the inhabitants of the small Swiss canton which served as the Protestant Rome happened to coincide with that of the most populous and powerful seventeenth-century realm. Whereas Calvin himself could not read Luther's German works, the Prussian Hohenzollerns could and did read Calvin in French. Partly because of the influence it had long exerted as the medieval *lingua franca*, partly because of the new radiation of Genevan culture in the age of Calvin but mainly because of the successful statecraft of the Bourbons, French *did* displace Latin as the international language for most purposes.[210] Nevertheless, Calvin's native tongue never achieved the cosmopolitan status which medieval Latin had achieved in religious affairs.

As a common sacred language, medieval Latin continued to unite Catholic Europe and 'Latin' America as well. Protestant churches were forever divided by early-modern linguistic frontiers, and here the Presbytery was caught up in the same contradictions as all other

---

[208] 'A Garland for Gutenberg,' the *Times Literary Supplement* (June 22, 1967), p. 561.
[209] Hexter, *Reappraisals*, p. 33.   [210] See chap. 2, above, n. 260.

Protestant churches. Its claims were universal, as Hexter says, but there was no way of making the Bible more 'universally' accessible without casting the scriptures into a more national mold. Thus the Genevan Bible which circulated among English and Scotch Puritans was written in a language that was foreign to the so-called 'Protestant Rome.'[211] A fund of lore based on Shakespeare, Blackstone and the King James version is often described by nostalgic Americans as providing 'a common culture' which the twentieth century has lost.[212] This reading matter did reach across the ocean, it is true, and linked backwoods lawyers in the New World with Victorian empire builders in the Old. It stopped at the water's edge, nonetheless. Across the Channel, on the continent among cultivated Europeans, this culture was not common at all. Outside Catholic Europe, then, a scriptural faith penetrated deeply into all social strata and provided the foundation for some sort of 'common culture.' But although a Bible Belt left permanent marks across many lands, the 'old time religion' was abruptly arrested at new linguistic frontiers.

It is worth noting in this regard that the Bible Belt is the product of the same forces that produced the Index. It is a mistake to couple biblical fundamentalism with Aristotelianism as 'obsolescent habits of thought' which seemed in retreat in the age of Erasmus, before religious warfare revived them.[213] The capacity of like-minded men to cite the same chapter and verse and to govern their daily lives accordingly, hinged on their access to identical copies of whole Bibles and hence on the output of sizable standard editions.

Medieval scribal culture did make more room for Bibles than conventional accounts often suggest.[214] But it also encouraged an intermingling of excerpts from the Bible with other matter. Printed editions lent themselves to a different cast of mind. During the middle ages 'most people had no means of knowing what was, and what was not in the Bible.'[215] The stories conveyed through mixed media by means

[211] On the production of this Bible by John Knox and his colleagues in the 1550s, its tremendous success during the seventeenth century, its influence on the Pilgrim fathers and Miltonic verse, see Berry's introduction to the *Geneva Bible*, and Hardin Craig, 'The Genevan Bible.'

[212] Bridenbaugh, 'The Great Mutation,' p. 320, thus laments the passing of 'the common religious and cultural bond of *Bible* reading.'

[213] Trevor-Roper, *The Crisis of the Seventeenth Century*, p. 161. Altick, *English Common Reader*, p. 38, also seems absent-minded when he refers to the Bible as providing 'immemorial fare' in English cottages. For 'immemorial' should we not substitute post-print?

[214] See warning given by Green, 'The Bible in Sixteenth Century,' p. 120.

[215] Greenslade, 'Epilogue,' p. 485.

of glass windows, wall-paintings, church portals, miracle plays, and the like, were of little help. Biblical anecdotes and biblical imagery intruded themselves into 'every nook and cranny' of medieval life. But by a seeming paradox, well described by Southern, the medieval Bible made its way 'into every corner and turn of speech at the very moment when the amount of the Bible which was read in church was falling away rapidly.'[216] The 'interjection of special lessons for a large number of saints' days' had already produced a state of affairs in the twelfth century that would give rise to the indignation expressed in the preface, attributed to Cranmer, of the Elizabethan Book of Common Prayer:

this godly and decent order of the ancient fathers…hath been so altered, broken and neglected by planting in uncertain stories, legends, responds, verses, vain repetitions, commemorations and synodals that commonly when any book of the Bible was begun, before three or four Chapters were read out, all the rest went unread.[217]

Popular preaching styles developed by the new mendicant orders helped to make matters worse. Congregations were captivated by colorful anecdotes designed to keep them awake. Writers like Chaucer, and later Rabelais, were provided with a rich fund of anecdotal material to draw on. But scripture was also mixed with more foreign matter than before.[218] If the laity rarely saw Bibles, the clergy, who were familiar with Peter Lombard's *Sentences* and preachers' manuals, were not much better off.[219] The idea that preachers should take their sermons directly from scripture, far from being 'obsolescent' in the age of Erasmus, was just beginning to come into its own. The same point applies to lay conduct – to the new dogged insistence on sticking with the Gospel and taking the Bible as one's only guide.

A variety of social and psychological consequences resulted from the new possibility of substituting Bible-reading for participation in traditional ceremonies – such as that of the mass. The slogan: 'sola scriptura,' as Bernd Moeller says, was equivocal. It could be used in an inclusive sense to mean 'not without scripture' or assigned the meaning

216 Southern, *The Making of the Middle Ages*, p. 217.
217 Preface to *The Book of Common Prayer* (1559) edited by John Booty, pp. 14–15.
218 Smalley, *English Friars* and Owst, *Literature and Pulpit* provide samples of anecdotal material employed by English friars. Krailsheimer, *Rabelais and the Franciscans*, does the same for the Franciscans in France and Italy.
219 The 'rarity of Bibles' in clerical possession before the Reformation and 'the rare use made of them,' even in the services by English parish priests is noted by Heath, *English Parish Clergy*, pp. 74–5.

that Luther gave it: 'with scripture alone.'[220] When taken in this latter sense, Bible-reading might take precedence over all other experiences to a degree and with an intensity that was unprecedented in earlier times. The idea of seeking the 'real presence' by reading scripture, it has been suggested, meant 'internalizing observance which formerly had been acted out publicly in sacraments and ceremonies.'[221] In view of the many new public ceremonies involving prayer meetings and joint singing of psalms that were developed by Protestants who rejected the mass, the point should not be pressed too far. When the art of preaching was overhauled by the Reformers, it was invigorated not weakened.

Nevertheless the act of putting Bibles in Everyman's hand did encourage a perpetual splintering of congregations and a new tendency toward religious self-help. It posed new questions concerning church attendance and group observance that had not been posed before. Stubbornly dogmatic and even obsessive religious attitudes were fostered among the new sects who elevated the infallible scripture to a more lofty position than Catholics ever elevated their popes. An introverted spiritual life developed among solitary readers who received silent guidance from repeatedly re-reading the same book on their own. In speaking of the self-taught preachers and religious fanatics who were common in Bunyan's day, Delaney comments, 'Scripture had an inordinately strong influence on half-educated men of this kind because they read little else.'[222] This still seems to be true, and it should be remembered that fundamentalist sects, like Gideon Bibles, have not ceased to proliferate in the present century. This is not the place to elaborate on the emergence of fundamentalism which, strictly speaking, was a nineteenth-century not a sixteenth-century development. I simply want to underline that biblical literalism, far from dying out in the age of Erasmus, was just beginning to assume its modern form. The rich and variegated communal religious experiences of the middle ages provided a different basis for the 'common culture' of Western man than did the new reliance on Bible-reading. Open books, in some instances, led to closed minds.

The impact of printing on the Western scriptural faith thus pointed in two quite opposite directions – toward 'Erasmian' trends and ulti-

[220] Moeller, *Imperial Cities*, p. 29.   [221] Delany, *British Autobiography*, p. 34.
[222] Delany, *British Autobiography*, p. 29.

mately higher criticism and modernism, and toward more rigid orthodoxy culminating in literal fundamentalism and Bible Belts. Vernacular Bible translation took advantage of humanist scholarship only in order to undermine it by fostering patriotic and populist tendencies. It has to be distinguished from scholarly attacks on the Vulgate because it was connected with so many non-scholarly anti-intellectual trends. Moreover, it coincided, as scholarly editions and 'profitless polyglots' did not, with the profit-making drives of early printers.[223] Not all printers were scholars, nor were all of them pious, but they had to make profits to stay in business at all. The Bible had always presented itself to devout readers as a holy book and to theologians as a guide to the science of God. It was only after the mid-fifteenth century, however, that it came to be viewed as a potential bestseller and could even be promoted among laymen on occasion as entertaining reading to help pass time.[224]

4. RESETTING THE STAGE FOR THE PROTESTANT REFORMATION

As these remarks suggest, I think printers did more than enable broadsides and tracts to be spread by heretics who had not commanded such organs of publicity before. Before the first Lutheran tract had been written – let alone printed and spread – scholars were being provided with Greek and Hebrew texts; vernacular Bibles in diverse languages and editions were being placed at the disposal of all. Reuchlin's rudiments of Hebrew and Erasmus' Greek New Testament were both in Luther's hands before the Ninety-Five Theses were composed.[225] Even before Luther arrived at the University of Wittenberg, the University library had acquired the most refined tools of scholarship available in

[223] Problems posed for scholar–printers who wanted to do more than turn out a pirated edition of a New Testament are noted by Black, 'The Printed Bible,' p. 431. But losses and risks incurred from scholarly publication programs could be compensated for by winning rich and powerful patrons who were often more helpful to a given firm than quick profits. See examples given by Hendricks, 'Profitless Printing.' How the London *Polyglotte* was supported by subscribers is noted by Sarah Clapp, 'The Subscription Enterprises of John Ogilby and Richard Blowe.'

[224] Black, 'The Printed Bible,' p. 423 cites a preface to a French Bible of 1510 which equates the work with 'a good tale' which could help pass time.

[225] In addition to Reuchlin's *De Rudimentis Hebraicis*, Luther also had a copy of a Hebrew Bible (first published by the Soncino press in 1488) in a Brescian edition of 1494 according to Box, 'Hebrew Studies,' p. 322. On his use of Reuchlin's work see Kooiman, *Luther and the Bible*, p. 74. His eager reception and 'almost instantaneous use' of Erasmus' Greek New Testament

the early sixteenth century. New acquisitions had been obtained on the advice of the greatest scholar–printer of the day.[226] Bibles had been translated into German and printed before Luther was born. The position of the Church and the quality of Christian faith was already in the process of being transformed by the shift from script to print before the Protestant revolt had begun.

Luther's Theses received top billing in their day and are still making headlines in our history books. The indulgences and Bibles that came from a Mainz workshop have seemed less newsworthy all along. Nevertheless, Bibles were being rapidly duplicated before Protestant tracts were. The dissemination of glad tidings by print preceded and helped to precipitate the Lutheran revolt. In dealing with that revolt it is conventional to postpone mention of printing until *after* theories of causation have been debated and we come to the question of results ('of consummation' as Dickens says). Socio-economic and political factors are discussed; theological issues and ecclesiastical abuses are explored. Charismatic leaders are analyzed and, in recent years, psycho-analyzed as well. But the new presses are rarely allowed to go into operation until after Luther has arrived at the Church door.

In this way, debates about the Reformation tend to conceal the changes wrought by printing, much as do debates about the Renaissance. In both instances, the function of the new technology is drastically restricted. It is given no part in shaping new views but only seen to diffuse them after they have been formed. Since the classical revival did begin under scribal auspices, it is understandable that Renaissance scholars postpone discussion of the new presses and are prone to underestimate their role. It is not as easy to explain why Reformation studies place first things last, given the interval between Gutenberg and Luther. One answer may be found in the way Renaissance and Reformation are currently defined and related to each other. Insofar as scribal ideas of a 'rinascita' are carried over into the concept of a 'reformatio,' the advent of printing (which could scarcely be foreseen

is noted by Bluhm, *Martin Luther*, pp. x–xi. How Erasmus was prodded by Froben to get this latter work done to meet a publication deadline and how he complained that the work was 'precipitated rather than edited' is noted by Jarrott, 'Erasmus' Biblical Humanism,' pp. 120–1. Jarrott also notes how Erasmus improved his fourth edition of 1527 after studying the *Complutensian Polyglot*. There is still much uncertainty as to which edition of Erasmus' Greek New Testament, which German vernacular Bibles and which editions of the Latin Vulgate Luther consulted when in the Wartburg. Clearly he was better equipped by printers than he would have been by scribes during this interval of enforced isolation.

[226] See chap. 3, n. 159 above.

in Petrarch's day) is likely to be omitted in discussion of the latter term. Debates about how to distinguish properly between Italian and Northern, Classical and Christian, quattrocento and cinquecento humanism are sufficiently absorbing to leave little room for discussion of differences between manuscript Bibles and printed ones. In most accounts, at any rate, the movement of humanism from Italy to the North and the shift from a 'classical' to a 'Christian renaissance' take precedence over the shift from script to print. Thus, arguments over setting the stage properly for Luther's appearance divert the spotlight of history from the presses of Mainz, Strasbourg and other German towns. The printer is left to slip into place behind the scenes, so to speak. He installs his machinery and goes into production so inconspicuously that his output goes unnoted until Lutherans enlist him in their cause.

Almost any description of pre-Reformation developments would serve to illustrate this point. *The Cambridge History of the Bible*, for example, sets the stage with Lefèvre d'Etaples's familiar celebration of the religious renewal which began in the West 'about the time Constantinople was captured by the enemies of Christ.' Then comes a discussion of the hopeful outlook of the Christian humanists:

This is something new and fundamental to the cultural world of the early sixteenth century: it cannot be set down as merely a further stage in the development of humanist studies which had begun in the fourteenth century or earlier. There was a *preparatio evangelica* in the first quarter of the sixteenth century for it was then and not before that there appeared in combination the achievements of the humanist scholar–printers; the fruits of intensive study in the grammar and syntax of the three languages; and the energy provided by the economic development and regional patriotism of the cities where *bonae litterae* flourished...

Further, it was in this period that was felt the full force of...an insistent demand...for a well grounded knowledge of the Bible...coming not only from a scholarly priest like Lefèvre, but also from the educated laity... An attempt to meet this increasing demand can be seen in the large number of vernacular translations from the Vulgate in Germany and France in the later fifteenth and earlier sixteenth centuries.[227]

In many ways, this passage provides welcome support for my views, for the advent of printing seems to underlie almost all the developments

[227] Basil Hall, 'Biblical Scholarship,' pp. 38–9.

that are mentioned. But this is by no means clear from the passage as it stands. We are not reminded, for example, that the event Lefèvre used to date the renewal – 'about the time Constantinople was captured' – coincided with the advent of printing. We are not encouraged to connect the more forceful insistent demand for well-grounded knowledge of the Bible with the increased output that was made possible by Gutenberg's invention. The large number of vernacular translations is not related to new profit-drives of book producers. The achievements of the 'humanist scholar–printers' are treated as discrete from such related developments as the systematic pursuit of trilingual studies, increased lay erudition, and the new burst of cultural energy combined with patriotic zeal that was manifested in urban centers where printing industries took their start.

Because the effects of the typographical revolution are muffled in treatments of the *preparatio evangelica*, its contribution to the Reformation cannot be properly assessed. Once printers have been restricted to the function of spreading Lutheran tracts, they will play at best a supporting role in the drama. In specialized studies it is not unusual to find that their part has been cut out altogether.

A detailed account of how the Reformation came to Strasbourg helps to illustrate this point. It shows that most of the pro-Lutheran tracts which were printed in Strasbourg appeared only after the actual conversion of townsmen had already begun, thus suggesting that 'the publishers mirrored the Reform rather than influenced it.'[228] Accordingly, the 'act of preaching' is stressed and the role of print played down in a way that leads a reviewer to remark, 'It was not the printed page but the spoken words of the Strasbourg reformers – Bucer, Hedio, Capito and Zell – which converted people to the Book and to the founding of parish schools.'[229] The conclusion that effective preaching played the key role in the conversion seems inescapable, for most townsmen could not read and could only be reached by the 'spoken word.'[230]

Yet it is also possible to argue that the publishers played a less passive role provided one looks beyond the spread of Lutheran tracts. Preaching and conversion came in 1520–2, as end-products of a process that had long been under way. Strasbourg was one of the cities, mentioned by

[228] Chrisman, *Strasbourg and the Reform*, chap. 7, pp. 98–117. See also appendix A-1.
[229] N. Z. Davis, review article, *Journal of Modern History* (1968), p. 589.
[230] Chrisman, *Strasbourg*, p. 99.

Hall, where *bonae litterae* had flourished and the cause of lay evangelism had been fostered by Gutenberg's earliest emulators. More than fifty years before they began to spread Lutheran tracts, Strasbourg presses had been in operation.[231] The very first German Bible to appear in print had been published in this city more than twenty years before Luther's birth. From 1480 to 1510, eminent scholars and literati throughout the Empire had gravitated to the city's presses to serve as compilers, translators, proof readers and advisors. Strasbourg print shops became gathering places for erudite laymen and served as focal points for opinion-forming groups. During the same interval and within the same milieux, new concepts of German history and national character were shaped and publicized; the civic and religious duties of Christian laymen were reevaluated; programs for a new system of public education were set forth. The latter in particular was urgently promoted. For 'without education,' as Wimpfeling noted, 'the people could not read the Holy Scripture or the laws of the city.'[232]

The reformers who directed people to the Book and parish schools were conveying a message which had already entered into printed literature even before it was conveyed by word of mouth. Of course the message was not really new any more than was lay piety among medieval German burghers. What was new was the chance to make the message stick; to bring Bible-reading and book learning within the reach of all. For purposes of persuasion, the reformers used the pulpit no less effectively than the press. But it was the latter rather than the former which enabled them to change the educational institutions of Strasbourg for good. The most lasting result of the Strasbourg Reformation was the establishment of a new municipal system of public education that markedly contrasted with medieval precedents. The educational reforms were pushed through in the face of strong opposition from conservative church officials who withheld books belonging to Cathedral and monastery schools.[233] If academic book provisions had remained under clerical supervision and supplies of texts had been governed by scribal regulations it seems doubtful that the opposition to the scheme could have been overcome. But if scribal book production had still been in effect, reforming zeal would probably have

[231] On Strasbourg presses, first established in 1458, see Benzing, *Buchdrucker-Lexicon*, pp. 157ff.
[232] Chrisman, *Strasbourg*, pp. 63–5.   [233] Chrisman, *Strasbourg*, pp. 264–8.

been focused on clerical education, as had been the case in the past.

As it was, fifty years of printing had changed the quality of clerical education and had extended new opportunities for young men of humble birth. The small group of priests who spearheaded the Strasbourg reformation were markedly different from the 'ignorant and inarticulate' priests who had served the townspeople in similar capacities before.[234] Although one was the son of a shoemaker and another that of a blacksmith, they were all steeped in the new learning and skilled in Greek and Hebrew. Their approach to the spoken word was affected by their access to the printed page and to trilingual studies. They brought to the pulpit an ideal of eloquence, derived from antiquity and revived by Italian literati, which was being turned to religious ends. They sought to drive their message deep into the human heart, not as Ciceronian orators to arouse support for a civil leader or instil patriotic fervor, but as Christian pastors to convey the Word of God and rekindle a faith which had (in their view) been comatose for hundreds of years.[235] Conservative members of the Cathedral chapter were disconcerted by the idea of preaching freely from the Gospel to laymen rather than following the safe topics set forth in preachers' manuals. The new priests had learned to be contemptuous of the 'mish-mash' contained in old manuals[236] and had heard the Gospel discussed by intelligent laymen before. Capito, for example, had worked beside Amerbach and Froben and had helped Erasmus edit the New Testament. He was not merely a bright blacksmith's son who had been recruited as a priest. He knew more than a 'smattering' of Latin. He had already published in Basel, before he preached in Strasbourg, his own Hebrew edition of the psalms.[237]

How some publishers influenced the Reform, even before others mirrored it, is also suggested by the activities of Matthäus Zell, who initiated the new style of preaching in Strasbourg and won a following

---

[234] Chrisman, *Strasbourg*, p. 81. How the advent of printing helped to heighten concern over problems posed by 'unreading priests' in England is noted by Heath, *English Parish Clergy*, pp. 73ff.

[235] The transposition of themes developed in the 'pursuit of eloquence' under the aegis of northern Christian humanists led by Erasmus is described by Scribner, 'The Social Thought.' (See especially pp. 8–9; 15.) See also data on Reuchlin's *Art of Preaching* and compilation by Albrecht von Eyb in Hirsch's 'Printing and the Spread of Humanism,' p. 35.

[236] Chrisman, *Strasbourg*, p. 120.

[237] On Capito's activities in Strasbourg, see Kittelson, 'Wolfgang Capito,' pp. 126ff.

despite opposition from the Cathedral chapter. As a defiant evangelist, Zell 'operated outside traditional institutions.'[238] Like most sixteenth-century rebels, he also had certain precedents to go by. His sermons not only recalled the legendary seventy-two preachers sent out by Christ but also the teachings of an earlier Strasbourg preacher: Geiler von Keysersberg. The written word could only reach a few in the early sixteenth century, but the message of a dead preacher could not be heard by anyone unless conveyed in written form. Geiler himself had combined publishing with preaching, and as a Strasbourg publisher had turned out the complete works of an earlier celebrated preacher, the conciliarist, Jean Gerson.[239] He himself achieved posthumous celebrity as the subject of two laudatory biographies[240] and his pulpit oratory gained added resonance by being transposed into print. Issued in numerous editions, his collected sermons became an early 'bestseller' and reached out to 'influence Zell' even from beyond the grave.[241] One is reminded of the exchange between Luther and another Stras-bourg reformer: 'When Martin Bucer of Strasbourg somewhat prig-gishly urged the Wittenberg theologians to get out into the world and preach, Luther replied in the pregnant words: "We do that with our books." He knew his century.'[242]

The exchange is not without irony. For one thing, Bucer also knew his century well enough. He managed to publish more than eighty books during his stay in Strasbourg.[243] For another thing, the idea of preaching with books was by no means peculiar to Luther's century or to print culture. As noted above, the tradition of an 'apostolate of the pen' went back to Cassiodorus' advice to monks:

to preach unto men by means of the hand, to untie the tongue by means of the fingers...to fight the Devil...with pen and ink. Every word of the Lord written by the scribe is a wound inflicted on Satan...Though seated in one spot, the scribe traverses diverse lands through the dissemination of what he has written.[244]

238 Chrisman, *Strasbourg*, p. 73.
239 Geiler's edition of the complete works of Jean Gerson is noted by Renaudet, *Préréforme et Humanisme*, pp. 101–2.
240 The two biographies, written by Wimpfeling and Beatus Rhenanus, were first published in 1510 and went through several editions. See Giesey, book review, *Bibliothèque d'Humanisme et Rénaissance*, p. 207.   241 Chrisman, *Strasbourg*, p. 78.
242 Dickens, *Reformation and Society*, p. 86.   243 Eels, *The Attitude*, p. 9.
244 Cited by Metzger, *Text of the New Testament*, p. 18. See also citation from Leclercq, above, pp. 316–17. Is Cassiodorus a source for Luther's flinging an inkpot at the Devil? No doubt John Foxe's notion of using the press to wound the papal anti-Christ derives from this tradition.

This advice held special significance for members of those ascetic orders who had shunned pulpit oratory and could only 'preach with their hands.' 'Since we cannot preach God's words by mouth,' wrote a twelfth-century prior of his order, which was sworn to silence, 'let us preach it with our hands. Every time we write a book, we make of ourselves heralds of the Truth...'[245] Compared to the Priors of the *Grande Chartreuse*, Luther was much more committed to the power of the spoken word and much less prepared to detach the work of the mouth from that of the hand. Printed publicity served preaching as it served vocal performances of many other kinds. This point is worth keeping in mind as a warning against oversimplifying the impact of printing and jumping to the conclusion that it invariably favored sight over sound, reading over hearing. 'To Luther (who wrote a good deal!) the Church is not a pen house but a mouth house. The Gospel proclaimed viva voce has converting-power; preaching is a means of grace; Word and sacrament must not be sundered.'[246] It is because the printed page amplified the spoken word and not because it silenced it that Luther regarded Gutenberg's invention as God's 'highest act of grace.' To set press against pulpit is to go against the spirit of the Lutheran Reformation. But it is also misguided to envisage sixteenth-century reformers addressing townsmen without first placing the new presses on the scene. The new invention affected the vocation of preachers and the outlook of German burghers even before a handful of reforming priests climbed onto available pulpits and set about converting the citizens of Strasbourg and other German towns.

If first things were placed first then, we would begin our description of how the Reformation came to Strasbourg with the printing of a German Bible in 1466 instead of with the preaching of a sermon in 1520.[247] We would investigate the formation of opinion-making groups and the articulation of new views by the literati who gravitated to new print shops, before estimating the output of Lutheran tracts. It would then be possible to show how the presses, which were indispensable to the *preparatio evangelica*, entered into its myriad aspects and phases. At the very least, it is clear that in Strasbourg the publishers

---

[245] Coutumes de Gigue I, Prieur de la Grande Chartreuse, 12ème Siècle (B. N. Mss. lat 4342) Item no. 410, *Le Livre* (Catalogue of *Bibliothèque Nationale* Exhibition), p. 134.
[246] Greenslade, 'Epilogue,' p. 485.
[247] Or perhaps one should begin with Mentelin's Latin Bible of 1460 rather than his German version six years later. See p. 440 below.

did much more than mirror the Reform; they prepared its way, they secured its results.

If first things were placed first, it would also be noted that indulgences got printed before getting attacked. The first dated printed product from Gutenberg's workshop was an indulgence.[248] More than half a century elapsed between the Mainz indulgences of the 1450s and Luther's attack on indulgences in 1517. During this interval the output of indulgences had become a profitable branch of jobbing-printing. 'When...Johann Luschner printed at Barcelona 18,000 letters of indulgence for the abbey of Montserrat in May 1498 this can only be compared with the printing of income tax forms by His Majesty's Stationery Office.'[249] Given mass production of this sort, high pressure salesmanship became more difficult to avoid. Middlemen were needed to unload the forms, and had to be paid off along with the printer. The latter also found a new and profitable sideline by turning out sales promotion pamphlets and leaflets providing sensational accounts of Christian exploits that indulgence sellers could use.[250] Of course commercial exploitation of indulgences had preceded printing – as Chaucer's Pardoner suggests.[251] But once trafficking in salvation was harnessed to a large scale profit-making enterprise, it could be used to subsidize larger schemes. As it became more attractive to officials who were hard pressed for cash, the professional money-raiser playing on fears about salvation became more ubiquitous and all the more aggravating to those believers who were genuinely concerned about their souls.

[248] On the Mainz indulgences of 1454–5, see Butler, *The Origin of Printing*, pp. 67–77. The reason why the advent of printing coincides in most texts with the fall of Constantinople is because the first dated printed product was issued in response to a request made of Gutenberg by an agent acting on behalf of the defenders of Cyprus against the Ottoman invaders. See McMurtrie, *The Book*, p. 149. Other indulgences issued in connection with the crusade against the Turks are noted by Hirsch, *Printing, Selling*, pp. 122–3. The first dated printed product from Caxton's press was also an indulgence (of 1476 for the Abbot of Abingdon). See J. Carter and P. Muir (eds.), *Printing and the Mind of Man*, p. 8. Subsequent issues by Caxton between 1476 and 1489 are noted by Blake, *Caxton and his World*, pp. 77–8; 232–3.

[249] Steinberg, *Five Hundred Years*, p. 139.

[250] A broadside printed by Michael Greyff, Reutlingen, 1480 entitled 'Miracula quae tempore obsidionis Rhodi Contingerunt' thus describes the sensational miracles that occurred during the Turkish siege of Rhodes, June–July 1480 for the benefit of indulgence sellers recruited to raise money for the defense of Rhodes.

[251] Thirteenth-century Dominican descriptions of transactions with the Church's Treasury of Merits and cash payments used to draw on good works deposited by saints are noted by J. H. Crehan, 'Indulgences,' pp. 84–90. See also article by Rosenwein and Little, 'Social Meaning in the Monastic and Mendicant Spiritualities,' pp. 4–33.

The ethical and theological bases of this fund raising were becoming dubious by any standards. In 1476, Sixtus IV had extended the scope of an Indulgence even to souls in purgatory, thus exploiting for cash the natural anxieties of simple people for their departed relatives. Luther's initial revolt was provoked by this spectacle of a salvation assurance company with branches in heaven, earth and purgatory.[252]

Even before the Mainz indulgences, block-printing had already pointed toward new abuses. The rogue in Heywood's play *Pardoner and the Friar* not only uses the language of printed indulgences but also speaks of the woodcuts of holy images which were sold as a sideline during the period.[253] Such images were duplicated by the dozens and sold along with playing cards by craftsmen who sought profits from things sacred as well as profane.[254] There had always been a certain ambivalence about permitting a cult of images in the Western Church. The popular cults must have seemed even less acceptable when exploited for profit and coupled with card games and fortune telling. Similarly, when sacred relics could be advertised like drugs on the market by printed publicity, their promotion probably appeared more offensive to reformers even while their ubiquity became more comical to the sceptically inclined. The multiplication of printed guides listing the same relics in different churches made it awkward even for true believers to decide just where the genuine articles could be seen.[255]

It was characteristic of Calvin that he grasped the potential usefulness of print for the elimination of false relics and acted decisively by publishing a tract in which he warned his readers against pretending 'any

252 Dickens, *Reformation and Society*, p. 35. The bulls of Sixtus IV were themselves better publicized than scribal edicts had been. Basel printers turned out 1,000 copies of a 1473 papal bull pertaining to indulgences according to Paulus, *Indulgences*, pp. 32–3. See also pp. 56–8 for data on how some printers were repaid (as copyists had been) by grants of indulgences which thus became almost equivalent to currency.

253 Kenneth Cameron, book review, *Renaissance Quarterly* (1971), p. 555.

254 The combined production of playing cards and holy images ('heilige') is noted by Carter and Goodrich, *The Invention of Printing*, p. 191. The early fifteenth-century output of block-prints is described by McMurtrie, *The Book*, p. 104. By 1441 the Venetian Council was already taking measures to arrest the local decline of 'the art and mystery of making cards and printed figures' by prohibiting imports from German towns such as Augsburg and Nuremberg, according to Clapham, 'Printing,' pp. 380–1.

255 An example of a guide listing relics in various churches and also itemizing the different indulgences to be gained by visits to each one is the *Indulgentiae Ecclesiarum Urbis Romae* issued by Guilleretus and Nani, Rome, 1511. Duplicate lists of this kind also fed the collectors' mania as is suggested by the huge relic collection amassed by Luther's protector the Elector of Saxony, Frederick the Wise. A catalogue of this collection, illustrated by woodcuts from Lucas Cranach's workshop was issued in 1509: as the 'Wittenberg Heiligtumsbuch.'

excuse of ignorance'. A short excerpt from an English translation of this tract seems worth citing:

Yea in the meantime as this book was a printing, one dyd shew me of the third foreskyn of our Lord Jesus, which is shewed at Heldesheim...There is an infinite number of such like...So it is of the relique: for all is so mingled and confused, that one can not worshyp the bone of a Marter, but he shall be in danger to worship the bones of some certain Murtherer or these, or else of an asse, or of a dog, or of a horsse, neither can one worshyp our ladyes ringes, or her comme, or girdell, but one shall be in danger of worshipping the ringes of some certaine hoore. Wherefore, take hede of the danger who so will for none from hence forth can pretende any excuse of ignoraunce.[256] (sig. H7^v).

After the duplication of indulgences and the promotion of relics were taken over by printers, traditional church practices became more obviously tainted with commercialism. But the same spirit of 'double entry bookkeeping,' which appeared to infect the Renaissance popes, also pervaded the movement which spearheaded the anti-papal cause. A resort to promotional literature and high pressure salesmanship which characterized the tactics of indulgence sellers, such as Tetzel, also characterized schemes developed by early reformers such as Beatus Rhenanus to publicize Luther's attacks on indulgence-selling. Even in Catholic countries, rural markets were opened to peddlers' books by sixteenth-century Protestant Bible-salesmen.[257] Indeed, however much they attacked 'mechanical devotions,' Protestants relied much more than did papists on the services of 'mechanick printers.' Insofar as their doctrine stressed an encounter with the Word and substituted reading scripture for participating in the mass, it bypassed the mediation of priests and the authority of the pope only to become more dependent on the efficiency of Bible printers and Bible-salesmen.

Even while describing the art of printing as God's highest act of grace, Luther also castigated printers who garbled passages of the Gospel and marketed hasty reprints for quick profit. In a preface to his Bible of 1541 he said of them, 'They look only to their greed.'[258]

---

[256] This passage from Calvin's *A very profitable treatise...declarynge what great profit might come... if there were a regester made of all reliques.* Translated by S. Wythers, London, 1561 (*STC* 4467) was given to me by David H. Stam.

[257] Natalie Z. Davis, 'Printing and the People,' pp. 202–3.

[258] Cited by Black, 'Printed Bible,' p. 432. Luther's objections to greedy printers who abused the divine art seem to echo the views expressed by the Archbishop of Mainz in his censorship edict of 1485. (See above, p. 347.) A study of ambivalent German attitudes toward the greatest 'German' invention might be worthwhile.

Nevertheless, by insisting on Bible-reading as a way of experiencing the Presence and achieving true faith,[259] Luther also linked spiritual aspirations to an expanding capitalistic enterprise. Printers and booksellers had to be enlisted in order to bypass priests and place the Gospels directly into lay hands. 'Hereby, tongues are known, knowledge groweth, judgment increaseth, books are dispersed, the Scripture is read, stories be opened, times compared, truth discerned, falsehood corrected and...all (as I said) through the benefit of printing.'[260] The tone of Foxe's tribute is remarkably similar to that of earlier treatises in praise of scribes. But print shop and monastery were worlds apart. Protestant doctrines harnessed a traditional religion to a new technology with the result that Western Christianity embarked on a course never taken by any world religion before and soon developed peculiar features which gave it the appearance, in comparison with other faiths, of having undergone some sort of historical mutation.[261]

5. RELATING THE PROTESTANT ETHIC TO A NEW CAPITALIST ENTERPRISE

As you may have guessed from the foregoing, I am inclined to regard debates over Max Weber's thesis[262] much as I do debates over Jacob Burckhardt's work. Although concerned with somewhat different problems, the two controversies share much in common. In both cases, an elusive modernizing process is debated even while the shift from script to print is concealed.

It seems especially regrettable that printing was assigned such an

259 According to Bainton (who draws on Erich Hassinger's study) the originality of Luther's theological position resides in his special emphasis on Gospel reading as a means of overcoming the distance between later generations and those privileged to be alive when Jesus was on earth. 'Interpretations of the Reformation,' p. 77. This view would make the interval between the Incarnation and the invention of printing seem like a dark age indeed to Luther.

260 Citation from 1641 edn. of Foxe's *Book of Martyrs* on flyleaf of Thomas F. Dibdin's *Typographical Antiquities* I. See, for comparison, Trithemius, *De Laude Scriptorum*, chap. 1, lines 10–20.

261 See Fenn, 'The Bible and the Missionary,' pp. 402–3, and Greenslade, 'Epilogue,' pp. 478–9, for suggestions concerning the world-wide impact of the continuous publication and translation of the Bible during the last five hundred years. By 1960, about 30,000,000 Bibles were circulating annually in over 1,100 languages and dialects.

262 For a favorable appraisal of Weber's oeuvre and good bibliography of relevant literature (up to 1970) see Nelson, 'Weber's Protestant Ethic.' In the author's introduction to Max Weber, *The Protestant Ethic*, pp. 13–16, there is one incidental mention of printed literature and the periodical press as peculiar to the Occident; it is given an inconspicuous place amid a large (jumbled) collection of phenomena, such as: rational chemistry, canon law, counterpoint, musical notation, Gothic vaulting, central perspective.

inconspicuous position in Weber's work, because he was concerned with the very developments (involving rationality and science) that were most strongly affected by the new medium. Those drives toward rationalization and systematic organization which were already present in Western culture could be much more effectively implemented after printing than before; while scientific data collection was placed on an entirely new basis by the communications shift. In a later section I will explore the possible relationship between printing and the rise of modern science as well as controversies over Protestantism and science. Here I will merely touch on a few of the issues raised in Weber's seminal essay on 'The Protestant Ethic,' in order to suggest how they might be related to changes ushered in by printing.

Let me start with the familiar issue of the concept of a 'special calling' which presumably left the monastery for the world.[263] One might note in passing that twelfth-century sermons already praised hard-working laymen who served faithfully in a given calling, whether as knights or merchants or peasants – so that one must be cautious about assigning too much novelty to later Protestant views consecrating work done in this world.[264] Moreover there could be no agreement among members of a variegated clergy as to just which form of consecrated service was most pleasing to God. As the very term suggests, the 'secular' clergy had been undertaking consecrated work outside the monastery and in the world at least since the days of Peter and Paul. Even if one follows the lead given by Weber and looks exclusively at monks, it is still clear that varied forms of specially consecrated work were allowed in different orders' rules. Nevertheless, a persistent distinctive feature of Western monasticism was the high value assigned to the work of the scribe. This was the work 'most fitting for cloistered monks,' according to repeated injunctions. The work which represented a 'special calling' (in the words of a Carthusian Prior as they were set down and preserved in the 'Customs' of his order) was the 'lasting rather than the passing work' of making books with one's hands.[265]

263 Weber, *Protestant Ethic*, pp. 121; 235, n. 79.

264 Chenu, *Nature Man and Society in the Twelfth Century*, p. 224 discusses relevant medieval sermon literature. Nelson, 'Weber's Protestant Ethic' sees Weber sharply distinguishing between lay work that might be viewed as useful, legitimate even honorable by the medieval preacher and the specially *consecrated* work of performing religious offices done by monks.

265 Citation from the sayings of Gigue (or Guigo) II, Fifth Prior of the Grande Chartreuse (d. 1180) from *Consuetudines* of the Order (in Migne, *Patrologia Latina*, t. 153) as noted by Marks, 'The Scriptorium and Library of St. Barbara's, Cologne.'

As we have seen, this concept was not challenged in the later middle ages even though book production did expand beyond the cloisters and moved further out into the world. The mendicant orders thus relied on hired copyists for book supplies; urban merchants also began to set themselves up as stationers in response to expanding academic needs, while independent manuscript bookdealers in Italy gained patrons and protectors by catering to the luxury book-trade. But none of these developments extinguished the idea that it was especially fitting for monks to copy books by hand. Not only was the idea retained in the rules observed by the older houses and reasserted by those newly formed – such as the Windesheim congregation – but consecrated space continued to be used for this long consecrated work.

The new presses, however, brought this 'lasting' work to an end. The Abbot of Sponheim sounded its death knell in the course of printing his *Praise of Scribes*. Some monasteries invited printers to set up presses within their walls. (Printing came to Italy in just this way.) Others farmed out projects to nearby local firms and lent manuscripts to printers for use as copy in return for receiving printed versions.[266] Whatever solution was adopted, an irreversible change had taken place. The long hallowed, consecrated work of making books was decisively removed from monkish hands while the contents of monastic libraries were disclosed to lay readers of all kinds. At the same time and by the same process, intense pressures were generated to expand book markets far beyond previous limits and to whip up a greater lay demand for Bibles and prayer books and for all the genres of devotional literature that the religious orders had previously consumed. Under these circumstances it would not be surprising to find that both monks and laymen began to think of their vocations in somewhat different terms, or that the latter, in particular, were increasingly attracted to new concepts involving religious 'self help.'

As book producers who took over work previously consecrated by monks, the activities of early printers seem especially relevant to the problems posed by Weber. They coupled capitalist enterprise with spiritual edification and evangelical drives in a way that provides one answer to the chief question the sociologist raised: 'How could activity that was at best ethically tolerated turn into a calling in the sense of Benjamin Franklin?'[267] One of the unfortunate consequences of

---

[266] See chap. I, n. 39 above.   [267] Weber, *Protestant Ethic*, p. 74.

analysis based on 'ideal types' is that it encourages attempts to answer this question without bothering to ascertain just what Franklin's actual calling was. Although Franklin's *ideas* about money-making are compared with those of a 'Renaissance man,' such as Alberti, the way Franklin actually made money is left out of Weber's account. If one sets out, as Weber says he does, to obtain an *historical* explanation of 'the ethic and manner of life' of an eighteenth-century Philadelphian printer, the very first point one might be expected to consider is how the occupation of the American differed from that of earlier times. General economic conditions in Renaissance Florence and Colonial Pennsylvania, however interesting, do not seem to be equally pertinent.[268] If Franklin's maxims reflect a new 'spirit' of capitalism, this could be related quite plausibly to the fact he was engaged in a new kind of capitalist enterprise. It makes such good sense to connect Franklin's views with his activities that it is particularly puzzling why we are called on to argue instead about Luther's use of the term *Beruf* or Calvin's views of usury.[269] To account for the 'spirit' expressed in *Poor Richard's Almanack* by looking always at Protestants and always overlooking printers is to side-track any investigation from the start.

Weber's many critics have done little more than his defenders to remedy this initial oversight. While arguing about Protestants and capitalists they leave the shift from script to print out of their accounts. Robertson's treatment of the importance of double-entry bookkeeping provides a good case in point. He mentions Sombart's suggestion that a possible 'birthdate for modern capitalism' would be 1202, when Leonardo of Pisa's *Liber Abaci* first appeared; talks of 'the slow spread

---

[268] See footnote comparing the 'ethic and manner of life,' of Franklin and Alberti; Weber, *Protestant Ethic*, pp. 194-6, n. 12. Weber's contrast between the 'highly capitalistic' Florentine 'money market' and the 'backwoods small bourgeois circumstances' of eighteenth-century Pennsylvania 'where business threatened...to fall back into barter' (p. 75) encourages argument about many irrelevant issues. Discussion focused on comparing the conditions of work of a Florentine manuscript bookdealer with that of an eighteenth-century Philadelphia printer, would, I think, prove more illuminating. For recent study of colonial printers, see Botein, 'Meer Mechanics.' Simpson, 'The Printer as Man of Letters,' pp. 1ff. provides welcome support for some of my views. A summary of Franklin's career as a Philadelphia printer and a description of the more than 800 items printed by his firm are given by C. W. Miller, *Benjamin Franklin's Philadelphia Printing*. For data on the printer, bookseller, stationer who was Franklin's partner, see Harlan's two articles 'David Hall and the Stamp Act'; 'David Hall and the Townshend Acts.'

[269] See long excursion into etymology of 'calling,' 'profession,' 'vocation,' etc. Weber, *Protestant Ethic*, pp. 204-11. Granted that such digressions have uncovered much of interest to historians; granted that Calvin's position on the issue of usury has been greatly clarified by recent careful research, much scholarly energy has also been dissipated in tracking down false leads.

of scientific book-keeping' as a 'chief cause' of medieval traditionalism in business affairs; and discusses how its rapid spread helped to quicken economic activity during the sixteenth century. By following 'the same lines as Weber, it would be very easy to substitute systematic books for the Protestant Ethic as the origin of the capitalist spirit,' he says. He concludes, however, that Weber's lines are too restricted:

The great cause of the rise of the spirit of capitalism has been capitalism itself; and it has been conditioned by general cultural conditions...more particularly by developments in business techniques and by governmental and legal institutions affecting commerce...[270]

To learn that 'the great cause of the rise of the spirit' is the 'ism itself' is to be reminded that historical explanations in this century are often still disconcertingly similar to medical explanations in Molière's day – the sleep-making properties of opium have something in common with phenomena which are 'conditioned by general cultural conditions.'

With regard to possible birthdates of modern capitalism, the difference between completing a manuscript and issuing a printed edition ought to be given some thought. The *Book of the Abacus*, a huge compendium, of which a 1228 copy is preserved, was not much easier to obtain than Ptolemy's *Almagest* during the thirteenth and fourteenth centuries.[271] In late medieval Florence, where commercial education was far in advance of other regions, merchants were still using wooden tables with counters for calculations and reckon masters were called in by builders when it came time for them to settle their accounts.[272]

The 'slow spread of scientific book-keeping' before the sixteenth century and its more rapid spread thereafter is probably related to the shift from script to print. During the later middle ages, there is evidence that commercial arithmetic was taught by private lessons given by masters in university towns, but for the most part future merchants learned the tricks of their trade from doing what their masters did.[273]

270 H. M. Robertson, 'A Criticism of Max Weber,' p. 81.
271 The medieval *Liber Abaci*, a 459 page manuscript compendium is discussed by Joseph and Frances Gies, *Leonardo of Pisa* and Karl Menninger, *Number Words and Number Symbols*, pp. 425 ff. The first printed arithmetic book (Treviso, 1478) is described; its first page (referring to the 'mercantile art') is reproduced and the early publication of other arithmetic books in different regions is discussed by Menninger, pp. 334ff. On this topic, see also Gordon, 'Books on Accountancy.'
272 Goldthwaite, 'Schools and Teachers.' See p. 420 on Sapori's findings, and p. 425, n. 20 on the importance of apprenticeship over schooling before 1500.
273 Beaujouan, 'Motives and Opportunities,' p. 235.

English apprentices, for example, joined the household of a Florentine merchant in Southampton in 1476, in order to learn the 'mysteries of his trade.'[274] After 'the secrets of the press' had been mastered by merchant adventurers such as Caxton,[275] the secrets of bookkeeping and business arithmetic became more accessible to the mercantile community at large.[276] Reckon masters and tutors found it profitable to turn out manuals and treatises which advertised their services and added luster to their names. They were especially likely to stress the usefulness of double-entry bookkeeping, partly because its elegance and precision appealed to their own aesthetic sense but also because it was still regarded as a 'mystery' by the ordinary merchant. The latter might wish to hire the services of trained accountants and professional bookkeepers if duly impressed by the advantages of the new art. Here as elsewhere the great merchant printer was out of the ordinary. The ledger used to keep the accounts of the far-flung concerns of Plantin's Antwerp firm reflects remarkably sophisticated cost accounting techniques. The expertise was not supplied by Plantin himself but by Cornelius von Bomberghen, whose great uncle Daniel had probably picked up a double-entry system as a master printer in Venice.[277] But for ordinary merchants, it is argued, double-entry bookkeeping was less important for early-modern business practices than the textbook promoters made it seem.[278]

The new proliferation of books on the business arts, at all events, did inject a new spirit into European *literary* culture. Readers were told that they might obtain 'peace and rest of mind such as is looked for in another world' by keeping systematic books. The advice was not unfamiliar to earlier merchants, but it did represent a somewhat different message than had been conveyed by previous literary genres. Doubtless such advice seemed especially suitable to early printers who had to worry about balancing their books. Yet it also reflected how arts of persuasion developed by preachers and teachers could be turned to new ends. As later discussion suggests, printing opened new careers

---

[274] Kenneth Charlton, *Education in Renaissance England*, pp. 258–60.

[275] Blake, *Caxton and His World*, p. 56, remarks on the difficulty of acquiring the 'secrets of the press' in Cologne in the 1460s and 70s.

[276] See relevant titles and discussion by Goldthwaite, 'Schools and Teachers' and Charlton, *Education in Renaissance England*, pp. 279; 298; also Curtis, 'Education and Apprenticeship,' pp. 68–70; Wright, *Middle-Class Culture*, p. 162.

[277] Raymond de Roover, 'The Business Organization of the Plantin Press'; Florence Edler (de Roover), 'Cost Accounting in the 16th Century'; Kingdon, 'Christopher Plantin and his Backers,' p. 309.   [278] Yamey, 'Scientific Bookkeeping.'

to Renaissance pedagogues who were able to teach with their pens. Friars who were gifted as popular preachers also helped to launch new genres of science writing and to popularize the *quadrivium* in print. An Italian friar and professor of sacred theology thus became the 'father of double entry book keeping' by producing the chief treatise on the topic in 1494.[279] When Defoe proclaimed in his *English Tradesman* that, before meeting one's maker, it was almost as important to have one's books in order as it was to have one's soul prepared, he was not necessarily reflecting a 'secularized Puritan' outlook. He was offering one more variation on a theme which had been used to promote sales of accountancy books from the first Renaissance blurb writer on.[280]

The promotional literature which accompanied early printed treatises on bookkeeping was only one of several new genres that might suggest to later scholars that a new capitalist 'spirit' had emerged. As Natalie Davis has shown, commercial arithmetic books also contained much that seemed to undercut the admonitions of preachers against sharp dealing and usury. Word problems illustrating different methods of calculation depicted businessmen driving hard bargains without any words of disapproval and almost as if in tacit agreement with readers that such practices took place every day. Even Catholic monks when serving as authors of such textbooks suspended their moral judgment and preserved a neutral tone. Procedures for calculating large profits or setting exorbitant interest rates were presented as lessons to be learned by attentive readers and not as actions that were displeasing to God.

These textbooks...taught business techniques and calculations generally *without* reference to religious-moral admonitions and to the stipulations of the canonists and Protestant theorists; the implied or explicit suggestion was that necessary business practice was the ordinary guide to behavior. Here lay one basis for a morally neutral attitude toward business. These works of instruction played no important role in that interesting process described by Max Weber – the marshaling of religious energy to the benefit (often unintended) of business life.[281]

---

279 R. E. Taylor, 'Luca Pacioli.' See also in same collection R. de Roover on 'Accounting Prior to Luca Pacioli,' pp. 114–74. The spread of the double-entry system outside Italy is attributed by de Roover to printing (p. 174.) On Pacioli and other popularizers of the *quadrivium*, see pp. 547ff., volume II below.

280 Yamey, 'Scientific Bookkeeping,' pp. 102–4 cites Defoe and his predecessors.

281 Natalie Z. Davis, 'Sixteenth Century French Arithmetics,' p. 43. The entire article pp. 18–48 should be consulted. Some writers did mention admonitions and prohibitions but only to override them by examples. The heterogeneous religious affiliations of the authors discussed are brought out (p. 44). They included both a Spanish and a French monk (p. 21).

These works did, however, show how the talents of members of the religious orders were deflected by new opportunities extended after printing toward instruction aimed at amoral secular ends.

A new drive toward uniformity and rationalization was also propelled by the output of printed arithmetics which were designed with large circulation figures in mind. Word problems had to be chosen with special care to be of use to readers located beyond local markets. Weights and measures or systems of coinage had to be selected that would be comprehensible beyond the special locality from which the author came.[282] Conversion tables were encouraged since they enabled the same text to sell in different regions. Such tables, of course, were also useful to all the wholesale merchants, factors or agents who had to move beyond local markets to sell their wares. Here as elsewhere the prospering publisher was himself a likely customer for the very products he purveyed.

The daily routines of the printer were obviously more compatible than those of monks or friars with the calculation of financial loss and gain. Insofar as he helped to edit and publish business manuals and arithmetic texts, he was passing on to others, for profit, lessons that he also had to learn himself. Accurate accounting had to be practiced as well as preached by successful textbook producers. Sixteenth-century printers, to be sure, also made money from publishing sermons, but they derived no pecuniary advantage from taking them to heart.

Long before *Poor Richard*, printers had learned from their daily experience that time was money and that profits and piety went together. They were carriers of a 'spirit of capitalism' for the simple reason that they were capitalists themselves. If they deserve to be singled out among contemporary entrepreneurs, it is because they were temporarily in command of the nascent communications industry and played a key role in reshaping cultural products and conveying ideas. Their outlook was reflected in handbooks like *The Merchants Mappe of Commerce* and in the advice such handbooks contained.[283] The tables and rules, the admonitions concerning extravagance and the advice as to the cumulative advantages of saving a farthing a day had already appeared in Italian merchant manuals before printing.[284] They were

[282] Pertinent data are given by Struik, 'Mathematics in the Netherlands.' (See esp. p. 52.)

[283] See works cited by Wright, *Middle-Class Culture*, p. 162.

[284] Sapori, *The Italian Merchant*, p. 102 discusses fourteenth-century 'commercial handbooks' which contained equivalents of weights and measures, formulas for calculations, details on currency regulations and customs as well as calendars.

probably not entirely new to Elizabethan merchants. But such instruction was being presented in a form that entered almost every English household – well before Philadelphia printers had set up shop. By the seventeenth century, in England at least, the almanack outsold the Bible. 'No other book in the English language had as large a circulation as the annual Almanack.'[285]

The contents of these almanacks diverged from scribal books of hours or shepherd's calendars in that they contained uniform tables for computing costs of goods and payments of wages, and lists converting weights and measures or providing distances between main towns. Granted that much misinformation, false remedies and useless prognostications were also being propagated, merchants could still handle their affairs more systematically when they no longer had to compute costs, distances, or wages for various transactions, by laborious and often faulty procedures on their own.

The same considerations also apply to all the other practical manuals, directories, maps and globes that proliferated after print. The increased output of practical handbooks, to be sure, is occasionally noted by social historians, but then it is almost always explained in terms of a new demand created by a 'rising middle class.' If we are dissatisfied with the way 'general cultural conditions' are used to explain early-modern developments, we will probably also share J. H. Hexter's critical view of 'the rising middle class.'[286] Indeed, the second explanatory principle seems to me to be as vacuous as the first. Instead of concentrating on a vaguely conceived, ever-expanding demand, more thought should be devoted to a specific transformation that affected production and supply.

Professor Lopez has shown that the Renaissance was on the whole a period of economic regression, yet the shopkeepers established in a great many cities had abundant arithmetical needs. Think only of the printing presses and the bookshops, which were particularly abundant in university towns...in Salamanca at the beginning of the sixteenth century there were already fifty-

---

[285] Bosanquet, 'English Seventeenth Century Almanacks,' p. 361. See also same author's *English Printed Almanacks*, and references given by Hetherington, 'Almanacs and...Knowledge of the New Astronomy...,' p. 275, n. 1. For other aspects of English almanac printing (in connection with the reception of the new astronomy) see pp. 631–2, volume II below. A comparison of this genre in different countries would be worthwhile. Data contained in French studies seem different (more archaic and oriented to a more rural and less literate public than the English almanacs), but this may be due to divergent approaches of authors rather than intrinsic differences in material. See Bollème, *Les Almanachs Populaires* and my review of this book in *The French Review*, pp. 777–8.   [286] Hexter, *Reappraisals*, chap. 5.

two printing presses and eighty-four book-shops...These petty merchants were not interested in the theory of numbers but they needed practical guidance for their accounts.[287]

Merchants needing practical guidance had not been lacking in earlier centuries. Lopez characterizes the thirteenth century as an interval of rapid economic growth and yet, as Sarton himself notes, the transmission of skills in commercial arithmetic (outside Northern Italy) during that interval was 'incredibly slow.' Even though the growth of towns and the expansion of trade created new demands from the eleventh century on, manuals of instruction, tables, maps and charts remained multiform and in short supply. The concentration of shopkeepers and petty merchants in particular sixteenth-century college towns did not in itself change this situation any more than did the 'rise of a middle class.' Expanding markets had long been in existence. What had changed were the products that could be supplied. Some of these products in turn were designed by printers with their own special needs in mind. The popular road-guide turned out by Charles Estienne in 1553: *Guide des Chemins de France* may serve as an example. This guidebook laid out routes long familiar to those who were engaged in the book-trade; routes which had been travelled for fifty years by members of the publishing dynasty to which Charles Estienne belonged.[288] The French merchants who followed the paths laid out by Estienne's road-guide will do nicely as symbols of the larger historic process that was at work. After the fifteenth century, Western businessmen, who launched various new enterprises and broke new paths in many fields, were often indebted in their pioneering endeavors to the early printers who first pointed the way.

With the establishment of printers' workshops, book production was lodged more decisively in the hands of profit-seeking capitalists who chafed at clerical regulations and controls. By acknowledging this shift more explicitly, one might illuminate the social background of the Reformation without having to fall back on overworked nineteenth-century schemes. These schemes have led to the kind of circular argument which Peter Burke has aptly summarized: 'Whenever a rational calculating approach is found, the man in question is described as a

---

[287] Sarton, *Appreciation*, p. 151.
[288] Armstrong, *Robert Estienne*, p. 34. On Charles Estienne's work as an anatomist–printer see p. 367, volume II below. His contribution to the spirit of improving landlords: *L'Agriculture et la Maison Rustique* also proved successful, running through many editions.

bourgeois' thus paving the way for the conclusion 'that the bourgeoisie were more rational and calculating than other social groups' and 'that their social rise caused the rise of a rational calculating world view.'[289]

Interpretations based on the dichotomies: feudal/capitalist; aristocracy/bourgeoisie were shaped by the political revolution in France and the industrialization of England. Perhaps they help to define social tensions observed on both sides of the channel by late eighteenth-century commentators. But they are not always helpful in describing pre-revolutionary or pre-industrial conditions and are likely to lead us astray in trying to explain how Christendom was disrupted in the sixteenth century. Although Weber sought to break away from Marx's scheme, his interpretation left the familiar polarities intact. By arguing that Protestant doctrines helped to fuel the driving force of capitalism he encouraged Marxists to play further variations on their favorite theme. Weber's essay could be used to drive home even harder a view of Calvinism as a class ideology which stiffened bourgeois resistance to the old order.

The idea that the disruption of medieval Christendom and the success of Protestant movements were related to the rise of a capitalist bourgeoisie at the expense of a feudal aristocracy is, of course, by no means confined to debates centered on Marx and Weber. The forces of Protestantism and of a 'rising middle class' were intertwined by earlier 'Whiggish' historians such as Macaulay and Guizot; and the equations: 'Catholic-feudal-medieval' and 'Protestant-middle-class-modern' still loom large in conventional non-Marxist works.[290] In criticizing these equations, J. H. Hexter suggests that there are many other polarities (he lists eight in all) that ought to be considered when dealing with sixteenth-century developments. They all resemble Catholic-Protestant divisions, in his view, because none of them 'fit the patterning of history that makes the sixteenth century the great divide between feudal-universal-medieval on the one hand and middle-class-national-modern on the other.'[291] It is significant that he excludes from his list divisions based on class, order, or status group, and thus ignores conflicts between nobles and commoners altogether. Hexter shows clearly just how conventional treatments strain the evidence to force connections that do not

[289] Burke, *Culture and Society*, p. 14.
[290] These equations are criticized by Hexter, *Reappraisals*, pp. 33–4. The contribution of Whig and Protestant writers to their formulation is noted by Trevor-Roper, *Crisis*, p. 193.
[291] Hexter, *Reappraisals*, p. 34.

seem plausible. But his own revised version seems to neglect some connections that do seem plausible and runs the risk of leaving us with no coherent pattern at all.

For example, as noted above, there are reasons (associated with vernacular Bible translation) for linking Protestantism with patriotic and democratic tendencies and for placing the Counter-Reformation Church on the opposite side.[292] As Hexter's refusal to distinguish between a Catholic and a Calvinist 'international' movement shows, these reasons have not yet received adequate consideration. They will never be considered if we insist on detaching sixteenth-century polarities from any larger, long-range trends. Indeed, to detach the Reformation so completely from periodization schemes seems to fly in the face of historical common sense. When evolutionary assumptions go out of favor, moreover, catastrophic explanations come into vogue – leaving historians somewhat worse off than before. Tiresome clichés about emerging nationalism and rising middle classes are in need of sharp criticism, but historical perspectives are also badly skewed when we are asked to think of every event as a discontinuous leap and every era as an 'age of crisis.'[293]

If we give...consideration to those varied polarities...the sense of inevitable straight-line trends...diminishes. The sense of the catastrophic...increases. For a while in the fifteenth century, tensions...stand in...complex balance ...Then a couple of wholly unpredictable things happen. Luther successfully defies the Pope; the conquistadors discover the...mines of America. Within a few decades these events drastically augment the tensions in the system... the stream of happenings flows not with glacial majesty but with devastating violence.[294]

Once again we are back, waiting for Luther to arrive at the church door, without first having established the printer in his workshop and without seeing how churchmen divided over the new issues printing posed. The shift from script to print is thus ignored by revisionist and conventional historians alike, and the relationship between the religious reformation and the advent of modern times remains a bone of contention provoking somewhat aimless dispute. It is particularly surprising that Marxists have not made more of this shift, in view of all that they

[292] See pp. 363–4 above.
[293] The succession of ages of 'crisis' from the fourteenth century on, is noted in my article: 'Clio and Chronos,' p. 38.
[294] Hexter, Reappraisals, p. 39.

have written about the importance of changing modes of production. Given general acceptance of this portion of Marxist theory, one might also expect even non-Marxist historians would display more curiosity about the transfer of power the advent of printing entailed.

As it is, there are few studies on the subject, and one must dig into the special literature on early printing to try to ascertain just what changes were involved. However one interprets these studies it seems evident that the transfer of book production is difficult to fit into patterns associated with prevailing historical schemes. Thus it was less at the expense of the feudal aristocracy and more at that of the clergy than is allowed for by most theories based on constitutional conflict or class struggle. When the body politic is divided between nobles and commoners or rich and poor, it is difficult to make room for tripartite arrangements associated with the three orders or Estates. Marxists are likely to bisect the clergy along class lines.[295] Constitutional historians, intent on dramas played out in representative assemblies, also subordinate divisions between laymen and churchmen to Lords versus Commons or Court versus Country disputes. When taxes and levies were at issue between 'those who fought' and 'those who paid', the clergy ('those who prayed') did in fact play a minor part. But prayers themselves became an issue once printers set to work. By the end of the fifteenth century, not only had the production of prayer books become a profit-making urban enterprise, but supply for the first time seemed to be capable of meeting lay demand. A formidable task for hardworking copyists barely able to fill clerical markets had become a privilege, keenly sought by printers who aimed at boosting sales. New controls had to be devised or priestly prerogatives would be undermined. The rapid formation of a far-flung syndicate which produced one hundred thousand Huguenot psalters for French markets in the course of one year and the publication of 22,000 breviaries, which enabled Philip II to assert his control of the Spanish clergy against papal claims,[296] indicate how the balance of power shifted, to favor anti-Roman trends, after the production of prayer books was taken into the capitalists' hands.

Once the fifteenth-century book revolution is more explicitly acknowledged, it may become somewhat easier to explain the down-

---

[295] See e.g. argument by Kaplow, 'Class in the French Revolution,' p. 500.
[296] Kingdon, 'Patronage, Piety, and Printing,' pp. 27-35.

grading of prayers and monkish ideals in favor of more worldly forms of asceticism involving hard work and utilitarian values. In most discussions of this shift in values, the most obvious and significant contrast is usually passed over. When 'middle class' thrift and industry are contrasted with 'aristocratic' leisure and largesse, the unstereotyped behavior of real people becomes troublesome. Problems accumulate, along with evidence concerning Catholic bankers, Huguenot nobles, improving landlords, idle rentiers, thrifty peasants. The shift from an ideal based on prayer and concern with salvation, to one based on useful work and concern with prosperity, cannot be adequately explained by methods developed by social and economic historians who investigate changes affecting the wool trade or estate management. Procedures employed by intellectual historians who compare Aquinas' statements with Calvin's are also unlikely to give satisfaction. By contrasting the life-styles and work-habits of scribes with printers we could probably come closer to our goal.

The copyist working in a monastery for remission of his sins or serving as a lay brother attached to a scriptorium might well take time out to compose a devotional work such as the *Imitation of Christ*.[297] The mendicant friar, organizing book provisions for members of his order, at a House of Studies in a major university town, might be expected to enthrone theology as queen of the sciences. When the profit-seeking printer handled devotional and theological works, however, he was more likely to assess them in terms of their prospective sales value. To keep his firm solvent and stay ahead of his creditors, the printer could not learn much from advice proffered by Thomas à Kempis or Thomas Aquinas. His ideas about Christian virtue did not necessarily coincide with those of monks.

At the same time, moreover, his new enterprise also helped to dignify commerce and trade. Saints' lives may have been tarnished by being put to commercial use, but commercial activities also gained new luster when associated by monks like Luther with 'God's highest act of Grace.' Partly because of its association with the 'opus dei' and service consecrated by monks, and partly because it also served lay philosophers and scholars, the 'divine art' was never relegated to the low servile status assigned by tradition to other mercenary trades.

---

[297] Delaissé, *Le Manuscrit Autographe*, provides a wealth of data on the composition of this celebrated work. That controversy over its authorship still persists is shown in Deschamps' book review, *Quaerendo* (1973), p. 78.

Early printers in their prefaces did all they could to reinforce the impression that theirs was an unusually elevated calling.[298] They cultivated all the arts of self-advertisement and pioneered as press agents on their own behalf. At the same time they catered to the needs of other merchants by issuing handbooks and manuals that were also dignified by the addition of poetical prefaces and an abundance of classical allusions. By artful references to Boethius, Pythagoras, and the muses, business arithmetic could be elevated to the rank of a liberal art and linked to the wisdom of ancient philosophers.[299] Even while the inhabitants of Grub Street proliferated, authors were being presented as immortals and placed on Olympian heights. Genteel publishers mingled easily with literati and patricians, won seats in city governments, and found favor at court. Even journeymen typographers chafed at patterns of subordination and demonstrated considerable self-esteem. In contrast to the slaves who served the book-trade of antiquity and the monks who stressed humility and sin, the mechanics who manned the sixteenth-century presses of Lyons saw themselves as 'freemen working voluntarily at an excellent and noble calling'; they took the Goddess of Wisdom as their patron saint and caused labor costs to soar by repeatedly striking for higher wages.[300]

Printers were particularly vulnerable to work stoppage provoked by strikes (and to delays provoked by the theological quibbles of censors). In contrast to seasonal rhythms which governed agricultural work, or the church bells which patterned the daily rounds of the clergy, the pace set by their machines was relentless and unceasing. Lay manuscript-book dealers had farmed out copying jobs on an irregular basis. Books were completed by scribes who needed to make extra money by copying between other jobs.[301] Early printers, however, had to develop some expertise in time–motion study, and try to keep their workers occupied all the time. Even after the cost of initial investment had been recouped, unyielding pressures persisted. Reams of paper had to be paid for, deadlines set by book fairs met. A steady flow of work was required to enable firms to prosper. Idle presses signified disaster.

---

298 For a convenient compilation, see Botfield, *Praefationes* which provides prefaces to the first editions of the chief Greek and Roman classical authors and of the Church fathers.

299 Natalie Z. Davis, 'Sixteenth Century French Arithmetics,' p. 29 brings this point out.

300 Natalie Z. Davis, 'Strikes and Salvation at Lyons,' p. 52. The high self-estimate of journeymen–typographers is also stressed by Febvre and Martin, *L'Apparition*, p. 201. The first strike by printing workers was in 1471 in Basel, Steinberg, *Five Hundred Years*, p. 48.

301 This is clear from de la Mare's studies cited above, chap. 1 and chap. 2.

Abhorrence of irregularity or interruption was built into the trade.[302] As one of Aldus' most celebrated prefaces makes clear, the printer was too busy to pass the time of day or even to extend courteous greetings to visitors.[303] The brusque manner he adopted to discourage aimless chatter, and his subordination of friendship to impersonal efficiency were as pronounced in sixteenth-century Venice as among business men in Victorian England.

As a hard-driving, self-made man of affairs, the printer not only shared with other urban merchants a natural antipathy for members of the begging orders; he had more reason than most businessmen to feel keen contempt for defects in monkish learning. Furthermore, he was uniquely well situated to make his views known. The prevalence of anti-clericalism throughout the middle ages can be richly documented from fabliaux, farces and Goliard poetry – not to mention the tales told by Franciscans about rival mendicant groups. Margins of manuscripts and capitals on columns also remain as visible tokens of a spirit of mischief that cast priests in grotesque roles and consigned bishops and popes to hell. Of course one must be alert, as are most authorities, to the difference between medieval satires – based on the gap between the office and the man or the ideal and the performance – and the more thorough-going rejection of both office and ideal expressed during the Enlightenment by such writers as Gibbon and Adam Smith: 'Penance, mortification…and the whole train of monkish virtues are everywhere rejected by men of sense.'[304] On the other hand, it is the nature of humor to elude general laws, and distinctions made by later historians were probably not always observed by anti-clerical wits. The greedy and lecherous monk who falls comically short of an ascetic ideal outlived the Age of Reason. I imagine that monkish ideals involving chastity and self-mortification were not always respected even in the middle ages, especially when ribald students gathered in medieval Latin quarters. The inversion of these ideals, illustrated by Rabelais' famous 'Abbey of Free Will,' was already implicit in some popular medieval texts which elevated classical virtues. That the Benedictine

---

[302] The complex allocation of work in a seventeenth-century print shop is vividly described by McKenzie, 'Printers of the Mind.' He stresses the diversity of operations and constant attention of master printer needed to keep crews busy. See also other references, cited above, chap. 2, n. 50.

[303] Preface to Cicero's *De Arte Rhetorica* (1514–1515) cited in *The Portable Renaissance Reader*, pp. 396–401.

[304] Cited by Raphael, 'Adam Smith,' p. 248.

Rule was a fit topic for irreverent humor is clear from tales re-told by writers such as Jean de Meung, Chaucer and Boccaccio.[305]

At all events, the printer not only helped to shape a competing hedonistic and utilitarian ethic; he also made possible a fuller orchestration of all the old anti-clerical themes. Especially after the replacement of hand illumination by woodcuts and engravings, anti-clerical forces were provided with organs of publicity that had not been at their disposal before. 'Increasingly the arts of a corrosive journalism would be directed against the shortcomings of the clergy both high and low.'[306] Private or 'in-group' jokes, as Peter Heath suggests, were amplified into 'public scandal' and anti-clericalism was 'transformed in scale, temper and conviction.'[307] It is one thing to laugh with some friends in a tavern over the latest misdemeanor of a local monk or to feel uncharitable when approached by a begging friar. It is another to find openly proclaimed in printed literature all one's secret antipathies to the tonsured and cowled figures who wandered in the streets, requesting alms as if it were their right. The impersonal medium of the printed page seemed to offer group support for antipathies that had hitherto been kept to oneself – if indeed one had not repressed forbidden thoughts entirely.

The attack on monks and friars found nobles and commoners, knights and tradesmen, even court and country for once, on the same side. In Hexter's terms, the polarities 'lay-clerical,' 'secular-religious,' 'Church-State' loomed large and cut across other divisions based on class or status group. The initial assault on monks and popes was by no means exclusively 'bourgeois' or 'middle class.' Aretino's anti-papal obscenities went down well with Italian patricians; Ulrich von Hutten joined German printers in assailing papal monopolies; Venetian oligarchs turned a deaf ear to complaints from insulted friars.[308] After the French Revolution, the priest and the aristocrat would be regarded as natural allies; but this was by no means true in Ulrich von Hutten's day.

---

305 Hodgart, *Satire*, pp. 44; 95. For precursors of Rabelais, see Krailsheimer, *Rabelais, passim* and Mohl, *The Three Estates*, p. 37. From the 'Goliard' poets on, it is worth noting that student quarters have often been closely allied with the output of satirical anti-establishment literature. Mordant wit directed against clerks is perhaps more likely to be found among academic 'lower classes' than in burgherly or artisanal milieux.

306 Dickens, *Reformation and Society*, p. 28.   307 Heath, *English Parish Clergy*, pp. 193–4; 196.

308 See Grendler, *Critics of the Italian World*, pp. 4–7, for data on Aretino and Venetians. Ulrich von Hutten's objection to the Italian monopoly that prevented German printers from publishing Tacitus is cited in Hillerbrand, ed. *The Reformation*, p. 77.

Nobles who were more skillful at dueling and hunting than in handling books suffered a loss of prestige, to be sure; for military strategists, learned councillors and bureaucrats gained favor at court at their expense.

In my day, gentlemen studied only to go into the Church and even then were content with Latin and their prayer book. Those who were trained for court or army service went, as was fitting, to the academy. They learned to ride, to dance, to handle weapons, to play the lute...a bit of mathematics and that was all...Montmorency, the late Constable, knew how to hold his own in the provinces and his place at court without knowing how to read.[309]

Once military command required mastering a 'copious flow of books' on weaponry and strategy[310] and royal councillors were called upon 'to think clearly, analyze a situation, draft a minute, know law's technicalities, speak a foreign language,'[311] it must have become more difficult to hold 'one's place in court' without knowing how to read. Possibly gunpowder outmoded chivalry. But literate royal councillors planned the strategy that tamed dueling nobles at home and implemented grand designs abroad. Failure to adopt new ways in some instances probably paved the way for the rise of new men.

Whether we describe it as a 'rise' or 're-grouping,' the increasing prominence assigned to robe nobles in France, for example, might be examined with this point in mind. Officials and magistrates who acquired landed estates and adopted a noble life-style from the sixteenth century on, apparently abandoned many of 'their bourgeois ways.'[312] Yet they did not relinquish them all. From the early sixteenth century on, robe nobles were acquiring private libraries, not only leaving the noblesse d'epée behind but also outstripping the clergy by the end of the sixteenth century.[313] Was it not largely because learning by reading was becoming as important as learning by doing that the robe took its place alongside the sword? New powers were lodged in the hands of a legal bureaucracy which defined and interpreted rules pertaining to

[309] Remarks of a seventeenth-century French nobleman, reported by Saint-Evremond, cited by Lough, *An Introduction to Seventeenth Century France*, p. 203.
[310] John Hale, 'War and Public Opinion,' pp. 20–2. See also discussion of military education of French nobles by Irene Q. Brown, 'Philippe Ariès,' pp. 364–5.
[311] Stone, *Crisis*, p. 673. See also, MacCaffrey 'Elizabethan Politics,' pp. 32–3; Stone, 'The Educational Revolution.'
[312] Major, 'Crown and Aristocracy in Renaissance France.'
[313] Febvre and Martin, *L'Apparition*, pp. 298–9; Ford, *Robe and Sword*, pp. 217–21; 246–52.

privileges, monopolies, patents and office-holding while seeking privileges, profits, and places itself. That Jansenist *parlementaires* resembled Protestant magistrates is probably not because a 'bourgeois' spirit was abroad but because similar attitudes were fostered by lay Bible-reading and legal training.

Nevertheless, the 'rise of a literate and educated lay establishment' (as J. H. Elliott suggests in a different connection) did not necessarily entail the 'rise of a new social class.'[314] Instead, it often meant merely a new kind of schooling for well-born offspring. From Froben's Basel press in 1517 came one of the most celebrated manifestoes of the new age, in the form of a dedication to the founder of Saint Paul's School from Richard Pace, secretary to Cardinal Wolsey and author of *De Fructu*:

> The occasion for its composition is described by the author in his dedication to Colet. While travelling...some years earlier, he had met at dinner [a]... gentleman [who]...burst into a tirade against scholarship...'All learned men are paupers – even Erasmus complains of poverty. By God's body, I would rather have my son hanged than that he should be studious. Gentlemen's sons should be able to sound the hunting horn, hunt cunningly, neatly train, and use a hawk. The study of literature should be left to the sons of peasants.' Pace is provoked into a sharp reply: 'when the King needs someone to reply to a foreign ambassador, he will turn not to the horn blowing gentleman but to the educated rustic.'[315]

Granted that Richard Pace had a special vested interest in giving the best of this exchange to himself, his point was well suited to the times. Indeed the same point was reportedly made to Spanish courtiers by the great Habsburg Emperor Charles V. Courtiers who complained about his choice of low-born councillors were told to see that their children were better educated.[316] Again the anecdote seems nicely calculated to serve the interests of tutors, schoolmasters and textbook publishers, and hence must be taken with caution. The point is that the sixteenth century was an age when schoolmasters and textbook publishers came into their own. This process needs to be distinguished from the rise of the bourgeoisie; for it contributed to the 'reconstruction' of the European aristocracy. In England, according to Hexter, not only was

---

[314] Elliott, 'Revolution and Continuity.'
[315] Hay, 'The Early Renaissance in England,' p. 105. Hay gives 1516 as the publication date in his text, but 1517 in his footnote. The Folger Library copy of *De Fructu qui ex doctrina, percipitur, liber* is also dated 1517.   [316] Kagan, *Students and Society*, p. xxi.

there a 'stampede to bookish education' which edged the clergy out of some schools, but books followed country gentry when they returned to manage their estates. '...men who received what was once called clerkly training no longer remained concentrated in schools nor did they make a beeline for the church or the offices of the central administration of the realm. Bookish learning had gone with them out into the shires and was widely scattered among the men who ruled the countryside.'[317]

The acquisition of bookish tastes by members of the aristocracy had important consequences for the literary culture of early-modern Europe and points to the fallacy of equating the 'rise of the reading public' with the 'rise of the middle class.' As patrons and purchasers of the output of early printers, European aristocrats left a lasting mark on the Republic of Letters – not only as freethinking libertines and daring atheists – but also as connoisseurs, dilettanti and amateurs who cared little for pedantry or professional jargon and favored vernacular as against Latin letters.[318]

It seems plausible that the First Estate would suffer more than the Second when book production was taken over by lay commoners. Those who had served as the principal custodians of scribal culture naturally had most to lose. Within the First Estate the regular clergy which had been heavily engaged in teaching, preaching and book provision, was particularly vulnerable. In earlier times, ruined abbeys meant a setback for book production, but this was not the case after print. Letters and learning certainly did not cease to flourish in Tudor England after the English monasteries had been despoiled and their manuscript collections dispersed. Members of teaching and preaching orders, who had been mobilized to meet the needs of growing medieval towns, also ran into more opposition after printers' workshops were set up. The production of textbooks and the shaping of curricula became subject to intense conflict between church and lay officials. The activities of militant new teaching orders (such as the Jesuits) showed that clerical supervision of education could no longer be taken for granted but had to be aggressively pursued. (It has remained a bone

317 Hexter, *Reappraisals*, p. 56.
318 The nobles of the sword thus achieved a kind of cultural ascendancy over the 'robins' in seventeenth-century France. They helped to dignify French belles lettres while downgrading Latin erudition and contributed to the ideal of the 'honnête homme,' according to Martin, *Livre à Paris* II, 964. The development of an English equivalent of the 'honnête homme' is described by Wilkinson, 'The Gentleman Ideal.'

of contention in Catholic realms down to the present.) The secular clergy was also drawn into the struggle as lay tutors and schoolmasters began to come into their own.[319] As we have seen, the Cathedral chapter of Strasbourg, which had previously handled book provision for local schools, became powerless to prevent the establishment of a lay system of public education.[320]

As the foregoing suggests, I think that the shift in book production dealt a relatively swift blow to ecclesiastical influence, which had remained strong despite the expansion of lay book production and the development of lay piety during the later middle ages. Several early presses were established under the aegis of the Church and the theological faculties. It was under ecclesiastical patronage (that of a German Benedictine monastery supervised by Cardinal Torquemada) that Sweynheim and Pannartz (both clerics in minor orders themselves) set up the first press in Italy. When these two pioneering printers left Subiaco, they followed the route taken by medieval churchmen and scribes, by going to Rome. Their firm did not prosper, however.[321] Some forty presses were established in Rome between 1460 and 1500; later on, a firm run by Aldus Manutius' son, Paul, profited from serving Counter-Reformation popes as assiduously as Aldus had earlier served humanist patrons. Nevertheless, Rome never became a major printing center. The expanding industry required much larger markets than the Church alone could provide and by the end of the fifteenth century, the most flourishing centers were at the crossroads of commerce and outside ecclesiastical control. Of the numerous presses operating in Venice at the turn of the century, very few were run by men who felt subservient to popes or cardinals, Dominican inquisitors or faculties of theology. Instead, authors were prodded by Venetian printers to exploit popular lay themes.

Venice dominated Italian printing: perhaps one half of all Cinquecento books were printed there...The Venetian printers reflected and reinforced changes ...led public taste...made popular vernacular literature commercially successful and provided Italian writers with a unique opportunity to live

---

[319] How the Spanish church became alarmed about the spread of unsupervised primary education after printing and moved toward rigorous inspection is noted by Kagan, *Students and Society*, p. 11.

[320] See p. 371 above. The establishment of lay schools in Protestant Strasbourg in the 1520s might be contrasted with the situation in Catholic Angers in the 1780s where church-run schools (from the elementary to university level) prevailed. See McManners, *French Ecclesiastical Society*, passim.   [321] Maas, 'German Printers,' pp. 118–26.

and write independently...Aretino's blistering criticism of the papal court went uncensored. Insult, slander, even obscenity against friars and priests were so common that anti-clericalism became a literary convention...authors avoided only criticism of things Venetian.[322]

French printers, whether in Paris, Meaux, or Lyons, ran into more difficulties with clerical censors than did the early printers in Venice. In the 1470s, the Sorbonne had briefly housed the first French press.[323] But for most of the early-modern era it was more hospitable to theological censors who held up publication and were viewed with antipathy by the French publishing trade.[324] The well-documented case of Robert Estienne offers a striking example of how circumstances had changed for the faculty of theology at the Sorbonne: 'A layman, a merchant craftsman was producing within their own university precincts works of European reputation which embodied the qualities which they were blamed for neglecting: devotion to the text of the Bible and the scientific study of language.'[325]

Whereas the shops and bookstalls of the Paris university stationers had been appendages of the colleges and designed to serve the needs of the arts and theological faculties, the workshops run by the scholar-

---

[322] Grendler, *Critics of the Italian World*, pp. 4–7.

[323] That the first Paris press was not a 'university press' but rather the private press of two Sorbonne masters is brought out by Hirsch, *Printing, Selling*, p. 51. Johann Heynlin, college librarian and co-sponsor went on to Basel, taking Amerbach and Reuchlin with him, thus contributing to the founding of the Amerbach-Froben firm. See Hilgert, 'Johann Froben,' pp. 141–9; Zeydel, 'Johann Reuchlin and Sebastian Brant,' p. 119. The other sponsor: Guillaume Fichet, the rector of the Sorbonne, went to Rome, leaving an influential group of followers behind. Among the 'Fichetistes' was Robert Gaguin, to whom Fichet addressed his celebrated praise of typography and who gave Erasmus his first chance to appear in print. Fichet's interest in bringing printers to the Sorbonne had little to do with theological studies but much with getting his own *Rhetorica* duplicated in advance of George of Trebizond's *Rhetorica* (Venice, 1472). How Fichet sided with Bessarion (and with de' Bussi, the editor for Sweynheim and Pannartz, and later Bishop of Aleria) against George of Trebizond is described in a new monograph: Monfasani, *George of Trebizond*, pp. 215–16; 227, 321–2. The tendency for the first presses at universities to be established as 'vanity presses' by officials who wanted to see their works in print is discussed by Goldschmidt, *The First Cambridge Press*, pp. 3–4. (Henry Bullock's speech of welcome to Cardinal Wolsey is thus the first printed work to come from Siberch's press at Cambridge in 1521.) The German printers who were brought by Fichet and Heynlin to Paris set up business for themselves on the Rue Saint Jacques in 1474 and catered to conventional academic taste – abandoning humanist types and texts in favor of preachers' manuals and canon law texts in Gothic styles. See Lucien Febvre, *Au Coeur Religieux*, p. 34; Renaudet, *Préréforme et Humanisme*, pp. 83–4; Tilley, *The Dawn*, pp. 88; 212–14, and bibliography in Febvre and Martin, *L'Apparition*, pp. 521–2.

[324] For evidence of repercussions on the book-trade of the Sorbonne condemnations of 1521, see Bietenholz, *Basle and France*, p. 30. Difficulties caused by simply having to wait for Sorbonne theologians to render opinions are noted in works cited above, chap. 2, n. 310.

[325] Armstrong, *Robert Estienne*, p. 203.

printers became independent centers conferring rewards and prestige. Engaged in far-flung operations, initiating advances in lay erudition, the print shops attracted wandering scholars much as monastic libraries and medieval colleges had. The heads of the new firms not only cultivated princely patrons but also dispensed patronage themselves, providing part-time jobs and room and board to impecunious students and clerks who had previously been more dependent on finding careers within the church. As one might expect, scholars became somewhat bolder about denouncing clerical monopolies of learning and pointing out the deficiencies resulting therefrom when benefices were no longer their chief means of support and a new kind of lay patronage could be obtained.[326]

Collaboration with printers made it possible for a new generation of men of letters to behave as did the German pamphleteers who ridiculed the professors of Cologne. Like the 'obscure men' who plagued Johann Reuchlin, the learned doctors at the Sorbonne soon became prime targets for Erasmian satire and Rabelaisian mirth. Not only had lay erudition overtaken that of schoolmen, but new opportunities were simultaneously opened for 'lowborn adventurers of the pen.' Obscure young monks like Erasmus and Rabelais could rise in the world without staying in clerical orders. They could find more congenial work in print shops and fully exploit the talents that won them patrons and fame.[327] The young monk François Rabelais could win freedom from monastic discipline by finding work with a Lyonnais printer while going through medical school. He later won a post as a municipal physician on the basis of the work he did for Gryphius, as an editor of ancient medical texts. That he found a new irreverent métier especially rewarding is suggested by his extravagant boast that 'more copies of *Gargantua* were sold in two months than Bibles in ten years.' Needless to say, this attitude did not endear him to scholarly Bible printers any more than it did to the theologians at the Sorbonne. Robert Estienne himself denounced the bestselling author as foul-mouthed, ungodly

---

[326] Attacks on clerical learning made by sixteenth-century French scholars such as Pithou and La Popelinière are cited by Huppert, *The Idea of Perfect History*, p. 20. How attacks on plural holdings and benefices may be related to new careers opened to clerics and preachers by printing was brought out in an exchange over Clichtove at the 1970 Meeting of the Canadian Historical Association. See Kraus, 'Patronage and Reform' and N. Z. Davis, 'New Monarchs,' pp. 46–73.

[327] The career of Ortensio Lando, a former monk who found employment with Gryphius in Lyons before serving Venetian printers and running into trouble with the Index as outlined by Grendler, *Critics of the Italian World*, pp. 26–37 fits a similar pattern.

and blasphemous.[328] But the politics of censorship made strange bed-fellows. Estienne's Bibles and Rabelais' bawdy tales, having been condemned alike by the Sorbonne censors, were commemorated alike by later freethinkers in France.

As a friendless young canon from Rotterdam, Erasmus also avoided having to defer to clerical superiors by taking full advantage of the new forms of patronage extended after print. After reading P. S. Allen's account of the obscure young Dutchman who tried every shift: pushing his name onto a blank space in the French scholar's book, currying favor with a kindly printer only to drop him when a better deal could be arranged; one finds it hard to reconcile the obnoxious young man on the make with the dignified 'Prince of Humanists' that the Republic of Letters revered.[329] The careerist portrayed by Allen is bad enough, but the later study by Hoyaux seems almost too much. It shows how the hundreds of complimentary copies given Erasmus by his printers were used by the wily author to fool hundreds of patrons into thinking of themselves as dedicatees and (hopefully) providing hundreds of pensions in return.[330] It is almost as difficult to imagine Thomas à Kempis adopting a similar stratagem as it is to envisage Erasmus serving meekly as a copyist in Deventer after he had completed his schooldays there. At all events, Erasmus showed how men of letters could be emancipated from client status – even before an author's copyright or royalties were dreamt of – by harnessing their pens to the new powers of the press. By garnering favors and pensions from innumerable lords and ladies, he freed himself from being dependent on any single one, and could use his considerable powers of persuasion to win support for causes that he himself held dear.[331]

It is intriguing to observe how the young Calvin started out to follow where Erasmus had led, with a controversial commentary on Seneca which he got published at his own expense in 1532 in the hope of creating a stir. When the work appeared, he wrote his friends to tell them, 'the die is cast' and to urge them to mention the book when they took

[328] Kline, 'Rabelais'; Armstrong, *Robert Estienne*, pp. 251–2 notes that Estienne's objections to Rabelais were coupled with a liking for his attack on the Sorbonne.

[329] Allen, 'Erasmus' Relations with his Printers,' pp. 297–323. Compare with Harbison, *Christian Scholar*, chap. 3 and Trevor-Roper's essay, 'Desiderius Erasmus.'

[330] Hoyaux, 'Les Moyens d'Existence d'Erasme.' Additional income came from sales of complimentary copies which were much more numerous (reaching as many as one hundred per edition) than one might expect.

[331] On Erasmus' peculiar blending of the roles of scholar and publicist, see also comments by Scribner, 'Social Thought of Erasmus,' pp. 24–6.

to pulpit or lectern.[332] In the 1530s, however, to take issue with Erasmus over Seneca was not the way to make one's name. Calvin's book on Seneca 'caused hardly a ripple of interest, so there seemed little hope of making a living as a writer.'[333] To say that Calvin's next effort was more successful would be to understate the case. The first version of the *Institutes of the Christian Religion* made the name of John Calvin as well known as any aspiring author could wish. By 1535, of course, Calvin was not merely an aspiring author but had undergone a religious conversion. His new work reflected his new sense of mission and evangelical zeal. It also marked the debut of a new kind of theologian, one who had taken no degree in theology and had never been ordained priest.

Printing had opened new opportunities to preachers and teachers who wished to address large congregations without ever taking orders or going through the schools. It made it possible for a small city in one Swiss canton to function as a Protestant Rome.[334] Like men of letters, reformers with a genuine spiritual vocation were emancipated from old dependencies by print. They could launch reform movements without going through traditional channels, without trying to curry favor at the curia and even without travelling over the Alps to visit Rome. To implement new programs they no longer had to wait for the Pope to approve the formation of a new order or the reformation of an old one. Their goals could be implemented instead by gaining the support of lay officials and collaborating with publishers and booksellers. The regular clergy had always been more at odds with lay officials and more directly obligated to popes than other groups in medieval society. The loyalties of Lyonnais or Venetian printers ran in precisely the opposite direction. Reformers who turned to new presses were not only less dependent on friars and popes, they were also in closer contact with men who, by the very nature of their trade, scorned monkish learning and favored lay literacy.

In trying to understand how values held in common by Erasmus and Calvin differed from those of earlier religious reformers, it seems worth pausing over their alliance with printers. Theologians and scholars were being introduced to a new dynamic business enterprise

---

[332] Citations from Calvin's letters given by Hillerbrand, ed. *The Reformation*, pp. 170-5.

[333] Harbison, *Christian Scholar*, p. 147.

[334] The remarkable role played by Geneva as a staging base for the upheaval in France is brought out most clearly by Kingdon, *Geneva and the Coming of the Wars of Religion*. That Geneva served both as 'Mecca and Moscow' has been stated by Donald Kelley. The propaganda that made it a kind of Moscow is well described by Kingdon.

and made acquainted with a new occupational culture when they took their texts into printers' workshops or lodged there for months at a time.[335]

6. FROM CATHOLIC SOUTH TO PROTESTANT NORTH: SEEDPLOTS OF ENLIGHTENMENT THOUGHT

In most accounts, the social context of Reformation thought is portrayed in such sweeping general terms that it seems to float loose of any time and place. Vaguely-conceived 'secular forces' are rendered in a way that leaves no room for visits to new workshops or for pausing over the significance of presses being established in certain towns.

> The new age was symbolized not by the grave and contemplative Deventer ...but by the international business world of Antwerp and Augsburg or by Dürer's Nuremberg, with its European commerce and its attractive fusion of Italianate humanism and German technology. The dominant elements of the new Europe were the lawyers, merchants, bankers, industrialists, bureaucrats, ambassadors, publicists, printers, designers and skilled craftsmen, men of courts and cities...[336]

It seems to be equally possible to take sixteenth-century Nuremberg, Augsburg and Antwerp as symbols not of a new age but of an older one when municipal corporations were still viable political units and medieval trade patterns still prevailed.[337] According to one study, for example, Nuremberg saw a 'shrinking of commercial horizons' in the 1550s. The age of the Reformation in Nuremberg marked the end of 'that long period of economic and political expansion which makes so remarkable a chapter in the history of the late Middle Ages in Germany.'

> By the 1570s, economic and political forces were at work in Europe and Germany for which tradition-bound urban patricians had little understanding and no sympathy...the independent city state had become an anomaly... Its self-contained system...of values and its parochial orientation...were soon to make it a museum piece.[338]

---

[335] A glimpse of how one Paris printer's shop (that of Vascosan, during the winter of 1547–8) served as the scene of daily discussion and argument is offered by Natalie Z. Davis, 'Peletier and Beza Part,' pp. 197–202. Discussion ranged over such topics as the merits and defects of vernacular translation, the timing of cultural reforms, which word problems should be put into books on business arithmetic, and the revolutionary consequences of printing itself. [336] Dickens, *Reformation and Society*, p. 44.

[337] On this point, see cogent comment by Luethy, *From Calvin to Rousseau*, p. 34 concerning the 'spirit of medieval urban republics' being perpetuated in the Reformation.

[338] Gerald Strauss, *Nuremberg in the Sixteenth Century*, p. 151.

Nuremberg's merchants prized stability, preferred to deal in safe commodities and for the most part 'avoided the slippery world of high finance.' There were very few entrepreneurs who 'practiced adventurous finance capitalism' or invested in the new oceanic trade. A notable exception was 'Jakob Cronberger who had gone to Seville as a printer' and, joined by his son and son-in-law, made money from the Caribbean trade.[339] At the beginning of the century however a large-scale cosmopolitan enterprise had already been launched – by the merchant publisher Anton Koberger, who played a significant role in Dürer's career. The difference between 'Dürer's Nuremberg' and that known to previous generations of artisans, who lived before the 1470s in the same town, was not made by commerce or humanism or technology in general. It was the establishment of printers' workshops in Nuremberg that provided the dominant element in the 'new Europe' that Dürer knew. A particular enterprise enabled him to make his mark on images that were seen around the world.

The same enterprise encouraged heterodoxy and toleration. When a papal legate visited Nuremberg in 1524 he expressed his surprise and displeasure at the willingness of the town government to permit the publication and sale of Lutheran books. Two centuries before Voltaire contrasted English toleration with French repression, the legate commented on the toleration of some forty different religious concepts that seemed to be on public display in the town.[340]

When a 'grave and contemplative' Deventer is contrasted with 'parochial' and 'tradition-bound' Nuremberg, it is not easy to find the appropriate social context within which to set Reformation thought. The problem seems closer to resolution when attention is focused more sharply on the establishment of new workshops near old churches, colleges, marketplaces and guild halls. Printers supplied a new dynamic element in small towns and large cities alike – in Deventer no less than in Nuremberg or Augsburg, Antwerp and Venice. Several studies of fifteenth-century Lyons show that the arrival of printers in a fairly large commercial town could still create a considerable stir. They transformed the culturally barren Rhone city into a fertile and flourishing intellectual center, attracting scholars and literati to a place that

---

[339] Gerald Strauss, *Nuremberg in the Sixteenth Century*, pp. 129–30.
[340] Bebb, 'The Lawyers,' p. 62.

had been dominated by money-making and litigation up to then.[341] Their presence in Luther's Wittenberg, Erasmus' Basel, Zwingli's Zürich and Calvin's Geneva is also worthy of note. In every town where the new presses were set up, some traditional barriers came down. New career opportunities were extended, not only to merchants and craftsmen but to professors and preachers as well. In fifteenth-century Augsburg, for example, a priest turned printer and then went abroad to serve as an agent for a large Basel firm.[342] In the field of Reformation studies, however, the occasional priest who turned printer may be of less interest than the forces which enabled many priests to persist as preachers even while breaking with Rome. In this massive irreversible movement, the seemingly old-fashioned particularistic orientation of numerous late medieval towns and principalities played a significant role.

Taking advantage of plural jurisdictions and diverse local regulations, enterprising printers established branch offices and outlets in different towns. They found it relatively easy to keep turning out banned books and tracts despite strong censorship edicts issued by the most powerful rulers in Europe who governed the Habsburg and Valois realms, and despite strenuous opposition from all the theologians and priests who remained loyal to Rome. In addition to access to good trade routes, cheap paper supplies, and money markets, the flourishing of the printed book-trade hinged on opportunities to market popular products without confronting the long delays, heavy fines and personal risks that censorship often entailed. Such opportunities were multiplied by the existence of late medieval walled cities and city-states, communes and petty principalities that acted as independent political units during the early-modern era.[343] We are accustomed to regarding large-scale commercial activity as an enemy of particularism but free-wheeling merchant publishers had good reasons to avoid well-ordered consolidated dynastic realms and to fear the extension of central control from Rome. There was money to be made from marketing vernacular Bibles and Psalters, the works of Erasmus, Rabelais and Aretino and controversial religious tracts. Profits were even greater when one's

[341] Fedou, 'Imprimerie et Culture.' *Cinq Etudes.* Other articles in this work are also relevant, as is Wadsworth, *Lyons 1473–1503.*   [342] Bietenholz, *Basle and France,* p. 26.
[343] On the inability of the imperial court to enforce anti-Lutheran edicts and the independence of German princes and municipalities with regard to censorship see Gravier, *Luther et L'Opinion Publique,* p. 60.

products were advertised throughout Europe without charge by printed lists of prohibited books.

Given the convergence of interests among printers and Protestants, given the way the new media implemented older evangelical goals, it seems pointless to argue whether material or spiritual, socio-economic or religious 'factors' were more important in transforming Western Christianity. Not only do these dichotomies seem to be based on spurious categories,[344] but they also make it difficult to perceive the distinctive amalgam which resulted from collaboration between diverse pressure groups. It is by no means pointless, however, to insist that printing be assigned a prominent position when enumerating 'factors' or analyzing causes. To leave the interests and outlook of printers out of the amalgam (as most accounts do) is to lose one chance of explaining how Protestant-Catholic divisions related to other concurrent developments that were transforming European society. Not all changes ushered in by print were compatible with the cause of religious reform; many were irrelevant to that cause, some, antipathetical to it. Pastors and printers were often at odds in regions governed by new consistories.[345] Nevertheless, Protestants and printers had more in common than Catholics and printers did. Religious divisions were of critical importance to the future development of European society partly because of the way they interacted with other new forces released by print. If Protestants seem to be more closely affiliated with certain 'modernizing' trends than do Catholics, it is largely because reformers did less to check these new forces and more to reinforce them at the start.

Thus when functions were transferred from churchmen to lay commoners, the balance between the three estates was changed in a way that undermined traditional hierarchies. The full consequences of this shift took centuries to spin out. Nevertheless, divergent religious reactions to its initial effects patterned later history. In Protestant regions, these effects were swiftly implemented. Regular orders were dissolved and the printer was encouraged to perform the apostolic mission of spreading glad tidings in different tongues. Within frontiers held by the Counter-Reformation Church, measures were taken to curtail and

---

[344] For spirited discussion of false dichotomies and spurious 'factor analysis,' see Fischer, *Historians' Fallacies*, pp. 8–12; 165–6.

[345] Examples of conflict are given by N. Z. Davis, 'Strikes and Salvation at Lyons,' pp. 58–64 and by Kingdon, 'The Business Activities,' p. 265.

counteract these effects. New orders, such as the Jesuits or the Congregation of the Propaganda, were created; teaching and preaching from other quarters were checked by Index and Imprimatur. Thereafter the fortunes of printers waned in regions where prospects had previously seemed bright and waxed in smaller, less populous states where the reformed religion took root.

The condemnation of Luther's teachings by the Sorbonne (15 April, 1521) coincided with extraordinary business opportunities in Basel where the proliferation of *Lutheriana* and other Evangelical literature was...tolerated and where book trading...with the French kingdom...had been favored ...by the political alliance.[346]

Before lines were drawn in the sixteenth century, men in Catholic regions appear to have been just as eager to read the Bible in their own tongues as were men in what subsequently became Protestant regions. Similarly, Catholic printers combined humanist scholarship with piety and profit-seeking. They were just as enterprising and industrious as Protestant printers. They also served the most populous, powerful and culturally influential realms of sixteenth-century Europe: Portugal and Spain (with their far-flung empires), Austria, France, Southern German principalities and Italian city states. But they do appear to have been less successful in expanding their markets and in extending and diversifying their operations during the sixteenth and seventeenth centuries.

The Lutheran Reformation had spent its impetus by the middle of the sixteenth century; but Protestantism, and consequently the Protestant book trade, maintained its ascendancy over the intellectual life of Germany well into the beginning of the nineteenth century. This, incidentally, meant the shift from the south to central and north Germany. The barriers erected by the Habsburg and Wittelsbach rulers against the danger of heretical writings, it is true, gave the publishers of Vienna and Munich a monopoly within these dominions; but their influence on German life and letters was nil...

From 1550 to 1800 typefounding, printing, publishing, and book-selling were almost Protestant preserves. This applies also to Frankfurt. Even when its book fair was ruined by Jesuit censorship, Frankfurt retained a leading role in the production and marketing of types and in the design and printing of illustrated books...[347]

Steinberg's description of developments in Germany is relevant to what happened throughout Europe as a whole during the second cen-

[346] Bietenholz, *Basle and France*, p. 30.   [347] Steinberg, *Five Hundred Years*, p. 194.

tury of printing. Perhaps the most dramatic shift from south to north occurred within the Spanish Habsburg Empire in the middle of the sixteenth century. 'In the 1550s, the world center for publishing books in the Spanish language moves from Spain itself (Seville, Alcalà, Salamanca) to the Netherlands.'[348] Plantin's firm in Antwerp thus gleaned a lion's share of rewards from the expansion of an overseas book trade in Spain's golden age. Plantin himself became not only Royal Typographer but chief censor of all his competitors' output while gaining a monopoly of all the liturgical books needed by priests throughout the far-flung Habsburg realms.

When generalizing about developments in different regions over the span of many decades, of course, one must allow for numerous qualifications and exceptions. Both in Germany and elsewhere on the continent there was a temporary spurt of activity in late sixteenth-century Catholic regions, where the religious renaissance kept Counter-Reformation presses busy.[349] Moreover, there were some Catholic firms which continued to flourish during the seventeenth century, not only in expanding urban centers such as Paris, but even in declining ones such as Antwerp.

Long after the 'golden age' of this Belgian port had ended, for example, the Plantin-Moretus *officina* remained solvent. It continued to profit from trade with Spanish dominions. It also turned out liturgical and devotional works for home markets along with beautifully illustrated emblem books for export. Artists of the caliber of Rubens were employed to decorate some of its magnificent volumes. But, although it contributed much to Catholic Baroque culture, the fate of the Plantin-Moretus firm nevertheless seems to prove the rule suggested above. After the Catholic recapture of Antwerp in 1585, the horizons of the firm began to shrink and its richly diversified and cosmopolitan publication policies came to an end. The search for expanding markets ended and the firm pursued a relatively cautious, safe course (in marked contrast to that followed by its buccaneering founder) by catering to regional markets and to the unvarying needs of wealthy Catholic clientèle.[350] Whereas Moretus, the Catholic, stayed in Antwerp and

---

[348] Beardsley, 'The Classics and Spanish Translators,' p. 5.

[349] See discussions by Hirsch, *Printing, Selling*, pp. 109–10. Febvre and Martin, *L'Apparition*, pp. 292–4. H. Martin, *Livre à Paris* I, 305–18.

[350] Voët, *Golden Compasses* I, 388–92. Voët's analysis of the contracting horizons of Plantin's Antwerp *officina* brings into sharper focus several issues that are raised by Smolar, 'Resiliency of Enterprise.'

adjusted printing policies to contracting markets, Frans Raphelengius, another of Plantin's sons-in-law, went to Leiden as a Calvinist convert. There he found more diverse opportunities on hand.[351] The victory of Catholics in Antwerp meant contracting horizons for Flemish printers, but with the victory of the Calvinists in Holland the golden age of Dutch printing had dawned. The position of university printer at Leiden held by Raphelengius was taken over by the Elseviers.

Louis Elsevier, that firm's founder, followed much the same course as Plantin's Protestant son-in-law, having worked in Antwerp (perhaps for Plantin at one point) and settling in Leiden after fleeing the Spanish fury. Unlike the Catholic firm of Moretus, the Elsevier enterprise was expansive, with windows that opened on many worlds. Especially after an Amsterdam branch was launched, the firm looked beyond the great Protestant university of Leiden and Dutch Calvinist markets toward a larger, more variegated community.[352] Very much as had Aldus in Venice, and Plantin in Antwerp, the Dutch firm served an ecumenical Commonwealth of Learning that was not contained within any religious, dynastic or linguistic frontiers. Thanks to the Elsevier presses in the Calvinist Netherlands, Catholic philosophers such as Galileo and Descartes could make major contributions to a new form of public knowledge that reshaped human culture throughout the entire world.

By the mid-seventeenth century, not only had Amsterdam emerged as the central city of the Republic of Letters but the once great centers of Venice and Lyons had experienced the same reversals as Antwerp. Throughout the continent, from 1517 on, the movement of printers toward Protestant centers and the tendency for markets to expand and diversify more rapidly under Protestant than Catholic rule seems marked enough to be correlated with other developments.

The movement of ideas that was traced by Paul Hazard, for example, and the related series of problems posed by Trevor-Roper might be illuminated by considering how the centers of the book-trade shifted during early-modern times:

---

[351] Voët, *Golden Compasses* I, 197. On Plantin's own activities in Leiden during 1583–5 see *ibid.* I, 105–16. Raphelengius, who had studied with Postel and worked on his father-in-law's polyglot Bible, also got a post on the Leiden faculty teaching oriental languages. Among other works he published the censored supplement on Hebrew vowel points, mentioned above, p. 332 and an edition of Lucretius' *De Rerum Natura* (1595).

[352] David W. Davies, *The World of the Elseviers, passim*. See also Dibon, 'L'Université de Leyde,' p. 19.

Just as the northern nations, in the first period looked for ideas to the Mediterranean, so the Mediterranean nations in the second period looked north... religion is deeply involved in this shift...the Renaissance was a Catholic, the Enlightenment a Protestant phenomenon. Both economically and intellectually, in the seventeenth century, the Protestant countries...captured the lead from the Catholic countries of Europe.[353]

Although one may be inclined to go along with the general thrust of this argument, one is also likely to question the assertion that the Renaissance was a Catholic, the Enlightenment a Protestant phenomenon. Indeed the difficulty of trying to connect the two cultural movements with the two churches may well lead one to doubt whether religion was involved after all. Even if one holds to the notion that there was some religious involvement, its character will remain vague and problematic unless the activities of printers are taken into account. Renaissance humanists and Enlightenment *philosophes* were too ecumenical and anti-dogmatic to be divided from each other along dogmatic confessional lines. Both groups, however, relied heavily on printers, and printers in turn did gravitate away from major commercial centers in Catholic Europe toward the Northern regions that broke away from Rome.

Needless to say, the fortunes of printing industries resembled those of other early capitalist enterprises in being affected by many different variables and concurrent changes. The expansion of Venice and Lyons as major early printing centers may be explained by examining late medieval trade patterns rather than religious affairs. On the other hand, one must take religion into account to understand why Wittenberg and Genevan presses began to hum. The first export industry to be established in Geneva was planted there by religious refugees from France: 'The French installed Geneva's first export industry, publishing... When Calvin died in 1564 the only exportable product which his Geneva produced – the printed book – was a religious as well as an economic enterprise.'[354] The influx of religious refugees into Calvin's Geneva in the 1550s 'radically' altered the professional structure of the city. The number of printers and booksellers jumped from somewhere between three and six to some three hundred or more.[355] As was the

---

353 Trevor-Roper, *Crisis*, p. 2. See also Hazard's chapter on the movement from South to North in *Crise de la Conscience* I, chap. 3, pp. 70–104.
354 Monter, *Calvin's Geneva*, p. 21.
355 Monter, *Calvin's Geneva*, pp. 5; 166. See also Kingdon, *Geneva and the Coming of the Wars*, pp. 98–9.

case with Basel after the Sorbonne condemnations of the 1520s, Geneva gained in the 1550s at French expense. 'Wealthy religious refugees surreptitiously transferred capital out of France.'[356] Major printing firms went. The movement of workers between Lyons and Geneva which had, until then, involved a two way traffic 'suddenly became one way and the proportions were reversed.'[357] Robert Estienne had moved from Paris but the main flight of labor and capital came from Lyons. By the time that Jean II de Tournes moved his firm from Lyons to Geneva in 1585, the firms that remained in the once great French printing center were engaged mainly in repackaging books printed in Geneva, adding title pages that disguised their Calvinist origins, before shipping them off to Catholic Italy and Spain. The reasons why Lyons printers became dependent on Genevan firms by the end of the century were many and complex. Labor costs, paper supplies and many other factors played important roles. But so too did religious affiliations and curbs on vernacular Psalters, Bibles and bestsellers of varied kinds.[358]

Like the printers of Lyons and Antwerp, those of Venice were caught up in a process of decline that had many diverse causes, including the vast movement from Mediterranean to oceanic trade.[359] But there, also, the free-wheeling operations of the early sixteenth century were curbed by the Counter-Reformation Church. Bible-printing came to a standstill.[360] Between 1570 and 1590 the Republic collaborated with Roman censors. Publication of works listed on the Index was prohibited by local officials and Venetian printing firms were dealt a lasting blow.[361] Even during later decades, when doges and popes were not collaborating, Italian vernacular Bibles still had to be smuggled into the Republic from abroad, lining the pockets of foreign competitors and not of Venetian firms. It was in Geneva, not Venice, that Giovanni

---

[356] The most thorough study is Bremme's *Buchdrucker und Buchhändler zur Zeit der Glaubenskämpfe*. See review by R. M. Kingdon in *American Historical Review* (1970) p. 1481.

[357] Geisendorf, 'Lyons and Geneva,' p. 150.

[358] On the decline of Lyons and flight of capital to Geneva; in addition to references given above, see also Martin, *Livre à Paris* I, 31–2.

[359] Pullan, *Crisis and Change in the Venetian Economy* and Rapp, *Industry and Economic Decline*, point to diverse problems entailed. Rapp argues that the 'decline' was relative and more a matter of self-definition than of objective indices. Venetian printers certainly had good cause for a 'troubled spirit' in my view.

[360] Armstrong, *Robert Estienne*, p. 254 attributes the decay of the Venetian book-trade to over-zealous censorship. The relocation of continental Bible-printing centers after Venetian activities were halted is described by Black, 'The Printed Bible,' pp. 440–51.

[361] This opinion has been amply documented in the recent book based on intensive archival research by Grendler, *The Roman Inquisition*. See also his earlier article: 'The Roman Inquisition.'

Diodati produced his Italian translation of the Scriptures and also in Geneva not Venice that he translated the famous Venetian attack on Catholic censors made by Galileo's friend, Paolo Sarpi, in his *History of the Council of Trent*. 'There never was a better scheme' than the Index, wrote Sarpi, for 'using religion to make men crazy.'[362] In assessing the position of Paolo Sarpi with regard to the free Republic of Venice and its policy toward Rome, surely something should be said about the changed status of printers in the city where Aldus Manutius had won world renown.

Sarpi's religious position appears...closer to Wittenberg and Geneva than to Rome...not because he was attracted by Protestantism as such but rather because the position expressed in the Protestant creeds seemed to him more consonant with the values he held so deeply as the free citizen of a free Republic. In this way, Sarpi can perhaps provide some insight into major tendencies of both the Renaissance and the Reformation and above all into their profound connection.[363]

In searching for elements that made Wittenberg and Geneva seem attractive to the Venetian friar, the movement of printers needs to be taken into account. Venetians might be proud to be described as free citizens of a free republic, yet they were well aware that they no longer enjoyed a free press. 'The modern reader may find it helpful' suggests Peter Burke, 'to think of those East European writers who have published books in the West in order to appreciate Sarpi's problems.'[364] Genevan printers served him better than did those of his own Republic; civic humanism was less helpful to him than appeals to foreign kings. The Anglican monarchy under James I gave him a chance of publication he could not obtain at home.[365] One could agitate against papal bulls and hostile friars within the Republic. But one could not get anti-papist treatises printed there. Like Galileo, Campanella and other compatriots, Sarpi had to resort to devious tactics. 'I am forced to wear a mask,' he said.[366]   Here as elsewhere his position seems to

---

362 From *History of the Council of Trent* (book 6, chap. 1) in *Sarpi: Selections* tr. Peter Burke, p. 207. That the seventeenth-century circulation of this work was 'largely Protestant' (twenty-four editions being published in Protestant regions as compared with five in Catholic ones) is noted by Burke in his introduction, p. xxiv. As one might expect, Catholic versions appeared in Gallican France during the intervals when it was quarreling with Rome.

363 Bouwsma, 'Venice, Spain,' p. 376.

364 Burke, introduction to *Sarpi*, p. xx.

365 For details concerning English reception of Sarpi's manuscript and its publication, see Yates, 'Paolo Sarpi's History'; Lievsay, *Venetian Phoenix*.

366 Burke, introduction to *Sarpi*, p. xvii.

be closer to that of enlightened *philosophes* who dealt with clandestine book agents than to the civic humanists of an earlier Renaissance Italy who did not have to reckon with an Index of Forbidden Books.

On this point, I cannot agree with the high estimate of Venetian liberty offered by Bouwsma: '...the Counter Reformation generally suppressed what was left of the culture that the older political order had supported. But Venice, as has been too little recognized, was a unique exception to the rule. Venice retained the liberty that was lost by the rest of Italy.'[367] In Aldus Manutius' day, Venetians did not have to smuggle out manuscripts to England or Geneva to get them printed. In Sarpi's day, they did.[368] As later discussion of Galileo's case also suggests, there is a significant distinction between free thought and free speech, on the one hand, and a free press on the other. In explaining why the central city of the Republic of Letters moved from Venice to Amsterdam, this distinction needs to be underlined.

Of course, trade in commodities other than books also moved North, and away from Mediterranean to Atlantic coasts, during the early-modern era. It is worth repeating that the movement of printing industries was affected by many factors other than religious divisions. If we want to understand how these divisions *did* affect an important early capitalist enterprise, however, this can be done better by looking at printing than at metallurgy, textiles, ship-building, or other such enterprises. Moreover, the expansion of the printing industry probably affected the rate of development of many other enterprises – not merely because typefounding is related to metallurgy; paper mills to textile manufacture; publicity and advertising to sales; but also because the rate of technological innovation and supplies of skilled labor were likely to develop most rapidly in regions where printers also flourished and book-markets were growing.

Between 1570 and 1630, Antwerp, which had dominated the Netherlands book-trade, lost ground to the Northern provinces which successfully rebelled against Spain. A recent study of the rapid growth

---

[367] Bouwsma, 'Venice, Spain,' p. 358. The same thesis is developed more fully in Bouwsma's book-length work: *Venice*.

[368] Two different versions of how the *History of Trent* was smuggled out are given by Burke, introduction to *Sarpi*, pp. xxiii–xxiv. That the Venetians disappointed their English champions by allowing Inquisition censors to operate in the Republic after the papal interdict was lifted is noted by Yates, 'Paolo Sarpi,' p. 134. Among other authors who suffered from this censorship was James I himself.

of the book industry in the latter region shows that the remarkable boom was primarily an import from the South. Not only did the emigrés supply at least sixty-eight per cent of the personnel studied but 'nearly all the bookmen most sophisticated in their technology and business arrangements came from the South.'[369] A similar movement of skilled technicians, which redounded to the special advantage of the Dutch, occurred when Huguenot paper-makers left France after the revocation of the Edict of Nantes.[370] When considering the phenomenon which preoccupied Max Weber: the prevalence of Protestants among 'higher technically and commercially trained personnel,'[371] the fact that so many printers and paper-makers 'voted with their feet' for Protestant regions deserves further thought.

So too does the question of varying incentives towards literacy extended by the diverse creeds. It is wise to sidestep problems associated with literacy rates whenever possible since inadequate data and uncertain criteria make all general statements suspect. Hard evidence for the interval before the eighteenth century is not only scarce, it tells us only about learning to write rather than learning to read – let alone learning *by* reading. Evidence gathered from richer documentation for later centuries indicates as sharp a difference between two regions of the single realm of France as one can find by contrasting any one realm with another – thus suggesting the complexity of the issue.[372] Certainly one cannot be satisfied with the flat assertion, often made, that 'literacy is the basic personal skill that underlies the whole modernizing sequence.'[373] Among other problems, the 'whole modernizing sequence' is notoriously difficult to define. But, as I have also noted earlier, one can err by being too cautious as well as by being too bold. That 'basic personal skills' were affected by divisions over vernacular

[369] Kingdon, book review, *Library Quarterly* (1976), pp. 210–11.
[370] The Dutch had previously imported supplies from France; after the expulsion of the Huguenots, Holland became a chief center of paper-manufacture, according to Verwey, 'The Netherlands Book,' p. 39. How the exodus of Huguenot paper-makers hurt French publishers and led to further decline of an already ailing industry is noted by Martin, *Livre à Paris* II, 690.
[371] Weber, *Protestant Ethic*, p. 35.
[372] In addition to references given by Cipolla, *Literacy and Development* and Stone, 'Literacy and Education,' there are several collaborative investigations currently underway. For reports of recent findings, see references given by Chartier, Compère, Julia, *L'Education en France*, chap. 3; the collected papers in *Literacy and Society in a Historical Perspective*; F. Furet and W. Sachs, 'La Croissance de l'alphabetisation.' I owe thanks to my Michigan colleagues, Raymond Grew, François Furet and Kenneth Lockridge for acquainting me with recent work on this topic.
[373] Lerner, 'Toward a Communication Theory,' p. 145.

Bible-reading seems sufficiently probable to be worth keeping in mind.[374]

The contrast registered on the title page illustration of Foxe's *Actes and Monuments* – showing devout Protestants with books on their laps and Catholics with prayer beads in their hands – [375] ought to be added to evidence gleaned from parish registers. In the course of the sixteenth century, vernacular Bibles that had been turned out on a somewhat haphazard basis in diverse regions were forbidden to Catholics and made almost compulsory for Protestants. 'From the time of the arrival of the Great Bible in parish churches, religious instruction and exhortations to read went hand in hand – as is evident from the Injunctions of 1538, 1547 and 1559.'[376] Well-to-do Scottish householders who did not have 'a Bible and a psalm book in the vulgar tongue in their homes' were subject to fines of ten pounds, and there is evidence the penalty was enforced.[377] An incentive to learn to read was, thus, eliminated among lay Catholics and officially enjoined upon Protestants. Book-markets were likely to expand at different rates thereafter. Bible-printing, once authorized, often became a special privilege, so that its decline in Catholic centers had a direct impact on a relatively small group of printers.[378] The entire industry, however, suffered a glancing blow from the suppression of the large potential market represented by a Catholic lay Bible-reading public. Furthermore, vernacular Bibles were by no means the only bestsellers that were barred to Catholic readers after the Council of Trent. Erasmus had made a fortune for his printers before Luther outstripped him. Both, along with many other popular authors, were placed on the Index.[379] Being listed as forbidden served as a form of publicity and may have

---

[374] For study of Protestant minorities in South America which offers a striking example of high literacy rates, see Willems, 'Cultural Change,' p. 198. For data on simultaneous penetration of Protestantism and literacy in a sixteenth-century French region see LeRoy Ladurie, *Paysans* I, chap. 1.

[375] Haller, *Elect Nation*, p. 118 and plate facing p. 25.

[376] M. Aston, review article, *Shakespeare Studies* (1968) p. 388.

[377] Berry, introduction to *Geneva Bible*, p. 21. See also Wright, *Middle-Class Culture*, pp. 106–7 for discussion of Elizabethan householders' duty to teach children, apprentices and servants to read.

[378] On the other hand it is indicative of the kind of loss suffered by Catholic printers that a fortune bequeathed to the cause of printing the Bible in his native tongue by a Spaniard, Juan Pérez de Pineda, landed in the hands of the Elizabethan printer, Richard Field. Dennis Woodfield, *Surreptitious Printing in England*, p. 39.

[379] That sales of prohibited works by Luther and Erasmus were regarded as necessary by sixteenth-century Paris printers to keep their firms solvent is noted by Febvre and Martin, *L'Apparition*, pp. 456ff.

spurred sales. It was, however, more hazardous for Catholic printers than for Protestant ones to profit thereby.

The fate of Erasmus' books offers a good illustration of the relocation of profits made from printing the works of a bestselling author:

The imprints of Paris, Augsburg, Mainz, Alcalà, Seville, Zaragoza, Venice, Modena gradually disappear from their title pages to be replaced by Basel, Geneva, Amsterdam, Leyden, Hanover, Heidelberg, Leipzig, Oxford, Stockholm, Aberdeen.[380]

Given the existence of profit-seeking printers outside the reach of Rome, Catholic censorship boomeranged in ways that could not be foreseen. Lists of passages to be expurgated, for example, directed readers to 'book, chapter, and line' where anti-Roman passages could be found; thus relieving Protestant propagandists of the need to make their own search for anti-Catholic citations drawn from eminent authors and respected works.[381] 'Early copies of all the original Indexes found their way as soon as they were produced to Leiden, Amsterdam and Utrecht and were promptly utilized by the enterprising Dutch publisher as guides.'[382] They were also deemed useful by Bodley's librarian. In 1627 he advised the curators of the Bodleian collection to look to the Index for those titles that were most worth collecting and preserving.[383]

Books that were known to be banned had a built-in attraction for buyers and could be brought out unhampered by competition from firms located in Catholic realms. In Elizabethan England, foreign trade in forbidden books provided a way for a newcomer to break into a business that was monopolized by privileged firms.

Faced with the continued opposition of vested interests and short of good copy, Wolfe hit on the idea of reprinting editions of popular and well known Italian works which could not be reprinted by Italian printers (as they normally would have been) because of their appearance in the newly established Roman Catholic *Index Librorum Prohibitorum*.[384]

---

[380] Trevor-Roper, 'Desiderius Erasmus,' p. 51. Problems created by the stringent ban on Erasmus' works in the Index of 1559 in South German, Bohemian and Polish regions, where schoolteachers had been accustomed to listing selections from Erasmus in textbooks are noted by S. Jackson, 'Printed Books,' p. 45. See also Paul and Marcella Grendler's ' The Survival of Erasmus in Italy.'

[381] Putnam, *Censorship* I, 12–13 cites Bishop Barlow in 1693 on the value of Indices as records of literature 'obnoxious to Rome.'   [382] Putnam, *Censorship* I, 40.

[383] Putnam, *Censorship* I, 12–13 cites Thomas James' preface to his treatise on the Index which was published at Oxford in 1627. James' earlier *Treatise of the Corruption of Scripture Councels, and Fathers...* (London, 1611) is also worth consulting.

[384] Dennis Woodfield, *Surreptitious Printing in England*, p. 8.

The chance to exploit the 'double market' provided by Catholic readers abroad and curious readers at home was especially attractive when all the reliable domestic staples: Bibles, prayer books, primers, grammars, law books, music books and the like were allocated by a system of privileges to existing firms.

What Wolfe needed, as an enterprising new printer–publisher in an area not already preempted by others – those 'monopolists' whom he so bitterly fought – was a roster of names of resounding international appeal. These he was quick to seek out; and one of the first he chose was one who was still in hot request almost a century later.[385]

He chose Aretino, who had once made money for Italian printers but now could cause them grief. For 'imbracing of men and women together in unusual manners begets a scandal and the Inquisition permits no such matters, it condemns all such sordid things, nay not so much, but the Amarous Adventures in Romances it condemns.'[386]

Traffic in such romances also must have seemed somewhat less 'sordid' to a patriotic English or Dutch printer than to an Italian or Spanish one. The former had the added satisfaction of frustrating the papists by interfering with their grand design. Thus along with the pecuniary advantages offered by free publicity and a virtual monopoly of foreign markets went the virtuous feeling of contributing to the patriotic anti-papist cause. The smuggling of forbidden books out of the country to foreign markets also helped to pave the way for winning friends in high office at home. Extra funds could be obtained by acting as a propagandist or foreign agent.[387] The printer who was familiar with clandestine book-trade networks on the continent was well placed to serve his country as an occasional intelligence agent on the side. In short, there was much to be gained and little to be lost for the Protestant printer who developed his list of forthcoming books with an eye on the latest issue of the Index. Decisions made by Catholic censors thus inadvertently deflected Protestant publication policies in the direction of foreign heterodox, libertine and innovative trends.

This deflecting action is worth pausing over. It suggests why printers

[385] Lievsay, *The Englishman's Italian Books*, p. 17. On Wolfe, Vautrollier, Field, Charlewood, Bill and others, discussed by Lievsay, see also Woodfield, *Surreptitious Printing in England*.
[386] Cited from Torriano's *Piazza Universale: Dialoghi* (1666) by Lievsay, *Englishman's Italian Books*, pp. 17–19.
[387] This is brought out by the discussion of Burghley's relations with Wolfe and Vautrollier in Woodfield, *Surreptitious Printing in England*, p. 25.

have to be treated as independent agents when trying to correlate Catholic – Protestant divisions with other developments. It was the profit-seeking printer and not the Protestant divine who published Aretino, Bruno, Sarpi, Machiavelli, Rabelais and all the other authors who were on Catholic lists. When the intervening agent is left out of account, it becomes difficult to explain why such a secular, freethinking and hedonist literary culture should have flourished in regions where pious Protestants were in control.

Protestants were just as dogmatic and bigoted as Catholics; and their doctrines were even more likely to stress predestination and original sin. Why then should the regions where they ruled have become 'seedplots' of Enlightenment thought?

Calvinist Holland, Puritan England, Calvinist Switzerland...if we look at the continuous intellectual tradition which led from the Renaissance to the Enlightenment – these Calvinist societies appear as the successive fountains from which that tradition was supplied, the successive citadels into which it retreated to be preserved. Without those fountains, without those citadels what we may ask would have happened to that tradition?...Grotius, Descartes, Richard Simon, John Locke, Pierre Bayle would still have been born, but would they have written as they did, could they have published what they wrote? And without predecessors, without publishers, what would have happened to the Enlightenment, a movement which owed so much of its character to the thought of the preceding century and to its own success in propaganda and publicity?[388]

This citation comes from an essay on the 'religious origins of the Enlightenment' which are traced back to Erasmian humanism and later Socinian–Arminian trends. According to Trevor-Roper, the heterodox precursors of Enlightenment rallied to support militant Calvinists under the 'pressure of fear' produced by the greater evil represented by Rome. Although Calvinism *per se* was an 'obscurantist deviation' it stiffened anti-papist resistance. Driven 'to the Left' by Catholic reaction, Erasmian humanists temporarily accepted 'Genevan leadership.' They only later revealed their true colors by proclaiming intellectual independence, emerging as Socinian or Arminian opponents of Calvinist doctrines in the end.[389]

This argument has the merit of distinguishing between dogmatic Protestant theology and more libertarian and ecumenical trends. Yet

[388] Trevor-Roper, *Crisis*, p. 197.   [389] Trevor-Roper, *Crisis*, p. 221.

it does not really explain the survival of the latter. How could Erasmian, Socinian or Arminian currents of thought be 'subsumed in Calvinism' and yet remain intact? Why should intolerant Calvinists permit so many heretics to perpetuate false doctrines in their midst? In fact, militant Calvinists were just as willing as Dominican inquisitors to resort to coercion and the stake. Arminians had reason to fear Calvinist synods which sent Grotius to prison. Servetus was closer to the Socinians than to the Calvinists who had him burned. When Castellio protested against the burning he was acting as a precursor of Enlightenment, but he was still *persona non grata* as far as Genevan Calvinists were concerned.

To understand how the 'continuous intellectual tradition which led from the Renaissance to the Enlightenment' was sustained, one must turn from Calvin's Geneva to Erasmus' Basel, where Castellio's protest was printed by Oporinus, whose firm also supported John Foxe during his exile and published the first European edition of the Koran.

Official Basle loyally backed the action taken against Servetus in Geneva; yet nobody could fail to notice that it also listened sympathetically to Castellio's pleas for toleration...Servetus had clearly been a heretic and was now dead. There was no point in weakening the authority of a sister church by denying that it had acted in good faith. Castellio however was alive within the city walls. His modesty and probity were generally known. There was no point in joining the witch hunt of the Genevans...Ambiguity seemed less dangerous than controversy. The printing industry must have welcomed this calculated indecision...It was on the side of Castellio and tolerance...[390]

From the days of Castellio to those of Voltaire, the printing industry was the principal natural ally of libertarian, heterodox, and ecumenical philosophers. Eager to expand markets and diversify production, the enterprising publisher was the natural enemy of narrow minds. If he preferred the Protestant Rome to the Catholic one, it was not necessarily because Geneva served him as a citadel (although it did serve some printers that way) but rather because it was not as powerful as papal Rome and could not control the book-trade beyond the confines of a single small town.[391]

When Beza himself was refused permission to publish a pioneering

[390] Bietenholz, *Basle and France*, p. 132.
[391] The relative impotence of the 'Protestant Rome' is shown by the way the Council of Leiden repudiated the 'inquisition of Geneva' in the 1580s in a case discussed by Trevor-Roper, *Crisis*, p. 170.

monarchomach tract in Geneva, he sent it to Heidelberg and had the first edition printed there.[392] When the intolerant *Consensus Helveticus* was later defeated in Geneva in 1706, the persuasive Arminian propaganda that carried the day had been turned out in Holland.[393] Here again it is worth noting that the absence of any one international control center left each Protestant community to go its own way. Official censors serving plural parochial interests often worked at cross-purposes, for they had no one list of prohibited books to act as a uniform guide. The only such list came from Catholic Rome and, as noted above, it encouraged Protestant printers to publish impious books.

When setting the stage for the Enlightenment, metaphorical 'citadels' and 'fountains' are too insubstantial to serve as props. Real presses and printing firms made it possible for Grotius, Descartes, Richard Simon and John Locke to make a permanent impression on the European mind. Most of these presses were located in the United Netherlands, where Amsterdam became the central city of the Republic of Letters after the presses of Antwerp had begun to decline. In this light, the counter-factual questions posed by Trevor-Roper do seem worth further thought. Had the Dutch lost their war of Independence the most seminal treatises of the pre-Enlightenment would have fallen on barren soil. With Dutch presses silenced, much of the new philosophy would have been deprived of publication outlets. Le Clerc's edition of Erasmus' collected works would have died stillborn. Pierre Bayle's career would have taken a different course and probably proved less inspiring to Voltaire.

It was in Rotterdam...that the volumes of Bayle's famous *Dictionnaire* appeared...not only was permission not given to reprint the first edition in French, but the mere entry of the book into France was forbidden...This important book...was not dedicated to any great aristocratic patron...The only patron Bayle needed was his publisher who, in turn relied on the existence of a sufficiently large reading public...[394]

---

392 Kingdon, 'Reactions to the St Bartholomew Massacres,' p. 28.

393 Barnes, *Jean Le Clerc*, pp. 200–1 notes that the influential *Histoire du Consensus* by Turretini was published in Holland, thanks to the efforts of Jean Le Clerc. Although the Consensus Helveticus was overturned in Geneva in 1706, most Swiss theologians in the Protestant cantons continued to hold to it. Moreover, the Synod of Dort, held soon after, represented a Calvinist victory and an Arminian defeat in the Netherlands. But decisions of Dutch synods still left the Dutch presses relatively free, as is noted by Haley, *The Dutch*, pp. 88; 123.

394 Haley, *The Dutch*, p. 173. On Bayle's experiences in Rotterdam and relations with his publisher, Reinier Leers, see also Labrousse, *Pierre Bayle* I, chap. 7, esp. pp. 167–83. A glimpse of the far-flung operations of the Leers' firm is offered by Martin, *Livre à Paris* II, 748.

For publishers who relied on the existence of a sizable reading public, Protestant realms (although smaller and less populous than those under Catholic rule) also provided a built-in guarantee. Whatever similarities there were between the persecutors of Servetus and Grotius on the one hand, of Bruno and Galileo on the other, the Calvinists never took any measures, as did the victorious Catholic party at Trent, to discourage vernacular book-reading or hold down levels of lay literacy. On the contrary, they actively promoted the cultivation of reading habits (to the point of subjecting young children to forced growth) with consequences unforeseen by all.

The merchant publishers of early-modern Europe thus had a particular special interest that aligned them with Protestants – a special interest that other capitalists of the same era did not necessarily share. If one fails to examine the special case presented by printing when considering possible connections between Protestants and capitalists, one may find it plausible, as does Herbert Luethy, to come up with a negative verdict and conclude that the Reformers simply did less to hurt nascent enterprise than did the Counter-Reformation Church. They 'interposed the least formidable obstacle to...the rise of innovating capitalism.'[395]

With respect to the expanding markets required by innovating printers, however, the Reformers played a more positive and actively energetic role. Not only did they interpose fewer obstacles, they provided powerful incentives. On the desirability of lay literacy, doctrinaire Calvinists and more tolerant Erasmians, ambitious men of letters, and profit-seeking printers were all in accord. On this point also the Calvinist presbyter provided the most extreme contrast with the Catholic priest. Cautious Anglicans, for example, objected, in 1543, to Bible-reading among 'women, apprentices, husbandmen.' No true Puritan would thus abandon the most vital principle of his creed.

The essential, imperative exercise of religious life, the one thing not to be omitted was for everyone the reading of the Bible. This was what the reformers put in place of the Mass as the decisive high point of spiritual experience – instead of participation in the sacrament of the real presence on one's knees in church, they put encounter with the Holy Spirit in the familiar language of men on the printed page of the sacred text...[396]

[395] Luethy, *From Calvin to Rousseau*, p. 38. Earlier in this essay, which was originally published in *Cahiers Vilfredo Pareto* (1961–3), the literacy of Protestant minorities in Catholic realms is noted in passing (pp. 30–1).
[396] Haller, *The Elect Nation*, p. 52.

7. ASPECTS OF THE NEW BOOK RELIGION

That Protestantism was above all a 'book religion' has certainly been noted repeatedly.[397] But this could be more fully exploited in comparative studies if it were related to other unevenly phased changes set in motion by printing. Given a clearly defined incentive to learn to read that was present among Protestants *qua* Protestants and not among Catholics *qua* Catholics, for example, one might expect to find a deeper social penetration of a distinctive literary culture among the former than among the latter during the second century of printing. Earlier lines dividing literate from unlettered social strata – magistrates, merchants, or masters, from journeymen artisans or yeomen – might grow fainter in Protestant regions and more indelible in Catholic ones between the 1550s and 1650s. This, in turn, would encourage the pooling of talents drawn from more varied social sectors among Protestants. Distinctions between Latin-reading élites and vernacular-reading publics would also be less sharp where clergy and laity shared in common vernacular prayer books and Bibles. In regions where artisans were encouraged to master letters, they were better able to enrich technical literature, to participate in large-scale data collection and to contribute to the cross-fertilization of ideas. As later chapters suggest, the opposition of the vernacular-writing artisan to the Latin-writing professional is often overplayed when considering scientific change in the early-modern era. Nevertheless newly literate artisans, mechanics, mariners and the like did make significant contributions to early-modern science, even while furnishing publishers with growing markets for technical works.

The variation in incentives toward literacy during the centuries of Bible-reading has important implications not only for the history of science or of ideas. Political consciousness and collective action were also entailed. The social penetration of literacy, which was linked with Bible-reading, changed the character of group identity and engendered 'revolutions of rising expectations.' Religious affiliation thus entered into diverse forms of social agitation and mobility, political cleavage and cohesion. We know that the mechanization of most modes of production came much more gradually in France than in England.

---

[397] See references in Altick, *English Common Reader*, pp. 24–5. Long before Gutenberg, of course, Christians (as well as Jews) were being described as 'people of the Book.' The phrase appears in the Koran. See Marrou, *A History of Education*, pp. xiv–xv.

The effects of the steam press, however, probably came more explosively. Certainly religion had not acted on Bible-reading German Anabaptists or English regicides as an opiate. Many low-born Londoners were already steeped in book learning, were turning out tracts and proclaiming themselves 'free-born,' before many Parisian sans-culottes had mastered letters.[398]

Where there was an uncompromising insistence on the duty of everyone to read the Bible, an early political maturation resulted. Even in the eighteenth century, some enlightened *philosophes* who were educated by Jesuits were afraid to speak freely in front of their servants. A century earlier, English Puritans, harking back to Lollard traditions, wanted books placed in the hands of serving maids and simple folk. They encouraged low-born men to defy the high and mighty and to fight as Christian soldiers against papists and monks. Successive editions of Foxe's *Book of Martyrs* were progressively enriched by dramatic accounts of fishermen, tailors, housewives and the like, who confounded learned churchmen and bested their persecutors before going heroically to face torture and death.[399] Foxe's massive work was immensely popular partly because it enabled ordinary men and women to participate vicariously in a great historic epic. They could learn of other ordinary people just like themselves who performed brave deeds in order to defeat the anti-Christ and enthrone a Virgin Queen. Once the common man could see himself not bowed down by Adam's sin but akin to an early Christian martyr, not comical like Bottom the weaver but as heroic as any of Arthur's knights, the stage was set for the reign of the latter-day saints. This kind of vicarious participation by a mass-reading public in a national historical drama has an equivalent in France – but not until the early nineteenth century – when catechisms

---

[398] In her biography of John Lilburne, Pauline Gregg brings out clearly how much he owed to the printing press. Is there any seventeenth-century French figure similar to 'free-born John'? Between a quarrelsome Huguenot like Etienne Dolet in the sixteenth century and a self-taught, self-appointed 'tribune of the People,' like 'Gracchus' Babeuf in the late eighteenth century, no one comes to mind. According to Soboul, *The Parisian Sans-Culottes*, pp. 240–3, there were many Parisian militants holding posts in the revolutionary sections during the Terror, who could neither read nor write. It seems unlikely that this could be said of the Puritan militants a century-and-a-half earlier in England, see E. P. Thompson, *The Making of the English Working Class*, part 1.

[399] The way Foxe put ordinary people into his epic is well brought out by Haller, *The Elect Nation*, pp. 251 ff. The outpouring of tracts contributing to a new Protestant martyrology which culminated in Foxe's successive editions is discussed by Fairfield, 'John Bale.' Foxe and Bale came in contact with the continental tradition in print shops such as that of Oporinus.

and epics reflected anti-clerical views – and adult education for working class Parisians was undertaken under radical republican auspices in post-Napoleonic France.[400] One might compare the silent war of words in seventeenth-century England with the efflorescence of *chansons* and festivals in revolutionary France. With regard to morals, the Jacobins were 'puritan'; with regard to oral and visual propaganda they were not. Methodism was the antidote for Jacobinism partly because an earlier Bible-reading culture had taken root. In brief, literacy rates among revolutionary 'crowds' on both sides of the channel are worth further thought.

Possibly the most fundamental divergence between Catholic and Protestant cultures may be found closest to home. The absence or presence of family prayers and family Bibles is a matter of some consequence to all social historians. 'Masters in their houses ought to be as preachers to their families that from the highest to the lowest they may obey the will of God' ran a marginal note in the Geneva Bible.[401] Where functions previously assigned to priests in the Church were also entrusted to parents at home, a 'spiritualization of the household' occurred. Unlike nobles who had family chaplains, ordinary householders of moderate means had relied on the parish church for spiritual guidance. Now they were told it was their duty to conduct family services and catechize children and apprentices. Ordinary husbands and fathers achieved a new position in Protestant households that Catholic family men entirely lacked.[402]

Since the Reformation the family had become the...most essential unit of government in the Church. The head of the household was required to see that his subordinates attended services and that children and servants were sent to be catechized. He was expected, moreover, particularly by Puritans, to conduct daily worship at home and to see to the general welfare of all his household...The master was both king and priest to his household...[403]

---

[400] My unpublished dissertation: Eisenstein, 'The Evolution of the Jacobin Tradition in France 1815–1848' (Radcliffe, 1952) contains data on popular manuals, republican tracts, and adult education courses devoted to French history which focused almost exclusively on the tri-colored epic of war and revolution between 1789–1815 and assigned leading roles to 'the people' and to the so-called 'martyrs of Thermidor.'

[401] See Hill, *Society and Puritanism*, chap. 13, title and epigraph.

[402] Hill, *Society and Puritanism*, p. 447 notes that 'The Household Philosophie' translated 'from the popish Italian of Tasso of 1588' omits to mention religious duties of heads of families.

[403] Thomas, 'Women and Civil War Sects,' p. 333. See also Walzer, *The Revolution of the Saints*, p. 190, on duties assumed by Puritan fathers.

Concepts of the family were probably also transformed where the Holy Spirit was domesticated.

Religion is for the Puritan, family religion. Divine worship is, not incidentally but primarily, family worship...

The home was deliberately and not illogically transformed into a church. It was no longer that the family went to the temple, rather the temple came to the family and fashioned it anew.[404]

The character of family life, to be sure, was also changed by various Protestant policies which had little to do with printed Bibles. The abandonment of matrimony as a sacrament, which paved the way for divorce; the sanctioning of clerical marriage, which helped to dignify the matrimonial state, are two examples that come to mind. Nevertheless, 'the temple' entered the family circle in the form of a printed Bible. Boundaries between priesthood and laity, altar and hearthside, were effectively blurred by placing Bibles and prayer books in the hands of every God-fearing householder. Here again, the printer was quick to encourage self-help: 'To help guide him, the father could rely on the numerous pocket-size manuals that came off the printing presses, such as *A Werke for Householders* (1530)...[405] or 'Godly private prayers for householders to meditate upon and to say in their families (1576).'[406]

Through prayer and meditation, models for which they could find in scores of books, the draper, the butcher...soon learned to approach God without ecclesiastical assistance...The London citizen learned to hold worship in his own household...the private citizen had become articulate in the presence of the Deity...[407]

Puritan tradesmen who had learned to talk to God in the presence of their apprentices, wives, and children were already on their way to self-government.[408] However low they were ranked among pari-

[404] Schücking, *The Puritan Family*, pp. 56–7. Schücking also contrasts the situation in Piers Plowman's day where lack of widespread educational facilities made home-services impossible (p. 65).
[405] Charlton, *Education in England*, p. 201. See also Hill, *Society and Puritanism*, pp. 446–7; and Laslett, *The World We Have Lost*, p. 241, n. 3 for other references.
[406] Cited by Wright, *Middle-Class Culture*, p. 245, along with many other relevant titles.
[407] Wright, *Middle-Class Culture*, pp. 239–41.
[408] Haller, *The Elect Nation*, pp. 182–3, stresses Bible-reading as source of new self-assertion on part of 'free-born Englishmen.' That a politically aggressive Puritan ministry contained a large proportion of autodidacts and that Gospel-reading was the key element in creating a sense of fellowship is noted by Walzer, *Revolution of the Saints*, pp. 135; 120–1, but unlike Haller he is not explicit about the role of the printed word in the formation of his Puritan 'new man' (p. 4).

shioners in church[409] they could find at home satisfying acknowledgement of their own dignity and worth.[410]

Catholic tradesmen and businessmen were deprived of the chance to conduct religious services at home.[411] The Bible should not be in French, ran a Catholic treatise of 1548 that went through many editions. The Scripture is obscure because God wanted it that way. Theologians and priests could be entrusted with the Holy Word but ordinary people should be instructed by intermediaries.[412] A Catholic cardinal during Mary Tudor's reign warned Londoners against reading Scripture for themselves. 'You should nott be your owne masters,' said Reginald Pole in his address to the citizens of London.[413] That 'household religion was a seed-bed of subversion' was taken for granted by the Counter-Reformation Church. It discouraged 'domestic bible reading' and created no effective substitute to ensure religious observances within the family circle.[414]

Perhaps the French businessman was more likely to aspire to noble status, and to spend his money not by reinvesting in business but by purchasing land and offices, partly because the stigma of being in trade had never been counterbalanced by the chance to play king and priest in his home.[415] One might also speculate that the threat of a Catholic

[409] Laslett, *The World We Have Lost*, p. 30, cites Sir Thomas Smith in the 1560s as testimony of the very low rank assigned 'merchants, tailors, shoemakers' etc. who 'have no free land...no voice nor authority in their commonwealth.' The arrangement of pews in Tudor and Stuart parish churches enabled the Church to serve 'not merely as a social centre but as a social register' according to C. V. Wedgwood, 'Rural England under the Stuarts,' p. 509.

[410] This seems to contradict Walzer's discussion *Revolution of the Saints* (pp. 248–9) of an 'uneasy literature of self-enhancement' composed by English merchants in response to status anxiety stimulated by the increased output of books on heraldry. He also cites books aimed specifically at 'would-be gentlemen' (p. 250). How references, in prefaces, blurbs, catalogues, etc., to different groups of readers affected class consciousness needs more study. Whatever anxiety or ambivalence about status was shared by Protestant and Catholic tradesmen, I still think the former (especially when of a Puritan persuasion) had a sturdier sense of self-respect than the latter. See Laslett's discussion in *The World We Have Lost* of how men got to be addressed as 'worshipful,' p. 27.

[411] Except in Jansenist circles where Bible-reading was stressed as a layman's duty (a proposition condemned by the Bull Ugenitus), see F. J. Crehan, 'The Bible in the Catholic Church,' p. 222.

[412] Droz, 'Bibles Françaises,' p. 213. The long (600-page) treatise: *Bouclier de la Foy* by Nicole Grenier took the form of a dialogue between 'Bien Allant' and 'Mal Allant' and provoked several Huguenot ripostes.

[413] Reginald Pole's 'Speech to the Citizens of London on behalf of religious houses' is cited in Blench, *Preaching in England*, pp. 50–1.

[414] Bossy, 'The Counter Reformation and the People of Catholic Europe,' pp. 68–9. Bossy's entire article (pp. 51–70) is relevant to above discussion.

[415] To forestall misunderstanding, please mentally underline 'partly.' Before comparing status instability or social mobility in France and England, many variables must be considered.

Restoration would arouse a keen and personal sense of concern on the part of any householder who had come to value being acknowledged as his 'owne master' in his own home. Several studies have illuminated the different elements that contributed to anti-Catholic sentiment in Tudor and Stuart England. They show how clever propagandists aroused mass hatreds and fears by evoking the specter of Catholic massacres and elaborating on the anti-Spanish Black Legend.[416] In addition to the concoction of atrocity literature, it has been suggested that Englishmen from all social sectors found apocalyptic and millennial fantasies compelling and that a kind of collective delusion led to persistent over-estimation of the Catholic menace and to repeated overreactions to any hint of a Popish plot.[417] Doubtless collective fantasies and manipulative propaganda played a part. The power of the press lent itself to such abuses from the first. But there were also more rational elements in the anti-Papist campaign and good reasons why ordinary people felt incapable of tolerating a Catholic king. Even without the threat of massacres and apocalyptic beasts, Catholic policies might still seem repugnant to Englishmen who had come to value their family Bibles as a source of new-found self-esteem. The more forbidding aspects of Calvinist doctrine – such as its insistence on human depravity and its tendency to encourage repression, anxiety and guilt – ought to be balanced against the opportunities it offered for the achievement of a new sense of self-mastery and self-worth.

The transformation of the home into a church and of the householder into a priest, at all events, seems to bear out Weber's suggestion that:

the Reformation meant not the elimination of the Church's control over daily life, but rather the substitution of a new form of control for the previous one. It meant the repudiation of a control that was very lax...in favor of a regulation of the whole of conduct which, penetrating to all departments of private and public life was infinitely burdensome and earnestly enforced.[418]

By thinking about Bible-reading in particular rather than the Reformation in general, one could become more specific about the difference between new and old controls. Instead of merely contrasting laxity

---

As C. B. A. Behrens points out, it was easier to enter and harder to leave the ranks of the nobility in *ancien régime* France than in Georgian England and there are many other differences to be noted. I merely want to suggest that variation in religious role-playing at home should also be taken into account when dealing with this complex comparative problem.

416 Clifton, 'The Popular Fear of Catholics.' 417 Wiener, 'The Beleaguered Isle.'
418 Weber, *Protestant Ethic*, p. 36.

with strictness, one might compare the effects of listening to a Gospel passage read from the pulpit with reading the same passage at home for oneself. In the first instance, the Word comes from a priest who is at a distance and on high; in the second it seems to come from a silent voice that is within.

This comparison, to be sure, needs to be handled with caution and should not be pressed too far. Informal gatherings assembled for Gospel readings were probably more significant in the birth of Protestant communities than solitary Bible-reading.[419] The latter, moreover, was not entirely a post-print development, for it had earlier been practiced by some medieval monks. The contrast between church-goer and solitary reader moreover should not be taken as pointing to mutually exclusive forms of behavior. During the sixteenth century, most Protestants listened to preachers in church *and* read the Gospels at home. Nevertheless I think that the 'deep penetration of new controls' to all departments of life becomes more explicable when we note that printed books are more portable than pulpits, more numerous than priests, and the messages they contain are more easily internalized.

The formation of a distinctive ethos within Puritan households may be partly explained by the fact that Puritans exploited most fully the new possibility of 'going by the book.' To understand the control over daily life exerted by Calvinist churches, it is worth looking more closely at certain examples of early book learning. In particular, it is worth pausing over domestic manuals and household guides (such as one issued 'For the ordering of Private Families according to the direction of God's word')[420] while recalling, once again, new features introduced by typography.

With regard to books on 'household government' and 'domesticall duties' some previous observations seem particularly cogent. Here, in particular, the superficial observer will see only evidence suggesting that printing contributed to cultural inertia. The domestic advice that was issued after print seems to vary not at all from that which was issued in the age of scribes. Those who look for novel views in sixteenth- and seventeenth-century conduct-books are likely to be disappointed. The same ancient wisdom is cited, the same cautions issued,

---

[419] Hauser, *Etudes*, pp. 86–7.
[420] Wright, *Middle-Class Culture*, p. 211, cites this sub-title of a book by Robert Weaver (1598).

428

the same morals drawn, by one generation after another.[421] In this instance, I must reluctantly admit that McLuhan's bold formula does seem to apply: It was not a new message but a new medium that changed the character of domestic life most profoundly. Along with cookbooks and herbals, domestic books were written in the age of scribes. They had not been duplicated in sizable quantities, however. Views of how family life should be conducted in a well ordered household were relatively casual and amorphous as long as reliance on unwritten recipes prevailed. Elizabethans who purchased domestic guides and marriage manuals were not being given new advice. But they were receiving old advice in a new way and in a format that made it more difficult to evade.

A much more limited and standardized repertoire of roles was extended to them than had been extended to householders before. Instead of a cross-fire of gossip conveying random impressions about what was expected, or haphazard interpretations of what a sermon meant, came books that set forth (with all the i's dotted and all the t's crossed) precise codes for behavior that godly householders should observe. These codes were known to others – to relatives and neighbors – as well as to oneself. Insofar as they were internalized by silent and solitary readers, the voice of individual conscience was strengthened. But insofar as they were duplicated in a standardized format, conveyed by an impersonal medium to a 'lonely crowd' of many readers, a collective morality was also simultaneously created. Type-casting in printers' workshops thus contributed to new kinds of role-playing at home. A 'middle class' morality which harked back to Xenophon and the Bible was fixed in a seemingly permanent mold.

In dealing with altered concepts of the family and the roles performed within it, we need then to consider the sort of cultural differentiation that came in the wake of the printing press. Books entered Protestant households more frequently than Catholic ones. Book learning among Protestants could be described as more homely and less courtly than among Catholics.[422] In all regions, however, primers and grammars, arithmetic books and writing manuals became more uniform and more abundant at more or less the same time. As Father

---

421 See Wright, *Middle-Class Culture*, pp. 226-7, for comment on the 'strange sameness' of domestic guidance offered to a burgher in 1558 and to his grandson in 1640.

422 See Wright, *Middle-Class Culture*, p. 203, no. 3, on limited vogue in England for translations of Castiglione's *Courtier* and other aristocratic guidebooks.

Ong points out, a new pedagogical method was entailed in asking students to 'look at page 7, line 3, fourth word.'[423] Home-work and learning processes were restructured by access to the printed page. Both the character of educational institutions and of child-rearing were transformed in a manner that affected well-nurtured youths in all realms.

'Upper-class' etiquette as well as 'middle-class' morality was fixed in a new way in the sixteenth century. The behavior of boys and girls became subject to rules and regulations which were not really new (since they were already present in medieval sermons and manuscripts), but which became much more difficult for parents and teachers to ignore. Erasmus' *De Civilitate Morum Puerilium*, first published by Froben (Basel, 1530), enjoyed an immediate success – a minimum of 47,000 copies are estimated to have been in circulation before 1600. Translated into diverse vernaculars, plagiarized, pirated and imitated, the work fixed a code of manners and introduced a new type-style ('civilité') which guided writing masters at the same time.[424] As a school book, it served the same double function (later carried on in nineteenth-century America by the McGuffey Reader) of inculcating sound Christian morals while teaching children to read. What may be most intriguing to child psychologists is the way outward appearance and body language were stressed. Children were instructed not only how to be 'correct' in their general conduct, table manners and apparel (along lines immortalized by Polonius' advice to Laertes) but also, in really remarkable detail, just how they must convey by their comportment and facial expressions that they were well bred. After reading about all the ways one's eye movements and eyebrows must be controlled in order to avoid giving the impression of being violent, arrogant, mad, up-to-mischief, idle, irascible etc. and going on to learn what one should do with one's cheeks, lips, limbs, one would expect to find that an increased self-consciousness would set off the early-modern from the medieval sensibility. One can also understand why so many Mannerist portraits convey a mask-like immobile expression and why social historians feel that school, parents and clergy alike seemed to be engaged in an effort to bring the child under more complete control. As noted earlier, it is a mistake to assume that the only

---

[423] Ong, *Ramus*, p. 314.
[424] Chartier, Compère, Julia, *L'Education en France*, pp. 136–7; Verwey, 'The First "Book of Etiquette" for Children', and also, by same author, 'Les Caractères de Civilité.'

audience for such books were the children to whom they were directed. Not only tutors but parents who consulted these etiquette books could not help but become more anxious about themselves, and more concerned about controlling the children whom they had in their charge. Such books seem to me to have exerted a truly relentless pressure upon helpless parents and children alike.

Changes affecting schooling and family life between the fifteenth and the eighteenth centuries have been examined in many separate studies since the appearance of Philippe Ariès' pioneering work on *ancien régime* France[425] – a seminal work which virtually founded a new scholarly industry and field of research. Many of these studies raise important questions about Ariès' methods and research, about the way he uses evidence and about its limited range.[426] But few have suggested the need to select a different point of departure for the changed approach to childhood Ariès discerned. Granted that criticism has eroded the notion that there was a 'discovery of childhood' in the early-modern era; most critics still agree that some sort of shift did occur and that children tended to be more segregated from the company of adults after the fifteenth century. 'If there is truth in the statement that "there is no place for children in the medieval world", it rests in the perception that children are to be found not in any well defined and fenced-off areas, such as nurseries, homes and schools.'[427] Insofar as there was a new tendency after the fifteenth century to segregate children from adults either by placing them in special institutions, or by assigning them a special kind of literature, it remains to be explained. The only clue provided comes in a passage toward the end of Ariès' book. There we are told that 'the great event was the revival at the beginning of modern times of an interest in education' – a revival sparked by churchmen, lawyers and scholars who were primarily moralists rather than humanists.[428] Yet a 'revival of an interest in education' is not the only possible point of departure. Why not consider first of all how child-rearing and schooling were affected by the shift from script to print?[429]

[425] Ariès, *Centuries of Childhood*, passim.
[426] Some of this later burgeoning literature is discussed in the author's preface to the new French edition: Ariès, *L'Enfant et La Vie Familiale sous L'Ancien Régime*, pp. i–xx. See also Stone, 'The Massacre of the Innocents,' pp. 25–31.
[427] McLaughlin, 'Survivors and Surrogates,' p. 102.
[428] Ariès, *Centuries of Childhood*, pp. 412–13.
[429] Since this was written, an article suggesting connections between printing and new attitudes toward children has come to my attention: Berry, 'The First English Pediatricians.'

Possibly no social revolution in European history is as fundamental as that which saw book learning (previously assigned to old men and monks) gradually become the focus of daily life during childhood, adolescence and early manhood. Ariès has described the early phases of this vast transformation: 'The solicitude of family, Church, moralists and administrators deprived the child of the freedom he had hitherto enjoyed among adults.' The school 'was utterly transformed' into 'an instrument of strict discipline.'[430] I would argue that such changes are probably related to the shift from 'learning by doing' to 'learning by reading.' Surely some sort of new discipline was required to keep healthy youngsters at their desks during daylight hours. As methods of transmitting skills were changed, so too were the functions assigned parents and pedagogues. Books outlining the duties of schoolmasters and book lists bearing titles aimed at different markets heightened consciousness of the difference between age grades. Textbooks were newly designed to take students in sequence from the most elementary to the most advanced level of a given skill.[431] Distinctions between levels of learning also were made sharper after textbook publishing became competitive, and different genres of texts – such as ABC books, Latin grammars, law books – were farmed out to different privileged firms. As a consumer of printed materials geared to a sequence of learning stages, the growing child was subjected to a different developmental process than was the medieval apprentice, ploughboy, novice or page.

Insofar as printing led to new forms of cumulative cognitive advance and incremental change, it also widened the gap between literate and oral cultures in a manner that placed the well-read adult at an increasing distance from the unschooled small child. More of an effort was required for grown men and women to make contact with the child in themselves, for authors to retell 'fairy tales' or for parents to participate spontaneously in child's play.[432] The growing concern of *ancien régime* officials 'with the behavior of the People seen as a "great child"' also may be related to the growing literacy gap. The same point applies to

---

[430] Ariès, *Centuries of Childhood*, p. 413.

[431] That the disciplines associated with the *trivium* and *quadrivium* could be taught at both elementary and advanced levels to young and mature students during the middle ages is noted in Ariès, *Centuries of Childhood*, pp. 145ff. The carefully ordered sequence of textbooks written by Robert Recorde which took the reader from the '*grounde* of arts' along the '*pathway* to knowledge' to the '*castle* of knowledge' has no counterpart among manuscript texts, as far as I know.

[432] This point seems relevant to the stimulating 'Débats et Combats' provoked by M. Soriano's 'Les Contes de Perrault.'

'the redefinition of "reason" and "unreason"; "sane" and "insane."'[433] Indeed the more adult activities were governed by conscious deliberation or going by the book, the more striking the contrast offered by the spontaneous and impulsive behavior of young offspring, and the more strenuous the effort required to remold young 'bodies and souls.' It was 'to gain a start on the devil' that the Puritan child 'was given the Bible to read at an early stage.'[434]

It may be partly because spontaneous and impulsive behavior had to be more sternly repressed, that Satanic forces appeared more threatening in the age of the Reformation. It is often noted that Protestants repudiated Mariolatry, attacked the cult of saints and scholastic angelology, even while accepting the views of Dominican friars on demonology. Belief in the Devil was shared by churchmen who were divided on many other doctrinal issues. Of course, religious warfare itself fostered preoccupation with Satan, who was assigned a commanding role in the enemy camp. But the forces of evil probably also loomed larger when efforts were bent to enforce a stricter, closer 'walk with God.' The new moral rigorism, shared by Catholics and Protestants alike, made particularly heavy demands on the clergy. Whether the duty of lay obedience or that of lay Bible-reading was stressed, sixteenth-century churchmen in all regions were subject to the stricter discipline that was associated with 'going by the book.' It is more than coincidence, I think, that the same interval saw the most prolonged and intensive witch-hunt Western Christendom had ever known.

The relationship between the shift from script to print and the incidence of witchcraft trials, however, is a much more complicated issue than the above paragraph suggests. Here again is a many-faceted topic which deserves a more extended study than can be provided here. Let me simply underline the need for further study, in view of the cavalier treatments the topic currently receives. A celebrated essay by Hugh Trevor-Roper provides a good case in point. The effects of print are reduced to the 'mere multiplication of evidence,' and then dismissed as too trivial to account for the rapid growth of the witch craze. 'Whatever allowance we may make for the mere multiplication of the evidence after the discovery of printing, there can be no doubt that the

---

[433] The problems considered by Foucault in *Madness and Civilization*, and in his more recent work on shifting views of 'words and things' seem to me to be related to the shift from script to print.   [434] Schücking, *Puritan Family*, p. 68.

witch craze grew, and grew terribly after the Renaissance.'[435] Printing is not mentioned again, despite its relevance to all the speculations which follow as to why 'organized systematic demonology' acquired a 'terrible momentum' during the sixteenth and seventeenth centuries.

The topic receives somewhat more attention in a review article by Pierre Chaunu, partly because the book under review (a study of French magistrates by Robert Mandrou) is exceptional in taking some aspects of the impact of print into account.[436] Thus something is said about the shift from the oral transmission of witchcraft lore to its codification in printed form. The contribution of publicity to the spread of the mania; the effect of law-printing and standardization on demonology in general, and French trials in particular, are also discussed. Finally, the eventual replacement of credulity by scepticism which results in changing the legal definition of sorcery (so that witches are linked with crooks and charlatans instead of demons by an edict of 1682) receives considerable attention. The problems posed by this significant change in attitudes (raised many years ago by Lucien Febvre)[437] are handled, however, without reference to the possible impact of printing. Cartesian rationalism is stressed, while the possible effects of a new publicity system on old forms of secrecy and on the position of sorcerers go unnoted.[438] Chaunu is prepared to agree with Mandrou that more efficient judicial machinery helped to increase the number of cases brought to trial. He also agrees that the authority conferred by the printed word and the diffusion of learned treatises helps to explain the increased preoccupation with the threat posed by witches. But in the end he decides (much as Trevor-Roper does) that mere duplication is too trivial to account for such a massive movement. 'Small cause, great effect?' he asks and concludes: 'One must search further.'[439]

Chaunu's further search takes him away from law courts and book-readers into the same rugged backwoods territory that Trevor-Roper and others have also profitably explored. I found his journey unusually rewarding partly because it suggests how much sixteenth-century missionary 'mopping up' operations (designed to complete the Christianization of the barbarian peoples in Europe) owed to printed

[435] Trevor-Roper, *Crisis*, p. 91.   [436] Chaunu, 'Sur la Fin des Sorciers.'
[437] Febvre, 'Sorcellerie.'
[438] For speculation about the effect of print on occult lore and the position of sorcerers, see above, pp. 276–7.   [439] Chaunu, 'Sur la Fin des Sorciers,' p. 906.

catechisms and service books, and also because it provides a fascinating preview of later clashes between the Western powers and native cultures. His vivid portrayal of the conflict provoked between clergymen with their intrusive civilizing mission and the insular resistant folk culture clinging to familiar procedures seemed analogous to me to more recent developments such as the revival of Mau Mau in Kenya or the resurgence of Voodoo in Haiti. He argues convincingly that stubborn resistance to *rigueurs puritains* – particularly to the attack on rituals designed to protect fertility – accounts for much of the data that entered the dossiers compiled by witch-hunters. When stern black-robed clergymen forced their way into secluded communities in the Scottish highlands or Vosges mountains and demanded the abandonment of age-old rituals in the name of Christ, they threatened practices associated with birth, copulation and death – with community preservation, in brief. That deep anxieties were aroused by the priestly intruders, that some midwives or herbalists refused to accept their authority or partake of their sacraments and instead furiously attacked Christian symbols and clung to their unwritten recipes, does not seem surprising. Nor does it seem unnatural that missionaries and magistrates would regard obdurate, blasphemous old women who spit on the cross as servants of Satan.[440]

Although it is not explicitly concerned with the advent of printing, Chaunu's discussion illuminates an aspect of the topic. The suppression of community practices based on oral transmission by a missionary movement, implemented by print and backed by law courts and magistrates, was (I think) associated with the same historic process as the repression of impulsive, spontaneous behavior among sixteenth-century Europeans at home – or at work and at school. Chaunu's sympathetic treatment of the deep anxieties the intrusive missionaries aroused seems to me to be more enlightening than Trevor-Roper's contemptuous reference to 'the mental rubbish of peasant credulity and feminine hysteria.'

The Hammerers of Witches built up their systematic mythology of Satan's kingdom and Satan's accomplices out of the mental rubbish of peasant credulity and feminine hysteria...the...mythology once launched acquired

---

[440] Chaunu stresses the Christian marriage ceremony as a focus of conflict because it interfered with rites designed to guard against sterility and ensure a fruitful match. I think it likely that anxieties would also be aroused by any move that weakened the authority of midwives who presided over childbirth itself or that of herbalists entrusted with power to kill or cure.

a momentum of its own. It became an established folklore generating its own evidence and applicable far outside its original home...[441]

Because the contribution of the new medium to the formal launching of the myths and to the momentum they acquired is left out of account, the timing of the witch craze becomes unnecessarily perplexing:

The duration of the witch craze is certainly surprising...In the fourteenth century, that century of plague and depression and social dislocation, the mental climate might be congenial; but the later fifteenth century which saw the craze formally launched was the beginning of a period of new European expansion...The Witch Bull and the Malleus appeared in an age of enlightened criticism...of Renaissance humanism...At a time when the older forgeries of the Church were being exposed and the text of scripture critically examined, why should the new absurdities escape scrutiny?[442]

Once we realize that 'formally launched' means to appear in print, the question posed becomes something of an absurdity, itself. In 1486, the first edition of the *Malleus Maleficarum*, an encyclopedia of demonology compiled by two Dominican inquisitors, was published. It contained the papal bull of 1484, which called for the extirpation of witches in Germany and thus helped to promote the Dominicans' book sales as well as their cause. The *Malleus* ran through nine editions in six years.[443] 'What the Dominicans had been doing hitherto was local... From now on a general mandate was given or implied...the persecution which had been sporadic...was made general.'[444] To ask why diffusion by means of print did not occur in the age of scribes is a waste of scholarly energy. Speculation about a 'congenial mental climate' provided by the plague-ridden fourteenth century seems pointless. The invention of print and not the outbreak of plague accounts for the timing of an event which 'advertised to all Europe...the new epidemic of witchcraft and the authority...given...to suppress it.'[445]

This point has a bearing on the speculation of scholars other than Trevor-Roper. In his special study of English developments, for example, Keith Thomas also wrestles with the problem of explaining why the witch craze assumed new dimensions after the middle ages had ended. Thomas notes that mid-sixteenth-century observers felt the witch problem was assuming frightening new proportions. At one

---

[441] Trevor-Roper, *Crisis*, p. 116. Monter, 'Chronique,' pp. 205–13, also finds Trevor-Roper's display of 'aristocratic disdain' objectionable (p. 209). [442] Trevor-Roper, *Crisis*, pp. 128–9.
[443] Steele, 'What Fifteenth Century Books Are About,' pp. 351–3.
[444] Trevor-Roper, *Crisis*, pp. 128–9. [445] Trevor-Roper, *Crisis*, p. 101.

point he seems to suggest that the new presses at work on the continent helped to create this impression. 'It was only when continental ideas poured into sixteenth-century England after the invention of printing, that witchcraft stood revealed as the greatest crime of all.'[446] But this suggestion is offered only to be dismissed, as one of several explanations that Thomas regards as inadequate.

Given the continental publication date of 1486 for the first edition of the *Malleus*, given the time required for importing and domesticating its contents, given the need for decades of 'pounding in,' it would seem plausible to correlate the new press output with the remarks of officials such as Bishop Jewel who, in 1559, 'asserted that during the previous reign "the number of witches and sorcerers had everywhere become enormous...this kind of people within these few last years are mar-vellously increased." '[447] Instead of starting with a post-print treatise, however, Thomas starts with the plague-ridden century when Domini-can inquisitors became active. The campaign launched by clerics and inquisitors, he says cannot explain witch-prosecution, for there was too long a 'time lag between the propagation of continental ideas in the fourteenth and fifteenth centuries and the beginnings of English prosecution well over a hundred years later.'[448] Yet the 'propagation of continental ideas' (as distinct from their formulation) could not have assumed new proportions until after the *Malleus* had been printed and its contents made known across the Channel – that is, until the fifteenth century was coming to an end.

If more attention was paid to the effect of print, moreover, one would not be surprised that humanist scholarship coexisted with efforts to codify demonology or increased concern about pacts with the Devil. As noted in the previous chapter, data inherited from the age of scribes came to sixteenth-century scholars in scrambled form and time was required to unscramble them. Mystification as well as enlightenment resulted from the output of early printers. Renaissance scholarship was by no means incompatible with belief in a spirit world. It entailed the acceptance of many 'forgeries' and false texts. It encompassed the hieroglyphics of 'Horapollo,' alchemy, astrology and learned treatises on the Cabala. Moreover, the expanded horizons of Renaissance bookworms were not irrelevant to suspicions of pacts with the Devil.

[446] Thomas, *Religion and the Decline of Magic*, p. 436.
[447] Thomas, *Religion and the Decline of Magic*, p. 455.
[448] Thomas, *Religion and the Decline of Magic*, p. 456.

The sort of book learning that was cultivated by Doctor Faustus was correctly perceived as endangering orthodoxy by theologians. Moreover, studies once regarded as innocuous came to seem more dangerous as time went on. The more the scriptural tradition was reconstituted and purified by textual analysis, the more pagan and Christian elements which had co-existed for millennia were forced into conflict, and the larger became the share of an ancient, Latin and barbarian heritage that got assigned to the Devil. Although Trevor-Roper strangely exempts belief in the hermetic texts from his category of 'new absurdities,' the hermetic vogue was no less vulnerable to critical textual analysis than Dominican demonology.[449] The spectacle of a learned man, such as Marsiglio Ficino, singing weird chants in his study in order to conjure up a demon[450] seems even stranger to incredulous moderns than that of old women spitting on priests. Hermeticists who boasted of their magical power may have, on occasion, attacked witch-hunters. But they certainly did not help to dispel fears of the demonic. Frances Yates has recently shown how the Rosicrucians, who exploited new publicity techniques to proclaim the arrival of 'the invisible ones' and to dramatize their special occult powers, were made the subject of an elaborate mythology centering on a Satanic organization dispersed throughout the world in groups of six.[451] The specter which began to haunt Europe with the Rosicrucian manifestoes – the specter of a cosmopolitan conspiracy with awesome powers capable of placing hidden agents everywhere to do its bidding – was linked to the early-modern witch-craze by more than mere analogy.

When all due allowance is made for backwoods resistance to Christianization there is still much that remains to be said about tensions within the academic community, about the mentality of Renaissance scholars and the battles of books in which they were engaged. It is well to remember in any case that peasants have no monopoly of credulity nor women of hysteria; particularly in periods of intellectual dislocation, both symptoms may be found among monks and pro-

---

449 Platonism and 'Hermetic mysticism' are associated by Trevor-Roper with the advancement of science and arbitrarily detached from 'vulgar,' 'ridiculous' and 'crude' forms of 'witch belief.' *Crisis*, pp. 132–3. Again I agree with Monter, 'Chronique,' that there is no basis for exempting Hermeticism from other kinds of sixteenth century credulity.

450 Walker, *Spiritual and Demonic Magic*, chap. 1.

451 Yates, *Rosicrucian Enlightenment*, pp. 103–7. Resemblances between the fears evoked in the 1623 pamphlet: 'Horrible Pacts made between the Devil and the pretended invisible ones' and later anti-semitic literature seem worth noting in connection with the approach to collective psychopathology suggested above, chap. 2, n. 322.

fessors. Learned Dominicans and not countryfolk set the witch-craze in motion, after all.

In dealing with sixteenth-century demonology, Trevor-Roper seems to make the same basic error that I have noted above in connection with literal fundamentalism. Indeed he couples them together: the 'dying witch craze' with 'biblical fundamentalism' in his list of 'obsolescent habits of thought' that were 'in retreat in the age of Erasmus.' I have already suggested that literal fundamentalism was a post-print phenomenon. I think the monster trials which followed publication of the *Malleus* were too.

The recrudescence of the absurd demonology of the *Malleus* was not the logical consequence of any religious idea...Perhaps on the eve of the Reformation the mythology was on its way out. Who can say what might have happened if Erasmus had triumphed instead of Luther and Loyola? Then the Renaissance might have led direct to the Enlightenment and the witch-craze have been remembered as a purely medieval lunacy.[452]

But the witch-craze that was 'formally launched' with the *Malleus* could never have been remembered as 'purely medieval.' Like literal fundamentalism and Erasmus' career, it was a by-product of Gutenberg's invention. According to John Wesley, 'giving up witchcraft is in effect giving up the Bible.' After printing, more people took up the Bible. The command in Exodus xxii, 18: 'Thou shalt not suffer a witch to live' was impressed on more readers than ever before.[453] To imagine that Bible-reading and witch burning were on their way out on the 'eve of the Reformation' is to overlook the very forces which propelled them; to overlook the same forces, be it noted, that shaped Erasmus' career and produced the Enlightenment.

The basic error is to point developments in a single direction so that we are given to understand there is a direct route from Renaissance to Enlightenment that only fools and fanatics failed to take. Movements that do not point in the designated direction are classified as retrograde, obsolescent or anomalous. Calvinism is thus dismissed as an 'obscurantist deviation,' Bible-reading relegated to the age of handwritten books,

[452] Trevor-Roper, *Crisis*, p. 140.
[453] Thomas, *Religion and the Decline of Magic*, p. 570. Thomas notes that literalists could be found among those who remained sceptical of witch hunters. As Protestants they objected to the pagan 'friarly' superstitions that changed Old Testament witches into devil worshipers. On the other hand there is the case of the Lutheran witch hunter who 'read the Bible from cover to cover 53 times...and procured the death of 20,000 persons,' which is noted by Trevor-Roper, *Crisis*, p. 159.

and the appearance of fundamentalism in the age of Darwin or the holding of a Scopes trial in the age of Ford become almost completely inexplicable.

One of the advantages of considering the effects produced by printing is that we can come to terms with the coexistence of incompatible views and the persistence of contradictory movements without treating any as anomalous and without forcing them into over-simple grand designs. The many changes introduced by the new technology far from synchronizing smoothly or pointing in one direction, contributed to disjunctions, worked at cross-purposes and operated out of phase with each other.

To illustrate this point, one more look at Bible-printing is in order. By the mid-sixteenth century, it was proceeding apace in Protestant regions while being arrested in Catholic ones with consequences unforeseen by all. Even with hindsight, no simple formula can be applied to these consequences. Not only did Protestant and Catholic cultures move apart, but within Protestant regions contrary tendencies were encouraged. The new mode of production had a different effect on printers and publishers than it had on consumers or purchasers. Men who saw copy through the stages of publication looked at texts differently than did those who received the finished products. To be enabled to read the holy words of God in one's own tongue was probably an awesome experience for a devout sixteenth-century reader. It seems quite likely that new forms of 'sect-type' Christianity and literal fundamentalism resulted from an increased consumption of vernacular Bibles. On the other hand, in workshops where texts were processed and copy-edited and among booksellers seeking new markets, printed Bibles were associated with other commodities produced for sale.

the first Strasbourg printer Johann Mentelin...was a careless printer but obviously a smart business man. His first publication was a Bible, issued in 1460–1 in direct competition with Mainz; but whereas the 42-line Bible occupied 1,286 pages, Mentelin succeeded in squeezing the work into 850 pages, thus saving almost a third of the paper. His next book again shows his sound commercial instinct. It was the first Bible printed in German or in any vernacular and, although full of school-boy howlers, it nevertheless remained the standard text of all German Bibles before Luther.[454]

[454] Steinberg, *Five Hundred Years of Printing*, p. 47.

There were, of course, some printers who were deeply devout; who took particular pains over holy books and considered their Bibles as the crowning glory of their career. Others were sufficiently zealous to risk torture and death, several were martyred for their faith.[455] Yet even the most pious printer had to keep his mind on his business much of the time. Markets had to be gauged, finances secured, privileges sought, Catholic friars and officials evaded, compositors supervised, distribution organized. What appeared to the devout reader in a quasi-miraculous guise involved an exercise in processing texts, shrewd politicking and practical problem-solving for the equally devout producer. Mammon as well as Caesar necessarily entered into the printer's calculations. So, too, did variant readings of the same sacred words.

Moreover, printers themselves did not share a 'common mind' and hence were diversely affected by involvement in a new mode of production. Some were fiery apostles wholly committed to serving one true church or one 'elect nation.' But others were not, and tried to serve many. The early Basel printers were especially flexible in their policies. As prudent operators they have been contrasted with Genevans who 'risked their necks' in 'boldly illegal' efforts to proselytize on behalf of the Calvinist cause.[456] Yet there were also Genevans who failed to exhibit a 'Calvinist sense of mission' and only wanted to take over the trade of Lyons. They surreptitiously turned out books that catered to the taste of Catholic markets in Southern Europe. Much as Henri IV felt Paris worth a mass, or Cardinal Richelieu that 'raison d'état' dictated alliance with infidel Turks, so too it seems that a Manutius, an Estienne, or a Plantin kept family firms solvent and presses in operation by alliances with Protestants, Catholics, Jews, Spaniards, Dutchmen, and all shades of Frenchmen alike.[457]

J. H. Hexter has pointed to the fallacy of assuming that an increase in secularism meant a decrease in religion. He suggests that both were intensified during the sixteenth century partly because they interacted with each other. Thus the more furious the battles between religious zealots, the greater the peril to the body politic and the more concerned statesmen became about securing a stable civil order.[458] This interpreta-

[455] See essays in Meylan, ed., *Aspects de la Propagande*, for examples.
[456] See Bietenholz, *Basle and France*, pp. 36–7.
[457] This is brought out in several articles by Kingdon: 'The Business Activities'; 'The Plantin Breviaries'; 'Christopher Plantin and His Backers'; 'Patronage, Piety and Printing.'
[458] Hexter, *Reappraisals*, p. 42.

tion is helpful; yet like other clear and logical schemes, it also has the defects of its virtues. Opposing factions are lined up so neatly – with secular-minded *politiques* set against fanatical *ligueurs* – that one looks in vain for run-of-the-mill, ambivalent, inconsistent human beings. Fickle printers 'who ran with the hares and hunted with the hounds,'[459] who catered to Catholic, Calvinist and secular markets alike help to remind us of human complexity. They do not fit easily into any simple two-fold scheme – or even into a three-fold one. Their rationale was often at odds with that of religious zealots; yet some were devout Christians and belonged to proscribed heterodox sects. Although they collaborated with Erastian rulers, their interests differed also from those of nation-building statesmen who raised armies and waged dynastic wars. Their business flourished better in loosely federated realms than in strongly consolidated ones, in small principalities rather than in large and expanding ones. The politics of censorship made them the natural opponents not only of church officials but also of lay bureaucrats, regulations and red-tape. As independent agents they supplied organs of publicity and covert support to a 'third force' that was not affiliated with any one church or one state.[460] When attempting to account for the 'rise of toleration,' the 'burghers of Zürich' and the 'landed aristocrats of England' may well be worth a closer look. Printers located in many other regions throughout Europe should not be ignored.[461]

459 Armstrong, *Robert Estienne*, pp. 13–14, uses the phrase in connection with Colines' policy of publishing both Lefèvre d'Etaples and the Sorbonnistes' attacks on him. Plantin's feat of serving the King of Spain as royal typographer and the Dutch Calvinists as official printer is only the most celebrated example of this kind. See p. 443 below.
460 The existence of this kind of 'third force' is noted by Vöet, *Golden Compasses* I, 29–30 in conjunction with Plantin's circle and the 'Family of Love.' The same phrase is used by Verwey, 'Trois Hérésiarques,' p. 329 in a pioneering article on the founders of the heterodox 'Familist' sect. See also Heer, *Die Dritte Kraft*.
461 Kamen, *The Rise of Toleration*, points to Zürich and England. On the aid given by Oporinus to Castellio and other advocates of toleration see Bietenholz, *Basle and France*, p. 131. This Basel firm provoked both the Calvinists in Geneva and the Counter-Reformation authorities in Rome. In 1559 it was one of fifteen firms blacklisted by the Council of Trent. Steinmann, *Oporinus*, pp. 97 ff. Plantin managed to stay on good terms with both Dirk Coornhert, who translated Castellio's work and believed forced conversion should be actively repudiated, and with Justus Lipsius who took a more passive, neo-Stoic 'politique' position. On debate between Coornhert and Lipsius in 1590 see Jellema's book review, *American Historical Review*, p. 1143 and Rekers, *Montano*, pp. 84–6 who underlines the strategic role of censorship in the debate. (New issues posed by censorship need more emphasis in studies dealing with religious toleration. See e.g. Lecler, *Toleration*.) Coornhert's relationship with the 'Family of Love' is discussed by Verwey, 'Trois Hérésiarques,' pp. 322–4 and his acquaintance with Plantin discussed by Vöet, *Golden Compasses* I, 385. Lipsius was so frequent a guest in Plantin's house that a special room was named for him.

The formation of syndicates of heterodox businessmen and printers linked to far-flung distribution networks indicates how the new industry encouraged informal social groupings that cut across traditional frontiers and encompassed varied faiths. It also encouraged the adoption of a new ethos which was cosmopolitan, ecumenical and tolerant without being secular, incredulous or necessarily Protestant – an ethos that seems to anticipate the creed of some of the masonic lodges during the Enlightenment, not least because of its secretive and quasi-conspiratorial character.

One main center for advocates of the new ethos in its fully mature phase was Plantin's *officina* in Antwerp, which retained its Catholic affiliations even while attracting support from scholars, merchants and statesmen of diverse confessions. Some members of the Plantin circle were also affiliated with the loosely organized 'Nicodemite' sect called the 'Family (or House) of Love.' Familist literature, turned out from Plantin's Antwerp press and also from that of Thomas and Govert Basson (an English printer and his son at Leiden who served the persecuted Dutch Arminian party later on) has attracted considerable attention in recent years,[462] and little wonder! Documents still being uncovered offer a unique chance to look into the workings of an unusually influential sixteenth-century underground that went undetected in its day. 'In Plantin's circle of friends and acquaintances, we have an almost unique example of a successful secret society and the resources of the Plantin-Moretus Museum...allow us to see something of what it was and how they avoided detection.'[463] Among other factors that enabled this network to expand while avoiding persecution was Plantin's superlative skill in winning friends who held key posts and in obtaining strategic positions for himself. Perhaps his most remarkable feat was to get Philip II to appoint him 'Proto-Typographer' thus making him responsible for supervising the printing industry throughout the Low Countries and for checking on the competence and religious orthodoxy of every printer in the region.[464] Almost equally remarkable was his achievement in winning over Philip II's councillor and most distinguished court scholar, Benito Arias Montano who was sent from Spain to supervise work on the Antwerp Polyglot and re-

---

[462] For review of literature up to 1965, see Kirsop, 'The Family of Love.' For an updated account, see Verwey, 'The Family of Love.' On the Basson firm, see chap. 2, n. 297, above.
[463] Kirsop, 'Family of Love,' p. 107.
[464] Kingdon, 'Patronage, Piety and Printing,' pp. 24–5.

turned to win new honors from Philip II even while maintaining a secret correspondence with his new-found circle of Netherlandish friends and altering the normal pattern of the book-trade in Spain for a time.

The scholarly contact between Spain and the Low Countries is best shown by the frequent shipments of books that the Spaniards received from the Antwerp press. Partly on account of Montano's influence the demand for foreign books increased appreciably. In 1586 Plantin decided to open a branch office in Salamanca...

Salamanca was a well chosen place for a branch office. The University had 8,000 students. The bookshop was ostensibly founded to facilitate the sale of prayer books which since 1569 by royal command could only be printed in Antwerp. Needless to say, this channel was used for distributing works of a different character as well...

The availability of this foreign learning was of course against official Inquisitorial policy. Since 1559 the ecclesiastical authorities had put a cordon sanitaire around the peninsula. Printing offices were watched closely and a license was required for imported volumes...[465]

But Arias Montano as royal chaplain and councillor had been given a special licence to handle banned books, and was appointed to serve as royal librarian in the Escorial. In that gloomy palace he gathered around him a group of disciples who helped to give a new lease on life to the so-called 'Erasmian' movement in Spain. Part of the fascination exerted by the story of the Plantin circle and the 'Family of Love' is its capacity to excite the paranoid imagination by revealing that an eminent Catholic official who was also a renowned Counter-Reformation scholar was actually engaged in organizing subversive 'cells' in the very depths of the Escorial.

Plantin's vast publishing empire, which was the largest in Europe at the time, owed much to his capacity to hedge all bets by winning rich and powerful friends in different regions who belonged to diverse confessions. The permission granted to members of 'Nicodemite' sects to obey whatever religious observances were common in the regions where they lived, also helped to smooth the way for the publishers' foreign agents and made it easier to hold potential persecutors at bay.[466] The ecumenical and Nicodemite character of Plantin's

---

[465] Rekers, *Montano*, p. 430.
[466] George H. Williams, *The Radical Reformation*, chaps. 19, 22, and 23, provides useful background on Familists and Nicodemites. According to Carlo Ginzburg, *Il Nicodemismo*, Otto

heterodox creed may thus be seen – as Robert Kingdon points out – as complementary to his activities as an early capitalist entrepreneur. His Antwerp circle offers 'yet another example of the ways in which religious conviction and economic self-interest can reinforce each other powerfully.'

> In Plantin and his creditors we have uncovered a group which resembles in miniature the...longer lasting group of financiers...known as 'la banque protestante'...and recently studied...by Herbert Lüthy...Perhaps we should conclude, as did Lüthy, that the primary forces binding people of this sort together in...financial combines are ties of blood and friendship. However, it seems to me that one can go further and find connections more analogous to those which...Max Weber sought...I would suggest that the beliefs of the members of the 'House of Love' were a positive economic advantage to businessmen operating in situations...ridden with ideological tensions...A set of beliefs, which were secretly 'nicodemite' and emphasized brotherly love, permitted its members to avoid the disasters which could overtake any businessman, particularly any printer...so committed...to a dogmatic position...that he could not accommodate himself to a...regime enforcing an opposite point of view.[467]

To forestall misunderstanding, we may assume that Kingdon does not mean Plantin chose his beliefs with their economic advantages in mind – a faith so rationally selected being almost a contradiction in terms. He is, instead, tracing an evolutionary pattern along Darwinian lines; suggesting that businessmen, particularly printers, with anti-dogmatic views, were most fit to survive and even to prosper amid the shifting fortunes of religious warfare. If they adopted a tolerant creed that could be covertly sustained they could avoid persecution by zealots even while attracting foreign financial support. The point is well taken. Still it leaves room for additional considerations.

Doubtless the cosmopolitan and ecumenical outlook of the successful merchant–publisher was related to his position as a capitalist entrepreneur in an era of shifting power centers and religious frontiers. But it was also related to the particular nature of the products he manufactured. Plantin's merchandise set him apart from other businessmen and tradesmen. It brought men of letters and learning into his shop. It

Brunfels, author of the celebrated pioneering herbal, was the first influential advocate of religious dissimulation in hostile realms – a practice that Calvin later denounced under the label 'Nicodemite.' Bainton has a useful review of Ginzburg's monograph in *The Journal of Modern History* (1971), p. 309. See also Walker, 'A Secret Conspiracy Exposed,' pp. 42–4.

[467] Kingdon, 'Plantin and his Backers,' p. 315.

encouraged him to feel more at ease with strange scholars, bibliophiles and literati than with neighbors or relatives in his native town. The prospering merchant publisher had to know as much about books and intellectual trends as a cloth merchant did about drygoods and dress fashions; he needed to develop a connoisseur's expertise about type-styles, book catalogues and library sales. He often found it useful to master many languages, to handle variant texts, to investigate antiquities and old inscriptions along with new maps and calendars. In short, the very nature of his business provided the merchant publisher with a broadly based liberal education. It also led toward a widened circle of acquaintances and included close contacts with foreigners. If emigrés or aliens were welcome in his workshop this was rarely because of previous ties of blood or friendship; and not always because foreign financing, new market outlets, patrons or privileges were being sought. Foreign experts were also needed as editors, translators, correctors and type designers. The demand for vernacular scriptures, psalters and service books among enclaves of Protestants on foreign soil also encouraged an interchange between printers and 'communities of strangers,' based on the religious needs of alien enclaves. The provision of service books for an Italian community in London, an English community in Geneva, a French church in Holland led not only to affiliations with foreign merchants but also to more awareness of the varieties of Christian religious experience and of the different nuances associated with liturgy in diverse tongues.

Foreigners engaged in translation were welcomed into homes as well as shops. They were often provided with room and board by the local printer and sometimes taken into his family circle as well. The names of those who were admitted to the Basel workshop of Vesalius' publisher Oporinus were perhaps even more remarkable than the circle formed around Plantin's Antwerp shop later on. Most of the leading lights of the 'radical reformation' lodged at some point with Oporinus: Servetus, Lelio Sozzini, Ochino, Postel, Castellio, Oecolampadius, Schwenckfelt – not to mention the Marian exiles such as John Foxe. The Basel printer was also on good terms with Paracelsus. He also provided a refuge for David Joris, one of the three heresiarchs who founded the 'Family of Love.'[468] Much later, among the Enlightenment

---

[468] On circles around Oporinus, see Bietenholz, *Basle and France*, pp. 124, 141, 203; Steinmann, *Oporinus*, pp. 76–7; Verwey, 'Trois Hérésiarques,' p. 315. On variety of scholars who visited with Plantin, see Vöet, *Golden Compasses* I, 367–9. An interesting link between various printers'

philosophes, and still later among the followers of Saint-Simon, the use of the term 'Family' to mean a joint intellectual commitment became more symbolic and metaphorical. But the translators, correctors and proof readers who lodged with printers did become temporary members of real families. Polyglot households were not uncommon where major scholarly publishing ventures took place.

Once again Bible-printing should be brought into the picture. The peculiar polyglot character of the Christian scriptures contributed to a rapid expansion of cultural contacts among scholar–printers who handled biblical editions and translations. Aldus Manutius' plans for a polyglot edition might be kept in mind when considering the circle around him.[469] Plantin's later Antwerp program brought together sophisticated scholars representing diverse realms and faiths. In order to complete the eight-volume project it was desirable to achieve smooth working relationships between the variegated editors. Domestic peace also hinged on encouraging toleration of varied views. The same consideration applies to the biblical editions turned out by Estienne. Representatives of ten different nationalities sat around the table of Robert Estienne and Perrette Badius. According to their son, Henri, even the Estiennes' servants picked up a smattering of Latin, the only tongue shared in common by all.[470] Similar heterodox and cosmopolitan circles were formed around the Amerbach-Froben shop in Basel,[471]

circles and several generations is supplied by the Bomberg or Bomberghen firm. Its founder, Daniel Bomberg, came from the Netherlands, pioneered in Hebrew Bible-printing in Venice but left sons and nephews in Antwerp who inherited his types, contributed to the export of Hebrew Bibles to North African Jewish communities and helped to finance Plantin's operations. A foreman of Bomberg's Venice firm, which operated from 1517 to 1459, was sent by Vesalius over the Alps to Oporinus in Basel carrying the precious plates for the *De Fabrica*. A corrector for the same firm, Elias Levita (d. 1549) was the foremost Hebrew scholar of the day. Levita's publication on vowel points in 1538 (which was reprinted by Sebastian Munster in 1539) set the stage for the later contributions of Arias Montano and Louis Cappel – according to Box, 'Hebrew Studies,' p. 333. Daniel Bomberg's aid to Postel and other scholars seeking help with Arabic as well as Hebrew is noted by Dannenfeldt, 'The Renaissance Humanists' (see esp. 101; 113). The Antwerp 'van Bomberghe' appear in the guise of 'rich merchants' who were among the first adherents of H. Niclaes, a founder of the Familist sect, in Verwey's 'Trois Hérésiarques,' p. 324. They became active members of the Calvinist church in Antwerp however and were forced to flee when the Duke of Alva's Council listed them as known heretics. See Kingdon, 'Plantin and his Backers,' pp. 309–10; Verwey, 'Family of Love,' p. 235.

[469] As is noted by Geanakoplos, *Greek Scholars in Venice* the very first polyglot edition edited under the supervision of Cardinal Ximenes at Alcalà was indebted to one of Aldus' chief editors for help with the Greek text.

[470] Armstrong, *Robert Estienne*, p. 15.

[471] Johann Amerbach's network of correspondence was no less remarkable than Plantin's. It included among others: Reuchlin, Lefèvre d'Etaples, Waldseemüller, Dürer, Trithemius, Koberger, thus linking Hebrew scholars, pioneering map-makers, engravers and savants

and around many other printing firms responsible for biblical editions
– in scattered cities throughout Europe. The notion of a single subversive cell in the depths of the grim Escorial may excite cloak-and-
dagger fantasies. The idea of many print shops located in numerous
towns, each serving as an intellectual cross-roads, as a miniature
'international house' – as a meeting place, message center, and sanctuary all in one – seems no less stimulating to the historical imagination.
In the late sixteenth century, for the first time in the history of any
civilization, the concept of a *Concordia Mundi* was being developed on
a truly global scale and the 'family of man' was being extended to
encompass all the peoples of the world.[472] To understand how this
happened, there is no better place to begin than with the hospitality
extended by merchant publishers and scholar–printers who plied their
trade during the religious wars. Plantin's correspondence shows him
requesting advice from Postel about Syriac typefonts, obtaining a
Hebrew *Talmud* for Arias Montano, responding to a request from
Mercator concerning the map of France, advising a Bavarian official
on which professor to appoint at Ingolstadt, asking for theological
guidance on how to illustrate a religious book.[473] To look over the
connections revealed in this correspondence is to see laid bare the
central nervous system or chief switchboard of the Republic of Letters
in its formative phase. Plantin's account-books provide a fine opportunity for economic historians to examine the operations of one early-
modern entrepreneur. But his correspondence also points to the
development of something other than early capitalism. All the elements
that will produce a later 'crisis of the European conscience' are already
drawn together there.

Here again, I think the suggestive analysis of Trevor-Roper would be

much as did the later Antwerp network. See list of names given by Febvre, *Au Coeur Religieux*,
p. 140. For a glimpse of a central-European network centered around the Wechel firm in
Frankfurt, see Evans' *Rudolf II*, p. 282 as well as his monograph on *The Wechel Presses*. Other
overlapping circles are delineated in the section on 'the little world of the book' in Febvre
and Martin, *L'Apparition*, chap. 5, section III.

472 The 'global scale' is provided by Ortelius, the pioneer atlas publisher, whose affiliations with
Plantin's circle are noted by Boumans, 'The Religious Views of Abraham Ortelius.' It is
intriguing to note that Ortelius was connected with biblical editions through his father and
uncle who translated Miles Coverdale's Bible. On the expanding concept of a 'Family of
Man,' see Bouwsma, *Concordia Mundi*, *passim*. Postel was a self-taught, low-born Norman
scholar who mastered Greek, Hebrew, Arabic and other exotic tongues and worked with
Bomberg in Venice and Oporinus in Basel. His correspondence with Plantin and Ortelius
included letters in which he mentioned the 'family of love' and described printing as 'the
lance and sword of Christ's victory' (pp. 240–2).

473 Vöet, *Golden Compasses* I, 383.

strengthened by giving more attention to the role of printers and publishers. In order to explain the growth of attitudes encouraging theological reconciliation, it is insufficient to point to three intervals when religious warfare was at a low ebb.[474] Even when the Spanish fury was at its height, an international peace movement was being quietly shaped. 'Erasmian' trends were persistently propelled throughout the entire century-and-a-half of religious warfare. Wandering scholars, intellectual emigrés and religious refugees not only found shelter in the homes of merchant publishers, they also found likeminded colleagues and publication outlets there. The problem of understanding the religious origins of the Enlightenment cannot be resolved by carving out an 'age of Erasmus' or an 'age of Bacon' to serve as a refuge for peace-loving philosophers. By taking into consideration the possibility that Bible-reading could intensify dogmatism even while Bible-printing might encourage toleration, the problem becomes somewhat easier to handle. The same approach may be helpful when dealing with other, similar problems relating to cross-currents and contradictory attitudes manifested during the Reformation.

It also seems worth giving more thought to the effects of printing when tackling the basic problems of causation which crop up repeatedly in Reformation studies:

The basic question can be formulated as follows: Were the ecclesiastical conditions of the early sixteenth century such as to denote a precarious equilibrium that necessitated some kind of revolutionary or reformatory upheaval? Was Europe in the early sixteenth century 'crying for the Reformation?'

...we know far too little...to offer more than tentative statements...Still the general conclusion at this point appears to be that European society was far more stable than has been traditionally assumed. In other words, if Luther and the other early reformers had died in their cradles, the Catholic church might well have survived the sixteenth century without a major upheaval.[475]

Granted that European society and ecclesiastical institutions seemed relatively stable around 1500, what about the state of the scriptural tradition fifty years after Gutenberg? As this chapter may suggest, it

---

[474] Trevor-Roper, *Crisis*, pp. 200–2, describes three periods: an age of Erasmus, of Bacon, and of Newton, as 'phases of light,' as intervals of 'cosmopolitan intellectual correspondence' which were immune from 'ideological war' whether 'hot or cold.'

[475] Hillerbrand, 'The Spread of the Protestant Reformation,' p. 270; see also Mueller, *Imperial Cities*, pp. 12–13.

was in a highly volatile state. Conflict over new questions pertaining to priestly prerogatives and sacred studies could not have been postponed indefinitely. Even if Luther, Zwingli and others had died in their cradles, it seems likely that some reformers would still have turned to the presses to implement long lived pastoral concerns and evangelical aims. Perhaps civil war in Christendom was not inevitable but the advent of printing did, at the very least, rule out the possibility of perpetuating the status quo.

On the whole, it seems safe to conclude that all the problems associated with the disruption of Western Christendom will become less baffling if we approach them by respecting the order of events and put the advent of printing ahead of the Protestant revolt.

PART THREE

THE BOOK OF NATURE
TRANSFORMED

5

INTRODUCTION;
PROBLEMS OF PERIODIZATION

I. INTRODUCTION: 'THE GREAT BOOK OF NATURE'
AND THE 'LITTLE BOOKS OF MEN'

Problems associated with the rise of modern science lend themselves to a similar argument. In other words, I think the advent of printing ought to be featured more prominently by historians of science when they set the stage for the downfall of Ptolemaic astronomy, Galenic anatomy or Aristotelian physics. This means asking for a somewhat more drastic revision of current guidelines than seems necessary in Reformation studies. In the latter field, the impact of printing may be postponed; but at least it is usually included among the agents that promoted Luther's cause. The outpouring of tracts and cartoons left too vivid and strong an impression for the new medium to be entirely discounted when investigating the Protestant Revolt. The contrary seems true in the case of the so-called 'scientific revolution.' Although a few authorities have suggested that sixteenth-century science was revolutionized by the 'cataclysmic' effect of printing, they do so by stressing a 'mass movement' which seems singularly unimpressive to other historians of science.[1] For exploitation of the mass medium was more common among prognosticators and quacks than among Latin-writing professional scientists, who often withheld their work from the press. When important treatises did appear in print, they rarely achieved the status of bestsellers. Given the limited circulation of works such as De Revolutionibus and the small number of readers able to understand them, it appears plausible to play down the importance of

[1] Price, Science since Babylon, pp. 98–9 stresses this popularizing theme and links the Reformation to it. See also passage cited in Conclusion, p. 691, below.

printing. Given the wider circulation of antiquated materials, many authorities are inclined to go even further and assign to early printers a negative, retrogressive role. 'There is no evidence that, except in religion, printing hastened the spread of new ideas...In fact the printing of medieval scientific texts may have delayed the acceptance of... Copernicus.'[2]

As the previous chapter may suggest, however, even in religion, the 'spread of new ideas' was only one of several new functions that deserve consideration. New functions performed by print affected orthodoxy as well as heresy. They changed the very nature of authority and authorship. They reoriented a sacred textual tradition. When seeking to understand scientific change we also need to look beyond the 'spread of new ideas' and to associate printers with other functions than popularization and propaganda. Textual traditions inherited from the Alexandrians, for example, were no more likely to continue unchanged after the shift from script to print than were scriptural traditions. For natural philosophers as for theologians, attempts at emendation and the pursuit of long-lived goals were likely to have a different outcome after printers replaced scribes.

At present, however, we are not only inclined to set the mass appeal of Lutheran tracts against the restricted appeal of Copernican treatises; we are also prone to discount textual traditions altogether when dealing with problems of scientific change. Conventional iconography encourages us to envisage Protestants with books in their hands (especially when we contrast them with Catholics holding rosaries). Early-modern scientists, however, are more likely to be portrayed holding plants or astrolabes than studying texts. Insofar as natural philosophers may have studied early printed editions of Ptolemy, Pliny, Galen or Aristotle,

2 McLean, *Humanism and the Rise of Science*, p. 22. McLean's opinion is derived from the passage in Febvre and Martin, *L'Apparition* cited above (see chap. 1 n. 85, volume I). The thesis of retrogression was initially set forth by Sarton, 'The Scientific Literature,' pp. 62–8, and strongly upheld by Lynn Thorndike, *A History of Magic*, pp. 5–6. Sarton, in his later works: *Six Wings*, pp. 3, 116–19; *Appreciation*, pp. xi, 89–95; and 'The Quest,' p. 56; forcefully asserted that printing made possible scientific advance without abandoning the view that it also produced a 'retrograde' movement. His final verdict is probably best summed up in his own words as 'ambivalent.' See *Appreciation*, p. 168 and discussion of 'cultural lag' problem below, pp. 508. Sarton's scattered aperçus as well as Price's remark about 'cataclysmic' effects suggest the need to qualify the verdict that *all* historians of science have treated the advent of printing as unimportant given by Drake, 'Early Science and the Printed Book: The Spread of Science Beyond the University.' As its subtitle indicates, Drake's article, like Price's comments, connects printing with diffusion and vernacular translation. The limitations of this approach are noted in chap. 6 below.

they are usually accused of looking in the wrong direction. 'One would have thought that the breathtaking discoveries of the navigators would have turned attention from the little books of men to the great book of Nature but this happened much less often than one might expect.'[3] Yet how could the 'great book of Nature' be investigated, one is tempted to ask, without exchanging information by means of the 'little books of men?' The question is worth posing if only to bring out our own tendency to look in the wrong direction when considering the rise of modern science and related trends. It is partly because we envisage the astronomer gazing always at unchanging heavens and the anatomist taking human bodies as his only books, that the conceptual revolutions of the sixteenth century – which came before methods of star-gazing or dissection had been altered – seem peculiarly difficult to explain.

In this regard, the long-lived metaphorical image of by-passing other books in order to read in the book of nature, 'that universal and publick manuscript that lies expans'd unto the Eyes of all' is a source of deception which needs further analysis. Conventional treatments of this metaphor by intellectual and cultural historians provide fascinating excursions into the history of ideas but rarely pause over the problem of making freshly recorded observations available 'unto the Eyes of all.'

there are two Books from whence I collect my Divinity; besides that written one of God, another of His servant Nature, that universal and publick Manu-script, that lies expans'd unto the Eyes of all: those that never saw Him in the one, have discover'd Him in the other...Surely the Heathens know better how to joyn and read these mystical Letters than we Christians, who cast a more careless Eye on these common Hieroglyphicks and disdain to suck Divinity from the flowers of Nature.[4]

When Sir Thomas Browne compared the Bible with the book of nature, he was not only reworking a theme favored by Francis Bacon,[5]

---

[3] Sarton, *Six Wings*, p. 6.

[4] Thomas Browne, *Religio Medici* (1643), pt. I, chap. 16. Cited by Curtius, *European Literature*, p. 323 (where it is, confusingly, run in with a citation taken from the first part of chap. 15 of *Religio Medici*). See *Prose of Browne* (Endicott, ed.), p. 21.

[5] In the first book of *The Proficience and Advancement of Learning Divine and Humane* (1605) Bacon couples the 'book of God's word' with 'the book of God's work' and later refers to 'our Savior...laying before us the books or volumes to study if we will be secured from error: first the Scriptures...and then the creatures,' *Francis Bacon A Selection of His Works*, pp. 205, 242. Browne was using a 'Baconian technique...in calling Nature a Scripture,' according to Willey, *The Seventeenth Century Background*, p. 51. Since the same theme occurs

but was also drawing on earlier sources. According to Ernst Curtius, the same two 'books' were mentioned in medieval sermons and derive ultimately from very ancient Near Eastern texts. This lineage is viewed by Curtius as evidence of cultural continuity, and he uses it to argue against Burckhardt's thesis (or at least, against vulgarized versions of it). 'It is a favorite cliché...that the Renaissance shook off the dust of yellowed parchments and began instead to read in the book of nature or the world. But this metaphor itself derives from the Latin Middle Ages...'[6] The mere fact that references to a 'book of nature' appear in medieval Latin texts, however, is not a valid objection to the otherwise objectionable cliché. The persistence of old metaphors often masks major changes. In this case, all the changes that were entailed by the shift from script to print have been concealed. A seventeenth-century author, who coupled scripture with nature, might echo older texts. But both the real and metaphorical 'books' he had in mind were necessarily different from any known to twelfth-century clerks.

Thus when Saint Bernard referred to a 'book of nature,' he was not thinking about plants and planets, as Sir Thomas Browne was. Instead he had in mind monastic discipline and the ascetic advantages of hard work in the fields.[7] When his fellow monks celebrated natural fecundity, they also had pious ends in view. Many different vivid images were needed to serve as memory aids when learning moral lessons. 'Mankind is blind,' noted a fourteenth-century preacher's manual, containing excerpts drawn from works on natural history.

The human soul is forgetful in divine matters; but examples from nature are excellent devices to seize the memory in inescapable fashion...to fix men's thoughts upon the Creator...natural *exempla* are indispensable for preachers. Not only do they serve to capture the attention, but such examples are more meaningful than exhortation.[8]

The preacher in search of meaningful *exempla* was well served by the

in works by Bacon's contemporaries – such as Raleigh, Campanella and Galileo (whom Browne also read) the label 'Baconian' probably has to be cautiously applied. See e.g. relevant passage in Sir Walter Raleigh's *History of the World* (London, 1614) 1, 2, referring to 'Hieroglyphical Characters written on these large volumes of the firmament...also on the earth and the seas by the letters of...living creatures and plants' and citation from Galileo noted on p. 458, below. For philosophical background on the use of the theme by virtuosi, see Nelson, 'The Quest for Certitude,' pp. 363–72.   [6] Curtius, *European Literature*, p. 319.

[7] Leclercq, *The Love of Learning*, p. 135.

[8] Rouse and Rouse, 'The Texts called "Lumen Anime,"' p. 28. Paraphrased translation of preface to text composed *c.* 1332, by a compiler who may have been an Augustinian canon named Godfrey of Vorau.

abundance of variegated forms.[9] In medieval sermons, where didactic purposes came first, Scripture and nature were not separate but were intertwined. The latter, swathed in allegory, played a subservient role.

> The remarks we find as to the behavior of animals...denote occasionally a certain sense of observation. Yet here again, allegories from the *Bestiary* are often superimposed on the things seen. In Nature, everything is symbolic. The symbols come either from biblical...or...classical tradition but they all have moral overtones.... works like the *Hortus deliciarum*...are used for teaching all the virtues through the imagery of the flowers that beautify a wholly spiritual garden. The meaning of the flowers and fruits lies...in their properties. No doubt few Western monks ever had any opportunity to see mandrake...or pomegranate but the plants which they did see, they saw through descriptions given by the *auctores*...[10]

When set against prefaces to medieval *florilegia*[11] Browne's reference to the 'heathens' who did not 'disdain' to 'suck Divinity' from real 'flowers of Nature' seems to indicate disenchantment with an earlier habit of mind. Much as Rabelais satirized those who assigned special 'virtues' to special plants, so too does Browne seem to be rejecting the literary allegorical conventions which had been cultivated by generations of monks.[12]

By the seventeenth century, the circumstances which had given rise to such conventions had been changed. Plant forms were no longer needed for memorizing moral lessons in Stuart England. When flowers

[9] The importance assigned to vivid, colorful and variegated objects in classical 'memory art' exercises is made clear by Yates, *The Art of Memory, passim*. She also describes how churchmen mobilized these arts to serve didactic Christian aims. How Erasmus prolonged this tradition by recommending the study of geography for oratory and composition is described by Watson, *The Beginnings of the Teaching of Modern Subjects in England*, p. 111.

[10] Leclercq, *The Love of Learning*, p. 137. It is important to note that this description is relevant to the Latin pulpit literature described by Curtius and characteristic of the monastic culture treated by Leclercq; but does not necessarily encompass the views of other medieval occupational groups, such as, e.g. merchants, woodcarvers, apothecaries *et al*. Late medieval natural philosophers were concerned with the properties of natural phenomena rather than their usefulness as mnemonic aids. Many other differences between scholastic and monastic views are underlined by Leclercq.

[11] Leclercq, *The Love of Learning*, pp. 186–7, discusses such prefaces. A typical example is offered by Herrade de Landsberg: 'This book was composed by me, a little bee...with the nectar from diverse flowers drawn from Holy Scripture...' Preface to *Hortus Deliciarum* attributed to Herrade de Landsberg (d. 1195) in Straub and Keller, *Herrade de Landsberg*, p. vi. The basic topos comparing the reader to a 'ruminating and selective' bee goes back at least to Plutarch and Basil. It also appears in one of Caxton's early prefaces. See Montgomery, 'William Caxton and the Beginnings of Tudor Critical Thought,' pp. 100–1. In transmuted form, it may be discerned in Matthew Arnold's celebrated discussion of 'sweetness and light.'

[12] Rabelais' satire, which appears in the seventh chapter of *Pantagruel* is discussed by Kline, 'Rabelais and the Age of Printing,' pp. 13 ff.

were associated with virtues or vices, it was more for poetic than for pedagogic effect. The Bible itself was no longer conveyed by a variety of 'mixed media' such as stained glass, altar-pieces, stone portals, choral music or mystery plays. Sacred stories could be more clearly separated from profane ones after the same authorized version had been placed in every parish church. To couple Bible reading and nature study, to link religious anthologies with botanical texts, no longer came naturally but required resorting to literary artifice, as is well demonstrated by Browne's Baroque prose.

When he reworked the old theme, did Browne have in mind a contrast between gardens of verses and real flower gardens? Was he underscoring the difference between 'Christian' florilegia and 'heathen' nature study? When he wrote of joining and reading 'mystical' letters or 'common Hieroglyphicks' was he referring to the heliocentric hypothesis, set forth in a treatise such as Thomas Digges' 'most auncient doctrine of Pythagoreans lately revived by Copernicus and by Geometricall Demonstrations approved'?[13] Did his paradoxical image of a 'universal public Manuscript' reflect an acquaintance with Galileo's celebrated reference to the 'grand book the universe which stands continually open to our gaze...written in the language of mathematics ...its characters are triangles, circles and other geometric figures'?[14]

Given the many levels of meaning that are compressed in his works, there is no easy way of answering such questions and several digressions would be required to attempt to reply. For my purpose it is enough to note that, whatever else was on his mind, Browne was familiar with the medium of print and with printed visual aids. In this regard, his book metaphors were based on objects Saint Bernard had never seen.

One might argue that this point is so obvious there is no need to restate it. Few surveys fail to remind us that science, like religion, underwent major changes during the early-modern era. Every schoolchild learns that the twelfth-century world picture was different from the seventeenth-century one. But beyond the textbook platitudes lies

13 On Digges' treatise, see Koyré, *From the Closed World*, p. 35 and chap. 7 n. 146 below.
14 From the *Assayer* (1623) in *Discoveries and Opinions of Galileo*, ed. and tr. by Stillman Drake, pp. 237-8. In the passage about his 'two books' cited above (n. 4), Browne relates the 'Scripture and Theology of the Heathens' to 'the naturall motion of the Sun' in contrast to the sun's 'Supernatural station' admired by 'the Children of Israel.' His cautious approach to Copernican views, his admiration for Galileo and his wide acquaintance with contemporary scientific literature are discussed by Chambers, 'Sir Thomas Browne.'

a vast literature of controversy over how to describe just what was different and how best to explain why a transformation occurred. In dealing with such questions I think there is much to be gained by placing more emphasis on the obvious, and pausing more carefully over the fact that the shift from script to print preceded a transformation of world views.

As things stand now, this seemingly obvious point is all too often obscured. To explain why Copernicus broke with the long prevailing geocentric theories; why observations made by Tycho Brahe and by William Harvey differed from those of previous investigators; why 'Galileo, Descartes and Newton were suddenly able to see well-known phenomena in a new way,' the historian of science, like the historian of the Reformation, is accustomed to consider a variety of factors. He is likely to pause over the 'problem of the Renaissance' and weigh the claims of Italians against Northerners, scholastics against lay humanists or Aristotelians against Platonists. Such 'novelties' as 'Neoplatonism,' the 'revival of ancient atomism' or the 'rediscovery of Archimedes' make demands on his attention.[15] As in dealing with the Reformation, he cannot overlook the possible significance of medieval 'precursors,' or the problems posed by individual 'genius.' He may be introduced, as are Lutheran scholars, to the findings of psychologists – not only to study the psychic life of 'young man, Newton,' but also to ponder the possibility of a collective 'gestalt-switch.'[16] He is also urged, mainly by Marxists, not to ignore socio-economic changes bearing on the commercial revolution and the rise of capitalism. He may well feel inclined to collaborate with sociologists and examine the 'Weber thesis' once again.[17] Whatever strategy is adopted however, the fifteenth-century communications revolution seems to require only the most casual glancing reference, if it is noticed at all.[18] Among new inventions or instruments, Galileo's telescope will loom larger than

---

[15] Thomas Kuhn, 'Science' (citations are from p. 78).

[16] Manuel, *A Portrait of Isaac Newton*; Thomas Kuhn, *The Structure of Scientific Revolutions*, pp. 111–14, 122–3.

[17] See especially Merton, *Science, Technology*. King, ('Reason, Tradition and the Progressiveness of Science') in discussing the approaches of Merton and Kuhn argues that 'the analysis of the formation [and] transmission...of research traditions' is a task for sociologists (p. 25). I hope this chapter will suggest why the help of historians is also needed.

[18] Basalla, *The Rise of Modern Science, External or Internal Factors?*, pp. ix–x, lists possible 'causal factors' currently proposed without mentioning the shift from script to print. As is suggested below, I think that the dichotomy implied by Basalla's subtitle would become less troublesome if more attention were given to the shift.

Gutenberg's movable type. If communications are considered in some detail, or the shift from script to print is assigned importance, the discussion is more likely to focus on seventeenth-century correspondence than on fifteenth-century books.

In most surveys dealing with early-modern science, European communications are handled in a way that postpones consideration of major change until the appearance of a periodical press, which replaced the 'letter box' of correspondents such as Friar Mersenne. Artificial barriers created by the practice of specializing in particular centuries often make it difficult to perceive cumulative continuous trends. In this instance, such barriers enclose the 'century of genius' in a way that seems to dam up a swelling stream of scientific publication and cut it off from the productive forces that brought it into the world. The development and improvement in postal service thus receives more attention than does the prior establishment of early printers' workshops, trade networks and book fairs.[19] 'During the seventeenth century, the printed word first assumed the importance which it is only now beginning to lose...The first of our learned journals the *Journal des Sçavans* and the *Philosophical Transactions* were both started in 1665.'[20]

These learned journals are singled out in standard accounts because they speeded up circulation of scientific news and enabled scattered virtuosi to keep abreast of each others' work. Periodical publication is thus viewed as a further extension of the kind of scientific reporting that had previously been conducted by handwritten correspondence.[21] It seems fair enough to place the shift from script to print in the seventeenth century when dealing with the limited topic of scientific journalism. But it is wrong to do this when one is concerned with the larger subject of the rise of modern science. Handwritten letters could keep correspondents informed about their colleagues' activities only up to a point. Handwriting was less helpful when it came to conveying actual research results. Doubtless news that Kepler was working on a new set of tables could be conveyed quite efficiently by handwritten

---

[19] On the 'rise of government postal services' as the one change in communications 'which truly deserves to be called revolutionary,' see Clark, *The Seventeenth Century*, p. 54. Similar emphasis on improved postal service (and better overland transportation) in promoting 'intercourse in the domain of thought' and facilitating 'the development of science' is in Merton, *Science, Technology*, p. 222.

[20] Vann (ed.), *Century of Genius*, part 1, 'The Medium and the Message,' p. 1.

[21] See e.g. Ornstein, *The Role of Scientific Societies*, p. 198.

correspondence. But this point does not apply to the *Rudolphine Tables* itself. When it came to distributing hundreds of copies of a work containing long lists of numbers, or diagrams, maps and charts, or even precise detailed verbal reports, hand-copying was vastly inferior to print. Kepler himself was well aware of the difference between manuscript and print.[22] As later discussion suggests, he was only one of many virtuosi who had made strenuous efforts to secure the services of printers. Even Mersenne took time out from letter-writing to help get Galileo's manuscripts to press. The historical significance of Galileo's trial is bound to be misconstrued if the printed word is held not to assume importance until the mid-1660s.[23] Since the printed word first assumed importance for the European scientific community in the 1470s when Regiomontanus established his Nuremberg press, the estimate is off by almost two hundred years.[24]

Doubtless the periodical publication which began in the 1660s affected the pace and character of scientific activities. Sociologists of science have good reason to argue that the functions performed by the new journals deserve close scrutiny.[25] At present, moreover, the scientific article and the scientific book often do seem to perform different functions; with the former playing a more innovative and the latter a more conservative role.[26] It is not clear, however, whether this holds true for nineteenth-century scientific publication, when significant innovative contributions by Lyell, Darwin, Maxwell and many others were made in books as well as in journals. The distinction, moreover, becomes ever more pointless as one moves back in time. It makes little

---

[22] A long passage in praise of printing by Kepler, taken from a 1606 publication, is cited by Rosen, 'In defense of Kepler,' pp. 141–9.

[23] On Kepler's struggles and activities of Mersenne and Galileo, see discussion in chap. 8 below.

[24] Stillwell, *The Awakening Interest*, pp. 32–4 offers data on the output of Regiomontanus' press in the 1470s. For further discussion see pp. 586 ff below.

[25] Merton and Zuckerman, 'Patterns of Evaluation in Science.'

[26] The 'conservative' function performed by scientific *textbooks* is emphasized by Thomas Kuhn, *Structure of Scientific Revolutions*, pp. 136–7, even as the innovative function performed by periodical articles is stressed by Merton and Zuckerman, 'Patterns of Evaluation.' Both pass over the category of *innovative books*. That such books may still get published in the present century primarily as *monographs* is suggested by Anthony Parker, 'The Difficult Publishing Art of Persuading Scientists to Sit Down and Write Books,' pp. 813–14. He cites G. N. Watson's monograph on *Bessel Functions* as a case in point. Dirac's *Quantum Mechanics* might be added to the list. The pace of scientific publication has accelerated to the point where the circulation of 'pre-prints' has taken over the place previously occupied by the periodical press and Toulmin's paradoxical comment 'only out-of-date ideas ever actually get into print' seems cogent (Stephen Toulmin, *Human Understanding*, p. 275). In one sense, of course, the paradox has always held good. Unless composing is done with a compositor's stick, press work always involves some kind of 'lag.'

sense in the late seventeenth century, when Newton's *Principia* was published and the first issues of the *Transactions* appeared. When considering earlier works produced during the 'century of genius' or when tracing the full sequence of the Copernican Revolution, opposing books to journals not only fails to clarify any issues but also makes many things unnecessarily obscure.

However one may assess the role played by the learned journal in scientific activity, it should not lead to discounting 'the mere printing of a scientific work.' The learned journal probably did contribute significantly to a sharper definition of the professional scientist, to new divisions of intellectual labor and to the creation of a 'referee system.' But it did not usher in serial publication, the preservation of data, the 'shift from motivated secrecy to motivated public disclosure,' or a feedback from informed readers to responsive authors and editors.[27] These features were already taking shape before 1500 – in the age of incunabula. They ought to be placed *before* Copernicus and not after Galileo – if we want to understand how scientific data collection was transformed.

When set beside the consequences of the new mode of book production, moreover, the results of improvements in postal service or overland transport appear trivial indeed. Letters exchanged by Europeans in the early-modern era did not travel much more rapidly than had letters sent out in ancient Rome, but the information flow had nevertheless been transformed. It was not a more efficient postal service or better roads that distinguished the facilities available to seventeenth-century European astronomers from those enjoyed by the Alexandrians. (Nor was it a money economy or urbanization.) In seeking to explain why the *Almagest* remained authoritative as an astronomical text for some fourteen hundred years, whereas *De Revolutionibus* was surpassed in less than one hundred years, the replacement of scribe by printer must be examined first of all.

To insist that one must distinguish more sharply between a system of 'written' and one of 'printed' interchange, to insist that this difference is more important than that which separates a 'printed' book from a 'published' article is not merely to quibble over fine distinctions. If we seek to answer the question posed by Whitehead as to why the pace of a hitherto 'languid' search 'suddenly quickened in the sixteenth and

27 Merton and Zuckerman, 'Patterns of Evolution,' p. 68.

seventeenth century,' then we have to be more careful and discriminating when considering how 'the mind of Europe' was prepared for its new adventure.

It is unnecessary to tell in detail the various incidents which marked the rise of science: the growth of wealth and leisure; the expansion of universities; the invention of printing; the taking of Constantinople; Copernicus; Vasco da Gama; Columbus; the telescope. The soil, the climate, the seeds were there, and the forest grew.[28]

Far from being unnecessary, I think it is essential to go into detail when discussing these assorted 'incidents,' and it is equally important to discriminate among them.

Every step of the remarkable 'adventure in ideas' which took educated Europeans from the *Almagest* to the *Principia* in less than two centuries was marked by the 'practice of merely putting manuscripts into print.' Because this practice was unknown before the fifteenth century, the ancients who had access to the special facilities for data collection provided in Alexandria, Pergamum and other great centers still had much to teach Europeans who lived in 1500. Given the difficulty of ensuring an adequate supply of specially trained copyists who could transcribe technical information, it is remarkable that a work such as the *Almagest* was preserved intact for so long an interval. Only the high priority Islam assigned to the study of astronomy can account for the work's preservation during those centuries when it was lost to the West. Islamic conquests embraced many ancient message centers. New observatories were constructed, old theories reformed and new data recorded by Arab astronomers. But no other great composition was produced to rival the authority possessed by the Alexandrian text in the Moslem world.[29]

Once recovered by the West and translated into Latin in the twelfth century, energies were necessarily absorbed there also in preserving and transmitting it. It was a very esoteric treatise throughout the age of scribes. Few copies of the full work were available at any one time.

---

[28] Whitehead, *Science and the Modern World*, pp. 27–8.
[29] The authority exerted by the *Almagest* among Arab astronomers is underlined by Sayili, *The Observatory in Islam*, p. 80, by Nasr, *Science and Civilization in Islam*, pp. 172–4, and by Watt, *The Influence of Islam on Medieval Europe*, pp. 24–5. All three point to numerous Arab critics and correctors of Ptolemy who seem to have played a role similar to the numerous scholastic critics of Aristotle in the West. Alternative models were occasionally proposed, additions and changes were often made but with the aim of explicating not discarding an inherited corpus of texts. On this point see also Pannekoek, *A History of Astronomy*, p. 169.

Few Western astronomers in any one generation were equipped to read the entire work or to instruct others in its use. The lifetimes of gifted astronomers were consumed, right down to Regiomontanus himself, making copies, recensions and epitomes of an initially faulty and increasingly corrupted twelfth-century translation from an Arabic text.

It is sometimes difficult to realize how much effort was needed to reconstitute the bodies of knowledge such as those of astronomy and arithmetic as they had been known in the ancient world. It was not a question of going beyond the ancients – the impulse to 'research' in the sense of extending the boundaries of scientific knowledge was only faintly stirring even in the twelfth century – but simply to learn what had been known and what the world had since lost was a stupendous task, demanding the labors of many scholars.[30]

For a full three hundred years *after* the twelfth century, the boundaries of scientific knowledge attained by Alexandrians continued to remain out of reach. The complete *Almagest* itself, it has been said, 'almost vanished from European astronomical literature until the sixteenth century.'[31] This may be somewhat overstated. In 1451 a new translation was made from the Greek; a carefully edited epitome based on the twelfth-century translation from Arabic was printed in 1496.[32] Nevertheless, the notion of an open-ended investigatory process, where increments of new information accumulate and the frontiers of the unknown recede, was still only 'faintly stirring' in the fifteenth century. The modern impulse to extend scientific knowledge had not yet been detached from the older impulse to retrieve and reconstitute it.

In the sixteenth century A.D. astronomers were still concerned with the very same problems that Ptolemy had tackled...To many people, this period of stagnation appears...inexcusably long, and they look for someone to blame ...To think in such terms is to miss two crucial points. The change-over to our modern views...called for a series of daring intellectual steps which could be taken only as new evidence gradually accumulated...This inevitably took time. In any case, the process could not begin at once. The

[30] Southern, *The Making of the Middle Ages*, p. 188.
[31] Ravetz, *Astronomy and Cosmology*, p. 21.
[32] George of Trebizond's translation from the Greek made in 1451 was printed in 1528. According to North, 'Medieval Background,' p. 8, Ravetz overstates the absence of knowledge of the complete *Almagest* until the sixteenth century. Gingerich's suggestion ('Crisis versus Aesthetic in the Copernican Revolution,' p. 88) that, in the 1460s, well-trained astronomers were just able to comprehend Ptolemy, seems fair enough.

young growth of Greek science, having been cut down...in Alexandria had to be transplanted.[33]

There is yet another 'crucial point' one must not miss when confronting the prolonged 'stagnation.' During the interval that elapsed between Ptolemy and Regiomontanus, new evidence was less likely to accumulate 'gradually' than to get corrupted or get lost and have to be retrieved or restored.[34] It is not so much 'stagnation' or even a slow rate of advance that needs explaining when dealing with conditions before printing. It is rather the manner in which a process of loss and corruption was temporarily arrested, and even on occasion reversed.

This reversal had occurred in ancient Alexandria where fresh data were preserved and did 'gradually accumulate' under the careful supervision of an élite corps of librarians.[35] Under these 'hothouse' conditions, fruitful work flourished for hundreds of years. Given such a long-lived collaborative enterprise and given its technical sophistication, one might question the notion of a 'young growth' and think instead about the unusual maturity that was achieved. The extensive facilities which made possible so much progress in mapping the earth and charting the planets seem to have been exceptional. Thereafter, some new ground was gained, but more old ground was lost. The feats of data collection achieved by ancient 'giants' remained beyond the reach of later 'dwarfs,' after the contents of Alexandrian libraries had been dispersed. Alexandrian achievements could not be surpassed, that is, until the process of textual transmission was transformed and data collection was placed on a new basis.

Once it is made clear that printing placed facilities which were

[33] Toulmin and Goodfield, *The Fabric of the Heavens*, p. 169. The significance of printing is more strongly asserted elsewhere in this book (see pp. 201–2) than in many other surveys.
[34] On the 'appallingly frequent scribal blunders...always present in medieval astronomical tables which have not been copied by astronomers' see Price (ed.) *The Equatorie of the Planetis*, p. 151. Note also references to frequent corruption of numerals as common scribal error and to 'contaminated' ms. tradition in Benjamin and Toomer, *Campanus of Novara*, pp. xii–xiii, n. 2.
[35] On this 'greatest library before the invention of printing' see Parsons, *The Alexandrian Library* who notes that the actual use made of it over the course of seven, possibly nine centuries, 'is still a virgin field of inquiry' (p. ix). Parsons' somewhat uncritical acceptance of ancient legends concerning Alexandria should be balanced against the more critical account by Pfeiffer, *History of Classical Scholarshp* (see especially pp. 236–7). Peiffer does note the absence of any central manuscript library on the scale of Alexandria even during the Renaissance (p. 110). When Zilsel, 'The Genesis of the Concept of Scientific Progress,' p. 328, discusses the lack of 'systematic organized collaboration' in antiquity he mentions Alexandria without appreciating its exceptional role and, here as elsewhere, fails to allow for the difference between conditions before and after print.

superior to those of Alexandria at the disposal of learned men, it may become somewhat easier to explain why their activities had such unprecedented results. Belief in mathematical order, 'a habit of definite exact thought,' and concern with precise measurement need not necessarily be seen as late medieval novelties that require explanation. In some cases they may be regarded as long prevailing attitudes held by different groups that were weakly implemented throughout the age of scribes. For example, there is evidence in the field of astronomy that 'the ambition to achieve ever increasing standards of accuracy' was 'as strong in ancient Mesopotamia as it is in the modern world.'[36] Given Copernicus' profession, medieval scholasticism is no more needed than is Renaissance neo-Platonism to account for his desire to achieve a mathematically elegant scheme. 'Copernicus was a dedicated specialist. He belonged to the revived Hellenistic tradition of mathematical astronomy.'[37] However theologians and philosophers differed about cosmology, the professional astronomer had always assumed the universe was designed according to some form of mathematical order.

Thus one might supplement Whitehead's suggestion that scholasticism implanted a habit of 'definite exact thought' in the European mind by considering how this same habit was inculcated in astronomers of all cultures. The preservation of the *Almagest* was as important for Islam as it was for Christendom. Concern with precise description of celestial phenomena took different forms in different cultures, however. It is worth noting that the Christian calendar posed peculiar problems – just as polyglot Scriptures did. Fixing the date of Easter involved much more complicated issues, for example, than did the yearly celebration of Ramadan. When he examined Alexandrian texts and Arabic star maps or took advantage of new work in trigonometry, Copernicus was pursuing a course similar to that followed by previous generations of Christian astronomers who had been recruited by churchmen to solve calendrical problems. But he was freed from the task of copying tables and charts, and thus had released time for reading and reflecting. He was also supplied with more treatises, records and linguistic tools. His successors had even greater advantages in the form of paper tools.

'Why in the world' asks Herbert Muller, 'should men want to

36 Hoyle, *Astronomy*, p. 35.
37 Thomas Kuhn, *The Copernican Revolution*, p. 183. For further discussion see chap. 7 below.

measure...things precisely as they had not in the past? By the end of the sixteenth century, men had somehow developed the itch to know exact times, distances, rates, quantities...'[38] Muller is referring not to the study of the heavens but to more mundane, terrestrial activities associated with 'the publication of tables for calculation of interest,' the invention of decimals and logarithms, the 'spread of business habits of close reckoning.' The same question is often posed in connection with the high degree of precision achieved by the naked-eye observations of Tycho Brahe. Whatever activities were affected by exact measurement, a different approach to the problem is worth trying out. Here again, before assuming that new 'desires' had developed, we might look longer at the way old ones had been met. An Anglo-Norman 'algorism' of the fourteenth century consisting of 137 rhymed couplets, 'mostly octo-syllabic in Old French' indicates 'a practical spirit in the midst of bestiaries, computs, divination books, etc.'[39] Reciting rhymed couplets, however helpful as a mnemonic aid, does not lend itself as does studying notation to innovative higher mathematics. Heavy wooden tables are cumbersome compared with paper ones. Counting on one's fingers or even using an abacus did not encourage the invention of Cartesian coordinates. Leonardo Fibonacci, to be sure, compiled a 'book of the abacus' in the early thirteenth century, but it was a 'difficult task to memorize the tables the book contained' and 'not until the fifteenth century when Hindu numerals were spread by the printing press' did the systems outlined in the famous *Liber Abaci* achieve widespread use.[40]

It would seem that the first factor limiting the introduction into scientific practice of higher standards of observation and measurement...lay in the nature of science itself. Only when the concept of scientific research had changed was it possible to pay attention to the attainment of these higher standards...[41]

The very first limiting factor, however, was probably outside 'the nature of science' and was set by the difficulty of duplicating tables, charts, diagrams and maps. Before the advent of printing, to call for

[38] Muller, *Freedom in the Western World*, p. 239.
[39] Karpinski and Staubach, 'An Anglo Norman Algorism,' p. 126.
[40] Joseph and Frances Gies, *Leonardo of Pisa*, p. 98. The re-entry of the abacus marked an advance in the eleventh century, as noted by Southern, *Making of the Middle Ages*, pp. 186-7. The inconclusive struggle between abacists and algorists until the advent of printing and the victory of the latter thereafter is noted by Dantzig, *Number: the Language of Science*, pp. 33-4.
[41] A. R. Hall, *The Scientific Revolution*, p. 234.

more precise and uniform standards was to indulge in wishful thinking rather than contribute to research. The closest navigators and surveyors could come to universal common units was by using their own hands and feet, pacing across boat decks while at sea or across fields when on land.[42] Observation and measurement became more precise when man ceased to be the literal measure of things; when tables, charts and detailed records could be exactly reproduced and drawings to scale did not blur or smudge over time. After early printers had made available handbooks such as Simon Stevin's 'decimall arithmetike' or Leonard Digges' *A Booke Named Tectonicon* (the latter with a subtitle referring to 'exact measuring and speedie reckoning of all manner of Land, Squares, Timber, Stone, Steeples, Pillers, Globes'),[43] the old limits could be transcended and higher standards attained.

According to Crombie, 'the elements, both intellectual and practical, that came to produce the Scientific Revolution had been incubating in Western civilization for several centuries.'[44] One might elaborate this suggestion by emphasizing how many different groups within late medieval society placed a high value on achieving greater accuracy and more precise results. 'To astrologers, land-measurers, measurers of tapestry and wine casks and stereometricians, in general, mint masters and merchants all,' Simon Stevin addressed his new 'decimall arithmetike.'[45] In view of present tendencies to stress divisions between practical and theoretical, artisan and academic groups, it seems worth noting that Stevin's decimals, like Napier's logarithms, were just as helpful to professors of mathematics as to military engineers. The use of printed tables cut across other barriers which separated town from gown. Unlike rhymed verses in old French, the new forms of silent non-phonetic communication transcended distinctions between learned and vulgar tongues.

This point applies also to the new repeatable pictorial statements that became increasingly common in printed technical reference works. Like decimals and logarithms, woodcuts and engravings travelled

---

[42] On how man served as 'a measure for all things' see Dupree, 'The Pace of Measurement from Rome to America,' pp. 19–40, and Boas, *The Scientific Renaissance*, p. 204. See also Boas, pp. 35–6 for interesting description of how sailors envisaged a human figure (with head pointing North; feet pointing South; and arms pointing East and West) for the purposes of celestial navigation.

[43] Boas, *Scientific Renaissance*, p. 200 cites Leonard Digges' subtitle. This is the father of Thomas Digges whose description of Copernicus' doctrine is noted above, p. 458.

[44] See Crombie (ed.) *Scientific Change*, pp. 316 ff.

[45] Sarton, 'The First Explanation,' p. 160.

across linguistic frontiers, providing the life sciences with 'one common measure which speaks universally to all mankind' – in the words of Sir Joseph Banks describing pictures made by the artists who were sent with Captain Cook.[46] With regard to 'the veins, tools, vessels, sluices, machines, furnaces,' wrote Agricola, 'I have not only described them, but have also hired illustrators to delineate their forms, lest descriptions which are conveyed by words should either not be understood by the men of our times, or should cause difficulty to posterity.'[47] The descriptions of the Alexandrians had often caused difficulty to Western scholars partly because the texts of Ptolemy, Vitruvius, Pliny and others had been transmitted without pictures to accompany the often copied and translated words. Vitruvius refers to diagrams and drawings, but after the tenth century they were detached from Vitruvian texts.[48] Ptolemy's work on geography was retrieved, but any accompanying maps had been lost long before.[49] Simple pictograms had a better survival value. In the sixteenth century, when the difficulties created by scribal transmission were not fully appreciated, it often seemed as though earlier authorities had been arbitrarily and deliberately obscure.

Agricola protests against this arbitrary character in the name of knowledge that is communicable and whose language has the character of precision and intersubjectivity. There are many other books on this subject, but all are difficult to follow because the writers on these things use strange names which do not properly belong to the metals and because some of them employ now one name and now another although the thing itself changes not...[50]

Views of 'animals, plants, metals and stones' which had been transmitted for centuries became unsatisfactory to Agricola and his contem-

[46] Bernard Smith, 'European Vision and the South Pacific,' p. 67 cites Sir Joseph Banks' remarks on the importance of engravings made from renderings of soil, rocks and plants observed on the expedition.

[47] Cited by Paolo Rossi, Philosophy, Technology, p. 48.

[48] Krinsky, 'Seventy-eight Vitruvius Manuscripts.' See also Zoubov, 'Vitruve et ses Commentateurs du XVIe Siècle,' pp. 69–70, concerning effort of illustrators to follow Vitruvius' description of the Tower of Winds in Athens. The effort to replace lost illustrations for Vitruvius and Ptolemy seems to me worth more attention as a powerful stimulus producing unexpected results. The invention of central perspective and of new map projection techniques, like that of the opera, may have resulted from attempts to redo what the ancients were (mistakenly) believed to have done before. See pp. 268 n, 281 above.

[49] That the text of Ptolemy's Geography when recovered had long since lost all its maps is noted by Boas, Scientific Renaissance, p. 33. That the relatively small 500-copy first edition of the Geographia (Bologna, 1477) conveyed to many Italians and Germans their first sight of a map of any kind is noted by Bagrow, History of Cartography, p. 89.

[50] Rossi, Philosophy, Technology, p. 53.

poraries. They attributed the deficiencies and inconsistencies they found to the 'linguistic barbarism' of the Gothic dark ages and to a prolonged 'lack of interest' in natural phenomena. Present evidence suggests that medieval natural philosophers were not lacking in curiosity. They were, however, lacking some essential investigative tools. Agricola's concern with 'communicable descriptive techniques' is certainly worth emphasizing but it also ought to be related to the new communications system of his day. The same point applies to Vesalius' 'acute sense of the importance of minutiae and...of precise and full reporting of observations.' Surely the new possibility of duplicating precise detailed reports alongside precise, detailed images deserves more attention when considering the shift that placed 'the traditional frames of...knowledge ...into a crisis situation.'[51] Similarly, the 'insistence that all experiments and observations be reported in full and naturalistic detail preferably accompanied by the names and credentials of witnesses'[52] needs to be related to the new kind of reporting that became possible only after the shift from script to print. As these comments may suggest, many different ancient and medieval scientific traditions were transformed by the capacity of printing to transmit records of observations without any loss of precision and in full detail. In view of the new equipment printing provided, it seems worth thinking longer about the new implementation of old aims before assuming that the significant change came from a shift of attitudes and goals. This approach, which seemed helpful when dealing with problems posed by the Reformation, ought to be equally useful when dealing with early-modern science.

By placing more emphasis on how print served to re-orient prevailing traditions, moreover, we might also be in a better position to relate religious and scientific changes to each other. Scriptural and scientific texts that had been transmitted by scribes were re-oriented at more or less the same time, under the aegis of printers. The fate of texts inherited from Aristotle, Galen and Ptolemy had something in common with that of texts inherited from Saint Jerome – a point to be discussed in the concluding chapter of this book.

[51] Rossi, *Philosophy, Technology*, pp. 47–9. In note 82 (p. 49), Rossi cites A. R. Hall on Vesalius and Sarton on how the new illustrations encouraged more awareness of 'stereotyped words.' But he does not deal explicitly with the way hand-copied illustrations had degenerated into stereotyped images before the advent of print.
[52] Thomas Kuhn, 'The Function of Measurement,' p. 192.

Insofar as Scripture and nature had been reoriented, their being coupled no longer meant the same thing. Browne kept up with the publications of the Royal Society and with the work of Bible scholars. Bible-reading and nature study were sufficiently distinguished in his mind that he could assign different functions and separate languages to each. Like his fellow virtuosi he was well aware of the thorny problems associated with deciphering God's words from ancient Hebrew texts.[53] Against the uncertain meanings and ambiguous allegories to be found in Scripture, he set the circles, triangles and other 'common hieroglyphicks' that 'heathen' philosophers – such as Euclid or Archimedes – knew how to join and read. When 'scriptural statements conflict with scientific truths,' notes Basil Willey, 'Browne will adhere unto Archimedes who speaketh exactly, rather than the sacred Text which speaketh largely.'[54]

In opposing Archimedes' formula to that provided by Solomon in the book of Chronicles, Sir Thomas Browne was not shaking off 'the dust of yellowed parchments' and taking a fresh look at the great outdoors. On the contrary he remained in the library with his eyes trained on old texts. But he *was* looking at texts which enabled Euclid and Archimedes to speak more 'exactly' (in Indo-Arabic numerals and by means of uniform diagrams) than had been the case before.[55] Similar analysis can be applied to the varied activities of the virtuosi who lived in Browne's day.

There is one very important feature of Kepler's actual procedure that I do not believe has ever come to light. It is, simply, that the hypotheses set forth were not developed inductively from an inspection of nature. Kepler was reading neither the Book of Nature nor the Book of Scripture but the books of ancient and contemporary writers...[56]

The notion that Renaissance men discarded 'dusty parchments' in favor of the 'book of nature' is not objectionable merely because previous book metaphors have been overlooked but mainly because the

---

[53] That Browne was thoroughly conversant with disputes over Hebrew vowel points and other controversies among seventeenth-century biblical scholars is shown in his tract, 'Of Language,' in *Prose of Browne* (Endicott, ed.) pp. 602 ff. In his introduction, Endicott also notes Browne's interest in Royal Society reports of Leeuwenhoek's work (p. xiii).

[54] Willey, *Seventeenth Century Background*, p. 68. The relevant passages are in Browne's *Pseudoxia Epidemica*, chap. 9 *Prose of Browne* (Endicott, ed.), p. 143.

[55] How a medieval copyist (of a twelfth-century Barcelona ms.) made Archimedes speak inexactly (by confusing a line drawn from point C to point L with a Roman numeral for 150) is noted by Clagett, *Archimedes*, p. 17.   [56] Westman, 'Kepler's Theory,' pp. 253–4.

investigation of natural phenomena has been misconstrued. The so-called cliché rests on a naive conception of scientific activity which is seen to consist of discarding old books or rejecting received opinion and making first-hand observations for oneself. 'He who wishes to explore nature must tread her books with his feet. Writing is learned from letters. Nature however by travelling from land to land: One land, one page. This is the Codex Naturae, thus must its leaves be turned.'[57] This naive view of science takes Browne's tricky image of a 'universal publick manuscript' at face value – as if any one observer could actually don 'seven-league boots' and see the whole world laid out before him, without recourse to maps and star catalogues, to atlases and travel guides; or, as if observations made in varied regions at different times did not have to be collected, preserved and correlated with each other, before plants or animals or minerals could be classified and compared; or finally, as if experiments did not have to be recorded in more than one notebook to be checked out and be of any scientific value at all.

sell your lands...burn up your books...buy yourself stout shoes, travel to the mountains, search the valleys, the deserts, the shores of the sea, and the deepest depressions of the earth; note with care the distinctions between animals, the differences of plants, the various kinds of minerals...Be not ashamed to study the astronomy and terrestrial philosophy of the peasantry. Lastly, purchase coal, build furnaces, watch and operate the fire...In this way and no other you will arrive at a knowledge of things and their properties.[58]

Insofar as it entails rejection of second-hand accounts and insistence on using one's own eyes, this naive view owes much to the arguments of sixteenth-century empiricists who set fresh observation and folk wisdom against the Latin book learning that was transmitted in the schools. The movement championed by these empiricists has been described by Whitehead as a 'recoil against the inflexible rationality of medieval thought.' 'The world required centuries of contemplation of irreducible and stubborn facts...after the rationalistic orgy of the middle ages...'[59]

To jump from the inflexibly rational schoolman to the nature-loving empiricist, however, is to pass over the intervening figure of the

[57] Cited from Paracelsus by Pagel and Rattansi, 'Vesalius and Paracelsus,' p. 316.
[58] Cited from Peter Severinus' *Idea Medicinae Philosophicae* (1660) by Debus, *English Paracelsians*, p. 20.   [59] Whitehead, *Science*, pp. 19; 28.

humanistic book-hunter. A 'recoil' against logic-chopping schoolmen had already occurred during the quattrocento, but it had often been on behalf of ancient authors and classical belles lettres rather than 'stubborn facts.'[60] Because of their attacks on scholasticism, their preference for examples over precepts and their interest in historical data, the quattrocento humanists are sometimes linked with sixteenth-century empiricists. Given the number of sixteenth-century humanists (such as Vives or Rabelais) who expressed empirical views, it seems that some sort of linkage did exist. Nevertheless, the humanist slogan, 'Back to the Sources!' led to Greek studies and library collections. It was quite compatible with fining professors who interpolated new material into fixed texts.[61] But it pointed in a different direction from the empiricist injunction to 'Burn up your books!' and learn from unlettered folk. 'The appearance of Paracelsus and the Aldine edition of Galen's works almost coincided...no two events could contrast more. Paracelsus had no use for the humanistic occupation with classical authors and with their words...to most of the humanistic Galenists Paracelsus and his whole following were an abomination.'[62] The humanist concern with rhetoric and the pursuit of eloquence, moreover, was not easily reconciled with the empiricist tendency to exalt the 'study of things' by deprecating the 'rabble of words.'[63]

All that is wanted is a certain power of observation. So will he observe the nature of things in the heavens in cloudy and clear weather, in the plains, on the mountains, in the woods. Hence he will seek out and get to know many things about those who inhabit those spots. Let him have recourse, for instance, to gardeners, husbandmen, shepherds, and hunters...For no man can possibly make all observations without help in such a multitude and variety of directions.[64]

It is noteworthy that Vives, even in this short passage, goes beyond a simple request for 'a certain power of observation' and in the end is

---

[60] Humanist objections to schoolmen posed by Salutati and his friends (who believed the cardinal sin was to argue without books or study of basic texts) are outlined by Gilbert, 'The Early Italian Humanists,' p. 219. The strongly anti-empirical position of Salutati vis-à-vis medical studies is brought out by Kemp, 'Il Concetto dell "Anima,"' p. 130.

[61] The case of John Geynes who was forced by the College of Physicians in 1559 to sign a recantation of his opinion that Galen was not infallible is cited by Debus, Science and Education, p. 6.

[62] Owsei Temkin, Galenism Rise and Decline of a Medical Philosophy, p. 132.

[63] Sir William Petty's dismissal of a 'rabble of words' is cited by R. F. Jones, Ancients and Moderns, p. 91. On the central role played by the pursuit of eloquence, see seminal essay by Gray, 'Renaissance Humanism.'

[64] Passage from Vives' De Anima (1538) cited by Haydn, The Counter Renaissance, p. 199.

envisaging a coordinator who correlates the findings of many observers. Still, he seems to think practical men unspoiled by book learning can provide adequate 'help.' The study of ancient languages aimed at mastery of technical literature produced by careful observers in the past finds no place in this program. Instead anti-intellectual and primitivist views are set forth which denounce all academic training, whether scholastic or humanist, or both. One authority has recently depicted the movement as directed against schoolmasters, textbooks and other restraints which print culture imposed.

When Libavius speaks of the Book of Nature he has in mind the clear-cut well ordered textbook of the class room. Croll's book on the other hand was...more mysterious...ultimately derived from the spoken word of God...intended for a largely illiterate audience with no access to the book of words...Paracelsus and Croll urge their followers to abandon the words ...in academic texts [and to] embrace the mentality of the illiterate peasant and artisan...[65]

In depicting the conflict between schoolmaster and Paracelsian, Hannaway appears to set the 'bourgeois' print culture of the former against the oral 'folk' culture of the latter. But this equation does not really work. For one thing, classroom procedures were geared to oral-aural modes of interchange – to dictation and recitation. For another thing, Croll (like Vives) belongs in the company of Renaissance scholars who were at home in the libraries and courts of princely patrons. He was affiliated with a court circle in Southern Bohemia which stood second only to that of Rudolph in Prague.[66] His major work, the *Basilica Chymica*, eventually issued by the Wechel press in Frankfurt, was designed for a Latin-reading, learned audience. It reflected a mentality which was quite remote from that of peasants and artisans. Paracelsus himself comes closer to being an autodidact and artisan-author. In this capacity he frequented the company of Basel printers, took full advantage of the new publicity system, and turned out a stream of publications – which suggests he had a flair for the metier of Aretino as well as for the healing arts. In short he too was a creature of print culture.

Attacking the academic establishment and satirizing pedants was indeed a common theme among Aretino's followers, the 'poligrafi' of

---

[65] Hannaway, *The Chemists and the Word*, p. 113.
[66] R. J. W. Evans, *Rudolf II and His World*, p. 142.

sixteenth-century Venice.[67] It seems plausible that students rather more than peasants provided the largest market for anti-establishment satires and polemics. (Do not many students belong within the category of 'bourgeois' print culture even when they chafe at the discipline that parents and teachers impose?) At all events, the sixteenth century did witness an unusually rich literary orchestration of anti-pedantic, primitivist themes which set the experience of simple folk against the foolishness of Latin pedants. The existence of a generalized rebellion against traditional academic pursuits and conventional bookish wisdom has been most amply illustrated by Hiram Haydn. Under the somewhat confusing rubric 'counter-Renaissance,' Haydn has collected a large number of citations from sixteenth-century theologians, philosophers, poets and other literati demonstrating that something more than either a 'recoil' from scholasticism or a rebellion against schoolmasters was at work.[68]

In my view the movement Whitehead describes as a 'recoil' and Haydn calls a 'counter-Renaissance' reflected disenchantment with those forms of teaching and book learning which had been inherited from the age of scribes. Insofar as memory training and 'slavish copying' became less necessary, while inconsistencies and anomalies became more apparent after printed materials began to be produced, a distrust of received opinion and a fresh look at the evidence recommended itself to all manner of curious men.

The difference between my philosophising and that of Pico is this: I learn more from the anatomy of an ant or a blade of grass...than from all the books which have been written since the beginnings of time. This is so, since I have begun...to read the book of God...the model according to which I correct the human books which have been copied badly and arbitrarily and without attention to the things that are written in the original book of the Universe...[69]

The idea of observing natural phenomena directly and carefully was as old as Aristotle or Galen. The phrase 'ego vidi' was not lacking in many scholastic commentaries.[70] Manuscript margins show skillful renderings of species of recognizable insects and birds. But the chance

[67] On Paracelsus see chap. 3, n. 337, volume I above. On Aretino's followers, see Grendler's *Critics of the Italian World*, chap. 1.
[68] See especially chap. 4 in Haydn, *Counter Renaissance*.
[69] Tommaso Campanella, Letter of 1607, cited by Garin, *Italian Humanism*, p. 215.
[70] The phrase 'ego vidi' is cited as 'Buridan's motto' and the frequency of its use in the fourteenth century is noted by Gabriel, *The College System*, p. 18.

to discard inherited schemes, collect fresh data and build improved models on them came only after print. In view of the output of corrupted data ('of human books copied badly') during the first century of printing and in view of the new possibility of duplicating fresh records, a reaction of some new kind against accepted texts, fixed lectures and received opinion was almost inevitable. But it would be wrong to assume that a rejection of technical literature paved the way for the rise of modern science. It was not the burning of books but the printing of them that provided the indispensable step.

In view of the errors inherited from scribal records and the way habits of 'slavish copying' persisted after they were no longer required, the empiricist reaction is understandable. It is easy to sympathize with those who placed more reliance on fresh observations than rote learning. Nevertheless insistence on going directly to the 'book of nature' soon took on the very attributes it was intended to repel. It became a ritualistic literary formula, devoid of real meaning.[71] 'As Olschki says of the natural philosophers: All of these thinkers who begin with the motto: "Away from books!"...know natural phenomena only from books! What they offer as observational material is merely anecdotes based on their own experience or known from hearsay...'[72] The unending stream of publications issued by exponents of the 'new philosophy' suggests that the virtuosi were not entirely consistent in attacking the written word.

When the Royal Society published a volume of 'Directions for Seamen, Bound for Far Voyages' in 1665, it defined its aim 'to study Nature rather than Books' but it also noted its intention 'from the Observations...to compose such a History of Her [i.e. Nature] as may hereafter serve to build a solid and useful Philosophy upon.'[73] Presumably Royal Society publications were designed to be read. Did not the Society actually aim at getting more of nature *into* books? However much they valued knowledge acquired through direct experience, members of the new scientific academies were still engaged in processing data and purveying it at second hand. Unlike shepherds or huntsmen, astronomers and anatomists could not really dispense with access to

[71] See e.g. Descartes' account of his decision to abandon 'the study of letters' and set out to study the 'great book of the world,' *A Discourse on Method*, part 1, pp. 6–7.
[72] Adelmann, Introduction to *The Embryological Treatises of Hieronymus Fabricius of Aquapendente*, p. 54.
[73] Notice appearing in the *Philosophical Transactions*, Jan. 8, 1665/6 cited by Bernard Smith, 'European Vision,' p. 65.

treatises and records. Insofar as they were involved in actual investigations, rather than philosophizing or propagandizing, they also had to master the technical literature available in their day. Indeed all work in science is incomplete until the report has been written *and* presented in published form. The irreducible 'fact,' the direct observation and any kind of raw data must be processed by being written down and made available for checking and confirmation by other eyes.

To most twentieth-century observers, it seems quite obvious that scientists must do more than make careful observations and show proper respect for 'stubborn facts.' When this point is made, however, it is usually to suggest that something more than induction is entailed in scientific activity. It is necessary, most authorities agree, to couple empiricism with rationalism and to develop theoretical frameworks for ordering collected facts. Both data collection and laboratory tests are often assigned a secondary role to the use of mathematical logic and resort to thought experiments. But there is yet another task that must be undertaken. It is too obvious, perhaps, ever to be spelled out. Before a scientist embarks on mental voyages or real ones, written records of previous undertakings have to be surveyed. A 'search of the literature' is so indispensable that an illiterate scientist is close to being a contradiction in terms. John Hale has suggested that the explorer may be distinguished from other voyagers because he works 'in the service of an organised vision of what might be found' and seeks 'to relate it to what is known. Unlike the wanderer...the explorer sees himself as contributing to a sum of knowledge he has assessed beforehand.'[74]

The point is relevant to the scientist as well. It is not only his command of technical literature – but also his capacity to put his findings in a form where they can be correlated with prior work – where they can be accepted or rejected by consensual validation – that helps to distinguish the scientist from the shrewd observer or from the speculative 'crank' and the ingenious gadgeteer.

the report of an experiment is a very long way...from that direct... wrestling with...Nature that the individual research worker experiences in his own laboratory.

When we say that scientific knowledge is...firmly based on empirical

[74] Hale, *Renaissance Exploration*, p. 9.

evidence, we do not mean that each scientist has seen with his own eyes all the wonders in which he believes. We mean that there exists a collection of reports of observations made by reliable witnesses and set out according to certain conventions...These reports...give...a carefully edited version of...events...by becoming part of the stock of public knowledge they have become...second-hand information, far removed from the direct experience of any one of us.[75]

This citation comes from an English physicist who agrees with Robert Merton that science is public rather than private knowledge and who also stresses the role of the printing press in making this form of knowledge possible. 'Modern science arose shortly after...printing ...this may have been no accident...the communications system needed in the scientific community could not have been provided by a less powerful technique.'[76]

After reading Professor Ziman's analysis, the paradox implicit in Browne's 'book of nature' becomes clear. The notion of a 'universal publick manuscript' may tickle our fancy as a Baroque conceit. But it is important to remember that there is no way of making fresh observations 'universal' and 'public' as long as they can be recorded only in manuscript form.

It is surprisingly easy to be absent-minded on this point. Most authorities either seem to forget that all records had to remain in manuscript form until the fifteenth century, or else they discount the importance of this fact. More often than not it seems sufficient to note that a 'collective memory' was transmitted first by word of mouth and then by writing without paying attention to the incapacity of scribal culture to make detailed records 'public' and at the same time preserve them intact. When Kenneth Boulding describes the emergence of a 'public image,' for example, he mistakenly assigns to manuscript maps the capacity to convey a uniform spatial reference frame. Although world maps before print actually came in oddly assorted shapes and sizes, Boulding seems to imagine them as being slightly fuzzier versions of our modern uniform outline maps. They were blurred around the edges, he suggests, until the voyages of discovery led to a 'closure of geographic space...looking over the long course of recorded history there is an orderly development in the...spatial image...early images

---

[75] Ziman, *Public Knowledge*, p. 35.
[76] Ziman, *Public Knowledge*, p. 45. For definition of science as 'public and not private knowledge,' see Merton, *Science, Technology*, p. 219.

can always be seen as partial unclear expressions of later more exact images...'[77]

When one places a reconstruction of a Ptolemaic world map derived from the second century A.D. beside mappaemundi designed later on, it becomes clear that this statement needs qualification. Instead of demonstrating 'orderly development' a sequence of hand-copied images will usually reveal degradation and decay. A survey of maps issued during a millennium or more shows how the 'course of recorded history' produced 'spatial images' that cannot be ordered even by taking full advantage of hindsight and present techniques of placing and dating past records.

More than 600 maps and sketches made between 300 and 1300 have survived the ravages of time...regardless of size and the quality of workmanship, it is impossible to trace in them a developmental process, a progression of thought...It is also impossible to grade them in terms of accuracy and utility.[78]

The 'disassociated transcript' that Boulding describes could emerge only after the shift from script to print. To confuse our modern uniform reference frame with the multiform 'world pictures' that hand-copying produced is to lose sight of the obstacles to systematic data collection in the past and to misconstrue what happened when such obstacles were removed.

We learn our geography mostly in school, not through our own personal experience. I have never been to Australia. In my image...however it exists with 100 percent certainty. If I sailed to the place where the map makers tell me it is and found nothing there but the ocean, I would be the most surprised man in the world. I hold to this part of my image...however purely on authority...what gives the map this extraordinary authority, an authority greater than that of the sacred books of all religions...is a process of feedback from the users of maps to the map maker. A map maker who puts out an inaccurate map will soon have this fact called to his attention by people...who find that it violates their...personal experience.[79]

The 'process of feedback' described in this passage was one of the more important consequences of printed editions. We have already noted how Ortelius' atlas was expanded and how the map-publisher

---

[77] Boulding, *The Image*, p. 77. This comment is cited with approval by Shera, 'An Epistemological Foundation for Library Science,' p. 23.

[78] Lloyd Brown, *The Story of Maps*, p. 94.

[79] Boulding, *The Image*, p. 66.

solicited data from informed readers throughout Europe.[80] The generation that followed Ortelius and Mercator saw further developments. After the 'golden age of Antwerp' had faded, new firms founded by Dutch map-publishers and globe-makers such as W. J. Blaeu and J. Hondius turned Amsterdam into the central city for data collection on a truly worldwide scale – a process which culminated in the twelve volume *Grand Atlas* of Joan Blaeu. Joan's father, Willem Janszoon, who founded the firm, is worth singling out for attention for his many contributions to the process described by Boulding, and for the way he exploited diverse advantages inherent in the new medium.

W. J. Blaeu started out as a clerk in the herring trade, then worked on Hven as one of Tycho Brahe's assistants in 1595–6, and finally established a thriving business in Amsterdam, making and selling astronomical and navigational instruments, sea charts and guidebooks from his shop on the waterfront. By 1637 his firm, with its sign of a golden sundial, was established in new premises (almost as elaborate as those of Plantin's 'Golden Compasses' in Antwerp) with nine presses for letterpress printing, six presses for copperplate work, a typefoundry, and rooms set aside for engravers. The bookshop, however, was left in the old store 'on the water near the old bridge.' Although he died (in 1638) before his son's grand atlas was published, he had lived to see the announcement of the forthcoming work appear in an Amsterdam newspaper of February 11, 1634.[81]

Blaeu's activities as instrument-maker ranged from designing an improved press (the first to improve on Gutenberg's design) to producing a huge quadrant, which spurred the building of the 'famous Observatory at Leiden.' As a publisher he preceded the Elseviers in issuing editions of contemporary heterodox authors, such as Grotius, in convenient small formats. His edition of Copernicus' *De Revolutionibus* was neatly timed to appear after the condemnation of 1616 had publicized the newly forbidden astronomical theory. At the same time that he served the Latin-reading Commonwealth of Learning he also furnished simplified latitude tables, vernacular pilot guides and printed sea charts to sailors – in the latter case offering the equivalent of a money-back guarantee that his printed cards were better than any

---

80 See pp. 109–10, volume 1 above.
81 For data see Keuning, *Willem Jansz. Blaeu*; Koeman, *Joan Blaeu and His Grand Atlas*. A special issue of *Quaerendo* (1973) III, 2 is devoted to W. J. Blaeu and contains useful articles by Wytze Hellinga, Ernst Crone, de la Fontaine Verwey *et al.*

hand-copied ones.[82] His role in publicizing 'Tycho's star' and in competing with his rival Hondius for the latest information about unchartered heavens belongs in a later chapter of this book. Here let me just underline the significance of finding Blaeu and his rivals jostling each other at the docks of Amsterdam while waiting for the return of an expedition, and plotting to secure the ship's log or its pilot or captain in order to place new data on their maps and globes.[83] We are thus provided with a glimpse of how the process of 'feedback' that Boulding seems to take for granted had begun to accelerate in the early seventeenth century.

This process has, indeed, never ceased; increments of information are still being added to geodetic surveys, and map-makers (as Boulding notes) are still being 'checked by the fact that it is possible to travel through space.' But this kind of checking could not occur until voyagers were provided with uniform maps and encouraged to exchange information with map-publishers. Even then it took many centuries and cost many lives to achieve the absolute confidence a modern atlas conveys.[84] The story of the prolonged impossible quest for a northwest passage indicates how difficult it was to achieve a final closure of geographic space and how important was the role played by communications in the process.

in spite of one fruitless or fatal voyage after another the expeditions still sailed on their impossible missions. The difficulties were not only physical... but also sprang from the inability of one explorer to pass on his knowledge to another...The outlines traced on a chart might be clear enough, but when this information came to be incorporated in a map covering a larger area, it might well be fitted into the wrong place in the jigsaw of straits, fjords and islands. Time after time the same mistakes were made, the same opportunities missed...[85]

---

[82] Blaeu discusses the advantages of his newly printed 'Sea-Cardes' in the 1612 edition of the *Light of Navigation* (the English translation of his popular pilot guide: *Het Licht.*) He notes that some pilots prefer the written ones 'dayly made and everie day corrected' but argues 'they cannot be made so sound nor with such speed' as printed ones and being often 'copied by the ignorant' are also more liable to error. He assures the reader that printed cards are 'as easie to correct.' Furthermore 'if any man can show us' an error to be corrected, it will be done 'at our charge.' W. J. Blaeu, *The Light of Navigation: Facsimile of 1612 Edition.* (Thanks are due to Rachel Doggett, of the Folger Library staff, for bringing this information to my attention.)

[83] In addition to discussion on p. 600 below, see Verwey, 'Willem Jansz. Blaeu,' pp. 87–105 for relevant material.

[84] How Kepler was misled by his favorite geographers Ortelius and Mercator is noted by Rosen, *Kepler's Somnium,* appendix 224–5.

[85] Hale, *Renaissance Exploration,* p. 75.

The recurrence of mistakes and missed opportunities was much more prevalent before the advent of printing. That many surprises were encountered by mariners in the fifteenth and sixteenth centuries is something even American schoolchildren are taught. The maps consulted in the 'age of discovery' entirely lacked the 'extraordinary authority greater than that of the sacred books of all religions,' which Boulding now consigns to his modern maps. This point is worth keeping in mind when considering changed attitudes toward divine revelation. Confidence in the sacred word was affected by the new authority assigned to literature which described the mundane.

Some of the greatest obstacles holding back the exploration of the globe... are psychological not technical. It was not so much men's inability to overcome natural barriers which prevented them from extending the range of their knowledge by new discoveries as the notions they had of the world around them.[86]

The statement goes on to note that Phoenicians and Vikings were not held back by the lack of technical equipment available to later mariners. Whatever landfalls were made, however, the goal of extending the range of knowledge by new discoveries was still technically as well as psychologically blocked throughout the age of scribes.

From 300 until 1300 there were many merchant adventurers, pious pilgrims, and fierce Norsemen who set out to sea or travelled overland. From evidence gathered after the thirteenth century, we know that trained cartographers took advantage of reports sent back to charthouses and merchant companies in the later middle ages. A special atlas once completed could not be 'published,' however. A fifteenth-century monastery near the University of Vienna served as a major center for the collection of geographic information and advanced cartography. Maps drawn in Klosterneuberg could be seen by visiting scholars and astronomers.[87] But however such exceptional manuscript maps were handled, they were unavailable to scattered readers for guidance, for checking and for feedback. The best maps, indeed, were

---

[86] Issawi, 'Arab Geography,' p. 117.

[87] Durand, *The Vienna-Klosterneuberg Map-Corpus, passim*. The scholarly circle at Klosterneuberg, where Augustinian friars, collaborating with scholars from Padua and Vienna imported manuscripts containing astronomic, geographic and mathematical data and had them copied by professional scribes, seems to represent a unique enterprise in the fifteenth century – unlike the competing map-publishing firms later on. By the seventeenth century there were no less than eighteen chief map-making centers in Europe according to Brown, *Story of Maps*, pp. 156-7.

often carefully hidden from view – like the map made for a fourteenth-century Florentine merchant which was placed in a warehouse 'secretly and well wrapped so that no man could see it.'[88] To make multiple copies would not lead to improvement but to corruption of data; all fresh increments of information when copied were subject to distortion and decay.

This same point also applies to numbers and figures, words and names. Observational science throughout the age of scribes was perpetually enfeebled by the way words drifted apart from pictures, and labels became detached from things. Uncertainty as to which star, plant, or human organ was being designated by a given diagram or treatise – like the question of which coastline was being sighted from a vessel at sea – plagued investigators throughout the age of scribes. No wonder it was believed that one of the greatest secrets God entrusted to Adam was how to go about naming all things!

Writing of Conrad Gesner's *History of Animals* Professor Thorndike makes the simple but fundamental observation that even it is primarily concerned with names and words and with information and allusions for the use and enjoyment of the scholar and literary reader rather than with the collection and presentation of facts for scientific purposes.[89]

In my opinion, this observation is *too* simple. Gesner and his contemporaries lived in an era when science and scholarship were necessarily interdependent. To collect and present 'facts' required mastery of records made by observers in the past. Sixteenth-century investigators had to be concerned with ancient languages and inscriptions, with 'names and words,' whether their interests were 'literary' or not. To classify flora and fauna or place them on maps meant sorting out the records left by previous observers as well as observing freshly for oneself. 'Historical' research and 'scientific' data collection were close to being identical enterprises. Thus, geographers, such as Ortelius, had to engage in research on old place-names and often inspired major studies in philology as well as topography. An astronomer such as Copernicus had to steep himself in ancient chronologies and master

---

[88] See reference in Datini's journal to a Florentine jewel merchant cited by Origo, *The Merchant of Prato*, p. 99. According to Penrose, *Travel and Discovery*, p. 25, the data contained in the now famous Catalan Atlas of 1375 would have 'surprised' Chaucer and Petrarch. See also reference to Dante's ideas of world maps gleaned from looking at monastery walls. Orr, *Dante and the Early Astronomers*, pp. 224–5. The crude pictogram available to readers of manuscript copies of Marco Polo's *Travels* is illustrated in Skelton's useful *Explorer's Maps*, fig. 3.
[89] Endicott, introduction, *Prose of Browne*, p. xv.

inscriptions on coins. As a celestial globe-maker, W. J. Blaeu learned Latin, Greek and even Arabic terms. Not even mythology could be ignored by astronomers trying to match Greek constellations with Arabic ones. If anatomists were not well trained in language studies, and lacked the experience of editing ancient texts, they were likely to have the sort of difficulty that Leonardo had, when he became puzzled as to just which organs Galen was describing. Even while noting how geography tended to become a branch of philology and how Boccaccio had devoted a treatise to diverse names assigned to bodies of water, George Sarton seems surprised at the way 'curiosity about natural phenomena' was combined with 'literary' and 'historical' research.[90]

The combination is no way surprising. Indeed many early scientific field trips were launched by publishers, editors and translators who were producing books for new markets and thus had strong 'literary' interests from the first.[91] The work of a 'naturalist' such as Pierre Belon, as presented by Sarton himself, provides a good case in point. Belon

who was planning to translate Dioscorides and Theophrastus into French, was inhibited at every step by the difficulty of identifying the plants and animals which were dealt with in the ancient books. He realized...the need of going to the East and seeing with his own eyes the...creatures which the Greek naturalists had described.[92]

He secured royal patronage for an expedition to the Near East and returned with an account of the plants and animals he had observed. His book became a landmark in natural history and was published in many editions and translations, after first being printed in Paris in 1553. Sarton's discussion seems unexceptionable up to this point, but then he comments:

As distinguished from the majority of his learned contemporaries Belon was primarily a naturalist, not a humanist...real naturalists caring for the objects of nature rather than for literal descriptions were very rare. It is passing strange that it took so long for intelligent men writing about nature to discover their opportunities.[93]

90 Sarton, *Six Wings*, p. 6.
91 The first example of such a 'field trip' known to me is the one so described by William Ivins which was sponsored in the 1480s by Gutenberg's erstwhile assistant Peter Schoeffer in connection with his herbal *Gart der Gesundheit*. See p. 266, volume 1 above.
92 Sarton, *Appreciation*, p. 57.　　　　93 Sarton, *Appreciation*, p. 60.

To oppose the 'objects of nature' to 'literal descriptions' of them is to adopt an approach that itself seems somewhat strange. Belon's point of departure, after all, was an effort to translate 'literal descriptions.' Had he not been trying to identify objects described by the ancients, his approach to natural phenomena would have taken a different form. Far from being indifferent to literal description he was frustrated precisely because he could not get it right.

The early editors of Theophrastus, Dioscorides, Pliny and Galen faced the usual problems of editing any classical work during the Renaissance. They had to work from manuscripts which were usually poor copies of earlier copies. The ravages of neglect and the ignorant mistakes of scribes turned every text into a series of puzzles for the diligent editor to solve by ingenious emendations. While Renaissance philologists generally had to rely on their knowledge of ancient languages...to make their textual corrections, with the botanical treatises they could make sense out of corrupt passages by inspecting the living plants in question.

The labor of collating classical botanical texts with nature flourished in the sixteenth century...The ancient authors provided a model through their accounts of the long journeys they had undertaken...

The lack of a technical descriptive vocabulary though made it very hard to identify the plants named...with living plants in the field. If living plants alone could not communicate...then the obvious alternative was to rely on pictures...[94]

The labor of collating 'classical texts with nature' thus led to departing from classical precedent by resorting to woodblocks and engravings. The decision to 'rely on pictures' was a radical departure in more than one respect. 'The weight of ancient opinion discouraged the use of illustrations to record and convey botanical knowledge.'[95] Ironically the slogan of the empiricists – that one should use one's own eyes and trust nature not books – derived from an experience which printing outmoded. Classical authorities had warned against trusting hand-copied pictures for the excellent reason that they degenerated over time.[96] When Galen said that 'the sick should be the doctor's books' he was justified by the circumstances of scribal culture. Paracelsians

[94] Reeds, 'Renaissance Humanism and Botany,' pp. 27–9.
[95] Reeds, 'Renaissance Humanism,' pp. 27–9.
[96] See William Ivins, *Three Vesalian Essays*, pp. 50–1 where relevant remarks from Pliny are cited and pertinent issues discussed. On botanical illustration, in addition to standard accounts by Singer, Nissen, Arber, Blunt *et al.* see Stannard, 'The Herbal as a Medical Document,' pp. 212 ff, where the medieval separation of textual and illustrative materials associated with the Dioscoridean herbal is described in interesting detail (p. 217).

who repeated the phrase were actually being less responsive to changed circumstances than Latin-writing professors such as Fuchs and Vesalius who had freshly rendered drawings transferred for duplication on durable woodblocks. Since the 'living plant alone could not communicate' as well as the repeatable image could, only a small fraction of the world's plants had been known to the ancients. After the talents of painters and woodcarvers were tapped, fresh information that lacked respectable classical ancestry began to make its way into scientific texts.

Elsewhere, Sarton again reproaches early-modern investigators for excessive concern 'with words rather than facts.' The editors of early printed editions of scientific treatises, he complains,

illustrate the relative weakness of the typical Renaissance approach...It was literary and wordy instead of being experimental and matter of fact. It took scholars an astonishing long time to discover that science could not be investigated profitably in any book except the Great Book of Nature. The few who realized this were more likely to be rebels like Bernard Palissy...[97]

Insofar as Bernard Palissy was a rebel, it was surely not as a potter trying out a new glaze; it was rather as a craftsman trying his hand at writing books. Generations of potters had been observed at their kilns, but none had contributed to French literature before. It was as an artisan author that Palissy was a pioneer. Partly because more men could serve in this capacity from the sixteenth century on, more of nature could be placed in books. Printing made it possible not only to sort out old records but also to secure fresh records and drawings made by careful observers in an easily portable form.

Well before printing, observations drawn from nature had been made by painters and woodworkers, goldsmiths and stone carvers who were unfamiliar with scribal conventions. Even in the sixteenth century, few had their eyes trained on books; before the advent of printing, most were entirely unlettered. Thereafter they rarely mastered the language which was used in the schools. They had not received university degrees after committing to memory the words of professors reciting from Galen while peering vaguely at the cadaver on the dissecting table. They did not know that only plants bearing Latin names were deemed worthy of inclusion in learned treatises. They carried out the instructions of editors and authors as carefully as they could, but, on occasion, they erred by turning out pictures that were 'truer to life' than the

[97] Sarton, *Appreciation*, p. 5.

texts they were intended to illustrate.[98] Field trips to distant regions and specimens sent in from scattered readers, thus were supplemented by a new look at ordinary garden variety plants grown for centuries at home.

As Karen Reeds points out, anatomists and botanists experienced the effect of the challenge to received opinion somewhat differently – the latter in a more gradual manner than the former. 'No botanist had to challenge the authority of Dioscorides in the way that Vesalius had to oppose Galen.' Nevertheless the limitations of the ancient authority who had described some 600 plants became increasingly apparent as the new process of data collection gathered momentum. By 1623, the number had grown from 600 to 6,000.

As botanists perfected their techniques for collecting and sharing their data and increased the geographical range of their botanical explorations they gradually realized that the ancients, far from being omniscient in botany, had named but a small fraction of the plants in the world...every day seemed to bring forth 'new founde Herbes wherof is no mention in any olde auncient writer.'[99]

As we noted in an earlier chapter, once fresh observations drawn from nature could be duplicated in printed books, they became available to scattered readers who could, at long last, check books against nature and feed back corrections with new observations to be incorporated into later editions. The 'information explosion in botany and zoology' that occurred during Captain Cook's voyages and the receipt of packages of seeds by Linnaeus from scattered members of the reading public (who hoped they might be immortalized in his next volume), represent later phases of a process that was already under way in the mid-sixteenth century.[100]

Indeed, plant observation from the mid-sixteenth century onward acquired much the same character as bird-watching does today and depended in somewhat the same way on visual aids in pocket-sized reference guides.[101] Botanical publication also began to take a serial form.

---

[98] Arber, 'From Medieval Herbalism,' pp. 322–3 describes how Weiditz drew plants, excluded from Brunfels' conventional scheme, for the celebrated herbal of 1530 which turned out to be landmarks in the history of plant delineation. A. R. Hall, *Scientific Revolution*, pp. 43, 47 notes that the cuts for Vesalius' *De Fabrica* were occasionally more accurate and less traditional than the text they illustrated. [99] Reeds, 'Renaissance Humanism,' p. 540.

[100] On public response to Linnaeus, see Eisley, *Darwin's Century*, p. 17. The process of feedback initiated in both botany and zoology is discussed in section 4, chap. 2, volume I above.

[101] See reference to pocket-sized edition of Fuchs' herbal in chap. 2, n. 308, volume I above.

Mattioli won fame for his commentaries on Dioscorides, first published in 1554 and reprinted in many editions, periodically revised and corrected, not only in Latin but in many vernaculars. Mattioli's commentary on Dioscorides became a treatise on botany just as a 'Ptolemy' was actually a new treatise on geography. His publications were immensely popular; some 32,000 copies of them were sold. His authority was so great that discoverers of new plants ...communicated their information to Mattioli to be included in his next edition.[102]

Mattioli's successive editions, which were periodically revised and corrected to take into account this feedback from readers, acted very much like later scientific periodicals. This sort of collaborative publication suggests why it is a mistake to delay the effects of printing until the late seventeenth century and learned periodicals such as the *Transactions* of the Royal Society.

In later sections, I hope to elaborate on some of these points. The main purpose of this introductory section has been to suggest that the views of natural philosophers were transformed by print in ways that have yet to be taken into account. The same point applies to activities pursued by late medieval craftsmen. The new technology equipped both groups to reach for old goals by new means. When considering the scientific revolutions of early-modern times, changes wrought by the new presses ought to receive higher priority. Insofar as a major turning point occurred in the late fifteenth century, I contend, it was not that men turned from books to nature, but rather that books went from script to print.

2. PROBLEMS OF PERIODIZATION REVISITED

(a) *Burckhardtians versus Medievalists*

At present this thesis is unconventional. Most historians who deal with the rise of modern science have to confront the issue of periodization, and at some point must pause to balance evidence of continuity against indications of change. The 'problem of the Renaissance' will loom large at such points for Burckhardt's claim that the Italians were the first-born sons of modern Europe explicitly encompassed the 'sphere of the natural sciences.'[103] In discussing the study of nature, Burckhardt

---

[102] Sarton, *Six Wings*, pp. 138–9. See also 144–6 concerning relevant role played by Plantin's firm in sponsoring botanical publication.

[103] See Burckhardt, *The Civilization of the Renaissance* II, part IV, 'The Discovery of the World and of Man,' especially chaps. I and 2. The view of Durand, 'Tradition and Innovation in 15th

distinguished sharply between the occasional medieval schoolman who managed to free himself from 'slavery to books and tradition' and the collective emancipation of a 'whole people' which occurred on the Italian peninsula. He also made an invidious comparison between the widespread delight taken by Italians in investigating nature and the indifference exhibited by other nations.[104] However defended or attacked, extended or delimited, the thesis has loomed large in subsequent treatments of Renaissance science. Indeed the 'primacy of Italy' has been assigned more attention when setting the stage for the 'rise of modern science' than the effects of the shift from script to print. Here, as elsewhere, when dealing with problems of 'modernization,' I think scholarly priorities ought to be revised.

Let me forestall misunderstanding: I am not denying that certain Italian developments ought to be singled out for special emphasis. When observing the sculpture and paintings that were produced by the Italians during the Renaissance, it seems quite legitimate to refer to a native genius. The nude figures rendered by Italian artists such as Mantegna or Pollaiuolo moreover were more important than those of other regions in shaping the new visual aids which were significant for the 'new' anatomy.[105] Similarly, when dealing with medical studies during the early-modern era, certain Italian universities have to be singled out for special notice. Given the sequence that runs from Vesalius to Harvey, one can scarcely avoid assigning a very special role to the University of Padua. Nevertheless the national pride of Flemings and Englishmen is needlessly offended when innovations associated with either of these celebrated figures are attributed to the native genius of Italians. It also becomes difficult to discern some of the significant new elements that characterized *De Fabrica* or *De Motu* when the Italianate theme is overplayed.

When Vesalius is portrayed as working near 'the countryside of Petrarch' and in Titian's Venetian studio and there is nothing said about the long line of Flemish physicians from whom he was descended, or about his studies at Louvain and Paris or his editing of medical texts, one senses that the theme is being overstressed. The suspicion deepens

century Italy,' p. 25, that Burckhardt ignored science 'almost completely in his periodization scheme' needs qualifying. Although Burckhardt treated science in a very cursory way, it was important 'in his periodization scheme,' as later debates suggest.

[104] Burckhardt, *Civilization of the Renaissance* II, 283.
[105] For relevant illustrations of engravings by Pollaiuolo and Mantegna, see Mayor, *Prints and People*, figures nos. 184–91.

when told that a reader of *De Fabrica*, unlike *De Revolutionibus* 'is not repelled by the crabbed Gothic lettering of the North but is invited by the bold clear typeface of Italian printing.'[106] After all, *De Fabrica* was actually printed under German Swiss auspices by the son of a Northern painter named Herbst. Vesalius went to much trouble to get heavy blocks carried out of Italy, over the Alps to Oporinus' famous workshop in Basel. The contrast with Copernicus' Northern 'Gothic' work also suggests how arbitrary this kind of pattern weaving can be, not only because the types used in *De Revolutionibus* do not fit the description, but also because Copernicus visited Italy and there are reasons for believing that he was influenced by the teacher he encountered there.

Especially when dealing with advances in astronomy, I think, insistence on Italian initiative comes close to being a distracting nuisance. The cosmopolitan Latin-writing élite to which professional astronomers belonged does not lend itself to efforts at separating out 'Italianate' elements from the rest. In extending his claims for 'the countrymen of Columbus'[107] Burckhardt unwittingly provoked an unending series of embittered 'Columbus Day' disputes with Germans, Danes and Poles. One reads: 'it was in Italy not Nürnberg that Copernicus' thoughts turned to astronomy'[108] and one finds it hard not to be distracted by thinking of the deluge of articles in Polish about the university of Cracow such a statement is likely to provoke. A Heilbronn printer of 1492 proudly claimed Regiomontanus for the Germans[109] whereas Burckhardt placed him alongside Copernicus and other learned men who confessed themselves 'to be Italy's pupils.'[110] Both views can be justified, but efforts to do so seem destined to generate more heat than light.

As these comments may suggest, exclusive emphasis on the genius of any one people or nation (however welcome to patriotic Italian scholars) can easily exacerbate national rivalries and rarely yields useful results. Furthermore, in the course of claiming that Italians took the lead in

---

106 Gillispie, *The Edge of Objectivity*, p. 57. Later on (p. 60) Brussels, Louvain and Paris are mentioned with a comment that Vesalius 'hated his teachers' but without noting how much he learned from their lectures or from helping them edit Galenic texts. That 'crabbed Gothic' was often easier to read than 'Italic' is also overlooked.
107 Burckhardt, *Civilization of the Renaissance* II, 281–2.
108 Wightman, *Science and the Renaissance* I, 111.
109 See discussion of Santritter of Heilbronn and other relevant material in Thorndike, *A History of Magic and Experimental Science*, pp. 332–7.
110 Burckhardt, *Civilization of the Renaissance* II, 286.

scientific pursuits, Burckhardt also stressed their empiricism and their collective commitment to investigation and exploration. The entire nation, he suggested 'took a natural delight in the study...of nature at a time when other nations were indifferent.' Here again I think he helped to sidetrack later studies. By setting the venturesome nature-lovers of Renaissance Italy against the sedentary schoolmen of medieval Europe, he incorporated the false dichotomy of books versus nature into his periodization scheme. Medieval man was, accordingly, portrayed as enslaved by 'books and tradition' and emancipation attributed to the 'nautical' nature-loving Renaissance Italians. To make a convincing case, however, the otherwise conspicuous role played by 'books and tradition' in quattrocento Italy had to be glossed over. Even latter-day Burckhardtians found this difficult. As one has confessed: although 'the Renaissance...brought a refreshing breeze into Christendom through contact with naturalistic paganism...it was more concerned with book-learning than with the first-hand study of nature...'[111] By emphasizing pagan and naturalistic elements in antiquity and by pitting them against Christian dogma, the classical revival could be partly modernized – a tactic Burckhardt's followers exploited to the hilt: 'Into this oppressive atmosphere, the recovered classics of Greece and Rome came like a refreshing sea breeze. Poets and painters...were inspired with a new interest in natural phenomena...In these respects modernism was essentially a revival of antiquity brought about with the aid of the literature of antiquity.'[112] Even when presented as an anti-clerical device, however, the cult of antiquity retained certain imitative and bookish tendencies. Burckhardt was never entirely able to reconcile the backward-looking veneration of the ancients with the forward-looking 'genius of the Italian people' and he argued against assigning too much significance to the classical revival while deliberately relegating the topic to a subordinate position in his book.[113]

Quattrocento bookworms were embarrassing to Burckhardt, and he was not entirely successful in fitting them into his scheme. By calling into question their contribution to early-modern science, he set the terms for future debate. However much one might stress the achieve-

111 Wolf, *A History of Science, Technology* I, 8.
112 Wolf, *A History of Science, Technology* I, 2. This view of 'modernism' is essentially the same as that of Gay – as is suggested by the subtitle of the first volume of the two-volume work: *The Enlightenment: An Interpretation I – The Rise of Modern Paganism.*
113 See Burckhardt, *Civilization of the Renaissance* I, part III, 175 ff.

ments of Renaissance artists and engineers, explorers and algorists, the fact remained that dusty parchments and ancient authors were no less highly valued in Medicean Florence and Rome than they had been in medieval Oxford or Paris. Indeed there were fewer books to be 'enslaved' by in the earlier era and less strict observance of ancient grammatical rules. Before Gutenberg also, there were more keen-eyed observers and intrepid voyagers who never consulted any books at all.

The dichotomy 'books versus nature' could thus be turned against the Burckhardt thesis by medievalists – as much of Lynn Thorndike's work shows. Thorndike was just as fond of denouncing bondage to old books as Burckhardt had been. He was much less ambivalent than the Burckhardtians about the role played by humanism. He went so far in derogating Renaissance book-hunters that he described the recovery of Ptolemy's treatise on geography as a setback while noting that medieval explorers had already ventured well beyond the Greek oecumene. Ignoring the problem of distinguishing 'Cathay' from 'China' or of locating either on oddly assorted scribal maps, he even claimed that 'the thirteenth century knew China better than we knew it in the nineteenth century.'[114] On such points one might object that enthusiasm for medieval accomplishments was pressed too far.[115] But it was difficult to find fault with the contention that medieval mariners and merchants were just as observant and venturesome, often better travelled, and certainly less bookish than were the contemporaries of Petrarch and his successors. Similar arguments were framed by others who learned, from studying art history, that medieval craftsmen had often taken nature as their guide. The 'astonishingly life-like' renderings of plants and animals in the sketchbooks of artists serving Hohenzollern emperors or Dukes of Milan were not completely incompatible with Burckhardt's very elastic periodization scheme. However, images found in more distant places and times (such as the famous 'leaves of Southwell' or the Bury Saint Edmunds herbal) suggested that careful observation and recording of natural forms simply did not originate with the Italians of the Renaissance.[116]

114 Thorndike, *Science and Thought*, pp. 19–20.
115 On confusion as to whether China and Cathay were the same and on earlier difficulties regarding 'Sina and the Seres,' see Needham, *Science and Civilisation in China* I, chap. 7, (d) (2), pp. 168–70.
116 Pächt, 'Early Italian Nature Studies.' On Southwell carvings and the twelfth-century herbal, see especially pp. 29–30.

Accordingly, when Whitehead came to the point of discussing the 'final ingredient necessary for the rise of modern science,' he moved into territory that was entirely foreign to Burckhardt's scheme since it was first occupied by Benedictines and then by stonecutters who worked outside Italy before Giotto's day.

Gregory and Benedict were practical men with an eye for the importance of ordinary things...The alliance of science and technology by which learning is kept in contact with irreducible and stubborn facts owes much to the practical bent of early Benedictines...

The influence of this contact between the monasteries and the facts of nature showed itself first in art. The rise of Naturalism in the later Middle Ages was the entry into the European mind of the final ingredient necessary for the rise of science. It was the rise of interest in natural objects and natural occurrences for their own sake. The natural foliage of a district was sculptured in out of-the-way spots...every art exhibited a direct joy in the apprehension of the things which lie around us. The craftsmen who executed the late medieval sculpture, Giotto, Chaucer, Wordsworth, Walt Whitman... Robert Frost are all akin to each other in this respect. The simple immediate facts are the topics of interest, and these reappear in the thought of science as the irreducible stubborn facts...[117]

It is noteworthy that nothing is said, in this famous passage, about how the craftsman's keen interest in natural forms came to be shared by philosophers to the point of checking their propensity for logic-chopping. Not only is the gap between craftsmen and schoolmen left open; the distance that separated the views of medieval artisans from those of nineteenth-century romantic poets has been incautiously closed. An introduction to a recent survey suggests how this sets perspectives askew: 'Medieval artists and craftsmen who turned from books to nature are sometimes credited with being initiators of the scientific revolution.'[118] Wordsworth, Goethe and other literati did, indeed, turn 'from books to nature,' from 'gray' theories to 'green' leaves. But 'medieval artists and craftsmen' were not well equipped to do this. Few possessed books from which to turn; many had not learned how to read.

Be that as it may, Whitehead's much quoted passage does serve to demonstrate how keen-eyed observers who took 'nature as a guide' could be seen at work in Europe outside Italy and before the Renais-

[117] Whitehead, *Science and the Modern World*, p. 27.
[118] Marsak (ed.) *The Rise of Science in Relation to Society*, introduction, p. 1.

sance. With much of Burckhardt's initial argument taken over by the enemy camp, his latter-day defenders often turn his thesis upside down. They thus stress the difference between framing a scientific theory and simply experiencing nature in the raw. They downplay naive empiricism while stressing the retrieval of Alexandrian texts. Against the medievalists who now echo the master's first verdict that humanism did 'injury to the inductive investigation of nature,'[119] they assign positive value to a classical revival which enriched scientific literature as well as belles lettres. By emphasizing the advantages of studying Euclid and Archimedes (rather than the negative effect of repeating errors drawn from Pliny or Galen) and by stressing 'Pythagorean' or 'neo-Platonic' concern with mathematics, book-hunting and Greek studies could be seen as helpful. 'In the realm of science, the outcome of this looking backward was a big leap forward...'[120] Or, as another authority put it: 'Il faut reculer pour mieux sauter.'[121]

In celebrating the rebirth of Alexandrian science under the aegis of Renaissance editors, the latter-day Burckhardtians were themselves reviving doctrines held by an earlier school. For much the same emphasis on the Alexandrian revival had been characteristic of those Victorians who had pioneered in the history of science.[122] In the days of William Whewell, however, it was commonly assumed that the middle ages were dark as far as the 'exact sciences' were concerned.[123] Poets and artists might find the Gothic revival congenial; but nineteenth-century historians of science, still under the spell of the Royal Society, believed the cause of science was bound to languish whenever belief in ghosts and spirits was sustained.[124] They saw no reason to question the claims that were made in the prefaces of early printed editions where editors and publishers congratulated themselves on

119 Burckhardt, *Civilization of the Renaissance* II, 286. This somewhat grudging concession to Libri's *Histoire des Sciences Mathématiques en Italie* (1838) is frequently repeated.
120 Rosen, 'Renaissance Science as Seen by Burckhardt and his Successors,' p. 79.
121 Boas, *Scientific Renaissance*, p. 27.
122 Whewell's description of the dark and barren 'Stationary Period of Science' between ancient Greece and modern Europe, is noted by Wightman, *Science and the Renaissance* I, 5. See also A. R. Hall, 'On the Historical Singularity,' p. 203.
123 This view is still reasserted by some historians of mathematics in the present century. See e.g. reference to 'thousand-year stupor' by Dantzig, *Number*, p. 129, and Unguru, 'Witelo and Thirteenth century Mathematics.'
124 Of course this view has also retained supporters down to the present. That the medieval Christian Church was a 'chief obstacle' to science is asserted by Wolf, *History of Science, Technology*, I, 8 among others. As is noted below, despite his viewing humanism as a curse, Randall, 'Scientific Method in the School of Padua,' departs from medievalists such as Duhem because he stresses lay, anticlerical elements.

restoring noble disciplines after centuries of neglect. That nothing of consequence had occurred in the exact sciences between the days of Ptolemy and those of Regiomontanus could be taken for granted. Needless to say this is no longer the case. A respected authority can state quite flatly 'It can no longer be held that the Middle Ages was a period of scientific stagnation...[125] Indeed Whewell's view has been vigorously assailed since the beginning of this century as a 'strange delusion.' 'The physicists of the sixteenth century were hailed as creators to whom the world owed the renaissance of the sciences. Very often they were only continuators and sometimes plagiarists.'[126]

Ever since Pierre Duhem's first volume appeared, more and more medieval commentaries and treatises have been uncovered showing that problems in 'exact sciences' were being tackled by medieval school-men by methods that came close to anticipating later innovations. In the eyes of Duhem and his successors, the Alexandrians had little need of being reborn. By encouraging continuous examination of Aristotle's physics, scholasticism had sown the seeds that were to flower in Western science, and the humanists did little save postpone fruitful results. Not only did their bookish revival point away from craft empiricism. Not only was it imbued with an élitist intellectual contempt for mechanical and manual work. It was also strongly biased against the exact sciences.

Many scholars now agree that 15th-century humanism...was an interruption in the development of science. The so-called 'revival of letters' deflected interest from matter to literary style and in turning back to Classical Anti-quity, its devotees affected to ignore the scientific progress of the previous three centuries. The same absurd conceit that led the humanists to abuse... their immediate predecessors...also allowed them to borrow from the scholastics without acknowledgement...[127]

In hailing medieval contributions to the exact sciences, some autho-rities stress the condemnation of Aristotle on theological grounds, the role played by friars at Oxford and Paris and the diffusion of major scholastic commentaries to other centers of Dominican and Franciscan learning until finally, the long ripening seeds flowered in Galileo's physics. Others (notably Randall) stay closer to anti-clerical Italianate

[125] Schmitt, 'Essay Review: A Fresh Look at Mechanics' I, 161.
[126] Pierre Duhem, cited and tr. by Rosen, 'Renaissance Science,' p. 94, from Duhem's *Système* VII, 3–4. Similar views attacking the sixteenth-century editors' prefaces are in Thorndike, *Magic and Experimental Science*, pp. 332–4. [127] Crombie, *Augustine to Galileo*, pp. 268–9.

themes by stressing the role played by lay faculties of medicine and the movement of dissident Averroists to Padua. Whether they stress theologians or lay faculties, the anti-humanists agree that attacks on scholasticism and the graduate faculties at the universities rendered a serious disservice to science by deprecating the very groups who were developing the most promising lines of inquiry. Thus the debate over the rise of modern science has become a vehicle for propelling old battles between scholastics and humanists, graduate studies and under-graduate 'liberal arts.' Instead of helping to bridge the gap between our so-called 'two cultures,' historical scholarship in this field has done much to perpetuate old feuds.

Mathematics and astronomy were assiduously cultivated...and great things were being done when humanism ushered in the anthropocentric Renais-sance and bid fair to crush all scientific interest in the world of nature.

Despite the popular legend to the contrary, for natural science, humanism was and has remained an almost unmitigated curse. Had it not centered the interests and energies of the best intellects upon the essentially unscientific... narrowly ethical classic Greeks and Romans, there is every possibility that a Galileo might have lived in the fourteenth century instead of the seven-teenth, and that scientific investigation and discovery might have been three hundred years further advanced than they are now.[128]

Humanism was *almost* an unmitigated curse because there was one alleviating factor, namely the 'revival of Alexandrian mathematical science.' By acquainting investigators with the 'methods of mathe-matical analysis and synthesis of Archimedes,' Randall admitted, quattrocento Greek studies did supply a missing ingredient.[129] Yet later research showed that even this ingredient was not completely lacking before the Renaissance. As Marshall Clagett has made clear, Archimedes was not unknown to the schoolmen and was, indeed, translated into Latin by the very same Fleming who also made Aristotle available to Aquinas. According to Clagett, Archimedes played a 'modest but nevertheless important part in that thin tradition of Greek mathematics and physics that trickled down through the Middle Ages

---

128 Randall, *The Making of the Modern Mind*, p. 212. See also passage in later rev. ed. (New York, 1940), 'by 1375 the genius of Descartes, Galileo and Copernicus had been anticipated' (p. 212).
129 Randall, *Modern Mind* (rev. ed.), pp. 215; 217. See also Randall, 'Scientific Method in the School of Padua,' p. 179. According to Butterfield, *The Origins of Modern Science*, p. 58, 'the last pocket of the science of antiquity...recovered in time to be...a factor in the formation of our modern science' was 'the works of Archimedes, made generally available in translation in 1543.' Here, as elsewhere, a key issue is how to define 'generally available.'

into modern times.'[130] A difference remained, nevertheless, between a thin trickle and a full-blown revival. The most 'advanced' work on statics in the middle ages for example was composed without Archimedes' help.[131] Although William of Moerbeke's late thirteenth-century translations made most of the corpus available (in the very form that was printed later on),[132] the more sophisticated texts tended to go unread. They could not be exploited by 'medieval mathematicians who had a rather elementary knowledge of geometry.'[133] Mastery of 'the *more advanced elements* of Archimedes', as Duhem himself noted, continued to elude the grasp of the schoolmen. Until this mastery was achieved, the 'doctrines whose seeds had been planted by Oresme and Buridan' could not 'flower or bear fruit.'[134] In addition to mathematical tools, moreover, Duhem noted that observational instruments were also lacking.

Duhem's efforts to explain why 'scholastic physics could not pass beyond the boundary to which fourteenth century Parisians had brought it' suggested that other factors than the 'curse' of humanism might have been at work. The existence of this boundary, and the incapacity of the schoolmen to traverse it, has been acknowledged by many medievalists. 'After the great beginnings in the fourteenth century' Clagett comments 'one might expect a further development at Paris in the fifteenth century. Such does not appear to be the case... Thomas Bricot's discussion suffers in comparison with the pristine account of Buridan.'[135] Similarly Moody notes that the fourteenth-century scholastics had not used 'the new ideas they had worked out

---

[130] Clagett, *Archimedes* I, 14.

[131] Clagett and Moody (ed.) *The Medieval Science of Weights* refer to the failure of Jordanus to use Moerbeke's translation in their introduction (p. 10). They also note that sixteenth-century authors such as Cardano, Tartaglia, and Benedetti, seem to borrow theorems from Jordanus without acknowledging their debt and even while criticizing his work (p. 20).

[132] According to Durand, 'Tradition and Innovation,' p. 45, the first printed editions (in 1503 and again in 1543) of Archimedes' work 'brazenly plagiarized' William of Moerbeke's text. Although accusations of plagiarism are common for the period, one may question its use before literary property rights were clearly fixed. At all events, Durand holds that Archimedes 'remained dormant' from Moerbeke's day until the sixteenth century.

[133] Clagett, *Archimedes*, p. ix. It should be noted that their 'elementary knowledge of geometry' still put the thirteenth-century schoolmen well ahead of those of the eleventh century who had no knowledge of Euclid and could not figure out what Boethius meant when he referred to the interior angles of a triangle, and – after consulting Fulbert at Chartres – were still none the wiser. See Southern, *Making of the Middle Ages*, pp. 201–2.

[134] Duhem, cited and tr. by Rosen, 'Renaissance Science,' p. 96 (from *Système* x, 45).

[135] Clagett, *The Science of Mechanics in the Middle Ages*, p. 638. See also similar comments on 'decline 'and 'stagnation' reflected in a treatise by Blasius of Parma written around 1400 in Clagett and Moody, *Medieval Science of Weights*, p. 20.

for special cases' to 'build a new science that would replace Aristotelian physics and cosmology...'[136] Even Crombie observes that 'there was no continuous mathematical tradition comparable with that in logic.'[137] Such admissions offered the latter-day Burckhardtians at least one issue they could still exploit with some success.

(b) The shortcomings of medieval science –
suggestions for a new approach

Much as the difference between transitory, limited revivals and a permanent total Renaissance was stressed by Panofsky, so too the difference between partial anticipations and actual breakthrough is underlined by those who regard Burckhardt's scheme as useful for the history of science.

Who extended the use of alphabetic letters after Jordanus Nemorarius introduced them to replace numbers in arithmetical calculations? Who developed Oresme's graphs? Why did the magnificent work of Frederick II on ornithology or of Peter the Stranger on the magnet, or of Theodore of Freiburg on the rainbow, find no worthy successor?[138]

In trying to explain why so many promising starts petered out, Rosen agrees with Duhem that medieval investigators were handicapped by the absence of certain essential pieces of equipment – such as mathematical skills and observational instruments. He also approves of Duhem's pointing to a craze for the dialectic as a major pitfall. Being trained to win 'victory in debate' rather than to 'search for the truth' deflected the talents of the schoolmen even before humanists had aroused interest in belles lettres.[139] Perhaps the most important obstacle of all, in Rosen's view, was the failure to distinguish between problems posed by falling angels and those posed by falling stones. Here the diagnosis departs sharply from that of Duhem's school by suggesting that theological concerns sidetracked medieval science from the start.[140]

---

136 Moody, 'Galileo and his Precursors,' p. 42.
137 Crombie, *Augustine to Galileo*, p. 269.
138 Rosen, 'Renaissance Science,' p. 95.
139 Rosen, 'Renaissance Science,' pp. 94–7. Duhem's objection to oral disputation (cited by Rosen from *Système* VII, 621–2) has been repeated by Dijksterhuis. See discussion, p. 506, below.
140 Rosen, 'Renaissance Science,' pp. 94–5. The extent to which mental energy was expended on describing the movements made by angels or the increase and decrease in the intensity of love seems to be brought out more clearly by Rosen than by other authorities, who often leave the supernatural context of much medieval speculation out of their accounts.

When confronted by the extreme verdict that 'humanism' was an 'unmitigated curse' for Western science, it is perhaps necessary to redress the balance by suggesting that the enthronement of theology was not an unmixed blessing. But it also seems that this particular debate has been conducted in a way that brings all kinds of prejudice into play. As long as the limitations imposed by the conditions of scribal culture go unnoted, less neutral agencies will go on being blamed. Efforts to account for the gap between medieval anticipations and seventeenth-century fulfillment seem to have reached the point where old debates are being perpetuated with diminishing returns.

The humanists turned the much praised subtle doctor of the late thirteenth century (Duns Scotus) into the nursery Dunce of the sixteenth. Modern historians, admiring the ingenuity of fourteenth-century mathematics and physics, deplore this antipathy and regard humanist worship of antiquity as having been harmful to the smooth advance of science. But however high the achievements of the fourteenth-century philosophers in certain directions, some other ingredient was needed to stimulate the development of modern science...the medieval inspiration was at a low ebb by the beginning of the fifteenth century and the Greek inspiration had, at the moment more to offer.[141]

If one is persuaded that a 'smooth advance of science' had not been possible before the advent of printing, then one may avoid assigning humanism too much credit as well as too much blame. To skip over the Latin–Arabic tradition and go more directly to the Greek sources probably did prove helpful for students of Euclid, Archimedes or Appollonius.[142] But the 'Greek inspiration' although important, was by no means the only significant ingredient that early printers supplied. The Greeks, for example, had no words for the ciphers and zeros that came via Moslem routes. The discarding of Roman numerals was an anti-classical act. The mixture of many ingredients was in itself a new source of inspiration and there were also significant changes in the way the mixture could be imbibed. By paying more attention to the enrichment of technical literature that came after printing, and by appreciating the widened range of materials that could be surveyed at one time, it might be possible to accommodate conflicting claims made

[141] Boas, *Scientific Renaissance*, p. 27.
[142] For a detailed, thoroughly documented discussion of the humanist retrieval of Greek mathematical texts in Italy see Rose, 'Humanist Culture and Renaissance Mathematics.' (A useful bibliography bearing on the debate is given in footnotes 2 and 3, pp. 46–7.)

for rival schools and to view the shortcomings of earlier scholars in a more sympathetic light.

'It was not medieval mathematicians who became oblivious of Archimedes' rule, but it was modern historians who became oblivious of medieval mathematicians' remarks a scholar who has uncovered evidence that a sophisticated mathematical tool (in the form of a theory of decimal fractions) was developed by Bonfils in the fourteenth century.[143] In fact, this tool, although invented, was never given to anyone to use. 'The theory was jotted down on a piece of paper in Hebrew, and put away. There it remained buried, for about six centuries. The old Hebrew copyist failed to grasp its meaning...Bonfils' invention exercised no influence on his contemporaries or successors...'[144] If we are trying to understand 'the rise of modern science' should we begin with Bonfils' well-kept fourteenth-century secret or Simon Stevin's well-advertised sixteenth-century work? Both started from more or less the same position – with a retrieval of Alexandrian texts. Bonfils passed nothing on to Stevin. Stevin, however, passed a great deal on to us.[145] Much the same problem is posed by Thorndike when he chides Dreyer and others for cutting Copernicus and Tycho off from their 'medieval background.' He points to a thirteenth-century treatise by Campanus of Novara arguing in favor of reducing the number of 'spheres' – a treatise that Dreyer failed to mention. Neither Copernicus nor Tycho knew of this treatise, but Thorndike believes that Dreyer, as a modern historian, ought to take 'a broader view.'[146]

Doubtless, it is useful to note that Copernicus was not the first Christian astronomer who sought to simplify the Ptolemaic scheme and that parsimony was valued by mathematical astronomers even before 'Occam's razor' had been described.[147] Nevertheless, Thorn-

---

[143] Gandz, 'The Invention of the Decimal Fractions,' p. 25. (Bonfils is better known for contributing a set of astronomical tables in his effort to help determine the Jewish calendar.)

[144] Gandz, 'The Invention of the Decimal Fractions,' p. 31.

[145] On Stevin's work, see Sarton, 'Simon Stevin of Bruges (1548–1620)'; and 'The First Explanation of Decimal Fractions and Measures (1585).' Also Dijksterhuis, Simon Stevin, and Struik, 'Mathematics in the Netherlands.'

[146] Thorndike, Magic and Experimental Science, pp. 407–8.

[147] That Copernicus' desire for simplicity is often overplayed to the point of falsifying the number of epicycles required by Ptolemaic astronomers is persuasively argued by Robert Palter, 'An Approach to the History of Early Astronomy.' When discussing the issue, the outlook of professional astronomers needs to be distinguished from that of the layman baffled by any sophisticated reckoning scheme as reflected in the oft-cited remark of the medieval king: When the complexity of drawing up tables was explained to King Alfonso, 'he remarked that it was too bad, God had failed to consult him when creating the universe.' (See Toulmin and Goodfield, The Fabric of the Heavens, p. 179; Thomas Kuhn, Structure, p. 69.)

dike's 'broader view' is too often ungenerous to sixteenth-century scientists who are seen as 'strangely deluded' because they failed to acknowledge medieval precursors whose treatises are now accessible to us but were not to them. Any adequate account of Copernicus' or Tycho's 'medieval background' must take into consideration that we now see more of the 'thin trickle' from Alexandria than did the generations before us. Sixteenth-century investigators did not have our capacity to 'search the literature.' They lacked the resources of a knowledge industry developed after four or more centuries of print. When they claimed to be 'restoring an art' or 'reviving a discipline' buried since Alexandrian days, they were not necessarily indulging an 'absurd conceit.'[148] They were often telling the truth as they saw it. The point is that they were bound to see things differently from us. To take a really 'broad view' one has to keep this difference in viewpoints constantly in mind. The technical literature inherited by sixteenth-century virtuosi was subject to discontinuities which have now been filled in. Insofar as modern historians are absent-minded on this point, they are 'strangely deluded' themselves.

In calling for more caution when extrapolating continuous lines between medieval 'precursors' and early-modern pioneers, I may seem to be simply repeating what others have already said. The fallacy of overestimating early-modern erudition has often been underscored. For example, Rosen questions the 'allegedly continuous development of modern mechanics from the thirteenth century on' on the grounds that many medieval solutions which are now seen as anticipations of Galileo's work were probably unknown to Galileo.

Galileo did not possess Duhem's enormous erudition. He was not an assiduous reader, preferring to consult what he liked to call the book of Nature …he felt little sympathy for the long-winded theological speculations, mythological allusions and autobiographical meanderings in which Kepler concealed his genuine achievement.[149]

As this citation shows, although others also object to tracing continuous lines, they usually do so without reference to the state of communications, and with the dichotomy 'books versus nature' featured prominently instead. Admittedly this dichotomy did loom large in Galileo's writings. He repeatedly urged that the book of nature was more

---

[148] Crombie, *Augustine to Galileo*, p. 269.
[149] Rosen, 'Renaissance Science,' p. 88.

trustworthy than the books of Aristotle and told his readers to turn their gaze away from pictures printed on paper to look at the real world instead.[150] With the advantage of hindsight, it is easy to understand his position and hard not to share it as well. Now that we know they were wrong, it is difficult to sympathize with those stubborn professors who seemed to trust Aristotle and Galen more than their own eyes. We are more likely to cheer on those bolder spirits who behaved like Paracelsus when he denounced Galen, burned Avicenna, and described the human body as the only trustworthy book.

Nevertheless, one must also consider that the destruction of ancient Greek and Arabic medical texts would have meant the onset of a new dark age for medieval faculties of medicine. It was not until after Avicenna's *Canon* had been secured by print that the act of discarding it could be taken as an advance. The publication of certain texts by Galen, far from perpetuating conventional views, broke new ground in the early sixteenth century. When a sixteenth-century anatomist stated that 'one ought to trust one's own eyes rather than anatomical books,' he may have been dutifully quoting from Galen himself.[151] To have burned any of Archimedes' texts, moreover, would at no point have been helpful to the budding science of mechanics. With his access to Archimedes safely secured, Galileo may have saved time by ignoring solutions buried amid 'errors and obscurities' in medieval Latin texts. But the case of Archimedes shows that reading the book of nature and studying ancient texts were by no means incompatible. And, of course, the same point applies to reading Apollonius' work on conic sections or plowing through Kepler's turgid prose. When it came to planetary astronomy, had he been as assiduous about studying certain texts as he was in training his telescope on the night skies, Galileo might have been spared some frustrating struggles with

[150] See e.g. citation in Garin, *Science and Civic Life*, p. 127. Galileo's instructions recall ancient warnings based on the corruption of hand-copied images. See pp. 485–6 above.

[151] The new awareness Vesalius achieved by careful study of each of Galen's works is stressed by Edwin Clarke, review, *Medical History* (1964), pp. 380–3. That a sixteenth-century anatomist was often merely repeating Galen's dictum when writing that 'he intended to trust his own eyes rather than books' is noted by Gernot Rath, 'Charles Estienne,' pp. 354–9. Rath also notes the fascinating problem presented by the 'rete mirabile' – a network of vessels at the base of the brain (actually found in cattle but not in man) which was described by Galen. Many Renaissance anatomists saw this 'rete' with their own eyes after dissecting human cadavers or so they said. The habit of keeping a head of an ox or lamb on hand when human dissection occurred in order to demonstrate certain arteries more clearly, helped to confuse matters. (See Boas, *Scientific Renaissance*, pp. 142–3 n.) At all events, the example shows why seeing 'with one's own eyes' is not sufficient to establish a scientific theory.

celestial mechanics.[152] Moreover, any seventeenth-century reader who took his advice too much to heart and turned away from all 'pictures printed on paper' would have lost track of all the new findings that were set forth on the sky maps, sea charts and great atlases of the day.[153]

As these comments suggest, when too much weight is placed on the antinomy: books versus nature, the crucial issue of access to technical literature is likely to be concealed. The importance of the issue is suggested by the fact that most of the great scientists of antiquity had access to the greatest libraries of antiquity. Galen of Pergamum was the foremost teacher of Vesalius, as Ptolemy of Alexandria was of Copernicus. Alexandrian achievements did not get surpassed until printing made it possible to put the 'world on paper' for all armchair travellers to see. Until the advent of printing, recovering and preserving what had been known to the ancients had to take precedence over any other task, and the chief function of a given graduate faculty was to serve as the custodian of a particular corpus of inherited texts.

Why these fourteenth-century scholastics did not exploit the new ideas they had worked out for special cases and build a new science that would replace Aristotelian physics and cosmology may well be asked. I would suggest that, as teachers in universities whose philosophical curriculum was built out of the books of Aristotle, they had neither opportunity nor motivation to overhaul; their job was to make the best sense they could out of their textbooks, not to abolish them.[154]

Insofar as they were chiefly responsible for preserving and transmitting inherited texts, natural philosophers were in much the same position as professors of the law faculties during the middle ages. As Butterfield puts it, they were 'for the most part...only playing on the margins' of Aristotle's system.[155] Much as generations of glossators and post-glossators played variations on themes set forth in the *Corpus Juris*, so too did commentators on Aristotle's physics spin off in certain new directions. In both instances, texts were reinterpreted under the

---

[152] That Galileo was alerted to Kepler's theory of elliptical orbits as early as 1612 but that he probably found Kepler's unsystematic clumsy presentation posed unsurmountable difficulties, is suggested by Father Russell. See Russell, 'Kepler's Laws of Planetary Motion, 1609–1666,' p. 6.

[153] Two recent publications issued by the Theatrum Orbis Terrarum in Amsterdam have cogent titles: de Vrij, *The World on Paper* (a descriptive catalogue of cartographical material published in seventeenth-century Amsterdam) and Koeman, *The Sea on Paper*.

[154] Moody, 'Galileo and his Precursors,' p. 42.

[155] Butterfield, *Origins of Modern Science*, p. 58.

impact of new circumstances and currents of thought. Whatever new paths were opened up in natural philosophy (as in law), however, the professors were at no time placed in a position where it would be feasible to discard rather than to explicate the corpus of inherited texts.

contrary to widely accepted opinion, there was no such thing as a fourteenth-century science of mechanics in the sense of a general theory of local motion applicable throughout nature and based on a few unified principles. By searching the literature of late medieval physics for just those ideas...that turned out, three centuries later, to be important...one can construct... a medieval science of mechanics that *appears* to form a coherent whole and to be built on new foundations replacing those of Aristotle's physics. But this is an illusion, and an anachronistic fiction, which we are able to construct only because Galileo and Newton gave us the pattern by which to select the right pieces and put them together...[156]

To imply, as does Randall, that fourteenth-century graduate faculties were on the verge of a 'breakthrough' such as the one which occurred in Galileo's day is to ignore all the limits imposed on the circulation of technical literature as long as hand-copying prevailed. If promising beginnings traced in manuscripts seemed to peter out with negligible results, if significant ancient work 'lay dormant' as did Archimedes' more difficult treatises, the conditions of scribal culture ought to receive at least some share of the blame. The many defects that plagued medieval investigations: a low level of mathematical skills, an absence of observational instruments, a tendency toward 'unbridled specula-tion' and so forth – may also be partly attributed to the state of communications.

It seems significant that Crombie refers to 'the medieval predicament of intellectual aspiration failing to get into communication with practical demand' and to 'an incomplete dialogue between theoretical concepts and practical quantifying procedures.'[157] Until print trans-formed conditions governing communication and dialogue, this kind of predicament was likely to persist. Thus 'theoretical concepts' could not make 'contact with the data of observation' until it became pos-sible to publish 'open letters' and take full advantage of reports sent from field trips by incorporating new data in updated editions of charts, maps and texts. Similarly instrument-makers had few incentives

---

[156] Moody, 'Galileo and his Precursors,' pp. 42–3.
[157] Crombie, 'Quantification in Medieval Physics,' pp. 158–9.

to make inventions known until new forms of publicity brought patronage and profits to their door.[158]

Dr. Crombie notes that the men he is considering made little contribution to the permanent body of scientific knowledge and that their actual researches are absurdly inadequate to the notions of scientific method they ostensibly entertained.

Now I find this discrepancy between alleged conception and actual performance puzzling...Dr. Crombie's only explanation...is that 'something seems to have kept the gaze [of the medieval thinkers] turned in a direction different from that which seventeenth-century science has taught us to seem obvious...'[159]

Given the difference between a sequence of corrupted copies and a sequence of improved editions of a given reference work, one might expect that scribal scholars would look in a 'different direction' from virtuosi who lived after printing. As long as energies were bent toward retrieval and preservation, little could be spared for moving ahead with new research. Careful observations once set down in writing were subject to loss or erosion over time. The feats of data-collection achieved at Alexandria represented the outermost limits of what successive generations could achieve. The recovery of Ptolemy's astronomy and later, of his geography, were naturally regarded as constituting significant advance.

Untenable and long refuted theories were revived time after time, to be refuted and rejected once again; in general this tended to foster a mental attitude which looked to the past rather than to the future and which, on the grounds that scientific truths had all been known in the past and that the only problem was to rediscover them, led investigators in precisely the wrong direction. They did not realize that science is always a thing of the future.[160]

But science was not 'always a thing of the future.' To scholars struggling over the meaning of Euclid's theorems or receiving Latin translations of the *Almagest* with gratitude, science was very much a thing of the past. Even a century-old treatise might be better than one newly composed, as an historian of medieval optics suggests.

The main optical activity of the fourteenth century was copying Pecham's

---

[158] For further discussion and examples, see p. 241, volume I above and pp. 556 ff. below.
[159] Nagel, comment in *Critical Problems* (ed. Clagett), pp. 153-4.
[160] Dijksterhuis, *The Mechanization of the World Picture*, p. 167, section II, no. 98.

Perspectiva Communis...We are no closer to the proper theory of pinhole images at the end of the fourteenth century; indeed we are possibly farther away...the thirteenth was not only clearer than the fourteenth on the problem to be solved, it was also clearer on the proper terms of the solution.[161]

In the same vein it seems unfair to complain of 'unbridled speculation' without pausing longer over the difficulty of preserving precise data against which theorizing could be checked. Similarly, the 'prominent place which oral disputation occupied in...teaching' needs to be related to the problems of providing students with books. Among other 'obstacles in the way of an unprejudiced study of nature,' Dijksterhuis singles out 'the immoderate application of an idea sound in itself, namely the stimulating and clarifying effect of an oral exchange of views.' Unfortunately, he says, echoing Duhem, oral exchange was overdone and thus

produced the reverse of the effect aimed at. The numerous disputes...on the success of which the student's career depended, inevitably resulted in arguments being conducted for the sake...of defeating one's opponents...the inquiry after truth becoming of secondary importance. In general the medieval method of university teaching had the serious disadvantage of appealing too much to human vanity...young scholars who wished for promotion had to shine in debate...[162]

It is difficult to ascertain when, if ever, scientists or academics generally ceased to engage in competitive displays of virtuosity, lost their propensity for polemics and became pure and disinterested seekers after truth. It is easier to determine when heavy reliance on verbal argument, unwritten recipes and mnemonic aids were reduced, and young scholars who were not gifted in verbal disputation could still 'shine' as authors of treatises. After the advent of printing, priority struggles could replace 'dialectical orgies' as the chief outlet for competitive drives.[163] The cause of science gained by this substitution, even if appeals to human vanity were not diminished. At all events, dependence on oral exchange was not an 'effect that anyone aimed at' during the fourteenth century nor was it peculiar to the schoolmen. It was shaped by material conditions that no one group of scholars controlled. By making the thin and unreliable flow of technical literature

161 Lindberg, 'The Theory of Pinhole Images in the 14th Century,' pp. 299; 323.
162 Dijksterhuis, *Mechanization of the World Picture*, pp. 167–8, section II, no. 99.
163 On priority struggles, see pioneering studies by Merton, collected in *The Sociology of Science*.

more responsible for the frail and often stunted character of medieval science, one might be less inclined to blame other scapegoats. Mixed motives could be more evenly distributed. The role played by theology on one hand and humanism on the other could be viewed with more equanimity and perhaps one could obtain agreement that neither served Western science as an unmixed blessing or as an unmitigated curse.

In suggesting that the advent of printing ought to figure much more prominently when setting the stage for the scientific revolutions of the early-modern era, I am not being entirely unconventional. Similar views have been set forth before – emphatically and repeatedly by the late George Sarton.

> The discovery of printing was one of the great turning-points in the history of mankind, and it was of special importance for the history of science. It changed the very warp and woof of history, for it replaced precarious forms of tradition (oral and manuscript) by one that was stable, secure, and lasting; it is as if mankind had suddenly obtained a trustworthy memory instead of one that was fickle and deceitful.[164]

Although often overlooked by other authorities, Sarton's later writings convey a sense of full awareness of the importance of printing for the history of science. Unlike either medievalists or Burckhardtians, Sarton firmly seized on the 'double invention of printing from movable type and engraving from copper plates' as an epoch-making event.[165] He pointed to the 'transmutation of values' the new technology entailed, and even went so far (too far in my opinion) as to state that 'the main event separating the period we call Renaissance from the Middle Ages was the invention of printing.'[166]

These bold assertions appear in at least three works by Sarton, and he is a founding father of the history of science. Yet they have not been taken up by others nor provoked sufficient controversy to attract attention in review articles. This may be partly because they take the form of scattered aperçus and glancing references which stop short of sustained discussion. More important, Sarton's strong positive assertions are counterbalanced by equally strong negative ones expressed in passages which underline 'the extraordinary incuriosity or inertia' of

---

[164] Sarton, *Six Wings*, p. 3.
[165] Sarton, *Six Wings*, pp. 116; 119.
[166] Sarton, *Appreciation*, p. xi; see also on p. 89; 'The age of incunabula was the infancy of the Renaissance itself.' As noted above (p. 171, volume I), to follow this suggestion would simply compound the confusion that has already surrounded the much used term.

early printers and the 'retrogressive' character of incunabula.[167] These passages reflect Sarton's repeated surprise at the way early printers perpetuated literary trends followed by copyists and overlooked new discoveries made by the *avant-garde* of the day. At one point, he refers to the 'ambivalent' effects of typography, which 'helped the birth and diffusion of new ideas but also gave a new lease on life to the old ones.'[168] His own ambivalence about the 'great turning point' was pronounced. One gains the impression of too high expectations being deflated over and over again.

One would have thought the breath-taking discoveries of the navigators... would have turned attention from the little books of men to the great book of Nature but this happened much less often than one might expect. More weight was given to Strabon's words than to those of Columbus...and the expedition of the Argonauts was considered more interesting than Magellan's.[169]

Such passages show that Sarton also undermined his positive thesis by endorsing the views of the extreme empiricist and thus discounting the significance of technical literature.[170] If science could advance only when the 'little books of men' were set aside; if 'science could not be investigated properly in any book' except the metaphorical 'great book of Nature,'[171] then shifts affecting real quartos and octavos could not be made to seem significant. In his earlier writings, at all events, the negative thesis that printing contributed to cultural inertia is so prominent, it is often (erroneously) cited as the only view of the impact of print Sarton had.

(c) *Corrupted materials duplicated: the illusion of cultural lag*

As Sarton's mixed verdict on the 'ambivalent' effects of typography may suggest, the distracting effect of debates over Burckhardt is not the only reason why the importance of printing is discounted by historians of science. The inferior quality of the materials that were duplicated by

---

167 Sarton, *Appreciation*, p. 92; *Six Wings*, pp. 27; 246, n. 14. As noted above (n. 2) the 'retrogressive character' of incunabula was first set forth by Sarton in his 1938 *Osiris* article on 'Scientific Literature' which was, in turn, inspired by the pioneering study by Klebs, 'Incunabula Scientifica et Medica.' The same view was again asserted in a 1943 article: 'The Study of Early Scientific Textbooks.'   168 Sarton, *Appreciation*, p. 168.

169 Sarton, *Six Wings*, p. 6.

170 See reference in *Appreciation*, p. 27, to physicians in Ferrara whose 'eyes were open' not just to 'Greek and Latin books in the library' but to 'the book of nature.' This passage also includes admiring references to the views of Paracelsus.   171 Sarton, *Appreciation*, p. 5.

many early printers also has to be considered. It is true that a few scholar–printers (such as Oporinus) worked closely with experts in several fields and there were some scientist–printers (such as Regio-montanus or Charles Estienne) who published innovative works themselves. In such cases, publication programs could and did take advantage of special technical expertise and thus contributed directly, as Sarton suggested, to 'the birth and diffusion of new ideas.' But most early printers and publishers simply duplicated somewhat indiscriminately whatever manuscript materials were already being circulated by stationers and scribes. They also began to put together their own collections of prophecies and prognostications and sought to exploit the appeal of the most sensational 'pseudo-science' – much as do tabloid journals even now. Thus a great deal of scientifically 'worthless' material was duplicated and gained a wide circulation during the first century of print. Even while much 'useless' stuff got printed in numerous editions; many treatises, now judged to be of unusual scientific value, suffered a fate similar to Leonardo's notebooks and 'circulated or remained stagnant' in manuscript form.[172] Because of his early death, some of Regiomontanus' work may have reached Copernicus in this form;[173] while Copernicus' own delayed appearance in print is often cited by those who caution us against exaggerating the positive function performed by the new medium. 'Scientific advance was not dependent on the printed word, indeed many scientists like Copernicus withheld their work from the press for many years...'[174]

Once his work did get printed, moreover, Copernicus' views were still slow to spread. Arthur Koestler has described *De Revolutionibus* as 'an all-time worst-seller' and scolds its author for failing to exploit publicity techniques.[175] One need not agree with Koestler in order to

[172] See Thorndike, *Magic and Experimental Science*, p. 6. In my view the 'stagnation' of innovative works in manuscript form during the sixteenth century is overplayed by Thorndike. The intervals between death and posthumous publication that he cites are not long – at least compared to those experienced by the Alexandrians. The terms 'worthless' and 'useless' have been put in quotes to convey the opinion of authorities, such as Thorndike. In my view the so-called 'rubbish' ought to be re-evaluated along the lines of analysis that anthropologists have developed.

[173] This possibility should not be exaggerated. Copernicus did *not* see a most important treatise by Regiomontanus until 1539, precisely because it remained in manuscript form, from the 1470s to the 1530s. (See p. 591 below.)

[174] Boas, *Scientific Renaissance*, p. 30. In a previous paragraph on 'printing and science' (pp. 29–30), Boas raises several pertinent issues.

[175] Koestler, *The Sleepwalkers*, p. 191. For sharp criticism of Koestler's ill-founded judgment, see Rosen, 'Biography of Copernicus,' *Three Copernican Treatises*, pp. 406–7. See also discussion in chap. 7, below.

acknowledge that printers were not mobilized by Latin-writing professional astronomers as they were by religious reformers. Evangelism came more naturally to clerics who inherited an apostolic tradition than to mathematicians who harked back to Pythagoras and temple scribes.[176] As agents of diffusion, at all events, printers snarled the periodization schemes of modern historians. For they did much in the second half of the sixteenth century to familiarize readers with the world-picture that emerged in Dante's era. It is the medieval 'Sphaera' of 'Sacrobosco' and not the *De Revolutionibus* (or the *Almagest*, for that matter) that proved 'supremely popular' and ran through hundreds of editions down to 1600 and beyond.[177]

As noted earlier, it is a mistake to imagine that 'medieval world pictures' merely 'survived' in Elizabethan times. Thanks to printers and engravers, Ptolemaic models of the movement of planets and distribution of land masses, along with Aristotle's cosmological schemes, were more often graphically conveyed and were much more widely distributed to sixteenth-century poets and playwrights than they had been to minstrels and mummers of Dante's own day. Insofar as we are likely when using the term to envisage the 'exactly repeatable' image that our textbooks contain, 'medieval' is a misleading adjective. Even the familiar geocentric diagram with its concentric circles representing celestial and infernal regions – although it had been sketched in medieval manuscripts – was not really fixed as a uniform world picture until post-medieval times.[178] Be that as it may, the reproduction of pre-Columbian maps beyond the completion of Magellan's voyages, and the duplication of pre-Copernican schemes down to Newton's day casts doubt on the proposition that printing 'hastened the trans-

---

[176] A contrast between the publicity assigned Christian themes and the secrecy that surrounded techniques and craft 'mysteries' is discussed in chap. 3, volume 1, above. See pp. 270.

[177] On the *Sphaera Mundi* by 'Sacrobosco' (sometimes called John of Holywood), see Thorndike (ed. and tr.), *The Sphere of Sacrobosco and Its Commentators*, introduction. Rosen, review of Thorndike's edition, *Isis* (1949), pp. 257–64, and entry no. 70 in Stillwell, *Awakening Interest*, p. 22. According to Johnson, 'Astronomical Textbooks in the Sixteenth Century,' pp. 293–4, 'There can be no complete census of editions of this supremely popular manual' because new versions 'are constantly turning up.' First printed in Venice in 1472, at least thirty editions were turned out before 1501 and at least 200 by 1600. As is noted below (p. 517) the 'Sphaera' like 'Ptolemy' became a vehicle for new commentaries and new data often carried in the form of appendices, supplements, etc.

[178] See reference to Tillyard, p. 79, volume 1, above. The misleading character of most modern diagrams depicting the so-called 'Ptolemaic system' is stressed by Hanson, 'The Copernican Disturbance and the Keplerian Revolution.' For description of degeneration of scribal diagrams see Van der Tak, 'Calcidius' Illustration of the Astronomy of Heracleides of Pontus,' *Mnemosyne* (1972).

mission of the new discoveries,' and leads most authorities to argue that the contrary was the case.[179] Some even argue that early printers initially limited, rather than extended, literary resources available to professional élites, because they duplicated such a small and inferior sample of extant fifteenth-century manuscripts.

Printing did not...in the first instance alter the cultural background of Europe. In fact...it may have initially limited it. Febvre and Martin have pointed out that the expense involved...made selection inevitable, so that although more copies of a given text were available, the range of texts was narrower and reflected the judgement of the printer-publisher.[180]

But manuscript books did not become less available simply because not all of them got into print at once. 'The printed book-trade did not immediately displace the ms. trade, but was simply added to it... The average library, whether public or private, contained mss. as well as printed books...a doctor might have one treatise of Aristotle in printed form and another in ms. form.'[181] However undiscriminating early printers may have been, they did not subtract from existing book supplies. They never narrowed, but continuously enlarged, the range of titles available in a given library.[182]

Perhaps printing failed to 'speed up' the adoption of 'new' theories, as Febvre and Martin assert. It is certainly difficult to measure acceleration (or even determine novelty), as one must do in order to test any proposition relating to relative speeds before and after print. (How 'rapidly' did manuscripts transmit news of Viking landfalls or theories of pinhole images? Should Ptolemy's geography be considered new or old in the 1420s?) It may be less troublesome to consider the rejection of old theories than the adoption of new ones. Perhaps we may agree that printing did 'speed up' the downfall of Ptolemaic astronomy, Galenic anatomy and Aristotelian physics. Given the authority exerted by Ptolemy's 'Great Composition' for more than a thousand years, surely the vitality of the *Almagest* in printed form is relatively short-lived. Much the same thing could be said of Galen's work on anatomy and embryology or of Aristotle's natural philosophy. The habit of citing medieval recensions and commentaries such as Sacrobosco's

179 Hellman, 'Science in the Renaissance', p. 186; Wightman, *Science and the Renaissance* I, 70; and Febvre and Martin, *L'Apparition*, p. 148.
180 McLean, *Humanism and the Rise of Science*, p. 22.   181 Sarton, *Appreciation*, p. 4.
182 Stillwell, *Awakening Interest in Science*, pp. ix–x comments on vast backlog made available by early printers.

Sphaera or Mondino's *Anatomia* as if they were independent compositions, ought not to be taken as a sign that Alexandrian works were at
any time outmoded or surpassed. Although much of the *Sphaera* was
not based directly on Ptolemy, for example, most of it did derive from
Arabic recensions of Ptolemy's great work. It is not entirely correct to
say its author 'slavishly copied an elementary Arabic treatise' since he
did draw on more than one Arab treatise and even drew on Martianus
Capella as well. Nevertheless, where the author departed from copying
others, it was usually to fall into error on his own (often by revealing
his 'pitiful ignorance of Greek').[183] Oddly enough, the same authority
who describes early printed maps as retrogressive because bound by
Ptolemaic conventions also describes this inferior medieval recension
as one of the 'most useful books of all time'.[184] The *Sphaera* may offer
valid evidence that the sphericity of the earth was known to the schoolmen well before the age of Columbus. But the superior technical
expertise of the Alexandrians, who were ultimately responsible for this
knowledge, must be kept in mind.

It is also important to note that during the later middle ages, the
effect of an astronomical text teaching that the world was round was
not reinforced by various scribal mappae mundi and crude, stylized
pictograms, which probably conveyed to 'the average uncritical copyist
or student' 'a flat disk-shaped' image of the earth.[185] According to
Bagrow, printing extended the life of the T-O diagram well into the
sixteenth century.[186] In the hands of copyists, however, this diagram
seemed to have an indefinitely long lease on life. How many armchair
travellers (before the sixteenth century) had a chance to see anything
else?

The mappae mundi survived for longer than might have been expected.
Competent portolani or coastal charts exist from the end of the thirteenth
century and probably existed even earlier, but though these might have

---

[183] See comment on John of Holywood who 'slavishly copied an elementary Arabic treatise,' in
Thomas Kuhn, *Copernican Revolution*, p. 123. Comment on ignorance of Greek comes from
Rosen's review of Thorndike's edition of Sacrobosco's work, p. 259. See also remarks on
Campanus of Novara's *Theorica Planetarum*: 'When Campanus does produce an original
argument, it can be a singularly poor one,' Benjamin and Toomer, *Campanus of Novara*, p. 25.
[184] Penrose, *Travel and Discovery*, p. 12.
[185] Durand, *Vienna-Klosterneuberg Map-Corpus*, p. 18. See also, Oakeshott, 'Some Classical and
Medieval Ideas in Renaissance Cosmography,' p. 248 where ignorance of spherical theories
among late medieval literati and many scribal illuminators is noted. Additional data is offered
in Penrose, *Travel and Discovery*, p. 25; Orr, *Dante and the Early Astronomers*, pp. 224-5 and
Skelton, *Explorer's Maps*, fig. 3.   [186] Bagrow, *History of Cartography* p. 91.

been useful to mariners, it did not follow that the learned would consent to take notice of them.[187]

How could the learned 'consent to take notice' of works that were forever kept out of their sight? Freshly drawn charts were no more immune to degradation by copying than any other scribal work. To be useful to a large number of scattered armchair travellers, maps had to be copied many times. Even portolani became stereotyped and increasingly less useful when subjected to repeated duplication.

As these remarks suggest, the average output of early printers can be described as retrogressive only when the materials they inherited from copyists are ignored. The output of copyists *is* usually ignored when developments are traced from the early middle ages onward. We are encouraged to move from one fresh composition to another – from one newly retrieved ancient masterpiece to another – until the age of Gutenberg arrives. The printer is expected to take over where culture heroes selected by hindsight – the most innovative thinker, learned scholar, or sophisticated draughtsman (as presently defined) – left off. Not surprisingly he falls short of these high expectations. In most cases he took over from the stationer and the 'slavish copyist' who handled materials which were in steady demand. The most useful and much used reference works were not only likely to be corrupted, but were also conveyed without title pages to help place or date them. They came to early printers in a state of disarray.

The Middle Ages is supposed to be a period of more or less complete stagnation. 'Progress' is thought to be solely a modern achievement. But could anyone put Isidore of Seville's *Etymologies* beside the great *Summa* of Thomas Aquinas and say there was no intellectual progress between the seventh century and the thirteenth?[188]

When instructed to think of medieval intellectual trends in this way, the late fifteenth-century printers who turned out editions of the seventh-century *Etymologies* will appear to be setting things back. In fact, they were merely continuing the work of previous copyists. They were duplicating a useful reference work that the *Summa* had not outmoded and that went on being used beyond Aquinas' day. The *Specu-*

[187] Hunter, 'Elizabethans and Foreigners,' p. 39.
[188] McIlwain, 'Medieval Institutions in the Modern World,' p. 73. A similar comment, contrasting Isidore's *Etymologies* with a late thirteenth-century *Compendium Philosophae* by a student of Albertus Magnus is made by Boüard, 'Encyclopédies Mediévales, Sur la 'Connaissance de la Nature et du Monde' au Moyen Age,' p. 301.

lum of Vincent of Beauvais and other later medieval 'encyclopedias' may 'replace' Isidore's work in modern surveys and texts. But in the late fifteenth century, habits of dating texts and arraying them in chronological sequence were just beginning to be formed. The late fifteenth-century Venetian bookseller who kept eighty copies of the *Etymologies* in stock[189] was not introducing a bizarre or anachronistic element into the bookish culture of the quattrocento. He was merely trying to continue, as earlier stationers had done, to serve a reading public that was oblivious to the kind of 'intellectual progress' modern scholars regard as obvious now.

The same point applies to the crude mappa mundi which illustrated the first edition of the *Etymologies* (printed in Augsburg in 1472) and is now registered in history books as the first world map to appear in print.[190] Although this woodcut simply duplicated the work-in-progress of contemporary copyists, it appears to be out of keeping with what we have come to expect of fifteenth-century cartography. In view of a 'continuous development' which modern scholars find 'conspicuous on manuscript maps' (after they have lined up a sequence of freshly drawn work) printed maps will seem to be regressive. This is especially true for the fifteenth and sixteenth centuries when hand-drawn mariners' charts were registering coastlines unknown to the ancient world and printed maps were just beginning to introduce Ptolemy's world to armchair travellers. When one surveys the first century of printed cartography, we are told, 'one is struck by the lack of continuous development so conspicuous in manuscript maps.'[191]

The epic discoveries of the Portuguese and Spaniards were recorded more quickly and more accurately in manuscript maps than they were in early printed maps, which were still bound by Ptolemaic conventions as well as even by those of the unrealistic mappae mundi.[192]

The advent of printing ushered in a century of cartographic retrogression marked by 'constant backslidings and bizarre anachronisms.'[193] It was not until the late sixteenth century that the work of Ortelius, Mercator and a new school of Dutch geographers finally emancipated printed cartography from archaic conventions.

---

[189] R. E. Taylor, *No Ryoal Road*, p. 200.   [190] Bagrow, *History of Cartography*, p. 91.
[191] Penrose, *Travel and Discovery*, p. 318. There is a basic paradox here for scribal cartographers were freer to make fresh maps and spend less time copying older ones after printed cartography got under way.   [192] Penrose, *Travel and Discovery*, p. 299.
[193] Penrose *Travel and Discovery*, p. 318.

The period of cartographic incunabula, characterized by a slavish following of old doctrines and strongly influenced by Ptolemy, was closed – to be succeeded by a new period, distinguished by an effort to found the knowledge of the earth not on the writings of the ancients but on first hand information and scientific investigation. Manuscript cartography had, as we have seen, freed itself long before...[194]

Insofar as printing affected developments in cartography one might conclude from Penrose's account that it introduced backslidings and anachronisms into a discipline previously subject to 'continuous development.' Yet the very fact that early printed maps were bound not only by recently recovered Ptolemaic conventions but also by those of the 'unrealistic mappae mundi' should serve as a reminder that not all of 'manuscript cartography' registered 'continuous development' in the age of Henry the Navigator.

Even when the world maps of the later Middle Ages, drawn for the most part in the scriptoria of monasteries, attempted a faithful delineation of known geographic facts...they still respected the conventional pattern [of] Christian cosmography... *Until the second half of the fifteenth century* the habitable world continued to be represented as a circular disc surrounded by the ocean sea, with Jerusalem at the center and east (with the Earthly Paradise) to the top; and the symmetrical pattern of the T-O diagrams was still reflected in the more elaborate mappae mundi...

Variations of this basic pattern were introduced to admit new geographical information or ideas or new cartographic concepts.[195]

The 'slavish following of old doctrines' registered on early printed maps reflected the prolongation of scribal conventions. Isolated portions of scribal culture had never been dominated by these conventions but, by the same token, these portions were isolated, fragmentary – largely composed of coastlines enclosing dark interiors – and destined to be garbled when assimilated into more comprehensive world pictures.

Cartographic incunabula appear bizarre because certain portions of scribal output, the very portions that were most accessible to fifteenth-century scholars, and to the printers who served them, have now slipped out of view. Once having been duplicated, diverse assorted and oddly-shaped images were later outmoded and are now concealed by print-made schemes. These schemes do not allow for localized methods of record keeping. Hence they overlook the coexistence of incongruous

[194] Penrose, *Travel and Discovery*, p. 325.
[195] Skelton, 'The Vinland Map,' p. 111. (Italics mine.)

images of the world and the prolonged absence of uniform conventions as to how to depict it. Continuous development appears conspicuous on late manuscript maps because the discontinuities that characterized scribal culture are left out of account. Hand-drawn charts accurately depicting new voyages are neither left in coastal charthouses nor transferred in garbled form onto mappae mundi nor even duplicated by early printers as up-to-date supplements to Ptolemies. Instead they are mentally transferred onto modern outline maps to mark steady advances in the age of discovery.[196] When the outlines of 'archaic' pictures are prematurely erased, the fifteenth-century vogue for Hellenistic geography is seen to be regressive. 'In the history of human knowledge there are few stranger chapters than that which records the influence of the Ptolemaic revival in delaying the formation of an accurate world map in the 15th, 16th and 17th centuries.'[197] This chapter seems strange because expectations formed by a print culture have been projected back into early-modern times. Just as Copernicus began where the *Almagest* left off, so too did Ortelius and Mercator find in the ancient *Geographia* a point of departure for their mid-sixteenth-century work. Before an 'accurate world map' could register new voyages, old rules governing the construction of world maps had to be studied and absorbed.

The Geographia is a complete cartographer's handbook. It states clearly the fundamental distinction between chorography and geography; it specifies the need of precise astronomical measurement and correct mathematical contraction, describes the method of making terrestrial globes and of projecting maps on a plane surface.[198]

The Ptolemaic revival was just as indispensable for Mercator and Ortelius as it was for Copernicus. The major achievements of the 'golden age' of map-publishing were predicated on thorough mastery of the Alexandrian heritage, which had to be assimilated before it could be surpassed. Moreover, successive editions of a 'Ptolemy' often contained surprising 'news' in the form of a preface, an extra supplement or appendix. Whereas modern publishers try to boost sales by

---

[196] See e.g. Stavrianos, *The World Since 1500*, where 'Western Man's Knowledge of the Globe' is graphically conveyed by an array of identical outline world maps with expanding knowledge indicated by spotlighting a small portion for the first century, a larger one for the fifteenth century and a still larger one for the sixteenth century. Actually no one saw any portion of the world represented in this way during the centuries indicated.

[197] C. R. Beazley, *The Dawn of Modern Geography* III, 517.

[198] Durand, *Vienna-Klosterneuberg Map-Corpus*, pp. 12–13.

tacking new titles on old textbooks, early printers served academic markets which valued ancient wisdom. New contents were often concealed in old wrappings. Counting the frequency with which old titles crop up on sixteenth-century book lists, although often taken as hard evidence of cultural lag, provides nothing of the kind. Even the much published *Sphaera* of Sacrobosco might be filled with fresh data before being issued by the early printers.[199]

Thus the duplication in print of extant scribal maps and ancient geographical treatises, even while seeming to provide evidence of 'backsliding,' also provided a basis for unprecedented advance. To found knowledge of the whole world 'on first-hand information' is, literally speaking, quite impossible. Access to a wide variety of second-hand information furnished by reports, ship's logs, charts, over the course of many generations is required. Above all, a uniform grid is needed for assimilating all the assorted information that may be supplied. Before the outlines of a comprehensive and uniform world picture could emerge, incongruous images had to be duplicated in sufficient quantities to be brought into contact, compared and contrasted.[200]

The production of an atlas such as the *Theatrum* with its alphabetical index, list of authors consulted, and orderly progression of maps which expanded in number over time, entailed an enterprise whose novelty needs underscoring. Collaborative ventures in large-scale data collection, which had been intermittent and limited to the facilities provided by one charthouse or manuscript library became continuous and ever-expanding. Here in particular it would be helpful to elaborate on comments made in passing, about the way new presses increased scholarly access to texts. 'The tyranny of major authorities inherent in small libraries was broken. The scholar could indulge in an ease of computation and cross-referencing formerly unthinkable.'[201]

Limits set by the very largest manuscript libraries were also broken. Even the exceptional resources which were available to ancient Alexandrians stopped short of those that were opened up after the shift from script to print. The new open-ended information-flow that

---

[199] Thus the second chapter of sixteenth-century editions of the *Sphaera* is a good place to look for early references to the 'new world' according to Goldschmidt, 'Not in Harrisse.' See also examples of new data given on p. 590, below.

[200] Brown, *Story of Maps*, pp. 160–1 discusses some of the problems entailed in the ten years spent by Ortelius and his collaborators planning and designing the novel publication.

[201] A. R. Hall, *Scientific Revolution*, p. 10.

commenced in the fifteenth century made it possible for fresh findings to accumulate at ever-accelerated pace. It extended the number of skilled investigators who could collaborate on large projects, such as mapping the earth and locating all the creatures, plants and rocks that could be found upon it. In this regard, the walled libraries of the age of scribes may be related to the closed cosmos envisaged by generations of philosophers. Limits had been set to the data that could be collected, preserved, and transmitted about distant landmasses and oceans, exotic flora and fauna, or constellations seen in Southern skies. Just as geographic space stopped short at the Pillars of Hercules, so too did human knowledge itself appear to stop short at fixed limits set by scribal data pools.

Note how frequently the Pillars of Hercules, with their supposed inscription 'ne plus ultra' are used to indicate the closed circle of ancient knowledge... the vast increase in geographical knowledge over that of the ancients operated consciously and unconsciously in undermining the supposed superiority of the classical writers, a fact later conspicuously revealed in various geographical figures of speech used to express modern progress in knowledge.[202]

With the shift from script to print, the closed circle was broken. Just as the number of known plants, having increased from 600 to 6,000, multiplied ever more rapidly thereafter, so too many other forms of data collection – entailing feedback from reader to publisher – pointed to an indefinite expansion. Concepts of limitlessness and infinity were not unfamiliar among Christian scribal scholars, to be sure, but such concepts were employed to contrast the limitations of human cognition with the ineffable, unknowable divine mysteries of the Godhead. When seventeenth-century natural philosophers titled their treatises 'Plus Ultra,' they were expressing something more than traditional Christian doctrines pertaining to Adam's dominion over nature. They were suggesting that limits previously set to human knowledge were illusory. They were laying claim in the name of future generations to all the unfathomed depths and celestial regions that had always before been reserved for God alone.

When engaged in comparing the limited Greek oecumene with the ever-widening horizons of the age of reconnaissance or when tracing the cosmological movement from 'a closed world to an infinite

---

[202] R. F. Jones, *Ancients and Moderns*, p. 290, n. 25.

universe,' it is worth devoting more thought to the appearance of a 'library without walls.' The large library, as Sarton noted, is just as much a scientific instrument as is the telescope or cyclotron.[203] Laboratory facilities were lacking to sixteenth-century observers. Star-gazers still had to rely only on their 'naked' eyes. But the flow of information had been re-oriented, and this had an effect on natural philosophy that should not go ignored.

[203] Sarton, 'A Summing Up,' p. 370.

6

TECHNICAL LITERATURE GOES
TO PRESS:
SOME NEW TRENDS IN SCIENTIFIC
WRITING AND RESEARCH

I. BRIDGING THE GAP BETWEEN TOWN AND GOWN

It is worth pausing over the fact that a new kind of collaborative venture in data collection had been set in motion even before laboratory facilities were built or new observational instruments had been invented. The shift from script to print helps to explain why old theories were found wanting and new ones devised even before telescopes, microscopes, and scientific societies had appeared. Gutenberg's invention not only preceded Galileo's tube; it was a more versatile aid and affected a wider range of data. Some professors shunned controversy and withheld treatises from the press just as some refused at first to look through the telescope. But none failed to consult printed reference guides or preferred to have to copy out tables by hand. Whatever views were held concerning Aristotle, Ptolemy or Galen, whatever objections were posed against using vernaculars or courting publicity; printed maps, charts, and diagrams found rapid acceptance from all. Indeed Latin-reading professional groups profited from new kinds of book learning just as much as did untutored artisans. In view of the many new printed treatises that William Gilbert consulted, for example, it is somewhat misleading to describe *De Magnete* as being based 'only on observations and experiment.'[1] Gilbert probably gleaned as much useful data from reading technical works composed by others as from observing and experimenting on his own. That Tycho Brahe and Isaac Newton could learn so much by reading on their own also had significant consequences for their work. Logarithms and slide-rules, moreover, served Latin-reading astronomers as well as vernacular-

[1] Zilsel, 'The Origins of William Gilbert's Scientific Method,' p. 17.

reading artisan-engineers. Charts and diagrams helped professors as well as surgeons, surveyors and merchant adventurers. Increased freedom from 'slavish copying' and fruitless book-hunting was particularly helpful to teachers and students. Until the recent advent of computers, has there been any other invention which saved so many man-hours for learned men?

It is also worth noting that professors were encouraged to spend more time in urban workshops with mechanics and merchants after bookhands were replaced by typefonts and master printers took over from university stationers and scribes. Professors and printers began to engage in fruitful collaboration almost as soon as the new presses were installed. The former were often hired by the latter to serve as editors, translators or correctors. They sometimes helped to finance and often supervised the output of medical and astronomical texts. As a young professor of mathematics at Ingolstadt, Apianus (Peter Bienewitz) also ran his own press. As royal professor of mathematics, Oronce Finé worked in several Paris print shops. New careers as science writers were opened to professors no less than to artisans, while the scientist–printer deserves to be placed alongside the scholar–printer as a new kind of protean, Renaissance man.

It seems necessary to pause over interchanges between printers and professors because current interpretations tend to keep them apart – even while conveying the impression that changes wrought by printing left academic science undisturbed. In this regard two opposite schools reinforce each other. On the one hand, those who stress problem-solving and the life of the mind when considering scientific change, are likely to exclude early printers and their presses along with other 'external' or 'socio-economic' factors. Even if they do not go as far as a review article suggests, by lumping the printing press with 'witchcraft and patent law' as 'alien to intellectual history,'[2] they are not likely to regard the establishment of printers' workshops as having a direct bearing on the technical and cerebral activities with which they are concerned.

On the other hand, those who stress the 'sociological roots' of early-modern science and try to integrate star-gazing with more mundane activities also drive a wedge between new workshops and old lecture halls.[3] Artist–engineers, merchants, mechanics, and other lay urban

---

[2] 'Toward a New History of the New Science,' *Times Literary Supplement* (Sept. 15, 1972).
[3] See e.g. Zilsel, 'The Sociological Roots'; Struik, 'Mathematics in the Netherlands'; Baron, 'Toward a More Positive Evaluation.'

groups are thus set against clerical Latin-reading élites. Insofar as a 'progressive' alliance of capitalists and artisans is arrayed against tradition-bound clerical–feudal ideologues, this alignment seems to owe something to Marxist schemes. It also fits well with the older polemic of lay humanists against scholastics and of artisan-authors against Sorbonnistes. It owes a special debt to attacks on Oxford and Cambridge by seventeenth-century Puritan pamphleteers. Whatever its sources, the dichotomized scheme often does more to hinder than to help us to see how social factors may be related to scientific change. 'Sociological roots' are artificially prevented from ever bearing anything but bitter fruit for Latin-reading learned men. The fact that early printers were close to merchants and mechanics is mistakenly taken to indicate that they were distant from professors and professional élites. When new contributions from non-academic milieux are stressed by historians of science, the importance of Gutenberg's invention is often acknowledged. But when dealing with theories that were developed or recast within libraries and lecture halls, the impact of printing is usually left out of account.

The misleading impression conveyed by this lopsided approach is akin to that developed in Reformation studies, where the impact of print on heresy is stressed while its impact on orthodoxy is ignored. As was the case with Thomist theology or Jerome's translation of Scripture, so too it seems likely that late medieval natural philosophy did not continue unchanged.[4] Much as theologians were divided over new issues posed when Bible study went from script to print, so too were other university faculties affected by new methods of processing Aristotelian and Alexandrian texts.

In the late fifteenth and sixteenth centuries various forces combined to undermine scholastic Aristotelianism as a dominant philosophy...

Mental horizons were extended...by the humanists who recovered a whole world of classical thought which however was now seen to exhibit far greater conflict and diversity than had been evident from the few ancients who dominated scholastic thinking...

---

4 For excellent summary of pertinent issues and suggestions for further research on Renaissance Aristotelianism, see monograph and article by Schmitt, *A Critical Survey and Bibliography*; 'Toward a Reassessment of Renaissance Aristotelianism.' How the Aristotelian tradition was affected by the shift from script to print seems to me to be worth further investigation. That many important scholastic scientific treatises by fourteenth-century Paris and Oxford masters were printed between 1470 and 1520 is documented by Clagett, *Science of Mechanics*, pp. 652–3 and by Schmitt, 'Essay Review,' p. 173, n. 10.

There was...a re-structuring of scholastic Aristotelianism to meet the new challenges...Protestant neoscholasticism borrowed...from learned Jesuit commentators of the Iberian peninsula. At some of the Italian universities notably Padua, a 'purified' Aristotelianism provided the background for important advances in the life sciences...[5]

Heightened awareness of 'conflict and diversity' in the classical tradition, surely owed something to the enrichment of literary diets that came with increased book production. The same point applies to clashes between 'Greeks' and 'Arabs.' Advanced instruction in Aristotle's physics was less likely to clash with Ptolemaic computations when complete manuscript copies of the *Almagest* were circulated among a small circle of professional astronomers and rarely seen by commentators on Aristotle.[6] Similarly, differences between Arabic and Galenic doctrines were less troublesome when the full Galenic corpus had not been retrieved. Once printed editions of Averroes and Ptolemy, Avicenna and Galen could be studied in the same place at the same time, contradictions previously concealed by glosses and commentaries and compilations were laid bare.[7] As was the case with the Scriptures, the process of copy-editing in the printers' workshops also encouraged a new awareness of internal inconsistency in a given textual tradition, forcing literalists and modernists apart.

Recent investigations would...tend to make one hesitant in concluding that the innovations and criticisms in the academic sciences – astronomy, physics, anatomy – which we call the scientific revolution, were the product solely or even chiefly of forces and changes operating outside the universities. Rather it would seem that in relation to these subjects it was a case of internal strife, one party of academic innovators trying to wrest the field from a more numerous one of academic conservationists. Certainly this was the case with Vesalius and his fellow anatomists, with Copernicus, with Galileo. It was the academic and professional world that was passionately divided on the question of the inviolability of the Galenic, Aristotelian or Ptolemaic doctrines; these quarrels of learned men had as little to do with capitalism as with the Protestant ethic.[8]

[5] Rattansi, 'The Social Interpretation of Science,' pp. 7–8.
[6] For data on Averroist critique of Ptolemy, printed in Padua in 1473, and Rheticus' plea for Ptolemy's return to his ancient place of honor after long exile from the schools, see Rosen, *Three Copernican Treatises*, pp. 132, 141, 195n, 251. See also chap. 7, n. 15, below.
[7] See e.g. discussion of 'gulf' between Arab commentators and texts of Galen and Hippocrates disclosed by Symphorien Champier in published texts of 1507–33. Holmes, 'A Brief Survey of the Use of Renaissance Themes,' pp. 38–9. See also Temkin, *Galenism*, pp. 126–9.
[8] A. R. Hall, 'The Scholar and the Craftsman,' p. 7.

If the effects of printing were more completely described, 'forces and changes operating outside the universities' could probably be more clearly related to the 'quarrels of learned men.' At the same time the position of 'academic innovators' and the disputes they provoked also might be clarified. Regulations fining professors for departing from a given text, for example, had served a useful purpose when lecturing was linked to dictating and students served as scribes; for the transmission of precise information was imperilled whenever a professor altered a passage or interpolated a comment. After the advent of printing, such rules lost much of their reason for being. Yet even as their vital functions ebbed, they were harder to evade and could be enforced more rigorously. The petrification of rules holding teachers to certain texts did not mean that universities were impervious to forces or changes operating outside. On the contrary! Petrification was itself a form of change and precipitated academic divisions of a new kind. Ciceronians, Bartholists, Peripatetics, and Galenists were placed in much the same position as orthodox churchmen who objected to revision of the Vulgate text when scholar–printers set to work.

But sixteenth-century universities also sponsored trilingual studies and produced polyglot scholars who edited and translated Bibles. It would be misguided to take official statements objecting to any tampering with the Vulgate as representing all biblical scholarship in the sixteenth century. To take regulations fining professors who departed from Galen as representing all academic science during the early-modern era seems no less unwarranted. At present, however, historians of science who deal with the effects of printing do seem to depict academic science as inflexibly set against innovation. A case in point is provided by Stillman Drake's pioneering essay on printing and the rise of early-modern science.[9] As a suggestive discussion of a much neglected topic, Drake's treatment is illuminating. Nevertheless, it discounts the impact of print on Latin-writing professional élites and conveys the impression that the 'spread of science beyond the Universities' left academic institutions untouched. An innovative 'non-u' science, spearheaded by early printers, is thus sharply contrasted with an older 'academic' science that resisted the winds of change and remained 'Aristotelian to the core.' 'Official science,' we are told, 'continued after the invention of printing much as it had before.'

9 Drake, 'Early Science,' *passim*.

Without pausing over the question whether academic Aristotelianism itself did not undergo change and without taking up other criticisms that have been directed at Drake's views,[10] it must be noted that he deals with the effects of print on a limited portion of early-modern science. Developments in mechanics pointing to the downfall of Aristotelian physics are stressed. Vernacular translation by self-taught artisan-authors, such as Tartaglia, loom large. But innovations in such fields as astronomy and anatomy, which were of equal significance in the so-called 'rise of modern science,' are set aside. Thus, although the resistance of Paduan professors to Galileo's views is stressed, the repudiation of Ptolemaic theories by Copernicus, Rheticus, Maestlin, Kepler et al. is passed over. The same point may be applied to the repudiation of Galenic theories by Latin-writing professors of anatomy, from Vesalius to Harvey. As these cases suggest, the portrayal of 'official science' as tradition-bound and impervious to print culture, which some authorities may find plausible when Galileo's assault on Aristotelian physics is stressed, becomes more implausible when the downfall of Ptolemy and Galen is also brought into view.

Even when discussion is restricted to Galileo's career, moreover, it seems unwise to place professors at too great a distance from printers. After all, Galileo was himself a Paduan professor when his first vernacular publication appeared.[11] His exploitation of publicity as a self-proclaimed inventor of the telescope also occurred while he was still holding an academic chair. His lectures at the university had to conform to fixed texts, but his freedom to publish was not thereby restrained. Interpretations based on the old polarities which set the lay humanists of Florence against the Aristotelian faculties of Padua are misleading in this regard. A recent article goes so far as to credit Florentine humanism with the capacity to have created a general reading public, to have provided Galileo with his audience and to have rendered

10 See Schmitt's 'Essay Review' for pertinent criticisms of Drake's general approach. Although issues pertaining to printing are not raised, Schmitt poses several objections that concur with views expressed here. See especially treatment of Latin versus vernaculars (p. 167) and of exclusive focus on mechanics (p. 175, n. 41 and 42).

11 This was a vernacular pamphlet 'Le Operazioni del compasso geometrico et militare' printed in 1606, on a press in Galileo's 'own house' and dedicated to Cosimo II. It described a 'proportional compass' or 'sector,' presumably 'invented in 1597' and gave rise to a priority dispute between Galileo and a rival claimant that was decided in favor of Galileo by the university officials. Galileo's printed defense against the 'calumnies and impostures' of his rival, in 1607, marks his debut as a formidable polemicist. See Drake, Discoveries and Opinions of Galileo, p. 16, and two essays in Galileo, Man of Science, (ed. McMullin): Bedini, 'The Instruments of Galileo,' pp. 256–92; Boyer, 'Galileo's Place in the History of Mathematics,' p. 237.

him independent of established authority. 'The public to which Galileo turned for support after 1610 was composed not of university professors but of ordinary citizens like Michelangelo Buonarroti Jr, Jacopo Nardi, Cosimo di' Bardi and, of course, Cosimo de Medici and Cristina of Lorraine.'[12] The names cited are not those of 'ordinary citizens' in most senses of the word. If a grand duke and a grand duchess are to be viewed as forming a 'general reading public,' then humanism may well deserve credit for this category. But Florentine princes and patricians (who did, after all, represent 'established authority' of a kind and who had supplied patronage to scribal scholars for centuries) probably ought to be distinguished from the even more 'general' reading public who purchased both the Latin version and the vernacular translations of the *Starry Messenger* in the early seventeenth century. At all events, Galileo was in some ways more independent of 'established authority' and more certain of reaching the 'general reading public' while he remained a Paduan professor than after he was assured of a living by the Grand Duke of Tuscany.

As a professor at Padua, Galileo had not been kept from association with Venetian merchants, mechanics, or men-of-affairs. Even while holding a university chair, he had been able to lay claim to new intellectual property-rights as an inventor and instrument-maker. He expressed a wish to devote himself more exclusively to writing books, in his letter requesting Medici patronage. Nevertheless he had managed quite well as a Paduan professor to get several works into print. News of Galileo's tube had travelled fast and far. When considering quattrocento trends, one may perhaps contrast the 'clerical atmosphere of medieval...universities' with the 'symbiosis of thought and action' in Florentine workshops. As an 'heir' of Florentine humanism, Galileo probably had such contrasts in mind.[13] Yet it seems doubtful that moving to Florence enabled Galileo to link 'the world of scientific research' with 'that of technology.'[14] The move brought him aristocratic

[12] Cochrane, 'Science and Humanism,' p. 1057. Since Galileo had already dedicated his 1606 pamphlet to Cosimo II, he was not really 'turning' to his former pupil, the Grand Duke of Tuscany, *after* 1610 'for support' but rather continuing to cultivate a potential patron whose favor he had long sought. For biographical data see Geymonat, *Galileo Galilei*.

[13] Baron, 'Toward a more Positive Evaluation,' stresses the university-workshop opposition and Eugenio Garin's two essays, 'Galileo and the Culture of His Age,' and 'Galileo the Philosopher,' in his *Science and Civil Life*, persuasively depict Galileo as an heir of the Florentine humanist tradition.

[14] Drake, introduction to 'Letters on Sunspots,' *Discoveries and Opinions*, p. 78. Drake's suggestion that men-of-affairs at the Florentine court made more suitable companions than Galileo's

patronage but took him away from easy access to Venetian presses – to the very workshops where the two worlds had already become one. When he left the university, he not only left Latin lectures, Aristotelian curricula and hostile colleagues behind; he also placed himself in a position that resulted in his house arrest. He moved to Florence partly, perhaps, because he was nostalgic about his native region; more certainly because he had finally secured Medici patronage. His preference for the vernacular was not accompanied by any democratic distaste for currying the favor of élites. When discussing mathematics, astronomy, or anatomy, Galileo could be quite contemptuous of the common man who relied on 'common sense' or sense impressions. In his insistence on the superiority of the trained investigator to the ordinary observer he often seems to be more of an élitist than some of his interpreters suggest.[15] His move to Florence won him princely patrons and audiences with popes. He also achieved membership in an early scientific society. But he lost immunity from the Inquisition and had to bow, in the end, to non-academic thought-control.

In Galileo's case, scientific innovation went together with a flair for publicity, a resort to vernacular pamphleteering, and attacks on Aristotelian professors. Yet others who contributed to the downfall of Ptolemy and Galen often shied away from publicity and wrote for Latin-reading peers. Galileo created the greatest stir, and his trial had spectacular historical consequences. Thereafter the 'quiet' rise of modern science was caught up in the 'noisy' clash of rival faiths. Galileo's case was exceptional, and exceptions – however spectacular – ought not to be taken as rules. This is especially true of efforts to relate print culture to early-modern science.

Reverberations from the seventeenth-century trial are likely to lead us astray when dealing with earlier developments. Even when dealing with the century of genius, a distorted view may result. In his persua-

'former professorial colleagues' also seems to me to overlook the diverse opportunities extended by the Venetian milieu. On pp. 70–1 Drake cites a passage from Doni's *I Marmi* contrasting the lively stimulating Florentine atmosphere with the 'dreamy' Venetian one. Yet Doni himself was better supported by Venetian presses than Florentine ones. Contrasts between the two city-states ought to allow for the changing position of printers and censors within them, especially when dealing with early-modern science.

15 See passages in 'Letter to the Grand Duchess Christina,' where he indicates the shortcomings of 'vulgar' and 'brutish views' (Drake, *Discoveries and Opinions*, pp. 196–7). See also comment by Shea, *Galileo's Intellectual Revolution*, p. 47, n. 36 questioning conventional view of Galileo appealing 'over the heads' of professors to 'ordinary' laymen.

sive account of 'Galileo and the Culture of His Age' for example, Eugenio Garin describes how the Italian universities, after welcoming censorship to crush anti-Aristotelians, taught 'a tired, used-up knowledge that found no echo anywhere.' At an earlier time, Garin suggests, a curriculum reform had seemed possible. 'The introduction of new texts' by Platonists and other innovators had begun to undermine ancient authorities and created a 'tension between the universities and the mental climate outside them.' But the invaders were repelled. Pisa and Padua became strongholds of reaction. A prolonged battle of books between the lay humanists of Florence and the scholastic professors of Padua ended in a defeat of the former. In Garin's version, which resembles that of Drake, the universities were left 'to propagate nothing but an utterly exhausted tradition.'[16]

When Galileo is made to share 'the culture of his age' with other contemporary scientists, the Italian academic climate appears in a somewhat different light. William Harvey was at Padua between 1592 and 1610, and studied under a professor who served as Galileo's doctor there. Harvey went to Padua on the advice of his mentors at Cambridge to take advantage of the superior training that was available on the continent. To the erstwhile Cambridge undergraduate, Paduan studies were notably innovative and experimental. Aristotle loomed in certain courses, to be sure. But this was probably more of a help than a hindrance in Harvey's work.[17]

A rigorous training in logical argument as well as in techniques of dissection were fruitfully combined in De Motu. It could be argued that required courses in logic actually sharpened Harvey's perception of contradiction. It is clear, at all events, that he did pay close attention to shaky arguments in newly printed anatomy texts (even pausing to correct an important misprint) and that the much abused universities

---

[16] Garin, *Science and Civil Life*, pp. 94–7, 101. In previous passages, pp. 80–9, Garin makes indirect references to the impact of print by bringing in the repressive effects of the Index on Italian cultural life. His condemnation of Paduan Aristotelianism is linked to his belief that the Paduan philosophers were spurious 'freethinkers' who took advantage of the Index to censor anti-Aristotelian opponents and thus stifle scientific advance. For different view of the University of Padua, see Randall's article, 'Scientific Method' and many later references cited by Schmitt, 'The Faculty of Arts at Pisa.' On p. 250, n. 24 Schmitt dismisses the notion of a university as 'a center of free inquiry' as a 'romantic ideal' rather than an historical reality.

[17] See Whitteridge, *William Harvey*, pp. 3–4. Whitteridge notes that the founder of Harvey's College at Cambridge, John Caius, had been friendly with Vesalius at Padua and had later attended dissections by the barber–surgeons of London even while serving as a fellow of the Royal College of Physicians, thereby bridging town–gown divisions. Harvey's use of Aristotle has been underlined in many studies by Walter Pagel. See e.g. 'William Harvey.'

had prepared him rather well for this task.[18] 'The doors of sixteenth century universities were closed to new scientific ideas from the outside,' according to one of Galileo's biographers.[19] Harvey's model of the circulation of the blood was a new scientific idea that came from the inside – after more than a half-century of almost exclusively academic debate. Harvey was not a proponent of vernacular science-writing, nor did he share Galileo's flair for publicity and distaste for academic life. On the contrary, he wrote in Latin for specialists and procrastinated about attacking Galen in print.[20]

To make too much of Harvey's Aristotelian Latin learning, however, would be just as misguided as to overplay Galileo's occasional use of the vernacular. Although Drake's discussion of printing seems to me to be one-sided it does nevertheless offer a necessary corrective to the disdainful treatment of the output of early printers by medievalists such as Lynn Thorndike. Thorndike briskly dismissed the 'bungling' of amateurs and the 'billingsgate' of Paracelsus. In his view, the new presses served only to spread a 'little learning' 'more thinly over a greater population.' They augmented superstition while obscuring genuine scientific work.[21] Contributions to the 'exact' sciences made by Northerners, such as Gemma Frisius or Simon Stevin and by the numerous Italians who are discussed by Drake – all of whom wrote in the vernacular for literate laymen – are simply left out of Thorndike's account. Yet these vernacular science-writers did more than spread a smattering of old learning thin. Granted that Latin remained the language of the cosmopolitan Commonwealth of Learning; vernacular science-writing aimed at non-academic readers (including prospective patrons and purchasers of instruments) probably did help to transform some older fields of learning. It attracted amateur interest in new discoveries while creating new disciplines, such as applied mathematics and mechanics, at the same time.

[18] Harvey's close study of the 1593 edition of Realdus Columbus' *De Re Anatomica* and his picking out an important misprint (of *systole* for *diastole*) is described by Whitteridge, pp. 49, 70–2, 92.
[19] Drake, 'Early Science,' p. 49. Here, as elsewhere, Drake agrees with Garin.
[20] Whitteridge, *William Harvey*, pp. 105–6. Harvey's choice of a relatively unknown foreign firm (run by an English relative of the de Bry family in Frankfurt) for the first edition of *De Motu* is attributed to persuasion exerted by Robert Fludd. Weil, 'William Fitzer,' pp. 142–3. Harvey's friendship with Fludd links him to heterodox Rosicrucian currents which seem to be excluded from Whitteridge's account. The first favorable notice of Harvey in print came from Fludd in a Frankfurt publication of 1629. The major boost came from Descartes in *Discours sur la Méthode* (1637). See Whitteridge, *William Harvey*, pp. 150–3.
[21] Thorndike, *History of Magic and Experimental Science*, pp. 5 ff.

The applied mathematicians of the sixteenth century, for example, helped to transform the language of numbers in a way that laid the basis for later innovations by virtuosi such as Fermat and Descartes. Members of this new occupational group, although eager to profit from publicity, ought not to be categorized as mere popularizers or publicists.[22] Nor does this point apply only to the new mathematical practitioners described by Dirk Struik or E. G. R. Taylor. It applies just as well to the 'chemical teachers' described by Owen Hannaway and Marie Boas. The latter points to 'simple, precise and detailed' works of instruction such as 'Chemistry for Beginners' which left 'no room for alchemical secretiveness' and won acceptance for a new field of study in the schools.[23] Similar developments affected other life-sciences, as numerous medical treatises and botany books attest. In all these fields, a new style of exposition, 'simple, precise and detailed' affected interpretations of natural phenomena and encouraged a deflation of overblown theories which Latin verbiage had previously concealed.

One may agree with Thorndike that printing opened up new opportunities for bunglers and braggarts to set forth absurd claims and for charlatans to profit from mass credulity. But one also ought to note that verbal confidence games had not been unknown in medieval lecture halls. Certain kinds of academic trickery became less feasible. Arguments aimed at intelligent practitioners, at architects, surveyors, surgeons, apothecaries, navigators and the like, were bound to be different from those which were designed to impress academic colleagues or to win a rhetorical contest held at papal and princely courts. The increased use of vernaculars sometimes did a disservice to the cosmopolitan Commonwealth of Learning.[24] It often owed much to an

22 On important contributions made by mathematical practitioners and instrument-makers in paving the way for later departures from 'traditional methods and standards of solution' associated with the work of Fermat and Descartes see Mahoney, *The Mathematical Career*, pp. 8–10; Struik, 'Mathematics in the Netherlands'; and E. G. R. Taylor, *The Mathematical Practitioners of Tudor and Stuart England*.

23 Boas, *Scientific Renaissance*, pp. 164–5; see also Hannaway's discussion of Libavius and his confrères.

24 In a letter to a Paduan friend about his *Letters on Sunspots*, Galileo shows the impossibility of writing for the vernacular-reading 'everyman' without excluding foreign scientists – such as his German Jesuit rival, Scheiner, who could not read Italian. See citation in Drake, introduction to *Letters on Sunspots*, in *Discoveries and Opinions*, p. 84. In the *Sidereus Nuncius*, where he wanted his message to reach beyond compatriots to 'astronomers and philosophers all over Europe as quickly as possible' (Drake, introduction to *The Starry Messenger*, p. 19) Galileo wrote in Latin. In either language, however, he employed a clear plain prose style, aimed at

insular, patriotic outlook that worked at odds with the authors' professed desire to serve humanity. It was partly propelled by the desire to profit from an invention or an instrument that could be bought at a given author's home. Nevertheless vernacular science-writing enlarged and democratized the Commonwealth of Learning. It extended the range of talents that were tapped, linked instrument-making with mathematical theorizing and helped to propel data collection in many new directions.

Yet although the increased use of vernaculars was a significant development, it was by no means the most important of the many changes undergone by scientific communications. For one thing, many of the new 'simple, precise and detailed' texts were first written in Latin and translated thereafter. For the most part, scientific textbook writing was done by authors (Agrippa, Robert Recorde, Pacioli *et al.*) who had command of both ancient and modern tongues. For another thing, the chief language of science (as Galileo pointed out) was neither Latin nor the 'Volgare,' but numbers and figures, circles, triangles, and squares. The discarding of Roman numerals or rhymed verses in old French represented changes that cut across town–gown divisions and penetrated college halls. These changes are well reflected in the new printed materials turned out by applied mathematicians, whose books often served to advertise their instruments. Thus diverse textual traditions, previously transmitted by separate channels, were freely combined. 'With the Greek rudiments, they freely mixed material taken from arabic texts and applied algebra.' The new possibility of printing tables and maps led to practical compromises that violated philosophical dogma but produced genuinely useful paper tools.

trigonometric theorems...meant little to the navigator until translated into computational techniques...the preparation of...tables in turn required that one surrender geometrical exactitude for accurate arithmetical approximation and interpolation...in contrast to the canons...the navigator, the map maker, the engineer...treated arithmetic and geometry as realms with a common open border...Stevin...honored Archimedes' geometry, devised...decimal place-value fraction...and did research in algebra... Napier...conceived of logarithms in terms of motions of points along a line but Euclid was ignored as ratios of these motions were computed in numbers

clarification rather than mystification. For discussion of his literary styles see D. Della Terza, 'Galileo, Man of Letters,' pp. 1–23.

and rounded off...The goal was not theoretical rigor but a sufficiently accurate technique for manipulating large numbers and trigonometrical functions.

The same practical spirit overrode the classical...distinction between the mathematical and mechanical and fostered increasing research on mathematical instruments...Within six years of the publication of Napier's... *Logarithms* and within three years of Briggs'...Richard Gunter and Edmund Wingate had reduced logarithmic computation to a small instrument, the first slide rule.[25]

Uniform mathematical symbols brought professors closer to reckonmasters. They did not separate academicians from artisans, although they did move scientists away from poets. To the warfare between scholastics and humanists was added a new schism, between the party of number and the party of words. Print insured a victory of the 'algorists' over the 'abacists.' It saw new arithmetic texts displace Boethius in the schools. Other branches of the *quadrivium* and more advanced mathematics were also transformed. The achievements of a sixteenth-century virtuoso such as Viète were not based on a critique of Aristotle's physics, but on manipulating Indo–Arabic symbols to solve problems that Aristotle had not posed. Higher mathematics was detached from the concerns of medieval natural philosophers, much as business arithmetic was taught without reference to moral or theological concerns. Both developments reflected the rapid expansion of a new knowledge industry after print. As was the case with classical archeology or locating plants, the language of number was propelled as an autonomous discipline and the solution of problems became subject to incremental change.

Let me note in passing that the way letters, numbers, and figures were pulled and pushed into new alignments by early printers and engravers is worth further thought. Human proportions were made to conform with letters once inscribed on ancient Roman arches, even while Roman numerals were being replaced by Arabic ones.[26] Solid geometrical forms were presented on two-dimensional planes and heavy wooden tables gave way to paper ones. In short, the basic 'building blocks' of the *quadrivium*: words and letters, numbers and figures,

---

[25] Mahoney, *The Mathematical Career*, pp. 9–10. How Latin-writing astronomers must have welcomed these 'practical' inventions is suggested by the enormous effort it cost Rheticus and his successors to compile tables of functions before Napier. See chap. 7, n. 162 below.

[26] For pertinent references, see later discussion of Luca Pacioli's work in this chapter, pp. 548–9 below.

even notes of music and lyrics for songs were rearranged, recast and almost literally thrown into a melting pot from whence they emerged in altered guise. To investigate how different branches of the *quadrivium* were affected by such changes is too formidable a task to be undertaken here. Let me merely suggest that each of the four disciplines underwent a complex metamorphosis after printing and their relationship to each other was also changed in various ways. Thus algebra moved closer to plane geometry; while the conic sections of solid geometry reshaped the music of the spheres.

Changes affecting different branches of the *quadrivium* could scarcely fail to penetrate Latin schools and college halls. The mistaken view that academic science was impervious to innovative trends has been traced, in a recent study of medical faculties in England, to false impressions left by statutory regulations that concealed the new content which was poured into old forms. 'Again and again, from the late Elizabethan period on, one finds countless examples of changeless academic...regulations and transformed subject matter.'[27] The same point applies to the contents of arithmetics, grammars, and other textbooks which often varied, after printing, from one edition to another.[28] 'A survey of works...published for academic use shows an overwhelming predominance of texts over a hundred years old... nothing could better illustrate the stagnation of scientific advance in the fifteenth century.'[29] Yet the stagnation may be illusory – based on failure to appreciate how often new contents were concealed by old labels.[30] At Copenhagen when the young Tycho Brahe was there, for example, students were presumably studying a traditional 'Aristotelian and conservative' curriculum.[31] Yet they were also furnished with new Greek and Hebrew grammars in accordance with Melanchthon's program of reform. Like earlier medieval students, they were being given Sacrobosco's *Sphaera* but in place of a medieval commentary

---

[27] R. G. Frank, 'Science, Medicine,' p. 200. This point needs to be balanced against the undeniable conservatism of statutory regulations which were not entirely without significance. See argument of Charles Webster, *The Great Instauration*, p. 199, defending the condemnation, by Puritan zealots, of 'scholastic' education.

[28] For a study of successive editions of Recorde's *Ground of Artes* see Easton, 'The Early Editions.'

[29] Goldschmidt, *Medieval Texts*, p. 23.

[30] See e.g. contrast drawn between the many early editions of Sacrobosco's *Sphaera* and the neglect of more noteworthy medieval scientific treatises by early printers serving academic markets in Wightman, *Science in a Renaissance Society*, p. 60. Actually editions of Sacrobosco could serve as vehicles for new information. See chap. 5, n. 199 above; p. 590 below.

[31] Christianson, 'Tycho Brahe.'

there was Regiomontanus' more sophisticated critique. Similarly a seemingly 'conservative' Ptolemaic text such as Apianus' *Cosmography* contained a new and useful supplement on triangulation supplied by Gemma Frisius.[32] Even while taking the traditional cycle of studies associated with the *trivium* and *quadrivium*, Tycho as a teenage student was mastering new mathematical and linguistic skills and being exposed to new data – albeit often in concealed form.

Although Struik suggests that 'the universities and the Latin schools were not the carriers of life in the exact sciences,' he also notes that the *Arithmetica* of Gemma Frisius found its way into almost every Latin school, while Gemma Frisius himself taught geography and mathematics at Louvain, the 'bulwark of theology and scholastic learning.'[33] Napier's work on logarithms was perfected and printed under the guidance of an eminent professor: Sir Henry Briggs. The academic posts held by men like Frisius and Briggs and the uses to which decimals and logarithms were put, point to the fallacy of over-playing the gap between 'the latinized university doctors' and the 'uncouth technicians and bookkeepers of the commercial cities.'[34]

The *Ground of Artes* by Robert Recorde known in twenty-eight editions... must have been 'read to pieces.'...Recorde was no 'rude mechanical' but a Fellow of All Souls, Oxford (1531) and a Doctor of Medicine, Cambridge (1545)...involved also in the 'modern' enterprise of mining and employed at the Bristol mint.[35]

---

32 Christianson, 'Tycho Brahe' notes that Tycho had a 1558 Wittenberg edition of Sacrobosco's *Sphaera* and Gemma Frisius' edition of Apianus' *Cosmography*. Struik notes that Gemma's new prescription for triangulation was attached to Apianus' text.

33 Struik, 'Mathematics in the Netherlands,' pp. 48–9. It was at Louvain, incidentally that Gemma Frisius and Vesalius met, thus suggesting how some 'scholastic' strongholds housed pioneers of early-modern science. In view of its trilingual curriculum, Louvain was also more unconventional than Struik's characterization suggests.

34 Struik, 'Mathematics in the Netherlands.' The versatile role played by Briggs, interchanges between Oxford and London, and the fallacy of portraying English universities as resistant to new philosophy are brought out by Shapiro, *John Wilkins*, p. 15 and *passim*. See also R. G. Frank's two-part article: 'Science, Medecine'.

35 Wightman, *Science in a Renaissance Society*, p. 101. On Recorde, see E. G. R. Taylor, *Mathematical Practitioners*, pp. 50–3. The successive editions of Recorde's first vernacular textbook, which are studied by Easton, culminate in an advertisement for *Decimals Made Easy* in 1699. Recorde's titles for his series of textbooks, beginning with *The Pathway to Knowledge* (1551) going on to *The Gate of Knowledge* and *The Castle of Knowledge* and ending with the uncompleted *Treasure of Knowledge*, suggest a kind of educational 'pilgrim's progress' – moving from 'ground' to 'pathway' to 'gate' to 'castle' (where Copernican doctrines are explained) to ultimate 'treasure' (along lines that point to the later 'Rosicrucian Enlightenment' as described by Frances Yates). Recorde and John Dee were fellow students at Cambridge and shared similar pedagogical concerns. Later editions of *The Ground of Artes* carried advertisements for Billingsley's English *Euclid* containing Dee's celebrated introduction.

The 'carriers of life in the exact sciences' consisted more and more of equations, diagrams, tables, maps and charts that could not be conveyed by lecture or disputation and that required silent scanning to be comprehended and absorbed. Instead of taking dictation from masters, college students became increasingly able to learn mathematics by teaching themselves. After 'silent instructors' had been produced in urban workshops, new lectureships in mathematics were introduced into the schools. Simon Stevin not only matriculated at Leiden, he ended by taking on a teaching post there. Stevin's appointment at Leiden was not the only sign that this famous Northern university was receptive to change. 'Universities in those days followed a traditional scheme of four faculties: law, medicine, theology, philosophy; but Leiden was not long in adding to these such appendages of modern universities as an engineering school, botanic garden, observatory and university press.'[36]

These signs of modernization were by no means peculiar to Leiden at the end of the sixteenth century. Earlier decades had seen the study of mathematics and botany flourish at new universities such as Wittenberg, while old university centers such as Paris and Padua acquired new facilities and faculty chairs. 'The Paduan school of anatomy owed its initial renown to Vesalius.'[37] His experiences at Paris and Louvain also placed Vesalius well within those academic circles, which are usually deemed tradition-bound. Yet the sixteenth-century Fleming also spent much time in the company of engravers and printers – where outsiders and mavericks, such as Paracelsus and Servetus, also could be found. For Vesalius, as for his printer Oporinus, there seems to be no clear division of work between academic circles and a reading public composed of surgeons, city physicians, artists, and literati. One of his earliest publications (in 1538) suggested how he helped to break down such divisions. Large placards or charts designed to be held up for audiences at his lectures were published as prints and were made available to interested observers in many towns.[38] Much as preachers extended their range by using presses as well as pulpits, so too did professors such as Vesalius reach a larger public outside college halls. As was the

[36] D. W. Davies, *The World of the Elseviers*, p. 12.
[37] Whitteridge, *William Harvey*, p. 15. On the University of Wittenberg see Dannenfeldt, 'Wittenberg Botanists' and Westman: 'The Melanchthon Circle,' 'Three Responses.'
[38] Saunders and O'Malley, *The Illustrations*, p. 16. The importance of anatomical prints such as these for the work of Rabelais is noted by Kline, 'Rabelais and Printing,' p. 50.

case with preachers also, the new publicity often generated new interest in watching celebrated authors perform. As Vesalius became something of a celebrity, anatomy lessons generated the same kind of excitement as other Baroque spectacles or theatrical events.[39]

When the discussion is broadened to include other figures than Galileo and other fields than mechanics and physics, moreover, clear-cut distinctions between academic and non-academic science become ever more blurred. The most advanced work in physics had taken the form of Latin commentaries on Aristotle's works and stemmed from courses in Natural Philosophy given by schoolmen. But advanced work in other fields often occurred outside lecture halls. The full text of Ptolemy's *Almagest* was probably harder for college students to obtain than Aristotle's *Physics*, for graduate faculties did not offer advanced instruction in astronomy.[40] Throughout the middle ages, most professional astronomers themselves were likely to be found outside college halls. They frequented courts, town halls, and charthouses. They cast horoscopes for princes or helped navigators and cartographers; advised on coinage or weights and measures; and worked with churchmen on calendrical problems. Town–gown divisions continue to seem irrelevant, and patronage by prelates and princes continues to dominate the scene after the end of the middle ages – from the days of Regiomontanus (who served a King of Hungary before obtaining a patron who financed his Nuremberg press) to those of Copernicus, Tycho, Kepler, and beyond. Whatever the impact of print on astronomy (and I believe it was considerable) it could not do very much to encourage professional astronomers to work on practical problems outside universities. Few astronomers had worked for long inside universities before.[41]

Much the same point may be made about developments in higher

---

[39] Cohen, 'Diagrams and Illustrations,' offered a graphic demonstration of new public interest in Vesalius' demonstrations as opposed to the bored and indifferent spectators at earlier anatomy lessons by contrasting the illustration in Ketham's *Fasciculus Medicinae* (Venice: Gregoriis, 1493/4) with the frontispiece of *De Fabrica*. Perhaps these renderings should be regarded less as accurate reports than as two artists' conceptions of how the scene *ought* to be represented. In either case, the contrast is worth noting.

[40] Crombie, *Augustine to Galileo*, p. 149, mentions Ptolemy's *Almagest* among 'texts prescribed' at medieval Oxford but other studies of medieval curricula seem to confirm above remarks. See e.g. Weisheipl, 'Curriculum at the Faculty of Arts,' pp. 142; 170; 172. Also Gabriel, *The College System*, pp. 19, 41 n, 140.

[41] Thus it is not clear whether Campanus of Novara ever did serve as a professor, while his services at the papal court are well documented. See Benjamin and Toomer, *Campanus of Novara*, p. 11.

mathematics. It is not at all surprising that Leonardo Fibonacci, the most accomplished Western mathematician of the thirteenth century, was linked with the astronomer Michael Scott through Frederick II's court rather than through university affiliations. Fibonacci's *Liber Abaci* seems to have been as little studied in the schools as was Ptolemy's full *Almagest*.[42] Simplified recensions by Sacrobosco served for teaching the rudiments of astronomy and arithmetic alike. Despite the brilliant work done on the margins of Aristotle's *Physics*, higher mathematics was assigned an extracurricular role in most medieval universities.[43] Formal instruction was limited to a cursory undergraduate 'eight-day' lecture course. While holding his 'chair' as a professor of mathematics, Galileo himself also gave private instruction at home.

It would be a mistake therefore to imagine that some sort of medieval academic monopoly had to be broken in order to release the talents of mathematical virtuosi such as Tartaglia, Cardano, Viète, Fermat, Pascal, Descartes, Leibniz *et al.* Before concluding that the 'new philosophy and science were forced to take root outside the academic garden where they should have found most fertile soil,'[44] it is worth noting that some hardy perennials had flourished for centuries outside university walls. The mathematical wizards of medieval and early-modern times had varied careers – ranging from merchant apprentices and self-taught reckon-masters to college professors and closet philosophers. They included doctors, lawyers, and clergymen who played with numbers in their spare time. However one may classify this variegated group, their academic affiliations (like their preference for Latin or vernaculars) often seem to be beside the point.[45]

The situation is somewhat different with regard to the life sciences, for medicine – unlike astronomy or mathematics – *was* taught by graduate faculties. Indeed, instruction in the *quadrivium* was mainly designed for undergraduates planning to take a medical degree. Advanced work in

[42] The composition and limited circulation of Fibonacci's treatises are covered by Rose, *The Italian Renaissance of Mathematics*, pp. 82–3. For interesting speculation on the circulation of his treatise on 'practical geometry' see Shelby, 'The Geometrical Knowledge,' p. 404. On Frederick II's court, see Haskins, *Studies*, p. 249.

[43] On private classes held for teaching mathematics and uncertainty about the academic status of Jordanus, Gerard of Brussels, etc. see Beaujouan, 'Motives and Opportunities' in Crombie (ed.) *Scientific Change*, p. 235. That mathematics was outside the regular university courses when Vittorino da Feltre was at Padua in the 1400s is noted by Woodward, *Vittorino da Feltre*, p. 7.

[44] A. R. Hall, 'The Scholar and the Craftsman,' p. 9.

[45] On the 'hodge-podge of varied activities' entailed in early-modern mathematics and absence of any term to cover them, see Mahoney, *The Mathematical Career*, p. 14.

medicine, as in law, was thus handled under academic auspices. Professors of medicine, however, also served as physicians and gained clinical experience at courts and in towns. Throughout the middle ages, moreover, there were branches of medicine practiced by surgeons and apothecaries that were excluded from the curriculum and had tenuous academic affiliations or none at all. It has been said, of medical studies during the later middle ages, that a 'tide of ink and parchment separated brain from hand.'[46] The influx of ancient texts in Latin translation probably increased divisions between professors and practitioners. Classical objections to scholars dirtying their hands were revived. Professors of medicine increasingly devoted themselves to study of Latin, Greek, and Arabic texts; surgeons and apothecaries were without Latin learning and worked outside the schools. As we have noted when discussing the problems of the Renaissance, the advent of printing helped to reverse these trends. Collaboration between the painter who belonged to the apothecary's guild and the learned physician was thus an important feature of early printed herbals. The output of vernacular texts for surgeons and the provision of anatomical illustrations for medical texts also brought 'hand and brain' together in new ways. Above all, the cause of literate surgery, which had received repeated setbacks during the middle ages, was finally secured.

In the later middle ages, Mondino's *Anatomia* had found a place in the schools, but Gui de Chauliac's *Chirurgia* had not. Gui himself was an academically trained man who studied at Bologna and Montpellier before serving the townsmen of Lyons and the Avignon Popes. He urged surgeons to master letters and study anatomy before setting out to practice their craft. Under the aegis of the Avignon Papacy, Gui collected a fine library and temporarily broke the monopoly of the Italians at Bologna where surgical texts were jealously guarded. But with the end of the Avignon Popes and the outbreak of the Hundred Years War, the library was dispersed, and the cause of literate surgery beyond the Alps received a setback again.[47] Gui's program was not implemented until the sixteenth century when the 'new anatomy'

---

[46] Lynn White, 'Pumps and Pendula,' p. 102. See also Singer, 'The Confluence,' p. 263.

[47] The difficulty of sustaining the cause of literacy for surgeons before printing is noted by Malgaigne, *Surgery and Ambroise Paré*, pp. 33; 63. See also Talbott and Hammond, *The Medical Practitioners*, pp. viii–lx. Many editions of Gui's work were printed before 1501 in French, Latin, Dutch, and German. See Sarton, *Six Wings*, p. 300, n. 71.

became an accepted part of the curriculum at universities. In the 1550s, a new course in anatomy given at Paris signalled the acceptance of Gui in French medical schools. Later in the century a Montpellier professor edited a new French edition of the *Chirurgia* so that 'those who have a natural bent for the surgeon's calling' could take advantage of 'books which are silent instructors' and 'nowadays carry farther than public lectures.'[48]

In the case of anatomy, one may see how courses and texts worked together and varied talents were pooled in new ways. But even while new forms of collaboration were encouraged, old rivalries were also exacerbated. Divisions of labor between surgeons, physicians, and apothecaries varied so greatly from region to region that few generalizations hold true. Still, it seems safe to suggest that changes wrought by print intensified wrangling between diverse groups almost everywhere. In England, for example, the seventeenth-century publication of the London *Pharmacopoeia*, even while dignifying the apothecary's craft, also precipitated vigorous attacks on the *status quo* by disclosing how many impossibly complicated, absurd and extravagant remedies had been passed down for centuries by 'slavish copyists' in the schools.[49] Attacks on money-grubbing physicians and claims made for cheap, sure-fire home remedies in some of the literature provoked by the *Pharmacopoeia* have a remarkably modern ring. So too does the promotional literature, issued outside the medical establishment, advertising pills and panaceas for sale. In a modern vein also, academic medicine proved sensitive to commercial pressures associated with new forms of publicity. Paracelsus' plans for an elaborate publication proving guaiac useless for treating syphilis led to trouble with the Leipzig medical faculty who feared loss of Fugger patronage if Fugger revenues from guaiac were imperilled.[50] Quarrels between physicians and surgeons seem to have been especially bitter and prolonged in France, where intermittent hostilities continued for three centuries or more.[51]

---

[48] Sherrington, *The Endeavour*, p. 111. The citation comes from Isaac Joubert who, along with his father, Laurent Joubert (Dean and Chancellor of the University) was on the Montpellier medical faculty. How these Protestant professors of medicine contributed to the vernacular translation movement (discussed in chap. 4, volume I above) is described by Sherrington, pp. 108–14. [49] Brockbank, 'Sovereign Remedies,' 1–13.

[50] Pagel, *Paracelsus*, pp. 24–5.

[51] Hostilities between French physicians and surgeons during the seventeenth and eighteenth centuries are noted in many studies. See e.g. Sherrington, *The Endeavour*, pp. 104–6; Solomon, *Public Welfare*, chapter 5; and Barber, *The Bourgeoisie*, p. 24. On appointment of Paré in sixteenth century Paris, see n. 58, below.

Prolonged struggles over status and role among members of the medical profession show, once again, that university faculties were not insulated from the winds of change. The University of Paris which had been the main center of the university book-trade in the age of scribes was particularly vulnerable to the new currents. The very closeness of print shops to colleges in Paris encouraged friction as well as new forms of interchange. In this regard the active role performed by Parisian printers needs to be contrasted with the more passive role previously performed by stationers and scribes. Here again too much emphasis on trends traced in Galileo studies are likely to lead us astray.

In France no second stream of science outside the universities seems to have flourished, perhaps because the University of Paris continued much longer than other universities to pursue the medieval tradition that linked mathematics to physics. Perhaps there is also a connection with the fact that printing in Paris was much more closely linked to the University than in any other city.[52]

In the age of the scribe, Parisian stationers, who handled the university book-trade, tended to play a subservient role. In the age of the printer, however, book provisions for faculties at the unversity were handled by more independent entrepreneurs. As is suggested by the case of Robert Estienne, Parisian printers did not necessarily pursue the same policy as Sorbonne theologians. On more than one occasion, the two groups sharply clashed. Paris printers were also more sensitive than earlier stationers had been to the demands of kings and parlements. The printed book-trade was too large and varied to be controlled by old university regulations. Although some Paris printers might still serve, as had the stationers, in the role of college officials, they were often linked with branches elsewhere in France and with foreign firms as well.[53] Their multifarious connections have to be examined before the strength of any one link can be made clear.

It is quite true that French printers sometimes served the University of Paris in official capacities.[54] It is also clear that certain Parisian colleges

52 Drake, 'Early Science,' p. 52. It seems doubtful that links were closer in Paris than in other university towns such as Wittenberg, Tübingen, Leiden or Cologne.
53 Bietenholz, *Basle and France* offers data on networks linking Paris firms to outside ones. Parent, *Les Métiers*, pp. 51, 124–5, 168 discusses the activities of some five hundred bookmen who inhabited university *quartiers* and notes the shift from the Sorbonne to royal regulatory power.
54 Sherrington, *The Endeavour*, pp. 3–4 describes services rendered to out-of-town students by de Colines and the Estiennes. The end papers of Sherrington's biography provide useful maps, pinpointing the numerous celebrated sixteenth-century print shops that clustered around the University of Paris.

held scholastic physics in high esteem – to the point of arranging for the early printing of treatises by Oxford and Paris schoolmen.[55] But although late medieval academic markets were important to early printers, tapping new markets was also profitable and was vigorously pursued. A so-called 'second stream' of non-academic publication may be found near the Seine (and the Rhône) throughout the first century of printing. Treatises by a new breed of vernacular science-writers came off French presses no less frequently than did Rabelaisian satires on pedants, priests, and Sorbonnistes. In Lyons, no less than London, practicing apothecaries broke into print by attacking 'The Abuses and Ignorance of Physicians.'[56] In Paris, no less than Nuremberg, engravers (such as Geoffroy Tory) also wrote treatises on geometry. As is noted below, French presses sponsored the debut of an anatomist–printer, Charles Estienne. They made it possible for artisans such as the potter Bernard Palissy to gain access to writings by Paracelsus and Cardano and to turn out popular attacks on the Sorbonne. Palissy's *Discours Admirables*, containing his lectures to Parisian 'physicians, dilettanti, and *gens du monde*' and inviting his readers to come to his shop for demonstrations of his work, epitomized the new genre of vernacular science-writing that was ushered in by printing.[57] So too did the works of the self-proclaimed barber–surgeon, Ambroise Paré. That Paré, who knew no Latin, was elevated to the rank of college professor (albeit at a college for surgeons, not physicians) suggests how some academic conventions were broken (to the consternation of some Paris professors) rather than inertly sustained.[58]

Moreover these trends encompassed mathematics as well as medicine. French engravers, no less than French barbers, became authors and professors. Euclid and Archimedes were translated into French as into other tongues. French tutors and reckon-masters were just as eager as their counterparts elsewhere to attract wealthy pupils and patrons while

---

[55] Clagett, *Science of Mechanics*, pp. 652–3 lists pertinent titles printed under the auspices of the College of Montaigu. The anti-humanist, Gallican and Ockhamist views of Montaigu's faculty are described by Renaudet, *Préreforme*, pp. 463 ff.

[56] On this Lyons publication by Pierre Braillier, an apothecary, see N. Z. Davis, 'Printing and the People,' p. 215.

[57] Rossi, *Philosophy Technology*, pp. 1–4 reviews recent literature on Palissy and discusses his possible influence on the young Francis Bacon. See also Sarton, *Six Wings*, pp. 164–71.

[58] Distinctions between Latin-reading, learned 'surgeons of the long-robe' at the Collège de Saint Côme and barber–surgeons are covered by Sarton, *Six Wings*, p. 197. Paré created a stir by being admitted to the St Côme faculty without Latin learning. For further references, see *Six Wings*, pp. 300–1, n. 75; n. 76.

achieving the more elevated status conferred by literary fame. There was no dearth of new arithmetic books in sixteenth-century France. The 'medieval tradition that linked mathematics to physics' and both to glosses on Aristotle's books was not a prominent feature in most of the texts, although many of them did attempt to dignify and elevate tricks of the reckon-master's trade. The same literary devices that had earlier adorned anthologies of devotional literature began to appear in arithmetic books which dealt with tables of interest and accounting. The importance of cultivating business arts by financiers and statesmen was stressed by authors with aspirations toward upward mobility who added particles to their own names while aiming their books at officials and governors. The same authors also found ways of dignifying applied or practical geometry. Its usefulness to gentry with landed estates and to nobles entrusted with military command could be underlined.[59]

As these comments suggest, the shadow of the Sorbonne did not prevent French publishers from issuing numerous texts that placed a new language of numbers at the disposal of merchants, surveyors, and military men. Nor did sixteenth-century French academies, which were affiliated with scholar–printers and editors, seem unwilling to press for curriculum reform. On the contrary, projects for reforming the teaching of mathematics went together with plans to reform orthography and grammar and with a celebration of the elegance of the French language itself. In this regard it may be a mistake to dismiss all the 'critiques of method' by 'anti-Aristotelian philosophers,' such as Francis Bacon and Peter Ramus as having little or no effect on university science.[60] Although Ramus contributed nothing to the 'new mechanics,' he did help to propel mathematics as a separate discipline. He also issued a challenge that captured the imagination of the young Kepler.[61] In his *Scholae Mathematicae*, published at Basel in 1569, he served mathematicians and atronomers – much as Vasari served painters and sculptors – thus elevating calculators to the dignity achieved by inspired poets and artists.[62] In developing new terms such

---

[59] For data see two articles by N. Z. Davis, 'Sixteenth-Century French Arithmetics'; and 'Mathematicians in the Sixteenth-Century French Academies.' The possible relevance of these texts to the 'spirit of capitalism' is noted on p. 384, volume 1 above.

[60] Drake, 'Early Science,' pp. 49–50.

[61] See p. 651 below.

[62] Rose, *Italian Renaissance of Mathematics*, p. 259, notes that Ramus was preparing an enlarged second edition when killed during the Massacre of St Bartholomew's eve and that his first edition was used by Bernardino Baldi for his large-scale *Lives of Mathematicians* (which covered some two hundred biographies but was never published).

as 'negative number' he could perhaps be said to have contributed something to the 'new math' of his day. Unlike Francis Bacon, at all events, Ramus was keenly aware of the significance of the language of numbers. He worked zealously to reform the French university curriculum, pointing to German achievements (especially to Melanchthon's reforms) as a spur to patriotic Valois kings.[63] At least one of his projects was crowned with some success, when new chairs in pure and applied mathematics were established at Paris. The French example in turn was used to prod English authorities by curriculum reformers there.

2. PUBLICIZING SCIENCE: NEW CAREERS OPEN TO VARIED TALENTS

In both medicine and mathematics, expanding academic opportunities went hand in hand with the chance to achieve literary fame. The new forms of authorship and intellectual property rights created by print proved no less attractive to would-be professors than to artisans and other groups. The chance to serve expanding book markets encouraged the adoption of new attitudes on the part of professors, tutors, and clerks. Literate élites underwent internal transformations as old pedagogical impulses were drawn into new channels. Science-writing provided sixteenth-century teachers with alternative ways of exerting their talents. They were confronted by a variety of conflicts and choices that had not confronted many clerks before.

The career of Jacques Peletier du Mans (as has been demonstrated by Professor Davis) offers a good illustration of this point.[64] Peletier moved in and out of teaching posts at Bayeux, Poitiers, and Bordeaux while turning out books on diverse branches of the *quadrivium* and collaborating with other members of the Pléiade in their projects for purifying and glorifying French. Intervals spent between teaching posts found him lodging with printers in Paris and Lyons while preparing treatises for

63 Hooykaas, *Humanisme, Science et Réforme*, chap. x, discusses Ramus' role as proselytizer for mathematical studies and his survey of the state of mathematics in sixteenth-century Europe. Ramus was especially impressed by developments in German cities and helped to propel the claim that Melanchthon was 'the preceptor of Europe' and that Wittenberg was the nursery of science. See also the facsimile of the 1569 Basel publication: Petrus Ramus, *Scholae in Liberales Artes*.
64 See N. Z. Davis, 'Peletier and Beza Part Company,' for above account.

their presses. In the winter of 1547–8, Vascosan's shop in the Rue Saint Jacques[65] was the scene of daily discussion and argument between Peletier and his learned friends (such as Theodore Beza) on the kind of problems that ought to go into arithmetic books, on using Latin as against French, and on the usefulness of devising a uniform orthography. In Lyons during most of the period from 1553 through 1555, Peletier made his headquarters at 'the atelier of Jean I de Tournes.' He tutored young Jean II in mathematics and saw some of his views on orthography incorporated into the handsome French Protestant Bible that de Tournes printed in 1554. Troubled by the outbreak of religious warfare, and determined to remain in the Catholic fold, Peletier later withdrew from association with Protestants, renounced vernacular science-writing and his projects for reform. But his experiences at Paris and Lyons suggest that printers played a larger role in shaping sixteenth-century academic careers than is noted in many accounts.

This point may be reinforced by taking as a second example the career of Oronce Finé, royal lecturer at the University of Paris in the 1530s. Although he has been described as the 'most lustrous mathematician of his day,'[66] Finé's work as an astronomer was technically inferior to that of many of his contemporaries. His skills seem to have been displayed to better advantage as a teacher, technician, and book illustrator. He was fond of parading his considerable fund of Latin learning and wrote several treatises against contaminating 'higher' mathematics with the vulgar problems posed in commercial arithmetics. Yet he also contributed to vernacular science-writing (probably with 'vulgar' commercial motives in mind) and expounded diverse branches of the *quadrivium* for early sixteenth-century laymen. His defense of the vernacular was characteristically élitist: 'because many noble and fine minds among the gentry and bourgeois no less than mechanics lack knowledge of Latin.' But he still made use of new presses to teach a wider public than could be taught in college halls. Moreover, he proved just as versatile as any other 'Renaissance man'

[65] In providing hospitality for Peletier, Vascosan was carrying on a family tradition. His father-in-law, Josse Bade (Badius) had been equally hospitable. See Parent, *Les Métiers*, p. 170.

[66] N. Z. Davis, 'Sixteenth Century French Arithmetics,' pp. 30–1. Finé's technical inferiority was pointed out to me by Owen Gingerich. For basic study of his work see Ross, 'Studies on Oronce Finé' and also by the same author, 'Oronce Finé's De Sinibus Libri II,' pp. 379 ff. Other useful references are offered by Hilliard and Poulle, 'Oronce Finé et L'Horloge Planétaire,' pp. 320–1; Brun, *Le Livre Français*, p. 43.

when advising François I on fortifications during the Italian campaign or when developing new techniques for cartographers and surveyors. Like most medieval mathematicians and astronomers, Finé was both willing and able to work with his hands, designing instruments and maps to rival those produced by other skilled craftsmen and even serving the Paris printer, Simon de Colines, as a designer of title borders in his spare time.

As these two examples may suggest, pedagogues were perhaps more likely than were craftsmen to take advantage of new careers opened by print and to contribute to the enrichment of technical literature. 'It is paradoxical that the first treatise on mining and metallurgy next to Biringuccio's in date but wider in scope was composed by a man who was neither a miner nor a metal worker but a physician and burgomaster; Agricola had been a teacher of Greek and Latin.'[67] What seems paradoxical is the assumption that teachers of Greek and Latin, who were friends of scholar–printers, were *not* going to be involved in a literary translation movement. Surely there were very few merchants, miners, or metal workers who might have had the leisure and requisite literary skills. Knowledge of Greek and Latin was obviously helpful for translating Greek and Latin technical texts. A town physician and schoolmaster like Erasmus' friend Georg Bauer seems to me to have just the right mix of talents to produce the famous handbook. Much as medieval kings had called on professors to convert certain texts into mother tongues, so too did printers have to turn to Latin scholars when making ancient treatises on arts and crafts available to lay readers. Artisan-authors were often encouraged by printers to write new texts in their own tongue, but a vernacular translator required some command of Latin in order to function at all. Moreover, vernacular translation was not always the best way to achieve widespread use. An English alchemist asserted he was employing 'blunt and rude English' in order 'to please ten thousand laymen' instead of 'ten able clerks.'[68] Yet Dutch and Flemish treatises on mathematics and on botany had to be

---

[67] Sarton, *Six Wings*, p. 125. In view of the tendency to underrate the extent to which the cult of antiquity was compatible with curiosity about metallurgy and mechanics it is worth noting that study of classical technical literature 'awakened and fortified' Agricola's 'scientific curiosity' according to Sarton, *ibid*. A recent detailed study of Renaissance editions of the pseudo-Aristotelian *Mechanica* offers useful evidence of the initiative supplied for these publications by classical scholars, literati, and printers (beginning with Cardinal Bessarion and Aldus Manutius). Rose and Drake, 'The Pseudo-Aristotelian "Questions."'

[68] Thomas Norton, *The Ordinall of Alchemy* (1477) cited by Jones, *Triumph*, p. 5, n. 8.

converted from a little-known vernacular into Latin in order to reach wider markets abroad.[69]

Furthermore, the use of vernaculars for the purpose of popularization had been a familiar resort of teachers and preachers before printing. Vernacular preaching had become an important branch of pulpit oratory in the age of scribes. A lively anecdotal style was increasingly cultivated when composing sermons designed to keep congregations awake.[70] That freshness and novelty were also prized is suggested by prefaces to preachers' anthologies.[71] Moreover, medieval texts for beginners in such fields as astronomy or optics had been written for the benefit of students attending the papal college and cathedral schools.[72] Private tutors and teachers trying to impart learning to young pupils had also anticipated later trends. Those who served in princely households or who taught in court schools also tried to simplify and enliven inherited materials as well as translate important works into vernacular tongues.

This is not to discount the significance of the new output of artisan-authors like Paré, Palissy, Dürer, Tartaglia *et al*. It is merely to note that learned men accustomed to teaching and preaching had been pioneering in translation and abridgement even before self-taught authors set to work. When one recalls that Nicole Oresme presented his royal master with French translations of Aristotle's *Politics* and *Ethics* one may be less inclined to regard Tartaglia's translation of Euclid as 'departing from ordinary scholarly practices' and less likely to assume that 'no professor would have bothered to make a vernacular translation.'[73] In fact, the idea of conveying Euclidean geometry to laymen

---

[69] Clusius' work for Plantin consisted partly of translating Dutch, Spanish, Portuguese, and French scientific works into Latin. See Sarton, *Six Wings*, pp. 143-4. Schmitt, 'Essay Review' I, 166-8, notes that Stevin was more influential in Latin than in Dutch. See also reference to Galileo's *Sidereus Nuncius*, n. 24 above.

[70] That English friars prized novel anecdotes that kept congregations awake (and were reluctant to share them with colleagues) is noted by Smalley, *English Friars*, pp. 37-44. Smalley also notes that despite new *exempla* the content of sermons remained traditional. Stale and hackneyed themes made it even more desirable to use fresh and novel anecdotes.

[71] A fourteenth-century collection of sermons thus contains a prologue by its compiler stating that 'modern man who admires novelty' was being given a 'novel collection in a novel style.' Rouse and Rouse, 'The Texts Called Lumen Anime,' p. 28. See also remarks about an 'avid public interest in novel things' made in connection with an Italian sermon of 1305-6 noted in Rosen, 'The Invention of Eyeglasses,' p. 34.

[72] This was the case with Pecham's *Perspectiva Communis*, according to Lindberg's introduction, *John Pecham*, p. 17.

[73] Drake, 'Early Science,' p. 51. On Oresme's translations, see references given by C. R. Sherman, 'Some Visual Definitions,' p. 319 n. Oresme's prefaces, cited by Sherman, contain the topoi which vernacular translators democratized after printing.

and of exploiting the new presses to do this was vigorously advocated fifty years before Tartaglia by Luca Pacioli, who was a doctor of divinity and on the faculty of several universities.

The celebrated portrait of Pacioli by Jacopo de' Barbari which shows the friar teaching Euclid to the future Duke of Urbino does not do justice to Pacioli's unconventional role as a pioneering public lecturer and science-writer whose work was ransacked by others for a century or more. As a pedagogue, the friar probably owed much to the Venetian 'school of the Rialto' where he had studied as a youth; as a publicist he was also clearly indebted to the Venetian presses.[74] At the same time, he reflected attitudes that had been common among Franciscan preachers in many regions from the thirteenth century on. 'Pacioli had the common touch. In his book, he turned away from scholars and directed his voice to the public.'[75] Far from considering vernacular translations beneath him, Pacioli urged that Euclid be made available in the vernacular because 'the subject matter will bear more fruit if there are more people to read it.'

Pacioli understood the need...for mathematics and a study of Euclid... He had the native good sense to see that a printed book in mathematics would not get far unless Arabic numerals were used and unless the native language was resorted to in order to reach the greatest number of students.[76]

Dedicated to a Duke of Urbino and partly subsidized by Marco Sanuto, Pacioli's major treatise, the *Summa de arithmetica, geometria et proportionate* (Venice: Paganini, 1494), was deliberately written in the vernacular for 'if written in Latin, each and everyman could not understand it.'[77] Thereafter, it was translated into Latin and numerous other tongues. It was excerpted in countless sixteenth-century works, including mathematics texts used in college courses. Its contents were

74 J. B. Ross, 'Venetian Schools,' p. 531 points to the key study by Nardi, 'La scuola di Rialto' which relates Pacioli's activities to the school of the Rialto and the latter to Paduan Aristotelianism. Dr Ross's own article contains a wealth of new data on a pedagogue who edited several volumes for the Aldine press: Giovanni Battista Egnazio.
75 R. E. Taylor, *No Royal Road*, p. 197. In a similar vein, see remarks of Alessandro Piccolomini, Archbishop of Patras on the need for vernacular translation to benefit Italian engineers and architects (as reported by Biringuccio), cited by Rose and Drake, 'The Pseudo-Aristotelian "Questions,"' p. 85.
76 R. E. Taylor, 'Luca Pacioli,' p. 183. Pacioli's revision of the Latin translation of Euclid done by Campanus of Novara for Pope Urban IV (first printed by Erhard Ratdolt, Venice, 1482 and used by Copernicus) appeared in Venice in 1509. It was done partly to rescue Campanus' reputation from attack. See Rose, 'Humanist Culture.' p. 99.
77 R. E. Taylor, *No Royal Road*, p. 187.

paraphrased by Bishop Tunstall and Jerome Cardano.[78] That Pacioli himself reproduced ('plagiarized'?) large portions of earlier scribal treatises was made clear by the author himself and is often noted in later literature.[79] Less often noted is the way this fifteenth-century encyclopedic work linked double-entry bookkeeping and business arithmetic with Pythagorean harmonies and the music of the spheres. Fibonacci's practical Book of the Abacus was thus brought together with treatises composed by commentators on Euclid, such as Campanus of Novara, who stressed divine proportion, golden sections and the like. As an eclectic mélange of classical and Arabic, scholastic and mercantile treatises, Pacioli's Summa represents something of a land-mark. Within the covers of this one book could be found all the varied aspects of mathematics known to his day. As a friar and theologian who numbered quattrocento artists among his close friends, Pacioli bridged the gulf between schoolmen and humanists. He paid homage in his preface not only to scholastic culture heroes such as Aristotle, Isidore of Seville, Boethius, Bartolus, and Duns Scotus, but also to Renaissance artists – to Verrocchio, Mantegna, Piero della Francesca and Alberti.[80] He converted Piero's treatise on perspective from script into print and from Latin into a vernacular tongue while inserting it as a section of his Italian treatise On Divine Proportion.[81] Just as he expounded the mys-teries of double-entry bookkeeping for merchants, so too he underlined the importance of the study of Euclid for surveyors, architects, and other 'universal men.'

Engravers and type designers – such as Dürer and Tory – were

---

78 For indications that parts of the Summa entered into the two chief arithmetic texts that replaced Boethius in sixteenth-century college courses, see remarks on Bishop Tunstall's De Arte Supputandi (1522) in Stillwell, Awakening Interest in Science, p. 71 and comments on Cardano's Ars Magna (1545) by Ore, foreword to G. Cardano, The Great Art, p. vii. On how Tunstall and Cardano replaced Boethius as required texts at Oxford by 1549 see Johnson, Astronomical Thought, pp. 83–4.

79 His discovery of a ms. version of Fibonacci's Liber Abaci in the Venetian library of San Antonio di Castello is noted by Rose, Italian Renaissance of Mathematics, p. 83.

80 See preface to Luca Pacioli's Summa (tr. R. E. Taylor), p. 191. In reconciling Plato with Aristotle and the schoolmen, Pacioli was following the path set forth by Cardinal Bessarion in his widely read In Calumniatorum Platonis (first printed in Latin in 1469). Kristeller, Renaissance Concepts, p. 101.

81 Sarton, Appreciation, p. 135. Pacioli is scolded by Vasari for stealing and publishing as his own Piero's treatise. Vasari, Lives, p. 93. Piero's treatise De Prospectiva Pingendi is described by Panofsky in Albrecht Dürer (1 vol. ed.), pp. 249, 251 as an unpublished work which did not get printed until 1899. Dürer's trip to Bologna in 1506 to learn the 'secret' of perspective from a master (who may have been Pacioli) is noted on pp. 251–2. Of course, the Italian edition of Piero's treatise was still in a foreign tongue to the Nuremberg artist.

especially attracted to this aspect of Pacioli's work. The effort to design letters that conformed to classical canons, and the belief that ancient lettering had been modelled on the same lines as Vitruvian man produced some remarkable human alphabets and experiments in type design.[82] According to Panofsky, Dürer's printed treatise on regular polygons helped to acquaint 'coopers and cabinet makers with Euclid and Ptolemy and...professional mathematicians with...workshop geometry.' The Italian friar performed a comparable service, and probably contributed something to Dürer's treatise itself. When considering the expanding vogue for Vitruvian man, the nesting 'perfect' solids that captivated Kepler throughout his life, the 'geometrical spirit' that Pascal opposed to intuition, or even ideal cities laid out with divine proportions in mind, Pacioli's early printed treatises are worth a longer look. As an editor of Euclid, his work also deserves more attention as providing themes reworked later by Elizabethans such as John Dee.[83]

In the year 1570...a very important book was printed by John Day in London. It was the first English translation of Euclid by H. Billingsley, citizen of London. The translation is preceded by a very long preface in English by John Dee in which Dee surveys all the mathematical sciences both from the point of view of Platonic and mystical theory of number and also with the purpose of being of practical utility to artisans. In this preface, Dee makes many quotations from Vitruvius...gives the Vitruvian theory of architecture ...using not only 'Vitruvius the Romaine' but also 'Leo Baptista Albertus a Florentine.'[84]

[82] Morison, *Fra Luca Pacioli*, p. 7. John Lewis, *Anatomy of Printing*, pp. 55–6 also offers relevant references and illustrations. Efforts to achieve the impossible task of reconciling human proportions with Roman inscriptions and Euclidean geometry, are described by Lewis (p. 56) as straining logic to the breaking point. Obsession with symmetry and insistence on perfect congruence leads, beyond the 'architecture of humanism,' to a kind of 'crazy' logic, reflected in the utopian schemes for perfect cities of the seventeenth century or in Kepler's preoccupation with perfect solids (see chap. 7, n. 43 below). Perspective renderings of alphabet forms and manuals on perspective partly inspired by Pacioli's work are also illustrated by Mayor, *Prints and People*, 173–8. Dürer's attempt to force Gothic letters into a system based on modules is well illustrated in Panofsky's *Albrecht Dürer* (1 vol. ed.), figures 6a–7b, pp. 258–9.
[83] See description of the plan of 'Christianopolis' in Yates, *The Rosicrucian Enlightenment*, pp. 147–8, where emphasis on the mathematical sciences is attributed partly to John Dee's influence. In considering the Euclidean and Vitruvian features that are prominent in continental utopian schemes in the seventeenth century, Pacioli's *Summa* and *Divine Proportion* seem to me to be more seminal than the later writings of Dee or Fludd. Dee's trips to Italy brought him into contact with Pacioli's successors such as Federico Commandino (who published a manuscript attributed to Euclid brought to him by Dee). See Rose, 'Notes and Correspondence.' On Dee's stay with his Antwerp printer, Sylvius, see chap. 2, n. 168, volume I above.
[84] Yates, *The Art of Memory*, p. 347.

In view of these references and of the contents of the work he was introducing, one might expect that Dee was not unfamiliar with Pacioli's eclectic work. Indeed he mentions 'Frater Lucas de Burgo' along with Tartaglia, Dürer *et al.* as precursors of his effort to bring Euclid to 'unlatined people.' The Italian universities, Dee argued, did not feel themselves 'disgraced or their studies anything hindered' by Pacioli's large volumes 'in vulgar speche.'[85]

Later on, to be sure, Dee's preface was put to anti-Aristotelian and anti-academic purposes that were quite alien to the Franciscan friar. Thus the 'preface before Euclide' by the 'expert and learned Dr John Dee' was used as ammunition by a Puritan divine, urging curriculum reform at the English universities while attacking 'Aristotelians' and the 'supine negligence of the schools.'[86] Pacioli, however, was writing before later battle lines were drawn. In keeping with his protean role as a 'father of double-entry bookkeeping,' translator of Piero della Francesca, mentor of Leonardo da Vinci and doctor of divinity, he displayed an ecumenical frame of mind. After the initial privilege granted to his wide-ranging work expired, sections of the *Summa* were published separately. 'The Perfect School for Merchants' and 'Divine Proportion' tended to go their separate ways. But for the ten-year interval, 1494–1504, a printed vernacular mathematical encyclopedia had managed to link the most heavenly with the most mundane concerns.

Pacioli was probably the most wide-ranging, influential and forceful advocate of mathematics for the layman during the first century of print. His work repeatedly stressed utilitarian, popular, and progressive themes. For Zilsel this indicates that Pacioli 'must have had close contacts with artist-engineers and merchants.'[87] In the Marxist scheme adopted by Zilsel, it is as if friars and scholars were not permitted to initiate 'progressive' trends once early capitalists had appeared on the

[85] John Dee, Preface, *The Elements of Geometrie of the Most Ancient Philosopher Euclide of Megara* (tr. and ed. Henry Billingsley) (London, John Day, 1570), pp. Aiij v–Aiiij r. (I am indebted to Alice McGinty for bringing this reference to my attention.) On John Day, see recent monograph by Oastler.

[86] John Webster, passages from *Academiarum Examen* (London, 1654). Cited by Pagel, 'News, Notes and Queries.' Webster's eulogy of Dee provoked a rebuke from an Oxford professor, Seth Ward, who likened Webster's 'canting discourse' to that of a 'moping Friar' while deprecating the school of mathematical enthusiasts such as Dee and Fludd and praising Baconian experimental philosophy. Yates, *Rosicrucian Enlightenment*, pp. 186–7. For full account of this debate see Debus, *Science and Education*.

[87] Zilsel, 'The Genesis,' p. 342, n. 31.

scene. The initial impulse to contribute to public knowledge always has to come from merchants and artisan-engineers. Yet priests often activated presses more readily than did guildsmen. There is no question that Pacioli was on friendly terms with artists such as Piero della Francesca and Leonardo da Vinci. But it was Piero who composed a Latin treatise and the friar who put it into the vernacular and got it circulated in print.[88] It is quite possible that Pacioli secured the help of Leonardo for the design of illustrations for his *Divine Proportion*,[89] but the initiative for making the work available to architects and surveyors came from the friar and not the artist-engineer.

The prominent role played by friars – such as Pacioli, Bruno, Foscarini, Campanella, Mersenne and others – as heterodox science-writers and publicists surely deserves more attention. The Franciscan tradition that transmitted the heritage of Grosseteste, Roger Bacon, and John Pecham is also worth noting when considering 'neo-Platonic' or 'Pythagorean' trends in the quattrocento. Pecham's *Perspectiva Communis* offers a good example of the kind of science-writing that provided Pacioli with a precedent. But it was designed for friars at Paris and Oxford and clerks at the papal university or monastic seminaries. The different public reached by treatises, such as Pecham's with the aid of early-modern printers is striking. An Italian edition of 1482 was probably consulted by Leonardo da Vinci as well as by other Renaissance artisan-engineers.[90]

The contrast between Pacioli's frequent resort to the new presses and Leonardo's predilection for ciphers and secrecy is also instructive. It underlines my point that the role of the publicist was often more easily assumed by teachers and preachers (by a bishop like Tunstall or a friar like Pacioli) than by artists and craftsmen who were untrained in

---

[88] See note 81 above. Note also that L. B. Alberti wrote his major architectural treatise *De Re Aedificatoria* not in Italian for architects but in Latin, under the patronage of Lionello d'Este, for presentation to Pope Nicholas V. This point is underlined by Krautheimer, 'Alberti's Templum Etruscum,' p. 328.

[89] According to Keele, 'Leonardo da Vinci's Influence,' p. 361, Leonardo probably learned how to manipulate mathematical roots while working for Pacioli. The extent of Leonardo's collaboration with Pacioli is as difficult to determine as that of Jan Stephan of Calcar with Vesalius. A printed copy of Pacioli's *Summa de Arithmetica* as well as an unidentified vernacular ms. Euclid is listed among Leonardo's books. See items No. 93 and No. 110 in Ladislao Reti, 'The Two Unpublished Manuscripts,' pp. 81 ff.

[90] Lindberg (tr. and ed.), *John Pecham*, p. 17. Keele, 'Leonardo da Vinci's Influence,' p. 364 cites Fazio Cardano's Italian translation of Pecham's treatise as influential in Leonardo's work. Eastwood, in a review of Lindberg's edition of Pecham (*Speculum* (1972) p. 324), contends that Pecham's influence on quattrocento artists, such as Ghiberti, has been overplayed. Of course, Ghiberti did not, like Leonardo, have printed vernacular works to consult.

rhetorical and scribal arts. The case of Tartaglia, so often singled out to illustrate 'the frame of mind of gun founders and military engineers,'[91] is also worth examining. The self-taught artisan-author pioneered with a vernacular translation of Euclid, yet he was unwilling to part with the most recent tricks of a reckon-master's trade. Indeed he was infuriated by Cardano's publication of his solution to a cubic equation – even though he was repeatedly credited with the discovery in three separate chapters of Cardano's book.[92]

To the modern scholar imbued with the notion that, as R. K. Merton has put it 'an idea is not really yours until you give it away' (i.e., through publication), Tartaglia's attitude seems strange. Yet...the very notion of individual ownership of ideas was itself novel and strange.[93]

In view of his objections to the publication of his mathematical solution there is need to qualify the familiar portrayal of Tartaglia as a representative of a new non-academic popularizing movement, associated with artisan-engineers and emergent capitalist enterprise. A more wholehearted acceptance of the 'novel and strange' uses of publicity was demonstrated by Jerome Cardano who, unlike Tartaglia, had gone through the schools. As a science-writer Jerome Cardano was following an example set by his natural father. Fazio Cardano was a university professor whose vernacular translation of Pecham's treatise on optics has already been noted as having been consulted by Leonardo da Vinci among others.[94] Leonardo took advantage of printed materials to increase his mastery of numerous fields. But he also retained the secretive habits of medieval craftsmen. His behavior – like that of Tartaglia – may remind us that Latin grammars had circulated more freely in the later middle ages than did 'mysteries' transmitted within guilds.

The desire to collaborate more closely with craftsmen had long been expressed by university scholars, such as Vincent of Beauvais, Albertus

---

91 Zilsel, 'Genesis,' pp. 337–8; see also Drake, 'Early Science,' pp. 50–2.

92 Ore, foreword to *The Great Art*, pp. ix–xi, offers a detailed account of this intriguing priority struggle. Tartaglia actually 're-discovered' the contested solution (for the special cubic equation $x^3 + ax = b$) and when imparting the secret to Cardano claimed he made Cardano swear an oath 'never to publish it and put it down in cipher.' The opening sentence of the *Ars Magna* (p. 7) suggests the rudimentary state of acknowledgments in the sixteenth century. 'This art originated with Mohamet, the son of Moses the Arab. Leonardo of Pisa is a trustworthy source for this statement.'

93 Mahoney, *The Mathematical Career*, p. 7.

94 See n. 90 above. On Leonardo's study of printed technical literature, see n. 135 below.

Magnus or Roger Bacon.[95] Medieval schoolmen indeed often seemed more eager to learn from guildsmen than the latter were to publicize what they knew. Here again it seems worth recalling that the spread of glad tidings was cultivated by medieval churchmen but guarding trade secrets was inculcated in medieval apprentices. Insofar as artisan-authors did contribute to sixteenth-century technical literature, they were risking the disapproval of colleagues who felt that guild 'mysteries' were not intended to be disclosed. Their prefaces show their felt need to justify themselves. In resorting to publicity, they were not perpetuating workshop traditions but breaking with them instead.

Even where secrecy had not been enforced during previous centuries, and where letters were mastered by shopkeepers' sons, apprenticeship learning and unwritten recipes were the customary channels for transmitting the tricks of all trades. New techniques or inventions might be mentioned in writing, but this was usually in a sermon that some clerk had transcribed. Before the advent of printing, events of significance, when reported at all, were usually conveyed from the pulpit. 'Lenses were already known in the thirteenth century...For three centuries a kind of conspiracy of silence was entered into concerning them... they became an object of theoretical study only in the sixteenth century.'[96] News of the invention of spectacles was not suppressed by 'a conspiracy' in the later middle ages. But it was conveyed by word of mouth somewhat vaguely in a sermon that was transcribed.[97] By the early seventeenth century, however, technology had gone to press. Reports of optical instruments which were being developed gave rise to priority struggles over inventions such as 'Galileo's tube.' As noted above, movable type had a unique advantage over the other late medieval inventions, for it alone was able to advertise itself. Hence the unusually rapid spread of printing and debates about its inventor's name. Inventors of compass or gunpowder might also be described as

95 Interchanges between the two groups based on personal contact rather than written materials are well described by Shelby, 'Education of Medieval Masons,' pp. 16–18, who suggests how masons and their patrons collaborated on Gothic cathedral building. For reference by Roger Bacon to Magister Petrus' desire to 'learn from metal workers' et al. see Zilsel, 'Origins of William Gilbert's Method,' p. 30. Other references are given by Crombie, 'Commentary,' Clagett (ed.) Critical Problems, p. 73.

96 Rossi, Philosophy, Technology, p. 35. Rossi refers to an article by V. Ronchi, who has underlined the prolonged failure to put lenses to use for scientific purposes (as in telescopes and microscopes) in numerous studies.

97 See Rosen, 'Invention of Eyeglasses' for data on the Lenten sermon delivered at Florence in 1306 by Friar Giordano of Pisa – one of the earliest extant specimens of a transcribed vernacular Italian sermon.

subject to a 'kind of conspiracy of silence.'[98] It was not that such technical inventions were despised or even undervalued until a new class of capitalists came along; it was rather that in the late fifteenth century, functions performed by the pulpit began to be taken over by the press. The advent of printing lessened reliance on oral transmission even while providing powerful new incentives to open closed sketch-books and publicize the tricks of various trades. The result was an avalanche of technical treatises and teach-yourself books, which had at least as much effect on advanced studies as on procedures followed in workshops.

Just how this early printed literature may have affected actual practices and techniques is a complex question. On the one hand there is evidence to support the sceptical opinion that 'teach-yourself' books proved more helpful to teachers than doers.[99] The opinion that books explaining double-entry bookkeeping were more helpful for teachers of accountancy than for merchants has already been noted.[100] A recent biographer of Fermat makes the same point concerning many presumably 'practical,' problem-solving sixteenth-century arithmetic texts.[101] Similarly Samuel Eliot Morison emphasizes how mariners went on using dead-reckoning and ignoring treatises presumably written for their benefit.

To assume that once an instrument is invented or a rutter or nautical almanac published, every offshore shipmaster is familiar with them is a complete fallacy. The very simple mathematical calculations involved in obtaining latitude from a meridional observation of the sun were too much for most sailors in 1550 and are still too much for many sailors in the present century.[102]

But although some scepticism concerning uncritical claims made for technical literature may be justified, it can also be carried too far.

---

98 For 'scraps of evidence' pertaining to the invention of the compass, see Kreutz, 'Mediterranean Contributions.' Diverse views on the origin of gunpowder are discussed by Hale, 'Gunpowder and the Renaissance,' pp. 115–17.

99 It is a mistake to assume as does McLean, Humanism and the Rise of Science, p. 142, that when John Dee directed his preface at technicians and artisans, he must have hit the target at which he presumably aimed. For useful discussions of general problems associated with relating technical literature to innovation, see Mathias, 'Who Unbound Prometheus?' chap. 3, Cipolla, Before the Industrial Revolution, chap. 6.

100 See above, p. 383, volume I. For good description of the professional 'overkill' in early treatises on bookkeeping see Yamey, 'Scientific Bookkeeping.'

101 Mahoney, The Mathematical Career, p. 6.

102 Morison, The European Discovery of America, pp. 141–2. See also discussion of tables carried by Columbus, pp. 582 ff below.

Whatever the case with double-entry bookkeeping or 'cossist algebra,' or nautical tables, there were printed materials – converting weights and measures, giving distances between important towns or guides to foreign languages and phrases – that probably did provide practical aid. Furthermore learned professional groups often profited from rule books, even though craftsmen went on using rules of thumb. Simple sailors might fail to master improved declination tables but what about cartographers, geographers and astronomers? Were they not likely to put such tables to good use? Even now, journals such as *Popular Mechanics* are rarely read by real mechanics; but they are studied with profit by students who are drawn toward some kind of scientific career. During the first centuries of printing, similar trends prevailed. The young Isaac Newton was stimulated by John Wilkins' *Mathematical Magick* – a 'popular science' treatise which owed something in turn to the works of Simon Stevin and to Galileo's early tracts.[103] Browsing at book fairs and reading at random probably helps to account for the proliferation of 'amateurs' and 'dilettanti' – who joined the scientific societies as gentlemen of leisure without any special institutional affiliations or professional roles. The same activity was common among professional scientists. As already noted, significant and novel services were rendered by technical handbooks which acted as 'silent instructors' during student years.

When dealing with the 'reaction of learned men to the state of technology' at all events, more consideration ought to be given to the precise state in question: had technology gone to press or was it still largely concealed? Beginning with early editions of Vitruvius and Valturius' first illustrated volume on military engines, going on to Biringuccio and Agricola, culminating in the late sixteenth-century works of Besson and Ramelli, the machines that men used in the great workshops and mines and arsenals of Western Europe were made increasingly visible to the armchair traveller. In this light it seems doubtful that the

philosopher of antiquity had as great an opportunity of appreciating the inventiveness of craftsmen as his successors of the sixteenth and seventeenth centuries...The success of craft empiricism was nothing new in...early-modern times...if the philosopher became conscious of its significance for

103 On young Newton, see Manuel, *Portrait*, p. 406 and citation on p. 245, volume I above. On Wilkins' work, see Shapio, *John Wilkins*, p. 43.

science it was not because such success was more dramatic now than in the past. It was always there to be seen by those who had eyes to see it, and the change was in the eyes of the beholder.[104]

Craft successes must have been more difficult to see as long as oral and scribal transmission prevailed. As discussion of Renaissance book illustration has already indicated, engravings which displayed the engines required to destroy a fortress or to erect an obelisk, did dramatize engineering feats. Readers who turned the pages of Jacques Besson's appropriately named *Theatre of Machines* were witnessing a dramatic spectacle that previous scholars had not seen, just as readers of Agricola and of Vesalius had their eyes opened to 'veins and vessels' that had been less visible before.[105]

In this regard, it is probably misleading to make too much of the continuous scholarly interest exhibited in technology since the twelfth century or to try to demonstrate the 'rising articulateness of higher artisans' by lining up a long series of 'technical treatises'

extending backwards to the sources behind the twelfth century chemical treatises of Adelard of Bath and of Theophilus the priest and forwards through the writings...of Walter of Henley...Cennini...Alberti and the other fifteenth-century German and Italian treatises on military engineering and architecture. The series continues through the sixteenth-century descriptions of crafts, and inventions by such writers as Agricola...and Ramelli down indeed to the Royal Society's projected History of Trades and the plates of the *Encyclopédie*.[106]

The path that led to the *Grande Encyclopédie* was not open in the days of Theophilus the priest. Instead of a gradually 'rising articulateness' there was a fairly abrupt change. Before printing, even the most 'articulate artisans' preferred to keep their sketchbooks closed. They might not have taken

the extra precaution of describing their designs in mirror-writing...but they were strongly inclined to keep their discoveries for themselves. In a world which knew little of copyrights or patents, the inventor had no interest in publicizing his work for others to steal. So long as their secrets remained secrets they were valuable, but once they became public property they were worthless. No wonder that few 'inventors' were prepared to expose their brain-children to the critical judgement of their peers.

104 A. R. Hall, 'The Scholar and the Craftsman,' p. 15.
105 See pp. 261–2, volume I above.
106 Crombie, 'Commentary,' Clagett (ed.) *Critical Problems*, p. 77

Even so a patent system was beginning to grow up. Monarchs had less interest...in keeping inventions private and...were ready to grant privileges of copyright as their ancestors had granted lands, making the reproduction of specified inventions illegal for the space of several years. Protected in this way, mechanicians might have begun to think it worth the risk of telling the world of their discoveries in books...The growing market for books of mathematical instruments...could have taught them that publicity was as good a servant as secrecy.[107]

The emergence of mathematical practitioners and instrument-makers as distinctive occupational groups is often associated with new demands for greater precision made by monarchs, bureaucrats and merchants during early-modern times and is accordingly related to middle-class enterprise and expanding dynastic states. The output of mathematical instruments, atlases, globes and 'theatres of machines' should also be related to the new possibility of profiting from disclosing instead of withholding the tricks of varied trades. The new publicity apparatus enabled ingenious individuals to satisfy the long-standing 'public' aims of bureaucrats and army engineers even while serving their own private needs as well. It was not so much that 'monarchs had less interest in keeping inventions private' but that inventors had been given new incentives for making their brain children public.

The reasons for the growing demand for instruments of navigation in the sixteenth century are obvious. But there was also a demand for instruments by surveyors, architects, and miners. The old rule-of-thumb methods were felt to be inadequate; greater precision was now demanded and precise instruments of calculation needed to attain it.[108]

It seems likely that old rule-of-thumb methods had been felt to be inadequate by some groups for many centuries. As Rupert Hall reminds us, interest in precisely predicting the motion of projectiles did not wait until the introduction of gunpowder and cannon into warfare. 'The simplest methods of hurling projectiles – the human arm, the sling, the bow – pose problems of motion no less emphatically than more complex or powerful devices.'[109] The desire to publicize devices and techniques for determining the trajectory of projectiles waited – not for the invention of gunpowder but for opportunities opened up by print.

[107] Keller, *A Theatre of Machines*, p. 3.   [108] Keller, *A Theatre of Machines*, p. 3.
[109] A. R. Hall, 'The Scholar and the Craftsman,' p. 16.

The effect of early printed technical literature on science and technology is open to question. That it served as a major vehicle for the expression of a new 'scientific ethos' seems less subject to doubt. The socially conscious, public-spirited and progressive themes sounded in numerous prefaces have been noted in many studies. In expressing a desire to serve the cause of posterity, in setting unselfish service to humanity against guild monopolies and the selfish pursuit of personal glory, sixteenth-century authors repeatedly anticipated later Enlightenment views.[110] But the new values expressed in the prefaces were derived less from old routines pursued in artisan workshops than from reactions to the publicity apparatus furnished by print. By a marvelous alchemy, print transmuted self-seeking activities into public good. To advertise an invention or sea chart did not render it worthless but attracted purchasers to the shops of instrument-makers and map-publishers.

In this respect I agree with those who question Zilsel's emphasis on the strategic role played by workshops and arsenals where men were accustomed to working together and were familiar with ideas of progress that applied to improvements in particular arts and crafts.[111] When accounting for the emergence of an idea of progress one ought not to overlook the accumulation of improvements leading to the perfecting of certain skills among artisans. But a significant strategic role must also be reserved for the shift from script to print. If one looks hard enough, one may find different kinds of progressive themes being played in a limited way in libraries and observatories as well as in workshops or mines during the age of scribes. Print encouraged a fuller orchestration of all such themes and for the first time enabled them to be continuously sustained,

'The idea that technology must be furthered through publication made head-way in the sixteenth century'[112] mainly because technology could be furthered by publication – could 'go to press,' that is – for the first time. Map-publishers such as Ortelius, Mercator, Blaeu, and Hondius sponsored new forms of intellectual cooperation and served astronomers and mariners, historians, and merchant adventurers in new ways – not because they were affiliated with painters and Netherlands guildsmen but because they could take advantage of a new

[110] In addition to Zilsel, Rossi *et al.*, see Houghton, 'The History of Trades.'
[111] See e.g. Keller, 'Zilsel, The Artisans,' pp. 281–6.   [112] Zilsel, 'Genesis,' p. 335.

medium for duplicating charts and books.[113] The 'fading of guild secrecy' was not due to the growth of large-scale enterprise in general but to a particular enterprise represented by the expanding printing industry, that made possible technical publication programs.

In other words, new attitudes toward publicity ought to be related to new forms of publicity. Discussion of how authors of technical treatises dealt with a so-called 'contribution process' should be related to the new kind of 'contribution,' authors who were served by printers could make.[114] Cooperation among artisans and between patrons had long been encouraged by large-scale endeavors. The construction of cathedrals no less than the later manufacture of cannons had called for a pooling of varied talents. Ventures in cooperative data collection, however, could not be continuously or systematically pursued until after printers had set to work.[115] Thereafter authors were likely to write prefaces in which they supplemented traditional scribal themes by expressing their hope that their work might contribute in some way to the betterment of mankind – to a collective and cumulative cognitive advance.

This new concern about making a contribution toward a collective goal, this new desire to serve humanity and posterity, is misinterpreted when described as peculiarly altruistic. 'Knowledge is no longer the business of literati greedy for personal fame and disputing schoolmen,' says Zilsel, in connection with the *Transactions* of the Royal Society.[116] One need only glance at the long list of priority struggles to see that the rise of science entailed no particular decrease in greed or vanity or contentiousness among men of knowledge or inventors of useful things. Socially useful techniques could be publicized in the sixteenth century not because of the rise of a new class but because of the advent of print. Artisan-authors were no less attracted by the lure of new intellectual property rights than were literati and schoolmen. Dürer's preface, which expressed the wish to contribute to a collective endeavor, to augment and improve the art of painting for the benefit

---

113 See Zilsel, 'Genesis,' pp. 344–5 where Zilsel singles out these map-publishers as exemplifying the new approach.

114 Over-emphasis on craft traditions and neglect of new trends launched by print seem marked in Lilley, 'Robert Recorde and the Idea of Progress.' Lilley's theories are invoked but fail to help Keith Thomas analyze certain 'puzzling phenomena' in *Religion and the Decline of Magic*, p. 430. See also discussion on pp. 245–6, volume 1 above.

115 Here again, an exception should be made to cover certain major scribal message centers such as the Alexandrian Museum.   116 Zilsel, 'Genesis,' p. 348.

of later generations,[117] was not unrelated to the output of sheets containing giant woodcuts which, 'like the ships of a great merchant, bearing a distinctive flag, carried his initials: 'A.D.' all over the world.'[118] Whatever prefaces said about the glory of God and the good of humanity, the fact remained that contributors to technical literature were not only better able to serve others after printing; they were also better able to serve themselves.

We can discern the first...rudimentary formulations of the new concept of ...scientific progress in many texts written by the 'master craftsmen' and the engineers of the sixteenth century. As justifications for their work the technicians advanced the glory of God and public utility. And this work was viewed as something that would be added to an already existing fund of knowledge destined to be prolonged, perfected and integrated in time through the cooperation of others. Edgar Zilsel in a felicitous image has contrasted the workshop arsenal and *bottega*...where men worked together, to a monk's cell and a humanist's study. Zilsel draws conclusions...that are not wholly acceptable. But we can agree...that the birth of capitalism and ...economic competition led those men to theorize goals...which were... very different and certainly more impersonal than those of individual sanctification or literary immortality.[119]

Even while 'theorizing' about impersonal goals, however, artisan-authors were achieving eponymity. The personal celebrity and literary immortality won by Dürer, Paré, Palissy *et al.* had not been within the reach of guildsmen before.

Not only did these authors seek fame much as had scribal poets, but they were no less attracted than any other social group by the prospect of pecuniary rewards and material gain. It is noteworthy that high-minded passages justifying the writing of books by 'humble' craftsmen often went together with appeals to the reader to visit the author's workshop where 'marvelous things can be seen' and with the inclusion of addresses where instruments were on sale.[120] The important point

[117] Cited by Lilley, 'Robert Recorde and the Idea of Progress,' p. 10.
[118] Panofsky, *Albrecht Dürer*, p. 44.
[119] Rossi, *Philosophy, Technology*, pp. 70–1. Rossi follows Zilsel in citing treatises written by a mixed group of authors ranging from vernacular writing artisans and/or engineers (Tartaglia, Dürer, Paré, Norman) to the Latin-reading astronomer–publisher 'Apianus' and map-publisher Mercator. See Zilsel, 'Genesis,' pp. 343–7.
[120] See examples given of Henry Lyte, Robert Norman, Bernard Palissy on p. 241, volume I above. W. J. Blaeu also made clear where his maps, globes, and sea charts could be found. Early printers' colophons and booksellers' catalogues were among the first printed materials to treat readers as potential purchasers and guide them to places of sale.

is that selfishness and altruism could be served at the same time. This capacity to satisfy mixed motives needs more attention because it helps to explain the driving power of the press.

This point is just as applicable to learned Latin treatises as to more popular vernacular ones; to the 'brain children' of professors as to those of instrument-makers – if, indeed, the two figures can be kept apart.[121] A certain ambivalence concerning new forms of publicity characterized academicians no less than artisans at first. Both groups contained men who expressed their desire to disclose information for virtuous motives and who became entangled in priority disputes. It has been suggested that 'the craft of philologists like Fichet and Budé was changed by the invention of printing in ways parallel to the crafts of barber surgeons and navigators following the introduction of gunpowder and the compass.'[122] I am arguing, however, that craftsmen *and* scholars, barber–surgeons *and* philologists were affected by the same invention at the same time. When a barber–surgeon like Paré could become a published author, his craft was changed perhaps even more fundamentally than was the case when wounds were made by bullets rather than arrows. In the early-modern era, 'scholarship had as much ground on which to base its view of cumulative advance as had technology' notes a critic of Zilsel.[123] But scholarship and technology also shared common ground, namely the early printers' workshops. The new flow of technical literature required skills cultivated in the schoolroom no less than in urban workshops or mines. In view of the significance assigned to 'rudimentary formulations' of 'the new concept of scientific progress' it is necessary to repeat that texts written *for* craftsmen and engineers were not always written *by* them. Granted that an 'awareness of the...necessity of intellectual cooperation and of the progressive character of knowledge in time is...evident in passages in many "technical" books written in the sixteenth century,' this awareness should not be viewed as peculiar to master craftsmen. It was shared by preachers, teachers, and other learned men.

When analyzing diverse approaches toward new forms of publicity,

---

121 Galileo combined both roles, inventing his 'proportional compass' while serving as a professor at Padua (see n. 11 above). So did his rival, the Jesuit astronomer, Christopher Scheiner, whose *Exegeses Fundamentorum Gnomonicorum* (Ingolstadt, 1615) contained a new design for an elliptical compass. Rose, 'Renaissance Italian Methods of Drawing the Ellipse,' pp. 399–400. In general the designing of scientific instruments seems to cut across town gown divisions.
122 Kinser, 'Ideas of Temporal Change,' p. 710.
123 Keller, 'Zilsel, the Artisans,' p. 286.

moreover, one must assign due weight to personal idiosyncrasies which often counted more than did occupational roles. Cardano's flair for self-advertisement probably owed as much to temperament as to parental example or professional status group. Vesalius 'rushed into print' but other professors of anatomy did not.[124] Whereas some mathematicians and astronomers ran new presses themselves, others were reluctant even to let their manuscripts get into printers' hands. That Paracelsians tended to favor a paradoxical mixture of publicity with secrecy has been already noted. Bishop Sprat's complaint on this point is worth citing:

This desire of glory and to be counted *Authors* prevails on all, even on many of the dark and reserv'd Chymists themselves: who are ever printing their greatest mysteries though indeed they seem to do it with so much reluctancy ...which makes their style to resemble the smoak in which they deal.[125]

One reason why early-modern trends are peculiarly confusing to the historian of science is that many charlatans and pseudo-scientists were eager publicity-hounds, and many gifted professionals clung to habits shaped by scribes. It took time before the magician could be distinguished from the scientist by his refusal to disclose all that was known about his arts, by his 'smoky' style, and by his reluctance to frame his theories in a form where they could be openly tested and accepted or rejected.

Furtiveness clung to alchemy. It thus sinned against the open altruism of the true scientific spirit. A precept of science is free interchange. 'Science' said Rutherford, 'depends on the combined wisdom of thousands of men all thinking about the same problem.' The alchemist concealed from others such knowledge as he thought he had. [He] devised secret systems. Cryptic alphabets...anagrams and acrostics masked [his] results.[126]

Rutherford's vision of a cooperative endeavor, which entailed the use of print, had been clearly articulated by Francis Bacon in the early seventeenth century. 'Knowledge of Nature was to be public; indeed, the jealously guarded secrets of craftsmen were to be set out in great collections of "histories." '[127] Bacon condemned magic for its 'non-

---

[124] See discussion of the ambitious but long delayed publication program, involving elaborate illustration, of Fabricius in Adelman, *Embryological Treatises of Fabricius*, p. 23. See also Whitteridge, *William Harvey*, p. 19.

[125] Sprat, *History of the Royal Society*, part 2, section viii, p. 74. See also discussion of secrecy and publicity, pp. 274 ff, volume 1 above.

[126] Sherrington, *The Endeavour*, p. 46.   [127] Rattansi, 'Alchemy and Natural Magic,' p. 135.

progressive, non-cooperative methods.' He attacked alchemy for placing too much stress on the 'solitary inspiration of the individual genius,' and for relying on 'special secret transmission' rather than 'normal public channels.' His program for human mastery of nature was predicated on a vast collaborative collective effort that required resort to publication at every stage of the game.[128]

Bacon's program was taken over by the Commonwealth of Learning and later became a hallmark of Enlightenment thought; yet it was by no means commonly shared by the learned men of his own day. Indeed Sir Walter Raleigh took the opposite side. Somewhat soured, no doubt, by confinement in the Tower, Raleigh praised Archimedes for withholding inventions designed 'to enrich a Mechanicall trade and teach the art of murdering men.' He defended 'alchymists and al others that haue...any secret skill,' for not wanting to 'cast away upon men of no worth the long travells of an understanding braine.'[129] As Raleigh's comments may suggest, in the early seventeenth century furtiveness was by no means a clear sign that charlatans were at work. Cryptic alphabets, anagrams and acrostics did not necessarily conceal trickery. The appearance of strange codes and ciphers might be a sign that a mathematical genius was inventing a new language or giving birth to the equivalent of the Pythagorean theorem. (That ancient Egyptians had concealed fundamental equations in their mysterious hieroglyphs continued to be believed until the deciphering of the Rosetta Stone.)[130] Bacon's opposition to secrecy went together with his antipathy to mathematicians and to a language of numbers whose significance he never understood. In the middle ages it should be remembered, secrecy was not peculiar to alchemists. It also characterized mathematicians and mechanics.[131] Acrostics and ciphers continued to attract many mathematicians down to Leibniz and beyond. There were still 'scientific societies' in the early seventeenth century which exchanged information by means of ciphers and codes.[132]

[128] Rossi, *Francis Bacon*, pp. 30–5.
[129] Cited from Raleigh's *History of the World* (book 1, part 5, chap. 3, section 15) by Rattansi, 'Alchemy and Natural Magic,' p. 136.
[130] See Sprat, *History of the Royal Society*, p. 5 on this point.
[131] See Gandz, 'Invention of the Decimal Fractions,' pp. 29–30, for description of how the medieval mathematician, Bonfils, deliberately concealed his procedures and substituted easily memorized but cumbersome inelegant 'rules of thumb.' See also references discussed on pp. 277 ff, volume 1 above.
[132] On use of ciphers and secret codes by Prince Cesi's Academy of the Lincei see Preserved Smith, *History of Modern Culture* 1, 155–6. The effect of print on codes and ciphers is worth

How furtiveness and the 'true scientific spirit' could still be combined in the early sixteenth century is shown by Leonardo da Vinci's work. The celebrated contrast drawn by George Sarton, between Dürer who turned to print and Leonardo who shunned it, seems instructive in this regard:

The comparison between these two men is valid because they were interested, roughly speaking, in the same things; the difference between them was that Leonardo accumulated notes and perplexities, while Dürer's thoughts though less deep were more fertile. Dürer would not bother much about a subject unless he had a practical purpose such as the writing of a book. He not only prepared his books as any bookmaker would but he printed them...

Dürer was always practical and earthbound. Leonardo was just the opposite. While Leonardo disdained typography and engraving, Dürer understood immediately the commercial possibilities of both arts...He established himself as printer, engraver, and bookseller...We are well informed about his business dealings because he kept careful accounts of all his receipts and expenditures...signed all his works and often added the date. Leonardo did not bother about such matters. He was as indifferent to chronology as the Hindus...

Dürer was a businessman...capable of taking some interest in scientific questions but he was not a man of science. Leonardo on the contrary was a pure artist, a distinterested inventor, a man of science.[133]

The contrast is vividly, but unfairly, drawn with anachronistic overtones developed at Dürer's expense. The German businessman is used merely as a foil for the romanticized portrayal of the Italian artist and one loses sight of the creative talents that produced the brooding figure of 'Melancholia I.' Dürer deserves no more to be stereotyped as a nineteenth-century bourgeois philistine than do other humanists and artists such as Erasmus or Raphael who also took full advantage of printing and engraving. Coming from an indefatigable and conscientious chronicler such as Sarton, whose many large volumes might well be condemned by romantics for dry-as-dust pedantry, the

separate study. Complex letter–number systems (not unlike those used in the Cabala) had been developed both in connection with scribal memory arts and also for the purpose of indexing or cross-referencing large compilations and anthologies. Handwriting manuals in print made it more difficult for diplomats to assume that written messages would be illegible if they fell into the wrong hands. Beginning with L. B. Alberti's invention of a 'cipher wheel' (which was perhaps inspired by movable type according to Gadol, pp. 207–8) going on to Trithemius' *Steganographia* and *Polygraphia* and culminating in the work of seventeenth-century virtuosi – such as John Wilkins and Leibniz – the arts of coding and decoding were propelled in new directions. David, *Le Débat sur les Ecritures*, pp. 26–7, 29.

133 Sarton, *Six Wings*, pp. 232–3.

portrayal of Leonardo as a 'capricious' bohemian poet and dreamer who turned out to be the true 'man of science' seems somewhat paradoxical. The paradox deepens when one notes that Sarton fully recognized that Leonardo, for all his brilliant scientific work, failed to contribute very much to the science of his day.

His love for science and his zeal need not be argued...but is it possible to ascribe to him a single discovery, except such as are contained implicitly in his drawings?

In order to receive credit for a discovery it is not enough to make it. One must explain it; one must prove very clearly that one has understood it... One might say that a discovery is not completed until it has been justified in public.

Leonardo's ideas were like seeds that failed to nurture. They remained buried in his notes and drawings...

The most elaborate part of Leonardo's scientific work is that on anatomy, yet this exerted little if any influence...One might say that the evolution of anatomy might be the same if Leonardo had never existed...

One of the greatest men of science in history...remained unknown by his own fault for he did nothing to publish his own discoveries; in most cases indeed he did not even bother to complete them...

Nothing is more curious and perplexing...than the caprices of the mechanical inventor. Leonardo invented and reinvented a whole series of machines, yet he overlooked two of the greatest inventions not only of his own time but of all time: printing and engraving.[134]

Actually Leonardo did not overlook advantages conferred by printed materials to the point of refusing to consult them. As noted earlier, he consulted a fair number of printed texts.[135] His lack of Latin learning limited his range. It led to struggles with word lists and slowed down the progress of his studies in technically sophisticated fields.

Compared to Vesalius, Leonardo was slow to gain a thorough acquaintance with classical anatomy at its best...Ignorance does not place Leonardo's

---

[134] Sarton, *Six Wings*, pp. 228–9.
[135] The list of Leonardo's collection of books, given by Reti, 'Two Unpublished Manuscripts of Leonardo da Vinci,' pp. 81 ff., shows how his library expanded in the decade after 1497. How the study of newly printed vernacular works by ancients and moderns (especially the illustrations in *De Re Militari* by Valturius) entered in his work as an engineer is well described by Gille, *Renaissance Engineers*, pp. 52–3, 122–3, 132, 144. See also Aiton, 'Essay Review,' *Studies in History and Philosophy of Science* (1970–1); Reti, 'Leonardo and Ramelli,' p. 577. How his anatomical studies were guided by his limited access to technical literature and how belated acquaintance with some of Galen's work enriched his later oeuvre is demonstrated by Kemp in two seminal essays: 'Il Concetto dell' Anima' and 'Dissection and Divinity.'

researches at an empirical advantage...His early dissections tend to reflect partial knowledge of debased traditions.[136]

His later studies show how his knowledge also was enriched by contacts with learned men and their works. But Leonardo himself did remarkably little to enrich the studies of others in turn. The many authorities who repeat Leonardo's favorite dictum 'painting is natural philosophy' might well pause over his own failure to serve the natural philosophers of his day. In view of his preference for 'mute' visual statements against 'blind' verbal ones, there is a certain irony in the fate of his own superbly rendered picture-sequences of embryonic development. These sequences were too 'silent' to speak to sixteenth-century scientists. One other point is worth underlining here: if the development of anatomy as a scientific discipline left Leonardo's observations out of account, this was not because university doors failed to open but because his remarkable sketchbooks remained closed.

3. GALENIC SCIENCE REVIVED AND SURPASSED: RESETTING THE STAGE FOR THE 'NEW ANATOMY'

In the history of anatomy Leonardo da Vinci, the great artist, probably made less of a mark than did the master-printer Charles Estienne. As a member of a scholar–printer dynasty, Estienne was a better Latinist and more erudite than either Leonardo or Dürer. Many of the same skills that were useful for producing polyglot Bibles and multi-lingual dictionaries were also helpful in handling Greco-Latin and Arabic terms used for parts of the body. Such terms, which proved to be a stumbling block for Leonardo, were more easily mastered by an editor and proof reader such as Servetus[137] or by a member of the scholar–printers' dynasty such as Estienne. This urban entrepreneur, who also composed a road guide for French merchants and a handbook

---

136 Kemp, 'Dissection and Divinity,' p. 201. Along with Keele, Kemp accepts Vasari's suggestion that Marcantonio della Torre, professor of anatomy at the University of Pavia, probably guided Leonardo's anatomical studies and was responsible for the Galenic influence that led to Leonardo's improved later work. On Leonardo's word lists, see references given by Augusto Marinoni, book review, *Technology and Culture* (1972).

137 Servetus followed Vesalius in Paris as an assistant to Guinther (or Winter) of Andernach and, like Rabelais, also worked for a Lyons publishing firm (Trechsel) in the 1530s. His work provides a good example of the overlap between Bible study and geographical and medical research. See O'Malley, *Michael Servetus*.

for landed proprietors, had close contacts with university science. When Vesalius as a student in Paris in the 1530s was assisting the distinguished Professor Guinther (or Winter) of Andernach who edited Galen's *Anatomical Procedures*, Estienne was assisting his relative, the Paris printer Simon de Colines, who had charge of publishing the first edition of this important Latin text.[138] Thereafter, Vesalius went on to become a professor while Estienne carried on in the publishing trade. As pioneering authors of new illustrated texts, however, the anatomist–printer and professor were close rivals and spurred each other on.[139]

Beginning about 1520 there was a great rush of anatomical works, one after another of varying degrees of originality. All are...more or less influenced by Galen. Each...has its own merits and its own discoveries; all together represent the 'new anatomy.' It is difficult to distinguish them chronologically for books were often years in publication; one of the distinctions of Vesalius was the way in which he rushed into print.[140]

As noted above, although Vesalius was a young man in a hurry, other anatomists were not. Yet most professors who contributed to this increasingly important academic science in the sixteenth century differed from prior generations in that they had had eventual publication in mind. Many of them helped to prepare plates, and process copy while others consulted printers, engravers, and artists as university professors had never done before. Whether they were engaged helping to supervise illustrations or in copy-editing medical manuscripts or in following polemical pamphleteers, all members of the new generation of anatomy students were encouraged to rethink familiar problems and to handle them along new lines. 'One wrong word may now kill

138 On Vesalius' study of the *Anatomical Procedures* which 'started him on his triumphant career' see Singer (ed. and tr.) *Galen on Anatomical Procedures*, pp. xiii, 2. Among other services rendered by Robert Estienne's stepfather, the printer, Simon de Colines, was that of helping Jean Fernel, the future 'father of physiology' on his way through medical school. See Sherrington, *The Endeavour*, pp. 3–4. Fernel's early publications stemming from his pre-medical work on the *quadrivium* included the *Monolasphaerium* (de Colines, 1526) (which had a title page border bearing *quadrivium* symbols attributed to Oronce Finé) and the *Cosmotheoria* (1527) which contained data on the measurement of the earth, later confirmed by Jean Picard in 1671. Fernel's 'Dialogue' of 1542 also contains a celebrated passage on printing as facilitating both recovery and discovery. See Sherrington, pp. 3–4, 12, 15–17, 21–2. Also Sarton, *Six Wings*, pp. 191–6.

139 See Kellett, 'Two Anatomies,' pp. 342–50 for discussion of litigation between Estienne and his collaborator, de la Rivière in 1539 which alerted Vesalius to their project. See also Rath, 'Charles Estienne.' Charles Estienne's road guide has been noted above, p. 387, volume 1. His *L'Agriculture et la Maison Rustique* (Paris: J Du Puys, 1564) ran through many editions. It was aimed at proprietors and land management agents.

140 Boas, *Scientific Renaissance*, p. 142.

thousands of men,' noted Rabelais in the course of collating texts by Hippocrates and Galen for the scholar–printer Gryphius who was eager to get editions out for the Lyons book fair of 1532.[141]

That professors had the preparation of a printed edition in mind helps to account for the marked change in attitude which differentiates Vesalius' school from that of previous professors of medicine. The 'attitude of scrupulous diligence' toward 'observation' and 'description of factual data' exhibited by Vesalius and some of his fellow anatomists has been singled out by many authorities. They tend to agree with Rossi that the new attitude placed 'traditional frames of knowledge...in a crisis situation.'[142] Although medievalists occasionally demur, for the most part there is agreement that Vesalius approached his field with a new insistence on 'systematic analytic and meticulous' description, and was less inclined to tolerate 'obscure and enigmatic terms.' Other features that are singled out include the new assertion of the dignity and value of mechanical arts, and the new use of

special illustrative techniques...to translate the results of observation into the clearest, and most comprehensive graphic images possible. It was this desire for clarity, this precise will to avoid mistakes, to place oneself deliberately at a distance from the fabulous view of things, that a work like Vesalius' *De Fabrica* and Agricola's *De Re Metallica* had in common...[143]

In addition to his own views, Rossi cites those of others on how Vesalius introduced 'an acute sense of the importance of minutiae, of the mastery of special methods and of precise and full reporting of observations' into biological science and how 'it became more objectionable to reproduce stereotyped words in the vicinity of correct images.'[144] As a description of new views and attitudes, Rossi's account cannot be faulted. But any explanation of how or why these new views appeared when they did must leave more room for the shift from script to print. Changed approaches to 'communicable knowledge' hinged on the transformation of communication techniques. The 'enormous distance' which separates the outlook of Vesalius or Agricola from that of medieval encyclopedists cannot be fathomed without prior consideration of the new features ushered in by print.

---

[141] Kline, 'Rabelais and the Age of Printing,' pp. 8–9. Kline also notes that Rabelais' work on Hippocrates and Galen helped win him a job as a doctor at the chief hospital in Lyons. He has cogent remarks on how assistants in Gryphius' workshop correlated work on medical texts with work on legal and biblical texts.   [142] Rossi, *Philosophy, Technology*, p. 49.
[143] Rossi, *Philosophy, Technology*, p. 49.   [144] Rossi, *Philosophy, Technology*, n. 82.

As discussion of Renaissance book illustration has already indicated, the new visual vocabulary developed by quattrocento draughtsmen and the new arts of engraving were of great importance in transforming the study of anatomy. But no less important was the reconstruction of the Galenic corpus that accompanied publication of all of Galen's works. The admission of barber–surgeons to certain college faculties although it created an uproar was probably of less consequence in reshaping medical school curriculum than was the re-editing of Galen and the output of pocket-sized texts.

in the anti-medieval and anti-Arabic climate of the period, every attempt was made to get...Galenic works into the hands of medical students: thus in 1528 there was published in Paris a series of four handy texts in pocket size ...The rise in importance of the medical school of the University of Paris dates from the renewed interest in Galen indicated by these publications. It was Johannes Guinther of Andernach...a professor at Paris who first published a Latin translation of the newly discovered and most important Galenic text: *On Anatomical Procedures*...Guinther was a medical humanist rather than a practicing anatomist but...[he] did perform...dissections as well as make translations. Vesalius as a student assisted Guinther in preparing the professor's own textbook.[145]

In the middle ages it had been customary also for students to help professors prepare texts as well as copy them out by hand. As a student in Paris in the early sixteenth century, however, Vesalius was less encumbered by the duties of a 'slavish' copyist and could devote more time to copy-editing. When his student days in Paris were over, he combined the activities of a professor with those of an author–editor who was in close contact with artists in Titian's workshop as well as the celebrated scholar–printers of the day.[146] He edited texts for major editions of Galen's collected works. After supervising preparation of the famous woodcuts that were made in Venice he got the manager of a distinguished printing firm to help him convey the finished blocks over the Alps to Oporinus in Basel where *De Fabrica* was seen through the press.[147] Oporinus, the son of a Strasbourg painter named Herbst,

[145] Boas, *Scientific Renaissance*, pp. 134–5.
[146] On questions raised about collaboration with Titian's assistants, see p. 267, volume 1 above, for pertinent references.
[147] See letter from Vesalius to Oporinus in Basel dated August 24, 1542 noting that blocks were being entrusted to Nicholas Stopius, manager of Daniel Bomberg's Venetian firm and 'well versed in the humanities.' Saunders and O'Malley, *Illustrations*, pp. 46 ff. See chap, 2, n. 39, volume 1 above for Herrlinger's discussion of refinement and durability of the blocks.

had mastered Latin, Greek, and Hebrew while working for the Amerbachs and Froben in Basel. He became an assistant to Paracelsus and served for a while as town physician and lecturer on medicine in Basel. He eventually formed his own Basel firm, in partnership with Thomas Platter. He extended hospitality to all the leading figures of the 'radical Reformation' and to the Marian exiles as well. He issued the first Latin edition of the Koran. He thus exemplified the protean character of the early scholar–printer. His workshop served as a cross-roads for all kinds of cultural exchange. He was superbly well equipped to supervise the varied tasks entailed in producing a work such as *De Fabrica*.[148]

Partly because it occurred under the aegis of scholar–printers in Venice, Lyons, Paris and Basel, the Galenic revival of the early sixteenth century took a different course than had similar revivals in prior centuries.

Humanism was another force...which played a part in bringing about the scientific revolution...improved editions and translations of...familiar works of Galen as well as the discovery and publication of a hitherto unknown Galenic text...gave a great boost to the study of anatomy...*De Fabrica*...one of the seminal works of the scientific revolution was itself founded to some extent on...Galen's works which [were]...virtually unknown before Vesalius' lifetime.

The rediscovery of classical scientific texts must therefore have a place in any discussion of the origins of the scientific revolution, but it is of course a limited place. The humanists looked back to classical antiquity as the golden age...this idea extends to the science of the ancients. A great feature of the scientific revolution however was that it did improve...upon the...ideas of the ancient world. The rediscovery of classical texts, which gave significant impetus to scientific studies cannot therefore account for the direction which these studies finally took.[149]

In my view the Galenic revival moved in a new direction because methods of transmission had been changed. Not humanism but printing gave the 'great boost' which led researchers to surpass the ancients and move toward new frontiers for the first time. The 'significant impetus'

---

148 Oporinus' circle is also discussed on p. 446, volume 1 above. Apart from Steinmann's biography, relevant data on his contacts with Vesalius are given by Pagel and Rattansi, 'Vesalius and Paracelsus'; O'Malley, *Andreas Vesalius*, pp. 131–3.

149 Alan G. R. Smith, *Science and Society*, pp. 45–6. For a similar statement concerning the relation between classical revivals and the surpassing of Greek science, see A. R. Hall, 'The Scholar and the Craftsman,' p. 11.

was provided by the new method of duplicating inherited technical literature which freed scholars from scribal labors and provided new means of achieving long sought goals. Vesalius' position *vis-à-vis* Galen was similar to that of Erasmus *vis-à-vis* St Jerome. He was aiming at reconstituting, reforming, and emending rather than replacing or discarding an ancient art. 'Anatomy will soon be cultivated in our academies,' he wrote hopefully, 'as it was of old in Alexandria.' He sought to 'restore from the world of the dead the knowledge of the parts of the human body that had died long ago' – to come closer to a 'pristine' knowledge that had become corrupted and confused. 'The notion of a *prisca medicina* and *anatomia* known to the ancients but lost from view after the Gothic invasions pervades the preface to the *De Fabrica*.'[150]

This notion (which was shared by Paracelsus, Agricola, and many others) seems to be yet another variation played on the familiar Petrarchan theme pertaining to rebirth, reconstruction and recall after an interval of darkness, destruction and forgetfulness. Petrarch, to be sure, had little use for medical studies and scornfully relegated ignoble bodies to doctors while reserving for philosophers and rhetoricians the more elevated education of minds.[151] Vesalius took the position adopted by many Renaissance physicians in the course of interdepartmental wars, that medical arts encompassed both theory and practice, philosophy and experience. The idealized Renaissance physician resembled Vitruvius' ideal architect. He claimed a superior role because his art encompassed all others and linked brain with hand.[152] Vesalius thus anticipated many recent interpretations by deploring the separation of mental from manual skills as indicative of the low state to which medicine had been brought by the ravages of the Goths. Nevertheless when he writes of the loss of the 'elegant compositions of the ancients' and their 'true knowledge of drugs,' when he castigates the 'barbarous names and false remedies' which had been left in the wake of the invasions, and when he celebrates the 'blessed age' which is emerging from 'utter darkness,' he does seem to be replaying a familiar Petrarchan theme.[153]

When trying to account for the ubiquity of this theme in the writings

[150] Pagel and Rattansi, 'Vesalius and Paracelsus,' p. 324.
[151] See chap. 3, n. 260, volume 1 above.
[152] On this topos, see references given in chap. 3, n. 251 and n. 257, volume 1 above.
[153] See Pagel and Rattansi, 'Vesalius and Paracelsus' for relevant citations.

of pioneers in early-modern science, the main features of scribal transmission deserve more attention than they usually receive. Many authorities seem to find it strange that so many early-modern scientists
thought that they were merely rediscovering 'ancient truths once
clearly perceived.' For the most part this belief is treated as a kind of
collective delusion and traced to some peculiar spell cast by a cult of
antiquity or of the hermetic tradition. There is much speculation, for
example, about the 'strange kind of historicism among the pioneers of
modern science which led them so far into the hermetic tradition...
that they conceived of their science as a rediscovery of ancient truths
once clearly perceived by the gifted and uncorrupted founders of
philosophy.'[154] Yet those virtuosi who believed they were rediscovering
what ancient sages knew were not necessarily being 'led far into
Hermeticism.' Rather they were reflecting long-prevailing attitudes
shaped by the repeated loss of manuscripts and reliance on evidence
supplied by scribes.

In view of what had happened to medical literature over the course
of time, the views expressed by anatomists such as Vesalius, at all events,
seem quite plausible. Anatomical data had been scrambled. Transmission of theoretical treatises on drugs had been separated from the living
experience of practicing apothecaries. Nomenclature had become
confused when manuscripts travelled along Greek–Arab–Latin routes.
Pictures of plants and animals had been corrupted and appropriate
labels had been lost. Certain important Galenic texts had almost
completely disappeared. In the 1530s, Galen's *Anatomical Procedures*
'broke entirely new ground.' Recovery of Galen meant discovery of
natural phenomena to professors and students in Vesalius' day.

Here as elsewhere, the transitory and incomplete revivals that had
occurred under the auspices of particular colleges during the middle
ages ought to be compared with the permanent, total process of recovery that occurred after printers set to work. It was not the practice
of dissection that distinguished sixteenth-century anatomy from that
of the thirteenth century. It was rather the retrieval of medical literature
and the way it was at last secured. The practice of dissection had been
revived at Bologna in the thirteenth century. There, a distinguished
professor of medicine, Mondino, not only used cadavers for demon-

---

154 A. R. Hall, 'Can the History of Science be History?' p. 208. Hall is referring especially to the
now celebrated interpretation of Newton offered by McGuire and Rattansi, 'Newton and the
"Pipes of Pan."'

stration but also prepared a useful and much used anatomy text. After Mondino's death, however, degeneration set in.

In Mondino dei Luzzi [c. 1275–1326] medieval anatomy reached its zenith. He dissected for research and...was probably the first teacher since the third century B.C. to demonstrate publicly on the human body. His *Anathomia*, which was printed many times, long remained a popular text. Eager to reconcile authorities he did not venture to assert his own views and perpetuated many mistakes. Good anatomists succeeded Mondino...but there was a general deterioration in the teaching of the subject...The body again became merely an illustration to the words of nobler men. Anatomy degenerated into the repetition of phrases and names.

The curve moves upward again toward the end of the fifteenth century. One factor in this seems to have been pressure in the medical schools for more demonstrative teaching...Another was recognition of human dissection...by the Papacy. The first printed anatomies with figures...in the last decade of the century and the first half of the sixteenth century show a whole group of able...anatomists at work.[155]

In my view, the curve did not merely 'move upward again.' It moved in a new direction, involving correction, feedback, and progressive improvement, rather than corruption and loss. Unlike medieval revivals, the sixteenth-century Galenic revival was not followed by a degenerate phase. On the contrary, full recovery of the Galenic corpus was merely a prelude to an era that saw Galen surpassed. Once the full corpus had been fixed in print it could be subjected to critical scrutiny. It became possible to perceive discrepancies between data and description that had not been perceived or disclosed before. Thus a major step was taken by Vesalius when he became aware that Galen was discussing a vertebra that could be found in the spine of a monkey but not in that of a man.[156] Moreover, the second edition of the *De Fabrica* was an improved version of the first.[157] The opposite was the case with copies of Mondino's long venerated text. *De Fabrica* itself was succeeded by even more elaborate publication programs aimed at surpassing Vesalius' treatise. By provoking a prolonged and vigorous

155 A. R. Hall, *Scientific Revolution*, p. 40. On Mondino's use of dissection as a way of merely demonstrating truths set down by Galenic texts see Singer, 'Confluence,' p. 265.
156 Edwin Clarke, book review, *Medical History* (1964), pp. 380–3, underlines the importance of the recovery of Galen's *Anatomical Procedures* in this connection. See also Pagel and Rattansi, 'Vesalius and Paracelsus,' p. 319.
157 In addition to the improved illustrations noted above, chap. 3, n. 39, volume 1, the merits of the second edition of *De Fabrica* (Basel: Oporinus, 1555) are noted by Adelman, *Embryological Treatises of Hieronymus Fabricius*, p. 60; and O'Malley, 'Vesalius,' p. 306.

debate, Vesalius' criticisms of Galen rendered much the same service to the next generations that was rendered by Copernicus' work.[158] Medical students were no longer presented with one single authoritative corpus of texts that they were expected to learn and then transmit to future generations in turn. They were confronted by alternative views that forced a reassessment of the evidence and encouraged further checking of data against description, leading to the overhauling of inherited schemes.

'Progress in anatomy before the sixteenth century is as mysteriously slow as its development after 1500 is startlingly rapid.'[159] If we are encouraged to regard academic science as impervious to changes wrought by printing, then this kind of reversal is bound to seem 'mysterious and startling.' The contrary is true, when the 'doors of the sixteenth century universities' however tightly 'closed to new scientific ideas' are nevertheless opened to early printers' workshops and to the new interchanges that took place in them.

[158] According to Whitteridge, *William Harvey*, p. 461, Vesalius expressed his growing doubts about the penetration of the septum by pores in the 1555 edition of *De Fabrica*. This probably alerted the next generation to a problem not thrashed out before. The diverse theories and debates that were put forth between the 1550s and 1620s and set the stage for *De Motu* are described by Whitteridge, p. 19 and Adelman, *Embryological Treatises of Hieronymus Fabricius*, p. 23.

[159] Boas, *Scientific Renaissance*, p. 130.

7

RESETTING THE STAGE FOR THE COPERNICAN REVOLUTION

In some ways the early stages of the Copernican Revolution resemble those just sketched in connection with the 'new anatomy.' Like anatomy, astronomy was initially transformed from within, so to speak, by members of a small Latin-writing élite engaged in preserving and transmitting sophisticated techniques first developed in antiquity and later retrieved in the twelfth century. *De Fabrica* and *De Revolutionibus* had more in common than their publication date of 1543.

Vesalius' role in the development of anatomy has many parallels to the role Copernicus played in the development of astronomy. Like Copernicus, Vesalius rejected certain crucial assumptions of his predecessors and replaced them with his own speculations...[Each man] produced a comprehensive text that was equal, if not superior to the text that it was designed to replace.[1]

By producing new technical treatises that were no less comprehensive than the old ones and yet diverged from the latter on certain major points, both authors presented the next generation of fellow professionals with alternatives that prior generations had not known. In this way both set in motion a revolutionary sequence whose outcome neither author could foresee. Insofar as they launched a new tradition even while aiming their work at emending an inherited one, both treatises seem to lend themselves to the line of analysis I have been trying out in this book. Both suggest, that is, how old pursuits produced new results after techniques of communication had been transformed.

Yet although the two authors shared some things in common, they reacted to the new arts of printing and engraving in a manner that sharply diverged. Unlike the young anatomist who 'rushed into print,'

1 Steneck, *The Scientific Press*, p. 12.

the ageing astronomer circulated handwritten texts, avoided the press and shunned publicity for most of his long life. This contrast seems worth pondering, because it has led many historians of the Copernican Revolution to underrate the printer's role. When dealing with Copernicus' seemingly negative reaction to the medium that Vesalius eagerly employed, several special circumstances need to be kept in mind.

For one thing, the pursuit of disparate disciplines has to be taken into account. Mathematical equations and diagrams were likely to have a more limited appeal than anatomical illustrations which artists as well as anatomists could use.[2] It is not unusual to find sixteenth-century authors of texts devoted to physics or astronomy or other mathematical sciences invoking the sign presumably posted over the entrance to Plato's Academy: 'Without a knowledge of geometry do not enter here.'[3] This warning was displayed on the title page of De Revolutionibus whereas the frontispiece of De Fabrica depicts a dissection being dramatized for all to see. This suggests that there may have been different assumed publics for the two works and that the astronomer envisaged a more restricted circle of readers than did the anatomist. Vesalius also may have been better attuned to publicity by the very nature of his profession being accustomed to perform anatomical demonstrations in front of large audiences. Although Copernicus may have given a few public lectures when visiting Italy, most of his life was spent working in a quiet study, far from theatres and crowds.

As an advocate of a theory presumably regarded as impious by the ancients, seemingly contrary to a literal reading of Scripture, and easily ridiculed by the wits of the day, Copernicus had additional special reasons for shunning publicity and for fearing the reaction it would bring.[4]

[2] This point is implied by Gillispie, *The Edge of Objectivity*, pp. 56–7, when he contrasts 'stunning woodcuts' with 'forbidding calculations.'

[3] See e.g. reproduction of title page – literally illustrating an 'inner circle' of geometers – from Niccolo Tartaglia, *Nova Scientia* (Venice, 1550; first ed. 1537) and discussion by Steneck, *The Scientific Press*, p. 9. This theme is discussed by Rosen, 'Copernicus's Attitude,' pp. 281–3. That Leonardo also said only mathematicians should read his work (see e.g. Kline, *Mathematics in Western Culture*, p. 133) suggests that this theme was favored by others than astronomers and physicists and that the contrast drawn above between exoteric anatomical illustration and esoteric mathematical tables can be overdone.

[4] For details on Copernicus' excision of a passage referring to Aristarchus, his reaction to ridicule presented in a school play, and to the condemnation of Wittenberg theologians, see Rosen, 'Biography of Copernicus,' *Three Copernican Treatises*, pp. 294; 375, and the same author's article on 'Copernicus' in *Dictionary of Scientific Biography*, p. 402. How Copernicus probably

I hesitated long whether on the one hand I should give to the light these my Commentaries written to prove the Earth's motion or whether, on the other hand it were better to follow the example of the Pythagoreans and others who were wont to impart their philosophic mysteries only to intimates and friends and then not in writing but by word of mouth...[5]

Apart from expecting adverse reactions to a theory that ran counter to both Scripture and common sense, Copernicus also seems to have had the kind of temperament one might describe as 'introverted.' At least he spent many decades leading a quiet, studious life. By contrast Vesalius appears to have been gregarious and to have relished working in public, close to noisy crowds. Probably such temperamental, as well as occupational, differences ought to be taken into account when considering time spent in printers' workshops, where silence and solitude were difficult to obtain. Copernicus certainly spent much less time in the company of printers and engravers than did other astronomers of note – yet another point of contrast with Vesalius who was often found in such company, as we know. As far as experience of printing went, the expertise commanded by Regiomontanus and the close supervision that later characterized the work of Tycho and Kepler had no counterpart in Copernicus' experience. He left everything in the hands of Rheticus – the printing of tables and texts, and even the choice of places and firms. This lack of interest in the way his data were processed may be related to the somewhat anomalous character of Copernicus' work.

As is often noted, *De Revolutionibus* was by no means a landmark in observational science, but relied on old tables and often corrupted data to support a new theory for computing the movement of the planets about the sun. Here also one may draw a contrast with *De Fabrica*. The carefully prepared and closely supervised illustrations for which Vesalius' work is celebrated indicate a concern with precise and detailed reporting of observed phenomena – a concern that was manifested by Tycho Brahe but was seemingly absent from Copernicus' work.

learned from Giorgio Valla's *De Rebus Expetendis* (Venice: Aldus, 1501) of a relevant passage in Plutarch referring to the ancient condemnation of Aristarchus as an impious heliocentric theorist is noted by Thomas Africa, 'Copernicus' Relation.' An intriguing account of how Galileo and Copernicus differed in their approach to Aristarchus and how a Baroque artist alluded to the condemnation of Copernican doctrines in a portrait of the ancient astronomer, is given by Askew, 'A Melancholy Astronomer.'

5 Cited by Steneck, *The Scientific Press*, p. 1. See also Rosen, *Three Copernican Treatises*, p. 401, who notes Copernicus' reference to keeping his book 'hidden' four times longer than the interval recommended by Horace.

Although his name has become more famous, Copernicus was in many ways less modern than Vesalius, in particular he had a far less acute sense of the reality of nature: like many medieval men he was far more concerned to devise a theory which should fit an uncritically collected series of observations than to examine the quality of observational material. Tycho Brahe half a century later was the Vesalius of astronomy.[6]

Yet Copernicus was by no means prepared to accept every 'uncritically collected series of observations.' In his *Letter against Werner*, for example, he was keenly critical of a colleague's procedures for dating and placing a particular observation made in the past, and elsewhere he seemed to be a keen-eyed observer of inconsistencies in prior reports.[7]

Here again one must make some allowance for the disparity between scientific disciplines. Unlike anatomists and unlike physicists as well, astronomers have to study observations made at different intervals over long periods of time. Data supplied by the Alexandrians and Arabs were indispensable for anyone concerned with the precession of the equinoxes, for example. The long-term cycles that had to be mastered to achieve successful calendar reform required lining up a series of observations made over the course of hundreds of years; and this task in turn required mastering diverse languages and systems for describing locations in time and space. In this respect, Copernicus' failure to supply the kind of fresh findings that were later provided by Tycho Brahe needs to be balanced against his sustained and zealous efforts to unscramble dusty records made by observers in the past.[8]

If the importance of archival research for astronomers were to receive more attention the early phases of the Copernican Revolution could be more clearly related to concurrent changes transforming libraries and book routes during the first century of print. As a post-print astronomer, Copernicus had an opportunity to survey a wider range of records and to use more reference guides than had any astronomer before him. This obvious point is often obscured by heated debates over the role played by one textual tradition as against another – over how much weight to assign continuous criticism of Aristotle,

---

[6] A. R. Hall, *Scientific Revolution*, pp. 51–2.

[7] How Copernicus' 'careful scrutiny' of predecessors' results led to his finding inconsistencies in the reports of 'two outstanding medieval Muslim observers' is described by Rosen, *Three Copernican Treatises*, p. 388. On *Letter against Werner*, see below, n. 13.

[8] For a different view, chiding Copernicus for failing to reject all earlier observations until he achieved the equivalent of Tycho's observational program see Swerdlow, 'On Copernicus' Theory of Precession,' esp. pp. 50–1.

as against a new revival of Plato or the vogue for Hermetic texts. Granted that such influences may be important in Copernicus' work and are worth investigating; it is also worth pausing over the interplay of many different texts upon his single mind. Given freedom from many hours of 'slavish' copying, given an increased output of dictionaries, and other reference guides; given title pages, book lists, and other rudimentary bibliographical aids, Copernicus was able to undertake a search of the literature on a vaster scale than had been possible before.

Increased access to a variety of records was not only useful when he decided 'to read again the works of all the philosophers upon whom I could lay hand...' in order to canvass possible alternatives to an 'uncertain mathematical tradition.'[9] Access to many records also enabled him to tackle certain technical problems relating to long-term cycles that had remained out of the reach of astronomers who were served by scribes.

My teacher made observations...at Bologna...at Rome...then here in Frauenberg when he had leisure for his studies. From his observations of the fixed stars he selected the one which he made...in 1525... *Then comparing all the observations of previous writers with his own* he found that a revolution of the...circle of inequality had been completed...

To reduce these calculations to a definite system in which they would agree with all the observations, my teacher computed that the unequal motion is completed in 1,717 Egyptian years...and the complete revolution of the mean motion will take 25,816 Egyptian years.[10]

To investigators concerned with celestial cycles that could take over 25,000 years, it must have been helpful to gain increased access to written records and to be supplied with bibliographical guides.

Copernicus undoubtedly learned much from a neo-Platonist professor at Bologna and from the debates conducted by Aristotelians at Padua as well. But Copernicus later abandoned the role of a wandering scholar for long years of study in Frombork. His work indicates that he was acquainted with a vast variety of texts – ranging from the Synoptic Gospels to tables of sines. He made a debut in print in 1509 with a Latin translation of a Greek work: the *Letters* of Theophilactus Simocatta, the first such translation to be printed in Cracow and one

---

[9] Prefatory Letter to *De Revolutionibus*, cited by Thomas Kuhn, *The Copernican Revolution*, p. 141.
[10] Excerpts from the *Narratio Prima* (1540) of Rheticus, in Rosen, *Three Copernican Treatises*, pp. 111–14. (Italics mine.)

that owed much to Aldus' Venetian press.[11] Although Simocatta is usually described as a minor Byzantine man of letters, students of medieval geography single him out as a seventh-century geographer who indicated knowledge of Asian territories. It seems likely that Copernicus' choice of this author was stimulated by curiosity about geography as well as about Byzantine Greek letters.[12] Certainly he was an assiduous investigator of place names and calendars, of ancient chronologies and coins, as indeed he had to be in order to unravel scribal confusion between 'Nebuchadnezzar' and 'Nabonassar,' or to ascertain the different points taken by past observers for the start of a new year. Neither the Platonic revival nor continued criticism of Aristotle enabled him to line up observations that went back to pre-Christian times, to compare observations made by Alexandrians and Arabs with his own, to establish the 'names of Egyptian months' and the length of 'Callippic cycles' or to point out that a colleague's dating of an autumnal equinox observed by Ptolemy was wrong by at least ten years.[13]

No fundamental astronomical discovery, no new sort of astronomical observation persuaded Copernicus of ancient astronomy's inadequacy or of the necessity for change. Until half a century after Copernicus' death no potentially revolutionary changes occurred in the data available to astronomers...[14]

Shortly before Copernicus was born, however, an actual revolution in book production had begun to affect the technical literature and mathematical tools available to astronomers. As a student at Cracow

[11] A facsimile of Copernicus' translation of the letters of Theophilactus Simocatta from Greek into Latin, first printed by Jan Haller (Kraków, 1509) was shown in the Library of Congress exhibition on Copernicus in 1973. The Greek text used by Copernicus comes from an anthology published in Venice by Aldus in 1499. See Rosen, *Three Copernican Treatises*, p. 325, where interesting connections are traced between the professor of Greek at Bologna (where Copernicus matriculated in 1496) and Aldus Manutius. See also Rose, *Italian Renaissance of Mathematics*, pp. 120–1.

[12] Kimble, *Geography in the Middle Ages*, p. 122 singles out Theophylactus [*sic*] Simocatta as an Egyptian Greek writing *c.* A.D. 678 about lands bordering on Turkish possessions. The fact that Copernicus' translation was prefaced by a long poem by his former Cracow instructor, George Rabe ('Corvinus') who was a geographer, also suggests that geographical curiosity helped to stimulate the work. On Rabe and printing of the *Letters*, see Rosen, *Three Copernican Treatises*, pp. 337–8.

[13] See *Letter against Werner* in Rosen, *Three Copernican Treatises*, pp. 94–8. A 'reminder that chronology was an important constituent of astronomy' is offered by Ravetz, *Astronomy and Cosmology*, p. 58. The 'immense effort' spent by Copernicus 'merely organizing the Egyptian month' is noted by Gingerich, Commentary, *The Copernican Achievement*, p. 104, n. 9.

[14] Thomas Kuhn, *Copernican Revolution*, p. 131.

in the 1480s, the young Copernicus probably found it hard to get a look at a single copy of Ptolemy's *Almagest* – even in a corrupted medieval Latin form.[15] Before he died, he had three different editions at hand. As a fourteen-year-old in Copenhagen in 1560, the young Tycho Brahe could purchase all of Ptolemy's work, including an improved translation of the full *Almagest* made from the Greek. Soon thereafter, while at Leipzig and still in his teens, Tycho picked up a copy of the *Prutenic Tables* that had recently been computed on the basis of Copernicus' major work.[16] No 'new sort of observation' had affected astronomy in this interval. Nevertheless, the transmission of old observations had undergone a major change. One need not wait until 'a half a century after Copernicus' death' to observe the effect of this change, for it had begun to affect the study of astronomy shortly before Copernicus was born. Copernicus was not supplied, as Tycho's successors would be, with precisely recorded fresh data. But he was supplied, as Regiomontanus' successor and Aldus Manutius' contemporary, with guidance to technical literature carefully culled from the best Renaissance Greek manuscript collections and, for the first time, made available outside library walls. 'By 1543, every

15 Ravetz, 'The Origins of the Copernican Revolution,' p. 92, states that no copy of the *Almagest* was available in Cracow during Copernicus' student days, but offers no evidence to back up the statement. Ms. copies of the *Almagest* of course are difficult to track down. Since advanced instruction in astronomy was given outside regular university courses in most regions, whatever copies there were, were likely to be less available in university libraries than the texts that were used for 'ordinary' lectures by medical, legal or theological faculties. See e.g. the case of the Swedish master cited by Gabriel, *The College System*, p. 19. That advanced instruction in Aristotle's physics was given in the schools whereas Ptolemaic computation was usually taught outside may help to explain how the two incompatible approaches could co-exist for so long. After printing, as noted in chap. 6, they came into closer contact and conflict. Albert of Brudzewo not only lectured on Peurbach's astronomy at the University of Cracow in 1482–3 but had his lectures printed (at Milan) in 1494–5. He also lectured on Aristotle's *De Caelo* in 1493 when Copernicus was a student at the University and pointed out how it contradicted Ptolemaic views. A Latin translation of Averroës' *Commentary* which described Ptolemaic astronomy as 'computing the nonexistent' was printed at Padua in 1473. That Ptolemy had been previously 'excluded from the schools' and ought to be 'restored' like a 'returned exile' to his 'ancient place of honor' was argued by Rheticus in the *Narratio Prima*. See Rosen, *Three Copernican Treatises*, pp. 132, 141, 195 n. 251, and 274.

16 Dreyer, *Tycho Brahe*, pp. 14–19. On pp. 81, 131, 135, Dreyer indicates Tycho's persistent concern about new books, his efforts to increase his library and his desire to take advantage of the Frankfurt book fairs. Gade, *The Life and Times of Tycho Brahe*, pp. 54–5, notes that Tycho hoped to meet Christopher Plantin when he went to the fair in 1575. See below, pp. 596–7 for uses to which Tycho put his teenage purchases. Tycho made a point of acquiring Copernicana. He owned and annotated the first and second editions of *De Revolutionibus* and procured the unprinted *Commentariolus* and *Letter against Werner* as well. On the uses of the printed edition of *De Revolutionibus* as a kind of 'textus receptus' among post-Copernican astronomers who glossed their copies and corresponded about passages, see Westman, 'Three Responses to the Copernican Theory,' appendix, pp. 342–3.

important work on ancient astronomy was available in printed editions.'[17]

Given the exaggerated claims made in prefaces to early printed books and given the righteous indignation they have provoked, one hesitates to assign too great a significance to Regiomontanus' role.

It was once usual to see such men as Nicholas of Cusa, Peurbach, and Regiomontanus in the fifteenth century as forerunners of a scientific revival, but more recent estimates of their works serve rather to emphasize the continuity to their thought than to indicate an incipient break with the past.[18]

No doubt the medieval translators of the *Almagest* and compilers of the *Alphonsine Tables* did at least as much to 'restore' astronomy in the West as did many boastful editors who converted medieval translations and tables into print.[19] Not only did a 'recovery' of the *Almagest* occur hundreds of years before Regiomontanus; he also had less to do with the 'discovery' made by Columbus than some of his later compatriots have maintained.

Kepler's tables...accompanied the men who went...on journeys of discovery just as...Regiomontanus' tables had accompanied Columbus... Without themselves having moved very far out into the world, these two Germans had performed important services in the conquest of the earth's globe.[20]

The publication of a so-called practical guide is one thing, putting it into practice is another. We have already noted Samuel Eliot Morison's cogent objections to the notion that sixteenth-century sailors skilled in dead reckoning could be persuaded to use new-fangled

---

[17] Francis Johnson, *Astronomical Thought*, p. 64, n. 62. The one exception: Archimedes' work was printed in Basel the following year and owed something to Regiomontanus' editing. See n. 33 below.

[18] A. R. Hall, *Scientific Revolution*, p. 11. The inflation and deflation of Peurbach and Regiomontanus is discussed by Wightman, *Science and the Renaissance* I, 103. The initial inflationary argument goes back to the sixteenth-century publications of Tanstetter (1514), Melanchthon (1545) and Rheticus who set a theme taken up later by Ramus. German efforts to counter Italian claims to have ended the Dark Ages were present in much of this early history of science literature.

[19] The early sixteenth-century prefaces that boasted of 'restoring' texts and tables (which were actually translated and/or computed during the medieval era) are cited by Thorndike, *History of Magic and Experimental Science*, chapter XVI, pp. 332–77. That sixteenth-century editors such as Tanstetter lacked historical information available to modern scholars and that their references to data 'almost obliterated from human memory' had some validity is not sufficiently appreciated by Thorndike. But the followers of Burckhardt are also prone to overlook the debt owed to medieval scholars for the retrieval and transmission of Alexandrian texts. On the defects of these two approaches, see pp. 300–3, above.

[20] Caspar, *Kepler*, p. 327.

printed devices. Granted Columbus carried a copy of the early printed tables on board, it remains to be shown that he was able to put them to good use.[21]

Here is a case that seems to support the warning issued by many authorities against exaggerating the 'effectiveness of the printed word as a channel for the diffusion of innovations.'[22] But although many sixteenth-century mariners did not put newly printed tables to good use, sixteenth-century astronomers surely did. In the year Columbus set off for the Indies, Copernicus matriculated at Cracow. 'As a student he was able to acquire and to annotate his own printed set of the *Alfonsine Tables* as well as Regiomontanus' *Ephemerides*.'[23] Unlike the stubborn mariners described by Morison, Tycho Brahe fully exploited all the mathematical tools and instruments that inventive printers and engravers advertised. Tycho's efforts to increase the precision of his observations 'would have been useless without trigonometric tables of corresponding accuracy.'[24] Where Regiomontanus pioneered, Ratdolt, Rheticus, Reinhold and others carried on. Lacking logarithms no less than the telescope, Tycho still had on hand paper instruments that astronomers had lacked before.[25] In guiding star-gazers, if not

21 See p. 554 above. See also data in Morison's *Admiral of the Ocean Sea*, pp. 185–6; 653–5. Columbus' exposure to printed materials (especially during his stay with his brother Bartholomew, who was 'a hawker of printed books' in Lisbon in the 1470s) and his expertise in chartmaking which are noted by Morison (p. 35) seem to be underplayed once the author gets him under sail. But in this book and others, Morison's distaste for 'armchair admirals' and admiration for unlettered mariners does lead him to raise important questions about the actual usefulness of the 'almanachs, textbooks, charts,' etc. that others stress: e.g. E. G. R. Taylor, *Mathematical Practitioners* (Morison's particular *bête noire*); Waters, 'Science and the Techniques of Navigation,' p. 233. Surprisingly Morison seems to credit the story of Columbus' use of Regiomontanus' tables to predict an eclipse and thus impress credulous Jamaican natives in 1504. 'Si non é vero é ben trovato!' The story shows a mentality Mark Twain later immortalized as that of a Connecticut Yankee emanating from Mediterranean Europe even before Luther's day. Thus the European is shown intimidating 'sullen' 'superstitious' natives, not by using gunpowder or invoking gospel truths, but by exploiting superior knowledge of celestial clockwork conveyed by the printed word.

22 Cipolla, 'The Diffusion of Innovations,' p. 47. See also p. 554 above.

23 Gingerich, 'Crisis versus Aesthetic.' On an early edition of the *Alphonsine Tables* printed by Ratdolt in 1483, see Stillwell, *Awakening Interest*, p. 8. According to Noel Swerdlow, 'The Derivation and First Draft of the Commentariolus,' (pp. 425–6) Copernicus used a 1492 edition (Venice: Johannes Hamman) of the *Alphonsine Tables* along with Ratdolt's 1490 Augsburg edition of Regiomontanus' *Tabulae Directionum* for his *Commentariolus*. See n. 53, below, concerning use of this same *Tabulae Directionum* while Copernicus was studying at Bologna in 1500. On Ratdolt, see pp. 587 ff. below.

24 Cajori, *A History of Mathematics*, p. 132.

25 See Dreyer, *Tycho Brahe*, p. 4; Pannekoek, *A History of Astronomy*, pp. 200–3. On Regiomontanus' pioneering work on trigonometry, see Rose, *Italian Renaissance of Mathematics*, p. 99 and Hughes, ed. and tr., *Regiomontanus on Triangles*; but note errors in Hughes underscored by Rosen, *Three Copernican Treatises*, p. 300, n. 1026.

navigators, the contribution made by the first astronomer–printer was large.

Historical perspectives may be skewed when the role played by early printers is inflated. But they can also be set awry if one goes too far in the opposite direction. Often deflationary tendencies have been carried too far.

No mutational elements of significance appear to have been introduced in the fifteenth century. There were no major translations or discoveries. The much vaunted version of the *Almagest* initiated by George Peurbach and completed by Regiomontanus was little more than an epitome with few alterations of substance. Both Toscanelli and Regiomontanus professed to be aware that the traditional Ptolemaic–Alphonsine astronomy stood in need of revision, but the observational data and the calculational theory at their disposal were insufficient for the task...[26]

The 'much vaunted version' of the *Almagest was* a noteworthy achievement, given the data which its two authors inherited and the circumstances under which they worked. For one thing, it was much more than a mere 'epitome.' It pointed to unresolved problems in Ptolemaic astronomy and also contained post-Alexandrian data, which Copernicus later put to good use.[27] For another thing, it provided many young astronomers with their first chance to examine specific details given in the *Almagest* – a chance very few astronomers had been granted for a millennium before. Insofar as some of it was based on a corrupted medieval translation from the Arabic and its second author did not fully exploit better versions in Greek, this was because the task of preservation was urgent and plans for future renovation were cut short by premature death.

Because a 'mutational element' was introduced in the fifteenth century – one which eventually doubled the lifetime of the astronomer[28] – renovation continued despite the short lives of Peurbach and

[26] Durand, 'Tradition and Innovation,' p. 35.

[27] As Durand notes, 'Tradition and Innovation,' p. 34, n. 21, this point was stressed by Zinner *Leben und Werken*, pp. 60-3. The argument between Thorndike and Zinner over Regiomontanus' significance is briefly described in Durand's annotations. According to Swerdlow, 'Derivation,' pp. 425-6, the virtues of the *Epytoma in Almagestum Ptolemai* 'cannot be overpraised.' It is the 'finest textbook of Ptolemaic astronomy' ever written. But Swerdlow also holds (p. 426, n. 5) that the first printed edition of 1496, done in Venice by Johannes Hamman, was 'very bad.' This was the version Copernicus used. According to Gingerich, 'Copernicus and the Impact of Printing,' p. 204, the student astronomer was indebted to the new medium for having access to the work, even in an impure form.

[28] Laplace's suggestion that logarithm tables 'by shortening the labors, doubled the life of the astronomer' is cited by A. G. R. Smith, *Science and Society*, p. 69.

of Regiomontanus. The publication of the *Epitome* was the beginning of a process of retrieval which made more of Alexandrian astronomy increasingly available and provided the next generation of astronomers with purified versions of Ptolemy's work. Before Copernicus died, a Greek text of the *Almagest* (the very same text that had been brought to Venice by Cardinal Bessarion and consulted by Regiomontanus more than a half-century earlier) was published in Basel and permanently secured.[29]

To the jaded modern scholar looking back over five hundred years, early printed editions of the *Almagest* are disappointing – even retrogressive – works.[30] But they opened up exciting new prospects to astronomers in Copernicus' day.

Copernicus studied the *Almagest* very carefully indeed. For the *De Revolutionibus* is the *Almagest*, book by book, section by section rewritten to incorporate the new Copernican theory but otherwise altered as little as might be. Kepler was to remark later that Copernicus interpreted Ptolemy, not nature, and there is some truth in the remark.[31]

Actually, the alternative to interpreting Ptolemy that Kepler had in mind was not really 'nature' but Tycho's data instead. By providing a fully worked out parallel text containing an alternate theory, Copernicus furnished Tycho with a motive for collecting the data Kepler used.[32] He did much to prepare the field, and should not be reproached for dying before others could reap the fruit. As a pre-Tychonic astronomer, he could not have consulted the 'nature' Kepler knew.

As a successor of Regiomontanus, however, Copernicus was better placed to recast the *Almagest* than earlier astronomers had been. He was not the first Western astronomer who had the good luck to gain access to a text setting forth the details of Ptolemaic astronomy. But he was the first for whom this initial stroke of good fortune was followed up by many more. Regiomontanus did little to guide Columbus over-

[29] For early printed editions of the *Almagest*, see Stillwell, *Awakening Interest*, pp. 30–1; 33–4. On lists of books owned by or available to Copernicus, see Gingerich, 'Copernicus and the Impact of Printing,' p. 204, n. 8.

[30] Swerdlow's disappointment (see n. 27 above) at the inferior printed version of Regiomontanus' fine ms. *Epitome* is characteristic of the reaction of most specialists who examine fifteenth-century mss. and then compare them with early printed versions.

[31] Boas, *Scientific Renaissance*, p. 74. According to Ravetz, *Astronomy and Cosmology*, p. 55, *De Revolutionibus* actually departs from the *Almagest* more frequently than this oft-cited description suggests. If he is right, it seems ironical that modern historians by themselves acting as 'slavish copyists' of earlier textbooks depict Copernicus as being more of a 'slavish copyist' than he was.

[32] See discussion below p. 597.

seas but he did much to steer Copernicus and his colleagues toward useful technical treatises not only by Ptolemy but also by Archimedes, Apollonius, Heron, Witelo *et al.* He had singled out such works with 'unerring judgement' after studying with Cardinal Bessarion and then serving as a librarian to Matthias Corvinus, King of Hungary, whose vast manuscript collection in Buda rivalled that of Bessarion and of Renaissance Popes. After the library in Buda – which contained many scientific texts taken from Athens and Constantinople among its 50,000 volumes – had vanished, Regiomontanus' book list survived to guide publication programs and armchair travellers for a century or more.[33]

A useful service might be performed by discriminating more clearly between the new functions performed by the first astronomer–printer and those previously performed when astronomers had had to serve as scribes. Until 1470, Regiomontanus pursued a course similar to that followed by his immediate predecessors such as Toscanelli or Peurbach who had also been wandering scholars and versatile servants of cardinals and kings. Insofar as he combined librarianship with astronomy, he followed a pattern that had been characteristic of Alexandrians and Arabs alike. When he left the library in Buda in 1470 to set up his Nuremberg press, however, Regiomontanus crossed an historical great divide. He had, up to then, served colleagues and patrons in

---

[33] For illustration of this famous book list, see Sarton, 'Scientific Literature,' pp. 115, 163 (figure 42). According to Gingerich, there are only two copies now available at the British Museum and at the Staatsbibliothek in Munich, 'Copernicus and the Impact of Printing,' p. 209, fig. 70. The rich material found in the library of Matthias Corvinus, is noted by Bühler, *Fifteenth Century Book*, pp. 18–19; 96. See also Csapodi, *The Corvinian Library History and Stock*. On Regiomontanus' stay there, his selection of titles for advance list and his posthumous contribution to the edition of Archimedes published in Basel, 1544, see Wightman, *Science and the Renaissance* I, 110; II, 13, n. 38. The edition of Witelo's *Perspectiva*, ed. by Tanstetter and Apianus, published in Nuremberg by Johannes Petreius in 1535 (in Stillwell, *Awakening Interest*, p. 75, n. 254) came two years after *De Triangulis* and eight years before *De Revolutionibus* were issued by the same printer. Regiomontanus' ties to Bessarion and the importance he assigned to using new presses for his program of 'restoring' astronomy are brought out by Rose's chapter on Regiomontanus, *Italian Renaissance of Mathematics*, chap. 4. Since he places 'Regiomontanus in Italy' and focuses exclusively on his Italian heirs, Rose's treatment does not bring out the important role of northern contributors to the trends he traces. In his 'Humanist Culture,' pp. 90–3, Rose also touches on the difficulty of gaining access to Bessarion's collection of scientific mss. after it was bequeathed to Venice and made the nucleus of the Biblioteca Marciana, and implies that there was something of a hiatus in the use made of the collection during the interval between Regiomontanus and the more liberal lending policy inaugurated by Bembo in 1532. The same point is made by Lowry, 'Two Great Venetian Libraries,' (see volume I, chap. 3, n. 164 above). The output of Ratdolt and his co-workers in Venice and Augsburg right after Regiomontanus' death, and that of Nuremberg printers in the early sixteenth century seem all the more important in this light.

a traditional fashion. By gaining the backing of a wealthy Nuremberg citizen to set up a press and observatory, by turning out duplicate tables of sines and tangents, series of Ephemerides and advertisements for instruments, by training apprentices to carry on with the printing of technical treatises and by issuing his own advance publication list, he served later generations in new ways. He died prematurely in 1476. Some of his manuscripts did not get printed until more than fifty years after his death. Others were lost so completely that his ultimate plans for reforming astronomy will never be known. Moreover the great library at Buda that he had culled had its contents dispersed and was sacked by the Turks in 1527. Similar catastrophes had set astronomy back in the past. The course pursued by Regiomontanus gained momentum instead. The serial publications he launched never stopped. Ephemerides and trigonometry tables flowed in an uninterrupted stream which seems to have no stopping point even now. His efforts to train assistants in scientific printing and instrument-making also produced increasingly useful results. Insofar as he embodied the roles of printer and scientist 'in one and the same person,' Regiomontanus was the first but not the last of a new breed.[34] Others carried on where he left off – as did those who prepared De Revolutionibus for a Nuremberg press more than sixty years after his death, and as Erhard Ratdolt and his co-workers did in Venice right away.[35]

Innovations associated with Ratdolt's press: the first 'modern' title page, the first use of Arabic numerals for dating a book, the earliest extant type-specimen sheet, the first list of errata, the first three-color

[34] Hirsch, Printing, Selling, p. 146, overdoes the uniqueness of Regiomontanus as a scientist-printer. J. Santritter of Heilbronn who followed Ratdolt in Venice and Peter Bienewitz (or 'Apianus') in Nuremberg are only two of many others who played the same role.

[35] On titles issued by Petreius, the Nuremberg printer of De Revolutionibus, see Shipman, 'Johannes Petreius.' Redgrave, Erwin Ratdolt, pp. 3–5, notes Ratdolt's probable connection with Regiomontanus in Nuremberg before he set up a press in Venice where he worked from 1476 to 1486, before returning to Augsburg, where he issued the Tabulae Directionum (1490) used by Copernicus (see n. 53 below). As noted above, many of Regiomontanus' intellectual heirs who consciously tried to carry on his publication program are omitted from Rose's Italian Renaissance of Mathematics which needs to be supplemented by a closer look at concurrent developments north of the Alps. Thus the series of ephemerides launched by Regiomontanus was continued by Johann Stöffler and Jacob Pflaum. Stöffler, a professor at Tübingen who taught Melanchthon, and Johannes Schöner, the Nuremberg mathematician to whom Rheticus addressed the Narratio Prima and who wrote a preface to Regiomontanus' treatise on the comet of 1472 (which was posthumously printed in Nuremberg in 1531) are but two of several non-Italian mathematicians who represent important links between Regiomontanus' and Copernicus' work. Eleven books listed on Regiomontanus' advance list which turned up in the library of Johan Scheubel, a professor of mathematics at Tübingen are noted by Hughes, 'The Private Library of J.S.,' p. 417, n. 1.

printed illustrations, the first engraved diagrams in a printed geometry book – are often noted in books aimed at bibliophiles.[36] But their broader significance for the history of science remains to be explored. Ratdolt's *editio princeps* of Euclid, for example, has been described as merely continuing a 'crabbed medieval' manuscript tradition going back to Adelard of Bath.[37] 'The splendour of Greek mathematics,' says Sarton, 'was dimly illustrated' by reproducing the 'poor translation' of Campanus of Novara.[38] Yet the *editio princeps* (which Ratdolt published in Venice in 1482 and Copernicus consulted as a young man) not only made the works of Euclid more available, it also arrested corruption of the text and introduced sharp-edged visual aids.[39] The six-hundred-odd diagrams, which were ingeniously devised for the *editio princeps*, illustrated Euclidean proofs somewhat less 'dimly' than had been done in many hand-copied books. Printed diagrams endowed the *Elements* with a clarity and uniformity that they had not possessed before.[40] Is it too fanciful to suggest that Euclid was associated, thereafter, less with Latin verbiage and more with triangles, circles and squares?

What Ratdolt's diagrams did for plane geometry, other early publication programs (beginning perhaps with Luca Pacioli) did for solid geometry – thereby making new use of the artistic invention of focused perspective developed in quattrocento Italy.[41] The sharp and clear perspective renderings of three-dimensional geometric forms that illustrate Pacioli's *Divina Proportione*[42] and other later sixteenth-century

---

[36] See e.g. Mayor, *Prints and People* (opposite plates no. 74 and 75); Updike, *Printing Types* I, 77.

[37] Durand, 'Tradition and Innovation,' p. 42.

[38] Sarton, 'Scientific Literature,' p. 64.

[39] Bühler, 'A Typographical Error,' pp. 102–4, describes how a compositor's slip was caught by Ratdolt who stopped the presses, made a correction and resumed printing, thereby eliminating the error from thirty-five out of thirty-nine copies seen by Bühler.

[40] On these diagrams and materials used to produce them, see Mayor, *Prints and People*, plates 74 and 75; Redgrave, *Ratdolt*, p. 16; and Thomas-Stanford, 'Early Editions of Euclid's *Elements*,' pp. 40–1.

[41] On Pacioli's relation to Piero della Francesca and other quattrocento artists and his concern with popularizing Euclid, see pp. 548, 551 above. Pacioli's own revision of Campanus of Novara's Latin *Euclid* was printed in Venice in 1509, partly as a riposte to a new translation produced by Zamberti in 1505 which assailed the 'barbarous' Campanus and boasted of the new translator's knowledge of Greek. Rose, 'Humanist Culture,' pp. 98–9. Did Pacioli's edition of the Campanus' *Euclid* also influence Candalla, the French mathematician who shared Kepler's fascination with the properties of regular solids and whose commentary on Euclid is cited by Kepler? See Westman, 'Kepler's Theory of Hypothesis,' p. 256.

[42] See e.g. Octahedron, woodcut from Pacioli's *Divina Proportione* (Venice, Pagano, 1509) in Mayor, *Prints and People*, fig. 174. On question of whether Leonardo da Vinci had a hand in designing these woodcuts in the 1490s while both men were in Milan, see chap. 6, n. 89 above. The effects produced by printed visual aids might be worth considering in connection with

books seem to have supplied the models Kepler had in mind when he envisaged the planetary orbits as a series of nesting 'perfect solids.'[43] It has been noted that *De Revolutionibus* also reflects a new concern with diagrammatic unity and visually symmetrical models.[44] Is it not possible that such concerns owed something to the new forms of book illustration that were ushered in by printing? The Platonic–Pythagorean tradition was not unfamiliar to medieval astronomers. Some Euclidean geometry had entered into the quadrivium as taught in the schools. Astrolabes and mechanical clocks proved mental and manual work could be ingeniously combined. Actual models of a clockwork universe were constructed and discussed.[45] But the visual aids supplied by copyists and illuminators had been infrequent and multiform. As noted above, even theoretical treatises showing that the world was round had not been reinforced by occasional T-O pictograms and sketches conveying flat discs.[46]

Insofar as Copernicus and Kepler shared a conviction that the design of the solar system had to conform to new requirements set by principles of 'fixed symmetry' the novelty of repeated encounters with

the issues raised by Giorgio de Santillana, 'The Role of Art in the Scientific Renaissance,' pp. 33–66. Some cogent remarks are made by Cyril Stanley Smith, 'Art Technology and Science,' but without assigning as much significance as I do to 'colorless linear diagrams' (p. 530).

43 For discussion of the inspiration which came to Kepler in July 1595 while drawing a figure on the blackboard for his class, and for illustrations designed by Kepler for his *Mysterium Cosmographicum* (Tübingen, 1596), see Koestler, *The Sleepwalkers*, pp. 247–61, and critique by Westman, 'Kepler's Theory of Hypothesis', p. 256. For a suggestive account of Kepler's visual imagination and its indebtedness to picture-books such as Wenzel Jamnitzer's *Perspectiva Corporum Regularum* (1568) see Benesch, *The Art of the Renaissance*, pp. 156–8, 183. Jamnitzer's debt to Dürer's *Unterweisung* seems clear from Benesch (n. 38), and Pacioli's *Summa* also crops up in the same connection.

44 This point is stressed by several authors. See e.g. Hanson, 'The Copernican Disturbance.' Hanson notes (p. 176) how modern textbook illustrations convey a misleading impression of a uniform 'Ptolemaic' system. The significance of Copernicus' reference to 'the design of the universe and the fixed symmetry of its parts' is also brought out by Gingerich, 'Crisis versus Aesthetic,' p. 6.

45 The most celebrated example is the 'Astrarium' that was constructed 1348–64 by Giovanni de' Dondi. See Bedini and Maddison, 'Mechanical Universe,' esp. p. 27, where interest at Cracow (stimulated by Regiomontanus' associate and his successor at Buda, Marcin Bylica) is noted and the copying of mss. of Dondi's treatise on his instrument is held to coincide with Copernicus' student days there. Horsky, 'Astronomy and the Art of Clockmaking,' pp. 25–34 stresses the large numbers of geared clocks in public places as affecting views of the 'machina mundi' among the learned in Copernicus' day. That Copernicus conceived of a divinely constructed clockwork, a 'machina mundi' in contrast to Ptolemy's more pulsating, voluntaristic 'anima mundi' is brought out in a paper by Curtis Wilson, 'Rheticus, Ravetz,' see esp. p. 37. But, of course, Ptolemaic schemes were not always incompatible with notions of clockwork, as is shown by Dondi's 'astrarium' itself. On the existence of ancient Greek geared clockwork calendrical mechanisms, see Price, 'Gears from the Greeks,' and review by Drachmann, *Technology and Culture*, pp. 112–16.   46 See p. 512, above.

identical symmetrical diagrams and with three-dimensional renderings of geometrical forms might be worth further thought. Beginning with early printed editions, new visual aids contained in manuals and textbooks made even 'medieval world pictures' easier to see.[47] The anatomy of the eye itself could be rendered by uniform diagrams for the first time.[48] In circulating large numbers of a medieval manual such as Sacrobosco's *Sphaera*, printers may be said to have done the same thing that copyists had been doing before. By supplying an edition of the *Sphaera* with identical polychrome printed diagrams, however, Erhard Ratdolt was doing something copyists had not done.[49]

The addition of polychrome diagrams, moreover, represented only one of several new features that Regiomontanus' former assistant added to technical texts. During the years that Copernicus was coming of age, successive editions of the *Sphaera* were being issued with supplementary data that helped to stimulate a reassessment of conventional views. Ratdolt's 1482 edition of Sacrobosco offers a case in point. He replaced the commentary of Gerard of Cremona by the most up-to-date and sophisticated critique of this same commentary – a critique composed by Regiomontanus himself.[50] This was only one of many instances where Regiomontanus, despite the early demise of his press, managed to exert a posthumous influence on the new generation that was coming of age. His advance book list of 1474 was characteristic of many early printed products in that it promised much more than the publisher actually delivered. But it also pointed the way to future scientific publication programs, setting guidelines that later publishers and vir-

---

[47] See Westman, 'Three Responses,' pp. 322–3 for an intriguing account of how schematic diagrams of the systems of Martianus Capella and Copernicus, which appeared in a text on astronomy published in Venice in 1573, stimulated Tycho Brahe when he was developing his own scheme.

[48] On the inadequacy of medieval drawings illustrating Pecham's *Perspectiva Communis* compared to the new illustrations reflecting Renaissance conceptions that accompanied printed editions of Witelo's, Alhazen's and Pecham's works on optics, see Lindberg, *John Pecham*, pp. 248–9. Lindberg's opinion is questioned by B. S. Eastwood, book review, *Speculum* (1972), p. 326, who sees medieval elements in the illustrations of the 1535 edition of Witelo's *Optics*.

[49] See figure facing p. 16 in Redgrave, *Erwin Ratdolt*. Redgrave notes that the 'beautiful' woodcut diagrams in the 1482 edition were hand-colored; polychrome printing was introduced in the 1485 edition (pp. 17–19).

[50] Redgrave, *Erhard Ratdolt*, p. 19 notes that Ratdolt's 1482 edition contained Regiomontanus' 'contra Cremonensia' along with Peurbach's 'Theoricae Novae.' R. E. Johnson 'Astronomical Textbooks,' p. 295, indicates that this set a vogue. At least eleven editions, issued from Venice between 1482 and 1518, contained Regiomontanus' critique – initially printed in Nuremberg in 1472–4. See Houzeau and Lancaster, *Bibliographie Générale de l'Astronomie* I, 1e partie, item 2256, p. 552.

tuosi pursued.[51] At the same time, it furnished astronomers who belonged to Copernicus' generation, and for whom bibliographies and reference works were hard to find, with a rudimentary reader's guide. Although the publication program that was launched by Regiomontanus in fifteenth-century Nuremberg was much less newsworthy than the expedition mounted by Columbus, it was more unprecedented than overseas voyages and probably had a more immediate impact on Copernicus' lifetime work. 'Copernicus was probably acquainted with every publication, written, edited or printed by Regiomontanus including, of course, his posthumous trigonometrical treatise *De Triangulis*.'[52]

There is no room in Sarton's brisk summary to note just how and when the astronomer became acquainted with different texts. In fact, Copernicus was unfamiliar with the major treatise *On Triangles* – the first full discussion of trigonometry to appear in the Western world – until he was over sixty-five years old. Only in 1539 did he have a chance to look over a copy which was brought to him by Rheticus at that time. The treatise had been left in manuscript for more than fifty years after its author's premature death. The first edition was issued by Petreius in Nuremberg, in 1533 – roughly a decade before *De Revolutionibus* came off the same press. That Copernicus had already finished his section on trigonometry without any knowledge of his predecessor's treatise suggests how scientific interchange was enfeebled when texts were left in manuscript form. How Regiomontanus' influence was extended by the use of a Nuremberg press is indicated by the fact that Copernicus overhauled his presentation of indispensable theorems after consulting the fifty-year-old work.[53]

In this regard, it is worth reaffirming that 'Europeans of Copernicus' generation' were practicing astronomy in an environment which differed from any in which astronomy had been practiced before. In trying to describe the distinguishing features of the new environment, however, it seems prudent to look more closely at the astronomer in his study before venturing too far outside.

[51] This point is overlooked by Thorndike, *History of Magic and Experimental Science*, p. 339, who makes much of the failure of the defunct Nuremberg press to produce the titles on the advance list. The usefulness of the book list as a guide to sixteenth-century Italian virtuosi and editors is spelled out by Rose, *Italian Renaissance of Mathematics*, pp. 64, 293.

[52] Sarton, *Six Wings*, p. 257, n. 105.

[53] Rosen, 'Biography of Copernicus,' *Three Copernican Treatises*, p. 326. Rosen also notes how Copernicus acquired a copy of Regiomontanus' *Tables of Directions* (Augsburg, 1490) in time to use it when making observations in Bologna in 1500.

Until a half a century after Copernicus' death no potentially revolutionary changes occurred in the data available to astronomers. Any possible understanding of the revolution's timing and of the factors that called it forth must therefore be sought principally outside of astronomy within the larger intellectual milieu inhabited by astronomy's practitioners.[54]

Once embarked on a search for new factors to be found 'outside astronomy' within a 'larger intellectual milieu,' the multivariable strategy currently favored by historians makes it difficult to stop short of describing everything that happened around the time Copernicus was born.

The Renaissance had happened...The Commercial Revolution had begun ...men's thoughts were becoming accustomed to a widening horizon. The earth was circumnavigated which proved in more popular fashion its rotundity. The antipodes were found to be quite inhabited...Further...unprecedented religious upheaval contributed to loosen men's thinking... There appeared a number of centres of religious life besides Rome. The rise of vernacular literatures...added their bit...In this ferment of strange and radical ideas, widely disseminated by the recent invention of printing it was not so difficult for Copernicus to consider...and suggest...a shift of the centre of reference in astronomy...London and Paris had become like Rome; in the absence of evidence to the contrary, it is to be conceived that the distant celestial bodies are like the earth...[55]

Granted that printing brought distant events closer, it still seems doubtful that the rise of the vernaculars, challenges to Rome or the consolidation of dynastic states had much effect on Copernicus' efforts to recast Ptolemy's work. To an astronomer engaged in trying to emend Ptolemaic theories, accounts of new-found lands were undoubtedly significant.[56] But even more important was access to data collected by past observers. Insofar as we lose sight of changes affecting the transmission of old records when searching for new factors, multivariable explanations are not much more helpful than monocausal ones. At many points such explanations seem to be positively unhelpful. Particularly where they touch on the problem of the Renaissance, they make it hard to avoid entanglement in a large number of counterproductive disputes.

At present, the two trips over the Alps made by Copernicus (like

---

54 Thomas Kuhn, *Copernican Revolution*, p. 131. 55 Burtt, *The Metaphysical Foundations*, p. 40.
56 One should not conclude however that news of overseas voyages invariably undermined confidence in Ptolemy's *Geography* and hence of his astronomy as well. Learned men, who believed Ptolemy knew better than the Genoese mariner how to calculate the dimensions of the globe, had their hunch confirmed after Magellan's voyage. See Morison, *Admiral*, p. 384.

countless astronomers before him) are deemed more significant than the three decades he spent in his Prussian study using facilities that had never been extended to armchair travellers before. We are encouraged to think of 'ten years in the sun and in the open intellectual climate of Italy' in connection with expanding mental horizons. Narrow-mindedness and Gothic gloom, by contrast are associated with the tower room in 'crabbed little Frauenburg' where Copernicus 'would peer through the mists and pore over Ptolemy and the tables of astronomy.'[57] Yet it was 'in Frauenburg when he had leisure for his studies' that Copernicus lined up key observations reported by Alexandrians and Arabs and drew conclusions from them.[58] It was there that Rheticus brought him Greek editions of Euclid and Ptolemy, and several other significant technical works.[59] Doubtless Copernicus' journey over the Alps was of major significance for his work. His studies at Bologna and Ferrara, his visit to papal Rome and his chance to learn some Greek supplemented his experience at Cracow in many important respects. Nevertheless the northern student who went to Italy for graduate studies or to learn Greek was a less remarkable phenomenon than the astronomer who could spend thirty-odd years studying a vast range of records without leaving home. It is significant that when a Greek teacher at Bologna died, the northern astronomer could go on mastering the difficult language with the aid of printed lexicons and guidebooks.[60]

Intellectual horizons probably expanded most rapidly when wandering scholars could stay longer in one place and, instead of setting out in search of 'walking encyclopedias' or manuscripts in scattered libraries, could get copies of books sent to them instead. Portable records combined with a fixed observation-post proved helpful to Tycho Brahe on his northern isle no less than to Copernicus in his Prussian tower study. Before trying to account for the achievements of either man, the question of possible changes affecting 'the data available to astronomers' needs to be thought through again. The 'larger intellectual milieu inhabited by astronomy's practitioners' is at present too vague a concept to be helpful and also too inclusive as a catch-all.

[57] Gillispie, *Edge of Objectivity*, pp. 21–2. See also deployment of familiar stereotypes setting the 'crabbed Gothic lettering of the North' against the 'bold clear typeface of Italian printing' despite its inappropriateness to editions involved – as noted on p. 490 above.
[58] Rheticus, 'Narratio Prima,' p. 111.
[59] Rosen, 'Biography of Copernicus,' *Three Copernican Treatises*, p. 393.
[60] See account of Copernicus' well-worn copy of Crestone's *Greek-Latin Dictionary* (Modena, 1499) in Rosen, 'Biography of Copernicus,' *Three Copernican Treatises*, p. 323.

This point may be illustrated by drawing on an otherwise very useful study of the Copernican Revolution.

To Europeans of Copernicus' generation, planetary astronomy was... practiced in an intellectual and social environment quite different from any in which astronomy had been practiced before. In part that difference arose from theological accretions...Even more essential changes were produced by the...criticism of men like Buridan and Oresme. But these were medieval contributions and Copernicus did not live during the Middle Ages. His lifetime, 1473–1543, occupied the central decades of the Renaissance and Reformation and novelties characteristic of this later age were also effective in inaugurating and shaping his work.[61]

This eclectic and multivariable approach is in keeping with a practice long honored by historians. Medieval contributions are not neglected; almost everything that happened in the Renaissance and Reformation is presented in review. Background and foreground are carefully distinguished – more carefully than usual, so that implausible far-fetched connections are avoided. The more distant repercussions produced by the Turkish threat, the Protestant revolt, the rise of nation states and of a new commercial aristocracy are assigned brief paragraphs. The voyages of exploration, which helped discredit Ptolemy's *Geography*; the agitation for calendar reform which spurred Copernicus' efforts to overhaul the *Almagest*; and the Greek revival, which contributed to the reconstitution of Ptolemy's texts are featured more prominently. Finally, Renaissance neo-Platonism is discussed at some length as a movement which 'gave a significant new direction to the science of the Renaissance and, in particular, shaped Copernicus' appreciation of mathematical elegance and his preference for a heliocentric hypothesis.'[62]

With the discussion of neo-Platonism, the 'conceptual stage setting' is deemed complete. All the 'novelties that were effective in inaugurating and shaping Copernicus' work' have presumably been introduced. Yet although distant repercussions from movements associated with Columbus, Luther, Machiavelli and Calvin have been duly acknowledged, the consequences of Gutenberg's invention are left out of account. Nothing is said about the installation of new presses, and one might well conclude that the technical literature consulted by sixteenth-century astronomers was still being copied out by hand.

[61] Thomas Kuhn, *Copernican Revolution*, p. 123.
[62] Thomas Kuhn, *Copernican Revolution*, pp. 123–31.

To say that the advent of printing ought to be featured more prominently than is done in this case, is not merely to advocate putting another prop on an already over-cluttered stage. I am not asking 'the over-burdened historian' to add yet another item to his long list of 'features of the Renaissance' or even to re-order items so as to give printing 'higher billing.'[63] Instead, I am suggesting that the entire problem of providing an appropriate setting for the Copernican Revolution has to be thought through again.

Once the shift from script to print has been taken into account, the setting which is currently provided appears to need re-adjustment at important points. For one thing, several of the 'novelties' singled out as most significant for Copernicus' work were not entirely novel and probably had been on the scene before. Thus overseas voyages had occurred before Columbus; medieval scholars in Sicily had studied Ptolemy in Greek; and pressure for calendar reform was almost as venerable as the Venerable Bede (a point to be discussed at more length below). For another thing, what was genuinely new about Copernicus' rejection of Ptolemaic astronomy cannot be perceived unless printing is brought into the picture. Insofar as he objected to 'the diffuseness and continued inaccuracy of the Ptolemaic tradition,'[64] Copernicus was objecting to features that characterized all textual traditions shaped by scribal transmission. If he differed from earlier astronomers who had perpetuated this tradition, this was partly because these 'monstrous' features had become more visible and also because he did not have to put up with them any more.

This is not to say that Renaissance 'intellectual currents' were insignificant in Copernicus' work. Scholastic criticism of Aristotle and neo-Platonist views undoubtedly helped to shape the solution he tried out. His recognition that some ancient authorities had believed in heliocentric and/or geokinetic theories owed much to Renaissance classical anthologies produced by Italian humanists, such as Giorgio Valla.[65] But of course his access to several humanist anthologies and

---

[63] Rabb, 'Debate: The Advent of Printing,' p. 139.

[64] According to Thomas Kuhn, *Copernican Revolution*, p. 140, 'these are the two principal characteristics' which Copernicus found objectionable. Other authorities differ on this point. See e.g. Gingerich 'Crisis versus Aesthetic,' pp. 85–97.

[65] See n. 4 above. That Copernicus found support for a sun-centered cosmology in many different ancient sources and that the one citation from the hermetic corpus which appears in *De Revolutionibus* has been overstressed in recent studies is persuasively argued by Rosen, 'Was Copernicus a Hermetist?' p. 171.

his expanded awareness of ancient cosmologies and astronomical theories also hinged on the output of printed editions.[66] Increased access to texts seems especially relevant to a heightened concern with 'inconsistency among the mathematicians.' Moreover something must be said about his chance to work out a new solution – his chance to rework all the Ptolemaic computations in full mathematical detail with the positions of sun and earth reversed. Had this kind of opportunity been extended to European astronomers before printing? Should we not at least pose this kind of question when seeking to understand 'the Revolution's timing and the factors that called it forth'?

The passage of time...presented a counterfeit problem which ironically was even more effective than the real motion of the planets in fostering recognition of errors in the Ptolemaic method. Many of the data inherited by Copernicus...were bad data...Some had been collected by poor observers; others had...been...miscopied or misconstrued during the process of transmission...The complexity of the problem presented by Renaissance data transcended that of the heavens themselves...[67]

It was not so much the 'passage of time' as it was the conditions of scribal culture that produced this 'counterfeit problem.' As long as these conditions persisted, the problem was not counterfeit, but all too real. Even when they were aware that they had inherited bad data, astronomers could do little to arrest scribal drift, and drifting texts were uncertain indicators of shifting stars. Moreover awareness of error was kept at a low level given necessary reliance on one seemingly authoritative corpus of texts. As long as planetary positions had to be computed on the basis of Ptolemy's instructions, there was no way of using the 'heavens themselves' to act as an independent check. By providing another complete set of instructions, the 'second Ptolemy' freed astronomers from their total dependance on the first.

How recognition of error was fostered by access to two Ptolemies instead of to one is implicit in the oft-cited anecdote about the young Tycho Brahe. Having taught himself astronomy by sneaking books past his tutor and poring over them alone at night, Tycho procured copies of the (Ptolemaic) *Alphonsine Tables*, the (Copernican) *Prutenic Tables* and Stadius' *Ephemerides* (which were based on the latter).

---

[66] The Aldine collection *Astronomici Veteres* (Venice, 1499) ought to be mentioned along with Giorgio Valla's *De Rebus* in this connection. See Rose, 'Humanist Culture,' p. 99, n. 241.
[67] Thomas Kuhn, *Copernican Revolution*, p. 140.

Tycho soon mastered the use of these tables and perceived that the computed places of the planets differed from the actual places in the sky...He even found out that Stadius had not computed his places correctly from Reinhold's tables. And already while Tycho was a youth only sixteen years of age his eyes were opened to the great fact which seems to us so simple to grasp but which escaped the attention of all European astronomers before him that only through a steadily pursued course of observations would it be possible to obtain a better insight into the motions of the planets.[68]

Tycho's 'eyes were opened' to the need for fresh data partly because he had on hand more old data than young students in astronomy had had before. Even as an untutored teenager he could compare Copernicus with Ptolemy and study tables derived from both.[69] Contradictory predictions concerning the conjunction of planets encouraged him to re-examine the 'writing in the skies.' For the purpose of gathering fresh data, he was also supplied with newly forged mathematical tools which increased his speed and accuracy when ascertaining the position of a given star. In these and in other respects, Tycho's case does not entirely fit that of 'an astronomer who saw new things while looking at old objects with old instruments.'[70] Printed sine tables, trigonometry texts, star catalogues did represent new objects and instruments in Tycho's day. As a self-taught mathematician who mastered astronomy out of books, Tycho was himself a new kind of observer.

Because he lacked recourse to a telescope and yet saw a different writing in the skies than star-gazers had seen before, the findings of the Danish astronomer pose a special problem for historians of science.

Brahe's fine instruments were not required to discover the superlunary character of novas and comets...Maestlin needed only a piece of thread to decide that the nova of 1572 was beyond the moon...The observations... which speeded the downfall of traditional cosmology...could have been made at any time since remote antiquity. The phenomena and the requisite instruments had been available for two millenniums before Brahe's birth, but the observations were not made or, if made, were not widely interpreted. During the last half of the sixteenth century age-old phenomena rapidly changed their meaning and significance. Those changes seem incompre-

---

[68] Dreyer, *Tycho*, pp. 18–19.

[69] In 1574–5, Tycho bought copies of the *Prutenic Tables* and distributed them among the poorest students while lecturing on Copernicus, as the 'second Ptolemy' at the University of Copenhagen. Moesgaard, 'Copernican Influence on Tycho Brahe,' p. 32.

[70] Thomas Kuhn, *Structure of Scientific Revolutions*, pp. 116–17.

hensible without reference to the new climate of scientific opinion one of whose first outstanding representatives is Copernicus.[71]

One wonders how the 'superlunary character of novas and comets' could, in fact, be established before scattered observations of transitory stellar events could be made simultaneously, coordinated with other findings, checked and confirmed. As long as accounts of separate stellar events were transmitted by scribes; as long as separate observers lacked uniform methods for placing and recording what they saw; as long as the most careful observers lacked mastery of trigonometry; how could falling stars be permanently located beyond the moon's sphere?[72] 'The desire to find an orbit for a *purely transitory, ephemeral* phenomenon marked an important shift in the theoretical, interpretation of comets.'[73] Maybe Tycho's 'fine instruments' were not needed, but certainly Maestlin's piece of thread was not enough to fix transitory, ephemeral stellar events so firmly that they could be seen to conflict with traditional cosmology.[74]

To understand why these 'age-old phenomena' rapidly changed their meaning in the sixteenth century at all events, it is worth going back, beyond Copernicus, to the thickening literature on comets that commenced shortly after the first press was established at Mainz.[75] Here again Regiomontanus appears as a significant pioneer, with his posthumously published treatise on the comet of 1472 and his sixteen-point program for ascertaining the distance of future comets from the earth. By Maestlin's day, much of the program had been fulfilled. Various

---

[71] Thomas Kuhn, *Copernican Revolution*, p. 209.

[72] That the phrase: 'length of a lance' was commonly used to describe the length of a comet's tail until Regiomontanus is noted by Hellman, 'The Role of Measurement,' p. 43. Tycho's use of Regiomontanus' spherical trigonometry is noted by Wightman, *Science and the Renaissance* I, 123 ff.

[73] Westman, 'The Comet and the Cosmos,' p. 11. (Italics mine.)

[74] That it took more than a piece of thread is suggested by the efforts of Regiomontanus' disciple Vogelinus who tried to work out the parallax of the comet of 1532 and by the sixteen-point program set forth by Regiomontanus himself. See Hellman, *The Comet*, pp. 81–2, 97. Maestlin's own research is described by Westman, 'The Comet and the Cosmos,' pp. 7–30.

[75] Hellman, *Comet*, pp. 74–6, 111–12, notes that the comet of 1472 inspired more treatises and had more observers than did those of 1456 and 1468 and that the volume of reports increased steadily thereafter, due 'partly to the use of printing' and 'partly to the fact that fewer of the later tracts were lost with time.' I think increased preservation was probably related to the new process of duplication and find it indicative that there was no similar continuous thickening of documentation for any interval between the twelfth and fifteenth centuries. According to Bernard Goldstein, 'Theory and Observation,' p. 46, comets did not 'formally enter the realm of astronomy' until Tycho but did 'begin to get treated as astronomical phenomena' in Regiomontanus' day. Goldstein stresses the absence of any 'textual evidence' to 'account for this change of attitude' and makes no reference to the advent of printing.

methods for determining parallaxes had been described by mathematicians, reports of comets had given rise to 'a flood of fugitive literature'
and to the compiling and publishing of comet catalogues as well. The
comet of 1533 provoked controversial pamphleteering on the part of
scattered observers. By 1541, Rheticus was writing a Wittenberg
colleague that, 'in this area,' it was known 'that comets originated
beyond the lunar sphere.'[76] Continuous publication increased interest
and curiosity. The nova of 1572 attracted more observers from all
parts of Europe than had ever gazed at a single star before.[77] When
Tycho announced his findings, he had to struggle 'to make his voice
heard above the din.'[78] He succeeded so well in this unprecedented
situation that long after the nova had faded, 'Tycho's star' gleamed too
brightly beyond the moon's sphere for cosmologists to ignore it or
chroniclers to shift it around. 'Almost every star chart and globe
between 1572 and the end of the 17th century showed where [it]...
had appeared, encouraging astronomers to watch for its return.'[79]

Stellar events that had been witnessed before the advent of printing
could not be pinpointed so precisely and permanently that one man's
name could be assigned to one such event. Nor could any one detailed
account avoid getting blurred in the course of entering into the public
domain. Much as was the case with mundane events when they were
woven into tapestries or noted in monkish chronicles, discrete separate
events merged into a single mythical category;[80] conventional images
and standard formulae smudged carefully observed detail. Jerusalem
stayed at the center of the world, comets stayed below the lunar sphere,
and neither could be permanently dislodged from their appointed
places until scribal transmission had come to an end.

'These stars marked out in gold are those of the Lord Tycho; the

---

[76] For controversy engendered by the Comet of 1533, in which Apianus (d. 1552), Jerome
Cardano, Gemma Frisius and Copernicus participated, see Rosen, 'Biography of Copernicus,'
Three Copernican Treatises, pp. 373–4, where citation from Rheticus' letter is also given.

[77] Hellman, *Comet*, pp. 80 ff, stresses Regiomontanus' pioneering role and criticizes Thorndike's
deprecatory remarks. She also describes how solutions to finding parallaxes were published by
Cardano and Gemma Frisius (pp. 91–6), how the comet of 1556 gave rise to the first publication of comet catalogues, how the Nova of 1572 gave rise to more tracts and observers than
any previous stellar event (pp. 110–11), and how Tycho at Hven and Hagecius at Prague were
alerted to coordinate their observations of the comet of 1577 (pp. 118 ff). Westman, 'Comet
and Cosmos,' p. 8, n. 20 notes that the six-year-old Kepler had been led by his mother to
a high place to view it.

[78] The phrase comes from Christianson, 'Astronomy and Printing.'

[79] Warner, 'The First Celestial Globe,' p. 36.

[80] This point is brought out by Nichols, Jr. 'The Interaction of Life,' pp. 51–77.

remaining ones correspond to those observed by the Ancients,' runs an English translation of the Latin text placed on a celestial globe produced by Willem Janszoon Blaeu between 1596 and 1599.[81] Blaeu's 'exceedingly accurate globe' not only made clear what the great modern astronomer had added to skies studied by the greatest star-gazers of antiquity; it also made clear that even more exciting news was destined to be forthcoming from intrepid explorers who had ventured beyond the edge of the known world.

Certain stars nearer to the Antarctic Pole, and avoiding our sight, are not less remarkable for their magnitude than those lying in the northern region, whether by report of the extent of their brilliances or by the annals of writers, nevertheless having delineation as uncertain, we have here omitted the measuring of them.[82]

What Blaeu cautiously omitted in the late 1590s a competitor was able to fill in by 1600, suggesting how competition between profit-driving printers – no less than collaboration among scattered observers – helped to accelerate data collection and push it along new paths. Just as Blaeu was finishing supervision of his plates, an expedition was returning carrying records of uncharted skies. 'At the very end of the century two Dutchmen...working sometimes together, made the first systematic attempt to organize and catalogue the southern stars.' Both men sailed on the 1595–7 voyage of the *Hollandia* and kept records of the observations of the southern skies they made while voyaging in the East Indies. One, the chief pilot, died at sea, but his data carried back to Amsterdam were exploited by Blaeu's chief competitor, Jocondus Hondius for his celestial globe of 1600. No less than fourteen new constellations were displayed on the Hondius globe.

So Blaeu who doubtless expected his first celestial globe to be widely acclaimed and distributed, instead saw it become obsolete just a short time after publication. There was nothing to do but to withdraw it from the market and begin again.[83]

To begin again in the age of print had a different meaning than had been the case in the age of scribes. By 1602, Blaeu turned out an up-dated smaller globe which contained all the fresh data brought back

---

[81] Warner, 'First Celestial Globe,' p. 36.

[82] According to Warner, 'First Celestial Globe,' p. 36, n. 24, Blaeu is echoing comments made in Tycho's *Astronomiae Instauratae Mechanica*.

[83] Warner, 'First Celestial Globe,' p. 37.

from the Dutch expedition and, in addition, registered a brand-new observation that was uniquely his own. In August, 1600 he had noted a new star of the third magnitude in the constellation Cygnus and this also he placed upon his globe – where it remained to be duplicated repeatedly – long after the star faded from everyone's view.[84] Moreover, he never really did begin all over again. In 1603 the large plates for his first globe, which had been too valuable to discard, were re-used after corrections had been made on them and resulted in the 'now justly famous 34 centimeter globe of 1603' with his own name prominently displayed alongside that of his former master, 'Lord Tycho,' on the revised title text.[85]

According to Wightman, Tycho Brahe was the first Western astronomer to pursue the kind of program that later became characteristic of the Royal Society.[86] He was the forerunner of a new breed of astronomers who were singled out by Bishop Sprat. They 'studied to make it not onely an enterprise of one season or of some lucky opportunity; but a business of time; a steddy, a lasting, a popular, an uninterrupted work.'[87] It does not detract from Tycho's justly distinguished position in the history of astronomy to suggest that he was favored by a 'lucky opportunity' by being born at the right time. No one man however gifted could put so vast a collaborative enterprise as astronomy on a new footing or live long enough to assure that it would be a steady, lasting, popular, uninterrupted enterprise. The 'business of time' lies outside the control of any one generation, let alone that of a single mortal creature. Geoffrey of Meaux's nightly observations of the comet of 1315 suggest that Tycho's program of steady observation to obtain fresh data was not unprecedented.[88] Much as Viking landfalls preceded Columbus, careful star-gazers had been at work before Tycho. What was unprecedented (with new stars

---

[84] After being visible for a few years, Warner says the star faded completely. It reappeared in 1657–8 before fading to the fifth magnitude. The capacity to fix a location for an invisible star so that its reappearance may be detected was greatly enhanced after printing.

[85] Warner, 'First Celestial Globe,' p. 38.

[86] Wightman, Science and the Renaissance I, 120.

[87] Sprat, Royal Society, part 2, sect. 5, p. 62.

[88] Hellman, Comet, pp. 47, 67 ff, describes medieval observations. In her 'Role of Measurement,' p. 43, she notes that Geoffrey's observations were 'unusual in the annals of the era.' Goldstein, 'Theory and Observation,' p. 47, shows that an observer of an eclipse in 1337 noted that the Alphonsine Tables were in error but left no evidence of trying to rectify the error. Unless associated with a special message center designed to correct and copy astronomical data, individual observers could do little to change such tables until after the advent of printing. Incentives to compile long lists of numbers in tables were also at a low ebb. See n. 162 below.

and new worlds alike) was the way observed phenomena could be recorded and confirmed.

As the foregoing may suggest, when trying to explain the new sixteenth-century view of 'age-old phenomena' such as novas and comets, the changes wrought by printing need to be taken into account. General references to a turbulent age or even more specific evocation of the 'new climate of scientific thought' represented by Copernicus do not help very much to explain phenomena such as Tycho's star. The neo-Platonic and Aristotelian currents that entered into Copernicus' studies with Italian masters, such as Domenico Maria de Novara, had no counterpart in the young Danish nobleman's case. Indeed Tycho set out to become an astronomer by defying his tutor and teaching himself. He by-passed the traditional master–apprentice relationship by taking advantage of printed materials. It seems likely that his freedom from prevailing cosmological assumptions owed something to his unusual position as a largely self-made astronomer.[89] Symmetry and sun-worship seem to have been subordinated to other concerns in Tychonic astronomy.[90] Its architect did not share Copernicus' aesthetic or metaphysical concerns. The two astronomers were not linked by mutual admiration for a particular classical or Christian textual tradition.[91] As sixteenth-century astronomers they may be distinguished from their predecessors not so much because they were influenced by one or another Renaissance current of thought but rather because they were freed from copying and memorizing and could make use of new paper tools and printed texts.

Whether the sixteenth-century astronomer confronted materials derived from the fourth century B.C. or freshly composed in the fourteenth century A.D., or whether he was more receptive to scholastic or humanist currents of thought seems of less significance in this particu-

[89] Tycho's position as an 'autodidact,' is of course a limited one since he did take the usual cycle of undergraduate courses. As noted (pp. 533–4) above, while taking the traditional cycle of studies associated with the *trivium* and *quadrivium*, Tycho was also exposed to new mathematical and linguistic training and some new information (albeit often in a concealed form).

[90] The fact that 'symmetry and proportionality' were not respected in the Tychonic scheme offended Maestlin. He strongly opposed Tycho's cosmology on that account. See Westman, 'Comet and Cosmos,' p. 27.

[91] One could elaborate on this point by noting that Copernicus had taken a degree in canon law at Ferrara whereas Tycho was trained at a 'Philipist' university where canon law was regarded as a diabolic instrument of the Papal anti-Christ. The possible influence of working with a 'concordance of discordant canons' on Copernicus' approach to discordant Ptolemaic and Arabic texts might be worth further thought – according to Schoeck's paper on 'Copernicus and Humanism.'

lar connection than the fact that all manner of diverse materials were being seen in the course of one lifetime by one pair of eyes. For Copernicus as for Tycho, the result was heightened awareness of, and dissatisfaction with, discrepancies in the inherited data.

For the first time a technically competent astronomer had rejected the time-honored scientific tradition for reasons internal to his science...The astronomical tradition had not previously seemed monstrous. By Copernicus' time a metamorphosis had occurred and Copernicus' preface brilliantly described the felt causes of that transformation.[92]

Copernicus' preface emphasizes the diversity of views held by the authorities who described 'the movements of the sun, moon and planets' according to incompatible schemes. His precursors were 'so unsure of the movement of the sun and the moon that they cannot even explain or observe the constant length of the seasonal year.' When set side by side their systems fail to cohere; 'they use neither the same principles and hypotheses nor the same demonstrations of apparent motions and revolutions.'[93] Too many textbooks have overplayed Copernicus' dissatisfaction with the purported complexity of Ptolemaic celestial machinery.[94] Only a few bring out clearly how his own words express 'nothing else than the knowledge that the mathematicians are inconsistent in these investigations.'[95] In many accounts indeed, Copernicus' dissatisfaction with Ptolemaic astronomy can scarcely be distinguished from that of an untrained layman, baffled by the intricacies of a sophisticated reckoning scheme. But Copernicus' reaction not only needs to be distinguished from that attributed to King Alfonso X; it also needs to be distinguished from that of later contributors to so-called scientific 'revolutions.' It was not predicated on an accumulation of minor discrepancies in the course of prolonged 'normal' research. Copernicus was not simply reacting, as did later critics of Newton, to the inadequacy of a given astronomical theory.[96] He was also expressing concern at his finding that no one theory had been *consistently* used.

His comments point both to the difficulty of lining up observations

---

[92] Thomas Kuhn, *Copernican Revolution*, p. 138.

[93] Citation from preface to *De Revolutionibus* in Thomas Kuhn, *Copernican Revolution*, p. 137.

[94] That this theme has been overdone (to the point of falsifying the number of epicycles required by Ptolemaic astronomers) is persuasively argued by Palter, 'An Approach to the History,' See also Gingerich, 'Crisis versus Aesthetic,' n. 7 and 8.

[95] Citation from preface to *De Revolutionibus*, in Thomas Kuhn, *Copernican Revolution*, p. 137.

[96] See Thomas Kuhn, *Structure of Scientific Revolutions*, pp. 68–9.

made by predecessors who used diverse reckoning schemes and to the monstrous model that was produced when trying to assemble separate parts 'each excellently drawn but not related to a single body.'[97] In both cases the chief irritant was supplied by inconsistency.

Copernicus and his contemporaries inherited not only the *Almagest* but also the astronomies of many Islamic and a few European astronomers who had criticized and modified Ptolemy's system...There was no longer any one Ptolemaic system, but a dozen or more and the number was multiplying rapidly with the multiplication of technically proficient astronomers.[98]

Insofar as there was a rapid multiplication of incongruous theories this was probably related to the fact that texts had become more numerous after printers set to work. However many colleagues Copernicus had, and however few professional astronomers Europe had known when Regiomontanus was alive, their number probably had not 'multiplied' as fast as had copies of astronomical texts after printers set to work. Although uncertain guidance is offered here, the number of technically proficient astronomers who were equipped to read the *Almagest* in the early sixteenth century actually seems to have been quite small.[99] 'To Europeans of Copernicus's generation, planetary astronomy was almost a new field.'[100]

Now if planetary astronomy was 'almost a new field' to Copernicus' generation it would seem to be an unlikely setting for a breakdown of

[97] Cited by Thomas Kuhn, *Copernican Revolution*, p. 138. This passage which invokes aesthetic canons seems to owe something to quattrocento theories developed by humanists such as Alberti, who transposed Aristotelian rules as set forth in the *Poetics* and other classical rhetorical conventions into visual terms and stressed compositional unity when judging a painting. See Baxandall, *Giotto*, *passim*. How Copernicus' view of God as 'the great artisan' who designed a perfect celestial machine contrasted with Ptolemy's view of the god-like wandering stars is well brought out by Curtis Wilson's paper, 'Rheticus, Ravetz.'

[98] Thomas Kuhn, *Copernican Revolution*, pp. 138–9. Just what is meant by a 'dozen or more' Ptolemaic systems in this passage is not entirely clear and entails using the term 'system' more loosely than may be deemed justified by other authorities. When Copernicus himself refers to something 'which the mathematicians call their system' (in the citation given by Kuhn on pp. 137–8) he seems to be implying that the term is not deserved. Previous authorities have questioned whether Ptolemaic astronomy can be associated with any 'system' but Goldstein, 'The Arabic Version of Ptolemy's *Planetary Hypotheses*,' part 4, *passim* shows that there was a definite order of planets set forth in the full Ptolemaic text.

[99] See references to the 'small group of Europeans' and 'small group equipped to read Ptolemy's treatise,' Thomas Kuhn, *Copernican Revolution*, p. 135, as against later passages asserting *De Revolutionibus* 'was widely read,' and that 'the book's large audience ensured it a small but increasing number of readers equipped to discover Copernicus's harmonies' (p. 186). The 'wildly diverse' estimates of the size of the first edition of *De Revolutionibus* which probably ranged between 500 and 800 copies, are discussed by Gingerich, 'Copernicus and the Impact of Printing,' p. 207.

[100] Thomas Kuhn, *Copernican Revolution*, p. 123.

'normal science' to occur. Jerome Ravetz has suggested that early sixteenth-century science was not well enough organized to fit a pattern followed in later scientific revolutions.[101] His suggestion fits in well with the views offered here. Scribal transmission produced a fundamentally different pattern from the flow of information after print. The conditions that permitted Alexandrian achievements were not 'normal' but exceptional. Accurately copied tables were exceptional as well. 'Firmly established expectations that things will go right' had not begun to characterize those who sought to chart every planet's wandering course.

Instead of confronting an unprecedented 'break*down*' of a 'normal research effort,'[102] in other words, sixteenth-century European astronomers were just beginning to take advantage of a technological break-*through* which set continuous problem-solving on its later 'normal' path. To depict Copernicus' preface as 'one of the classic descriptions of a crisis state' in astronomy and to attribute his rejection of Ptolemy to a 'breakdown in normal technical puzzle-solving'[103] seems ill-suited to a situation when 'normal' puzzle-solving was barely getting under way, corrupted scrambled records were just beginning to get sorted out and fresh data had not yet been systematically collected.

By the early sixteenth century an increasing number of Europe's best astronomers were recognizing that the astronomical paradigm was failing in application to its own traditional problems. That recognition was prerequisite to Copernicus' rejection of the Ptolemaic paradigm and his search for a new one.[104]

The chief 'traditional' problem for astronomers in Western Christen-

---

101 Ravetz, *Astronomy and Cosmology*, p. 44. Ravetz is referring specifically to the kind of 'normal science' that is described in Kuhn's *Structure of Scientific Revolutions* as I am also doing throughout this discussion.

102 'As time went on...the net result of the normal research effort of many astronomers' pointed toward a crisis for the Ptolemaic paradigm according to Thomas Kuhn, *Structure of Scientific Revolutions*, pp. 68–9.

103 Thomas Kuhn, *Structure of Scientific Revolutions*, p. 69.

104 Thomas Kuhn, *Structure of Scientific Revolutions*. When Kuhn says (p. 67), 'On this point historical evidence is entirely unequivocal, the state of Ptolemaic astronomy was a scandal before Copernicus' announcement,' the actual 'point' that provoked scandal seems to be unclear. In his footnote, Kuhn refers the reader to A. R. Hall's discussion of how tables of eclipses and church calendars were awry. On the question of the calendar which was 'the most notorious,' according to Hall, historical evidence is not unequivocal and the scandal is centuries-old. The role of calendar reform in 'intensifying the crisis' is also underlined by Kuhn in 'The Function of Measurement,' 181, no. 39. A very long-simmering 'steady-state' crisis seems to be entailed. (The validity of Kuhn's use of the term 'crisis' is also questioned by Gingerich in 'Crisis versus Aesthetic.')

dom was posed by church calendars failing to align Easter with the vernal equinox. Awareness of this failure may have served as a prerequisite for the Copernican Revolution. But it did not take 'an increasing number of Europe's best astronomers' in the sixteenth century to recognize the problem. It had been a concern of Christian Churchmen from the early middle ages on.

Had 'normal' puzzle-solving been feasible for the astronomers of Latin Christendom, it seems likely that calendar reform would have been accomplished well before Copernicus was born. Full technical mastery of Alexandrian and Arabic computations represented a relatively recent achievement for a sixteenth-century Western astronomer. In contrast, pressure for calendar reform, 'a pressure that made the puzzle of precession particularly urgent' had been a significant feature of the culture of Latin Christendom in Roger Bacon's day. Indeed the Church's sponsorship of the study of astronomy and its contribution to the retrieval of Alexandrian scientific texts was partly predicated on the need for help with this perennial problem. A 'long list of Christian scholars had called for calendar reform.' Many popes took a special interest in the matter. It loomed large at various church councils.[105]

One is reminded of repeated efforts to establish trilingual studies. There was nothing new about perceiving that the calendar was awry in Copernicus' day; just as there was nothing new about acknowledging the need of help from trilingual scholars to emend the Vulgate.[106] As in the latter case, so too in the former, novelty lay in the steps that were taken to achieve a long-desired goal. Although agitation for calendar reform had persisted for centuries, implementation had been frustrated for reasons that have yet to be made clear.

On this issue no two specialists seem to agree. (It is even difficult to discover whether Copernicus' work was helpful or irrelevant to the Gregorian reform that was finally carried through.)[107] Most accounts

[105] Sarton, Six Wings, p. 70. For repeated church requests, see also Thorndike, History of Magic and Experimental Science, p. 18.

[106] See p. 340, volume I above.

[107] Ravetz, Astronomy and Cosmology, p. 40, says that calendar reform 'was impossible before Copernicus' who provided the methods and data which rendered the Alphonsine Tables obsolete. Rosen, 'Galileo's Misstatements About Copernicus,' pp. 328–9, says, 'the Gregorian Calendar owed nothing to Copernicus' and was not based on the Prutenic Tables but rather on the mean tropical year as defined in the Alphonsine Tables. A seemingly authoritative reference from the journal of the Pontificia Academia Scientiarum, kindly supplied by Robert Palter, helps to clarify this question. According to de Kort, 'Astronomical Appreciation,' the length of the Gregorian Year was based on a value adopted from the Alphonsine Tables but the length of the month 'was taken from Copernicus's data as used in the Prutenian Tables' (p. 57).

imply that official inertia was primarily responsible. Unsolved astronomical problems are rarely discussed, and it is difficult for the non-specialist to ascertain whether they played an important role or indeed any role at all. Some studies state that only 'simple arithmetic and common sense' were required,[108] and others imply that the technical problems had been surmounted several centuries before Copernicus set to work. 'The reform of the Julian calendar was a limited and quantitative problem which medieval writers set out to solve and in fact solved.'[109] It is clear that a short-term reform of the Julian calendar was undertaken in the thirteenth century and that guidelines for further reform were also proposed.[110] Tinkering with the ancient Roman calendar was not quite the same as replacing it, however, and medieval calendar reform seems to have left the latter task unfulfilled. 'In improving the calendar' Rheticus complained on his teacher's behalf, 'most scholars enumerate various lengths of the years as computed by writers. But they do this in a confused way and come to no conclusion...'[111]

To arrive at a firm conclusion on an issue of this kind would have been exceedingly difficult in the age of scribes. According to Jerome Ravetz, most accounts tend to underestimate the technical difficulties that had to be surmounted in order to achieve the Gregorian reform. It was not as easy a task, Ravetz argues, as hindsight (based on Gauss' eighteenth-century formula) makes it appear. In his view, the Gregorian reform could not occur until after 'inequalities appearing from records of the past' had been mastered – as Copernicus set out to do.[112] If Ravetz is right, the conditions of scribal culture ought to be featured more prominently for having frustrated previous efforts at thoroughgoing reform.

It does seem misleading, at all events, to attribute the prolonged delay to 'institutional reluctance to apply scientific results' and to draw

Of course using the *Prutenic Tables* does not imply acceptance of Copernican geokinetic theories. Erasmus Reinhold who compiled the *Tables*, for example, did so without accepting the Copernican scheme.

[108] Sarton, *Six Wings*, p. 70.
[109] Crombie, 'Rejoinder,' pp. 318–19.
[110] See e.g. account of later adjustments in the calendar which had already been reformed by Grosseteste, made by Peter Nightingale in 1292. Nightingale's program encompassed a seventy-six-year period and detailed instructions for re-adjustment thereafter (which were followed in 1369 and 1440) according to Pedersen, 'The Life and Work of Peter Nightingale,' p. 6.
[111] Rheticus, 'Narratio Prima,' p. 127.
[112] Ravetz, *Astronomy and Cosmology*, pp. 7, 9, 38–9, 51–2. On p. 38, n. 23, Ravetz suggests that Sarton's approach is too naive.

analogies with the English postponement until 1752 and the Russian failure to move until 1918.[113] Even apart from uncertainty about 'scientific results,' medieval officials were handicapped by the difficulty of 'publishing' such results and of ensuring their uniform adoption. Institutional incapacity as well as possible reluctance must be taken into account.

It would have been an extremely simple matter once in every 308 years to prepare and publish a new table of Golden Numbers giving effect to this simple correction. But this was not done. The dread of innovation or some sort of superstitious regard for the established table apparently prevented any change.[114]

For one thing, this particular correction appears 'simple' only after the proper formula has been devised – after it is known that '235 lunations fell short of 19 Julian years by 1 hour and 29 minutes every 308 years.'[115] Before there was agreement on just these points, the case was not simple at all. For another thing, reluctance to instruct officials to change numerical tables every three centuries and eight years would have been sensible, not 'superstitious' in an era when there was no way of publishing 'errata' of any kind, when copies of written instructions were likely to drift over the course of a single century and when heavy reliance on oral transmission meant one had to arrange for changing memorized formulae – a dangerous procedure indeed. It became relatively easy to train clerks to handle Dominical letters after they were laid out in printed tables. But formidable mnemonic feats were required of the Oxford clerks who studied the computus from the thirteenth to the sixteenth centuries. To help them learn the required 260 lines of hexameter, each finger was assigned six joints and all sixty joints were used.[116] Before printed calendars, it was 'an arduous mathematical feat' merely to 'find a day that corresponded to a given date.'[117]

In view of the difficulty of ensuring conformity with the existing system any 'dread of innovation' was soundly based. It seems mis-

---

[113] Crombie, 'Rejoinder,' pp. 318–19.   [114] Philip, *The Calendar*, p. 68.
[115] Philip, *The Calendar*, p. 68.
[116] Bosanquet, *English Printed Almanacks*, p. 59. See also discussion of vernacular rhymes in a manual on the *Computus* written by Alexander de Villedieu and taught to students at the Paris college of Ave Maria in the fourteenth century, Gabriel, *Garlandia*, p. 110.
[117] D. E. Smith, *Le Comput*, p. 13. This publication also contains a discussion of early printed versions (beginning with a Strasbourg manual of 1488), of other medieval mnemonic works, and of finger exercises such as those illustrated in a 1504 Lyons publication (pp. 28, 49).

guided, at all events, to attribute postponement of reform to 'inner quarrels of the Church' which prevented any measure being taken until the late sixteenth century. When the measure was finally taken, Western Christendom was no less quarrelsome than it had been before. The more plausible explanation offered by Kuhn, who points to the expansion of dynastic states and burgeoning bureaucracy, also seems somewhat doubtful to me. To suggest that the '...size of political, economic and administrative units placed a new premium upon an efficient and uniform means of dating' seems to put the cart before the horse.[118] It was not the high value assigned to calendar reform but the means of achieving this long-desired goal that was new in the sixteenth century. Calendar reform had been a church-sponsored project at the outset, and remained one to the end. It was so little valued by secular statesmen that Protestant officials in well-consolidated realms were willing to bow to anti-Papist sentiment and postpone its adoption for many decades.

That the project was assigned high priority by medieval churchmen rather than by early-modern state officials is worth underlining, for it points to some neglected religious roots of Western science. Investigation into calendrical problems was the accidental by-product of sacred concerns that were peculiar to the Christian faith and that centered on commemorating the miracle of the Resurrection. The definition of Easter made at the Council of Nicea kept Western mathematicians and astronomers at work on a set of problems that evaded solution throughout the age of scribes. Was there any other religious community that celebrated a sacred festival so peculiarly sensitive to errors in solar and lunar tables or so insistent that the puzzle of the precession of equinoxes be solved?[119]

The complexity of the Christian Church calendar, like that of its polyglot Bible, can best be appreciated when set against Moslem simplicity. 'We are a people who do not write and do not count' said Mohammed. Not sixty knuckles and hundreds of lines of hexameter but only ten fingers shown three times with the thumb folded on the third time were needed by the faithful of Islam to measure the passing

[118] Thomas Kuhn, *Copernican Revolution*, p. 124. Pannekoek, *History of Astronomy*, p. 219 attributes the delay to 'inner quarrels' of the Church.
[119] Calendrical problems spurred the development of mathematical science in China according to Needham, *Science and Civilisation* III, 152. But successful reform was achieved only after the arrival of Western missionaries in the seventeenth century. See d'Elia, *Galileo in China*, appendix, pp. 61 ff.

of the months.[120] The same Semitic calendar that was complicated by the Christians at Nicea was drastically simplified by Mohammed who eliminated intercalations and ignored the solar cycle. The length of every year was arbitrarily fixed at twelve lunar months, and seasonal changes were irrelevant to the celebration of Ramadan. Over the course of centuries the Moslem calendar became increasingly out of phase with the solar cycle (by now it is forty years off) but the growing discrepancy did not serve as an irritant. Moslems 'simply ignored the law of nature in their regulation of their time scheme.'[121] This is not to say that *all* the sacred concerns of the Moslems were indifferent to the laws of nature. Problems posed by orienting all mosques toward Mecca in an expanding empire, for example, may have spurred study of astronomy and geography among the Arabs.[122] But a different set of problems was posed for Christians by a celestial clockwork that perversely moved out of phase with annual commemoration of the central miracle of their faith.

Throughout the middle ages, the movable feast of Easter, indeed, served as a focal point where studies of astronomy and of chronology, of sacred history and of profane all converged. Not only were solar and lunar cycles difficult to reconcile, but Passover also had to be kept out of Easter's way. Ancient Jewish and Roman time schemes had to be mastered. The puzzling precession of the vernal equinox could not be set aside nor could contradictions in the gospels be left out of account.[123] The problems posed by Easter help to explain why Chris-

---

[120] Sayili, *The Observatory in Islam*, p. 22, cites Al Bîrûnî's version of Mohammed's statement in this connection.

[121] Philip, *The Calendar*, p. 26. Data on how the Christians complicated and the Moslems simplified a luni-solar calendar inherited from the Jews are also contained in Archer, *The Christian Calendar*, pp. 39-52.

[122] According to Sayili, *The Observatory in Islam*, pp. 23-5, taxes and harvests were affected by the absence of a solar calendar or of any intercalated years in Islam. For a brief interval in the eleventh century, the Malikshâh Observatory introduced reckoning according to a solar calendar but this lasted only twenty years (1072-92). The orientation of mosques allowed for so much latitude (up to forty-five degrees error or more) that this problem provided less impetus to astronomy than might be thought. Non-sacred concerns, such as desert navigation, *did* stimulate the Arabs, however, to develop some observational techniques well in advance of those available in the West in Columbus' era. (See e.g. Morison, *Admiral*, p. 184.)

[123] The additional complications posed by the Council of Nicea's insistence on avoiding 'judaising Easter' are described by Philip, *The Calendar*, pp. 63, 78. Archer, *The Christian Calendar*, pp. 18, 53, argues that the decision was predicated, not on animosity toward the Jews, but to avoid the inconsistency of celebrating the Resurrection before or on the same day as the slaying of the Paschal Lamb which prefigured the crucifixion. One need not adopt an either/or approach. Probably both anti-Semitism and allegorical consistency played a role. The fact that no calendar can avoid Easter's occasionally coinciding with Passover is only one of many complications that persistently challenged the ingenuity of Christian clerks.

tian astronomers down to Newton's day were so often preoccupied with biblical chronology,[124] and why Christian churchmen going back to Bede's time, devoted so much effort to graphing the planets, compiling tide-tables and instructing future priests in the mysteries of the computus.

computistical material did much to stimulate the use of tables and diagrams. Although the tables abound in error...their construction stimulated at least scientific ratiocination...It is possible but by no means proved that such astronomical graphing influenced the application of graphing techniques to problems of local motion and qualitative changes in the fourteenth century.[125]

The early medieval graphs described by Clagett did not merely have some indirect bearing on the future development of fourteenth-century mechanics. They also point more directly to the inclusion of planetary astronomy in the sacred concerns of Christians even during the early middle ages. They offer evidence that concern with uniformity, regularity and a mathematical order in nature was manifested in church schools even before Aristotle's *Logic* re-entered the West. The 'craze for the dialectic' came well after a strong 'habit of definite exact thought' had been implanted in Christian culture. Among professional astronomers, of course, this habit went back to pre-Christian times. But even after ancient astronomy had been lost and before it was again retrieved, the same habit was being inculcated among novices who tried to master the computus in order to become Christian priests. By a seeming paradox, their most sacred festival kept Christian energies bent toward puzzle-solving of a purely scientific kind.

In this regard one might take issue with modern writers who project a more recent warfare between science and theology into earlier eras. 'Comets and monsters were of greater moment to medieval piety than the daily sunrise and normal offspring.'[126] The news value of the odd as opposed to the ordinary event is still rated high even in these impious days. Insofar as they viewed dog-biting men as more newsworthy than man-eating dogs, monkish chroniclers had more in common with modern journalists than with medieval natural philoso-

[124] Kepler's many references to J. J. Scaliger's *De Emendatione Temporum* (1583) and his correspondence with the author about ancient chronology are noted by Palter (ed.) *Johannes Kepler 1571–1630*, Catalogue, item no. 118. An entire section in this catalogue: *VI. Calendars and Chronology* points to many other relevant titles. The case of Newton has inspired a special study: Manuel, *Isaac Newton Historian.* On Scaliger's work see Grafton, 'Joseph Scaliger and Historical Chronology.'   [125] Clagett, *Greek Science*, pp. 162–5.
[126] Zilsel, cited by Lewis Feuer, *The Scientific Intellectual*, p. 249.

phers who graphed planetary movements and studied the tides. Insofar as the daily sunrise was part of a celestial clockwork that was persistently out of phase with Easter, it could not be ignored by pious clerics and was a source of constant concern. Their very belief in a supernatural event encouraged learned churchmen to persist with investigations of the order of nature. The desire to commemorate a miracle on the proper holy day forced repeated inquiries into cyclical movements of a non-miraculous kind.

Until the advent of printing, scientific inquiries about 'how the heavens go' went hand-in-hand with religious concerns about 'how to go to heaven.' Astronomers were needed to help commemorate Gospel truths. After printing, however, the study of celestial mechanics was propelled in a new direction and soon reached levels of sophistication that left calendrical problems far behind. With the output of printed tables, moreover, training priests to master the computus lost many of the virtues it had formerly possessed. Complex mnemonics, parchment volvelles and other devices designed to help with 'Easter date computation, Golden Numbers, Sunday Letters and all the rigamaroles of the passion for calendrics that afflicted the scholarly church'[127] eventually receded into a dimly remembered Gothic past. That intelligent adults had actually been preoccupied with child-like jingles such as 'Thirty days hath September...' made medieval men seem strangely 'retarded' to scholars who lived in an 'enlightened' age. Churchmen and astronomers continued to move apart to the point where it now seems odd to think of their having ever been committed to a joint enterprise.

The calendrical problems posed by Easter – like the linguistic ones posed by the Bible – turned out to be peculiarly sensitive to changes wrought by print. The Koran did not provide the same incentive that the Vulgate did to master strange tongues or dig up ancient scrolls. The observance of Ramadan did not supply the religious motives that Easter did to go beyond the *Almagest* and ascertain the long-term slow-motion movements of the stars. Their most sacred festival as well as their holy scriptures acted to keep Christian men of learning constantly pressing against the limits imposed by scribal culture. Special religious motives helped to provide the initial impetus for what later appeared to be an almost sacriligious 'Faustian' quest.

127 Price, 'The Book as a Scientific Instrument,' p. 102.

Evidence of this special concern was clearly present in the book that launched the Copernican Revolution. Even though Copernicus originally set out to emend Ptolemaic astronomy without giving much thought to calendrical problems,[128] a concern with these problems did play a significant part in guiding his research during the last thirty years he spent revising his *magnum opus*. For a decade he 'concentrated on the unequal length of the seasons and explanations of this inequality.'[129] His prolonged investigation was not without a significant result:

In Copernicus's mature *Revolutionibus*, this fixed apsidal line was replaced by a moving terrestrial aphelion.

This discovery, doubtless connected with Copernicus's intensified investigation of the length of the year was based in part on a careful scrutiny of the results obtained by his predecessors. It is sometimes said that Copernicus had too much faith in the observations of earlier astronomers. But in this instance he could not be incredulous, since he found an incompatibility in the position of the solar apogee as reported by two of the most outstanding medieval Muslim observers between whom he had to choose.[130]

The recruitment of mathematicians and astronomers to help with calendar reform thus acted very much as did the use of trilingual scholars to help with scriptural emendation. In urging Copernicus to work further on the calendrical problems that the fifth Lateran Council had not solved, Paul of Middelburg was doing something many other learned churchmen had done before. In accepting the assignment Copernicus was also serving in a conventional role.[131] For astronomers as for biblical scholars, however, unanticipated consequences resulted when new means came to the aid of those who were pursuing old goals. Copernicus set out to reform Ptolemy much as Erasmus had set out to re-do Saint Jerome – in order to serve the Church, not subvert it.

---

[128] Rosen, 'Biography of Copernicus,' *Three Copernican Treatises*, p. 360, points out that the *Commentariolus* was undertaken before Copernicus was asked to help with calendar reform and indicates little concern with the topic. Other good reasons for rejecting Ravetz's suggestion 'that Copernicus' reconstruction of astronomy sprang from the problem of calendar reform' are set forth by Wilson, 'Rheticus, Ravetz,' pp. 4–5. The problem *did* enter into Copernicus' revision of Ptolemaic astronomy, but at a later stage. See n. 131 below.

[129] Rosen, 'Biography of Copernicus,' *Three Copernican Treatises*, p. 362.

[130] Rosen, 'Biography of Copernicus,' *Three Copernican Treatises*, p. 388.

[131] On the invitation addressed to Paul of Middelburg (1445–1533) Bishop of Fossebrone, by Pope Leo X to help with calendar reform and on how Copernicus was 'spurred' by the urging of Paul of Middelburg in 1515 to investigate the topic more closely see Rosen, 'Biography of Copernicus,' *Three Copernican Treatises*, pp. 359–62. How Paul of Middelburg's own calendrical research led him toward Hebrew studies is discussed by Offenberg, 'The first use of Hebrew.'

'Never, perhaps, has such a conservative and quiet thinker had such an upsetting effect upon men's minds and souls...'[132]

De Revolutionibus itself must be a constant puzzle and a paradox for...it is a relatively staid, sober and unrevolutionary work...In every respect except the earth's motion the De Revolutionibus seems more closely akin to the works of ancient and medieval astronomers...than to the writings of succeeding generations...who made explicit the radical consequences that even its author had not seen in his work...[133]

The 'radical consequences' that ensued from Copernicus' 'sober and unrevolutionary work' might seem somewhat less puzzling if the new powers of print were taken into account. As things stand now, however, these powers tend to be mainly confined to functions associated with publicity and propaganda. Accordingly, they seem to loom large in the early stages of the Lutheran revolt and to recede to the point of vanishing in the first phases of the Copernican Revolution. Whether they are called into play to spread Lutheran tracts or Copernican theories, it should be noted, the new presses make a belated appearance as agents of change. But although early printers have to wait until 1517 before their presence on the stage of history is acknowledged in Reformation studies, they are assigned significant functions thereafter. News of the ninety-five Theses spread far and fast; Luther's German Bible set records as a bestseller. Whether one is willing to accept Arthur Koestler's verdict or not, one must admit that by contrast with the stir Luther made, the reception of Copernicus was very subdued. According to Koestler, this posthumous publication 'created less of a stir than Rheticus' First Account of it. Rheticus had promised that the book would be a revelation; it turned out to be a disappointment... it raised no particular controversy either in public or among professional astronomers...[134]

Many authorities, to be sure, regard Copernicus' failure to attract

---

[132] Boas, Scientific Renaissance, p. 69.

[133] Thomas Kuhn, Copernican Revolution, p. 134.

[134] Koestler, Sleepwalkers, p. 213. The 'book that nobody read' is so described on p. 191. For sharp attack on Koestler's 'ludicrously unhistorical' judgment, see Rosen, 'Biography of Copernicus,' Three Copernican Treatises, pp. 406–8. Actually, sufficient controversy was created for the Italian publicist, Doni, to portray two Florentines disputing the hypothesis as a theory refuted in sermons – in I Marmi (Venice, 1552) and for Du Bartas to include verses ridiculing it in his popular poem: 'La Semaine' of 1587. See Preserved Smith, Origins of Modern Culture, pp. 52–3. A full account of sixteenth-century publicity pro and con cannot be given here. Recent studies have outdated the pioneering monograph by Dorothy Stimson, The Gradual Acceptance of the Copernican Theory of the Universe (New York, 1917) as noted in a review by Erna Hilfstein and Edward Rosen of a recent Polish book by Barbara Bienkowska.

publicity as less deplorable than does Koestler. When Whitehead, for example, contrasts the 'quiet' rise of modern science with the 'popular' religious uprising that 'drenched Europe in blood,' it is to suggest that diffident scientists were really better Christians than were quarrelsome monks: 'Since a babe was born in a manger, it may be doubted whether so great a thing happened with so little stir.'[135] Kuhn regards the 'quiet' reception of De Revolutionibus as useful for the purposes of subversion. By making his work 'unreadable to all save the most erudite,' Kuhn suggests, Copernicus actually fashioned 'an almost ideal weapon' for the struggle that lay ahead. By the time opposition was mobilized, professional astronomers had come to rely on Copernicus' mathematical techniques and had become accustomed to computing planetary positions from a moving earth. The geokinetic theory had already achieved 'victory by infiltration' before it came under strong official attack. Kuhn even argues that printing helped to consolidate this victory by making it more difficult 'to suppress the work completely' – a somewhat debatable point.[136]

Whether effective opposition was eventually blunted because De Revolutionibus was printed and not copied out by hand is a matter for debate. There can be no dispute, at any rate, that early printers play a much less conspicuous and much more problematic role in the Copernican Revolution than in the Reformation. Not only did sixteenth-century printers fail to rally behind the Copernican cause as they did behind the Lutheran one, they also did much to popularize Ptolemaic views.[137] As noted above, their propensity for backing the 'wrong' astronomical theory is repeatedly used as a warning not to

---

[135] Whitehead, *Science and the Modern World*, pp. 11–12. Particularly after Galileo turned to print, the 'quiet rise of modern science' was less remote from the noisy clash of rival faiths than this passage suggests. See chap. 8, below, for critique of Whitehead's view.

[136] Thomas Kuhn, *Copernican Revolution*, p. 185. Given the technical nature of the work, and given the less rigorous character of censorship before printing, it seems unlikely that an attempt would have been made 'to suppress the work completely' had it been in ms. form. As it was, *De Revolutionibus* lent itself easily to expurgation thus rendering 'complete' suppression unnecessary. That it could be used *without accepting the earth's motion* should also be kept in mind. See n. 107 above on Reinhold's work as an example.

[137] Koestler, *Sleepwalkers*, p. 191 points to fifty-nine editions of Sacrobosco's *Sphaera*, nineteen reprints of Clavius's *Treatise*, nine reprints of Melanchthon's textbook and other reprints of Ptolemy's *Almagest* and Peurbach's *Planetary Theory* to come up with a total of 'a hundred reprints in Germany' before 1600 as against the one reprint of *De Revolutionibus* and thus validate his description of a 'worst seller.' This is somewhat like comparing the number of editions of Einstein's *Die Allgemeine Relativitätstheorie* with those of all textbooks and popularizations based on 'classical' Newtonian theories during the past fifty years. As noted above, moreover, many editions of old titles contained supplements which pointed toward a new astronomy.

exaggerate the effects of print. The most debased version of this over-done thesis appears in a well reviewed volume by a former curator of prints at the Metropolitan Museum of Art:

Before the age of Galileo, Descartes and Newton, printers tended to leave scientific innovations in manuscript. Commercially they were right, for in 1543 when Johann Kepler [sic] proved that the planets circle around the sun and not around the earth, his founding treatise of modern astronomy sold so slowly that it did not need reprinting for 23 years.[138]

As long as functions performed by early printers are confined to the 'spread of new ideas,' as long as they are associated with conversion and propaganda (or even with subversion and infiltration) they are bound to seem less effective when dealing with the new astronomy than with new approaches to the Gospel. Of course *De Revolutionibus* does appear to be a 'worst seller' when set against Lutheran Bibles and tracts. But this kind of juxtaposition would also make Vesalius appear to have produced a 'worst seller.'

Vesalius's work did not at once have the important success that it deserved; only with difficulty and slowly were the truths established that he had audaciously put forth...the teachings of Galen continued to occupy an important place in the universities for another century...[139]

In many surveys, sixteenth-century anatomy books are just as likely as astronomical treatises to be subjected to a 'cultural lag' – an illusory lag, which is based on ignoring all the advantages that hindsight has con-ferred. If the 'wrong' theories of Galen and Ptolemy continued to circulate and be taught in the second half of the sixteenth century this was partly because the 'right' theories developed by Kepler and Harvey had not been spelled out fully. Sixteenth-century printers and pro-fessors naturally failed to anticipate what Kepler and Newton would make of Copernicus' work. Given the difficult technical nature of *De Revolutionibus* and given the fact that five editions of the *Narratio Prima* were also being put on the market during the same century, it seems remarkable that the Basel printer 'Henricpetreius' thought a second

---

[138] Mayor, *Prints and People*, text below fig. 108. Page references cannot be given, for there are no page numbers in this book – which may help to explain how the substitution of Kepler for Copernicus went uncorrected. This kind of boner is too obvious to do much harm (apart from reinforcing two-culture divisions). But the false opinion that scientific innovation did not get into print until the seventeenth century is more insidious and skews perspectives on the 'century of genius.'

[139] Castiglioni, *A History of Medicine*, p. 425. On the debates engendered by *De Fabrica*, see above, p. 574.

edition was worth issuing twenty-three years after the first[140] and that a third one was deemed worthwhile by W. J. Blaeu's Amsterdam firm in 1617.[141]

As we have seen, there are significant differences between *De Fabrica* and *De Revolutionibus* and between the two authors' attitudes toward print. Nevertheless it seems more appropriate to compare two scientific treatises published in 1543 than to set Copernicus next to Darwin and Marx – and throw in Luther for good measure as well!

The Darwinian revolution struck like lightning, the Marxian took three-quarters of a century to hatch. The Copernican revolution...spread in a slower and more devious manner than all. Not because the printing press was new, or the subject obscure; Luther's theses created an immediate all-European turmoil though they were less easy to compress into a single slogan than 'the Sun does not go round the Earth but the Earth goes round the Sun.'[142]

Actually, geokinetic theories had been publicized by slogans decades before the publication of *De Revolutionibus*. The view 'that the earth moves but the sun stands still' was assigned to a pamphlet written by Copernicus as early as 1514.[143] Koestler himself mentions the relatively catchy title of Calcagnini's treatise 'concerning how the Heavens rest; the Earth moves' – a treatise probably inspired by Cusa and 'echoing an idea...much in the air.'[144] It was not the lack of a catchy slogan but the presence of lengthy and complicated calculations that prevented *De Revolutionibus* from achieving bestsellerdom. Nothing suggests that Copernicus' few readers were disappointed or that hopes raised by Rheticus seemed to be betrayed when the large work was finally

140 The *Narratio Prima* was printed first at Danzig and then at Basel, 1540–1. A third edition was coupled with the 1566 Basel *De Revolutionibus*; a fourth and fifth with Kepler's *Mysterium Cosmographicum*, Tübingen, 1596 (under Maestlin's supervision) and at Frankfurt, 1621. Rosen, *Three Copernican Treatises*, p. 11; Dreyer, *A History of Astronomy*, p. 349. On the decision to print a second edition of *De Revolutionibus* see Rosen, 'Biography of Copernicus,' pp. 406–7 and on Heinrich Petri, 'Henric-petri' or 'Henricpetreius' (1527–79) heir to a distinguished Basel dynasty and husband of a Froben widow, see entry no. 16 in Benzing, *Buchdrucker-lexicon*, p. 24 and chap. 2, n. 175, volume I above.

141 Koestler, *Sleepwalkers*, p. 458 passes over this important third edition, published by Blaeu in 1617 soon after *De Revolutionibus* was condemned. He gives uninformed readers the mistaken impression that no one bothered to reprint *De Revolutionibus* since it was outdated by Tycho's observations, Kepler's discoveries and Galileo's telescope. On the timing of Blaeu's

143 publication, see discussion, below, p. 676.   142 Koestler, *Sleepwalkers*, p. 149. According to Rosen, 'Biography of Copernicus,' *Three Copernican Treatises*, p. 343, there is no question that this description of a pamphlet which is contained in an inventory of a Cracow doctor's library referred to the *Commentariolus*, i.e., the first draft of Copernicus' 'geokinetic and heliostatic theory.'   144 Koestler, *Sleepwalkers*, p. 209.

published. On the contrary, the evidence suggests the magnitude of the task performed by the 'second Ptolemy' impressed even those sixteenth-century astronomers who failed to adopt Copernican views.[145] (That an 'unreadable' work often commands more awe and respect than an easy-to-read one is suggested by the reception of Einstein's 'general theory of relativity.') It is the twentieth-century science reporter who experiences disappointment when looking over the book that purportedly started it all. In the 1550s and 1560s, heliocentricity was not devoid of intriguing implications and Elizabethans who read about the 'most aunciente doctrine of the Pythagoreans lately revived by Copernicus' do not seem to have been disappointed.[146] Nevertheless the Copernican hypothesis did not stir readers' interest in the same way as did the latest news about a royal marriage or the election of a Pope. Insofar as the heavens were deemed newsworthy, controversy over the meaning of a given planetary conjunction was likely to attract the largest number of pamphleteers.

To historians of science, Regiomontanus is 'newsworthy' for having edited an epitome of the *Almagest*, for launching a continuous series of *Ephemerides* or for posthumously providing a pioneering text on trigonometry. Almost a century after his death, the work of his that was most exciting to Elizabethan literati was an astrological verse concern-

[145] Tycho's tribute in a Copenhagen lecture to the 'second Ptolemy' in 1574 is noted above, n. 68. Dreyer, *History of Astronomy*, p. 349 cites Urstisius' praise of Copernicus as a 'truly divine genius' in a work printed in 1573; Ravetz, *Astronomy and Cosmology*, p. 49 notes that even Clavius hailed Copernicus as the 'restorer of astronomy.' Westman's 'Three Responses' brings out the respectful attention as well as the diverse reactions elicited by *De Revolutionibus* as viewed by professional astronomers who belonged to the circle around Melanchthon and who transmitted diverse aspects of the Copernican heritage to the next generation.

[146] Thomas Digges, *A Perfit Description of the Caelistiall Orbes according to the Most Aunciente Doctrine of the Pythagoreans, lately Revived by Copernicus and by Geometrical demonstrations approved* was first published in 1576 as a supplement to a reissue of his father's (Leonard Digges) ephemerides: *The Prognostication Everlasting* and was reprinted at least six times by 1605. See Johnson, *Astronomical Thought*, pp. 100–2. Since this treatise contained large portions of Book I of *De Revolutionibus* it also argues against the 'worst-selling' thesis. The printer of the *Prognostication Everlasting*, Thomas Marsh (or Marshe) also published in 1556 the celebrated *Ephemeris Anni 1557* which contained the *Prutenic Tables* (issued only five years previously) rearranged for the meridian of London by John Feild and containing a preface by John Dee, mentioning Copernicus and Reinhold. See Bosanquet, *English Printed Almanacks*, pp. 33–4; Dreyer, *History of Astronomy*, pp. 346–7. When Koestler, *Sleepwalkers* says the Copernican theory 'was practically ignored until Kepler and Galileo' (p. 213) he sets Thomas Digges aside as a 'non-astronomer' although Digges contributed to Tycho's work on the Nova of 1572. The early interest in the Copernican theory shown by English Cantabrigians who matriculated in the 1540s and frequented the libraries of Cheke and Sir Thomas Smith is underlined by Johnson, *Astronomical Thought*, p. 89. The 1556 catalogue of Sir Thomas Smith's library testifies to the innovative role of early printers and the long reach of Regiomontanus.

ing the world's end.[147] The outpouring of sixteenth-century printed material devoted to portents and prognostication ought not to be dismissed as sheer rubbish. As previous discussion of Tycho's star suggests, useful observations might come as by-products of the mounting public excitement. Markets for *Ephemerides* were enlarged, astronomical instrument-makers could flourish and serial publication was encouraged by intense interest in eclipses and conjunctions.[148] Moreover, the sheer volume of conflicting prophecies and predictions may have helped eventually to undermine the confidence of some readers in the validity of astrology.[149] Nevertheless, there is no positive correlation between the publicity value and the scientific worth of any treatise in any age.

Even after Galileo stirred the Republic of Letters, and scientific curiosity was stimulated among princes and poets, the news value of the oddity outstripped that of the ordinary. Sober discussion of celestial or terrestrial mechanics still did not achieve the same sales as did more sensational 'pseudo-scientific' reports. Moreover, the scientist never did achieve the same position as the evangelist. Even in the heyday of Enlightenment, Methodist tracts and hymnals kept presses humming and new Bible societies used the powers of print to the full. Furthermore, entertainment was never outsold by instruction. The Royal Society celebrated the banishing of ghosts and goblins from its precincts. Romantic novelists, visionaries, and Grub Street hacks found a large reading public who were more entranced than disenchanted by such stuff.

It may be worth noting that the situation has not changed much over the course of recent centuries. The number of astronomers and mathematical physicists has greatly increased. It still remains proportionately small compared to the audience tapped by Gothic tales of witchcraft, reports of flying saucers, and the like. The news value of a weeping statue or of a haunted house is still likely to hold its own against a

[147] Aston, 'The Fiery Trigon,' n. 66.
[148] According to Bosanquet, *English Printed Almanacks*, p. 4, few prognostications were issued in written form before print. See Keith Thomas, *Religion and the Decline of Magic*, pp. 283–389 on the outpouring of fugitive literature in Tudor and Stuart England.
[149] Thomas, *Religion and the Decline of Magic*, pp. 335 ff says that 'massive and repeated errors' did not diminish the demand for prognostications but also notes (p. 300) that a Council of State in 1652 issued a paper, stating that eclipses were natural events without political implications, in order to counteract the impact of anonymous pamphlets. The effectiveness of prognostications was also diminished according to Thomas, p. 350, by increasingly accurate predictions, such as that offered by Halley's comet.

treatise on astrophysics or a story about a quasar. However popular the American journal, *Popular Mechanics*, its sales never rivalled those of printed horoscopes – or of Bibles for that matter.

It is also worth noting that spreading news came naturally to six-teenth-century evangelists whereas keeping secrets was conventional among the followers of Pythagoras. This situation *did* change. Trade secrets were advertised, arcana were disclosed. Unwritten recipes entered the public domain. Science became 'public knowledge' and as such was separated from 'furtive' magic. Yet even after this trans-formation it is interesting to observe that scientists are still more uneasy about publicity than are evangelists (or journalists or performing artists of any kind). Secretive attitudes, at all events, were entirely conven-tional in Copernicus' day (even Newton retained them much later on). It seems unwarranted to expect a sixteenth-century astronomer to share the attitudes of the modern science reporter.[150]

Kepler, whom Koestler does not describe as 'timid' or 'devious,' also had a thesis that could be compressed into a simple statement. Yet Kepler's demonstration that planets do not move in circles caused little more of a stir than did the heliocentric views Copernicus had pre-viously set forth. At least the thesis set forth in *De Revolutionibus* managed to reach Kepler. The latter's work was so 'supremely un-readable' that its important contents passed Galileo by.[151] Elliptical orbits failed to make contact with parabolic curves until later on.[152]

---

[150] Koestler, *Sleepwalkers*, pp. 149–50 accuses Copernicus of being 'infatuated with the Pythago-rean cult of secrecy,' 'arrogantly obscurantist' and 'anti-humanist' in contrast to Erasmus, Reuchlin, von Hutten, Luther *et al.* That the Pythagorean cult was quite compatible with many forms of Northern humanism and shared by Reuchlin among others is clear from many studies. See e.g. Spitz, *The Religious Renaissance*, and 'Reuchlin's Philosophy.'

[151] See chap. 5 above, pp. 501–3; n. 152. How other readers were eventually persuaded to study Kepler's difficult prose and to extricate important theorems from them is discussed below, p. 631.

[152] See Boyer, *History of Mathematics*, p. 358 for suggestive remarks about ellipses and parabolas and also for a relevant discussion of Kepler's work on the measurement of the volume of liquid in barrels. Here again, the addition of uniform sharp-edged diagrams to texts needs more attention. Problems associated with conic sections must have been clarified thereby. 'How many mathematicians are there who will undertake the labor of reading through the Conics of Apollonius of Perga?' asked Kepler (Boas, *Scientific Renaissance*, p. 305). In medieval Latin manuscripts the theorems of Apollonius (like those of Euclid) could not speak unam-biguously and directly to 'reason's inner ear' partly because they were not presented clearly to the eye. The transmission of Apollonius' *Conics* is well covered by Rose, 'Renaissance Italian Methods of Drawing the Ellipse,' where Rose notes the 'weak' medieval tradition, the plans of Regiomontanus to publish a new translation based on the Greek text, the printing of excerpts by Giorgio Valla in his *De Rebus* (1501) and other editions up to that of Commandino (Bologna, 1566). Rose's article also contains valuable data on methods of constructing conic sections and new instruments devised for this purpose. Koestler, *Sleepwalkers*, pp. 330–1,

Whereas Copernicus' failure to attract as many followers as Luther did is attributed to a cowardly penchant for secrecy, contemporary neglect of elliptical orbits is seen merely as the price Kepler paid for being ahead of his time. The double standard is particularly inconsistent because Copernicus had even fewer contemporaries who could follow his arguments with Ptolemy than Kepler did. Only astronomers who were equipped to read the *Almagest* could be expected to judge the 'Second Ptolemy's' work. As noted above, the number of astronomers who were thus equipped probably was not large.[153]

It is indeed mainly because Copernicus belonged to such a restricted professional group that historians rarely think about the impact of printing when dealing with his work. If the effects of printing are confined to dissemination, and circulation figures are stressed, it will scarcely seem to matter whether the *De Revolutionibus* was printed or not. Much useful astronomical data continued to be transmitted during the early-modern era without getting into print. Copernicus is often said to have studied some of Regiomontanus' works before they went to press;[154] Tycho obtained some of Copernicus' manuscripts; Kepler inherited all of Tycho's papers. Until as late as 1854, the posthumous circulation of Copernicus' 'Letter against Werner' was handled by scribal transmission.[155] Is it not conceivable that copies of *De Revolutionibus* might have reached the restricted group equipped to make use of it by the same means?

Many authorities seem inclined to answer this question affirmatively. Accordingly, they postpone considering changes in communications until the appearance of learned periodicals in the seventeenth century. They may argue, as does Thorndike, that since professional scientists

speculates about Kepler's unconscious 'fixation' or 'biological bias' because of his failure to recognize ellipses in egg-shaped curves. It might be more helpful to investigate the presence or absence of clear diagrams of conic sections in early mathematical texts.

153 See n. 99 above.
154 But see evidence provided by Rosen and discussed above, p. 591 showing that *On Triangles* was *not* seen by Copernicus until Rheticus brought him the first printed edition on his visit to Frombork in 1539.
155 See Rosen, introduction, *Three Copernican Treatises*, p. 8 for suggestion that such sixteenth-century hand-copied letters served the function later performed by printed articles and book reviews. That Tycho obtained a second- or third-hand transcription of the *Letter Against Werner* and that mss. turned up both in Berlin and Vienna in the nineteenth century is also noted (pp. 8–9, n. 15). Swerdlow, 'Derivation of Commentariolus' also notes that a ms. of Copernicus' *Commentariolus*, which was owned by Tycho, served as the basis for further copies. His comments on the corrupt texts of the later copies are indicative of problems posed by scribal transmission at any time. Since the data inherited from Tycho by Kepler was in fresh, uncopied form, scribal transmission is irrelevant to this latter case.

could serve each other adequately by handwritten interchange, early printing merely propagated error, spreading a little learning more thinly over a greater surface of the public-at-large. Or they may take a more positive view as does Stillman Drake, who welcomes the breaking of an academic monopoly and the tapping of scientific talents outside university walls. Whether Latin-reading professional élites are regarded as progressive or reactionary, there seems to be agreement that they were fairly adequately served by scribes.

The medieval university community was clearly relatively small and homogeneous... A large number of copies of any given work was never necessary within that community whether we think of this as a single university, of several universities in a geographical area, or even as all the universities in Europe. It was unlikely that a person living in the university community would long remain unaware of the existence of a significant work related to his particular interests. If a copy was not immediately at hand, it is probable that the scholar who told him of the existence of the work would also be able to outline the nature of its contents.[156]

The argument seems sufficiently plausible to win general assent. Yet I think it neglects the obstacles posed by scribal culture and seriously overestimates the services it rendered academic élites. Even the most intrepid 'wandering scholars' seeking access to highly valued technical texts had much more difficulty than we are likely to recognize, given problems posed by books locked in chests or chained in collegiate and ducal libraries. Throughout the later middle ages, teaching and preaching orders kept copies in different places but use was confined exclusively to fellow friars. Lay faculties were equally reluctant to allow important texts to circulate outside cloistered walls.[157] Given restricted access to diverse collections, there was little more free trade in ideas than there was open interchange of guild secrets. The academic community was not homogeneous and the texture of learning was remarkably variegated. The high level of sophistication achieved by one group of fellows in a particular college or a monastic order often went unshared in other lecture halls. Regional barriers were much more formidable in the age of scribes than they were after annual book

---

156 Drake, 'Early Science,' p. 48.
157 See Gabriel, *College System*, p. 28; Humphreys, *The Book Provisions of the Medieval Friars 1215–1400*, *passim*. See also problem of gaining access to the Bessarion manuscripts in the Marciana experienced by Poliziano in 1491 (Rose, 'Humanist Culture,' p. 93) and experience of Budé viewing the Florentine codex of the *Digest* as noted on p. 103, volume I above.

fairs began. During the later middle ages, for example, knowledge of tangent functions scarcely moved beyond Paris and Oxford.[158] Before the advent of printing the full *Almagest* was rarely available in any college libraries at all.

It would not be of much help to a student of astronomy to know that there was in existence a great composition by an ancient hand. His imagination might be stimulated from hearing someone outline its contents, but his capacity to make use of the work would go unfulfilled. Could Tycho have 'taught himself' astronomy merely by overhearing astronomers converse? Further, would he have felt compelled to re-appraise the evidence without having two conflicting tables to ex-amine? The difference between having a full treatise on hand when drawing diagrams and compiling tables and having to go by a report about its contents is worth pausing over. It helps to explain why as-tronomy remained in a pre-Copernican state for so long. Even Koestler grudgingly admits that Copernicus' 'disappointing' treatise won for its author a 'certain repute' because it served as a basis for the *Prutenic Tables* which Erasmus Reinhold published eight years after *De Revolutionibus*. However unsatisfactory as popular reading matter, these tables were 'welcomed' as a 'long overdue replacement for the Alphonsine Tables.' As previous remarks suggest, the new tables may have been historically significant not so much as a 'replacement' for the old ones but rather as an alternative set that encouraged further checking against the writing in the sky. At all events, they were put into use very quickly – as the case of the young Tycho Brahe shows:

> On 17 August, 1563 at the age of seventeen while Vedel was asleep he noticed that Saturn and Jupiter were so close together as to be almost in-distinguishable. He looked up his planetary tables and discovered that the Alphonsine tables were a whole month in error...and the Copernican tables by several days.[159]

Koestler not only provides a retelling of Gassendi's often-told tale, he

---

[158] Hughes, introduction, Regiomontanus' *On Triangles*, p. 7. Northern Europe was poorly supplied with trigonometry texts for a long time. Even after his student days at Tübingen in the late sixteenth century, Kepler remained ignorant of the 'science of the sine' and the 'computation of triangles' until he borrowed a text from a doctor traveling through Gratz from Italy. Only later on did he gain access to copies of Euclid and Regiomontanus. See Koestler, *Sleepwalkers*, p. 583, n. 20. Rheticus' undertaking the separate publication (by Luther's favorite firm) of the first two chapters (on plane and spherical trigonometry) of Book I of *De Revolutionibus: De Lateribus et Angulis Triangulorum* (Wittenberg: Johannes Lufft, 1542) probably performed a more useful service than is often recognized.

[159] Koestler, *Sleepwalkers*, p. 287. The *Prutenic Tables* are discussed on p. 213.

also offers an equally familiar gloss.[160] Tycho's shock at the disparity between predictions and outcome is taken to indicate a new habit of mind. It is also contrasted with the 'almost hypnotic submission to authority,' associated with reliance on Ptolemy and inherited data, manifested by all previous astronomers, including Copernicus.[161] In 1563 the *Prutenic Tables* were twelve years old. Before puzzling over why Tycho had put his two sets of tables to a new use, it ought to be noted that no one had been supplied with two full sets of tables to put to use before.[162]

It was not because he gazed at night skies instead of at old books that Tycho Brahe differed from star-gazers of the past. Nor do I think it was because he cared more for 'stubborn facts' or precise measurement than had the Alexandrians or the Arabs. But he did have at his disposal, as few had before him, two separate sets of computations based on two different theories, compiled several centuries apart which he could

---

[160] On Gassendi's efforts to amass biographical data while assembling Tycho's works see Christianson, 'Tycho Brahe's Facts of Life,' pp. 21–2. Gassendi's role as a kind of latter-day Vasari to the chief Renaissance astronomers is worth further study. See his *Tychonis Braheii ...Vita. Accessit Nicolai Copernici, Georgii Peurbachii et Joannis Regiomontanii* (The Hague: A. Vlacq, 1654). According to Dreyer, *Tycho*, p. 127, Gassendi also got data on Tycho from Willem Janzoon Blaeu, the founder of the Dutch map-publishing dynasty, whose work is discussed above, pp. 480, 600–1. With his own engraved icons of the great astronomers and printed output, Tycho helped to create his own posterity. He is also included in Ramus' *Scholarum Mathematicarum* (Basel, 1569) (having made that author's acquaintance in Augsburg). From Ramus to Gassendi to Fontenelle and ultimately to Voltaire's eulogy of Newton, members of the French Republic of Letters (often propelled by Huguenot or foreign presses), took the lead in celebrating the star-gazers who produced the new astronomy. Italian initiative in this field represented by Bernardo Baldi's *Vite dei Matematici* composed between 1587–95, failed, characteristically, to be fully implemented by print. See Rose's *Italian Renaissance of Mathematics*, chap. 11. Italian presses were responsible for immortalizing Tycho, Kepler, Galileo (as well as Ptolemy, Sacrobosco, Kircher, Scheiner *et al.*) by placing them on a moon map in an anti-Copernican work by an Italian Jesuit: Giovanni Battista Riccioli's *Almagestum Novum Astronomiam Veterem* (Bologna, 1651). That Riccioli's work fixed the nomenclature of lunar formations until recently is noted by Van de Vyer, 'Original Sources.'

[161] Koestler, *Sleepwalkers*, p. 199.

[162] In addition to working with Reinhold in Wittenberg and probably helping in the preparation of the *Prutenicae Tabulae Coelestium Motuum* (Tübingen: Ulricus Morhardus, 1551) Rheticus also began several monumental projects, entailing diverse series of trigonometric tables that were extended and completed by such successors as Viète, L. Valentine Otho and Bartholomaeus Pitiscus. Sarton, *Appreciation*, p. 161 marvels at the amount of labor involved in compiling such tables by hand. So does Koestler, *Sleepwalkers*, p. 189, who suggests Rheticus needed this kind of 'occupational therapy' to keep sane. The new freedom from having to copy out earlier tables and the knowledge that new ones once compiled could be preserved by print ought to be taken into account. The interval between Regiomontanus and Napier – a pre-logarithmic but post-print interval – might be singled out as a distinctive phase in the history of mathematical sciences, since it inspired a special kind of intellectual labor. No doubt desk calculators will soon lead future historians to marvel at how much was accomplished in the way of dreary labor with slide rules, during the last few centuries. Like the logarithm, the slide rule is another much neglected print-made innovation.

compare with each other. The study of records was no less important for Tycho than it had been for the astronomers of the past. Like his predecessors he had no telescope to aid him. But his observatory, unlike theirs, included a library well stocked with printed materials as well as assistants trained in the new arts of printing and engraving. For he took care (and went to much trouble and expense) to install printing presses and a paper mill on the island of Hven.[163]

Given the more than fifty assistants at work on the island, and the stream of publications that issued forth, Tycho's 'Uraniborg' has been suggested as a possible prototype for Bacon's 'Salomon's House' and for the later Royal Society[164] 'Uraniborg' did see collaboration and publication applied to astronomical observation on a scale the Western world had not seen before. Insofar as Tycho's observations were made with the aid of instruments, he could tap the talents of engravers who 'knew the meaning of "within a hair's breadth." '[165] He also exploited the arts of engraving to display astronomical instruments for readers of his books. His own printing press is displayed in his most celebrated self-portrait.[166] Ever since he started to sneak books past his tutor, he profited greatly from the product of other presses. In these respects, he differed from his predecessors in ways that need to be underlined. The deliberate use of publicity to channel excitement about ephemeral stellar events and thus encourage precise recording of fresh observations on a vast scale was one of Tycho's most lasting and unheralded accomplishments. The Danish astronomer was not only the last of the great naked-eye observers; he was also the first careful observer who took full advantage of the new powers of the press – powers which enabled astronomers to detect anomalies in old records, to pinpoint more precisely and register in catalogues the location of each star, to enlist collaborators in many regions, fix each fresh observation in

[163] Gade, The Life, p. 102 describes the 'blank check' given Tycho by the Danish King for paper supplies throughout Denmark and Norway, which turned out to be inadequate, leading to the establishment of a mill on the island of Hven. Dreyer, Tycho, pp. 239 ff, describes Tycho's remarkable trip, made with the printing press loaded on to the baggage van, to Copenhagen and Rostock in 1597–8. [164] Christianson, 'Astronomy and Printing.'

[165] It is intriguing to note the line which reaches from Tycho to Moxon's Mechanick Exercises via W. J. Blaeu who worked for Tycho and instructed Moxon in the more advanced typographical arts of the day. E. G. R. Taylor, Mathematical Practitioners, pp. 92, 231–3. Moxon was one of the few instrument-makers and printers who was admitted as a fellow to the Royal Society.

[166] This engraving of Tycho showing his great mural quadrant and assistants at work is in his Astronomiae Instauratae Mechanica which was dedicated to Rudolph II and was printed by a Hamburg printer in 1598. See easily available illustration in Boas, Scientific Renaissance, pp. 96–7.

permanent form and make necessary corrections in successive editions.

The unusual fate of Tycho's star has already been noted. The expansion of his star catalogue is equally worthy of note.

The *Tabulae Rudolphinae* remained for more than a century an indispensable tool for the study of the skies...The bulk of the work consists of...rules for predicting the positions of the planets and of Tycho's catalogue of 777 star places enlarged by Kepler to 1,005. There are also refraction-tables and logarithms put for the first time to astronomic uses; and a gazeteer of the towns of the world, their longitudes referred to Tycho's Greenwich – the meridian of Uraniborg on Hveen.[167]

Koestler's estimation of the value of printing 'unreadable' technical works seem to change after his hero Kepler has set to work. One might compare his high opinion of the *Rudolphine Tables* with his deprecatory references to Copernicus' *De Revolutionibus*, while keeping in mind that he assumes both works were published in first editions of the same size.[168]

Kepler's heroic struggles over the course of four years to get his valuable work into print during the turmoil of the Thirty Years War, suggest how political and religious events impinged on scientific developments – much as they did on biblical scholarship. The *Rudolphine Tables*, very much like the Antwerp Polyglot produced by Plantin's press, indicates how rapidly new and precise information accumulated after print and how many obstacles had to be overcome by the masterbuilders of the new monuments of erudition.[169] As an overseer of a technical publication program, who saw a manuscript of 568 pages

---

167 Koestler, *Sleepwalkers*, pp. 410–11. The improvements made by Tycho's 777 star catalogue over that of Ptolemy and the Arabs are noted by Warner, 'First Celestial Globe,' p. 30. On the composition and contents of *Rudolphine Tables*, see also Caspar, *Kepler*, p. 327, who notes that a plan to add a world map was frustrated at the last minute. The 'refraction tables' owed much to the publication of various works on optics, particularly Witelo's which, having been on Regiomontanus' advance list, was printed by Petreius in Nuremberg in 1535, and was among the books Rheticus brought to Copernicus in 1539.

168 According to Koestler, *Sleepwalkers*, pp. 191; 410, each edition consisted of one thousand copies but there seems to be no sound basis for this guess. The estimates of Gingerich are noted above, n. 99.

169 On research spurred by publication of polyglot Bibles, see Preserved Smith, *Origins of Modern Culture*, p. 251, and discussion, pp. 337 ff, volume 1 above. Kepler's biblical research and work on technical chronology is discussed by Caspar, *Kepler*, pp. 317–19. That chronological tables and gazeteers were necessary supplements to both types of publication and that both also required mastery of trilingual studies points to the overlapping of research interests among biblical scholars and astronomers. The latter were among the first group of scholars to raise questions about the dating of the birth of Jesus, for example. See Caspar, *Kepler*, p. 228. Both studies of Newton by Manuel: *Portrait of Newton* and *Isaac Newton, Historian* contain a wealth of data on Newtonian research into scriptural chronology and calendrical problems.

through the press, the dreamy, mystical, 'sleepwalking' astronomer also seems to be cast in an uncharacteristic role. Kepler spent many hours of each day in the printing house, coped successfully with political emergencies and personnel problems, procured adequate supplies of paper, supervised the punch-cutting of symbols, the setting of type and finally – in the guise of a travelling salesman – set out in the company of tradesmen to peddle his finished products at the Frankfurt book fair. While he was at Ulm during the final stages of the four-year ordeal, Kepler found time to help local officials solve problems pertaining to weights and measures. As an ingenious gadgeteer, he provided Ulm with a new standard measuring device.[170] That he was capable of using his hands as well as his head is also shown by the fact that he himself designed the frontispiece to his massive work.[171]

The House of Astronomy as envisaged by Kepler is modelled on Baroque lines that may seem somewhat dream-like – even surreal – to modern eyes. Like the memory theatres described by Frances Yates, it presents oddly assorted motifs closely juxtaposed. Ancient sages and modern masters are displayed in a temple of eclectic design. Muses representing the mathematical sciences stand around the dome, while the German imperial eagle hovering above (hopefully) furnishes patronage and gold. Not only the reference to financial sponsorship from on high but also the instruments hanging on pillars and the printing press engraved on a wall at the base suggest that the 'sleepwalker' had his practical side.[172]

It seems significant that Koestler's romantic biography contains a

[170] Caspar, *Kepler*, pp. 317–24. Kepler's previous work on barrels: the *Stereometria*, also indicates his skill in solving practical problems. Koestler, *Sleepwalkers*, pp. 406–9, also describes the long ordeal and (p. 415) notes Kepler's later, eighteen-month long struggle to procure type and machinery and install a press in his own lodgings in Sagan, in order to publish *Ephemerides* for the years 1629–36.

[171] The actual engraving was made by a Nuremberg craftsman: Georg Coler, who placed his name at the base. As noted above, both practical and manual tasks had been undertaken by astronomers and mathematicians in the middle ages. They had helped to design astrolabes and sundials and had served as mint masters even before the advent of printing. Thereafter they collaborated closely with instrument-makers, engravers and type-designers and often turned their own talents to such work. Thus it seems unnecessary to invoke a 'puritanical' ethos to account for such a phenomenon as Newton's willingness to grind lenses (see e.g. Manuel, *Portrait of Newton*, p. 47).

[172] The print shop actually occupies two of the five panels visible at the base. Immediately to the right of the central panel (showing the isle of Hven) are two printers at a press and beyond, the extreme right-hand panel shows a compositor at work with pieces of type and a wooden frame. Kepler's high regard for the new art of printing (which he associated with the revival of ancient writers and the advent of new theology, medicine, astronomy *et al.*) is clear from citation in Rosen, 'In Defense of Kepler,' pp. 141–9.

description of this same frontispiece which omits the press and the other instruments. Despite his praise of the '*Tabulae Rudolphinae*' as an 'indispensable tool,' and as Kepler's 'crowning achievement in practical astronomy,' Koestler seems almost contemptuous of the tedious 'herculean donkey work' such tables entailed. One can understand why he might sympathize with Kepler's weary reaction to the 'treadmill of mathematical computation,'[173] but it seems unfair to withhold sympathy from Kepler's predecessors, who deserved it perhaps even more. The compiling of hand-copied tables had much more of a 'treadmill' character than was the case after print. The herculean analogy also seems to be better suited to labors performed in the age of scribes, when astronomers knew that their tables would be refilled with errors almost as soon as they had been cleansed.

As is often the case, when the shift from script to print is ignored, the incapacity to achieve precise error-free results is attributed to indifference or stupidity. Earlier astronomers are belabored for wasting their 'life work' by providing seafarers and star-gazers with bad tables instead of good.[174] Kepler is commiserated with for toiling away at his dreary task, and little or nothing is said about the labor-saving devices that came to his aid. Napier's name is not in the index; his logarithms are not mentioned in the text. Only a footnote preserves Maestlin's grudging comment, 'It is not fitting for a professor of mathematics to manifest childish joy just because reckoning is made easier.'[175] But although some astronomers may have been inhibited about expressing their joy, it is incumbent on historians to take note of it. To compare Kepler's tables with those derived from Copernicus' work, without pausing over the new tools that had been supplied in the interim is not only unfair; it is to miss a chance of understanding how Alexandrian astronomy came to be surpassed.

For it is really beside the point whether Copernicus was timid and devious or Kepler frank and bold. The point is, rather, that the flow of information had been reoriented to make possible an unprecedented cumulative cognitive advance. In using Napier's logarithms for the *Rudolphine Tables* Kepler was doing something his master could not do. Although Tycho had hoped to put such tables to use, they were not

---

[173] Koestler, *Sleepwalkers*, p. 407. On p. 411 the frontispiece is described without mention of the two panels containing printing equipment. A similar omission is in Caspar's description upon which Koestler's account relies.   [174] Koestler, *Sleepwalkers*, p. 124.
[175] Koestler, *Sleepwalkers*, p. 590, n. 5.

published until the Danish astronomer had died. Tycho had, however, been able to compare the *Prutenic Tables* with the *Alphonsine Tables* as Copernicus could not do, for the latter were compiled from the older man's posthumous work. In reworking all of Ptolemy's computations, in charting every planet's course as from a moving earth, did Copernicus also achieve something that could not have been accomplished in the age of scribes? The answer is necessarily speculative, yet it seems likely that a complete recasting of the *Almagest* – like a thorough-going calendar reform – required freedom from hours of copying and access to reference works that were rarely available to astronomers after Alexandrian resources had been dispersed.

Perhaps the most significant contribution made by Copernicus was not so much in hitting on the 'right' theory as in producing a fully worked out *alternative* theory and thus confronting the next generation with a problem to be solved rather than a solution to be learned. In the frontispiece to Riccioli's *Almagestum Novum* of 1651, the Copernican and Tychonic schemes are diagrammed on either side of a scale held by a muse while the Ptolemaic scheme is displayed on the ground with the notation: 'I will arise only if I am corrected.' The fact that the balance is tilted in favor of Tycho or that the notion of 'restoring' Ptolemy is retained should not distract attention from the novelty of presenting three clearly diagrammed alternative planetary models within a single frame.[176] Much as contradictory scriptural commentaries encouraged recourse to the text of the Good Book itself, so too did conflicting verdicts rendered by the 'little books of men' encourage a persistent checking against the 'great book of Nature.'

By the time Kepler was a student at Tübingen, astronomers had to choose between three different theories. A century earlier, when Copernicus was at Cracow, students were fortunate to gain access to one. The fact that Kepler's teacher Maestlin gave instruction in all three schemes has been cited to show that university instruction was backward and resistant to innovating currents from outside.[177] That a given student at one university was being instructed in three different ways of positioning the sun and earth when computing planetary orbits seems to me to indicate a remarkable change.[178] All three authorities

176 For more conventional treatment of Riccioli's work see Stimson, *Gradual Acceptance*, pp. 77–8.
177 Drake, 'Early Science,' p. 49.
178 By Newton's day, undergraduates in English colleges could study contradictory versions by reading Gassendi's *Institutio Astronomica*, which went through at least six editions between

fell short of correctly describing planetary orbits. Tycho's brand-new scheme no less than Ptolemy's very old one was destined to be discredited later on. But after 1543, commentaries, epitomes, or addenda devoted to one master's work had been superseded by a confrontation with alternatives that forced some sort of choice. Given the hundreds of years that had been spent compiling, retrieving and preserving the *Almagest*, the appearance of two alternative full fledged planetary theories in the course of a single century does not point toward cultural lag or the presence of an inertial force. On the contrary, it points toward a cognitive breakthrough of an unprecedented kind.[179]

Furthermore it should be noted that alternative theories were accompanied by alternative sets of tables which also forced astronomers to make choices and focused special attention on key stellar events. Exclusive reliance on the *Alphonsine Tables* until the 1540s might be contrasted with the array of six different sets of tables confronting astronomers in the 1640s. Detailed instructions in the use of six different sets were actually provided by Galileo's friend Rienieri in a single work: the *Tabulae Medicae* of 1639. By then, the idiosyncratic experience of the young Tycho, who checked two conflicting tables against the writing in the skies, was becoming commonplace. The accuracy of competing tables was tested by simultaneous observations made from different places and by many eyes. Challenges were being issued in the form of open letters alerting all European astronomers to observe a particular stellar event and recheck their findings against different predictions.

Astronomers could compare the predictions of the tables with the actual observed positions of the sun, moon and planets and could then compare the results with those of rival astronomical theories...could decide whether it was worth while to undertake the difficult and laborious work of mastering Kepler's methods...[180]

1647 to 1702 and was later used as a textbook in eighteenth-century Harvard and Yale. See Palter (ed.), Kepler Catalogue, item no. 93. Stimson, *Gradual Acceptance*, p. 90, notes that 'spheres according to the Ptolmean, Tychonean and Copernican systems with books for their use' were available at a London bookseller in 1670.

[179] See Thomas Kuhn, *Structure of Scientific Revolutions*, p. 77 for comment on importance of confrontation with alternative theories.

[180] Russell, 'Kepler's Laws,' p. 7. See also p. 13 for data on contrast between one set of tables available in 1550 as against six sets in 1660. The long struggle of one astronomer, Peter Cruger, with Kepler's 'obscure' writings which moved him to pray, like King Alfonso, for some simpler solution and his eventual conversion in 1629 which led him to reappraise Kepler's important *Epitome Astronomiae Copernicanae* 'previously read and thrown aside' is recounted in fascinating detail on p. 8.

In 1631 Gassendi, following a suggestion made by Kepler, published an open letter to the astronomers of Europe asking them to observe the transit of Mercury across the sun and noting it was due to take place on November 7, 1631. Here is an example of a collaborative effort in simultaneous observation that was made possible by print and had been impossible in the age of scribes. The new process of feedback operated in this instance as well. A German observer who accepted the challenge not only found the *Rudolphine Tables* gave the most accurate prediction. He also published a pamphlet in 1632 which informed the reading public of his findings, outlined Kepler's theory and referred interested readers to Kepler's publications for further details.[181]

To return for a moment to the problem posed by Galileo's neglect of Kepler's discovery of elliptical orbits. According to Rosen, Galileo felt a natural reluctance to struggle with Kepler's turgid prose. He was put off by 'the longwinded theological speculations, mythological allusions and autobiographical meanderings in which Kepler concealed his genuine achievement.'[182] If we accept this explanation, then the question remains as to how this sort of reluctance was overcome so that the 'genuine achievement' was finally disclosed. From recent accounts describing how astronomers became convinced of the superiority of the *Rudolphine Tables*, one may see the important role played by the publishers and editors of *Almanacks* and *Ephemerides* who were spurred by competitive conditions to investigate rival claims made by different astronomers and who were eager to hit on the most foolproof schemes. Resistance to strange logarithms and seemingly cumbersome procedures, as well as reluctance to struggle with Kepler's formidable prose were overcome once a given publisher became persuaded by demonstrations (such as Gassendi's) that better tables could be printed only by mastering Kepler's techniques.[183] One English almanack publisher who entered flourishing popular markets during the English civil war concluded that Kepler was the 'most subtile mathematician

[181] Russell, *Kepler's Laws*, pp. 10–11.   [182] See citation above, p. 501.

[183] In addition to data given in Father Russell's article cited above, see Curtis Wilson, 'From Kepler's Laws,' where the 'open' dispute over elliptical orbits between Ismael Boulliau and Seth Ward in the 1630s and 40s is described (pp. 100–19) and the conversion of Noel Duret, a publisher of *Ephemerides* is noted (p. 100, n. 29). The articles of Wilson, Russell and Whiteside contain evidence which runs counter to views expressed by Hetherington 'Almanacs,' pp. 275–9. Hetherington deprecates Wing's 'sketchy' treatment (p. 277), whereas Whiteside 'Before the Principia,' shows how Newton picked up Wing's references (to Salusbury's translation of Galileo, for example) and used them to guide his reading.

that ever was' and described his work as 'the most admirable and best restoration of astronomy of any that did precede him.'[184] This publisher was Vincent Wing, author of the *Astronomia Britannica* that was later read and annotated by Newton.[185] By the time Newton had come of age, the *Rudolphine Tables* and the *Epitome Astronomiae Copernicae* had begun to drive out competitors – at least in regions where there was a free trade in ideas. Elliptical orbits, at long last, could make contact with parabolic curves.

Shortly before Copernicus was born, Regiomontanus left his post as chief librarian to the King of Hungary to set up in Nuremberg the first scientific press known to the world. Soon after Copernicus died, Tycho Brahe sent off to Wittenberg to secure expert help so that he could set up a printing office, and when he left Denmark he brought a press along. That the struggle to get his tables into print loomed large among Kepler's many ordeals has already been outlined above. From his youthful quarrels over priority to his last smuggled manuscript, Galileo's career hinged on exploiting the new powers of the press. When such examples are invoked it is relatively easy to see that the new presses were important in the activities of many who helped to shape the Copernican Revolution. It seems plausible to argue that they ought to figure more prominently in our accounts. But the case seems more doubtful when we think about Copernicus in his tower or all the manuscripts stuffed in Newton's desk drawer. The two men who inaugurated and completed the Copernican Revolution not only wrote for Latin-reading colleagues. They both procrastinated about seeing their manuscripts into print, shied away from publicity and spent little time in the printing-house, if any at all.

The fact that they exhibited ambivalence toward the printing press and retained esoteric, élitist attitudes does not mean that Copernicus and Newton were unaffected by the shift from script to print. On the contrary, secretive philosophers who set out to voyage on strange seas of thought were much better equipped for their long journeys by printers than they had been by scribes, as the following comments suggest:

at the beginning of Newton's final year as an undergraduate (1664) his notebooks give us...different signs...he gave up an exclusive diet of reading

---

[184] Russell, 'Kepler's Laws,' pp. 18–19.
[185] Wilson, 'From Kepler's Laws,' pp. 123–4. Whiteside, 'Before the Principia,' pp. 5ff.

the ancients...and plunged into the moderns...we can trace the...
flowering of...genius as he came to know the scientific writings of the men
of his own century...He devoured books by Boyle and Hooke...took
careful notes on his reading in the *Philosophical Transactions*...read and
made notes on Galileo's *Dialogues*...and Descartes' *Principles of Philosophy*;
from Descartes he copied out an English version of the principle of inertia...
As we turn the pages of his notebooks we can see his mind leap from summaries of his reading to his own new principles and results...He began to
think of gravity as a force extending as far as the moon...Newton's chief
mentor was Descartes. From the latter's *Geometrie*, a veritable mathematical
bible in Schooten's richly annotated second Latin edition, he drew continuous
inspiration over the two years from the summer of 1664...In those two
years a mathematician was born...His only earnest regret must have been
that he had yet found no outlet for communicating his achievement to
others. The papers...throb with energy and imagination but yet convey the
claustrophobic air of a man completely wrapped up in himself, whose only
real contact with the external world was through his books...[186]

The image of Newton in his mother's apple orchard at Woolsthorpe
is so full of mythical overtones[187] that trips made to bookstalls or to a
neighboring rector's library are likely to get overlooked.

In recent years, Pope's couplet on Newton: 'Nature and Nature's laws lay
hid in night;/God said, Let Newton be!–And all was light,' has become
unconvincing even as poetic hyperbole. The *Principia* did not spring full
blown...Newton's...process of discovery was often tortuous...While the
story of the apple may be true, it was a long way from the initial insight in
his mother's garden to the finished mathematical proofs.[188]

Perhaps the story of the apple also should be demythologized. The
'initial insight in a maternal garden' might be reinterpreted in the light
of Whiteside's careful review of Newton's miraculous years.[189] This is
not to deprecate the importance of time spent in a maternal garden
watching apples fall. Idle reveries release unconscious energies that

[186] Whiteside (ed.), *The Mathematical Papers of Isaac Newton I: 1664–1666*, cited by I. B. Cohen, book review, *The Scientific American*, pp. 139–44. In an additional passage, Cohen refers to 'the arithmetical symbols of Oughtred' which seems to support the suggestion by Taylor, *Mathematical Practitioners*, p. 347, that Oughtred's *Clavis Mathematica* had replaced Recorde's sixteenth-century textbook in mid-seventeenth century English schools.
[187] For a glimpse at some of the myth-making entailed (by Voltaire and Hegel among others) see Robert Gorham Davis, 'Speak of the Devil,' p. 55.
[188] Manuel, *Portrait*, p. 151.
[189] On Newton's visits to the library of Humphrey Babington, rector of Boothby Pagnell which was three miles north-east of Woolsthorpe manor house; on his use of Isaac Barrow's fine private library in Cambridge and on his book purchases, compare Manuel, *Portrait*, pp. 81–2, 98; with Whiteside, 'Newton's Marvellous Year.'

seem essential for many creative acts. But it was the library not the orchard that had undergone the greatest change and that furnished the shy undergraduate with his chief means of making 'contact with the external world.' Even more than Tycho Brahe, Newton was 'uniquely a self-taught man' who seems to have learned more by reading on his own than from talking to tutors or attending lectures in the schools. His observations of falling bodies, like his experiments with prisms, were shaped by close study of many printed texts, beginning with childish experiments with recipes for making paints.[190] Given his intense curiosity and introverted personality, silent scanning probably offered a welcome substitute for verbal interchange. At all events, it seems desirable to think of the young Newton as being equipped with more than 'his prism and silent face.' If we want to know why the fall of the apple and the colors thrown on the wall conveyed patterns that had been unperceived before, then we ought to note the unprecedented free mental play with printed tables and formulas, diagrams, and equations that marked his apprenticeship years.

It is also worth remarking that Copernicus in his isolated tower and Newton in his lonely chamber were persuaded in the end to part with their manuscripts and thus make their contributions to the science of their day. Thanks in large part to good offices performed by intermediaries such as Rheticus and Halley, public knowledge was vastly enriched. When he was over sixty years old, Rheticus welcomed the young Otho who had come to work for him: 'You come to see me at the same age as I myself went to Copernicus. If I had not visited him, none of his works would have seen the light.'[191] Insofar as 'nature and nature's laws' were contained in Newton's mass of notes, Halley also deserves considerable credit for bringing them 'to light.'

It was he who first undertook to report Newton's solution to the Society and he who undertook to bear both the cost and burden of publication when the Society had drained its treasury in printing Willoughby's *De Historia Piscium*.[192]

The importance of these expensive ventures in scientific publication is too often discounted. The willingness to undertake them in certain

---

190 Lohne, 'Isaac Newton,' offers a description of the teenage Newton in Woolsthorpe, studying recipes for mixing paints, preparing dyes and printing ink (p. 128). Whiteside, 'Before the Principia,' describes the 'self-taught' Newton's reading in detail.
191 Koestler, *Sleepwalkers*, p. 190.
192 Manuel, *Portrait*, p. 154.

realms and the reluctance to do so in others is worth further thought. For the problem of gaining access to publication outlets forced science into contact with religion and politics in a manner that remains to be assessed. To a preliminary exploration of this issue, the following chapter is addressed.

8

SPONSORSHIP AND CENSORSHIP
OF SCIENTIFIC PUBLICATION

I. INTRODUCTION

This chapter serves as a companion piece to the previous one. There I argued for the need to reset the stage for the Copernican Revolution. Here I will employ a similar approach to Galileo's trial. There will be no attempt at detailed coverage of the episode itself or at a comprehensive survey of all the issues it raised. My main purpose in dealing with the trial is to show that the problem of access to publication outlets was a pivotal issue – one that has been unduly neglected and needs to be given more weight. I also hope to show how this same issue enters into other related problems and provides a kind of missing link between episodes on battlefields and adventures in ideas. In the following discussion, special consideration will be given to two interrelated problems.

First, there is the problem of connections between the Reformation and early-modern science. Second, there is the relevance of external social institutions to the internal, relatively autonomous, life of science. By bringing out the significance of the role of publication, I hope to suggest a fresh approach to both problems. I hope, that is, to throw some new light on connections between Protestants and scientists, and also to suggest how the external regulation of the book-trade impinged on scientific theories and creative acts.

Let me start with the vivid contrast drawn by Whitehead and others between the quiet, peaceful rise of science with its world-wide repercussions and the bloody clash of rival faiths that disrupted Western Christendom alone. According to Whitehead, the rise of science contrasts 'in every way' with the contemporary religious movement.[1] The

---

[1] Whitehead, *Science and the Modern World*, p. 12.

new philosophy won adherents without resort to fire or sword, without forced conversion or any manipulation of mass minds; whereas the Reformation unleashed a popular uprising that drenched Europe in blood for a century and a half. George Sarton draws the same lesson from observing the peaceful collaboration between the Catholic Copernicus and the Protestant Rheticus during the mid-sixteenth century when religious zeal was at its height. The 'sublime' quest for truth, Sarton says, placed the activities of scientists 'au-dessus de la mêlée.'[2] Finally, when Sir Herbert Butterfield views the scientific revolution in the perspective of world history, he says it outshines everything since the rise of Christianity and reduces the Reformation to the rank of a 'mere episode, a mere internal displacement within the system of Medieval Christendom.'[3]

Such contrasts, however valid, seem to be carried so far that they detach early-modern science from its historical moorings and cut all its connections with the forces that brought it forth. A most significant connection from my point of view was provided by the felt need of scientists to publish their results. By placing more emphasis on access to publication outlets and on the fate of the firms which got the printing done, one may see how even minor episodes on the battle-fields of Western Europe could affect major achievements of the human mind.

'In a generation which saw the Thirty Years War and remembered Alva in the Netherlands,' says Whitehead, 'the worst thing that happened to men of science was that Galileo suffered an honorable detention and a mild reproof before dying peacefully in his bed.'[4] One would scarcely imagine from this passage that there might be some connection between troop movements in the Netherlands and what Galileo achieved. Yet because the Dutch won their war of independence (a very minor scuffle, from world history's view) scientific publication outlets were open to Galileo that might otherwise have been closed. Worse things *could* happen to men of science in the seventeenth century than being 'honorably detained and mildly reproved' for a given publication. One might not be able to publish at all. Galileo, whose last major treatise had been smuggled out to Holland, could probably die with his mind at peace. But there were less fortunate investigators who

[2] Sarton, 'Quest for Truth,' p. 62.
[3] Butterfield, *The Origins of Modern Science*, p. viii.
[4] Whitehead, *Science and the Modern World*, p. 12.

went to their graves with thousands of manuscripts left to gather dust.

In this regard, Whitehead's celebrated dictum ought to be emended: 'In the year 1500, Europe knew less than Archimedes. . .yet in the year 1700, Newton's *Principia* had been written.'[5] In 1700, the *Principia* had not merely 'been written.' Thanks to Halley, who stepped in when the Royal Society's publication funds were exhausted, it had been issued in printed editions and discussed in all the major learned journals of Europe. It had been made known throughout the Commonwealth of Learning in a Latin review which stimulated major revisions in the second edition of 1713, and which led Leibniz to turn out three articles even before he had seen Newton's work. It had been publicized for the Republic of Letters in a French translation of a long review-essay which may have been written by John Locke.[6]

To stop short before Halley's intervention is to leave the revolution launched by Copernicus still incomplete, with Newton's papers still piled in disarray on his desk. Many accounts do stop short in just this way. They follow the activities of virtuosi up to the point where experiments are performed, observations recorded, theories framed and treatises composed. But they stop short of the point where manuscripts are handed over to printers and actual publication occurs. In this way the 'internal' life of science is disconnected from the external social forces which shaped it from birth. Even the most elegant experiments were destined to wither on the vine if cultivated too long in private and deprived of exposure in the end. That publication will be forthcoming is too often taken for granted. It is simply assumed that intermediaries such as Rheticus or Halley will perform whatever tasks are needed, or that scientists themselves will see to it that the services of printers are

---

5 Whitehead, *Science and the Modern World*, p. 16.
6 Axtell, 'Locke's Review of the *Principia*,' pp. 152–61, describes the English pre-publication notice by Halley in the *Philosophical Transactions*; the Latin review in the *Acta Eruditorum* and the French review in the *Journal des Sçavans* as well as the unsigned French review, which upheld Newton against the Cartesians, and appeared in Jean LeClerc's *Bibliothèque Universelle*. Axtell's attribution of this unsigned review to Locke and his high estimation of its significance is questioned by I. B. Cohen, *Introduction*, p. 46, n. 9. In an evaluation of the early reviews (pp. 145–62) Cohen argues that the long Latin review in the *Acta* is more worthy of attention. As noted by Aiton, 'Essay Review,' *History of Science*, the *Acta Eruditorum* account not only led Newton to revise his text, but stimulated Leibniz to publish three papers even before he read the *Principia* itself. Yet the review which appeared in LeClerc's journal, however unworthy, was more likely to attract attention from the chief publicists of the Republic of Letters. It set a theme that Enlightenment *philosophes* exploited to advantage for the next century and makes one question the verdict of Jacob, 'Early Newtonianism,' pp. 142–6, that one must wait for the Boyle lectures before Europeans learned of Newton's scientific accomplishments.

secured. These necessary services, however, hung in the balance for many virtuosi three centuries ago.

While Kepler was busy with the publication of his presentation of the Copernican theoretical structure...Copernicus' work was banned. In the summer of 1619...he received...news that the first part of his *Epitome* which appeared in 1617 likewise had been placed on the Index of prohibited books. The news alarmed Kepler...He feared that should censorship be granted in Austria also, he could no longer find a printer there...He pictured the situation so black that he supposed he would be given to understand he should renounce the calling of astronomer...[7]

Kepler was reassured by his friends that his worst fears were exaggerated. They wrote to tell him that his book could be read, even in Italy, by learned men who secured special permits. One Venetian correspondent suggested, shrewdly, that authors often benefited from having their books banned. In Italy, he wrote, 'books by distinguished German scholars even if prohibited would be secretly bought and read so much the more attentively.'[8]

Similar reassurances are still being issued by historians who discount the significance of the Catholic condemnation of pro-Copernican works.[9] Once publication has been assured, it may well be advantageous to have one's book banned in certain regions. But when one is having trouble getting technical printing completed, official proclamations aimed at frightening printers are not advantageous at all.[10] As these remarks suggest, to understand the circumstances confronting seventeenth-century scientists we need to assign more significance to the act of publication and to the role of intermediaries who got the printing done. If this were done, moreover, one might be able to draw significant connections between the rise of modern science and seemingly extraneous political events. For the outcome of dynastic and religious wars obviously affected the kind of publication-programs that could be undertaken in a given realm. It determined the degree of risk that printing a given work entailed. Forms of piety and patronage, licensing and censorship, literacy and book-reading habits varied from region to region in accordance with this outcome. Since the distribution of

---

[7] Caspar, *Kepler*, p. 298.   [8] Caspar, *Kepler*, p. 299.
[9] See e.g. citations from Ben-David given in text below (pp. 654, 656) and comment by A. R. Hall, *Scientific Revolution*, p. 77 that 'the significance of Galileo's summons to Rome is easily exaggerated.'
[10] Kepler's difficulties during the Thirty Years War in trying to obtain printers and keep necessary presswork going are described by Caspar, *Kepler*, pp. 310–22.

printing industries can be determined with a fair degree of accuracy, the 'geography of the book' can be mapped out; and the movement of printing centers can be correlated with the fixing of religious and dynastic frontiers.

What about the movement of scientific centers? Obviously it is more difficult to trace. Indeed it is open to question whether there were any real centers of scientific activity when clusters of print shops were first formed. The printer can be readily identified before the role of the scientist had clearly emerged. The latter is still a problematic creature, as current definitions suggest. In the early-modern era, it may be a mistake to use the label at all.[11] The distribution of talents contributing to 'scientific' advances in the early-modern era hinges on a wide variety of activities (mathematical techniques, instrument-making, data collection and so forth). The question of where and how to apply the term 'scientist' to men who did not regard themselves as such is open to dispute. Furthermore, from the 1500s to the 1640s, investigations now regarded as 'scientific' were still largely un-coordinated. Scattered regions containing varied clusters of talents – an observatory on a Danish island, groups of instrument-makers in Nurem-berg, lens-grinders in Amsterdam or Jesuit astronomers in Rome – dot the map somewhat randomly. Some highly energetic 'centers,' such as Tycho's Uraniborg or Mersenne's 'Letterbox' or Rudolph II's court at Prague, were so short-lived and so dependent on the movements of a particular individual that their location cannot be taken as proving any rule.[12]

Given inevitable uncertainty over the location of the 'main centers' of scientific activity, there is bound to be disagreement over the factors that encouraged their formation and early growth. There are those who argue that a prime role during the strategic 'take-off' phase was played in Catholic regions, especially in Italy where the Platonic revival flourished, the study of natural philosophy was propelled by lay university faculties, and the first scientific societies appeared.[13]

[11] The 'scientist' – a term first popularized by William Whewell – has been plausibly defined (by Derek da Solla Price) as anybody who has contributed at least one article to a professional scientific journal. But by this definition, the creature is called into being only after the appearance of a learned periodical press. This seems to put Descartes, Galileo, Kepler and Harvey in an occupational limbo and to bisect the 'century of genius' in an unhelpful way.

[12] How the cluster of talents mobilized by Rudolph II evaporated after his death is well described by Evans, *Rudolf II and His World*, p. 192.

[13] On the primacy of Italy, see references in chap. 5, section 2, above.

There are those who look instead to regions that broke away from Rome. They believe Protestant teachings spurred a new systematic investigation of God's open book. Some single out Wittenberg, rather than Padua, as *the* university which served as the seed-bed for modern science; while others play variations on Max Weber's theme by emphasizing Calvinist centers such as Leiden and Puritan academies established elsewhere.[14] Yet another school regards all universities and confessions as too conservative and tradition-bound, and looks to heterodox circles and non-academic groups, represented by 'invisible colleges' and 'schools of the night.' 'The presence or absence of Protestantism' is thus regarded by Frances Yates as less significant than the 'Hermetic–Cabalist' tradition. Virtuosi such as Newton owed less to Anglican bishops and Puritan divines than to the Renaissance Magus who sought to play the 'pipes of Pan.'[15] Yet others argue that Newton's mathematical physics ought not to be confused with his alchemy or theology, and agree with Edward Rosen: 'out of Renaissance magic... came not modern science, but modern magic.'[16] They stress the demystifying aspects of the new philosophy, its open and public character, and the predictive powers that made it useful to practical men. For the most part, they identify science with materialism and regard it as incompatible with belief in a spirit world. Anti-clerical circles and libertine groups are thus singled out, along with the revival of pre-Christian pagan views associated with atomism and hedonism.[17]

[14] Dannenfeldt, 'Wittenberg Botanists' cites a relevant passage from Ferdinand Cohrs, *Philipp Melanchthon, Deutschlands Lehrer*: 'At no other university did mathematics and the natural sciences bloom as at Wittenberg' (p. 242). (This view goes back to Peter Ramus who praised German efforts in order to spur French kings.) For opinion that the main centers later passed from Catholic Italy and Lutheran Germany to Calvinist circles elsewhere in Europe, see Mason, 'The Scientific Revolution,' and Hooykaas, 'Science and the Reformation,' which also offers a good summary of Lutheran and Calvinist views. In his *Humanisme*, p. 86, Hooykaas cites Ramus' praise of Germany as the 'nursery of mathematics' and his tributes to Melanchthon and the Wittenberg school. The more insular debate over Anglican, Puritan, Latitudinarian, deist, academic and non-academic influences in the Royal Society has given rise to a large literature – too large to be covered here. The updated bibliography (up to 1970) given in the 1970 edition of Merton, *Science, Technology*, pp. 266–73, may be consulted along with essays collected by Webster, ed. *The Intellectual Revolution*.

[15] In addition to Yates, *Rosicrucian Enlightenment*, p. 227, McGuire and Rattansi, 'Newton and the "Pipes of Pan,"' and Rattansi's several articles, see also critical essays by A. R. Hall, 'Magic, Metaphysics,' and Rossi 'Hermeticism,' both in *Reason, Experiment and Mysticism* (ed. Righini Bonelli and Shea).

[16] Rosen, 'Was Copernicus a Hermetist?' p. 171. Westman's 'Magical Reform' is a devastating critique of Yates.

[17] Demystification and disenchantment are themes that go back at least to the Enlightenment *philosophes* and their nineteenth-century admirers: Comte and Marx. The rejection of the occult and the shift away from magic is stressed by Rossi in his book on *Francis Bacon* as well

Finally there are the eclectics who find some truth in all views even while holding to a multivariable approach. No one region or institution, tradition, creed or class played a strategic role in the great collaborative venture, which was itself composed of diverse methods and pursuits.[18] Competing claims for the primacy of diverse 'external' forces when taken all together tend to cancel each other out. The way is paved for a reassertion of the autonomy of activities which owed something to all groups but nothing special to any one. We are back to Sarton's 'sublime quest for truth,' envisaged as a neutral and non-partisan cerebral activity unaffected by the clash of warring creeds and conducted 'au-dessus de la mêlée.'

Although all these arguments have some merit, none in my opinion goes far enough. Discussion of research activities ought to be accompanied by consideration of publication of results. In the search for seedbeds or nurseries, moreover, early printers' workshops deserve a closer look. So too does the problem of how scattered circles were linked and how they began to cooperate on many different fronts. However they differ, the various interpretations now offered share in common a tendency to assume that coordination was inevitable and that the flow of information would not be disrupted or cut off. As we have seen modern authorities take more for granted than a seventeenth-century printer or virtuoso could.

The issues of communication and coordination are not neglected in all studies, to be sure. But when they are raised, it is usually in a form that detaches research from publication and leaves the role of intermediaries out of account.

From a convent in Paris, Mersenne...drew into his epistolary network most of the leading scientists of his day irrespective of religion or nationality, even to the extent of admiring the work of Bacon, Harriott and Oughtred. Though based in Paris, the circle was Western European in scope. It connected Descartes in Holland, Gassendi and Peiresc in Provence, Schickard

---

as in his other essays. Anti-clerical views are prominent in Andrew White's old *Warfare of Science with Theology* which more recent works still cite although it is misleading on Protestant censure of Copernicus (see strictures offered by Hooykaas, 'Science and Reformation,' pp. 238–9, n. 100; 104). Anti-clericalism is also evident in many later positivist accounts, such as those of Wolf and Randall cited above in chapter 5. Feuer borrows from Randall *et al.* in order to stress materialist and epicurean currents in *The Scientific Intellectual*.

[18] The need for a multivariable approach is underscored by A. R. Hall, 'On the Historical Singularity.' That the English use of the singular form 'science' (in contrast to the European preference for 'les sciences') obscures the diversity of plural enterprises is suggested by Charles Schmitt's 'Essay Review' on 'Mechanics in 16th Century Italy,' p. 175, n. 45.

in Tübingen, Hortensius in Leyden, Galileo in Florence and Van Helmont in Brussels...It was upon these foundations and not upon economic developments confined to particular geographical areas that scientific research advanced...

The intellectual Europe of the age of Galileo took no account of later national boundaries. Nor, curiously enough, do religious differences seem relevant, despite the shadow of the Thirty Years War.[19]

By conducting his wide-ranging correspondence, Mersenne undoubtedly helped to coordinate the varied activities of scattered virtuosi, and he did so while steering clear of trouble with authorities. Yet the fact that Mersenne's letterbox was located in Paris does not really offer an adequate clue to its celebrated contents. Private correspondence had been handled by friars in Paris convents for centuries. It was the open letter addressed to Europe at large that was new. Mersenne's letterbox was distinctive because it was plugged into a much larger communications network created by print. This larger network had several nodal points – all located outside Paris in northern Protestant regions, beyond the borders of France.

The mistaken impression that a network centered in Paris provided the foundations for seventeenth-century scientific advance derives from the common practice of detaching early scientific communications and organization from the output of the scientific press. Centers are located by considering all the diverse forms of interchange and research activities which stop short of publication. Thus encounters at Peiresc's residence in Provence and at the Paris 'Cabinet des Frères Dupuy,'[20] taken together with Minorite Friar's letterbox, give rise to the impression that there was a 'translatio studii' from Galileo's Italy (where the first societies were formally organized) to Mersenne's France. But although a few promising scientific publication programs were initiated by enterprising Frenchmen during the age of Mersenne, none received continuous support; all were at some point interrupted or curtailed.[21]

[19] Kearney, 'Puritanism and Science,' pp. 108–9.
[20] Harcourt Brown, *Scientific Organizations*, discusses these meeting places.
[21] Difficulties experienced by Théophraste Renaudot (whose 'Feuilles du Bureau d'Addresse' may be described as the 'first scientific periodical,' according to Harcourt Brown) and by Denis de Sallo who launched the *Journal des Sçavans* are noted in Brown, *Scientific Organizations*, pp. 21–4; 195. On Renaudot's career as an enterprising pioneer in scientific journalism (who influenced Samuel Hartlib among others) see also Solomon, *Public Welfare, passim*. On de Sallo and his Journal see Birn, 'Journal des sçavans.'

Mersenne's own efforts were so frequently blocked that he has been described in a recent study as a 'publicist manqué.'[22] By remaining publicly discreet on the burning issues of the day (to the point of doctoring a publication sent to Rome) even while condemning 'mystical-magical' practices, the friar did what he could to neutralize science and set suspicions at rest.[23] But he was not really able to remain 'au-dessus de la mêlée.' Rather he was forced into contact with underground channels, becoming involved in a clandestine book-trade that got works listed on the Index quickly translated and into print.[24]

In these clandestine efforts the key role of intermediary was not played by Mersenne but by a Genevan diplomat who was stationed in Paris. Elias (Élie) Diodati did as much to bring Galileo's work 'to light' as Rheticus did for Copernicus or Halley for Newton. A member of the celebrated Protestant family which had left northern Italy for Geneva in the sixteenth century; a cousin of the Diodati who translated the Bible,[25] Elias also belonged to an inner circle of erudite 'free-thinking' Frenchmen. He participated actively in the meetings held at Peiresc's residence in Provence and at the Paris 'Cabinet des Frères Dupuy.' Pierre Gassendi, Gabriel Naudé and La Mothe Le Vayer were his three closest friends.[26] Travelling frequently on commercial and

---

[22] Whitmore, The Order of Minims, p. 21. The conflict between Mersenne's potential for pioneering in 'haute vulgarization' and his need to preserve a measure of clandestinity is also brought out on p. 150.

[23] On Mersenne's preparing a special version of the Questions Théologiques – which substituted passages on music for astronomy – to be sent to Rome after his hearing of Galileo's condemnation, see two articles by Hine, 'Mersenne and Copernicanism,' p. 30; 'Mersenne Variants.' Mersenne's efforts to separate magic from science are noted by Yates, Giordano Bruno, chap. 22. On this point the pioneering study is Lenoble, Mersenne.

[24] The French translation of Herbert of Cherbury's deist treatise: De Veritate, was made by Mersenne and 'printed clandestinely through his good offices' shortly after the work was placed on the Index, as is noted in a letter of 1640 sent to Comenius, according to D. P. Walker, Ancient Theology, p. 170. The route by which De Veritate travelled to Peiresc in Aix, Campanella in Rome, Mersenne and Gassendi in Paris is noted by Krivatsky, 'Herbert of Cherbury's De Veritate.' Elias Diodati, in London during 1632–3, took copies back with him to France. On other useful services performed by Diodati and Mersenne see Ornstein, The Role of Scientific Societies, pp. 140–1; Hine, 'Mersenne,' p. 30; Drake, Discoveries and Opinions, p. 171, n. 33.

[25] When de Santillana, The Crime of Galileo, p. 173 describes Elias Diodati both as Galileo's Paris correspondent and as the Tuscan emigré 'who had had a great part in the French translation of the Bible,' one wonders if he has confused Elias with his cousin Jean (or Giovanni) who had 'a great part' in the Italian translation of the Bible (1605) and who also prepared a French translation of Sarpi's History of the Council of Trent (1621) as noted on p. 412, above.

[26] See Pintard, Le Libertinage Erudit I, 129–30; 175–6. Elias Diodati's contributions to the Strasbourg publication of the censored Lettera of Foscarini and Galileo's Letter to the Grand Duchess are noted in II, 593. Readers of Spink, French Free Thought, are left unaware of Elias Diodati's existence. Whereas Pintard includes him in the close-knit quartet whose other three members

diplomatic missions to the central cities of Western Europe, he developed useful contacts with publishers, booksellers, couriers and postal officials. He served in Pintard's words as a 'colporteur de la République des Lettres' well before the era of Jean LeClerc and Pierre Bayle. In this capacity he brought the 'new philosophy' out of convents and secluded villas and into contact with the world of the Elseviers – acting more boldly than his French Catholic comrades dared. He accompanied Grotius on a voyage, sustained Campanella in Paris, publicized Francis Bacon and won a following for Lord Herbert of Cherbury, the 'father of Deism,' in France. Although his name often appears in small print in Galileo studies, he seldom receives adequate recognition for his energetic and successful efforts to get the works of the imprisoned virtuoso translated, printed, and well publicized abroad.

The same thing can be said of Diodati's most important ally, the Dutch printer Louis Elsevier. Among visits made to Galileo's residence in Arcetri, where he was confined as a political prisoner, few were as historically significant as the visit made by this member of the great Dutch publishing firm.[27] Yet few of the visitors who saw the celebrated prisoner have been so neglected in later accounts.

'Intellectual Europe in the age of Galileo' was fundamentally affected by the movement of printing industries away from older cultural centers. The seventeenth-century knowledge industry was not based in Paris, nor did villas in Florence and Provence contribute as much as did the presses of the Dutch Netherlands to sustaining scientific research. Indeed Colbert was dissuaded from prohibiting the entry of Dutch printed books into France, despite his concern about their subversive content and adverse impact on the Paris printing industry, by the argument that French *savants* could not do without them.[28] During the seventeenth century, it has been suggested, more books were printed in the United Provinces than in all other countries taken together.[29] The

were Gassendi, Naudé, and Le Vayer; Spink discusses the same trio and substitutes Gui Patin for Diodati as the fourth member.

[27] Elias Diodati's correspondence with Galileo concerning Louis Elsevier's visit in 1635 and Elsevier's contacts with Mersenne are described in the editors' introduction to Mersenne's *Les Nouvelles Pensées de Galilée*, ed. Costabel and Lerner 1, 17–24. On the Elsevier firm and its founder's links with Plantin, see D. W. Davies, *The World of the Elseviers, passim*.

[28] Febvre and Martin, *L'Apparition*, pp. 374–5. The preference for Dutch printers and their products exhibited by Englishmen under Charles I which provoked a complaint from Laud is noted by Haley, *The Dutch*, p. 123.

[29] This statement, made by de La Fontaine Verwey, 'The Netherlands Book,' p. 29, is based on guesswork, as is noted by Haley, *The Dutch*, p. 123.

contrast between the meagre scientific output of the most populous, powerful, well-consolidated realm in Europe and the abundant one of the small, loosely federated Dutch realm underscores a point made in an earlier chapter, that nation-building worked at cross-purposes with the expansion of printing industries. It was the powerlessness of central courts and the strength of the towns which secured for Dutch entre-preneurs a *de facto* if not a *de jure* free press.[30]

The significance of Dutch presses for the expansion of Western science is obliquely acknowledged by Sir Herbert Butterfield in a passage which, however, places them on the stage of history almost one hundred years too late.

In this period the changes were not by any means confined to France... The movement was localized however and it is connected with a humming activity which was taking place, say from 1660 not only in England, Holland and France but also actually between these countries – the shuttle running to and fro and weaving what was to become a different kind of Western culture. At this moment the leadership of civilization...moved in a definite manner from the Mediterranean...to the regions farther north...

Not only did England and Holland hold a leading position, but that part of France which was most active in promoting the new order was the Huguenot or ex-Huguenot section, especially the Huguenots in exile... who... – after 1685 – after the Revocation of the Edict of Nantes – ...fled to England or became the intermediaries for the publication in Holland of journals written in French communicating English ideas...[31]

The important role played by a French language press, run by exiles in the Netherlands, in publicizing the 'new philosophy' and in forcing a 'crisis of the European conscience' is certainly worth underlining; for it is too often ignored. 'French Huguenots made no mark scien-tifically' argues Kearney. 'In Holland Cartesianism came under heavy fire.'[32] Yet French Huguenots manning Dutch presses provided some Cartesians, such as Malebranche, with important opportunities to make their mark.[33] Nevertheless, the 'humming activity' that occurred

---

[30] See p. 405, volume I, above. J. L. Price, *Culture and Society*, chapter 7 brings this point out more clearly than do other authorities writing about the Dutch press.

[31] Butterfield, *Origins of Modern Science*, pp. 140–1. This description is based on Hazard, *La Crise de la Conscience*. See especially I, chapter III where Hazard describes the movement of culturally influential centers from Catholic South to Protestant North.

[32] Kearney, 'Puritanism and Science,' p. 109.

[33] Martin, *Livre à Paris* II, 874–9, offers pertinent data about Malebranche. Haley's account of what the support of his Rotterdam printer, Reiner Leers, meant to Pierre Bayle is cited on p. 420, volume I above.

in the late seventeenth century also needs to be related to events that preceded the Revocation of the Edict of Nantes in France (and that also antedated the establishment of the Royal Society in England). The seventeenth-century cosmopolitan French language press which conveyed the ideas of Newton and Locke to the Republic of Letters was really a latecomer to the 'world of the Elseviers.' The wars of Dutch independence had ushered in a golden age of printing in Holland (and had established at Leiden a great Protestant university) before the Edict of Nantes had even been proclaimed. A third edition of Copernicus' prohibited *De Revolutionibus*, the works of Descartes and Galileo (and of Bacon, Comenius, Hobbes, Grotius, Gassendi *et al.*) were being turned off Dutch presses before this Edict had been revoked.[34] The 'humming activity' that propelled scientific advances toward the end of the seventeenth century did not originate in a Paris convent. Nor did it start with the Huguenot exodus of the 1680s or even with earlier programs launched by Francis Bacon, Galileo and Descartes. It began with defeats suffered by the Spanish Habsburgs in the sixteenth-century Dutch wars – minor scuffles on a corner of the globe, to be sure, but with world-wide repercussions nonetheless.

The divergent publication programs pursued by Plantin's two sons-in-law – by the Catholic Jan Moretus, who stayed in Antwerp; and the Protestant Frans Raphelengius, who went to Leiden – point to differences characterizing publication policies in Catholic and Protestant Europe as a whole.[35] When considering problems associated with such divergence, it seems odd to find that Jesuit publishers in Peking (where Jesuit policy soon led to condemnation from Rome) attract more attention than do the successors of Plantin who worked so much closer to home.[36] During the age of Galileo, Catholic Antwerp specialized in serving the needs of Catholic churchmen. Protestant Amsterdam diversified and served lay readers all over the globe. Insofar

[34] The penetration of French cultural influences into Holland before the 1680s is described by Haley, *The Dutch*, pp. 190 ff. See also Gustave Cohen, *Ecrivains Français en Hollande, passim*. Italian Protestant refugees who (like the Diodati clan) prospered in Geneva after their mid-sixteenth-century exodus, also contributed something to the cosmopolitan French language press that developed in Holland. See Barnes, *Jean LeClerc, passim*.

[35] On these divergent policies as delineated by Vöet, *The Golden Compasses* I, 197, see pp. 408–9, volume I above.

[36] Both Rabb, 'Religion and the Rise of Modern Science,' p. 117 and Koestler, *The Sleepwalkers*, p. 495 discuss Jesuit astronomical publication in seventeenth-century China as if it was pertinent to Protestant–Catholic policies in Europe. Yet Jesuit teachings in China brought them into disrepute in Rome (as is shown by Hazard, *La Crise* I, 29).

as the pace of scientific publication quickened in the seventeenth century, it did so outside regions that followed the Counter-Reformation policies set in Rome.

This is not to say that the activities of Jesuit astronomers and missionaries in China should be overlooked. It is useful to recall that the intellectual conquest of Asia by Western science was inaugurated under Catholic auspices and connected with calendar reform.[37] Jesuit successes in China help to remind us what the previous chapter has tried to bring out; namely, that the study of astronomy had long been encouraged by the Roman Church. Religious motives for deciphering the writing in the sky pre-dated the Reformation. So too did belief that God, as the Author of Nature, was pleased by study of His work. Religious motives for scientific inquiry, in other words, were too deeply rooted in Western Christendom to be regarded as a special by-product of Protestantism.

2. DIVERGENT PROTESTANT AND CATHOLIC PUBLICATION POLICIES

By stressing the new implementation rather than the older motivation, one might be in a better position to handle the much-debated question of how Catholic–Protestant divisions were related to early scientific advance.

After all, the rise of science is the topic under discussion. The question is not why Protestantism proved to be more flexible in the long run, but rather what part religion played in stimulating the great advances in anatomy, physics and astronomy which are known as the scientific revolution. Most of these advances had taken place by the end of the 1630's. By 1640, with the work of Galileo, Harvey and Descartes virtually complete, one can safely say that science had risen...[38]

Instead of looking for direct connections between Protestantism and

---

[37] Rabb, 'Religion and the Rise of Modern Science,' p. 133 says that Counter-Reformation popes, such as Paul III and Gregory XIII, 'at least welcomed the findings of the new astronomy which paved the way for calendar reform.' But the connection between Copernicus' work and the Gregorian Reform is very tenuous, as is noted in chap. 7, n. 107, above. To my knowledge there is no evidence of any pope welcoming 'the findings of the new astronomy' (unless one interprets 'new' to include data incorporated into Ptolemaic or Tychonic schemes). According to the introduction (by Donald Menzel) to Pasquale D'Elia, Galileo in China, p. vii, the Jesuits did circulate news of Galileo's discoveries and helped with reform of the Chinese calendar but because of the Injunction of 1616 and Sentence of 1633, they never did teach a heliocentric system in their Chinese publications.

[38] Rabb, 'Religion and the Rise of Modern Science,' p. 112.

science, it might be more helpful to begin by considering the role played by printers 'in stimulating the great advances.' Once this role has been brought out, the 'part played by religion' is more likely to fall into place. For example, it becomes easier to see that a more positive role was played by Protestant publishers than by Catholic ones in bringing the work of Galileo and Harvey and Descartes to the point of being 'virtually complete.' One is also less likely to feel safe about assuming that 'science had risen' in 1640 when the fate of continental publishing centers was still being affected by the shifting fortunes of the Thirty Years War. Finally one will probably be inclined to go beyond the mere acknowledgement that 'Protestantism proved more flexible in the long run,' and note that Catholic policy was less stimulating from the first.

When the new presses are left out of account, it may seem plausible to argue: 'It is only by ignoring the enormous Catholic scientific activity' between the 1540s and 1640s that 'major claims can be made for the importance of Protestantism.'[39] Once technical publication is brought into the picture one may fully acknowledge Catholic activity and still make 'major claims' for the way Protestants encouraged and Catholics discouraged its development and expansion. 'The lack of noticeable difference between Protestant and Catholic resistance to change... must be explained away if the reformed religion is considered inherently more conducive to science or in any way responsible for the rise of the new form of inquiry.'[40] When resistance to changes wrought by printing is brought into the picture, the difference between the two confessions is not merely noticeable: it is striking. The common practice of treating anti-Copernican *statements* made by sixteenth-century Protestants as if they were equivalent to anti-Copernican *measures* taken by seventeenth-century Catholics is, in this regard, misleading. It leads many historians astray. For example, Bronowski and Mazlish seriously misinform their readers by asserting that Luther's contempt for Copernicus 'strangled' the scientific revolution in Germany.[41] (The achievements of Rheticus, Reinhold, Maestlin, Kepler notwithstanding !) Theological statements do not represent the same

39 Rabb, 'Religion and the Rise of Modern Science,' p. 117.
40 Rabb, 'Religion and the Rise of Modern Science,' p. 113.
41 Bronowski and Mazlish, *The Western Intellectual Tradition*, p 124. The assertion is coupled with a remark that 'in 1596, Kepler had taken refuge with the Jesuits.' But this was the date when Kepler's first work was published under Maestlin's sponsorship in Tübingen – scarcely an indication of how the Copernican Revolution was being strangled.

kind of resistance to change as do measures taken to prevent publication.[42] The latter threatened the life of science as the former did not.

Protestant printers often ran afoul of authorities by producing political or theological tracts, but when serving mathematicians and astronomers they were left in relative peace. This was not merely true in late seventeenth-century England when (it is often said) religious zeal had begun to lose its force. It was also true in the age of Luther and Melanchthon when zeal was at its height. The evangelical drive which powered the presses of Wittenberg and other centers of the Reformed religion encouraged the expansion of book markets from the first. At the same time the theology of the reformers, drawing on older Christian traditions, also promoted scientific research.[43] The positive impulse thus given both to the establishment of printers' workshops and to scientific publication programs was, to my knowledge, never checked or reversed. Thus anti-Copernican pronouncements made by Luther and Melanchthon did not deter the Wittenberg professor Rheticus or the Nuremberg printer Petreius from getting the Catholic astronomer's work into print.[44] The Protestant theologian Andreas Osiander, who

[42] See Rabb, 'Religion and the Rise of Modern Science,' p. 122 where the 'earlier hostility of the Protestants' is balanced against later Catholic 'official opposition' with the suggestion that 'roles were reversed.' Kepler's sufferings 'at the hands of German theologians and professors' and the fact that the leading reformers 'openly and vehemently' opposed the heliocentric theory is made equal to the condemnation of 1616 and Galileo's forced recantation. Yet the reformers' 'open, vehement' opposition consisted of one statement by Luther (possibly made in 1539 and later recorded in the Table Talk) and one by Melanchthon made in 1541 along with a later criticism of Copernican theory in Melanchthon's published textbook. At no point did this opposition lead to arresting or even delaying publication of the three editions of De Revolutionibus or of works promoting and publicizing its contents. On Kepler's troubles with the Tübingen faculty see p. 654 below.

[43] Hooykaas, 'Science and Reformation,' p. 214 contains relevant discussion on Protestant views. The positive role played by German Lutherans is documented by J. W. Montgomery, 'Cross, Constellation and Crucible' (not to be confused with same author's two-volume biography of Andreae: Cross and Crucible). The promotion of botanical and astronomical studies by northern universities, subject to Melanchthon's reforms which was publicized by Peter Ramus is described by several authorities. See n. 14 above. Westman, 'The Melanchthon Circle' offers the most thorough recent investigation into the complex positions of members of the Wittenberg school of astronomers.

[44] Rosen, Three Copernican Treatises, pp. 400–1 speculates that the hostile statements did deter Rheticus from going on beyond the preliminary trigonometry section with a Wittenberg printer and caused him to turn to Petreius in Nuremberg instead. (He had used Luther's printer, Hans Lufft, for the separate section: 'Sides and Angles of Triangles' (Wittenberg, 1542) and Lufft later printed Melanchthon's Initia Doctrinae Physicae, which contained an anti-Copernican passage.) But Petreius had indicated interest in publishing De Revolutionibus as early as 1540 and his previous output and reputation made him a logical choice. (See Shipman, 'Johannes Petreius.') Moreover, Petreius himself was closely linked to the Wittenberg theologians and collaborated with one of them, Osiander, in preparing De Revolutionibus for publication. The question of Rheticus' departure from Wittenberg has been examined by

took over editorial chores, did connive with the publisher to add prefatory remarks: 'Ad Lectorem' which implied that the author was setting forth a purely fictitious scheme.[45] Osiander's position is taken by many authorities to indicate that Protestant theology, just like Catholic theology, prevented astronomers from attempting to do more than 'save the appearances' and forbade assigning any physical reality to a given planetary model. Yet Osiander's comments did not deter Protestants from publishing different views. On the contrary, it provoked Peter Ramus into issuing a celebrated challenge, offering his chair at the Collège Royale to anyone who could devise an 'astronomy corresponding to the truth of the heavens'; to anyone, that is, who could avoid resorting to 'false' hypotheses, such as those described in Osiander's 'Ad Lectorem.' The Ramean challenge, in turn, spurred Kepler to claim that he had earned the right to the French chair by demonstrating the physical truth of the geokinetic scheme.[46] Thus although Protestant and Catholic theologians did adopt very much the same position – both assigning a provisional hypothetical status to geokinetic theories – Protestant publicists and astronomers were not deterred from rejecting this position, in marked contrast to Catholics after the condemnation of 1616.

Even before the 1616 condemnation and after Luther and Melanchthon's pronouncements, Catholic publishers still did less than did Protestants to promote the Copernican cause. In this regard, too much emphasis on Copernicus' position as a Catholic canon who relied on Church patronage most of his life can be misleading: 'While Copernicus was aided by a Protestant mathematician,' says Sarton, 'he received his greatest encouragement from prelates...His book was published

45 Elert, *The Structure of Lutheranism*, pp. 420–2, who concludes that Rheticus' espousal of Copernicanism was unrelated to this move.
45 Osiander's positive contributions to the publication of *De Revolutionibus* and his intention of safeguarding the work by tacking on the celebrated 'Ad Lectorem,' which assigned a purely hypothetical status to the Copernican system, is brought out by Wrightsman, 'Andreas Osiander's Contribution.' That the 'Ad Lectorum' (although anonymously presented) was by Osiander (who openly admitted authorship to Petrus Apianus) was known to many of the professional astronomers and astronomical publishers of the next generation. See Rosen, *Three Copernican Treatises*, p. 404 and Alexandre Koyré, *La Révolution Astronomique*, p. 99, n. 13.
46 Curtis Wilson, 'Newton and Some Philosophers.' See esp. pp. 246; 250–2 where relevant citations are discussed. Kepler had written to Maestlin about the Ramean challenge in 1597 but made his claim in print with the *Astronomia Nova* of 1609. There also he made the first public disclosure that Osiander had falsified Copernicus' views by tacking on unauthorized remarks to the *De Revolutionibus*. In this way, he publicly aired the chief issues that provoked the condemnation of 1616.

under the highest Catholic auspices.'[47] In his career as a churchman, Copernicus was aided by several Catholic prelates and he had his major treatise dedicated to a Catholic pope.[48] Nevertheless the actual work of publishing *De Revolutionibus* was done under *Protestant* auspices. Beginning with Rheticus' *First Narration*, works describing or promoting Copernican theories, whether under the guise of a new astronomy or as 'the ancient doctrine of the Pythagoreans lately revived,' never ceased to come from Protestant presses. It is worth noting that this point applies just as well to the mystical Copernicanism of Catholic friars such as Giordano Bruno and Tommaso Campanella as to such English virtuosi as Thomas Digges and William Gilbert. The imprints of Venice and Paris on the first editions of Bruno's works were fictitious. It was during Bruno's stay in London between 1583 and 1585 that the English printer John Charlewood printed his six major treatises. Charlewood belonged to a group of London publishers who obtained both profits and patronage by taking advantage of free publicity provided by the Index. He engaged in 'surreptitious' operations, turning out works in foreign vernaculars, bearing foreign imprints and aimed at continental markets.[49]

In contrast to the active role played by Protestant firms in propelling early Copernicanism, Catholic presses seem to have been relatively inactive – until Galileo's *Sidereus Nuncius* was published in the spring of 1610. An overnight sensation, *The Starry Messenger* not only catapulted its author into the position of an international celebrity, it also did for astronomy what had been done for theology by Luther's early tracts – stimulating literary excitement and generating publicity of a new kind. 'The extent and rapidity of the spread of Galileo's telescopic discoveries can scarcely be exaggerated. Only five years after *The Starry Messenger* appeared, the principal facts announced by Galileo were published by a Jesuit missionary in Peking.'[50] Not only were Jesuit presses in China activated, but so too were Italian printers in Venice and Rome. The

---

[47] Sarton, *Six Wings*, p. 61.
[48] Rosen, *Three Copernican Treatises*, p. 406 suggests that the dedication to Pope Paul III taken together with Osiander's 'Ad Lectorem' saved *De Revolutionibus* from being placed on the Index sooner than it was. Copernicus' rejection of Cardinal Schönberg's request to have his writings copied and of his friend Bishop Tiedemann Giese's plans to get his work published is noted by Rosen, *Three Copernican Treatises*, p. 393. When de Santillana says *De Revolutionibus* was 'sponsored' by Schönberg and that Giese 'assisted at its publication' (*The Crime of Galileo*, p. 22, n. 14) he seems, like Sarton, to overplay Catholic involvement in the actual publication.
[49] Woodfield, *Surreptitious Printing*, p. 20.
[50] Drake, *Discoveries and Opinions*, p. 59, n. 1.

Republic of Letters, which had previously looked to Wittenberg and other northern centers for the most sensational fast-breaking stories, began to turn back toward Italy once more. Even in England the accomplishments of earlier English virtuosi were overshadowed by literary excitement generated by reports of what could be seen through 'Galileo's tube.' 'It is "the Italian's moon" and the "Florentine's new world" we find in English poetry, not the same moon as it had appeared to Hariot in London and to Lower in Wales.'[51] For the first time in many decades, Italian publishers were able to take advantage of the excitement generated by a new bestselling author who appealed to a vernacular-reading public.[52] A flurry of pamphlets brought profits to local firms, and probably helped to spur fresh observations along with sales of instruments and books. But this promising windfall for Italian publishers lasted only five or six years. The stimulus supplied by Galileo ricocheted to the benefit of foreigners in the end. The 'dangerous consequences' of 'spreading' Copernican views 'among the people by writing in the vernacular'[53] were arrested by the decree of the Congregation of the Index in 1616. Open promotion of Copernican theories and indeed any vernacular treatise dealing with astronomy or physics became risky for Catholic printers and thus all the more profitable for Protestant ones. This occurred in the early seventeenth century, it should be noted – well before the works of Descartes et al. were 'virtually complete.'

One may agree that Galileo's *Letter to the Grand Duchess Christina* reflected a 'long-standing continental tradition' and expressed views that were by no means peculiar to Protestants like Francis Bacon, but were common among many Catholic virtuosi as well.[54] But it should also be noted that had Galileo had only Catholic compatriots to aid him, this very same *Letter* would have never seen the light of day. In 1635–6, Elias Diodati and Louis Elsevier, aided by other friendly

---

[51] Nicolson, *Science and Imagination*, p. 34.

[52] The *Letters on Sunspots* which contained Galileo's first unequivocal endorsement of the geokinetic theory in print (and was published in Rome in 1613 under the auspices of the Lincean Academy) was deliberately written in the vernacular. Galileo knew that he could not only appeal to potential Italian patrons in this way but could also delay swift retaliation from his foreign rival, the Jesuit father Christopher Scheiner (who was using the pseudonym, 'Apelles'), by writing in a 'colloquial tongue' the Latin-reading, German Jesuit could not understand. See letter to Paolo Gualdo, cited by Drake, *Discoveries and Opinions*, pp. 84–5.

[53] Citation from the letter sent to Kepler, August 13, 1619, which described the 'practical effect of the prohibition' aimed at Foscarini's vernacular work in Langford, *Galileo, Science*, p. 104.

[54] Rabb, 'Religion and the Rise of Modern Science,' p. 117.

virtuosi and Strasbourg printers, collaborated to make *Letter to the Grand Duchess Christina* along with the forbidden *Dialogues* available in Latin to the Commonwealth of Learning.[55] This collaborative effort has been deemed significant by a sociologist of science because it marked the emergence of 'an active "scientific lobby" in Protestant Europe.' In Ben-David's view, the trial of Galileo was blown up by scientific publicists in Protestant regions simply in order to gain more substantial official patronage for their cause. Although the case provided an occasion of energetic lobbying and thus helped to heighten the collective consciousness of the growing scientific community, he believes that it was insignificant in and of itself.

The first notable opportunity for the emergence of a distinctly Protestant science policy was provided by the persecution of Galileo...A group of Protestant scholars in Paris, Strasbourg, Heidelberg, and Tübingen decided ...to translate Galileo's work into Latin. In this endeavor they received general support from several Protestant communities otherwise not notable for their tolerance of Copernican ideas. Copies of the original work were obtained through doctrinally rigid Geneva; one member of the group was from Tübingen University where only some time before Kepler had been prevented from earning a theological degree...It is difficult to conclude how long the Galileo case was used to link science with Protestantism: It was not in any case a major factor in the establishment of science...[56]

As far as I know, there is no evidence that 'Protestant communities' such as Geneva or Tübingen had ever been notable for their *in*tolerance of 'Copernican ideas.' Kepler's troubles with the Tübingen faculty came chiefly from his Calvinist leanings and from scruples that prevented him from adhering to the Lutheran Formula of Concord.[57] It was via lectures given at Tübingen, after all, that Michael Maestlin first opened Kepler's eyes to the defects of Ptolemaic astronomy and to the advantages of the Copernican scheme. As a professor at Tübingen also, Maestlin obtained the University Senate's approval for the publication of Kepler's first book and spent many days in the workshop personally supervising the actual printing of his student's work. When the *Mysterium Cosmographicum* was published in 1596, it was accompanied by a fourth edition of the *Narratio Prima*. Rheticus' brief de-

---

55 See Drake, *Discoveries and Opinions*, p. 171, n. 33 for discussion of Elias Diodati's role in the Strasbourg printing of this tract in 1636 and of rigorous Catholic efforts to suppress it. Costabel and Lerner note (p. 17) that Louis Elsevier bore the cost of the Strasbourg publication.
56 Ben-David, 'The Scientific Role', p. 571.
57 See Caspar, *Kepler*, pp. 52, 188, 205, 258–9.

scription of the Copernican theory was thus published under the auspices of Tübingen, twenty years before Copernicus went on the Index and forty years before a so-called 'Protestant lobby' was formed.

As for 'doctrinally rigid Geneva,' the myth that Calvin was anti-Copernican has been discredited for some time.[58] Calvin was too ignorant of Copernicus to have taken any stand on his work. He supported Aristotelian theories since they seemed to be accepted by the scientific experts of his day. But in supporting the ancient philosophers, he also argued against using the Bible to serve as a guide to astronomy and thus helped to pave the way for the eventual separation of theology from scientific research. Far from supporting a rigid anti-Copernicanism, Calvinist arguments were used by Kepler and by pro-Copernican Dutch theologians – not only by Remonstrants but also by some of the more zealous anti-Arminian leaders who won out at the Synod of Dort.[59]

Unlike Tübingen and several other Lutheran centers, Geneva produced little in the way of scientific publication. But Calvinist Holland produced a great deal. In view of the services rendered by Dutch printers to virtuosi of all lands, it seems misleading to say that in 'small self-contained Protestant communities such as those in Geneva...in most places in Germany and later in the seventeenth century, in Holland, science fared worse than in the great Catholic centers of Italy, France and Central Europe.'[60] For virtuosi seeking publication outlets the great Catholic realms offered very little, the smaller Protestant communities offered much more.

There were Dutch Calvinists, to be sure, who refused to regard the Bible as irrelevant to any concern and who opposed the new philosophy as contrary to Scripture. The Voetian party, headed by the rector of Utrecht, thus denounced Cartesians and Copernicans and found them guilty of associating with Arminians and libertines. At no point, however, did the quarrels of theologians prevent Dutch printers from serving Copernicans, Cartesians and scientific investigators of all kinds.[61] In small German Protestant communities such as Strasbourg and Frankfurt, printers were also much better able to serve scientists (as well

---

[58] Rosen, 'Calvin's Attitude.' (See also exchange in *J. of the History of Ideas* (1961) XXII, 382–8.)
[59] Hooykaas, 'Science and Reformation,' pp. 227; 234–5.
[60] Ben-David, 'The Scientific Role,' p. 570.
[61] See Hooykaas, 'Science and Reformation,' pp. 234–5 for discussion of the position of the two Dutch Calvinist groups: the anti-Copernican Voetians and the pro-Copernican Cocceians and p. 239, n. 104, for objections to A. D. White's misleading account of this issue.

as a wide variety of heterodox groups) than was the case in the larger realms that were on friendly terms with Counter-Reformation Rome. That Galileo's friends turned to Leiden and Strasbourg in the 1630s was not the result of some new development but of book-trade patterns that had long since been laid down.

Many Protestant professors and churchmen objected to the new astronomy. Several Catholic virtuosi presided at its birth. The fact remains that Protestant authorities interposed few obstacles in the way of scientific publication and actively encouraged (however inadvertently) expanding lay book markets which attracted printers to Protestant realms. The Counter-Reformation Church pursued a contrary course. Beginning with the banning of vernacular Bibles and the prohibitions issued against other secular bestselling works, Catholic printers were subject to pressures that worked against diversification and that led to greater and greater reliance on turning out 'safe' devotional literature and on serving a clerical clientèle.

Here again a word of warning is needed. Serving a clerical clientèle did not invariably render a disservice to science. Seventeenth-century Jesuits furnished much useful data for serious astronomers. Profit-driving lay printers who served vast markets by churning out prognostications were not invariably helpful to scientific advance. Parallels often drawn between the 'Protestant who interpreted God's word for himself' and the scientist who interpreted nature for himself' need to be handled with caution. 'Everyman his own scientist' is a slogan that Puritan pamphleteers often seemed to push too far. 'Culpeper translated into English the sacred text of the College...He hoped it would make everyman his own physician as the Bible made everyman his own theologian...'[62] Culpeper was neither the first nor the last to question the usefulness of Latin prescriptions and medical degrees or to encourage more self-help among long-suffering patients.[63] In the early-modern era, doctors rarely did more good than harm, and there was

[62] Hill, *The World Turned Upside Down*, p. 240. For further discussion of these trends see Brockbank, 'Sovereign Remedies,' two articles by Rattansi, 'Paracelsus and the Puritan Revolution' and 'The Helmontian-Galenist Controversy in Restoration England,' Debus, *Science and Education* and now Charles Webster, *The Great Instauration, passim.*

[63] For examples of sixteenth-century vernacular translations being promoted on behalf of French surgeons, see references to the Jouberts, father and son, chap. 6, n. 48, above. Renaudot's 'Présence des Absens' discussed by Solomon, *Public Welfare*, pp. 17; 175–6 (and described pp. 246–7, volume 1 above) is a fine example of the same trend (described by Webster and Hill in connection with Puritan revolutionaries) being promoted by a French Protestant publicist in Richelieu's pay who provoked hostility from the French medical establishment.

every reason to be critical about the way physicians were trained. Yet even in that benighted era, the advancement of medical science still owed much to Latin treatises on anatomy, physiology and embryology.

Insofar as they encouraged literacy among surgeons and apothecaries and pressed for more mathematics as against Greek and Latin in the schools, the campaigns led by the more radical Protestant pamphleteers were not unhelpful to science. But they could also take an excessively anti-intellectual form. As previous chapters suggest, there is a difference between surpassing the ancients after mastering their technical literature and simply attacking the ancients while imitating Paracelsus and burning old books.[64]

The Protestant doctrine...proclaimed the duty of everybody to read the book of Scripture for himself. As a consequence...the duty to read the book of nature without regard to the authority of...Aristotle, Pliny, Ptolemy, Galen was put forward...everybody...might be a priest to the book of creation in defiance...of the ancient authorities. When Palissy was derided because of his ignorance of the classical languages...he proudly answered... I have no book but heaven and earth and it is given to everyman to know and read this beautiful book.[65]

As an artisan-author Palissy both contributed to public knowledge and produced a new ceramic glaze. In his public lectures he spelled out a program that was taken up by Francis Bacon and proved highly significant later on. Nevertheless, the attack on learned authorities and the defense of everyone's right to read the 'book of nature' for himself was not always helpful to the advancement of science. Did not later fundamentalists stand on much the same ground, when they claimed the right to judge Darwin's teachings for themselves? Even Galileo, who appealed on occasion over the heads of Latin-reading professors to the ordinary 'horse sense' of intelligent compatriots, pointed out that understanding the organs of the human body or the movement of the stars called for special training and required much more than merely looking with untutored eyes.

The eyes of an idiot perceive little by beholding the external appearance of a human body, as compared with the wonderful contrivances which a careful

Such phenomena provide necessary background for dealing with the later pre-revolutionary struggle between Mesmerists and physicians in which Marat figured prominently – as described by Darnton, *Mesmerism, passim.*

[64] See pp. 472, above. On Paracelsus' burning of Avicenna's *Canon* in 1527 (in imitation of Luther's burning of a Papal bull) reported by Sebastian Franck in his *Chronica* (Strasbourg, 1531), see Pagel, *Paracelsus*, pp. 20–1.   [65] Hooykaas, 'Science and Reformation,' pp. 215–16.

and practiced anatomist or philosopher discovers...Likewise that which presents itself to mere sight is as nothing in comparison with the...marvels that the ingenuity of learned men discovers in the heavens by long and accurate observation...[66]

In another celebrated passage, Galileo again underlined his conviction that the 'book of nature' although always open to public inspection, was not really 'given to everyman to know and read.'

Philosophy is written in this grand book, the universe which stands continually open to our gaze. But the book cannot be understood unless one first learns to comprehend the language and read the letters in which it is composed. It is written in the language of mathematics.[67]

The language of mathematics certainly differed from Latin or Greek, but not because it was as easy to learn as one's mother tongue. On the contrary, it became increasingly sophisticated in the course of the seventeenth century and was subject to incremental change. 'Newton was as incomprehensible to the average mechanic as Thomas Aquinas. Knowledge was no longer shut up in the Latin Bibles which priestly scholars had to interpret; it was increasingly shut up in the technical vocabulary of the sciences which the new specialists had to interpret.'[68] There are not only affinities but there are also contradictions that have to be considered when applying a 'priesthood of all believers' doctrine to the study of nature. As Rabb suggests, the parallels and analogies that are frequently drawn between early Protestant and early scientific thought 'do not prove the existence of any significant connection between the two movements.'[69]

I agree that mere analogies prove nothing and believe they are sometimes pushed too far. Yet here again by assigning more significance to publication programs one may find some valid connections that still remain to be drawn. For example, the larger the vernacular reading public, the larger the pool of potential scientific talent that could be tapped, and the more craftsmen would be encouraged to disclose trade secrets by printing treatises and attracting purchasers to their shops.

[66] 'Letter to the Grand Duchess Christina' in Drake, *Discoveries and Opinions*, p. 196. Galileo's use of the term 'horse sense' in his explanation of why he was using the vernacular in the *Letters on Sunspots* is in his letter to Paolo Gualdo, Drake, *Discoveries and Opinions*, p. 85. (On this letter, see also n. 52, above.)
[67] 'The Assayer,' in Drake, *Discoveries and Opinions*, pp. 237–8.
[68] Hill, *World Turned Upside Down*, p. 239.
[69] Rabb, 'Religion and the Rise of Modern Science,' p. 120.

New and useful interchanges between publishers and readers were also encouraged by the social penetration of literacy. When authors of atlases and herbals called on their readers to send in notes about coastlines or dried plants and seeds, a form of data collection was launched in which 'everyman' *could* play a supporting role. Pliny's *Natural History* and Ptolemy's *Geography* were not burned by Paracelsians or Puritans. Yet they were permanently outmoded in the end. Even the output of prognostications probably stimulated sales of almanacs and ephemerides and may have encouraged some readers to buy telescopes, thereby stimulating instrument-makers to turn out more pamphlets designed to bring purchasers to their shops.[70]

The expansion of a large and variegated public for their products was especially important for booksellers, map-publishers, instrument-makers, mathematical practitioners, and other contributors to applied sciences, whose prefaces are often cited when the new scientific ethos is described. Reijer Hooykaas has described how

The defenders of the 'new' science called upon the unlearned to contribute to the knowledge of natural history, geography and physics by communicating their observations on birds and flowers, on ebb and flood tide, on celestial phenomena and the...magnetic needle. Travellers and mariners especially were invited to do so.[71]

Hooykaas plausibly links such invitations to Protestant notions pertaining to a priesthood of believers and to the belief that 'everyone should read the book of nature according to his capacities.' Yet the men who solicited responses from readers were not all of them devout Protestants or conscious defenders of a 'new science.' In many instances they were acting rather as conscientious manufacturers of globes, maps and almanacs or of other guidebooks or instruments, who hoped to attract purchasers, outdo competitors and ensure steady sales by building up their reputation as makers of reliable and useful products.

In repudiating vulgar Marxism, Hooykaas writes, somewhat indignantly, that Protestant insistence:

[70] Copernican doctrines were thus publicized by Leonard Digges' *Prognostications Everlasting*. The 1595 Catalogue of Andrew Maunsell (noted above, pp. 106–7, volume I for defining 'science' along modern lines) carried mention of 'Leon. Diggs gent. his Prognostication everlasting... whereunto is added by T. Diggs his sonne A perfect description of the Celestiall Orbes according to the most ancient doctrine of the Pythagorians. Latelie revived by Copernicus & etc. Reprinted by Tho. Orwin 1592.' (Thomas Digges' celebrated translation of the first part of *De Revolutionibus* first appeared in 1576 as is noted in chap. 7, n. 146, above).

[71] Hooykaas, 'Science and Reformation,' p. 216.

on the benefit that may come to mankind from useful inventions...is not a manifestation of the capitalistic mentality of a rising merchant class hiding mammonistic intentions behind a pious pretence. Genuine love for God and one's fellow beings is the main driving force...[72]

Here again it seems mistaken to set one motive against another, when 'having it both ways' is what most human beings seek. Insofar as technical publication was spurred, the driving force was fueled not by love of God *or* Mammon but by love of God *and* Mammon – and of one's compatriots and of oneself – in short by the very same powerful mixture of altruistic and self-serving motives which propelled early Bible-printing along with map-publishing and instrument-making. (For some time indeed the two activities went hand in hand, for new gazeteers and other technical guides were often prepared to supplement Bible editions.) I would imagine that the chance to serve God and help mankind, even while making money and establishing one's name was just as attractive to instrument-makers, reckon-masters, and map-publishers in Catholic realms as in Protestant ones. But official Church policies diverged significantly. Catholic enterprise was braked in a manner that encouraged Protestants to move into high gear. Thus the same censorship policies that discouraged Catholic Bible printers and curtailed their markets, later closed up scientific publication outlets in Catholic lands. The same forces that encouraged expanding markets for vernacular Bibles also favored interchanges between readers and publishers of useful vernacular works.

3. BLOCKING THOUGHT EXPERIMENTS, SPONSORING CREATIVE ACTS

Of course, some authorities question whether useful vernacular treatises and Baconian programs should be linked to true scientific advance. They stress a series of creative acts by a small group of virtuosi who gave the century of genius its name. Collecting facts or promoting 'useful knowledge' are set aside by this school as irrelevant to the investigations of Pascal, Harvey, Kepler, Galileo, Malpighi, and other great men.

The Scientific Revolution was surely utilitarian only to a limited degree. The classical experiments were anything but useful in their application... The improvement of man's lot on earth was an irrelevant consideration...

---

[72] Hooykaas, 'Science and Reformation,' p. 216.

What has been said about Pascal applies equally to Kepler's planetary investigations, Galileo's mechanics, Mersenne's study of music, the Cartesian theory of the universe, Harvey's discovery of the circulation of the blood and Newton's *Principia*. Intellectual curiosity is relevant here, not crude utilitarianism...A sociological investigation...must concentrate attention not upon technology and economic need but upon the social and intellectual conditions which favored the development of originality.[73]

Once again it seems possible to avoid an either-or approach. Intellectual curiosity *and* useful trigonometry texts entered into 'Kepler's planetary investigations.' In laboring over the *Rudolphine Tables* during the Thirty Years War, Kepler himself produced a work that was designed to do more than satisfy 'intellectual curiosity,' a work that proved useful to editors of ephemerides and publishers of sky maps. Activities such as compiling tables of functions, or developing logarithms and slide rules also involved the production of useful tools and at the same time spurred new creative acts.

In this connection it is worth recalling Laplace's dictum that logarithm tables doubled the life of the astronomer. Consideration of the intellectual labor saved by printed materials points to aspects of early-modern scientific activities which are neglected by those sociologists of science who emphasize the Puritan work ethic. Present guidelines, derived from Max Weber, focus attention on the appearance of a set of values that discouraged unrelieved idleness on the part of a leisure class.[74] Something more should be said about the new *leisure* that printing gave to a *learned* class. Within the Commonwealth of Learning, systematic work habits were coupled with released time *from* grinding labor. Thought experiments required time off from slavish copying and freedom from compiling long tables of numbers by hand. Less reliance on memory work and rote repetition in lecture halls also brought new mental talents into play. Printing enabled natural philosophers to spend more time solving brain teasers, designing ingenious experiments and new instruments; or even chasing butterflies and collecting bugs if they wished.

In this particular connection I agree with Lewis Feuer (although elsewhere I think he overdoes the theme) that it is a mistake to dwell only on the ascetic attitudes scientists displayed.[75] Cardano's anticipation of

[73] Kearney, 'Puritanism and Science,' p. 108.
[74] Merton, *Science, Technology*, p. 96.
[75] Feuer, *Scientific Intellectual, passim.*

probability theory which stemmed from his own penchant for gambling did not found a new science since his *De Ludo Aleae* (unlike his *Ars Magna*) was not published until after Pascal's and Fermat's works. Nevertheless card playing, betting and dice throwing (which were notoriously antipathetical to Puritanism) contributed to the development of probability theory in the seventeenth century.[76] Pascal's Jansenism linked him with Puritan theology but his celebrated 'wager' about the existence of God had distinctly *un*Puritan overtones. The pleasure principle should not be ruled out when considering the rapid development of new puzzle-solving techniques by men who were aptly described as *dilettanti* and *amateurs*. 'Homo Ludens' as well as 'Homo Faber' was encouraged after printing to use his mental energies in new ways – as the modern chess player or bird watcher may suggest. Early-modern science owed something to playfulness and 'idle' curiosity as well as to piety and profit-seeking drives.

Even black-robed Latin-writing professional lawyers, physicians, and astronomers took advantage of new leisure by browsing at book fairs and indulging in mathematical fun and games. The use of print to mobilize European talents by issuing open letters and challenges was not confined to sponsoring inventions deemed useful by bureaucrats and capitalists, such as methods of finding longitude at sea. Newton's image of himself as a child playing on the seashore diverting himself 'by finding a smoother pebble or prettier shell than ordinary' seems to be singularly at odds with a work ethic and even somewhat pagan in its implications.[77] The satisfaction of pure intellectual curiosity, as Hugh Kearney says, needs to be given due weight.

[76] Ore, *Cardano: The Gambling Scholar*, pp. 176–7. The *Ars Magna* was published in 1545 by the same Nuremberg firm of Petreius which published *De Revolutionibus* in 1543.

[77] This celebrated metaphor may have been picked up from a sermon by John Donne (as suggested by Christopher Hill, 'Newton and His Society,' p. 46, n. 96) or both Donne and Newton may have been drawing on common classical-Christian topoi. The Renaissance humanist Vergerius was fond of referring to the practice favored by Scipio and Laelius 'who sought rest for exhausted minds in aimless walks along the shore, picking up pebbles and shells as they went' in order to refute this idle indulgence and suggest (à la Dr Arnold) that strenuous recreation and purposeful work were better as restoratives. See Woodward, *Vittorino*, p. 116. (Ironically the humanist seems fonder of the work ethic than the presumably puritanical seventeenth-century scientist.) Newton's further comment that 'the great ocean of truth lay all undiscovered around him' evokes a favorite theme of Baroque engravers: i.e. the legend of St Augustine who, while pondering the mystery of the Trinity beheld a child with a seashell trying to empty the ocean and realized that his human efforts to comprehend the divine mystery were equally hopeless. The first graphic rendition was in the third (illustrated) edition of Cesare Ripa's *Iconologia* (Rome, 1603), p. 109. See *Baroque and Rococo Pictorial Imagery*, Item no. 3, 'The Deity.'

Nevertheless, even the most seemingly impractical cerebral feats and all the 'classical experiments' mentioned by Kearney required repeated recourse to various printed materials. Tables and charts were not turned out in idle moments by members of a leisured class. The output of better maps and globes, the new ventures in data collection which led to improved estimates of the dimensions of the earth were helpful to pure science as well as to applied.[78] When publishers competed to get news from an expedition the minute it docked or instrument makers took time off to advertise their wares, such actions contributed to *all* kinds of scientific experiments – whether they were aimed at bearing fruit or intended only to shed light.

Even when considering only the light-shedding experiments performed by a very small number of highly gifted men, the many practical problems posed by publication still have to be taken into account. Where publication outlets were imperiled, speculative freedom was also endangered. Official censorship could affect even the hidden life of the mind. One wonders, for example, whether the 'Cartesian Theory of the Universe' was ever fully disclosed, even to Descartes himself. When hearing of Galileo's fate in 1633, he stopped working on his grand cosmological treatise and perhaps clipped the wings of his own imagination by this negative act.[79] Newton's creative energies could be given freer rein. Conditions that guarantee speculative freedom are probably related to the 'development of originality.' They are also related to mundane matters involving economics, technology, and affairs of church and state.

[78] W. J. Blaeu's contributions to terrestrial measurement are described by Keuning, *Willem Jansz. Blaeu*, pp. 22–4 who notes the use made of them by Jean Picard. The latter's 1672 expedition (which had simultaneous measurements of the altitude of Mars taken in Cayenne and in Paris and secured more accurate estimates of the sun's mean distance from the earth) is cited in Newton studies by many authorities (see Butterfield, *Origins of Modern Science*, p. 120) who suggest Newton delayed final calculations for the *Principia* until seeing Picard's results in a publication of 1684. (This suggestion was queried by Florian Cajori in his appendix to *Sir Isaac Newton's Mathematical Principles*, p. 663 who shows Newton already had used a fairly accurate value derived from an earlier Dutch measurement by Snell (in 1617) and by Norwood, when correcting a table of distances in his emended version of Varenius' *Geographia Generalis emendata et illustrata ab Isaaco Newton* (Cambridge, 1672). But, of course, Newton may well have waited for Picard's well substantiated verdict while using those of Snell and Norwood as the most reliable to date. Newton's work on Varenius' *Geographia* is described by Manuel, *Portrait*, p. 117 as useful for his chronological research. It entered into his astronomical calculations as well.

[79] Descartes' letter to Mersenne describing his decision to withdraw his treatise on 'Le Monde' from publication after learning of Galileo's recantation is discussed by Hine, 'Mersenne and Copernicanism,' p. 30. His prudent handling of problems posed by French censorship and use of Dutch firms is described by Martin, *Livre à Paris* II, 874–6.

By 1640, we are told, 'science had risen.' The work of Descartes, Galileo and Harvey was 'virtually complete.' But Descartes' work was surely incomplete. The complete *Monde* was never issued, even in a posthumous form. By 1640, moreover, Kepler's laws had not won acceptance. Three alternative planetary models and six sets of conflicting tables were in circulation. Elliptical orbits were still far from making contact with parabolic curves. During the same interval, the fate of the continental publishing firms that were used by Kepler, Galileo, and Harvey also hung in the balance and hinged on the shifting fortunes of war. Perhaps it is *un*safe to say that science had risen – especially in those regions where printers were being subject to new controls. In Italy, for example, a clandestine book-trade had taken hold, and scientific publication programs were winding down. One might be better advised to think less of science as 'rising' among Galileo's compatriots than of its going underground. At least it was able to go abroad, thanks to the help provided by the Royal Society, whose efforts at underwriting foreign work deserve to be better known.

For it was not just large and costly volumes of English virtuosi, such as Willoughby, that made the financing of the *Principia* difficult for the Royal Society. It was also the expense of undertaking to publish (and illustrate lavishly) significant contributions by Italians who worked in their native land and yet found it awkward to publish there. For example, all the major treatises of Marcello Malpighi, indeed every work that he published after 1669, were published by the Royal Society.[80] Much as Copernicus was served by Rheticus, Galileo by Diodati or Newton by Halley, so too was Malpighi served, not by Italian colleagues, but by Henry Oldenburg and by Robert Hooke. These Secretaries of the Royal Society furnished the great embryologist with the most recently published technical literature. (It was easier to wait for books from England than to turn to local booksellers by that time.) They solicited contributions and assured him repeatedly of the fine reception accorded his papers by the 'company of philosophers abroad.'[81] In general, they provided the Italian virtuoso with the en-

---

[80] Adelman, *Marcello Malpighi* 1, 669–726. Kearney, 'Puritanism and Science,' p. 109 cites Malpighi's contributions as evidence that Italian scientific activity was not affected by religious and political events. See also Rabb, 'Religion and the Rise of Modern Science,' p. 123, for a similar interpretation of Italian academies and virtuosi, which overlooks the question of publication outlets.

[81] Adelman, *Marcello Malpighi* 1, 670. See pp. 712–15 for discussion of new treatises sent by Oldenburg, all in Latin so that Malpighi could read them.

couragement and group support he lacked at home. That the atmosphere in Italy was less receptive, Malpighi's many letters show. Even while expressing some concern about possible reprisals for engaging in the 'commerce with Protestants' Malpighi also commented that a friend had mentioned there were advantages in having works 'condemned by Italian censors sail to England to be printed.'[82]

This opportunity was advantageous not only to Malpighi but to the Commonwealth of Learning at large, as Oldenburg recognized at the time. His correspondence with the Italian embryologist shows that the Secretary of the Royal Society was fully aware of the special service the press was rendering to scientific advance.[83] Having assured the anxious author that his history of the silkworm was to be published 'in splendid style,' Oldenburg noted that publication would 'bring out the opinion of all the learned, and perhaps where you have not yet seen clearly, they will shed fuller light.'[84] With these words, Oldenburg underscored a theme which has been running through this book; namely that printing rendered a special service to the learned Latin-reading community. Publication would not serve to acquaint 'everyman' with Malpighi's highly technical treatise on the silkworm. But it would 'bring out the opinion of all the learned,' that is, it would elicit contributions from other qualified investigators who could check observations, repeat experiments or devise new tests and present fresh data. Given Oldenburg's clear understanding of the value of scientific publication and the vigorous efforts he made on its behalf, it seems odd that this aspect of his activities is not acknowledged more often.

As things stand now, recognition of the important services rendered by printing to the scientific community, a recognition that was shared by Renaudot as well as by the founders of the Royal Society, is likely to be obscured by the debate over the so-called 'Baconian' movement and whether it was peripheral or central to seventeenth-century scientific advance. Those who scornfully dismiss the 'Baconians' as promoters rather than as real scientists and those who uphold the same group (while depicting them as embattled Puritans trying to bring down

[82] Adelman, *Marcello Malpighi* i, 347. Malpighi was not the only Italian virtuoso who turned to England for help. A 1661 letter from Vicenzo Viviani to Robert Southwell, a future president of the Royal Society, urging promotion of Viviani's work reads like 'the letter of a sales manager to a favorite travelling salesman,' according to Middleton, *The Experimenters*, p. 282.
[83] Oldenburg's appreciation of the uses of publicity and of the need to improve scientific communications systems was also shared by others associated with the Royal Society. See Shapiro, *John Wilkins*, pp. 32; 223.   [84] Adelman, *Marcello Malpighi* i, 674 (Letter of March 25, 1669).

Latin-reading élites) serve to reinforce each other. The special functions rendered by the underwriting of costly technical publications tend to be discounted by both sides.

Along with the special services rendered by Royal Society publications, the special threats posed by press censorship also are likely to be discounted. It has become increasingly fashionable to muffle the repercussions of Galileo's trial and to view the stir it caused as a consequence of clever Protestant propaganda.

> It is very doubtful whether the dramatic events of the condemnation of Galileo were in themselves of far-reaching significance. The indignation aroused...probably increased the popularity of science. There is no sign of cessation of scientific activity following the condemnation...It is true that the activities of the Lincei were curtailed...but some of its members... continued to be active...and participated in the foundation...of the Cimento...[85]

Although scientific activity did not cease in Italy after 1632, studies of the *Lincei*, the *Cimento*, the *Investiganti*, and of individual members of these societies show how it was being crippled. The *Lincei* had to discontinue the study of physics and astronomy; its short-lived successor, the *Cimento*, which relied entirely on the personal patronage of a Medici duke, was disbanded ten years after its formation. Two of its members were imprisoned by the Inquisition. Its collective papers: the 'Saggi' ('Examples' or 'Samples') were published in 1667, but could not be purchased in Italian bookshops.[86] Indeed it required action once again by the Royal Society for the *Saggi* to become known abroad.[87]

A brief comparison of the policy of the Royal Society with that of its Italian counterpart, the *Cimento*, in the 1660s seems worth making if only to suggest how divergent publication policies might serve to stimulate or to stifle scientific advance. With the *Transactions*, the Royal Society launched a continuous series[88] that attracted an expanding list

---

[85] Ben-David, 'The Scientific Role,' p. 571.

[86] Ornstein, *The Role of Scientific Societies*, pp. 76, 78–9, 812; Middleton, *The Experimenters, passim*.

[87] The *Saggi* was translated into English by Richard Waller and published by the Royal Society in 1684. Oldenburg's impatient and eager letters awaiting receipt of copies of the Italian version in 1665–6 are in Middleton, *The Experimenters*, p. 289.

[88] The series was *almost* uninterrupted. There was a hiatus between 1687 and 1691 before Richard Waller took over and previous difficulties were experienced between 1665 and 1669 due to plague, the fire of London, and Oldenburg's imprisonment in the Tower (for corresponding in French with a virtuoso). See Stimson, *Scientists and Amateurs*, pp. 107–8; Margaret Espinasse, 'Decline and Fall of Restoration Science,' pp. 347–69.

of subscribers and readers all over the world. The *Cimento* issued only one single compendium, whose first edition could not be locally bought or sold. The *Transactions* encouraged signed contributions and attracted authors even from abroad with the lure of fame. Its editors took measures to ensure the protection of intellectual property rights by dating contributions and adjudicating priority disputes. The *Saggi* tried to protect contributors from persecution by leaving them anonymous. It thereby deprived them of the incentive to make a public contribution while achieving personal fame.[89]

As an institution which failed to survive... [the *Cimento*] shows us something interesting about...the 'reward structure' of science. Within the social system of modern science, one of the primary incentives for...original research is the desire for recognition and status...The Academy failed... because the enthusiasm of its most talented researchers was dampened by the anonymity of its only publication.[90]

Adverse publication policies also hurt the chief scientific society of Naples, as Max Fisch's article on the Academy of the Investigators suggests. Its members were often on the verge of publication but almost never ventured over the brink. One of them, Tommaso Cornelio, postponed publication to the point where he 'lost credit' for significant work in anatomy and physiology. English virtuosi, although slower in their research, were quicker to win eponymous fame.[91] It has been suggested that Naples should have a place alongside Padua, Florence, Copenhagen, Paris, and London as a center of seventeenth-century scientific activity.[92] Seventeenth-century Naples contained many distinguished virtuosi. But it was not a good location for any scientist who hoped to get his major works into print before he himself expired. Cornelio's master, Marco Aurelio Severino, left seventy-seven volumes of unpublished manuscript materials behind him when he died of the plague in 1656. As a host to many English visitors and a careful reader of Harvey's pioneering studies, he had

[89] See Ornstein, *The Role of Scientific Societies*, pp. 88–90 on first edition of the *Saggi* and p. 130 on Oldenburg's handling of problem of 'plagiary.' For sophisticated sociological analysis of the role played by the *Transactions* editors, see Merton and Zuckerman, 'Patterns of Evaluation in Science.'

[90] Westman, book review, *Renaissance Quarterly* (1974) p. 223.

[91] Fisch, 'The Academy of the Investigators' I, 528. See also discussions of constant postponement of publication by another member of the *Investiganti* (Joseph Valetta) on pp. 544–5. A similar pattern is traced by Whitmore, *The Order of Minims*, with regard to the friars of Mersenne's order in France. See n. 128 below.

[92] Schmitt, 'A Garin Compendium,' p. 420.

written hopefully to England in search of publication outlets there.[93] Severino's former mentor, Tommaso Campanella, was eventually rescued from his Neapolitan prison by the good offices of a pope and he found refuge in a Parisian convent not far from Mersenne. But his *Apologia Pro Galileo*, written in Naples in the fateful year 1616, had to be smuggled out by German disciples to be published under Rosicrucian auspices in Frankfurt.[94]

In the year 1616 the head of the Carmelite Order, Foscarini, was silenced for arguing that Copernicanism might be in harmony with Scripture. The Anglican bishop, Thomas Sprat, who said much the same thing later in the century, also provoked opposition. Thus Henry Stubbe, an English physician, was moved to write: 'A Censure upon Certaine Passages Contained in the *History of the Royal Society* As being Destructive to the Established Religion and the Church of England.'[95] Unlike Foscarini and his printer, however, Bishop Sprat and his colleagues could afford to view this kind of 'censure' with relative equanimity. Controversy attracted publicity and helped to boost sales. The author of the *History of the Royal Society* was protected by all the forces that rallied Englishmen behind the anti-Papist cause. 'Without a doubt,' ran one of the arguments which allowed press censorship to lapse in England, 'if the late King James had continued on the throne ...books against Popery would have...been deemed offensive...'[96] Unlike members of the *Cimento*, the apologist for the Royal Society could draw on the heritage of biblical humanists and vernacular translators to provide religious sanction for the new undertaking. The Anglican Church and the Royal Society may both lay claim to the achievement of a 'Reformation' said Sprat:

both have taken a like course to bring this about; each of them passing by the corrupt copies and referring themselves to the perfect originals for instruc-

---

93 Schmitt and Webster, 'Harvey and M. A. Severino.'

94 The disciples were Tobias Adami and Wilhelm Wense, both friends of Andreae who got the *City of the Sun* also printed in Frankfurt. Yates, *Rosicrucian Enlightenment*, pp. 137–8. On Frankfurt firm associated with Rosicrucians, see Evans, *The Wechel Presses*, pp. 281–2. On Campanella's *Apologia Pro Galileo* see also Grant McColley's introduction to *The Defense of Galileo of Thomas Campanella* and McColley, 'The Debt of Bishop John Wilkins.' On Boyle's approval of Hartlib's plan to produce English translations of Campanella's *City of the Sun* and Andreae's *Christianopolis* see Rattansi, 'Social Interpretation of Science,' p. 20

95 Ornstein, *Role of Scientific Societies*, p. 132. R. F. Jones, *Ancients and Moderns*, pp. 249–62 has long excerpts from Stubbe's 'Censure.' That Stubbe was ironically attacking, not defending, the Anglican church is argued in James Jacob's forthcoming study.

96 Item no. 15, 'The House of Commons' Reasons for Not Renewing the Licensing Act (1695)' cited from *Lords' Journals* xv, 545 by Vann, ed. *Century of Genius*, p. 7.

tion; the one to Scripture, the other to the huge Volume of Creatures. They are both accused unjustly by their enemies of the same crimes, of having forsaken the Ancient Traditions and ventured on Novelties. They both suppose alike that their Ancestors might err; and yet retain a sufficient reverence for them...[97]

Sprat's reference to retaining 'a sufficient reverence' suggests that the establishment of public knowledge entailed some measure of prudence and self-restraint. Even in England, protection and patronage were likely to be withheld from those who pressed controversial causes too far. This was especially true during the Restoration when men were weary of civil war. Virtuosi, who were easily confused with magicians and sorcerers, and who still numbered some astrologers and alchemists in their midst, had particular reasons to be prudent in pressing their cause. The claim to bring about a 'Reformation' was associated with Rosicrucian and revolutionary manifestos and was by no means free of political implications.[98] Moreover, there was still a residual confusion between the 'true experiments' of virtuosi and the charlatan's mystico-magical tricks. The experimenters were also vulnerable as 'amateurs' and as founders of unauthorized 'invisible colleges' to being classed with zealous Puritans and levellers who had attacked Latin learning, university faculties and the granting of any professional degrees.[99]

In securing support for the new form of 'public knowledge,' the founders of the Royal Society used tactics similar to those deployed by Mersenne.[100] They took care to present the study of nature in its most neutral, innocuous guise; treading a cautious middle path between Hobbist 'atheistical materialism' on the one hand and occult 'Familias-tical-levelling Magical' trends on the other.[101] Even while upholding

---

[97] Sprat, History of Royal Society, part 3, sect. 23, p. 371.

[98] See passage calling for a 'general reformation of the world' in Boccalini's Ragguagli di Parnaso (Venice, 1612–13) translated as Advertisements from \Parnassus by the Earl of Monmouth (London, 1669) as cited by Yates, Giordano Bruno, pp. 408–11. As Yates shows, Boccalini's tract was translated into German and incorporated into the first Rosicrucian Manifesto (Cassel, 1614). See also Yates, The Rosicrucian Enlightenment, chap. x. Special insular concerns also entered into the effort to disassociate the Royal Society from belief in occult and hermetic texts. Early reactions to James I's Demonologie are described by Rattansi, 'Alchemy and Natural Magic.' (See also n. 101, below.)

[99] See n. 62 above for coverage of attacks on English universities by Puritan sectaries.

[100] According to Yates, Rosicrucian Enlightenment, p. 111, the 'Mersenne-Fludd controversy held the attention of all Europe.' It was set off by Mersenne's Questione in Genesim of 1623. How this landmark in 'demythologization' was related to the Rosicrucian furore is also discussed by Yates in her Giordano Bruno, pp. 435 ff.

[101] Prior, 'Joseph Glanvill,' suggests how one effort to disassociate English science from atheism and materialism (à la Hobbes) led, paradoxically, to the claim that belief in witchcraft was scientifically valid.

claims to Reformation, welcoming contributions from artisans, and advocating the use of unadorned vernacular prose, Bishop Sprat emphasized the apolitical non-partisan character of the Society. Not only poetry and magic, but also religion and politics were banned. There is more than a hint of a suggestion in Sprat's apologia that the neutral scientific society had taken over functions once assigned to the medieval Church by providing a peaceful sanctuary for factions who were otherwise at each other's throats. Later Addison asserted that the Society was established less to promote natural knowledge than 'to keep out of politics many of the greatest Geniuses of the age who might otherwise have set their country in a flame.'[102] The 'innocent amusements' which diverted the virtuosi were depicted in a manner calculated to distract attention from earlier Puritan zeal and in a way that evoked an Edenic freedom from original sin. Within the refuge provided by the study of nature, Anglicans and Puritans could behave as did inhabitants of a 'peaceable kingdom' where lions lay down with lambs. 'The Beautiful Bosom of *Nature* will be Expos'd to our view; we shall enter into its *Garden* and taste of its *Fruits* and satisfy ourselves with its plenty.'[103] The heretical implications of this vision of science as restoring the prelapsarian paradise on earth have been brought out by many authorities. The paradoxical implications of associating large-scale data collection, expanding knowledge industries and periodical publication with medieval images of enclosed gardens, modest maidens and forbidden fruit remain to be explored.

4. RESETTING THE STAGE FOR GALILEO'S TRIAL

For Italian virtuosi, at all events, no similar refuge could be constructed; flaming swords still barred the way. The 'book of nature' was not open to public inspection, but was subject to expurgation, and large tracts were declared out of bounds. Libraries were ransacked and printers were imprisoned. Fear of persecution led to a different kind of self-censorship than that enjoined upon members of the Royal Society, who had to stay clear of politics and theology but could wander freely within nature's realm.

historians have not thrown much light upon the rise of the Index. They have not brought out the actual differences it made in each case in each place...

---

[102] From *The Spectator* 262 (31 Dec., 1711), cited by Espinasse, 'Decline and Fall,' p. 353.
[103] Sprat, *History of The Royal Society*, part 3, section 1, p. 327.

the silent battles that were...fought behind the scenes about certain works, publishing houses, the sales and the circulation of books brought in from abroad...Everything vital and new that had been produced during a century and half of cultural effort was now being mutilated and suppressed...

The secret history of the great battle which was supposed to protect the Catholic world from the progress of European knowledge is still to be written...it is difficult to understand the atmosphere of suspicion, secretiveness and suppression which dominated the world of culture in the age of Galileo. Everything became dangerous...Heresy was ferreted out from dictionaries and traced in the collections of apothegms; it was believed to be hidden in the very names of the printers and had to be exterminated there...[104]

Since 1965 when Garin published the above passages, several historians have thrown more light on the 'silent battle' as it was fought out in particular regions of Italy. Thus John Tedeschi has studied documents pertaining to the situation in Florence between 1592 and 1606 and has described the 'unmitigated confusion' and interminable delays which led to the ruin of booksellers and printers. Tedeschi agrees with Garin concerning the 'devastating effects on Italian culture of Roman censorship practices.'[105] Paul Grendler, who has followed the situation in Venice over a longer interval (1540–1605), draws a picture that is somewhat less black-and-white; for Venetian policy was often at odds with that of Rome. Thus Grendler describes both the initial delay in implementing Roman edicts when they were first issued and the eventual curtailment of the power of clerical censors by officials who weathered the interdict crisis. He also suggests that 'mutilation and suppression' of innovative literature was not entirely successful, even when collaboration with Roman inquisitors was the order of the day. Between 1570 and 1590, Venetian virtuosi continued to obtain forbidden works. 'The Inquisition was unable to stop illicit traffic' and could not 'halt clandestine importation of ultramontane titles.' Profits from this traffic, however, did not line the pockets of Venetian printers. The latter were hard hit by the two decades of collaboration with Rome which benefited their foreign competitors. The 'ban on publication of prohibited titles was almost totally effective' and this 'dealt a lasting blow' to local booksellers and publishing firms.[106]

[104] Garin, *Science and Civic Life*, pp. 85–6.
[105] Tedeschi, 'Florentine Documents,' pp. 579–605.
[106] Grendler, 'The Roman Inquisition,' pp. 48–66. (This article summarizes the findings which are now spelled out in more detail in Grendler's book by the same title.)

Italian virtuosi, in sixteenth-century Venice at least, seem to have kept in touch with innovative literature from abroad. Later Venetian literati contributed much to pro-republican and anti-papist propaganda and also to the prolonged struggle for a free press. But what about the access of virtuosi and literati to funds for publication programs and to printers and patrons willing to risk carrying them out? Because this question is rarely posed, the most telling blows to early-modern science dealt by clerical censorship are often overlooked. Instead of pointing to the clear and present threats posed by the decree of 1616 and the trial of 1633, careful distinctions are drawn between different theological positions taken by churchmen on the two occasions. These theological subtleties, however intrinsically interesting, still strike me as being somewhat beside the point.[107]

The decree of 1616 described the doctrine of Copernicus as contrary to Scripture and therefore not to be defended or held. Nevertheless, we are told, the Copernican theory could still be presented as an hypothesis (albeit as an indefensible and absurd one). Moreover, 'if there were any Catholic astronomers who had no doubt that the Copernican system was true' they did not have to violate their inner conviction of certitude. The decree requiring 'interior assent' came from a fallible authority and those who had no doubt 'were excused.'[108] Interior assent could be withheld. But what about external dissent? On the strategic issue of publication, recent Catholic apologists have singularly little to say. Catholic scientists who had no inner doubts (and were certain that Copernicus was right) were still expected to remain silent, or pay a high price for failure to prove their case. At least this conclusion seems to follow from Galileo's trial.

Galileo had... openly disobeyed the express prohibitions against his theory and plainly failed in his attempt to prove the Copernican astronomy. Still it is hard to see the logic of the sentence. There was no reason to condemn the *Dialogue* outright. It... defended the new astronomy as true on physical grounds. If this was objectionable, Galileo's book, like Copernicus' *De Revolutionibus*, should have been suspended until corrected and made more hypothetical. As for Galileo personally the most that should have been given

---

[107] See for example, Langford, *Galileo, Science*, pp. 98–104. For a good summary of literature on the diverse theological and philosophical positions that are entailed, see Nelson, 'The Early Modern Revolution' pp. 1–40 (see esp. bibliography and appendices). Nelson does more to bring out the revised opinions of Cardinal Bellarmine's biographer, Father Brodrick, than other authorities do.

[108] Langford, *Galileo, Science*, p. 103, n. 50.

him was a penance for disobeying Bellarmine's admonition...As for the decree of the Index, it was aimed at books, not authors.[109]

Obviously the prelates who presided over the condemnation of 1633 did not view the issues in quite the same light as does a modern Catholic scholar such as Langford. Although the latter contends that the case of Galileo is too often lifted out of its historical context, his difficulty in understanding 'the logic of the sentence' suggests an incomplete success in reconstructing the mentality of seventeenth-century churchmen. At all events, any decree that was aimed at books was bound to hit printers and authors as well. Whatever interpretation is placed on the edicts of 1616 and 1633, it can scarcely be doubted that they had an inhibiting effect on scientific publication programs in Catholic lands. When it asserted that the old world-system had to be maintained as long as the new one was inadequately proved, and when it forbade further 'attempts to demonstrate' that the new system was 'true in fact'[110] the Church was not encouraging suspension of judgment or urging further investigation of the matter. The condemnations not only curtailed scientific publication programs, they also did much to block 'thought experiments' based on envisaging the Copernican scheme as physically real.

Poor Borelli! He was truly on the road to the great discovery...He renounced all theory beyond the brute, experimental fact and by this very means barred the road to progress. Hooke and Newton had more courage. It is the intellectual audacity of Newton just as much as his genius which permitted him to overcome the obstacles that stopped Borelli ...[111]

When comparing Hooke and Newton with Borelli, one cannot afford to confine the terms of discussion to 'internal' factors alone. Of course, the state of the art and the special talents of the gifted puzzle-solvers have to be considered. But one must also give due weight to unevenly distributed 'external' forces. Otherwise an unfair comparison will result. Borelli may or may not have been less courageous and less audacious than Newton. Surely he had fewer incentives to spur him on and more formidable obstacles to surmount.

Insofar as anti-Copernican edicts might be taken as a challenge to come up with more adequate proof of heliocentric schemes, they were much more likely to be taken in this way by Protestant than by Catho-

[109] Langford, *Galileo, Science*, pp. 150–1.   [110] Langford, *Galileo, Science*, pp. 98–9.
[111] Koyré, *La Révolution Astronomique*, p. 506 (translation mine).

lic scientists. Ramus had taken Osiander's preface as a challenge. His open letter to Europe's astronomers helped to spur Kepler on. But when Galileo failed to come up with certain proof, the case was closed – at least as far as papal writ could reach. It is difficult to envisage a member of an Italian scientific society acting as Halley did, urging Newton to overcome his hesitations and to bring his grand design to completion, and then supervising its publication and assuring it favorable publicity. Friends of Catholic virtuosi were more likely to dissuade them from taking the condemned theory too seriously. Even without friends to dissuade them, devout Catholics would feel qualms about moving ahead on their own.

Thus members of the *Cimento* devoted themselves to careful laboratory experiments while avoiding large-scale theories and holding thought-experiments in check. 'It is dangerous to make original conjectures, so look again before giving it to a printer,' ran a note found among the papers of those responsible for preparing the *Saggi* for publication in Italy.[112] The fear of publishing subversive subject-matter led to excluding from the *Saggi* potentially interesting investigations and discussions of comets. Not only cosmology but also astronomy represented a potentially dangerous field after 1633. Even Borelli, who chafed at anonymity and eventually left Tuscany in order to publish on his own, resorted to a pseudonym when publishing one treatise on comets and masked the Copernican implications of a passage before releasing his *Theoricas Mediceorum Planetarum*.[113] The defense of plain-speaking by spokesmen for the Royal Society such as Sprat was not aimed only at excluding poets, rhetoricians and fabulists from the Commonwealth of Learning. It had positive as well as negative aspects. It reflected a recognition that 'Aesopian' language, when effective enough to fool censors, often deceived fellow scientists and sometimes inhibited clear thinking by oneself.

Perhaps enough has been said to suggest that the picture of flourishing Italian scientific activity drawn by several authorities needs to be qualified. Even though the *Cimento* was founded and did important

---

[112] Middleton, *The Experimenters*, p. 72.
[113] Settle, 'Borelli, Giovanni Alfonso, 1608–1679,' *Dictionary of Scientific Biography* II, 306–14. Although he did win patronage and publication support from Queen Christina after her conversion to Catholicism, Borelli's career ended badly – as a poverty-stricken political suspect teaching elementary mathematics in Rome. Settle's description of the setbacks suffered by seventeenth-century Italian science (p. 306) should be contrasted with the bland dismissal by other authorities of the impact of the anti-Copernican decrees.

work, its own scientific publication program was crippled; others in Italy had suffered damaging blows. But then Italian technical publication had already experienced many set-backs in the past. A recent account of the fate of the mid-sixteenth-century *Accademia Venetiana* is instructive in this respect. The *Accademia* had an ambitious program to 're-establish Venice's reputation as the leading publishing center.' It planned to enlist the aid of Paul Manutius' publishing firm and to issue editions of many important scientific works. Founded in 1557, the *Accademia* was incapable of meeting the high costs entailed in securing supplies of paper, the services of printers, editors, and rentals of bookshops and went bankrupt in 1561.[114] Given the pressure being exerted from the Papacy in the 1550s to control printing firms and bring Venetian censorship in line with the Index; given the difficulties experienced by Venetian bookmen stemming from official policies during subsequent decades, it would seem the founders of *Accademia* had chosen the wrong time for launching their ambitious project. But when one surveys developments over the course of the next century, it seems that the time never did come when Italian publication outlets were free of the risk of being abruptly closed off.

In this regard, the stage is set just as awkwardly for Galileo's trial as for other major historical events. The placing of *De Revolutionibus* on the Index by the decree of 1616, and the prohibition of the *Lettera* by Paolo Antonio Foscarini (a sixty-four page treatise published in 1615 by a Carmelite friar, which argued that the Copernican theory was physically plausible and theologically sound) are discussed in many studies. The hard lesson learned by Foscarini's printer, Lazaro Scoriggio, however, is rarely taken into account. 'By the beginning of February 1616 Galileo...felt...victory was in sight. He wrote to secure permission...for a visit to Naples, probably to see Foscarini and if possible Campanella and to organize the campaign in favor of Copernicus...'[115]

On March 5 the decree pertaining to Copernican doctrines was officially published. Foscarini's *Lettera*, which sought to reconcile Copernican views with Scripture, was 'altogether prohibited and condemned.' *De Revolutionibus*, however, was merely 'suspended until it be corrected.' The distinction between the prohibition of the theologi-

---

[114] Rose, 'The Accademia Venetiana.' In his *Italian Renaissance of Mathematics*, Rose has a chapter on Bernardino Baldi (d. 1617) who set out to be the Vasari of mathematicians, collected 200 or so 'Lives' but failed to get his *Vite de' Matematici* into print.

[115] Drake, *Discoveries and Opinions*, pp. 218–20.

cal argument and the suspension of the astronomical treatise is frequently stressed by Catholic apologists and by others who try to soften
the effect of the blow. Thus Langford suggests that it was 'not really
a serious setback to progress in astronomy' and Koestler argues that,
despite the mistaken impression of 'the man in the street,' the 'effect of
the decree on scientific discussion and research was to leave things
almost exactly where they had been.'[116] Neither notes, that in 1617,
one year after the decree, the Amsterdam printing firm (run by the
noted Dutch astronomer, globe-maker and map-publisher, Willem
Janszoon Blaeu) brought out a third edition of *De Revolutionibus*.[117]
Perhaps Blaeu, like many of his competitors was hoping to trade on the
advantages of being listed on the Index. Perhaps he had laid plans for
a 1617 publication date long before. Whatever the case, Blaeu's edition
appeared at a time when scientific publication programs bearing on
physics and astronomy were being caught up in a familiar pattern –
one that had already affected Erasmus, Boccaccio, Rabelais, Luther,
and Machiavelli. New opportunities to profit from banned titles were
extended to Protestant firms. At the same time new risks and un-
certainties were posed for scientific publishers in Catholic lands.
Virtuosi engaged in scientific research were not unaffected by this turn
of events. A member of the *Lincei* resigned, accusing Galileo of upholding forbidden views.[118] Galileo withdrew his plan to visit Naples
ostensibly because of 'bad roads.' As Drake suggests, after March 5,
1616, the 'road to Naples was...bad...in more than one sense.' 'The
printer who had published Foscarini's book there was soon to be
imprisoned and the author died that same year under obscure
circumstances.'[119] The road to Naples never did improve, so far as
scientific publication programs were concerned.

Very much like Luther during the decade after 1517, Galileo during
the decade after 1633 could count on the support of numerous publishers, printers, and booksellers to render papal actions ineffective even
while they made profits on the side. The fate of the banned *Dialogue*
demonstrated once again the advantage that accrued to Protestant
publishers from purveying titles listed on the Index, and the attraction

---

[116] Langford, *Galileo, Science*, pp. 58–9; Koestler, *The Sleepwalkers*, p. 458.
[117] The editor of this edition which bore the title *Astronomia Instaurata* was Nicolas Müller,
a professor of mathematics at Gröningen. According to various authorities, Müller was not
a Copernican himself but his corrections made the third edition an improvement over the
previous versions.   [118] Ornstein, *Role of Scientific Societies*, p. 76.
[119] Drake, *Discoveries and Opinions*, pp. 219–20.

exerted even by fairly recondite scientific treatises that were designated as forbidden fruit.[120] According to de Santillana's colorful account, the black market profits made by the *Dialogue* were high:

priests, monks, prelates even, vie with each other in buying up copies of the *Dialogue* on the black market...the black market price of the book rises from the original half-scudo to four and six scudi [almost a hundred dollars in American currency] all over Italy.[121]

Galileo's *Dialogue on Two World Systems* was such a provocative and polemical treatise, however, it almost seemed to court censorship in a way that is quite atypical of most serious scientific work. The same thing cannot be said of his later treatise which helped to found classical physics: the *Discourses on Two New Sciences*.

No great cosmic or philosophical questions intrude into this unimpassioned treatise...it is about as controversial and stirring as some freshman lecture on mechanics, of which indeed, it is the ultimate source.

The crowning irony of Galileo's career is that the failure of the great *Dialogues* should be so much more interesting than the success of the unobjectionable *Discourses*.[122]

It is hard to think of a better example of the kind of 'pure science' that is naturally placed 'au-dessus de la mêlée' than the 'ultimate source' of a 'freshman lecture on mechanics.' Yet the dull 'unobjectionable' *Discourses* were also caught up in the fray. They were not deemed unobjectionable by those who kept Galileo under house arrest; their success was not uninteresting when one considers the means by which it was brought out. Given an ageing but resolute political prisoner, whose captors had forbidden him to publish or even write anything ever again; a Dutch printer's visit to Italy and the smuggling of a manuscript in a diplomat's pouch, the ingredients do not lack interest. They could be woven into a narrative involving considerable suspense.

---

[120] A key figure in the English exploitation of the publicity value of Galileo's being on the Index was Thomas Salusbury who (copying a procedure used for expurgated passages in Scripture by Bodley's Librarian, Thomas James) translated the treatises (and expurgated passages from works designated as forbidden in the Indexes of 1616 and 1619) and published them by popular subscription soon after the Restoration of 1660. See Stimson, *The Gradual Acceptance*, p. 90. According to Nicolson, 'English Almanachs,' pp. 22–3, Salusbury's English translations from the Italian and Latin versions of Galileo's works were advertised by Vincent Wing, the almanac publisher, whose work was annotated by Newton. Since the latter came into contact with Galileo's work through the Salusbury translation, the propagandist accomplished a useful task.   [121] de Santillana, *The Crime of Galileo*, p. 325.

[122] Gillispie, *The Edge of Objectivity*, p. 52.

The book was completed in 1636 when Galileo was seventy-two. As he could not hope for an imprimatur in Italy, the manuscript was smuggled out to Leiden and published by the Elseviers. But it could also have been printed in Vienna where it was licensed, probably with imperial consent, by the Jesuit Father Paulus.[123]

One wonders what grounds there are for Koestler's optimism concerning possible Viennese publication, in view of the risk of reprisals Viennese printers would have to run. There were, after all, many powerful officials in Vienna who disapproved of the licensing and viewed any support of Galileo as a subversive act. Koestler's account, here as elsewhere, seems to underrate the forces of reaction and needs to be balanced against evidence supplied by other accounts.

as soon as the *Discourses on Two New Sciences* is licensed in Olmutz by the bishop and then in Vienna, obviously under direct imperial orders by the Jesuit Father Paulus, the other Jesuits start in hot pursuit after the book. 'I have not been able' writes Galileo...in 1639, 'to obtain a single copy of my new dialogue...Yet I know that they circulated through all the northern countries. The copies lost must be those which, as soon as they arrived in Prague were immediately bought up by the Jesuit fathers so that not even the Emperor was able to get one.' The charitable explanation would be that they knew what they were doing. Someone at least may have understood that Galileo's work in dynamics went on quietly establishing the foundations of the system that he had been forbidden to defend. But they were like that gallant man of whom Milton speaks who thought to pound in the crows by shutting the park gate.[124]

When considering factors that affected the quiet establishment of the foundations of modern science, the difference between getting published by the Elseviers in Holland and being licensed by Father Paulus in Vienna is worth keeping in mind.

'Fortunate Newton!' Einstein exclaimed, 'Happy childhood of science! To him nature was an open book whose letters he could read without effort.' As the case of 'poor Borelli' may suggest, Newton was fortunate not only in being a genius who was born in the right century. He was lucky to be born in the right country as well. After the advent of printing, all talents alike had been freed from certain previous limits set by hand-copying and memory work. But unevenly distributed

---

[123] Koestler, *The Sleepwalkers*, p. 494. For account of complex negotiations between Galileo and François de Noailles which disguised the handing of the *Discourses* over to Louis Elsevier, see Costabel and Lerner, pp. 18–20.   [124] de Santillana, *The Crime of Galileo*, p. 326.

literacy rates governed access to the new form of public knowledge and even among literate élites incentives, penalties and rewards varied in accordance with divergent policies pursued by varying régimes. 'Sir Isaac,' wrote his nephew, Conduitt, 'had the happiness of being born in a land of liberty where he could speak his mind – not afraid of Inquisition as Galileo...not obliged as Descartes was to go into a strange country and to say he proved transubstantiation by his philosophy.' There is a certain irony here, for Newton was much more averse to 'speaking his mind' than was Galileo. Even in the *Principia*, he told a friend, he intentionally wrote in 'a cryptic and complicated manner to discourage ignorant quibblers.'[125] Like Copernicus, he was by nature secretive and inclined toward the old esoteric scribal tradition. All the more reason to give credit to the enthusiastic sponsors of scientific publication who encouraged these reticent geniuses to expose their writings to many eyes.

In analyzing the remarkable cluster of talents that marked the century of genius, consideration of random elements supplied by a gene pool may be usefully supplemented by closer study of specific historical determinants.[126] The *Académie des Sciences*, writes Charles Gillispie, was a better-designed and more professional organization than the Royal Society.

But this admirable design was frustrated by the waywardness of genetics. The scientific minds which matured in France under Louis XIV were far less fertile than those of the generation of Descartes and Pascal, far less productive than the cluster of English genius which crowded in upon the Royal Society in Newton's time.[127]

In addition to the 'waywardness of genetics,' one ought to consider the exodus of Huguenot printers and paper-makers, and the press policies adopted by both King and Académie. Did they not help to set back scientific productivity? Neither Descartes nor Pascal had felt free of constraint. During the last third of the century the odds were, if anything, stacked even higher against virtuosi seeking publication outlets in France. Manuscripts containing ample evidence of 'fertile minds' tended to pile up in Paris convents as they did in Naples and

---

[125] Manuel, *Portrait*, pp. 267, 365.
[126] See cogent remarks by Merton, *Science, Technology*, chap. 9. Merton's treatment of social interaction and communication on pp. 220–4 needs to be supplemented in my view by further consideration of the consequences of printing.
[127] Gillispie, *Edge of Objectivity*, p. 112.

Rome.[128] Even closet philosophers taking up residence abroad were necessarily sensitive to decisions made by censors in Rome; although they were often indifferent to the nature of the political régime and welcomed patronage from all quarters, including Catholic prelates, aristocrats or kings.

In this regard, it seems necessary to qualify the usual description of science as an enterprise that was especially characteristic of bourgeois capitalism, sober Puritans and a 'rising middle class.'[129] One may grant that a deeper social penetration of literacy encouraged the tapping of more talents and more chance for useful feedback. One may grant also that expanding mercantile enterprise was linked to the expansion of data collection. One may grant finally that many major scientific publication programs were launched by prospering firms such as those of the Estiennes, Oporinus, Plantin, the Elseviers and the Blaeus – few of whom were orthodox Catholics, all of whom were sober business-men and profit-driving entrepreneurs. Nevertheless the support of royal, aristocratic and clerical patrons was also of great importance both to the early printers and to the virtuosi they served. Mechanical toys and ingenious gadgeteers had long been welcome at different courts. Mathematical wizardry along with botanical gardens and zoos continued to flourish under princely protection (as the names of Leibniz and Gauss may suggest). The rulers of several minor principalities on the fringes of the large Bourbon realm were often more helpful to the cosmopolitan French language press than were the entrepreneurs who monopolized the French book-trade in Paris. Despite the com-bination of Puritan attacks on Charles I and Laud with attacks on Ptolemaic and Galenic theories, the connection between early-modern political revolutions and scientific ones is tenuous at best. When Galileo appealed over the heads of Latin-writing professors to the lay vernacular

---

[128] According to Sauvy, *Livres saisis à Paris*, 1678–1701 was the most rigorous period of press censorship during the Ancien Régime. Martin, *Livre à Paris* II, chap. IV also contains relevant data. Hahn, *The Anatomy of a Scientific Institution*, chap. I describes the adverse policy of anonymity and other difficulties which inhibited publication down to 1699. The visit to Charles Plumier in his Paris convent in 1698 by the English zoologist, Martin Lister, seems similar to visits by English virtuosi to Severino and other members of the *Investiganti* in Naples earlier in the century. Friar Plumier (who belonged to the same order as Mersenne) had trouble finding a publisher for his work on American voyages and left masses of un-published manuscripts at his death. See Whitmore, *The Order of Minims*, pp. 186–97. Whit-more also notes difficulties with publication experienced by the *Académie des Sciences*, its inability to get any copies of the *Philosophical Transactions* sent to it during war time, and the damaging effects of excluding friars, such as Plumier, from membership (pp. 109; 189–90).

[129] See e.g. Gillispie, *The Edge of Objectivity*, pp. 114–15.

reading public, he was not enlisting the support of commoners against aristocrats. On the contrary, he repeatedly solicited help from princely patrons to free him from clerkly academic chores and, not incidentally, to protect him from the enemies his publications might provoke.[130]

The need for official protection and for official approval of publication programs probably contributed to the movement to purify science of associations with sorcery and magic. Calvinist disapproval of magic, along with prayers for intercession by supernatural powers, has been plausibly related to this movement by followers of Max Weber. But Anglican and Catholic campaigns against witches and sorcerers also need to be taken into account. When searching for connections between 'religion and the decline of magic,' pressures exerted by censorship deserve consideration. Concern about censorship probably encouraged Catholic virtuosi to press the cause of mechanism especially hard. Mersenne, Gassendi and Descartes thus cast the soul out of nature with particular zeal. When royal controls over printing were swept away during the Commonwealth, however, the more radical English Puritans sided with the Paracelsians and believers in the occult.[131] As was the case with the Mesmerists in eighteenth-century France, these English revolutionaries contributed little if anything to the 'disenchantment of the world.' Even after the Restoration, the 'new philosophy' that was promoted by the Protestant Royal Society was somewhat less mechanistic than the Catholic Cartesian version. Newtonian theories left more leeway for attractive and repulsive forces and more room for Nature's God to behave in mysterious ways.[132]

It was undoubtedly easier for English authorities – whether Puritan, Anglican or both – to regard scientific pursuits as innocuous than was the case in realms where clandestine book routes carried lectures on physics along with all kinds of subversive stuff. Although French Cartesians went further in purging science of magic and tried hard to stay clear of theological debate, they were less successful in neutralizing the new vocation than were the turncoat Puritans who became bishops

130 See e.g. Galileo's complaints to his prospective Medici patron about his teaching chores and his statement, 'I should like my books (dedicated always to my lord) to become my source of income' in his 'Letters on Sunspots,' Drake, *Discoveries and Opinions*, p. 62.

131 See Debus, *Science and Education*; Webster, *The Great Instauration*, and two essays by Rattansi: 'Paracelsus and the Puritan Revolution,' p. 28, 'The Social Interpretation of Science,' pp. 1–33.

132 Westfall, 'Newton and the Hermetic Tradition,' *passim*, discusses the non-mechanistic elements in Newton's ideas of force. Burtt, *Metaphysical Foundations* and Koyré, *From the Closed World* deal with neo-Platonic concepts associated with 'action at a distance' and 'absolute space.'

under the restored Stuart king. In the 'English rehearsal for the European Enlightenment of the eighteenth century, only one feature was missing. There was no hostility to Christianity.'[133] There was also less trouble with clerical censors. Indeed, after the Glorious Revolution, freedom of the press came to England for good. Across the Channel in France, as Voltaire noted, things were ordered differently. Programs associated with the advancement of learning, the spread of literacy and instruction in 'popular mechanics' were not neutral or peaceful in the Bourbon realm. To appreciate the difference one need only compare the quiet reception of Chambers' *Cyclopedia* in England with what happened to the project to translate it into French.

At all events, the description of science as a neutral, value-free enterprise 'au-dessus de la mêlée' was developed by men who were far from neutral on issues pertaining to press censorship and who were committed to achieving a free trade in ideas.[134] Did this commitment disguise an ulterior motive associated with the vested interests of a 'capitalistic bourgeoisie'? It may be easier to agree that it constituted an accurate appraisal by virtuosi of conditions that were essential for their work.

On this one issue the currently unfashionable and undeniably old-fashioned 'Whig interpretation of history' may still have a useful message to convey. Milton's plea for the 'liberty of Unlicenc'd Printing' and his comments in *Areopagitica* about visiting Galileo 'grown old as a prisoner of the Inquisition for thinking in Astronomy otherwise than the Dominican licensers thought' ought not to be lightly dismissed as *nothing* but anti-Papist propaganda – although it certainly was that. Granted that the case of Galileo was exploited to the hilt by Protestant publicists and pamphleteers such as Milton himself, it was not merely used to link science with Protestantism. It disclosed a link that had been forged ever since printing industries had begun to flourish in Wittenberg and Geneva and had begun to decline in Venice and Lyons. The continuous operation of printing firms beyond the reach of Rome was of vital concern to Western European scientists. The case of Galileo simply drove this lesson further home.

[133] Gillispie, *Edge of Objectivity*, p. 114.
[134] In his *History of The Royal Society*, part 2, p. 64, Sprat expressed the desire of the virtuosi to make the Society 'the general Banck and Freeport of the World.'

CONCLUSION:
SCRIPTURE AND NATURE
TRANSFORMED

The elements which go into the making of 'modernity' may be seen...
first...in the sixteenth and seventeenth centuries. Some historians attributed
the change to the liberation of men's minds during the Renaissance and the
Reformation. Today many historians would be more likely to stress the
conservatism of these two movements...Their emphasis tends instead to
fall on...'the Scientific Revolution.'

By this is meant above all the imaginative achievements associated with
the names of Copernicus, Galileo and Newton...Within the space of a century and a half a revolution had occurred in the way in which men regarded
the universe. Most of this was made possible by the application of mathematics to the problems of the natural world...

All this is by now well known...though many of the details are still to
be worked out...What is not clear is how it all came about...[1]

This book has been aimed at developing a new strategy for handling the
issues posed by the above citation. It seems futile to argue over 'the
elements which go into the making of modernity,' for 'modernity'
itself is always in flux; always subject to definitions which have to be
changed in order to keep up with changing times. As the age of Planck
and Einstein recedes into the past, 'achievements associated with Copernicus, Galileo and Newton' will probably come to share the fate of the
achievements of earlier Renassiance humanists and Protestant reformers.
Indeed recent interpretations of Copernicus show that his work is
already coming to seem more and more conservative; less and less
associated with emancipation from traditional modes of thought.
Pointing early-modern science toward an elusive modernity leads to
invidious comparisons between 'liberating' later movements and

[1] Kearney, introduction, *Origins of the Scientific Revolution*, p. xi.

earlier 'conservative' ones and brings us no closer to understanding 'how it all came about.'

To ask historians to search for elements which entered into the making of an indefinite 'modernity' seems somewhat futile. To consider the effects of a definite communications shift which entered into each of the movements under discussion seems more promising. Among other advantages this approach offers a chance to uncover relationships which debates over modernity only serve to conceal. Thus one may avoid entanglement in arguments over whether the first-born sons of modern Europe were to be found among the humanists of Renaissance Italy, or whether we must wait for the Pope to be defied by Luther, or for the Calvinists to turn Geneva into a Protestant Rome; or whether genuine modernity came with the scientific revolution or should be postponed even further until industrialization. Energies can be directed toward the more constructive task of discerning, in each of the contested movements, features which were not present in earlier epochs and which altered the textual traditions upon which each movement relied.

By setting aside the quest for theoretical 'modernizing' processes and focusing attention on the paradoxical consequences of a real duplicating process, it should be possible to handle periodization problems more deftly. We may see how movements aimed at returning to a golden past (whether classical or early Christian) were reoriented in a manner that pointed away from their initial goal and how the very process of recovering long-lost texts carried successive generations ever farther away from the experience of the Church Fathers and of the poets and orators of antiquity. We may also see how lay humanists, priests and natural philosophers alike shared the common experience of acquiring new means to achieve old ends and that this experience led in turn to a division of opinion and ultimately to a reassessment of inherited views.

To adopt this strategy does not make it possible to provide a complete answer to questions of 'how it all came about' but does open the way to supplying more adequate answers than have been offered up to now. Thus we would be in a better position to explain why long-lived scientific theories were deemed less acceptable even before new observations, new experiments, or new instruments had been made.

It is one of the paradoxes of the whole story with which we have to deal that the most sensational step leading to the scientific revolution in astronomy was taken long before the discovery of the telescope – even before... improvement...in observations made with the naked eye...William Harvey...carried out his revolutionary work before any serviceable kind of microscope had become available...even Galileo discusses the ordinary phenomena of everyday life[and]...plays with pellets on inclined planes in a manner that had long been customary...[2]

Current efforts to account for this seeming paradox do not take us very far. We are asked to guess about a transformation that took 'place inside the minds of the scientists themselves,' when they 'put on new thinking caps' to gaze at the unchanging heavens. Yet the technical literature upon which astronomers relied had undergone change even before the 'new thinking caps' were put on. More careful consideration of the shift that altered the output and intake of this literature would help to explain the timing of the 'sensational step' and also help us analyze its relationship to other 'modernizing' trends.

When considering Copernicus' intellectual environment, changes wrought by printing deserve a more central place. Present tactics either encourage us to wander too far afield compiling lists of everything that happened and marvelling at the general turbulence of the times, or else trap us into prolonging old debates – between Platonists and Aristotelians, scholastics and humanists; Catholics and Protestants, Anglicans and Puritans, even, on occasion, between Italians, Germans, Danes and Poles. By placing more emphasis on the shift from script to print, many diverse trends may be accommodated without resort to an indiscriminate mélange and in a way that avoids prolongation of intellectual feuds. The sixteenth-century astronomer may be seen to owe something to the neo-Platonists and to the Renaissance Aristotelians; to his masters in Catholic Poland and Italy and to a disciple from Protestant Wittenberg later on; to calculations made by ancient Alexandrians, observations made by medieval Arabs and to a trigonometry text compiled in Nuremberg around the time he was born.

We are less likely to set Plato against Aristotle or any one textual tradition against another when we appreciate the significance of setting many disparate texts side by side. The character of Copernicus' studies and of the currents of thought which influenced him are certainly

[2] Butterfield, *Origins of Modern Science*, p. 1.

worth studying. But this investigation should not divert us from recognizing the novelty of being able to assemble diverse records and reference guides, and of being able to study them without having to transcribe them at the same time. If we want to explain heightened awareness of anomalies or discontent with inherited schemes then it seems especially important to emphasize the wider range of reading-matter that was being surveyed at one time by a single pair of eyes.

Similarly in seeking to explain why naked-eye observation produced unprecedented results, it is worth paying more attention to the increased output of materials relating to comets and conjunctions and the increased number of simultaneous observations made of single celestial events. Nor should we neglect to note how stars which faded from the heavens (and brief landfalls made on distant shores) could be fixed permanently in precise locations after printed maps began to replace hand-copied ones. Although inferior maps continued to be duplicated and many map-publishers perpetuated errors for a century and more, a process of transmission had been fundamentally reoriented when this replacement occurred. Analogies with inertial motion do not apply to this sort of reversal. When considering a shift in direction it is misleading to draw analogies with uniform motion in a straight line. Since corrupt data were duplicated and thus perpetuated by print, one may say that scribal corruption was prolonged for some time. But one must also take into account that an age-old process of corruption was being decisively arrested and was eventually reversed. With proper supervision, fresh data could at long last be duplicated without being blurred or blotted out over the course of time.

By making more room for new features introduced by typography we would also be better situated to explain the timing of 'the application of mathematics to the problems of the natural world.' By considering the difficulties faced by astronomers, assayers, surveyors, merchants, mint masters and all others who tried to use the language of number in the age of scribes, and by recognizing how new incentives encouraged instrument-makers and reckon-masters to publicize their wares, the victories won by quantitative analysis could be better explained. By paying more attention to the duplication of pictorial statements, we might see more clearly why the life sciences no less than the physical ones were placed on a new footing and how the authority of Pliny, no less than that of Galen and Ptolemy, was undermined.

Even while acknowledging the importance of the empirical movement and of the slogan 'from books to nature' it should be noted that dissatisfaction with literature inherited from scribes coincided with the development of new forms of data collection. The advent of printing made it possible for more of nature to be put into books. Here as elsewhere, claims made for the significance of particular developments in special fields such as Renaissance art or Renaissance Aristotelianism need to be coupled with more consideration of how separate developments (the separate talents of painters and physicians, for example) could be coordinated and combined. When Agricola and Vesalius hired illustrators to render 'veins' or 'vessels' for their texts, they were launching an unprecedented enterprise and not simply continuing trends that manuscript illuminators had begun.

The advantages of issuing identical images bearing identical labels to scattered observers who could feed back information to publishers enabled astronomers, geographers, botanists and zoologists to expand data pools far beyond all previous limits – even those set by the exceptional resources of the long-lasting Alexandrian Museum. Old limits set by the pillars of Hercules and the outermost sphere of the Grecian heavens were incapable of containing findings registered in ever expanding editions of atlases and sky maps. The closed world of the ancients was opened, vast expanses of space (and later of time) previously associated with divine mysteries became subject to human calculation and exploration. The same cumulative cognitive advance which excited cosmological speculation also led to new concepts of knowledge. The closed sphere or single corpus, passed down from generation to generation, was replaced by an open-ended investigatory process pressing against ever advancing frontiers.

In attempting to explain 'how it all came about,' finally, new elements involving coordination and cooperation deserve not only more attention but also a more central place. When searching for the nurseries of a new philosophy, it seems unprofitable to linger too long in any one region, university, court or town – or focus too much attention on any one special skill or special scientific field. Certain universities, ateliers or lay academies may be singled out for special contributions. But the chief new feature that needs further attention is the simultaneous tapping of many varied talents at the same time. As the chief sponsors of field trips, open letters, advertisements for instruments and technical handbooks of all kinds, early printers ought to receive as much attention as is currently given to special occupational groups such as Paduan professors, Wittenberg botanists or quattrocento artist-engineers. Publication programs launched from urban workshops in many regions made it possible to coordinate scattered efforts and to expand the scope of investigations until (like the Blaeu *Grand Atlas*) they became truly world-wide.

Attempts to account for the rapid growth and expansion of scientific enterprise during the century of genius may be handled in much the same manner as treatments of nurseries, seed-beds and births. In explaining the 'acceleration of scientific advance,' there is much disagreement over whether to stress the role played by individual genius, the internal evolution of a speculative tradition, a new alliance between intellectuals and artisans, or a host of concurrent socio-economic or religious changes affecting the 'environment against which these discoveries took place.'[3] To say that argument over such issues is pointless, because *all* these 'factors' were at work, still leaves open the question of how and why they became operative when they did. Unless some new strategy is devised to handle this question, the old argument will break out once again. Since it perpetually revolves about the same issues, diminishing returns soon set in. One advantage of bringing printing into the discussion is that it enables us to tackle the open question directly without prolonging the same controversy *ad infinitum*.

As previous remarks suggest, the effects produced by printing may be plausibly related to an increased incidence of creative acts, to internally transformed speculative traditions, to exchanges between intellectuals and artisans, and indeed to each of the contested factors in current disputes. Thus we need not invoke some sort of 'mutation in the human gene pool' to explain an entire 'century of genius' nor do we need to deny that random motives (both personal and playful) entered into the successful puzzle-solving of the age. Without detracting from the strong personal flavor of each separate creative act, we may also make room for the new print technology which made food for thought much more abundant and allowed mental energies to be more efficiently used.

A similar approach would also take us further toward bridging the false dichotomy between the life of science and that of society at large.

<hr/>

[3] Kearney, 'Puritanism, Capitalism and the Scientific Revolution,' p. 81.

Changes wrought by printing had a more immediate effect on cerebral activities and on the learned professions than did many other kinds of 'external' events. Previous relations between masters and disciples were altered. Students who took full advantage of technical texts which served as silent instructors were less likely to defer to traditional authority and more receptive to innovating trends. Young minds provided with updated editions, especially of mathematical texts, began to surpass not only their own elders but the wisdom of ancients as well. Methods of measurement, records of observations and all forms of data collection were affected by printing. So too were the careers that could be pursued by teachers and preachers, physicians and surgeons, reckon-masters and artist-engineers. 'It is easy to agree with...contentions that a neat separation of internal and external factors is out of the question...but, as G. R. Elton wrote several years ago, there is work to be done rather than called for.'[4]

Before work can be done, however, some promising avenues of inquiry have to be opened up and more attention given to the presence of new workshops alongside older lecture halls. Printed materials should be allowed to affect thought-patterns, facilitate problem-solving, and, in general, penetrate the 'life of the mind.' Printers themselves must be allowed to work with Latin-writing professors as well as with vernacular-writing publicists and pamphleteers. In other words, the divisions that are often assumed to separate scholars from craftsmen, universities from urban workshops need to be reappraised.

This point applies to theories which internalize scientific problem-solving to the extent of ignoring the communications revolution and neglecting its possible relevance to the lectures and studies of learned men. It also applies to theories which deny that churchmen and schoolmen are capable of launching innovating trends. In this respect, Marxist theories of class struggle seem to be more of a hindrance than a help. To set an avant garde of early capitalists against a rear guard of Latin-reading clerks does little to clarify medieval developments and much to conceal the new interchanges that came after print shops spread. There are perfectly good reasons for associating printers with merchants and capitalists. There are none for detaching them from association with professors and friars – especially in the age of scholar-printers, when close collaboration was the rule. Indeed preachers and

4 'Toward a New History,' *Times Literary Supplement.*

teachers often turned to new forms of publicity with less conflict than did artisans accustomed to preserving trade secrets. Early printers were invited to set up presses in monasteries and colleges, while schoolmasters and tutors were much in demand as editors and translators. The formation of lay cultural centers outside universities and of the vernacular translation movement was of major significance. But no less significant were changes that affected university faculties and students seeking professional degrees. When Latin-writing professional élites are insulated from the effects of the new technology, internal divisions within the scholarly community become more puzzling than they need be and a rare opportunity to watch 'external' forces enter into the 'internal' life of science is lost.

These points carry beyond the special field of the history of science to the more general problem of relating socio-economic and political developments to intellectual and cultural ones. Attention focused on a communications shift encourages us to relate mind to society and at the same time to avoid forcing connections between economic class and intellectual superstructure, in order to fit a prefabricated scheme. Plausible relationships can be traced by taking into account the connecting links provided by a new communications network which coordinated diverse intellectual activities while producing tangible commodities to be marketed for profit. Since their commodities were sponsored and censored by officials as well as consumed by literate groups, the activities of early printers provide a natural connection between the movement of ideas, economic developments and affairs of church and state.

The policies pursued by merchant publishers offer a useful corrective to the conventional wisdom which opposes 'forward-looking' centralizing rulers and nation-building statesmen to 'backward' petty principalities and late medieval walled city states. The printing industries represented a 'forward-looking,' large-scale enterprise which flourished better in small loosely federated realms than in well consolidated larger ones. Printers also injected into diverse Protestant literary cultures foreign secular ingredients which will appear anomalous unless the peculiar workings of a censored book-trade are taken into account. When tracing the movement of ideas from Catholic South to Protestant North, factors which led to the prior movement of printing industries ought to be given due weight. How the center of gravity of the Republic of Letters shifted from sixteenth-century Venice to late seventeenth-century Amsterdam warrants special consideration in any social history of ideas.

When searching for the 'seedplots of Enlightenment thought' the *modus operandi* of the more celebrated master printers (such as Aldus Manutius, Robert Estienne, Oporinus, Plantin) deserves a closer look and so too does the relatively aristocratic nature of their clientèle. As Martin Lowry's forthcoming biography of Aldus points out; when the Venetian printer discarded the large folio in favor of a smaller octavo format he was aiming at serving the convenience of scholar–diplomats and patrician councillors of state. He was not thinking, somewhat absurdly, of tapping popular markets with texts devoted to classical Greek works. From the Aldine octavo of the 1500s to the Elsevier duodecimo of the 1630s the circulation of convenient pocket-sized editions altered circumstances within the Commonwealth of Learning, first of all. Before assuming that an altered world view implies the rise of a new class, it seems worth devoting more thought to intellectual regroupment among Latin-reading élites. By this means we may also rectify an imbalance created by current emphasis on popularizing trends and mass movements.

In this age when the paperback book is probably doing more to change the process of science education than all the new teaching methods, it should not be difficult to appreciate the intimate connection between the printer's craft and that of science...

If science helped give birth to the printed book, it was clearly the printed book that sent science from its medieval habits straight into the boiling scientific revolution...It was of course the rapid dissemination of knowledge to whole new classes that created the modern new attitudes to both science and religion at the end of the fifteenth century.[5]

This statement may have some validity with regard to the religious Reformation, but does not seem to apply to early-modern science. Mentelin's German Bible appeared in 1460, and forty years of vernacular Bible-printing (along with the increased output of other devotional literature) need to be considered when setting the stage for the Lutheran Revolt. But despite the early date of Regiomontanus' Nuremberg press (1474), the end of the fifteenth century still seems much too early to think of scientific knowledge being 'rapidly disseminated to whole new classes' by means of the printed word. Even later on, as we have

---

[5] Price, 'The Book as a Scientific Instrument,' pp. 102–4.

noted, Latin treatises by Copernicus, Harvey and Kepler were not disseminated in the same manner as Lutheran Bibles, broadsides and tracts. Bestsellerdom was reserved for prognostications and Sacrobosco's *Sphaera*. In 1500, Latin-learning was still restricted, scientific translation movements were just getting under way, the corrupted materials which were being duplicated had not yet been sorted out. To jump from 'the birth of the printed book' to the creation of 'modern new attitudes' so precipitously and by means of popularization raises doubts about assigning any significance to the advent of printing for scientific change. The precipitous jump also detaches the Reformation from the Copernican Revolution, while reinforcing the view that mobilization of 'whole new classes' is the only conceivable motor of major historical change.

The evangelical impulse which powered early presses had the most rapid spectacular consequences and provoked mass participation of new kinds. But this should not divert attention from more subtle yet equally irreversible transformations which altered the world view of Latin-reading élites. Several new features other than dissemination which were introduced by printing entered into the scientific revolution and played an essential part in the religious reformation as well. In relating the two movements we need to consider the way old attitudes were being implemented within learned communities, before expecting new attitudes to be created, let alone knowledge to be disseminated to whole new classes. Even when dealing with evangelical trends, this approach has merit. Earlier attitudes exhibited by Lollards, Waldensians, Hussites and the Brethren of the Common Life were being newly implemented by printing before full-fledged Protestant doctrines were born. In setting the stage for the Reformation, moreover, some attention must be given to those many pre-Reformation controversies which had less to do with vernacular translation than with trilingual studies and learned exegesis of Latin texts. In the scholar–printer's workshop, editors of patristic and of Alexandrian texts had a common point of encounter. More attention to changes affecting textual transmission among learned élites should bring us closer to understanding how different strands of early-modern intellectual history may be related to each other. In particular, it may help to clarify the relationship between religious and scientific change.

Thus we may see that the fate of texts inherited from Aristotle,

Galen and Ptolemy had much in common with that of texts inherited from Saint Jerome. Just as scribal scholars had all they could do to emend Saint Jerome's version and to protect it from further corruption, so too did medieval astronomers labor to preserve and emend Ptolemy's *Great Composition*. Much as trilingual studies, repeatedly called for, did not get launched until after the advent of printing; so too was reform of the Julian calendar frequently requested and never obtained. After the advent of printing, Jerome's version was protected from further corruption only to be threatened by the annotations of scholars who had acquired mastery of Hebrew and Greek. Similarly, Ptolemy's work was no sooner emended and purified than it too came under attack. As the 'second Ptolemy,' Copernicus (despite his personal distance from print shops) was cast in much the same role as was Erasmus who had set out to re-do the work of Saint Jerome. Both men set out to fulfill traditional programs: to emend the Bible and reform the Church; to emend the *Almagest* and help with calendar reform; but both used means that were untraditional and this propelled their work in an unconventional direction, so that they broke new paths in the very act of seeking to achieve old goals.

The new issues posed by sixteenth-century path-breaking works also led natural philosophers and theologians to divide along similar lines. Conservatives within both groups were placed in the awkward position of departing from precedents even while defending the *status quo*. Defenders of Aristotle and Galen who sought to fine professors for departing from fixed texts resembled those defenders of Jerome's translation who censored scholars for annotating scriptural editions. At the same time many churchmen and lay professors were attracted by new opportunities extended by printers to reach a wider audience, win new patrons and achieve celebrity. Members of both groups contributed their services as editors, translators, and authors to popular as well as to scholarly trends. Theologians who argued for a priesthood of all believers and translated Bibles were in much the same position as the friars, physicians and schoolmasters who compiled craft manuals and translated mathematical and medical texts. The vernacular translation movement not only enabled evangelists to bring the Gospel to Everyman but also tapped a vast reservoir of latent scientific talent by eliciting contributions from reckon-masters, instrument-makers and artist-engineers. Protestant encouragement of lay reading and self-help was especially favorable for interchanges between readers and publishers – which led to the quiet displacement of ancient authorities, such as Pliny, and to expansive data collection of a new kind. Finally the same censorship policies and élitist tendencies that discouraged Catholic Bible-printers eventually closed down scientific publication outlets in Catholic lands.

But although Protestant exploitation of printing linked the Reformation to early-modern science in diverse ways, and although scientific publication was increasingly taken over by Protestant printing firms, evangelists and virtuosi were still using the new powers of print for fundamentally different ends. The latter aimed not at spreading God's words but at deciphering His handiwork. The only way to 'open' the book of nature to public inspection required (paradoxically) a preliminary encoding of data into ever more sophisticated equations, diagrams, models and charts. For virtuosi the uses of publicity were much more problematic than for evangelists. The case of Galileo may be misleading in this regard. Exploiting his flair for publicity and gifts as a polemicist, he *did* act as a proselytizer for the Copernican cause. Catholic friars such as Bruno, Campanella and Foscarini also exhibited a kind of evangelical zeal in the same cause. So, too, did Rheticus, in his master's behalf. Nevertheless the downfall of Ptolemy, Galen and Aristotle did not come about as a result of cartoons and pamphleteering. Scientific change follows a different pattern than religious revivals. Publication was indispensable for anyone seeking to make a scientific contribution but the kind of publicity which made for bestsellerdom was often undesirable. Even now, reputable scientists fear the sensational coverage which comes from premature exposure of their views. Early-modern virtuosi had even better reasons for such fears. Many Copernicans (including Copernicus himself) took advantage of printed materials while shrinking from publicity. Many Puritan publicists and disciples of Francis Bacon proselytized on behalf of a 'new science' without favoring or even comprehending the technical Latin treatises which marked significant advance.

Visionary schemes for promoting useful knowledge, belief in science for the citizen and mathematics for the millions did, to be sure, enter into the views of the group responsible for launching the *Transactions* of the Royal Society. Nevertheless, contributions to this pioneering scientific journal were of significance insofar as they accomplished the purpose Oldenburg conveyed in his letter to Malpighi: to 'bring out the opinion of all the learned.' To make possible consensual validation by trained observers, experimenters and mathematicians entailed a different use of the press than efforts to spread glad tidings to all men. Eventually, access to scientific journals and societies was shut to all save a professionally trained élite. The rise of modern science entailed the discrediting, not only of Aristotelians, Galenists or Ptolemaists but also of self-proclaimed healers, 'empirics' and miracle workers who attacked book learning while publicizing themselves. From Paracelsus through Mesmer and on to the present, the press has lent itself to the purposes of pseudo-scientists as well as those of real scientists, and it is not always easy to tell the two groups apart. Distinguishing between scientific journals and sensational journalism is relatively simple at present. But during the early years of the Royal Society when sightings of monsters and marvels were still being credited and recorded, the two genres were easily confused. Confusion was further compounded by the workings of the Index which lumped dull treatises on physics with more sensational forbidden tracts and transformed advocacy of Copernicanism into a patriotic Protestant cause.

Thus an English Paracelsian did not find it incongruous to place the secretive Latin-writing Catholic Copernicus in the company of Lutheran reformers for having 'brought Ptolemeus' Rules Astronomicall and Tables of Motions' to 'their former puritie.' His argument suggests that Protestants linked the fate of the Vulgate with that of the *Almagest* – along lines which are by now familiar to the readers of this book. Much as the Protestants had purified Scripture, he said, 'by expelling the clowdes of Romish religion which had darkened the trueth of the worde of God,' so too Copernicus had purified tables which had become corrupted 'by a long excesse of time.'[6] Copernicus was thus cast in much the same conservative role as the editor of the London 'Polyglotte' who claimed in his Prospectus to have freed the Scriptures 'from error, from the negligence of scribes, the injury of times, the wilful corruption of sectaries and heretics.'[7] This relatively

---

[6] Cited by Allen Debus, *The English Paracelsians*, p. 59, from a treatise by 'R. Bostocke Esq.,' London, 1585. Although Bostocke's comment seems to be pointed at the *Prutenic Tables* which were compiled by Erasmus Reinhold who used calculations in Copernicus' *De Revolutionibus* but rejected the geokinetic hypothesis, it probably implied, in the author's mind, support of the latter hypothesis.

[7] Brian Walton's *Prospectus* for the London 'Polyglotte' of 1657 is cited by Hendricks, 'Profitless Printing.'

conservative Erasmian theme with its emphasis on emendation and purification also lent itself to the purposes of those who sought to legitimize the Royal Society, as is suggested by the often-cited comment from Bishop Sprat's *History of the Royal Society*. The Royal Society and the Anglican Church, the Bishop said, 'both may lay equal claim to the word Reformation,'

the one having compassed it in Religion, the other purposing it in Philosophy...They both have taken a like course to bring this about each of them passing by the corrupt copies and referring themselves to the perfect originals for their instruction; the one to Scripture the other to the huge Volume of Creatures...[8]

It seems significant that when such remarks are cited by historians they are not seen to relate to the shift from script to print (despite the reference to the passing by of 'corrupt copies') but are used instead to reiterate the Bishop's three-hundred-year-old claim that the Reformation and the scientific revolution are somehow connected. As long as printing is left out of account this thesis seems destined to engender an inconclusive debate. To leave printing out of the picture is not only to conceal significant links but also to overlook equally important disjunctions.

Scriptural and scientific traditions had taken a 'like course' in the age of scribes. By the time of the Reformation, however, they had come to a parting of the ways. Even while providing both biblical scholars and natural philosophers with new means of achieving long-lived goals, the new technology had driven a wedge between the two groups and was propelling them in different directions.

Until the advent of printing, scientific inquiries about 'how the heavens go' were linked with religious concerns about 'how to go to heaven.' Erasmus and Copernicus had shared a common interest in deciphering ancient place names and dating old records. Insofar as the movable holy festival of Easter posed problems, astronomers were needed to help the Church commemorate Gospel truths. After the advent of printing, however, the study of celestial mechanics was propelled in new directions and soon reached levels of sophistication that left calendrical problems and ancient schemes of reckoning far behind. The need to master philology or learn Greek became ever more

---

[8] Sprat, *History of the Royal Society*, part 3, section 23, p. 371. This citation appears in works by S. F. Mason, D. S. Kemsley, R. Hooykaas and others mentioned in chap. 8 above.

important for Bible study and ever less so for nature study. Indeed, difficulties engendered by diverse Greek and Arabic expressions, by medieval Latin abbreviations, by confusion between Roman letters and numbers, by neologisms, copyists' errors and the like were so successfully overcome that modern scholars are frequently absent-minded about the limitations on progress in the mathematical sciences which scribal procedures imposed.[9] From Roger Bacon's day to that of Francis Bacon, mastery of geometry, astronomy or optics had gone together with the retrieval of ancient texts and pursuit of Greek studies. But by the seventeenth century, Nature's language was being emancipated from the old confusion of tongues. Diverse names for flora and fauna became less confusing when placed beneath identical pictures. Constellations and landmasses could be located without recourse to uncertain etymologies, once placed on uniform maps and globes. Logarithm tables and slide rules provided common measures for surveyors in different lands. Whereas the Vulgate was followed by a succession of polyglot editions and multiplying variants; the downfall of the *Almagest* paved the way for the formulation by Newton of a few elegant simple universal laws. The development of neutral pictorial and mathematical vocabularies made possible a large-scale pooling of talents for analyzing data, and led to the eventual achievement of a consensus that cut across all the old frontiers.

Vesalius' recourse to pictorial statements like Galileo's preference for circles and triangles suggests why it is unwise to dwell too long on whether treatises were written in the vernacular or in Latin, and why parallels between evangelical reformers and early-modern scientists should not be pressed too far. Many proponents of the new philosophy favored plain speaking and opposed mystification just as did evangelical reformers. Nevertheless the language employed by new astronomers and anatomists was still incomprehensible to the untutored layman and did not resemble anything spoken by the man in the street. For the most part, it was an *unspoken* language quite unlike that favored by

9 Such absent-mindedness is reinforced by modern editions such as the splendid volume on medieval manuscript versions of Archimedes by Clagett, *Archimedes* where the author has taken pains to exclude 'corrupt and senseless readings,' to reconstruct diagrams where figures were obscure and incorrect, to convert a mixture of Roman numerals and rhetorical expressions into consistently used Indo-Arabic numerals, etc. (pp. xv, 36–7); in short: to eliminate just those aspects of major technical works which gave the most trouble before print. On confusion over terms such as cipher and zero which came from the same Arabic word, see Dantzig, *Number*, p. 32.

Protestants who preserved links between pulpit and press in seeking to spread the Word. Recourse to 'silent instructors' conveying precisely detailed non-phonetic messages helped to free technical literature from semantic snares. 'The reign of words' had ended, noted Fontenelle in 1733, 'things' were now in demand. Two hundred years earlier, verbal dispute was already being abandoned in favor of visual demonstration.

> I dare affirm a man shall more profit in one week by figures and charts well and perfectly made than he shall by the only reading or hearing the rules of that science by the space of half a year at the least.

So wrote Thomas Elyot in 1531, in the course of recommending courses in drawing to educators.[10]

Publication before printing had often entailed giving dictation or reading aloud. In contrast to scribal culture which had fostered 'hearing the rules of a given science,' print culture made possible the simultaneous distribution of 'well made figures and charts.' In this way, it not only transformed communications within the Commonwealth of Learning, but laid the basis for new confidence in human capacity to arrive at certain knowledge of the 'laws of Nature and of Nature's God.'

> What threatened the very foundations of the Church was the new concept of truth proclaimed by Galileo. Alongside the truth of revelation comes now an independent and original truth of nature. This truth is revealed not in God's words but in his work; it is not based on the testimony of Scripture or tradition but is visible to us at all times. But it is understandable only to those who know nature's handwriting and can decipher her text. The truth of nature cannot be expressed in mere words...[but]...in mathematical constructions, figures and numbers. And in these symbols nature presents itself in perfect form and clarity. Revelation by means of the sacred word can never achieve...such precision, for words are always...ambiguous... Their meaning must always be given them by man...In nature...the whole plan of the universe lies before us.[11]

This famous passage brilliantly describes a major intellectual transformation but stops short of explaining why it happened when it did. Cassirer's description needs to be supplemented by noting that 'mathematical constructions, figures and numbers' had not always presented themselves 'in perfect form and clarity.' 'To discover the truth of

[10] Cited from *Boke called the Gouvernour* (1531) by Watson, *The Beginning of Teaching*, p. 136.
[11] Cassirer, *The Philosophy of the Enlightenment*, p. 43.

propositions in Euclid,' wrote John Locke, 'there is little need or use of revelation, God having furnished us with a natural and surer means to arrive at knowledge of them.'[12] In the eleventh century, however, God had not furnished Western scholars with a natural or sure means of grasping a Euclidean theorem. Instead the most learned men in Christendom engaged in a fruitless search to discover what Euclid meant when referring to interior angles.[13]

A new confidence in the accuracy of mathematical constructions, figures and numbers was predicated on a method of duplication that transcended older limits imposed by time and space and that presented identical data in identical form to men who were otherwise divided by cultural and geographical frontiers. The same confidence was generated by pictorial statements which, as Sir Joseph Banks observed, provided a common measure which spoke 'universally to all mankind.' It was conveyed by the maps to which Kenneth Boulding assigns an 'extraordinary authority greater than that of all sacred books.'[14] But it was not generated by the scholarly controversies which accompanied the expanding editions of the sacred book of Western Christendom.

Even while the study of nature was increasingly freed from translation problems, the study of Scripture was becoming more ensnared. Not only did vernacular translations fragment the religious experience of the peoples of Latin Christendom and help to precipitate prolonged civil wars; but successive polyglot versions brought the erudite scholars of the Commonwealth of Learning no closer to finding the pure original words of God. Tycho Brahe, confronted by conflicting astronomical tables based on corrupted data, could carry out his vow to check both versions against a 'pure original' – against fresh observation of uncorrupted 'writing in the sky.' But dissatisfaction with corrupted copies of Saint Jerome's Latin translation could not be overcome in the same way. Instead it led to multilingual confusion and a thickening special literature devoted to variants and alternative theories of composition. The mystical illumination which had presided over creation flickered ever more dimly as pedants argued about how to date the event and how to authenticate versions of Genesis. Baroque monuments of erudition, which had been designed to obtain a clear view of the

---

[12] John Locke, *An Essay on Human Understanding*, book IV, chap. XVIII.

[13] See chap. 5 n. 133, above, for reference to Southern's account of Fulbert of Chartres.

[14] See chap. 5 n. 46, above, for reference to Sir Joseph's comment. For discussion of Boulding's disassociated transcript, see pp. 478 ff, above.

divine will, not only fell short of their objective. In the end, they made it seem more elusive than before.

It is surely one of the ironies of the history of Western civilization that Bible studies aimed at penetrating Gothic darkness in order to recover pure Christian truth – aimed, that is, at removing glosses and commentaries in order to lay bare the pure 'plain' text – ended by interposing an impenetrable thicket of recondite annotation between Bible-reader and Holy Book. In his inaugural lecture at Wittenberg, the young Philip Melanchthon scornfully referred to the neglect of Greek studies by angelic doctors, to the superficial glosses of ignorant scribes and to the soiling of sacred Scriptures with foreign matter. He called for a return to the 'pure' Greek and Hebrew sources.[15] But the more trilingual studies progressed, the more scholars wrangled over the meaning of words and phrases and even over the placement of vowel points. The very waters from which the Latinists drank became roiled and muddy as debates among scholars were prolonged. Hobbes and Spinoza both plunged into Bible study and found in the sharp clarity of Euclidean proofs a refreshing contrast to the murky ambiguities of scriptural texts. Sir William Petty protested against teaching boys 'hard Hebrew words in the Bible' and contrasted the profitable 'study of things to a Rabble of Words.'[16] We have already encountered Sir Thomas Browne's preference for 'Archimedes who speaketh exactly' as against 'the sacred text which speaketh largely.' Robert Boyle might endow a lecture series to reconcile scriptural revelation with the mathematical principles of natural philosophy; Isaac Newton might struggle to prove Old Testament tales conformed to a chronology that meshed with celestial clockwork. God's 'two books,' nevertheless, had come to a parting of the ways.

One day in the eighteenth century, some Swedish scientists discovered a certain alteration in the shores of the Baltic...the theologians of Stockholm made representations to the Government that 'this remark of the... scientists, not being consistent with Genesis must be condemned.' To whom reply was made that God had made both the Baltic and Genesis...if there was any contradiction between the two works, the error must lie in the copies we have of the book than in the Baltic Sea of which we have the original.[17]

[15] Melanchthon's lecture is cited in Hillerbrand (ed), *The Reformation*, pp. 59–60.
[16] Petty's comments, are cited by Jones, *Ancients and Moderns*, p. 91.
[17] Arthur Wilson, *Diderot*, p. 143.

Thus the effect of printing on Bible study was in marked contrast with its effect on nature study. This contrast is concealed when one places an exclusive emphasis on popularizing themes, and couples the spread of vernacular Bibles with that of technical texts. It is also obscured by the anti-papist propaganda which linked the emendation of the *Almagest* with that of the Vulgate. Corruption by copyists had provided churchmen and astronomers with a common enemy; but once this enemy was vanquished, former collaborators took divergent paths. To observe this divergence requires studying internal transformations within a Commonwealth of Learning where Latin Bibles had long been studied although full polyglot editions had not been seen. In addition to new problems posed for this community by polyglot versions of sacred words, old limits set on data collection and new advantages provided by printed tables, charts and maps also need to be taken into account. One may then set the stage for Enlightenment thought without resorting to vague concepts such as 'modernity' or becoming entangled in debates over bourgeois ideology. At least in my view the changes wrought by printing provide the most plausible point of departure for explaining how confidence shifted from divine revelation to mathematical reasoning and man-made maps.

The fact that religious and scientific traditions were affected by printing in markedly different ways points to the complex and contradictory nature of the communications shift, and suggests the futility of trying to encapsulate its consequences in any one formula. When considering Protestant iconoclasm or increased Bible-reading, it may seem useful to envisage a movement going from 'image to word'; but one must be prepared to use the reverse formula 'word to image' when setting the stage for the rise of modern science. In the latter case, printing reduced translation problems, transcended linguistic divisions and helped to bridge earlier divisions between university lectures and artisan crafts. In religious affairs, however, the communications shift had a divisive effect; permanently fragmenting Western Christendom along both geographic and sociological lines. Not only were Catholic regions set off from Protestant ones but within different regions religious experience was also internally bifurcated. Loss of confidence in God's words among cosmopolitan élites was coupled with enhanced opportunities for evangelists and priests to spread glad tidings and rekindle faith. Enlightened deists who adhered to the 'Laws of Nature and Nature's

God' were thus placed at a distance from enthusiasts who were caught up in successive waves of religious revivals.

In all regions the ebb and flow of religious devotion affected diverse social strata at different times. But the Bible became 'the treasure of the humble,' with unpredictable consequences only in Protestant realms. Among Protestants, the universalistic impulse to spread the Gospel far and wide had special paradoxical results. Vernacular Bibles authorized by Protestant rulers helped to Balkanize Christendom and to nationalize what had previously been a more cosmopolitan sacred book. Bible-reading householders acquired an enhanced sense of spiritual dignity and individual worth. An 'inner light' kindled by the printed word became the basis for the shared mystical experiences of separate sects. Yet even while spiritual life was being enriched, it was also being tarnished by commercial drives. Where indulgence sellers were discredited, Bible salesmen multiplied.

In print shops especially, old missionary impulses were combined with the demands imposed by an expanding capitalist enterprise. In the early-modern print shop, however, several other impulses also converged. Was the driving power of capitalism stronger than the long-lived drive for fame? Both together surely were stronger than either one alone. Did not the presses also offer rulers a way of extending their charisma and furnish significant help to impersonal bureaucrats as well? Among map-publishers, reckon-masters and artisans, as we have seen, printing acted by a kind of marvelous alchemy to transmute private interest into public good. It also catered to the vanity of pedants, artists and literati. When dealing with the new powers of the press, one may make a sound case for a multivariable explanation even while stressing the significance of the single innovation. The mixture of many motives provided a more powerful impetus than any single motive (whether that of profit-seeking capitalist or Christian evangelist) could have provided by itself. In this sense the use of early presses by Western Europeans was 'over-determined.' The convergence of different impulses proved irresistible, producing a massive irreversible cultural 'change of phase'.

The early presses which were first established between 1460 and 1480 were powered by many different forces which had been incubating in the age of scribes. In a different cultural context, the same technology might have been used for different ends (as was the case in China and

Korea) or it might have been unwelcome and not been used at all (as was the case in many regions outside Europe where Western missionary presses were the first to be installed). In this light one may agree with authorities who hold that the duplicating process which was developed in fifteenth-century Mainz, was *in itself* of no more consequence than any other inanimate tool. Unless it had been deemed useful to human agents it would never have been put into operation in fifteenth-century European towns. Under different circumstances, moreover, it might have been welcomed and put to entirely different uses – monopolized by priests and rulers, for example, and withheld from free-wheeling urban entrepreneurs.

Such counter-factual speculation is useful for suggesting the importance of institutional context when considering technological innovation. Yet the fact remains that once presses were established in numerous European towns, the transforming powers of print did begin to take effect. The new shops themselves interacted with the urban élites who received them in a manner that produced occupational mutations and intellectual regroupment. Here again, one may agree that even when acting as agents of change, early printers could be effective only in combination with other forces. Indeed, the very fact that they functioned as catalysts and as coordinators was of special significance. However much one may wish to stress reciprocal interaction and avoid a simplistic 'impact' model; one must leave room for the special features which distinguish the advent of printing from other innovations.

One cannot treat printing as just one among many elements in a complex causal nexus for the communications shift transformed the nature of the causal nexus itself. It is of special historical significance because it produced fundamental alterations in prevailing patterns of continuity and change. On this point one must take strong exception to the views expressed by humanists who carry their hostility to technology so far as to deprecate the very tool which is most indispensable to the practice of their own crafts.

The powers which shape men's lives may be expressed in books and type, but by and of itself printing... is only a tool, an instrument, and the multiplication of tools and instruments does not of itself affect intellectual and spiritual life.[18]

[18] Archer Taylor, 'The Influence of Printing,' p. 13.

Intellectual and spiritual life, far from remaining unaffected, were profoundly transformed by the multiplication of new tools for duplicating books in fifteenth-century Europe. The communications shift altered the way Western Christians viewed their sacred book and the natural world. It made the words of God appear more multiform and His handiwork more uniform. The printing press laid the basis for both literal fundamentalism and for modern science. It remains indispensable for humanistic scholarship. It is still responsible for our museum-without-walls.

SOME FINAL REMARKS

This book has stopped short in the age of the wooden hand press. It has barely touched on the industrialization of paper-making and the harnessing of iron presses to steam. Nothing has been said about the railway tracks and telegraph wires which linked European capitals in the mid-nineteenth century, or about the Linotype and Monotype machines which went together with mass literacy and tabloid journalism. The typewriter, the telephone, and a vast variety of more recent media have been entirely ignored. Too much territory has been traversed too rapidly as it is. Because contrary views have been expressed, however, it is necessary to point out that the process that began in the mid-fifteenth century has not ceased to gather momentum in the age of the computer print-out and the television guide. Indeed the later phases of an on-going communications revolution seem altogether relevant to what is happening within our homes, universities, or cities at present. In particular, they are relevant to apocalyptic pronouncements about contemporary Western culture delivered by modern intellectuals and literati.

Since the advent of movable type, an enhanced capacity to store and retrieve, preserve and transmit has kept pace with an enhanced capacity to create and destroy, to innovate or outmode. The somewhat chaotic appearance of modern Western culture owes as much, if not more, to the duplicative powers of print as it does to the harnessing of new powers in the past century. It may yet be possible to view recent developments in historical perspective provided one takes into account neglected aspects of a massive and decisive cultural 'change of phase' that occurred five centuries ago.

Some of the unanticipated consequences that came in the wake of Gutenberg's invention are now available for retrospective analysis – certainly more than could be seen in Bacon's day. Others are still unfolding, however, and *these* unanticipated consequences are, by definition, impossible to gauge at present. Few, if any, of the changes we have outlined could have been predicted. Even with hindsight they are difficult to describe. Clearly, more study is needed, if only to counteract premature leaps in the dark. A continuous accumulation of printed materials has certain disadvantages. (The voracious appetite of Chronos was feared in the past. A monstrous capacity to disgorge poses more of a threat at present.) But the capacity to scan accumulated records also confers certain modest advantages. We may examine how our predecessors read various portents and auguries and compare their prophecies with what actually occurred. We may thus discern over the past century or so a tendency to write off by premature obituaries the very problems that successive generations have had to confront.

This impulse to end tales that are still unfolding owes much to the prolongation of nineteenth-century historical schemes, especially those of Hegel and Marx which point logical dialectical conflicts toward logical dialectical ends. The possibility of an indefinite prolongation of fundamentally contradictory trends is not allowed for in these grand designs. Yet we still seem to be experiencing the contradictory effects of a process which fanned the flames of religious zeal and bigotry while fostering a new concern for ecumenical concord and toleration; which fixed linguistic and national divisions more permanently while creating a cosmopolitan Commonwealth of Learning and extending communications networks which encompassed the entire world. At the very least, this book may have indicated the premature character of prevailing grand designs and of the fashionable trend-spotting that extrapolates from them. For the full dimensions of the gulf that separates the age of scribes from that of printers have yet to be fully probed. The unevenly phased continuous process of recovery and innovation that began in the second half of the fifteenth century remains to be described.

To draw any further conclusions about the force, effect, or consequences of the advent of printing on the basis of these chapters would also be premature. My conjectures have been based on uneven knowledge of pertinent data, much of it drawn from unreliable general accounts, and all of it relevant to very few regions. Too many gaps have been filled in by logical inference. To set forth views that may be invalid can be justified when it paves the way for more educated guess-work based on more empirical evidence. A more troublesome issue is posed by speculations that resist invalidation because imponderables are involved. However many crude generalizations may be discarded or refined, there seems to be no way of excluding such imponderables when dealing with this particular topic. One might conceivably measure the varying output of different kinds of printed materials, analyze their contents, examine their distribution, estimate their rate of consumption. There is no way of measuring what may be 'read into' any given text or to assess the effect of 'action at a distance' without resorting to speculation. No one may claim to read the minds of other readers without leaving room for uncertainty; it is even more difficult to read the minds of those who have long since gone to their graves. Imponderables of this kind have, however, to be included in any effort to find out how things happened as they did. When silent, invisible interactions are ignored because they defy precise analysis, more mysterious spirits, ethics, and isms are likely to take their place. There are advantages in defining margins of uncertainty with some precision and thereby holding conspiratorial myth-makers at bay.

'He would be a bold man' says Somervell in discussing certain popular nineteenth-century English novelists, who would deny them 'an influence on general elections.'[19] Historians who exclude reading habits and belles lettres from their work appear to be cautiously avoiding intractable data where firm conclusions are impossible. Yet it may be rash, not cautious, to base analyses on 'hard facts' while leaving 'soft' or 'mushy' issues to others. Possibly such issues appear softer and mushier than need be because most practitioners of *Ideengeschichte*, literary historians, and belles lettrists, have inherited a venerable tradition of proud ignorance of matters material, mechanical, or commercial. It is futile to condemn intellectual divisions of labor. The 'universal bibliography' compiled by Conrad Gesner in the sixteenth century was not only the first of its kind. It was also the last attempt by a single scholar to achieve comprehensive coverage of every work in print. Increasing specialization is inevitable, given an expanding knowledge industry. Granted that intensive cultivation of different fields must be separately undertaken, there is still no warrant for

[19] Somervell, *English Thought*, p. 8.

allocating all the 'hard' facts to some fields; all the 'soft' ones to others. Specialists must reckon with both, whatever historical changes they may choose to explore.

Those who are concerned with the 'shaping of the modern mind' might profitably focus more attention on data-processing within early workshops where laboratories of advanced erudition were maintained and where tangible commodities were produced and distributed in measurable quantities. Despite invented accommodation addresses, most publications may be placed and dated with a fair degree of accuracy. Their contents may be tabulated and analyzed. Shifting centers of production and distribution networks may also be located on real maps. Studies pertaining to the 'social history of ideas' and comparative studies of many other kinds would probably be illuminated by more precise analysis of these matters. Those who are concerned with the shaping of modern society – with political economy, legal institutions, or affairs of church and state – however, have to deal with issues that cannot be handled by rigorous quantitative analysis. For they are confronted by the more indirect effects of the consumption of printed materials. Problematic issues pertaining to literacy, book-reading, and new mental habits cannot be avoided when dealing with 'rationalization,' 'modernization,' 'centralization,' élite regroupment, religious divisions, upward mobility, rising expectations, or entrepreneurial organization. While changes affecting paper production, credit or contracts may be related fairly directly to the expansion of printing industries, the same is not true of changes associated with class consciousness or, indeed, any form of group identity. Scepticism is called for about theories pertaining to a meeting of minds or a touching of hearts. Such theories must nonetheless be framed in order to come to terms with changes that affected consciousness and identity and hence necessarily engaged human thoughts and feelings. Thus a salutary inversion of customary alignments might result from exploring the consequences that came in the wake of the printing press. A greater respect for hard facts and material technologies among humanist scholars and intellectual historians; more appreciation of the role played by imponderables and the reality of intangible phenomena among those who investigate socio-economic, political, or institutional changes could, conceivably, lead to more fruitful collaboration between groups of specialists.

Many advantages would, I believe, be gained by following Bacon's advice. Of them all none seems more important than seeing how many of the facts of life that are presently being kept apart actually belong together.

BIBLIOGRAPHICAL INDEX

Given the survey of relevant literature in the first chapter of this book and the space devoted to historiography in other sections, it seemed redundant to supply a bibliographical essay. A conventional comprehensive bibliography was also ruled out on the grounds that more than a hundred pages of book titles constituted an inefficient use of space. This index will enable readers to retrieve full titles of all the works cited in the footnotes while displaying the full range of studies used for my book. Important works that were consulted but are not cited in specific footnotes have been listed without entries. Readers who want to keep up with the most recent work should note that 1976 is my cut-off date and should consult the special periodicals cited in chapter 1 (note 2) volume I, where notices of relevant new studies are to be found.

Adams, Henry. *The Education of Henry Adams: An Autobiography* (Cambridge, Mass., 1918). **x.**

Adamson, J. W. *The Illiterate Anglo Saxon and Other Essays* (Cambridge, 1956). Consulted but not cited.

  'The Extent of Literacy in England in the Fifteenth and Sixteenth Centuries: Notes and Conjectures,' *The Library*, 4th ser. x (1929) 163–93. **62.**

Adelmann, Howard B. Introduction to *The Embryological Treatises of Hieronymus Fabricius of Aquapendente* (Ithaca, New York, 1942). **476, 562, 573-4.**

  Marcello Malpighi and the Evolution of Embryology (5 vol. Ithaca, New York, 1967). **664-5.**

Adhémar, J. 'L'Estampe et la Transmission des Formes Maniéristes,' *Le Triomphe du Maniérisme Européen* (Amsterdam, 1955). **82.**

Africa, Thomas. 'Copernicus' Relation to Aristarchus and Pythagorus,' *Isis* 52 (1961) 403–9. **577.**

Aidan, Francis (Cardinal Gasquet). 'Roger Bacon and the Latin Vulgate,' *Roger Bacon Essays*, ed. A. G. Little (Oxford, 1914) 89–99. **339.**

Aiton, E. J. 'Essay Review,' *History of Science* 11 (1973) 217–30. **638.**

  'Essay Review,' *Studies in History and Philosophy of Science* I (1970–71) 265–73. **565.**

Allen, P. S. *The Age of Erasmus* (Oxford, 1914). **19, 175.**

  Erasmus: Lectures and Wayfaring Sketches (London, 1934). **81.**

'Erasmus' Relations with his Printers,' *Transactions of the Bibliographical Society* XIII (Oct. 1913–March 1915) 297–323. **401.**

Allen, Ward, tr. and ed. *Translating for King James: Notes Made by a Translator of the King James Bible* (Vanderbilt University Press, 1969). **360.**

Allison, A. F. and Rogers, D. M. *A Catalogue of Catholic Books in English Printed Abroad or Secretly in England, 1558–1640* (London, 1964). **354.**

Altick, R. *The English Common Reader. A Social History of the Mass Reading Public 1800–1900* (Chicago, 1963). **65, 130–1, 134, 149, 153, 361, 364, 422.**

Ames, Joseph. *See* Thomas F. Dibdin.

Arber, Agnes. 'From Medieval Herbalism to the Birth of Modern Botany,' *Science, Medicine, and History. Essays . . . In Honor of Charles Singer,* ed. E. A. Underwood (2 vol. Oxford, 1953) I, 317–36. **266, 487.**

Archer, Peter, S.J. *The Christian Calendar and the Gregorian Reform* (New York, 1941). **610.**

Ariès, Philippe. *Centuries of Childhood: A Social History of Family Life,* tr. R. Baldick (New York, 1962). **431-2.**

L'Enfant et La Vie Familiale sous L'Ancien Régime (Paris, 1973). **431.**

Armstrong, Elizabeth. *Robert Estienne, Royal Printer* (Cambridge, 1954). **75, 87, 387, 399, 401, 411, 442, 447.**

Arnold, Klaus, ed. and introduction to Johannes Trithemius, *In Praise of Scribes – De Laude Scriptorum,* tr. R. Behrendt (Lawrence, Kansas, 1974). **14-15, 94-5, 97, 200.** *See also* Johannes Trithemius.

Artz, Frederick. *The Development of Technical Education in France, 1500–1850* (Cambridge, Mass., 1966). **351.**

Askew, Pamela. 'A Melancholy Astronomer by Giovanni Serodine,' *The Art Bulletin* XLVII (March 1965) 121–8. **577.**

Aston, Margaret. *The Fifteenth Century: The Prospect of Europe* (London, 1968). **310.**

'The Fiery Trigon Conjunction: An Elizabethan Astrological Prediction,' *Isis* 61 (1970) 159–87. **619.**

'John Wycliffe's Reformation Reputation,' *Past and Present* 30 (April 1965) 23–52. **304, 345.**

'Lollardy and the Reformation: Survival or Revival?' *History* XLIX (1964) 149–70. **304.**

Review article, *Shakespeare Studies* IV (1968) 388. **415.**

Atkinson, Geoffroy. *Les Nouveaux Horizons de la Renaissance Française* (Paris, 1935). **303.**

Auerbach, Erich. *Literary Language and its public in late Latin Antiquity and in the Middle Ages,* tr. R. Manheim (New York, 1965). **334.**

'The Author and his Ghosts,' *Times Literary Supplement* (Sept. 22, 1972) 1121. **122.**

Axtell, J. L. 'Locke's Review of the *Principia*,' *Notes and Records of the Royal Society of London,* XX (1965) 152–61. **638.**

Bachman, A. *Censorship in France from 1715 to 1750* (New York, 1934). **145.**

Bacon, Francis. *Francis Bacon. A Selection of His Works,* ed. S. Warhaft (College Classics in English, ed. H. Northrop Frye) (Toronto, 1965). **455.**

Bagrow, Leo. *History of Cartography,* rev. and ed. R. A. Skelton (Cambridge, Mass., 1964). **53, 469, 512, 514.**

Bailey, John E. 'Dee and Trithemius' Steganography,' *Notes and Queries* (May 24, 1879), 5th ser. XI, 401–2, 422–3. **96, 137.**

Bainton, Roland. *Here I Stand: A Life of Martin Luther* (New York, 1950). **307.**

'Interpretations of the Reformation,' *The American Historical Review* LXVI (Oct. 1960) 74–84. **378.**

'Man, God and Church,' *The Renaissance: Six Essays* (New York, 1962) 77–96. **238.**

Review, *The Journal of Modern History* 43 (June 1971) 309–10. **445.**

Baker, Herschel. *The Wars of Truth* (Cambridge, Mass., 1952). **321.**

Baldwin, T. W. *William Shakespere's Small Latine & Lesse Greeke* (2 vol. Urbana, Ill., 1944). **350.**

Barber, Elinor. *The Bourgeoisie in Eighteenth Century France* (Princeton, 1955). **539.**

Barnes, Annie. *Jean Le Clerc et la République des Lettres* (Paris, 1938). **137, 321, 332, 420, 647.**

Barnett, S. W. 'Silent Evangelism: Presbyterians and the Mission Press in China, 1807–1860,' *Journal of Presbyterian History* 49 (Winter 1971) 287–302. **317.**

Baron, Hans. *The Crisis of the Early Italian Renaissance* (rev. edn, 1 vol. Princeton, New Jersey, 1966). **185.**

'The *Querelle* of the Ancients and Moderns as a Problem for Renaissance Scholarship,' *Journal of the History of Ideas* XX (Jan. 1959) 3–22. **123, 185.**

'Toward a More Positive Evaluation of the Fifteenth Century Renaissance,' *Journal of the History of Ideas* IV (Jan. 1943) 21–49. **251, 521, 526.**

Baroni, Victor. *La Contre Réforme devant la Bible* (Thèse de Doctorat) (Lausanne, 1943). **349.**

Baroque and Rococo Pictorial Imagery: The 1758–1760 Hertel edition of Ripa's Iconologia, ed. E. A. Moser (New York, 1971). **662.**

Basalla, George, ed. and introduction. *The Rise of Modern Science: External or Internal Factors?* (Lexington, Mass., 1968). **459.**

Bataillon, Marcel. *Erasme et L'Espagne. Recherches sur l'Histoire Spirituelle du XVIe Siècle* (Paris, 1937) chap. xi. Consulted but not cited.

Etudes sur le Portugal au Temps de l'Humanisme (Coimbra, 1952). Consulted but not cited.

'Philippe Galle et Arias Montano,' *Bibliothèque d'Humanisme et Renaissance* II (1942) 132–60. **20.**

Bate, W. Jackson. *The Burden of the Past and the English Poet* (Cambridge, Mass., 1970). **192.**

'Battle of the Senses,' *Times Literary Supplement* (March 1, 1963) 156. **40.**

Baumann, F. E. 'Mutianus Rufus and Natural Religion: A Test Case,' *Renaissance Quarterly* XXIX (1976) 567–98. **273.**

Baxandall, Michael. *Giotto and the Orators: Humanist Observers of Painting in Italy and the Discovery of Pictorial Composition 1350–1450* (Oxford, 1971). **232, 293, 604.**

Painting and Experience in 15th Century Italy (Oxford, 1972). **293.**

Beardsley, Theodore S. 'The Classics and Their Spanish Translators in the Sixteenth Century,' *Renaissance and Reformation* VIII (Toronto, 1971) 2–9. **360, 408.**

Beaujouan, Guy. 'Motives and Opportunities for Science in the Medieval University,' *Scientific Change: Symposium on the History of Science*, ed. A. C. Crombie (New York, 1963) 219–36. **382, 537.**

Beazley, C. R. *The Dawn of Modern Geography* (3 vol. Oxford, 1906). **516.**

Bebb, P. N. 'The Lawyers, Dr. Christoph Scheurl and the Reformation in Nürnberg,'

The Social History of the Reformation (Festschrift for Harold Grimm) ed. L. P. Buck and J. W. Zophy (Columbus, Ohio, 1972) 52–73. **308, 404.**

Bec, Christian. *Les Marchands Ecrivains; Affaires et Humanisme à Florence 1375–1434* (Paris, 1967). **62.**

Bedini, S. A. 'The Instruments of Galileo,' *Galileo, Man of Science*, ed. Ernan McMullin (New York, 1967) 256–92. **525.**

Bedini, S. A. and Maddison, F. R. 'Mechanical Universe,' *Transactions of the American Philosophical Society* 56 (Oct. 1966) 3–67. **589.**

Ben-David, Joseph. 'The Scientific Role; The Conditions of Its Establishment in Europe' (1st pub. in *Minerva* IV (1965) 15–20), *Western Civilization: Recent Interpretations*, ed. C. D. Hamilton (2 vol. Chicago, 1973) 556–78. **654-5, 666.**

Benesch, Otto. *The Art of the Renaissance in Northern Europe* (rev. edn, London, 1965). **589.**

Benjamin, F. S. and Toomer, C. J. *Campanus of Novara and Medieval Planetary Theory* (Madison, Wis., 1971). **465, 512, 536.**

Bennett, H. S. *English Books and Readers 1475–1557* (Cambridge, 1952). **62, 104-5, 127, 130, 139, 358, 361.**
English Books and Readers 1558–1603 (Cambridge, 1965). **358.**
'The Production and Dissemination of Vernacular Manuscripts in the Fifteenth Century,' *The Library*, 5th ser. I (1947) 167–78. **11.**

Benton, John, ed. and introduction. *Self and Society in Medieval France: The Memoirs of Abbot Guibert of Nogent (1064?–c. 1125)* (New York, 1970). **236.**

Benzing, Josef. *Buchdrucker-Lexicon des 16 Jahrhunderts* (Deutsches Sprachgebiet) (Frankfurt, 1952). **99, 206, 307, 371, 617.**

Berelson, Bernard and Janowitz, Morris. *Reader in Public Opinion and Communication* (Glencoe, Ill., 1953). **8.**

Bergendorff, C. *See* Luther. *Luther's Works.*

Berger, Samuel. *Histoire de la Vulgate pendant les premiers siècles du Moyen Age* (Paris, 1893). **328.**

Berkvens-Stevelinck, Christiane. 'Prosper Marchand, Auteur et Editeur,' *Quaerendo* v (1975) 218–34. **143.**

Berry, B. M. 'The First English Pediatricians and Tudor Attitudes toward Childhood,' *Journal of the History of Ideas* XXXV (1974) 561–77. **431.**

Berry, Lloyd, introduction. *The Geneva Bible: A Facsimile of the 1560 Edition* (Madison, Wis., 1969). **305, 360, 364, 415.**

Berry, W. T. and Poole, H. W. *Annals of Printing: A Chronological Encyclopaedia from Earliest Times to 1950* (London, 1966). **4.**

Besson, Jacques. *A Theatre of Machines* (1579) ed. Alexander G. Keller (New York, 1965). **240, 262, 557.**

Besterman, Theodore. *The Beginnings of Systematic Bibliography* (Oxford, 1936). **94, 98.**

Bevan, E. R. and Singer, Charles, eds. *The Legacy of Israel* (Oxford, 1927). Includes articles by Box, G. H.; Singer, Charles.

Bietenholz, P. G. *Basle and France in the Sixteenth Century: The Basle Humanists and Printers in their contacts with Francophone Culture* (University of Toronto Press, 1971). **187, 399, 405, 407, 419, 441-2, 446, 540.**

Billanovich, R. 'Petrarch and the Textual Tradition of Livy,' *Journal of the Warburg and Courtauld Institutes* XIV (1951) 137–208. Consulted but not cited.

Bohnstedt, J. W. *The Infidel Scourge of God.* Transactions of the American Philosophical Society (Philadelphia, 1968). **303.**

Bolgar, R. R. *The Classical Heritage and Its Beneficiaries: From the Carolingian Age to the End of the Renaissance* (New York, 1964). **181, 212, 217, 222, 224, 244, 272.**

    ed. *Classical Influences on European Culture A.D. 500–1500* (Cambridge, 1971). Includes article by Gerlo, A.

    ed. *Classical Influences on European Culture A.D. 1500–1700* (Cambridge, 1976). Includes article by Oestreich, G.

Bollème, Geneviève. *Les Almanachs populaires aux XVIIe et XVIIIe siècles* (Paris, 1969). **386.**

Bonelli Righini, M. L. and Shea, W. R., eds. *Reason, Experiment and Mysticism in the Scientific Revolution* (New York, 1975). **641.** Includes articles by Debus, A.; Hall, A. R.; Rossi, P.

The Book of Common Prayer (1559) ed. John Booty (Charlottesville, Va., 1976). **365.**

Borchardt, F. 'Etymology in Tradition and in the Northern Renaissance,' *Journal of the History of Ideas* XXIX (July–Sept. 1968) 415–29. **277.**

Bosanquet, E. F. *English Printed Almanacks and Prognostications, A Bibliographical History to the Year 1600* (London, 1917). **386, 608, 618-19.**

    'English Seventeenth-Century Almanacks,' *The Library,* 4th ser. X (1930) 361–97. **386.**

Bossy, John. 'The Counter Reformation and the People of Catholic Europe,' *Past and Present* 47 (May 1970) 51–70. **426.**

Botein, Stephen. 'Meer Mechanics and an Open Press,' *Perspectives in American History* IX (1975) 127–225. **381.**

Botfield, Beriah, ed. *Praefationes et Epistolae Editionibus Principus Auctorum Veterum* (Cambridge, 1861). **20, 320, 392.**

Boüard, Michel de. 'Encyclopédies Médiévales, Sur la "Connaissance de la Nature et du Monde" au Moyen Age,' *Revue des Questions Historiques* 58 (1930) 258–305. **513.**

Boulding, Kenneth. *The Image* (Ann Arbor, Mich., 1961). **81, 479.**

Boumans, René. 'The Religious Views of Abraham Ortelius,' *Journal of the Warburg and Courtauld Institutes* XVII (July–Dec. 1954) 374–7. **448.**

Bouwsma, William. *Concordia Mundi: The Career and Thought of Guillaume Postel (1510–1581)* (Cambridge, Mass., 1957). **340, 343, 448.**

    Venice and the Defense of Republican Liberty: Renaissance Values in the Age of the Counter Reformation (Berkeley, 1968). **353, 413.**

    'Venice, Spain and the Papacy: Paolo Sarpi and the Renaissance Tradition,' *The Late Italian Renaissance 1525–1630,* ed. Eric Cochrane (New York, 1970) 353–77. **412-13.**

Bouyer, Louis. 'Erasmus in Relation to the Medieval Biblical Tradition,' *Cambridge History of the Bible,* Vol. 2. *The West from the Fathers to the Reformation,* ed. G. W. H. Lampe (Cambridge, 1969) 492–505. **338.**

Box, G. H. 'Hebrew Studies in the Reformation Period and After,' *The Legacy of Israel,* ed. E. R. Bevan and Charles Singer (Oxford, 1927) 315–75. **224, 367, 447.**

Boxer, C. R., et al. *Exotic Printing and the Expansion of Europe, 1492–1840,* catalogue of Exhibition, Lilly Library, Indiana University, 1972. **317.**

Boyd, Julian. 'These Precious Monuments of ... Our History,' *The American Archivist* XXII, 2 (1959) 175–6. **116.**

Boyer, Carl. *History of Mathematics* (New York, 1968). **620.**

'Galileo's Place in the History of Mathematics,' *Galileo, Man of Science*, ed. Ernan McMullin (New York, 1967) 232–55. **525.**

Brann, Noel. 'The Shift from Mystical to Magical Theology in the Abbot Trithemius.' Paper given May 5, 1976, 11th Conference on Medieval Studies (Kalamazoo, Mich.). **95.**

Branner, Robert. 'Manuscript Makers in Mid-thirteenth Century Paris,' *The Art Bulletin* XLVIII (March 1966) 65–7. **11, 13, 46.**

'The Soissons Bible Paintshop in Thirteenth-Century Paris,' *Speculum* XLIV (Jan. 1969) 13–34. **11, 13, 46, 328.**

Braudel, Fernand. *Capitalism and Material Life, 1400–1800*, tr. M. Kochon (1st Fr. edn 1967, New York, 1974). **27.**

Bredvold, L. I. *The Intellectual Milieu of John Dryden* (Ann Arbor, 1956). **323, 326.**

Bréhier, Émile. 'The Formation of our History of Philosophy,' *Philosophy and History: The Ernst Cassirer Festschrift*, ed. R. Klibansky and H. J. Paton (rev. edn, New York, 1963) 159–73. **333.**

Bremme, H. J. *Buchdrucker und Buchhandler zur Zeit der Glaubenskämpfe: Studien zur Genfer Druckgeschichte, 1565–1580* (Geneva, 1969). **411.**

Bridenbaugh, Carl. 'The Great Mutation,' *The American Historical Review* LXVIII (Jan. 1963) 315–31. **ix, 364.**

Briel, J. G. C. A. *See* Kingdon, R. M.

Brinton, Crane. *The Anatomy of Revolution* (New York, 1938). **136.**

Brockbank, William. 'Sovereign Remedies: A Critical Depreciation of the Seventeenth Century London Pharmacopoeia,' *Medical History* VIII (1964) 1–13. **539, 656.**

Bronowski, Jacob and Mazlish, Bruce. *The Western Intellectual Tradition: From Leonardo to Hegel* (New York, 1960). **649.**

Bronson, Bernard. 'The Writer,' *Man Versus Society in Eighteenth Century Britain*, ed. J. L. Clifford (Cambridge, 1968) 102–32. **322.**

Brown, Harcourt. *Scientific Organizations in 17th Century France 1620–1680* (New York, 1934). **643.**

Brown, Irene Q. 'Philippe Ariès on Education and Society in Seventeenth and Eighteenth Century France,' *History of Education Quarterly* (Fall 1967) 357–68. **395.**

Brown, Lloyd. *The Story of Maps* (Boston, 1959). **110, 479, 482, 517.**

Browne, Sir Thomas. *The Prose of Sir Thomas Browne*, ed. Norman Endicott (New York, 1967). **18, 471, 483.**

Brun, Robert. *Le Livre Français Illustré de la Renaissance* (Paris, 1969). **544.**

Buck, L. P. and Zophy, J. W., eds. *The Social History of the Reformation* (Festschrift for Harold Grimm) (Columbus, Ohio, 1972). Includes articles by Bebb, P. N.; Cole, R.; Dannenfeldt, Karl.

Bühler, Curt. *The Fifteenth Century Book, the Scribes, the Printers, the Decorators* (Philadelphia, 1960). **6, 14, 19, 49–51, 72, 83, 139, 206, 250, 586.**

Fifteenth Century Books and the Twentieth Century: An Address and a Catalogue of an Exhibition at the Grolier Club (April–June 1952) (New York, 1952). **167–8.**

The University and the Press in 15th Century Bologna, Texts and Studies in the History of Medieval Education, vol. VII (South Bend, Indiana, 1958). **56.**

Review article. *The Library*, 5th ser. VIII (1953) 53–6. **38.**

'Roman Type and Roman Printing in the Fifteenth Century,' *Bibliotheca Docet: Festgabe für Carl Wehmer*, ed. S. Joost (Amsterdam, 1963) 101–10. **204-5.**

'A Typographical Error in the Editio Princeps of Euclid,' *Gutenberg-Jahrbuch* (1966) 102–4. **588.**

Burckhardt, Jacob. *The Civilization of the Renaissance in Italy*, tr. S. G. C. Middlemore, ed. B. Nelson and C. Trinkaus (2 vol. New York, 1958). **45, 48, 221, 226, 228, 237-8, 243, 300, 488-91, 494.**

Burke, Peter. *Culture and Society in Renaissance Italy 1420–1540* (London, 1972). **45, 88.**

Introduction, *A New Kind of History and Other Essays from the Writings of Lucien Febvre* (New York, 1973). **41.**

The Renaissance (Problems and Perspectives in History, ed. H. F. Kearney) (London, 1964). **177.**

The Renaissance Sense of the Past (Documents of Modern History, ed. A. G. Dickens and A. Davies) (New York, 1970). **257, 300.**

'Fanfare for Princes,' *Times Literary Supplement* (Sept. 10, 1976). **133.**

Burns, Howard. 'Quattrocento Architecture and the Antique,' *Classical Influences on European Culture A.D. 500–1500*, ed. R. R. Bolgar (Cambridge, 1971) 269–89. **83.**

Burns, R. E. Book review. *American Historical Review* LXXIV (Oct. 1968) 181. **290.**

Burrow, John. 'The Medieval Compendium,' *Times Literary Supplement* (May 21, 1976) 615. **122.**

Burtt, E. A. *The Metaphysical Foundations of Modern Science* (1st edn 1932, rev. edn, New York, 1955). **592, 681.**

Butler, Pierce. *The Origin of Printing in Europe* (Chicago, 1940). **6, 17, 89, 95-6, 113, 119, 163, 375.**

Butterfield, Herbert. *The Origins of Modern Science 1300–1800* (rev. edn, New York, 1951). **496, 503, 637, 646, 663, 685.**

The Statecraft of Machiavelli (New York, 1960). **291.**

Butterworth, C. *The English Primers (1529–1545)* (Philadelphia, 1953). **350.**

Cajori, Florian. *A History of Mathematics* (New York, 1919). **583.**

See also Newton, Isaac.

Cambridge History of the Bible (3 vol. Cambridge, 1963–70). Vol. 2. *The West from the Fathers to the Reformation*, ed. G. W. H. Lampe (Cambridge, 1969). Vol. 3. *The West from the Reformation to the Present Day*, ed. S. L. Greenslade (Cambridge, 1963). Includes articles by Black, M. H.; Bouyer, Louis; Crehan, F. J.; Fenn, Eric; Foster, Kenelm; Greenslade, S. L.; Hall, Basil; Jones, D. R.; Lockwood, W. B.; Loewe, R.; Milburn, R. L. P.; Richardson, A.; Robson, C. A.; Sayce, R. A.; Sutcliffe, E. F.; Sykes, N.

Cambridge Modern History, New (14 vol. Cambridge, 1957–79). Vol. I. *The Renaissance, 1493–1520*, ed. G. R. Potter (Cambridge, 1957). Vol. II. *The Reformation, 1520–59*, ed. G. R. Elton (Cambridge, 1958). Includes articles by Hall, A. R.; Hay, Denys; Weiss, R.

Cameron, Kenneth W. Book review. *Renaissance Quarterly* XXIV (Winter 1971) 555. **376.**

Cameron, Richard. 'The Attack on the Biblical Work of Lefèvre d'Etaples (1514–1521),' *Church History* XXXVIII (1969) 9–24. **331.**

Campbell, Anna M. *The Black Death and Men of Learning* (New York, 1966). **295.**

Cardano, G. *The Great Art*, tr. and ed. T. R. Witmer (Cambridge, Mass., 1968). **548, 552.**

Carter, Charles Howard, ed. *From the Renaissance to the Counter Reformation. Essays in Honor of Garrett Mattingly* (New York, 1965). Includes articles by Hale, J. R.; Hay, Denys; Hill, Christopher; Kristeller, P. O.; Smolar, F. J.; Strauss, G.

Carter, Harry. *A View of Early Typography up to about 1600* (Oxford, 1969). **55, 203, 205-7.**

Carter, Harry and Vervliet, H. D. L. *Civilité Types* (Oxford Bibliographical Society Publications, New Ser. XIV) (Oxford, 1966). **202, 205-6.**

Carter, J. W. and Muir, P. H., eds. *Printing and the Mind of Man* (London, 1967). **375.**

Carter, T. F. and Goodrich, C. L. *The Invention of Printing in China and Its Spread Westward* (1st edn 1925, New York, 1955). **27, 376.**

Caspar, Max. *Kepler*, tr. C. Doris Hellman (London, 1948, rev. edn 1959). **582, 626-7, 639, 654.**

Cassirer, Ernst. *The Philosophy of the Enlightenment*, tr. F. Koelln and J. Pettegrove (Princeton, 1951). **698.**

'On the Originality of the Renaissance,' *Journal of the History of Ideas* IV (Jan. 1943) 49-56. **229, 230.**

Castiglioni, A. *A History of Medicine*, tr. E. B. Krumbhaar (rev. edn, New York, 1958). **616.**

Cavallera, Ferdinand. 'La Bible en Langue Vulgaire au Concile de Trente: IVe Session,' *Mélanges E. Podechard* (Lyon, 1945) 37-56. **329, 343-4.**

Chabod, Frederico. *Machiavelli and the Renaissance*, tr. David Moore, introduction, A. P. d'Entrèves (New York, 1965). **185, 293.**

Chalotais, Louis René de Caradeuc de la. *Essay on National Education, or Plan of Studies for the Young*, tr. H. R. Clark (London, 1934). **351.**

Chambers, G. K. 'Sir Thomas Browne, True Scientist,' *Osiris* II (1936) 28-79. **458.**

Chambers, R. W. 'The Lost Literature of Medieval England,' *The Library*, 4th ser. V (1925) 293-321. **115.**

Charlton, Kenneth. *Education in Renaissance England* (London, 1965). **243, 383, 425.**

Chartier, R., Compère, M. M., Julia, D. *L'Education en France du XVIe au XVIIIe Siècle* (Paris, 1976). **350, 414, 430.**

Chastel, André. 'What is Mannerism?' *Art News* (Dec. 1965), 64. **82.**

Chaucer, G. *The Equatorie of the Planetis*, ed. Derek de Solla Price (Cambridge, 1955). **277, 465.**

Chaunu, Pierre. 'Sur la Fin des Sorciers au XVIIe Siècle,' *Annales: Economies Sociétés Civilisations* XXIV (July-Aug. 1969) 895-911. **434.**

Chaytor, H. J. *From Script to Print* (Cambridge, 1945). **10, 121, 171, 227, 299, 319.**

Chenu, M. D. *Nature, Man and Society in the Twelfth Century*, ed. and tr. J. Taylor and Lester Little (Chicago, 1968). **184-5, 251, 290, 379.**

Chester, Alan G. 'The New Learning: A Semantic Note,' *Studies in the Renaissance* II (1955) 139-47. **174.**

Chrisman, Miriam Usher. *Strasbourg and the Reform: A Study in the Process of Change* (New Haven, 1967). **370-3.**

Christianson, John. 'Astronomy and Printing,' paper presented at Sixteenth Century Studies Conference, October 26, 1972, Concordia Seminary, St Louis, Mo. **599, 625.**

'Tycho Brahe at the University of Copenhagen 1559–1562,' *Isis* 58 (1967) 198–203. **533-4.**

'Tycho Brahe's Facts of Life,' *Fund og Forskning i Det Kongelige Biblioteks* 17 (1970). **624.**

Cipolla, Carlo M. *Before the Industrial Revolution* (New York, 1976). **244, 554.**

Literacy and Development in the West (London, 1969). **61, 414.**

'The Diffusion of Innovations in Early Modern Europe,' *Comparative Studies in Society and History* 14 (1972) 46–52. **583.**

Clagett, Marshall. *Archimedes in the Middle Ages I: The Arabo-Latin Tradition* (Madison, Wis., 1964). **471, 497, 697.**

ed. *Critical Problems in the History of Science* (Proceedings of the Institute of the History of Science, Sept. 1957) (Madison, Wis., 1959). Includes articles by Crombie, A. C.; Santillana, G. de; Hall, A. R.; Nagel, E.

Greek Science in Antiquity (London, 1957). **611.**

The Science of Mechanics in the Middle Ages (Madison, Wis., 1959). **497, 522, 541.**

Clagett, M. and Moody, E., eds. *The Medieval Science of Weights* (Madison, Wis., 1952). **497.**

Clair, Colin. *Christopher Plantin* (London, 1960). **100.**

'Willem Silvius,' *The Library* 5th ser. XIV (1959) 192–205. **96.**

Clapham, Michael. 'Printing,' *A History of Technology* II *From the Renaissance to the Industrial Revolution*, ed. Charles Singer, E. J. Holmyard, A. R. Hall and Trevor Williams (4 vol. Oxford, 1957) 377–411. **21, 31, 45, 273, 376.**

Clapp, Sarah L. C. 'The Beginnings of Subscription in the Seventeenth Century,' *Modern Philology* XXIX (1931) 199–224. Consulted but not cited.

'The Subscription Enterprises of John Ogilby and Richard Blowe,' *Modern Philology* XXXI (May 1933) 365–79. **367.**

Clapp, V. W. 'The Story of Permanent Durable Book Paper, 1115–1970,' *Scholarly Publishing, A Journal for Authors and Publishers* II (Toronto, 1971) 108 ff. **14, 115.**

Clark, Sir George N. *Early Modern Europe from about 1450 to about 1720* (revised excerpt from *The European Inheritance*, ed. E. Barker and P. Vaucher) (Oxford Paperbacks University Series no. 4) (Oxford, 1966). **169.**

The Seventeenth Century (rev. edn, Oxford, 1947). **29, 460.**

Clarke, Edwin. Review, *Medical History* VIII (1964), 380–3. **502, 573.**

Clifton, Robin. 'The Popular Fear of Catholics in England,' *Past and Present* 52 (Aug. 1971) 23–55. **427.**

Clough, C. H. *Machiavelli Researches* (Naples, 1967). **100.**

Introduction. *The Discourses of Niccolò Machiavelli*, tr. Leslie J. Walker (2 vol. London, 1965). **100.**

Cochin, Augustin. *Les Sociétés de Pensée et la Révolution en Bretagne 1788–1789* (2 vol. Paris, 1925). **149.**

Cochrane, Eric. Book review. *The American Historical Review* 82 (Feb. 1977) 88. **314.**

'Science and Humanism in the Italian Renaissance,' *American Historical Review* 81 (Dec. 1976) 1039–57. **526.**

Cochrane, J. A. *Dr. Johnson's Printer: The Life of William Strahan* (London, 1964). **112.**

Cohen, Gustave. *Ecrivains Français en Hollande dans la Première Moitié du XVIIe Siècle* (Paris, 1920). **647.**

Cohen, I. Bernard. *Introduction to Newton's 'Principia'* (Cambridge, 1971). **638.**

Curtis, Mark. *Oxford and Cambridge in Transition 1558–1642* (Oxford, 1959). **134.**
'The Alienated Intellectuals of Early Stuart England,' *Past and Present* 23 (Nov. 1962) 25–41. **136.**
'Education and Apprenticeship,' *Shakespeare Survey* XVII (1964) 53–72. **243, 383.**
Curtius, Ernst. *European Literature and the Latin Middle Ages*, tr. W. Trask (1st edn 1948; New York, 1963). **6, 123, 455–6.**

Dahl, Folke. *Dutch Corantos 1618–1650. A Bibliography* (The Hague, 1946). **138.**
Daly, Lloyd W. *Contributions to a History of Alphabetization in Antiquity and the Middle Ages* (Brussels, 1967). **89–90, 92.**
Daniélou, J., Contratin, A. H. and Kent, John. *Historical Theology* (The Pelican Guide to Modern Theology) (London, 1969). **313.**
Daniel-Rops, Henri. *The Protestant Reformation*, tr. A. Butler (New York, 1961). **330.**
Dannenfeldt, Karl. 'The Renaissance Humanists and the Knowledge of Arabic,' *Studies in Renaissance* II (1955) 96–117. **224, 447.**
'Wittenberg Botanists during the Sixteenth Century,' *The Social History of the Reformation*, ed. L. P. Buck and J. W. Zophy (Columbus, Ohio, 1972) 223–46. **98, 535, 641.**
Dantzig, Tobias. *Number: The Language of Science* (4th edn, New York, 1967). **467, 494, 697.**
Darlowe, T. H. and Moule, H. T. *Historical Catalogue of the Printed Editions of Holy Scripture in the Library of the British and Foreign Bible Society* (London, 1903). **337.**
Darnton, Robert. *Mesmerism and the End of the Enlightenment in France* (Cambridge, Mass., 1968). **657.**
'The Encyclopédie Wars of Prerevolutionary France,' *American Historical Review* 78 (1973) 1331–52. **29, 139.**
'The Grub Street Style of Revolution,' *Journal of Modern History* XL (1968) 301–27. **29.**
'The High Enlightenment and the Low Life of Literature . . .,' *Past and Present* 51 (1971) 81–115. **29.**
'Reading, Writing and Publishing in Eighteenth Century France,' *Daedalus* (1971) 214–57. **29.**
David, Madeleine. *Le Débat sur les Ecritures et l'Hiéroglyphe aux XVIIe et XVIIIe Siècles* (Paris, 1965). **279, 284, 564.**
Davies, David W. *The World of the Elseviers, 1580–1712* (The Hague, 1954). **409, 535, 645.**
Davies, H. W., ed. and introduction. *Bernhard von Breydenbach and His Journey to the Holy Land 1483–4: A Bibliography* (London, 1911). **86.**
Davis, Hugh H. Book review, *Renaissance Quarterly* XXVIII (Autumn 1975) 353. **33.**
Davis, Natalie Zemon. 'Mathematicians in the Sixteenth-Century French Academies: Some Further Evidence,' *Renaissance News* XI (Spring 1958) 3–10. **542.**
'New Monarchs and Prudent Priests,' *Canadian Journal of History* VI (March 1971) 46–73. **400.**
'Peletier and Beza Part Company,' *Studies in the Renaissance* XI (1964) 188–222. **403, 543.**
'Printing and the People,' *Society and Culture in Early Modern France: Eight Essays* (Palo Alto, California, 1975). **xiii, 63–5, 130, 234, 241–2, 362, 377, 541.**

'The Protestant Printing Workers of Lyons in 1551,' *Aspects de la Propagande Religieuse*, ed. H. Meylan (Geneva, 1957) 247–57. **130, 352.**

'Publisher Guillaume Rouillé, Businessman and Humanist,' *Editing Sixteenth Century Texts*, ed. R. J. Schoeck (Toronto, 1966) 72–112. **87-8, 234.**

Review article, *Journal of Modern History* xxx (Dec. 1968) 589. **370.**

'Sixteenth-Century French Arithmetics on the Business Life,' *Journal of the History of Ideas* xxi (1960) 18–48. **384, 392, 542, 544.**

'Strikes and Salvation in Lyons,' *Archiv für Reformationsgeschichte* lvi (1965) 48–64. **87, 250, 392, 406.**

Davis, Robert Gorham. 'Speak of the Devil,' *The New York Times Book Review* (March 25, 1972) 55. **633.**

Deanesly, Margaret. *The Lollard Bible* (Cambridge, 1920). **345, 357.**

'Débats et Combats'. *See* Soriano, M.

Debus, Allen. *The English Paracelsians* (New York, 1966). **472.**

  Science and Education in the Seventeenth Century: The Webster–Ward Debate (London, 1970). **275, 473, 550, 656, 681.**

  'The Chemical Debates of the Seventeenth Century,' *Reason, Experiment and Mysticism*, ed. M. L. Bonelli Righini and W. R. Shea (New York, 1975) 19–44. **275.**

  ed. *Science, Medicine and Society in the Renaissance* (Essays to Honor Walter Pagel) (New York, 1974). Includes articles by Keller, A.; Westfall, Richard.

Dechend, Hertha von. *See* de Santillana, G.

De Frede, Carlo. 'Per la Storia della Stampa nel Cinquecento in Rapporto con la Diffusione della Riforma in Italia,' *Gutenberg-Jahrbuch* (1964) 175–84. **311, 348.**

Degering, H. *Lettering: Modes of Writing in Western Europe from Antiquity to the Eighteenth Century* (London, 1929). **205.**

Delaissé, L. M. J. *A Century of Dutch Manuscript Illumination* (Berkeley, Calif., 1968). **259, 339.**

  Le Manuscrit Autographe de Thomas A Kempis et 'L'Imitation de Jésus Christ' (2 vol. Brussels, 1952). **12, 121, 391.**

  Book review of Millard Meiss' work, *The Art Bulletin* lii (1970) 206–12. **13.**

De la Mare, Albinia. 'Bartolomeo Scala's Dealings with Booksellers, Scribes and Illuminators, 1459–63,' *Journal of the Warburg and Courtauld Institutes* xxxix (1976) 237–45. **48-9.**

  'Messer Piero Strozzi, A Florentine Scribe,' *Calligraphy and Paleography. Essays Presented to A. J. Fairbank*, ed. A. S. Osley (London, 1965) 55–68. **13.**

  'The Shop of a Florentine "cartolaio" in 1426,' *Studi Offerti a Roberto Ridolfi* (Florence, 1973) 237–48. **47.**

  'Vespasiano and the Library of the Badia at Fiesole' to be published by the Warburg Institute. Forthcoming. **45.**

  'Vespasiano da Bisticci Historian and Bookseller' (unpublished doctoral dissertation, London University, 1965). **12-13, 45-6, 48-50, 217.**

Delany, Paul. *British Autobiography in the Seventeenth Century* (London, 1969). **229-30, 236, 366.**

D'Elia, Pasquale. *Galileo in China. Relations Between Galileo and the Jesuit-Scientist-Missionaries 1610–1640*, tr. R. Suter and M. Sciascia (Cambridge, Mass., 1960). **609.**

Delof, G. Turbet. 'Comment déjouait-on la censure en France au XVIIe siècle?' *Revue Française d'Histoire du Livre* III (1975) 113–15. **138.**

Delumeau, Jean. *Le Catholicisme entre Luther et Voltaire* (Paris, 1971). **314.**

DeMolen, Richard L. 'The Age of the Renaissance and Reformation,' *The Meaning of the Renaissance and Reformation*, ed. R. L. DeMolen (Boston, 1974) 1–25. **178.**

ed. *The Meaning of the Renaissance and Reformation* (Boston, 1974). Includes articles by DeMolen, R.; Reed, R. B.

Denholm-Young, N. *History and Heraldry 1254–1310* (Oxford, 1965). **134.**

Descartes, René. *A Discourse on Method*, tr. John Veitch, introduction A. D. Lindsay (Everyman's Library edn, 1912). **476.**

Deschamps, J. Book review, *Quaerendo* III (1973) 78. **391.**

Destrez, Jean. *La 'Pecia' dans les Manuscrits Universitaires du XIIIe et du XIVe Siècle* (Paris, 1935). **6, 13–14, 19, 103, 203, 216, 259.**

Deuel, Leo. *Testaments of Time: The Search for Lost Manuscripts and Records* (New York, 1965). **209, 211, 222.**

Deutsch, Karl. *Nationalism and Social Communication: An Inquiry into the Foundations of Nationality* (Cambridge, Mass., 1953). **118.**

Devereux, E. J. 'English Translators of Erasmus 1522–1557,' *Editing Sixteenth Century Texts*, ed. R. J. Schoeck (Toronto, 1966) 45–58. **357–8.**

Dibdin, Thomas F. *Typographical Antiquities or the History of Printing in England Scotland and Ireland...begun by the late Joseph Ames, augmented by William Herbert and Greatly Enlarged by the Reverend Thomas Frognell Dibdin* (4 vol. London, 1810). **ix, 378.**

Dibon, Paul. 'L'Université de Leyde et la République des Lettres au 17e Siècle,' *Quaerendo* V (Jan. 1975) 25–32. **137, 140, 409.**

Dickens, Arthur Geoffrey. *The Counter-Reformation* (London, 1969). **315, 353.**

The English Reformation (New York, 1964). **310, 324.**

Reformation and Society in Sixteenth Century Europe (New York, 1968). **303, 359, 373, 376, 394, 403.**

Thomas Cromwell and the English Reformation (London, 1959). **356.**

Dijk, S. J. P. von. 'An Advertisement Sheet of an Early 14th Century Writing Master at Oxford,' *Scriptorium* x (1956) 47–64. **82.**

Dijksterhuis, E. J. *The Mechanization of the World Picture*, tr. C. Dikshoorn (Oxford, 1961). **505–6.**

Simon Stevin (The Hague, 1943). **500.**

See also Forbes, R. J.

Diringer, David. *The Hand Produced Book* (London, 1953). **22.**

The Illuminated Book (London, 1958). **22.**

Dorsten, Jan van. *The Radical Arts* (London, 1973). Consulted but not cited.

Thomas Basson 1555–1613: English Printer at Leiden (Sir Thomas Browne Institute) (Leiden, 1963). **140.**

'Garter Knights and Familists,' *Journal of European Studies* 4 (1974) 178–88. **140, 143.**

Drachmann, A. G. Review, *Technology and Culture* 17 (Jan. 1976) 112–16. **589.**

Drake, Stillman, ed. and tr. *Discoveries and Opinions of Galileo* (New York, 1957). **458, 525, 526–7, 530, 644, 652–4, 658, 675–6, 681.**

'Early Science and the Printed Book: The Spread of Science Beyond the University,' *Renaissance and Reformation* (University of Toronto) 6 (1970) 38–52. **454, 524, 529, 540, 542, 546, 552, 622, 629.**

See also Rose, P. L.

Dreyer, J. L. E. *History of Astronomy, From Thales to Kepler* (rev. edn, New York, 1953). **617-18.**

Tycho Brahe (Edinburgh, 1890). **581, 583, 597, 624-5.**

Droz, Eugénie. 'Bibles Françaises après le Concile de Trente,' *Journal of Warburg and Courtauld Institutes* XXVIII (1965) 210-15. **334, 342-4, 349, 426.**

Dudek, Louis. *Literature and the Press* (Toronto, 1960). **153, 157.**

Dupree, Hunter. 'The Pace of Measurement from Rome to America,' *The Smithsonian Journal of History* III (1968) 19-40. **468.**

Dupront, Alphonse. 'Livre et Culture dans la Société Française au XVIIIe Siècle – Réflexions sur une Enquête,' *Annales: Economies Sociétés Civilisations* (1965) 867-98. **29, 149.**

Durand, Dana B. *The Vienna-Klosterneuberg Map Corpus: A Study in the Transition from Medieval to Modern Science* (Leiden, 1952). **21, 482, 512, 516.**

'Tradition and Innovation in 15th Century Italy: "Il Primato dell'Italia" in the Field of Science,' *Toward Modern Science*, ed. R. Palter (2 vol., New York, 1961) II, 25-48. **170, 488, 497, 584, 588.**

Durant, Will and Ariel. *The Story of Civilization*, Vol. 6 *The Reformation* (New York, 1957). **250.**

Durme, M. van, ed. *Correspondance Mercatorienne* (Antwerp, 1959). **110.**

Easton, J. B. 'The Early Editions of Robert Recorde's Ground of Artes,' *Isis* 58 (1967) 515-32. **533-4.**

Eastwood, B. S. Review of Lindberg's edition of Pecham, *Speculum* XLVII (1972) 324. **551, 590.**

Ebel, J. G. 'Translation and Cultural Nationalism in the Reign of Elizabeth,' *Journal of the History of Ideas* XXX (Oct.–Dec. 1969) 593-602. **360.**

Echeverria, Durand. *Mirage in the West* (Princeton, 1957). **149.**

Edgerton, Samuel. *The Renaissance Rediscovery of Linear Perspective* (New York, 1975). **192, 268.**

Edler de Roover, F. 'Cost Accounting in the Sixteenth Century,' *Accounting Review* 12 (1937) 226-37. **22, 383.**

'New Facets on the Financing and Marketing of Early Printed Books,' *Bulletin of the Business Historical Society* 27 (1953) 222-30. **22.**

'Per la Storia dell'arte della Stampa in Italia: come furono stampati a Venezia tre dei primi libri in volgare,' *La Bibliofilia* LV (1953) 107-15. **38.**

Eels, Hastings. *The Attitude of Martin Bucer toward the Bigamy of Philip of Hesse* (New York, 1924). **373.**

Egbert, Virginia Wylie. *The Medieval Artist at Work* (Princeton, 1967). **82.**

Ehrman, Albert. 'The Fifteenth Century,' in Ehrman and Pollard, *The Distribution of Books by Catalogue* (Roxburghe Club, Cambridge, 1965). **22.**

Ehrman, Albert and Pollard, Graham. *The Distribution of Books by Catalogue from the Invention of Printing to A.D. 1800* (Roxburghe Club, Cambridge, 1965). **58, 91.**

Eisenstadt, S. N. ed. *The Protestant Ethic and Modernization* (New York, 1968). Includes articles by Hooykaas, R.; Willems, E.

Eisenstein, E. L. 'The Advent of Printing and the Problem of the Renaissance,' *Past and Present* (Nov. 1969) 19-89. **xi.**

'L'Avènement de l'Imprimerie et la Réforme,' *Annales: Economies Sociétés Civilisations* (Nov.–Dec. 1971) 1355–882. **xi.**

'Clio and Chronos,' *History and Theory*, Beiheft 6 (1966) 36–65. **xi, 9, 17, 21, 24, 31, 289, 389.**

'The Evolution of the Jacobin Tradition in France 1815–1848' (unpublished dissertation, Radcliffe, 1952). **424.**

'The Position of the Printing Press in Current Historical Literature,' *American Historical Review* LXXV (Feb. 1970) 727–43. **xi.**

'Some Conjectures about the Impact of Printing on Western Society and Thought,' *Journal of Modern History* 40 (March 1968) 1–56. **xi.**

Book review, *The American Historical Review* 78 (October 1973) 1049–50. **149.**

Book review, *The French Review* (March 1971) 777–8. **386.**

Eisley, Loren. *Darwin's Century* (New York, 1958). **487.**

Elert, Werner. *The Structure of Lutheranism*, tr. W. A.Hansen (St Louis, Mo., 1962). **651.**

Elliott, J. H. 'Revolution and Continuity in Early Modern Europe,' *Past and Present* 42 (Feb. 1969) 34–56. **396.**

Elliott, J. H. and Koenigsberger, H. G., eds. *The Diversity of History; Essays in Honor of Sir Herbert Butterfield* (Ithaca, New York 1970). Includes article by Hall, A. R.

Elton, G. R. *Policy and Police: The Enforcement of the Reformation in the Age of Thomas Cromwell* (Cambridge, 1972). **135, 312.**

Reformation Europe 1517–1559 (New York, 1966). **306, 310.**

Endicott, Norman, ed. See Browne, Sir Thomas.

Erasmus. *The 'Adages' of Erasmus: A Study with Translations*, tr. and ed. Margaret Mann Phillips (Cambridge, 1964). **219, 223, 280.**

The Colloquies of Erasmus, tr. and ed. Craig Thompson (Chicago, 1965). **72.**

Escarpit, Robert. *Sociologie de la Littérature* (Paris, 1958). **153.**

Espinasse, Margaret. 'Decline and Fall of Restoration Science,' *The Intellectual Revolution*, ed. C. Webster (London, 1974) 347–69. **666, 670.**

Estienne, Henri. *The Francofordiense Emporium of Henri Estienne*, ed. J. W. Thompson (Chicago, 1911). Consulted but not cited.

Evans, R. J. W. *Rudolf II and His World: A Study in Intellectual History 1576–1612* (Oxford, 1973). **448, 474, 640.**

'The Wechel Presses: Humanism and Calvinism in Central Europe 1572–1627,' *Past and Present*, Sup. 2 (Oxford, 1975). **141, 275, 448, 668.**

Evennett, H. O. *The Spirit of the Counter Reformation*, ed. John Bossy (Cambridge, 1968). **315, 354.**

Fairfield, Leslie P. *John Bale: Mythmaker for the English Reformation* (W. Lafayette, Indiana, 1976). **112.**

'John Bale and the Development of Protestant Hagiography in England,' *Journal of Ecclesiastical History* XXIV (April 1973) 145–60. **423.**

'The Vocacyon of Johan Bale and Early English Autobiography,' *Renaissance Quarterly* XXIV (Autumn 1971) 327–39. **229.**

Febvre, Lucien. *Au Coeur Religieux du XVIe Siècle* (Paris, 1957). **15, 94, 399, 448.**

Le Problème de l'incroyance au XVIe siècle: la Religion de Rabelais (Evolution de L'Humanité LIII) (Paris, 1942). **10, 187.**

'Sorcellerie, Sottise ou Révolution Mentale?' *Annales: Economies Sociétés Civilisations* III (Jan.–March 1968) 9–15. **434.**

Frankl, Paul. *The Gothic: Literary Sources and Interpretations through Eight Centuries* (Princeton, 1960). **201.**

Franklin, Julian. *Jean Bodin and the Sixteenth Century Revolution in the Methodology of Law and History* (New York, 1963). **103, 200-1.**

Franklin, Ralph. 'Conjectures on Rarity,' *The Library Quarterly* (Chicago) 44 (1974) 309–31. **20.**

French, Peter. *John Dee: The World of an Elizabethan Magus* (London, 1972). **96.**

Frumkin, Maximilian. 'Early History of Patents for Invention,' *Transactions of the Newcomen Society for the Study of the History of Engineering and Technology* XXVI (1947–9) 47–56. **240, 251.**

Fuhrman, Otto W. 'The Invention of Printing,' *A History of the Printed Book*, ed. L. C. Wroth (New York, 1938) 25–57. **27.**

Furet, F. and Sachs, W. 'La Croissance de l'alphabétisation en France, XVIIIe-XIXe Siècles,' *Annales: Economies Sociétés Civilisations* (1974) 714–37. **414.**

Fussner, F. Smith. *The Historical Revolution: English Historical Writing and Thought 1580–1640* (London, 1962). **14, 113.**

Gabriel, Astrik. *The College System in the Fourteenth Century Universities* (Baltimore, Md., n.d.). **475, 536, 581, 622.**

Garlandia: Studies in the History of the Medieval University (Frankfurt, 1969). **608.**

Gade, J. A. *The Life and Times of Tycho Brahe* (Princeton, 1947). **581, 625.**

Gadol, Joan. *Leon Battista Alberti* (2nd edn, Chicago, 1973). **192, 268, 564.**

Galilei, Galileo. 'Letter to the Grand Duchess Christina' (1615), *Discoveries and Opinions of Galileo*, tr. and ed. Stillman Drake (New York, 1957) 175–216. **78, 527.** (*See also* entries under Drake.)

Gallick, Susan. 'A Look at Chaucer and His Preachers,' *Speculum* L (July 1975) 456–76. **236.**

Gandz, Solomon. 'The Dawn of Literature: Prolegomena to a History of Unwritten Literature,' *Osiris* VII (1939) 261–515. **9, 334.**

'The Invention of the Decimal Fractions and the Application of the Exponential Calculus by Immanuel Bonfils of Tarascon (c. 1350),' *Isis* XXV (May 1936) 16–45. **500, 563.**

Gardiner, Stephen. *The Letters of Stephen Gardiner*, ed. J. A. Muller (Cambridge, 1933). **68.**

Garin, Eugenio. *Italian Humanism: Philosophy and Civic Life in the Renaissance*, tr. P. Munz (New York, 1965). **100, 252, 475.**

Science and Civic Life in the Italian Renaissance, tr. P. Munz (New York, 1969). **502, 526, 528, 671.**

'A Garland for Gutenberg,' *Times Literary Supplement* (June 22, 1967) 561. **363.**

Gaskell, Philip. *A New Introduction to Bibliography* (Oxford, 1972). **4.**

Gautier, Théophile. Preface to *Mademoiselle de Maupin* (1835) tr. F. de Sumichrast, in *Paths to the Present*, ed. E. Weber (New York, 1960). **157.**

Gay, Peter. Introduction, *Deism: An Anthology* (Princeton, N. J., 1968). **323-4.**

The Enlightenment: An Interpretation (2 vol. New York, 1966). **209, 299, 491.**

The Party of Humanity (New York, 1964). **146.**

Geanokoplos, Deno J. *Greek Scholars in Venice: Studies in the Dissemination of Greek Learning from Byzantium to Western Europe* (Cambridge, Mass., 1962). **221, 223, 447.**

'Commentary,' *The Copernican Achievement*, ed. R. S. Westman (Los Angeles, 1975) 99–108. **580.**

'Copernicus and the Impact of Printing,' *Vistas in Astronomy* 17, ed. A. Beer and K. A. Strand (Oxford, 1975) 201–9. **584-6, 604.**

'Crisis versus Aesthetic in the Copernican Revolution,' *Vistas in Astronomy* 17, ed. A. Beer and K. A. Strand(Oxford, 1975) 85–95. **464, 583, 589, 595, 603, 605.**

Ginzburg, Carlo. *Il Nicodemismo: Simulazione e Dissimulazione religiosa nell'Europa del '500* (Turin, 1970). **141, 444-5.**

'High and Low: The Theme of Forbidden Knowledge,' *Past and Present* 73 (1976) 28–42. **147.**

Goldschmidt, E. P. *The First Cambridge Press in Its European Setting* (Cambridge, 1955). **399.**

Gothic and Renaissance Bookbindings (2 vol. Amsterdam, 1967). **49.**

Medieval Texts and Their First Appearance in Print (London, 1943). **10, 45, 115, 168, 211, 533.**

The Printed Book of the Renaissance: Three Lectures on Type, Illustration, Ornament (Cambridge, 1950). **82, 204, 206, 248, 280.**

'Not in Harrisse,' *Essays Honoring Lawrence C. Wroth* ed. F. Goff (Portland, Maine, 1951) 129–43. **517.**

Goldstein, B. R. 'The Arabic Version of Ptolemy's Planetary Hypotheses,' *Transactions of the American Philosophical Society* 57 (1967) part 4, 1–55. **604.**

'Theory and Observation in Medieval Cosmology,' *Isis* 63 (1972) 39–47. **598, 601.**

Goldthwaite, Richard. 'Schools and Teachers of Commercial Arithmetic in Renaissance Florence,' *The Journal of European Economic History* I (Fall 1972) 418–33, **382-3.**

Golino, C. L., ed. *Galileo Reappraised* (Berkeley, Calif., 1966). Includes articles by Moody, E. A.; Terza, D. D.; White, Lynn.

Gombrich, E. H. *Art and Illusion. A Study in the Psychology of Pictorial Representation* (rev. edn, Princeton, 1972). **268.**

In Search of Cultural History (Oxford, 1969). **25, 226, 295.**

'The Renaissance Conception of Artistic Progress and its Consequences,' *Norm and Form: Studies in the Art of the Renaissance* (London, 1966) 1–10. **83, 293.**

'Art and Scholarship,' *Meditations on a Hobby Horse* (London, 1963) 106–19. **232.**

'Icones Symbolicae: The Visual Image in Neo-Platonic Thought,' *Journal of the Warburg and Courtauld Institutes* XI (1948) 163–92. **280, 288.**

'The Leaven of Criticism in Renaissance Art,' *Art, Science, and History in the Renaissance*, ed. C. S. Singleton (Baltimore, 1967) 3–43. **254.**

Goodfield, J. *See* Toulmin, S.

Goodrich, C. L. *See* Carter, T. F.

Goody, Jack, ed. *Literacy in Traditional Societies* (Cambridge, 1968). **9.**

Goody, Jack and Watt, Ian. 'The Consequences of Literacy,' *Comparative Studies in Society and History* v (1963) 304–45. **9, 114.**

Gordan, Phyllis W. G., ed. *Two Renaissance Book Hunters: The Letters of Poggius Bracciolini to Nicolaus de Niccolis* (New York, 1974). **137, 189, 221.**

Gordon, Cosmo. 'Books on Accountancy 1494–1600,' *Transactions of the Bibliographical Society* XIII (1916) 145–70. **382.**

Gordon, D. J., ed. *Fritz Saxl 1890–1948: A Volume of Memorial Essays* (London, 1957). Includes articles by Oakeshott, W.; Pächt, O.; Singer, Charles.

Gossman, Lionel. *Medievalism and the Ideologies of the Enlightenment: The World and Work of La Curne de Sainte-Palaye* (Baltimore, 1968). **201, 338.**

Goudy, Frederick. *The Capitals from the Trajan Column at Rome* (New York, 1936). **82.**

Grabois, Aryeh. 'The *Hebraica Veritas* and Jewish-Christian Intellectual Relations in the Twelfth Century,' *Speculum* L (Oct. 1975) 613–34. **224.**

Grafton, Anthony T. 'Joseph Scaliger and Historical Chronology,' *History and Theory* XIV (1975) 156–85. **611.**

Graham, H. J. ' "Our Tong Maternall Marvellously Amendyd and Augmentyd": The First Englishing and Printing of the Medieval Statutes at Large, 1530–1533,' *UCLA Law Bulletin* XIII (Nov. 1965) 58–98. **105, 119, 360.**

'The Rastells and the printed English Law Book of the Renaissance,' *Law Library Journal* 47 (1954). **105.**

Graña, César. *Bohemian versus Bourgeois* (New York, 1964). **153, 156.**

Gravier, Maurice. *Luther et l'Opinion Publique* (Paris, 1942). **310–11, 354, 405.**

Gray, Hanna. 'Renaissance Humanism: The Pursuit of Eloquence,' *Journal of the History of Ideas* XXIV (1963) 497–514. **296, 473.**

'Valla's Encomium ... and the Humanist Conception of Christian Antiquity,' *Essays in History and Literature Presented to Stanley Pargellis*, ed. Heinz Bluhm (Chicago, 1965) 37–51. **195, 323.**

Green, Lowell C. 'The Bible in Sixteenth Century Humanist Education,' *Studies in the Renaissance* XIX (1972). 112–34. **364.**

Greenslade, S. L. 'English Versions of the Bible A.D. 1525–1611,' *Cambridge History of the Bible*, Vol. 3. *The West from the Reformation to the Present Day*, ed. S. L. Greenslade (Cambridge, 1963) 141–74. **358.**

'Epilogue,' *Cambridge History of the Bible*, Vol. 3. 476–519. **343, 364, 374, 378.**

Gregg, Pauline. *Free-born John: A Biography of John Lilburne* (London, 1961). **362, 423.**

Grendler, Paul F. *Critics of the Italian World* (Madison, Wis., 1969). **137, 139, 228, 394, 399, 400.**

The Roman Inquisition and the Venetian Press 1540–1605 (Princeton, 1977). **348, 411, 671.**

'Francesco Sansovino and Italian Popular History 1560–1600,' *Studies in the Renaissance* XVI (1969) 139–80. **360.**

'The Rejection of Learning in Mid-Cinquecento Italy,' *Studies in the Renaissance* XIII (1966) 230–49. **228.**

'The Roman Inquisition and the Venetian Press 1540–1605,' *Journal of Modern History* 47 (March 1975) 48–66. **341, 348, 411, 671.**

Grendler, Paul and Marcella. 'The Survival of Erasmus in Italy,' *Erasmus in English Newsletter* (University of Toronto) No. 8 (1976) 2–22. **145, 416.**

Grimm, Harold J. Introduction to Ninety-Five Theses, *Career of the Reformer I* (*Luther's Works* XXXI, ed. H. T. Lehman) (Philadelphia, 1957) 19–23. **306–7.**

Grimm, Heinrich. 'Luther's "Ablassthesen" und die Gegenthesen von Tetzel-Wimpina in der Sicht der Druck- und Buchgeschichte,' *Gutenberg-Jahrbuch* (1968) 139–50. **306–8.**

Grossmann, Maria. *Humanism in Wittenberg 1485–1517* (Nieuwkoop, 1975). **221.**

'Wittenberg Printing, Early Sixteenth Century,' *Sixteenth Century Essays and Studies* (St Louis, Mo., 1970), I, 53–74. **307–8.**

1974). 5, 6, 13, 15, 34, 37, 44, 50, 52, 55–60, 64, 80, 85, 168, 176, 206, 263, 316, 346–7, 360, 375, 399, 405, 587.

'Bulla Super Impressione Librorum, 1515,' *Gutenberg-Jahrbuch* (1973) 248–51. 317, 347.

'Pre-Reformation Censorship of Printed Books,' *The Library Chronicle* XXI (University of Pennsylvania, 1955) 100–5. 347.

'Printing and the Spread of Humanism in Germany: The Example of Albrecht Von Eyb,' *Renaissance Men and Ideas*, ed. R. Schwoebel (New York, 1971) 23–39. 180, 372.

Hodgart, Matthew. *Satire* (World University Library) (New York, 1969). 394.

Hofer, Philip. 'Variant Issues of the First Edition of Ludovico Arrighi Vicentino's "Operina",' *Calligraphy and Paleography. Essays Presented to A. J. Fairbank*, ed. A. S. Osley (London, 1965) 95–107. 82.

Holborn, Hajo. *Ulrich von Hutten and the German Reformation*, tr. Roland Bainton (New Haven, 1937). 243, 304.

Holborn, Louise. 'Printing and the Growth of a Protestant Movement in Germany from 1517–1524,' *Church History* XI (June 1942) 1–15. 303, 354.

Holmes, Margaret L. 'A Brief Survey of the Use of the Renaissance Themes in Some Works of the Lyonese Doctor ... Symphorien Champier,' *Cinq Etudes Lyonnaises (Histoire et Civilisation du Livre – VI)* (Geneva, 1966) 27–55. 523.

Holt, J. C. *Magna Carta* (Cambridge, 1965). 119.

Holznecht, Karl. *Literary Patronage in the Middle Ages* (1st edn, 1923; New York, 1966). 228.

Hooykaas, Reijer. *Humanisme, Science et Réforme: Pierre de la Ramée 1515–1572* (Leiden, 1958). 543, 641.

Religion and the Rise of Modern Science (Edinburgh, 1972; rev. edn, 1973). Consulted but not cited.

'Science and the Reformation,' *The Protestant Ethic and Modernization*, ed. S. N. Eisenstadt (New York, 1968) 211–39. 641–2, 650, 655, 657, 659–60.

Horsky, Zdenek. 'Astronomy and the Art of Clockmaking in the fourteenth, fifteenth, and sixteenth centuries,' *Vistas in Astronomy* 9, ed. A. Beer (Oxford, 1967) 25–35. 589.

Houghton, Walter. 'The History of Trades: Its Relation to Seventeenth Century Thought as Seen in Bacon, Petty, Evelyn, and Boyle,' *Journal of the History of Ideas* II (1941) 33–60. 558.

Houzeau, J. C. and Lancaster, A. *Bibliographie Générale de l'Astronomie* (3 vol. Brussels, 1889). 590.

Hoyaux, Jean. 'Les Moyens d'Existence d'Erasme,' *Bibliothèque d'Humanisme et Renaissance* V (1944) 7–59. 401.

Hoyle, Fred. *Astronomy* (London, 1962). 466.

Huffines, Marion L. 'Sixteenth Century Printers and Standardization of New High German,' *Journal of English and Germanic Philology* LXXIII (Jan. 1974) 60–72. 117.

Hufstader, Anselm. 'Lefèvre d'Etaples and the Magdalen,' *Studies in the Renaissance* XVI (1969) 31–60. 331.

Hughes, Barnabas, 'The Private Library of Johan Scheubel, sixteenth century mathematician,' *Viator* III (1972) 417–32. 587.

ed. and tr. See Regiomontanus.

733

Karpinski, L. C. and Staubach, C. N. 'An Anglo Norman Algorism of the Fourteenth Century,' *Isis* XXIII (1935) 121–52. **467.**

Katzman, Natan. 'The Impact of Communication Technology: Promises and Prospects,' *Journal of Communication* (University of Pennsylvania) 24 (1974) 47–59. **39.**

Kearney, Hugh F. Introduction, *Origins of the Scientific Revolution* (Problems and Perspectives in History) (London, 1966). **683.**

'Puritanism and Science: Problems of Definition,' *Past and Present* 29 (July 1965) 104–10. **643, 646, 661, 664.**

'Puritanism, Capitalism and the Scientific Revolution,' *Past and Present* 28 (July 1964) 81–101. **688.**

Keele, K. D. 'Leonardo da Vinci's Influence on Renaissance Anatomy,' *Medical History* VIII (1964) 360–70. **551.**

Keller, Alexander G. 'Mathematical Technologies and the Growth of the Idea of Technical Progress in the Sixteenth Century,' *Science, Medicine and Society in the Renaissance*, ed. Alan Debus (New York, 1974) 11–27. **20, 27, 261.**

'A Renaissance Humanist Looks at "New" Inventions: The Article "Horlogium" in Giovanni Tortelli's *De Orthographia*,' *Technology and Culture* 11 (1970) 345–65. **20, 252.**

'Zilsel, The Artisans and the Idea of Progress in the Renaissance,' *Roots of Scientific Thought*, ed. Wiener and Noland (New York, 1957) 281–6. **558, 561.**

ed. *See* Besson, Jacques.

Kellett, C. E. 'Two Anatomies,' *Medical History* VIII (Oct. 1964) 342–50. **567.**

Kelley, Donald R. *Foundations of Modern Historical Scholarship* (New York, 1970). **103-4, 189, 191, 195, 201, 218.**

'Faces in Clio's Mirror,' *Journal of Modern History* 47 (Dec. 1975) 679–90. **218.**

'Martyrs, Myths and the Massacre: The Background of St. Bartholomew,' *American Historical Review* 77 (Dec. 1972) 1323–42. **133.**

Kemp, Martin. 'Dissection and Divinity in Leonardo's Late Anatomies,' *Journal of the Warburg and Courtauld Institutes* XXXV (1972) 200–25. **565-6.**

'A Drawing for the De Fabrica and some thoughts upon the Vesalius Muscle-Men,' *Medical History* XIV (July 1970) 277–88. **267.**

'"Il Concetto dell'Anima," in Leonardo's Early Skull Studies,' *Journal of the Warburg and Courtauld Institutes* XXXIV (1971) 115–34. **251, 473, 565.**

Kemsley, Douglas S. 'Religious Influences in the Rise of Modern Science,' *Annals of Science* XXIV (1968) 199–226. **696.**

Kenney, E. J. *The Classical Text: Aspects of Editing in the Age of the Printed Book* (Berkeley, Calif., 1974). **81, 108, 113, 209, 338.**

Kent, John. *See* Daniélou, J.

Kenyon, Frederick G. *Books and Readers in Ancient Greece and Rome* (Oxford, 1951). **15, 22, 334.**

Kermode, Frank. 'Between Two Galaxies,' *Encounter* 113 (Feb. 1963) 76–82. **x.**

Keuning, J. *Willem Jansz. Blaeu*, rev. and ed. M. Donkerslootde Vrij (Amsterdam, 1973). **480, 663.**

Khan, M. S. 'The Early Bengali Printed Books,' *Gutenberg-Jahrbuch* (1966) 200–8. **317.**

Kimble, George H. T. *Geography in the Middle Ages* (London, 1938). **580.**

King, M. D. 'Reason, Tradition and the Progressiveness of Science,' *History and Theory* 10 (1971) 3–32. **459.**

Kooiman, Willem Jan. *Luther and the Bible* (Philadelphia, 1961). **367.**

Kort, J. de. 'Astronomical Appreciation of the Gregorian Calendar,' *Pontificia Academia Scientarium, Acta* XIII 4, 55–62. **606.**

Kortepeter, Max. 'German Zeitung Literature in the Sixteenth Century,' *Editing Sixteenth Century Texts*, ed. R. J. Schoeck (Toronto, 1966) 113–29. **307.**

Koyré, Alexandre. *From the Closed World to the Infinite Universe* (Baltimore, 1957). **219, 458, 468, 681.**

La Révolution Astronomique: Copernic, Kepler, Borelli (Paris, 1961). **651, 673.**

Krailsheimer, A. J. *Rabelais and the Franciscans* (Oxford, 1963). **365, 394.**

Kraus, M. J. 'Patronage and Reform in the France of the Prereforme: The Case of Clichtove,' *Canadian Journal of History* VI (March 1971) 45–73. **400.**

Krautheimer, Richard. 'Alberti's Templum Etruscum' (1961), *Studies in Early Christian, Medieval and Renaissance Art* (New York, 1969) 333–45. **551.**

'The Beginnings of Art Historical Writing in Italy' (1929), *Studies in Early Christian, Medieval, and Renaissance Art* (New York, 1969) 257–75. **232.**

Krautheimer, Richard and Krautheimer-Hess, T. *Lorenzo Ghiberti* (Princeton, 1956). **232.**

Kreutz, B. M. 'Mediterranean Contributions to the Medieval Mariner's Compass,' *Technology and Culture* XIV (1973) 367–83. **554.**

Krinsky, Carol H. 'Seventy-eight Vitruvius Manuscripts,' *Journal of the Warburg and Courtauld Institutes* XXX (1967) 36–70. **211, 469.**

Kristeller, Paul. *Early Florentine Woodcuts* (London, 1897). **86.**

Kristeller, Paul Oskar. *Iter Italicum: A Finding List of Uncatalogued Humanistic Mss* (2 vol. London and Leiden, 1963–67). I, preface, xi–xxviii. **47, 171.**

Latin Manuscript Books before 1600 (New York, 1965). **47.**

Renaissance Concepts of Man and Other Essays (New York, 1972). **548.**

Renaissance Thought: The Classic, Scholastic and Humanist Strains (New York, 1961). **47, 174, 183, 188, 208, 210–11, 213, 218, 222.**

Le Thomisme et la Pensée Italienne de la Renaissance (Montreal, 1967). **314.**

'Bartolomeo Facio and his Unknown Correspondence,' *From the Renaissance to the Counter-Reformation*, ed. C. H. Carter (New York, 1965) 51–65. **233.**

'The Contribution of Religious Orders to Thought and Learning,' *Medieval Aspects of Renaissance Learning: Three Essays*, ed. E. P. Mahoney (Durham, N.C., 1974) 95–159. **15, 46, 94.**

'The European Diffusion of Italian Humanism,' *Renaissance Thought II* (New York, 1965) 69–89. **177.**

'The Modern System of the Arts,' *Renaissance Thought II* (New York, 1965) 163–228. **251, 253.**

Krivatsky, Nati H. 'Herbert of Cherbury's "De Veritate" (1633) Given to Leiden Professor by English Pupil,' *Quaerendo* VI (1976) 197–9. **644.**

Kronenberg, M. E. 'Forged Addresses in Low Country Books in the Period of the Reformation,' *The Library*, 5th ser. II (1947) 81–94. **138.**

Kruitwagen, B. 'Het Schrijven op Feestdagen in de Middeleuwen,' *Tijdschrift voor boek en bibliotheek wezen* V (1907) 97–120. **59.**

Kubler, George. *The Shape of Time* (New Haven, Conn., 1962). **255.**

Kuhn, Sherman. 'The Preface to a Fifteenth Century Concordance,' *Speculum* XLIII. (April 1968) 258–73. **90.**

Review of Daly's *Contributions, Speculum* XLVII (1972) 300–3. **90.**

Lopez, Robert. 'Hard Times and Investment in Culture,' *The Renaissance: Six Essays* (New York, 1962) 29–55. **21.**

Lough, John. *Essays on the Encyclopédie of Diderot and d'Alembert* (Oxford, 1968). **147.**
An Introduction to Seventeenth Century France (London, 1960). **155, 395.**

Louis Philippe. *Mémoires de Louis Philippe* (2 vol. Paris. 1973). **19.**

Lovejoy, A. O. *The Great Chain of Being: A Study in the History of an Idea* (Cambridge, Mass., 1948). **215.**

Lowinsky, Edward. 'Music in the Culture of the Renaissance,' *Journal of the History of Ideas* IX (1954) 509–53. **249.**
'Music of the Renaissance as Viewed by Renaissance Musicians,' *The Renaissance Image of Man and the World*, ed. B. O'Kelly (Columbus, Ohio, 1966) 129–77. **249.**

Lowry, M. J. C. 'The "New Academy" of Aldus Manutius,' *Bulletin of the John Rylands University Library of Manchester* 58 (Spring 1976) 378–420. **222.**
'Two Great Venetian Libraries in the Age of Aldus Manutius,' *Bulletin of the John Rylands University Library of Manchester* 57 (Autumn 1974) 128–66. **222, 586.**

Luethy, Herbert. *From Calvin to Rousseau*, tr. S. Attanasio (New York, 1970). **403, 421.**

Luther, Martin. 'Against the Heavenly Prophets in the Matter of Images and Sacraments' (1525), *Luther's Works*, ed. C. Bergendorff and H. T. Lehmann, XL (Philadelphia, 1958) 99–100. **68.**

Lutz, Cora E. 'Manuscripts Copied from Printed Books,' *Essays on Manuscripts and Rare Books* (Hamden, Conn., 1975) 129–39. **51, 52.**

MacCaffrey, W. T. 'Elizabethan Politics: The First Decade 1558–1568,' *Past and Present* 24 (April 1963) 25–43. **395.**

McColley, Grant, Introduction, *The Defense of Galileo of Thomas Campanella* (Smith College Studies in History XXII) (Northampton, Mass., 1937). **668.**
'The Debt of Bishop John Wilkins to the "Apologia Pro Galileo",' *Annals of Science* IV (April 1939) 150–69. **668.**

McConica, James K. *English Humanists and Reformation Politics Under Henry VIII and Edward VI* (Oxford, 1965). **331.**

McDonald, E. E. 'The Modernizing of Communication: Vernacular Publishing in Nineteenth Century Maharashtra,' *Asian Survey* VIII (July 1968) 589–607. **317.**

McGuire, J. E. and Rattansi, P. M. 'Newton and the "Pipes of Pan",' *Notes and Records of the Royal Society* 21 (Dec. 1966) 108–43. **286, 572, 641.**

McIlwain, Charles. 'Medieval Institutions in the Modern World,' *The Twelfth Century Renaissance*, ed. Warren Hollister (New York, 1969) 72–81. **513.**

McKenzie, D. F. 'Printers of the Mind: Some Notes on Bibliographical Theories and Printing House Practices,' *Studies in Bibliography* XXII (Charlottesville, Va., 1969) 1–75. **11, 56, 393.**

McKerrow, R. B. 'Booksellers, Printers, and the Stationers Trade,' *Shakespeare's England* II (2 vol. Oxford, 1916) chap. 23, 212–39. **120.**

MacKinney, Loren. *Medical Illustrations in Medieval Manuscripts* (London, 1965). Consulted but not cited.

McLaughlin, Mary M. 'Survivors and Surrogates: Children and Parents from the Ninth to the Thirteenth Centuries,' *The History of Childhood*, ed. Lloyd de Mause (New York, 1974) 101–83. **431.**

McLean, Antonia. *Humanism and the Rise of Science in Tudor England* (London, 1972). **34, 35, 454, 511, 554.**

McLuhan, Marshall. *The Gutenberg Galaxy: The Making of Typographical Man* (Toronto, 1962). **16, 35, 122, 129, 151, 159, 186, 258.**

Understanding Media: The Extensions of Man (New York, 1965). **16, 159.**

McManners, John. *French Ecclesiastical Society under the Ancien Regime* (Manchester, 1960). **398.**

The French Revolution and the Church (New York, 1970). **352.**

McMullin, Ernan, ed. *Galileo, Man of Science* (New York, 1967). Includes articles by Bedini, S. A.; Boyer, Carl.

McMurtrie, Douglas. *The Book* (Oxford, 1943). **7, 167, 375-6.**

McNair, Philip. *Peter Martyr in Italy: An Anatomy of Apostasy* (Oxford, 1967). **348.**

McNally, R. L. 'The Ninety-five Theses of Martin Luther,' *Theological Studies* XXVIII (1967) 439–80. **306.**

McPherson, David. 'A Possible Origin for Mopsa in Sidney's Arcadia,' *Renaissance Quarterly* XXI (Winter 1968) 420–9. **259-60.**

Maas, Clifford. 'German Printers and the German Community in Renaissance Rome,' *The Library*, 5th ser. XXXI (June 1976) 118–26. **398.**

Machiavelli, Bernardo. *Libro di Ricordi*, ed. C. Olschki (Florence, 1954). **100.**

Machiavelli, Niccolò. *The Discourses of Niccolò Machiavelli*, tr. Leslie J. Walker (1950) with new introduction by C. H. Clough (2 vol. London, 1975). **100.**

Maddison, F. R. *See* Bedini, S. A.

Mahoney, Michael S. *The Mathematical Career of Pierre de Fermat (1601–1665)* (Princeton, N.J., 1973). **530, 532, 537, 552, 554.**

Major, J. Russell. 'Crown and Aristocracy in Renaissance France,' *American Historical Review* LXIX (April 1964) 631–45. **395.**

Malgaigne, J. F. *Surgery and Ambrose Paré*, tr. W. B. Hamby (Norman, Okla., 1965). **538.**

'The Man Behind the Sermon,' *Times Literary Supplement* (Feb. 27, 1964) 175. **337.**

Mandrou, Robert. *De la Culture Populaire aux 17e et 18e Siècles: La Bibliothèque Bleue de Troyes* (Paris, 1964). **130.**

'Le Livre: Ce Ferment,' *Revue Française d'Histoire du Livre* I (1971) 1–9. **29.**

'La Transmission de l'Hérésie à l'époque moderne,' *Hérésies et Sociétés dans l'Europe pré-industrielle, 11e–18e Siècles* (Colloque de Royaumont, 1962) ed. Jacques Le Goff (Civilisations et Sociétés 10) (The Hague, 1968) 281–9. **311.**

Mann, E. L. 'The Problem of Originality in English Literary Criticism, 1750–1800,' *Philological Quarterly* XVIII (1939) 97–118. **192.**

Mannheim, Karl. *Essays on the Sociology of Culture*, ed. and tr. E. Manheim (Oxford, 1956). **18, 154.**

Manuel, Frank. *The Eighteenth Century Confronts the Gods* (Cambridge, Mass., 1959) **282-3.**

Isaac Newton Historian (Cambridge, 1963). **611, 626.**

A Portrait of Isaac Newton (Cambridge, Mass., 1968). **283, 459, 555, 626-7, 633-4, 663, 679.**

Mardersteig, Giovanni. *The Remarkable Story of a Book Made in Padua in 1477*, tr. H. Schmoller (London, 1967). **56.**

Margolin, Jean-Claude. 'La Réalité Sociale dans l'Univers d'Albert Dürer,' *Individualisme et Société* (Brussels Colloquium) 215–56. **247-8.**

Marinoni, Augusto. Book review, *Technology and Culture* XIII (1972) 301–9. **566.**

Marks, Richard B. *The Medieval Manuscript Library of the Charterhouse of Saint Barbara in Cologne* (*Analecta Cartusiana* vol. 21–2) (Salzburg, 1974). **15.**

   'The Scriptorium and Library of St. Barbara's Cologne,' lecture at Catholic University of America, July 9, 1974. **379.**

   'The Significance of Fifteenth-Century Hand Corrections in the Düsseldorf Exemplars of Some of Therhoernen's editions of the Works of Werner Rolevinck,' *Gutenberg-Jahrbuch* (1977) 49–56. **316.**

Marrou, H. I. *A History of Education in Antiquity*, tr. George Lamb (1st edn, 1948; New York, 1956). **422.**

Marsak, L. M., ed. *The Rise of Science in Relation to Society* (New York, 1964). **493.**

Martin, H.-J. *Livre, Pouvoirs et Société à Paris au XVIIe Siècle* (2 vol. Geneva, 1969). **5, 135, 315, 333, 337, 349-50, 397, 408, 411, 414, 420, 646, 663, 680.**

   See also Febvre, Lucien.

Masai, François. *See* Gilissen, John.

Maslen, K. I. D. and Gerritsen, John. Correspondence, *The Library* XXX (June 1975) 81–94, 134–6. **56.**

Mason, S. F. 'The Scientific Revolution and the Protestant Reformation,' *Annals of Science* IX (1953) 64–88. **641.**

Mathias, Peter. 'Who Unbound Prometheus?' *Science and Society 1600–1900*, ed. P. Mathias (Cambridge, 1972) 54–81. **554.**

   ed. *Science and Society 1600–1900* (Cambridge, 1972). Includes articles by Mathias, P.; Rattansi, P. M.

Maunsell, Andrew. *Three Part Catalogue of English Printed Bookes* (London, 1595). **106, 107.**

Mayer, C. A. 'The Problem of Dolet's Evangelical Publications,' *Bibliothèque d'Humanisme et Renaissance* XVII (1955) 405–14. Consulted but not cited.

Mayor, A. Hyatt. *Prints and People* (New York, 1971). **489, 549, 588, 616.**

Mazlish, Bruce. *See* Bronowski, Jacob.

Mehl, James V. 'Ortwin Gratius: Cologne Humanist' (unpublished dissertation, University of Missouri, Columbia, Mo., 1975). **206.**

Meiss, Millard. *Painting in Florence and Siena After the Black Death* (Princeton, N.J., 1951). **297.**

Menninger, Karl. *Number Words and Number Symbols: A Cultural History of Numbers*, tr. Paul Broneer (rev. edn, Cambridge, Mass., 1969). **382.**

Menzel, Donald. Introduction to Pasquale D'Elia, *Galileo in China: Relations between Galileo and the Jesuit-Scientist-Missionaries 1610–1640*, tr. R. Suter and M. Sciascia (Cambridge, Mass., 1960). **648.**

Mersenne, Marin. *Les Nouvelles Pensées de Galilée*, ed. and introduction by P. Costabel and M.-P. Lerner (2 vol. Paris, 1973). **645.**

Merton, Robert K. *On the Shoulders of Giants: A Shandean Postscript* (New York, 1965). **121-2.**

   Science, Technology and Society in Seventeenth Century England (rev. edn offset reprint, New York, 1970). **459-60, 478, 641, 661, 679.**

   The Sociology of Science (Chicago, 1973). **506.**

Merton, Robert K. and Zuckerman, H. 'Patterns of Evaluation in Science: Institutionalisation, Structure and Functions of the Referee System,' *Minerva* 9 (1971) 63–102. **461-2, 667.**

Mesnard, Pierre. 'Le Commerce Epistolaire comme Expression Sociale de l'Individualisme Humaniste,' *Individu et Société à la Renaissance: Colloque International-1965* (Brussels, 1967) 15-21. **228-9.**

Metzger, Bruce M. *The Text of the New Testament, Its Transmission, Corruption and Restoration* (Oxford, 1968). **338, 373.**

Meyer, Carl S., ed. *Luther for an Ecumenical Age: Essays* (St Louis, Mo., 1967). Includes articles by Bluhm, H.; Schweibert, E. G.

Meyer, R. W. *Leibniz and the Seventeenth Century Revolution,* tr. J. P. Stern (Cambridge, 1952). **245.**

Meylan, Henri, ed. *Aspects de la Propagande Religieuse (Travaux d'Humanisme et Renaissance* xxvIII) (Geneva, 1957). **441.** Includes articles by Davis, N. Z.; Kingdon, R. M.

Michelangelo. *The Divine Michelangelo: The Florentine Academy's Homage on his Death in 1564* (a facsimile edition of the 'Esequie del Divino Michelangelo Buonarroti', Florence, 1564), introduction, tr., annot. Rudolf and Margot Wittkower (London, 1964). **254.**

Michelet, Jules. *Histoire de France: VII Renaissance* (16 vol.) (Oeuvres Complètes de J. M. 40 vol.) (Paris, Flammarion, 1893–99). **300.**

Middleton, W. E. K. *The Experimenters: A Study of the Accademia del Cimento* (Baltimore, 1971). **107, 665-6, 674.**

Milburn, R. L. P. 'The "People's" Bible: Artists and Commentators,' *Cambridge History of the Bible,* Vol. 2. *The West from the Fathers to the Reformation,* ed. G. W. H. Lampe (Cambridge, 1969) 280–308. **257, 355.**

Miller, C. William. *Benjamin Franklin's Philadelphia Printing 1728–1766: A Descriptive Bibliography* (American Philosophical Society Memoir: 102) (Philadelphia, 1974). **381.**

Miller, Edwin H. *The Professional Writer in Elizabethan England: A Study of Non Dramatic Literature* (Cambridge, Mass., 1959). **137.**

Miller, P. J. 'Eighteenth Century Periodicals for Women,' *History of Education Quarterly* (Fall 1971) 279-86. **134.**

Miner, Dorothy. *The Giant Bible of Mainz: 500th Anniversary: 4 April 1952.* Library of Congress Pamphlet, Washington, D.C. **82.**

Moeller, Bernd. *Imperial Cities and the Reformation: Three Essays,* tr. H. E. Midelfort and M. U. Edwards (Philadelphia, 1972). **366, 449.**

Mohl, Ruth. *The Three Estates in Medieval and Renaissance Literature* (New York, 1933). **394.**

Molho, A. and Tedeschi, J. ed. *Renaissance: Studies in Honor of Hans Baron* (DeKalb, Ill., 1971). Includes articles by Gilbert, N.; Kinser, S.; Nauert, C.; Strauss, G.; Zimmerman, T. P.

Molnar, Thomas. *The Decline of the Intellectuals* (New York, 1961). **153.**

Momigliano, Arnaldo. 'Ancient History and the Antiquarian' (1950), *Studies in Historiography* (New York, 1966) 1–40. **186, 190, 218, 325.**

Mommsen, Theodor E. 'Petrarch's Conception of the "Dark Ages",' *Speculum* xVII (April 1942) 226-42. **185, 294-5, 298.**

Monfasani, John. *George of Trebizond: A Biography and a Study of His Rhetoric and Logic* (Columbia Studies in the Classical Tradition 1) (Leiden, 1976). **399.**

Monter, E. William. *Calvin's Geneva* (New York, 1967). **410.**

O'Connell, Marvin. *The Counter Reformation 1559–1610* (The Rise of Modern Europe) (New York, 1974). **314.**

Oestreich, G. 'Die Antike Literatur als Vorbild der Praktischen Wissenschaften im 16 and 17 Jahrhundert,' *Classical Influences on European Culture AD 1500–1700*, ed. R. R. Bolgar (Cambridge, 1976) 315–25. **194.**

Offenberg, Adri. 'The First Use of Hebrew in a Book Printed in the Netherlands,' *Quaerendo* IV (1974) 44–54. **613.**

Olin, John C., ed. and tr. *See* 'The Life of Erasmus by Beatus Rhenanus.'

Olschki, C., ed. *See* Machiavelli, Bernardo.

O'Malley, C. D. *Andreas Vesalius of Brussels 1514–1564* (Berkeley, Calif., 1964). **267, 570.**
'Andreas Vesalius 1514–1564: In Memoriam,' *Medical History* VIII (Oct. 1964) 299–308. **573.**
See also Saunders and O'Malley.

Ong, Walter J., S.J. *The Presence of the Word* (New Haven, Conn., 1967). **41, 319.**
Ramus: Method and the Decay of Dialogue. From the Art of Discourse to the Art of Reason (Cambridge, Mass., 1958). **41, 92, 102, 275, 430.**
Rhetoric Romance and Technology (Ithaca, N.Y., 1971). **41, 92.**
'From Allegory to Diagram in the Renaissance Mind,' *Journal of Aesthetics and Art Criticism* XVII (June, 1959) 423–40. **92.**
'System Space and Intellect in Renaissance Symbolism,' *Bibliothèque d'Humanisme et Renaissance* XVIII (1956) 222–40. **92.**

Ore, Oyestein. *Cardano: The Gambling Scholar* (Princeton, N.J., 1953). **236, 662.**

Origo, Iris. *The Merchant of Prato* (rev. edn, London, 1963). **483.**

Ornstein, Martha. *The Role of Scientific Societies in the Seventeenth Century* (Chicago, 1928). **460, 644, 667–8, 676.**

Orr, M. A. *Dante and the Early Astronomers* (London, 1913). **483, 512.**

Ortelius, Abraham. 'Message to the Reader,' *Theater of the Whole World* (London, 1606) (Facsimile edn, Antwerp: Theatrum Orbus Terrarum Ltd, 1968). **88, 193, 227.**

Osley, A. S., ed. *Calligraphy and Paleography. Essays Presented to A. J. Fairbank* (London, 1965). Includes articles by de la Mare, A.; Hofer, P.; Wolpe, B. L.

Overfield, James. 'A New Look at the Reuchlin Affair,' *Studies in Medieval and Renaissance History* (University of Nebraska) VIII (1971) 165–207. **305.**

Owst, G. R. *Literature and Pulpit in Medieval England* (Oxford, 1966). **365.**

Ozment, Steven. *The Reformation in the Cities* (New Haven, Conn., 1975). **318.**

Pächt, Otto. 'Early Italian Nature Studies and the Early Calendar Landscape,' *Journal of the Warburg and Courtauld Institutes* XIII (1950) 13–47. **82, 233, 264, 492.**
'Notes and Observations on the Origin of Humanist Book Decoration,' *Fritz Saxl Memorial Essays*, ed. D. J. Gordon (London, 1975) 184–94. **204.**

Pagel, Walter. *Paracelsus: An Introduction to Philosophical Medicine in the Era of the Renaissance* (Basel, 1958). **286, 539, 657.**
'News, Notes and Queries,' *Medical History* VIII (1964) 78–83. **550.**
'William Harvey: Some Neglected Aspects of Medical History,' *Journal of the Warburg and Courtauld Institutes* VII (1944) 144–53. **528.**

Pagel, W. and Rattansi, P. 'Vesalius and Paracelsus,' *Medical History* VIII (Oct. 1964) 309–34. **472, 570–1, 573.**

Painter, George D. *William Caxton: A Quincentenary Biography* (London, 1976). **38.**

Peyre, Henri. 'The Influence of Eighteenth Century Ideas on the French Revolution,' *Intellectual Movements in Modern European History*, ed. Franklin L. Baumer (*Main Themes in European History*, ed. B. Mazlish) (New York, 1965) 63–85. **148.**

Pfeiffer, Rudolf. *History of Classical Scholarship From the Beginnings to the End of the Hellenistic Age* (Oxford, 1968). **22, 465.**

Philip, Alexander. *The Calendar: Its History, Structure and Improvement* (Cambridge, 1921). **608, 610.**

Phillips, W. A. 'Faust,' *Encyclopedia Britannica* x (28 vol. 11 edn, London, 1910–11) 210–11. **50.**

Pintard, René. *Le Libertinage Erudit dans la Première Moitié du XVIIe Siècle* (2 vol. Paris, 1943). **644.**

Plant, Marjorie. *The English Book Trade* (London, 1939). Consulted but not cited.

Plumb, J. H. 'The Public, Literature and the Arts in the 18th Century,' *The Emergence of Leisure*, ed. M. M. Marrus (New York, 1974) 11–37. **131.**

Pocock, J. G. A. *The Ancient Constitution and the Feudal Law* (Cambridge, 1957). **201, 224.**

The Machiavellian Moment (Princeton, New Jersey, 1975). **189–90.**

Pollack, Michael. 'The Performance of the Wooden Printing Press,' *Library Quarterly*, vol. 42 (April 1972) 218–64. Consulted but not cited.

'Production Costs in Fifteenth Century Printing,' *Library Quarterly* xxxix (Oct. 1969) 318–30. Consulted but not cited.

Pollard, Graham. 'The University and the Book Trade in Medieval Oxford,' *Miscellanea Mediaevalia* iii (Berlin, 1964) 336–46. **14.**

See also Ehrman, Albert.

'Pontiff says Media Lead Youth Astray,' *The Washington Post* (Tuesday, May 5, 1970) A14. **355.**

Poole, H. W. *See* Berry, W. T.

Popkin, Richard. *The History of Scepticism from Erasmus to Descartes* (New York, 1964). **231, 326.**

The Portable Renaissance Reader, ed. and tr. J. B. Ross and M. M. McLaughlin (New York, 1969). **27, 166, 217, 320, 393.**

Post, R. R. *The Modern Devotion: Confrontation with Reformation and Humanism* (Leiden, 1968). **16, 346.**

Potter, G. R. 'Zwingli and His Publisher,' *The Library Chronicle* xl (Winter 1974) 108–17. **99.**

Pottinger, David. *The French Book Trade in the Ancien Regime 1500–1791* (Cambridge, Mass., 1958). **128, 145–7, 399.**

Poulle, E. *See* Hilliard, D.

Praz, Mario. *Studies in Seventeenth Century Imagery* (Rome, 1964). **280.**

Preus, R. *The Inspiration of Scripture* (Edinburgh, 1957). **319, 323, 326, 332.**

Price, Derek de Solla. *Science since Babylon* (enlarged edn, New Haven, 1975). **453–4.**

'The Book as a Scientific Instrument,' *Science* 158 (6 Oct. 1967) 102–4. **612, 691.**

'Gears from the Greeks: The Antikythera Mechanism,' *Transactions of the American Philosophical Society* 64 (Philadelphia, 1974) part 7, 1–70. **589.**

'Geometrical and Scientific Talismans,' *Changing Perspectives in the History of Science: Essays in Honor of Joseph Needham*, ed. M. Teich and R. Young (London, 1973) 250–64. **55.**

ed. *See* Chaucer.

Price, Hereward T. 'Grammar and the Compositor in the Sixteenth and Seventeenth Centuries,' *Journal of English and Germanic Philology* XXXVIII (1939) 540–8. **87.**

Price, J. L. *Culture and Society in the Dutch Republic during the Seventeenth Century* (London, 1974). **646.**

'Printing and the Mind of Man,' Catalogue of Exhibition at the British Museum and Earl's Court July 16–27, 1963. **59.**

 See also Hay, Denys.

Prior, Moody. 'Joseph Glanvill, Witchcraft and 17th Century Science,' *Modern Philology* 30 (1932–3) 167–93. **669.**

Proctor, Robert. *The Printing of Greek in the Fifteenth Century* (London, 1900). **222.**

Proust, Jacques. *Diderot et l'Encyclopédie* (Paris, 1967). **262.**

Pullan, Brian. *Crisis and Change in the Venetian Economy* (*Debates in Economic History*, ed. Peter Mathias) (London, 1968). **411.**

Putnam, G. H. *Authors and Their Public in Ancient Times* (New York, 1894). **22.**

 Books and Their Makers in the Middle Ages (2 vol. New York, 1896). **22.**

 The Censorship of the Church of Rome and Its Influence upon the Production and Distribution of Literature (2 vol. New York, 1906). **347-8, 416.**

Quinn, David B. *England and the Discovery of America 1481–1620* (New York, 1974). **105.**

 'The New Horizons of Geographical Literature,' Paper given at Conference on First Images of America, UCLA, Feb. 7, 1975, subsequently published in *First Images of America*, ed. F. Chiappelli (Berkeley, Calif., 1975). **120.**

Rabb, T. K. 'Debate, The Advent of Printing and the Problem of the Renaissance,' *Past and Present* 52 (August 1971) 135–44. **101, 595.**

 'Religion and the Rise of Modern Science,' *Past and Present* 31 (July 1965) 110–26. **647-50, 653, 658, 664.**

Ramus, Petrus. *Scholae in Liberales Artes*, introduction by W. J. Ong (facsimile edn of Basel, 1569, New York, 1970). **543.**

Randall, J. H. *The Making of the Modern Mind* (Cambridge, Mass., 1926). **178, 496.**

 'The Development of Scientific Method at the School of Padua,' *The Journal of the History of Ideas*, I (1940) 177–206. **494, 496, 528.**

Raphael, D. D. 'Adam Smith and "The Infection of David Hume's Society",' *The Journal of the History of Ideas* XXX (April–June 1969) 225–48. **393.**

Rapp, R. T. *Industry and Economic Decline in Seventeenth Century Venice* (Cambridge, Mass., 1976). **411.**

Rashdall, H. *The Universities of Europe in the Middle Ages*, ed. F. M. Powicke and A. B. Emden (3 vol. Oxford, 1936). **103.**

Rath, Erich von. 'The Spread of Printing in the Fifteenth Century,' *History of the Printed Book*, ed. Lawrence C. Worth (The Dolphin no. 3) (New York, 1938). 59–80. **37.**

Rath, Gernot. 'Charles Estienne: Contemporary of Vesalius,' *Medical History* VIII (Oct. 1964) 354–9. **502, 567.**

Rattansi, P. M. 'Alchemy and Natural Magic in Raleigh's "History of the world",' *Ambix* XIII (Oct. 1966) 122–38. **562-3, 669.**

 'The Helmontian–Galenist Controversy in Restoration England,' *Ambix* XII (Feb. 1964) 1–24. **656.**

 'Paracelsus and the Puritan Revolution,' *Ambix* XI (Feb. 1963) 24–33. **656, 681.**

'Galileo's Misstatements About Copernicus,' *Isis* 49 (1958) 319–30. **606.**

'The Invention of Eyeglasses,' *Journal of the History of Medicine and Allied Sciences* XI (1956) 13–46, 183–218. **119, 123, 240, 546.**

'Renaissance Science as Seen by Burckhardt and His Successors,' *The Renaissance: A Reconsideration*, ed. T. Helton (Madison, Wis., 1964) 77–103. **494-5, 497-8, 501.**

Review of Thorndike's edition of Sacrobosco's 'Sphera,' *Isis* XXXX (1949) 257–64. **510, 512.**

'Was Copernicus a Hermetist?' *Historical and Philosophical Perspectives of Science*, ed. R. H. Stuewer (Minnesota Studies v) (Minneapolis, Minn., 1970) 163–71. **595, 641.**

See also Hilfstein, Erna.

Rosenberg, Eleanor. *Leicester: Patron of Letters* (New York, 1955). **360.**

Rosenthal, Earl. 'The Renaissance in the History of Art,' *The Renaissance: A Reconsideration*, ed. T. Helton (Madison, Wis., 1964) 53–77. **260.**

Rosenwein, B. H. and Little, Lester K. 'Social Meaning in the Monastic and Mendicants Spiritualities,' *Past and Present* 63 (May, 1974) 4–33. **375.**

Ross, D. J. A. 'A Late Twelfth Century Artist's Pattern Sheet,' *Journal of the Warburg and Courtauld Institutes* XXV (1962) 119–28. **82.**

Ross, J. B. 'Venetian Schools and Teachers, Fourteenth to Early Sixteenth Century,' *Renaissance Quarterly* XXXIX (1976) 521–60. **547.**

See also *The Portable Renaissance Reader.*

Ross, Lillian. 'Our Far-Flung Correspondents: The Bible in Dinocittà, Rome, Sept. 15,' *The New Yorker* (Sept. 25, 1965) 197. **348.**

Ross, Richard P. 'Oronce Fine's *De Sinibus Libri II*,' *Isis* 66 (1975) 379–86. **544.**

'Studies on Oronce Fine (1494–1555),' Columbia University Dissertation, 1971. **544.**

Rossi, Paolo. *Francis Bacon: From Magic to Science*, tr. S. Rabinovich (Chicago, 1968). **272-4, 276, 285, 563.**

Philosophy, Technology and the Arts in the Early Modern Era, tr. S. Attansio, ed. Benjamin Nelson (1st Italian edn, 1962; New York, 1970). **241, 243, 469-70, 541, 553, 560, 568.**

'Hermeticism, Rationality and the Scientific Revolution,' *Reason Experiment and Mysticism*, ed. M. L. Bonelli Righini and W. R. Shea (New York, 1975) 247–83. **641.**

Rothkrug, Lionel. *Opposition to Louis XIV Political and Social Origins of the French Enlightenment* (Princeton, New Jersey, 1965). **135.**

Rouse, Mary A. See Rouse, Richard H.

Rouse, Richard H. 'The Archeology of the Book,' Medieval Academy Summer Institute Lecture, Catholic University, 1974. **67.**

Rouse, Richard H. and Mary A. 'The Texts Called Lumen Anime,' *Archivum Fratrum Praedicatorum* XLI (1971) 4–113. **294, 456, 546.**

Rubinstein, Nicolai. 'Il Medioevo nella Storiagraphia Italiana della Rinascimento,' *Concetto, Storia Miti e Immagini del Medio Evo*, ed. Vittore Branca (Florence, 1973) 429–48. **191.**

Rud, Einar. *Vasari's Life and Lives*, tr. R. Spink (London, 1923). **233.**

Rupp, Gordon. *Luther's Progress to the Diet of Worms, 1521* (Chicago, 1951). **310.**

Russell, J. L. 'Kepler's Laws of Planetary Motion, 1609–1666,' *The British Journal for the History of Science* II (June 1964) 1–24. **503, 630-2.**

Sachs, W. *See* Furet, E.

Saenger, Paul. 'Colard Mansion and the Evolution of the Printed Book,' *The Library Quarterly* 45 (Oct. 1975) 405–18. **37-8, 80.**

Sailor, Danton B. 'Moses and Atomism,' *Journal of the History of Ideas* XXV (Jan.–March 1964) 3–16. **209.**

St John, N. Book review, *The American Journal of Sociology* 73 (1967). **3.**

Santillana, Giorgio de. *The Age of Adventure* (New York, 1956). **165.**

    The Crime of Galileo (Chicago, 1955). **644, 652, 677-8.**

    Book review, *American Historical Review* LXX (1965) 455. **279.**

    'The Role of Art in the Scientific Renaissance,' *Critical Problems in the History of Science*, ed. Marshall Clagett (Madison, Wis., 1959) 33–66. **249, 589.**

Santillana, Giorgio de and Dechend, Hertha von. *Hamlet's Mill. An Essay on Myth and the Frame of Time* (Boston, 1969). **279.**

Sapori, Armando. *The Italian Merchant in the Middle Ages*, tr. P. A. Kennen (New York, 1970). **62, 385.**

Sarpi, Paolo. *Sarpi: History of Benefices and Selections from History of the Council of Trent*, ed. and tr. by Peter Burke (*The Great Histories*, ed. H. Trevor-Roper) (New York, 1967). **412-13.**

Sarton, George. *Appreciation of Ancient and Medieval Science During the Renaissance 1450–1600* (New York, 1958, 2nd edn). **55, 69, 98-9, 171, 194, 454, 484, 486, 507-8, 511, 548, 624.**

    Six Wings (Bloomington, Indiana, 1957). **20, 111, 234, 267, 454-5, 484, 488, 507-8, 538, 541, 545-6, 564-5, 567, 591, 606-7, 652.**

    'The First Explanation of Decimal Fractions and Measures (1585),' *Isis* 23 (1935) 153–245. **241, 468, 500.**

    'Incunabula Wrongly Dated,' *Sarton on the History of Science*, ed. D. Stimson (Cambridge, Mass., 1962) 320–5. **106.**

    'The Quest for Truth: Scientific Progress during the Renaissance,' *The Renaissance: Six Essays* (New York, 1962) chap. 3. **27, 75, 79, 81, 113, 124, 454, 637.**

    'The Scientific Literature transmitted through the Incunabula,' *Osiris* 5 (1938) 62–8. **454, 508, 586, 588.**

    'Simon Stevin of Bruges (1548–1620),' *Isis* 21 (1934) 241–303. **500.**

    'The Study of Early Scientific Textbooks', *Sarton on the History of Science*, ed. D. Stimson (Cambridge, Mass., 1962) 339–54. **508.**

    'A Summing Up,' *Sarton on the History of Science*, ed. D. Stimson (Cambridge, Mass., 1962) 367–70. **519.**

Saunders, J. B. and O'Malley, C. D. *The Illustrations from the Works of Andreas Vesalius of Brussels* (Cleveland, Ohio, 1950). **535, 569.**

    eds *Leonardo da Vinci on the Human Body* (New York, 1952). **267.**

Saunders, J. W. 'From Manuscript to Print: A Note on the Circulation of Poetic Manuscripts in the Sixteenth Century,' *Proceedings of the Leeds Philosophical and Literary Society* VI (May 1951) 507–28. **65.**

Sauvy, Anne. *Livres saisis à Paris entre 1678 et 1701* (The Hague, 1972). **680.**

Saxl, Fritz. 'A Spiritual Encyclopedia of the Later Middle Ages,' *Journal of the Warburg and Courtauld Institutes* V (1942) 82–136. **92, 259.**

'Reuchlin's Philosophy, Pythagoras and Cabala for Christ,' *Archiv für Reformationsgeschichte* 47 (1956) 1–20. **278, 620.**

Sprat, Thomas. *History of the Royal Society* (1667) ed. J. I. Cope and H. W. Jones (St Louis, Mo., 1958). **283, 562, 563, 601, 669–70, 682.**

Stannard, Jerry. 'The Herbal as a Medical Document,' *Bulletin of the History of Medicine* XLIII (May–June 1969) 212–20. **265, 485.**

Starnes, DeWitt T. *Robert Estienne's Influence on Lexicography* (Austin, Texas, 1963). **91, 336.**

Staubach, C. N. *See* Karpinski, L. C.

Stavrianos, L. S. *The World Since 1500: A Global History* (Englewood, New Jersey, 1966). **516.**

Steele, Robert. 'What Fifteenth Century Books are About,' *The Library*, 2nd ser. IV (Oct. 1903) 337–55; V (Oct. 1904) 337–56; VI (Jan. 1905) 137–55; VIII (July 1907) 225–38. **169, 346, 436.**

Steinberg, S. H. *Five Hundred Years of Printing* (rev. edn, Bristol, 1961). **5, 7, 32–3, 44, 52, 59, 80–2, 89, 113, 117, 128, 138, 202, 204, 206, 259, 326, 359, 375, 392, 407, 440.**

Steiner, George. *After Babel: Aspects of Language and Translation* (Oxford, 1975). **287.**
'The Retreat from the Word,' *Kenyon Review* (Spring 1961) 187–216. **159.**

Steinmann, Martin. *Johannes Oporinus: Ein Basler Buchdrucker um die Mitte des 16. Jahrhunderts* (Basel, 1967). **442, 446, 570.**

Steneck, N. H. *The Scientific Press at the Time of Copernicus, 1530–1550* (Catalogue of Exhibition held at Ann Arbor, Michigan, April 3–5, 1973). **575–7.**

Stephenson, Carl. *A Brief Survey of Medieval Europe* (New York, 1941). **36.**

Stevens, Henry N. *Ptolemy's Geography A Brief Account of all the Printed Editions down to 1730* (London, 1908). **110.**

Stillwell, Margaret Bingham. *The Awakening Interest in Science During the First Century of Printing, 1450–1550. An Annotated Checklist of First Editions* (New York: Bibliographical Society of America, 1970). **461, 510–11, 548, 583, 585–6.**
The Beginning of the World of Books 1450 to 1470. A Chronological Survey of the Texts Chosen for Printing . . . With a Synopsis of the Gutenberg Documents (New York, 1972). **44, 50.**

Stimson, Dorothy. *The Gradual Acceptance of the Copernican Theory of the Universe* (New York, 1917). **614, 629–30, 677.**
Scientists and Amateurs, A History of the Royal Society (New York, 1948). **666.**

Stone, Lawrence. *The Crisis of the Aristocracy 1558–1641* (Oxford, 1965). **136, 395.**
Social Change and Revolution in England 1540–1640 (Problems and Perspectives in History, ed. H. F. Kearney) (London, 1966). **310.**
'The Educational Revolution in England, 1560–1640,' *Past and Present* 28 (July 1964) 41–80. **395.**
'Literacy and Education in England 1640–1900,' *Past and Present* 42 (Feb. 1969) 69–139. **61, 67, 330, 414.**
'The Massacre of the Innocents,' *The New York Review of Books* (Nov. 14, 1974) 25–31. **431.**

Strachan, James. *Early Bible Illustrations: A Short Study* (Cambridge, 1957). **64, 108 257.**

Strauss, Gerald. *Nuremberg in the Sixteenth Century* (New York, 1966). **308, 403–4.**
'The Course of German History: The Lutheran Interpretation,' *Renaissance:*

Tory, Geoffroy. *Champ Fleury*, tr. George B. Ives (New York, 1967) (republication of Grolier Club edn, 1927). **203-4.**

Toulmin, Stephen. *Human Understanding* (Princeton, 1972). **461.**

Toulmin, S. and Goodfield, J. *The Fabric of the Heavens* (London, 1963). **465, 500.**

'Toward a New History of the New Science', *Times Literary Supplement*, Sept. 15, 1972, 1058. **521.**

Tracy, James D. 'Erasmus becomes a German,' *The Renaissance Quarterly* XXI (Autumn 1968) 281–8. **309.**

Trapp, J. B. 'The High Renaissance at Harvard,' *Times Literary Supplement*, Jan. 14, 1977, 41. **261.**

Trattner, W. I. 'God and Expansion in Elizabethan England: John Dee 1527–1583,' *Journal of the History of Ideas* XXV (Jan.–March 1964) 17–34. **274.**

Trénard, Louis. 'L'Histoire des Mentalités Collectives: Les Livres: Bilan et Perspective,' *Revue d'Histoire Moderne et Contemporaine* 15 (1968) 691–703. **29.**

'La Presse Française des Origines à 1788,' *Histoire Générale de la Presse Française*, ed. C. Bellanger *et al.* (4 vol. Paris, 1974) 27–376. **131, 134, 138, 147, 259.**

Trevor-Roper, Hugh R. *The Crisis of the Seventeenth Century: Religion, the Reformation and Social Change* (New York, 1968). **364, 388, 410, 418–19, 434, 436, 438–9, 449.**

'Desiderius Erasmus,' *Men and Events* [English title: *Historical Essays*] (New York, 1957) 35–61. **145, 401, 416.**

Review essay, *History and Theory* V (1966) 61–82. **281.**

Trimpi, Wesley. 'The Meaning of Horace's "Ut Pictura Poesis",' *Journal of the Warburg and Courtauld Institutes* XXXVI (1973) 1–34. **230, 256, 319, 322.**

Trinkaus, Charles. *In Our Image and Likeness, Humanity and Divinity in Italian Humanist Thought* (2 vol. Chicago, 1970). **298.**

'Humanism, Religion, Society: Concepts and Motivations of some Recent Studies,' *Renaissance Quarterly* XXIX (Winter 1976) 676–714. **298.**

Trithemius, Johannes. *In Praise of Scribes – De Lande Scriptorum*. **14–15, 50, 378.** *See* Klaus Arnold, ed.

Tuchman, Barbara. 'Hazards on the Way to the Middle Ages,' *The Atlantic Monthly* (Dec. 1975) 72–8. **236.**

Uhlendorf, B. A. 'The Invention and spread of printing till 1470 with special reference to social and economic factors,' *The Library Quarterly* II (1932) 179–231. **6, 44.**

Ullman, B. L. *The Origin and Development of Humanistic Script* (Rome, 1960). **45, 203, 205.**

Ullmann, Walter. *The Individual and Society in the Middle Ages* (Baltimore, 1966). **229.**

Underwood, E. A., ed. *Science, Medicine and History. Essays . . . In Honor of Charles Singer* (2 vol. Oxford, 1953). Includes articles by Arber, A.; Fisch, M.; Johnson, R. F.

Unguru, Sabetai. 'Witelo and Thirteenth century Mathematics: An Assessment,' *Isis* 63 (Dec. 1972) 496–508. **494.**

Updike, D. B. *Printing Types: Their History Forms and Use: A study in Survivals* (2 vol. Cambridge, Mass., 1937). **203, 224, 250, 588.**

Vaassen, Elgin. *Die Werkstatt der Mainzer Riesenbibel in Würzburg und Ihr Umkreis* (Frankfurt-am-Main, 1973). **54.**

Woodbridge, John. 'Censure Royale et Censure Episcopale, le Conflict de 1702,' *Dix-Huitième Siècle* (1976) 333–55. **333.**

Woodfield, Dennis. *Surreptitious Printing in England 1550–1690* (New York, 1973). **415, 416, 417, 652.**

Woodward, W. H. *Vittorino da Feltre and Other Humanist Educators*, ed. Eugene Rice (New York, 1963 [reprint of 1897 edn]). **175, 190, 537, 662.**

Worden, Blair. 'Edmund Ludlow: the Puritan and the Whig,' *Times Literary Supplement* (Jan. 7, 1977) 15–16. **142.**

Wormald, F. and Wright, C. E., eds. *The English Library before 1700* (London, 1958). Includes articles by Ivy, G. S.; Irwin, R.; Wilson, R. M.

Wright, C. E., ed. *See* Wormald, F.

Wright, Louis B. *Middle Class Culture in Elizabethan England* (Chapel Hill, N.C., 1935). **130, 243, 361, 383, 385, 415, 425, 428–9.**

Wrightsman, Bruce. 'Andreas Osiander's Contribution to the Copernican Achievement,' *The Copernican Achievement*, ed. R. S. Westman (Los Angeles, 1975) 213–43. **651.**

Wroth, Lawrence C., ed. *A History of the Printed Book* (The Dolphin no. 3) (New York, 1938). Includes articles by Fuhrman, O. W.; Lehmann-Haupt, H.; Rath, Erich von.

Yamey, B. S. 'Scientific Bookkeeping and the Rise of Capitalism,' *The Economic History Review* I (1949) 99–114. **383–4, 554.**

ed. *See also* Littleton, A. C.

Yardeni, Myriam. 'Journalisme et Histoire Contemporaine à l'Epoque de Bayle,' *History and Theory* XII (1973) 208–29. **138.**

Yates, Frances. *The Art of Memory* (London, 1966). **23, 66–7, 69, 92, 123, 189, 272, 286, 296–7, 457, 549.**

Giordano Bruno and the Hermetic Tradition (London, 1964). **77, 274, 275, 276, 278, 281, 282, 286, 644, 669.**

The Rosicrucian Enlightenment (London, 1972). **97, 141, 275, 276, 286, 438, 534, 549, 550, 641, 668, 699.**

The Valois Tapestries (London, 1959). **84.**

'The Hermetic Tradition in Renaissance Science,' *Art, Science and History in the Renaissance*, ed. C. S. Singleton (Baltimore, 1967) 259–60. **272.**

'Paoli Sarpi's History of the Council of Trent,' *Journal of the Warburg and Courtauld Institutes* VII (1944) 123–44. **412–13.**

Zervas, D. F. 'The *Trattato dell'Abbaco* and Andrea Pisano's Design for the Florentine Baptistery Door,' *Renaissance Quarterly* XXVIII (Winter 1975) 483–504. **252.**

Zeydel, E. H. 'Johann Reuchlin and Sebastian Brant: A Study in Early German Humanism,' *Studies in Philology* LXVII (April 1970) 117–39. **94, 399.**

Zilsel, Edgar. 'The Genesis of the Concept of Scientific Progress,' *Journal of the History of Ideas* VI (1945) 325–49. **112, 248, 465, 550, 552, 558–60.**

'The Origins of William Gilbert's Scientific Method,' *Journal of the History of Ideas* II (1941) 1–32. **23, 241, 520.**

'The Sociological Roots of Science,' *American Journal of Sociology* 47 (1942) 544–60. **521.**

Ziman, John. *Public Knowledge: The Social Dimension of Science* (Cambridge, 1968). **478.**

Zimmerman, T. P. 'Confession and Autobiography in the Early Renaissance,' *Renaissance: Studies in Honor of Hans Baron* (DeKalb, Ill., 1971) 121–40. **229.**

Zinner, Ernst. *Leben und Werken des Johannes Müller von Königsberg, genannt Regiomontanus* (Munich, 1938). **584.**

Zophy, J. W. *See* Buck, L. P.

Zoubov, V. P. 'Vitruve et ses Commentateurs du XVIe Siècle,' *La Science au Seizième Siècle* (Colloque de Royaumont) (Paris, 1960). 69-90. **469.**

Zuckerman, H. *See* Merton, Robert K.

GENERAL INDEX